For Students

MEANINGFUL HELP AND FEEDBACK

- Personalized interactive learning aids for point-of-use help and immediate feedback. These learning aids include:

  - "Help Me Solve This" walks students through solving an algorithmic version of the questions they are working, with additional detailed tutorial reminders. These informational cues assist the students and help them understand concepts and mechanics.

  - "Accounting Simplified" videos give students a 3- to 5-minute lesson on concepts. Our new videos are engaging whiteboard animations that help illustrate concepts for students.

  - eText links students directly to the concept covered in the problem they are working on.

  - Homework and practice exercises with additional algorithmically generated problems for further practice and mastery.

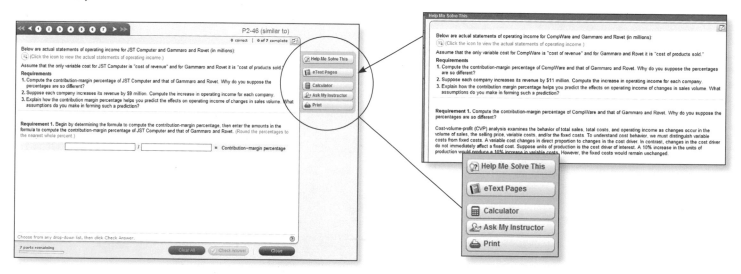

PERSONALIZED STUDY PATH

- Assists students in monitoring their own progress by offering them a customized study plan based on Homework, Quiz, and Test results.

- Includes regenerated exercises with unlimited practice and the opportunity to prove mastery through Quizzes on recommended learning objectives.

SIXTEENTH EDITION

Introduction to

MANAGEMENT ACCOUNTING

Charles T. Horngren
Stanford University

Gary L. Sundem
University of Washington – Seattle

David Burgstahler
University of Washington – Seattle

Jeff Schatzberg
University of Arizona

PEARSON

Boston Columbus Indianapolis New York San Francisco Upper Saddle River
Amsterdam Cape Town Dubai London Madrid Milan Munich Paris Montréal Toronto
Delhi Mexico City São Paulo Sydney Hong Kong Seoul Singapore Taipei Tokyo

*To our spouses and children,
and to all our students, past and
present.*

Editor-in-Chief: Donna Battista
Acquisitions Editor: Ellen Geary
Director of Editorial Services: Ashley Santora
Editorial Project Manager: Nicole Sam
Editorial Assistants: Jane Avery and Lauren Zanedis
Director of Marketing: Maggie Moylan Leen
Marketing Manager: Alison Haskins
Marketing Assistant: Kimberly Lovato
Managing Editor, Production: Jeff Holcomb
Sr. Production Project Manager: Roberta Sherman
Manufacturing Buyer: Carol Melville

Sr. Art Director: Anthony Gemmellaro
Cover Design: Anthony Gemmellaro
Interior Design: 511 Design and Anthony Gemmellaro
Cover Photo: Pete Gardner/Photographer's Choice/Getty Images
Media Project Manager, Editorial: James Bateman
Media Project Manager, Production: John Cassar
Full-Service Project Management: GEX Publishing Services
Composition: GEX Publishing Services
Printer/Binder: RR Donnelley Harrisonburg
Cover Printer: RR Donnelley Harrisonburg
Text Font: 10/12 Times

Credits and acknowledgments borrowed from other sources and reproduced, with permission, in this textbook appear on appropriate page within text.

Library of Congress Cataloging-in-Publication Data
Horngren, Charles T.
  Introduction to management accounting / Charles T. Horngren, Stanford University; Gary L. Sundem,
University of Washington - Seattle; David Burgstahler, University of Washington - Seattle; Jeff Schatzberg,
University of Arizona. -- Sixteenth edition.
      pages cm
  Includes index.
  ISBN 978-0-13-305878-9 (casebound)
1. Managerial accounting. I. Title.
  HF5635.H814 2014
  658.15'11--dc23
                        2012047454

11   16

ISBN 13: 978-0-13-305878-9
ISBN 10: 0-13-305878-6

About the Authors

Charles T. Horngren was the Edmund W. Littlefield Professor of Accounting, emeritus, at Stanford University. A graduate of Marquette University, he received his MBA from Harvard University and his PhD from the University of Chicago. He also received honorary doctorates from Marquette University and DePaul University.

A certified public accountant, Horngren served on the Accounting Principles Board, the Financial Accounting Standards Board Advisory Council, and the Council of the American Institute of Certified Public Accountants and served as a trustee of the Financial Accounting Foundation, which oversees the Financial Accounting Standards Board and the Government Accounting Standards Board. He is a member of the Accounting Hall of Fame.

Horngren served the American Accounting Association as its president and as director of research. He received the association's first annual Outstanding Accounting Educator Award. He also received its Lifetime Contribution to Management Accounting Award.

The California Certified Public Accountants Foundation gave Horngren its Faculty Excellence Award and its Distinguished Professor Award. He is the first person to have received both awards. The American Institute of Certified Public Accountants presented him with its first Outstanding Educator Award. He was also named Accountant of the Year, Education, by the national professional accounting fraternity, Beta Alpha Psi.

Professor Horngren was a member of the Institute of Management Accountants, where he received its Distinguished Service Award. He was a member of the Institute's Board of Regents, which administers the Certified Management Accountant examinations.

Horngren authored several other accounting books published by Prentice Hall: *Cost Accounting: A Managerial Emphasis*, *Introduction to Financial Accounting*, *Accounting*, and *Financial Accounting*. He was also the Consulting Editor for the Charles T. Horngren Series in Accounting.

Gary L. Sundem is professor of accounting emeritus at the University of Washington, Seattle. He received his BA from Carleton College and his MBA and PhD from Stanford University.

Professor Sundem has served as President of the American Accounting Association, Executive Director of the Accounting Education Change Commission, and Editor of *The Accounting Review*. He is currently president of the International Association for Accounting Education and Research.

Sundem is a past president of the Seattle chapter of the IMA (formerly the Institute of Management Accountants). He has served on IMA's national board of directors and chaired its Academic Relations and Professional Development committees. He has chaired the AACSB's Accounting Accreditation Committee He currently serves on the Board of Trustees of Rainier Mutual Funds and the Board of Trustees of Carleton College, where he chairs the audit committee. He received the Carleton College Outstanding Alumni award in 2002.

Professor Sundem has numerous publications in accounting and finance journals including *Issues in Accounting Education*, *The Accounting Review*, *Journal of Accounting Research*, and *Journal of Finance*. He was selected as the Outstanding Accounting Educator by the American Accounting Association in 1998 and by the Washington Society of CPAs in 1987.

David Burgstahler is the Julius A. Roller Professor of Accounting at the University of Washington, Seattle. He received his BA degree from the University of Minnesota–Duluth, and his PhD from the University of Iowa. He has been associate dean for masters programs and executive education and acting dean at the University of Washington Business School. He has served on more than 40 PhD supervisory committees and has been recognized multiple times as Beta Alpha Psi Professor of the Year and as MBA Professor of the Quarter at the University of Washington.

Professor Burgstahler was 2007–2009 vice president of publications of the American Accounting Association and has served on a number of Association committees.

Professor Burgstahler received the American Accounting Association's American Institute of Certified Public Accountants Notable Contributions to Accounting Literature Award in 2002. He has numerous publications in journals including *The Accounting Review, Journal of Management Accounting Research, Journal of Accounting Research, Journal of Accounting and Economics, Contemporary Accounting Research, Auditing: A Journal of Practice and Theory, Behavioral Research in Accounting,* and *The CPA Journal.*

Jeff Schatzberg is the Vice-Dean and Eller Professor of Accounting in the Eller College of Management at the University of Arizona. Professor Schatzberg received his BA (in philosophy), MA (in accounting), and PhD (in business administration), all at the University of Iowa. Professor Schatzberg has numerous publications in the most prestigious accounting and business journals, including the *Journal of Accounting Research, The Accounting Review, Contemporary Accounting Research, Auditing: A Journal of Practice and Theory, Journal of Management Accounting Research,* and *Issues in Accounting Education.* His teaching and research interests are in managerial accounting and auditing. He has given numerous seminars at several U.S. universities and international schools in Canada, England, Wales, Norway, France, Germany, and Switzerland. Schatzberg has also served on the editorial board of several scholarly accounting journals.

Professor Schatzberg has been teaching undergraduate, graduate, and MBA managerial accounting courses at the University of Arizona for the past 26 years. He has extensive experience in executive education worldwide (e.g., United States, China, Korea, Taiwan, Mexico, and Peru), has developed customized managerial accounting programs and performed consulting for numerous companies (e.g., Raytheon, Honeywell, Microsoft, and Intel), and has taught executives from many multinational firms (e.g., IBM, Motorola, LG, BenQ, Acer, and Mattel). Professor Schatzberg has received the MBA Faculty of the Year Award from the Eller Graduate School of Business at the University of Arizona on seven occasions and is the recipient of the Arizona Society of CPA's Excellence in Teaching Award. He is a CPA and worked for several years as an auditor and tax accountant in the Phoenix office of KPMG Peat Marwick. His work experience includes both manufacturing and service industry firms, as well as not-for-profit institutions.

Brief Contents

PART 1   Focus on Decision Making

Chapter 1   Managerial Accounting, the Business Organization, and Professional Ethics   2

Chapter 2   Introduction to Cost Behavior and Cost-Volume-Profit Relationships   36

Chapter 3   Measurement of Cost Behavior   86

Chapter 4   Cost Management Systems and Activity-Based Costing   122

Chapter 5   Relevant Information for Decision Making with a Focus on Pricing Decisions   180

Chapter 6   Relevant Information for Decision Making with a Focus on Operational Decisions   226

PART 2   Accounting for Planning and Control

Chapter 7   Introduction to Budgets and Preparing the Master Budget   270

Chapter 8   Flexible Budgets and Variance Analysis   310

Chapter 9   Management Control Systems and Responsibility Accounting   352

Chapter 10   Management Control in Decentralized Organizations   390

PART 3   Capital Budgeting

Chapter 11   Capital Budgeting   434

PART 4   Product Costing

Chapter 12   Cost Allocation   480

Chapter 13   Accounting for Overhead Costs   532

Chapter 14   Job-Order Costing and Process-Costing Systems   576

PART 5   Basic Financial Accounting

Chapter 15   Basic Accounting: Concepts, Techniques, and Conventions   618

Chapter 16   Understanding Corporate Annual Reports: Basic Financial Statements   660

Chapter 17   Understanding and Analyzing Consolidated Financial Statements   716

Appendix A   Recommended Readings   A1

Appendix B   Fundamentals of Compound Interest and the Use of Present-Value Tables   A5

Appendix C   Excerpts from Form 10-K of Nike, Inc.   A11

Glossary   G1

Subject Index   I1

Company Index   I11

Contents

Preface   *xiv*
Acknowledgements   *xviii*

PART 1   Focus on Decision Making

Chapter 1   Managerial Accounting, the Business Organization, and Professional Ethics   2

Starbucks   2

Management Accounting and Your Career   3

Roles of Accounting Information   4

Management by Exception   6

Cost-Benefit and Behavioral Considerations   9

Planning and Control for Product Life Cycles and the Value Chain   9

Accounting's Position in the Organization   12

Adaptation to Change   15

Ethical Conduct for Professional Accountants   18

Accounting Vocabulary   24   •   Fundamental Assignment Material   24   •   Additional Assignment Material   26

Chapter 2   Introduction to Cost Behavior and Cost-Volume-Profit Relationships   36

Boeing Company   36

Identifying Activities, Resources, Costs, and Cost Drivers   37

Variable-Cost and Fixed-Cost Behavior   39

Cost Behavior: Further Considerations   42

Cost-Volume-Profit Analysis   45

Additional Uses of CVP Analysis   55

Contribution Margin and Gross Margin   58

Appendix 2A: Sales-Mix Analysis   61

Appendix 2B: Impact of Income Taxes   62

Accounting Vocabulary   63   •   Fundamental Assignment Material   64   •   Additional Assignment Material   67

Chapter 3   Measurement of Cost Behavior   86

America West   86

Cost Drivers and Cost Behavior   87

Management Influence on Cost Behavior   88

Cost Functions   90

Methods of Measuring Cost Functions   93

Appendix 3: Use and Interpretation of Least-Squares Regression   102

Accounting Vocabulary   106   •   Fundamental Assignment Material   106   •
Additional Assignment Material   107

Chapter 4   **Cost Management Systems and Activity-Based Costing   122**

Dell   122

Cost Management Systems   123

Cost Accounting Systems   124

Cost Terms Used for Strategic Decision Making and Operational Control
Purposes   126

Cost Terms Used for External Reporting Purposes   131

Traditional and Activity-Based Cost Accounting Systems   134

Activity-Based Management: A Cost Management System Tool   142

Appendix 4: Detailed Illustration of Traditional and Activity-Based Cost
Accounting Systems   145

Accounting Vocabulary   154   •   Fundamental Assignment Material   154 •
Additional Assignment Material   160

Chapter 5   **Relevant Information for Decision Making with a Focus on
Pricing Decisions   180**

Grand Canyon Railway   180

The Concept of Relevance   181

Pricing Special Sales Orders   186

Basic Principles for Pricing Decisions   191

Influences on Pricing in Practice   194

Cost-Plus Pricing   195

Target Costing   201

Accounting Vocabulary   205   •   Fundamental Assignment Material   205   •
Additional Assignment Material   209

Chapter 6   **Relevant Information for Decision Making with a Focus on
Operational Decisions   226**

Nantucket Nectars   226

Analyzing Relevant Information: Focusing on the Future and Differential
Attributes   227

Make-or-Buy Decisions   229

Deletion or Addition of Products, Services, or Departments   234

Optimal Use of Limited Resources: Product-Mix Decisions   236

Joint Product Costs: Sell or Process Further Decisions   238

Keeping or Replacing Equipment   240

Identify Irrelevant or Misspecified Costs   242

Conflicts Between Decision Making and Performance Evaluation   244

Accounting Vocabulary   246   •   Fundamental Assignment Material   246   •
Additional Assignment Material   250

PART 2   Accounting for Planning and Control

Chapter 7   Introduction to Budgets and Preparing the Master Budget   270

Ritz-Carlton   270

Budgets and the Organization   271

Types of Budgets   277

Preparing the Master Budget   279

Budgets as Financial Planning Models   290

Appendix 7: Use of Spreadsheet Models for Sensitivity Analysis   292

Accounting Vocabulary   294   •   Fundamental Assignment Material   294   •
Additional Assignment Material   296

Chapter 8   Flexible Budgets and Variance Analysis   310

McDonald's   310

Using Budgets and Variances to Evaluate Results   311

Revenue and Cost Variances   316

The Role of Standards in Determining Variances   318

Finding Explanations for Variances   319

More Detailed Analysis of Flexible-Budget Variances   322

Overhead Variances   327

Accounting Vocabulary   331   •   Fundamental Assignment Material   332   •
Additional Assignment Material   334

Chapter 9   Management Control Systems and Responsibility Accounting   352

Health Net   352

Management Control Systems   353

Management Control Systems and Organizational Goals   353

Designing Management Control Systems   355

Controllability and Measurement of Financial Performance   360

Measurement of Nonfinancial Performance   365

The Balanced Scorecard   370

Management Control Systems in Service, Government, and Nonprofit Organizations 372

Future of Management Control Systems 373

Accounting Vocabulary 374 • Fundamental Assignment Material 375 • Additional Assignment Material 377

Chapter 10   Management Control in Decentralized Organizations 390

NIKE 390

Centralization Versus Decentralization 391

Performance Metrics and Management Control 393

Measures of Segment Performance 396

Economic Profit and Economic Value Added (EVA) 400

Incentives from Income, ROI, or Economic Profit 402

Transfer Pricing 404

Keys to Successful Management Control Systems 413

Accounting Vocabulary 416 • Fundamental Assignment Material 416 • Additional Assignment Material 419

PART 3   Capital Budgeting

Chapter 11   Capital Budgeting 434

Toyota Motor Corporation 434

Capital Budgeting for Programs or Projects 435

Discounted-Cash-Flow Models 435

Sensitivity Analysis and Risk Assessment in DCF Models 439

The NPV Comparison of Two Projects 440

Relevant Cash Flows 443

Income Tax Effects 445

Other Models for Analyzing Long-Range Decisions 452

Performance Evaluation 454

Appendix 11: Capital Budgeting and Inflation 457

Accounting Vocabulary 459 • Fundamental Assignment Material 460 • Additional Assignment Material 462

PART 4   Product Costing

Chapter 12   Cost Allocation 480

L.A. Darling 480

A General Framework for Cost Allocation 481

Allocation of Service Department Costs 483

Allocation of Costs to Product or Service Cost Objects 490

An ABC Approach 495

Allocation of Costs to Customer Cost Objects to Determine Customer Profitability 498

Allocation of Central Corporate Support Costs 506

Allocation of Joint Costs and By-Product Costs 507

Accounting Vocabulary 510 • Fundamental Assignment Material 510 • Additional Assignment Material 513

Chapter 13   Accounting for Overhead Costs 532

DELL 532

Accounting for Factory Overhead 533

Illustration of Overhead Application 534

Problems of Overhead Application 536

Variable Versus Absorption Costing 539

Fixed Overhead and Absorption Costs of Product 544

Effect of Other Variances 548

Appendix 13: Comparisons of Production-Volume Variance with Other Variances 552

Accounting Vocabulary 554 • Fundamental Assignment Material 554 • Additional Assignment Material 557

Chapter 14   Job-Order Costing and Process-Costing Systems 576

Jelly Belly 576

Distinction Between Job-Order Costing and Process Costing 577

Illustration of Job Costing 577

Activity-Based Costing/Management in a Job-Costing Environment 582

Job Costing in Service and Nonprofit Organizations 585

Process Costing Basics 586

Application of Process Costing 591

Physical Units and Equivalent Units (Steps 1 and 2) 591

Calculation of Product Costs (Steps 3 to 5) 592

Effects of Beginning Inventories: Weighted-Average Method 594

Transferred-In Costs 595

Costing in a JIT System: Backflush Costing 598

Accounting Vocabulary 601 • Fundamental Assignment Material 601 • Additional Assignment Material 604

PART 5   Basic Financial Accounting

Chapter 15   Basic Accounting: Concepts, Techniques, and Conventions 618

General Mills 618

The Need for Accounting 619

Financial Statements—Balance Sheet and Income Statement 619

Accrual Basis and Cash Basis   624

Adjustments to the Accounts   625

Adjustment Type I: Expiration of Unexpired Costs   625

Adjustment Type II: Recognition (Earning) of Unearned Revenues   629

Adjustment Type III: Accrual of Unrecorded Expenses   629

Adjustment Type IV: Accrual of Unrecorded Revenues   631

Dividends and Retained Earnings   632

Preparing Financial Statements   633

Sole Proprietorships and Partnerships   634

Generally Accepted Accounting Principles   635

Three Measurement Principles   638

Appendix 15A: Additional Accounting Concepts   641

Appendix 15B: Using Ledger Accounts   643

Accounting Vocabulary   646   • Fundamental Assignment Material   647   • Additional
Assignment Material   649

Chapter 16   Understanding Corporate Annual Reports: Basic Financial Statements   660

NIKE   660

Classified Balance Sheet   661

Income Statement   669

Statement of Changes in Stockholders' Equity   671

Statement of Cash Flows   674

Cash Flow from Operating Activities   680

Interpreting the Cash Flow Statement   685

Annual Reports   687

Appendix 16A: Accounting for Inventory   691

Appendix 16B: Shareholder Reporting, Income Tax Reporting, and
Deferred Taxes   696

Accounting Vocabulary   698   • Fundamental Assignment Material   698   • Additional
Assignment Material   701

Chapter 17   Understanding and Analyzing Consolidated Financial Statements   716

Berkshire Hathaway   716

Part One: Intercorporate Investments Including Consolidations   717

Market-Value and Equity Methods   717

Consolidated Financial Statements   719

Recognizing Income after Acquisition   720

Part Two: Analysis of Financial Statements   728

Component Percentages 730

Uses of Ratios 731

Efficient Markets and Investor Decisions 735

Accounting Vocabulary 738 • Fundamental Assignment Material 738 • Additional
Assignment Material 743

Appendix A: *Recommended Readings A1*
    Periodicals A1
    Books in Management Accounting A1
    Online Resources A4

Appendix B: *Fundamentals of Compound Interest and the Use of Present-
Value Tables A5*
    The Nature of Interest A5

Appendix C: *Excerpts from Form 10-K of NIKE, Inc. A11*
    Part 1 A11
    **Management's Annual Report on Internal Control Over Financial
Reporting A37**
    Report on Independent Registered Public Accounting Firm A37
    NIKE, Inc., Notes to Consolidated Financial Statements A44

Glossary G1
Subject Index I1
Company Index I11

Preface

Now more than ever, managers have to understand how their decisions affect costs.

Management accounting is an essential tool that enhances a manager's ability to make effective economic decisions. Because understanding concepts is more important than memorizing techniques, *Introduction to Management Accounting*, 16th edition, describes both theory and practice so students understand how to produce and apply information that's useful in day-to-day decision making. From the first chapter, we encourage students to think about the advantages and disadvantages of various techniques, not to simply memorize and apply the techniques.

Introduction to Management Accounting, 16th edition, deals with all business sectors—nonprofit, retail, wholesale, service, selling, and administrative situations—as well as manufacturing. The focus is on planning and control decisions, not on product costing for inventory valuation and income determination.

Our Philosophy

Introduce concepts and principles early, then revisit them at more complex levels as students gain understanding, and provide appropriate real-company examples at every stage.

In management accounting courses students learn how managers use accounting information to help make better business decisions. They begin their understanding of managerial decisions by asking, "How will my decisions affect the costs and revenues of the organization?" Students then progress to more complex questions: "What is the most appropriate cost-management system for the company?" "What products or services should we emphasize?" "What do our budget variances mean?" Introduction to Management Accounting presents the most basic cost concepts in chapters 1–6 and adds more complex analyses that build on these concepts in the remaining chapters.

Our goals are to choose relevant subject matter and to present it clearly and accessibly, using many examples drawn from actual companies. Examples from companies, such as Starbucks, Boeing, AT&T, McDonald's, Microsoft, and more, help students understand management accounting concepts in a real-company context.

Introduction to Financial Accounting, 11th edition, and *Introduction to Management Accounting*, 16th edition, together provide a seamless presentation for any first-year accounting course. Please contact your Pearson representative about cost-saving discounts when adopting both books.

New Edition Enhancements and Updates

The authors have made changes to both update the topic coverage and to add clarity to the discussion of various topics. Some noteworthy changes include the following:

- **New and revised "Business First" boxes** provide insights into operations at well-known organizations, including Microsoft, General Electric, Southwest Airlines, Harley-Davidson, Nortel Networks, and Harvard University.
- **New and revised chapter-opening vignettes** help students understand accounting's role in current business practice. We revisit the chapter-opening company throughout the chapter so that students can see how accounting influences managers in real companies. Students will recognize many of the companies, such as Starbucks, Boeing, US Airways, McDonald's, Nike, and Dell.
- **A problem** in each chapter based on Nike's SEC Form 10-K. These problems illustrate how publicly available information can lead to insights about a company, its costs, and its management decisions.

- **Increased coverage of ethics**, including an ethics problem in each chapter's assignment material.
- **End-of-chapter material** includes new and significantly revised exercises and problems to provide fresh, new examples.

Chapter-Specific Updates

Chapter 1 emphasizes the importance of accounting information for decision makers and the role of accounting systems in control. The chapter continues to emphasize the importance of ethics in business, with a section devoted to "Ethical Conduct for Professional Accountants." We shortened the discussion of entry-level careers in accounting and expanded the discussion of trends in management accounting.

Chapter 2 is a major update in the 16th edition. The discussion of mixed-cost and step-cost behavior has been moved up to this chapter, immediately following the discussion of fixed- and variable-cost behavior. Also, degree of operating leverage is defined and illustrated with an example.

Chapter 3 has been reorganized and provides a more focused discussion of cost behavior and cost estimation, as well as an enhanced examination of regression analysis.

Chapter 4 uses Dell as the primary example throughout the chapter, and in this edition we discuss Dell's strategic decision to shift their product mix away from consumer sales and toward enterprise solutions and services. We describe how cost management systems at Dell support strategic decisions as well as operational control. The discussion of cost categories and cost terminology has been rewritten and refined.

In **Chapter 5** we enhanced the pricing focus of the chapter, and further refined our discussion of the accounting formats that aid in such decision making, namely the absorption versus contribution margin approaches. We compare and contrast these two approaches throughout the chapter.

Chapter 6 has been edited to enhance operating decisions and the incremental analysis framework. The decision-making focus was further emphasized and related examples and problems were revised and updated.

Chapter 7 emphasizes the importance of budgets for both planning and control. The second half of the chapter illustrates the details of preparing a budget using the Cooking Hut example used in previous editions.

Chapter 8 has been reorganized to develop variance concepts in smaller steps. Basic variance concepts and terminology are introduced at the beginning of the chapter. The example introduced at the beginning of the chapter is first used to illustrate the static-budget variances for income. Then the static-budget variance is analyzed as the sum of activity-level and flexible-budget variances. Then, income variances are analyzed as more detailed revenue and cost variances. Finally, flexible-budget variances are divided into price and quantity variances (for materials and labor) or spending and efficiency variances (for variable overhead).

Chapter 9 includes multiple examples of performance evaluation and incentive issues for service organizations such as health-care organizations and hotels. We use the balance scorecard as an integrated framework to consider both financial and nonfinancial performance measures. The penultimate section of the chapter outlines issues of designing and implementing management control systems for service and nonprofit organizations.

In **Chapter 10**, learning objectives 4 and 5 have been revised, where objective 5 now focuses on the incentives created by alternative performance measures. We also revised the discussion of alternative measures of performance and profitability.

Chapter 11 includes a detailed, step-by-step example of calculation of net present value (NPV). The discussion of the internal rate of return formulation and its relation to the NPV formulation has also been expanded, though the chapter continues to primarily focus on the NPV model. The discussion of tax effects has also been further clarified.

Chapter 12 includes extensive revisions for clarity throughout the chapter. The general guidelines for allocating service department costs have been revised and condensed and the section showing how to apply the guidelines has been reorganized. The steps in ABC cost allocation were reduced from 4 to 3 and their description extensively revised. Finally, the discussion of which department to allocate first in step-down allocations moved from a footnote to the text.

Chapter 13 includes an enhanced discussion of overhead cost allocation and disposition of overhead variances. The complex discussion of variances was clarified as were the related problems and examples.

Chapter 14 has been revised to clarify the discussion throughout the chapter, especially regarding job-order costing and process costing. These two systems are explained in more detail and are compared and contrasted in a more meaningful way.

Chapter 15 includes updates to the General Mills examples throughout the chapters as well as to the Business First box on corporate citizenship awards. Revisions for clarity include an expanded discussion of accrued revenues and accrued expenses, a major revision of the presentation of the first 7 transactions of King Hardware, an added balance sheet after transaction 2 to show how a balance sheet changes with each transaction, and a revision of the section on non-profit organizations.

In Chapter 16, in addition to updating the Nike examples throughout, there is a revised discussion of goodwill, an expanded coverage of diluted EPS, and coverage of the FASB/IASB proposal that would mandate the direct method for the cash flow statement.

Chapter 17 includes a new learning objective on using financial statement analysis, a new section showing how income statements and balance sheets show noncontrolling interests, and a new line in all consolidation tables to clarify the totals before eliminating entries. Finally, we have updated all financial statement references throughout.

Supplements for Instructors and Students

INSTRUCTOR'S RESOURCE MANUAL Substantially revised, this resource manual provides insightful and useful tips on how to best manage course content when using *Introduction to Management Accounting*, 16th edition, in class. Chapter-by-chapter explanations and pedagogical philosophies are clearly delineated and oriented to greatly aid the teaching process.

SOLUTIONS MANUAL Comprehensive solutions, prepared by the authors, are provided for all end-of-chapter material. The Solutions Manual includes a listing of problems covering each learning objective, sample assignment schedules, a linking of 15th edition problems to those in this edition, comments on choices of problems in each chapter, and key amounts from suggested solutions to selected problems.

TEST ITEM FILE This is a ready-to-use bank of testing material that contains, for each chapter, a variety of types of questions, including true/false, multiple-choice, and critical thinking problems. For ease of use, each question is linked to chapter objectives and also provides a suggested difficulty level and references to text pages where answers can be found.

TESTGEN This testing software is designed to aid in creating custom tests in minutes. Features include question randomization, a point-and-drag interface, and extensive customizable settings.

POWERPOINT PRESENTATION Complete PowerPoint presentations are provided for each chapter. Instructors may download and use each presentation as is or customize the slides. Each presentation allows instructors to offer an interactive presentation using colorful graphics, outlines of chapter material, and graphical explanations of difficult topics. This is available online at http://www.pearsonhighered.com/horngren.

COURSE WEB SITE AT HTTP://WWW.PEARSONHIGHERED.COM/HORNGREN This complete online resource offers a variety of Internet-based teaching and learning support. It provides a wealth of resources for students and faculty, including Excel spreadsheet templates.

MyAccountingLab MyAccountingLab provides students with a personalized interactive learning environment where they can learn at their own pace and measure their progress.

HALLMARK FEATURES

- **Personalized help** is available on MyAccountingLab whenever students need it with the interactive "Help Me Solve This" tool. This tool automatically generates algorithmic versions of a particular problem and provides step-by-step assistance until the solution is obtained.
- **Dynamic learning resources** found in MyAccountingLab cater to students' individual learning styles. All Learning Aids can be turned off by the instructor.
- **A personalized Study Plan**, for self-paced learning, links students directly to MyAccountingLab's interactive tutorial exercises on the topics they have yet to master.

NEW FEATURES FOR 2012

- **Excel Integration**. MyAccountingLab now allows students to work through end-of-chapter or quiz problems in an Excel simulated environment. Their work is then automatically scored and reported to the MyAccountingLab Gradebook.
- **Open-response Questions**.

Acknowledgments

We have received ideas, assistance, miscellaneous critiques, and assorted assignment material in conversations with and by mail from many students, professors, and business leaders. Each has our gratitude, but the list is too long to enumerate here. We wish to thank the following reviewers whose feedback was helpful in this and previous editions:

Jim Carroll, Georgian Court University
James Chiafery, University of Massachusetts Boston
Constance J. Crawford, MBA, CPA, Ramapo College of New Jersey
William Creel, Herzing College
Stan Davis, Indiana University – Purdue University Fort Wayne
Chris Gilbert, Glendale Community College
Valerie Goodwin, Olean Business Institute
Lawrence Grasso, Central Connecticut State University
Henry Huang, Butler University
Agatha Jeffers, Montclair State University
Cody King, Georgia Southwestern State University
Roman J. Klusas, University of Indianapolis
Chuo-Hsuan (Jason) Lee, Plattsburgh State University of New York
Lisa Martin, Hampton College
Maureen Mascha, Marquette University
Jerold R. Miller, Chaparral College
David Mona, Champlain College
Julian Mooney, Georgia Southern University
Behnaz Quigley, Marymount University
Bill Rankin, Colorado State University
Patrick Rogan, Cosumnes River College
Walter Smith, Siena College
Ken Snow, Kaplan University & Florida Community College at Jacksonville
John Stancil, Florida Southern College
Vic Stanton, Stanford Graduate School of Business
Holly Sudano, Florida State University
Diane Tanner, University of North Florida
Geoffrey Tickell, Indiana University of Pennsylvania
Michael Tyler, Barry University
Karen Wisniewski, County College of Morris

Students in our classes have provided invaluable feedback on previous editions, for which we are grateful.

Many people at Pearson also earn our deepest thanks for their thoughtful contributions, including Stephanie Wall, Ellen Geary, Nicole Sam, Jane Avery, Lauren Zanedis, Roberta Sherman, Anthony Gemmellaro, James Bateman, and Carol Melville.

Finally, the authors greatly appreciate the contributions that Bill Stratton made to the development of the book over many years.

Charles T. Horngren
Gary L. Sundem
David Burgstahler
Jeff Schatzberg

Introduction to

MANAGEMENT
ACCOUNTING

1

Managerial Accounting, the Business Organization, and Professional Ethics

LEARNING OBJECTIVES

When you have finished studying this chapter, you should be able to:

1. Explain why accounting is essential for decision makers and managers.

2. Describe the major users and uses of accounting information.

3. Explain the role of budgets and performance reports in planning and control.

4. Describe the cost-benefit and behavioral issues involved in designing an accounting system.

5. Discuss the role accountants play in the company's value-chain functions.

6. Identify current trends in management accounting.

7. Explain why ethics and standards of ethical conduct are important to accountants.

▶ STARBUCKS

If you had asked most people a decade or two ago whether consumers around the world would pay a premium price for a "better" cup of coffee, few would have answered yes. Nevertheless, the expansion of Starbucks since its founding in 1971 in Seattle's Pike Place Market has been nothing short of phenomenal. In 2011, Starbucks' total revenues—the amount the company received for all items sold— were $11.7 billion, compared with only $700 million in 1996. Net income—the profit that Starbucks made—was $1.7 billion, up from only $42 million in 1996. Total assets—the recorded value of the items owned by Starbucks—grew from less than $900 million in 1996 to more than $7.3 billion in 2011. These numbers are accounting measures of the cumulative success of numerous managers of Starbucks stores in many countries. Managers use these figures, along with more detailed accounting numbers, to make day-to-day decisions and to measure performance.

Starbucks has established a worldwide reputation to match its financial success. Interbrand ranked Starbucks among the 100 best global brands for 2011. Starbucks ranked seventy-third on *Fortune* magazine's "100 Best Companies to Work For." *Corporate Responsibility* magazine placed it thirty-ninth in its list of "100 Best Corporate Citizens." Finally, in 2011 *Fortune* named Starbucks the sixteenth most admired company in the world and named founder and CEO Howard Schultz the businessperson of the year.

How did Starbucks accomplish all this? As we embark on our journey into the world of management accounting, we will explore what it takes for a company such as Starbucks to ensure that when Mei-Hwa Zhang walks into a Starbucks in Beijing, she has much the same quality experience as Mohammad Kumar does in a Starbucks in Kuwait or Franz Mueller does in Zurich. All Starbucks' managers, from baristas to store managers to the chief executive officer, use accounting reports to assess how well their units meet corporate goals and objectives. Accounting provides a common language to help managers around the world communicate and coordinate their actions. By the time you finish reading this book, you will be comfortable with the language of accounting. You will know why it is necessary to understand accounting information in order to use it wisely in your decisions. You will also understand the role of performance evaluation systems in communicating strategy and coordinating actions throughout an organization.

Managerial accounting information is used in all sorts of decisions. For example, consider decisions you might face as a manager in the following situations:

- Suppose you are a Boeing engineer preparing manufacturing specifications for a component of its new 787 Dreamliner airplane. There are three possible ways to organize the assembly of the component. Which is the most cost-effective approach?
- Suppose you are a product manager at General Mills and you are designing a new marketing plan for Cheerios. Market research predicts that distributing free samples in the mail will increase annual sales by 4%. Will profits from the added sales be more than the cost of producing and distributing the free samples?
- Bank of America offers free checking to customers with no minimum balance requirement in their MyAccess™ checking account. How much does it cost the bank to provide this free service?
- Kitsap County Special Olympics holds a series of athletic events for disabled youth. As executive director, you must set a goal for the group's annual fund drive based on the estimated cost to support its planned activities.
- Madison Park Cafe currently is open only for dinner, but the owner is considering opening for lunch. The average lunch is priced at about $15, and the café expects to serve about 40 lunches per day. Can the chef produce a luncheon menu that meets the café's quality standards at an average cost that yields a reasonable profit?
- Amazon.com offers free 2-day shipping on all orders for subscribers that pay a single $79 annual fee. Does the fee plus the profits from increased sales to subscribers exceed the cost of providing free shipping?

For all these decisions, managers rely on managerial accounting information.

In this chapter, we provide an overview of management accounting in all types of organizations. Larry White, former chair of the **Institute of Management Accountants (IMA)**, the largest U.S. professional organization focused on internal accounting, sums up the role of management accounting as follows: "Management accountants are committed to helping their organization achieve its strategic goals by providing decision support, planning, and control for business operations with a high level of ethics and professional competence." ■

© Richard Ellis/ZUMA Wire Service/Newscom

Starbucks' coffee shops have strategic locations throughout the world, including this one in Beijing.

Institute of Management Accountants (IMA)
The largest U.S. professional organization of accountants focused on internal accounting.

management accounting
The branch of accounting that produces information for managers within an organization. It is the process of identifying, measuring, accumulating, analyzing, preparing, interpreting, and communicating information that helps managers fulfill organizational objectives.

Management Accounting and Your Career

In this book we focus on **management accounting**, which is the process of identifying, measuring, accumulating, analyzing, preparing, interpreting, and communicating information that helps managers fulfill organizational objectives. In contrast, **financial accounting** produces information for external parties, such as stockholders, suppliers, banks, and government regulatory agencies. Exhibit 1-1 summarizes the major differences between management accounting and financial accounting.

This book is written primarily for managers who are not accounting specialists. All managers use information from accounting systems. By learning about accounting systems, you will better understand the relationships among different components of an organization. You also learn why it is essential to understand the system that generates accounting information in order to use that information in any of a wide variety of functional decisions (including purchasing, manufacturing, inventory management, hiring, marketing, and pricing, among others). You will learn to evaluate whether your accounting system is providing the information you need for your decisions. You will learn to evaluate performance measures generated by your accounting system and assess whether the performance measures create appropriate incentives. In sum, a thorough understanding of accounting is essential for managers in any organization.

When accounting is mentioned, most people think first of financial accounting. Independent auditors—**certified public accountants (CPAs)** in the United States and **chartered accountants (CAs)** in many other nations—provide assurance to external users about the reliability of companies'

financial accounting
The branch of accounting that develops information for external decision makers, such as stockholders, suppliers, banks, and government regulatory agencies.

certified public accountant (CPA)
In the United States, independent accountants who assure the reliability of companies' published financial statements.

	Management Accounting	Financial Accounting
Primary users	Organization managers at various levels	Outside parties such as investors and government agencies but also organization managers
Freedom of choice of accounting measures	No constraints other than requiring the benefits of improved management decisions to exceed information costs	Constrained by generally accepted accounting principles (GAAP)
Behavioral implications in selecting accounting measures	Choice should consider how measurements and reports will influence managers' daily behavior	Choice based on how to measure and communicate economic phenomena; behavioral considerations are secondary, although executive compensation based on reported results may have behavioral impacts
Time focus of reports	Future orientation: formal use of budgets as well as historical records. Example: 20X2 budget versus 20X2 actual performance	Past orientation: historical evaluation; example: 20X2 actual performance versus 20X1 actual performance
Time span of reports	Flexible, varying from hourly to 10–15 years	Less flexible; usually one year or one quarter
Types of reports	Detailed reports include details about products, departments, territories, etc.	Summary reports: primarily report on the entity as a whole
Influence of other functional areas	Field is less sharply defined; heavier use of economics, decision sciences, and behavioral sciences	Field is more sharply defined; lighter use of related disciplines

Exhibit 1-1
Distinctions Between Management Accounting and Financial Accounting

chartered accountant (CA)
In many countries, the equivalent to the CPA in the United States—independent accountants who assure the reliability of companies' financial statements.

certified management accountant (CMA)
The management accountant's counterpart to the CPA.

published financial statements. Another, even larger, group of people work in private industry and government as management accounting specialists. Though management accountants often help to produce financial statements for external users, they primarily produce accounting information for internal users. The **certified management accountant (CMA)** designation is the management accountant's counterpart to the CPA. The Institute of Management Accountants (IMA) oversees the CMA program. CMAs must pass an examination covering (1) financial planning, performance, and control, and (2) financial decision making.[1] Like the CPA designation, the CMA confers status and often opens the door to higher-level positions. A survey by *Financial Executive* magazine showed that 33% of CEOs in companies with revenues greater than $500 million had risen through the finance/accounting ranks, compared with 26% from operations and 21% from sales and marketing.

Roles of Accounting Information

One basic purpose of accounting information is to help you make decisions. Every day, you and your organization face a new and continually changing set of decisions, and many of these decisions rely on accounting information. When you understand how your decisions affect costs and revenues, you will be a better decision maker.

A second basic purpose of accounting is to help you plan and control your organization's operations. Plans describe how the organization will achieve its objectives. Control is the process of implementing plans and evaluating whether your organization is achieving its objectives. When you understand how people respond to the incentives created by performance evaluation and control systems, you will be better able to assess which system creates the most appropriate incentives.

Objective 2

Describe the major users and uses of accounting information.

[1]For information about the IMA and the CMA exam, see www.imanet.org.

Organizations address these two purposes by designing and implementing **accounting systems**, which are formal mechanisms for gathering, organizing, and communication information about an organization's activities. The organization of this book reflects how accounting systems address these two basic purposes. Part 1, Chapters 2 through 6, focuses on the decision-making purpose of accounting information. These chapters help you determine what costs are relevant for different decisions and how accounting systems generate relevant costs for managers, demonstrating a key concept in management accounting: "Different costs for different purposes." Part 2, Chapters 7 through 10, deals with planning and control systems. These chapters show how measuring performance affects managers' incentives, leading to a second key concept: "You get what you measure." Parts 3 and 4 explore these concepts in still more depth, as Part 3, Chapter 11, focuses on relevant costs for long-term capital investment decisions and Part 4, Chapters 12 through 14, describes systems to generate detailed product costing information.

accounting system
A formal mechanism for gathering, organizing, and communicating information about an organization's activities.

As you progress in your study of management accounting and in your career, you move from understanding how to use information from existing accounting systems to creating systems that produce information useful to your particular decisions. Early in your studies, you initially react to the systems that are described to you, making sure that you understand how each system works and how to use the information it produces in your decisions. Early in your career, you may have little opportunity to influence the management accounting system, and your initial goal is simply to understand and use the information from the accounting system. As you advance in your studies, you learn about increasingly complex systems designed to provide information for a variety of purposes. As you learn about specific alternatives, you also develop the ability to design new alternatives that provide better information for your decision-making and performance evaluation purposes. Finally, you develop the proficiency and understanding required to evaluate the relative advantages of alternative accounting systems. You will likely see a parallel progression in the use of management accounting in your career. As you advance, you are able to suggest changes to improve the existing systems, and eventually you may be in a position to influence the systems implemented by your organization. The more you can influence management accounting systems, the more important it is to understand their role.

Information for Decision Making and Planning and Control

What types of accounting information do managers need for decision making and performance evaluation and control? For **decision making**—choosing among alternative courses of action to achieve some objective—accounting information helps answer problem-solving questions. For performance evaluation and control, accounting helps answer scorecard and attention-directing questions:

decision making
Choosing among alternative courses of action designed to achieve some objective.

1. Scorecard questions: Is the company doing well or poorly? **Scorekeeping** is the accumulation, classification, and reporting of data that help users understand and evaluate organizational performance. Scorekeeping information must be accurate and reliable to be useful. For example, Starbucks produces numerous reports to evaluate results for stores and divisions.
2. Attention-directing questions: Which areas require additional investigation? **Attention directing** involves reporting and interpreting information that helps managers to focus on operating problems, imperfections, inefficiencies, and opportunities. For example, a manager who sees that a Starbucks store has reported profits of $120,000 when budgeted profit was $150,000 will look for explanations as to why the store did not achieve its budget.
3. Problem-solving questions: Of the alternatives being considered, which is the best? The **problem-solving** aspect of accounting involves analysis of alternative courses of action and identification of the best course to follow. For example, Starbucks experiments with adding various items to its menu. After an analysis of how a new product will affect revenues and costs, management decides which items to add and which to delete.

scorekeeping
The accumulation, classification, and reporting of data that help users understand and evaluate performance.

attention directing
Reporting and interpreting information that helps managers to focus on operating problems, imperfections, inefficiencies, and opportunities.

problem solving
Analysis of possible courses of action and identification of the best course to follow.

The scorecard and attention-directing uses of information are closely related. The same information that helps a manager understand and evaluate performance may also serve an attention-directing function for the manager's superior. For example, by pinpointing where actual results differ from plans, performance reports show managers how they are doing and where to take action. Companies produce most scorecard and attention-directing information on a routine basis every day, month, quarter, or year.

In contrast, specific decisions often require problem-solving information beyond the information routinely generated for scorekeeping and attention directing. When organizations make decisions (such as how to price products and special orders, whether to make or to buy components, whether to add or drop a product, how to adjust product mix, or whether to keep or replace equipment), specially-prepared information is often required. For example, Starbucks uses problem-solving information when deciding whether to run ads during the Super Bowl™ broadcast.

Decision making is the core of the management process. Decisions range from the routine (setting daily production schedules) to the non-routine (launching a new product line), and accountants are information specialists who aid the decision makers. Managers use accounting information for all types of decisions. Accountants must make sure that they produce information that is useful for these decisions and managers must work with accountants to get the information that is needed.

Making Managerial Decisions

What type of information—scorekeeping, attention-directing, or problem-solving—would managers use for each of the following decisions? Why?

1. Deciding whether to replace a traditional assembly line with a fully automated robotic process
2. Evaluating the performance of a division for the preceding year
3. Identifying which products exceeded their budgeted profitability and which ones fell short of their budgets

Answers

1. Problem-solving. This is a one-time decision for which managers need information about the potential impacts of each of the alternatives under consideration.
2. Scorekeeping. This is a routine evaluation of an organizational unit for which managers want systematic data on a regular basis.
3. Attention-directing. To identify products that need attention, managers want information that highlights deviations of actual results from pre-specified expectations in the budget.

planning
Setting objectives for an organization and determining how to attain them.

control
Implementing plans and using feedback to evaluate the attainment of objectives.

Another essential element of the management process is planning and controlling the organization's operations. **Planning** provides the answers to two questions: What objectives does the organization want to achieve? When and how will the organization achieve these objectives? **Control** refers to implementing plans and using feedback to evaluate the attainment of objectives. Thus, feedback is crucial to the cycle of planning and control. Planning determines action, action generates feedback, and the control phase uses this feedback to influence further planning and actions. Timely, systematic reports provided by the accounting system are a primary source of useful feedback.

The left side of Exhibit 1-2 demonstrates the planning and control cycle of current operations that could be used by a particular Starbucks store. The planning section in Exhibit 1-2 shows an objective for the store (increase profitability) and how it will be attained (product growth and improved marketing). The control section shows the actions that are intended to increase profitability and how Starbucks will evaluate the actions. The Starbucks store will implement its plan to expand the number of drinks on its menu and increase advertising. Management will evaluate these actions based on three performance measures, the increase in drinks sold, increase in advertising expenditures, and the increase in revenue. Managers will then use the performance evaluation results for further planning and implementation.

Management by Exception

Objective 3

Explain the role of budgets and performance reports in planning and control.

The right side of Exhibit 1-2 shows that the accounting system formalizes plans by expressing them as budgets. A **budget** is a quantitative expression of a plan of action and an aid to coordinating and implementing plans. Budgets are the chief devices for disciplining management planning. Without budgets, planning may not get the front-and-center focus that it deserves. The Starbucks store expresses its plan for product growth and improved marketing through revenue and advertising budgets.

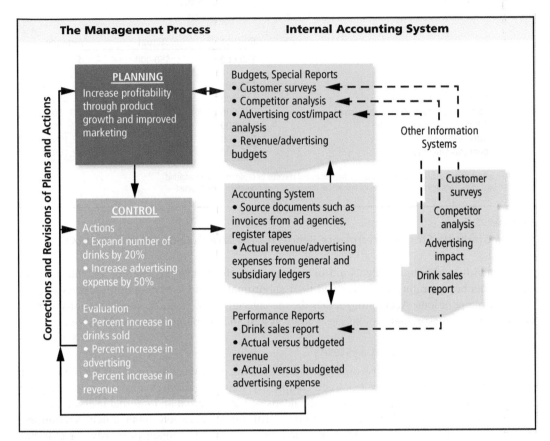

The accounting system records, measures, and classifies actions to produce performance reports (the last box in Exhibit 1-2). **Performance reports** provide feedback by comparing results with plans and by highlighting **variances**, which are deviations from plans. Organizations use performance reports to judge managers' decisions and the productivity of organizational units. Performance reports compare actual results to budgets, thereby motivating managers to achieve the objectives. For example, managers of the Starbucks store evaluate the effectiveness of its advertising plan by comparing the increase in revenue and profits to the increase in advertising costs. Based on their evaluation, managers at Starbucks make corrections and revisions to their plans.

Exhibit 1-3 shows a simple performance report for a hypothetical Starbucks store, the Mayfair Starbucks. The first column of Exhibit 1-3 is the budget for March 20X1. It is based on a predicted level of sales and the estimated costs needed to support that level of sales. After managers and their superiors agree on a budget, it becomes the managers' target for the month. As the store sells its products and incurs costs, Starbucks' accounting system collects the revenue and cost information. At the end of each month (or more often if managers need more frequent feedback), the accounting department prepares a store-level performance report, such as the one in Exhibit 1-3. Managers use the performance report to help evaluate the store's operations.

The Mayfair store report shows that the store met its targeted sales, but the $2,500 unfavorable variance for ingredients shows that these costs were $2,500 over budget. Other variances show that store labor costs were $400 under budget and other labor was $50 over budget. At the Mayfair store, management would undoubtedly focus attention on ingredients, which had by far the largest unfavorable variance. However, it may also be worthwhile to investigate the $400 favorable labor variance. By investigating favorable variances, managers may find better ways of doing things.

Performance reports spur investigation of exceptions—items for which actual amounts differ significantly from budgeted amounts. Managers then revise operations to conform with the plans or revise the plans. This process is **management by exception**, which means concentrating more on areas that deviate from the plan and less on areas that conform with plans. Thus, the management-by-exception approach frees managers from needless concern with those phases of operations that adhere to plans and are running smoothly. However, well-conceived plans incorporate enough discretion or flexibility so that the manager feels free to pursue any unforeseen opportunities.

budget
A quantitative expression of a plan of action and an aid to coordinating and implementing the plan.

performance reports
Feedback provided by comparing results with plans and by highlighting variances.

variances
Deviations from plans.

management by exception
Concentrating more on areas that deviate from the plan and less on areas that conform with plans and are presumed to be running smoothly.

	Budget	Actual	Variance
Sales	$50,000	$50,000	$ 0
Less:			
Ingredients	$22,000	$24,500	$2,500 U
Store labor (baristas, etc.)	12,000	11,600	400 F
Other labor (managers, supervisors)	6,000	6,050	50 U
Utilities, maintenance, etc.	4,500	4,500	0
Total expenses	$44,500	$46,650	$2,150 U
Total operating income	$ 5,500	$ 3,350	$2,150 U

U = unfavorable—actual cost greater than budgeted; actual revenue or profit less than budgeted
F = favorable—actual cost less than budgeted; actual revenue or profit greater than budgeted

Exhibit 1-3
Mayfair Starbucks Store—Performance Report for the Month Ended March 31, 20X1

Notice that although budgets aid planning and performance reports aid control, it is not accountants but operating managers and their subordinates who use accounting reports to plan and control operations. Accounting assists the managerial planning and control functions by providing prompt measurements of actions and by systematically pinpointing trouble spots.

Influences on Accounting Systems

generally accepted accounting principles (GAAP)
A set of standards to which public companies' published financial statements must adhere.

Accounting systems vary across organizations—systems must meet the needs of each particular organization. In order to reduce costs and complexity, many organizations use a general-purpose accounting system that attempts to meet the needs of both external and internal users. However, as outlined in Exhibit 1-1, there are important differences between management accounting information and financial accounting information. Systems developed primarily for external reporting may not produce the most useful information for managers.

There are three categories of requirements imposed on accounting systems designed to meet the requirements of external users. First, public companies' financial reports for external users must adhere to a set of standards known as **generally accepted accounting principles (GAAP)** as determined by the Financial Accounting Standards Board (FASB) in the United States and the International Accounting Standards Board (IASB) in most of the rest of the world. Second, every company is also subject to various taxes, and therefore subject to various reporting requirements specified by tax rules and regulations. Third, many companies are subject to other government regulations.

Sarbanes-Oxley Act
A 2002 law that requires top-management oversight of a company's accounting policies and procedures.

There are many other governmental regulations that influence accounting systems. For example, in 2002 the **Sarbanes-Oxley Act** added several levels of regulation in the United States. Driven by corporate bankruptcies blamed in part on accounting lapses (as well as deficiencies in corporate governance, lax securities regulation, and executive greed), the act requires more top-management oversight of a company's accounting policies and procedures. By requiring chief executive officers to sign a statement certifying the accuracy of the company's financial statements, the act makes accounting numbers the concern of all managers, not just the accountants. Sarbanes-Oxley requires external auditors to examine and prepare a separate report on a company's system of **internal controls**—policies to protect and make the most efficient use of an organization's assets.

internal controls
Policies to protect and make the most efficient use of an organization's assets.

Foreign Corrupt Practices Act
A U.S. law forbidding bribery and other corrupt practices. The law also requires all publicly held companies to maintain their accounting records in reasonable detail and accuracy and have an appropriate system of internal controls.

Another example of broad regulation is the **Foreign Corrupt Practices Act**, a U.S. law forbidding bribery and other corrupt practices but also requiring companies to maintain reasonably detailed accounting records and to have an appropriate system of internal controls. The word *Foreign* in the title is somewhat misleading because the act's provisions apply to all publicly held companies, even if they do not conduct business outside the United States. This law requires that companies maintain their accounting records in reasonable detail and accuracy. Most companies have **internal auditors** who review and evaluate accounting systems, including companies' internal controls, and conduct **management audits**—reviews to determine whether managers are implementing the policies and procedures specified by top management. A final specific area of regulation is government contracting. Universities, defense contractors, and others contracting with the U.S. government must comply with numerous reporting requirements.

internal auditors
Accountants who review and evaluate accounting systems, including their internal controls.

management audit
A review to determine whether managers are implementing the policies and procedures specified by top management.

The requirements of external reporting should not take precedence over the scorekeeping, attention-directing, and problem-solving information that is generated to meet the needs of internal users. In later chapters, we will see many examples where a general-purpose accounting system designed to meet external reporting requirements does not generate the information needed for management decisions. As a decision-maker, you must recognize when information from the existing accounting system is not sufficient for your decision and be prepared to ask for additional information to be generated. Your requests for more information should be balanced against the cost of obtaining the information. As explained in the following section, you should only incur the cost to acquire additional information when the expected benefit of an improved decision exceeds the cost of the information.

Cost-Benefit and Behavioral Considerations

Managers should keep two important ideas in mind when designing accounting systems: (1) the cost-benefit balance and (2) behavioral implications.

The **cost-benefit balance**—weighing estimated costs against probable benefits—is the primary consideration in choosing among accounting systems and methods. We will refer again and again to cost-benefit considerations throughout this book. Accounting systems are economic goods—like office supplies or labor—available at various costs. Which system does a manager want to buy: a simple file drawer for amassing receipts and canceled checks, an elaborate budgeting system based on computerized models of the organization and its subunits, or something in between?

The answer depends on a straightforward concept that often becomes complex when applied to real decisions. The concept is that the manager should purchase the system that provides the largest excess of benefits over cost. Real-world applications of this concept are often complex because the expected benefits are difficult to assess. For example, consider a manager at University Clinic who is considering installing a HorizonMIS®-computerized system from American Medical Systems of Ohio for managing a medical practice. With this system, users enter a piece of information only once and the system automatically integrates it with billing, insurance claims, and patient history records. Such a system is efficient and is subject to few errors, but should it be purchased? The expected benefits from the new system come from improved decisions or better controls, and it can be very difficult to develop a comprehensive assessment of these benefits, a point that will be illustrated repeatedly in later chapters.

Management accounting reports influence the decisions of managers. The system must provide accurate, timely reports in a form useful to managers. If a report is too complex, too difficult to use, or arrives too late, the manager may not use the report in making decisions. A report that goes unused creates no benefits.

Managers should also consider **behavioral implications**, that is, the system's effect on employees' decisions and behavior. For example, consider a performance report that a manager's superiors use to evaluate the operations for which the manager is responsible. If the report unfairly attributes excessive costs to the manager's operations, the manager may lose confidence in the system and not let it influence future decisions.

In a nutshell, think of management accounting as a balance between costs and benefits of accounting information coupled with an awareness of the importance of behavioral effects. Therefore, management accountants must understand related disciplines, such as economics, the decision sciences, and the behavioral sciences, to make intelligent decisions about the best information to supply to managers.

Planning and Control for Product Life Cycles and the Value Chain

To effectively plan and control production of goods or services, accountants and other managers must consider the product's life cycle. **Product life cycle** refers to the various stages through which a product passes: conception and product development; introduction into the market; maturation of the market; and, finally, withdrawal from the market. At each stage, managers face differing costs and potential returns. Exhibit 1-4 shows a typical product life cycle.

In the planning process, managers predict revenues and costs over the entire life cycle—however long or short. Then accounting systems track actual costs and revenues throughout the life cycle. Periodic comparisons between planned costs and revenues and actual costs and revenues allow managers to assess the current profitability of a product, determine its current product life-cycle stage, and make any needed changes in strategy.

Objective 4

Describe the cost-benefit and behavioral issues involved in designing an accounting system.

cost-benefit balance
Weighing estimated costs against probable benefits, the primary consideration in choosing among accounting systems and methods.

behavioral implications
The accounting system's effect on the behavior, specifically the decisions, of managers.

product life cycle
The various stages through which a product passes, from conception and development to introduction into the market to maturation and, finally, withdrawal from the market.

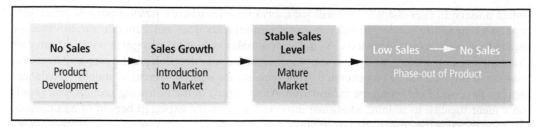

Exhibit 1-4
Typical Product Life Cycle

For example, suppose **Pfizer** is developing a new drug to reduce high blood pressure. There will be substantial development costs and no revenue during the product development stage. Most of the revenues from the product will be received during the introduction and mature market stages when there will also be production costs. During the phase-out of the product, there will be little revenue, but Pfizer will need to keep the drug on the market for those who have come to rely on it. Thus, the product pricing strategy must recognize the need for revenues during the introduction and mature market stages to cover both development and phase-out costs as well as the direct costs of producing the drug.

Product life cycles range from a few months (for fashion clothing or faddish toys) to many years (for automobiles or refrigerators). Some products, such as many computer software packages, have long development stages and relatively short market lives. Others, such as **Boeing** 737 airplanes, have a market life many times longer than their development stage. Many companies are working to shorten the product development phase, both to reduce the time during which a product generates no revenue and to bring products to market on a more timely basis.

The Value Chain

Objective 5

Discuss the role accountants play in the company's value-chain functions.

value chain

The set of business functions or activities that add value to the products or services of an organization.

In addition to considering a product's life cycle, managers must recognize those activities necessary for a company to create the goods or services that it sells. These activities comprise the **value chain**, the set of business functions or activities that add value to the products or services of an organization. As shown in Exhibit 1-5 these functions include the following:

- Research and development: generation of ideas related to new products, services, or processes
- Design: detailed design and engineering of products, services, or processes
- Production: coordination and assembly of resources to produce a product or deliver a service
- Marketing: methods by which customers learn about the value and features of products or services (for example, advertising or selling activities)
- Distribution: mechanisms by which a company delivers products or services to the customer
- Customer service: support activities provided to the customer

Not all functions are of equal importance to the success of a company. Senior management must decide which functions enable the company to gain and maintain a competitive edge. For example, managers at **Dell Computers** consider the design function a critical success factor. The features designed into Dell's computers create greater value and higher quality. In addition, the design of efficient processes used to make and deliver computers lowers costs and speeds up delivery to its customers. Dell also performs the other value-chain functions, but it concentrates on being the best process designer in the computer market.

Accountants play a role in supporting all the value-chain functions. Most obvious is the production stage, where accountants facilitate cost planning and control through the use of budgets and performance reporting and help track the effects of continuous improvement programs. However, accounting can also have a great influence on the two pre-production value-chain functions. For example, accountants provide estimated revenue and cost data during the research and development stage and during the design stage of the value chain. Managers use these data to decide which ideas will move to the production stage and which will be dropped. These data also

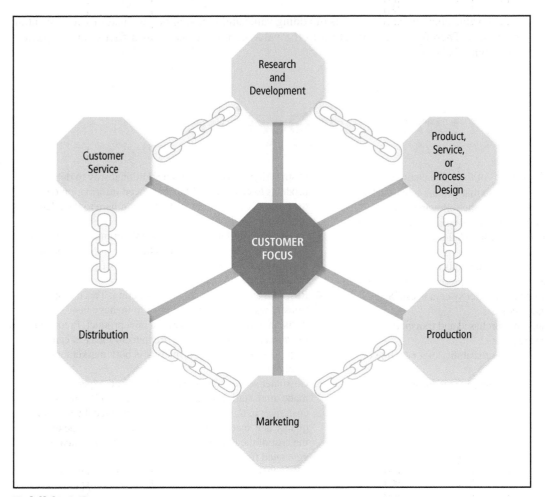

Exhibit 1-5
The Value Chain of Business Functions

enable managers and engineers to reduce the life-cycle costs of products or services by changing product and process designs. Accountants can give managers feedback on ideas for cost reductions long before the company must make a commitment to purchase expensive equipment.

Accountants also play a role in post-production value-chain functions. For example, accountants analyze the trade-off between the increased revenue expected from a marketing program and its cost. In addition, accounting information can influence decisions about distributing products or services to customers. Should a company sell its products directly to a chain of retail stores, or should it sell to a wholesaler? What transportation system should be used—trucks or trains? Accountants provide important information about the costs of each alternative. Finally, accountants provide cost data for customer service activities, such as warranty and repair costs and the costs of goods returned. Managers compare these costs to the benefits generated by better customer service. As you can see, cost management is important throughout the value chain.

Note that customer focus is at the center of Exhibit 1-5. Each value-chain function should focus on activities that create value for the customer. Successful businesses never lose sight of the importance of maintaining a focus on the needs of their customers. For example, one of the main principles in Starbucks' mission statement is to "develop enthusiastically satisfied customers all of the time." Customers are also the focus at Wal-Mart, as explained by Sam Walton, founder and former chairman:

There is only one boss—the customer. Customers can fire everybody in the company from the chairman on down, simply by spending their money somewhere else.

The value chain and the concepts of adding value and focusing on the customer are essential for success. Therefore, we will return to the value chain and use it as a focus for discussion throughout this book.

Making Managerial Decisions

Measuring costs at various stages of the value chain is important to **Starbucks**. Suppose that you are a Starbucks manager or accountant. For each of the following activities, indicate the value-chain function that is being performed and what accounting information might be helpful to managers in the function:

1. Process engineers investigate methods to reduce the time to roast coffee beans and to better preserve their flavor.
2. A direct-to-your-home mail-order system is established to sell custom-blended coffees.
3. Arabica coffee beans are purchased and transported to company processing plants.
4. Focus groups investigate the feasibility of a new line of Frappuccino drinks.
5. A telephone hotline is established for mail-order customers to call with questions and comments on the quality and speed of delivery.
6. Each company-owned retail store undertakes a campaign to provide information to customers about the processes used to make its coffee products.

Answers

1. Research and development or design. Both the generation of ideas for new processes and the design of new production processes are important parts of the value chain. Managers need the costs of various possible production processes to decide among the alternatives.

2. Distribution. This provides an additional way to deliver products to customers. Managers need information on the costs of a mail-order system to compare to the added profit from mail-order sales.
3. Production. Starbucks purchases only premium beans, but the company is still concerned about the purchase price of beans and transportation. These are part of product costs incurred during production.
4. Research and development or marketing. These costs (mostly wages) are incurred prior to management's final decision to design and produce a new product. Predicted revenues and costs from the Frappuccino market can help managers design a drink that is both marketable and profitable.
5. Customer service. These costs include all expenditures made after Starbucks has delivered the product to the customer; in this case, Starbucks obtains feedback on the quality and speed of delivery. Managers will trade off the cost of the hotline and the value of the information generated from the calls.
6. Marketing. These costs are for activities that enhance the existing or potential customers' awareness and opinion of the product. Like many advertising expenses, it is easy to estimate the costs of such a program but hard to quantify the benefits.

Accounting's Position in the Organization

How do management accountants fit into an organizational structure? Consider the following four work activities of management accountants:

- Collecting and compiling information
- Preparing standardized reports
- Interpreting and analyzing information
- Being involved in decision making

The role of management accountants in organizations is evolving. Management accountants are spending less time on the first two, data collection and reporting activities, and more time on the last two, analysis and decision-making activities. In essence, the management accountant is becoming an internal consultant on information-related issues—that is, an advisor for managers about what information is available, what additional information would be useful, and how to analyze the information and use it in decision making.

Line and Staff Authority

As an organization grows, it must divide responsibilities among a number of managers and executives, each with specific responsibilities. **Line managers** are directly involved with making and selling the organization's products or services. Their decisions lead directly to meeting (or not meeting) the organization's objectives. In contrast, **staff managers** are advisory—they have no authority over line managers, but they support the line managers by providing information and advice. The organization chart in Exhibit 1-6 shows how a traditional manufacturing company divides responsibilities between line and staff managers. The line managers in manufacturing are supported by corporate-level staff (in sales, engineering, human resources, and finance) and by factory-level staff (in receiving, inspection, tool room, purchasing, production control, and maintenance).

Many modern organizations have abandoned the type of hierarchical structure shown in Exhibit 1-6 in favor of a "flatter" organization. For example, W. L. Gore & Associates, maker of GORE-TEX® and other products using fluoropolymer technologies, has gone so far as to eliminate all job titles so everyone shares the same title, "associate." Gore also limits the size of organizational units to 150 associates. In these flatter organizations, specialization by individuals is giving way to decision making by cross-functional teams. In such an organization, management accountants are still the information specialists. However, they are not isolated in one branch of the organization chart and do not sit in their offices and issue reports. Instead, the management accountants are physically located with the line managers, and they work together to determine the optimal information support for the managers. We highlight some other recent changes in the role of accountants in the Business First box on p. 14.

line managers
Managers who are directly involved with making and selling the organization's products or services.

staff managers
Managers who are advisory to the line managers. They have no authority over line managers, but they support the line managers by providing information and advice.

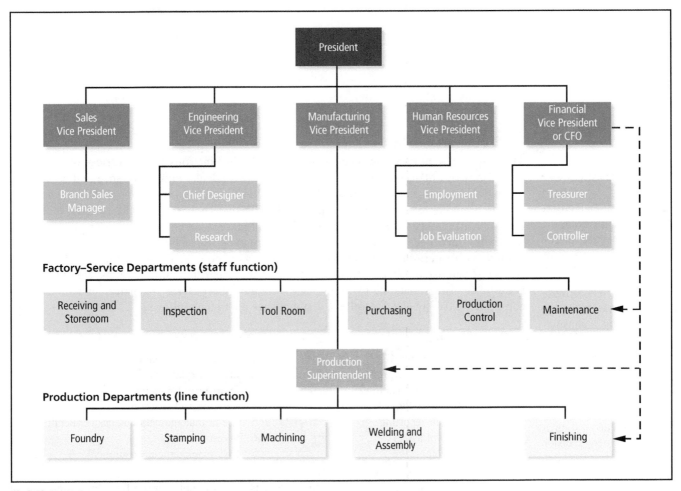

Exhibit 1-6
Partial Organization Chart of a Manufacturing Company

Business First

The Accountant's Role at the Marmon Group

The Marmon Group illustrates nearly all the reasons why management accounting is a vital and growing function in today's leading companies. Marmon, a Berkshire Hathaway company, is an international association of about 140 manufacturing, distribution, and service companies that employ more than 16,000 people and operate primarily in North America, Europe, and China. Because operations are spread over many different countries with thousands of diverse products and services (such as workers' gloves, water coolers, railroad tank cars, medical products, and credit services for banks), managers at Marmon make extensive use of management accounting information when undertaking important decisions.

What exactly is the role of management accountants at Marmon? According to Jim Smith, Marmon's former director of cost management, "The role of the management accountant is changing dramatically in most of our companies." In the past, Marmon's management accountants were basically clerical workers who spent most of their time analyzing monthly cost variances. Now, however, Marmon's management accountants work closely with operating and sales managers, providing cost information in a format that makes sense to those managers. Says Smith, "In the past few years the management accountant has become much more of a

financial and business strategy adviser to senior management. Operating and sales managers are demanding meaningful cost information, and management accountants are helping them see how their actions affect costs and the bottom line."

Management accountants have become more important to Marmon because recessions and foreign competition have awakened the understanding in most managers that managing costs is an important function. Measurement of product costs or the cost of servicing a particular customer has become essential to Marmon's profitability.

"To help manage costs," says Smith, "accountants and managers are shying away from using one cost, often the cost used for financial reporting purposes, as the only important cost." Instead, they are now using costs relevant for each specific decision. As Smith said, "Depending on the decision, any of the cost methods described in *Introduction to Management Accounting* are relevant." He believes this is a very positive change, "since it allows and, in fact, requires the management accountant to understand all of the functions in a business and how each one adds value to the product or service."

Source: The Marmon Group Web site (www.marmon.com); discussions with James Smith, former director of cost management, the Marmon Group.

Controller and Treasurer Functions

chief financial officer (CFO)
The top executive who deals with all finance and accounting issues in an organization. The CFO generally oversees the accounting function.

treasurer
The executive who is concerned mainly with the company's financial matters, such as raising and managing cash.

controller (comptroller)
The accounting officer of an organization who deals mainly with operating matters, such as aiding management decision making.

The employees carrying out management accounting functions have a variety of titles. The **chief financial officer (CFO)**, the top executive who deals with all finance and accounting issues in an organization, oversees the accounting function in most organizations. Both the treasurer and controller generally report to the CFO, as shown in Exhibit 1-6. The **treasurer** is concerned mainly with the company's financial matters such as raising and managing cash, while the **controller** (also called **comptroller** in many government organizations) is concerned mainly with operating matters such as aiding management decision making. In a small company, one person may perform both treasury and controllership functions. Nevertheless, it is useful to differentiate the two roles. The Financial Executives Institute, an association of corporate treasurers and controllers, distinguishes the two as follows:

Controllership

1. Planning for control
2. Reporting and interpreting
3. Evaluating and consulting
4. Tax administration
5. Government reporting
6. Protection of assets
7. Economic appraisal

Treasurership

1. Provision of capital
2. Investor relations
3. Short-term financing
4. Banking and custody
5. Credit management and cash collections
6. Investments
7. Risk management (insurance)

Management accounting is the primary means of implementing the first three functions of controllership, including advice and help in budgeting, analyzing variances, pricing, and making special decisions.

Adaptation to Change

Businesses in the twenty-first century differ from those in the twentieth century. Markets have become more competitive, and access to information has become more important. Many companies today derive their competitive advantage from their information, not their physical facilities. Companies such as **Amazon.com** and **Netflix** pride themselves on managing the information obtained from their customers and suppliers. Such companies work to continually improve their accounting information. The information that supported traditional companies in the 1980s and 1990s does not adequately support the modern business environment.

Objective 6

Identify current trends in management accounting.

We next discuss four major business trends that are influencing management accounting today:

1. Shift from a manufacturing-based to a service-based economy in the United States
2. Increased global competition
3. Advances in technology
4. Changes in business process management

Service Sector

Accountants in manufacturing organizations developed many of the basic ideas of management accounting. These ideas, however, have evolved so that they apply to all types of organizations, including service and nonprofit organizations. **Service organizations**, for our purposes, are organizations that do not make or sell tangible goods but instead provide other forms of value. Public accounting firms, law firms, management consultants, real estate firms, transportation companies, banks, insurance companies, and hotels are examples of profit-seeking service organizations. Most nonprofit organizations, such as hospitals, schools, libraries, museums, and government agencies, are also service organizations.

service organizations
Organizations that do not make or sell tangible goods but instead provide other forms of value.

Common characteristics of service organizations include the following:

1. *Labor is a major component of costs:* The highest proportions of expenses in service organizations, such as schools and law firms, are typically wages, salaries, and payroll-related costs, not the costs relating to the use of equipment and physical facilities.
2. *Output is usually difficult to measure:* Because service outputs are intangible, they are often hard to measure. For example, the output of a university might be defined as the number of degrees granted, but many contend that the real output is the knowledge and beliefs the students develop during their time at the university.
3. *Service organizations cannot store their major inputs and outputs:* Services cannot usually be stockpiled. For example, an airline cannot save an empty airline seat for a later flight, and a hotel's available labor force and rooms are either used or unused as each day passes.

The service sector now accounts for more than 80% of the employment in the United States. Service industries are extremely competitive, and their managers increasingly rely on accounting information. Many examples in this book are from service companies.

Managers and accountants in service companies, whether profit-seeking or nonprofit organizations, have much in common. They raise and spend money. They prepare budgets and design and implement control systems. They have an obligation to use resources wisely. Used intelligently, accounting information contributes to efficient operations and helps organizations achieve their objectives.

Simplicity is the watchword for accounting systems in service industries and nonprofit organizations. Why? Because many of the decision makers using these systems, such as physicians, professors, or government officials, are too busy to try to grapple with a complex system. For them to use the information, it must be in a form that is easy to understand. In fact, simplicity is an important consideration in the design of any accounting system. Complexity generates costs of gathering and interpreting data, and the costs of complexity often exceed the prospective benefits.

Global Competition

Global competition has increased in recent years as many countries have lowered international barriers to trade, such as tariffs and duties. In addition, there has been a worldwide trend toward deregulation. The result has been a shift in the balance of economic power in the world.

electronic commerce (e-commerce)
Conducting business online.

business-to-consumer (B2C)
Electronic commerce from business to consumer.

business-to-business (B2B)
Electronic commerce from one business to another business.

enterprise resource planning (ERP) systems
Integrated information systems that support all functional areas of a company.

eXtensible Business Reporting Language (XBRL)
An XML-based accounting language that helps communicate financial information electronically.

business process reengineering
The fundamental rethinking and radical redesign of business processes to improve performance in areas such as cost, quality, service, and speed.

computer-aided design (CAD)
The use of computer technology for the design of real or virtual objects.

computer-aided manufacturing (CAM)
The use of computer-based software tools in manufacturing or prototyping.

computer-integrated manufacturing (CIM) systems
Systems that use computer-aided design, computer-aided manufacturing, robots, and computer-controlled machines.

just-in-time (JIT) philosophy
A philosophy to eliminate waste by reducing the time products spend in the production process and eliminating the time products spend on activities that do not add value.

Nowhere has this been more evident than in the United States. To regain their competitive edge, many U.S. companies redesigned their accounting systems to provide more accurate and timely information about the cost of activities, products, or services. Improved cost information helps managers better understand and predict the effects of their decisions.

Advances in Technology

The dominant influence on management accounting over the past two decades has been technological change, affecting both the production and the use of accounting information. The increasing capabilities and decreasing cost of computer processing and storage has changed how accountants gather, store, manipulate, and report data. In many cases, databases allow managers to access data directly and to generate their own reports and analyses. Today managers and accountants work together to assure the availability of the data needed for decisions and to be sure managers know how to assemble and use the data.

Electronic commerce, or **e-commerce**—conducting business online—including both **business-to-consumer (B2C)** and **business-to-business (B2B)** transactions—continues to grow at nearly 50% a year. The growth in B2B activities is especially significant as many companies have discovered that B2B creates real savings. For example, some companies have reduced procurement processing costs by as much as 70% by automating the process.

A major effect of technology on accounting systems has been the growing use of **enterprise resource planning (ERP)** systems—integrated information systems that support all functional areas of a company. Accounting is just one part of such a system. For example, Oracle describes its JD Edwards EnterpriseOne ERP system as one that "helps you integrate all aspects of your business—including customer relationship management, enterprise asset management, enterprise resource planning, supply chain management, and supplier relationship management." Other well-known ERP system providers are SAP, Microsoft Dynamics, and The Sage Group. Accountants must work with managers throughout the organization to ensure that the ERP system provides the financial information that managers need.

Finally, the development and widespread adoption of **eXtensible Business Reporting Language (XBRL)**, an XML-based accounting language, helps communicate financial information electronically. This language is greatly influencing both internal and external reporting by making comparisons across companies much simpler.

Changes in Business Process Management

Because management accounting supports business decisions, accounting systems must adapt to changes in management practices. Some companies implement sweeping changes in operations through **business process reengineering**, the fundamental rethinking and radical redesign of business processes to improve performance in areas such as cost, quality, service, and speed. Companies reduce process time by redesigning, simplifying, and automating the production process. They use **computer-aided design (CAD)** to design products that can be manufactured efficiently and **computer-aided manufacturing (CAM)** to direct and control production equipment. **Computer-integrated manufacturing (CIM) systems** use CAD, CAM, robots, and computer-controlled machines. The costs of such a system are quite different from those of a less-automated system. Companies that install a full CIM system use very little labor. Instead, they acquire the robots and computer-controlled machines needed to perform the routine jobs that were previously accomplished by assembly-line workers.

One management change leading to increased efficiency in business processes has been the adoption of a **just-in-time (JIT) philosophy**. Originally, JIT referred to an inventory system that minimized inventories by arranging for materials and subcomponents to arrive just as they were needed for production and for goods to be made just in time to ship them to customers—no sooner and no later. But JIT has become the cornerstone of a broad management philosophy. It originated in Japanese companies such as Toyota and Kawasaki. Now many large U.S. companies use JIT, including Hewlett-Packard, Goodyear, General Motors, Intel, and Xerox, as well as many smaller firms. The essence of the JIT philosophy is to eliminate waste by (1) reducing the time that products spend in the production process and (2) eliminating the time that products spend in activities that do not add value (such as inspection and waiting time).

Another management approach focused on efficiency is **lean manufacturing**, which applies continuous process improvements to eliminate waste from the entire enterprise.

For example, Matsushita Electric's Saga plant on Japan's Kyushu island decreased the time it takes to produce a finished product from $2\frac{1}{2}$ days to 40 minutes by replacing conveyor belts with clusters of robots. As with JIT, lean ideas are now being extended beyond manufacturing to other business processes.

A focus on quality is also important in today's competitive environment. Many companies have implemented **total quality management (TQM)** initiatives. TQM minimizes costs by maximizing quality. It focuses on prevention of defects and customer satisfaction. Recently the focus on quality has shifted to **Six Sigma**, a disciplined, *data-driven approach* to eliminating defects in any process. Used by about 35% of major U.S. companies, Six Sigma is essentially a continuous process-improvement effort designed to reduce costs by improving quality. Pioneered in the 1980s by Motorola, Six Sigma has also been implemented by companies such as General Electric in the United States and Samsung in Korea to transform their business. Six Sigma seeks to ensure that internal processes are running as efficiently as possible. Staff functions, such as legal departments, also use Six Sigma today. For example, law departments in both DuPont and Tyco use Six Sigma to "improve compliance, reduce risk, contain costs, and align the law department more closely with the objectives of the business." Management accountants play a major role in Six Sigma applications as both the experts on the measurements being used and as full members of the cross-functional teams that lead the efforts.

Why do these business process changes affect management accounting? They all directly affect costs, and accountants often measure the actual cost savings, predict anticipated cost savings, and develop costs for products or services for different production environments. For example, one midwestern factory saved production time by redesigning its plant layout to reduce the distance products traveled from one operation to the next during production from 1,384 feet to just 350 feet. Accountants measured the cost the company saved by the reduced production time. As another example, a British company reduced the time to manufacture a vacuum pump from 3 weeks to 6 minutes by switching from long assembly lines to manufacturing cells that accomplish all production steps in quick succession. Again, accountants measured the benefits created by the reduced production time. In general, when companies change their production processes to accomplish economic objectives, accountants predict and measure the economic impact.

lean manufacturing
Applying continuous process improvements to eliminate waste from the entire enterprise.

total quality management (TQM)
An approach to quality that focuses on prevention of defects and on customer satisfaction.

Six Sigma
A data-driven continuous process improvement effort designed to eliminate defects and improve quality.

Making Managerial Decisions

Suppose you are a manager of a DuPont chemical plant. The plant has just undertaken a business process reengineering project and, as a result, has substantially changed its production process. It is much more automated, with newly acquired equipment replacing labor-intensive operations. The plant is also making more use of electronic commerce and moving toward a JIT inventory policy. You have a meeting with your accountant to discuss possible changes in your accounting system. What types of accounting-system changes might be warranted?

Answer
Major changes in production processes generally lead to different information needs. The old accounting system may have focused on accounting for labor, while the new system should focus on the use of the automated equipment. This will direct attention to the most important costs in the process and make sure that they are monitored and controlled. Problem-solving needs will also be different. Initially, the plant's managers will probably want comparative data on the cost of the new process versus the cost of the old. In the future, they will need information about how best to use capacity that the plant owns (the equipment) rather than how much labor to use for the planned level of production.

Implications for the Study of Management Accounting

As you read the remainder of this book, remember that accounting systems change as the world changes. Companies currently apply the techniques described in this book. However, to adapt to changes, you must understand why companies are using the techniques, not just how they are using them. Resist the temptation to simply memorize rules and techniques, and instead develop your understanding of the underlying concepts and principles. This understanding will continue to be useful no matter what new conditions you encounter.

Ethical Conduct for Professional Accountants

Objective 7

Explain why ethics and standards of ethical conduct are important to accountants.

ethics

The field that deals with human conduct in relation to what is morally good and bad, right and wrong. It is the application of values to decision making. These values include honesty, fairness, responsibility, respect, and compassion.

Business processes and accounting systems change. However, the need for accountants to maintain high ethical standards of professional conduct will never change. The Institute of Management Accountants says that **ethics** "deals with human conduct in relation to what is morally good and bad, right and wrong. It is the application of values to decision making. These values include honesty, fairness, responsibility, respect, and compassion."

We like to think of ethics as simply doing what is right. One way to decide whether an action is unethical is to ask yourself whether you would be embarrassed to read about your action in the newspaper the next day. Another warning sign that an action may be unethical is when the justification for the action is "Everybody else is doing it," the phrase Warren Buffett has described as "the five most dangerous words in business." He goes on to say that this excuse should always raise a red flag: "Why would somebody offer such a rationale for an act if there were a good reason available? Clearly the advocate harbors at least a small doubt about the act if he utilizes this verbal crutch."

Why is it so important for accountants to have integrity? Think of it this way: If you buy a car, you can see many of the quality details. Further, if something goes wrong with the car, you will certainly know it. But accounting information is different. Users can't see its quality. Users might not know for years that something was wrong with the information—probably not until it's too late to do anything about it. Thus, users rely on the integrity of accountants to assure the integrity of information. If you cannot trust the information, then it is nearly worthless.

In the remainder of this section, we discuss ethical standards and formal codes of conduct that often help resolve ethical issues. We also provide examples of clearly unethical behavior. Finally, we turn to the difficult issue of ethical dilemmas, situations where conflicting values make it unclear which is the ethical action.

Standards of Ethical Conduct

IMA Statement of Ethical Professional Practice

A code of conduct developed by the Institute of Management Accountants; this code includes competence, confidentiality, integrity, and credibility.

code of conduct

A document specifying the ethical standards of an organization.

Ethical standards require CPAs and CMAs to adhere to codes of conduct regarding competence, confidentiality, integrity, and credibility. Exhibit 1-7 contains the **IMA Statement of Ethical Professional Practice**, a code of conduct developed by the Institute of Management Accountants. Professional accounting organizations have procedures for reviewing alleged behavior that is not consistent with the standards.

The ethical organization also has policies in place to motivate ethical actions. Integrity and outspoken support for ethical standards by senior managers, in both word and deed, are the greatest motivators of ethical behavior throughout an organization. A **code of conduct**—a document specifying the ethical standards of an organization—is the centerpiece of most ethics programs. (See the Business First box, "Ethics and Corporate Codes of Conduct," on p. 21.) But having a code is not sufficient. Actual policies and practices influence behavior. This means that managers' evaluations must include an assessment of ethical conduct. Organizations cannot tolerate unethical behavior, even if it appears to lead to great financial performance. For example, Enron, WorldCom, Tyco, Global Crossing, Adelphia, Xerox, and others were accused of creating accounting entries to make their financial reports look better than their actual performances. In some cases, accountants participated in these fraudulent activities. In other cases, they simply did not step up and challenge what they surely knew (or at least should have known) was misleading information.

Fortunately, there are also many examples of accountants who stood up and reported wrongdoing to their supervisors despite the personal costs. In the spring of 2001, Sherron Watkins began working directly for Enron CFO Andrew Fastow. When she discovered the off-the-books liabilities that have now become famous, she wrote a memo to CEO Kenneth Lay and met with him personally, explaining to him "an elaborate accounting hoax." Later she discovered that, rather than the hoax being investigated, her report had generated a memo from

Members of IMA shall behave ethically. A commitment to ethical professional practice includes: overarching principles that express our values and standards that guide our conduct.

Principles

IMA's overarching ethical principles include: Honesty, Fairness, Objectivity, and Responsibility. Members shall act in accordance with these principles and shall encourage others within their organizations to adhere to them.

Standards

A member's failure to comply with the following standards may result in disciplinary action.

I Competence

Each member has a responsibility to:
1. Maintain an appropriate level of professional expertise by continually developing knowledge and skills.
2. Perform professional duties in accordance with relevant laws, regulations, and technical standards.
3. Provide decision support information and recommendations that are accurate, clear, concise, and timely.
4. Recognize and communicate professional limitations or other constraints that would preclude responsible judgment or successful performance of an activity.

II Confidentiality

Each member has a responsibility to:
1. Keep information confidential except when disclosure is authorized or legally required.
2. Inform all relevant parties regarding appropriate use of confidential information. Monitor subordinates' activities to ensure compliance.
3. Refrain from using confidential information for unethical or illegal advantage.

III Integrity

Each member has a responsibility to:
1. Mitigate actual conflicts of interest. Regularly communicate with business associates to avoid apparent conflicts of interest. Advise all parties of any potential conflicts.
2. Refrain from engaging in any conduct that would prejudice carrying out duties ethically.
3. Abstain from engaging in or supporting any activity that might discredit the profession.

IV Credibility

Each member has a responsibility to:
1. Communicate information fairly and objectively.
2. Disclose all relevant information that could reasonably be expected to influence an intended user's understanding of the reports, analyses, or recommendations.
3. Disclose delays or deficiencies in information, timeliness, processing, or internal controls in conformance with organizational policy and/or applicable law.

Resolution of Ethical Conflict

In applying the Standards of Ethical Professional Practice, you may encounter problems identifying unethical behavior or resolving an ethical conflict. When faced with ethical issues, you should follow your organization's established policies on the resolution of such conflict. If these policies do not resolve the ethical conflict, you should consider the following courses of action:
1. Discuss the issue with your immediate supervisor except when it appears that the supervisor is involved. In that case, present the issue to the next level. If you cannot achieve a satisfactory resolution, submit the issue to the next management level. If your immediate superior is the chief executive officer or equivalent, the acceptable reviewing authority may be a group such as the audit committee, executive committee, board of directors, board of trustees, or owners. Contact with levels above the immediate superior should be initiated only with your superior's knowledge, assuming he or she is not involved. Communication of such problems to authorities or individuals not employed or engaged by the organization is not considered appropriate, unless you believe there is a clear violation of the law.
2. Clarify relevant ethical issues by initiating a confidential discussion with an IMA Ethics Counselor or other impartial advisor to obtain a better understanding of possible courses of action.
3. Consult your own attorney as to legal obligations and rights concerning the ethical conflict.

Source: IMA (Institute of Management Accountants, www.imanet.org). Adapted with permission.

Exhibit 1-7
IMA Statement of Ethical Professional Practice

Enron's legal counsel titled "Confidential Employee Matter" that included the following: "... how to manage the case with the employee who made the sensitive report.... Texas law does not currently protect corporate whistle-blowers...." In addition, her boss confiscated her hard drive, and she was demoted. In the end, Watkins proved to be right. Watkins made the ethical decision to reveal the wrongdoings and did not look back. In June 2002, Cynthia Cooper, vice president of internal audit for WorldCom, told the company's board of directors that fraudulent accounting entries had turned a $662 million loss into a $2.4 billion profit in 2001. This disclosure led to additional discoveries totaling $9 billion in erroneous accounting entries—the largest accounting fraud in history. Cooper was proud of WorldCom and highly committed to its success. Nevertheless, when she and her internal audit team discovered the unethical actions of superiors she admired, she did not hesitate to do the right thing.

Most companies make ethics a top priority. For example, **Starbucks** includes ethical principles in the first line of its mission statement: "To establish Starbucks as the premier purveyor of the finest coffee in the world while maintaining our uncompromising principles as we grow." **Ben & Jerry's**, the ice cream company, has a reputation for high ethical standards that focus on its external social obligations, as recognized in its mission statement: "To operate the Company in a way that actively recognizes the central role that business plays in the structure of society by initiating innovative ways to improve the quality of life of a broad community— local, national, and international." There are many more companies with high ethical standards than there are with ethical violations, though the latter receive most of the publicity.

Ethical Dilemmas

The ethical standards of the profession leave much room for individual interpretation and judgment. A first step is to ask two questions: Is this action unethical? Would it be unethical not to take this action? If the answers to these questions are clear, then the ethical action is clear. For example, if WorldCom's accountants had asked whether their recording of expenses as assets was unethical, they would have answered "yes." However, a manager's ethical choice becomes more complex when there are no legal guidelines or clear-cut ethical standards. Ethical dilemmas exist when managers must choose an alternative and there are (1) significant value conflicts among differing interests, (2) several alternatives are justifiable, and (3) there are significant consequences for stakeholders in the situation.

Suppose you are an accountant and your boss has asked you to supply the company's banker with a profit forecast for the coming year. A badly needed bank loan rides on the prediction. Your boss is absolutely convinced that profits will be at least $500,000—anything less than that and the loan is not likely to be approved.

Your analysis reveals three possible outcomes: First, if the planned introduction of a new product goes extraordinarily well, profits will exceed $500,000. Second, if there is a modestly successful introduction, there will be a $100,000 profit. You believe this is the most likely outcome. Third, if the product fails, the company stands to lose $600,000. Without the loan, the new product cannot be taken to the market, and there is no way the company can avoid a loss for the year. Bankruptcy is a real possibility.

What forecast would you make? The ethical dilemma arises here because of uncertainty and disagreement about the prospects for the new product. If your boss is correct that profits will exceed $500,000, it would be unethical to make a forecast of less than $500,000. Such a forecast seems to guarantee that the loan will not be obtained, leading to financial problems, perhaps even bankruptcy. This would hurt stockholders, management, employees, suppliers, and customers. On the other hand, if you are correct that the most likely outcome is a profit of $100,000, a forecast of $500,000 may not be fair and objective. It may mislead the bank.

There is no easy answer to this dilemma. It is one of those gray areas where either action includes risks. But remember that a series of gray areas can create a black area. That is, a series of actions that push the boundary of ethical behavior can add up to a clearly unethical situation. Accountants must draw the line someplace, and it is usually better to err on the side of full disclosure than to withhold important information. Enron repeatedly pushed boundaries by reporting only optimistic information. If its managers had done this once or twice, it might not have created a problem. But the pattern of exclusively optimistic projections eventually deteriorated into completely unrealistic, and unethical, projections.

Business First

Ethics and Corporate Codes of Conduct

The Sarbanes-Oxley Act of 2002 requires companies "to disclose whether or not, and if not, the reason therefore, such issuer has adopted a code of ethics for senior financial officers, applicable to its principal financial officer and comptroller or principal accounting officer, or persons performing similar functions." This has created increased interest in corporate codes of conduct. However, a code of conduct means different things to different companies. Some of the items included in companies' codes of conduct include maintaining a dress code, avoiding illegal drugs, following instructions of superiors, being reliable and prompt, maintaining confidentiality, not accepting personal gifts from stakeholders as a result of company role, avoiding racial or sexual discrimination, avoiding conflict of interest, complying with laws and regulations, not using an organization's property for personal use, and reporting illegal or questionable activity. Even before Enron and other corporate scandals, more than 80% of U.S. companies had a code of conduct, according to a survey by the Financial Executives Institute (FEI). But the codes differed in type and in level of enforcement.

One company had only one rule: "Don't do anything you would be embarrassed to read about in tomorrow's newspaper." Others have detailed lists of dos and don'ts. Some companies use consulting firms to advise them on their codes. Although the codes and their development differ, the goal is generally the same—to motivate employees to act with integrity.

To encourage development of codes of conduct, the FEI includes examples of codes on its Web site. Two extremes among those presented are those of Wiremold and CSX Corporation. Wiremold has a simple, seven-point code: (1) respect others, (2) tell the truth, (3) be fair, (4) try new ideas, (5) ask why, (6) keep your promises, and (7) do your share. In contrast, CSX has 26 paragraphs detailing expectations of employees under the following headings: Employee Relationships and Conflicts of Interest, Political Contributions and Public Service Involvement, Misrepresentations and False Statements, Employee Discrimination and Harassment, Competition, and Safety and the Environment.

FEI also lists inquiries about corporate codes of conduct among the questions to expect at shareholder annual meetings. As stated on FEI's Web site, "If there's any single issue that overlays the recent corporate and accounting scandals, it is a deficiency in ethical behavior among some company executives. Corporate governance consultants and academics agree that a company needs to have a code of conduct and ethics in place, by which the entire staff and management should conduct themselves in relation to their business activities.... In all probability, shareholders will ask questions relating to board committees or subcommittees focused on ethical matters."

While having a code of conduct is important, it is not sufficient. After all, Enron's code of conduct specified that "business is to be conducted in compliance... with the highest professional and ethical standards." Top management must set the tone and get out the message. Management must recognize and reward honesty and integrity. As Clarence Otis, CFO of Darden Restaurants, says, "Our senior managers care about honesty and integrity and doing things right, and that influences how they do their job." The corporate culture, more than codes of conduct, is the real influence on the ethical climate of an organization. Codes of conduct can be a part, but only a part, of developing a culture of integrity.

Sources: Sarbanes-Oxley Act of 2002, HR 3763; RedHawk Productions Web site (http://redhawkproductions.com); Financial Executives Institute Web site (www.fei.org); D. Blank, "A Matter of Ethics," *Internal Auditor*, February 2003, pp. 27–31; Enron Corporation, *2000 Corporate Responsibility Report*, p. 3.

To maintain high ethical standards, accountants and others need to recognize situations that create pressures for unethical behavior. Four such temptations, summarized in *Financial Executive*, are as follows:

1. *Emphasis on short-term results.* This may have been the largest issue in the recent spate of ethical breakdowns. If "making the numbers" is goal number one, accountants may do whatever is necessary to produce the expected profit numbers.

2. *Ignoring the small stuff.* Most ethical compromises start out small. The first step may seem insignificant, but large misdeeds are often the result of many small steps. Toleration of even small lapses can lead to large problems.

3. *Economic cycles.* A down market can reveal what an up market conceals. When Enron was flying high at the turn of the century, no one seemed to question its financial reports. When the economy took a downward turn, managers made ethical compromises to keep pace with expectations of an up market. The result was a huge crisis when scrutiny revealed many questionable practices. Similarly, later in the decade companies such as AIG, Fannie Mae, and Freddie Mac were accused of accounting compromises after the

economy started to sour in 2008. Companies need to be especially vigilant to prevent ethical lapses in good times when such lapses are more easily concealed, and thereby avoid revelation of lapses in bad times when their effects are especially damaging.

4. *Accounting rules.* Accounting rules have become more complex and less intuitive, making abuse of the rules harder to identify. Ethical accountants do not just meet the "letter of the law," they seek full and fair disclosure—conveying to users the real economic performance and financial position of the company.

Few organizations are intentionally unethical. Even Arthur Andersen, the accounting firm destroyed by failed audits at Enron, Sunbeam, Global Crossing, and others, had a formal ethical structure, including a partner in charge of ethics. Nevertheless, other pressures, especially the pressure for growing revenues, overrode some of the ethical controls and caused bad decisions.

Resolution of Ethical Conflicts

Ethical dilemmas also arise when you only observe, rather than commit, unethical behavior. If you discover unethical behavior in an organization, you are obligated to try to halt that behavior. However, you still have confidentiality issues to confront. The section on Resolution of Ethical Conflict in Exhibit 1-7 provides guidance. Most often you can bring the issue to the attention of your supervisor or a special ethics officer (often called an ombudsperson) in the organization. However, if there is not an ethics officer and you suspect your supervisor is involved in unethical activity, your decision becomes more complex. As was the case for Cynthia Cooper at WorldCom described on p. 20, you may need to go all the way to the board of directors. If the case involves legal issues and the board is not responsive, approaching the Securities and Exchange Commission (the body that regulates corporate reporting) or other legal authorities may be necessary.

Summary Problem for Your Review

PROBLEM

Yang Electronics Company (YEC) developed a high-speed, low-cost copying machine marketed primarily for home use. However, as YEC customers learned how easy and inexpensive it was to make copies with it, sales to small businesses soared. Unfortunately, the heavier use by these companies caused breakdowns in a component of the equipment that had been designed only for light use. The copiers were warranted for 2 years, regardless of the amount of usage. Consequently, YEC began to experience high costs for replacing the damaged component.

As the quarterly meeting of YEC's board of directors approached, the CFO asked Mark Chua, assistant controller, to prepare a report on the situation. It was hard to predict the exact effects, but it seemed that many business customers were starting to switch away from the YEC copier to more expensive copiers sold by competitors. It was also clear that the increased warranty costs would significantly affect YEC's profitability. Mark summarized the situation in writing as best he could for the board.

Alice Martinez, YEC's CFO, was concerned about the impact of the report on the board. She did not disagree with the analysis, but she thought it would make management look bad and might even lead the board to discontinue the product. She was convinced from conversations with the head of engineering that the copier could be slightly redesigned to meet the needs of high-volume users, so discontinuing it may pass up a potentially profitable opportunity.

Martinez called Chua into her office and asked him to delete the part of his report dealing with the component failures. She said it was all right to mention this orally to the board, noting that engineering is nearing a solution to the problem. However, Chua felt strongly that such a revision in his report would mislead the board about a potentially significant negative impact on the company's earnings.

Use the IMA Statement of Ethical Professional Practice in Exhibit 1-7 to explain why Martinez's request to Chua is unethical. How should Chua resolve this situation?

SOLUTION

Martinez's request violates requirements for competence, integrity, and credibility. It violates competence because she is asking Chua to prepare a report that is not complete and clear, and omits potentially relevant information. Therefore, the board will not have all the information it should to make a decision about the component failure problem.

The request violates integrity because the revised report may subvert the attainment of the organization's objectives to achieve Martinez's objectives. Management accountants are specifically responsible for communicating unfavorable as well as favorable information.

Finally, the revised report would not be credible. It would not disclose all relevant information that could be expected to influence the board's understanding of operations and, therefore, its decisions.

Chua's responsibility is to discuss this issue with increasingly higher levels of authority within YEC. First, he should let Martinez know about his misgivings. Possibly the issue can be resolved by her withdrawing the request. If not, he should inform her that he intends to take up the matter with the company president, and even the board, if necessary, until the issue is resolved. So that Chua does not violate the standard of confidentiality, he should not discuss the matter with persons outside of YEC.

Highlights to Remember

1. **Explain why accounting is essential for decision makers and managers.** Decision makers in all functional areas of an organization must understand the accounting information that they are using in their decisions and the incentives created by accounting systems.

2. **Describe the major users and uses of accounting information.** Internal managers use accounting information for making short-term planning and control decisions, for making nonroutine decisions, and for formulating overall policies and long-range plans. External users, such as investors and regulators, use published financial statements to make investment decisions, regulatory rulings, and many other decisions. Managers use accounting information to answer scorekeeping, attention-directing, and problem-solving questions.

3. **Explain the role of budgets and performance reports in planning and control.** Budgets and performance reports are essential tools for planning and control. Budgets result from the planning process. Managers use them to translate the organization's goals into action. A performance report compares actual results to the budget. Managers use these reports to monitor, evaluate, and reward performance and, thus, exercise control.

4. **Describe the cost-benefit and behavioral issues involved in designing an accounting system.** Management accounting information systems should be judged by a cost-benefit criterion—the benefits of better decisions and better incentives should exceed the cost of the system. Behavioral factors—how the system affects managers and their decisions—greatly influence the benefits from a management accounting system.

5. **Discuss the role accountants play in the company's value-chain functions.** Accountants play a key role in planning and control. Throughout the company's value chain, accountants gather and report cost and revenue information for decision makers.

6. **Identify current trends in management accounting.** Many factors have caused changes in accounting systems in recent years. Most significant are a shift to a service-based economy, increased global competition, advances in technology, and changed business processes. Without continuous adaptation and improvement, accounting systems would soon become obsolete.

7. **Explain why ethics and standards of ethical conduct are important to accountants.** Users of accounting information expect accountants to adhere to high standards of ethical conduct. Most users cannot directly assess the quality of that information, and if they cannot rely on accountants to produce unbiased information, the information will have little value to them. That is why professional accounting organizations, as well as most companies, have codes of ethical conduct. Many ethical dilemmas, however, require more than codes and rules. They call for value judgments, not the simple application of standards.

Accounting Vocabulary

Vocabulary is an essential and often troublesome phase of the learning process. A fuzzy understanding of terms hampers the learning of concepts and the ability to solve accounting problems. Before proceeding to the assignment material or to the next chapter, be sure you understand the words and terms in the Accounting Vocabulary section of each chapter. Their meaning is explained within the chapter and in the glossary at the end of this book.

accounting system, p. 5
attention directing, p. 5
behavioral implications, p. 9
budget, p. 7
business process reengineering, p. 16
business-to-business (B2B), p. 16
business-to-consumer (B2C), p. 16
certified management accountant (CMA), p. 4
certified public accountant (CPA), p. 3
chartered accountant (CA), p. 3
chief financial officer (CFO), p. 14
code of conduct, p. 18
computer-aided design (CAD), p. 16
computer-aided manufacturing (CAM), p. 16

computer-integrated manufacturing (CIM) systems, p. 16
control, p. 6
controller (comptroller), p. 14
cost-benefit balance, p. 9
decision making, p. 5
electronic commerce (e-commerce), p. 16
enterprise resource planning (ERP) system, p. 16
ethics, p. 18
eXtensible Business Reporting Language (XBRL), p. 16
financial accounting, p. 3
Foreign Corrupt Practices Act, p. 8
generally accepted accounting principles (GAAP), p. 8
IMA Statement of Ethical Professional Practice, p. 18
Institute of Management Accountants (IMA), p. 3
internal auditors, p. 8

internal controls, p. 8
just-in-time (JIT) philosophy, p. 16
lean manufacturing, p. 17
line managers, p. 13
management accounting, p. 3
management audit, p. 8
management by exception, p. 7
performance reports, p. 7
planning, p. 6
problem solving, p. 5
product life cycle, p. 9
Sarbanes-Oxley Act, p. 8
scorekeeping, p. 5
service organizations, p. 15
Six Sigma, p. 17
staff managers, p. 13
total quality management (TQM), p. 17
treasurer, p. 14
value chain, p. 10
variances, p. 7

MyAccountingLab # Fundamental Assignment Material

The assignment material for each chapter is divided into two groups: fundamental and additional. The fundamental assignment material consists of two sets of parallel problems that convey the essential concepts and techniques of the chapter. The additional assignment material covers the chapter in more detail and includes questions, critical thinking exercises, exercises, problems, cases, a problem based on Nike's 10-K, an Excel application exercise, a collaborative learning exercise, and an Internet exercise.

1-A1 Scorekeeping, Attention Directing, and Problem Solving

For each of the following activities, identify the primary function that the accountant is performing—scorekeeping, attention directing, or problem solving—and explain why it best fits that category.

1. Preparing a schedule of depreciation for forklift trucks in the receiving department of a **General Electric** factory in Scotland
2. Analyzing, for a **Sony** production superintendent, the impact on costs of purchasing some new assembly equipment
3. Preparing a scrap report for the finishing department of a **Toyota** parts factory
4. Interpreting why the **Colville Timber Resource Company** did not adhere to its production schedule
5. Explaining the stamping department's performance report
6. Preparing a monthly statement of European sales for the **Ford Motor Company**'s vice president of marketing
7. Preparing, for the manager of production control of a **Mittal Steel** plant, a cost comparison of two computerized manufacturing control systems

8. Interpreting variances on the performance report for the University of Michigan's purchasing department.
9. Analyzing, for an Airbus manufacturing manager, the desirability of having some parts for the A380 airplane made in Korea
10. Preparing the budget for the dermatology department of Providence Hospital

I-A2 Management by Exception

Beta Alpha Psi, the accounting honorary fraternity, held a homecoming party. The fraternity expected attendance of 80 persons and prepared the following budget:

Room rental	$ 170
Food	660
Entertainment	570
Decorations	210
Total	$1,610

After Beta Alpha Psi paid all the bills for the party, the total cost came to $1,885, or $275 over budget. Details are $170 for room rental; $875 for food; $570 for entertainment; and $270 for decorations. Ninety-six persons attended the party.

1. Prepare a performance report for the party that shows how actual costs differed from the budget. That is, include in your report the budgeted amounts, actual amounts, and variances.
2. Suppose the fraternity uses a management-by-exception rule. Which costs deserve further examination? Why?

I-A3 Professional Ethics

Exhibit 1-7 on page 19 lists four main categories of ethical standards for management accountants: competence, confidentiality, integrity, and credibility. For each of the following situations, indicate which of these four should influence the manager and what the appropriate action should be:

1. At a dinner party, a guest asked a General Mills manager how a major new cereal was doing. The manager had just read a report that said sales lagged much below expectation. What should he say?
2. Felix just graduated from business school with an accounting major and joined the controller's department of Pioneer Enterprises. His boss asked him to evaluate a market analysis for a potential new product prepared by the marketing department. Felix knows very little about the industry, and he never had a class to teach him how to make a market analysis. Should he just do the best he can on the analysis without asking for help?
3. Mary Sue prepared a budget for a division of Southeastern Electronics. Her supervisor, the division manager, was not happy that she included results for an exciting new product that was to be introduced in a month. He asked her to leave the results for the product out of the budget. That way, the financial results for the product would boost actual profits well above the amount budgeted, resulting in favorable reviews for the division and its managers. What should Mary Sue do?

I-B1 Scorekeeping, Attention Directing, and Problem Solving

For each of the following activities, identify the function the accountant is performing—scorekeeping, attention directing, or problem solving. Explain each of your answers.

1. Estimating the operating costs and outputs that could be expected for each of two large metal-stamping machines offered for sale by different manufacturers; only one of these machines is to be acquired by your company
2. Recording daily material purchase vouchers
3. Analyzing the expected costs of acquiring and using each of two alternate types of welding equipment
4. Preparing a report of overtime labor costs by production department
5. Estimating the costs of moving corporate headquarters to another city
6. Interpreting increases in nursing costs per patient-day in a hospital
7. Analyzing deviations from the budget of the factory maintenance department
8. Assisting in a study by the manufacturing vice president to determine whether to buy certain parts needed in large quantities for manufacturing products or to acquire facilities for manufacturing these parts

9. Preparing estimated costs for a new marketing campaign
10. Recording overtime hours of the product finishing department
11. Compiling data for a report showing the ratio of advertising expenses to sales for each branch store
12. Investigating reasons for increased returns and allowances for drugs purchased by a hospital
13. Preparing a schedule of fuel costs by months and government departments
14. Computing and recording end-of-year adjustments for expired fire insurance on the factory warehouse

I-B2 Management by Exception

The Skokomish Indian tribe sells fireworks for the 5 weeks preceding July 4. The tribe's stand on Highway 101 near Hoodsport had budgeted sales of $80,000. Expected expenses were as follows:

Cost of fireworks	$40,000
Labor cost	10,000
Other costs	7,000
Total costs	$57,000

Actual sales were $79,440, almost equal to the budget. The tribe spent $39,400 for fireworks, $13,100 for labor, and $6,900 for other costs.

1. Compute budgeted profit and actual profit.
2. Prepare a performance report to help identify those costs that were significantly different from the budget.
3. Suppose the tribe uses a management-by-exception rule. What costs deserve further explanation? Why?

I-B3 Ethical Code of Conduct

According to the Financial Executives Institute, "corporate governance consultants and academics agree that a company needs to have a code of conduct" for its employees. Most companies, even many of those who experienced ethical breakdowns, have such a code. Answer the following questions about corporate codes of conduct.

1. What is a corporate code of conduct?
2. What types of issues are covered in a corporate code of conduct? At what level of detail?
3. In some cases, codes of conduct were not effective. What, besides simply having a code, is necessary for a code of conduct to be effective?

MyAccountingLab ## Additional Assignment Material

QUESTIONS

I-1 Who uses information from an accounting system?

I-2 "The emphases of financial accounting and management accounting differ." Explain.

I-3 "The field is less sharply defined. There is heavier use of economics, decision sciences, and behavioral sciences." Identify the branch of accounting described in the quotation.

I-4 Distinguish among scorekeeping, attention directing, and problem solving.

I-5 "Generally accepted accounting principles (GAAP) assist the development of management accounting systems." Do you agree? Explain.

I-6 "The Foreign Corrupt Practices Act applies to bribes paid outside the United States." Do you agree? Explain.

I-7 Why is the Sarbanes-Oxley Act controversial?

I-8 Why is integrity so important to accountants?

I-9 "Integrity is more important for business professionals than it is for business students." Do you agree? Explain.

I-10 Give three examples of service organizations. What distinguishes service organizations from other types of organizations?

I-11 What two major considerations affect the design of all accounting systems? Explain each.

I-12 "The accounting system is intertwined with operating management. Business operations would be in a hopeless tangle without the recordkeeping that is so often regarded with disdain." Do you agree? Explain, giving examples.

1-13 Distinguish among a budget, a performance report, and a variance.

1-14 "Management by exception means abdicating management responsibility for planning and control." Do you agree? Explain.

1-15 Why are accountants concerned about product life cycles?

1-16 Name the six primary business functions (excluding support functions) that make up the value chain, and briefly describe each.

1-17 "Accountants in every company should measure and report on every function in the company's value chain." Do you agree? Explain.

1-18 Distinguish between the duties of line managers and staff managers.

1-19 The role of management accountants is changing, especially in companies with a "flatter" organizational structure. What are some of the changes?

1-20 Does every company have both a controller and a treasurer? Explain.

1-21 Describe the two parts of the qualifying examination for becoming a CMA.

1-22 "The problem with accounting is that accountants never get to become top managers such as CEOs." Do you agree? Explain.

1-23 How are changes in technology affecting management accounting?

1-24 What is the essence of the JIT philosophy?

1-25 Briefly describe how a change in a plant's layout can make its operation more efficient.

1-26 Standards of ethical conduct for management accountants have been divided into four major responsibilities. Describe each of the four in 20 words or fewer.

1-27 "Why are there ethical dilemmas? I thought accountants had standards that specified what ethical behavior is." Discuss this quote.

CRITICAL THINKING EXERCISES

1-28 Finance and Management Accounting

Often there is confusion between the roles played by the controller and treasurer in an organization. In many small companies, a single person performs activities related to both functions.

Distinguish between the controller and the treasurer functions by listing typical activities that are associated with each.

1-29 Accounting's Position in the Organization: Controller and Treasurer

For each of the following activities, indicate whether it is more likely to be performed by the controller or by the treasurer. Explain each answer.

1. Prepare divisional financial statements.
2. Help managers prepare budgets.
3. Advise which alternative action is least costly.
4. Meet with financial analysts from Wall Street.
5. Arrange short-term financing.
6. Prepare tax returns.
7. Arrange insurance coverage.
8. Prepare credit checks on customers.

1-30 Marketing and Management Accounting

A cross-functional team of managers, including the management accountant, performs each of the following activities. However, depending on the nature of the decision to be made, one functional area will take the leadership role. Which of these activities is primarily a marketing decision? What would the management accountant contribute to each of the marketing decisions?

1. **Porsche Motor Company** must decide whether to buy a part for one of its cars or to make the part at one of its plants.
2. **Airbus** must decide the price to charge for spare parts it sells over the Internet using its Spare Parts Web site.
3. **St. Luke's Hospital** must decide how to finance the purchase of expensive new medical analysis equipment.
4. **Amazon.com** must forecast the impact on video sales of a new advertising program.
5. **Mission Foods**, a leading producer and distributor of tortillas to retail and food service industries, must decide whether to accept a special order for tortilla chips by a large, national retail chain.
6. **Target Stores** must decide whether to close one of its retail stores that is currently operating at a loss.

1-31 Production and Management Accounting

A cross-functional team of managers, including the management accountant, performed each of the following activities. However, depending on the nature of the decision to be made, one functional area will take the leadership role. Which of these activities is primarily a production decision? What would the management accountant contribute to each of the production decisions?

1. **Saab Automobile AB** must decide whether to buy a part for one of its cars or to make the part at one of its plants.
2. **Boeing Company** must decide the price for spare parts it sells over the Internet using its Spare Parts Web site.
3. **St. Mary's Hospital** must decide how to finance the purchase of expensive new medical analysis equipment.
4. **Amazon.com** must forecast how a new advertising program will affect DVD sales.
5. **Mission Foods**, a leading producer and distributor of tortillas to retail and food service industries, must decide whether to accept a special order for tortilla chips by a large, national retail chain.
6. **Kmart** must evaluate its overall vision and strategic goals in the light of competitive pressures from **Target**, **Sears**, and **Wal-Mart**.
7. **Dell Computers** must decide whether to spend money on training workers to perform setups and changeovers faster. This will free up capacity to be used to make more computers without purchasing more equipment.
8. **Ford Motor Company** must decide whether to keep or replace 4-year-old equipment used in one of its Escape plants.

EXERCISES

1-32 Management Accounting and Financial Accounting

Consider the following short descriptions. Indicate whether each of the following descriptions more closely relates to a major feature of financial accounting or management accounting:

1. Field is less sharply defined
2. Provides internal consulting advice to managers
3. Has less flexibility
4. Is characterized by detailed reports
5. Has a future orientation
6. Is constrained by GAAP
7. Behavioral impact is secondary

1-33 Planning and Control, Management by Exception

Study the framework for planning and control of a **Starbucks** store in Exhibit 1-2 on page 7 . Suppose that for next year a particular store budgeted revenue of $356,400, an 8% increase over the current revenue of $330,000. The actions listed in Exhibit 1-2 resulted in six new budgeted products and a total advertising budget of $33,000. Actual results were as follows:

New products added	7
Advertising	$ 35,640
Revenues	$351,400

1. Prepare a performance report for revenues and advertising costs using the format of Exhibit 1-3 on page 8.
2. Suppose the remaining cost elements of net income were not available until several months after the store implemented the plan. The net income results were disappointing to management—profits declined even though revenues increased because costs increased by more than revenues. List some factors that might have caused costs to increase so much and that management may not have considered when it formulated the store's plan.

1-34 Line Versus Staff and Value-Chain Responsibility

For each of the following, indicate whether the employee has line or staff responsibility. Also indicate whether the employee primarily provides support for other value-chain functions or performs a specific value-chain business function.

1. President
2. District sales manager
3. Market research analyst
4. Cost accountant
5. Head of the legal department
6. Production superintendent

1-35 Microsoft's Value Chain

Microsoft is the world's largest software company. For each of the following value-chain functions, discuss briefly what Microsoft managers would do to achieve that function and how important it is to the overall success of Microsoft.

R&D	Product (service) and process design
Production	Marketing
Distribution	Customer service
Support functions	

1-36 Objectives of Management Accounting

The Institute of Management Accountants (IMA) is composed of nearly 70,000 members. The IMA "Objectives of Management Accounting" states, "The management accountant participates, as part of management, in assuring that the organization operates as a unified whole in its long-run, intermediate, and short-run best interests."

Based on your reading in this chapter, prepare a 100-word description of the principal ways that accountants participate in managing an entity.

1-37 Cost-Benefit of the Ethical Environment

A poor ethical environment results in costs to the company. On the other hand, a good ethical environment creates benefits. List several costs of a poor ethical environment and benefits of a good ethical environment.

1-38 Early Warning Signs of Ethical Conflict

The following statements are early warning signs of ethical conflict:

- "I don't care how you do it, just get it done!"
- "No one will ever know."

List several other statements that are early warning signs of ethical conflict.

PROBLEMS

1-39 Management and Financial Accounting

Lillian Choi, an able mechanical engineer, was informed that she would be promoted to assistant factory manager. Lillian was pleased but uncomfortable. In particular, she knew little about accounting. She had taken one course in financial accounting.

Lillian planned to enroll in a management accounting course as soon as possible. Meanwhile, she asked Walt Greenspan, a cost accountant, to state three or four of the principal distinctions between financial and management accounting.

Prepare Walt's written response to Lillian.

1-40 Use of Accounting Information in Hospitals

Most U.S. hospitals do not derive their revenues directly from patients. Instead, revenues come through third parties, such as insurance companies and government agencies. Until the 1980s, these payments generally reimbursed the hospital's costs of serving patients. Such payments, however, are now generally flat fees for specified services. For example, the hospital might receive $7,000 for an appendectomy or $28,000 for heart surgery—no more, no less.

How might the method of payment change the demand for accounting information in hospitals? Relate your answer to the decisions of top management.

1-41 Costs and Benefits

Marks & Spencer, a huge retailer in the United Kingdom with sales of more than £9 billion, was troubled by its paper bureaucracy. Looked at in isolation, each document seemed reasonable, but overall a researcher reported that there was substantial effort in each department to verify the information. Basically, the effort seemed out of proportion to any value received, and, eventually, the company simplified or eliminated many of the documents.

Describe the rationale that should govern systems design. How should a company such as Marks & Spencer decide what documents it needs and which can be eliminated?

1-42 Importance of Accounting

Some companies are run by engineers and other technical specialists. For example, a manager in a division that is now part of **ArvinMeritor**, an automotive parts supplier, once said that "there'd be sixty or seventy guys talking technical problems, with never a word on profits." Other companies, especially consumer products companies such as **General Mills**, fill top management positions primarily with marketing executives. And still others, like **Berkshire Hathaway** with Warren Buffett as CEO, have top managers with strong finance skills.

How might the role of management accountants differ in these types of companies?

1-43 Changes in Accounting Systems

In the last decade, **Boeing** has made several significant changes to its accounting system. None of these changes were for reporting to external parties. Management believed, however, that the new system gave more accurate costs of the airplanes and other products produced.

1. Boeing had been a very successful company using its old accounting system. What might have motivated it to change the system?
2. When Boeing changed its system, what criteria might its managers have used to decide whether to invest in the new system?
3. Is changing to a system that provides more accurate product costs always a good strategy? Why or why not?

1-44 Value Chain

Nike is an Oregon-based company that focuses on the design, development, and worldwide marketing of high-quality sports footwear, apparel, equipment, and accessory products. Nike is the largest seller of athletic footwear and athletic apparel in the world. The company sells its products to more than 20,000 retail accounts in the United States and through a mix of independent distributors, licensees, and subsidiaries in approximately 170 countries around the world. Nike contracts with hundreds of factories around the world to manufacture virtually all the company's products. Nike produces most footwear and branded apparel products outside the United States.

1. Identify one decision that Nike managers make in each of the six value-chain functions.
2. For each decision in requirement 1, identify one piece of accounting information that would aid the manager's decision.

1-45 Role of Controller

Juanita Veracruz, newly hired controller of Braxton Industries, had been lured away from a competitor to revitalize the controller's department. Her first day on the job proved to be an eye-opener. One of her first interviews was with Adrian Belton, production supervisor in the Cleveland factory. Belton commented, "I really don't want to talk to anyone from the controller's office. The only time we see those accountants is when our costs go over their budget. They wave what they call a 'performance report,' but it's actually just a bunch of numbers they make up. It has nothing to do with what happens on the shop floor. Besides, my men can't afford the time to fill out all the paperwork those accountants want, so I just plug in some numbers and send it back. Now, if you'll let me get back to important matters...." Veracruz left quickly, but she was already planning for her next visit with Belton.

1. Identify some of the problems in the relationship between the controller's department and the production departments (assuming that the Cleveland factory is representative of the production departments).
2. What should Juanita Veracruz do next?

1-46 The Accountant's Role in an Organization

The Business First box on page 14 described the role of accountants in the **Marmon Group**, a collection of operating companies that manufacture such diverse products as copper tubing, water purification products, railroad tank cars, and store fixtures, and provide services such as credit information for banks. Others have described accountants as "internal consultants." Using the information in the Business First box, discuss how accountants at Marmon can act as internal consultants. What kind of background and knowledge would an accountant require to be an effective internal consultant?

1-47 Ethics and Accounting Personnel

McMillan Shipping Company has an equal opportunity employment policy. This policy has the full support of the company's president, Rosemary Creighton, and is included in all advertisements for employee positions.

Hiring in the accounting department is done by the controller, D. W. "Butch" Brigham. The assistant controller, Jack Merton, also interviews candidates, but Brigham makes all decisions. In the last year, the department hired 5 new people from a pool of 175 applicants. Thirteen had been interviewed, including four minority candidates. The five hired included three sons of Brigham's close friends and no minorities. Merton had felt that at least two of the minority candidates were very well qualified and that the three sons of Brigham's friends were definitely not among the most qualified.

When Merton questioned Brigham concerning his reservations about the hiring practices, he was told that these decisions were Brigham's and not his, so he should not question them.

1. Explain why Brigham's hiring practices were probably unethical.
2. What should Merton do about this situation?

1-48 Ethical Issues

Suppose you are controller of a medium-sized oil exploration company in western Texas. You adhere to the standards of ethical conduct for management accountants. How would those standards affect your behavior in each of the following situations?

1. Late one Friday afternoon you receive a geologist's report on a newly purchased property. It indicates a much higher probability of oil than had previously been expected. You are the only one to read the report that day. At a party on Saturday night, a friend asks about the prospects for the property.
2. An oil industry stock analyst invites you and your spouse to spend a week in Tahiti free of charge. All she wants in return is to be the first to know about any financial information your company is about to announce to the public.
3. It is time to make a forecast of the company's annual earnings. You know that some additional losses will be recognized before the company prepares final statements. The company's president has asked you to ignore these losses in making your prediction because a lower-than-expected earnings forecast could adversely affect the chances of obtaining a loan that is being negotiated and that will be completed before actual earnings are announced.
4. You do not know whether a particular expense is deductible for income tax purposes. You are debating whether to research the tax laws or simply to assume that the item is deductible. After all, if you are not audited, no one will ever know the difference. If you are audited, you can plead ignorance of the law.

1-49 Hundred Best Corporate Citizens

Each year *Corporate Responsibility* magazine publishes its list of the 100 best corporate citizens. The magazine rates companies on performance in seven stakeholder categories: (1) environment, (2) climate change, (3) human rights, (4) employee relations, (5) corporate governance, (6) philanthropy, and (7) financial. In 2011, the top 10 corporate citizens were **Johnson Controls, Campbell Soup, International Business Machines, Bristol-Myers Squibb, Mattel, 3M, Accenture, Kimberly-Clark, Hewlett-Packard,** and **Nike.**

For each of the seven dimensions on which the magazine reported ratings, give a one-sentence description of what you think would make for good corporate citizenship. Based on your knowledge of these 10 companies, however limited that is, predict the top 2 companies in each of the seven rated categories.

CASES

1-50 Line and Staff Authority

Fidelity Leasing Company (FLC) leases office equipment to a variety of customers. The company's organization chart is shown on the following page. The responsibilities of the four positions in blue in the chart are:

- J. P. Chen, assistant controller—special projects. Chen works on projects assigned to him by the controller. The most recent project was to design a new accounts payable system.
- Betty Hodge, leasing contracts manager. Hodge coordinates and implements leasing transactions. Her department handles all transactions after the sales department gets a signed contract. This includes requisitioning equipment from the purchasing department, maintaining appropriate insurance, delivering equipment, issuing billing statements, and seeking renewal of leases.

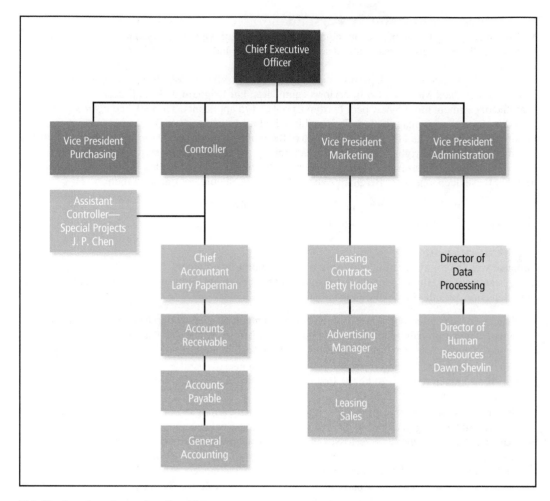

Fidelity Leasing Organization Chart

- Larry Paperman, chief accountant. Paperman supervises all the accounting functions. He produces reports for the four supervisors in the functional areas.
- Dawn Shevlin, director of human resources. Shevlin works with all departments of FLC in hiring personnel. Her department advertises all positions and screens candidates, but the individual departments conduct interviews and make hiring decisions. Shevlin also coordinates employee evaluations and administers the company's salary schedule and fringe benefit program.

1. Distinguish between line and staff positions in an organization and discuss why conflicts might arise between line and staff managers.
2. For each of the four managers described, identify whether their position is a line or staff position and explain why you classified it that way. Also, indicate any potential conflicts that might arise with other managers in the organization.

1-51 Professional Ethics and Toxic Waste

Alberta Mining Company extracts and processes a variety of ores and minerals. One of its operations is a coal-cleaning plant that produces toxic wastes. For many years, the wastes have been properly disposed of through Canadian Disposal, an experienced company. However, disposal of the toxic wastes is becoming an economic hardship because increasing government regulations caused the cost of such disposal to quadruple in the last 6 years.

Rachel O'Casey, director of financial reporting for Alberta Mining, was preparing the company's financial statements for the current year. In researching the material needed for preparing a footnote on environmental contingencies, Rachel found the following note scribbled in pencil at the bottom of a memo to the general manager of the coal-cleaning plant. The body of the memo gave details on the increases in the cost of toxic waste disposals:

> *Ralph—We've got to keep these costs down or we won't meet budget. Can we mix more of these wastes with the shipments of refuse to the Oak Hill landfill? Nobody seems to notice the coal-cleaning fluids when we mix it in well.*

Rachel was bothered by the note. She considered ignoring it, pretending that she had not seen it. But after a couple of hours, her conscience would not let her do it. Therefore, she pondered the following three alternative courses of action:

- Seek the advice of her boss, the vice president of finance for Alberta.
- Anonymously release the information to the local newspaper.
- Give the information to an outside member of Alberta's board of directors, whom she knew because he lived in her neighborhood.

1. Discuss why Rachel has an ethical responsibility to take some action about her suspicion of the illegal dumping of toxic wastes.
2. For each of the three alternative courses of action, explain whether the action is appropriate.
3. Assume that Rachel sought the advice of the vice president of finance and discovered that he both knew about and approved of the dumping of toxic wastes. What steps should she take to resolve the conflict in this situation?

NIKE 10K PROBLEM

1-52 Information in Nike's 10K Report
U.S. companies file 10K reports annually with the SEC. These reports contain the company's annual financial reports and much additional information about the company. Examine **Nike's** 10K report that is presented in Appendix C. Answer the following questions about Nike:

1. What is Nike's principal business activity?
2. What proportion of Nike revenue comes from sales in the United States? What proportion from other countries? How many retail outlets does Nike have in the United States?
3. Who is Nike's CFO? What is his accounting background?
4. Where does Nike manufacture most of its footwear? What ethical issues might result from this manufacturing philosophy?

EXCEL APPLICATION EXERCISE

1-53 Budgets and Performance Evaluation
Goal: Create an Excel spreadsheet to prepare a performance report, and use the results to answer questions about your findings.
Scenario: Beta Alpha Psi, the accounting honorary fraternity, has asked you to prepare a performance report about a homecoming party that it recently held. The background data for Beta Alpha Psi's performance report appears in the Fundamental Assignment Material 1-A2.
When you have completed your spreadsheet, answer the following questions:

1. Based on the formatting option used in the exercise, do the negative (red) variances represent amounts that are over or under budget?
2. Which cost/costs changed because the number of attendees increased?
3. Did the fraternity stay within the budgeted amount for food on a per person basis?

Step-by-Step:
1. Open a new Excel spreadsheet.
2. In column A, create a bold-faced heading that contains the following:
   Row 1: Chapter 1 Decision Guideline
   Row 2: Beta Alpha Psi Homecoming Party
   Row 3: Performance Report
   Row 4: Today's Date
3. Merge and center the date across columns A–D.
4. In row 7, create the following bold-faced, right-justified column headings:
   Column B: Budget
   Column C: Actual
   Column D: Variance

5. In column A, create the following row headings:
Row 8: Room rental
Row 9: Food
Row 10: Entertainment
Row 11: Decorations
Row 12: Total costs
Skip a row.
Row 14: Attendees
Skip a row.
Row 16: Food per person

6. Use the data from Fundamental Assignment Material 1-A2 and enter the budget and actual amounts for room, food, entertainment, decorations, and attendees.

7. Use budget minus actual formulas to generate variances for each of the cost categories.

8. Use the SUM function to generate total costs for the budget, actual, and variance columns.

9. Use a formula to generate the "per person" food amount for the budget and actual columns.

10. Format all amounts as follows:

Number tab:	Category:	Currency
	Decimal places:	0
	Symbol:	None
	Negative numbers:	Red with parentheses

11. Change the format of the food per person amounts to display two decimal places and a dollar symbol.

12. Change the format of the room rental and total cost amounts to display a dollar symbol.

13. Change the format of the total costs data (row 12) to display as bold faced.

14. Change the format of the total costs heading to display as indented:

Alignment tab:	Horizontal:	Left (Indent)
	Indent:	1

15. Save your work, and print a copy for your files.

COLLABORATIVE LEARNING EXERCISE

1-54 The Future Management Accountant

Students should gather in groups of three to six. One-third of each group should read each of the following articles. (Alternatively, you can do this exercise as a whole class, with one-third of the class reading each article.)

- Roth, R. T., "The CFO's Great Balancing Act," *Financial Executive*, July/August 2004, pp. 60–61.
- Johnsson, M, "The Changing Role of the CFO," *Strategic Finance*, June 2002, pp. 54–57, 67.
- Russell, K., G. Siegel, and C. Kulesza, "Counting More, Counting Less: Transformations in the Management Accounting Profession," *Strategic Finance*, September 1999, pp. 39–44.

1. Individually, write down the three most important lessons you learned from the article you read.

2. As a group, list all the lessons identified in requirement 1. Combine those that are essentially the same.

3. Prioritize the list you developed in requirement 2 in terms of their importance to someone considering a career in management accounting.

4. Discuss whether this exercise has changed your impression of management accounting and, if so, how your impression has changed.

INTERNET EXERCISE

1-55 Institute of Management Accountants

The Institute of Management Accountants (IMA) is a major professional organization geared toward managerial accounting and finance. The IMA has chapters throughout the United States as well as international chapters. The IMA is very concerned about ethics. Log on to www.imanet.org, the Web site for the IMA.

1. Click on About IMA and follow the link that shows the mission statement for the IMA. What is the mission of the IMA?
2. Click on IMA Membership, then Resources and Benefits, and then on the Professional Development link. How many courses does IMA offer to enhance effectiveness on the job, satisfy CPE requirements, and advance careers of members?
3. Click on the Ethics Center & Helpline link under Resources and Publications. Follow the Learn More link under the Ethical Practices heading to the Statement of Ethical Professional Practice. Read the code and comment on its importance to management accountants.

Introduction to Cost Behavior and Cost-Volume-Profit Relationships

LEARNING OBJECTIVES

When you have finished studying this chapter, you should be able to:

1. Explain how cost drivers affect cost behavior.

2. Show how changes in cost-driver levels affect variable and fixed costs.

3. Explain step- and mixed-cost behavior.

4. Create a cost-volume-profit (CVP) graph and understand the assumptions behind it.

5. Calculate break-even sales volume in total dollars and total units.

6. Calculate sales volume in total dollars and total units to reach a target profit.

7. Differentiate between contribution margin and gross margin.

8. Explain the effects of sales mix on profits (Appendix 2A).

9. Compute cost-volume-profit (CVP) relationships on an after-tax basis (Appendix 2B).

▶ BOEING COMPANY

In 1915, William Boeing, a Seattle timberman, assembled his first airplane in a boathouse. In 1954 Boeing introduced its first four-engine 707. The Boeing family of jets has grown to include the 727, 737, 747, 757, 767, 777, and the company delivered its first 787-Dreamliner in 2011. Today, the Boeing Company is the world's largest aerospace company, the second largest producer of commercial jets, and the second largest military contractor. Boeing builds 40 to 50 commercial jetliners each month and had annual revenue of $68.7 billion in 2011. The company produces aircraft that carry from about 100 to well over 500 passengers and has about half of the world's market share in airplane sales.

How will Boeing maintain its competitive edge and profitability? With intense competition from Airbus, Boeing knows that it can improve profits more by controlling (reducing) costs than by increasing prices to customers—especially when many of its customers are only beginning to recover from the steep decline in airline profits in 2008 and 2009. So, should Boeing develop new and bigger airplanes or produce more of its current line of planes with improvements in features and efficiencies that will lower customers' operating costs? Which alternative has lower costs for Boeing and its customers? To answer these questions, Boeing has to understand its own costs as well as the costs of its customers.

Consider a recent Boeing decision regarding development and production of a new airplane. Back in 1999, the company started an R&D program for the Sonic Cruiser. The Sonic Cruiser emphasized speed—it was designed to reduce travel time by about 20%. An important part of the development decision was the assessment of customers' costs—both of operating their existing fleet of planes and of the costs of the new Sonic Cruisers. In early 2001, discussions with airlines in North America, Asia, and Europe confirmed the design offered exactly what airlines and passengers were looking for: the ability to fly quickly and directly to their destinations while avoiding time-consuming and costly stops at major hubs. In late 2002, after more than 3 years of research, the company had completed the design of the new airplane and was faced with the final decision to launch. A decision to launch would involve a huge immediate investment in costly plant and equipment resources. To pay for these assets and make a profit, Boeing had to be confident that its customers would be willing to pay more for the airplane than it cost Boeing to design, produce, and sell it.

But production ultimately hinged on whether customers were willing to pay enough to cover the cost of producing a faster airplane that used the most up-to-date technology. Despite the years of development activities, Boeing decided not to proceed with the Sonic Cruiser. Why? Boeing made its decision after a careful analysis of its own production costs and the airlines' operating costs. According to Alan Mulally, CEO of Boeing Commercial Airplanes at the time, the airlines made it clear that they wanted a cheaper plane rather than a faster plane. Therefore, Boeing management decided to dedicate its resources to developing the 787-Dreamliner—a "super-efficient" jetliner constructed primarily from composite materials rather than aluminum and other metals.

© European Pressphoto Agency (EPA)/Alamy

The design and production of an airplane is a complex process. This is the first assembled Boeing 787 Dreamliner airplane at its production facility at Everett, Washington.

This chapter begins your study of costs. One of the main goals of management accounting is to help managers understand **cost behavior**—how the activities of an organization affect its costs—as they make crucial decisions about their production and service activities. For example, how much would it cost Boeing to produce each 787? How much cost does Delta Airlines incur when it adds one more passenger at the last moment to an existing flight, or when it adds one more flight to the schedule? What does it cost Toyota to develop a new line of luxury autos, as it did with Lexus? How much does it cost to produce one more Prius? How will an increase in Arizona's population affect the costs to run the state's department of motor vehicles? What does it cost Nestlé Purina to meet Wal-Mart's specifications for shipments of pet-care products? What activities contribute most to Nestlé Purina's cost to serve Wal-Mart stores? These are all specific forms of the general question: What will be the incremental effects if an organization changes its activities? ■

cost behavior
How the activities of an organization affect its costs.

Identifying Activities, Resources, Costs, and Cost Drivers

Different types of costs behave in different ways. Consider the costs of making the 737-MAX— Boeing's newest version of the most popular single-aisle airplane ever produced. As Boeing produces more airplanes, it buys and uses more resources, such as electrical wire, seats, aluminum, and labor. Therefore, each additional airplane requires Boeing to incur more of these resource costs. In contrast, the cost of other resources such as the factory and salaries of key managers stay the same, regardless of the number of airplanes made. To predict costs for decision making and to control costs on a day-to-day basis, Boeing managers identify

Objective 1

Explain how cost drivers affect cost behavior.

- key activities performed,
- resources used in performing these activities,
- costs of the resources used, and
- **cost drivers**, measures of activities that require the use of resources and thereby cause costs.

Exhibit 2-1 shows how activities link resources and their costs with the output of products or services. For example, an activity that requires resources and therefore causes costs for Boeing is installing seats. This activity uses many resources, but let's consider just two: 1) the seats themselves, which Boeing purchases from a subcontractor, and 2) labor for installing the seats. One measure of activity, number of seats installed, is an appropriate cost driver for the cost of the seats. A different measure of activity, labor hours used in installing the seats, is a cost driver for the cost of labor resources.

An organization may have many activities as part of its value chain and many cost drivers for those activities. For example, one manufacturer of pet foods has a plant in Denver with more

cost driver
A measure of activities that requires the use of resources and thereby cause costs.

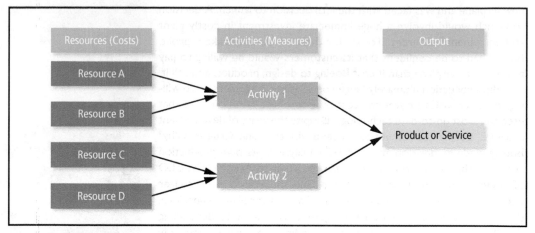

Exhibit 2-1
Linking Resource Costs to Outputs via Activities

than 50 production activities and a total of 21 cost drivers. Exhibit 2-2 lists examples of resource costs and potential cost drivers for activities in each of the value-chain functions. How well we identify the most appropriate cost drivers determines how well managers understand cost behavior and how well managers can control costs.

In this chapter we focus on a simple situation of one activity and one cost driver for the production of a particular product or service. The activity includes all aspects of the production and sale of the product or service. The cost driver is the number of units produced and sold, which we assume drives all the resource costs. Therefore, the analysis will examine how decisions about the volume of production and sales affect costs. This simplified analysis is useful to managers who want an estimate of the general relationship between production volume and costs. In later chapters, we will consider more specific and detailed analysis of costs.

Value-Chain Functions and Resource Costs	Example Cost Drivers
Research and development	
• Salaries of sales personnel, costs of market surveys	Number of new product proposals
• Salaries of product and process engineers	Complexity of proposed products
Design of products, services, and processes	
• Salaries of product and process engineers	Number of engineering hours
• Cost of computer-aided design equipment used to develop prototype of product for testing	Number of distinct parts per product
Production	Labor hours
• Labor wages	Number of people supervised
• Supervisory salaries	Number of mechanic hours
• Maintenance wages	Number of machine hours
• Depreciation of plant and machinery, supplies	Kilowatt hours
• Energy cost	
Marketing	Number of advertisements
• Cost of advertisements	Sales dollars
• Salaries of marketing personnel, travel costs, entertainment costs	
Distribution	Labor hours
• Wages of shipping personnel	Weight of items delivered
• Transportation costs including depreciation of vehicles and fuel	
Customer service	Hours spent servicing products
• Salaries of service personnel	Number of service calls
• Costs of supplies, travel	

Exhibit 2-2
Examples of Value-Chain Functions, Resource Costs, and Cost Drivers

Variable-Cost and Fixed-Cost Behavior

Accountants classify costs as variable or fixed depending on whether the cost changes with respect to a particular cost driver. A **variable cost** changes in direct proportion to changes in the cost driver. In contrast, changes in the cost driver do not affect a **fixed cost**. Suppose the cost driver is units of goods or services produced. A 10% increase in units produced would result in a 10% increase in variable costs. However, the fixed costs would remain unchanged.

Consider an example of variable costs for Watkins Products, the 140-year-old health food company. If Watkins pays its sales personnel a 20% straight commission on sales, the total cost of sales commissions to Watkins is 20% of sales dollars—a variable cost with respect to sales revenues. Or suppose Long Lake Bait Shop buys bags of fish bait from a supplier for $2 each. The total cost of fish bait is $2 times the number of bags purchased—a variable cost with respect to units (number of bags) purchased. Notice that variable costs do not change *per unit of the cost driver*, but the *total variable costs* change in direct proportion to the cost-driver activity.

Now consider an example of a fixed cost. Suppose Sony rents a factory for $500,000 per year to produce DVD players. The number of DVD players produced does not affect the *total fixed cost* of $500,000. The *unit cost* of rent applicable to each DVD player, however, does depend on the total number of DVD players produced. If Sony produces 50,000 DVD players, the unit cost will be $500,000 ÷ 50,000 = $10. If Sony produces 100,000 DVD players, the unit cost will be $500,000 ÷ 100,000 = $5. Therefore, while the fixed cost *per-unit of the cost-driver* becomes progressively smaller as the volume increases, the *total fixed cost* does not change with volume.

The term "fixed cost" describes the behavior of cost with respect to the cost driver, but a fixed cost can change due to factors other than changes in the cost driver. For example, heating costs are commonly fixed and do not change with respect to the production volume cost driver. Nonetheless, heating costs change with respect to factors not related to the cost driver, such as changes in the price of oil or electricity, or unusually warm or unusually cold weather.

Pay special attention to the fact that the terms "variable" or "fixed" describe the behavior of the total dollar cost, not the per-unit cost, which has the opposite behavior. Total variable costs increase as the cost driver increases but variable costs per unit remain constant. Total fixed costs remain constant as cost driver activity increases but fixed costs per unit decrease. Exhibit 2-3 summarizes these relationships.

Objective 2

Show how changes in cost-driver levels affect variable and fixed costs.

variable cost
A cost that changes in direct proportion to changes in the cost-driver level.

fixed cost
A cost that is not affected by changes in the cost-driver level.

Making Managerial Decisions

Test your understanding of the distinction between variable and fixed costs by answering the following questions.

1. A producer of premium ice cream uses "gallons of ice cream produced" as a cost driver for the production activity. One of the main resources this activity uses is dairy ingredients. Is the cost of dairy ingredients a variable or a fixed cost with respect to production volume?
2. Another resource used by this activity is supervisory salaries. If supervisory salaries do not change with the level of production of ice cream, is the supervisory salaries cost variable or fixed with respect to production volume?

Answer

The way to determine whether the cost of a resource is fixed or variable with respect to a cost driver is to ask the question, "If the level of the cost driver changes, what will happen to the cost?"

If the company increases or decreases its production of ice cream, the cost of dairy ingredients will increase or decrease in proportion to production volume. Thus, the cost of dairy ingredients is a variable cost. If the production of ice cream increases or decreases, supervisory salaries will not change. Thus, the cost of supervisory salaries is a fixed cost.

Exhibit 2-3
Cost Behavior of Fixed and Variable Costs

Type of Cost	If Cost-Driver Level Increases (or Decreases)	
	Total Cost	Cost per Unit*
Fixed costs	No change	Decrease (or increase)
Variable costs	Increase (or decrease)	No change

*Per unit of activity volume, for example, product units, passenger-miles, orders processed, or sales dollars

To plan and control costs, managers focus on the activities required to make, sell, and deliver products or services and the resources needed to support these activities. Consider one of the many activities performed as part of the production function at Boeing's plant—receiving parts that production workers install on an airplane. Managers need to know how the receiving activity affects production costs. For example, how does the increase or decrease in receiving activity affect the lease payment for renting the equipment used to move parts from the receiving area to the production floor? How does it affect the cost of fuel for the moving equipment? Similarly, how does it affect costs of receiving labor, supplies, and other resources?

Consider the behavior of just two of these resource costs, equipment and fuel costs, ignoring other resource costs such as labor and supplies. Suppose equipment costs of $45,000 are fixed and do not vary with increases or decreases in the number of parts received, while fuel cost is a variable cost that increases or decreases by $.80 with each part received. Exhibit 2-4 shows how these resource costs relate to the receiving activity.

Exhibit 2-5 illustrates the relationship between the receiving activity and resource costs. The equipment costs represent the total fixed lease cost of $45,000. The fuel costs are variable at $0.80 per part received. We can use the descriptions of cost behavior in Exhibits 2-4 and 2-5 to find total fuel and equipment cost at any other level of receiving activity. For example, the total equipment and fuel costs of receiving 30,000 parts is $45,000 + (30,000 × $.80) = $69,000. Similarly, the total cost of receiving 27,500 parts is $45,000 + (27,500 × $.80) = $67,000. Notice how we used the respective costs in these calculations. We used the total cost of $45,000 for the fixed equipment lease cost and the unit cost of $.80 for variable fuel cost.

Exhibit 2-4
Receiving Activity and Resources Used

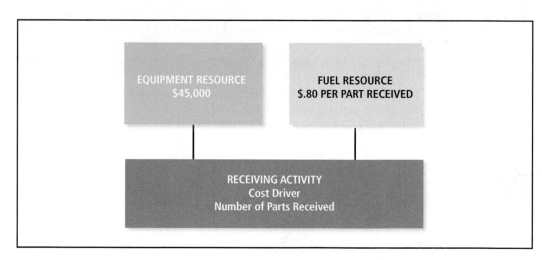

Exhibit 2-5
Total Fuel and Equipment Lease Costs

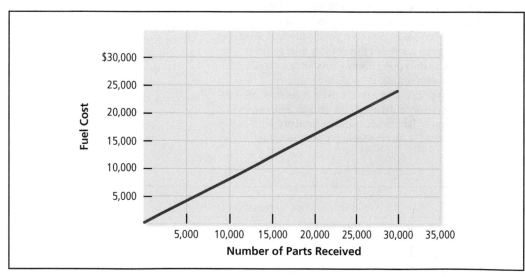

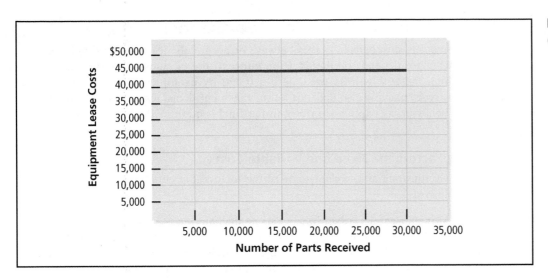

Exhibit 2-5
(continued)

Summary Problem for Your Review

PROBLEM

The manager at the **Boeing** plant is looking at a monthly report of plant costs. He notices that the receiving activity costs vary substantially from month to month and is interested in knowing more about why the total cost and unit cost of the receiving activity change. The number of parts received has ranged from 10,000 to 30,000 parts per month over the last several months.

1. Prepare a table that shows the cost of equipment, the cost of fuel, the total of equipment and fuel costs, and the cost per-part-received for 10,000 to 30,000 parts per month, using increments of 5,000 parts per month.

2. Prepare brief explanations of why the total and unit cost patterns change.

SOLUTION

1. The table can be developed using the relationships shown in Exhibit 2-5.

(1) Parts Received	(2) Equipment Cost	(3) $.80 × (1) Fuel Cost	(4) (2) + (3) Total Cost	(5) (4) ÷ (1) Cost per Part Received
10,000	$45,000	$ 8,000	$53,000	$5.30
15,000	45,000	12,000	57,000	3.80
20,000	45,000	16,000	61,000	3.05
25,000	45,000	20,000	65,000	2.60
30,000	45,000	24,000	69,000	2.30

2. Column (4) shows the total cost of the receiving activity, which shows a pattern of increasing total cost. The increase in total cost is less than proportional to the activity cost driver because total cost includes both the fixed cost component from Column (2) as well as the variable cost component from Column (3). For example, a 50% increase in the number of parts received from 10,000 parts to 15,000 parts results in a 50% increase in the variable cost component in column (3) but the total cost in column (4) increases by far less than 50% because the fixed cost in column (2) does not change.

   Column (5) shows the cost per part received, which shows a pattern of decreasing cost per part. The decreasing cost per part is entirely due to the fixed equipment cost being spread over increasing numbers of parts received, the cost driver. For example, consider the change in cost per part as the number of parts received increases from 10,000 to 15,000 parts. The fixed cost per part moves from $4.50 at 10,000 parts received ($45,000 ÷ 10,000) to $3.00 at 15,000 parts received ($45,000 ÷ 15,000). The variable cost per part remains constant at $0.80. Thus, the sum of the fixed and variable costs per part in column (5) decreases from $5.30 ($4.50 + $.80) to $3.80 ($3.00 + $.80) due entirely to the decline in the fixed cost per part.

Cost Behavior: Further Considerations

decision context
The circumstances surrounding the decision for which the cost will be used.

For a variety of reasons, cost behavior cannot always be accurately described as simply variable or fixed. Cost behavior depends on the **decision context**, the circumstances surrounding the decision for which the cost will be used, as illustrated by examples in the discussion that follows. Further, cost behavior also depends on management decisions—management choices determine cost behavior, as explained briefly in the final section of this chapter and in more detail in Chapter 3.

Complicating Factors for Fixed and Variable Costs

In this section, we illustrate and explain some of the factors that complicate cost behavior for fixed and variable costs.

FIXED COSTS   Although we described fixed costs as unchanging regardless of changes in the cost driver, this description holds true only within limits. For example, rent costs for a production building are generally fixed within a limited range of activity but may rise if activity increases enough to require additional rental space or may decline if activity decreases so much that it allows the company to rent less space. The **relevant range** is the limits of the cost-driver level within which a specific relationship between costs and the cost driver is valid.

relevant range
The limits of the cost-driver level within which a specific relationship between costs and the cost driver is valid.

Suppose that total monthly fixed costs are $100,000 for a General Electric lightbulb plant as long as production is between 40,000 and 85,000 cases of lightbulbs per month. However, if production falls below 40,000 cases, changes in production processes will slash fixed costs to $60,000 per month. On the other hand, if operations rise above 85,000 cases, rentals of additional facilities will boost fixed costs to $115,000 per month. Exhibit 2-6 graphs these assumptions about cost behavior. The top figure shows a refined analysis that reflects all the complexities described previously. The bottom figure shows a simplified analysis that focuses only on the cost in the relevant range, ignoring the issue of cost behavior outside the relevant range. Within the relevant range highlighted in yellow, the refined and simplified analyses coincide. However, the refined description at the top of Exhibit 2-6 explicitly shows the rental costs at the levels of activity outside the relevant range. The simplified description at the bottom of the exhibit shows only the rental costs for the relevant range and uses a dashed line outside the relevant range to remind the user that the graphed cost is outside the limits of the relevant range.

Exhibit 2-6
Fixed Costs and Relevant Range

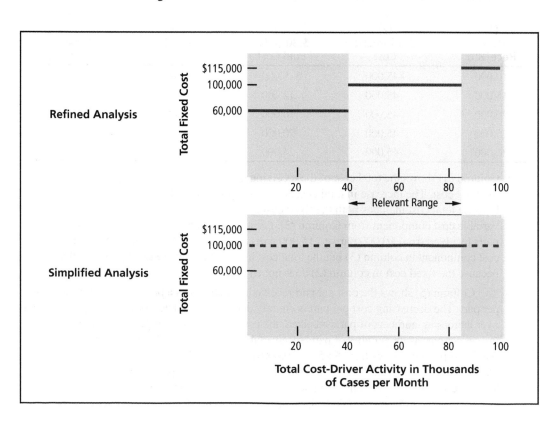

As a decision maker, it is essential to recognize when your decision will move outside the relevant range. In that case, it is essential that you obtain the information included in the refined analysis, showing how costs behave outside the relevant range.

VARIABLE COSTS   The idea of a relevant range is obviously important for fixed costs, but a corresponding issue may also arise for variable costs. For example, if **GE** obtains volume discounts for purchasing larger quantities of input materials such as glass and tungsten, the materials cost per case for the GE lightbulb plant would be lower, and the slope of the variable cost function would be lower, at higher levels of production. As another example, labor cost per case will decrease at higher levels of production if expansion to achieve higher levels of production results in a new production process with higher labor efficiency. When costs vary with changes in the cost driver but not in direct proportion to the change in the cost driver, the variable cost function does not produce a straight-line graph.

Step- and Mixed-Cost Behavior Patterns

Some costs are neither purely fixed nor purely variable. For example, two types of costs that combine characteristics of both fixed- and variable-cost behavior are step costs and mixed costs.

STEP COSTS   Costs that change abruptly at different levels of activity because the resources are available only in indivisible chunks are **step costs**. For decisions where the range of activity is limited to a single step of the cost function, we consider the cost a fixed cost. For decisions where the range of activity encompasses many steps, the cost behaves more like a variable cost.

Panel A of Exhibit 2-7 illustrates a decision where a step cost could be treated as a fixed cost. In this example, when oil and gas exploration activity reaches a certain level, the company must lease an additional rig. Each additional rig leased defines a new step in the cost function, which supports a new, higher volume of exploration activity. This step cost behaves as a fixed cost as long as all the decision alternatives remain within the relevant range of a single step, such as within the highlighted relevant range of the second step in the cost function shown in Panel A of Exhibit 2-7.

Panel B of Exhibit 2-7 illustrates a decision where a step cost could be treated as a variable cost. The cost function shows the wage cost of cashiers at a supermarket where the individual cost steps are uniform. Each cashier can serve an average of 20 shoppers per hour. In a decision about staffing, where the number of shoppers is expected to range from 40 per hour to 440 per hour, the required number of cashiers to match the number of shoppers would range between 2 and 22. Because the range of the number of shoppers in this decision spans a large number of equal-sized steps, this step cost behaves much like a variable cost, and for this decision there is only a small loss of accuracy when we assume the step cost is variable.

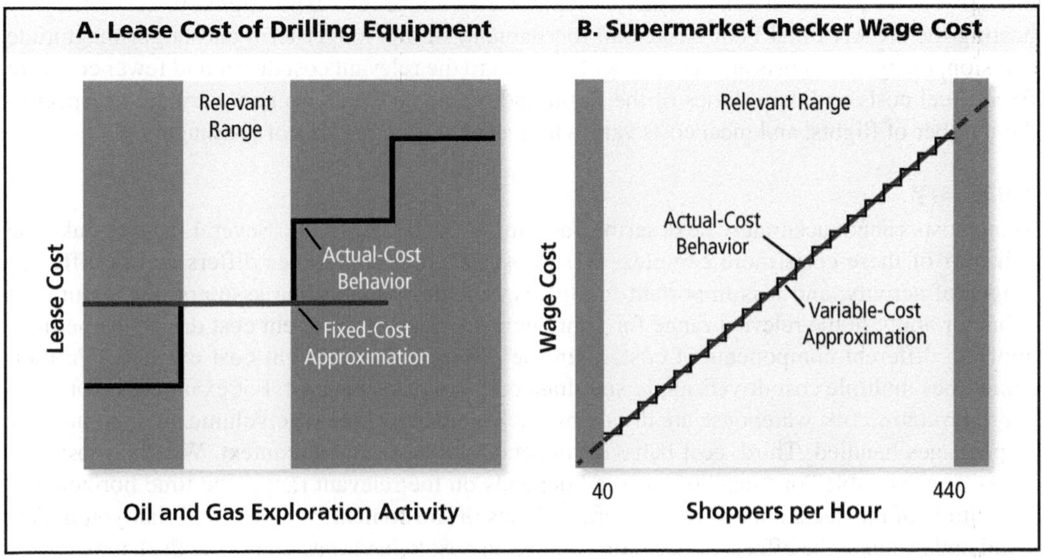

Objective 3

Explain step- and mixed-cost behavior.

step cost
A cost that changes abruptly at different intervals of activity because the resources and their costs come in indivisible chunks.

Exhibit 2-7
Step-Cost Behavior

Note that the decision context dictates whether a step cost can be treated as fixed or variable. For example, in the cashier staffing example, suppose we are deciding whether to implement a promotional offer expected to attract 5 more shoppers per hour during mid-afternoon when there are currently about 70 shoppers per hour. Because this decision will not span more than one step in the cashier cost function, for this decision we can assume cashier wages are a fixed cost.

mixed cost

A cost that contains elements of both fixed- and variable-cost behavior.

MIXED COSTS   Many costs are **mixed costs**, which contain elements of both fixed- and variable-cost behavior. The fixed-cost element is unchanged over the relevant range of activity levels while the variable-cost element of the mixed cost varies proportionately with cost-driver activity. You might think of the fixed cost element as the cost of creating the capacity to operate and the variable cost element as the additional cost of actually using that capacity.

For example, the cost of providing diagnostic imaging services at the Mayo Clinic is a mixed cost. There is a substantial fixed cost of having expensive imaging equipment available and ready for use. There is also a variable cost associated with actual use of the equipment, such as the costs of power, technicians to operate the equipment, and physicians to interpret the results. As another example, the cost of running an evening dinner cruise on the Seine River in Paris is a mixed cost. There is a fixed cost of having the boat and crew available to travel along the river. There is also a variable cost of having service staff, food, and beverages to match the number of passengers on the cruise.

Effect of Time Horizon and Magnitude on Cost Behavior

Whether costs behave as fixed or variable often depends on the time frame affected by a decision and on the magnitude of the change in cost-driver activity. For long time spans or large changes in activity level, more costs behave as variable. For short time spans or small changes in activity level, more costs behave as fixed. The preceding discussion of step costs shows how cashier wage costs can be variable in large magnitude decisions about staffing but fixed in small magnitude decisions.

To illustrate the effects of time horizon, suppose a United Airlines plane with several empty seats is scheduled to depart from its gate. A potential passenger is running down a corridor bearing a transferable ticket from a competing airline. Unless the gate attendant holds the airplane for an extra 2 minutes, the passenger will miss the departure and will not switch to United for the planned trip. What are the variable costs in the gate agent's decision whether to delay the departure and place one more passenger in an otherwise empty seat? Virtually all the costs in this situation are fixed. The number of passenger meals carried on the flight will not change at the last moment, and the flight crew salaries and maintenance costs will not change. Only the cost of jet fuel will change, but this change will be relatively small, and the additional fuel used when one more passenger is added is far less than proportional to the increase in the number of passengers. This is a decision that has a short time horizon, a small change in the cost driver (number of passengers), and therefore mainly fixed costs.

Now consider decisions that United makes that involve longer time horizons and larger magnitudes, such as the decision whether to temporarily add a few extra flights to serve the city hosting the NCAA Final Four basketball tournament. In this longer term and larger magnitude decision, many more costs are variable with respect to the relevant cost driver and fewer costs are fixed. Fuel costs and the salaries of the flight and maintenance crews now vary with respect to the number of flights, and meal costs vary with respect to the number of passengers.

Summary

Many costs cannot accurately be described as simply fixed or variable. Several factors make the behavior of these costs more complex. First, cost behavior sometimes differs across different ranges of activity, and it is important to always consider whether the assumptions about cost behavior apply in the relevant range for your decision. Second, different cost drivers sometimes apply to different components of cost, as in the United Airlines flight cost example. Further, sometimes multiple cost drivers apply simultaneously to the same cost. For example, labor costs at an Amazon.com warehouse are driven by package weight, package volume, and the number of packages handled. Third, cost behavior depends on the decision context. Whether costs are "fixed" or "variable" or "step" or "mixed" depends on the relevant range, the time horizon and magnitude of the decision, and other characteristics of the context. It is essential that you understand and evaluate the effects of decision context on cost behavior as you make decisions.

Cost-Volume-Profit Analysis

For the remainder of this chapter, we consider only decisions where costs are fixed, variable, or mixed. The models developed assume the fixed cost components of cost do not change with the cost driver and the variable cost components change in direct proportion to a single cost driver. These models serve as useful starting points in decisions where the assumptions do not hold exactly but are reasonable approximations. For example, the models apply to step costs where the decision spans a large enough number of steps and the steps in the cost function are proportional to the cost driver so that the steps can be reasonably approximated as a variable cost.

Consider situations where managers are trying to evaluate the effects of changes in the volume of goods or services produced. For example, managers might be interested in upward changes such as increased sales expected from increases in promotion or advertising. On the other hand, managers might be interested in downward changes such as decreased sales expected due to a new competitor entering the market or due to a decline in economic conditions. While such changes in volume have many effects, managers are always interested in the relationship between volume and revenue (sales), expenses (costs), and net income (net profit). We call this **cost-volume-profit (CVP) analysis**.

cost-volume-profit (CVP) analysis
The study of the effects of output volume on revenue (sales), expenses (costs), and net income (net profit).

CVP Scenario

Amy Winston, the manager of food services for one of Boeing's plants, is trying to decide whether to rent a line of snack vending machines. Although individual snack items have various acquisition costs and selling prices, Winston has decided that an average selling price of $1.50 per unit and an average acquisition cost of $1.20 per unit will suffice for purposes of this analysis. She predicts the following revenue and expense relationships:

	Per Unit	Percentage of Sales
Selling price	$1.50	100%
Variable cost of each item	1.20	80
Selling price less variable cost	$ .30	20%
Monthly fixed expenses		
Rent	$ 3,000	
Wages for replenishing and servicing	13,500	
Other fixed expenses	1,500	
Total fixed expenses per month	$18,000	

Graphing the CVP Relationship

Exhibit 2-8 is a graph of the cost-volume-profit relationship in our vending machine example. Most students find it easiest to begin the study of CVP relationships with graphs. After introducing the relationships with a graph, we will turn to equations that describe the same CVP concepts. The equations are usually the better way to find the quantitative answer to a specific question. On the other hand, when you need to explain a CVP model to an audience, graphs more quickly convey the break-even point and more easily show profits expected over a range of volume.

As you read the following procedure for constructing the graph, visualize the revenues and costs that correspond to the points and lines you are plotting.

1. Draw the axes. The horizontal axis is sales volume and the vertical axis is dollars of cost and revenue.
2. Plot revenue. Select a convenient value at the upper end of the relevant range for sales volume, say, 100,000 units, and plot point A for total sales dollars at that volume: 100,000 × $1.50 = $150,000. Draw the revenue line from the origin (the point corresponding to $0 and 0 units) to point A.
3. Plot fixed costs. Draw the horizontal line showing the $18,000 fixed portion of cost. The point where the horizontal fixed cost line intersects the vertical axis is point B.

Objective 4

Create a cost-volume-profit (CVP) graph and understand the assumptions behind it.

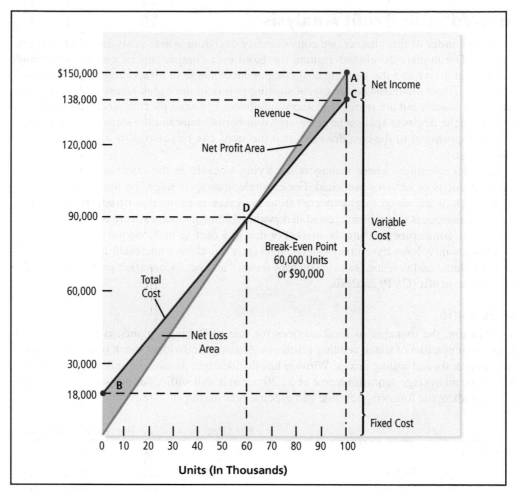

Exhibit 2-8
Cost-Volume-Profit (CVP) Graph

4. Plot fixed costs plus variable costs. Determine the variable portion of cost at the volume you used to plot point A: 100,000 units × $1.20 = $120,000. Plot point C, the fixed plus variable costs for 100,000 units, $18,000 + $120,000 = $138,000. Then draw a line between this point and point B, the fixed plus variable costs for 0 units, $18,000 + $0 = $18,000. This line shows the total cost (fixed cost plus variable cost) at volumes between 0 and 100,000 units.

break-even point
The level of sales at which revenue equals total cost and net income is zero.

5. Locate the **break-even point**—the volume of sales at which revenue equals total cost and therefore income is zero. Graphically, this is the point at 60,000 units where the sales revenue line and the total cost line cross. At 60,000 units, total revenue (60,000 × $1.50 = $90,000) is equal to total cost ([60,000 × $1.20] + $18,000 = $90,000). On the graph, the break-even point is labeled point D.

CVP analysis is sometimes also referred to as break-even analysis. However, this term is misleading. Why? Because CVP analysis reveals more than just the break-even point. At any volume of activity, the vertical distance between the revenue line and the total cost line represents the profit or loss at that volume.

Throughout the remainder of the book, we will see that CVP analysis plays an important role in management decision making and in planning for the effects of changes in competitive and economic conditions on sales, costs, and net income. The business press frequently discusses break-even points, especially during economic downturns. The Business First box on p. 47 describes efforts to lower break-even points by some high-tech and auto-industry firms.

Tech Firms and Auto Makers Lower Break-Even Points During Economic Recession

One might think that because the goal of business is to make a profit, not just break even, the term breakeven would not often be used in business. However when economic conditions result in declining sales, companies are keenly aware of the break-even point.

In the recession that began in 2008, many companies reported on their attempts to achieve profitability in spite of declining sales. They often focused on how their efforts to control costs reduced their break-even points. If a company faces rapidly falling sales, it must restructure its costs to be able to break even at a lower volume. Restructuring costs can involve reducing both fixed and variable costs.

Consider Sony's PlayStation 3. It costs Sony about $500 to make a PS3 but the sales price is about $300 and with competitive pressure from Nintendo Wii and Microsoft Xbox 360, raising the price was not an option. So how could Sony lower its costs to break even? The two actions Sony considered were reducing variable cost and fixed cost. To lower its variable cost, Sony reduced the number of parts and the cost for the console's central processing unit. Reducing the number of parts also lowered Sony's fixed costs, such as assembly equipment and salaries of purchasing agents responsible for vendor negotiations.

At the same time, automakers worldwide faced dramatic declines in sales, forcing equally dramatic restructuring of their operations to lower their costs in hopes of breaking even. For example, to deal with the ongoing downturn in auto sales, "Toyota embarked on efforts to make its domestic factory lines more flexible and introduce other changes to be able to break even at capacity utilization of 70 percent, equivalent to daily production of 12,000 units." Until the recession, the break-even level of car sales for the "Big Three" U.S. automakers was about 16 million per year. By early 2009, the annual sales rate was at a pace of 9 million, far below the break-even point. Among the actions taken to reduce the break-even sales level by GM, Chrysler, and Ford were massive plant closings, layoffs, and reduction of the number of models produced. Many of the associated costs were fixed and thus not dependent on unit sales. The main idea for automakers was to reduce both fixed costs and variable costs, thus lowering breakeven and eventually returning to profitability.

Sources: "Sony PS3 Costs Less To Make, But Still A Money Loser," *Techweb*, December 30, 2008; "Car Sales Not as Horrid In March," *USA Today*, April 2, 2009; "Toyota aims to lower break-even point for Japan operations," *Reuters*, December 24, 2010.

It is important to remember that CVP analysis is based on a set of important assumptions. Some of these assumptions follow:

1. We can classify costs into variable and fixed categories. The variable costs vary in direct proportion to activity level. Fixed costs do not change with activity level.
2. We expect no change in costs due to changes in efficiency or productivity.
3. The behavior of revenues and costs is linear over the relevant range. This means that selling prices per unit and variable costs per unit do not change with the level of sales. Note that almost all break-even graphs show revenue and cost lines extending back to the vertical axis as shown in Exhibit 2-8. As illustrated by the earlier discussion of Exhibits 2-6 and 2-7, this approach is misleading in cases where the relevant range does not extend all the way back to zero volume.
4. In multiproduct companies, the sales mix remains constant. The **sales mix** is the relative proportions or combinations of quantities of different products that constitute total sales. (See Appendix 2A for more on sales mixes.)
5. The inventory level does not change significantly during the period. That is, the number of units sold equals the number of units produced.

sales mix
The relative proportions or combinations of quantities of products that constitute total sales.

Computing the Break-Even Point

We next illustrate how to compute the break-even point using an equation that describes the CVP relationship. The discussion begins with the general approach, and then moves to a method that focuses on the contribution margin, which often leads more quickly to solutions.

Objective 5

Calculate break-even sales volume in total dollars and total units.

GENERAL EQUATION APPROACH   We begin with a general approach that you can adapt to any conceivable cost-volume-profit situation. You are familiar with a typical income statement. We can express an income statement in equation form as follows:

$$\text{sales} - \text{variable expenses} - \text{fixed expenses} = \text{net income} \qquad (1)$$

That is,

$$\left(\frac{\text{Unit sales}}{\text{price}} \times \frac{\text{number}}{\text{of units}}\right) - \left(\frac{\text{unit}}{\text{variable cost}} \times \frac{\text{number}}{\text{of units}}\right) - \frac{\text{fixed}}{\text{expenses}} = \frac{\text{net}}{\text{income}}$$

To find the break-even point, set net income on the right-hand-side of the equation to zero:

$$\text{sales} - \text{variable expenses} - \text{fixed expenses} = 0$$

Let N = number of units to be sold to break even. Then, for the vending machine example,

$$\$1.50\,N - \$1.20\,N - \$18,000 = 0$$
$$\$.30\,N = 18,000$$
$$N = \$18,000 \div \$.30$$
$$N = 60,000 \text{ units}$$

To express the break-even point in terms of dollar sales rather than number of units, multiply the number of units (60,000) by the selling price per unit ($1.50) to find the break-even point in terms of dollar sales, $90,000.

CONTRIBUTION-MARGIN METHOD The general equation can also be reformulated in terms of the **unit contribution margin** or **marginal income per unit** that every unit sold generates, which is the unit sales price minus the variable cost per unit. For the vending machine snack items, the unit contribution margin is $.30:

unit contribution margin (marginal income per unit)
The sales price per unit minus the variable cost per unit.

Unit sales price	$1.50
− Unit variable cost	1.20
= Unit contribution margin	$ .30

total contribution margin
Total number of units sold times the unit contribution margin.

When do we reach the break-even point? When we sell enough units to generate a **total contribution margin** (total number of units sold × unit contribution margin) that is sufficient to cover the total fixed costs. Think about the contribution margin of the snack items. Each unit sold generates extra revenue of $1.50 and extra cost of $1.20. Fixed costs are unaffected. If we sell zero units, we incur a loss equal to the fixed cost of $18,000. Each additional unit sold reduces the loss by $.30 until sales reach the break-even point. After that point, each unit sold adds (or contributes) $.30 to profit.

To find the break-even number of units, divide the fixed costs of $18,000 by the unit contribution margin of $.30. The number of units that we must sell to break even is $18,000 ÷ $.30 = 60,000 units. The sales revenue at the break-even point is 60,000 units × $1.50 per unit, or $90,000.

Instead of using per unit variable costs and contribution margins, it is sometimes more convenient to use percentages. The variable cost percentage and the contribution margin percentage can be computed using either total or per unit costs:

variable-cost percentage
Total variable costs divided by total sales.

$$\textbf{Variable-cost percentage} = \text{total variable costs} \div \text{total sales}$$
$$= \text{variable cost per unit} \div \text{sales price per unit}$$

contribution-margin percentage
Total contribution margin divided by sales or 100% minus the variable cost percentage.

$$\textbf{Contribution-margin percentage} = \text{total contribution margin} \div \text{total sales}$$
$$= \text{contribution margin per unit} \div \text{sales price per unit}$$

Note that the contribution-margin percentage = 100% − variable cost percentage. We can also express these percentages as ratios, the **variable-cost ratio** and **contribution-margin ratio**, which are simply the percentages multiplied by 100.

Now let's solve for break-even sales dollars in our vending machine example without computing the unit break-even point by using the contribution-margin ratio or percentage:

variable-cost ratio
Variable cost percentage expressed as a ratio.

contribution-margin ratio
Contribution margin percentage expressed as a ratio.

$$\frac{\text{contribution margin}}{\text{ratio or percentage}} = \frac{\text{contribution margin per unit}}{\text{sales price per unit}} = \frac{\$.30}{\$1.50} = .20 \text{ or } 20\%$$

Let S = sales in dollars needed to break even. Then variable expenses = .80S. Setting the right-hand-side of equation (1) to the break-even level of zero net income,

$$\text{sales} - \text{variable expenses} - \text{fixed expenses} = 0$$
$$S - .80S - \$18,000 = 0$$
$$.20S = \$18,000$$
$$S = \$18,000 \div .20$$
$$S = \$90,000$$

The 20% contribution-margin ratio or percentage implies that $.20 of each sales dollar is available for the recovery of fixed expenses. Thus, we need $18,000 ÷ .20 = $90,000 of sales to break even.

The condensed income statement at the break-even point is

	Total	Per Unit	Percentage
Units	60,000		
Sales	$90,000	$1.50	100%
Variable costs	72,000	1.20	80
Contribution margin*	$18,000	$ .30	20%
Fixed costs	18,000		
Net income	$ 0		

*Sales less variable costs

The preceding income statement shows three different ways the term **contribution margin** can be used. The term can refer to total contribution margin ($18,000), unit contribution margin ($.30 per unit), or contribution-margin ratio or percentage (.20 or 20%). The context generally makes it clear which meaning is intended.

The contribution margin method is often used to evaluate the overall effect of changes in volume for companies that sell multiple products with different unit prices and different unit variable costs. You can use the preceding formula to assess the effect of a change in dollar volume of sales. For example, you can use the formula to assess the effect of an increase in dollar sales for a grocery store selling hundreds of products at many different prices assuming that the variable-cost percentage stays the same. Note that the variable-cost percentage might change if the sales mix changes, an issue that we discuss further in Appendix 2A.

contribution margin
A term used for either total contribution margin, unit contribution margin, or contribution margin percentage.

RELATIONSHIP BETWEEN THE TWO METHODS   The contribution-margin method is a specific version of the general equation method. Look at the last three lines in the two solutions given for equation 1. They read

Break-Even Volume	
Units	Dollars
$.30N = \$18,000$	$.20S = \$18,000$
$N = \dfrac{\$18,000}{\$.30}$	$S = \dfrac{\$18,000}{.20}$
$N = 60,000 \text{ units}$	$S = \$90,000$

From these equations, we can derive the following shortcut formulas:

$$\text{break-even volume in units} = \frac{\text{fixed expenses}}{\text{unit contribution margin}} \qquad (2)$$

$$\text{break-even volume in dollars} = \frac{\text{fixed expenses}}{\text{contribution-margin ratio}} \qquad (3)$$

Should you use the general equation method or the contribution-margin method? Use whichever is easier for you to understand or apply to a particular case. Both yield the same results, so the choice is a matter of personal preference.

Making Managerial Decisions

Managers use CVP analysis to predict the effect of changes in sales or costs on the break-even point. Using shortcut formulas (2) and (3), answer the following questions. Remember that the contribution margin per unit equals the sales price per unit minus the variable costs per unit.

1. What would be the effect on the unit and dollar break-even level if fixed costs increase (and there are no other changes)?
2. What would be the effect on the unit and dollar break-even level if variable cost per unit decreases (and there are no other changes)?
3. What would be the effect on the unit and dollar break-even level if sales volume increases? (Think carefully before answering this question.)

Answers

1. The break-even level in both units and sales dollars would increase if fixed costs increase.
2. The break-even level in both units and sales dollars would decrease if variable cost per unit decreases.
3. The actual (or even planned) volume of sales in units has nothing to do with determining the break-even point. This is why unit sales volume does not appear in either equation (2) or (3).

Effects of Changes in Fixed Expenses or Contribution Margin

In addition to determining profit at various volume levels, we can use CVP to examine the effects of changes in fixed costs, variables costs, or selling prices.

CHANGES IN FIXED EXPENSES   Changes in fixed expenses cause changes in the break-even point. For example, if we double the $3,000 monthly rent of the vending machines, what is the monthly break-even point in number of units and dollar sales?

The fixed expenses increase from $18,000 to $21,000, so

$$\text{break-even volume in units} = \frac{\text{fixed expenses}}{\text{unit contribution margin}}$$

$$= \frac{\$21,000}{\$.30}$$

$$= 70,000 \text{ units}$$

$$\text{break-even volume in dollars} = \frac{\text{fixed expenses}}{\text{contribution-margin ratio}}$$

$$= \frac{\$21,000}{.20}$$

$$= \$105,000$$

Note that a one-sixth increase in fixed expenses increases the break-even point by one-sixth, from 60,000 to 70,000 units and from $90,000 to $105,000. This type of relationship always exists between fixed expenses and the break-even point, assuming everything else remains constant.

Companies frequently lower their break-even points by reducing their total fixed costs. For example, when demand for cars fell because of the slumping economy in 2008 and 2009, the "Big Three" auto companies closed factories to decrease fixed costs such as property taxes, insurance, depreciation, and managers' salaries. If they had merely produced fewer cars and trucks with the same fixed costs, their volume would have fallen below the break-even point. By reducing fixed costs, the companies lowered their break-even points and reduced their losses.

CHANGES IN UNIT CONTRIBUTION MARGIN   Companies can also reduce their break-even points by increasing their unit contribution margins, by either increasing unit sales prices or decreasing unit variable costs, or both.

For example, assume the fixed costs for the vending machine example remain at $18,000. (1) If Winston increases the selling price from $1.50 to $1.60 per unit and the original variable costs per unit are unchanged at $1.20 per unit, find the monthly break-even point in number of units and in dollar sales. (2) If Winston reduces variable costs per unit by $.10 per unit and the selling price remains unchanged at $1.50 per unit, find the monthly break-even point in number of units and in dollar sales.

Here's what happens to the break-even point:

1. If Winston increases the selling price from $1.50 to $1.60 per unit and the original variable expenses are unchanged, the unit contribution margin would increase from $1.50 − $1.20 = $.30 to $1.60 − $1.20 = $.40, and the break-even point would fall to $18,000 ÷ $.40 = 45,000 units. The break-even point in dollars would also change because of the selling price per unit and contribution-margin ratio change. The contribution-margin ratio would be $.40 ÷ $1.60 = .25. The break-even point in dollars would be 45,000 units × $1.60 = $72,000 or, using the formula,

$$\text{break-even volume in dollars} = \frac{\$18,000}{.25} = \$72,000$$

2. The variable expenses decrease from $1.20 to $1.10 per unit, the unit contribution margin increases from $.30 to $.40, and the contribution-margin ratio become $.40 ÷ $1.50 = .26667. The original fixed expenses of $18,000 would stay the same, but the denominators would change from those previously used. Thus,

$$\text{break-even point in units} = \frac{\$18,000}{\$.40} = 45,000 \text{ units}$$

$$\text{break-even point in dollars} = \frac{\$18,000}{.26667} = \$67,500$$

Note that the break-even point in units in (2) is the same as the break-even point in units in (1), because both examples have the same fixed costs and the same contribution margin. However, the break-even points in dollars differ, because the selling prices per unit differ.

You can see that small percentage changes in price or variable costs can lead to large percentage changes in the unit contribution margin and, hence, to large changes in the break-even point.

Target Net Profit and an Incremental Approach

Managers also use CVP analysis to determine the sales volume needed to reach a target profit. For example, in our vending example, suppose Winston considers $1,440 per month the minimum acceptable net income. How many units will she have to sell to justify the adoption of the vending machine plan? How does the number of units "translate" into dollar sales?

Objective 6

Calculate sales volume in total dollars and total units to reach a target profit.

To compute the target sales volume in units needed to meet the desired or target net income, we adapt the general approach (equation 1 on p. 47) by setting profit on the right-hand side to the target net income:

$$\text{target sales} - \text{variable expenses} - \text{fixed expenses} = \text{target net income} \qquad (4)$$

or

$$\text{target sales volume in units} = \frac{\text{fixed expenses} + \text{target net income}}{\text{unit contribution margin}}$$

$$= \frac{\$18,000 + \$1,440}{\$.30} = 64,800 \text{ units} \qquad (5)$$

The only real difference from the normal break-even analysis is that we are solving for a target net income of $1,440 instead of a target of $0, which is the definition of break-even net income.

Another way of finding the volume required to achieve a target level of net income is to start with the break-even point and adopt an incremental approach. The phrase **incremental effect** refers to the change in total results (such as revenue, expenses, or income) under a new condition in comparison with some given or known condition. In this case, the known condition is the 60,000-unit break-even point. The change or increment in net income for every unit of sales beyond 60,000 is the unit contribution margin of $1.50 − $1.20 = $.30. The incremental volume required to generate incremental profit of $1,440 is $1,440 ÷ $.30 = 4,800 units. Thus, the volume required to achieve target profit of $1,440 must exceed the break-even volume by 4,800 units; it would therefore be

incremental effect
The change in total results (such as revenue, expenses, or income) under a new condition in comparison with some given or known condition.

60,000 + 4,800 = 64,800 units. Multiply 64,800 units by sales price of $1.50 per unit to get the volume in dollar sales, $97,200.

To solve directly for sales dollars with the incremental approach, start at the break-even point in dollar sales of $90,000. Every sales dollar beyond that point contributes $.20 to net profit. Divide $1,440 by $.20 to find the incremental dollar sales ($7,200) required to produce incremental net profit of $1,440. Thus, the total dollar sales is $90,000 + $7,200 = $97,200.

Finally, you can solve directly for the volume in dollar sales using the formula

$$\text{target sales volume in dollars} = \frac{\text{fixed expenses} + \text{target net income}}{\text{contribution-margin ratio}}$$

$$= \frac{\$18,000 + \$1,440}{.20} = \$97,200 \tag{6}$$

The following table summarizes these alternative computations:

	Break-Even Point	Increment	New Condition
Volume in units	60,000	4,800	64,800
Sales	$90,000	$7,200	$97,200
Variable expenses	72,000	5,760	77,760
Contribution margin	$18,000	$1,440	$19,440
Fixed expenses	18,000	—	18,000
Net income	$ 0	$1,440	$ 1,440

Multiple Changes in Key Factors

So far, we have seen changes in only one CVP factor at a time. In the real world, managers often make decisions about the probable effects of multiple factor changes. For example, Boeing may cut the price of its airplanes to increase sales volume, affecting total revenue and total variable costs. Mars might decrease the size of its Snickers candy bar, saving variable costs and increasing the unit contribution margin, but also decreasing sales volume. Or Medtronic might automate the production of its insulin infusion pump, replacing variable costs of labor with fixed costs of equipment.

Consider our vending example. Suppose Winston is considering locking the vending machines from 6:00 PM to 6:00 AM, which she estimates will save $2,460 in wages monthly. However, she also estimates the cutback from 24-hour service would reduce volume by 10,000 units because many nighttime employees use the machines. Should the machines remain available 24 hours per day? We will perform the analysis for two months representing the lowest and highest predicted sales volume: (1) 62,000 units and (2) 90,000 units.

We will consider two approaches. The first is to construct and solve equations for conditions that prevail under each alternative and select the volume level that yields the highest net income.

Regardless of the current volume level, be it 62,000 or 90,000 units, if we accept the prediction that sales will decline by 10,000 units, closing from 6:00 PM to 6:00 AM will decrease net income by $540:

	Decline from 62,000 to 52,000 Units		Decline from 90,000 to 80,000 Units	
Units	62,000	52,000	90,000	80,000
Sales	$93,000	$78,000	$135,000	$120,000
Variable expenses	74,400	62,400	108,000	96,000
Total contribution margin	$18,600	$15,600	$ 27,000	$ 24,000
Fixed expenses	18,000	15,540	18,000	15,540
Net income	$ 600	$ 60	$ 9,000	$ 8,460
Change in net income		($540)		($540)

A second approach—an incremental approach—is quicker and simpler. Simplicity is important to managers because it keeps the analysis from being cluttered by irrelevant and potentially confusing data.

What does the insightful manager see in this situation? The effect of a 10,000 unit decline in volume does not depend on whether the initial volume is 62,000 or 90,000 units. The essence of this decision is whether the savings in fixed costs exceed the loss in total contribution-margin dollars.

Savings in fixed expenses	$2,460
Less: Lost contribution margin, 10,000 units at $.30	−3,000
Prospective decline in net income	$ −540

As in the first analysis, the incremental analysis also shows that locking the vending machines from 6:00 PM to 6:00 AM would cause a $540 decrease in monthly net income. Whichever way you analyze it, locking the machines is not a sound financial decision.

Nonprofit Application

The managers of nonprofit organizations also benefit from the study of CVP relationships. For example, administrators of nonprofit hospitals are concerned about the behavior of costs as the volume of patients fluctuates. Many nonprofit organizations do not derive revenue from selling goods or services, so their revenue function is not simply number of units sold multiplied by selling price per unit. For example, some nonprofit organizations receive a fixed allocation of funds to cover their costs, and must plan operations based on that fixed budget. Other nonprofit organizations use CVP analysis to plan how to adjust operations in response to changes in the level of donations received. Still other nonprofits receive a fixed allocation of funds and a revenue subsidy that covers a portion of the cost of the services provided. CVP analysis can be adapted to reflect the source or form of the organization's revenue.

To illustrate CVP analysis for a nonprofit organization with a fixed budget allocation, suppose a city has a $100,000 lump-sum budget appropriation to conduct a counseling program for drug addicts. The variable costs for counseling are $400 per patient per year. Fixed costs are $60,000 in the relevant range of 50 to 150 patients. If the city spends the entire budget appropriation, how many patients can it serve in a year?

We can use the break-even equation to solve the problem. Let N be the number of patients, substitute the $100,000 lump-sum budget for sales, and note that the lump-sum budget equals variable expenses plus fixed expenses if the city completely spends its budget.

$$\text{sales} = \text{variable expenses} + \text{fixed expenses}$$
$$\$100,000 \text{ lump sum} = \$400N + \$60,000$$
$$\$400N = \$100,000 - \$60,000$$
$$N = \$40,000 \div \$400$$
$$N = 100 \text{ patients}$$

The city can serve 100 patients. Now, suppose the city cuts the total budget appropriation for the following year by 10%. Fixed costs will be unaffected, but service will decline.

$$\text{sales} = \text{variable expenses} + \text{fixed expenses}$$
$$\$90,000 = \$400N + \$60,000$$
$$\$400N = \$90,000 - \$60,000$$
$$N = \$30,000 \div \$400$$
$$N = 75 \text{ patients}$$

The percentage reduction in service is $(100 - 75) \div 100 = 25\%$, which is more than the 10% reduction in the budget. Unless the city restructures its operations, the service volume must fall by 25% to stay within budget.

A graphical presentation of this analysis is in Exhibit 2-9. Note that lump-sum revenue is a horizontal line on the graph.

CVP Analysis and Spreadsheets

Spreadsheets simplify analysis of multiple changes in key factors in a CVP model. Managers use a spreadsheet-based CVP modeling program to study combinations of changes in selling prices,

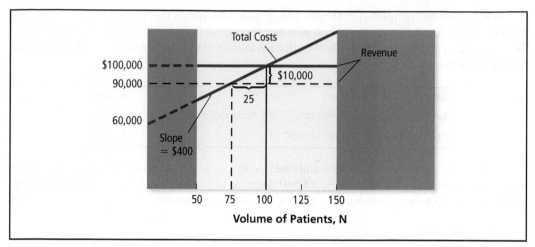

Exhibit 2-9
Graphical Presentation of Nonprofit Application

unit variable costs, fixed costs, and desired profits. Spreadsheets quickly calculate results for alternative assumptions and can display results both numerically and graphically.

Consider Exhibit 2-10, which is a sample spreadsheet that computes the required sales level for all possible combinations of three fixed cost levels ($4,000, $6,000, or $8,000), three variable cost percentages (40%, 44%, or 48% of sales), and three target income levels ($2,000, $4,000, or $6,000). For the 27 different combinations of fixed costs, variable costs, and target income, the spreadsheet calculates the required sales levels rapidly and without error. Further, managers can quickly substitute different numbers for fixed costs (column A), variable cost percentage (column B), and target net income (row 3 of columns C, D, and E) and the spreadsheet will immediately re-compute the required sales level.

In addition to speed and accuracy, spreadsheets allow a more sophisticated approach to CVP analysis than the one illustrated in this chapter. The assumptions we listed on page 47 are necessary to simplify the analysis enough to construct a CVP model by hand. Computer models can be more complex and include multiple cost drivers, nonlinear relationships between costs and cost drivers, varying sales mixes, and analyses for multiple relevant ranges.

	A	B	C	D	E
1				Sales Required to Earn	
2	Fixed	Variable Cost		Annual Net Income of	
3	Cost	as % of Sales	$ 2,000	$ 4,000	$ 6,000
4					
5	$4,000	0.40	$10,000*	$13,333	$16,667
6	$4,000	0.44	$10,714*	$14,286	$17,857
7	$4,000	0.48	$11,538*	$15,385	$19,231
8	$6,000	0.40	$13,333	$16,667	$20,000
9	$6,000	0.44	$14,286	$17,857	$21,429
10	$6,000	0.48	$15,385	$19,231	$23,077
11	$8,000	0.40	$16,667	$20,000	$23,333
12	$8,000	0.44	$17,857	$21,429	$25,000
13	$8,000	0.48	$19,231	$23,077	$26,923

*(A5 + C3)/(1 − B5) = ($4,000 + $2,000)/(1 − $.40) = $10,000
(A6 + C3)/(1 − B6) = ($4,000 + $2,000)/(1 − $.44) = $10,714
(A7 + C3)/(1 − B7) = ($4,000 + $2,000)/(1 − $.48) = $11,538

Exhibit 2-10
Spreadsheet Analysis of CVP Relationships

The use of computer models is a cost-benefit issue. The validity of these models depends on the accuracy of the underlying assumptions about revenue and cost behavior. More complex models often require fewer assumptions and, thus, are valid in more general circumstances. However, sometimes the costs of modeling exceed the value of the improved quality of management decisions. In small organizations, simplified CVP models often are accurate enough; the cost of more sophisticated modeling may exceed the benefit.

Additional Uses of CVP Analysis

Margin of Safety

CVP analysis can help managers assess risk. One measure of risk is the **margin of safety**. The margin of safety measures how far sales can fall before losses occur and is the difference between the level of planned sales and the break-even point. The margin of safety can be defined in either units or dollars:

> margin of safety in units = planned unit sales − break-even unit sales
>
> margin of safety in dollars = planned dollar sales − break-even dollar sales

For example, if Amy Winston in our vending machine example predicts sales volume of 80,000 units or $120,000, the margin of safety in units is 20,000 units and the margin of safety in dollars is $30,000:

> margin of safety in units = 80,000 units − 60,000 units = 20,000 units
>
> margin of safety in dollars = $120,000 − $90,000 = $30,000

The larger the margin of safety, the less likely it is that volume will fall to the point where the company has an operating loss, that is, below the break-even point. Conversely, a smaller margin of safety indicates greater risk of incurring a loss.

margin of safety
Planned unit sales less the break-even unit sales; a measure of how far sales can fall below the planned level before losses occur.

Operating Leverage

In addition to weighing the varied effects of changes in fixed and variable costs, managers need to consider the firm's **cost structure**—the combination of variable- and fixed-cost resources used to carry out the organization's activities. There is typically a tradeoff between variable and fixed costs in choosing a cost structure. Lower variable costs are often achieved by incurring higher fixed costs. For example, highly-automated factories with high fixed overhead costs typically have lower variable labor costs compared to less automated factories. Firms with higher fixed costs and lower variable costs are said to have greater **operating leverage**—the sensitivity of a firm's profit to changes in volume of sales. In highly leveraged companies with lower variable costs, small changes in sales volume result in large changes in net income. In companies with less leverage and higher variable costs, changes in sales volume have a smaller effect on income.

Exhibit 2-11 shows cost behavior relationships at two firms, one with higher operating leverage and one with lower leverage. The firm with higher leverage has fixed costs of $14,000 and variable cost per unit of $.10. The firm with lower leverage has fixed costs of only $2,000 but variable costs of $.25 per unit. For both firms, the sales price is $.30 per unit.

The amount by which profit changes with sales volume is determined by the respective contribution margins. The contribution margin per unit for the firm with higher operating leverage is $.30 − $.10 = $.20 per unit. The contribution margin per unit for the firms with lower operating leverage is $.30 − $.25 = $.05 per unit. Thus, each unit change in sales results in a $.20 change in profit for the firm with higher operating leverage and a $.05 change in profit for the firm with lower operating leverage.

To illustrate the effect of operating leverage in the preceding example, suppose expected sales at both companies are 80,000 units. At this sales level, both firms have net incomes of $2,000. If sales fall short of 80,000 units, profits drop more sharply for the more highly leveraged cost structure. If sales exceed 80,000 units, however, profits also increase more sharply. For example, at sales of 70,000 units, the higher-leveraged firm has zero profits, compared to $1,500 for the lower-leveraged firm. At sales of 90,000 units, however, net income is $4,000 for the higher-leveraged firm but only $2,500 for the lower-leveraged firm.

cost structure
The combination of variable- and fixed-cost resources used to carry out the organization's activities.

operating leverage
The sensitivity of a firm's profit to changes in volume of sales.

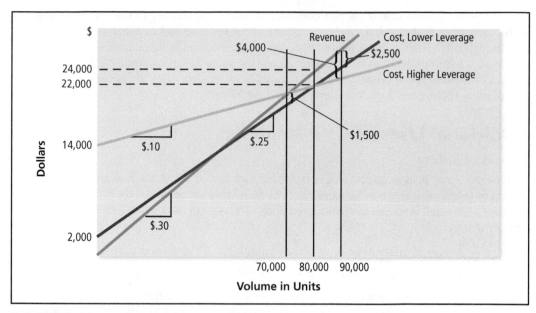

Exhibit 2-11
High Versus Low Operating Leverage

degree of operating leverage

The ratio of contribution margin to profit, defined at a specific volume of sales.

The effect of operating leverage on the variability of profit is captured by **degree of operating leverage**—the ratio of contribution margin to profit, defined at a specific volume of sales. The degree of operating leverage at a specific volume describes how a percentage change in sales will translate into a percentage change in profit.

For example, for the firm with lower operating leverage in Exhibit 2-11, the degree of operating leverage at 80,000 units is contribution margin at 80,000 units (80,000 × $.05) divided by profit at 80,000 units ($2,000), or $4,000/$2,000 = 2. In our example, a degree of operating leverage of 2 means that the percentage change in profit will be 2 times the percentage change in sales. If sales volume increases by 12.5%, increasing by 10,000 units from 80,000 units to 90,000 units, profit will increase by 2 × 12.5% = 25%, moving from $2,000 at 80,000 units to $2,500 at 90,000 units. Similarly, if sales volume decreases by 12.5%, decreasing from 80,000 units to 70,000 units, profit will decrease by 2 × −12.5% = −25%, moving from $2,000 to $1,500.

For the firm with higher operating leverage in Exhibit 2-11, the degree of operating leverage at 80,000 units is $16,000/$2,000 = 8, which means that the percentage change in profit will be 8 times the percentage change in sales. If sales volume increases by 12.5%, increasing by 10,000 units from 80,000 units to 90,000 units, profit will increase by 8 × 12.5% = 100%, moving from $2,000 at 80,000 units to $4,000 at 90,000 units. Similarly, if sales volume decreases by 12.5%, profit will decrease by 8 × −12.5% = −100%, moving from $2,000 to $0.

The higher-leverage cost structure is more risky. Why? Because it results in more variability of income—it might lead to a higher net income but it also might lead to a larger net loss. The lower-leverage alternative is less risky because variations in sales volume lead to smaller variability in net income. Is lower risk always better? Not necessarily. Suppose in the preceding example that managers are sure that volume will be greater than 80,000 units. Then the higher operating leverage (and higher risk) cost structure is better because it will yield higher profits. On the other hand, suppose there is a possibility that volume will be lower than 80,000 units. For volume lower than 80,000 units, the lower operating leverage (and lower risk) cost structure yields higher profits. Thus, if managers are unsure whether volume will be greater or lower than 80,000 units, they should evaluate the expected profit and should also take into account the effects of risk.

Best Cost Structure

Analyzing and managing the organization's cost structure is an important management responsibility. For example, purchasing automated machinery may raise fixed costs but reduce the variable cost, labor cost per unit. Conversely, it may be wise to reduce fixed costs to obtain a more favorable combination. For example, a company may decide to compensate its sales force via sales commissions rather than pay them salaries, thus reducing salaries (a fixed cost) but increasing sales commissions (a variable cost). Another example of exchanging a fixed cost for a variable cost is a contract Blockbuster signed with Disney and other major studios. Instead of buying video tapes for $65 each, a fixed cost for each tape, Blockbuster paid only a $7 fixed cost and an additional variable cost equal to a percentage of the rental revenues. You can see one result of this contract in the Business First box on p. 59.

A thorough understanding of cost-volume-profit relationships is essential in choosing a cost structure. The best combination of variable- and fixed-cost resources depends on many factors—the current level of sales, expected level of future sales, and the set of alternatives available now and in the future.

Generally, companies that spend heavily on the fixed costs of advertising are willing to do so because they have high contribution-margin percentages (e.g., airlines, cigarette, and cosmetic companies). Conversely, companies with low contribution-margin percentages usually spend less for advertising and promotion (e.g., manufacturers of industrial equipment). As a result, two companies with the same unit sales volumes at the same unit prices could have different attitudes toward risking an advertising outlay. Assume the following:

	Perfume Company	Janitorial Service Company
Unit sales volume	200,000 bottles	200,000 square feet
Dollar sales at $10 per unit	$2,000,000	$2,000,000
Variable costs	200,000	1,700,000
Total contribution margin	$1,800,000	$ 300,000
Contribution-margin percentage	90%	15%

Suppose each company can increase sales volume by 10% by spending $100,000 for advertising:

	Perfume Company	Janitorial Service Company
Increase in sales volume, 20,000 × $10	$200,000	$200,000
Increase in total contribution margin, 90%, 15%	180,000	30,000

By spending $100,000 on advertising, the perfume company would increase the total contribution margin by $180,000, thus increasing total profit by $180,000 − $100,000 = $80,000. In contrast, the janitorial service company would increase the total contribution margin by only $30,000, resulting in a change in total profit of $30,000 − $100,000 = −$70,000.

Note that when the contribution margin as a percentage of sales is low, large increases in volume are necessary to generate increases in net profits. At the same time, decreases in volume also generate smaller decreases in profit when contribution-margin percentages are low. High contribution-margin ratios have the opposite effect—large increases in profits if sales grow but large decreases in profits if sales fall.

The best cost structure depends on multiple factors. The best cost structure is not necessarily the cost structure with the greatest margin of safety, or the lowest break-even point, or the highest operating leverage, or the lowest operating leverage. The best cost structure depends on the impact of risk and on the expected volume of sales, both in the current time period and in future time periods. Further, as explained in later chapters, the expected volume of sales may be different for different cost structures. Managers must have a thorough understanding of all these factors in order to choose the best cost structure.

Contribution Margin and Gross Margin

Objective 7

Differentiate between contribution margin and gross margin.

gross margin (gross profit)
The excess of sales over the total cost of goods sold.

cost of goods sold
The cost of the merchandise that a company acquires or produces and sells.

This chapter has focused on the contribution margin. However, accountants also use a similar term, *gross margin*, to mean something quite different. Too often people confuse the terms *contribution margin* and *gross margin*. **Gross margin**, also called **gross profit**, is the excess of sales over the cost of goods sold. **Cost of goods sold** is the cost of the merchandise that a company acquires or produces and then sells. Compare the gross margin with the contribution margin:

gross margin = sales price − cost of goods sold

contribution margin = sales price − all variable expenses

Exhibit 2-12 shows costs divided on two different dimensions. As shown at the bottom of the exhibit, the gross margin uses the division on the production or acquisition cost versus selling and administrative cost dimension, and the contribution margin uses the division based on the variable-cost versus fixed-cost dimension.

In our vending-machine illustration, the contribution margin and the gross margin are identical because the cost of goods sold is the only variable cost:

Sales	$1.50
Variable costs: acquisition cost of unit sold	1.20
Contribution margin and gross margin are equal	$ .30

Now, suppose the firm had to pay a commission of $.12 per unit sold:

		Contribution Margin	Gross Margin
Sales		$1.50	$1.50
Acquisition cost of unit sold	$1.20		1.20
Variable commission	.12		
Total variable expense		1.32	
Contribution margin		$ .18	
Gross margin			$ .30

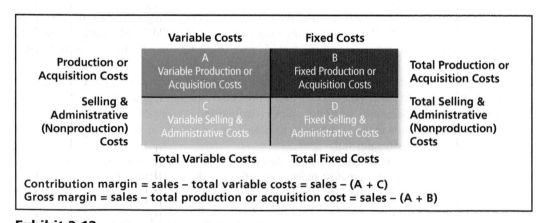

Exhibit 2-12
Costs for Gross Margin and Contribution Margin

Business First

Did Blockbuster Violate Disney Contract? Accounting Disagreement or Ethical Issue?

In early 2003, the Walt Disney Company sued Blockbuster, claiming that Blockbuster had violated a 1997 agreement between the two companies. Prior to the agreement, Blockbuster purchased videos from Disney for about $65 each and kept all the rental revenue. Under the pact, Blockbuster agreed to purchase movies from Disney for $7 a copy and then pay the studio a portion of the revenue from each rental.

The contract allowed Blockbuster to buy more copies of each video, which led to the guarantee that customers could rely on Blockbuster to have a copy of any movie the customer wanted or else the rental was free. With this policy, Blockbuster increased its market share of the video rental market from 28% to 40%. Essentially, Blockbuster turned a fixed cost, $65 per tape, into primarily a variable cost, with a small $7 fixed-cost portion and a larger variable-cost portion that depended on how much revenue Blockbuster generated from its rentals.

The arrangement was similar to that between the owners of shopping malls and many of their retail store tenants. Each store pays a monthly rental fee plus a percentage of its sales. Just as shopping mall owners rely on their tenants to truthfully report their sales, Disney relied on Blockbuster to correctly account for its video rentals.

In addition, Blockbuster and Disney also agreed on when Blockbuster could sell old rental tapes. Since these were so inexpensive for Blockbuster, selling them could be a lucrative business. But Disney did not want these low-cost tapes competing with its own videotape sales. Thus, it placed restrictions on when Blockbuster could sell them.

In the suit, Disney claimed that Blockbuster improperly deducted "promotional" credits from its gross rental fees, failed to account for "hundreds of thousands" of missing videos, and sold videos prematurely. Disney had to rely on Blockbuster to correctly account for its rental revenues and inventory of tapes. Blockbuster claimed that its accounting was in accordance with the original agreement.

This is an example where good ethics and good accounting are both important. The original agreement promised benefits to both companies—more rental income for Disney on hit movies and a lower operating leverage cost-structure for Blockbuster. But such a contract will not work if each party cannot trust the other. It's not clear who is right in this case, but both companies were hurt by the allegations. At a minimum, both will need to include better monitoring provisions in future contracts because other companies will suspect Disney of trying to get more than it deserves and Blockbuster of playing accounting tricks to minimize its payment to Disney.

Source: "Disney Sues Blockbuster Over Contract," *New York Times*, January 4, 2003; "Disney Sues Top Video Chain," *Los Angeles Times*, January 3, 2003.

Summary Problem for Your Review

PROBLEM

The budgeted income statement of Port Williams Gift Shop follows:

Net revenue	$800,000
Less expenses, including $400,000 of fixed expenses	880,000
Net loss	$(80,000)

The manager believes that an additional outlay of $200,000 for advertising will increase sales but is wondering how much sales will have to increase in order to achieve 1) breakeven, or 2) a $40,000 profit.

1. At what sales volume in dollars will the shop break even after spending $200,000 on advertising?
2. What sales volume in dollars will result in a net profit of $40,000 after spending the $200,000 on advertising?

SOLUTION

1. Note that all data are in dollars, not units. The variable costs are $880,000 − $400,000 = $480,000 and the variable-cost ratio is $480,000 ÷ $800,000 = .60.

(Remember to divide variable costs by sales, not by total costs.) Therefore, the contribution-margin ratio is .40. Let S = break-even sales in dollars. Then

$$\text{Sales} - \text{variable costs} - \text{fixed costs} = \text{net profit}$$

$$S - .60S - (\$400,000 + \$200,000) = 0$$

$$.40S = \$600,000$$

$$S = \frac{\$600,000}{.40} = \frac{\text{fixed costs}}{\text{contribution-margin ratio}}$$

$$S = \$1,500,000$$

2.
$$\text{required sales} = \frac{(\text{fixed costs} + \text{target net profit})}{\text{contribution-margin ratio}}$$

$$\text{required sales} = \frac{(\$600,000 + \$40,000)}{.40} = \frac{\$640,000}{.40}$$

$$\text{required sales} = \$1,600,000$$

Alternatively, we can use an incremental approach and reason that all dollar sales beyond the $1.5 million break-even point will result in a 40% contribution to net profit. Divide $40,000 by .40. Therefore, sales must be $100,000 beyond the $1.5 million break-even point to produce a net profit of $40,000.

Highlights to Remember

1. **Explain how cost drivers affect cost behavior.** A cost driver is an output measure that causes the use of costly resources. When the level of an activity changes, the level of the cost driver or output measure will also change, causing changes in costs.

2. **Show how changes in cost-driver levels affect variable and fixed costs.** Cost behavior refers to how costs change as levels of an organization's activities change. If the cost of the resource used changes in proportion to changes in the cost-driver level, the resource is a variable-cost resource (its costs are variable). If the cost of the resource used does not change because of cost-driver level changes, the resource is a fixed-cost resource (its costs are fixed).

3. **Explain step- and mixed-cost behavior.** Step and mixed costs combine aspects of variable- and fixed-cost behavior. Graphs of step costs look like steps. Costs remain fixed within a given range of activity or cost-driver level, but then rise or fall abruptly when the cost-driver level moves outside this range. Mixed costs involve a fixed element and a variable element of cost behavior. Unlike step costs, mixed costs have a single fixed cost at all levels of activity and in addition have a variable cost element that increases proportional to the level of activity.

4. **Create a cost-volume-profit (CVP) graph and understand the assumptions behind it.** We can approach CVP analysis (sometimes called break-even analysis) graphically or with equations. We create a CVP graph by drawing revenue and total cost lines as functions of the volume of activity. Be sure to recognize the limitations of CVP analysis and that it assumes efficiency, sales mix, and inventory levels are all held constant.

5. **Calculate break-even sales volume in total dollars and total units.** To calculate the break-even point in total units, divide the fixed costs by the unit contribution margin. To calculate the break-even point in total dollars (sales dollars), divide the fixed costs by the contribution-margin ratio.

6. **Calculate sales volume in total dollars and total units to reach a target profit.** Managers use CVP analysis to compute the sales needed to achieve a target profit or to examine the effects on profit of changes in factors such as fixed costs, variable costs, or cost-driver volume.

7. **Differentiate between contribution margin and gross margin.** The contribution margin—the difference between sales price and variable costs—is an important concept. Do not confuse it with gross margin, the difference between sales price and cost of goods sold.

Appendix 2A: Sales-Mix Analysis

The cost-volume-profit analysis in this chapter focused on the case of a single product. However, nearly all companies produce more than one product or service. For these companies, volume is determined not just by total sales but also by sales mix, which you will recall from p. 47 is the relative proportions or combinations of quantities of products that comprise total sales. If the proportions of the mix change, the cost-volume-profit relationships also change.

Objective 8

Explain the effects of sales mix on profits.

Suppose Ramos Company has two products, wallets (W) and key cases (K) and the following budget:

	Wallets (W)	Key Cases (K)	Total
Sales in units	300,000	75,000	375,000
Sales @ $8 and $5	$2,400,000	$375,000	$2,775,000
Variable expenses @ $7 and $3	2,100,000	225,000	2,325,000
Contribution margins @ $1 and $2	$ 300,000	$150,000	$ 450,000
Fixed expenses			180,000
Net income			$ 270,000

What is the break-even point for Ramos? The answer depends on the mix of products. For example, you can use the approach outlined in the chapter to find the break-even point if the mix is 100% W or 100% K. For instance, suppose Ramos Company sells only key cases, and fixed expenses stay at $180,000.

$$\text{break-even point in units of K} = \frac{\text{fixed expenses}}{\text{contribution margin per unit}}$$

$$= \frac{\$180,000}{\$2}$$

$$= 90,000 \text{ key cases}$$

If Ramos sells only wallets,

$$\text{break-even point in units of W} = \frac{\$180,000}{\$1} = 180,000 \text{ wallets}$$

We can also generalize the approach used in the chapter to find breakeven for any other fixed proportion of key cases and wallets. For example, consider a sales mix of four wallets for every key case. Letting K and W denote the number of units of key cases and wallets, respectively, the assumed sales mix implies $W = 4K$. The calculation of total volume to break even is as follows:

$$\text{sales} - \text{variable expenses} - \text{fixed expenses} = \text{zero net income}$$

$$[\$8(4K) + \$5(K)] - [\$7(4K) + \$3(K)] - \$180,000 = 0$$

$$\$32K + \$5K - \$28K - \$3K - \$180,000 = 0$$

$$\$6K = \$180,000$$

$$K = 30,000$$

$$W = 4K = 120,000$$

The break-even point for a sales mix of four wallets for every key case is 30,000 key cases and 120,000 wallets, or 150,000 total units.

These examples show that each sales mix has a break-even point. The break-even point if Ramos produces only wallets is 180,000 wallets, the break-even point if Ramos produces only key cases is 90,000 key cases, and the break-even point if Ramos produces four wallets for every key case is a total of 150,000 units (30,000 key cases and 120,000 wallets).

Changes in sales mix affect the break-even point and the expected net income at various sales levels. For example, consider a revised Ramos budget where the budgeted number of units remains at 375,000 units but the mix is revised to 325,000 wallets and 50,000 key cases:

	Wallets (W)	Key Cases (K)	Total
Sales in units	325,000	50,000	375,000
Sales @ $8 and $5	$2,600,000	$250,000	$2,850,000
Variable expenses @ $7 and $3	2,275,000	150,000	2,425,000
Contribution margins @ $1 and $2	$ 325,000	$100,000	$ 425,000
Fixed expenses			180,000
Net income			$ 245,000

The revised budget shows that the change in sales mix results in net income of $245,000, rather than $270,000 for the original mix of 300,000 wallets and 75,000 key cases. Although both budgets have identical total numbers of units, the revised budget has a smaller proportion of sales of the product bearing the higher unit contribution margin, key cases. Relative to the original budget, the revised budget has 25,000 fewer key cases with a contribution margin of $2 per unit ($5 − $3) and 25,000 more wallets with a contribution margin of $1 per unit ($8 − $7). As a result, budgeted net income is $25,000 lower in the revised budget.

The effect of sales mix on profit is often an important element of strategy. For example, a recent annual report for **Neenah Paper Inc.** described the role of product mix in its strategy to grow margins and improve profitability: "Margin improvement will come through optimizing our product mix, faster growth of higher margin products, new product sales generated through innovation/R&D efforts and overall benefits of volume and scale efficiencies."

Contribution margins help guide executives who must decide to emphasize or deemphasize particular products. For example, given limited production facilities or limited time of sales personnel, should we emphasize wallets or key cases? Contribution margins, along with other factors, affect these decisions. Chapter 5 explores these factors, including the importance of the contribution margin per unit of time (or per unit of other constrained resource) rather than per unit of product.

Appendix 2B: Impact of Income Taxes

Objective 9

Compute cost-volume-profit (CVP) relationships on an after-tax basis.

Thus far we have ignored income taxes, but most companies must pay income taxes. Income taxes do not affect the break-even point. Why? Because there is no income tax at a level of zero income. However, income taxes do affect calculation of the volume required to achieve a specified after-tax target profit.

Reconsider the vending machine example from earlier in this chapter. If the vending machine company pays income tax at a rate of 40%, the before-tax income of $1,440 corresponds to after-tax net income of $864, as shown by the following calculations:

Income before income tax	$1,440	100%
Income tax	576	40%
After-tax net income	$ 864	60%

This example illustrates the general relationship between income before tax and net income after tax:

$$\text{after-tax net income} = \text{income before income taxes} \times (1 - \text{tax rate})$$

or

$$\text{income before income taxes} = \frac{\text{after-tax net income}}{1 - \text{tax rate}}$$

The only change required to introduce taxes into the general equation illustrated in the chapter for calculation of volume required to achieve a given target income is to substitute $\frac{\text{target after-tax net income}}{1 - \text{tax rate}}$ on the right-hand side of the equation:

$$\text{target sales} - \text{variable expenses} - \text{fixed expenses} = \frac{\text{target after-tax net income}}{1 - \text{tax rate}}$$

Return to the target income example from the chapter where selling price is $1.50 per unit, variable cost is $1.20 per unit, and total fixed cost is $18,000. Assume that target after-tax net income is $864. The equation to find N, the number of units to be sold to achieve the after-tax income target of $864 is as follows:

$$\$1.50N - \$1.20N - \$18,000 = \frac{\$864}{1 - .4}$$

$$\$0.30N - \$18,000 = \$1,440$$

$$\$0.30N = \$1,440 + \$18,000$$

$$\$0.30N = \$19,440$$

$$N = 64,800 \text{ units}$$

Sales of 64,800 units produce an after-tax profit of $864 as shown here, which of course corresponds to the volume required to produce before-tax profit of $1,440, as shown in the chapter.

Now suppose the target after-tax net income is $1,800. The volume required for this higher level of after-tax income would rise to 70,000 units:

$$\$1.50N - \$1.20N - \$18,000 = \frac{\$1,800}{1 - .4}$$

$$\$0.30N - \$18,000 = \$3,000$$

$$\$0.30N = \$3,000 + \$18,000$$

$$\$0.30N = \$21,000$$

$$N = 70,000 \text{ units}$$

The formula from the chapter for the effect of a change in volume on income can also be adapted to show the effect on after-tax net income:

$$\text{change in net income} = \left(\begin{array}{c}\text{change in volume}\\ \text{in units}\end{array}\right) \times \left(\begin{array}{c}\text{contribution margin}\\ \text{per unit}\end{array}\right) \times (1 - \text{tax rate})$$

Apply this formula to verify how net income should change when we increase volume from a level of 64,800 units (which produced $864 after-tax net income) to a level of 70,000 units in our example:

$$\text{change in net income} = (70,000 - 64,800) \times \$.30 \times (1 - .4)$$

$$= 5,200 \times .30 \times .60 = 5,200 \times \$.18$$

$$= \$936$$

The formula verifies our earlier calculations. When volume increases from 64,800 units to 70,000 units, after-tax net income increases by $936, moving from $864 to $1,800.

Accounting Vocabulary

break-even point, p. 46
contribution margin, p. 49
contribution-margin
   percentage, p. 48
contribution-margin
   ratio, p. 48
cost behavior, p. 37
cost driver, p. 37
cost of goods sold, p. 58
cost structure, p. 55
cost-volume-profit (CVP)
   analysis, p. 45

decision context, p. 42
degree of operating
   leverage, p. 56
fixed cost, p. 39
gross margin, p. 58
gross profit, p. 58
incremental effect, p. 51
margin of safety, p. 55
marginal income
   per unit, p. 48
mixed cost, p. 44
operating leverage, p. 55

relevant range, p. 42
sales mix, p. 47
step cost, p. 43
total contribution
   margin, p. 48
unit contribution
   margin, p. 48
variable cost, p. 39
variable-cost
   percentage, p. 48
variable-cost ratio, p. 48

CHAPTER 2

MyAccountingLab   # Fundamental Assignment Material

2-A1 Fixed- and Variable-Cost Behavior

Maintaining a clean working environment is important to Napco, an industrial parts manufacturer. Cleaning the plant is the responsibility of the maintenance department. The 50,000 square foot plant is thoroughly cleaned from four to eight times a month depending on the level and stage of production. For the most recent month, March, the plant was cleaned four times. The production schedule for the next quarter (April through June) indicates that the plant will need to be cleaned five, six, and eight times respectively.

Two of the resources needed to clean the plant are labor and cleaning supplies. The cost driver for both resources is number of times the plant is cleaned. Plant cleaning laborers are full-time employees who are paid the same wages regardless of the number of times the plant is cleaned. Cleaning supplies is a variable cost. The March cost of labor was $21,000 and cleaning supplies used cost $8,000.

1. Prepare a table that shows how labor cost, cleaning supplies cost, total cost, and total cost per cleaning changes in response to the number of times the plant is cleaned. What is the predicted total cost of plant cleaning for the next quarter?
2. Suppose Napco can hire an outside cleaning company to clean the plant as needed. The charge rate for cleaning is $5,700 per plant cleaning. If the outside cleaning company is hired, Napco can lay off the workers who are now cleaning the plant and will spend nothing for cleaning supplies. Will Napco save money with the outside cleaning company over the next quarter? Prepare a schedule that supports your answer.

2-A2 Cost-Volume-Profit and Vending Machines

Vendmart Food Services Company operates and services snack vending machines located in restaurants, gas stations, and factories in four southwestern states. The machines are rented from the manufacturer. In addition, Vendmart must rent the space occupied by its machines. The following expense and revenue relationships pertain to a contemplated expansion program of 80 machines.

Fixed monthly expenses follow:

Machine rental: 80 machines @ $22.10	$1,768
Space rental: 80 locations @ $20.00	1,600
Part-time wages to service the additional 80 machines	500
Other fixed costs	132
Total monthly fixed costs	$4,000

Other data follow:

	Per Unit (Snack)	Per $100 of Sales
Selling price	$1.00	100%
Cost of snack	.68	68
Contribution margin	$.32	32%

These questions relate to the given data unless otherwise noted. Consider each question independently.

1. What is the monthly break-even point in number of units (snacks)? In dollar sales?
2. If 45,000 units were sold, what would be the company's net income?
3. If the space rental cost was doubled, what would be the monthly break-even point in number of units? In dollar sales?
4. Refer to the original data. If, in addition to the fixed space rent, Vendmart Food Services Company paid the vending machine manufacturer $.07 per unit sold, what would be the monthly break-even point in number of units? In dollar sales?
5. Refer to the original data. If, in addition to the fixed rent, Vendmart paid the machine manufacturer $.11 for each unit sold in excess of the break-even point, what would be the new net income be if 45,000 units were sold?

2-A3 Exercises in Cost-Volume-Profit Relationships

Upcraft Moving Company specializes in hauling heavy goods over long distances. The company's revenues and expenses depend on revenue-miles, a measure that combines both weights and mileage.

Summarized budget data for next year are based on predicted total revenue miles of 500,000. At that level of volume, and at any level of volume between 300,000 and 700,000 revenue miles, the company's fixed costs are $50,000. The selling price and variable costs are as follows:

Per Revenue-Mile	
Average selling price (revenue)	$2.00
Average variable expenses	1.60

1. Compute the budgeted net income. Ignore income taxes.
2. Management is trying to decide how various possible conditions or decisions might affect net income. Compute the new net income for each of the following changes. Consider each case independently.
   a. A 30% increase in sales price.
   b. A 30% increase in revenue miles.
   c. A 30% increase in variable expenses.
   d. A 30% increase in fixed expenses.
   e. An average decrease in selling price of $.05 per revenue mile and a 15% increase in revenue miles. Refer to the original data.
   f. An average increase in selling price of $.01 and a 30% decrease in revenue miles.
   g. A 30% increase in fixed expenses in the form of more advertising and a 15% increase in revenue miles.

2-A4 Types of Cost Behavior

Identify the following planned costs as (a) variable costs, (b) fixed costs, (c) mixed costs, or (d) step costs. For variable costs and mixed costs, indicate the most likely cost driver.

1. Public relations employee compensation to be paid by Intel
2. Crew supervisor in a Lands' End mail-order house; a new supervisor is added for every 12 workers employed
3. Sales commissions based on revenue dollars; payments to be made to advertising salespersons employed by radio station WCCO, Minneapolis
4. Jet fuel costs of Southwest Airlines
5. Total costs of renting trucks by the city of Nashville; charge is a lump sum of $300 per month plus $.20 per mile
6. Straight-line depreciation on desks in the office of an attorney
7. Advertising costs, a lump sum, planned by ABC, Inc.
8. Rental payment by the Internal Revenue Service on a five-year lease for office space in a private office building
9. Advertising allowance granted to wholesalers by 7-Up Bottling on a per-case basis
10. Compensation of lawyers employed internally by Microsoft
11. Total repairs and maintenance of a university classroom building

2-B1 Fixed- and Variable-Cost Behavior

Applejack Fine Dining has 970 restaurants across the United States. Maintaining a clean environment for customers is a key success factor at Applejack. Each restaurant is cleaned regularly after closing. In addition to regular cleaning, from 5 to 20 times a month, depending on various factors including the amount of business, a special treatment is given to the floors consisting of breaking down the old wax and rewaxing. So the total number of times a restaurant is cleaned varies from 35 to 50 times a month.

The two most costly resources needed to clean an Applejack restaurant are labor and supplies. The cost driver for both resources is number of times a restaurant is cleaned. Cleaning laborers are paid the same wages regardless of the number of times a restaurant is cleaned. Cleaning supplies is a variable cost. The cost of supplies used per regular cleaning and per special cleaning is about the same.

Suppose one of the local Applejack restaurants in Orlando has 6,000 square feet. In October, the restaurant was cleaned 35 times. The cost of cleaning labor was $21,000 for October, and cleaning supplies cost $16,800. The months of November and December are typically much busier, so the restaurant manager expects to clean 45 times and 50 times in November and December, respectively.

1. Prepare a table that shows how labor cost, cleaning supplies cost, total cost, and total cost per cleaning changes in response to number of times the restaurant is cleaned. Use volumes of 35, 40, 45, and 50 times cleaned. What is the predicted total cost of cleaning for November and December?

2. Suppose Applejack can hire an outside cleaning company to clean the restaurant as needed. The charge rate for cleaning is $.25 per square foot. If the outside cleaning company is hired, Applejack can lay off the workers who are now cleaning and will spend nothing on cleaning supplies. Will Applejack save money with the outside cleaning company over the next two months? Prepare a schedule that supports your answer. What information would you need to make a recommendation about hiring the outside cleaning company on a permanent basis?

2-B2 Cost-Volume-Profit at a Day Care Facility

Luke Morrison opened Luke's Corner, a small day care facility, just over 2 years ago. After a rocky start, Luke's Corner has been thriving. Morrison is now preparing a budget for November 20X7.

Monthly fixed costs for Luke's Corner are as follows:

Rent	$ 800
Salaries	1,400
Other fixed costs	140
Total fixed costs	$ 2,340

The salary is for Anna Dukes, the only employee, who works with Morrison by caring for the children. Morrison does not pay himself a salary, but he receives the excess of revenues over costs each month.

The cost driver for variable costs is "child-days." One child-day is one day in day care for one child, and the variable cost is $12 per child-day. The facility is open from 6:00 AM to 6:00 PM weekdays (that is, Monday–Friday), and there are 22 weekdays in November 20X7. An average day has 8 children attending Luke's Corner. State law prohibits Luke's Corner from having more than 14 children, a limit it has never reached. Morrison charges $30 per day per child, regardless of how long the child is at the facility.

1. What is the break-even point for November in child-days? In revenue dollars?
2. Suppose attendance for November 20X7 is equal to the average, resulting in $22 \times 8 = 176$ child-days. What amount will Morrison have left after paying all expenses?
3. Suppose both costs and attendance are difficult to predict. Compute the amount Morrison will have left after paying all expenses for each of the following situations. Consider each case independently.
    a. Average attendance is 9 children per day instead of 8, generating 198 child-days.
    b. Variable costs increase to $14 per child-day.
    c. Rent increases by $220 per month.
    d. Morrison spends $300 on advertising (a fixed cost) in November, which increases average daily attendance to 9.5 children.
    e. Morrison begins charging $33 per day on November 1, and average daily attendance slips to 7 children.

2-B3 Exercises in Cost-Volume-Profit Relationships

Each problem is unrelated to the others.

1. Given: Selling price per unit, $25; total fixed expenses, $9,100; variable expenses per unit, $18. Find break-even sales in units.
2. Given: Sales, $43,000; variable expenses, $30,100; fixed expenses, $8,400; net income, $4,500. Find break-even sales in dollars.
3. Given: Selling price per unit, $29; total fixed expenses, $30,400; variable expenses per unit, $13. Find total sales in units to achieve a profit of $8,000, assuming no change in selling price.
4. Given: Sales, $51,000; variable expenses, $18,000; fixed expenses, $18,000; net income, $15,000. Assume no change in selling price; find net income if activity volume increases by 20%.
5. Given: Selling price per unit, $48; total fixed expenses, $106,000; variable expenses per unit, $36. Assume that variable expenses are reduced by 25% per unit, and the total fixed expenses are increased by 15%. Find the sales in units to achieve a profit of $23,000, assuming no change in selling price.

2-B4 Identifying Cost Behavior Patterns

At a seminar, a cost accountant spoke on identification of different kinds of cost behavior. Tammy Li, a hospital administrator who heard the lecture, identified several hospital costs of concern to her. After her classification, Li presented you with the following list of costs and asked you to (1) classify its behavior as one of the following: variable, step, mixed, or fixed; and (2) identify a likely cost driver for each variable or mixed cost.

1. Operating costs of X-ray equipment ($95,000 a year plus $3 per film)
2. Health insurance for all full-time employees
3. Costs incurred by Dr. Rath in cancer research
4. Repairs made on hospital furniture
5. Training costs of an administrative resident
6. Straight-line depreciation of operating room equipment
7. Costs of services of King Hospital Consulting
8. Nursing supervisors' salaries (a supervisor is needed for each 45 nursing personnel)

Additional Assignment Material

MyAccountingLab

QUESTIONS

2-1 "Cost behavior is simply identification of cost drivers and their relationships to costs." Comment.

2-2 Give two rules of thumb to use when analyzing cost behavior.

2-3 Give three examples of variable costs and of fixed costs.

2-4 Why is the word *immediately* used in the definition of *fixed cost* and not in the definition of *variable cost*?

2-5 "It is confusing to think of fixed costs on a per-unit basis." Do you agree? Why or why not?

2-6 "All costs are either fixed or variable. The only difficulty in cost analysis is determining which of the two categories each cost belongs to." Do you agree? Explain.

2-7 "The relevant range pertains to fixed costs, not variable costs." Do you agree? Explain.

2-8 Identify the major simplifying assumption that underlies CVP analysis.

2-9 "Classification of costs into variable and fixed categories depends on the decision situation." Explain.

2-10 "Contribution margin is the excess of sales over fixed costs." Do you agree? Explain.

2-11 Why is *break-even analysis* a misnomer?

2-12 "Companies in the same industry generally have about the same break-even point." Do you agree? Explain.

2-13 "It is essential to choose the right CVP method—equation, contribution margin, or graphical. If you pick the wrong one, your analysis will be faulty." Do you agree? Explain.

2-14 Describe three ways of lowering a break-even point.

2-15 "Incremental analysis is quicker, but it has no other advantage over an analysis of all costs and revenues associated with each alternative." Do you agree? Why or why not?

2-16 Define operating leverage and explain why a highly leveraged company may be risky.

2-17 Suppose a company with high operating leverage is also operating at near capacity for all its fixed-cost resources. How could an increase in sales volume result in decreasing economies of scale for this company?

2-18 What is the relationship between the margin of safety and the break-even point?

2-19 "The contribution margin and gross margin are always equal." Do you agree? Explain.

2-20 "CVP relationships are unimportant in nonprofit organizations." Do you agree? Explain.

2-21 Study Appendix 2A. A company sold two products. Total budgeted sales and total actual sales in number of units were identical. Actual unit variable costs and sales prices were the same as budgeted. Actual total contribution margin was lower than budgeted. What could be the reason for the lower contribution margin?

2-22 Study Appendix 2B. Given a target after-tax net income, present the CVP formula for computing the income before income taxes.

2-23 Study Appendix 2B. Present the CVP formula for computing the effects of a change in volume on after-tax income.

CRITICAL THINKING EXERCISES

2-24 Mixed Costs and the Sales Force
Wysocki Company pays its sales force a fixed salary plus a 5% commission on all sales. Explain why sales force costs would be considered a mixed cost.

2-25 Marketing Function of Value-Chain and Cost Behavior
Refer to Exhibit 2-2. For the two examples of marketing costs given in Exhibit 2-2, describe their cost behavior in relation to the cost driver listed.

2-26 Production Function of Value-Chain and Cost Behavior
Refer to Exhibit 2-2. For the labor wages and depreciation of plant and machinery examples of production costs given in Exhibit 2-2, describe their cost behavior in relation to the cost driver listed.

2-27 Tenneco Automotive's Value Chain

Tenneco is a leading auto parts company that makes Walker exhaust systems and Monroe ride-control equipment (shocks, struts) for vehicle manufacturers and the replacement market, with annual revenues in excess of $5.9 billion. After reporting weak earnings, the company undertook a strategy to reduce its break-even point by 25% by selling excess capacity, reducing head count, and introducing new high-contribution-margin products. The company's senior vice president listed the key elements of the company's strategy, stating, "We are gaining momentum and transforming our North American aftermarket business with new products, new technology, new positioning strategies, and new pricing." For each of these "new" elements of Tenneco's aftermarket business strategy, list the value-chain function that is most applicable.

EXERCISES

2-28 Identifying Cost Drivers

The following list identifies several potential cost drivers for a manufacturing company that makes eight products. The company uses a JIT production system so it stores finished products for a very limited time. The eight products vary substantially in size from small (plastic casings for pens) to large (plastic casings for truck instrument panels). The company uses order-processing labor to process all orders from customers.

- Number of setups
- Setup time
- Square feet
- Cubic feet
- Cubic feet weeks
- Number of orders
- Number or order line items

For each of the following situations (activity and related resource), identify the best cost driver from the list and briefly justify your choice.

1. To produce a product, production mechanics must set up machinery. It takes about the same time to set up for a production run regardless of the product being produced. What is the best cost driver for the resources used during the setup activity?
2. Instead of the situation described in number 1, what driver should the company use for the setup activity if it takes longer to set up for complex products, such as the instrument panel casings, than for simple products, such as pen casings?
3. What driver should the company use for warehouse occupancy costs (depreciation and insurance)? The company uses the warehouse to store finished products.
4. What driver should the company use for the warehouse occupancy costs if it did not use a JIT system (that is, the company maintains inventories), and upon inspection one of the products had a thick layer of dust on it?
5. What driver should the company use for order processing cost? All orders are similar in terms of types of products ordered and it takes about the same time to process each type of product.
6. What driver should the company use for order processing cost if orders vary substantially in terms of types of products ordered and it takes about the same time to process each type of product?

2-29 Basic Review Exercises

Fill in the blanks for each of the following independent cases (ignore income taxes):

	Sales	Variable Expenses	Contribution Margin	Fixed Expenses	Net Income
1.	$960,000	$533,000	$ —	$310,000	$ —
2.	550,000	—	300,000	—	46,000
3.	—	500,000	520,000	200,000	—

2-30 Variable- and Fixed-Cost Behavior

Refer to Exhibits 2-2 and 2-3 on pages 38 and 39. Part of a company's marketing function is as described in Exhibit 2-2. Two of the many marketing-function activities are advertising and selling. The annual cost behavior of the resources used to perform the advertising activity is depicted in the following diagram. With respect to the cost driver number of advertisements, which of the two costs is fixed? Which cost is variable? What is the total cost of advertising if the number of advertisements is 46? 92? Does the total cost of advertising double in response to a doubling of the cost driver level? Why or why not?

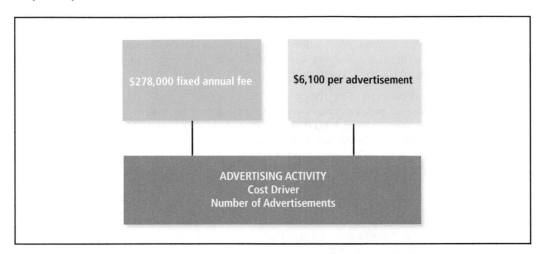

2-31 Variable- and Fixed-Cost Behavior

Refer to Exhibits 2-2 and 2-3 on pages 38 and 39. Part of a company's marketing function is as described in Exhibit 2-2. Two of the many marketing-function activities are advertising and selling. The annual cost behavior of the resources used to perform the selling activity is depicted in the following diagram. With respect to the cost driver sales dollars, which of the two costs is fixed? Which cost is variable? What is the total cost of the selling activity if sales dollars are $24,000,000? What is the total cost of selling if sales dollars are $12,000,000? Does the total cost of selling decrease by half in response to a 50% decrease in the cost driver level? Why or why not?

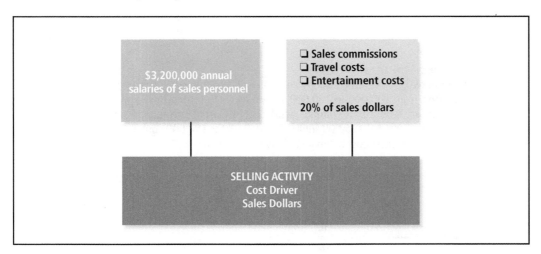

2-32 Basic Review Exercises

Fill in the blanks for each of the following independent cases:

Case	(a) Selling Price per Unit	(b) Variable Cost per Unit	(c) Total Units Sold	(d) Total Contribution Margin	(e) Total Fixed Costs	(f) Net Income
1	$26	$—	125,000	$750,000	$675,000	$ —
2	10	6	100,000	—	320,000	—
3	21	18	—	63,000	—	14,000
4	30	20	60,000	—	—	12,000
5	—	12	86,000	172,000	125,000	—

2-33 Basic Cost-Volume-Profit Graph

Refer to Exercise 2-32. Construct a cost-volume-profit graph for Case 2 that depicts the total revenue, total variable cost, total fixed cost, and total cost lines. Estimate the break-even point in total units sold and the net income for 100,000 units sold.

2-34 Basic Cost-Volume-Profit Graph

Refer to Exercise 2-32. Construct a cost-volume-profit graph for Case 4 that depicts the total revenue, total variable cost, total fixed cost, and total cost lines. Estimate the break-even point in total units sold and the net income (loss) for 50,000 units sold.

2-35 Basic Cost-Volume Graphs

From the following two graphs, construct two graphs that depict the cost behavior on a per-square-foot basis for volumes ranging from 100,000 to 200,000 square feet. (Note that the Total Labor Cost in these graphs is $24,000 for all volumes, while Total Supplies Cost ranges from $5,000 for 100,000 square feet to $10,000 for 200,000 square feet.) Which of the two constructed graphs show fixed-cost behavior? Variable-cost behavior?

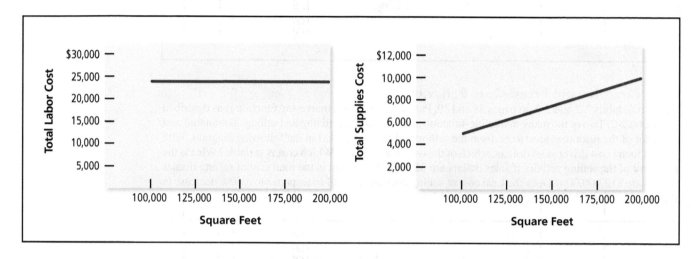

2-36 Basic Cost-Volume Graphs

From the following two graphs, construct two graphs that depict the cost behavior on a total cost basis for volumes ranging from 100,000 to 150,000 square feet. (Note that the Supplies Costs Per Square Foot in these graphs are $.06 for all volumes, while Labor Costs Per Square Foot range from $.12 for 100,000 square feet to $.096 for 125,000 square feet to $.08 for 150,000 square feet.) Which of the two constructed graphs show fixed-cost behavior? Variable-cost behavior?

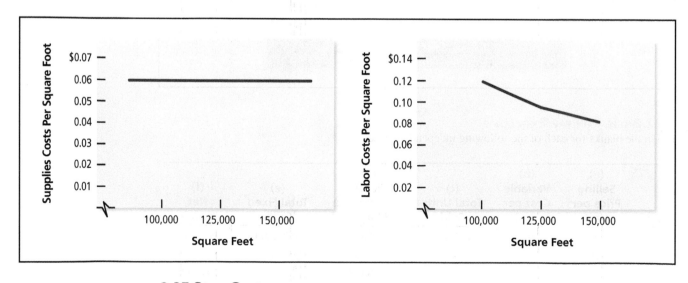

2-37 Step Costs

Which of the following are step costs? Why?

a. Rent on a warehouse that is large enough for all anticipated orders
b. Teachers for a private elementary school; one teacher is needed for every 15 students

c. Sheet steel for a producer of machine parts; steel is purchased in carload shipments, where each carload contains enough steel for 1,000 parts

2-38 Mixed Costs

The following cost function is a mixed cost. Explain why it is a mixed cost and not a fixed, variable, or step cost.

$$\text{Total cost} = \$8,000 + \$52 \times \text{units produced}$$

2-39 Various Cost-Behavior Patterns

In practice, there is often a tendency to simplify approximations of cost-behavior patterns, even though the "true" underlying behavior is not simple. Choose from the following graphs A–H the one that matches the numbered items. Indicate by letter which graph best fits each of the situations described. Next to each number-letter pair, identify a likely cost driver for that cost.

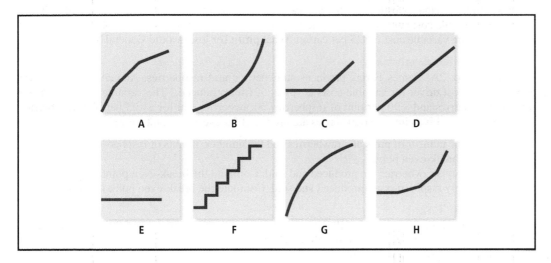

The vertical axes of the graphs represent total dollars of costs incurred, and the horizontal axes represent levels of cost driver activity during a particular time period. The graphs may be used more than once.

1. Cost of machining labor that tends to decrease as workers gain experience
2. Price of an increasingly scarce raw material as the quantity used increases
3. Guaranteed annual wage plan, whereby workers get paid for 40 hours of work per week even at zero or low levels of production that require working only a few hours weekly
4. Water bill, which entails a flat fee for the first 10,000 gallons used and then an increasing unit cost for every additional 10,000 gallons used
5. Availability of quantity discounts, where the cost per unit falls as each price break is reached
6. Depreciation of office equipment
7. Cost of sheet steel for a manufacturer of farm implements
8. Salaries of supervisors, where one supervisor is added for every 12 phone solicitors
9. Natural gas bill consisting of a fixed component, plus a constant variable cost per thousand cubic feet after a specified number of cubic feet are used

2-40 Hospital Costs and Pricing

Olympia Hospital has overall variable costs of 25% of total revenue and fixed costs of $45 million per year.

1. Compute the break-even point expressed in total revenue.
2. A patient-day is often used to measure the volume of a hospital. Suppose there are to be 37,500 patient-days next year. Compute the average daily revenue per patient-day necessary to achieve the break-even total revenue computed in item 1.

2-41 Cost-Volume-Profit at a Hospital

Children's Hospital predicts variable costs of 70% of total revenue and fixed costs of $42 million per year for the coming year.

1. Compute the break-even point expressed in total revenue.
2. Children's Hospital expects total revenue of $150 million from 200,000 patient-days. Compute expected profit (a) if costs behave as expected, and (b) if variable costs are 10% greater than predicted.

2-42 Motel Rentals

Super 8, the world's largest budget hotel chain, was founded in 1972. It now has more than 120,000 rooms in more than 2,000 locations (average is 61 rooms) in the United States and Canada. Suppose a particular

Super 8 has annual fixed costs of $900,000 for its 100-room motel, average daily room rents of $54, and average variable costs of $9 for each room rented. It operates 365 days per year.

1. How much net income on rooms will Super 8 generate (a) if the motel is completely full throughout the entire year and (b) if the motel is half full?
2. Compute the break-even point in number of rooms rented. What percentage occupancy for the year is needed to break even?

2-43 Variable Cost to Break Even

General Mills makes Nature Valley granola bars, Cheerios cereal, Yoplait yogurt, Häagen-Dazs ice cream, and many other food products. Suppose the product manager of a new General Mills cereal has determined that the appropriate wholesale price for a carton of the cereal is $48. Fixed costs of the production and marketing of the cereal are $19 million.

1. The product manager estimates that she can sell 800,000 cartons at the $48 price. What is the largest variable cost per carton that General Mills can pay and still achieve a profit of $1 million?
2. Suppose the variable cost is $25 per carton. What profit (or loss) would General Mills expect?

2-44 Sales-Mix Analysis

Study Appendix 2A. Eames Farms produces strawberries and raspberries. Annual fixed costs are $15,300. The cost driver for variable costs is "pints of fruit produced." The variable cost is $.85 per pint of strawberries and $.90 per pint of raspberries. Strawberries sell for $1.05 per pint, raspberries for $1.30 per pint. Five pints of strawberries are produced for every two pints of raspberries.

1. Compute the number of pints of strawberries and the number of pints of raspberries produced and sold at the break-even point.
2. Suppose only strawberries are produced and sold. Compute the break-even point in pints.
3. Suppose only raspberries are produced and sold. Compute the break-even point in pints.

2-45 Income Taxes

Review the illustration in Appendix 2B. Suppose the income tax rate were 25% instead of 40%. How many units would the company have to sell to achieve a target after-tax net income of (a) $864 and (b) $1,440? Show your computations.

2-46 Income Taxes and Cost-Volume-Profit Analysis

Study Appendix 2B. Suppose Wooliscroft Construction Company has a 32% income tax rate, a contribution-margin ratio of 45%, and fixed costs of $664,000. What sales volume is necessary to achieve an after-tax income of $136,000?

PROBLEMS

2-47 Terry's Pub, Cost-Volume-Profit Analysis in a Small Business

Terry Shevlin recently opened Terry's Pub in the University District. Because of licensing restrictions, the only liquor he can sell is beer. The average price of beer at Terry's Pub is $5.00 per glass, and each glass costs Terry an average of $4.10. Terry has hired a bartender and waiter at $3,000 and $4,000 per month, respectively. His rent, utilities, and other fixed operating costs are $3,000 per month.

Terry is considering selling hamburgers during the lunch hour. He feels that this will increase his daytime business, which is currently quite small. It will also allow him to be more competitive with other local bars that offer a wider variety of food and beverages.

Terry would like to sell the hamburgers for $1.24 each in order to be attractive to customers. Terry will buy buns for $1.44 a dozen and ground beef for $1.20 per pound. Each pound of ground beef will make three hamburgers. Other ingredients will cost an average of $.12 per hamburger. Terry will also need to hire a part-time cook at $1,200 per month. Other additional fixed costs will run about $360 a month.

1. If Terry sells only beer, how many glasses of beer does he have to sell each month to make a monthly profit of $500?
2. If Terry sells only beer, how many glasses of beer does he have to sell each month to make a monthly profit of 5% of sales?
3. Suppose Terry decides to add hamburgers to his menu. How many hamburgers does he need to sell to break even on the hamburgers? Assume that there is no effect on beer sales.
4. The main reason Terry wanted to add hamburgers was to attract more customers. Suppose that 3,000 extra customers per month came for lunch because of the availability of hamburgers and that each bought an average of 1 hamburger and 1.6 beers. Compute the added profit (or loss) generated by these extra customers.
5. Terry was not sure how many new customers would be attracted by the hamburgers. Give Terry some advice about how many new customers would be needed to just break even on the new business if each new customer bought one hamburger and one beer. Include an assessment of the consequences of volume falling below or above this break-even point.

6. Terry could offer a higher quality hamburger if he spends 50% more on the ingredients. He could then charge $2.24 for them. Explain how Terry could determine whether the higher quality hamburgers would be more profitable than the regular hamburgers.

2-48 Super Valu Grocery Chain, Variable and Fixed Costs

Maintaining a clean shopping environment is a key success factor for **Super Valu**, a large grocery chain based in Minnesota. Three of the most costly resources needed to clean a supermarket are labor, equipment, and cleaning supplies. The cost driver for all these resources is "number of times cleaned." Wages for cleaning laborers (called porters) and rent for cleaning equipment are the same regardless of the number of times the supermarket is cleaned. Supplies used for each regular daily cleaning and for each special cleaning are about the same.

A typical store has 48,000 square feet. Regular cleaning is performed each day from midnight until 7:00 AM. Special cleaning of floors and fixtures is performed in the various departments as needed. Special cleaning varies from 10 to 30 times a month depending on the amount of traffic through the store. Thus, the number of times a store is cleaned varies from 40 to 60 times a month.

Suppose that in one of Super Valu's stores in Minneapolis, cleaning was performed 60 times during March. For the month, the cost of labor and rent on equipment was $21,000 and cleaning supplies used cost $12,000. The sales budget for the next quarter (April through June) and better weather conditions indicate that the store will need to be cleaned 50, 46, and 35 times in April, May, and June respectively.

1. Prepare a table that shows how labor cost, rent, cleaning supplies cost, total cost, and total cost per cleaning changes in response to the number of times the store is cleaned. Show costs for 35, 40, 45, 50, 55, and 60 cleanings. What is the predicted total cost of cleaning the Minneapolis store for the next quarter?
2. Prepare a single graph that can be used to predict the fixed, variable, and total cleaning cost of the Super Valu store.
3. Suppose the manager of the Super Valu store can hire an outside cleaning company to clean the store as needed. The charge rate is $720 per cleaning. If the outside cleaning company is hired, Super Valu can lay off the workers who are now cleaning the store, eliminate the need for equipment rent, and stop purchasing cleaning supplies. Will Super Valu save money with the outside cleaning company over the next quarter? Prepare a schedule that supports your answer.

2-49 Fixed Costs and Relevant Range

Bridger Canyon Systems Group (BCSG) has substantial year-to-year fluctuations in billings to clients. Top management has the following policy regarding the employment of key professional personnel:

If Gross Annual Billings Are	Number of Persons to Be Employed	Key Professional Annual Salaries and Benefits
$2,000,000 or less	10	$1,000,000
$2,000,001–2,400,000	11	$1,100,000
$2,400,001–2,800,000	12	$1,200,000

Top management believes that the group should maintain a minimum of 10 individuals for a year or more even if billings drop drastically below $2 million.

For the past 5 years, gross annual billings for BCSG have fluctuated between $2,020,000 and $2,380,000. Expectations for next year are that gross billings will be between $2,100,000 and $2,300,000. What amount should the group budget for key professional personnel salaries? Graph the relationships on an annual basis, using the two approaches (refined and simplified) illustrated in Exhibit 2-6 on page 42. Indicate the relevant range on each graph. You need not use graph paper; simply approximate the graphical relationships.

2-50 Comparing Contribution Margin Percentages

Following are actual statements of operating income for **Microsoft** and **Procter & Gamble** (in millions):

Microsoft		Procter & Gamble	
Revenues	$60,420	Net sales	$83,503
Cost of revenue	11,598	Cost of products sold	40,695
Research and development	8,164	Selling, general, and administrative expenses	25,725
Sales and Marketing	13,039		
General and administrative	5,127	Operating income	$17,083
Operating income	$22,492		

Assume that the only variable cost for Microsoft is "cost of revenue" and for Procter & Gamble the only variable cost is "cost of products sold."

1. Compute the contribution-margin percentage of Microsoft and that of Procter & Gamble. Why do you suppose the percentages are so different?
2. Suppose each company increases its revenue by $10 million. Compute the increase in operating income for each company.
3. Explain how the contribution margin percentage helps you predict the effects on operating income of changes in sales volume. What assumptions do you make in forming such a prediction?

2-51 Cost Structure and Risk Sharing

Marge Porter is the manager of Stanford's traditional Sunday Flicks, sponsored by the Stanford Student Association. The admission price is deliberately set at a very low $3. Each Sunday, a film has two showings and a maximum of 500 tickets can be sold for each showing. The rental of the auditorium is $330 and labor is $435, including $90 for Porter. Porter must pay the film distributor a guarantee, ranging from $300 to $900, or 50% of gross admission receipts, whichever is higher.

Before and during the show, she sells refreshments; these sales average 12% of gross admission receipts and yield a contribution margin of 40%.

1. On June 3, Porter screened *The Descendants*. The film grossed $2,250. The guarantee to the distributor was $750, or 50% of gross admission receipts, whichever is higher. What operating income was produced for the Student Association?
2. Recompute the results if the film grossed $1,400.
3. The "four-wall" concept is increasingly being adopted by movie producers. In this plan, the movie's producer pays a guaranteed fixed rental to the theater owner for, say, a week's showing of a movie and the producer receives the ticket receipts less the fixed rental. As a theater owner, how would you evaluate a "four-wall" offer?

2-52 CVP for Promotion of a Rock Concert

TJB Productions, Ltd., is promoting a rock concert in London. The bands will receive a flat fee of £7.3 million. The concert will be shown worldwide on closed-circuit television. TJB will collect 100% of the receipts and will return 20% to the individual local closed-circuit theater managers. TJB expects to sell 1.3 million seats at a net average price of £15 each. TJB will also receive £270,000 from the London arena (which has sold out its 19,700 seats, ranging from £175 for box seats to £20 for general admission, for a gross revenue of £1.2 million); TJB will not share the £270,000 with the local promoters.

1. The general manager of TJB Productions is trying to decide what amount to spend for advertising. What is the most TJB could spend and still break even on overall operations, assuming sales of 1.3 million tickets?
2. If TJB desires an operating income of £490,000, how many seats would it have to sell? Assume that the average price is £15 and fixed costs consist of the £7.3 million fee for the bands and £3.7 million for advertising, for total fixed costs of £11 million.

2-53 Cost Drivers at Boeing

Consider the Boeing plant discussed on pages 36–37. Suppose Boeing has a cost-reduction program for this plant to reduce the costs of activities, such as receiving parts for its airplanes, by 10%.

At a meeting of the receiving department operating managers and the accounting staff, complaints were made that cost-reduction was not completely the responsibility of the receiving department because some factors were beyond the department's control. Managers pointed out that the total cost of fuel is a function of fuel price per gallon and the gallons used. Furthermore, neither the price paid for fuel nor the lease cost is controllable by receiving department employees. Managers argue that the factors such as fuel and equipment usage were not explicitly tracked and costed. These operating measures were the ones managers believed to be the ones that should be used as cost drivers.

You have been asked to refine the way variable and fixed costs are calculated by using the more relevant cost drivers for fuel and equipment—"gallons" and "hours operated." You have collected the following data for the most recent period.

Equipment cost	$45,000
Fuel cost	$24,000
Hours equipment operated	1,500
Gallons of fuel used	6,000
Parts received	30,000
Target cost goal after 10% cost reduction (90% × $69,000)	$62,100

1. Draw a diagram similar to Exhibit 2-4 on page 40 that shows the relationships between the receiving activity and the resources used and that incorporates the new cost drivers recommended by operating

managers. On the diagram, show the total level of each cost driver, the fuel consumption rate in gallons used per part received, and the equipment consumption rate in hours per part received.

2. Refer to your answer to requirement 1. If the number of parts received increased from 30,000 to 40,000, which number(s) would most likely change: total gallons used, total hours operated, or gallons per part received? Derive an equation that calculates total fuel cost as a function of fuel cost per gallon and fuel consumption rate. Predict the total cost of the receiving activity if the number of parts received is 40,000.

3. The managers in the receiving department have a plan that will improve fuel efficiency. What is the predicted total cost of receiving 30,000 parts if the fuel consumption rate is reduced by 20% (assume fuel costs per gallon will not change)? Will the receiving department achieve Boeing's 10% cost-reduction goal? Why or why not?

4. Comment on the benefits of the new cost-driver model compared to the one based solely on one cost driver—"number of parts received."

5. Can you think of other refinements in the cost-driver model based on the data that are given?

2-54 Basic CVP Relationships, Restaurant

Joann Swanson owns and operates a restaurant. Her fixed costs are $17,000 per month. She serves luncheons and dinners. The average total bill (excluding tax and tip) is $18 per customer. Swanson's present variable costs average $9.50 per meal.

1. How many meals must she serve to attain a profit before taxes of $8,500 per month?
2. What is the break-even point in number of meals served per month?
3. Suppose Swanson's rent and other fixed costs rise to a total of $25,420 per month and variable costs also rise to $11.40 per meal. If Swanson increases her average price to $22, how many meals must she serve to make $8,500 profit per month?
4. Assume the same situation described in requirement 3. Swanson's accountant tells her she may lose 15% of her customers if she increases her prices. If this should happen, what would be Swanson's profit per month? Assume that the restaurant had been serving 3,000 customers per month.
5. Assume the same situation described in requirement 4. To help offset the anticipated 15% loss of customers, Swanson hires a pianist to perform for 4 hours each night for $2,300 per month. Assume that this would increase the total monthly meals from 2,550 to 2,800. Would Swanson's total profit change? By how much?

2-55 Changing Fixed Costs to Variable Costs at Blockbuster Video

When John F. Antioco took charge of Blockbuster Video, he changed the company's strategy. Traditionally, Blockbuster had bought videos from the movie studios for an average cost of about $65 each, planning to rent them out often enough to make a profit. Mr. Antioco replaced this strategy with one that allows Blockbuster to purchase videos for an average of $7 each and pay the studio 40% of any rental fee received. With this arrangement, Blockbuster can afford to stock more copies of each video and guarantee customers that the movie they want will be in stock—or the rental is free. Suppose that Blockbuster rents videos for $2 a day. In each of the following questions, consider only the direct costs of the videos, not the costs of operating the rental store.

1. Under the traditional strategy, how many days must each video be rented before Blockbuster will break even on the video?
2. Under the new strategy, how many days must each video be rented before Blockbuster will break even on the video?
3. Suppose customers rented a particular copy of *Moneyball* for 50 days. What profit would Blockbuster make on rentals under the traditional strategy? Under the new strategy?
4. Suppose customers rented a particular copy of *The Descendants* for only 6 days. What profit would Blockbuster make on rentals under the traditional strategy? Under the new strategy?
5. Comment on how the new arrangement affects the risks Blockbuster accepts when purchasing an additional copy of a particular video.

2-56 CVP and Financial Statements for a Mega-Brand Company

Procter & Gamble Company is a Cincinnati-based company that produces household products under brand names such as Gillette, Bounty, Crest, Folgers, and Tide. The company's 2011 income statement showed the following (in millions):

Net sales	$82,559
Costs of products sold	40,768
Selling, general, and administrative expense	25,973
Operating income	$15,818

Suppose that the cost of products sold is the only variable cost; selling, general, and administrative expenses are fixed with respect to sales.

Suppose Procter & Gamble has a 10% decrease in sales next year and there is no change in costs except for decreases associated with the lower volume of sales. Compute the predicted operating income for Procter & Gamble and its percentage decrease. Explain why the percentage decrease in income differs from the percentage decrease in sales.

2-57 Bingo and Operating Leverage

Many churches sponsor bingo games, a tradition stemming from the time when only specific nonprofit institutions were allowed to sponsor games of chance. Reverend Donovan Dukes, the pastor of a new parish in Orange County, is investigating the desirability of conducting weekly bingo nights. The parish has no hall, but a local hotel would be willing to commit its hall for a lump-sum rental of $950 per night. The rent would include cleaning, setting up and taking down the tables and chairs, and so on.

1. A local printer would provide bingo cards in return for free advertising. Local merchants would donate door prizes. The services of clerks, callers, security force, and others would be donated by volunteers. Admission would be $8.00 per person, entitling the player to one card; extra cards would be $.50 each. Many persons buy extra cards so there would be an average of five cards played per person. What is the maximum in total cash prizes that the church may award and still break even if 200 persons attend each weekly session?

2. Suppose the total cash prizes are $1,050. What will be the church's operating income if 50 persons attend? If 200 persons attend? If 350 persons attend? Briefly explain the effects of the cost behavior on income.

3. After operating for 10 months, Reverend Dukes is thinking of negotiating a different rental arrangement but keeping the prize money unchanged at $1,050. Suppose the rental arrangement is $700 per night plus $1 per person. Compute the operating income for attendance of 50, 200, and 350 persons, respectively. Explain why the results differ from those in requirement 2.

2-58 Operating Leverage at eBay

In 2011, eBay had $11.6 billion in revenue and net income over $3.2 billion. eBay's mission is to "provide a global trading platform where practically anyone can trade practically anything." However, eBay has not always had profits in the billions.

Consider eBay's situation during the early years. In the first quarter of 2001, eBay reported revenue of $154 million and operating expenses of $123 million, for an operating profit of $31 million. In the first quarter of 2002, eBay reported that revenue had increased 59%, to $245 million. Assume that during both years, eBay's fixed costs were $37 million and all other costs were variable costs.

1. Compute eBay's operating income for the first quarter of 2002 assuming that variable costs were the same percentage of revenue in 2002 as in 2001. Compute the percentage increase in operating income between 2001 and 2002.

2. Explain how eBay managed to increase its income so much with only a 59% increase in revenue.

2-59 Adding a Product

Arnold's Brew Pub, located near Southwestern State University, serves as a gathering place for the university's more social scholars. Arnold sells draft beer and all brands of bottled beer at a contribution margin of $.72 a beer.

Arnold is considering also selling hamburgers during selected hours. His reasons are twofold. First, sandwiches would attract daytime customers. A hamburger and a beer are a quick lunch. Second, he has to meet competition from other local bars, some of which provide more extensive menus.

Arnold analyzed the costs of adding hamburgers as follows:

Per Month		Per Hamburger	
Monthly Fixed Expenses		**Variable Expenses**	
Wages of part-time cook	$1,452	Rolls	$.11
Other	330	Meat @ $2.66 per pound (seven hamburgers per pound)	.38
Total	$1,782		
		Other	.22
		Total	$.71

Arnold planned a selling price of $1.25 per hamburger to lure many customers. For all questions, assume a 30-day month.

1. What are the monthly and daily break-even points, in number of hamburgers?
2. What are the monthly and daily break-even points, in dollar sales?
3. At the end of 2 months, Arnold finds he has sold 3,800 hamburgers. What is the operating profit per month on hamburgers?
4. Arnold thinks that at least 75 extra beers are sold per day because he has these hamburgers available. This means that 75 extra people come to the bar or that 75 buy an extra beer because they are attracted by the hamburgers. How does the sale of hamburgers combined with the accompanying effect on beer sales affect Arnold's monthly operating income?
5. Refer to requirement 3. How many extra beers would have to be sold per day so that the overall effect of the hamburger sales on monthly operating income would be zero?

2-60 Government Organization

A social welfare agency has a government budget appropriation for 20X7 of $900,000. The agency's major mission is to help disabled persons who are unable to hold jobs. On the average, the agency supplements each person's income by $5,000 annually. The agency's fixed costs are $280,000. There are no other costs.

1. How many disabled persons were helped during 20X7?
2. For 20X8, the agency's budget appropriation has been reduced by 15%. If the agency continues the same level of monetary support per person, how many disabled persons will be helped in 20X8? Compute the percentage decline in the number of persons helped.
3. Assume a budget reduction of 15%, as in requirement 2. The manager of the agency has discretion as to how much to supplement each disabled person's income. She does not want to reduce the number of persons served. On average, what is the amount of the supplement that can be given to each person? Compute the percentage decline in the annual supplement.

2-61 Gross Margin and Contribution Margin

Eastman Kodak Company is a provider of imaging technology products and services to the photographic, graphic communications, and health-care markets. A condensed 2011 income statement follows (in millions):

Sales	$6,022
Cost of goods sold	5,135
Gross margin	887
Other operating expenses	1,487
Loss from continuing operations	$ (600)

Assume that $1,400 million of the cost of goods sold is a fixed cost representing depreciation and other production costs that do not change with the volume of production. In addition, $1,000 million of the other operating expenses is fixed.

1. Compute the total contribution margin for 2011 and the contribution margin percentage. Explain why the contribution margin differs from the gross margin.
2. Suppose that sales for Eastman Kodak are predicted to increase by 10% and that the cost behavior is expected to continue. Compute the predicted operating income (loss).
3. What assumptions were necessary to compute the predicted operating income in requirement 2?

2-62 Choosing Equipment for Different Volumes

MetroCinemas owns and operates a nationwide chain of movie theaters. The 500 properties in the chain vary from low-volume, small-town, single-screen theaters to high-volume, big-city, multiscreen theaters.

The management is considering installing machines that will make popcorn on the premises. These machines would allow the theaters to sell freshly popped popcorn rather than the prepopped, prebagged corn that it currently sells. This proposed feature would be properly advertised and is intended to increase patronage at the company's theaters.

The machines can be purchased in several different sizes. The annual rental costs and operating costs vary with the size of the machines. The machine capacities and costs are as follows:

	Popper Model		
	Standard	**Deluxe**	**Jumbo**
Annual capacity	50,000 boxes	120,000 boxes	300,000 boxes
Costs			
Annual machine rental	$7,840	$11,200	$20,200
Popcorn cost per box	.14	.14	.14
Cost of each box	.09	.09	.09
Other variable costs per box	.22	.14	.05

1. Calculate the volume level in boxes at which the standard and deluxe poppers would earn the same operating profit (loss).
2. The management can estimate the number of boxes to be sold at each of its theaters. Present a decision rule that would enable MetroCinemas management to select the most profitable machine without having to make a separate cost calculation for each theater. That is, at what anticipated range of unit sales should the theater use the standard model? The deluxe model? The jumbo model?
3. Could the management use the average number of boxes sold per seat for the entire chain and the capacity of each theater to develop this decision rule? Explain your answer.

2-63 Sales Compensation, Variable/Fixed Costs, and Ethics

Most companies compensate their sales forces with a combination of a fixed salary and a commission that is a percentage of sales. Consider two companies competing for the same customers—for example, Kellogg's and Post cereals. Suppose that Kellogg's pays its sales force a large fixed salary and a small commission, while Post pays its sales force a small fixed salary and a large commission. The total pay on average was the same for both companies.

1. Compare the sales cost structure of Kellogg's with that of Post. Which has the larger fixed cost? Which has the larger variable cost? How will this affect each company's risk? (Focus on how the company's profits change with changes in volume.)
2. What incentives does each pay system provide for the sales force?
3. Might either incentive system create potential ethical dilemmas for the sales personnel? Explain.

2-64 Sales-Mix Analysis

Study Appendix 2A. The Colorado Catering Company specializes in preparing Mexican dinners that it freezes and ships to restaurants in the Denver area. When a diner orders an item, the restaurant heats and serves it. The budget data for 20X5 are as follows:

	Product	
	Chicken Tacos	**Beef Enchiladas**
Selling price to restaurants	$4	$5
Variable expenses	3	3
Contribution margin	$1	$2
Number of units	200,000	100,000

The company prepares the items in the same kitchens, delivers them in the same trucks, and so forth. Therefore, decisions about the individual products do not affect the fixed costs of $680,000.

1. Compute the planned net income for 20X5.
2. Compute the break-even point in units, assuming that the company maintains its planned sales mix.
3. Compute the break-even point in units if the company a) sells only tacos, or b) sells only enchiladas.
4. Suppose the company sells 225,000 units of tacos and 75,000 units of enchiladas, for a total of 300,000 units. Compute the net income. Compute the new break-even point with this new sales mix. What is the major lesson of this problem?

2-65 Hospital Patient Mix

Study Appendix 2A. Hospitals measure their volume in terms of patient-days. We calculate patient-days by multiplying the number of patients by the number of days that the patients are hospitalized.

Suppose a large hospital has fixed costs of $52.8 million per year and variable costs of $750 per patient-day. Daily revenues vary among classes of patients. For simplicity, assume that there are two classes: (1) self-pay patients (S) who pay an average of $1,250 per day and (2) non–self-pay patients (G) who are the responsibility of insurance companies and government agencies and who pay an average of $950 per day. Twenty-five percent of the patients are self-pay.

1. Compute the break-even point in patient-days, assuming that the hospital maintains its planned mix of patients.
2. Suppose that the hospital achieves 172,000 patient-days but that 40% of the patient-days were self-pay (instead of 25%). Compute the net income. Compute the break-even point.

2-66 Income Taxes on Hotels
Study Appendix 2B. The Regal Hotel in downtown Phoenix has annual fixed costs applicable to rooms of $8.7 million for its 570-room hotel, average daily room rates of $90, and average variable costs of $42 daily for each room rented. It operates 365 days per year. The hotel is subject to an income tax rate of 25%.

1. How many rooms must the hotel rent to earn a net income after taxes of $801,000? Of $400,500?
2. Compute the break-even point in number of rooms rented. What percentage occupancy for the year is needed to break even?
3. Assume that the volume level of rooms rented is 200,000. The manager is wondering how much income could be generated if 6,000 additional rooms are rented. Compute the additional net income after taxes.

2-67 Tax Effects
Study Appendix 2B. Decca Company is a wholesaler of compact discs. The projected after-tax net income for the current year is $90,000, based on a sales volume of 170,000 CDs. Decca has been selling the CDs at $15 each. The variable costs consist of the $8 unit purchase price and a handling cost of $4 per unit. Decca's annual fixed costs are $714,000, and the company is subject to a 40% income tax rate.

Management is planning for the coming year when it expects that the unit purchase price will increase 25%.

1. Compute Decca Company's break-even point for the current year.
2. An increase of 15% in projected unit sales volume for the current year would result in an increased after-tax income for the current year of how much?
3. Compute the volume of sales in dollars that Decca Company must achieve in the coming year to maintain the same after-tax net income as projected for the current year if unit selling price remains at $15.
4. To cover a 25% increase in the unit purchase price for the coming year and still maintain the current contribution-margin ratio, Decca Company must establish a selling price per unit for the coming year of how much?

CASES

2-68 Hospital Costs
Gother City Hospital is unionized. In 20X6, nurses received an average annual salary of $45,000. The hospital administrator is considering changes in the contract with nurses for 20X7. In turn, the hospital may also change the way it charges nursing costs to each department.

The hospital holds each department accountable for its financial performance, and it records revenues and expenses by departments. Consider the expenses of the obstetrics department in 20X6.

Variable expenses (based on 20X6 patient-days) are as follows:

Meals	$ 610,000
Laundry	260,000
Laboratory	900,000
Pharmacy	850,000
Maintenance	150,000
Other	530,000
Total	$3,300,000

Fixed expenses (based on number of beds) are as follows:

Rent	$3,000,000
General administrative services	2,200,000
Janitorial	200,000
Maintenance	150,000
Other	350,000
Total	$5,900,000

Management assigns nurses to departments on the basis of annual patient-days as follows:

Volume Level in Patient-Days	Number of Nurses
10,000–12,000	30
12,001–16,000	35

Total patient-days are the number of patients multiplied by the number of days they are hospitalized. The hospital charges each department for the salaries of the nurses assigned to it.

During 20X6, the obstetrics department had a capacity of 60 beds, billed each patient an average of $810 per day, and had revenues of $12.15 million.

1. Compute the 20X6 volume of activity in patient-days.
2. Compute the 20X6 patient-days that would have been necessary for the obstetrics department to recoup all fixed expenses except nursing expenses.
3. Compute the 20X6 patient-days that would have been necessary for the obstetrics department to break even including nurses' salaries as a fixed cost.
4. Suppose obstetrics must pay $200 per patient-day for nursing services. This plan would replace the two-level, fixed-cost system employed in 20X6. Compute what the break-even point in patient-days would have been in 20X6 under this plan.

2-69 CVP in a Modern Manufacturing Environment

A division of Hewlett-Packard Company changed its production operations from one where a large labor force assembled electronic components to an automated production facility dominated by computer-controlled robots. The change was necessary because of fierce competitive pressures. Improvements in quality, reliability, and flexibility of production schedules were necessary just to match the competition. As a result of the change, variable costs fell and fixed costs increased, as shown in the following assumed budgets:

	Old Production Operation	New Production Operation
Unit variable cost		
Material	$ .88	$ .88
Labor	1.22	.22
Total per unit	$2.10	$1.10
Monthly fixed costs		
Rent and depreciation	$450,000	$ 875,000
Supervisory labor	80,000	175,000
Other	50,000	90,000
Total per month	$580,000	$1,140,000

Expected volume is 600,000 units per month, with each unit selling for $3.10. Capacity is 800,000 units.

1. Compute the budgeted profit at the expected volume of 600,000 units under both the old and the new production environments.
2. Compute the budgeted break-even point under both the old and the new production environments.

3. Discuss the effect on profits if volume falls to 500,000 units under both the old and the new production environments.
4. Discuss the effect on profits if volume increases to 700,000 units under both the old and the new production environments.
5. Comment on the riskiness of the new operation versus the old operation.

2-70 Multiproduct Break Even in a Restaurant

Study Appendix 2A. An article in *Washington Business* included an income statement for **La Brasserie**, a French restaurant in Washington, D.C. A simplified version of the statement follows:

Revenues	$2,098,400
Cost of sales, all variable	1,246,500
Gross profit	851,900
Operating expenses	
Variable	222,380
Fixed	170,940
Administrative expenses, all fixed	451,500
Net income	$ 7,080

The average dinner tab at La Brasserie is $40, and the average lunch tab is $20. Assume that the variable cost of preparing and serving dinner is also twice that of a lunch. The restaurant serves twice as many lunches as dinners. Assume that the restaurant is open 305 days a year.

1. Compute the daily break-even volume in lunches and dinners for La Brasserie. Compare this to the actual volume reflected in the income statement.
2. Suppose that an extra annual advertising expenditure of $15,000 would increase the average daily volume by three dinners and six lunches, and that there is plenty of capacity to accommodate the extra business. Prepare an analysis for the management of La Brasserie, explaining whether this would be desirable.
3. La Brasserie uses only premium food, and the cost of food makes up 25% of the restaurant's total variable costs. Use of average rather than premium ingredients could cut the food cost by 20%. Assume that La Brasserie uses average-quality ingredients and does not change its prices. How much of a drop-off in volume could it endure and still maintain the same net income? What factors in addition to revenue and costs would influence the decision about the quality of food to use?

2-71 Effects of Changes in Costs, Including Tax Effects

Study Appendix 2B. Pacific Fish Company is a wholesale distributor of salmon. The company services grocery stores in the Chicago area.

Average selling price per pound	$ 5.00
Average variable costs per pound	
Cost of salmon	$ 2.50
Shipping expenses	.50
Total	$3.00
Annual fixed costs	
Selling	$ 210,000
Administrative	356,250
Total	$ 566,250
Expected annual sales volume (390,000 pounds)	$1,950,000
Tax rate	40%

Small but steady growth in sales has been achieved by Pacific Fish over the past few years, while salmon prices have been increasing. The company is formulating its plans for the coming fiscal year. Presented next are the data used to project the current year's after-tax net income of $128,250.

Fishing companies have announced that they will increase prices of their products by an average of 15% in the coming year, owing mainly to increases in labor costs. Pacific Fish Company expects that all other costs will remain at the same rates or levels as in the current year.

1. What is Pacific Fish Company's break-even point in pounds of salmon for the current year?
2. What selling price per pound must Pacific Fish Company charge to cover the 15% increase in the cost of salmon and still maintain the current contribution-margin ratio?
3. What volume of sales in dollars must the Pacific Fish Company achieve in the coming year to maintain the same net income after taxes as projected for the current year if the selling price of salmon remains at $5 per pound and the cost of salmon increases 15%?
4. What strategies might Pacific Fish Company use to maintain the same net income after taxes as projected for the current year?

NIKE 10-K PROBLEM

2-72 Operating Leverage

Examine Nike's 10K report in Appendix C.

1. In Item 7 of the 10K, review the section titled Operating Segments. Prepare a table that compares the percent change in "Total revenue" to the change in "Pre-tax income" from 2010 to 2011 for the six major regions (ignore the Global Brand Divisions segment). Note that generally earnings before interest and taxes changes by a larger percentage than revenue. For example, in Western Europe, revenue declined by 2% but earnings declined by 16%. (The exception to this general observation is the "Central and Eastern Europe" region where revenue and earnings moved in opposite directions—revenue increased but earnings before interest and taxes decreased). How can operating leverage help explain the greater percent change in earnings than the percent change in total revenues?
2. What might explain the decrease in income despite the increase in revenue for the Central and Eastern region?
3. Would you expect Nike's operating leverage to be high or low? Explain. Which assets do you think contribute to Nike's ability to leverage operating overhead?

EXCEL APPLICATION EXERCISE

2-73 CVP and Break Even

Goal: Create an Excel spreadsheet to perform CVP analysis and show the relationship between price, costs, and break-even points in terms of units and dollars. Use the results to answer questions about your findings.

Scenario: Phonetronix is a small manufacturer of telephone and communications devices. Recently, company management decided to investigate the profitability of cellular phone production. They have three different proposals to evaluate. Under all the proposals, the fixed costs for the new phone would be $110,000. Under proposal A, the selling price of the new phone would be $99 and the variable cost per unit would be $55. Under proposal B, the selling price of the phone would be $129 and the variable cost would remain the same. Under proposal C, the selling price would be $99 and the variable cost would be $49.

When you have completed your spreadsheet, answer the following questions:

1. What are the break-even points in units and dollars under proposal A?
2. How did the increased selling price under proposal B impact the break-even points in units and dollars compared to the break-even points calculated under proposal A?
3. Why did the change in variable cost under proposal C not impact the break-even points in units and dollars as significantly as proposal B did?

Step-by-Step:
1. Open a new Excel spreadsheet.
2. In column A, create a bold-faced heading that contains the following:
   Row 1: Chapter 2 Decision Guideline
   Row 2: Phonetronix
   Row 3: Cost-Volume-Profit (CVP) Analysis
   Row 4: Today's Date
3. Merge and center the four heading rows across columns A–D.

4. In row 7, create the following bold-faced, right-justified column headings:
   Column B: Proposal A
   Column C: Proposal B
   Column D: Proposal C

   Note: Adjust cell widths when necessary as you work.

5. In column A, create the following row headings:
   Row 8: Selling price
   Row 9: Variable cost
   Row 10: Contribution margin
   Row 11: Contribution-margin ratio
   Skip a row.
   Row 13: Fixed cost
   Skip a row.
   Row 15: Breakeven in units
   Skip a row.
   Row 17: Breakeven in dollars

6. Use the scenario data to fill in the selling price, variable cost, and fixed cost amounts for the three proposals.

7. Use the appropriate formulas from this chapter to calculate contribution margin, contribution-margin ratio, breakeven in units, and breakeven in dollars.

8. Format all amounts as follows:

Number tab:	Category:	Currency
	Decimal places:	0
	Symbol:	None
	Negative numbers:	Red with parenthesis

9. Change the format of the selling price, contribution margin, fixed cost, and breakeven in dollars amounts to display a dollar symbol.

10. Change the format of both contribution margin headings to display as indented:

Alignment tab:	Horizontal:	Left (Indent)
	Indent:	1

11. Change the format of the contribution-margin amount cells to display a top border, using the default line style.

Border tab:	Icon:	Top Border

12. Change the format of the contribution-margin ratio amounts to display as a percentage with two decimal places.

Number tab:	Category:	Percentage
	Decimal places:	2

13. Change the format of all break-even headings and amounts to display as bold-faced.

14. Activate the ability to use heading names in formulas under Tools → Options:

Calculation tab:	Check the box:	Accept labels in formulas

15. Replace the cell-based formulas with "word-based" equivalents for each formula used in Proposal A.

    Example: Contribution margin for proposal B would be:
    = ('Selling price' 'Proposal B') − ('Variable cost' 'Proposal B')

    Note: The tic marks used in the example help avoid naming errors caused by data having similar titles (i.e., "contribution margin" and "contribution-margin ratio"). The parentheses help clarify groupings.

    Help: Ask the Answer Wizard about "Name cells in a workbook."

    Select "Learn about labels and names in formulas" from the right-hand panel.

16. Save your work, and print a copy for your files.

COLLABORATIVE LEARNING EXERCISE

2-74 CVP for a Small Business
Form into groups of two to six students. Each group should select a very simple business, one with a single product or one with approximately the same contribution-margin percentage for all products. Some possibilities are

> A child's lemonade stand
> A retail DVD rental store
> An espresso cart
> A retail store selling compact discs
> An athletic shoe store
> A cookie stand in a mall

However, you are encouraged to use your imagination rather than just select one of these examples. The following tasks might be split up among the group members:

1. Make a list of all fixed costs associated with running the business you selected. Estimate the amount of each fixed cost per month (or per day or per year, if one of them is more appropriate for your business).
2. Make a list of all variable costs associated with making or obtaining the product or service your company is selling. Estimate the cost per unit for each variable cost.
3. Given the fixed and variable costs you have identified, compute the break-even point for your business in either units or dollar sales.
4. Assess the prospects of your business making a profit.

INTERNET EXERCISE

2-75 Cost Behavior at Southwest Airlines
It is critical that managers understand how costs and revenues behave. One company that is affected by changes in costs and may not have the capability to rapidly change revenues because of competition is **Southwest Airlines**. Let's take a closer look at SWA and its costs and revenues. Log on to SWA's Web site at www.southwest.com. This Web site serves many purposes for the airline, such as providing flight schedules, making reservations and selling tickets, and displaying vacation and airfare specials.

1. Click on the Air icon and then on "See Where We Fly," which provides a map showing the cities served by Southwest. What is the closest city to your current location served by SWA? Click on that city as the departure city and then select any city you like for the arrival city. Now select a date about a month from now for leaving and one for returning. Click to continue to the next screen. What types of fares are available? Why do you think that there are different types of fares offered? Click on one of the fare-type captions to see if Southwest places any restrictions on this fare. If there are any restrictions, what purpose do they serve?
2. Return to the reservations screen and select a departure date that is less than a week away. What types of fare choices are available now? Are the rates the same as those that you found for a trip more than a month away? Why do you think that the choices remaining are for the most part the higher-priced ones? Is there any advantage to the fare(s) still available? Who is the most likely user of a ticket purchased at the last minute?

3. Now that you have looked at the revenue side, let's focus on the expense side. Individuals on the same flight may pay different prices for the ticket. Do you think that the cost of flying a passenger differs because of the price that he or she pays for the ticket? Why or why not?

4. Return to SWA's home page. Take a look at the costs that SWA actually incurs. Find the list of information available "About Southwest" near the bottom of the page and click on "Investor Relations." Click on the most recent "Annual Report" icon, which takes you to Southwest's most recent 10-K report. Open the 10K report and notice the summary information that the company has provided in the "Selected Financial Data" section. Give the most recent year's operating revenues and operating expenses. How much has each changed over the prior year? What does this imply for Southwest's profitability?

5. Now look further down the page and find "Operating Expenses per ASM." (ASM stands for *available seat miles*, a measure of capacity.) What kinds of costs do you suppose are included in operating expenses per ASM? Which of these costs is primarily fixed with respect to ASM? Which is primarily variable? What other cost drivers might be important causes of costs for Southwest?

Measurement of Cost Behavior

LEARNING OBJECTIVES

When you have finished studying this chapter, you should be able to:

1. Explain management influences on cost behavior.

2. Measure and mathematically express cost functions and use them to predict costs.

3. Describe the importance of activity analysis for measuring cost functions.

4. Measure cost behavior using the engineering analysis, account analysis, high-low, visual-fit, and least-squares regression methods.

► AMERICA WEST

US Airways and America West came together in 2006 to create the fifth largest domestic airline. US Airways, US Airways Shuttle, and US Airways Express now operate approximately 3,000 flights per day and serve more than 200 communities in the United States, Canada, Mexico, the Caribbean, Latin America, Europe, and the Middle East. Before its merger with US Airways, America West rode the wave of a booming economy to increased revenues in the late 1990s. As a result, management decided to expand by introducing service to new destinations including Acapulco, Miami, and Detroit, and by adding more daily flights to existing markets including Las Vegas, Mexico City, and Boston. To accomplish this, the company had to expand its labor force, add new aircraft, and spend more than $40 million on new technology.

Management took very seriously the decision to invest large amounts of money in aircraft and equipment. It knew that the decision would have a significant influence on costs, and thus profits, for many years. Management also knew that most of the costs would be fixed but the revenues would fluctuate with the economy. If the economy were bad, revenues would decline and may not cover these costs.

How does an airline protect itself against losses when the economy experiences a downturn? According to Richard Goodmanson, former president and chief executive officer of America West, "management has a goal to have from 5% to 10% of the fleet of aircraft leased and thus subject to annual renewal. This enhances the company's ability to decrease capacity (and related costs) in the event of an industry downturn." This example illustrates that understanding how costs behave, as well as how managers' decisions can influence costs, helped the airline improve its cost control.

Chapter 2 demonstrated the importance of understanding the cost structure of an organization and the relationships between an organization's activities and its costs, revenues, and profits. This chapter focuses on the **measurement of cost behavior**, which means understanding and quantifying how an organization's activities affect its costs. Recall that activities use resources, and these resources have costs. We measure this relationship between activity and cost using cost drivers. Understanding relationships between costs and their cost drivers allows managers in all types of organizations—profit seeking, nonprofit, and government—to do the following:

measurement of cost behavior
Understanding and quantifying how activities of an organization affect its levels of costs.

- Evaluate strategic plans and operational improvement programs. (Chapter 4)
- Make proper short-run pricing decisions. (Chapter 5)
- Make short-run operating decisions. (Chapter 6)
- Plan or budget the effects of future activities. (Chapters 7 and 8)

- Design effective management control systems. (Chapters 9 and 10)
- Make proper long-run decisions. (Chapter 11)
- Design useful and accurate product costing systems. (Chapters 12–14)

As you can see, understanding cost behavior is fundamental to management accounting. There are numerous real-world cases in which managers have made very poor decisions to drop product lines, close manufacturing plants, or bid too high or too low on jobs because they had erroneous cost-behavior information. This chapter, therefore, deserves careful study. ■

Cost Drivers and Cost Behavior

Accountants and managers often assume that cost behavior is linear over some relevant range of activity or cost-driver levels. We can graph **linear-cost behavior** with a straight line because we assume each cost to be either fixed or variable. Recall that the relevant range specifies the interval of cost-driver activity within which a specific relationship between a cost and its driver will be valid. Managers usually define the relevant range based on their previous experience operating the organization at different levels of activity.

In this chapter, we focus on costs for which the primary cost driver is the volume of a product produced or service provided, as such costs are easy to trace to products or services. Examples of volume-driven costs include the costs of printing labor, paper, ink, and binding to produce all the copies of this textbook. The number of copies printed affects the total printing labor, paper, ink, and binding costs. We can trace the use of these resources to the number of copies of the text printed by using schedules, payroll records, and other documents that show how much of each resource was used to produce the copies of this text.

Activities not directly related to volume also affect costs. Such costs often have multiple cost drivers. For the publisher of this textbook, the wages and salaries of the editorial staff are not easy to trace to outputs. These editorial personnel produce many different textbooks, and it would be very difficult to determine exactly what portion of their wages and salaries went into a specific book, such as *Introduction to Management Accounting.*

Understanding and measuring costs that are difficult to trace to outputs is a challenging exercise. In practice, many organizations use a linear relationship with a single cost driver to describe each cost, even though many costs have multiple causes. This approach is easier and less expensive than using nonlinear relationships or multiple cost drivers. If we use it carefully, this method often provides cost estimates that are sufficiently accurate for most decisions. This scheme may seem at odds with reality and economic theory, but the added benefit of understanding "true" cost behavior may be less than the cost of determining it, which is consistent with the cost-benefit approach to decision making.

Accountants often describe cost behavior in visual or graphical terms. Exhibit 3-1 shows linear-cost behavior, the relevant range, and an activity or resource cost driver. Note the similarity to the cost-volume-profit (CVP) graphs of Chapter 2.

Additionally, many cost graphs display mixed-cost behavior. For example, consider the monthly facilities maintenance department cost of the Parkview Medical Center (PMC), shown in Exhibit 3-2. Salaries of the maintenance personnel and costs of equipment are fixed at $10,000 per month. In addition, cleaning supplies and repair materials vary at a rate of $5 per patient-day[1] delivered by the hospital.

The chief administrator at PMC used knowledge of the facilities maintenance department cost behavior to do the following:

1. Plan costs: In May, the hospital expected to service 3,000 patient-days. May's predicted facilities maintenance department costs are $10,000 fixed costs plus the variable cost of $15,000 (3,000 patient-days times $5 per patient-day) for a total of $25,000.
2. Provide feedback to managers: In May, the actual facilities maintenance costs were $34,000 in a month when PMC serviced 3,000 patient-days as planned. The administrator wanted to know why the hospital overspent by $9,000 ($34,000 less the planned $25,000) so that managers could take corrective action.

© Marianna Day Massey/Newscom

America West airplanes on the ground at the company's Phoenix hub.

linear-cost behavior
Activity that can be graphed with a straight line because costs are assumed to be either fixed or variable.

---
[1]A patient-day is one patient spending 1 day in the hospital. One patient spending 5 days in the hospital is 5 patient-days of service.

Exhibit 3-1
Linear-Cost Behavior

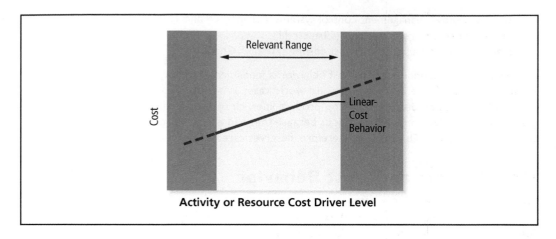

3. Make decisions about the most efficient use of resources: For example, managers might weigh the long-run trade-offs of increased fixed costs of highly efficient floor cleaning equipment against the variable costs of extra cleaning supplies needed to clean the floors manually.

We can see that managers not only passively measure how costs behave, they also actively influence the cost structure of an organization. Let's explore in more detail how managers influence cost behavior.

Management Influence on Cost Behavior

Objective 1

Explain management influences on cost behavior.

In addition to measuring and evaluating current cost behavior, managers can influence cost behavior through decisions about such factors as product or service attributes, capacity, technology, and policies to create incentives to control costs.

Product and Service Decisions and the Value Chain

Throughout the value chain, managers influence cost behavior. This influence occurs through their choices of process and product design, quality levels, product features, distribution channels, and so on. Each of these decisions contributes to the organization's performance, and managers should consider the costs and benefits of each decision. For example, Hertz, the car rental company, would add a feature to its services only if the cost of the feature—for example, GPS navigation systems in its vehicles—could be more than recovered in profit from increased business and/or extra fees it could charge for the feature.

capacity costs
The fixed costs of being able to achieve a desired level of production or to provide a desired level of service while maintaining product or service attributes, such as quality.

Capacity Decisions

Strategic decisions about the scale and scope of an organization's activities generally result in fixed levels of capacity costs. **Capacity costs** are the fixed costs of being able to achieve a desired level of production or service while maintaining product or service attributes, such as quality. Most companies make a capacity decision infrequently. They consider capacity decisions

Exhibit 3-2
Mixed-Cost Behavior

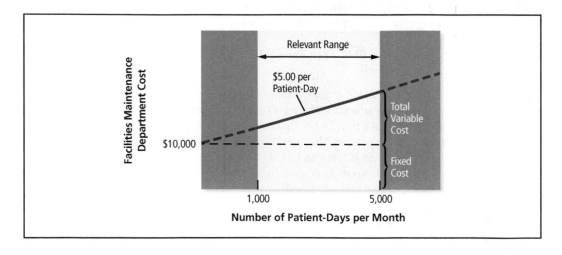

as strategic because large amounts of resources are involved. An incorrect capacity decision can have serious consequences for the competitiveness of a company. However, some companies make capacity decisions so frequently that they almost become routine operating decisions, such as opening a new Starbucks or McDonald's. In this case, the decision to open a new Starbucks is still strategic, but it becomes highly structured.

Companies in industries with long-term variations in demand must be careful when making capacity decisions. Companies may not be able to fully recover fixed capacity costs when demand falls during an economic downturn. Additionally, capacity decisions can entail an ethical commitment to a company's employees. Most companies try to keep a stable employment policy so that they do not need to fire or lay off employees unless there are huge shifts in demand. In the economic downturn of 2008, news stories about companies "downsizing" and initiating extensive layoffs abounded. But other companies managed the decrease in demand without imposing large financial and emotional costs on their employees. Companies that plan their capacity to allow flexibility in meeting demand generally are better able to survive economic hard times, without the upheaval caused by widespread firings and layoffs.

Committed Fixed Costs

Even if a company has chosen to minimize fixed capacity costs, every organization has some costs to which it is committed, perhaps for quite a few years. A company's **committed fixed costs** usually arise from the possession of facilities, equipment, and a basic organizational structure. They include mortgage or lease payments, interest payments on long-term debt, property taxes, insurance, and salaries of key personnel. Only major changes in the philosophy, scale, or scope of operations could change these committed fixed costs in future periods. Recall the example of the facilities maintenance department for the Parkview Medical Center. The capacity of the facilities maintenance department was a management decision, and in this case the decision determined the magnitude of the equipment cost. Suppose PMC were to increase permanently its patient-days per month beyond the relevant range of 5,000 patient-days. Because PMC would need more capacity, the committed equipment cost would rise to a new level per month.

committed fixed costs
Costs arising from the possession of facilities, equipment, and a basic organization.

Discretionary Fixed Costs

Some costs are fixed at certain levels only because management decided to incur these levels of cost to meet the organization's goals. These **discretionary fixed costs** have no obvious relationship to levels of capacity or output activity. Companies determine them as part of the periodic planning process. Each planning period, management will determine how much to spend on discretionary items such as advertising and promotion costs, public relations, research and development costs, charitable donations, employee training programs, and management consulting services. These costs then become fixed until the next planning period.

discretionary fixed costs
Costs determined by management as part of the periodic planning process in order to meet the organization's goals. They have no obvious relationship with levels of capacity or output activity.

Managers can alter discretionary fixed costs—up or down—even within a budget period, if they decide that different levels of spending are desirable. Conceivably, managers could eliminate such discretionary costs almost entirely for a given year in dire times, whereas they could not reduce committed costs. Discretionary fixed costs may be essential to the long-run achievement of the organization's goals, but managers can vary spending levels broadly in the short run.

Consider Marietta Corporation, which is experiencing financial difficulties. Sales for its major products are down, and Marietta's management is considering cutting back on costs temporarily. Marietta's management must determine which of the following fixed costs it can reduce or eliminate and how much money each would save:

Fixed Costs	Planned Amounts
Advertising and promotion	$ 50,000
Depreciation	400,000
Employee training	100,000
Management salaries	800,000
Mortgage payment	250,000
Property taxes	600,000
Research and development	1,500,000
Total	$3,700,000

Can Marietta reduce or eliminate any of these fixed costs? The answer depends on Marietta's long-run outlook. Marietta could reduce costs but also greatly reduce its ability to compete in the future if it cuts fixed costs carelessly. Suppose rearranging these costs by categories of committed and discretionary costs yields the following analysis:

Fixed Costs	Planned Amounts
Committed	
Depreciation	$ 400,000
Mortgage payment	250,000
Property taxes	600,000
Total committed	$1,250,000
Discretionary (potential savings)	
Advertising and promotion	$ 50,000
Employee training	100,000
Management salaries	800,000
Research and development	1,500,000
Total discretionary	$2,450,000
Total committed and discretionary	$3,700,000

Eliminating all discretionary fixed costs would save Marietta $2,450,000 per year. However, Marietta might be unwise to cut all discretionary costs completely. This could severely impair the company's long-run prospects and its future competitive position. Nevertheless, distinguishing committed and discretionary fixed costs would be the company's first step in identifying where costs could be reduced.

Technology Decisions

One of the most critical decisions that managers make is choosing the type of technology the organization will use to produce its products or deliver its services. Choice of technology (for example, labor-intensive versus robotic manufacturing, personal banking services versus automated tellers, or online versus in-store sales) positions the organization to meet its current goals and to respond to changes in the environment (for example, changes in customer needs or actions by competitors). The use of high-technology methods rather than labor usually means a much greater fixed-cost component and higher operating leverage, as discussed in Chapter 2. Higher operating leverage creates greater risks for companies with wide variations in demand.

Cost-Control Incentives

Finally, the incentives that management creates for employees can affect future costs. Managers use their knowledge of cost behavior to set cost expectations, and employees may receive compensation or other rewards that are tied to meeting these expectations. For example, the administrator of Parkview Medical Center could give the supervisor of the facilities maintenance department a favorable evaluation if the supervisor maintained quality of service and kept department costs below the expected amount for the actual level of patient-days. This feedback motivates the supervisor to watch department costs carefully and to find ways to reduce costs without reducing service quality.

Cost Functions

As a manager, you will use cost functions often as a planning and control tool. A few of the reasons why cost functions are important are listed here:

1. Planning and controlling the activities of an organization require useful and accurate estimates of future fixed and variable costs.
2. Understanding relationships between costs and their cost drivers allows managers in all types of organizations—profit seeking, nonprofit, and government—to make better operating, marketing, and production decisions; to plan and evaluate actions; and to determine appropriate costs for short-run and long-run decisions.

The first step in estimating or predicting costs is **cost measurement**—measuring cost behavior as a function of appropriate cost drivers. The second step is to use these cost measures to estimate future costs at expected levels of cost-driver activity. We begin by looking at the form of cost functions and the criteria for choosing the most appropriate cost drivers.

Form of Cost Functions

To describe the relationship between a cost and its cost driver(s), managers often use an algebraic equation called a **cost function**. When there is only one cost driver, the cost function is similar to the algebraic CVP relationships discussed in Chapter 2. Consider the mixed cost graphed in Exhibit 3-2 on page 88, the facilities maintenance department cost:

$$\begin{array}{l} \text{monthly facilities} \\ \text{maintenance} \\ \text{department costs} \end{array} = \begin{array}{l} \text{monthly fixed} \\ \text{maintenance cost} \end{array} + \begin{array}{l} \text{monthly variable} \\ \text{maintenance cost} \end{array}$$

$$= \begin{array}{l} \text{monthly fixed} \\ \text{maintenance cost} \end{array} + \left(\begin{array}{l} \text{variable cost per} \\ \text{patient-day} \end{array} \times \begin{array}{l} \text{number of patient-days} \\ \text{in the month} \end{array} \right)$$

Let

Y = monthly facilities maintenance department cost

F = monthly fixed maintenance cost

V = variable cost per patient-day

X = cost-driver activity in number of patient-days per month

We can rewrite the mixed-cost function as

$$Y = F + VX \tag{1}$$

or

$$Y = \$10{,}000 + \$5.00X$$

This mixed-cost function has the familiar form of a straight line—it is called a linear cost function. When we graph a cost function, F is the intercept—the point on the vertical axis where the cost function begins. In Exhibit 3-2, the intercept is the $10,000 fixed cost per month. V, the variable cost per unit of activity, is the slope of the cost function. In Exhibit 3-2, the cost function slopes upward at the rate of $5 for each additional patient-day.

In our example, we use patient-days as the relevant cost driver. How did we choose this cost driver? Why not use number of patients, or number of operations, or facility square footage? In general, how do we develop cost functions?

Developing Cost Functions

Managers should apply two criteria to obtain useful and accurate cost functions: plausibility and reliability.

1. The cost function must be plausible, that is, believable. Personal observation of costs and activities, when it is possible, provides the best evidence of a plausible relationship between a resource cost and its cost driver. Some cost relationships, by nature, are not directly observable, so the cost analyst must be confident that the proposed relationship is valid. Many costs may move together with a number of cost drivers, but no cause-and-effect relationships may exist. A cause-and-effect relationship (that is, the cost driver causes the organization to incur the resource cost) is desirable for cost functions to be useful and accurate. For example, consider three possible cost drivers for the total cost of a **US Airways** round-trip flight from Phoenix to San Diego: miles flown, number of passengers, and passenger-miles (number of passengers times miles flown). Which of these possible cost drivers makes most sense, if only one cost driver were used for total cost? The answer is passenger-miles—the cost driver used by almost all airlines because both distance AND number of passengers flown impact cost incurrence.

cost measurement

Estimating or predicting costs as a function of appropriate cost drivers.

cost function

An algebraic equation used by managers to describe the relationship between a cost and its cost driver(s).

2. In addition to being plausible, a cost function's estimates of costs at actual levels of activity must reliably conform to observed costs. We assess reliability in terms of "goodness of fit"—how well the cost function explains past cost behavior. If the fit is good and conditions do not change in the future, the cost function should be a reliable predictor of future costs.

Managers use these criteria together in choosing a cost function. Each is a check on the other. A manager needs to fully understand operations and the way accountants record costs to determine a plausible and reliable cost function that links cause and effect. For example, companies often perform maintenance when output is low because that is the best time to take machines out of service. Therefore, daily or weekly records of maintenance costs and outputs may show that higher maintenance costs occur when output is low. However, lower output does not cause increased maintenance costs, nor does increased output cause lower maintenance costs. A more plausible explanation is that over a longer period increased output causes higher maintenance costs. Understanding the nature of maintenance costs should lead managers to a plausible and reliable estimate of the long-run cost function.

Making Managerial Decisions

A cost function is a mathematical expression of how cost drivers affect a particular cost. However, an intuitive understanding of cost functions is just as important as being able to write the mathematical formula. Suppose you have been using a cost function to predict total order-processing activity costs. The cost function is total costs = $25,000 + $89 × (number of orders processed). This formula is based on data that are in the range of 0–700 orders processed. Now, you want to predict the total cost for 680 orders. You have a few fundamental questions to answer before you are comfortable using the cost function in this situation. What does it mean when a cost function is linear? Why do managers want to know whether a cost is linear? What is the importance of the relevant range?

Answer

A linear cost function means that there are two parts to the cost. One part is fixed—that is, it's independent of the cost driver. The other part varies in proportion to the cost driver—that is, if the cost driver increases by X%, this part of the cost also increases by X%. Knowing that a cost is linear allows a manager to separate the cost into fixed and variable components—a simplification that helps you understand how decisions will affect costs. Incidentally, the predicted total cost for 680 orders is $25,000 + ($89 × 680) = $85,520. As long as the operating conditions that existed when the data were collected have not changed significantly, then knowing that the number of orders processed is within the relevant range—0–700, in this case—gives you confidence in the predicted total cost.

Choice of Cost Drivers: Activity Analysis

Objective 3

Describe the importance of activity analysis for measuring cost functions.

activity analysis
The process of identifying appropriate cost drivers and their effects on the costs of making a product or providing a service.

How do managers construct plausible and reliable cost functions? Well, you cannot have a good cost function without knowing the right cost drivers, so constructing a cost function starts with choosing cost drivers—the X in equation (1) on page 91. Managers use **activity analysis** to identify appropriate cost drivers and their effects on the costs of making a product or providing a service. The final product or service may have several cost drivers because production may involve many separate activities. The greatest benefit of activity analysis is that it helps management accountants identify the appropriate cost drivers for each cost.

Consider Northwestern Computers, which makes two products for personal computers: a plug-in music board (Mozart-Plus) and a hard-disk drive (Powerdrive). These two products consist of material costs, labor costs, and support costs. In the past, most of the work on Northwestern's products was done by hand. In such a situation, labor costs were the primary driver of support costs. Support costs were twice as much as labor costs, on average.

Northwestern has just finished upgrading the production process. Now the company uses computer-controlled assembly equipment, which has increased the costs of support activities, such as engineering and maintenance, and has reduced labor cost. Its cost function has now changed; specifically, labor cost is now only 5% of the total costs at Northwestern. An activity analysis has shown that the number of components added to products (a measure of product complexity), not labor cost, is the primary cost driver for support costs. Northwestern estimated support costs to be $20 per component. Mozart-Plus has five component parts, and Powerdrive has nine.

Suppose Northwestern wants to predict how much support cost it will incur in producing one Mozart-Plus and how much for one Powerdrive. Using the old cost driver, labor cost, the prediction of support costs would be as follows:

	Mozart-Plus	Powerdrive
Prior labor cost per unit	$ 8.50	$130.00
Predicted support cost		
2 × direct labor cost	$17.00	$260.00

Using the more appropriate cost driver based on the new production process, the number of components added to products, the predicted support costs are as follows:

	Mozart-Plus	Powerdrive
Predicted support cost at $20 per component		
$20 × 5 components	$100.00	
$20 × 9 components		$180.00
Difference in predicted support cost between the old and new cost function	$ 83.00 higher	$ 80.00 lower

By using an appropriate cost driver, Northwestern can predict its support costs much more accurately. Managers will make better decisions with this more accurate information. For example, they can relate prices charged for products more closely to the costs of production. To see how an actual organization uses activity analysis, see the Business First box on page 94.

One major question remains in our discussion of the measurement of cost behavior: How are the estimates of fixed costs and variable cost per cost-driver unit determined? Equation (1) on page 91 denotes these amounts by F = monthly fixed maintenance cost and V = variable cost per patient-day. In practice, organizations use several methods of measuring cost functions and determining values for F and V. Let's look at each of these methods.

Methods of Measuring Cost Functions

After determining the most plausible drivers behind different costs, managers can choose from a broad selection of methods for approximating cost functions. These methods include (1) engineering analysis, (2) account analysis, (3) high-low analysis, (4) visual-fit analysis, and (5) least-squares regression analysis. These methods are not mutually exclusive; managers frequently use two or more together to confirm conclusions about cost behavior. The first two methods rely primarily on logical analysis of the cost environment, whereas the last three involve explicit analysis of prior cost data.

Engineering Analysis

The first method, **engineering analysis**, measures cost behavior according to what costs should be in an on-going process. It entails a systematic review of materials, supplies, labor, support services, and facilities needed for products and services. Analysts can even use engineering analysis successfully for new products and services, as long as the organization has had experience with similar costs. Why? Because they can base measures on information from personnel who are directly involved with the product or service. In addition to actual experience, analysts learn about new costs from experiments with prototypes, accounting and industrial engineering literature, the experience of competitors, and the advice of management consultants. From this information, cost analysts estimate what future costs should be. If the cost analysts are experienced and understand the activities of the organization, then their engineering cost predictions may be quite useful and reliable for decision making. The disadvantages of engineering cost analysis are that the efforts are costly and may not be timely.

Objective 4

Measure cost behavior using the engineering analysis, account analysis, high-low, visual-fit, and least-squares regression methods.

engineering analysis
The systematic review of materials, supplies, labor, support services, and facilities needed for products and services; measuring cost behavior according to what costs should be, not by what costs have been.

Business First

Activity Analysis in Health-Care Organizations

Manufacturing companies were the first organizations to use activity analysis. However, its use has spread to many service industries and nonprofit organizations. For example, Hosparus (formerly called the Alliance of Community Hospices and Palliative Care Services), a health-care organization formed by the merger of two hospices in Kentucky and one in Indiana, has used activity analysis to better understand its costs.

Hosparus is a Medicare/Medicaid-certified program providing medical care to the terminally ill. In addition to seeing to the medical needs of its patients, Hosparus has social workers, home health aides, volunteers, and chaplains. It also provides an 18-month bereavement program for families of patients.

Many of Hosparus's costs were related directly to patients, and understanding these costs posed no problems. However, support costs were large, and Hosparus had little information about what caused these costs.

The organization undertook an activity analysis to determine the appropriate cost drivers for support costs. This consisted of two basic tasks: (1) identify the activities being performed and (2) select a cost driver for each activity.

To identify the activities and the costs related to each activity, Hosparus formed a cross-functional team. The team identified 14 activities. The next step was to select a cost driver for each activity. Some of the activities and their related cost drivers were as follows:

Activity	Cost Driver
Referral	Number of referrals
Admission	Number of admissions
Bereavement	Number of deaths
Accounting/finance	Number of patient-days
Billing	Number of billings
Volunteer services	Number of volunteers

Using the cost information from the activity analysis, management was able to learn how much each different activity cost and could recognize that patients requiring use of expensive activities were more expensive to treat.

Another organization, a retirement and assisted-living community with 70 living units, took such an activity analysis one step further. Using an activity analysis similar to that of Hosparus, this organization took the resultant detailed cost information and conducted sensitivity analysis on profitability. Using optimization software called "Solver" from Microsoft Excel the organization was able to construct modified income statements that explicitly displayed how changes in its underlying cost activities would affect its profits. It was subsequently able to maximize its profits by optimizing the levels of these various activities, thus developing an organizational strategy that was best for its cost environment.

Sources: Adapted from Sidney J. Baxendale and Victoria Dornbusch, "Activity-Based Costing for a Hospice," *Strategic Finance*, March 2000, pp. 65–70; Sidney J. Baxendale, Mahesh Gupta, and P. S. Raju, "Profit Enhancement: Using an ABC Model," *Management Accounting Quarterly*, Winter 2005, pp. 11–21; and Hosparus's Web site (http://www.hosparus.org).

Nearly any organization can use this approach to measuring cost behavior. For example, Weyerhaeuser Company, producer of wood products, used engineering analysis to determine the cost functions for its 14 corporate service departments. These cost functions measure the cost of corporate services used by three main business groups. For example, Weyerhaeuser found that its accounts payable costs for each division are a function of three cost drivers: the number of hours spent on each division, number of documents, and number of invoices.

Now consider Parkview Medical Center, introduced earlier in the chapter. An assistant to the hospital administrator interviewed facilities maintenance personnel and observed their activities on several random days for a month. From these data, she confirmed that the most plausible cost driver for facilities maintenance cost is the number of patient-days. She also estimated from current department salaries and equipment charges that monthly fixed costs approximated $10,000 per month. Using interviews and observing supplies usage during the month, she estimated that variable costs are $5 per patient-day. She gave this information to the hospital administrator but cautioned that the cost measures may be incorrect for the following reasons:

1. The month observed may be abnormal.
2. The facilities maintenance personnel may have altered their normal work habits because the assistant was observing them.

3. The facilities maintenance personnel may not have told the complete truth about their activities because of their concerns about the use of the information they revealed.

However, if we assume the observed and estimated information is correct, we could predict facilities maintenance costs in any month by first forecasting that month's expected patient-days and then entering that figure into the following algebraic, mixed-cost function:

$$Y = \$10,000 \text{ per month} + (\$5 \times \text{patient-days})$$

For example, if the administrator expects 3,000 patient-days next month, the prediction of facilities maintenance costs would be as follows:

$$Y = \$10,000 + (\$5 \times 3,000 \text{ patient-days}) = \$25,000$$

Account Analysis

In contrast to engineering analysis, users of **account analysis** look to the accounting system for information about cost behavior. The simplest method of account analysis classifies each account as a variable or fixed cost with respect to a selected cost driver. The cost analyst then looks at each cost account balance and estimates either the variable cost per unit of cost-driver activity or the periodic fixed cost.

account analysis
Classifying each account as a variable cost or as a fixed cost with respect to a selected cost driver.

To illustrate this approach to account analysis, let's return to the facilities maintenance department at Parkview Medical Center and analyze costs for a recent month. The following table shows costs recorded in a month with 3,700 patient-days:

Monthly Cost	January Amount
Supervisor's salary and benefits	$ 3,800
Hourly workers' wages and benefits	14,674
Equipment depreciation and rentals	5,873
Equipment repairs	5,604
Cleaning supplies	7,472
Total facilities maintenance cost	$37,423

Recall that the most plausible and reliable driver for these costs is the number of patient-days serviced per month. Next, the analyst determines which costs may be fixed and which may be variable. Assume that the analyst has made the following judgments:

Monthly Cost	Amount	Fixed	Variable
Supervisor's salary and benefits	$ 3,800	$3,800	
Hourly workers' wages and benefits	14,674		$14,674
Equipment depreciation and rentals	5,873	5,873	
Equipment repairs	5,604		5,604
Cleaning supplies	7,472		7,472
Total facilities maintenance costs	$37,423	$9,673	$27,750

Measuring total facilities maintenance cost behavior, then, requires only simple arithmetic. First add up all the fixed costs to get the total fixed cost per month. Then divide the total variable costs by the units of cost-driver activity to get the variable cost per unit of cost driver.

$$\text{Fixed cost per month} = \$9,673$$

$$\text{Variable cost per patient-day} = \$27,750 \div 3,700 \text{ patient-days}$$

$$= \$7.50 \text{ per patient-day}$$

The algebraic, mixed-cost function, measured by account analysis, is

$$Y = \$9,673 \text{ per month} + (\$7.50 \times \text{patient-days})$$

Account analysis methods are less expensive to conduct than engineering analyses, but they require recording of relevant cost accounts and cost drivers. In addition, like engineering analysis, account analysis is subjective because the analysts decide whether each cost is variable or fixed based on their own judgment.

Summary Problem for Your Review

PROBLEM

The Dependable Insurance Company processes a variety of insurance claims for losses, accidents, thefts, and so on. Account analysis using one cost driver has estimated the variable cost of processing the claims for each automobile accident at 0.5% (.005) of the dollar value of all claims related to a particular accident. This estimate seemed reasonable because high-cost claims often involve more analysis before settlement. To control processing costs better, however, Dependable conducted an activity analysis of claims processing. The analysis suggested that there are three main cost drivers for the costs of processing claims for automobile accidents. The drivers and cost behavior are as follows:

0.2% of Dependable Insurance policyholders' property claims
+ 0.6% of other parties' property claims
+ 0.8% of total personal injury claims

Data from two recent automobile accident claims follow:

	Automobile Claim No. 607788	Automobile Claim No. 607991
Policyholder claim	$ 4,500	$23,600
Other party claim	0	3,400
Personal injury claim	12,400	0
Total claim amount	$16,900	$27,000

1. Estimate the cost of processing each claim using data from (a) the single-cost-driver analysis and (b) the three-cost-driver analysis.
2. How would you recommend that Dependable Insurance estimate the cost of processing claims?

SOLUTION

1. Costs are summarized in the table here.

	Automobile Claim No. 607788		Automobile Claim No. 607991	
	Claim Amount	Processing Cost	Claim Amount	Processing Cost
Using single-cost-driver analysis				
Total claim amount	$16,900		$27,000	
Estimated processing cost at 0.5%		$ 84.50		$135.00
Using three-cost-driver analysis				
Policyholder claim	$ 4,500		$23,600	
Estimated processing cost at 0.2%		$ 9.00		$ 47.20
Other party claim	0		3,400	
Estimated processing cost at 0.6%		0		20.40
Personal injury claim	12,400		0	
Estimated processing cost at 0.8%		99.20		0
Total estimated processing cost		$108.20		$ 67.60

2. The three-cost-driver analysis estimates of processing costs are considerably different from those using a single cost driver. If the activity analyses are reliable, then automobile claims that include personal injury losses are more costly to process than property damage claims. If these estimates are relatively inexpensive to keep current and to use, then it seems reasonable to adopt the three-cost-driver approach. Dependable will have more accurate cost estimates and will be better able to plan its claims processing activities. However, Dependable processes many different types of claims. Extending activity analysis to identify multiple cost drivers for all types of claims would result in a complicated system for predicting costs—much more complex (and costly) than simply using the total dollar value of claims. Whether to undertake an activity analysis for all types of policies depends on cost-benefit considerations. Managers can address such considerations by first adopting activity analysis for one type of claim and assessing the usefulness and cost of the more accurate information.

High-Low, Visual-Fit, and Least-Squares Methods

When enough relevant cost data are available, we can use historical data to estimate the cost function mathematically. Three popular methods are the high-low, visual-fit, and least-squares methods. All three methods are more objective than the engineering-analysis and account-analysis methods. Each is based on hard evidence and uses cost and activity information from multiple periods. In particular, least-squares regression is a powerful statistical tool that yields both accurate estimates of the cost function and precise measures of probable error inherent in the estimation.

While there are situations where one of the three data-based methods is the best way to develop estimates of the cost function, account analysis and engineering analysis will probably remain popular methods of estimating cost behavior because the three mathematical methods require relevant past cost data. Products, services, technologies, and organizations are changing rapidly in response to increased global competition and technological advances. In some cases, by the time enough historical data are collected to support these analyses, the data are obsolete—the organization has changed, the production process has changed, or the product has changed. These methods should only be used when the historical data are from a past environment that still closely resembles the future environment for which a manager wants to predict costs. Another concern is that historical data may hide past inefficiencies that the company could reduce if it could identify them. That being said, the three mathematical methods have their advantages when relevant data exist, in particular the least-squares analysis.

DATA FOR ILLUSTRATION In discussing the high-low, visual-fit, and least-squares regression methods, we will continue to use the Parkview Medical Center's facilities maintenance department costs. The following table shows monthly data collected on facilities maintenance department costs and on the number of patient-days serviced over the past year:

Facilities Maintenance Department Data

Month	Facilities Maintenance Department Cost (Y)	Number of Patient-Days (X)
January	$37,000	3,700
February	23,000	1,600
March	37,000	4,100
April	47,000	4,900
May	33,000	3,300
June	39,000	4,400
July	32,000	3,500
August	33,000	4,000
September	17,000	1,200
October	18,000	1,300
November	22,000	1,800
December	20,000	1,600

HIGH-LOW METHOD When sufficient cost data are available, the cost analyst may use historical data to measure the cost function mathematically. The simplest of the three methods to measure a linear-cost function from past cost data is the **high-low method** shown in Exhibit 3-3.

The first step in the high-low method is to plot the historical data points on a graph. This visual display helps the analyst see whether there are obvious errors in the data. Even though many points are plotted, the focus of the high-low method is normally on the highest and lowest activity points. However, if one of these points is an outlier that seems in error or non-representative of normal operations, we should use the next-highest or next-lowest activity point. For example, we should not use a point from a period with abnormally low activity caused by a labor strike or fire. Why? Because that point is not representative of a normal relationship between cost and cost driver.

After selecting the representative high and low points, we can draw a line between them, extending the line to the vertical (Y) axis of the graph. Note that this extension in Exhibit 3-3 is a dashed line, as a reminder that costs may not be linear outside the range of activity for which we have data (the relevant range). Also, managers usually are concerned with how costs behave within the relevant range, not with how they behave either at zero activity or at impossibly high activity levels. Cost measurements within the relevant range may not be reliable measures or predictors of costs outside the relevant range.

The point at which the line intersects the Y-axis is the intercept, F, or estimate of fixed cost. The slope of the line measures the variable cost, V, per patient-day. The clearest way to measure the intercept and slope with the high-low method is to use algebra:

Month	Facilities Maintenance Department Cost (Y)	Number of Patient-Days (X)
High: April	$47,000	4,900
Low: September	17,000	1,200
Difference	$30,000	3,700

Variable cost per patient-day,

$$V = \frac{\text{change in costs}}{\text{change in activity}} = \frac{\$47,000 - \$17,000}{4,900 - 1,200 \text{ patient-days}}$$

$$V = \frac{\$30,000}{3,700} = \$8.1081 \text{ per patient-day}$$

Exhibit 3-3
High-Low Method

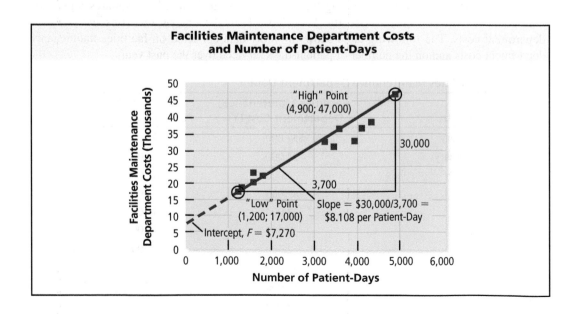

Facilities Maintenance Department Costs and Number of Patient-Days

Fixed cost per month, F = total mixed cost less total variable cost

$$\text{At X (high): } F = \$47,000 - (\$8.1081 \times 4,900 \text{ patient-days})$$
$$= \$47,000 - \$39,730$$
$$= \$7,270 \text{ per month}$$
$$\text{At X (low): } F = \$17,000 - (\$8.1081 \times 1,200 \text{ patient-days})$$
$$= \$17,000 - \$9,730$$
$$= \$7,270 \text{ per month}$$

Therefore, the facilities maintenance department cost function, measured by the high-low method, is

$$Y = \$7,270 \text{ per month} + (\$8.1081 \times \text{patient-days})$$

The high-low method is easy to apply and illustrates mathematically how a change in a cost driver can change total cost. The cost function that resulted in this case is plausible. Before the widespread availability of computers, managers often used the high-low method to measure a cost function quickly. Today, however, the high-low method is not used as often because it makes inefficient use of information, basing the cost function on only two periods' cost experience, regardless of how many relevant data points have been collected.

Summary Problem for Your Review

PROBLEM

The Reetz Company has its own photocopying department. Reetz's photocopying costs include costs of copy machines, operators, paper, toner, utilities, and so on. We have the following cost and activity data:

Month	Total Photocopying Cost	Number of Copies
1	$25,000	320,000
2	29,000	390,000
3	24,000	300,000
4	23,000	310,000
5	28,000	400,000

1. Use the high-low method to measure the cost behavior of the photocopy department in formula form.
2. What are the benefits and disadvantages of using the high-low method for measuring cost behavior?

SOLUTION

1. The lowest and highest activity levels are in months 3 (300,000 copies) and 5 (400,000 copies).

$$\text{Variable cost per copy} = \frac{\text{change in cost}}{\text{change in activity}} = \frac{\$28,000 - \$24,000}{400,000 - 300,000}$$

$$= \frac{\$4,000}{100,000} = \$0.04 \text{ per copy}$$

Fixed cost per month = total cost less variable cost

at 400,000 copies: $28,000 − ($0.04 × 400,000) = $12,000 per month

at 300,000 copies: $24,000 − ($0.04 × 300,000) = $12,000 per month

Therefore, the photocopy cost function is

Y(total cost) = $12,000 per month + ($0.04 × number of copies)

2. The benefits of using the high-low method are as follows:
- The method is easy to use.
- Not many data points are needed.

The disadvantages of using the high-low method are as follows:
- The choice of the high and low points is subjective.
- The method does not use all available data.
- The method may not be reliable.

visual-fit method

A method in which the cost analyst visually fits a straight line through a plot of all the available data.

VISUAL-FIT METHOD In the **visual-fit method**, we draw a straight line through a plot of all the available data, using judgment to fit the line as close as possible to all the plotted points. If the cost function for the data is linear, it is possible to draw a straight line through the scattered points that comes reasonably close to most of them and thus captures the general tendency of the data. We can extend that line back until it intersects the vertical axis of the graph.

Exhibit 3-4 shows this method applied to the facilities maintenance department cost data for the past 12 months. By measuring where the line intersects the cost axis, we can visually estimate the monthly fixed cost—in this case, about $10,000 per month. To find the variable cost per patient-day, select any activity level (for example 1,000 patient-days) and visually find the total cost at that activity level ($17,000). Then, divide the variable cost (which is total cost less fixed cost) by the units of activity.

Variable cost per patient-day = ($17,000 − $10,000) / 1,000 patient-days

= $7 per patient-day

The linear-cost function measured by the visual-fit method is

Y = $10,000 per month + ($7 × patient-days)

Although the visual-fit method uses all the data, the placement of the line and the measurement of the fixed and variable costs are subjective. This subjectivity is the main reason that many companies with sufficient data prefer to use least-squares regression analysis rather than the visual-fit method.

least-squares regression (regression analysis)

Measuring a cost function objectively by using statistics to fit a cost function to all the data.

LEAST-SQUARES REGRESSION METHOD Least-squares regression (or simply **regression analysis**) measures a cost function more objectively and explicitly than does the visual-fit method. Least-squares regression analysis uses statistics rather than human eyesight to fit a cost function to all the historical data. A simple regression uses one cost driver to measure a cost function, while a multiple regression uses two or more cost drivers. We will discuss only simple regression analysis in this chapter.

Exhibit 3-4
Visual-Fit Method

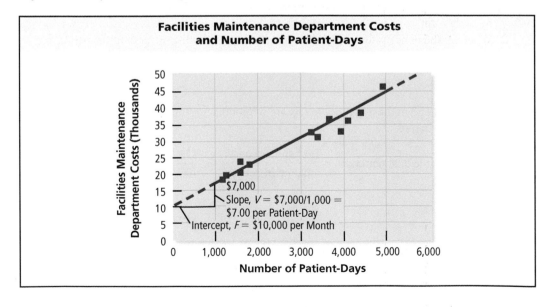

Facilities Maintenance Department Costs and Number of Patient-Days

Appendix 3 presents some statistical properties of regression and shows how to use spreadsheet software to conduct a regression analysis.

Regression analysis measures cost behavior more reliably than other data-based cost measurement methods. It also yields important statistical information about the reliability of its cost estimates. These statistics allow analysts to assess their confidence in the cost measures and thereby select the best cost driver. One such measure of reliability, or goodness of fit, is the **coefficient of determination, R^2** (or R-squared), which measures how much of the fluctuation of a cost is explained by changes in the cost driver. Appendix 3 explains R^2 and discusses how to use it to select the best cost driver.

Exhibit 3-5 shows the linear, mixed-cost function for facilities maintenance costs as measured mathematically by regression analysis. The fixed-cost measure is $9,329 per month. The variable-cost measure is $6.951 per patient-day. The linear-cost function is as follows:

Facilities maintenance department cost = $9,329 per month + ($6.951 × number of patient-days)

or

$$Y = \$9,329 + (\$6.951 \times \text{patient-days})$$

Compare the cost measures produced by each of the five approaches:

Method	Fixed Cost per Month	Variable Cost per Patient-Day
Engineering analysis	$10,000	$5.000
Account analysis	9,673	7.500
High-low	7,270	8.108
Visual-fit	10,000	7.000
Regression	9,329	6.951

Because the regression-cost measures are grounded in statistical theory, they are more reliable than those obtained from the other data-based methods. Thus, managers have more confidence in cost predictions from the regression-cost function.

coefficient of determination (R^2)

A measurement of how much of the fluctuation of a cost is explained by changes in the cost driver.

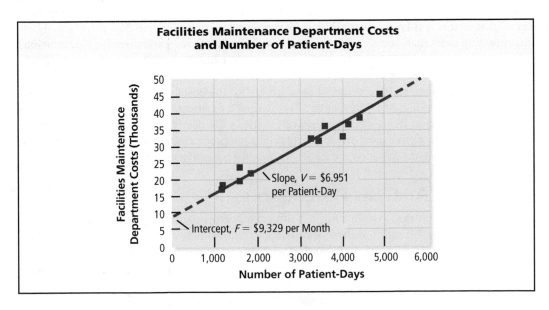

Facilities Maintenance Department Costs and Number of Patient-Days

Slope, V = $6.951 per Patient-Day

Intercept, F = $9,329 per Month

Number of Patient-Days

Exhibit 3-5
Least-Squares Regression Method

Highlights to Remember

1. **Explain management influences on cost behavior.**   Managers can affect the costs and cost behavior patterns of their companies through the decisions they make. Decisions on product and service features, capacity, technology, and cost-control incentives, for example, can all affect cost behavior.

2. **Measure and mathematically express cost functions and use them to predict costs.**   The first step in estimating or predicting costs is measuring cost behavior. This is done by finding a cost function. This is an algebraic equation that describes the relationship between a cost and its cost driver(s). To be useful for decision-making purposes, cost functions should be plausible and reliable.

3. **Describe the importance of activity analysis for measuring cost functions.**   Activity analysis is the process of identifying the best cost drivers to use for cost estimation and prediction and determining how they affect the costs of making a product or service. This is an essential step in understanding and predicting costs.

4. **Measure cost behavior using the engineering analysis, account analysis, high-low, visual-fit, and least-squares regression methods.**   Once analysts have identified cost drivers, they can use one of several methods to determine the cost function. Engineering analysis focuses on what costs should be by systematically reviewing the materials, supplies, labor, support services, and facilities needed for a given level of production. Account analysis involves examining all accounts in terms of an appropriate cost driver and classifying each account as either fixed or variable with respect to the driver. The cost function consists of the variable cost per cost-driver unit multiplied by the amount of the cost driver plus the total fixed cost. The high-low, visual-fit, and regression methods all use historical data to determine cost functions. Of these three methods, regression is the most reliable.

Appendix 3: Applying and Interpreting Least-Squares Regression

While we can perform regression analysis of historical cost data by hand, it would be unusual to find cost analysts doing so. Rather, spreadsheets or statistical analysis software are almost always used because they are faster, less prone to error, and produce explicit statistical analyses of the results. Therefore, we focus on interpreting regression results from a spreadsheet analysis.

This appendix is not a substitute for a good statistics class. More properly, think of it as a motivator for studying statistics so that you can better interpret regression cost estimates. Recall that in this text book we consider only simple regression (a single cost driver) analysis. Incorporating more than one cost driver into a cost function via regression (multiple regression) is beyond the scope of this text, and you should consult a statistics textbook to learn about this more advanced form of regression.

Assume that there are two potential cost drivers for the costs of the facilities maintenance department in Parkview Medical Center: (1) number of patient-days and (2) total value of hospital room charges. Regression analysis can assist in the determination of which activity is the better (more descriptive) cost driver in explaining and predicting costs. Exhibit 3-6 shows the past 12 months' cost and cost-driver data for the facilities maintenance department.

Regression Analysis Procedures

Most spreadsheet software available for PCs offers basic regression analysis in the data analysis or tools commands. We will use these spreadsheet commands to illustrate regression analysis because many readers will already be familiar with spreadsheet software.

Entering Data

First, create a spreadsheet with the historical cost data in rows and columns. Each row should be data from one period. Each column should be a cost category or a cost driver. For ease of analysis, all the potential cost drivers should be in adjacent columns. Each row and column should be complete (no missing data) and without errors.

Exhibit 3-6
Facilities Maintenance
Department Data

Month	Facilities Maintenance Cost (Y)	Number of Patient-Days (X_1)	Value of Room Charges (X_2)
January	$37,000	3,700	$2,183,000
February	23,000	1,600	2,735,000
March	37,000	4,100	2,966,000
April	47,000	4,900	2,846,000
May	33,000	3,300	2,967,000
June	39,000	4,400	2,980,000
July	32,000	3,500	3,023,000
August	33,000	4,000	2,352,000
September	17,000	1,200	1,825,000
October	18,000	1,300	1,515,000
November	22,000	1,800	1,547,000
December	20,000	1,600	2,117,000

Plotting Data

There are two main reasons why the first step in regression analysis should be to plot the cost against each of the potential cost drivers. First, plots may show obvious nonlinear trends in the data; if so, linear regression analysis may not be appropriate for the entire range of the data. Second, plots help identify outliers that should be excluded from the analysis—costs that are in error or are otherwise obviously inappropriate. For example, costs may have been abnormally high (or abnormally low) in one month because of an unusual event such as a strike or mechanical breakdown, in which case the abnormal cost for that month should not be used in estimating the normal cost relation.

Plotting with spreadsheets uses graph commands on the columns of cost and cost-driver data. These graph commands typically offer many optional graph types (such as bar charts and pie charts), but the most useful plot for regression analysis usually is called the XY graph. This graph is the type shown earlier in this chapter—the X-axis is the cost driver, and the Y-axis is the cost. The XY graph should be displayed without lines drawn between the data points (called data symbols)—an optional command. (Consult your spreadsheet manual for details because each spreadsheet program is different.)

Regression Output

The format of the regression output is different for each software package. However, every package will identify the cost to be explained ("dependent variable") and the cost driver ("independent variable") in the cost function.

Producing regression output with spreadsheets is simple: Just select the regression command, specify (or highlight) the X-dimension(s) (the cost driver[s]), and specify the Y-dimension or "series" (the cost). Next, specify where the output will be displayed on the spreadsheet, and select Ok. The following is a regression analysis of facilities maintenance department costs using one of the two possible cost drivers, number of patient-days, X_1.

Facilities Maintenance Department Cost Explained by Number of Patient-Days

Regression Output	
Constant	9,329
R^2	0.955
X coefficient(s)	6.951

Interpretation of Regression Output

The fixed-cost measure, labeled "constant" or "intercept" by most programs, is $9,329 per month. The variable cost measure, labeled "X coefficient" (or something similar in other spreadsheets), is $6.951 per patient-day. The linear cost function is

$$Y = \$9,329 \text{ per month} + (\$6.951 \times \text{patient-days})$$

As mentioned in the chapter, it is important to consider plausibility and reliability in evaluating a cost function and its estimates. Plausibility simply refers to whether the estimated cost function makes economic sense. We can assess this by examining the sign of the variable cost estimate. In the preceding cost function, this estimate is +$6.951. The positive sign in this cost function implies that as patient-days increase, facilities maintenance costs also increase (specifically, by $6.951 per patient-day). We assess the economic plausibility of this positive relationship by asking ourselves whether it makes economic sense that an increase in patient-days should increase facilities maintenance costs. Based on our economic intuition, a positive relationship appears to make sense (that is, we would expect that increasing patient-days would increase the cost of cleaning supplies and repair materials such that total facilities maintenance costs increase). While plausibility appears to be a simple and straightforward item to assess, it is the most important element to assess in a cost function. We would not want to use a cost function to estimate and predict costs if it did not exhibit plausibility (even if it displayed good reliability) because, without plausibility, we do not fundamentally understand the cost function, which makes cost estimation and prediction suspect.

Regarding reliability, the computer output usually gives a number of statistical measures that indicate how well each cost driver explains the cost and how reliable the cost predictions are likely to be when using the cost function. A full explanation of the output is beyond the scope of this text. However, one of the most important statistics, the coefficient of determination, or R^2, is an important measure of reliability—how well the cost function fits the actual cost data. In general, the better a cost driver is at explaining a cost, the closer the data points will lie to the line, and the higher will be the R^2, which varies between 0 and 1. An R^2 of 0 means that the cost driver does not explain variability in the cost data, whereas an R^2 of 1 means that the cost driver explains the variability perfectly. The R^2 of the relationship measured with number of patient-days as the cost driver is 0.955, which is quite high. This value indicates that the number of patient-days explains facilities maintenance department cost extremely well. In fact, the number of patient-days explains 95.5% of the past fluctuations in facilities maintenance department cost. Such a regression is highly reliable.

In contrast, performing a regression analysis on the relationship between facilities maintenance department cost and value of hospital room charges produces the following results:

Facilities Maintenance Department Cost Explained by Value of Hospital Room Charges

Regression Output	
Constant	$ 924
R^2	0.511
X coefficient(s)	0.012

While the positive sign of the variable cost estimate (+.012) appears to satisfy plausibility (that is, as hospital room charges increase we would expect facilities maintenance costs to also increase), the R^2 value, 0.511, indicates that the cost function using value of hospital room charges fits the facilities maintenance department cost worse than does the cost function using number of patient-days.

To use the information generated by regression analysis fully, an analyst must understand the meaning of the statistics and must be able to determine whether the statistical assumptions of regression are satisfied by the cost data. Indeed, one of the major reasons why cost analysts study statistics is to understand the assumptions of regression analysis better. With this understanding, analysts can provide their organizations with the best estimates of cost behavior.

Summary Problem for Your Review

PROBLEM

Comtell makes computer peripherals (disk drives, tape drives, and printers). Until recently, managers predicted production scheduling and control (PSC) costs to vary in proportion to labor costs according to the following cost function:

$$\text{PSC costs} = 200\% \text{ of labor cost}$$

or

$$Y = 2 \times \text{labor cost}$$

Because PSC costs have been growing at the same time that labor cost has been shrinking, Comtell is concerned that its cost estimates are neither plausible nor reliable. Comtell's controller has just completed regression analysis to determine the most appropriate drivers of PSC costs. She obtained two cost functions using different cost drivers:

$$Y = 2 \times \text{labor cost}$$
$$R^2 = 0.233$$

and

$$Y = \$10,000 \text{ per month} + (11 \times \text{number of components used})$$
$$R^2 = 0.782$$

1. How should the controller determine which cost function better predicts PSC costs?
2. During a subsequent month, Comtell's labor costs were $12,000, and it used 2,000 product components. Actual PSC costs were $31,460. Using each of the preceding cost functions, prepare reports that show predicted and actual PSC costs and the difference or variance between the two.
3. What is the meaning and importance of each cost variance?

SOLUTION

1. The controller should examine both the plausibility and the reliability of each cost function. Both costs seem plausible with positive signs on their respective variable cost estimates as we would expect. Regarding reliability, a statistical test of which function better explains past PSC costs compares the R^2 of each function. The second function, based on the number of components used, has a considerably higher R^2, so it better explains the past PSC costs. If the environment is essentially unchanged in the future, the second function probably will predict future PSC costs better than the first.

   A useful predictive test would be to compare the cost predictions of each cost function with actual costs for several months that were not used to measure the cost functions. The function that more closely predicted actual costs is probably the more reliable function.

2. Note that more actual cost data would be desirable for a better test, but the procedure would be the same. PSC cost predicted on a labor-cost basis follows:

Predicted Cost	Actual Cost	Variance
2 × $12,000 = $24,000	$31,460	$7,460 underestimate

   PSC cost predicted on a component basis follows:

Predicted Cost	Actual Cost	Variance
$10,000 + ($11 × 2,000) = $32,000	$31,460	$540 overestimate

3. The cost function that relies on labor cost underestimated PSC cost by $7,460. The cost function that uses the number of components closely predicted actual PSC costs (off by $540). Planning and control decisions would have been based on more accurate information using this prediction than using the labor-cost-based prediction. An issue is whether the benefits of collecting data on the number of components used exceeded the added cost of the data collection.

Accounting Vocabulary

account analysis, p. 95
activity analysis, p. 92
capacity costs, p. 88
coefficient of determination
  (R^2), p. 101
committed fixed costs, p. 89

cost function, p. 91
cost measurement, p. 91
discretionary fixed
  costs, p. 89
engineering analysis, p. 93
high-low method, p. 98

least-squares regression, p. 100
linear-cost behavior, p. 87
measurement of cost
  behavior, p. 86
visual-fit method, p. 100

MyAccountingLab # Fundamental Assignment Material

3-A1 Activity Analysis

Dogwood Signs makes customized wooden signs for businesses and residences. These signs are made of wood, which the owner glues and carves by hand or with power tools. After carving the signs, she paints them or applies a natural finish. She has a good sense of her labor and materials cost behavior, but she is concerned that she does not have good measures of other support costs. Currently, she predicts support costs to be 75% of the cost of materials. Close investigation of the business reveals that $70 times the number of power tool operations is a more plausible and reliable support cost relationship.

Consider estimated support costs of the following two signs that Dogwood Signs is making:

	Sign A	Sign B
Materials cost	$300	$800
Number of power tool operations	10	2
Support cost	?	?

1. Prepare a report showing the support costs of both signs using each cost driver and showing the differences between the two.
2. What advice would you give Dogwood Signs about predicting support costs?

3-A2 Division of Mixed Costs into Variable and Fixed Components

Molly Flutie, president of First Tool, Co., has asked for information about the cost behavior of manufacturing support costs. Specifically, she wants to know how much support cost is fixed and how much is variable. The following data are the only records available:

Month	Machine Hours	Support Costs
May	1,700	$ 22,000
June	1,600	21,000
July	1,500	19,500
August	1,400	18,500
September	1,300	18,000

1. Find monthly fixed support cost and the variable support cost per machine hour by the high-low method.
2. Explain how your analysis for requirement 1 would change if new October data were received and machine hours were 1,650 and support costs were $24,000.
3. A least-squares regression analysis gave the following output:

$$\text{Regression equation: } Y = \$4,050 + \$10.50X$$

What recommendations would you give the president based on these analyses?

3-B1 Activity Analysis

DeHart Technology, an Idaho manufacturer of printed circuit boards, has always estimated the support cost of its circuit boards with a 100% "markup" over its material costs. An activity analysis suggests that support costs are driven primarily by the number of manual operations performed on each board, estimated at $6 per manual operation. Compute the estimated support costs of the following two typical circuit boards using the traditional markup and the activity analysis results:

	Board Z15	Board Q52
Material cost	$46.00	$65.00
Manual operations	19	8

Why are the cost estimates different?

3-B2 Division of Mixed Costs into Variable and Fixed Components

The president and the controller of Toluca Transformer Company (Mexico) have agreed that refinement of the company's cost measurements will aid planning and control decisions. They have asked you to measure the function for mixed-cost behavior of repairs and maintenance from the following sparse data. Currency is the Mexican peso (P).

Monthly Activity in Machine Hours	Monthly Repair and Maintenance Cost
7,900	P202,000,000
11,900	P272,000,000

Additional Assignment Material

MyAccountingLab

QUESTIONS

3-1 What is a cost driver? Give three examples of costs and their possible cost drivers.

3-2 Explain linear-cost behavior.

3-3 "Step costs can be fixed or variable, depending on your perspective." Explain.

3-4 Explain how mixed costs are related to both fixed and variable costs.

3-5 How do management's product and service choices affect cost behavior?

3-6 Why are fixed costs also called capacity costs?

3-7 How do committed fixed costs differ from discretionary fixed costs?

3-8 Why are committed fixed costs the most difficult of the fixed costs to change?

3-9 What are the primary determinants of the level of committed costs? Discretionary costs?

3-10 "Planning is far more important than day-to-day control of discretionary costs." Do you agree? Explain.

3-11 How can a company's choice of technology affect its costs?

3-12 Explain the use of incentives to control cost.

3-13 Why is it important for managers and accountants to measure cost functions?

3-14 Explain plausibility and reliability of cost functions. Which is preferred? Explain.

3-15 What is activity analysis?

3-16 What is engineering analysis? Account analysis?

3-17 Describe the methods for measuring cost functions using past cost data.

3-18 How could account analysis be combined with engineering analysis?

3-19 Explain the strengths and weaknesses of the high-low and visual-fit methods.

3-20 In the high-low method, does the high and low refer to cost-driver levels or to total cost levels? Explain.

3-21 Why is regression analysis usually preferred to the high-low method?

3-22 "You never know how good your fixed- and variable-cost measures are if you use account analysis or if you visually fit a line on a data plot. That's why I like least-squares regression analysis." Explain.

3-23 (Study Appendix 3) Why should an analyst always plot cost data in addition to applying least-squares regression analysis?

3-24 (Study Appendix 3) What can we learn from R^2, the coefficient of determination?

3-25 At a conference, a consultant stated, "Before you can control, you must measure." An executive complained, "Why bother to measure when work rules and guaranteed employment provisions in labor contracts prevent discharging workers, using part-time employees, and using overtime?" Evaluate these comments.

CRITICAL THINKING EXERCISES

3-26 Committed and Discretionary Fixed Costs in Manufacturing

Among the fixed costs of Howarth Company are depreciation and research and development (R&D). Using these two costs as examples, explain the difference between committed and discretionary fixed costs.

3-27 Cost Functions and Decision Making

Why is it important that decision makers in a corporation know the cost function for producing the company's products?

3-28 Statistical Analysis and Cost Functions

What advantages does using regression analysis have over the visual-fit method for determining cost functions?

EXERCISES

3-29 Plotting Data

The following graph was constructed and data plotted to apply the visual-fit method. Then, the predicted total order-department costs for processing 90 orders was computed. Comment on the accuracy of the analysis. Do your own analysis and explain any differences. Assume the data in parentheses are accurate in thousands of dollars and number of orders.

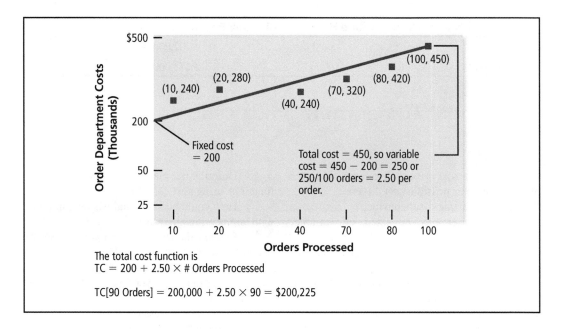

3-30 Cost Function for Travel Services

One Travel provides travel services on the Internet. 2011 was an important year for One Travel as it reported positive operating income after 3 years of operating losses. In the first quarter of 2010, One Travel reported an operating loss of $11 million on sales revenue of $74 million. In the first quarter of 2011, sales revenue had more than doubled to $154 million, and One Travel had operating income of $61 million. Assume that fixed costs were the same in 2011 as in 2010.

1. Compute the operating expenses for One Travel in the first quarter of 2010 and in the first quarter of 2011.
2. Determine the cost function for One Travel, that is, the total fixed cost and the variable cost as a percentage of sales revenue. Use the same form as equation (1) on page 91.
3. Explain how One Travel's operating income could increase by $72 million with an increase in sales of $80 million, while it had an operating loss of $11 million on its $74 million of sales in the first quarter of 2010.

3-31 Predicting Costs

Given the following four cost behaviors and expected levels of cost-driver activity, predict total costs:

1. Fuel costs of driving vehicles, $0.40 per mile, driven 16,000 miles per month
2. Equipment rental cost, $5,000 per piece of equipment per month for seven pieces for 3 months
3. Ambulance and EMT personnel cost for a soccer tournament, $1,200 for each 200 tournament participants; the tournament is expecting 2,400 participants
4. Purchasing department cost, $7,500 per month plus $5 per material order processed at 4,000 orders in one month

3-32 Identifying Discretionary and Committed Fixed Costs

Identify and compute total discretionary fixed costs and total committed fixed costs from the following list prepared by the accounting supervisor for Kasay Building Supply:

Advertising	$21,000
Depreciation	48,000
Health insurance for the company's employees	24,000
Management salaries	87,500
Payment on long-term debt	48,500
Property tax	30,000
Grounds maintenance	7,000
Office remodeling	24,000
Research and development	45,500

3-33 Cost Effects of Technology

American Sports, an outdoor sports retailer, is planning to add a Web site for online sales. The estimated costs of two alternative approaches are as follows:

	Alternative 1	Alternative 2
Annual fixed cost	$155,000	$315,000
Variable cost per order	$ 9	$ 7
Expected number of orders	45,000	45,000

At the expected level of orders, which online approach has the lower cost? What is the indifference level of orders, or the "break-even" level of orders? What is the meaning of this level of orders?

3-34 Mixed Cost, Choosing Cost Drivers, and High-Low and Visual-Fit Methods

Cedar Rapids Implements Company produces farm implements. Cedar Rapids is in the process of measuring its manufacturing costs and is particularly interested in the costs of the manufacturing maintenance activity, since maintenance is a significant mixed cost. Activity analysis indicates that maintenance activity consists primarily of maintenance labor setting up machines using certain supplies. A setup consists of preparing the necessary machines for a particular production run of a product. During setup, machines must still be running, which consumes energy. Thus, the costs associated with maintenance include labor, supplies, and energy. Unfortunately, Cedar Rapids' cost accounting system does not trace these costs to maintenance activity separately. Cedar Rapids employs two full-time maintenance mechanics to perform maintenance. The annual salary of a maintenance mechanic is $42,000 and is considered a fixed cost. Two plausible cost drivers have been suggested: "units produced" and "number of setups."

Data had been collected for the past 12 months and a plot was made for the cost driver—units of production. The maintenance cost figures collected include estimates for labor, supplies, and energy. Cory Fielder, controller at Cedar Rapids, noted that some types of activities are performed each time a batch of goods is processed rather than each time a unit is produced. Based on this concept, he has gathered data on the number of setups performed over the past 12 months. The plots of monthly maintenance costs versus the two potential cost drivers follow:

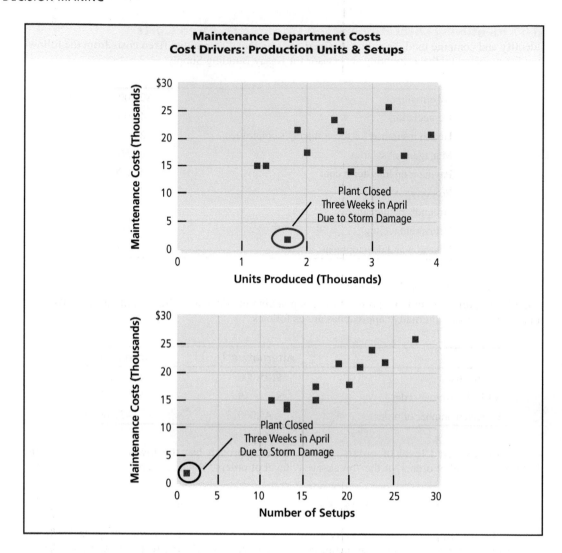

1. Find monthly fixed maintenance cost and the variable maintenance cost per driver unit using the visual-fit method based on each potential cost driver. Explain how you treated the April data.
2. Find monthly fixed maintenance cost and the variable maintenance cost per driver unit using the high-low method based on each potential cost driver.
3. Which cost driver best meets the criteria for choosing cost functions? Explain.

3-35 Account Analysis

Heavenly Computers is a company started by two engineering students to assemble and market personal computers to faculty and students. The company operates out of the garage of one of the students' homes. From the following costs of a recent month, compute the total cost function and total cost for the month:

Telephone	$ 60, fixed
Utilities	250, fixed: 30% attributable to the garage, 70% to the house
Advertising	85, fixed
Insurance	110, fixed
Materials	5,500, variable, for five computers
Labor	2,150: $1,400 fixed plus $750 for hourly help for assembling five computers

3-36 Linear Cost Functions

Let Y = total costs, X_1 = production volume, and X_2 = number of setups. Which of the following are linear cost functions? Which are mixed cost functions?

a. $Y = \$8X_1$

b. $Y = \$1,500$

c. $Y = \$8,500 + \$1.50X_1$

d. $Y = \$3,000 + \$6X_1 + \$30X_2$

e. $Y = \$9,000 + \$3(X_1 \times X_2)$

f. $Y = \$5,000 + \$4.00X_1$

3-37 High-Low Method

North Manchester Foundry produced 55,000 tons of steel in March at a cost of £1,150,000. In April, the foundry produced 35,000 tons at a cost of £950,000. Using only these two data points, determine the cost function for North Manchester.

3-38 Economic Plausibility of Regression Analysis Results

The head of the warehousing division of Lachton, Co., was concerned about some cost behavior information given to him by the new assistant controller, who was hired because of his recent training in cost analysis. His first assignment was to apply regression analysis to various costs in the department. One of the results was presented as follows:

A regression on monthly data was run to explain building maintenance cost as a function of direct labor hours as the cost driver. The results are

$$Y = \$7,810 - \$.47X$$

I suggest that we use the building as intensively as possible to keep the maintenance costs down.

The department head was puzzled. How could increased use cause decreased maintenance cost? Explain this counterintuitive result to the department head. What step(s) did the assistant controller probably omit in applying and interpreting the regression analysis?

PROBLEMS

3-39 Controlling Risk, Capacity Decisions, Technology Decisions

Consider the following hypothetical situation in the computer industry. HP had been outsourcing production to Acer and using overtime for as much as 20% of production—HP's plants and assembly lines were running at 100% of capacity and demand was sufficient for an additional 20%. HP had considered increasing its capacity by building new, highly automated assembly lines and plants. However, the investment in high technology and capacity expansion was rejected.

Assume that all material and labor costs are variable with respect to the level of production and that all other costs are fixed. Consider one of HP's plants that makes the Pavillion model. The increase in annual fixed costs to convert the plant to use fully automated assembly lines is $20 million. The resulting labor costs would be significantly reduced and there would be no need for overtime or outsourced production. The annual costs, in millions of dollars, of the build option and the existing costs that include outsourcing and overtime are given in the following tables:

	Build Option		
Percent of current capacity	60	100	120
Material costs	$18	$30	$36
Labor costs	6	10	12
Other costs	40	40	40
Total costs	$64	$80	$88

	HP's Existing Costs Using Outsourcing/Overtime		
Percent of current capacity	60	100	120
Material costs	$18	$30	$ 36
Labor costs	18	30	44
Other costs	20	20	20
Total costs	$56	$80	$100

1. Prepare a line graph showing total costs for the two options: (a) build new assembly lines, and (b) continue to use overtime and outsource production of Pavillions. Give an explanation of the cost behavior of the two options.
2. Which option enables HP's management to control risk better? Explain. Assess the cost-benefit trade-offs associated with each option.
3. A solid understanding of cost behavior is an important prerequisite to effective managerial control of costs. Suppose you are an executive at HP. Currently the production (and sales) level is approaching the 100% level of capacity, and the economy is expected to remain strong for at least 1 year. While sales and profits are good now, you are aware of the variability inherent in the computer business. Would you recommend committing HP to building automated assembly lines in order to service potential near-term increases in demand? Or would you recommend against building, looking to the possible future downturn in business? Discuss your reasoning.

3-40 Step Costs

Algona Beach Jail requires a staff of at least 1 guard for every 4 prisoners. The jail will hold 48 prisoners. Algona Beach attracts numerous tourists and transients in the spring and summer. However, the town is rather sedate in the fall and winter. The jail's fall–winter population is generally between 12 and 16 prisoners. The numbers in the spring and summer can fluctuate from 12 to 48, depending on the weather, among other factors (including phases of the moon, according to some longtime residents).

Algona Beach has four permanent guards, hired on a year-round basis at an annual salary of $36,000 each. When additional guards are needed, they are hired on a weekly basis at a rate of $600 per week. (For simplicity, assume that each month has exactly 4 weeks.)

1. Prepare a graph with the weekly planned cost of jail guards on the vertical axis and the number of prisoners on the horizontal axis.
2. What would be the budgeted amount for jail guards for the month of January? Would this be a fixed or a variable cost?
3. Suppose the jail population of each of the 4 weeks in July was 25, 38, 26, and 43, respectively. The actual amount paid for jail guards in July was $19,800. Prepare a report comparing the actual amount paid for jail guards with the amount that would be expected with efficient scheduling and hiring.
4. Suppose Algona Beach treated jail-guard salaries for nonpermanent guards as a variable expense of $150 per week per prisoner. This variable cost was applied to the number of prisoners in excess of 16. Therefore, the weekly cost function was as follows:

$$\text{Weekly jail-guard cost} = \$3{,}000 + \$150 \times (\text{total prisoners} - 16)$$

Explain how this cost function was determined.
5. Prepare a report similar to that in requirement 3 except that the cost function in requirement 4 should be used to calculate the expected amount of jail-guard salaries. Which report, this one or the one in requirement 3, is more accurate? Is accuracy the only concern?

3-41 Government Service Cost Analysis

Auditors for the Internal Revenue Service (IRS) scrutinize income tax returns after they have been prescreened with the help of computer tests for normal ranges of deductions claimed by taxpayers. The IRS uses an expected cost of $5 per tax return, based on measurement studies that allow 15 minutes per return. Each agent has a workweek of 5 days of 8 hours per day. Eighteen auditors are employed at a salary of $790 each per week.

The audit supervisor has the following data regarding performance for the most recent 4-week period, when 8,300 returns were processed:

Actual Cost of Auditors	Expected Cost for Processing Returns	Difference or Variance
$56,880	?	?

1. Compute the expected cost and the variance.
2. The supervisor believes that audit work should be conducted more productively and that superfluous personnel should be transferred to field audits. If the foregoing data are representative, how many auditors should be transferred?
3. List some possible reasons for the variance.
4. Describe some alternative cost drivers for processing income tax returns.

3-42 Cost Analysis at US Airways

US Airways is one of the nation's leading commercial air carriers, with hubs in Phoenix and Las Vegas. The following are some of the costs incurred by US Airways. For each cost, select an appropriate cost driver and indicate whether the cost is likely to be fixed, variable, or mixed in relation to your cost driver.

    a. Airplane fuel
    b. Flight attendants' salaries
    c. Baggage handlers' salaries
    d. In-flight meals
    e. Pilots' salaries
    f. Airplane depreciation
    g. Advertising

3-43 Separation of Mixed Costs into Variable and Fixed Components

A staff meeting has been called at SportsLab, a drug-testing facility retained by several professional and college sports leagues and associations. The chief of testing, Dr. Hyde, has demanded an across-the-board increase in prices for a particular test because of the increased testing and precision that are now required.

    The administrator of the laboratory has asked you to measure the mixed-cost behavior of this particular testing department and to prepare a short report she can present to Dr. Hyde. Consider the following limited data:

	Average Test Procedures per Month	Average Monthly Cost of Test Procedures
Monthly averages, 20X7	400	$ 60,000
Monthly averages, 20X8	500	80,000
Monthly averages, 20X9	600	140,000

3-44 School Cost Behavior

Oceanview School, a private high school, is preparing a planned income statement for the coming academic year ending August 31, 2013. Tuition revenues for the past two years ending August 31 were as follows: 2012, $840,000; and 2011, $880,000. Total expenses for 2012 were $830,000 and in 2011 were $844,000. No tuition rate changes occurred in 2011 or 2012, nor are any expected to occur in 2013. Tuition revenue is expected to be $830,000 for 2013. What net income should be planned for 2013, assuming that the implied cost behavior remains unchanged?

3-45 Activity Analysis

Washta Software develops and markets computer software for the agriculture industry. Because support costs are a large portion of the cost of software development, the director of cost operations of Washta, Vera Soren, is especially concerned with understanding the effects of support cost behavior. Soren has completed a preliminary activity analysis of one of Washta's primary software products: FertiMix (software to manage fertilizer mixing). This product is a software template that is customized for specific customers, who are charged for the basic product plus customizing costs. The activity analysis is based on the number of customized lines of FertiMix code. Currently, support cost estimates are based on a fixed rate of 65% of the basic cost. Data are shown for two recent customers:

	Customer	
	Mystical Plants	Todal Blooms
Basic cost of FertiMix	$8,000	$8,000
Lines of customized code	520	160
Estimated cost per line of customized code	$ 20	$ 20

  1. Compute the support cost of customizing FertiMix for each customer using each cost-estimating approach.
  2. If the activity analysis is reliable, what are the pros and cons of adopting it for all Washta's software products?

3-46 High-Low, Regression Analysis

On November 15, 2009, Sandra Cook, a newly hired cost analyst at Peterson Company, was asked to predict overhead costs for the company's operations in 2010, when 530 units are expected to be produced. She collected the following quarterly data:

Quarter	Production in Units	Overhead Costs
1/06	73	$ 715
2/06	76	709
3/06	68	640
4/06	133	1,124
1/07	122	995
2/07	125	1,105
3/07	122	1,113
4/07	130	1,036
1/08	121	982
2/08	126	1,060
3/08	112	990
4/08	81	951
1/09	81	829
2/09	119	1,044
3/09	87	985

1. Using the high-low method to estimate costs, prepare a prediction of overhead costs for 2010.
2. Sandy ran a regression analysis using the data she collected. The result was

$$Y = \$347 + \$5.76X$$

Using this cost function, predict overhead costs for 2010.
3. Which prediction do you prefer? Why?

3-47 Interpretation of Regression Analysis

Study Appendix 3. The tent division of New York Outdoor Equipment Company has had difficulty controlling its use of supplies. The company has traditionally regarded supplies as a purely variable cost. Nearly every time production was above average, however, the division spent less than predicted for supplies; when production was below average, the division spent more than predicted. This pattern suggested to Winnie Tsang, the new controller, that part of the supplies cost was probably not related to production volume, or was fixed.

She decided to use regression analysis to explore this issue. After consulting with production personnel, she considered two cost drivers for supplies cost: (1) number of tents produced, and (2) square feet of material used. She obtained the following results based on monthly data.

	Cost Driver	
	Number of Tents	Square Feet of Material Used
Constant	2,500	2,000
Variable coefficient	0.071	0.073
R^2	0.803	0.485

1. Which is the preferred cost function? Explain.
2. What percentage of the fluctuation of supplies cost depends on square feet of materials? Do fluctuations in supplies cost depend on anything other than square feet of materials? What proportion of the fluctuations is not explained by square feet of materials?

3-48 Regression Analysis

Study Appendix 3. Mr. Liao, CEO of a manufacturer of fine china and stoneware, is troubled by fluctuations in productivity and wants to compute how manufacturing support costs are related to the various sizes of batches of output. The following data show the results of a random sample of 10 batches of one pattern of stoneware:

Sample	Batch Size, X	Support Costs, Y
1	15	$180
2	12	140
3	20	230
4	17	190
5	12	160
6	25	300
7	22	270
8	9	110
9	18	240
10	30	320

1. Plot support costs, Y, versus batch size, X.
2. Using regression analysis, measure the cost function of support costs and batch size.
3. Predict the support costs for a batch size of 25.
4. Using the high-low method, repeat requirements 2 and 3. Should the manager use the high-low or regression method? Explain.

3-49 Choice of Cost Driver

Study Appendix 3. Richard Ellis, the director of cost operations of American Micro Devices, wishes to develop an accurate cost function to explain and predict support costs in the company's printed circuit board assembly operation. Mr. Ellis is concerned that the cost function that he currently uses—based on direct labor costs—is not accurate enough for proper planning and control of support costs. Mr. Ellis directed one of his financial analysts to obtain a random sample of 25 weeks of support costs and three possible cost drivers in the circuit-board assembly department: direct labor hours, number of boards assembled, and average cycle time of boards assembled. (Average cycle time is the average time between start and certified completion—after quality testing—of boards assembled during a week.) Much of the effort in this assembly operation is devoted to testing for quality and reworking defective boards, all of which increase the average cycle time in any period. Therefore, Mr. Ellis believes that average cycle time will be the best support-cost driver. Mr. Ellis wants his analyst to use regression analysis to demonstrate which cost driver best explains support costs.

Week	Circuit Board Assembly Support Costs, Y	Direct Labor Hours, X_1	Number of Boards Completed, X_2	Average Cycle Time (Hours), X_3
1	$66,402	7,619	2,983	186.44
2	56,943	7,678	2,830	139.14
3	60,337	7,816	2,413	151.13
4	50,096	7,659	2,221	138.30
5	64,241	7,646	2,701	158.63
6	60,846	7,765	2,656	148.71
7	43,119	7,685	2,495	105.85
8	63,412	7,962	2,128	174.02
9	59,283	7,793	2,127	155.30
10	60,070	7,732	2,127	162.20
11	53,345	7,771	2,338	142.97
12	65,027	7,842	2,685	176.08
13	58,220	7,940	2,602	150.19
14	65,406	7,750	2,029	194.06
15	35,268	7,954	2,136	100.51
16	46,394	7,768	2,046	137.47
17	71,877	7,764	2,786	197.44
18	61,903	7,635	2,822	164.69
19	50,009	7,849	2,178	141.95
20	49,327	7,869	2,244	123.37
21	44,703	7,576	2,195	128.25
22	45,582	7,557	2,370	106.16
23	43,818	7,569	2,016	131.41
24	62,122	7,672	2,515	154.88
25	52,403	7,653	2,942	140.07

1. Plot support costs, Y, versus each of the possible cost drivers, X_1, X_2, and X_3.
2. Use regression analysis to measure cost functions using each of the cost drivers.
3. According to the criteria of plausibility and reliability, which is the best cost driver for support costs in the circuit board assembly department?
4. Interpret the economic meaning of the best cost function.

3-50 Use of Cost Functions for Pricing

Study Appendix 3. Read the previous problem. If you worked that problem, use your measured cost functions. If you did not work the previous problem, assume the following measured cost functions:

$$Y = \$9,000/\text{week} + (\$6 \times \text{direct labor hours}); R^2 = .10$$

$$Y = \$20,000/\text{week} + (\$14 \times \text{number of boards completed}); R^2 = .40$$

$$Y = \$5,000/\text{week} + (\$350 \times \text{average cycle time}); R^2 = .80$$

1. Which of the support cost functions would you expect to be the most reliable for explaining and predicting support costs? Why?
2. Assume that American Micro Devices prices its products by adding a percentage markup to its product costs. Product costs include assembly labor, components, and support costs. Using each of the cost functions, compute the circuit board portion of the support cost of an order that used the following resources:

    a. Effectively used the capacity of the assembly department for 3 weeks
    b. Assembly labor hours: 20,000
    c. Number of boards: 6,000
    d. Average cycle time: 180 hours

3. Which cost driver would you recommend that American Micro Devices use? Why?
4. Assume that the market for this product is extremely cost competitive. What do you think of American Micro Devices' pricing method?

3-51 Review of Chapters 2 and 3

Curtis Institute of Music (CIM) provides instrumental music education to children of all ages. Payment for services comes from two sources: (1) a contract with Imagine That School to provide private music lessons for up to 140 band students a year (where a year is 9 months of education) for a fixed fee of $150,000, and (2) payment from individuals at a rate of $120 per month for 9 months of education each year. In the 2012–2013 school year, CIM made a profit of $1,000 on revenues of $270,000:

Revenues:		
Imagine That School contract	$150,000	
Private students	120,000	
Total revenues		$270,000
Expenses:		
Administrative staff	$ 64,000	
Teaching staff	100,000	
Facilities	51,000	
Supplies	54,000	
Total expenses		269,000
Profit		$ 1,000

CIM conducted an activity analysis and found that teaching staff wages and supplies costs are variable with respect to student-months. (A student-month is one student educated for 1 month.) Administrative staff and facilities costs are fixed within the range of 1,800–2,300 student-months. At volumes between 2,300 and 2,800 student-months, an additional facilities charge of $2,800 would be incurred. During the last year, a total of 2,200 student-months of education were provided, 1,000 of which were for private students and 1,200 of which were offered under the contract with Imagine That School.

1. Compute the following using cost information from year 2012–2013 operations:
   Fixed cost per year
   Variable cost per student-month

2. Suppose that in 2013–2014 Imagine That School decreased its use of CIM to 90 students (that is, 810 student-months). The fixed contract price of $150,000 was still paid. If everything else stayed as it was in 2012–2013, what profit or loss would be made in 2013–2014?
3. Suppose that at the beginning of 2013–2014 Imagine That School decided not to renew its contract with CIM, and the management of CIM decided to try to maintain business as usual with only private students. How many students (each signing up for 9 months) would CIM require to continue to make a profit of $1,000 per year?

CASES

3-52 Government Health Cost Behavior
Dr. Stephanie White, the chief administrator of Uptown Clinic, a community mental health agency, is concerned about the dilemma of coping with reduced budgets in the next year and into the foreseeable future, despite increasing demand for services. In order to plan for reduced budgets, she first must identify where costs can be cut or reduced and still keep the agency functioning. The following are some data about fixed costs from the past year:

Program Area	Costs
Administrative salaries	
Administrator	$60,000
Assistant	35,000
Two secretaries	42,000
Supplies	35,000
Advertising and promotion	9,000
Professional meetings, dues, and literature	14,000
Purchased services	
Accounting and billing	15,000
Custodial and maintenance	13,000
Security	12,000
Consulting	10,000
Community mental health services	
Salaries (two social workers)	46,000
Transportation	10,000
Outpatient mental health treatment	
Salaries	
Psychiatrist	86,000
Two social workers	70,000

1. Identify which costs you think are likely to be discretionary costs and which are committed costs.
2. One possibility is to eliminate all discretionary costs. How much would be saved? What do you think of this recommendation?
3. How would you advise Dr. White to prepare for reduced budgets?

3-53 Activity Analysis
The costs of the systems support (SS) department (and other service departments) of Southeast Pulp and Paper have always been charged to the three business divisions (forest management, lumber products, and paper products) based on the number of employees in each division. This measure is easy to obtain and update, and until recently none of the divisions had complained about the charges. The paper products division has recently automated many of its operations and has reduced the number of its employees. At the same time, however, to monitor its new process, paper products has increased its requests for various reports provided by the SS department. The other divisions have begun to complain that they are being charged more than their fair share of SS department costs. Based on activity analysis of possible cost drivers, cost analysts have suggested using the number of reports prepared as a means of charging for SS costs and have gathered the following information:

	Forest Management	Lumber Products	Paper Products
2011 number of employees	762	457	502
2011 number of reports	410	445	377
2011 SS costs: $300,000			
2012 number of employees	751	413	131
2012 number of reports	412	432	712
2012 SS costs: $385,000			

1. Discuss the plausibility and probable reliability of each of the cost drivers—number of employees or number of reports.
2. What are the 2011 and 2012 SS costs per unit of cost driver for each division using each cost driver? Do the forest management and lumber products divisions have legitimate complaints? Explain.
3. What are the incentives that are implied by each cost driver?
4. Which cost driver should Southeast Pulp and Paper use to charge its divisions for SS services? For other services? Why?

3-54 Identifying Relevant Data

eComp.com manufactures personal digital assistants (PDAs). Because these very small computers compete with laptops that have more functions and flexibility, understanding and using cost behavior is very critical to eComp.com's profitability. eComp.com's controller, Kelly Hudson, has kept meticulous files on various cost categories and possible cost drivers for most of the important functions and activities of eComp.com. Because most of the manufacturing at eComp.com is automated, labor cost is relatively fixed. Other support costs comprise most of eComp.com's costs. Partial data that Hudson has collected over the past 25 weeks on one of these support costs, logistics operations (materials purchasing, receiving, warehousing, and shipping), follow:

Week	Logistics Costs, Y	Number of Orders, X
1	$23,907	1,357
2	18,265	1,077
3	24,208	1,383
4	23,578	1,486
5	22,211	1,292
6	22,862	1,425
7	23,303	1,306
8	24,507	1,373
9	17,878	1,031
10	18,306	1,020
11	20,807	1,097
12	19,707	1,069
13	23,020	1,444
14	20,407	733
15	20,370	413
16	20,678	633
17	21,145	711
18	20,775	228
19	20,532	488
20	20,659	655
21	20,430	722
22	20,713	373
23	20,256	391
24	21,196	734
25	20,406	256

1. Plot logistics costs, Y, versus number of orders, X. What cost behavior is evident? What do you think happened in week 14?

2. What is your recommendation to Kelly Hudson regarding the relevance of the past 25 weeks of logistics costs and number of orders for measuring logistics cost behavior?

3. Hudson remarks that one of the improvements that eComp.com has made in the past several months was to negotiate JIT deliveries from its suppliers. This was made possible by substituting an automated ordering system for the previous manual (labor-intensive) system. Although fixed costs increased, the variable cost of placing an order was expected to drop greatly. Do the data support this expectation? Do you believe that the change to the automated ordering system was justified? Why or why not?

NIKE 10-K PROBLEM

3-55 Step and Mixed Costs and Cost Drivers

Refer to Nike's 10-K report in Appendix C and "Item 1. Business." Nike's contract manufacturers make the vast majority of Nike's footwear. Assume these costs are variable to Nike. Nike's largest fixed costs are associated with its distribution system. Consider one of Nike's three distribution and customer service facilities in the United States. List several examples of step-fixed costs and mixed costs at these centers. For each of the following activities at a distribution center, list one plausible cost driver:

1. Receiving activity
2. Unpacking incoming cases of footwear
3. Picking and packing cases of footwear for shipment to retail accounts
4. Processing orders from retail accounts
5. Providing customer service to retail accounts
6. Processing order changes from retail accounts

EXCEL APPLICATION EXERCISE

3-56 Fixed and Variable Cost Data

Goal: Create an Excel spreadsheet to calculate fixed and variable cost data for evaluating alternative approaches. Use the results to answer questions about your findings.

Scenario: American Sports has asked you to evaluate two alternative cost approaches for its new Web site. It would like you to calculate fixed and variable costs at different numbers of orders. The background data for your analysis appear in Exercise 3-33, on page 109.

When you have completed your spreadsheet, answer the following questions:

1. At what number of orders are the total costs for the two approaches the same? What does this mean?

2. Which alternative should be selected if the expected number of orders is less than the break-even level of orders? If the expected number of orders is greater than the break-even level of orders?

3. What conclusion regarding cost predictions can be drawn from your analysis?

Step-by-Step:

1. Open a new Excel spreadsheet.
2. In column A, create a bold-faced heading that contains the following:
   Row 1: Chapter 3 Decision Guideline
   Row 2: American Sports
   Row 3: Analysis of Alternative Cost Approaches
   Row 4: Today's Date
3. Merge and center the four heading rows across columns A–K.
4. In row 7, create the following bold-faced, right-justified column headings:
   Column A: Number of Orders
   Column B: Alternative 1
   Column C: Alternative 2

   Note: Adjust column widths as necessary.

5. In column A, rows 8–12, enter order levels from 40,000 to 80,000 in 10,000-unit increments.

6. Use the scenario data to create formulas in columns B and C for calculating the total costs (fixed plus variable costs) for each alternative at the order level in column A.

7. Format all amounts as follows:

Number tab:	Category:	Number
	Decimal places:	0
	Use 1000 Separator (,):	Checked

8. Modify the Page Setup by selecting File, Page Setup.

Page tab:	Orientation:	Landscape
Margins tab:	Top:	.5
	Bottom:	.5

9. Select the data in columns A–C, rows 7–12, and start the Chart Wizard either by inserting a chart (Insert, Chart) or by clicking the Chart Wizard icon on the toolbar.

Step 1 of 4—Chart Type

a. **Custom Types tab:**
b. Chart Type: Smooth Lines
c. Click "Next >" button

Note: List is alphabetical.

Step 2 of 4—Chart Source Data

d. **Data Range tab:**
e. Modify Data range to: = *SheetName*!$B$7:$C$12
f. Series in: Columns
g. **Series tab:**
h. Category (X) axis labels: = *SheetName*!$A$8:$A$12
i. Click "Next >" button

Step 3 of 4—Chart Options

j. **Titles tab:**
k. Chart Title: Analysis of Alternative Cost Approaches
l. Category (X) axis: Number of Orders
m. Value (Y) axis: Total Costs
n. **Gridlines tab:**
o. Category (X) axis: Major Gridlines (checked)
p. Value (Y) axis: Major Gridlines (checked)
q. Click "Next >" button

Step 4 of 4—Chart Location

r. As object in SheetName Checked
s. Click "Finish" button

10. Move the chart so the upper-left corner is on the left margin, row 14.
Left-click the upper-left handle and drag it to the designated location.

11. Resize the chart so the lower-right corner fills cell K37.
Left-click the lower-right handle and drag it to the designated location.

12. Format the Y-axis amounts (Total Costs) to display a dollar symbol by doing the following:
Double-click any cost amount on the Y-axis to open the "Format Axis" dialog box.

Scale tab:	Minimum:	300,000
Number tab:	Category:	Currency
	Decimal Places:	0
	Symbol:	$

13. Save your work, and print a copy for your files.

Note: Select cell A8 before printing if you want both the data and the chart to print. If you want only the chart to print, ignore the "Select cell A8" instruction.

Print your spreadsheet using landscape in order to ensure that all columns appear on one page.

COLLABORATIVE LEARNING EXERCISE

3-57 Cost-Behavior Examples

Select about 10 students to participate in a "cost-behavior bee." The game proceeds like a spelling bee—when a participant is unable to come up with a correct answer, he or she is eliminated from the game. The last one in the game is the winner.

The object of the game is to identify a type of cost that fits a particular cost-behavior pattern. The first player rolls a die.[2] If a 1 or a 6 comes up, the die passes to the next player (and the roller makes it to the next round). If a 2, 3, 4, or 5 comes up, the player has to identify one of the following types of costs:

If a 2 is rolled, identify a variable cost.
If a 3 is rolled, identify a fixed cost.
If a 4 is rolled, identify a mixed cost.
If a 5 is rolled, identify a step cost.

A scribe should label four columns on the board, one for each type of cost, and list the costs that are mentioned for each category. Once a particular cost has been used, it cannot be used again.

Each player has a time limit of 10 seconds to produce an example. (For a tougher game, make the time limit 5 seconds.) The instructor is the referee, judging if a particular example is acceptable. It is legitimate for the referee to ask a player to explain why he or she thinks the cost mentioned fits the category before making a judgment.

After each player has had a turn, a second round begins with the remaining players taking a turn in the same order as in the first round. The game continues through additional rounds until all but one player has failed to give an acceptable answer within the time limit. The remaining player is the winner.

INTERNET EXERCISE

3-58 Cost Behavior at Southwest Airlines

In this exercise, we will look at some costs and see if we can determine the type of behavior associated with those costs. While firms are concerned about trying to label costs as either variable or fixed to help in planning, very few costs are completely variable or fixed. The information provided by firms to external users also often precludes a user from determining specifics about the cost behaviors—they don't want to give the competitors too much information!

Log on to the **Southwest Airlines** Web site at www.southwest.com. Click on the information icon "About Southwest," and then click on "Investor Relations." This will take you to the site where you can then access the financial information.

1. Click on the most recent "Southwest Airlines One Report" tab. Then click on the "performance" tab, then "past performance," and find the page where the 10-year summary starts. Go to this section of the report. What type of information do you find there?
2. When you look at the operating revenue information, what do you see? Look at the information provided concerning operating expenses. Is it categorized in the same manner as the revenues? If the information is not in the same categories, why do you think Southwest did not match it up in the same manner?
3. Now look at the section on consolidated operating statistics. Southwest measures activity in revenue passenger miles (RPMs) and capacity in available seat miles (ASMs). Which of these is larger? How are the RPM and ASM determined? Is it possible for the two numbers to be the same? What information is provided for each of these items in the consolidated operating statistics section?
4. Using data from 2008 through 2011 and employing the high-low method, compute the fixed operating expense per year and the variable operating expense per RPM. Assume that half of the increase in operating expenses between 2008 and 2011 represents increases in fuel prices, which should be omitted from the analysis. Compare the total operating expense after omitting the increase caused by higher fuel prices and the variable expense for 2011. Is this relationship what you expected? Why or why not?
5. Airlines are often considered to be high-fixed-cost companies. Is this consistent with your findings in requirement 4? Explain why the high-low method this time might overestimate the amount of variable costs.

---

[2]Instead of rolling a die, players could draw one of the four cost categories out of a hat (or similar container) or from a deck of four 3 × 5 cards. This eliminates the chance element that can let some players proceed to a later round without having to give an example of a particular cost behavior. However, the chance element can add to the enjoyment of the game.

Cost Management Systems and Activity-Based Costing

LEARNING OBJECTIVES

When you have finished studying this chapter, you should be able to:

1. Describe the purposes of cost management systems.

2. Explain the relationship among cost, cost object, cost accumulation, and cost assignment.

3. Distinguish between direct and indirect costs.

4. Explain the major reasons for allocating costs.

5. Identify the main types of manufacturing costs: direct materials, direct labor, and indirect production costs.

6. Explain how the financial statements of merchandisers and manufacturers differ because of the types of goods they sell.

7. Understand the main differences between traditional and activity-based costing (ABC) systems and why ABC systems provide value to managers.

8. Use activity-based management (ABM) to make strategic and operational control decisions.

9. Describe the steps in designing an activity-based costing system (Appendix 4).

▶ **DELL**

Michael Dell founded Dell Inc. in 1984 while still a student at the University of Texas. He originally called the company PC's Limited but changed the name to Dell Computer Corporation in 1988, the same year the company issued its first shares to the public, and to Dell Inc. in 2003. Dell pioneered the selling of personal computers directly to end users by selling computers over the Internet. By waiting to produce a computer until it received an order and applying just-in-time manufacturing (see p. 16), Dell achieved a cost structure that gave it an advantage over its competitors.

In the 10 years leading up to 2011, revenues increased from $32 billion to $62 billion, but toward the end of the decade market share declined. In 2001 Dell was the world's largest seller of personal computers. In 2002, Dell temporarily slipped to second place after the merger of two major competitors, Hewlett-Packard and Compaq. However, Dell regained the lead the next year and held it through 2006. Dell lost the market-share lead to Hewlett-Packard in 2007 as global market share fell from 16% to 14%, and by 2011 Dell's market share had declined further to 12%.

In 2004 Michael Dell had stepped down as CEO. Shortly thereafter, Dell begain experiencing difficulties—quality problems and declining sales. Michael Dell stepped back in as CEO in early 2007 and summarized Dell's problems: "As we evolved we lost focus and allowed our cost structure to become non-competitive."

How could Dell regain its competitive cost structure? By better understanding and controlling its costs. Michael Dell described the company's renewed focus on cost control:

> Our strategy is focused on competitiveness and growth. To achieve the former, we comprehensively reviewed costs across all processes and organizations, which resulted in actions to reduce:
> - product and procurement costs by more closely matching our product design to customer segments and eliminating embedded costs associated with features not valued by our customers;
> - operating expenses, including a reduction of global employee headcount; and,
> - manufacturing and logistics costs by optimizing our global manufacturing network.

To accomplish these objectives, Dell had to develop systems to better measure and report the costs of producing products and serving customers. This chapter focuses on many of the issues Dell faced. Managers need information about costs to make good decisions in any organization, ranging from large corporations such as Dell or Hewlett-Packard to small businesses such as the local bakery or auto repair shop to nonprofit organizations such as hospitals or food banks. Managers need to know how decisions will affect their organization's costs. ■

© Kimihiro Hoshino/AFP/Getty Images/Newscom

Dell has focused on cost control and shifted its product mix toward services and solutions.

Cost Management Systems

To support managers' decisions, accountants develop **cost management systems (CMS)**—collections of tools and techniques that identify how decisions affect costs. A cost management system provides

1. cost information for strategic management decisions;
2. cost information for operational control; and
3. measures of inventory value and cost of goods sold for financial reporting to investors, creditors, and other external stakeholders.

External users need *aggregate* measures of inventory value and the cost of goods sold. Internal managers need more detailed cost information on individual products or services.

The need for sophisticated cost management systems is driven by the strategic and operational decisions faced by managers. Managers need accurate and timely cost information for strategic decisions, such as deciding on the optimal product and customer mix or investment decisions. For these decisions, managers want to know the costs of individual products, services, customers, and processes. For example, Dell's strategy has shifted its product mix away from consumer sales and toward services and enterprise solutions where expected margins are higher. In a recent interview, Michael Dell described this strategy: "Today, roughly 80 percent of our business is with businesses and public-sector organizations. Ninety-five percent of all Fortune 500 companies and 100 percent of G20 governments are Dell customers. While we have a strong consumer presence and will continue to compete in that space, it's important to focus and commercial is where we expect most of our growth will come from. Ours is a $3 trillion industry and only about $250 billion of it is consumer. We're laser-focused on the $2.75 trillion opportunity that is commercial." This strategic decision relied on cost information about both production costs and distribution costs.

Managers also strive for efficiency by controlling costs. For example, CFO Brian Gladden recently listed a number of cost improvements at Dell, including:

Reduced number of configurations resulting in materials reduction and faster time to market

Better products with reduced warranty expense and less obsolete inventory

Lower manufacturing and freight costs

Reduced overhead

Building and shipping in bulk based on better forecasts and enabling ocean shipment

To implement sustainable cost control programs, managers need accurate and timely feedback on costs.

Objective 1

Describe the purposes of cost management systems.

cost management system (CMS)
A collection of tools and techniques that identify how management's decisions affect costs.

Throughout this text, we describe many CMS tools and techniques that help managers make decisions. Examples include the contribution margin technique and cost-volume-profit analysis you read about in Chapter 2. All of these tools and techniques have one thing in common—the need for accurate information about costs. This chapter focuses on **cost accounting**, the part of a cost management system that measures costs for the purposes of management decision making and financial reporting.

Cost Accounting Systems

We define **cost** as a sacrifice or giving up of resources for a particular purpose. Consider the cost of labor resources. An organization pays (gives up) cash or its equivalent to employees in exchange for their work. We measure the cost of labor resources by the dollars (or other monetary units such as yen or euros) paid to obtain the labor resources. However, managers generally want more from their accountants than simply the cost of the resources used. They often want to know the cost of something in particular, such as a product or a service. Anything for which decision makers desire a separate measurement of costs is a **cost object** (or **cost objective**). Although managers most often want to know the cost of a product or service, there are many other possible cost objects. Examples include customers, departments, territories, and activities such as processing orders or moving materials. For example, one large manufacturer of pet food products recently changed its cost management system to report both the cost of products it makes and the cost to serve the company's major retail customers such as Wal-Mart and PETCO. It discovered that although the selling price exceeded the production cost for all its products, the cost to service some customers was greater than the excess of selling price above production cost, making these customers unprofitable. Knowing this, the company was able to develop a strategy to reduce costs to service these customers and transform them into profitable customers.

The cost data that managers use for decision making come from the **cost accounting system**—the techniques used to determine the cost of a product, service, customer, or other cost object. The cost accounting system is the most fundamental component of a cost management system. It supports all other cost management system tools and techniques.

Cost accounting systems need to provide accurate and timely cost information to help managers make decisions. Without accurate and timely cost information, many decisions can be downright harmful. For example, several years ago a large U.S. grocery chain, A&P, ran into profit difficulties and began retrenching by closing many stores. Management's lack of adequate cost information about individual store operations made the closing program a hit-or-miss affair. A news story reported the following:

> *Because of the absence of detailed profit-and-loss statements, and a [cost accounting] system that did not reflect true costs, A&P's strategists could not be sure whether an individual store was really unprofitable. For example, distribution costs were shared equally among all the stores in a marketing area without regard to such factors as a store's distance from the warehouse. Says one close observer of the company: "When they wanted to close a store, they had to wing it. They could not make rational decisions, because they did not have a fact basis."*

All kinds of organizations—manufacturing firms, service companies, and nonprofit organizations—need some form of cost accounting. Consider the following commentaries on the modern role of management accountants and cost accounting systems:

> *We [management accountants] have to understand what the numbers mean, relate the numbers to business activity, and recommend alternative courses of action. Finally, we have to evaluate alternatives and make decisions to maximize business efficiency.*

> —South Central Bell

> *Because the [cost accounting] system now mirrors the manufacturing process, the engineers and production staff believe the cost data produced by the cost accounting system. Engineering and production regularly ask accounting to help find the product design combination that will optimize costs.... The accountants now participate in product*

---

cost accounting

That part of the cost management system that measures costs for the purposes of management decision making and financial reporting.

Objective 2

Explain the relationship among cost, cost object, cost accumulation, and cost assignment.

cost

A sacrifice or giving up of resources for a particular purpose.

cost object (cost objective)

Anything for which decision makers desire a separate measurement of costs. Examples include departments, products, activities, and territories.

cost accounting system

The techniques used to determine the cost of a product, service, customer, or other cost object.

design decisions. They help engineering and production understand how costs behave.... The system makes the professional lives of the accountants more rewarding.

—Hewlett-Packard Company

A cost accounting system typically includes two processes:

1. **Cost accumulation**: Collecting costs by some "natural" classification, such as materials or labor, or by activities performed such as order processing or machine processing.
2. **Cost assignment**: Attaching costs to one or more cost objects, such as activities, processes, departments, customers, or products.

Exhibit 4-1 is a simple illustration of these two basic processes for materials costs. First, the system collects the costs of all materials. Then, it assigns these costs to the departments that use the materials and further to the specific activities performed in these departments. Last, the system assigns the accumulated costs to the products made—cabinets, tables, and desks. The total materials cost of a particular product is the sum of the materials costs assigned to it in the various departments. For example, the cost of a finished desk would include the following materials costs:

- Metal top, sides, and legs produced by the various activities in the machining department
- Bolts, brackets, screws, drawers, handles, and knobs pieced together by finishing department activities

Managers rely on the accuracy of the cost accounting system. In today's business environment, characterized by highly-competitive global markets and complex production processes, designing cost accounting systems that provide accurate and useful information is a key success factor for all types of organizations. The financial vice president of a major manufacturing firm recently told one of the authors that the company's main competitive advantage was its financial information system, not its manufacturing or distribution capabilities.

cost accumulation
Collecting costs by some natural classification, such as activities performed, labor, or materials.

cost assignment
Attaching costs to one or more cost objects, such as activities, departments, customers, or products.

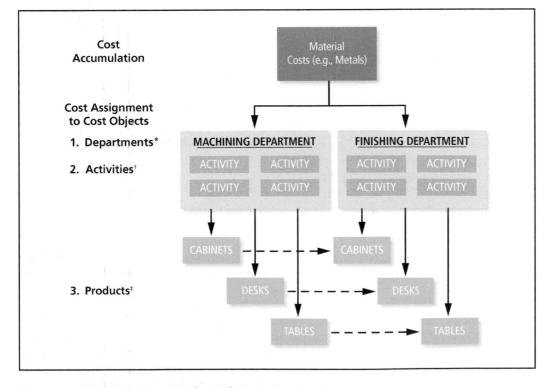

Exhibit 4-1
Cost Accumulation and Assignment

*Purpose: to evaluate performance of manufacturing departments
†Purpose: to measure and evaluate the efficiency of various activities
‡Purpose: to obtain costs of various products for valuing inventory, determining income, and judging product profitability

This chapter describes some major types of cost accounting systems. However, before describing the systems, we need to develop an understanding of the various cost terms that managers and accountants commonly use.

Cost Terms Used for Strategic Decision Making and Operational Control Purposes

Objective 3

Distinguish between direct and indirect costs.

Accountants have their own language laced with jargon. As a manager, you will need to understand the basics of this language. This section focuses on three key terms: direct costs, indirect costs, and cost allocation.

Direct Costs, Indirect Costs, and Cost Allocation

direct costs

Costs that accountants can identify specifically and exclusively with a given cost object in an economically feasible way.

tracing

Physically identifying the amount of a direct cost that relates exclusively to a particular cost object.

indirect costs

Costs that accountants cannot identify specifically and exclusively with a given cost object in an economically feasible way.

Costs may be direct or indirect with respect to a particular cost object. Accountants can identify **direct costs** specifically and exclusively with a given cost object in an economically feasible way. Parts and materials included in a product are the most common types of direct cost. For example, to determine the cost of parts assembled into a Dell laptop computer, Dell's accountants can determine the cost of the specific parts used. A key characteristic of direct costs is that accountants can physically identify the amount of the cost that relates exclusively to a particular cost object. We call this **tracing** the direct cost to the cost object. In contrast, accountants cannot specifically and exclusively identify the amount of **indirect costs** related to a given cost object in an economically feasible way. Examples of indirect costs include facilities rental costs, depreciation on equipment, and many staff salaries.

To further illustrate the distinction between direct and indirect cost, consider the cost of labor. Some employees work specifically on particular products. These labor costs are direct to those products because the costs can be traced to the products. Other employees, such as supervisors, general managers, accountants, and legal staff, do not work on individual products. Because these costs cannot be traced to the products, they are indirect costs.

Over time, the mix is shifting toward more indirect costs. A century ago, a large proportion of labor costs were direct. Most companies had a labor-intensive production process where a majority of the workers had hands-on involvement with producing their company's products. To produce 10% more units of a particular product, a company typically needed about 10% more workers. Today the situation is different. Automated production processes have eliminated many hands-on jobs, and more employees just oversee automated processes that make many different products. Increases or decreases in production, or changes in the product mix do not directly affect this labor cost.

Just because a cost is indirect does not mean it is unimportant. Companies cannot continue to make products without indirect costs. Further, in many companies today, indirect costs exceed 50% of total costs, so accurate assignment of indirect costs is crucial. Decision makers who ignore indirect costs or receive inaccurate measures of indirect costs often make poor decisions. One of the most challenging tasks of a cost accounting system is to assign indirect costs to cost objects.

cost allocation

Assigning indirect costs to cost objects in proportion to the cost object's use of a particular cost-allocation base.

cost-allocation base

A measure of input or output that determines the amount of cost to be allocated to a particular cost object. An ideal cost-allocation base measures how much of the particular cost is caused by the cost object.

To assign indirect costs to cost objects, we use **cost allocation**, which assigns indirect costs to cost objects in proportion to the cost object's use of a particular cost-allocation base. A **cost-allocation base** is some measure of input or output that determines the amount of cost to be allocated to a particular cost object. An ideal cost-allocation base measures how much of the particular cost is *caused by* the cost object. Note the similarity of this definition to that of a cost driver—a factor that causes costs. Therefore, *most cost-allocation bases are cost drivers*.

Consider how Dell's accountants assign assembly-equipment depreciation to a particular model of laptop. They might allocate this indirect cost based on the allocation base "machine hours," a measure of the amount of assembly equipment time used to make a particular computer. If making a Latitude laptop uses two machine hours while making an Ultrabook laptop uses only one, then Dell would allocate twice as much machine depreciation cost to the Latitude. An *allocated* cost is an indirect cost assigned to a cost object using a cost-allocation base.

Decision makers should be cautious in using allocated indirect costs. When the allocation base measures how much cost is *caused by* the cost objects, allocated costs will be relevant for many decisions. When the allocation is not related to the cause of the costs, managers have reason to suspect the resulting costs are inaccurate.

Because cost allocations are so important to cost measurement in today's companies, let's look more deeply into why and how companies allocate their indirect costs.

Purposes of Cost Allocation

What logic should we use for allocating costs? The answer depends on the purpose(s) of the cost allocation. In short, there are no firm rules that we can rely on—there is no universally best cost-allocation system. Instead of cost allocation rules, we focus on general concepts that provide guidance when managers design these systems. You will be a better decision maker if you use these concepts to evaluate the system generating the information you are using in your decisions.

Objective 4

Explain the major reasons for allocating costs.

Recall that cost allocations support a company's CMS—the system providing cost measurements for strategic decision making, operational control, and external reporting. Following are four purposes of cost allocation. The first two support strategic decision making and operational control, the third supports external reporting, and the fourth supports the previous three.

1. ***To predict the economic effects of strategic and operational control decisions:*** Major strategic decisions include setting the optimal product and customer mix, establishing pricing policy, and setting policy about which value-chain functions to develop as core competencies. Managers also need to predict the economic effects—both benefits and costs—of process improvement efforts. Managers within an organizational unit should be aware of all the consequences of their decisions, even consequences outside of their unit. Examples are the addition of a new course in a university that causes additional work in the registrar's office, the addition of a new flight or an additional passenger on an airline that requires reservation and booking services, and the addition of a new specialty in a medical clinic that produces more work for the medical records department.

2. ***To provide desired motivation and to give feedback for performance evaluation:*** Companies often hold managers responsible for total costs that include allocated costs. Therefore, cost allocations influence management behavior and can help motivate managers to make decisions that are in the company's best interests. For example, some organizations allocate the costs of legal services or internal management consulting services to spur managers to make sure the benefits of the services exceed the costs. Other organizations do not allocate such costs because top management wants to encourage their use.

3. ***To compute income and asset valuations for financial reporting:*** Companies allocate costs to products to measure inventory costs for their balance sheets and cost of goods sold for their income statements.

4. ***To justify costs or obtain reimbursement:*** Sometimes organizations base prices directly on costs. For example, government contracts often specify a price that includes reimbursement for costs plus some profit margin. In these instances, cost allocations directly determine the revenue received from a product or service.

Ideally, a single cost allocation would serve all four purposes simultaneously. But thousands of managers and accountants will agree that most systems fail to achieve this ideal. Instead, cost allocations are often a major source of discontent and confusion. Allocating fixed costs usually causes the greatest problems. Why? Because fixed costs by definition do not change with the level of activity or production, yet the allocated fixed costs are often misinterpreted as a measure of how costs change with the level of activity. At the same time, fixed costs are often necessary to run a business and systems that do not allocate these fixed costs can also be misinterpreted, creating the misimpression that all products or services that sell for more than their direct, variable costs are profitable. Because both systems that allocate costs and systems that do not allocate costs can lead to misinterpretation, managers and accountants need to decide which approach is preferable in a particular situation.

Often external reporting rules for measuring inventory and cost of goods sold dominate by default because they are externally imposed. For example, generally accepted accounting principles (GAAP) require a company to assign all production-related costs and only production-related costs to its products. On the other hand, managers may prefer not to allocate all production-related indirect fixed costs for some decision-making purposes. If a particular management decision does not affect such fixed costs, it can be misleading to include them as part of the cost of the product. In addition, managers may want to allocate major costs from nonproduction parts of the value chain, such as R&D, marketing, or administrative expenses. Thus, the product or customer costs managers need for decision making and performance evaluation often are different from the costs allocated under GAAP. The decision should be made to create a system of allocations that differ from those used for inventory-costing purposes when the benefits of the system exceed the added cost of the system.

Methods of Cost Allocation

Now let's turn to the question of how companies allocate costs. Because final products or services are important cost objects to nearly all organizations, we focus on how companies trace direct costs and allocate indirect costs to these cost objects. Examine Exhibit 4-2 to see the difference between tracing direct costs and allocating indirect costs to final products.

Physically tracing the direct costs is usually straightforward. For example, the cost accounting system can measure the amount and cost of each material added to a product. Workers can record the time spent on each product and the system can value each hour at the worker's appropriate wage rate. Systems to accurately measure direct costs have been available for decades, even centuries.

Allocating indirect costs is more complex. Because indirect costs are substantial for most companies, allocation choices are especially important. Allocation is a four-step process:

cost pool

A group of individual costs that a company allocates to cost objects using a single cost-allocation base.

1. Accumulate indirect costs into one or more cost pools. A **cost pool** is a group of individual costs that a company allocates to cost objects using a single cost-allocation base. Many simple cost accounting systems place all indirect production costs in a single cost pool.
2. Select an allocation base for each cost pool. If possible, the allocation base should be a cost driver—a measure that causes the costs in the cost pool. However, in many cases it is not possible to find a clear cost driver, and therefore companies resort to using an allocation base that has little to do with the cause of costs in the cost pool. For example, companies that have a single cost pool for indirect costs often use direct-labor hours or direct-labor cost as the cost-allocation base.
3. Measure the units of the cost-allocation base used for each cost object (for example, the number of direct-labor hours used on a particular product) and compute the total units used for all cost objects.
4. Multiply the percentage of total cost-allocation base units used for each cost object by the total costs in the cost pool to determine the cost allocated to each cost object.

Consider the depreciation on Dell's assembly equipment. How would Dell's accountants allocate $400,000 of depreciation for July to Ultrabook and Latitude laptop computers? Let's apply the four steps:

1. In July accountants measured the depreciation cost, the only cost in this cost pool, at $400,000.
2. The cost-allocation base selected is machine hours.

Exhibit 4-2

Assignment of Direct and Indirect Costs to Products, Services, Customers, or Activities

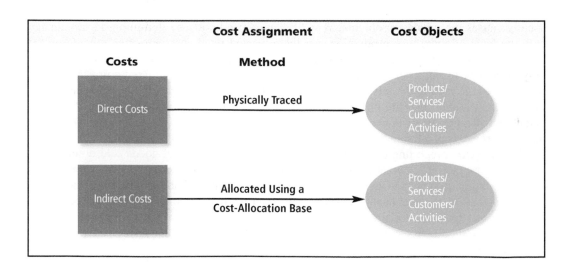

3. Dell used 2,000 machine hours in July to make Ultrabook laptops and 3,000 machine hours to make Latitude laptops, for a total of 5,000 machine hours.

4. This means that Dell used $2,000 \div 5,000 = 40\%$ of the machine hours for Ultrabook and $3,000 \div 5,000 = 60\%$ of the machine hours for Latitude, so the depreciation cost allocated to Ultrabook is $40\% \times \$400,000 = \$160,000$, and the cost allocated to Latitude is $60\% \times 400,000 = \$240,000$.

An alternative way to describe this allocation is to compute the depreciation cost per machine hour or $\$400,000 \div (3,000 + 2,000) = \$80$. The allocation to Ultrabook is $\$80 \times 2,000 = \$160,000$ and the allocation to Latitude is $\$80 \times 3,000 = \$240,000$.

Companies also use cost allocation to assign indirect costs to cost objects other than products or services. For example, suppose we are allocating costs to departments. A logical cost-allocation base for allocating rent costs to departments is the number of square feet that each department occupies. Other logical cost-allocation bases include cubic feet for allocating depreciation of heating and air conditioning equipment and total direct cost for allocating general administrative expense.

You will see varying terminology used to describe cost allocation. You may encounter terms such as *allocate, apply, absorb, attribute, reallocate, assign, distribute, redistribute, load, burden, apportion*, and *reapportion* being used interchangeably to describe the allocation of indirect costs to cost objects.

Unallocated Costs

Some costs lack an identifiable relationship to a cost object. Often it is best to leave such costs unallocated. **Unallocated costs** are costs that an accounting system records but does not allocate to any cost object. They might include research and development (R&D), process design, legal expenses, accounting, information services, and executive salaries. Keep in mind, though, that an unallocated cost for one company may be an allocated cost or even a direct cost for another. Why? Because businesses vary considerably in their value chains and operating processes. For example, product design is a critical success factor for some businesses, and therefore, managers in such companies are willing to spend the time and effort to deploy sophisticated accounting systems to allocate or even directly trace product design costs. For other companies, this cost is not important enough to warrant special treatment.

unallocated costs
Costs that an accounting system records but does not allocate to any cost object.

Consider the statement of operating income for Li Company in Panel A of Exhibit 4-3. Li Company makes cabinets, tables, and chairs. Each item in Panel A represents accumulated totals for all products sold for an entire reporting period. To help make a strategic decision regarding which of the three products to emphasize, it would be useful to "unbundle" these totals to find the profitability of each product. How can we do this?

Consider cost of goods sold, which includes all manufacturing costs. Like most companies, Li Company finds that it is easy to trace direct-material costs to individual products. However, other manufacturing costs are difficult to trace directly, so Li Company treats them as indirect and allocates them to products.

Let's assume that Li Company uses machine hours to allocate all indirect manufacturing costs. Last year Li Company used 9,000, 6,000, and 7,000 machine hours to make cabinets, tables, and chairs, respectively—a total of 22,000 machine hours. Therefore, the allocation of the $110,000 indirect manufacturing costs to cabinets is $\$110,000 \times (9,000 \div 22,000) = \$45,000$, to tables is $\$110,000 \times (6,000 \div 22,000) = \$30,000$, and to chairs is $\$110,000 \times (7,000 \div 22,000) = \$35,000$, as shown in Panel B of Exhibit 4-3. If managers responsible for each of the products believe the use of machine hours is closely related to the amount of indirect costs incurred, they would be satisfied that the cost of goods sold and gross profit amounts in Panel B are accurately measured.

Li Company also has both direct and indirect selling expenses. It can directly trace sales salaries to individual products because the company pays its sales force commissions based on individual sales and no fixed salaries. In addition, it allocates the expenses for the distribution of products to warehouses in a fair manner based on weight. Last year, shipments of cabinets, tables, and chairs weighed 6,000, 4,000, and 5,000 pounds, respectively, for a total of 15,000 pounds. Consequently, the allocation of the $30,000 total distribution costs to cabinets is $\$30,000 \times (6,000 \div 15,000) = \$12,000$, to tables is $\$30,000 \times (4,000 \div 15,000) = \$8,000$, and to chairs is $\$30,000 \times (5,000 \div 15,000) = \$10,000$.

Panel A Statement of Operating Income [External Reporting Purpose]		Panel B Contribution to Corporate Costs and Profit [Internal Strategic Decision-Making Purpose]			
		Cabinets	Tables	Chairs	Cost Type, Assignment Method
Sales	$470,000	$ 280,000	$100,000	$90,000	
Cost of goods sold:					
Direct material	120,000	50,000	30,000	40,000	Direct, direct trace
Indirect manufacturing	110,000	45,000	30,000	35,000	Indirect, allocation based on machine hours
Total cost of goods sold	230,000	95,000	60,000	75,000	
Gross profit	240,000	185,000	40,000	15,000	
Selling expenses:					
Sales salaries	47,000	28,000	10,000	9,000	Direct, direct trace
Distribution	30,000	12,000	8,000	10,000	Indirect, allocation based on
Total selling expenses	77,000	40,000	18,000	19,000	weight
Contribution to corporate expenses and profit	**163,000**	**$145,000**	**$ 22,000**	**$(4,000)**	
Corporate expenses (unallocated):					
Administrative salaries	40,000				
Other administrative expenses	60,000				
Total unallocated expenses	100,000				
Operating income	$ 63,000				

Exhibit 4-3
Direct, Indirect, and Unallocated Costs for Li Company

Because Li Company's allocation bases are good measures of what causes the indirect costs, managers are likely to view the allocated costs as fair. While the managers in charge of chairs may not be happy with the reported loss of $4,000, they would feel that it is a reasonable measure of profitability.

Li Company could find no reasonable means to allocate administrative salaries or other administrative expenses. Therefore, these corporate-level expenses remain unallocated. Why not allocate the administrative salaries and other administrative expenses to the products by using some simple measure, such as "percent of total revenue generated" or "number of units sold"? Because managers generally want allocations to be a fair measure of the costs incurred on their behalf. If administrative salaries and expenses are not closely related to the allocation base such as "percent of revenue" or "number of units sold," the allocations are arbitrary. Managers will not trust allocations that are arbitrary and may make decisions based on other less relevant information. Therefore, companies that cannot find cost drivers that are directly related to costs often choose not to allocate the costs.

Assigning a cost as direct, indirect, or unallocated requires judgment. Such judgments are based on the type of cost, its magnitude, and how expensive it is to implement a system to trace or allocate the cost. For direct costs, judgments required are generally fairly easy to make with the main issue being whether the cost of a system for tracing costs to cost objects is greater than its expected benefits. For example, a system for tracing the exact cost of products sold by Amazon.com to individual orders is likely to be worth its cost. However, it may be too expensive to trace the exact cost of packing and preparing each order for shipment, even though such a tracing is technically possible. For indirect costs, the judgments required are more difficult. Much of the remainder of this book deals with judgments about allocating indirect costs.

Frequently, managers want to know the costs of more than one cost object, such as departments, products, services, activities, or resources. In these cases, companies allocate costs to multiple cost objects. For example, suppose the manager of a local telephone company is faced with two decisions: 1) what price to charge for installing new phone service and 2) what costs to include in the installation department's budget. Among the various costs relevant to both decisions is the salary of a supervisor in the installation department who oversees both phone installations and routine service calls. For the pricing decision, the supervisor's salary is an indirect cost. Why? Because accountants cannot physically trace this cost to the phone installations or service calls and therefore must allocate the cost. However, for the department budget, the supervisor's salary is a direct cost. Why? Because accountants can physically identify 100% of the cost as belonging to the department. This is an example of a cost that is both direct (to the department) and indirect (to the product or service). In general, many more costs are direct when the cost object is a department than when it is a product or service.

Cost Terms Used for External Reporting Purposes

While this text focuses mostly on costs used by managers, it is important to recognize that cost accounting systems also support the financial reporting process. One of the four purposes of cost management systems is to provide aggregate measures of inventory value and cost of goods manufactured for external reporting to investors, creditors, and other external stakeholders. We will discuss four attributes of these costs: manufacturing costs, product versus period costs, costs on the balance sheet, and costs on the income statement.

Objective 5

Identify the main types of manufacturing costs: direct materials, direct labor, and indirect production costs.

Categories of Manufacturing Costs

Manufacturing companies accumulate and report the cost of inventories in a different way than merchandising companies. Manufacturing operations transform **raw materials**—the basic materials from which a product is made—into other goods through the use of labor and factory facilities. In manufacturing companies, products are frequently the cost object. Manufacturing companies classify production costs as either (1) direct-material costs, (2) direct-labor costs, or (3) indirect production costs:

1. **Direct-material costs** include the acquisition costs of raw materials that a company can trace to the products in an economically feasible way. Examples of materials that are typically considered direct-material costs are iron castings, lumber, aluminum sheets, and subassemblies. Examples where it is typically not economically feasible to trace materials cost to products are costs of solder, glue, or tape.
2. **Direct-labor costs** include the wages (and, in some companies, related benefits) paid to employees that a company can trace specifically and exclusively to the manufactured goods. Examples are the wages of machine operators and assemblers. In highly automated factories with a flexible workforce, there may not be any direct-labor costs. Why? Because all workers may spend time overseeing numerous products, making it economically infeasible to physically trace any labor cost directly to specific products.
3. **Indirect production costs** (also called **indirect manufacturing costs, factory overhead, factory burden**, or **manufacturing overhead**) include all costs associated with the production process that a company cannot trace to products or services in an economically feasible way. Examples of indirect production costs are power, supplies, supervisory salaries, property taxes, rent, insurance, and depreciation. Supplies or indirect materials are also part of indirect production costs. Supplies are materials used in the manufacturing process that do not become part of the product, such as sandpaper or cleaning materials. Minor items, such as tacks or glue, are also often treated as indirect materials even though they become part of the manufactured product because the cost of tracing these items is greater than the benefit of having more precise product costs. Similarly, accountants consider many labor costs, such as costs of janitors, forklift truck operators, plant guards, and storeroom clerks, to be indirect labor because it is impossible or economically infeasible to trace such activities to specific products.

raw material
The basic material from which a product is made.

direct-material costs
The acquisition costs of raw materials that a company traces to the manufactured goods.

direct-labor costs
The wages of all labor that a company can trace specifically and exclusively to the manufactured goods.

indirect production costs (indirect manufacturing costs, factory burden, factory overhead, manufacturing overhead)
All costs associated with the production process that a company cannot trace to the goods or services produced in an economically feasible way; usually all production costs except direct materials and direct labor.

Product Costs and Period Costs

When preparing income statements and balance sheets, accountants frequently distinguish between product costs and period costs. **Product costs** are costs identified with products manufactured or purchased for resale. In a manufacturing company, product costs include direct-materials costs, direct-labor, and indirect production costs. These costs first become part of the inventory; thus, we call them **inventoriable costs**. These inventoriable costs become expenses in the form of cost of goods sold when the company sells the inventory.

In contrast, **period costs** become expenses during the current period without becoming part of inventory. Period costs are associated with nonproduction value-chain functions (research and development, design, marketing, distribution, and customer service). Most firms' financial

product costs (inventoriable costs) Costs identified with goods produced or purchased for resale.

period costs
Costs that become expenses during the current period without becoming part of inventory.

statements report these costs as selling and administrative expenses. In short, these costs do not become a part of the reported inventory cost of the manufactured products for financial reporting purposes.

Exhibit 4-4 illustrates product and period costs. The top half shows a merchandising company, such as a retailer or wholesaler, that acquires goods for resale without changing their basic form. The only product cost is the purchase cost of the merchandise. The company holds unsold goods as merchandise inventory and shows their costs as an asset on a balance sheet. As the company sells the goods, their costs become expenses in the form of "cost of goods sold." A merchandising company also has a variety of selling and administrative expenses. These costs are period costs because the company deducts them from revenue as expenses without ever being regarded as a part of inventory.

The bottom half of Exhibit 4-4 shows product and period costs in a manufacturing company. Note that the company incurs direct-labor costs and indirect production costs to transform direct materials into salable items. You can see that the balance sheets of manufacturers and merchandisers differ with respect to inventories. Instead of one inventory account, a manufacturing concern has three inventory accounts that help managers trace all product costs through the production process to the time of sales. These accounts are as follows:

raw-material inventory
Raw material on hand and awaiting use in the production process.

- **Raw-material(direct-material) inventory:** Raw material on hand and awaiting use in the production process.
- **Work-in-process inventory:** Goods undergoing the production process but not yet fully completed. Costs include appropriate amounts of the three major manufacturing costs: direct-material costs, direct-labor costs, and indirect production costs.
- **Finished-goods inventory:** Goods fully completed but not yet sold.

work-in-process inventory
Goods undergoing the production process but not yet fully completed.

finished-goods inventory
Goods fully completed but not yet sold.

The only accounting difference between manufacturing and merchandising companies is in the composition of product costs. A merchandising company includes in product cost only the cost to acquire the merchandise it sells. In contrast, a manufacturing company includes in product cost such items as insurance, depreciation, and wages that are incurred in the production process in addition to the cost of materials. Although merchandising and manufacturing companies differ in how they account for product costs, they account for period costs the same. Regardless of the type of company, period costs never become part of inventory.

Balance Sheet and Income Statement Presentation of Costs

Objective 6

Explain how the financial statements of merchandisers and manufacturers differ because of the types of goods they sell.

How do published financial statements of merchandising and manufacturing companies differ in presenting costs? Let's first examine balance sheets and notice the extra detail provided by a manufacturer:

Current Asset Sections of Balance Sheets

Manufacturer			Retailer or Wholesaler	
Cash		$ 4,000	Cash	$ 4,000
Receivables		25,000	Receivables	25,000
Finished goods	$32,000			
Work in process	22,000			
Raw material	23,000			
Total inventories		77,000	Merchandise inventories	77,000
Other current assets		1,000	Other current assets	1,000
Total current assets		$107,000	Total current assets	$107,000

The difference between the balance sheet of a manufacturer and that of a merchandiser (retailer or wholesaler) is apparent from the inventory accounts from the 2011 annual reports of **Cisco Systems** (a manufacturer) and **Costco Wholesale** (a merchandiser), amounts in millions:

Cisco Systems, Inc.		Costco Wholesale Corporation	
Raw materials	$ 219	Merchandise inventories	$6,638
Work in process	52		
Finished goods	1,215		
Total inventories	$1,486		

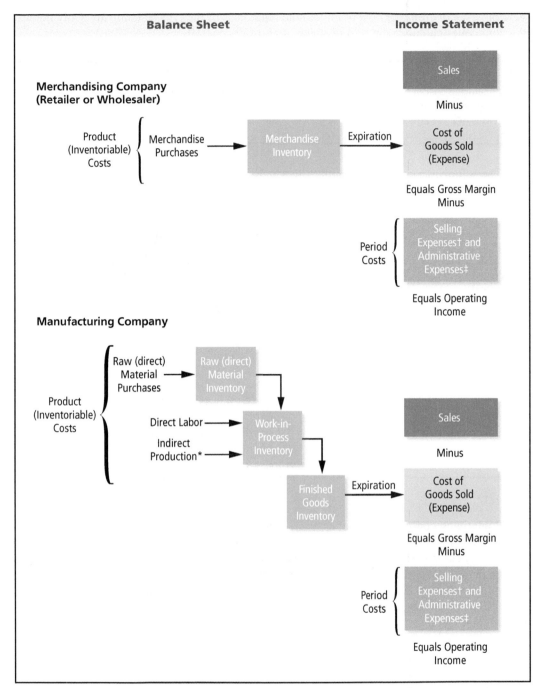

Exhibit 4-4
Relationships of Product Costs and Period Costs

*Examples: indirect labor, factory supplies, insurance on inventories, and depreciation on plant
†Examples: insurance on salespersons' cars, depreciation on salespersons' cars, salespersons' salaries
‡Examples: insurance on corporate headquarters building, depreciation on office equipment, clerical salaries
Note particularly that when insurance and depreciation relate to the manufacturing function, they are inventoriable, but when they relate to selling and administration, they are not inventoriable.

Now consider income statements. We have already mentioned that the reporting of selling and administrative expenses is typically the same for manufacturing and merchandising organizations. What about the cost of goods sold? In published financial statements you will generally see one line for cost of goods sold regardless of the type of company. Only the way the companies calculate the cost of goods sold differs, as follows:

Manufacturer	Retailer or Wholesaler
Manufacturing cost of goods produced and then sold, usually composed of the three major categories of cost: direct-material costs, direct-labor costs, and indirect production costs	Merchandise cost of goods sold, usually composed of the purchase cost of items that are acquired and then resold

The following shows how manufacturers and retailers or wholesalers calculate their cost of goods sold (numbers assumed):

Cost of Goods Sold Section of the Income Statement

Manufacturer			Retailer or Wholesaler	
Beginning finished goods inventory		$ 4,000	Beginning merchandise inventory	$ 4,000
Cost of goods manufactured:			Purchases	40,000
Direct materials used	$20,000			
Direct labor	12,000			
Indirect production	8,000	40,000		
Cost of goods available for sale		44,000	Cost of goods available for sale	44,000
Ending finished goods inventory		8,000	Ending merchandise inventory	8,000
Cost of goods sold		$36,000	Cost of goods sold	$36,000

Sometimes confusion arises because accountants and managers use the terms *costs* and *expenses* loosely. *Cost* is a broad term that describes the amount paid for an activity, product, or service. *Expenses* specifically denote the costs deducted from revenue on an income statement in a given period. All costs eventually become expenses, but they are not expenses until accountants deduct them from revenue in the income statement. Thus, product manufacturing costs become an expense on an income statement (called cost of goods sold) via the multistep inventory procedure shown earlier in Exhibit 4-4. In contrast, selling and administrative costs become expenses immediately in all types of companies.

Traditional and Activity-Based Cost Accounting Systems

Objective 7

Understand the main differences between traditional and activity-based costing (ABC) systems and why ABC systems provide value to managers.

There are many different types of cost accounting systems, but most of the important features of these systems can be described in terms of two general types—traditional and activity-based cost accounting systems.

Until the 1990s, almost all U.S. companies used **traditional costing systems**—those that do not accumulate or report costs of individual activities or processes. Traditional costing systems often use a single cost pool for all indirect production costs. Traditional systems allocate this pool of costs to products using a single cost-allocation base, such as labor cost or labor hours.

Traditional systems work well with simple production processes. Consider a company that makes only a few products for which indirect production costs are a small percentage of total costs so the system combines them into a single cost pool and allocates them to products using only one cost-allocation base, direct-labor hours. Such a company can achieve a reasonable level of accuracy of product costs with a traditional costing system because direct-material and direct-labor costs are a high percentage of total costs.

As companies grow, as they face increasing global competition, and as their operations become more complex, indirect costs become increasingly important. Companies often refine their traditional costing systems to increase the accuracy of product or service costs. They do this by accumulating indirect costs into multiple cost pools. For example, consider a company that has two operating departments, assembly and finishing. The resources in the assembly department are mainly large, expensive machines. The finishing department has only a few machines but many employees. Because operations within each department are relatively simple, the company might choose a traditional costing system that allocates manufacturing overhead using machine hours as an allocation base in the assembly department and labor hours as an allocation base in the finishing department.

But what about a still more complex situation where a company makes hundreds or thousands of different products and indirect production costs are a large percentage of total costs? What if the many different products consume resources at widely varying rates? Achieving a high level of cost accuracy in such an operating environment requires a more elaborate cost accounting system such as an **activity-based costing (ABC) system**—a system that first accumulates indirect resource costs for each of the *activities* of a particular plant, department, value-chain function, or organization and then assigns the cost of each activity to the products, services, or other cost objects that require that activity. Most ABC systems provide highly accurate product or customer costs that a company can use for strategic decisions. Further, information about the costs of activities helps managers to understand the cause and effect relationships between day-to-day activities and product or customer costs and thereby aids the operational control purpose of cost management systems. Many managers believe that ABC systems help them better manage their organizations. The Business First box on page 136 explains why some companies use ABC.

Companies adopt cost accounting systems that are consistent with their management philosophies and their production and operating technologies. Changes in philosophies or technologies often prompt corresponding changes in cost accounting systems. For example, when BorgWarner's automotive chain systems operation transformed its manufacturing operation to a just-in-time manufacturing system with work cells, it also changed its cost accounting system. The transformation in the way BorgWarner operated made the existing cost accounting system obsolete. According to management, the new cost accounting system, coupled with the new production systems, "improved the overall reporting, controls, and efficiency dramatically."

Comparing Activity-Based and Traditional Costing

Let's take a closer look at how ABC differs from traditional costing. Traditional systems generally focus on allocating only production costs—and not the costs of other value-chain functions—to the products. Why? Because traditional systems often focus on simply measuring inventory values for financial reporting purposes, and GAAP does not allow companies to include nonproduction costs in the inventory value of a product. ABC systems, in contrast, consider a broader range of costs that are important to decision makers. They often allocate the costs of value-chain functions such as design, marketing, order processing, and customer service in addition to production costs. As a result, ABC systems are more complex but provide more accurate costs to aid managerial decision making.

Activity-based costing also causes managers to look closely at the relationships among resources, activities, and cost objects—essentially analyzing the unit's production process. Many ABC teams find it useful to develop a **process map**—a schematic diagram that captures the interrelationships among cost objects, activities, and resources. These maps can help accountants and managers to better understand the company's operations.

traditional costing systems
Accounting systems that do not accumulate or report costs of individual activities or processes. They often use a single cost pool for all indirect production costs with a labor-based cost-allocation base.

activity-based costing (ABC) system
A system that first accumulates indirect resource costs for each of the activities of the area being costed, and then assigns the costs of each activity to the products, services, or other cost objects that require that activity.

process map
A schematic diagram capturing interrelationships between cost objects, activities, and resources.

Business First

Use of Activity-Based Costing

Why do managers use ABC? The most frequent applications are for product and service costing, process and activity analysis, and performance measurement. These are the primary purposes of strategic decision making and operational control that we discussed at the beginning of this chapter. A recent survey asked companies that use ABC to indicate how many managers routinely used the ABC system. The vast majority, 62%, indicated that from 10 to 24 managers used ABC; 23% of the companies reported that between 25 and 99 managers used ABC information.

BlueCross BlueShield of Florida (BCBSF) is an example of one company that uses ABC. BCBSF's major customers include local groups (persons in companies with headquarters in Florida), direct pay (individuals), national and corporate accounts (persons in companies with headquarters outside Florida), and government programs (persons 65 years or older with Medicare benefits). During the early 1990s, BCBSF faced increased competition for its health-care products and services. But its cost management system did not adequately meet the needs of managers.

The primary goal of BCBSF's management was to develop a new cost management system that would help identify opportunities for increased operating control and cost reduction in administrative expenses. Administrative expenses—all the costs of doing business other than claims payments—were

$588 million, or 20% of total revenue. The company goal was to reduce administrative costs from 20% of revenue to less than 10%. The cost-management-system technique BCBSF used was an ABC system. This new cost accounting system provided more accurate and timely measurements of

1. customer and product profitability—a strategic purpose,
2. activities that provided the most value to managers and customers—an operational control purpose, and
3. costs of non-value-added activities—an operational control purpose.

Another health-care organization using ABC is Froedtert Memorial Lutheran Hospital in Milwaukee. For example, the hospital uses ABC strategically to determine the costs of various levels of anesthesia care so that prices can be set based on solid cost data. It also uses ABC for control purposes. An example is determining the cost of various activities used in knee replacement surgery. The hospital used ABC information to reengineer the process to reduce operating room time by 37 minutes and resource costs by $828 per procedure.

Sources: Mohan Nair, "Activity-Based Costing: Who's Using It and Why?" *Management Accounting Quarterly*, Spring 2000, pp. 29–33; K. Thurston, D. Keleman, and J. MacArthur, "Cost for Pricing at BlueCross BlueShield of Florida," *Management Accounting Quarterly*, Spring 2000, pp. 4–13; and Cherly Grandlich, "Using Activity-Based Costing in Surgery," *AORN Journal*, January 2004, pp. 189–192.

The two examples in Exhibit 4-5 illustrate how to draw process maps. We depict resources by the ▲ symbol. When a product, service, or customer is the cost object, we use the ◗ symbol for the cost object. When the cost object is an activity we use a ▬.

When a resource supports only one activity or an activity applies to only one product, the entire cost of the resource or activity flows to the activity or product. In Exhibit 4-5, the costs of resource B and activity 1 flow entirely to activity 3 and product T, respectively. When a resource supports two or more activities or an activity applies to two or more products, we must divide the cost among the activities or products. In some cases we can physically trace the costs, but in many cases the costs must be allocated. In Exhibit 4-5 we assume that the costs of resource A, activity 2, and activity 3 are each allocated to two cost objects. The process map identifies the cost-allocation base on the arrow between the resource or activity cost and the cost object.

An Illustration of Traditional and ABC Systems

Now let's look at a simple example that demonstrates the main differences between traditional and ABC systems and shows the reasons why many managers prefer ABC systems. Lopez Plastics Company makes just two product lines, plastic casings for pens and plastic casings for cell phones. Last quarter, the company had an operating loss of $64,500. Management needs to take immediate actions to improve profitability.

You are the vice president of operations. You have to decide which of the two product lines to emphasize to improve profitability. You also wish to reduce costs—especially in the production function of the value chain. Lopez Plastics currently uses a traditional cost accounting system, but you are considering deploying an ABC system to support strategic decision making and operational control.

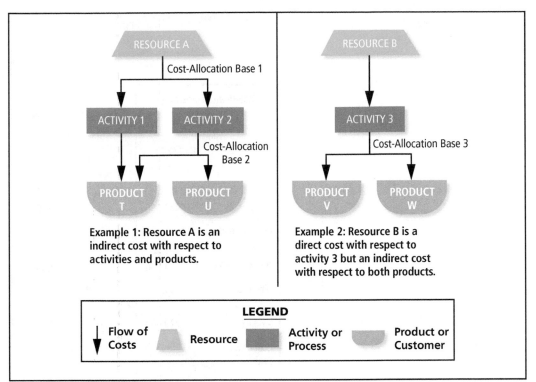

Exhibit 4-5
Basic Concepts for Process
Maps

Exhibit 4-6 shows the company's traditional cost accounting system in panel A and two financial reports based on the traditional system in panel B. Notice the three types of costs: direct, indirect, and unallocated. Direct-materials costs and direct-labor costs are shown with a symbol. The traditional costing system traces direct-materials costs and direct-labor costs to the products. It allocates the indirect production costs ($220,000) to each product in proportion to a single allocation base, the direct-labor hours consumed in making the product. Last period, the company used 4,500 and 500 direct-labor hours to make pen casings and cell phone casings, respectively, for a total of 5,000 hours. So the traditional system allocated (4,500 ÷ 5,000) = 90% of the indirect costs to pen casings and (500 ÷ 5,000) = 10% to cell phone casings. Finally, the system does not assign the unallocated value-chain costs ($100,000) to either product. The gross profit and gross profit margin lines for both products, shown at the bottom of the two right-hand columns of panel B, indicate that cell phone casings is the more profitable product line.

When does a traditional costing system that uses only one cost driver as a basis for allocating indirect production costs, like that of Lopez Plastics, provide accurate product costs? When there is a plausible and reliable relationship between the single cost driver and all the indirect resource costs being allocated. In today's complex business environments, this is rare.

Let's take a careful look at Lopez Plastics' production process to see if the traditional cost accounting system is providing the costing accuracy required for strategic decision making and operational control. Pen casings have a simple design and a simple production process. The company produces them in high volumes, using 90% of its direct-labor time. Pen casings rarely require special customer support or engineering work. This means that indirect production-support costs, such as design engineering of the pen casings, are small.

In contrast, cell phone casings have a more complex design, and the company produces them in small volumes, accounting for only 10% of its direct-labor time. Customers who buy cell phone casings have specific design requirements that cause much production engineering work. Most of the engineering work performed at Lopez Plastics supports the production of cell phones. How significant is the cost of engineering-related work? Of the $220,000 total indirect cost, engineering-related costs are $40,000.

Lopez Plastics' traditional cost system does not separately identify or report the indirect costs of the engineering activity. Instead, the $40,000 of resources used for engineering activity—such as engineer salaries and depreciation of computer-aided design (CAD) equipment—is part of the single indirect resource cost pool. The company allocates all $40,000 of these indirect costs using the cost driver direct-labor time as the cost-allocation base. Thus, it allocates only 10% of

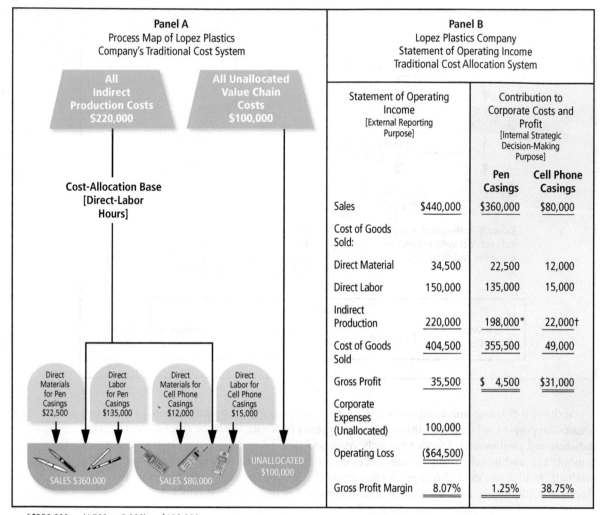

*$220,000 × (4,500 ÷ 5,000) = $198,000
†$220,000 × (500 ÷ 5,000) = $22,000

Exhibit 4-6
Lopez Plastics Company's Traditional Costing System and Statement of Operating Income

the engineering costs to the cell phone casings. However, the fact that most of the engineering work supports production of cell phones tells us that most of the costs of engineering should be allocated to the cell phone casings. We conclude that the traditional system probably does not provide the level of costing accuracy needed. How can we improve Lopez Plastics' costing accuracy? How can we design the company's cost accounting system to better support strategic decision making and operational control?

We could use an ABC system to 1) identify a cost pool for each significant production activity, including engineering activity as one cost pool; 2) assign each indirect resource cost to the appropriate cost pool; and 3) allocate the costs in each activity-cost pool to products using plausible and reliable cost drivers as allocation bases. Exhibit 4-7 depicts a **two-stage ABC system**, which uses two stages of allocation to get from the original indirect resource cost to the final product or service cost. (At this point, Lopez Plastics uses the ABC system only for production costs, so the $100,000 of nonproduction value-chain costs remains unallocated.) The first stage allocates indirect resource costs to two activity-cost pools, processing activity costs and production-support activity costs. The second stage allocates activity costs to the products or services. In essence, the cost objects in the first stage are the activities, and the cost objects in the second stage are the products. You will find a more detailed example of a two-stage ABC system in Appendix 4 on pages 145–146.

In the first stage, Lopez Plastics allocates the cost of two resources, (1) plant and machinery and (2) engineers and CAD equipment to two activities, (1) processing and (2) production support, as shown in Exhibit 4-7. The cost allocated to processing is ($135,000 + $8,000) = $143,000 and the cost allocated to production support is ($45,000 + $32,000) = $77,000, as explained in the next two paragraphs.

two-stage ABC system

A costing system with two stages of allocation to get from the original indirect resource cost to the final product or service cost. The first stage allocates indirect resource costs to activity-cost pools. The second stage allocates activity costs to products or services.

Exhibit 4-7
Lopez Plastics Company's ABC System

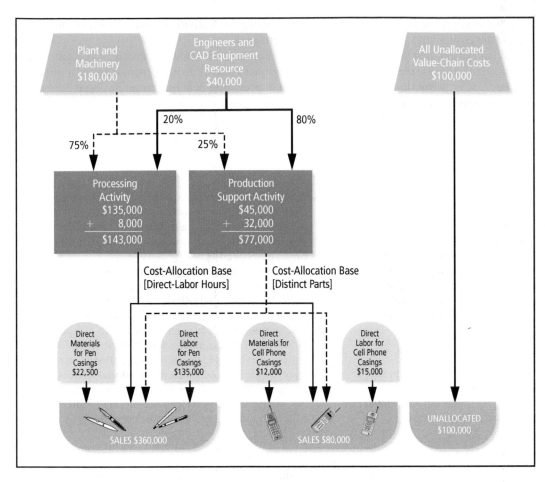

The cost of plant and machinery depends mostly on the square feet of space used. Processing uses 75% of the space and production support uses 25%. Therefore, we allocate 75% of the plant and machinery cost or $135,000 to the processing activity. Similarly, we allocate 25% or $45,000 to production support.

The cost of engineers and CAD equipment depends mainly on the amount of time engineers spend on a product. Engineers spend, on average, about 48 minutes each hour performing production-support activities, such as designing casings. They spend the other 12 minutes supervising the processing activity. Thus, we allocate $(48 \div 60) = 80\%$ of the cost of engineers and CAD equipment to the production-support activity and $(12 \div 60) = 20\%$ to processing. The resulting allocations are $80\% \times 40,000 = \$32,000$ to production support and $20\% \times 40,000 = \$8,000$ to processing.

The second stage allocates the costs of the two activities, processing and production support, to the two products, pen casings and cell-phone casings. There are several possible cost-allocation bases for the production-support activity costs, including "number of customer-generated engineering changes" and "number of distinct parts." The cost-allocation base should be a measure of the consumption of production-support activity. Let's assume this is "number of distinct parts." Suppose pen casings have only 5 distinct parts compared to 20 for cell phone casings. We would allocate $[20 \div (20 + 5)] \times \$77,000 = \$61,600$ of the production-support activity costs to cell phone casings and the remaining $[5 \div (20 + 5)] \times \$77,000 = \$15,400$ to pen casings. The ABC allocation better represents the use of engineering services than does the allocation based on the traditional system. Why? Because cell phone casings cause $(20 \div 25) = 80\%$ of the production-support activity costs, but the traditional system allocates only 10% of such costs to cell phone casings. In contrast, the ABC system allocates the appropriate 80% of the production-support activity costs to cell phone casings.

We will continue this example in the Summary Problem for Your Review, but first let's consider one more advantage of ABC systems. In many companies, managers try to gain cost savings by efficiently managing activities. If Lopez Plastics wants its managers to reduce the cost of producing cell phone casings, the managers will probably focus on possible cost savings in either processing or production support. They may also redesign the product to reduce direct materials costs or reengineer the production process to reduce direct-labor costs. But often the largest potential savings are in the indirect costs. By carrying out activities more efficiently, managers reduce the costs of the products that use those activities.

What information do managers need to examine the efficiency of activities? At a minimum, they need to know the cost of each activity. Traditional systems do not generate this cost information but ABC systems do. Therefore, in addition to providing better information about the cost of products, ABC systems can also promote better operating efficiency.

Making Managerial Decisions

Suppose you have been asked to attend a meeting of top management of your company. When the meeting begins, you are asked to explain in general terms the main differences and similarities in traditional and ABC systems and why managers might prefer ABC costs for decision-making purposes. You have only Exhibits 4-6 and 4-7 as a guide, so you quickly display these side-by-side on a PowerPoint slide, and, after taking a deep breath, you begin to talk. What similarities and differences would you point out? What advantages do ABC costs have?

Answer

1. Traditional costing systems are much simpler than ABC systems and are usually less costly to maintain.
2. Traditional systems and ABC systems both have all three types of costs: direct, indirect, and unallocated.
3. Traditional systems use only one cost pool that includes all indirect resource costs. ABC systems identify multiple cost pools, each representing a particular production activity. This allows ABC systems to better match costs with the causes of those costs.
4. ABC systems require many more cost-allocation bases than do traditional systems. When these cost-allocation bases are both plausible and reliable cost drivers, the overall accuracy of product, service, or customer cost is improved.
5. ABC systems assign indirect resource costs to cost objects in two stages of allocation, where the first stage allocates costs to activities and the second stage allocates activity costs to final cost objects such as products, services, or customers. Thus, ABC systems provide information about the costs of activities, which managers can use to reduce costs by improving operating efficiencies for activities.

We now are in a position to complete our ABC analysis and answer our strategic issue regarding our product mix strategy. We do this in the following Summary Problem for Your Review. It is important for you to carefully work this problem to gain a clear understanding of the basic concepts and value of an ABC system.

Summary Problem for Your Review

PROBLEM

Refer to the Lopez Plastics illustration, starting with the financial reports based on the traditional cost accounting system in panel B of Exhibit 4-6, p. 138. Based on these reports, a marketing manager has proposed a plan that emphasizes cell phone casings due to their large gross profit margin (38.75%) compared to that of pen casings (1.25%).

Now, management implements the ABC system shown in Exhibit 4-7, p. 139. The first stage of the two-stage ABC system has been completed, and the results are the activity-cost-pool figures given in Exhibit 4-7—processing activity costs of $143,000 and production-support activity costs of $77,000. You need to perform the second-stage allocations to determine the profitability of each product line. The cost-allocation base for processing activity is direct-labor hours and the cost-allocation base for production-support activity is number of distinct parts. Data on the use of these cost-allocation bases for the last quarter are as follows:

	Pen Casings	Cell Phone Casings
Direct-labor hours	4,500	500
Distinct parts	5	20

1. Calculate the gross profit and gross profit margin for each product based on ABC.
2. Explain why your results differ significantly from those based on the traditional cost accounting system in Exhibit 4-6, p. 138.
3. Evaluate marketing's plan.
4. Propose a product-mix strategy for the company.

SOLUTION

1. The table that follows shows the gross profit for each product using ABC costs.

Financial Reports for Lopez Plastics Company's Activity-Based Cost Allocation System

	Panel A Statement of Operating Income [External Reporting Purpose]	Panel B Contribution to Corporate Costs and Profit [Internal Strategic Decision-Making and Operational-Control Purposes]	
		Pen Casings	*Cell Phone Casings*
Sales	$440,000	$360,000	$ 80,000
Cost of goods sold:			
Direct material	34,500	22,500	12,000
Direct labor	150,000	135,000	15,000
Processing activity	143,000	128,700*	14,300
Production-support activity	77,000	15,400†	61,600
Cost of goods sold	404,500	301,600	102,900
Gross profit	35,500	$ 58,400	$(22,900)
Corporate expenses			
(Unallocated):	100,000		
Operating loss	$(64,500)		
Gross profit margin	8.07%	16.22%	(28.63%)

* The cost driver is direct-labor hours. The company used $4,500 \div (4,500 + 500) = 90\%$ of direct-labor hours to produce pen casings. Thus, the allocation is $\$143,000 \times .90 = \$128,700$.
† The cost driver is distinct parts. The company used $5 \div (20 + 5) = 20\%$ of distinct parts to make pen casings. Thus, the allocation is $\$77,000 \times .20 = \$15,400$.

2. The ABC system gives results that are dramatically different from those of the traditional cost allocation system. Pen casings are generating substantial profits for the company, while cell phone casings are losing money. Why is there such a dramatic difference between the two cost accounting systems? It's because the traditional cost accounting system doesn't recognize differences in the production process for each of the two products. The ABC system separates the processing-related costs from the production-support costs and allocates each activity cost to the products based on the proportion of the activity used by each product. Only the cell phone casings require large amounts of the production-support activity. The ABC system correctly allocates most of this cost to the cell phone casings, while the traditional system allocates most of it to the pen casings.

3. Marketing's plan most likely will result in significantly lower profitability. The company's top management should make the strategic decision to emphasize pen casings because of its large gross profit margin when accurately measured.

4. The cell phone casings are losing money, so management should carefully evaluate that product line. Possible actions include raising prices, changing the design by reducing the number of distinct parts, working with suppliers to reduce the cost of direct materials, improving the efficiency of direct labor, or dropping the product line.

Objective 8

Use activity-based management (ABM) to make strategic and operational control decisions.

activity-based management (ABM)

Using the output of an activity-based cost accounting system to aid strategic decision making and to improve operational control of an organization.

value-added cost

The necessary cost of an activity that cannot be eliminated without affecting a product's value to the customer.

non-value-added costs

Costs that a company can eliminate without affecting a product's value to the customer.

benchmarking

The continuous process of comparing products, services, and activities against the best industry standards.

Activity-Based Management: A Cost Management System Tool

Because ABC systems focus on costs of activities (as well as costs of products), they are a very useful tool in cost management systems. **Activity-based management (ABM)** uses the output of an activity-based cost accounting system to aid strategic decision making and to improve operational control of an organization. The strategic decision to emphasize pen casings at Lopez Plastics is an example of ABM. In the broadest terms, ABM aims to improve the value received by customers and to improve profits by identifying opportunities for improvements in strategy and operations.

One of the most useful applications of ABM is distinguishing between value-added and non-value-added costs. A **value-added cost** is the cost of an activity that a company cannot eliminate without affecting a product's value to the customer. Value-added costs are necessary (though there may be ways to lower value-added costs by performing activities more efficiently). In contrast, companies try to eliminate (or at least minimize) **non-value-added costs**, costs that a company can eliminate without affecting a product's value to the customer. Activities such as handling and storing inventories, transporting partly finished products from one part of the plant to another, and changing the setup of production-line operations to produce a different model of the product are all non-value-adding activities. A company can often reduce, if not eliminate, some of these costs by careful redesign of the plant layout and the production process.

Another useful management technique is **benchmarking**, the continuous process of comparing products, services, and activities to the best industry standards. Benchmarking is a tool to help an organization measure its competitive posture. Benchmarks can come from within the organization, from competing organizations, or from other organizations having similar processes.

Consider the production of laptops at Dell. Unit costs for key activities provide the basis for benchmarking the work groups in one production facility with those at others and possibly with industry standards. In addition, Dell can use the cost-allocation bases for key activities—for example, the time to assemble a motherboard—as operational benchmarks. The most efficient work groups and centers can share their ideas for process improvements with other groups and centers.

Companies must exercise caution when benchmarking, especially when using financial benchmarks. For example, consider comparison of branches in Chico and San Francisco for a California bank. The bank's benchmarking system uses the financial benchmark *cost per deposit* to measure deposit-processing efficiency. The San Francisco branch managers pointed out at least two problems that put them at a disadvantage. First, costs, especially labor costs, differ between Chico and San Francisco. Employees in metropolitan areas generally receive higher salaries because of their higher cost of living. Therefore, higher teller salaries in San Francisco increase the cost per deposit. Second, different branches can implement an ABC system in different ways. In this case, Chico's ABC system does not allocate equipment depreciation to the deposit-processing activity; these costs remain unallocated. In contrast, the San Francisco branch allocates this cost to the processing activity. This causes the cost per deposit to be higher at the San Francisco branches. As a result, even if the tellers process deposits faster and more accurately at the San Francisco branch, their performance will not appear to be as good as that of the tellers at the Chico branch. A better measure of the deposit process might be the *time to process* a *deposit*, a nonfinancial benchmark that is more directly controllable by the respective branch managers.

Benefits of Activity-Based Costing and Activity-Based Management

Activity-based costing systems are more complex and costly than traditional systems. Thus, companies that have relatively simple operations may not realize sufficient benefits to warrant the additional cost of an ABC system. But more organizations in both manufacturing and non-manufacturing industries are adopting activity-based costing systems for a variety of reasons:

- Fierce competitive pressure has resulted in shrinking profit margins. Companies may know their overall margin, but they often do not have confidence in the accuracy of the margins for individual products or services. Some are winners and some are losers—but which ones are which? Accurate costs are essential for answering this question. Consider Taylor Corporation, one of the largest specialty printers in the United States with annual sales of more than $1.3 billion. One of its operating divisions implemented an ABC system to provide better information on the profitability of more than 3,500 products. Managers used the ABC information to set an optimal product mix and to estimate the profit margins of new products.

- Greater diversity in the types of products and customers results in greater operating complexity. Often in such situations the consumption of a company's shared resources also varies substantially across products and customers—a condition that adds to the value of ABC systems.
- Indirect costs are far more important in today's automated world-class manufacturing environment than they have been in the past. In many industries, automated equipment is replacing direct labor. Indirect costs are sometimes more than 50% of total cost. Because ABC systems focus on indirect costs, they are more common in companies with automated production processes.
- The rapid pace of technological change has shortened product life cycles. Hence, companies do not have time to make price or cost adjustments once they discover costing errors. The accurate costs produced by ABC systems are essential.
- The costs associated with bad decisions that result from inaccurate cost estimates are substantial. Examples include bids lost due to overcosted products, hidden losses from undercosted products, and failure to detect activities that are not cost effective. Companies with accurate ABC product costs have a competitive advantage over those with inaccurate costs.
- Computer technology has reduced the costs of developing and operating ABC systems. Most ERP systems (see p. 16) routinely include ABC modules.

While many companies throughout the world are adopting ABC systems, some German companies, including Gruen Telekom and DaimlerChrysler, have gone a step further. They use a cost accounting system called **Grenzplankostenrechnung (GPK)**. Most GPK systems use between 400 and 2,000 cost pools to allocate indirect manufacturing costs. The Business First box on p. 144 summarizes some of the characteristics of GPK.

Grenzplankostenrechnung (GPK)
A German cost accounting system that goes a step further than ABC systems.

Highlights to Remember

1. **Describe the purposes of cost management systems.** Cost management systems provide cost information for external financial reporting, for strategic decision making, and for operational cost control.

2. **Explain the relationship among cost, cost object, cost accumulation, and cost assignment.** Cost accounting systems provide cost information about various types of objects—products, customers, activities, and so on. To do this, a system first accumulates resource costs by natural classifications, such as materials, labor, and energy. Then, it assigns these costs to cost objects, either tracing them directly or assigning them indirectly through allocation.

3. **Distinguish between direct and indirect costs.** Accountants can specifically and exclusively identify direct costs with a cost object in an economically feasible way. When this is not possible, accountants may allocate costs to cost objects using a cost driver. Such costs are called indirect costs. The greater the proportion of direct costs, the greater the accuracy of the cost system. When the proportion of indirect costs is significant, accountants must take care to find the most appropriate cost drivers.

4. **Explain the major reasons for allocating costs.** The four main purposes of cost allocation are to predict the economic effects of planning and control decisions, to motivate managers and employees, to measure the costs of inventory and cost of goods sold, and to justify costs for pricing or reimbursement. Some costs remain unallocated because the accountants can determine no plausible and reliable relationship between resource costs and cost objects.

5. **Identify the main types of manufacturing costs: direct-materials costs, direct-labor costs, and indirect production costs.** Accountants can trace direct-materials costs and direct-labor costs to most cost objects, but they allocate indirect production costs using a cost-allocation base.

Business First

GPK and ABC: Support for Short-Term and Long-Term Decisions

Many companies throughout the world have developed sophisticated cost accounting systems. While many U.S. companies have adopted ABC, many northern European companies, especially in France, Norway, Sweden, the Netherlands, and Germany, are increasingly using GPK, a system first developed 50 years ago in Germany. Among the GPK companies are **Porsche**, **STIHL**, **Gruen Telekom**, and **DaimlerChrysler**.

Advances in computer technology have made widespread use of these cost accounting systems more practical. When companies adopt Enterprise Resource Planning (ERP) systems that include software for ABC and GPK, they can upgrade their cost accounting systems without a huge additional investment. The ERP system of **SAP**, a German software company that helped pioneer such systems, offers the framework for GPK as part of its management accounting module, a main factor in the expanding use of GPK.

ABC and GPK embody both similarities and differences. Both allocate costs to products, services, or customers using multiple cost pools with various cost-allocation bases. A main difference is that GPK separates fixed and variable costs and applies only variable costs to products or services. Although the ABC approach could do the same, most ABC systems focus on applying all production-related costs (and, often, some nonproduction value-chain costs). Thus, GPK systems measure profitability on a contribution-margin basis, while ABC systems generally produce full-cost margins. Another difference between ABC and GPK is how they define cost pools for allocation. ABC companies focus on activities, with only a few major identified activities. In contrast, GPK companies focus on cost centers and may have thousands of them. Gruen Telekom has about 20,000, although Porsche has only 450,

and most companies have between 400 and 2,000. Most cost centers are work units of only a few people, often 10 workers or fewer. In both systems, the cost center or activity is the focus of day-to-day cost control. The GPK systems bring this focus down to a much lower level than do most ABC systems.

Which is best, ABC or GPK? Like many management accounting issues, the answer is "it depends." Because GPK focuses on contribution margins, it provides information that is more relevant for short-term decisions. In contrast, ABC starts with a long-term perspective and produces information more suited to strategic decisions. However, GPK systems can add a full-cost calculation for long-term decision purposes, and many ABC systems can separate fixed and variable costs for short-term decisions. Further, the difference between cost-center and activity-based cost pools may not be especially significant because underlying cost pools and cost drivers can be similar in both systems. Although there remain basic philosophical differences related to allocation of fixed costs and definitions of cost pools, in practice companies that use a combination of GPK and ABC principles may find the best of both worlds. For example, the **Hospital for Sick Children** in Toronto merged GPK with its ABC system to produce financial information that was more useful to management.

Sources: G. Frield, H. Kupper, and B. Pedell, "Relevance Added: Combining ABC with German Cost Accounting," *Strategic Finance*, June 2005, pp. 56–61; K. Krumwiede, "Rewards and Realities of German Cost Accounting," *Strategic Finance*, April 2005, pp. 27–34; Carl S. Smith, "Going for GPK," *Strategic Finance*, April 2005, pp. 36–39; Brian Mackie, "Merging GPK and ABC on the Road to RCA," *Strategic Finance*, November 2006, pp. 33–39; P. Sharman and B. Mackie, "Grenzplankostenrechnung (GPK): German Cost Accounting, Flexible Planning and Control," IMA Web site, http://www.imanet.org/pdf/3202.pdf.

6. **Explain how the financial statements of merchandisers and manufacturers differ because of the types of goods they sell.** The primary difference between the financial statements of a merchandiser and a manufacturer is the reporting of inventories. A merchandiser has only one type of inventory, whereas a manufacturer has three types of inventory—raw materials, work in process, and finished goods.

7. **Understand the main differences between traditional and activity-based costing (ABC) systems and why ABC systems provide value to managers.** Traditional systems usually allocate only the indirect costs of the production function. ABC systems often allocate many of the costs of other value-chain functions. Traditional costing accumulates costs using categories such as direct material, direct labor, and production overhead. ABC systems accumulate costs by activities required to produce a product or service. The key value of ABC systems is in their increased costing accuracy and better information provided that can lead to process improvements.

8. **Use activity-based management (ABM) to make strategic and operational control decisions.** Activity-based management is using ABC information to improve operations. A key advantage of an activity-based costing system is its ability to aid managers in decision making. ABC improves the accuracy of cost estimates, including product and customer costs and the costs of value-added versus non-value-added activities. ABC also improves managers' understanding of operations. Managers can focus their attention on making strategic decisions, such as product mix, pricing, and process improvements. ∎

Appendix 4: Detailed Illustration of Traditional and Activity-Based Cost Accounting Systems

As we mentioned in the chapter, ABC systems are more complex than traditional systems. In this appendix, we go more in depth than in the Lopez Plastics Company example. You will notice, however, that the main concepts are exactly the same—only the details will change.

Suppose the billing department of one of **AT&T**'s smaller customer care centers requires accurate and useful information about the cost of providing account inquiry and bill printing services for its 120,000 residential and 20,000 commercial customer accounts. A local service bureau has offered to provide all the services currently performed by the billing department at $4.30 per residential account and $8.00 per commercial account. To make informed decisions, AT&T's managers need accurate estimates of the billing department's cost per residential account and cost per commercial account. They also need to know the costs of the key activities performed in the department to determine whether they can achieve cost savings through better control of their activities.

Exhibit 4-8 depicts the residential and commercial customer classes (cost objects) and the resources used to support the billing department. All the costs incurred in the department

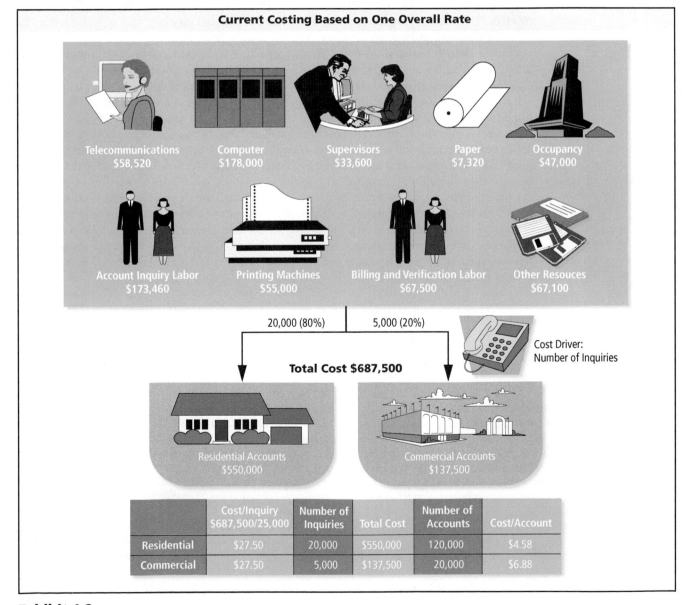

Exhibit 4-8
Traditional Costing System at the Billing Department

are indirect. There are no direct costs and no unallocated costs. The billing department currently uses a traditional costing system that allocates all indirect production costs based on the number of account inquiries.

Exhibit 4-8 shows that the cost of resources used in the billing department last month was $687,500. The traditional cost accounting system simply allocates this entire pool of indirect costs based on the number of inquiries the department receives from each customer class. The billing department received 25,000 account inquiries during the month, so the cost per inquiry was $687,500 ÷ 25,000 = $27.50. There were 20,000 residential account inquiries, 80% of the total. Thus, the traditional system assigns 80% of the indirect production cost to residential accounts and 20% to commercial accounts. The resulting cost per account is ($687,500 × 80%) ÷ 120,000 = $4.58 and ($687,500 × 20%) ÷ 20,000 = $6.88 for residential and commercial accounts, respectively. Does this traditional cost accounting system provide managers with accurate estimates of the cost to serve residential and commercial customers? If the answer is yes, the billing department management should accept the service bureau's proposal to service residential accounts because of the apparent savings of $4.58 − $4.30 = $.28 per account. The billing department should continue to service its commercial accounts because its costs are $8.00 − $6.88 = $1.12 less than the service bureau's bid. However, if the estimates of the cost to serve customers are not accurate, managers should develop more accurate cost estimates.

Suppose you are the billing department manager and you know that billing employees spend much of their time verifying the accuracy of commercial bills and very little time verifying residential bills. Yet the traditional cost accounting system allocates 80% of the costs of this work to residential customers. Does this make sense to you? Are you starting to doubt the accuracy of the cost-per-account data? Do you see a way to improve the assignment of billing labor costs to customers?

Suppose you also know that commercial accounts average 50 lines or two pages per bill, compared with only 12 lines or one page for residential accounts. This means that the billing department uses much more paper, computer time, and printing machine time for each commercial account. Further, suppose you believe that the actual consumption of support resources for commercial accounts is much greater than 20% because of their complexity. Again, your understanding of what drives costs does not fit with the traditional system allocation of 80% of costs to residential accounts and 20% to commercial accounts based on number of inquiries.

In summary, you would probably conclude that AT&T needs to improve the billing department's traditional cost accounting system because it is not providing managers with useful information for strategic decisions. You might also believe that a better cost accounting system would help management understand the relationships among key activities and resource costs. This is exactly what AT&T's management concluded. So, next we will design an activity-based costing system for the billing department.

Making Managerial Decisions

Suppose **AT&T**'s management retains its traditional cost accounting system but believes that a more plausible and reliable cost driver is "number of printed lines." Each residential bill averages 12 lines and each commercial bill averages 50 lines. What would be the new cost per account for residential and commercial customers based on number of lines per bill? How would this new cost accounting information affect the outsourcing decision?

Answer
The allocation of the total cost to each customer class would change. Instead of allocating 80% of total costs to residential customers, we would allocate only (12 × 120,000) ÷ [(12 × 120,000) + (50 × 20,000)] = 59% of total costs to residential customers and the other 41% to commercial accounts. The cost per account for residential customers would then be (59% × $687,500) ÷ 120,000 = $3.38, and the cost per commercial account would be (41% × $687,500) ÷ 20,000 = $14.09. The outsourcing decision would change because the cost per residential account is now less than the cost of outsourcing, and the cost per commercial account is not greater than the cost of outsourcing. Thus, we would outsource commercial accounts but not residential accounts. This example illustrates again how different costing systems can lead to very different decisions.

Design of an Activity-Based Cost Accounting System

Describe the steps in designing an activity-based costing system.

How do managers actually design ABC systems? At the billing department of AT&T's customer-care center, a team of managers from the billing department and AT&T's regional controller used the following four-step procedure to design their new cost accounting system.

Step 1: Determine the Key Components of the Activity-Based Cost Accounting System

The key components of an activity-based cost accounting system are cost objects, key activities, resources, and related cost drivers. These components, together with the purpose of the new system, determine the scope of the ABC system. Management at AT&T wanted the system to (1) determine the billing department cost per account for each customer class to better support the strategic decision regarding outsourcing accounts to the local service bureau and (2) enhance the managers' understanding of key billing department activities to support operational cost control. Because the bid from the local service bureau includes performing all the activities of the department, the ABC system must include all department costs. Further, because management wants to understand the key activities and related costs, the team designed an activity-based system.

Through interviews with the department supervisors, management identified the following activities and related cost drivers to use as cost-allocation bases for the billing department.

Activity	Cost-Allocation Base
Account billing	Number of printed pages
Bill verification	Number of accounts verified
Account inquiry	Number of inquiries
Correspondence	Number of letters
Other activities	Number of printed pages

The four key billing department activities are account billing, bill verification, account inquiry, and correspondence. These activities require the vast majority of the work done in the billing department. There are other activities performed in the billing department, such as routine printer and computer maintenance, training, and preparing monthly reports. Management did not identify these as individual activities. Instead, the team lumped them together and labeled them "other activities." Why? Because the cost of the resources used for each of these individual activities was relatively small, the team could not find plausible and reliable cost drivers for them, or the cost of collecting data was too high. The cost-allocation base selected for the "other activities" cost pool is number of printed pages because most of the other activities, such as maintenance and training, are associated in some way with the printing function.

Step 2: Determine the Relationships Among Cost Objects, Activities, and Resources

An important phase of any activity-based analysis is identifying the relationships among key activities and the resources consumed. The management team does this by interviewing personnel and analyzing various internal data. AT&T interviewed all employees as part of its ABC study. For example, the company asked supervisors how they spend their time. Based on time records, the supervisors estimated that they spend most of their time (40%) supervising account inquiry activity. They also estimated that they spend about 30% of their time supervising billing activity and about 10% of their time reviewing and signing correspondence. They spend the remaining 20% of their time on all other department activities. Exhibit 4-9 shows the results of the interviews.

Implementing an ABC system requires a careful study of operations. As a result, managers often discover that they can trace directly to cost objects some previously indirect or even unallocated costs, thus improving the accuracy of product or service costs. During interviews with the billing department supervisors, the ABC team learned that several of the billing employees work exclusively on verification of commercial bills. Thus, the team could separate the $67,500 of Billing and Verification Labor shown in Exhibit 4-8 into two cost pools. The first pool is the salaries of the employees that work exclusively on verification of commercial bills—$11,250. The team could trace this cost pool, now labeled as Verification Labor, directly to the commercial customer cost object. Let's examine the second pool, the remaining $56,250, now labeled as Billing Labor Expenses.

Look at the Computer resource row in Exhibit 4-9. The supervisor indicated that 45% of this resource supports account inquiry, 5% supports correspondence, and so on. How did the supervisor determine these percentages? Initially, he or she might simply estimate them. Later, the supervisor might gather data to support the estimates. Now consider the Occupancy resource row. The percentages used to allocate this resource might be based on the square feet used by the various employees for each activity compared to the total square feet in the department.

Next, the team determined which activities were needed by each cost object. The supervisors indicated that residential customers needed account inquiry, correspondence, and billing activities. Commercial customers needed account inquiry, correspondence, billing, and verification activities. Both also need other activities.

The process map in Exhibit 4-10 incorporates the information gathered from interviews. We allocate the costs of the 10 resources to the 5 activities based on the percentage of each resource used by each activity. For example, account inquiry activity consumes 40% of supervisor resources, 90% of account inquiry labor, 45% of computer resources, 90% of telecommunication resources, and 65% of occupancy costs. Then, we allocate the costs of the five activities to the two customer cost objects—residential and commercial. For example, commercial accounts require account inquiry, correspondence, billing, verification, and other activities. We allocate the activity costs based on a measure of the amount of activity that each customer uses. For example, we allocate the account inquiry activity cost pool based on the number of inquiries received from residential and commercial accounts.

Process maps can be a key tool for managers to gain an understanding of operations. For example, AT&T's managers considered this process map critical because it revealed how AT&T conducted business. Managers were able to see how operating activities consume costly resources. The ABC team used the process map as a guide for the next step in designing the ABC system—data collection. (Note that Exhibit 4-10 includes data on costs and cost drivers that is collected in Step 3, described next.)

Step 3: Collect Relevant Data Concerning Costs and the Physical Flow of the Cost-Driver Units Among Resources and Activities

Using the process map as a guide, billing department managers collected the required cost and operational data by further interviews with relevant personnel. Sources of data include the accounting records, special studies, and sometimes "best estimates of managers." The managers collected resource cost information from the general ledger (Exhibit 4-8) and data on the flow of cost drivers from various operational reports (Exhibits 4-9 and 4-11). Exhibit 4-10 shows the data collected. Management can now use the completed process map to determine costs for the strategic and operational decisions that they must make.

Resource Used to Perform Activity	Activity Performed					
	Account Inquiry Activity	Correspondence Activity	Billing Activity	Verification Activity	All Other Activities	Total
Supervisor	40%	10%	30%		20%	100%
Account inquiry labor	90	10				100%
Billing labor			30	70		100%
Verification labor				100		100%
Paper			100			100%
Computer	45	5	35	10	5	100%
Telecommunications	90				10	100%
Occupancy	65		15		20	100%
Printing machines		5	90		5	100%
All other department resources					100	100%

Exhibit 4-9

Analysis of Interviews with Supervisors from the Billing Department

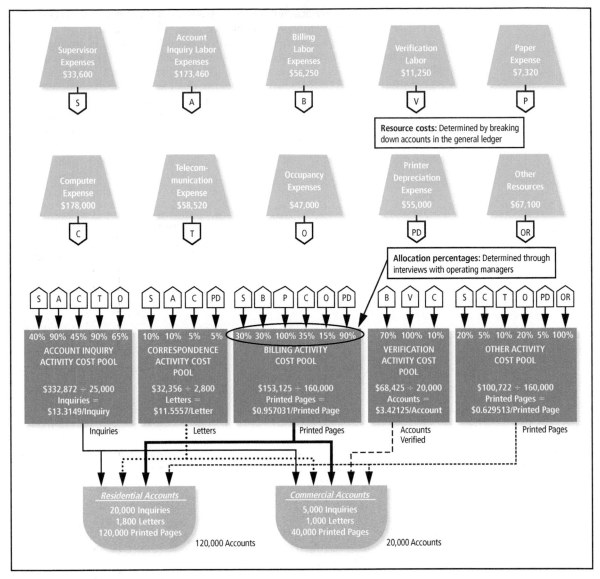

Exhibit 4-10
Two-Stage Cost Allocation for Billing Department Operations

		Number of Cost Driver Units		
Activity	Cost Driver Units	Residential	Commercial	Total
Account inquiry	Inquiries	20,000	5,000	25,000
Correspondence	Letters	1,800	1,000	2,800
Billing	Printed pages	120,000	40,000	160,000
Verification	Accounts verified		20,000	20,000
Other activities	Printed pages	120,000	40,000	160,000

Exhibit 4-11
Number of Cost Driver Units for the Billing Department

Step 4: Calculate and Interpret the New Activity-Based Cost Information

After collecting all required financial and operational data, we can calculate the new activity-based information. Exhibit 4-12 summarizes stage 1 allocations. It shows the total costs for each of the five activity cost pools. Notice that the total costs of $332,872 + $32,356 + $153,125 + $68,425 + $100,722 = $687,500 in Exhibit 4-12 equals the total indirect costs in Exhibit 4-8. Now we can determine the activity-based cost per account for each customer class (stage 2 allocations) from the data in step 3. Exhibit 4-13 shows the computations.

Examine the last two rows in Exhibit 4-13. Notice that traditional costing overcosted the high-volume residential accounts and substantially undercosted the low-volume, complex commercial accounts. The cost per account for residential accounts using ABC is $3.98, which is $0.60 (or 13%) less than the $4.58 cost generated by the traditional costing system. The cost per account for commercial accounts is $10.50, which is $3.62 (or 53%) more than the $6.88 cost from the traditional costing system. The analysis confirms management's belief that the traditional system undercosted commercial accounts. AT&T's management now has more accurate cost information for strategic decision-making and cost-control purposes.

Resource	Cost (from Exhibit 4-8)	Account Inquiry	Correspondence	Billing	Verification	Other
			Activity Cost Pool			
Supervisors	$ 33,600	$ 13,440*	$ 3,360**	$ 10,080***		$ 6,720****
Account inquiry labor	173,460	156,114	17,346			
Billing labor	56,250			16,875	$39,375	
Verification labor	11,250				11,250	
Paper	7,320			7,320		
Computer	178,000	80,100	8,900	62,300	17,800	8,900
Telecommunication	58,520	52,668				5,852
Occupancy	47,000	30,550		7,050		9,400
Printers	55,000		2,750	49,500		2,750
Other resources	67,100					67,100
Total cost	$687,500	$332,872	$32,356	$153,125	$68,425	$100,722

*From Exhibits 4-9 and 4-10, account inquiry activity uses 40% of the supervisor resource. So the allocation is 40% × $33,600 = $13,440.
**10% × $33,600
***30% × $33,600
****20% × $33,600

Exhibit 4-12
Total Cost of Each Activity in the Billing Department

Strategic Decisions, Operational Cost Control, and ABM

Now let's see how billing department managers can use the ABC system to improve their strategic decisions and operational cost control. Suppose that the billing department needed to find a way to increase its capacity to handle more accounts due to an expected large increase in demand from a new housing development and a business center. Managers proposed a strategic action—outsource certain customer accounts to a local service bureau. Billing department managers were also interested in reducing the operating costs of the department while not impairing the quality of the service it provided to its customers. To address both of these issues, they used the ABC information from Exhibit 4-13 to identify non-value-added activities that had significant costs. Account inquiry and bill verification activities are non-value-added and costly so management asked for ideas for cost reductions. The new information provided by the ABC system generated the following ideas:

- Use the service bureau for commercial accounts because of the significant cost savings. From Exhibit 4-13, the service bureau's bid is $8.00 per account, compared to the billing department's activity-based cost of $10.50, a potential savings of $2.50 per account! In addition, department managers would try to eliminate or reduce bill verification, commercial account inquiry, and commercial account correspondence activities, all non-value-adding activities.

	Driver Costs		
Activity (Driver Units)	Total Costs (from Exhibit 4-12) (1)	Total Number of Driver Units (From Exhibit 4-11) (2)	Cost per Driver Unit (1) ÷ (2)
Account inquiry (inquiries)	$332,872	25,000 Inquiries	$13.314880
Correspondence (letters)	$ 32,356	2,800 Letters	$11.555714
Account billing (printed pages)	$153,125	160,000 Printed pages	$ 0.957031
Bill verification (accounts verified)	$ 68,425	20,000 Accounts verified	$ 3.421250
Other activities (printed pages)	$100,722	160,000 Printed pages	$ 0.629513

		Cost per Customer Class			
		Residential		Commercial	
	Cost per Driver Unit	Number of Driver Units	Cost	Number of Driver Units	Cost
Account inquiry	$13.314880	20,000 Inquiries	$266,298	5,000 Inquiries	$ 66,574
Correspondence	$11.555714	1,800 Letters	20,800	1,000 Letters	11,556
Account billing	$ 0.957031	120,000 Pages	114,844	40,000 Pages	38,281
Bill verification	$ 3.421250			20,000 Accts.	68,425
Other activities	$ 0.629513	120,000 Pages	75,541	40,000 Pages	25,181
Total cost			$477,483		$210,017
Number of accounts			120,000		20,000
Cost per account			$ 3.98		$ 10.50
Cost per account, traditional system from Exhibit 4-8			$ 4.58		$ 6.88

Exhibit 4-13
Key Results of Activity-Based Costing Study

Suppose AT&T outsourced commercial customers to the service bureau. Would actual costs immediately decrease by $50,000 ($2.50 for each of 20,000 commercial accounts)? No, only the variable portion of resource costs, such as paper, variable telecommunication charges, variable computer charges, and overtime or part time labor, would decrease immediately. The fixed portion of resource costs would not change without some specific management actions. For example, suppose billing labor used for verification is a fixed-cost resource. The change in this cost will depend on whether management decides to lay off billing employees or to keep them in anticipation of the increase in printing activity due to the expected increase in residential customers.

- Exhibit 4-13 indicates that account inquiry activity is very costly, accounting for a significant portion of total billing department costs. A benchmarking analysis showed the cost per inquiry of $13.31 was unusually high compared to similar measures at other customer care centers. By meeting with managers from centers that had significantly lower activity cost rates, the billing department managers developed ideas for process improvements. One idea that resulted from these meetings was to implement a Web-based inquiry system to handle routine questions about bills.

The billing department, like so many companies that have adopted ABC and ABM, improved both strategic and operating decisions.

Summary Problem for Your Review

PROBLEM

Refer to the billing department illustration. Suppose that management at **AT&T**'S Youngstown area customer care center is implementing an ABC system. The center has 98,000 residential customers and 25,000 commercial customers. An ABC team has collected the data shown in Exhibit 4-14. Management has decided not to allocate the other resource costs.

Resource	Monthly Cost	Percent of Resource Used in Activity				
		Billing	Account Inquiry	Correspondence	Verification	Other
Supervisors	$ 30,500	40%	35%	8%		17%
Account inquiry labor	102,000		85	15		
Billing labor	45,000	70			30	
Paper	5,800	100				
Computers	143,000	30	48	7	10	5
Telecommunications	49,620		85			15
Occupancy	56,000	15	70			15
Printers	75,000	80		5		15
Other	59,000					100
Total	$565,920					

Activity	Cost Driver	Monthly Number of Cost Driver Units		
		Residential	Commercial	Total
Billing	Lines	1,176,000	1,250,000	2,426,000
Account inquiry	Inquiries	9,800	7,500	17,300
Correspondence	Letters	1,960	2,500	4,460
Verification	Accounts verified	49,000	12,500	61,500

Exhibit 4-14
First Stage Percentage Allocations and Monthly Number of Cost Driver Units

1. Using the same format as Exhibits 4-12 and 4-13, prepare schedules to determine the cost per driver unit for each activity and the activity-based cost per account for each customer type.
2. Consider the verification activity. Suppose the cost per account verified is $0.45. The center verifies 50% of residential and commercial bills. Given that there are, on average, 50 lines on each commercial bill and only 12 lines on each residential bill, criticize the use of accounts verified as a cost driver and suggest a more plausible and reliable cost driver.

SOLUTION

1. Exhibit 4-15 is a schedule showing the total cost of each activity of the billing department. From this we can determine the cost per driver unit and the activity-based cost per account for each customer class, as shown in Exhibit 4-16.
2. The ABC system allocates 49,000 ÷ (49,000 + 12,500) = 79.7% of verification costs to residential accounts based on the number of accounts verified. However, the work performed to verify a bill is probably closely related to the number of lines on the bill. Using "accounts verified" assumes that employees expend the same amount of effort verifying residential accounts and commercial accounts, even though there are many fewer lines on residential bills. Thus, the cost driver "lines verified" is more plausible and reliable. The number of lines verified for commercial accounts are 50 lines per

account × 12,500 accounts = 625,000 lines and for residential accounts are 12 lines per account × 49,000 accounts = 588,000 lines. Thus, we allocate 588,000 ÷ (588,000 + 625,000) = 48.5% of verification costs to residential accounts based on lines verified. ABC teams should always exercise care when choosing cost drivers to use as allocation bases. The Youngstown team might also want to investigate the plausibility and reliability of the "number of inquiries" cost driver because this assumes that residential and commercial customer inquiries require the same amount of work.

		Activity				
Resource	Cost (from Exhibit 4-14)	Billing	Account Inquiry	Correspondence	Verification	Other
Supervisors	$ 30,500	$ 12,200 *	$ 10,675**	$ 2,440***		$ 5,185****
Account inquiry labor	102,000		86,700	15,300		
Billing labor	45,000	31,500			$13,500	
Paper	5,800	5,800				
Computer	143,000	42,900	68,640	10,010	14,300	7,150
Telecommunication	49,620		42,177			7,443
Occupancy	56,000	8,400	39,200			8,400
Printers	75,000	60,000		3,750		11,250
Other resources	59,000					59,000
Total cost	$565,920	$160,800	$247,392	$31,500	$27,800	$98,428

*40% × $30,500
**35% × $30,500
***8% × $30,500
****17% × $30,500

Exhibit 4-15
Total Cost of Each Activity in the Billing Department

	Driver Costs		
Activity (Driver Units)	Total Costs (From Exhibit 4-15) (1)	Total Number of Driver Units (From Exhibit 4-14) (2)	Cost per Driver Unit (1) ÷ (2)
Account inquiry (inquiries)	$247,392	17,300 Inquiries	$14.300116
Correspondence (letters)	$ 31,500	4,460 Letters	$ 7.062780
Account billing (lines)	$160,800	2,426,000 Lines	$ 0.066282
Bill verification (accounts verified)	$ 27,800	61,500 Accounts Verified	$ 0.452033

	Cost per Customer Class				
		Residential		Commercial	
	Cost per Driver Unit	Number of Driver Units	Cost	Number of Driver Units	Cost
Account inquiry	$14.300116	9,800 Inquiries	$140,141	7,500 Inquiries	$107,251
Correspondence	$ 7.062780	1,960 Letters	13,843	2,500 Letters	17,657
Account billing	$ 0.066282	1,176,000 Lines	77,947	1,250,000 Lines	82,853
Bill verification	$ 0.452033	49,000 Accounts	22,149	12,500 Accounts	5,650
Total cost			$254,081		$213,411
Number of accounts			98,000		25,000
Cost per account			$ 2.59		$ 8.54

Exhibit 4-16
Cost Per Driver Unit and Activity-Based Cost Per Account

Accounting Vocabulary

activity-based costing (ABC)
    system, p. 135
activity-based management
    (ABM), p. 142
benchmarking, p. 142
cost, p. 124
cost accounting, p. 124
cost accounting system, p. 124
cost accumulation, p. 125
cost allocation, p. 126
cost assignment, p. 125
cost management system
    (CMS), p. 123
cost object, p. 124
cost objective, p. 124
cost pool, p. 128
cost-allocation base, p. 126

direct costs, p. 126
direct-labor costs, p. 131
direct-material costs, p. 131
direct-material
    inventory, p. 132
factory burden, p. 131
factory overhead, p. 131
finished-goods
    inventory, p. 132
Grenzplankostenrechnung
    (GPK), p. 143
indirect costs, p. 126
indirect manufacturing costs,
    p. 131
indirect production costs,
    p. 131
inventoriable costs, p. 131

manufacturing
    overhead, p. 131
non-value-added costs, p. 142
period costs, p. 131
process map, p. 135
product costs, p. 131
raw material, p. 131
raw-material inventory, p. 132
tracing, p. 126
traditional costing
    system, p. 135
two-stage ABC system, p. 138
unallocated costs, p. 129
value-added cost, p. 142
work-in-process
    inventory, p. 132

MyAccountingLab # Fundamental Assignment Material

4-A1 Direct, Indirect, and Unallocated Costs, Process Map

Penguin Window Company makes and sells three product lines—custom detailed windows, large standard windows, and small standard windows. The statement of operating income for the most recent period is shown below.

Penguin uses a traditional cost accounting system. A process map developed to describe this system is shown in Exhibit 4-17. To aid in the company's analysis of its product mix strategy, you have been asked to determine operating income (loss) for each product line. Use a format similar to Exhibit 4-3 on page 130 in the text.

Penguin Window Company Statement of Operating Income		
		Total
Sales		$307,900
Cost of goods sold		
Direct material	$47,800	
Indirect production costs	50,000	97,800
Gross profit		210,100
Selling and administrative expenses:		
Commissions	14,800	
Distribution to warehouses	10,900	25,700
Income before unallocated expenses		184,400
Unallocated expenses		
Administrative salaries	8,200	
Other administrative expenses	4,500	12,700
Operating income before taxes		$ 171,700

4-A2 Financial Statements for Manufacturing and Merchandising Companies

Annandale, Inc., produces and sells wireless reading devices. A competitor, Danube Electronic Products, sells similar wireless reading devices that it purchases at wholesale from Sonex

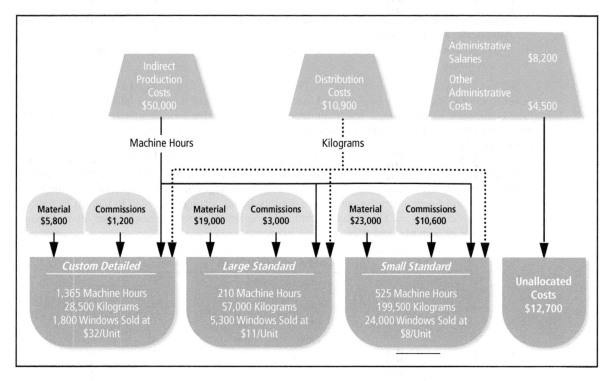

Exhibit 4-17

Process Map for Penguin Window Company's Traditional Cost Allocation System

for $75 each. Both sell the devices for $180. In 20X9 Annandale produced 12,000 devices at the following costs:

Direct materials purchased		$530,000
Direct materials used		$490,000
Direct labor		200,000
Indirect production:		
Depreciation	$ 35,000	
Indirect labor	20,000	
Other	155,000	210,000
Total cost of production		$900,000

Assume that Annandale had no beginning inventory of direct materials. Neither company had any beginning inventory of finished devices, but both had ending inventory of 2,500 finished devices. Ending work-in-process inventory for Annandale was negligible.

Each company sold 9,500 devices for $1,710,000 in 20X9 and incurred the following selling and administrative costs:

Sales salaries and commissions	$110,000
Depreciation on retail store	45,000
Advertising	10,000
Other	5,000
Total selling and administrative cost	$170,000

1. Prepare the inventories section of the balance sheet for December 31, 20X9, for Danube.
2. Prepare the inventories section of the balance sheet for December 31, 20X9, for Annandale.
3. Using the cost of goods sold format on page 134 as a model, prepare an income statement for the year 20X9 for Danube.
4. Using the cost of goods sold format on page 134 as a model, prepare an income statement for the year 20X9 for Annandale.

5. Summarize the differences between the financial statements of Danube, a merchandiser, and Annandale, a manufacturer.
6. What purpose of a cost management system is being served by reporting the items in requirements 1–4?

4-A3 Activities, Resources, Cost Drivers, and the Banking Industry

Silver Springs Bank is a local bank located in a residential area, and it services mostly individuals and local businesses. Silver Springs' four main services are transaction processing (withdrawals, checks, currency exchange), loans, simple investments (individual clients), and complex investments (portfolios of large businesses).

To support these activities, Silver Springs employs 10 front-office staff, 12 back-office staff dealing with loan applications and investments, and 2 people to consult with customers and manage complex portfolio investments. A team of 3 supervisors manages the overall operations of the bank. As part of Silver Springs' implementation of activity-based costing, it needed to identify activities, resources, and cost drivers. The following table summarizes the cost-allocation bases Silver Springs has chosen for its activities and resources:

Cost-Allocation Base
number of investments
number of applications
number of loans
number of person hours
number of minutes
number of computer transactions
number of square feet
number of loan inquiries
number of transactions
number of schedules
number of securities

For each of the brief descriptions that follows, indicate whether it is an activity (A) or a resource (R). For each activity or resource, choose the most appropriate cost-allocation base from the preceding list and indicate for each resource whether it is a fixed-cost (F) or variable-cost (V) resource. The first item is completed as a guide.

a. Contract maintenance of building (R; number of square feet; F)
b. Staff for front-line customer service
c. External computing services
d. Development of repayment schedules
e. Staff for consulting with customers and arranging the portfolios
f. External service bureau providing customer credit checks for loan applications
g. Preparing investment documents for customers
h. Research to evaluate a loan application
i. Overtime by back-office staff
j. Telephones/facsimile
k. Staff for service and background research
l. Establish customer collateral for approved loans

4-A4 Activity-Based Costing in an Electronics Company

The wireless phone manufacturing division of a consumer electronics company uses activity-based costing. For simplicity, assume that its accountants have identified only the following three activities and related cost drivers for indirect production costs:

Activity	Cost Driver
Materials handling	Direct-materials cost
Engineering	Engineering change notices
Power	Kilowatt hours

Three types of cell phones are produced: Senior, Basic, and Deluxe. Direct costs and cost-driver activity for each product for a recent month are as follows:

	Senior	Basic	Deluxe
Direct-materials cost	$25,000	$ 60,000	$135,000
Direct-labor cost	$14,546	$ 3,762	$ 6,772
Kilowatt hours	230,000	220,000	100,000
Engineering change notices	21	20	69

Indirect production costs for the month were as follows:

Materials handling	$ 15,400
Engineering	99,000
Power	11,000
Total indirect production cost	$125,400

1. Compute the indirect production costs allocated to each product with the ABC system.
2. Suppose all indirect production costs had been allocated to products in proportion to their direct-labor costs. Compute the indirect production costs allocated to each product.
3. In which product costs, those in requirement 1 or those in requirement 2, do you have the most confidence? Why?

4-B1 Direct, Indirect, and Unallocated Costs

Cambridge Tool Co. is a supplier that assembles purchased parts into components for three distinct markets—scooter parts, lawn mower parts, and hand tool parts. Following is the statement of operating income for the most recent period:

Cambridge Tool: Statement of Operating Income

		Total
Sales		$1,221,500
Cost of goods sold		
Direct material	$410,000	
Indirect production (allocated based on machine hours)	60,000	470,000
Gross profit		751,500
Selling and administrative expenses:		
Commissions	73,900	
Distribution to warehouses (allocated based on weight in kilograms)	135,000	208,900
Income before unallocated expenses		542,600
Unallocated expenses		
Corporate salaries	10,000	
Other general expenses	17,000	27,000
Operating income before taxes		$ 515,600

Cambridge Tool uses a traditional cost accounting system. Operating data used in the cost accounting system are as follows:

	Scooter Parts	Lawn Mower Parts	Hand Tool Parts
Purchase cost of parts assembled	$145,000	$175,000	$90,000
Machine hours	8,950	1,650	1,400
Weight of parts shipped to distributors (kilograms)	60,000	505,000	110,000
Sales commissions per unit	$ 4.30	$ 1.00	$ 0.40
Units assembled and sold	7,000	21,000	57,000
Sales price per unit	$ 80.00	$ 16.30	$ 5.60

You have been asked to determine operating income (loss) for each product line. Use a format similar to Exhibit 4-3 on p. 130.

4-B2 Allocation, Department Rates, and Direct-Labor Hours Versus Machine Hours

The Hernandez Manufacturing Company has two producing departments, machining and assembly. Mr. Hernandez recently automated the machining department. The installation of a CAM system, together with robotic workstations, drastically reduced the amount of direct labor required. Meanwhile, the assembly department remained labor intensive. The company had always used one firm-wide rate based on direct-labor hours as the cost-allocation base for applying all costs (except direct materials) to the final products. Mr. Hernandez was considering two alternatives: (1) continue using direct-labor hours as the only cost-allocation base, but use different rates in machining and assembly, and (2) using machine hours as the cost-allocation base in the machining department while continuing with direct-labor hours in assembly. Budgeted data for 20X0 are as follows:

	Machining	Assembly	Total
Total cost (except direct materials)	$540,000	$494,000	$1,034,000
Machine hours	90,000	*	90,000
Direct-labor hours	12,000	38,000	50,000

*Not applicable.

1. Suppose Hernandez continued to use one firm-wide rate based on direct-labor hours to apply all manufacturing costs (except direct materials) to the final products. Compute the cost-application rate that would be used.
2. Suppose Hernandez continued to use direct-labor hours as the only cost-allocation base but used different rates in machining and assembly.
   a. Compute the cost-application rate for machining.
   b. Compute the cost-application rate for assembly.
3. Suppose Hernandez changed the cost accounting system to use machine hours as the cost-allocation base in machining and direct-labor hours in assembly.
   a. Compute the cost-application rate for machining.
   b. Compute the cost-application rate for assembly.
4. Three products use the following machine hours and direct-labor hours:

	Machine Hours in Machining	Direct-Labor Hours in Machining	Direct-Labor Hours in Assembly
Product A	10.0	2.5	13.0
Product B	18.0	3.0	3.3
Product C	11.0	2.7	8.5

   a. Compute the manufacturing cost of each product (excluding direct materials) using one firm-wide rate based on direct-labor hours.
   b. Compute the manufacturing cost of each product (excluding direct materials) using direct-labor hours as the cost-allocation base, but with different cost-allocation rates in machining and assembly.
   c. Compute the manufacturing cost of each product (excluding direct materials) using a cost-allocation rate based on direct-labor hours in assembly and machine hours in machining.
   d. Compare and explain the results in requirements 4a, 4b, and 4c.

4-B3 Traditional Versus ABC Costing Systems

Yoko Iwabuchi is the controller of Kondo, Inc., an electronic controls company located in Osaka. She recently attended a seminar on activity-based costing (ABC) in Tokyo. Kondo's traditional cost accounting system has three cost categories: direct materials, direct labor, and indirect production costs. The company allocates indirect production costs on the basis of direct-labor cost. The following is the 20X0 budget for the automotive controls department (in thousands of Japanese yen):

Direct materials	¥ 55,000
Direct labor	28,368
Indirect production costs	21,276
Total cost	¥104,644

After Ms. Iwabuchi attended the seminar, she suggested that Kondo experiment with an ABC system in the Automotive Controls Department. She identified four main activities that cause indirect production costs in the department and selected a cost driver as a cost-allocation base for each activity as follows:

Activity	Cost-Allocation Base	Predicted 20X0 Cost (¥000)
Receiving	Direct-materials cost	¥ 6,600
Assembly	Number of control units	9,900
Quality control	QC hours	1,456
Shipping	Number of boxes shipped	3,320
TOTAL		¥21,276

In 20X0 the Automotive Controls Department expects to produce 99,000 control units, use 560 quality control hours, and ship 8,300 boxes.

1. Explain how Kondo, Inc., allocates its indirect production costs using its traditional cost system. Include a computation of the allocation rate used.
2. Explain how Kondo, Inc., would allocate indirect production costs under Ms. Iwabuchi's proposed ABC system. Include a computation of all the allocation rates used.
3. Suppose Kondo prices its products at 40% above total production cost. An order came in from Mazda for 9,000 control units. Iwabuchi estimates that filling the order will require ¥4,500,000 of direct-materials cost and ¥1,800,000 of direct labor. It will require 60 hours of QC inspection time and will be shipped in 670 boxes.
   a. Compute the price charged for the 9,000 control units if Kondo uses its traditional cost accounting system.
   b. Compute the price charged for the 9,000 control units if Kondo uses the ABC system proposed by Ms. Iwabuchi.
4 Explain why costs are different in the two costing systems. Include an indication of which costs you think are most accurate and why.

4-B4 Traditional Costing and ABC, Activity-Based Management

Refer to the text discussion of Lopez Plastics Company on pages 136–140. Assume that the company has the traditional cost accounting system described in Exhibit 4-6. The top management team wants to reverse the pattern of quarterly losses. The company president, Angie Oaks, has emphasized the importance of profit improvement by linking future pay raises of the two product-line managers to their respective gross profit margins. She is concerned about the profitability of the pen casing product line, while pleased with the profitability of the cell phone casing line. She also believes that the unallocated costs of the company are too high compared to competitors. The office of controller, whose costs are included in the unallocated costs, is responsible for vendor relations and purchasing of direct materials. The controller and head of the engineering department proposed 1) a price reduction, and 2) use of more standard parts:

> *We should use more standard parts in cell phone casings, which will dramatically reduce the purchasing department's work required for purchasing. I believe this should cut our office's costs by as much as $20,000 per quarter. Product engineering agrees that this idea is not only feasible but, if implemented, would substantially reduce the design work required for cell phone casings. Quality would also improve.*

Action	Predicted effects of action
Reduce prices of cell phone casings 25%.	The vice president of sales estimates that the improved quality of cell phone casings combined with the price reduction will yield a 100% increase in demand for cell phone casings per quarter.
Use standard parts wherever possible in cell phone casings.	The use of fewer suppliers will reduce vendor-relations work by the purchasing department. This will result in unallocated costs decreasing by $20,000.
	One of the two engineers can be let go at an annual cost savings of $80,000, which is $20,000 quarterly.
	Less of the plant and machinery will be used by production support so the allocation percentages will change from 75% and 25% to 80% and 20%. Much less engineer and CAD equipment costs will be needed for production support so these percentages will change from 80% and 20% to 50% and 50%.
	Processing time, measured in direct-labor hours, will increase by 500 hours due to an expected 100% increase in sales and production of cell phone casings, but there is adequate capacity of labor and machine time. Direct-labor costs are fixed as are all of the indirect production costs.
	Quality of cell phone casings will improve due to reduced complexity of processing.

1. Evaluate this idea using the traditional cost allocation system shown in Exhibit 4-6 on page 138. What would be the predicted profitability for each product line and the company as a whole? What would be the most likely level of support for the controller's idea by the product managers of the pen casing product line and the cell phone casing product line? What would be the level of support by the president?

2. Assume that you have the ABC system described in Exhibit 4-7 on page 139 with the gross margin percentages as shown in the table in the solution to the first Summary Problem for Your Review on page 140. Often, managers with ABC systems can anticipate more effects of improvement ideas because of their increased understanding of the operating system. In this case, although the total number of parts used would not change, the idea would reduce the number of distinct parts for cell phone casings from 20 to 11. Evaluate the controller's idea using the ABC system described in Exhibit 4-7. What would be the predicted profitability for each product line and the company as a whole? What would be the most likely level of support for the controller's idea by the product managers of the pen casing product line and the cell phone casing product line? What would be the level of support by the president?

3. As vice president, you have expressed concern about the traditional cost-allocation system's product-cost accuracy and its ability to provide relevant information for operational control. Does the new ABC system satisfy your concerns? Explain.

MyAccountingLab ## Additional Assignment Material

QUESTIONS

4-1 Define a cost management system and give its three purposes.

4-2 Cost management systems have three primary purposes. For each of the decisions listed next, indicate the purpose of the CMS being applied.

a. A production manager wants to know the cost of performing a setup for a production run in order to compare it to a target cost established as part of a process improvement program.

b. Top management wants to identify the profitability of several product lines to establish the optimum product mix.

c. Financial managers want to know the manufactured cost of inventory to appear on the balance sheet of the annual report.

4-3 Name four examples of cost objects.

4-4 "Products are the main cost objects. Departments are seldom cost objects." Do you agree? Explain.

4-5 What is the major purpose of detailed cost accounting systems?

4-6 What are the two major processes performed by a cost accounting system? Describe both of them.

4-7 Why are cost accounting systems critically important to managers?

4-8 Distinguish between direct, indirect, and unallocated costs.

4-9 "The same cost can be direct and indirect." Do you agree? Explain.

4-10 How does the idea of economic feasibility relate to the distinction between direct and indirect costs?

4-11 What are four purposes for cost allocation?

4-12 Why do companies assign all production costs and only production costs to products for external reporting purposes?

4-13 "A cost pool is a group of costs that accounting systems physically trace to the appropriate cost objective." Do you agree? Explain.

4-14 List five terms that are sometimes used as substitutes for the word *allocate*.

4-15 "The typical traditional accounting system does not allocate costs associated with value-chain functions other than production to units produced." Do you agree? Explain.

4-16 "It is better not to allocate some costs than to use a cost-allocation base that does not make any sense." Do you agree? Explain.

4-17 Production equipment maintenance, sales commissions, and process design costs are part of a company's costs. Identify which of these costs are most likely direct, indirect, and unallocated with respect to the products manufactured.

4-18 "For a furniture manufacturer, glue or tacks become an integral part of the finished product, so they would be direct material." Do you agree? Explain.

4-19 "Depreciation is a period expense for financial statement purposes." Do you agree? Explain.

4-20 Distinguish between costs and expenses.

4-21 Distinguish between manufacturing and merchandising companies. How do their accounting systems differ?

4-22 Why is there a direct-materials inventory account but no direct-labor inventory account on a manufacturing company's balance sheet?

4-23 "ABC systems are always more accurate than traditional costing systems." Do you agree? Explain.

4-24 Contrast activity-based costing (ABC) with activity-based management (ABM).

4-25 Explain how the layout of a plant's production equipment can reduce non-value-added costs.

4-26 Why do managers want to distinguish between value-added activities and non-value-added activities?

4-27 What is benchmarking? What do companies use it for? How do they determine benchmarks?

4-28 Why should caution be exercised when comparing company performance to benchmarks?

4-29 Why are more organizations adopting ABC systems?

4-30 (Appendix 4) Name four steps in the design and implementation of an ABC system.

CRITICAL THINKING EXERCISES

4-31 Marketing and Capacity Planning

A company has just completed its marketing plan for the coming year. When the company's management accountant entered the projected increases in sales volume into a process map (which relates activities and resources), the accountant discovered that the company will exceed several key resource capacities. What are three alternative courses of action to solve this dilemma?

4-32 ABC and ABM Compared

During seminars on ABM, participants often ask about the difference between ABC and ABM. Explain briefly. Why is this important to managers?

4-33 ABC for Product Costing and Operational Control

When companies implement an ABC system, they often use it first for product costing. Some managers think that is the only use for an ABC system. A typical comment is, "Activity-based allocation is useful for product costing, but not for operational control." Do you agree? Explain.

4-34 ABC and Cost Management Systems

Cost management systems have three primary purposes. Two of these are providing information for strategic and operational purposes. Companies often adopt ABC systems to increase the accuracy of cost information used by managers for strategic and operational decisions. Suppose a company produces only one product. This means that 100% of its costs are direct with respect to the product cost object. The accurate product unit cost is simply all costs incurred divided by the total units produced. Might this company be interested in an ABC system? Why or why not?

4-35 ABC and Benchmarking

Suppose that **AT&T** used benchmarking to compare the activity-based costs among its various divisions. As part of its benchmarking efforts, AT&T compared the activity cost per driver unit for similar activities and cost per customer for its billing departments in various geographic regions. For example, AT&T compared the costs at the Youngstown area billing department with the similar costs in the Los Angeles area. Are these meaningful comparisons? Why or why not?

EXERCISES

4-36 Classification of Manufacturing Costs

Costs are either direct or indirect depending on whether they can be traced to a cost object, and are either variable or fixed depending on whether they vary with changes in volume. Classify each of the following as direct (D) or indirect (I) with respect to a product as the cost object and as variable (V) or fixed (F). For each of the 10 items you will have two answers, D or I and V or F.

1. Factory rent
2. Salary of a factory storeroom clerk
3. Cement for a road builder
4. Supervisor training program
5. Abrasives (e.g., sandpaper)
6. Cutting bits in a machinery department
7. Food for a factory cafeteria
8. Workers' compensation insurance in a factory
9. Steel scrap for a blast furnace
10. Paper towels for a factory washroom

4-37 Confirm Your Understanding of the Classification of Manufacturing Costs

Classify each of the following as direct or indirect with respect to traceability to product and as variable or fixed with respect to whether the costs fluctuate in total as volume of production changes over wide ranges. Explain your classifications.

1. The cost of components that are assembled into a final product
2. The cost of supplies consumed when maintenance is performed on machines
3. The wages of machine operators who work on only one product
4. The cost of training mechanics who service processing machinery

4-38 Variable Costs and Fixed Costs; Manufacturing and Other Costs

For each of the numbered items, choose the appropriate classifications from the lettered items for a manufacturing company. If in doubt about whether the cost behavior is basically variable or fixed, decide on the basis of whether the total cost will fluctuate substantially over a wide range of volume. Most items have two answers among the following possibilities:

a. Manufacturing costs, direct
b. Manufacturing costs, indirect
c. General and administrative cost
d. Selling cost
e. Fixed cost
f. Variable cost
g. Other (specify)

Examples:

Direct material	a, f
President's salary	c, e
Bond interest expense	e, g (financial expense)

Items for your consideration:

1. Welding supplies
2. Salespersons' commissions
3. Salespersons' salaries
4. Supervisory salaries, production control
5. Supervisory salaries, assembly department
6. Supervisory salaries, factory storeroom
7. Factory power for machines
8. Fire loss
9. Sandpaper
10. Company picnic costs
11. Overtime premium, punch press
12. Idle time, assembly
13. Freight out
14. Property taxes
15. Paint for finished products
16. Heat and air conditioning, factory
17. Materials-handling labor, punch press
18. Straight-line depreciation, salespersons' automobiles

4-39 Direct, Indirect, and Unallocated Costs

Refer to the Lopez Plastics Company example on pages 136–140 and to Exhibit 4-7. The following list gives various resources used by Lopez Plastics Company. Use the letters *D*, *I* and *U* to indicate how the cost of each resource would be classified with respect to products manufactured: *D* = direct, *I* = indirect, and *U* = unallocated.

1. Depreciation of the plant
2. Resin used to make pen casings
3. Salary of plant manager
4. Salaries of cost accountants
5. Depreciation on computers used by engineers to design cell phone casings
6. Salaries of engineers
7. Salaries of operating labor processing pen casings
8. Travel costs of purchasing agent while investigating potential new suppliers of resin

4-40 Cost Allocation in ABC

Refer to the Lopez Plastics Company illustration on pages 136–140 and to Exhibit 4-7. Also see the table in the solution to the first Summary Problem for Your Review on page 140. Based on new information, management has adjusted the percentages that apply to the first stage of the ABC system as shown in the following table. Prepare a schedule that shows the gross margins for both products.

	Indirect Resource	
Percent of Resource Used in	**Plant and Machinery**	**Engineers and CAD Equipment**
Processing activity	90%	30%
Production support activity	10%	70%

4-41 Activity-Based Costing

The Gruen Toy Company makes a variety of dolls at its operation in Munich.

Its manufacturing process is highly automated. A recently installed ABC system has four activity centers:

	Indirect Resource	
Activity Center	**Cost Driver**	**Cost per Driver Unit**
Materials receiving and handling	Kilograms of materials	€.80 per kg
Production setup	Number of setups	€55 per setup
Cutting, sewing, and assembly	Number of units	€.50 per unit
Packing and shipping	Number of orders	€7 per order

Two dolls are called "Ann" and "Andy." They require .10 and .20 kg of materials, respectively, at a materials cost of €.75 for Ann and €1.10 for Andy. One computer-controlled assembly line makes all dolls. When a production run of a different doll is started, a setup procedure is required to reprogram the computers and make other changes in the process. Normally, 550 Ann dolls are produced per setup, but for Andy dolls, only 110 are produced per setup. Products are packed and shipped separately so a request from a customer for, say, three different products is considered three different orders.

Suppose the gift shop at the Munich Toy Museum (Spielzeugmuseum) just placed an order for 165 Ann dolls and 110 Andy dolls.

1. Compute the cost of the products shipped to the Munich Toy Museum gift shop.
2. Suppose the products made for the Munich Toy Museum gift shop required "Spielzeugmuseum" to be printed on each doll. Because of the automated process, printing the letters takes no extra time or materials, but it requires a special production setup for each product. Compute the cost of the products shipped to the Munich Toy Museum gift shop.
3. Explain how the activity-based-costing system helps Gruen Toy Company to measure costs of individual products or orders better than a traditional system that allocates all non-materials costs based on direct labor.

4-42 Two-Stage Activity-Based Costing—Stage One

The Maple Lake branch of Buffalo State Savings Bank (BSSB) is a retail branch in a rapidly growing residential area. It services individuals and local businesses. To support its services, the branch employs 14 tellers, 3 retail sales managers (RSMs), and the branch managing officer. The branch services about 3,100 customers. Each of the 70 branches of BSSB is implementing ABC in order to improve profitability. BSSB's branch managing officers have been given the responsibility to implement activity-based costing. The managing officer at the Maple Lake branch decided to implement a two-stage ABC system. Exhibit 4-18 depicts its two-stage ABC system.

The Maple Lake branch has the following cost data for the last year:

Teller wages	$ 370,000
RSM salaries and benefits	220,000
Managing officer salary and benefits	120,000
Other bank costs	400,000
Total	$1,110,000

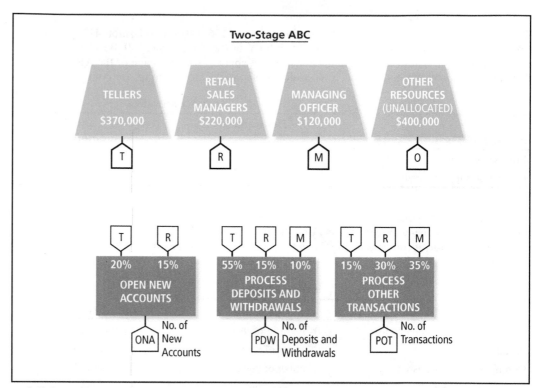

Exhibit 4-18
Two-Stage ABC at the Maple Lake Branch of BSSB

The "other bank costs" include depreciation on the facility including furniture, building, equipment, insurance, rentals of computers, contracted computer services, telecommunications, and utilities. These costs cannot be directly or indirectly related to routine bank activities, such as processing new accounts or processing deposits or withdrawals, and, thus, are unallocated. There are no costs that can be traced directly to customers so the Maple Lake branch has just two types of costs—indirect and unallocated. All employees have been interviewed as part of the ABC study. For example, tellers were asked how they spent their time. Three major activities were identified. They said that they spent most of their time (55%) processing deposits and withdrawals. They also estimated that they spent about 20% of their time processing new accounts and about 15% of their time processing other transactions. The remaining 10% of their time was spent on all other banking activities. The complete results of the interviews are presented in the following table:

Internal Activity Analysis

	Open New Accounts	Process Deposits and Withdrawals	Process Other Transactions	All Other Banking Activities	Total
Teller wages	20%	55%	15%	10%	100%
Retail sales manager salary	15%	15%	30%	40%	100%
Managing officer salary	0%	10%	35%	55%	100%

Determine the total cost of each of the three major activities conducted at the Maple Lake branch of BSSB. Use Exhibit 4-18 as a guide. (Note that this represents the first stage in the two-stage ABC method.)

4-43 Two-Stage Activity-Based Costing, Banking, Benchmarking
(This exercise is a continuation of Exercise 4-42 and should be assigned only if Exercise 4-42 is also assigned.)

A part of the activity analysis conducted at the Maple Lake branch of Buffalo State Savings Bank (BSSB) was identifying potential cost drivers for each major activity. The following cost drivers were chosen because they were both plausible and reliable and data were available:

Activity	Cost Driver	Annual Flow of Cost Driver
Process new accounts	Number of new accounts	580
Process deposits and withdrawals	Number of deposits and withdrawals	166,000
Process other transactions	Number of other transactions	46,000

Of the 3,100 customers of the branch, only 400 are local businesses. The business-customer class generated 20 new accounts, 89,000 deposits and withdrawals, and 22,000 other transactions. The implementation of ABC at all branches of BSSB provided sufficient data for internal benchmarking. The following are the lowest activity costs among all branches implementing two-stage ABC systems:

Activity	Lowest Activity Cost per Driver Unit
Open new accounts	$204.73 per new account
Process deposits and withdrawals	$ 2.25 per deposit or withdrawal
Process other transactions	$ 3.83 per transaction

Customer Class	Lowest Customer Cost per Account
Retail	$126.85
Commercial	$593.83

1. Determine the allocated (indirect) cost per account for retail and commercial accounts. Use Exhibit 4-18 as a guide.
2. Under what conditions would benchmarking between the Maple Lake branch of BSSB and the other branches be inappropriate?
3. What do the results of the ABC study suggest?

4-44 Direct, Indirect, and Unallocated Costs

Listed next are several activities and related costs that have been observed at Santana Company, a manufacturing company. The company makes a variety of products and currently uses a traditional costing system that allocates only production overhead based on direct-labor hours. It is implementing an ABC system for the design, production, and distribution functions of its value chain. You have been asked to complete the following table by indicating for each activity whether the related cost is direct, indirect, or unallocated. For each indirect cost, indicate one appropriate cost-allocation base (more than one cost-allocation base may be appropriate). The first two items have been completed for you.

Activity	Related Cost	Traditional	ABC
Supervising production	Supervisor salaries	Indirect (direct-labor hours)	Indirect (people supervised)
Designing a prototype for new product	Depreciation of computers	Unallocated	Indirect (number of parts)
Setting up for a production run	Mechanic wages		
Purchasing materials and parts to be used in products	Materials and parts cost		
Shipping sold products to customers (distributors)	Fuel used on company's fleet of trucks		
Market research study conducted by marketing staff to assess demand for potential new product	Salaries of market research staff		
Production scheduling	Salaries of production scheduling managers		
Purchasing materials and parts to be used in products	Salaries of purchasing agents		
Order processing of customer orders	Salaries of order processing staff		
Preparing cost analyses	Cost accountant salary		
Designing a new product	Salaries of design engineers that are fully dedicated to this new product		
Managing overall operations	Salary of executive of company		

PROBLEMS

4-45 Cost Accumulation and Allocation

Saouma Manufacturing Company has two departments, machining and finishing. For a given period, the following costs were incurred by the company as a whole: direct material, $400,000; direct labor, $90,000; and indirect production, $40,000. The grand total was $530,000.

The machining department incurred 50% of the direct-material costs, but only 10% of the direct-labor costs. Indirect production costs amounted to $10,000 in the machining department and $30,000 in finishing.

Three products were produced using the following proportions of direct material and direct labor in the two departments.

Product	Direct Material	Direct Labor
Alpha	20%	50%
Beta	40%	10%
Gamma	40%	40%
Total for the machining department	100%	100%
Alpha	60%	10%
Beta	30%	20%
Gamma	10%	70%
Total added by finishing department	100%	100%

As is commonplace, indirect production costs incurred by each department were allocated to products in proportion to the direct-labor costs of products within the departments.

1. Compute the total costs incurred by the machining department and added by the finishing department.
2. Compute the total costs of each product that would be shown as finished-goods inventory if all the products were transferred to finished stock on completion. (There were no beginning inventories.)

4-46 Hospital Allocation Base

Emilio Moreno, the administrator of Cook Community Hospital, has become interested in obtaining more accurate cost allocations on the basis of cause and effect. The $227,360 of laundry costs had been allocated on the basis of 784,000 pounds processed for all departments, or $.29 per pound.

Moreno is concerned that government health care officials will require weighted statistics to be used for cost allocation. He asks you, "Please develop a revised base for allocating laundry costs. It should be better than our present base, but it should not be overly complex either."

You study the situation and find that the laundry processes a large volume of uniforms for student nurses and physicians and for dietary, housekeeping, and other personnel. In particular, the coats or jackets worn by personnel in the radiology department take an unusual amount of handwork.

A special study of laundry for radiology revealed that 7,000 of the 23,000 pounds were jackets and coats that were five times as expensive to process as regular laundry items. Several reasons explained the difference, but it was principally because of the handwork involved.

Assume that no special requirements were needed in departments other than radiology. Revise the cost-allocation base to take into account that jackets in the radiology department use five times as much of the laundry resources as regular laundry items and compute the new cost-allocation rate. Compute the total cost charged to radiology using pounds and using the new base.

4-47 Traditional and ABC Cost Accounting, Activity-Based Management

Refer to the text discussion of Lopez Plastics Company on pages 136–140. Assume that the company has the traditional cost accounting system described in Exhibit 4-6. The top management team wants to reverse the pattern of quarterly losses. The company president, Angie Oaks, has emphasized the importance of profit improvement by linking future pay raises of the two product-line managers to their respective gross profit margins. She is concerned about the profitability of the pen casing product line while pleased with the profitability of the cell phone casing line. She also believes that the unallocated costs of the company are too high compared to those of competitors. The office of controller, whose costs are included in the unallocated costs, is responsible for vendor relations and purchasing of direct materials. The controller presents the following idea:

We should use more standard parts in cell phone casings, which will dramatically reduce the purchasing department's work required for purchasing. I believe this *should cut our office's costs by as much as $25,000 per quarter. In addition, using standard parts eliminates the need to purchase several expensive resins. The larger volume of purchases of less costly resin from fewer vendors will cut the cell phone casing direct-material cost by 10%. Product engineering agrees that this idea is not only feasible but, if implemented, would improve the overall quality of cell phone casings.*

The controller and marketing manager provided the following summary of actions and related effects:

Action	Expected effects
Reduce prices of cell phone casings 25%.	The vice president of sales estimates that the improved quality of cell phone casings combined with the price reduction will yield a 100% increase in demand for cell phone casings per quarter.
Use standard parts wherever possible in cell phone casings.	Total number of parts for each cell phone casing will not change, but the direct-material cost per casing will be reduced by 10% due to volume discounts from preferred vendors. The use of fewer suppliers will reduce vendor-relations work by the purchasing department. This will result in unallocated costs decreasing by $25,000.
	Processing time, measured in direct-labor hours, will increase by 500 hours due to expected 100% increase in sales and production of cell phone casings, but there is adequate capacity of labor and machine time. Direct-labor costs are fixed as are all of the indirect manufacturing costs.
	Quality of cell phone casings will improve due to reduced complexity of processing.

1. Evaluate this idea using the traditional cost allocation system shown in Exhibit 4-6 on page 138. What would be the predicted profitability for each product line and the company as a whole? What would be the most likely level of support for the controller's idea by the product managers of the pen casing product line and the cell phone casing product line? What would be the level of support by the president?
2. Assume that you have the ABC system described in Exhibit 4-7 on page 139 with the gross profit margins shown in the table in the solution to the first Summary Problem for Your Review on page 140. Often, managers with ABC systems can anticipate more effects of improvement ideas because of their increased understanding of the operating system. In this case, although the total number of parts would not change, the idea would reduce the number of distinct parts for cell phone casings from 20 to 9. Evaluate the controller's idea using the ABC system described in Exhibit 4-7. What would be the predicted profitability for each product line and the company as a whole? What would be the most likely level of support for the controller's idea by the product managers of the pen casing product line and the cell phone casing product line? What would be the level of support by the president?
3. As vice president, you have expressed concern about the traditional cost-allocation system's product-cost accuracy and its ability to provide relevant information for operational control. Does the new ABC system satisfy your concerns? Explain.

4-48 Activity-Based Costing and Product Line Profitability

SuperSol is a grocery company with stores throughout Spain. Suppose the company is planning an expansion of its store in central Madrid. A preliminary analysis has shown the packaged food department to be the most profitable, so the company plans to increase its space the most.

Assume that the Madrid store has just three departments: produce, packaged food, and meat. The most recent annual report for the store showed sales of €4,160,100, which generated a gross margin of €960,100. Sales and gross margins of the three departments were as follows:

	Produce	Packaged Food	Meat	Total
Revenues	€497,700	€2,100,000	€1,562,400	€4,160,100
Cost of products sold	320,000	1,600,000	1,280,000	3,200,000
Gross margin	€177,700	€ 500,000	€ 282,400	€ 960,100

In addition to cost of products sold, the store has €800,000 of support costs, so operating income is €960,100 − €800,000 = €160,100. SuperSol currently uses an accounting system that uses cost of products sold as a cost-allocation base for allocating support costs.

Francisco Ramirez, controller of SuperSol, recently attended a seminar on activity-based costing. He suggests that SuperSol management should undertake further analysis before deciding which product gets the largest increase in space in the expansion. He has asked you, his assistant, to lead this analysis.

1. The starting point of your analysis is to determine product profitability under the existing cost accounting system. Compute the operating income and the operating income as a percent of sales for each department using SuperSol's existing system. Use this information to assess the relative profitability per euro of sales of each of the three departments.

2. Ramirez asks you next to develop product costs using an activity-based accounting system. You determine that there are five major activities, each with a different cost driver to be used as a cost-allocation base:

   a. Ordering—Placing of orders for purchases
   b. Delivery—Physical delivery and receipt of merchandise
   c. Shelf-stocking—Stocking of merchandise on store shelves, including ongoing restocking
   d. Customer support—Assistance to customers, including check out and bagging
   e. Produce monitoring—Constantly checking on the stacking and freshness of produce

The cost drivers for each activity are as follows:

Ordering	Number of purchase orders
Delivery	Number of deliveries
Shelf-stocking	Hours of stocking time
Customer support	Number of items sold
Produce monitoring	Direct trace to the Produce Department

You have determined the following information about the cost drivers:

	Produce	Packaged Food	Meat	Total
Number of purchase orders	1,400	3,300	1,470	6,170
Number of deliveries	1,240	8,770	1,190	11,200
Hours of shelf-stocking	218	2,120	1,053	3,391
Items sold	50,100	440,800	122,700	613,600

The total cost of each activity was as follows:

Ordering	€ 67,870
Delivery	179,200
Shelf-stocking	128,858
Customer support	245,440
Produce monitoring	178,632
Total	€800,000

Using these data and activity-based costing, calculate the operating income and operating income as a percent of sales for each product. (For example, note that each purchase order costs €67,870 ÷ 6,170 = €11 to process.)

3. Propose a strategy for expansion. Which information, that based on the current costing system or that based on the activity-based costing system, is most useful? Why? What additional information would you like to have before making a more definitive recommendation on an expansion strategy?

4-49 Activity-Based Costing and Activity-Based Management, Automotive Supplier

O'Hanlon Company is an automotive component supplier. O'Hanlon has been approached by Chrysler's Ohio plant to consider expanding its production of part 24Z2 to a total annual quantity of 2,800 units. This part is a low-volume, complex product with a high gross margin that is based on a proposed (quoted) unit sales price of $8.20. O'Hanlon uses a traditional costing system that allocates indirect manufacturing costs based on direct-labor costs. The rate currently used to allocate indirect manufacturing costs is 500% of direct-labor cost. This rate is based on the $4,121,000 annual factory overhead cost divided by $824,200 annual direct-labor cost. To produce 2,800 units of 24Z2 requires $6,160 of direct materials and $1,960 of direct labor. The unit cost and gross margin percentage for part 24Z2 based on the traditional cost system are computed as follows:

	Total	Per Unit (÷2,800)
Direct material	$ 6,160	$2.20
Direct labor	1,960	.70
Indirect production: (500% of direct labor)	9,800	3.50
Total cost	$17,920	$6.40
Sales price quoted		8.20
Gross margin		$1.80
Gross margin percentage		22.0%

The management of O'Hanlon decided to examine the effectiveness of their traditional costing system versus an activity-based costing system. The following data have been collected by a team consisting of accounting and engineering analysts:

Activity Center	Factory Overhead Costs (Annual)
Quality	$ 880,000
Production scheduling	72,000
Setup	880,000
Shipping	384,000
Shipping administration	105,000
Production	1,800,000
Total indirect production cost	$4,121,000

Activity Center: Cost Drivers	Annual Cost-Driver Quantity
Quality: Number of pieces scrapped	16,000
Production scheduling and set up: Number of setups	800
Shipping: Number of containers shipped	64,000
Shipping administration: Number of shipments	1,500
Production: Number of machine hours	12,000

The accounting and engineering team has performed activity analysis and provides the following estimates for the total quantity of cost drivers to be used to produce 2,800 units of part 24Z2:

Cost Driver	Cost-Driver Consumption
Pieces scrapped	150
Setups	5
Containers shipped	12
Shipments	7
Machine hours	16

1. Prepare a schedule calculating the unit cost and gross margin of part 24Z2 using the activity-based costing approach. Use the cost drivers given as cost-allocation bases.

2. Based on the ABC results, which course of action would you recommend regarding the proposal by Chrysler? List the benefits and costs associated with implementing an ABC system at O'Hanlon.

4-50 Research in Activity-Based Costing or Activity-Based Management

Select an article from *Strategic Finance, Cost Management*, or *Management Accounting Quarterly* (an online journal) or any other journal that describes a particular company's application of either (a) an activity-based costing system, or (b) activity-based management. Prepare a summary of 300 words or fewer that includes the following:

- Name of the company (if given)
- Industry of the company
- Description of the particular application
- Assessment of the benefits the company received from the application
- Any difficulties encountered in implementation

4-51 Review of Chapters 2, 3, and 4

The Sharma Company provides you with the following miscellaneous data regarding operations in 20X9:

Gross profit	$ 40,000
Net profit	15,000
Sales	120,000
Direct material used	35,000
Direct labor	25,000
Fixed manufacturing overhead	15,000
Fixed selling and administrative expenses	12,000

There are no beginning or ending inventories.

Compute (a) variable selling and administrative expenses, (b) contribution margin in dollars, (c) variable manufacturing overhead, (d) break-even point in sales dollars, and (e) manufacturing cost of goods sold.

4-52 Review of Chapters 2, 3, and 4

Kyu Lee Corporation provides you with the following miscellaneous data regarding operations for 20X0 (in thousands of South Korean won, ₩):

Break-even point in sales	₩ 84,000
Direct material used	29,000
Gross profit	20,000
Contribution margin	25,000
Direct labor	30,000
Sales	100,000
Variable manufacturing overhead	5,000

There are no beginning or ending inventories.

Compute (a) the fixed manufacturing overhead, (b) variable selling and administrative expenses, and (c) fixed selling and administrative expenses.

4-53 Review of Chapters 2, 3, and 4

Dover High Fashions Company manufactured and sold 1,000 leather handbags during July. Selected data for this month follow:

Sales	$130,000
Direct materials used	35,000
Direct labor	11,000
Variable manufacturing overhead	18,000
Fixed manufacturing overhead	13,000
Variable selling and administrative expenses	?
Fixed selling and administrative expenses	?
Contribution margin	55,000
Operating income	33,000

There were no beginning or ending inventories.

1. What were the variable selling and administrative expenses for July?
2. What were the fixed selling and administrative expenses for July?
3. What was the cost of goods sold during July?
4. Without prejudice to your earlier answers, assume that the fixed selling and administrative expenses for July amounted to $6,250.
   a. What was the break-even point in units for July?
   b. How many units must be sold to earn a target operating income of $17,600?
   c. What would the selling price per unit have to be if the company wanted to earn an operating income of $62,650 on the sale of 910 units?

CASES

4-54 Multiple Allocation Bases

The Liverpool Company produces three types of circuit boards: Alpha, Beta, and Gamma. The cost accounting system used by Liverpool until 2012 applied all costs except direct materials to the products using direct-labor hours as the only cost driver. In 2012, the company undertook a cost study. The study determined that there were six main factors that incurred costs. A new system was designed with a separate cost pool for each of the six factors. The factors and the costs associated with each are as follows:

1. Direct-labor hours—direct-labor cost and related fringe benefits and payroll taxes
2. Machine hours—depreciation and repairs and maintenance costs
3. Pounds of materials—materials receiving, handling, and storage costs
4. Number of production setups—labor used to change machinery and computer configurations for a new production batch
5. Number of production orders—costs of production scheduling and order processing
6. Number of orders shipped—all packaging and shipping expenses

The company is now preparing a budget for 2013. The budget includes the following predictions:

	Alpha	Beta	Gamma
Units to be produced	10,000	800	5,000
Direct-materials cost	£70/unit	£88/unit	£45/unit
Direct-labor hours	4/unit	18/unit	9/unit
Machine hours	7/unit	15/unit	7/unit
Pounds of materials	3/unit	4/unit	2/unit
Number of production setups	100	50	50
Number of production orders	300	200	70
Number of orders shipped	1,000	800	2,000

The total budgeted cost for 2013 is £3,866,250, of which £995,400 was direct-materials cost, and the amount in each of the six cost pools defined previously is as follows:

Cost Pool*	Cost
1	£1,391,600
2	936,000
3	129,600
4	160,000
5	25,650
6	228,000
Total	£2,870,850

*Identified by the cost driver used.

1. Prepare a budget that shows the total budgeted cost and the unit cost for each circuit board. Use the new system with six cost pools (plus a separate direct application of direct-materials cost).
2. Compute the budgeted total and unit costs of each circuit board if the old direct-labor-hour system had been used.
3. How would you judge whether the new system is better than the old one?

4-55 Traditional Versus ABC Systems

Northwest Desserts, Inc., (NDI) produces a variety of premium cheesecakes and sells them in individual packages directly to retail customers and in packages of 10 cakes to restaurants in Washington, Oregon, Idaho, and Northern California. NDI started as a small retail outlet, where it developed a superb reputation for quality. In the late 1990s it opened a chain of retail outlets. Only recently it started selling cheesecakes to restaurants. Its penetration into the restaurant market has been slower than predicted.

Although NDI produces several types of cheesecakes, all are about the same size and are considered a single product for costing purposes. NDI's existing costing system has a single direct-cost category—ingredients—and a single indirect-cost pool—production overhead. The system does not trace labor costs to the products; it considers them part of production overhead. Production overhead is allocated on the basis of number of cheesecakes produced. The 2013 budget projected production of 500,000 cheesecakes, 400,000 for the retail market and 100,000 for restaurants. Predicted costs were as follows:

Ingredients	$ 900,000
Production overhead	2,216,000
Total	$3,116,000

In early 2012 NDI had unsuccessfully bid for a large restaurant contract from the Applebee's chain. Its bid had been 30% above that of the successful bidder. This came as a shock because NDI had budgeted only a small profit into the bid. In addition, the NDI plant was one of the newest and most efficient in the industry.

Before completing the budget for 2013, top management of NDI asked Naomi Lester, controller of NDI, to examine the company's cost accounting system. Naomi had attended a short course by the Institute of Management Accountants on activity-based costing (ABC), and she thought some of the principles of ABC might apply to NDI. She felt that accounting for the ingredients was not a problem; the ingredients cost the same whether a cheesecake was produced for retail or restaurant markets. However, when she analyzed production overhead costs, she saw several possible improvements.

Naomi found that production overhead costs could be divided into cost pools for four activities: 1) administration, 2) facilities operations and maintenance, 3) mixing/baking, and 4) decorating/packaging. The activities in administration and facilities operations and maintenance do not involve working directly on cheesecakes, but they support the areas in which the cheese-cakes are produced. Mixing/baking and decorating/packaging are the activities that directly produce the cheesecakes. Naomi described the four activities as follows:

Administrative: Three administrative employees work in a 600 sq. ft. office providing a variety of services to NDI, including accounting, personnel, etc. It is difficult to measure the amount of administrative services provided to each product, but they are roughly proportional to the number of employees. The administrative costs are budgeted at $140,000.

Facilities Operations and Maintenance: Two employees, located in an 800 sq. ft. office wing, operate and maintain the facilities. In addition, rent and depreciation charges and the cost of supplies for operating and maintaining the facilities are included in this cost pool. These facilities operations and maintenance costs are closely related to the number of square feet of space used. Budgeted facilities operations and maintenance costs are $320,000.

Mixing and Baking: Five employees are located in 4,000 sq. ft. of space with a capacity to produce 600,000 cheesecakes per year. Much of the mixing and baking operation is the same for all cheesecakes produced. However, the cheesecakes sold through NDI's own retail outlets require some special handling to give them a distinctive quality. The production line produces 80 retail cheesecakes per processing hour and 100 restaurant cheesecakes per processing hour. Costs are driven by the number of processing hours. Budged costs in mixing and baking are $540,000.

Decorating and Packaging: Decorating and packaging require two employees and 1,000 sq. ft. of space. There are two separate decorating/packaging lines. Only 10 retail cheesecakes can be decorated and packaged per hour, while 50 restaurant cheesecakes can be decorated and packaged in the same amount of time. Costs vary with the number of decorating/packaging hours. Budgeted costs are $1,216,000. Of this total cost, $376,000 is for packaging materials that could be traced to individual products, $360,000 to retail, and $16,000 to restaurants sales.

1. Use the existing costing system to find the budgeted cost per cheesecake for (a) the retail market and (b) the restaurant market. Comment briefly on the weaknesses of this system.
2. Use the ABC system to find the budgeted cost per cheesecake for (a) the retail market and (b) the restaurant market.
3. Prepare a memo from Naomi Lester to the president of NDI commenting on the differences in the costs between the traditional and ABC systems. Why are they different? What decisions should be made differently now that NDI has the information from the ABC system rather the information from the traditional system? How should managers use the ABC information to make better decisions?

4-56 ABC and Customer Profitability in Financial Services

To increase its share of the checking account market, Columbia City Bank in Seattle took two actions: It established a customer call center to respond to customer inquiries about account balances, checks cleared, fees charged, etc. Columbia paid year-end bonuses to branch managers who met their branch's target increase in the number of customers. While 80% of the branch managers met the target increase in the number of customers, Columbia City Bank's profits continued to decline. John Diamond, the CEO, didn't understand why profits were declining even though the bank was serving more customers. The Pierce County branch manager, Rose Perez, noticed that while small retail customers flocked to the bank, the number of business customers was declining.

Columbia City Bank's costing system, developed back in 1988, is straightforward. No costs are traced directly to customers. The bank simply assigns the total indirect costs to customer lines (retail customer line or business customer line) based on the total number of checks processed.

Perez suspected that Columbia City Bank's cost system might be part of the problem. Perez learned about ABC in school, but the applications involved manufacturing firms. She wonders whether Columbia City Bank could develop an ABC system, with the customer line as the primary cost object.

Rose's boss was skeptical. ("Our profits are going down the tubes and you want me to spend money developing a new accounting system?") However, Rose persuaded her boss to allow a pilot ABC study, using the three Tacoma branches for the pilot test.

The ABC implementation team included Perez, the managers of each of the three Tacoma branches, a bank teller, and a customer service representative from the customer call center. The team began by identifying the following three activities:

- Check payments
- Teller withdrawals and deposits
- Customer service call center

The ABC team then scrutinized the Tacoma branches' total indirect cost of $2,850,000. They classified the components of this total indirect cost into the appropriate activity pool, coming up with the following estimates (in thousands of dollars):

Cost	Activity Cost Pool to Which Cost Is Assigned	Estimated Total Costs for Tacoma Branches
Salaries of check-processing personnel	Check payments	$ 440
Depreciation on check-processing equipment	Check payments	700
Teller salaries	Teller withdrawals and deposits	1,200
Salaries of customer representatives at call center	Customer service call center	450
Toll-free phone lines at customer call center	Customer service call center	60
Total indirect costs		$2,850

The team then identified the following cost drivers for each activity cost pool:

Activity Cost Pool	Activity Cost Driver
Check payments	number of checks processed
Teller withdrawals and deposits	number of teller transactions
Customer service call center	number of calls

The ABC team estimated that for the Tacoma branches, the retail customer line and the business customer line would require the following total resources (in thousands):

Activity Cost Driver	Number of Units of Activity Cost Driver Used by Business Customers	Number of Units of Activity Cost Driver Used by Retail Customers	Total
Checks processed	2,280	9,120	11,400
Teller transactions	320	80	400
Customer calls to call center	95	5	100
Checking accounts	150	50	200

That is, the retail customers have 320,000 teller transactions, make 95,000 calls to the customer service center, and so on.

On average, Columbia City Bank earns revenue from each type of account (from interest earned on checking account balances) as follows:

Average revenue per retail customer account $10
Average revenue per business customer account $40

1. Using the original (old) cost system complete the following:

a. Compute the indirect cost allocation rate.
b. Determine the total indirect cost assigned to the retail customer line and the business customer line.
c. Compute the proportion of the total indirect cost assigned to the retail customer line and the business customer line.
d. Determine the indirect cost per retail account and the indirect cost per business account.
e. Assuming that there are no direct costs, compute the average profit per account for retail customers and for business customers.
f. Assess the likely business strategy that might be adopted by managers using data from this original cost system.

2. What are the signs that Columbia City Bank's original cost system was broken or in need of refinement?
3. Using the new activity-based costing system complete the following:

   a. Compute the indirect cost allocation rates for each of the three activities:
   - Check payments
   - Teller withdrawals and deposits
   - Customer call center

   b. Use the following schedule to compute the total indirect cost allocated to each customer line:

Activity	Total Indirect Cost Assigned to Retail Customer Line	Total Indirect Cost Assigned to Business Customer Line
Check payments		
Teller withdrawals and deposits		
Customer call center		
Total indirect costs		

   c. What proportion of each activity's resources is used by the retail customer line and the business customer line?
   d. Using the ABC data from requirement 3b, compute the indirect cost per retail customer account and the indirect cost per business customer account.
   e. Explain why the results in requirement 1d and requirement 3d differ. Be precise and specific.
   f. Using the new ABC data, compute the average profit per account for both retail and business customers. Assess the likely business strategy that might be adopted by managers using data from this ABC cost system.

4. Be prepared to discuss the following questions:

   a. Was Columbia City Bank's bonus-based incentive plan to increase the number of checking account customers a wise strategy? Would you suggest any change in the strategy based on the ABC analysis?
   b. What benefits can Columbia City Bank reap from the ABC analysis?
   c. Why might Rose Perez have suspected that the benefits of ABC would likely outweigh the costs of implementing ABC at Columbia City Bank?
   d. Why is it important for nonaccounting managers to understand ABC?

4-57 Identifying Activities, Resources, and Cost Drivers in Manufacturing

International Plastics is a multinational, diversified organization. One of its manufacturing divisions, Northeast Plastics, has become less profitable due to increased competition. The division produces three major lines of plastic products within its single plant. Product line A is high-volume, simple pieces produced in large batches. Product line B is medium-volume, more complex pieces. Product line C is low-volume, small-order, highly complex pieces.

Currently, the division allocates indirect production costs based on direct-labor cost. The vice president of manufacturing is uncomfortable using the traditional cost figures. He thinks the company is underpricing the more complex products. He decides to conduct an ABC analysis of the business.

Interviews were conducted with the key managers in order to identify activities, resources, cost drivers, and their interrelationships.

INTERVIEWEE: PRODUCTION MANAGER

Q1. *What activities are carried out in your area?*
A1. All products are manufactured using three similar, complex, and expensive molding machines. Each molding machine can be used in the production of the three product lines. Each setup takes about the same time irrespective of the product.
Q2. *Who works in your area?*
A2. Last year, we employed 30 machine operators, 2 maintenance mechanics, and 2 supervisors.
Q3. *How are the operators used in the molding process?*
A3. It requires nine operators to support a machine during the actual production process.
Q4. *What do the maintenance mechanics do?*
A4. Their primary function is to perform machine setups. However, they are also required to provide machine maintenance during the molding process.

Q5. Where do the supervisors spend their time?

A5. They provide supervision for the machine operators and the maintenance mechanics. For the most part, the supervisors appear to spend the same amount of time with each of the employees that they supervise.

Q6. What other resources are used to support manufacturing?

A6. The molding machines use energy during the molding process and during the setups. We put meters on the molding machines to get a better understanding of their energy consumption. We discovered that for each hour that a machine ran, it used 6.3 kilowatts of energy. The machines also require consumable shop supplies (e.g., lubricants, hoses, and so on). We have found a direct correlation between the amount of supplies used and the actual processing time.

Q7. How is the building used, and what costs are associated with it?

A7. We have a 100,000 sq. ft. building. The total rent and insurance costs for the year were $675,000. These costs are allocated to production, sales, and administration based on square footage.

1. Identify the activities and resources for the division. For each activity, suggest an appropriate cost driver.

2. For each resource identified in requirement 1, indicate its cost behavior with respect to the activities it supports (assume a planning period of 1 month).

NIKE 10-K PROBLEM

4-58 Nike's Cost Accounting System

Examine the inventory account in the balance sheet in **Nike**'s 10-K report in Appendix C and read Note 2 – Inventories. What does the statement about the composition of Nike's inventory imply about the company's manufacturing operations? Is Nike primarily a manufacturer or merchandiser? Can you confirm this elsewhere in the 10-K?

EXCEL APPLICATION EXERCISE

4-59 Traditional Costing Versus Activity-Based Costing

Goal: Create an Excel spreadsheet to compare traditional costing versus activity-based costing. Use the results to answer questions about your findings.

Scenario: Suppose Sunstar Corporation is one of **Dell**'s circuit board suppliers. Sunstar currently uses traditional costing for making business decisions. At the urging of Dell, however, the company has decided to move to activity-based costing for circuit board production related to products PCB124 and PCB136. As one of the company's accountants, you have been asked to prepare a spreadsheet comparing the two costing methods for the next company board meeting. Your supervisor has given you the following quarterly data:

Total Indirect Costs for the Quarter:

Assembly	$630,000
Soldering	$270,000
Inspection	$160,000

	PCB124	PCB136
Direct costs (materials, labor)	$162,400	$178,240
Machine hours (assembly)	480	1,080
Number of units produced (soldering)	6,000	4,000
Testing hours (inspection)	6,000	8,000

When you have completed your spreadsheet, answer the following questions:

a. What is the total manufacturing cost per unit using traditional costing for PCB124? For PCB136? Use machine hours as the cost-allocation base.

b. What is the total manufacturing cost per unit using activity-based costing for PCB124? For PCB136?

c. What conclusions can be drawn from your spreadsheet results?

Step-by-Step:

1. Open a new Excel spreadsheet.
2. In column A, create a bold-faced heading that contains the following:
   Row 1: Chapter 4Decision Guideline
   Row 2: Sunstar Corporation
   Row 3: Traditional Versus Activity-Based Costing
   Row 4: Today's Date

   Note: Adjust column widths as follows: Column A (41.57), Columns B, C, and D (21.0). Column D is for check figures only. The column widths have been designed to ensure that Column D will not print on the final version of the spreadsheet if only page 1 is printed.

3. Merge and center the four heading rows across columns A–C.
4. In column A, create the following row headings:
   Row 7: Raw data
   Row 8: Indirect costs for the quarter:
   Row 9: Assembly
   Row 10: Soldering
   Row 11: Inspection
   Row 12: Total indirect costs
   Skip two rows.
   Row 15: Direct costs (Materials, labor)
   Row 16: Machine hours (Assembly)
   Row 17: Number of units produced (Soldering)
   Row 18: Testing hours (Inspection)
   Skip two rows.
   Row 21: Traditional costing system
   Row 22: Indirect cost driver (machine hours)
   Row 23: Allocated indirect costs
   Skip a row.
   Row 25: Cost per product
   Row 26: Direct costs
   Row 27: Manufacturing overhead
   Row 28: Total manufacturing costs per product
   Skip a row.
   Row 30: Number of units
   Row 31: Total manufacturing costs per unit
   Skip two rows.
   Row 34: Activity-based costing system
   Row 35: Assembly cost driver (machine hours)
   Row 36: Allocated assembly cost
   Row 37: Soldering cost driver (units)
   Row 38: Allocated soldering cost
   Row 39: Inspection cost driver (testing hours)
   Row 40: Allocated inspection cost
   Skip a row.
   Row 42: Cost per product
   Row 43: Direct costs
   Row 44: Manufacturing overhead
   Row 45: Assembly
   Row 46: Soldering
   Row 47: Inspection
   Row 48: Total manufacturing costs per product
   Skip a row.
   Row 50: Number of units
   Row 51: Total manufacturing costs per unit
5. Change the format of Raw data (row 7), Traditional costing system (row 21), and Activity-based costing system (row 34) to bold-faced headings.

   Hint: Use the control key for highlighting multiple cells or rows when making changes.

6. Change the format of Cost per product (rows 25 and 42) to underlined headings.
7. In rows 14, 21, 25, 34, and 42 create the following bold-faced, right-justified column headings:

Column B: PCB124
Column C: PCB136

8. In rows 21 and 34 create the following bold-faced, right-justified column headings:
   Column D: Total

9. Use the scenario data to fill in the Raw data section.
   Use the SUM function to calculate Total indirect costs (row 12).

10. Traditional costing system:
    Fill in rows 26 and 30 with information from the Raw data section.
    Use appropriate formulas from this chapter to calculate the cost driver and allocated costs.
    Use the SUM function to calculate the Total column for manufacturing overhead costs.
    Complete the remainder of the Cost per product data using formulas and calculations.
    Calculate the Total manufacturing costs per product.

11. Activity-based costing system:
    Fill in rows 43 and 50 with information from the Raw data section.
    Use appropriate formulas from this chapter to calculate the cost drivers and allocated costs.
    Use the SUM function to calculate the Total columns for all allocated costs.
    Complete the remainder of the Cost per product data using formulas and calculations.
    Calculate the Total manufacturing costs per product.

    Hint: If using the SUM function to calculate Total manufacturing costs, verify range.

12. Format all amounts as follows:

Number tab:	Category:	Currency
	Decimal places:	2
	Symbol:	None
	Negative numbers:	Red with parentheses

13. Change the format of hours and units in rows 16–18, 30, and 50 to display no decimal places.

14. Change the format of the amounts in rows 9, 12, 15, 23, 26, 28, 31, 36, 38, 40, 43, 48, and 51 to display a dollar symbol.

15. Change the format of the row headings in rows 9–11, 15–18, 23, 36, 38, 40, and 45–47 to display as indented.

Alignment tab:	Horizontal:	Left (Indent)
	Indent:	1

16. Change the format of the amounts in rows 12, 28, and 48 to display a top border, using the default Line Style.

Border tab:	Icon:	Top Border

17. Change the format of the cost driver calculations in rows 22, 35, 37, and 39 to display as left-justified percentages with two decimal places.

Number tab:	Category:	Percentage
	Decimal places:	2
Alignment tab:	Horizontal:	Left (Indent)
	Indent:	0

18. Accentuate the Cost per product information for each costing method by applying cell shading to columns A, B, and C of rows 25–31 and 42–51.

Patterns tab:	Color:	Lightest grey

19. Save your work, and print a copy for your files.

Note: The final version of the spreadsheet will be on page 1. You do not need to print page 2 as it should contain only the check figures.

COLLABORATIVE LEARNING EXERCISE

4-60 Internet Research, ABC, and ABM

Form groups of three to five people each. Each member of the group should pick one of the following industries:

- Manufacturing
- Insurance
- Health care
- Government
- Service

Each person should explore the Internet for an example of a company that implemented activity-based costing and activity-based management. Prepare and give a briefing for your group. Do this by completing the following:

1. Describe the company and its business.
2. What was the scope of the ABC/ABM project?
3. What were the goals for the ABC/ABM project?
4. Summarize the results of the project.

After each person has briefed the group on his or her company, discuss within the group the commonalities between the ABC/ABM applications.

INTERNET EXERCISE

4-61 Vermont Teddy Bear Factory

Costs are important to any manager. Managers focus on trying to keep costs as low as possible. There are many ways to report costs, such as the total amount that is often seen on the income statement or an individual cost for a particular component part.

1. Go to the home page at www.vermontteddybear.com. When you click onto the Web site, what does it suggest that you should do? What is the current headline offering on the site?
2. Click the "What is a Bear-Gram?" icon under "Customer Services" at the bottom of the page. What is a Bear-Gram gift and what does it contain?
3. Take a tour of the factory by clicking on "Visit Our Factory" under About Us near the bottom of the home page and then clicking "Online Factory Tour." Take the online tour. List several activities shown in the tour. What are some resources that are consumed by these activities? For one of the activities you listed, give at least one fixed-cost and one variable-cost resource. Suggest a cost driver for one of the activities you listed.
4. Do you think that the Vermont Teddy Bear factory would be a good candidate for using activity-based costing? Explain.
5. From the description of the Vermont Teddy Bear Company, is it a manufacturer or merchandiser? If you looked at the details of its balance sheet, what would you expect to find under Inventories? Do you expect Vermont Teddy Bear Company to have large work-in-process inventories or finished-goods inventories?

Relevant Information for Decision Making with a Focus on Pricing Decisions

LEARNING OBJECTIVES

When you have finished studying this chapter, you should be able to:

1. Discriminate between relevant and irrelevant information for making decisions.

2. Apply the decision process to make business decisions.

3. Construct absorption and contribution-margin income statements, and identify their relevance for decision making.

4. Decide to accept or reject a special order using the contribution-margin approach.

5. Explain why pricing decisions depend on the characteristics of the market.

6. Identify the factors that influence pricing decisions in practice.

7. Compute a sales price by various methods, and compare the advantages and disadvantages of these methods.

8. Use target costing to decide whether to add a new product.

▶ GRAND CANYON RAILWAY

While you are on vacation, the last thing you want to worry about is transportation. For visitors to Grand Canyon National Park, the **Grand Canyon Railway** provides a relaxing alternative to driving to the canyon. Why drive when you can sit back and enjoy the scenery across 65 miles of beautiful Arizona countryside from the comfort of a fully reconditioned steam-powered train? Strolling musicians serenade you, and western characters stage attacks, holdups, and shootouts that offer a glimpse into what train travel might have been like for Old West loggers, miners, and ranchers at the turn of the century. The Grand Canyon Railway offers a ride not only to the canyon itself but into the past as well.

Rides into the past aren't exactly cheap. Tracks for the narrow-gauge train as well as the authentic steam engines and passenger cars required an investment of more than $20 million. Recovering that initial investment while earning a profit is not easy. According to the company CFO, Kevin Call, "Pricing is really the key in running a successful operation."

The railway offers four different classes of service, and setting the pricing on each one determines the company's profit. To set prices, management uses the contribution-margin approach introduced in Chapter 2. Among the influences on pricing discussed in this chapter, costs and customer demands are the most important to the railway. The prices charged must not only ensure a reasonable profit, they also must be attractive to the customer.

Costs are important in the pricing decisions of many types of companies. What price should a **Safeway** store charge for a pound of hamburger? What should **Boeing** charge for a 787 airplane? Should a clothing manufacturer accept a special order from **Wal-Mart**? Managers rely on accounting information to answer these questions and to make important decisions on a daily basis. However, not all accounting information applies to each type of decision. In this chapter, we'll focus on identifying relevant information for decision making and apply what we learn to pricing decisions. The ability to separate relevant from irrelevant information is often the difference between success and failure in modern business. ■[1]

© Stephen Bay/Alamy

Riding the Grand Canyon Railroad is like going back in time to the grand era of train travel.

The Concept of Relevance

What information is relevant to a decision maker? That depends on the decision being made. Decision making is essentially choosing among several alternative courses of action. Decision makers identify the available alternatives by an often time-consuming search and screening process, perhaps carried out by a company team that includes engineers, accountants, and operating executives. The accountant's role is primarily that of a technical expert on financial analysis who provides information that may be useful to the decision maker. However, the decision maker, who has the best understanding of the decision and the available alternatives, must understand what information is relevant.

What Is Relevance?

Making business decisions requires managers to compare two or more alternative courses of action. Two criteria determine whether financial information is relevant: (1) Information must be an expected future revenue or cost, and (2) it must have an element of difference among the alternatives. That is, **relevant information** is the predicted future costs and revenues that will differ among the alternatives.

Note that relevant information is a prediction of the future, not a summary of the past. Historical (past) information has no direct bearing on a decision. Such information can have an indirect bearing on a decision because it may help in predicting the future. But past figures, in themselves, are irrelevant to the decision itself. Why? Because the decision cannot change the past. Decisions affect the future. Nothing can alter what has already happened.

Of the expected future information, only data that will differ across alternatives are relevant to the decision. Any item that will remain the same regardless of the alternative selected is irrelevant. For instance, if a department manager's salary will be the same regardless of the products produced, the salary is irrelevant to the selection of products. Here are some examples to help you clarify the sharp distinctions between relevant and irrelevant information.

Suppose you always buy gasoline from either of two nearby gasoline stations. Yesterday you noticed that one station was selling gasoline at $3.90 per gallon. The other was selling it at $3.80. Your automobile needs gasoline today, and in making your choice of stations, you assume that these prices have not changed. The relevant costs are $3.90 and $3.80, the expected future costs that will differ between the alternatives. You use your past experience (that is, what you observed yesterday) for predicting today's price. Note that the relevant cost is not what you paid in the past, or what you observed yesterday, but what you expect to pay when you drive in to get gasoline. This cost meets our two criteria: (1) It is the expected future cost, and (2) it differs between the alternatives.

You may also plan to buy a bag of potato chips when you stop for gasoline. Suppose you expect the price of a bag of chips to be the same at either station. This expected future cost is irrelevant to your decision about which station to stop at because it will be the same under either alternative. It does not meet our second criterion.

On a business level, consider the following decision. A food container manufacturer is thinking of using aluminum instead of tin in making a line of large cans. The cost of direct material is expected to decrease from $.30 per can if tin is used to $.20 per can if the manufacturer uses aluminum. The direct-labor cost will continue to be $.70 per unit regardless of the material used. Direct-labor cost is irrelevant because our second criterion—an element of difference between the alternatives—is not met.

relevant information
The predicted future costs and revenues that will differ among alternative courses of action.

---

[1]Throughout this and the next chapter, to concentrate on the fundamental ideas, we ignore the time value of money and income taxes (discussed in Chapter 11).

	Aluminum	Tin	Difference
Direct material	$.20	$.30	$.10
Direct labor	.70	.70	—

In this example, the relevant cost is the cost of direct materials. We can safely exclude direct labor from the comparison of alternatives because it does not differ between the alternatives.

A Decision Model

Exhibit 5-1 illustrates this simple decision process, and it serves to show the appropriate framework for more complex decisions. Box 1(A) represents historical data from the accounting system. Box 1(B) represents other data, such as price indices or industry statistics, gathered from outside the accounting system. Regardless of their source, the data in step 1 help the formulation of predictions in step 2. (Remember that historical data are only relevant as a guide to predicting future costs and revenues. In the large-can manufacturing example, the historical costs of tin and aluminum are only relevant as predictors of future prices.)

decision model

Any method for making a choice, sometimes requiring elaborate quantitative procedures.

In step 3, these predictions become inputs to the decision model. A **decision model** is any method used for making a choice. Such models sometimes require elaborate quantitative procedures, such as a petroleum refinery's mathematical method for choosing what products to manufacture for any given day or week. A decision model, however, may also be simple. It may be confined to a single comparison of costs for choosing between two materials, as in the

Exhibit 5-1
Decision Process and Role of Information

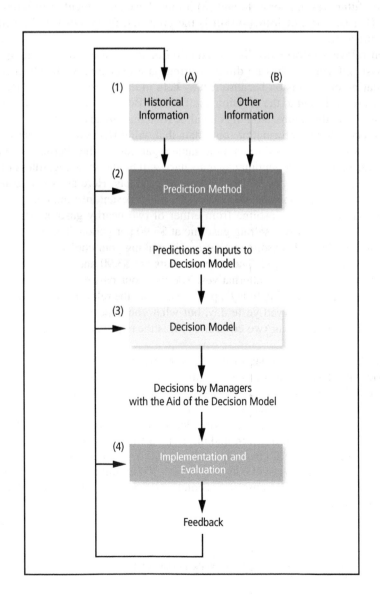

previous example of the tin versus aluminum cans. In this example, our decision model is to compare the predicted unit costs and, assuming that everything else is equal, select the alternative with the lower cost.

The decision process in Exhibit 5-1 applies to all business decisions, no matter how simple or complicated they may be. By using this process, you will be able to focus squarely on the relevant information—the predicted future differences between alternatives—in any decision. In the rest of this chapter, we will use this decision process to apply the concept of relevance to several specific pricing decisions.

Accuracy and Relevance

In the best of all possible worlds, decision-making information would always be both perfectly relevant and precisely accurate. However, in reality, such information is often too difficult or too costly to obtain. Accountants are sometimes forced to choose between more relevance or more accuracy.

Precise but irrelevant information is worthless for decision making. For example, a university president's salary may be $450,000 per year, to the penny, but may have no bearing on the question of whether to buy or rent data-processing equipment. In contrast, imprecise but relevant information can be useful. For example, sales predictions for a new product may be subject to error, but they are still helpful in deciding whether to manufacture the product. Relevant information must be reasonably accurate but not precisely so.

The degree to which information is relevant or precise often depends on the degree to which it is qualitative or quantitative. Qualitative aspects are those for which measurement in financial terms is difficult and imprecise; quantitative aspects are those for which financial measurement is easy and precise. Accountants, statisticians, and mathematicians try to express as many decision factors as feasible in quantitative terms. Why? Because this approach reduces the number of qualitative (subjective) factors they need to consider. Just as we noted that relevance is more crucial than precision in decision making, so may qualitative aspects dominate quantitative (financial) impacts in many decisions. For example, the extreme opposition of a militant labor union to new labor-saving machinery may cause a manager to forgo installation of such machinery even if it would reduce manufacturing costs. In a similar way, a company may pass up the opportunity to purchase a component from a supplier at a price below the cost of producing it themselves to avoid a long-range dependence on that particular supplier.

Likewise, managers sometimes introduce new technology (for example, advanced computer systems or automated equipment) even though the immediate quantitative results seem unattractive. Managers defend such decisions on the grounds that long-term financial results, although hard to predict, are likely to be improved by the technology.

The Relevance of Alternative Income Statements

In many cases, income statement information is relevant to decision making because it specifies how alternative choices impact income. Additionally, since executives use income statements to evaluate performance, managers need to know how their decisions will affect reported income. There are different ways to organize income statement information. Some income statements track fixed and variable costs using the contribution approach, whereas others adopt the absorption approach used in reporting to external parties.

Objective 3

Construct absorption and contribution-margin income statements, and identify their relevance for decision making.

Let's examine the relevance of contribution and absorption income statements. To highlight the different effects of these approaches, consider the Cordell Company. Suppose Cordell produces and sells 1,000,000 units of seat covers for seats on airplanes, buses, and railroad passenger cars. Cordell sells these to companies such as **US Airways** and the **Grand Canyon Railway Company**. The total manufacturing cost of making 1,000,000 seat covers is $30,000,000. The unit manufacturing cost of the product is $30,000,000 ÷ 1,000,000, or $30 per unit. We will assume that in 20X1 the Cordell Company has direct-materials costs of $14 million, direct-labor costs of $6 million, indirect manufacturing costs as illustrated in Exhibit 5-2, selling and administrative expenses as illustrated in Exhibit 5-3, and no beginning or ending inventories. Total sales are predicted at $40 million.

Note that Exhibits 5-2 and 5-3 subdivide costs as variable or fixed. As explained next, most companies do not make such subdivisions in their absorption income statements for external reporting. However, many companies use such partitioning in contribution income statements to align with the information managers often use in decision making.

Exhibit 5-2

Cordell Company
Schedules of Predicted Indirect Manufacturing Costs for the Year Ended December 31, 20X1 (thousands of dollars)

Schedule 1: Variable Costs		
Supplies (lubricants, expendable tools, coolants, sandpaper)	$ 600	
Materials-handling labor (forklift operators)	2,800	
Repairs on manufacturing equipment	400	
Power for factory	200	$ 4,000
Schedule 2: Fixed Costs		
Managers' salaries in factory	$ 400	
Factory employee training	180	
Factory picnic and holiday party	20	
Factory supervisory salaries	1,400	
Depreciation, plant, and equipment	3,600	
Property taxes on plant	300	
Insurance on plant	100	6,000
Total indirect manufacturing costs		$10,000

Exhibit 5-3

Cordell Company
Schedules of Predicted Selling and Administrative Expenses for the Year Ended December 31, 20X1 (thousands of dollars)

Schedule 3: Selling Expenses		
Variable		
Sales commissions	$1,400	
Shipping expenses for products sold	600	$2,000
Fixed		
Advertising	$1,400	
Sales salaries	2,000	
Other	600	4,000
Total selling expenses		$6,000
Schedule 4: Administrative Expenses		
Variable		
Some clerical wages	$ 160	
Computer time rented	40	$ 200
Fixed		
Office salaries	$ 200	
Other salaries	400	
Depreciation on office facilities	200	
Public-accounting fees	80	
Legal fees	200	
Other	720	1,800
Total administrative expenses		$2,000

absorption approach (absorption costing)
A costing approach that considers all indirect manufacturing costs (both variable and fixed) to be product (inventoriable) costs that become an expense in the form of manufacturing cost of goods sold only as sales occur.

Absorption Approach

Exhibit 5-4 presents Cordell's income statement using the **absorption approach** (or **absorption costing**), the method used by companies for external financial reporting. Firms that take this approach consider all direct and indirect manufacturing costs (both variable and fixed) to be product (inventoriable) costs that become an expense in the form of manufacturing cost of goods sold only when the firm sells the related product.

Note that gross profit or gross margin is the difference between sales and the manufacturing cost of goods sold. Note too that the primary classifications of costs on the income statement are by three major management functions: manufacturing, selling, and administrative.

Sales		$40,000
Less: Manufacturing cost of goods sold		
Direct materials	$14,000	
Direct labor	6,000	
Indirect manufacturing (Schedules 1 plus 2)*	10,000	30,000
Gross margin or gross profit		$10,000
Selling expenses (Schedule 3)	$ 6,000	
Administrative expenses (Schedule 4)	2,000	
Total selling and administrative expenses		8,000
Operating income		$ 2,000

*Schedules 1 and 2 are in Exhibit 5-2. Schedules 3 and 4 are in Exhibit 5-3.

Exhibit 5-4

Cordell Company

Predicted Absorption Income Statement for the Year Ended December 31, 20X1 (thousands of dollars)

Contribution Approach

In contrast, Exhibit 5-5 presents Cordell's income statement using the **contribution approach** (also called variable costing or direct costing). For decision purposes, the major difference between the contribution approach and the absorption approach is that the former emphasizes the distinction between variable and fixed costs. Its primary cost classification is by variable- and fixed-cost behavior patterns, not by business functions. Note that it is difficult to classify a given cost as variable, fixed, or mixed (for example, repairs), so often approximations must suffice.

The contribution income statement provides a contribution margin—revenue less all variable costs, including variable selling and administrative costs. This approach makes it easier to understand the impact of changes in sales volume on operating income. It also dovetails nicely with the cost-volume-profit (CVP) analysis illustrated in Chapter 2 and the decision analyses in this chapter and Chapter 6.

Another major benefit of the contribution approach is that it stresses the role of fixed costs in operating income. Before a company can earn income, its total contribution margin must exceed the fixed costs it has incurred for manufacturing and other value-chain functions. This highlighting of contribution margin and total fixed costs focuses management attention on cost behavior and control in making both short-run and long-run decisions. Remember that advocates of the contribution approach do not maintain that fixed costs are unimportant or irrelevant. They do stress, however, that the distinctions between behaviors of variable and fixed costs are crucial for certain decisions. Decisions usually affect fixed costs in a different way than they affect variable costs.

contribution approach
A method of internal (management accounting) reporting that emphasizes the distinction between variable and fixed costs for the purpose of better decision making.

Sales		$40,000
Less: Variable expenses		
Direct materials	$14,000	
Direct labor	6,000	
Variable indirect manufacturing costs (Schedule 1)*	4,000	
Total variable manufacturing cost of goods sold	$24,000	
Variable selling expenses (Schedule 3)	2,000	
Variable administrative expenses (Schedule 4)	200	
Total variable expenses		26,200
Contribution margin		$13,800
Less: Fixed expenses		
Manufacturing (Schedule 2)	$ 6,000	
Selling (Schedule 3)	4,000	
Administrative (Schedule 4)	1,800	11,800
Operating income		$ 2,000

*Note: Schedules 1 and 2 are in Exhibit 5-2. Schedules 3 and 4 are in Exhibit 5-3.

Exhibit 5-5

Cordell Company

Predicted Contribution Income Statement for the Year Ended December 31, 20X1 (thousands of dollars)

The distinction between the gross margin (from the absorption approach) and the contribution margin (from the contribution approach) is important, especially for manufacturing companies. Consider the following computations of contribution margin (CM) and gross margin (GM):

CM/unit = Price − (Variable manufacturing cost/unit + Variable selling & admin. cost/unit)

GM/unit = Price − (Variable manufacturing cost/unit + Fixed manufacturing cost/unit)

The variable selling and administrative cost per unit affects the contribution margin but not the gross margin, while the fixed manufacturing cost affects the gross margin but not the contribution margin. Because fixed manufacturing costs do not change with small changes in volume of units, it can be misleading to express such costs on a per unit basis. Thus, it can be misleading to use gross margin to predict the effect of changes in volume.

Comparing Contribution and Absorption Approaches

The contribution approach separates fixed costs from variable costs. It deducts variable costs from sales to compute a contribution margin and then deducts fixed costs to measure profit. In contrast, the absorption approach separates manufacturing costs from nonmanufacturing costs. It deducts manufacturing costs from sales to compute a gross margin and then deducts nonmanufacturing costs to measure profit. Both formats can be relevant for decision making, depending on the type of decision being contemplated. In situations where decisions affect variable costs differently than they affect fixed costs, such as the short-run pricing decisions we will discuss in this chapter, the contribution approach will yield great value. In contrast, the absorption approach is well suited for long-run pricing decisions, where it is important that the prices over a product's life cover all manufacturing costs, including fixed costs.

Regulators do not allow the contribution approach for external financial reporting. However, many companies use the contribution approach for internal decision-making purposes and an absorption format for external purposes. Why? Because they expect the benefits of making better decisions using the contribution approach to exceed the extra costs of using two different reporting systems simultaneously.

Pricing Special Sales Orders

Before considering more general approaches to pricing, it is helpful to examine how a manager might approach a specific pricing decision—whether to accept a special sales order. We will highlight the value of the contribution approach in such a decision.

Illustrative Example

In our illustration, we'll focus again on the Cordell Company. Suppose Branson Gray Line Tours offered Cordell $26 per unit for a 100,000-unit special order of seat covers that (1) would not affect Cordell's regular business in any way, (2) would not affect total fixed costs, (3) would not require any additional variable selling and administrative expenses, (4) would use some otherwise idle manufacturing capacity, and (5) would not raise any antitrust issues concerning price discrimination. Should Cordell sell the 100,000 seat covers for the price of $26 each?

Perhaps we should state the question more precisely: What is the difference in the short-run financial results between not accepting and accepting the order? As usual, the key question is as follows: What are the differences between alternatives? Exhibit 5-5 presents the income statement of the Cordell Company without the special order, using the contribution approach. Let's see how Cordell's operating income would change if it accepts the special order.

Correct Analysis—Focus on Relevant Information and Cost Behavior

Objective 4

Decide to accept or reject a special order using the contribution-margin approach.

The correct analysis focuses on determining relevant information and cost behavior. It employs the contribution-margin technique. As Exhibit 5-6 shows, this particular order affects only variable manufacturing costs, at a rate of $24 per unit. All other variable costs and all fixed costs are unaffected and, thus, irrelevant. Therefore, a manager may safely ignore them in making this special-order decision. Note how the distinction between variable- and fixed-cost behavior patterns in the contribution-margin technique aids the necessary cost analysis. Total short-run income will increase by $200,000 if Cordell accepts the order—despite the fact that the unit selling price of $26 is less than the total unit manufacturing cost of $30.

	Without Special Order 1,000,000 Units	Effect of Special Order, 100,000 Units		With Special Order, 1,100,000 Units
		Total	Per Unit	
Sales	$40,000,000	$2,600,000	$26	$42,600,000
Less: Variable expenses				
Manufacturing	$24,000,000	$2,400,000	$24	$26,400,000
Selling and administrative	2,200,000	—	—	2,200,000
Total variable expenses	$26,200,000	$2,400,000	$24	$28,600,000
Contribution margin	$13,800,000	$ 200,000	$ 2	$14,000,000
Less: Fixed expenses				
Manufacturing	$ 6,000,000	—	—	$ 6,000,000
Selling and administrative	5,800,000	—	—	5,800,000
Total fixed expenses	$11,800,000	—	—	$11,800,000
Operating income	$ 2,000,000	$ 200,000	$ 2	$ 2,200,000

Exhibit 5-6

Cordell Company
Comparative Predicted Income Statements, Contribution-Margin Technique for Year Ended December 31, 20X1

Why did we deduct fixed costs in Exhibit 5-6? After all, they are irrelevant because they do not differ across the alternatives considered in this decision. We included them because management often focuses on the bottom line—operating income. Both the contribution margin and the operating income increase by $200,000, so we could ignore the fixed costs and come to the same conclusion. However, management may prefer to see the effect of its decisions on operating income, so we include the irrelevant fixed costs in the presentation.

Note that our conclusion is that *short-run* income will increase by $200,000. In this example, we assumed that this special order would neither affect Cordell's regular business nor cause any additional fixed costs. These assumptions may be appropriate in the short run, but they may not hold in the long run. Accepting the special order may eventually affect sales to other customers, and it may at some time entail additional fixed costs for expanded capacity. If there are any expected long-run differences between accepting versus not accepting the special order, those differences should also be incorporated in the analysis.

Making Managerial Decisions

Suppose you are at a meeting of Cordell Company managers and someone asked the following questions. Some of the answers given by your colleagues follow:

Q: What will be the change in the contribution margin if we accept this order?

A: The contribution margin will increase to $14,000,000.

Q: In your analysis (Exhibit 5-6), you show that fixed costs do not change if we accept the order. Are these costs relevant?

A: No. Fixed costs are not relevant.

Q: OK. But do incurred fixed costs have an effect on the bottom line of our company?

A: Certainly. That is why we deduct fixed costs from the contribution margin to get operating income.

Q: Well, if fixed costs affect the bottom line, how can you say they are not relevant?

Comment on your colleague's answers, and answer the last question.

Answer

Your colleague's answer to the first question is technically incorrect. The question asks for change, not the new total contribution margin. The correct answer to this question is that contribution margin will increase by $200,000 (and therefore become $14,000,000 in total). Be careful to differentiate between terms that imply totals and terms that imply changes. In this case, $14,000,000 is the answer to "What is the new total contribution margin if we accept the order?"

Your colleague's responses to the second and third questions are correct. The fixed costs of Cordell are not relevant for this particular special order situation. Nevertheless, the bottom line—operating income—includes all costs and revenues. Do not confuse this with relevant costs—a term we associated with this specific decision. In a decision situation, relevant costs include only those future costs that differ between alternatives. If a manager wants to know the "bottom line" after accepting the order, we would need to include the fixed cost. However, the fixed costs do not affect the difference between the preorder bottom line and the bottom line after accepting the order. The difference is the same $200,000 amount by which the contribution margin increases.

Incorrect Analysis—Misuse of Unit Cost

Faulty cost analysis sometimes occurs because of misinterpreting unit fixed costs, especially with an absorption approach. For instance, Cordell's managers might erroneously use the $30 per-unit total manufacturing cost under the absorption approach ($30,000,000 ÷ 1,000,000 units per Exhibit 5-4) to make the following prediction for the year:

Incorrect Analysis	Without Special Order 1,000,000 Units	Incorrect Effect of Special Order 100,000 Units	With Special Order 1,100,000 Units
Sales	$40,000,000	$2,600,000	$42,600,000
Less: Manufacturing cost of goods sold at $30	30,000,000	3,000,000	33,000,000
Gross margin	10,000,000	(400,000)	9,600,000
Selling and administrative expenses	8,000,000	—	8,000,000
Operating income	$ 2,000,000	$ (400,000)	$ 1,600,000

The incorrect prediction of a $3 million increase in costs results from multiplying 100,000 units by $30. The fallacy in this approach is that it treats a fixed cost (fixed manufacturing cost) as if it were variable. Avoid the mistake of using total unit costs as a basis for predicting how total costs will behave. Unit costs are useful for predicting variable costs, but can be misleading when used to predict fixed costs.

Confusion of Variable and Fixed Costs

Consider the relationship between total fixed manufacturing costs and a fixed manufacturing cost per unit of product (per Exhibit 5-5):

$$\frac{\text{fixed manufacturing cost}}{\text{per unit of product}} = \frac{\text{total fixed manufacturing costs}}{\text{some selected volume level as the denominator}}$$

$$= \frac{\$6,000,000}{1,000,000 \text{ units}} = \$6 \text{ per unit}$$

As we noted in Chapter 1, the typical cost accounting system serves two purposes simultaneously: (1) planning and control and (2) product costing. We can graph the total fixed cost for planning and control purposes as a lump sum:

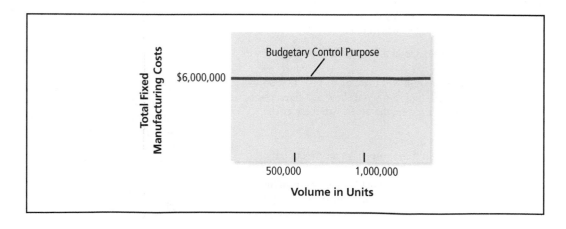

For product-costing purposes, however, it is easy to misinterpret the fixed unit manufacturing cost—to act as if these fixed costs behave as if they are variable costs, which is contrary to fixed-cost behavior:

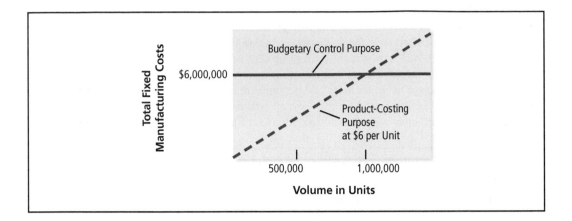

The addition of 100,000 units will not add any fixed costs as long as total output is within the relevant range. The incorrect analysis, however, includes $100,000 \times \$6 = \$600,000$ of additional fixed cost in the predictions of increases in total costs.

In short, we should compute the increase in manufacturing costs by multiplying 100,000 units by only the variable cost portion of cost, $24, not by $30. The $30 includes a $6 fixed-cost-per-unit component that will not affect the total manufacturing costs as volume changes within the relevant range. Alternatively, one way to avoid this misinterpretation is to use the contribution approach, which does not unitize fixed costs, as illustrated in Exhibit 5-6.

Making Managerial Decisions

We have discussed two key lessons so far in this chapter: relevant information and misuse of unit costs. We cannot stress enough how important it is to clearly understand the definition and concept of relevant information. It is also important to understand why the use of unit fixed costs can lead to an incorrect analysis.

Suppose you are a manager in a company that makes small appliances. You are deciding whether to accept or reject a special order for 1,000 units. (Assume there is sufficient excess capacity available for the order.)

1. Which of the following costs are relevant: (a) parts for the order, (b) supervisor's salary, (c) assembly equipment depreciation, (d) power to operate the assembly equipment?
2. Suppose the total unit manufacturing cost for the 1,000 units is $100 per unit. We determined this amount by dividing the total cost by 1,000 units. If the customer decided to double the order to 2,000 units, which costs listed in number 1 would change? Which costs per unit would change? Would the total cost of the order double?

Answers

1. Relevant costs and revenues are predicted future costs and revenues that differ among alternative courses of action. In this case, the cost of parts and power would increase if management accepts the order, and, thus, they are relevant. The other costs are fixed costs that would not change because excess capacity is available.
2. Only the relevant costs, in this case the total variable costs of parts and power, would change. Doubling production would cause these costs to double. In contrast, total fixed costs would be unaffected. However, the fixed cost per unit will decrease, whereas the variable cost per unit will stay the same. For example, fixed supervisory salaries and assembly equipment depreciation will be divided by 2,000 units instead of by only 1,000 units. Therefore, the per-unit supervisory cost will decrease while the per-unit cost of parts and power would stay the same. So, the total cost per unit would fall, and the total cost of the order would increase but by less than double the cost of 1,000 units.

Activity-Based Costing, Special Orders, and Relevant Costs

To identify relevant costs affected by a special order (or by other special decisions), many firms extend their analysis beyond simply identifying fixed and variable costs. As we pointed out in Chapters 3 and 4, a company's operations include many different activities. Businesses that have identified all their significant activities and related cost drivers can produce more detailed relevant information to predict the effects of special orders more accurately.

Suppose the Cordell Company examined its $24 million of variable manufacturing costs using activity-based costing (ABC) and identified two significant activities and related cost drivers: $21 million of processing activity that varies directly with units produced ($14 million in direct materials, $6 million in direct labor, and $1 million of variable manufacturing overhead) at a rate of $21 per unit and $3 million of setup activity (the remainder of variable manufacturing overhead) that varies with the number of production setups. Normally, Cordell produces 2,000 units per setup. Therefore, for processing 1,000,000 units, Cordell has 500 setups at a cost of $6,000 per setup, which explains the total setup cost of $3 million. Additional sales generally require a proportional increase in the number of setups.

Now suppose the special order is for 100,000 units that vary only slightly in production specifications. Instead of the normal 50 setups, Cordell will need only 5 setups for the special order. So processing 100,000 units will take only $2,130,000 of additional variable manufacturing cost:

Additional unit-based variable manufacturing cost, 100,000 × $21	$2,100,000
Additional setup-based variable manufacturing cost, 5 × $6,000	30,000
Total additional variable manufacturing cost	$2,130,000

Instead of the original estimate of 100,000 × $24 = $2,400,000 additional variable manufacturing cost, ABC shows the special order will cost only $2,130,000, or $270,000 less than the original estimate. Therefore, ABC allows managers to realize that the special order is $270,000 more profitable than predicted from the simple unit-based assessment of variable manufacturing cost.

A special order may also be more costly than predicted by a simple fixed- and variable-cost analysis. Suppose the 100,000-unit special order calls for a variety of models and colors delivered at various times so that it requires 100 setups. The variable cost of the special order would be $2.7 million, $300,000 more than the original estimate of $2.4 million:

Additional unit-based variable manufacturing cost, 100,000 × $21	$2,100,000
Additional setup-based variable manufacturing cost, 100 × $6,000	600,000
Total additional variable manufacturing cost	$2,700,000

ABC systems often provide more detailed and relevant information for special-order decisions, but the fundamental concepts remain the same—focus your attention on future costs and revenues that differ because of the special order. Also, be careful to recognize and properly use terms such as *impact, change,* and *total.* The summary problem for your review that follows gives you more practice at analyzing a special order.

Summary Problem for Your Review

PROBLEM

1. Suppose Nike produces and sells 500,000 units of the LeBron James "Fearless Lion Edition" basketball shirt. The selling price is $35, and there is excess capacity to produce an additional 300,000 shirts. The absorption cost of the shirts is $10,000,000 ÷ 500,000, or $20 per shirt, consisting of variable manufacturing costs of $7,000,000 ($7,000,000 ÷ 500,000 or $14 per shirt) and fixed manufacturing costs of $3,000,000 ($3,000,000 ÷ 500,000 or $6 per shirt). Variable selling and administrative costs are $3 per shirt, and fixed selling and administrative costs are $2,000,000. Assume Nike receives an offer from Sports Authority to buy 100,000 shirts at a price of $18.00 per shirt. If Nike accepts the order it would not incur any additional variable selling and administrative costs, but it would have to pay a flat fee of $80,000 to the manufacturer's agent who had obtained the potential order. Should Nike accept the special order?

2. What if the order was for 250,000 units at a selling price of $13.00 and there was no $80,000 agent's fee? One manager argued for acceptance of such an order as follows: "Of course, we will lose $1.00 each on the variable manufacturing costs ($13 – $14),

but we will gain $2.00 per unit by spreading our fixed manufacturing costs over 750,000 shirts instead of 500,000 shirts. Consequently, we should take the offer because it represents an advantage of $1.00 per shirt." The manager's analysis follows:

Old fixed manufacturing cost per unit, $3,000,000 ÷ 500,000	$6.00
New fixed manufacturing cost per unit, $3,000,000 ÷ 750,000	4.00
"Savings" in fixed manufacturing cost per unit	$2.00
Loss on variable manufacturing cost per unit, $13.00 − $14.00	1.00
Net savings per unit in manufacturing cost	$1.00

Explain why this is faulty thinking.

SOLUTION

1. Focus on relevant information—the differences in future revenues and costs. In this problem, in addition to the difference in variable costs, there is a difference in fixed costs between the two alternatives.

Additional revenue, 100,000 units at $18.00 per shirt	$1,800,000
Less: Additional costs	
Variable costs, 100,000 units at $14 per unit	1,400,000
Fixed costs, agent's fee	80,000
Increase in operating income from special order	$ 320,000

So, from a strictly financial perspective, Nike should accept the special order.

2. The faulty thinking comes from attributing a "savings" to the decrease in unit fixed costs. Regardless of how we "unitize" the fixed manufacturing costs or "spread" them over the units produced, the special order will not change the total of $3 million. Remember that we have a negative contribution margin of $1.00 per unit on this special order. Thus, there is no way we can cover any amount of fixed costs! Fixed costs are not relevant to this decision.

Basic Principles for Pricing Decisions

One of the major decisions managers face is pricing. Pricing decisions can take many forms in addition to pricing special orders. For example, managers make the following pricing decisions:

1. Setting the price of a new or refined product
2. Setting the price of products sold under private labels
3. Responding to a new price of a competitor
4. Pricing bids in both sealed and open bidding situations

Pricing decisions are so important that we will spend the rest of the chapter discussing the many aspects of pricing. Let us now consider some of the basic concepts behind pricing.

Pricing Under Perfect and Imperfect Competition

Pricing decisions depend on the market characteristics in which a firm operates. In **perfect competition** all competing firms sell the same type of product at the same price. Thus, a firm can sell as much of a product as it can produce, all at a single market price. If it charges more, no customer will buy. If it charges less, it sacrifices profits. Therefore, every firm in such a market will charge the market price, and the only decision for managers is how much to produce.

Objective 5

Explain why pricing decisions depend on the characteristics of the market.

perfect competition
A market in which a firm can sell as much of a product as it can produce, all at a single market price.

Exhibit 5-7
Marginal Revenue and Cost
in Perfect Competition

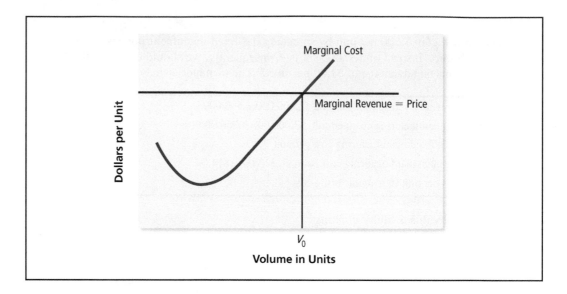

marginal cost

The additional cost resulting
from producing and selling one
additional unit.

Although costs do not directly influence prices in perfect competition, they do affect the
production decision. Consider the marginal cost curve in Exhibit 5-7. The **marginal cost** is the
additional cost resulting from producing and selling one additional unit—for the **Grand Canyon
Railway**, it's the cost of serving one additional passenger; for **General Motors**, it's the cost of
producing one additional car. With a fixed set of production facilities, the marginal cost often
decreases as production increases up to a point because of efficiencies created by larger volumes.
At some point, however, marginal costs begin to rise with increases in production because facilities become overcrowded or overused, resulting in inefficiencies.

marginal revenue

The additional revenue
resulting from the sale of an
additional unit.

Exhibit 5-7 also includes a marginal revenue curve. The **marginal revenue** is the additional
revenue resulting from the sale of an additional unit. In perfect competition, the marginal revenue curve is a horizontal line equal to the price per unit at all volumes of sales.

As long as the marginal cost is less than the marginal revenue (price), additional production
and sales are profitable. When marginal cost exceeds price, however, the firm loses money on
each additional unit. Therefore, the profit-maximizing volume is the quantity at which marginal
cost equals price. In Exhibit 5-7, the firm should produce V_0 units. Producing fewer units passes
up profitable opportunities, and producing more units reduces profit because each additional unit
costs more to produce than it generates in revenue.

imperfect competition

A market in which the price a
firm charges for a unit influences
the quantity of units it sells.

In **imperfect competition**, the price a firm charges for a unit influences the quantity of
units it sells. At some point, the firm must reduce prices to generate additional sales. Exhibit 5-8
contains a *demand curve* (also called the *average revenue curve*) for imperfect competition that

Exhibit 5-8
Marginal Revenue and Cost
in Imperfect Competition

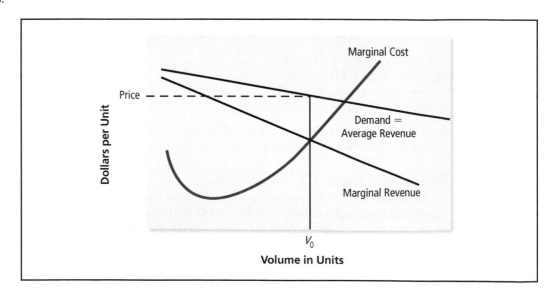

Units Sold	Price per Unit	Total Revenue			Marginal Revenue			Marginal Cost	Profit from Production and Sale of Additional Unit		
10	$50	10 ×	$50 =	$500							
11	49	11 ×	49 =	539	$539 −	$500 =	$39	$35	$39 −	$35 =	$4
12	48	12 ×	48 =	576	576 −	539 =	37	36	37 −	36 =	1
13	47	13 ×	47 =	611	611 −	576 =	35	37	35 −	37 =	(2)

Exhibit 5-9
Profit Maximization in Imperfect Competition

shows the volume of sales at each possible price. To sell additional units, the firm must reduce the price of all units sold. Therefore, the *marginal revenue curve*, also shown in Exhibit 5-8, is below the demand curve. That is, the marginal revenue for selling one additional unit is less than the price at which the company sells it because the price of all other units falls as well. For example, suppose a firm can sell 10 units for $50 per unit. However, the firm must drop the price to $49 per unit to sell 11 units, to $48 to sell 12 units, and to $47 to sell 13 units. The fourth column of Exhibit 5-9 shows the marginal revenue for units 11–13. Notice that the marginal revenue decreases as volume increases.

To estimate marginal revenue, managers must predict the **price elasticity**—the effect of price changes on sales volume. If small price increases create large volume declines, demand is highly elastic. If prices have little or no effect on volume, demand is highly inelastic.

price elasticity
The effect of price changes on sales volume.

For the marginal costs shown in the fifth column of Exhibit 5-9, the optimal production and sales level is 12 units. The last column of that exhibit illustrates that the eleventh unit adds $4 to profit, and the twelfth adds $1, but production and sale of the thirteenth unit would decrease profit by $2. In general, firms should produce and sell units until the marginal revenue equals the marginal cost, represented by volume V_0 in Exhibit 5-8. The optimal price charged will be the amount that creates a demand for V_0 units.

Notice that the marginal cost is relevant for pricing decisions. In managerial accounting, we often use variable cost as an approximation for marginal cost. What is the major difference between marginal cost and variable cost? Accountants assume that variable cost is constant within a relevant range of volume, whereas marginal cost may change with each unit produced. Within large ranges of production volume, however, changes in marginal cost are often small. Therefore, variable cost can be a reasonable approximation of marginal cost in many situations.

Pricing and Accounting

Accountants seldom compute marginal revenue and marginal cost curves. Instead, they use estimates based on judgment to predict the effects of additional production and sales on profits. In addition, they examine selected volumes, not the whole range of possible volumes. Such simplifications are justified because the cost of a more sophisticated analysis would exceed the benefits.

Consider a division of General Electric (GE) that makes microwave ovens. Suppose market researchers estimate that GE can sell 700,000 ovens at $200 per unit and 1,000,000 ovens at $180. The variable cost of production is $130 per unit at production levels of both 700,000 and 1,000,000. Both volumes are also within the relevant range so that changes in volume do not affect fixed costs. Which price should GE charge?

GE's accountant would determine the relevant revenues and costs. Relative to selling 700,000 ovens at $200, the additional revenue and extra costs of selling 1,000,000 ovens at the $180 price are as follows:

Additional revenue: (1,000,000 × $180) − (700,000 × $200) =	$40,000,000
Additional costs: 300,000 × $130 =	39,000,000
Additional profit	$ 1,000,000

So the $180 price is optimal since it generates $1,000,000 more profit. On the other hand, the accountant could compare the total contribution for each alternative:

Contribution at $180: ($180 − $130) × 1,000,000 =	$50,000,000
Contribution at $200: ($200 − $130) × 700,000 =	49,000,000
Difference	$ 1,000,000

Notice that comparing the total contributions is essentially the same as computing the additional revenues and costs—both use the same relevant information. Further, both approaches correctly ignore fixed costs, which are unaffected by this pricing decision.

Influences on Pricing in Practice

Several factors interact to shape the market in which managers make pricing decisions. Legal requirements, competitors' actions, and customer demands all influence pricing.

Legal Requirements

predatory pricing
Establishing prices so low that they drive competitors out of the market. The predatory pricer then has no significant competition and can raise prices dramatically.

discriminatory pricing
Charging different prices to different customers for the same product or service.

Managers must consider constraints imposed by United States and international laws when making pricing decisions. These laws often protect consumers, but they also help protect competing companies from predatory and discriminatory pricing.

Predatory pricing means firms set prices so low that they drive competitors out of the market, after which the firm faces no significant competition and can raise prices dramatically. For example, lawsuits have accused Wal-Mart of predatory pricing—selling at low cost to drive out local competitors. However, in a 4-to-3 vote, the Arkansas Supreme Court ruled in favor of Wal-Mart. Courts in the United States have generally ruled that pricing is predatory only if companies set prices below their average variable cost and actually lose money in order to drive their competitors out of business.

Discriminatory pricing is charging different prices to different customers for the same product or service. For example, a large group of retail druggists and big drugstore chains sued several large drug companies. The drugstores alleged that the drug companies' practice of allowing discounts—some as large as 40%—to mail-order drug companies, health maintenance organizations, and other managed-care entities constitutes discriminatory pricing. However, pricing is not discriminatory if it reflects a cost differential incurred in providing the good or service.

Both predatory and discriminatory pricing practices are not only illegal but unethical business practices. Management accountants have an ethical obligation to perform their duties in accordance with relevant laws and to refrain from engaging in or supporting any activity or practice that would discredit the profession.

Competitors' Actions

Competitors usually react to the price changes of their rivals. Many companies gather information regarding a rival's capacity, technology, and operating policies. In this way, managers make more informed predictions of competitors' reactions to a company's prices. The study of game theory focuses on predicting and reacting to competitors' actions.

A manager's expectations of competitors' reactions and of the overall effects of price changes on an industry's demand heavily influence pricing policies. For example, an airline might cut prices even if it expects matching price cuts from its rivals, hoping that total customer demand for the tickets of all airlines will increase sufficiently to offset the reduction in the price per ticket.

Competition is becoming increasingly global in its scope. Overcapacity in some countries often causes aggressive pricing policies for a company's exported goods. For example, companies might "dump" products by selling them at a low price in a foreign market that is isolated from its other markets. As you can imagine, when companies' markets expand globally, their pricing policies become more complex.

Customer Demands

More than ever before, managers are recognizing the needs of customers. Pricing is no exception. If customers believe a price is too high, they may turn to other sources for the product, substitute a different product, or decide to produce the item themselves. As the controller for the Grand Canyon Railway states, "... prices charged must be attractive to the customer." If not, customers can simply drive their own cars to the Grand Canyon or choose to ride a bus.

Cost-Plus Pricing

Accounting influences pricing by providing costs. The exact role costs play in pricing decisions depends on both the market conditions and the company's approach to pricing. This section discusses cost-plus pricing, the most common use of costs in pricing decisions.

What Is Cost-Plus Pricing?

Many managers set prices by "cost-plus" pricing. For example, Grand Canyon Railway sets its prices by computing an average cost and then adding a desired **markup**—the amount by which price exceeds cost—that will generate a desired level of income. The key is how to determine the "plus" in cost plus. Instead of being a fixed markup, the "plus" will usually depend on both costs and the demands of customers. For example, a lakeside resort may have a standard price (the rack rate) that does not change during the year, but it may offer discounts during the slow winter season.

markup
The amount by which price exceeds cost.

The most direct case of cost-plus pricing is in industries where revenue is based on cost reimbursement. Cost-reimbursement contracts generally specify how to measure costs and what costs are allowable. For example, the U.S. Defense Department has specific rules on reimbursable costs that determine a defense contractor's revenue on military contracts.

Ultimately, in most cases the market sets prices. Why? Because companies inevitably adjust the price as set by a cost-plus formula "in light of market conditions." The maximum price a company can charge is the one that does not drive the customer away. The minimum price might be considered to be zero (for example, companies may give out free samples to gain entry into a market).

A practical guide is that, in the short run, the minimum price sales personnel should quote on an order is the marginal cost that the company incurs if it gets the order (in effect its relevant costs of filling the order)—often all variable costs of producing, selling, and distributing the good or service. However, in the long run, the price must be high enough to cover all costs, including fixed costs. Therefore, many companies add an allocation of fixed costs per unit to the variable cost per unit to get a minimum price they want to achieve in the long run. They acknowledge that market conditions sometimes dictate sales at a price lower than this minimum price. Yet, to continue to produce and sell such a product in the long run, there must be a prospect of eventually achieving a price at or above the long-run minimum.

Cost Bases for Cost-Plus Pricing

To set a desired price for products or services, managers often add a markup to some measure of costs—thus, the term *cost plus*. The size of the "plus" depends on the definition of cost and the desired operating income. Prices can be based on a host of different markups that are in turn based on a host of different definitions of cost. Thus, there are many ways to arrive at the same price.

Objective 7

Compute a sales price by various methods, and compare the advantages and disadvantages of these methods.

Exhibit 5-10 displays the relationships of costs to selling prices, assuming a desired operating income of $1 million on a volume of 1 million units. The exhibited percentages represent four popular markup formulas for pricing based on percentages of four different measures of cost: (1) variable manufacturing costs, (2) total variable costs, (3) total manufacturing cost, and (4) full costs. Notice that the first two formulas are consistent with the contribution approach and the latter two are based on absorption costing numbers. Note also that **full cost** means the total of all manufacturing costs plus the total of all selling and administrative costs. As noted in earlier chapters, we use "selling and administrative" to include all value-chain functions other than production.

full cost
The total of all manufacturing costs plus the total of all selling and administrative costs.

To achieve the same prices, the percentages in Exhibit 5-10 differ for each definition of cost. For instance, the markup on variable manufacturing costs is 66.67%, and on full costs it is only 5.26%. Regardless of the formula used, the decision maker setting prices will be led toward the same $20 price. If the decision maker is unable to obtain such a price consistently, the company will not achieve its goal of $1 million in operating income.

Exhibit 5-10
Relationships of Costs to
Same Target Selling Price

			Alternative Markup Percentages to Achieve Same Sales Price
	Sales price	$20.00	
	Variable cost:		
(1)	Manufacturing	$12.00	($20.00 − $12.00) ÷ $12.00 = 66.67%
	Selling and administrative*	1.10	
(2)	Unit variable costs	$13.10	($20.00 − $13.10) ÷ $13.10 = 52.67%
	Fixed costs:		
	Manufacturing†	$ 3.00	
	Selling and administrative	2.90	
	Unit fixed costs	$ 5.90	
(4)	Full costs	$19.00	($20.00 − $19.00) ÷ $19.00 = 5.26%
	Desired operating income	$ 1.00	

*Selling and administrative costs include costs of all value-chain functions other than production.
†(3) A frequently used formula is based on total manufacturing costs: [$20.00 − ($12.00 + $3.00)] ÷ $15.00 = 33.33%.

We have seen that managers can base prices on various types of cost information, from variable manufacturing costs to full costs. Each of these costs can be relevant to the pricing decision. Each approach has advantages and disadvantages.

Advantages of the Contribution Approach in Cost-Plus Pricing

Prices based on variable costs represent a contribution approach to pricing. When used intelligently, the contribution approach has some advantages over the total-manufacturing-cost and full-cost approaches because the latter two often fail to highlight different cost behavior patterns.

The contribution approach offers more detailed information because it displays variable- and fixed-cost behavior patterns separately. Because the contribution approach is sensitive to cost-volume-profit relationships, it is a helpful basis for developing pricing formulas. As a result, this approach allows managers to prepare price schedules at different volume levels.

The correct analysis in Exhibit 5-11 shows how changes in volume affect operating income. The contribution approach helps managers with pricing decisions by readily displaying the inter-relationships among variable costs, fixed costs, and potential changes in selling prices.

In contrast, pricing with full costing presumes a given volume level. When the volume changes, the unit cost used at the original planned volume may mislead managers. Managers sometimes erroneously assume that they can compute the change in total costs by multiplying any change in volume by the full unit cost.

	Correct Analysis			Incorrect Analysis		
Volume in units	900,000	1,000,000	1,100,000	900,000	1,000,000	1,100,000
Sales at $20.00	$18,000,000	$20,000,000	$22,000,000	$18,000,000	$20,000,000	$22,000,000
Unit variable costs at $13.10*	11,790,000	13,100,000	14,410,000			
Contribution margin	6,210,000	6,900,000	7,590,000			
Fixed costs†	5,900,000	5,900,000	5,900,000			
Full costs at $19.00*				17,100,000	19,000,000	20,900,000
Operating income	$ 310,000	$ 1,000,000	$ 1,690,000	$ 900,000	$ 1,000,000	$ 1,100,000

*From Exhibit 5-10.
†Fixed manufacturing costs $3,000,000
   Fixed selling and administrative costs   2,900,000
   Total fixed costs $5,900,000

Exhibit 5-11
Analyses of Effects of Changes in Volume on Operating Income

The incorrect analysis in Exhibit 5-11 shows how using the $19 full cost per unit (based on a volume of 1,000,000 units from Exhibit 5-10) to predict effects of volume changes on operating income can mislead managers. Suppose a manager incorrectly uses the $19 figure to predict an operating income of $900,000 if the company sells 900,000 instead of 1,000,000 units. However, since the correct analysis predicts operating income of $310,000, the manager may be stunned by the actual results—and possibly be looking for a new job. Notice the only volume where the incorrect analysis is actually appropriate is at the 1 million unit volume level, which is also the only volume where the $19 full cost per unit is valid.

The contribution approach also offers insight into the short-run versus long-run effects of cutting prices on special orders. For example, recall the 100,000 unit special order at a lower than normal selling price ($26 versus $40) for Cordell Company displayed in Exhibit 5-6 (page 187). As you saw earlier, the contribution approach generated the most relevant information, showing that accepting this special order yielded a short-run advantage of $200,000.

However, the manager should also consider long-run effects. Will acceptance of the offer undermine the long-run price structure? In other words, is the short-run advantage of $200,000 more than offset by highly probable long-run financial disadvantages? The manager may think so and, thus, reject the offer. But—and this is important—by doing so the manager is, in effect, forgoing $200,000 now to protect certain long-run market advantages. Generally, the manager can assess problems of this sort by asking whether the probability of long-run benefits is worth an "investment" equal to the forgone contribution margin ($200,000, in this case). Under full-cost approaches, the manager must ordinarily conduct a one-time special study to find the short-run effects of a volume increase associated with a special order. Under the contribution approach, the manager has a system that will routinely provide such information.

Advantages of Absorption-Cost Approaches in Cost-Plus Pricing

Frequently, companies do not employ a contribution approach because they fear that managers will indiscriminately substitute variable costs for full costs and will, therefore, lead to suicidal price cutting. This problem should not arise if managers use the data wisely. However, if top managers perceive a pronounced danger of underpricing when they disclose variable-cost data, they may justifiably prefer an absorption-cost approach (either total manufacturing costs or full costs) for guiding pricing decisions.

Actually, in practice more companies use absorption cost than the contribution approach. Why? In addition to the reasons we have already mentioned, managers have cited the following:

1. In the long run, a firm must recover all costs to stay in business. Additionally, fixed costs eventually fluctuate as volume changes (all costs are variable in the long run, even if some are fixed in the short run). Therefore, it is prudent to emphasize the absorption-cost approach over the contribution approach.
2. Computing prices based on absorption cost may indicate what competitors might charge, especially if they have approximately the same level of efficiency as you and also aim to recover all costs in the long run.
3. Absorption-cost formula pricing meets the cost-benefit test. It is too expensive to conduct individual cost-volume analyses for the many products (sometimes thousands) that a company offers.
4. There is much uncertainty about the shape of demand curves and the correct price-output decisions. Absorption-cost pricing copes with this uncertainty by not encouraging managers to take too much marginal business.
5. Absorption-cost pricing tends to promote price stability. Managers prefer price stability, primarily because it makes planning more dependable.
6. Absorption-cost pricing provides the most defensible basis for justifying prices to all interested parties, including government antitrust regulators.
7. Absorption-cost pricing provides convenient reference points to simplify hundreds or thousands of pricing decisions.

Using Multiple Approaches

To say that either a contribution approach or an absorption-cost approach provides the "best" guide to pricing decisions is a dangerous oversimplification of one of the most perplexing issues in business. Lack of understanding and judgment can lead to unprofitable pricing regardless of the kind of cost data available or cost accounting system used.

No single method of pricing is always best. Many companies use both full-cost and variable-cost information in pricing decisions. Modern accounting systems, such as ERP systems, often identify variable and fixed costs, producing both full-cost and variable-cost information. This allows assessment of both short-run and long-run effects. In contrast, most older systems focus on absorption-cost and do not organize their data collection to distinguish between variable and fixed costs. When using such older systems, managers must use special studies or educated guesses to designate costs as variable or fixed.

Managers are especially reluctant to focus on variable costs and ignore allocated fixed costs when their performance evaluations, and possibly their bonuses, are based on income shown in published financial statements. Why? Because companies base such statements on absorption costing, and thus allocations of fixed costs affect reported income.

Formats for Pricing

Exhibit 5-10 showed how to compute alternative general markup percentages that would produce the same selling prices if used day after day. In practice, the format and arithmetic of quote sheets, job proposals, or similar records vary considerably.

Exhibit 5-12 is from an actual quote sheet used by the manager of a small job shop that bids on welding machinery orders in a highly competitive industry. The approach in Exhibit 5-12 is a tool for making informed pricing decisions. Notice that the maximum price is not a matter of cost at all. It is what you think you can obtain. The minimum price is the total variable cost.

The manager will rarely bid the minimum price. Businesses do need to make a profit. Still, the manager wants to know the effect of a job on the company's total variable costs. Occasionally, a company will bid near or even below that minimum price to establish a presence in new markets or with a new customer, especially when the company expects to receive cost reductions in the future or when the new product is tied to other products that generate profits for the firm, as in the Business First box on page 199 regarding Microsoft's Xbox 360.

Note that Exhibit 5-12 classifies costs specifically for the pricing task. More than one person may make pricing decisions in a particular company. The accountant's responsibility is to prepare an understandable format that requires a minimum of computations. Exhibit 5-12 combines direct labor and variable manufacturing overhead. It lumps together all fixed costs—whether manufacturing, selling, or administrative—and applies them to the job using a single fixed-overhead rate per direct-labor hour. If the company wants more accuracy, it could formulate many more detailed cost items and overhead rates. To obtain the desired accuracy, many companies are turning to activity-based costing.

Some managers, particularly in construction and in service industries (such as auto repair), compile separate categories of costs of (1) direct materials, parts, and supplies and (2) direct labor. These managers then use different markup rates for each category. They

Exhibit 5-12

Quote Sheet for Pricing

Direct materials, at cost	$25,000
Direct labor and variable manufacturing overhead, 600 direct-labor hours × $30 per hour	18,000
Sales commission (varies with job)	2,000
Total variable costs—minimum price*	45,000
Add fixed costs allocated to job, 600 direct-labor hours × $20 per hour	12,000
Total costs	57,000
Add desired markup	30,000
Selling price—maximum price that you think you can obtain*	$87,000

*This sheet shows two prices, maximum and minimum. Any amount you can get above the minimum price provides contribution margin.

Business First

Xbox 360 Pricing

Despite all the hype surrounding the Xbox 360 video game console in May of 2005, Microsoft didn't initially make any money on the machine itself. A tear-down analysis by market researcher iSuppli of the high-end Xbox 360 found that the materials (e.g., hard drive, computer chip, cables, etc.) cost Microsoft $525 before assembly. The console initially sold at retail for $399, for a loss of $126 per unit. iSuppli analyst Chris Crotty said efficiency gains would shave $50 off chip costs, which, with other reductions over time, would get Microsoft closer to breakeven. Microsoft expected that, including sales of its own game software, the Xbox line would start out "gross margin neutral"—breakeven—and would eventually turn a profit.

Microsoft continued this low-price strategy by reducing the price of its Xbox 360 Arcade system to less than $200 in 2008. As a result, Asian shipments of the Xbox in October 2008 grew by 53% compared to the prior month. Microsoft officials claim "...what is really driving our growth momentum right now is how we are broadening our consumer base to include not only hardcore gamers but also individuals who would have previously not thought about buying a game

console." Microsoft also commented that "...current shipment volumes had reached such high levels that the company could afford to depend on volume to rake in a profit despite the lower prices." This pricing strategy also boosted company profits from related software-game sales, additional equipment, and internet products for the Xbox, which is consistent with its fundamental claim that "Microsoft is a software company at heart, and we will continue to work with our partners and by ourselves to develop new software for the market." In fact, for calendar year 2011, Microsoft reported that the Xbox 360 was the fastest-growing console in the United States, with an industry-leading $6.7 billion in sales (more than $2.1 billion on consoles and $4.6 billion on games and accessories). The firm also reported more than 66 million Xbox 360 consoles and 16 million Kinect sensors sold worldwide, and almost 40 million Xbox Live memberships.

Sources: Adapted from Paul Lilly, "Xbox 360 Sales Smoked the Competition in 2011, Microsoft Says," MAXIMUMPC, January 13, 2012; Reuters, "Microsoft Eyes '09 Market-Beating Xbox Sales," December 17, 2008; Arik Kesseldahl, "For Every Xbox, A Big Fat Loss," Business Week, December 5, 2005.

use these rates to provide enough revenue to cover both indirect and unallocated costs and operating profit. For example, an automobile repair shop might have the following format for each job:

	Billed to Customers
Auto parts ($200 cost plus 40% markup)	$280
Direct labor (Cost is $20 per hour. Bill at 300% to recover indirect and unallocated costs and provide for operating profit. Billing rate is $20 × 300% = $60 per hour. Total billed for 10 hours is $60 × 10 = $600.)	600
Total billed to customer	$880

Another example is an Italian printing company in Milan that wants to price its jobs so that each one generates a margin of 28% of revenues—14% to cover selling and administrative expenses and 14% for profit. To achieve this margin, the manager uses a pricing formula of 140% times predicted materials cost plus €25 per hour of production time. The latter covers labor and overhead costs of €18 per hour. For a product with €400 of materials cost and 30 hours of production time, the price would be €1,310:

	Cost	Price	Margin
Materials	€400	€ 560	€160
Labor and overhead	540	750	210
Total	€940	€1,310	€370

The margin of €370 is approximately 40% of the cost of €940 and 28% of the price of €1,310.

You can see there are numerous ways to determine selling prices. However, some general words of caution are appropriate here. Managers are better able to understand their options and the effects of their decisions on profits if they know their costs. That is, it is more informative to pinpoint costs first, before adding markups, than to have a variety of markups already embedded in the "costs" used as guides for setting selling prices. For example, if materials cost $1,000, a price quotation guide should show them at $1,000, not at, for example, a marked-up $1,400 because that is what the seller hopes to receive.

Summary Problem for Your Review

PROBLEM

Custom Graphics is a Chicago printing company that bids on a wide variety of design and printing jobs. The owner of the company, Janet Solomon, prepares the bids for most jobs. Her cost budget for 20X1 follows:

Materials		$ 350,000
Labor		250,000
Overhead		
Variable	$300,000	
Fixed	150,000	450,000
Total production cost of jobs		1,050,000
Selling and administrative expenses*		
Variable	$ 75,000	
Fixed	125,000	200,000
Total costs		$1,250,000

*These expenses include costs of all value-chain functions other than production.

Solomon has a target profit of $250,000 for 20X1.

Compute the average target markup percentage for setting prices as a percentage of the following:

1. Materials plus labor
2. Variable production cost of jobs (assume labor is a variable-cost resource)
3. Total production cost of jobs
4. All variable costs
5. All costs

SOLUTION

The purpose of this problem is to emphasize that many different approaches to pricing might be used that would achieve the same selling price. To achieve $250,000 of profit, the desired revenue for 20X1 is $1,250,000 + $250,000 = $1,500,000. The required markup percentages are as follow:

1. Percent of materials and labor $= \dfrac{(\$1,500,000 - \$600,000)}{\$600,000} = 150\%$

2. Percent of variable production cost of jobs $= \dfrac{(\$1,500,000 - \$900,000)}{\$900,000} = 66.7\%$

3. Percent of total production cost of jobs $= \dfrac{(\$1,500,000 - \$1,050,000)}{\$1,050,000} = 42.9\%$

4. Percent of all variable costs $= \dfrac{(\$1,500,000 - \$975,000)}{\$975,000} = 53.8\%$

5. Percent of all costs $= \dfrac{(\$1,500,000 - \$1,250,000)}{\$1,250,000} = 20\%$

Target Costing

The pricing approaches so far have all developed a price based on measures of costs. Another approach to the relationship between costs and prices is to take a product's market price as given and determine the maximum cost the company can spend to make the product and still achieve the desired profitability. We call this **target costing**.

Consider a company that is deciding whether to develop and market a new product. In evaluating the feasibility of the new product, management must predict both the cost to produce the product and the price at which it will sell. The degree to which management actions can affect price and cost determines the most effective approach to use for pricing and cost management purposes. Companies use cost-plus pricing for products where management actions (for example, advertising) can influence the market price. Although cost management is important in this case, there is a strong focus on marketing and the revenue side of the profit equation.

But what if the market conditions are such that management cannot influence prices? If a company is to achieve management's desired profit, it must focus on the product's cost. What management needs is an effective tool to reduce costs without reducing value to the customer. A growing number of companies faced with this situation are adopting target costing. Based on the product's predicted price and the company's desired profit, managers set a desired, or target, cost before creating or even designing the product. Managers must then design the product and manufacturing process so that the product's cost does not exceed its target cost. Why focus on the product design phase? Because the design affects a vast majority of costs. For example, the design of the product and the associated production process largely determines the costs of resources, such as new machinery, materials, parts, and even future refinements. It is not easy to reduce these costs once production begins. So, the emphasis of target costing is on proactive, up-front planning throughout every activity of the new-product development process.

Target Costing and New Product Development

Exhibit 5-13 shows a real company's target costing process for a new product. Based on the existing technology and related cost structure, the new product has three parts, requires direct labor, and has four types of indirect costs. The first step in the target-costing process is to determine the market price. The market sets this price. So why does management have to determine it?

Objective 8

Use target costing to decide whether to add a new product.

target costing
Taking a product's market price as given and determining the maximum cost the company can spend to make the product and still achieve the desired profitability.

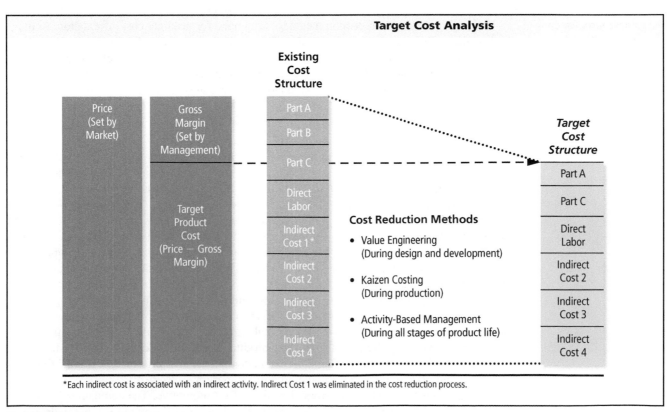

Exhibit 5-13
The Target Costing Process

Remember that the product is new and has not actually been on the market. So, management has to estimate what the market will pay for the product. There are several tools, such as market focus group studies and surveys, that a firm can use to determine this price. Management also sets a desired gross margin for the new product. The market price less the gross margin is the target cost for the new product. The company determines the existing cost structure for the product by building up costs on an individual component level. This product has two components. Component 1 consists of parts A and B. Component 2 is part C. Both components and the final assembly use direct labor. Finally, the activities necessary to plan and process the product create indirect costs.

Marketing plays a large role in target costing. Market research in the early planning stages guides the whole product development process by supplying information about customer demands and requirements. One of the key characteristics of successful target costing is a strong emphasis on understanding customer demands. Many companies actively seek customer input on the design of product features. Then, they compare the cost of each feature to its value to determine whether to add it to the product. For example, one of Boeing's customers wanted heated floors in its airplanes. However, the cost of the heated floors was too high, and the customer reconsidered.

In the example in Exhibit 5-13, the existing cost is too large to generate the desired profit. Does this mean that the new product is not feasible? Not necessarily. A cross-functional team consisting of engineers, sales personnel, key suppliers, and accountants now must determine if the company can implement cost reductions large enough to meet the target cost. In the example in Exhibit 5-13, the company reduced the cost of parts by changing the design of the product so that it could use part C in place of part B. The company also asked suppliers of parts A and C to reduce their costs. Design and process engineers were also able to eliminate the activity that generated one type of indirect cost (Indirect Cost 1). These cost reductions resulted from **value engineering**—a cost-reduction technique, used primarily during the design stage, that uses information about all value-chain functions to satisfy customer needs while reducing costs. In total, the planned cost reductions were adequate to reduce costs to the target.

Not all the reductions in cost have to take place before production begins. For example, **kaizen costing** is the Japanese term for continuous improvement during manufacturing. How do companies apply kaizen costing? They establish kaizen goals each year as part of the planning process. Examples include the continual reduction in setup and processing times due to increased employee familiarity with the procedure. In total, target costing during design and kaizen costing during manufacturing may allow the firm to achieve the target cost over the product's life, even if initial cost predictions look too high.

Underlying these cost-reduction methods is the need for accurate cost information. Activity-based costing often provides this information. Companies can then use activity-based management (ABM) to identify and eliminate non-value-added activities, waste, and their related costs. ABM is applied throughout both the design and manufacturing stages of the product's life. For examples of how accountants are using ABC and ABM in target costing, see the Business First box on page 203.

Illustration of Target Costing

Consider the target-costing system used by ITT Automotive—one of the world's largest automotive suppliers. The company designs, develops, and manufactures a broad range of products including brake systems, electric motors, and lamps. Also, the company is the worldwide market leader in antilock braking systems (ABS), producing 20,000 such systems per day.

What pricing approach does ITT Automotive use for the ABS? The pricing process starts when one of ITT's customers, for example Mercedes-Benz, sends an invitation to bid. The market for brake systems is so competitive that very little variance exists in the prices companies can ask (bid). ITT then forms a target-costing group and charges it with determining whether the price and costs allow for enough of a profit margin. This group includes engineers, management accountants, and sales personnel. Factors the group considers in their determination include competitor pricing, inflation rates, interest rates, and potential cost reductions during both the design (value engineering) and production (kaizen costing) stages of the ABS product life. ITT purchases many of the component parts that make up the ABS. Thus, the target-costing group works closely with suppliers. After making product and process design improvements and receiving commitments from suppliers, the company has the cost information needed to decide whether the bid price will provide the required profit margin.

The target-costing system has worked well at ITT Automotive. The company's bid for the ABS resulted in Mercedes-Benz U.S. International selecting ITT Automotive as the developer and supplier of ABS for the automaker's M-Class All-Activity Vehicle.

---

value engineering
A cost-reduction technique, used primarily during design, that uses information about all value-chain functions to satisfy customer needs while reducing costs.

kaizen costing
The Japanese term for continuous improvement during manufacturing.

Business First

Target Costing, ABC, and the Role of Management Accounting

The Consortium for Advanced Manufacturing—International defines target costing as a set of management tools that (1) guide design and planning activities for new products, (2) provide a basis for controlling subsequent operational phases, and (3) ensure that products achieve their profitability targets. Many companies use target costing together with an ABC system. ABC provides data on the costs of the various activities needed to produce the product. Knowing the costs of activities allows product and production process designers to predict the effects of their designs on the product's cost. Target costing essentially takes activity-based costs and uses them for strategic product decisions.

For example, Culp, a North Carolina manufacturer of furniture upholstery fabrics and mattress fabrics, uses target costing and ABC to elevate cost management into one of the most strategically important areas of the firm. Culp found that 80% of its product costs are predetermined at the design stage, but earlier cost control efforts had focused only on the other 20%. By shifting cost management efforts to the design stage and getting accurate costs of the various activities involved in production, cost management at Culp evolved into a process of cutting costs when engineers design a product, not identifying costs that are out of line after the production is complete.

A basic goal of target costing is to reduce costs before they occur. After all, once a company has incurred costs, it cannot change them. Such a strategy is especially important when product life cycles are short. Because most product life cycles are shrinking, use of target costing is expanding. Target costing focuses on reducing costs in the product design and development stages—when costs can really be affected. For example, target costing heavily influenced Boeing's pricing of specialized design features in its planes, and Procter & Gamble's CEO credits target costing for helping eliminate costs that could cause managers to price products too high for the market to bear. According to Ron Gallaway, CFO of Micrus Semiconductors (now part of NXP Semiconductors), "The design process is where you can truly leverage [reduce] your costs."

What role does management accounting play in target costing? At Micrus, management accountants are responsible for setting final target costs for all components and processes. One survey reports that 86% of companies using target costing take data directly from their cost systems to estimate product costs during product design. At Eastman Kodak, management accountants were a vital part of the cross-functional team that implemented target costing. This team included design and manufacturing engineers, procurement, and marketing, as well as management accounting. Peter Zampino, director of research at the Consortium for Advanced Manufacturing—International, stated, "It's like anything else; if finance doesn't bless the numbers, they won't have the credibility throughout the organization."

Sources: Adapted from R. Banham, "Off Target," CFO, May 2000; M. Kocakulah and A.D. Austill, "Product Development and Cost Management Using Target Costing: A Discussion and Case Analysis," Journal Of Business and Economics Research, February, 2006, pp. 61–72; D. Swensen, S. Anasri, J. Bell, and I. Kim, "Best Practices in Target Costing," Management Accounting Quarterly, Winter, 2003, pp. 12–17; G. Boer and J. Ettlie, "Target Costing Can Boost Your Bottom Line," Strategic Finance, July 1999, pp. 49–52; J. Brausch, "Target Costing for Profit Enhancement," Management Accounting, November 1994, pp. 45–49; G. Hoffman, "Future Vision," Grocery Marketing, March 1994, p. 6.

Target Costing and Cost-Plus Pricing Compared

Successful companies understand the market in which they operate and use the most appropriate pricing approach. To see how target costing and cost-plus pricing can lead to different decisions, suppose that ITT Automotive receives an invitation from Ford to bid on the ABS to be used in a new model car.

Assume the following data apply:

- The specifications contained in Ford's invitation lead to an estimated current manufacturing cost (component parts, direct labor, and manufacturing overhead) of $154.
- ITT Automotive had a desired gross margin rate of 30% on sales, which means that actual cost should make up 70% of the price.
- Highly competitive market conditions exist and have established a sales price of $200 per unit.

If ITT had used cost-plus pricing to bid on the ABS, the bid price would be $154 ÷ .7 = $220. Ford would most likely reject this bid because others are likely to bid $200. ITT Automotive's pricing approach would lead to a lost opportunity.

Suppose that managers at ITT Automotive recognize that market conditions dictate a set price of $200. If ITT used a target-costing system, what would be its pricing decision? The target cost is $140 (that is, $200 × .7) so a required cost reduction of $14 per unit is necessary. The target-costing group would work with product and process engineers and suppliers to determine if they could reduce the average unit cost by $14 over the product's life. Note that it is not necessary to get costs down to the $140 target cost before production begins if the company expects additional cost reductions during the production period. For example, an initial unit cost of $145 is acceptable if continuous improvement over the product's life will result in an additional $5 of cost reductions. If the managers receive commitments for cost reductions, they will decide to bid $200 per unit. Note that if ITT Automotive wins the bid, it must carry through with its focus on cost management throughout the life of the product.

Target costing originated in Japan and is a common practice there. However, a growing number of companies now use it worldwide, including **Boeing**, **Eastman Kodak**, **Honda of America**, **Mercedes-Benz**, **Procter & Gamble**, and **Caterpillar**, as well as ITT Automotive. Even some hospitals use target costing.

Why the increasing popularity of target costing? With increased global competition in many industries, companies are increasingly limited in influencing market prices. Cost management then becomes the key to profitability. Target costing forces managers to focus on costs to achieve the desired profits.

Highlights to Remember

1. **Discriminate between relevant and irrelevant information for making decisions.** To be relevant to a particular decision, a cost (or revenue) must meet two criteria: (1) It must be an expected future cost (or revenue), and (2) it must have an element of difference between the alternative courses of action.

2. **Apply the decision process to make business decisions.** All managers make business decisions based on some decision process. The best processes help decision making by focusing the manager's attention on relevant information.

3. **Construct absorption and contribution-margin income statements, and identify their relevance for decision making.** The major difference between the absorption and contribution approaches for the income statement is that the contribution approach focuses on cost behavior (fixed and variable), whereas the absorption approach reports costs by business functions (manufacturing versus nonmanufacturing). The contribution approach makes it easier for managers to evaluate the effects of changes in volume on income and thus is well suited for shorter-run decision making.

4. **Decide to accept or reject a special order using the contribution-margin approach.** Decisions to accept or reject a special sales order should use the contribution-margin technique and focus on the additional revenues and additional costs of the order.

5. **Explain why pricing decisions depend on the characteristics of the market.** Market demand and supply, the degree of competition, and marginal revenue and marginal cost concepts impact market price and must be incorporated into any pricing decision.

6. **Identify the factors that influence pricing decisions in practice.** Market conditions, the law, customers, competitors, and costs influence pricing decisions. The degree that management actions can affect price and cost determines the most effective approach to use for pricing and cost-management purposes.

7. **Compute a sales price by various methods, and compare the advantages and disadvantages of these methods.** Companies use cost-plus pricing for products when management actions can influence the market price. They can add profit markups to a variety of cost bases including variable manufacturing costs, all variable costs, full manufacturing costs, or all costs. The contribution approach to pricing has the advantage of providing detailed cost behavior information that is consistent with cost-volume-profit analysis.

8. **Use target costing to decide whether to add a new product.** When market conditions are such that management cannot significantly influence prices, companies must focus on cost control and reduction. They use target costing primarily for new products, especially during the design phase of the value chain. They deduct a desired target margin from the market-established price to determine the target cost. Cost management then focuses on controlling and reducing costs over the product's life cycle to achieve that target cost.

Accounting Vocabulary

absorption approach, p. 184
absorption costing, p. 184
contribution approach, p. 185
decision model, p. 182
discriminatory pricing, p. 194
full cost, p. 195

imperfect competition, p. 192
kaizen costing, p. 202
marginal cost, p. 192
marginal revenue, p. 192
markup, p. 195
perfect competition, p. 191

predatory pricing, p. 194
price elasticity, p. 193
relevant information, p. 181
target costing, p. 201
value engineering, p. 202

Fundamental Assignment Material

MyAccountingLab

5-A1 Straightforward Income Statements

The Liberty Company had the following manufacturing data for the year 2012 (in thousands of dollars):

Beginning and ending inventories	None
Direct material used	$410
Direct labor	330
Supplies	25
Utilities—variable portion	42
Utilities—fixed portion	17
Indirect labor—variable portion	93
Indirect labor—fixed portion	51
Depreciation	215
Property taxes	18
Supervisory salaries	59

Selling expenses were $296,000 (including $76,000 that were variable) and general administrative expenses were $149,000 (including $21,000 that were variable). Sales were $2.5 million.

Direct labor and supplies are regarded as variable costs.

1. Prepare two income statements, one using the contribution approach and one using the absorption approach.
2. Suppose that all variable costs fluctuate directly in proportion to sales and that fixed costs are unaffected over a very wide range of sales. What would operating income have been if sales had been $2.3 million instead of $2.5 million? Which income statement did you use to help obtain your answer? Why?

5-A2 Special Order

Consider the following details of the income statement of the McGregor Pen Company (MPC) for the year ended December 31, 20X0:

Sales	$15,900,000
Less cost of goods sold	9,450,000
Gross margin or gross profit	$ 6,450,000
Less selling and administrative expenses	4,350,000
Operating income	$ 2,100,000

MPC's fixed manufacturing costs were $3.6 million and its fixed selling and administrative costs were $3.3 million. Sales commissions of 3% of sales are included in selling and administrative expenses.

The division had produced and sold 3 million pens. Near the end of the year, **Pizza Hut** offered to buy 140,000 pens on a special order. To fill the order, a special Pizza Hut logo would have to be added to each pen. Pizza Hut intended to use the pens for special promotions in an eastern city during early 20X1.

Even though MPC had some idle plant capacity, the president rejected the Pizza Hut offer of $610,400 for the 140,000 pens. He said,

> *The Pizza Hut offer is too low. We'd avoid paying sales commissions, but we'd have to incur an extra cost of $.35 per pen to add the logo. If MPC sells below its regular selling prices, it will begin a chain reaction of competitors' price cutting and of customers wanting special deals. I believe in pricing at no lower than 8% above our full costs of $13,800,000 ÷ 3,000,000 units = $4.60 per unit plus the extra $.35 per pen less the savings in commissions.*

1. Using the contribution-margin technique, prepare an analysis similar to that in Exhibit 5-6 on page 187. Use four columns: without the special order, the effect of the special order (one column total and one column per unit), and totals with the special order.
2. By what percentage would operating income increase or decrease if the order had been accepted? Do you agree with the president's decision? Why?

5-A3 Formulas for Pricing

Gavin Petrosino, a building contractor, builds houses in tracts, often building as many as 20 homes simultaneously. Petrosino has budgeted costs for an expected number of houses in 20X0 as follows:

Direct materials	$ 3,000,000
Direct labor	2,000,000
Job construction overhead	2,500,000
Cost of jobs	$ 7,500,000
Selling and administrative costs	4,500,000
Total costs	$12,000,000

The job construction overhead includes approximately $1,500,000 of fixed costs, such as the salaries of supervisors and depreciation on equipment. The selling and administrative costs include $2,250,000 of variable costs, such as sales commissions and bonuses that depend fundamentally on overall profitability.

Petrosino wants an operating income of $1.2 million for 20X0.

Compute the average target markup percentage for setting prices as a percentage of the following:

1. Direct materials plus direct labor
2. The full "cost of jobs"
3. The variable "cost of jobs"
4. The full "cost of jobs" plus selling and administrative costs
5. The variable "cost of jobs" plus variable selling and administrative costs

5-A4 Target Costing

Dan's Discount Corporation uses target costing to aid in the final decision to release new products to production. A new product is being evaluated. Market research has surveyed the potential market for this product and believes that its unique features will generate a total demand over the product's life of 65,000 units at an average price of $380. The target costing team has members from market research, design, accounting, and production engineering departments. The team has worked closely with key customers and suppliers. A value analysis of the product has determined that the total cost for the various value-chain functions using the existing process technology are as follows:

Value-Chain Function	Total Cost over Product Life
Research and development	$ 2,100,000
Design	250,000
Manufacturing (40% outsourced to suppliers)	5,000,000
Marketing	1,400,000
Distribution	1,500,000
Customer service	3,070,000
Total cost over product life	$13,320,000

Management has a target contribution to profit percentage of 50% of sales. This contribution provides sufficient funds to cover corporate support costs, taxes, and a reasonable profit.

1. Should the new product be released to production? Explain.
2. Approximately 40% of manufacturing costs for this product consists of materials and parts that are purchased from suppliers. Key suppliers on the target-costing team have suggested process improvements that will reduce supplier cost by 15%. Should the new product be released to production? Explain.
3. New process technology can be purchased at a cost of $220,000 that will reduce non-outsourced manufacturing costs by 30%. Assuming the supplier's process improvements and new process technology are implemented, should the new product be released to production? Explain.

5-B1 Contribution and Absorption Income Statements

The following information is taken from the records of the Zealand Manufacturing Company for the year ending December 31, 2012. There were no beginning or ending inventories.

Sales	$14,000,000	Long-term rent, factory	$ 85,000
Sales commissions	470,000		
Advertising	430,000	Factory superintendent's salary	31,000
Shipping expenses	320,000	Factory supervisors' salaries	105,000
		Direct materials used	3,500,000
Administrative executive salaries	100,000	Direct labor	1,700,000
		Cutting bits used	53,000
Administrative clerical salaries (variable)	370,000	Factory methods research	42,000
		Abrasives for machining	99,000
Fire insurance on factory equipment	4,000	Indirect labor	950,000
Property taxes on factory equipment	26,000	Depreciation on factory equipment	430,000

1. Prepare a contribution income statement and an absorption income statement. If you are in doubt about any cost behavior pattern, decide on the basis of whether the total cost in question will fluctuate substantially over a wide range of volume. Prepare a separate supporting schedule of indirect manufacturing costs subdivided between variable and fixed costs.
2. Suppose that all variable costs fluctuate directly in proportion to sales, and that fixed costs are unaffected over a wide range of sales. What would operating income have been if sales had been $12 million instead of $14 million? Which income statement did you use to help get your answer? Why?

5-B2 Special Order, Terminology, and Unit Costs

Following is the income statement of Pelle Company, a manufacturer of men's blue jeans:

Pelle Company Income Statement for the Year Ended December 31, 20X0		
	Total	**Per Unit**
Sales	$77,000,000	$35.00
Less: Cost of goods sold	46,200,000	21.00
Gross margin	$30,800,000	$14.00
Less selling and administrative expenses	28,600,000	13.00
Operating income	$ 2,200,000	$ 1.00

Pelle had manufactured 2.2 million pairs of jeans, which had been sold to various clothing wholesalers and department stores. At the start of 20X0, the president, Ruth Catone, died unexpectedly. Her son, Chuck, became the new president. Chuck had worked for 15 years in the marketing phases of the business. He knew very little about accounting and manufacturing, which were his mother's strengths. Chuck has several questions, including inquiries regarding the pricing of special orders.

1. To prepare better answers, you decide to recast the income statement in contribution form. Variable manufacturing cost was $35.2 million. Variable selling and administrative expenses, which were mostly sales commissions, shipping expenses, and advertising allowances paid to customers based on units sold, were $16.5 million. Prepare the revised income statement.

2. Chuck asks, "I can't understand financial statements until I know the meaning of various terms. In scanning my mother's assorted notes, I found the following pertaining to both total and unit costs: full manufacturing cost, variable cost, full cost, fully allocated cost, gross margin, and contribution margin. Using our data for 20X0, please give me a list of these costs, their total amounts, and their per-unit amounts."

3. He also says, "Near the end of 20X0, I brought in a special order from Costco for 140,000 jeans at $34 each. I said I'd accept a flat $47,600 sales commission instead of the usual 5% of selling price, but my mother refused the order. She usually upheld a relatively rigid pricing policy, saying that it was bad business to accept orders that did not at least generate full manufacturing cost plus 65% of full manufacturing cost.

    That policy bothered me. We had idle capacity. The way I figured, our manufacturing costs would go up by $140,000 \times \$21 = \$2,940,000$, but our selling and administrative expenses would go up by only $47,600. That would mean additional operating income of $140,000 \times (\$34 - \$21)$ minus $47,600, or $1,820,000 minus $47,600, or $1,772,400. That's too much money to give up just to maintain a general pricing policy. Was my analysis of the impact on operating income correct? If not, please show me the correct additional operating income."

4. After receiving the explanations offered in number 2 and 3, Chuck said, "Forget that I had the Costco order. I had an even bigger order from Lands' End. It was for 600,000 units and would have filled the plant completely. I told my mother I'd settle for no commission. There would have been no selling and administrative costs whatsoever because Lands' End would pay for the shipping and would not get any advertising allowances.

    Lands' End offered $15.00 per unit. Our fixed manufacturing costs would have been spread over 2.8 million instead of 2.2 million units. Wouldn't it have been advantageous to accept the offer? Our old fixed manufacturing costs were $5.00 per unit. The added volume would reduce that cost more than our loss on our variable costs per unit.

    Am I correct? What would have been the impact on total operating income if we had accepted the order?"

5-B3 Cost-Plus Pricing and Target Costing

A Fortune 100 company, Caterpillar is the world's leading manufacturer of construction and mining equipment, diesel and natural gas engines, and industrial gas turbines. Caterpillar also manufactures custom piston pins for other manufacturers in the same facility used to make pins for its own heavy-duty engines. Piston pins are made with cost effective CNC bar feeders and multispindle barstock machines. This process is a high-output, high-efficiency operation that eliminates the added costs of purchasing special cut-to-length barstock or cutting barstock to specific lengths.

The market research department has indicated that a proposed new piston pin for a manufacturer of truck engines would likely sell for $46. A similar piston pin currently being produced has the following manufacturing costs:

Direct materials	$24.00
Direct labor	10.00
Overhead	16.00
Total	$50.00

Assume that Caterpillar desires a gross margin of 30% of the manufacturing cost.

1. Suppose Caterpillar used cost-plus pricing, setting the price 30% above the manufacturing cost. What price would be charged for the piston pin? Would you produce such a piston pin if you were a manager at Caterpillar? Explain.

2. Caterpillar uses target costing. What price would the company charge for a piston pin? What is the highest acceptable manufacturing cost for which Caterpillar would be willing to produce the piston pin?

3. As a user of target costing, what steps would Caterpillar managers take to try to make production of this product feasible?

Additional Assignment Material

QUESTIONS

5-1 Describe the accountant's role in decision making.

5-2 "Any future cost is relevant." Do you agree? Explain.

5-3 Why are historical or past data irrelevant to special decisions?

5-4 Describe the role of past or historical costs in the decision process. That is, how do these costs relate to the prediction method and the decision model?

5-5 "The distinction between precision and relevance should be kept in mind." Explain.

5-6 Distinguish between the quantitative and qualitative aspects of decisions.

5-7 What is the advantage of the contribution approach as compared with the absorption approach?

5-8 "The primary classifications of costs are by variable and fixed-cost behavior patterns, not by business functions." Name three commonly used terms that describe this type of income statement.

5-9 "There is a commonality of approach to various special decisions." Explain.

5-10 "Fixed costs are not relevant costs." Do you agree? Explain.

5-11 Why are customers one of the factors influencing pricing decisions?

5-12 "Basing pricing on only the variable costs of a job results in suicidal underpricing." Do you agree? Why?

5-13 Provide three examples of pricing decisions other than the special order.

5-14 List three popular markup formulas for pricing.

5-15 Describe two long-run effects that may lead to managers' rejecting opportunities to cut prices and obtain increases in short-run profits.

5-16 Give two reasons why full costs are more widely used than variable costs for guiding pricing.

5-17 What is target cost per unit?

5-18 What is value engineering?

5-19 What is kaizen costing?

5-20 "In target costing, prices determine costs rather than vice versa." Explain.

5-21 Many companies that use target costing involve both customers and suppliers in product and process design. Explain why.

5-22 If a target-costing system is used and the existing cost cannot be reduced to the target cost through cost reductions, management should not produce and sell the product. Do you agree? Explain.

CRITICAL THINKING EXERCISES

5-23 Fixed Costs and the Sales Function

Many sales managers have a good intuitive understanding of costs, but they often are imprecise in how they describe the costs. For example, one manager said the following: "Increasing sales will decrease fixed costs because it spreads them over more units." Do you agree? Explain.

5-24 Income Statements and Sales Managers

Suppose Chee Wong is in charge of selling Nantucket Nectars' juice cocktails. What type of income statement, absorption or contribution, would Wong find most useful for his decisions? Why?

5-25 The Economics of the Pricing Decision

Economic theory states that managers should set price equal to marginal cost in perfect competition. Accountants use variable cost to approximate marginal costs. Compare and contrast marginal cost and variable cost, and explain whether using variable costs as an approximation for marginal cost is appropriate for making pricing decisions.

5-26 Pricing Decisions, Ethics, and the Law

Managers should base pricing decisions on both cost and market factors. In addition, they must also consider ethical and legal issues. Describe the influence that ethics and the law have on pricing decisions.

5-27 Target Costing and the Value Chain

According to Keith Hallin, program affordability manager (target costing) for Boeing's MMA Program in Integrated Defense Systems, reaching target costs is a challenge for the company's entire value chain. Explain how managers of the various value-chain functions at Boeing might be involved in the target costing process.

EXERCISES

5-28 Pinpointing Relevant Costs

Today you are planning to see a motion picture, and you can attend either of two theaters. You have only a small budget for entertainment so prices are important. You have attended both theaters recently. One charged $5 for admission; the other charged $7. You habitually buy popcorn in the theater—each theater charges $3. The motion pictures now being shown are equally attractive to you, but you are virtually certain that you will never see the picture that you reject today.

Identify the relevant costs. Explain your answer.

5-29 Information and Decisions

Suppose the historical costs for the manufacture of a calculator by Radio Shack were as follows: direct materials, $5.00 per unit; and direct labor, $6.00 per unit. Management is trying to decide whether to replace some materials with different materials. The replacement should cut material costs by 10% per unit. However, direct-labor time will increase by 5% per unit. Moreover, direct-labor rates will be affected by a recent 10% wage increase.

Prepare an exhibit like Exhibit 5-1 (p. 182), showing where and how the data about direct material and direct labor fit in the decision process.

5-30 Identification of Relevant Costs

Brian and Tammy Ricci were trying to decide whether to go to the symphony or to the baseball game. They already have two nonrefundable tickets to "Pops Night at the Symphony" that cost $42 each. This is the only concert of the season they considered attending because it is the only one with the type of music they enjoy. The baseball game is the last one of the season, and it will decide the league championship. They can purchase tickets to the game for $18 each.

The Riccis will drive 50 miles round-trip to either event. Variable costs for operating their automobile are $.18 per mile, and fixed costs average $.13 per mile for the 15,000 miles they drive annually. Parking at the symphony is free, but it costs $5 at the baseball game.

To attend either event, Brian and Tammy will hire a babysitter at $10 per hour. They expect to be gone 4 hours to attend the baseball game but only 2 hours to attend the symphony.

Compare the cost of attending the baseball game with the cost of attending the symphony. Focus on relevant costs. Compute the difference in cost, and indicate which alternative is more costly to the Riccis.

5-31 Straightforward Absorption Statement

The Kerwin Company had the following data (in thousands) for a given period:

Sales	$780
Direct materials	180
Direct labor	230
Indirect manufacturing costs	210
Selling and administrative expenses	130

There were no beginning or ending inventories. Compute the (1) manufacturing cost of goods sold, (2) gross profit, (3) operating income, and (4) conversion cost (total manufacturing cost less materials cost).

5-32 Straightforward Contribution Income Statement

Masa, Ltd., had the following data (in millions of yen) for a given period:

Sales	¥990
Direct materials	250
Direct labor	140
Variable factory overhead	65
Variable selling and administrative expenses	115
Fixed factory overhead	110
Fixed selling and administrative expenses	75

There were no beginning or ending inventories. Compute the (a) variable manufacturing cost of goods sold, (b) contribution margin, and (c) operating income.

5-33 Straightforward Absorption and Contribution Statement

Anzola Company had the following data (in millions) for a recent period. Fill in the blanks. There were no beginning or ending inventories.

a.	Sales	$920
b.	Direct materials used	350
c.	Direct labor	210
	Indirect manufacturing costs:	
d.	Variable	100
e.	Fixed	50
f.	Variable manufacturing cost of goods sold	—
g.	Manufacturing cost of goods sold	—
	Selling and administrative expenses:	
h.	Variable	90
i.	Fixed	80
j.	Gross profit	—
k.	Contribution margin	—

5-34 Absorption Statement

Peterson Jewelry had the following data (in thousands of South African Rands, ZAR) for a given period. Assume there are no inventories. Fill in the blanks.

	ZAR ___
Sales	
Direct materials	355
Direct labor	—
Indirect manufacturing	—
Manufacturing cost of goods sold	745
Gross margin	135
Selling and administrative expenses	—
Operating income	30
Prime cost (direct materials + direct labor)	575

5-35 Contribution Income Statement

Spadoni Company had the following data (in thousands) for a given period. Assume there are no inventories.

Direct labor	$165
Direct materials	160
Variable indirect manufacturing	100
Contribution margin	185
Fixed selling and administrative expenses	105
Operating income	45
Sales	855

Compute the (a) variable manufacturing cost of goods sold, (b) variable selling and administrative expenses, and (c) fixed indirect manufacturing costs.

5-36 Special-Order Decision

Belltown Athletic Supply (BAS) makes game jerseys for athletic teams. The F. C. Kitsap soccer club has offered to buy 100 jerseys for the teams in its league for $15 per jersey. The team price for such jerseys normally is $18, an 80% markup over BAS's purchase price of $10 per jersey. BAS adds a name and number to each jersey at a variable cost of $2 per jersey. The annual fixed cost of equipment used in the printing process is $6,000, and other fixed costs allocated to jerseys are $2,000. BAS makes about 2,000 jerseys per year, so the fixed cost is $4 per jersey. The equipment is used only for printing jerseys and stands idle 75% of the usable time.

The manager of BAS turned down the offer, saying, "If we sell at $15 and our cost is $16, we lose money on each jersey we sell. We would like to help your league, but we can't afford to lose money on the sale."

1. Compute the amount by which the operating income of BAS would change if it accepted F. C. Kitsap's offer.
2. Suppose you were the manager of BAS. Would you accept the offer? In addition to considering the quantitative impact computed in requirement 1, list two qualitative considerations that would influence your decision—one qualitative factor supporting acceptance of the offer and one supporting rejection.

5-37 Unit Costs and Total Costs

You are a CPA who belongs to a downtown business club. Annual dues are $150. You use the club solely for lunches, which cost $9 each. You have not used the club much in recent years, and you are wondering whether to continue your membership.

1. You are confronted with a variable-cost plus a fixed-cost behavior pattern. Plot each on a graph, where the vertical axis is total cost and the horizontal axis is annual volume in number of lunches. Also plot a third graph that combines the previous two graphs.
2. What is the cost per lunch if you pay for your own lunch once a year? Twelve times a year? Two hundred times a year?
3. Suppose the average price of lunches elsewhere is $10. (a) How many lunches must you have at the luncheon club so that the total costs of the lunches would be the same, regardless of where you ate for that number of lunches? (b) Suppose you ate 200 lunches a year at the club. How much would you save in relation to the total costs of eating elsewhere?

5-38 Advertising Expenditures and Nonprofit Organizations

Many colleges and universities have been extensively advertising their services. For example, a university in Philadelphia used a biplane to pull a sign promoting its evening program, and one in Mississippi designed bumper stickers and slogans as well as innovative programs.

Suppose Hilliard College charges a comprehensive annual fee of $14,800 for tuition, room, and board, and it has capacity for 2,000 students. The admissions department predicts enrollment of 1,700 students for 20X1. Costs per student for the 20X1 academic year are as follows:

	Variable	Fixed	Total
Educational programs	$5,200	$ 3,900	$ 9,100
Room	1,100	2,300	3,400
Board	2,500	500	3,000
	$8,800	$ 6,700[*]	$15,500

*Based on 1,700–2,000 students for the year.

The assistant director of admissions has proposed a 2-month advertising campaign using radio and television advertisements, together with an extensive direct mailing of brochures.

1. Suppose the advertising campaign will cost $1.41 million. What is the minimum number of additional students the campaign must attract to make the campaign break even?
2. Suppose the admissions department predicts that the campaign will attract 335 additional students. What is the most Hilliard should pay for the campaign and still break even?
3. Suppose a 3-month (instead of 2-month) campaign will attract 440 instead of 335 additional students. What is the most Hilliard should pay for the 1-month extension of the campaign and still break even?

5-39 Variety of Cost Terms

Consider the following data:

Variable selling and administrative costs per unit	$ 7.00
Total fixed selling and administrative costs	$810,000
Total fixed manufacturing costs	$500,000
Variable manufacturing costs per unit	$ 12.00
Units produced and sold	100,000

Compute the following per unit of product: (a) total variable costs, (b) full manufacturing cost, (c) full cost.

5-40 Acceptance of Low Bid

The Velasquez Company, a maker of a variety of metal and plastic products, is in the midst of a business downturn and is saddled with many idle facilities. Columbia Health Care has approached Velasquez to produce 300,000 nonslide serving trays. Columbia will pay $1.50 each.

Velasquez predicts that its variable costs will be $1.60 each. Its fixed costs, which had been averaging $1 per unit on a variety of other products, will now be spread over twice as much volume. The president commented, "Sure we'll lose $.10 each on the variable costs, but we'll gain $.50 per unit by spreading our fixed costs. Therefore, we should take the offer because it represents an advantage of $.40 per unit."

Suppose the regular business had a current volume of 300,000 units, sales of $600,000, variable costs of $480,000, and fixed costs of $300,000. Do you agree with the president? Why?

5-41 Pricing by Auto Dealer

Many automobile dealers have an operating pattern similar to that of Austin Motors, a dealer in Texas. Each month, Austin initially aims at a unit volume quota that approximates a break-even point. Until the break-even point is reached, Austin has a policy of relatively lofty pricing, whereby the "minimum deal" must contain a sufficiently high markup to ensure a contribution to profit of no less than $400. After the break-even point is attained, Austin tends to quote lower prices for the remainder of the month.

What is your opinion of this policy? As a prospective customer, how would you react to this policy?

5-42 Pricing to Maximize Contribution

Reynolds Company produces and sells picture frames. One particular frame for 8 × 10 photos was an instant success in the market, but recently competitors have come out with comparable frames. Reynolds has been charging $12.50 wholesale for the frames, and sales have fallen from 10,000 units last year to 7,000 units this year. The product manager in charge of this frame is considering lowering the price to $10 per frame. He believes sales will rebound to 10,000 units at the lower price, but they will fall to 6,000 units at the $12.50 price. The unit variable cost of producing and selling the frames is $6, and $60,000 of fixed cost is assigned to the frames.

1. Assuming that the only prices under consideration are $10 and $12.50 per frame, which price will lead to the largest profit for Reynolds? Explain why.
2. What subjective considerations might affect your pricing decision?

5-43 Target Selling Prices

Consider the following data from Henderson Company's budgeted income statement (in thousands of dollars):

Target sales	$96,750
Variable costs	
Manufacturing	32,250
Selling and administrative	6,450
Total variable costs	38,700
Fixed costs	
Manufacturing	8,600
Selling and administrative	6,450
Total fixed costs	15,050
Total of all costs	53,750
Operating income	$43,000

Compute the following markup percentages that would be used for obtaining the same target sales as a percentage of (1) total variable costs, (2) full costs, and (3) variable manufacturing costs.

5-44 Competitive Bids

Griffy, Rodriguez, and Martinez, a CPA firm, is preparing to bid for a consulting job. Although Alicia Martinez will use her judgment about the market in finalizing the bid, she has asked you to prepare a cost analysis to help in the bidding. You have estimated the costs for the consulting job to be as follows:

Materials and supplies, at cost	$ 30,000
Hourly pay for consultants, 2,000 hours at $35 per hour	70,000
Fringe benefits for consultants, 2,000 hours at $12 per hour	24,000
Total variable costs	124,000
Fixed costs allocated to the job	
Based on labor, 2,000 hours at $10 per hour	20,000
Based on materials and supplies, 80% of 30,000	24,000
Total cost	$168,000

Of the $44,000 allocated fixed costs, $35,000 will be incurred even if the job is not undertaken.

Alicia normally bids jobs at the sum of (1) 150% of the estimated materials and supplies cost and (2) $75 per estimated labor hour.

1. Prepare a bid using the normal formula.
2. Prepare a minimum bid equal to the additional costs expected to be incurred to complete the job.
3. Prepare a bid that will cover full costs plus a markup for profit equal to 20% of full cost.

5-45 Target Costing

Premium Corporation believes that there is a market for a portable electronic toothbrush that can be easily carried by business travelers. Premium's market research department has surveyed the features and prices of electronic brushes currently on the market. Based on this research, Premium believes that $75 would be about the right price. At this price, marketing believes that about 78,000 new portable brushes can be sold over the product's life cycle. It will cost about $1,170,000 to design and develop the portable brush. Premium has a target profit of 25% of sales.

Determine the total and unit target cost to manufacture, sell, distribute, and service the portable brushes.

5-46 Target Costing

Best Cost Corporation has an aggressive research and development (R&D) program and uses target costing to aid in the final decision to release new products to production. A new product is being evaluated. Market research has surveyed the potential market for this product and believes that its unique features will generate a total demand of 50,000 units at an average price of $230. Design and production engineering departments have performed a value analysis of the product and have determined that the total cost for the various value-chain functions using the existing process technology are as follows:

Value-Chain Function	Total Cost over Product Life
Research and Development	$ 1,500,000
Design	750,000
Manufacturing	5,000,000
Marketing	800,000
Distribution	1,200,000
Customer Service	750,000
Total Cost over Product Life	$10,000,000

Management has a target profit percentage of 20% of sales. Production engineering indicates that a new process technology can reduce the manufacturing cost by 40%, but it will cost $1,100,000.

1. Assuming the existing process technology is used, should the new product be released to production? Explain.
2. Assuming the new process technology is purchased, should the new product be released to production? Explain.

PROBLEMS

5-47 Pricing, Ethics, and the Law
Great Lakes Pharmaceuticals, Inc. (GLPI), produces both prescription and over-the-counter medications. In January, GLPI introduced a new prescription drug, Capestan, to relieve the pain of arthritis. The company spent more than $50 million over the last 5 years developing the drug, and advertising alone during the first year of introduction will exceed $10 million. Production cost for a bottle of 100 tablets is approximately $12. Sales in the first 3 years are predicted to be 500,000, 750,000, and 1,000,000 bottles, respectively. To achieve these sales, GLPI plans to distribute the medicine through three sources: directly to physicians, through hospital pharmacies, and through retail pharmacies. Initially, the bottles will be given free to physicians to give to patients, hospital pharmacies will pay $25 per bottle, and retail pharmacies will pay $40 per bottle. In the second and third year, the company plans to phase out the free distributions to physicians and move all other customers toward a $50-per-bottle sales price.

Comment on the pricing and promotion policies of GLPI. Pay particular attention to the legal and ethical issues involved.

5-48 Analysis with Contribution Income Statement
The following data have been condensed from LaGrande Corporation's report of 2012 operations (in millions of euros):

	Variable	Fixed	Total
Manufacturing cost of goods sold	€300	€280	€580
Selling and administrative expenses	140	60	200
Sales			900

1. Prepare the 2012 income statement in contribution form, ignoring income taxes.
2. LaGrande's operations have been fairly stable from year to year. In planning for the future, top management is considering several options for changing the annual pattern of operations. You are asked to perform an analysis of their estimated effects. Use your contribution income statement as a framework to compute the estimated operating income (in millions) under each of the following separate and unrelated assumptions:
   a. Assume that a 10% reduction in selling prices would cause a 30% increase in the physical volume of goods manufactured and sold.
   b. Assume that an annual expenditure of €30 million for a special sales promotion campaign would enable the company to increase its physical volume by 10% with no change in selling prices.
   c. Assume that a basic redesign of manufacturing operations would increase annual fixed manufacturing costs by €80 million and decrease variable manufacturing costs by 15% per product unit, but with no effect on physical volume or selling prices.
   d. Assume that a basic redesign of selling and administrative operations would double the annual fixed expenses for selling and administration and increase the variable expenses for selling and administration by 25% per product unit; it would also increase physical volume by 20%. Selling prices would be increased by 5%.
   e. Would you prefer to use the absorption form of income statement for the preceding analyses? Explain.
3. Discuss the desirability of alternatives a–d in number 2. If only one alternative could be selected, which would you choose? Explain.

5-49 Pricing and Contribution-Margin Technique
The Transnational Trucking Company has the following operating results to date for 20X1:

Operating revenues	$50,000,000
Operating costs	40,000,000
Operating income	$10,000,000

A large Boston manufacturer has inquired about whether Transnational would be interested in trucking a large order of its parts to Chicago. Steve Goldmark, operations manager, investigated the situation and estimated that the "fully allocated" costs of servicing the order would be $45,000. Using his general pricing formula, he quoted a price of $50,000. The manufacturer replied, "We'll give you $39,000, take it or leave it. If you do not want our business, we'll truck it ourselves or go elsewhere."

A cost analyst had recently been conducting studies of how Transnational's operating costs tended to behave. She found that $30 million of the $40 million could be characterized as variable costs. Goldmark discussed the matter with her and decided that this order would probably generate cost behavior about the same as Transnational's general operations.

1. Using a contribution-margin technique, prepare an analysis for Transnational.
2. Should Transnational accept the order? Explain.

5-50 Cost Analysis and Pricing

The budget for the Oxford University Printing Company for 20X1 follows:

Sales		£1,128,600
Direct material	£295,000	
Direct labor	340,000	
Overhead	391,000	1,026,000
Net income		£ 102,600

The company typically uses a so-called cost-plus pricing system. Direct-material and direct-labor costs are computed, overhead is added at a rate of 115% of direct-labor costs, and 10% of the total cost is added to obtain the selling price.

Edith Smythe, the sales manager, has placed a £23,000 bid on a particularly large order with a cost of £5,300 direct material and £6,200 direct labor. The customer informs her that she can have the business for £16,000, take it or leave it. If Smythe accepts the order, total sales for 20X1 will be £1,144,600.

Smythe refuses the order, saying, "I sell on a cost-plus basis. It is bad policy to accept orders at below cost. I would lose £2,630 on the job."

The company's annual fixed overhead is £170,000.

1. What would operating income have been with the order? Without the order? Show your computations.
2. Give a short description of a contribution-margin technique to pricing that Smythe might follow to achieve a price of £23,000 on the order.

5-51 Pricing of Education

You are the director of continuing education programs for a state university. Courses for executives are especially popular, and you have developed an extensive menu of one-day and two-day courses that are presented in various locations throughout the state. The performance of these courses for the current fiscal year, excluding the final course, which is scheduled for the next Saturday, is as follows:

Tuition revenue	$2,000,000
Costs of courses	800,000
Contribution margin	1,200,000
General administrative expenses	400,000
Operating income	$ 800,000

The costs of the courses include fees for instructors, rentals of classrooms, advertising, and any other items, such as travel, that can be easily and exclusively identified as being caused by a particular course.

The general administrative expenses include your salary, your secretary's compensation, and related expenses, such as a lump-sum payment to the university's central offices as a share of university overhead.

The enrollment for your final course of the year is 30 students, who have paid $200 each. Two days before the course is to begin, a city manager telephones your office. "Do you offer discounts to nonprofit institutions?" he asks. "If so, we'll send 10 managers. But our budget will not justify our spending more than $100 per person." The extra cost of including these 10 managers would entail lunches at $20 each and course materials at $30 each.

1. Prepare a tabulation of the performance for the full year including the final course. Assume that the costs of the final course for the 30 enrollees' instruction, travel, advertising, rental of hotel classroom, lunches, and course materials would be $3,000. Show a tabulation in four columns: before final course, final course with 30 registrants, effect of 10 more registrants, and grand totals.

2. What major considerations would probably influence the pricing policies for these courses? For setting regular university tuition in private universities?

5-52 DVD Sales and Rental Markets

Is it more profitable to sell your product for $45 or $12? This is a difficult question for many movie studio executives. Consider a movie that cost $60 million to produce and required another $30 million to promote. After its theater release, the studio must determine whether to sell DVDs directly to the public at a wholesale price of about $12 per DVD or to sell to video rental store distributors for about $45 per DVD. The distributors will then sell to about 13,000 video rental stores in the United States.

Assume that the variable cost to produce and ship 1 DVD is $2.00.

1. Suppose each video rental store would purchase 5 DVDs of this movie. How many DVDs would need to be sold directly to customers to make direct sales a more profitable option than sales to video store distributors?
2. How does the cost of producing and promoting the movie affect this decision?
3. Walt Disney Co. elected to sell *The Lion King* directly to consumers, and it sold 33 million copies at an average price of $12.30 per DVD. How many DVDs would each video rental store have to purchase to provide Disney as much profit as the company received from direct sales? Assume that Disney would receive $45 per DVD from the distributors.

5-53 Use of Passenger Jets

In a recent year Continental Airlines filled about 50% of the available seats on its flights, a record about 15% below the national average.

Continental could have eliminated about 4% of its runs and raised its average load considerably. The improved load factor would have reduced profits, however. Give reasons for or against this elimination. What factors should influence an airline's scheduling policies?

When you answer this question, suppose that Continental had a basic package of 3,000 flights per month, with an average of 100 seats available per flight. Also suppose that 52% of the seats were filled at an average ticket price of $200 per flight. Variable costs are about 70% of revenue.

Continental also had a marginal package of 120 flights per month, with an average of 100 seats available per flight. Suppose that only 20% of the seats were filled at an average ticket price of $100 per flight. Variable costs are about 50% of this revenue. Prepare a tabulation of the basic package, marginal package, and total package, showing percentage of seats filled, revenue, variable expenses, and contribution margin.

5-54 Effects of Volume on Operating Income

The Hester Division of Melbourne Sports Company manufactures boomerangs, which are sold to wholesalers and retailers. The division manager has set a target of 220,000 boomerangs for next month's production and sales has developed an accurate budget for that level of sales. The manager has also prepared an analysis of the effects on operating income of deviations from the target:

Volume in units	170,000	220,000	260,000
Sales at $3.20	$544,000	$704,000	$832,000
Full costs at $2.10	357,000	462,000	546,000
Operating income	$187,000	$242,000	$286,000

The costs have the following characteristics: Variable manufacturing costs are $.85 per boomerang; variable selling costs are $.65 per boomerang; fixed manufacturing costs per month are $109,000; and fixed selling and administrative costs per month are $23,000.

1. Prepare a correct analysis of the changes in volume on operating income. Prepare a tabulated set of income statements at levels of 170,000, 220,000, and 260,000 boomerangs. Also show percentages of operating income in relation to sales.
2. Compare your tabulation with the manager's tabulation. Why is the manager's tabulation incorrect?

5-55 Pricing at the Grand Canyon Railway

Suppose a tour agent approached the general manager of the Grand Canyon Railway with a proposal to offer a special guided tour to the agent's clients. The tour would occur 20 times each summer and be part of a larger itinerary that the agent is putting together. The agent presented two options: (a) a special 65-mile tour with the agent's 30 clients as the only passengers on the train, or (b) adding a car to an existing train to accommodate the 30 clients on an already scheduled 65-mile tour.

Under either option, Grand Canyon would hire a tour guide for $200 for the trip. Grand Canyon has extra cars in its switching yard, and it would cost $40 to move a car to the main track and hook it up. The extra fuel cost to pull one extra car is $.20 per mile. To run an engine and a passenger car on the trip would cost $2.20 per mile, and an engineer would be paid $400 for the trip.

Depreciation on passenger cars is $5,000 per year, and depreciation on engines is $20,000 per year. Each passenger car and each engine travels about 50,000 miles a year. They are replaced every 8 years.

The agent offered to pay $32 per passenger for the special tour and $15 per passenger for simply adding an extra car.

1. Which of the two options is more profitable to Grand Canyon? Comment on which costs are irrelevant to this decision.
2. Should Grand Canyon accept the proposal for the option you found best in number 1? Comment on what costs are relevant for this decision but not for the decision in number 1.

5-56 Pricing of Special Order

The Drosselmeier Corporation, located in Munich, makes Christmas nutcrackers and has an annual plant capacity of 2,400 product units. Suppose its predicted operating results (in euros) for the year are as follows:

Production and sales of 2,000 units, total sales	€180,000
Manufacturing costs	
Fixed (total)	70,000
Variable (per unit)	25
Selling and administrative expenses	
Fixed (total)	30,000
Variable (per unit)	10

Compute the following, ignoring income taxes:

1. If the company accepts a special order for 300 units at a selling price of €40 each, how would the total predicted net income for the year be affected, assuming no effect on regular sales at regular prices?
2. Without decreasing its total net income, what is the lowest unit price for which the Drosselmeier Corporation could sell an additional 100 units not subject to any variable selling and administrative expenses, assuming no effect on regular sales at regular prices?
3. List the numbers given in the problem that are irrelevant (not relevant) in solving number 2.
4. Compute the expected annual net income (with no special orders) if plant capacity can be doubled by adding additional facilities at a cost of €500,000. Assume that these facilities have an estimated life of 4 years with no residual scrap value, and that the current unit selling price can be maintained for all sales. Total sales are expected to equal the new total plant capacity each year. No changes are expected in variable costs per unit or in total fixed costs except for depreciation.

5-57 Pricing and Confusing Variable and Fixed Costs

Kister Electronics had a fixed factory overhead budget for 20X0 of $72 million. The company planned to make and sell 9 million units of a particular communications device. All variable manufacturing costs per unit were $18. The budgeted income statement contained the following:

Sales	$252,000,000
Manufacturing cost of goods sold	234,000,000
Gross margin	18,000,000
Deduct selling and administrative expenses	9,000,000
Operating income	$ 9,000,000

For simplicity, assume that the actual variable costs per unit and the total fixed costs were exactly as budgeted.

1. Compute Kister's budgeted fixed factory overhead per unit.
2. Near the end of 20X0, a large computer manufacturer offered to buy 150,000 units for $3.45 million on a one-time special order. The president of Kister stated, "The offer is a bad deal. It's foolish to sell below full manufacturing costs per unit. I realize that this order will have only a

modest effect on selling and administrative costs. They will increase by a $10,000 fee paid to our sales agent." Compute the effect on operating income if the offer is accepted.

3. What factors should the president of Kister consider before finally deciding whether to accept the offer?

4. Suppose the original budget for fixed manufacturing costs was $72 million, but budgeted units of product were 4.5 million. How would your answers to numbers 1 and 2 change? Be specific.

5-58 Demand Analysis

Rouse Manufacturing Limited produces and sells one product, a three-foot Canadian flag. During 20X0, the company manufactured and sold 65,000 flags at $27 each. Existing production capacity is 75,000 flags per year.

In formulating the 20X1 budget, management is faced with several decisions concerning product pricing and output. The following information is available:

1. A market survey shows that the sales volume depends on the selling price. For each $1 drop in selling price, sales volume would increase by 10,000 flags.

2. The company's expected cost structure for 20X1 is as follows:
   a. Fixed cost (regardless of production or sales activities), $345,000
   b. Variable costs per flag (including production, selling, and administrative expenses), $14

3. To increase annual capacity from the present 75,000 flags to 105,000 flags, additional investment for plant, building, equipment, and the like of $610,000 would be necessary. The estimated average life of the additional investment would be 10 years, so the fixed costs would increase by an average of $61,000 per year. (Expansion of less than 30,000 additional units of capacity would cost only slightly less than $610,000.)

Indicate, with reasons, what the level of production and the selling price should be for the coming year. Also indicate whether the company should approve the plant expansion. Show your calculations. Ignore income tax considerations and the time value of money.

5-59 Target Costing

Memphis Electrical makes small electric motors for a variety of home appliances. Memphis sells the motors to appliance makers, who assemble and sell the appliances to retail outlets. Although Memphis makes dozens of different motors, it does not currently make one to be used in garage-door openers. The company's market research department has discovered a market for such a motor.

The market research department has indicated that a motor for garage-door openers would likely sell for $26. A similar motor currently being produced has the following manufacturing costs:

Direct materials	$13.00
Direct labor	6.00
Overhead	8.00
Total	$27.00

Memphis desires a gross margin of 20% of the manufacturing cost.

1. Suppose Memphis used cost-plus pricing, setting the price 20% above the manufacturing cost. What price would be charged for the motor? Would you produce such a motor if you were a manager at Memphis? Explain.

2. Suppose Memphis uses target costing. What price would the company charge for a garage-door-opener motor? What is the highest acceptable manufacturing cost for which Memphis would be willing to produce the motor?

3. As a user of target costing, what steps would Memphis managers take to try to make production of this product feasible?

5-60 Target Costing and ABM

Cleveland Plastics makes plastic parts for other manufacturing companies. Cleveland has an ABC system for its production, marketing, and customer service functions. The company uses target costing as a strategic decision-making tool. One of Cleveland's product lines—consumer products—has over 100 individual products with life cycles of less than 3 years. This means that about 30–40 products are discontinued and replaced with new products each year. Cleveland's top management has established the following tool to be used by the target-cost team for evaluating proposed new products:

Required Cost Reduction (RCR) as a Percent of Market Price	Action
RCR $\leq$ 0%	Release to production
0 < RCR $\leq$ 5%	Release to production and set kaizen improvement plan
5% < RCR $\leq$ 25%	Product and process redesign
RCR > 25%	Abandon subject to top management review and approval

The following operational and ABC data are for four proposed new products:

Value-Chain Function	Cost per Driver Unit	Estimated Number of Driver Units over Product Life Cycle			
		C-200472	C-200473	C-200474	C-200475
Production					
Direct material	$1.60 per pound	2,000	1,000	4,000	800
Setup/Maintenance	$1,015 per setup	10	4	12	5
Processing hour	$370 per machine	20	12	32	12
Marketing	$860 per order	30	10	50	16
Customer service	$162 per sales call	55	35	20	28
Estimated life-cycle demand in units		2,000	1,400	4,000	600
Estimated market price per unit		$39	28	35	50

Top management has set a desired contribution to cover unallocated value-chain costs, taxes, and profit of 40% of the estimated market price.

Prepare a schedule that shows for each proposed new product, the target cost, estimated cost using existing technology, and any required cost reduction as a percent of the estimated market price. Use the evaluation tool to make a decision regarding the four proposed new products.

5-61 Target Costing over Product Life Cycle

Central Equipment makes a variety of motor-driven products for homes and small businesses. The market research department recently identified power lawn mowers as a potentially lucrative market. As a first entry into this market, Central is considering a riding lawn mower that is smaller and less expensive than those of most of the competition. Market research indicates that such a lawn mower would sell for about $980 at retail and $795 wholesale. At that price, Centeral expects life-cycle sales as follows:

Year	Sales
20X1	1,600
20X2	5,500
20X3	10,600
20X4	10,600
20X5	8,800
20X6	6,300
20X7	4,300

The production department has estimated that the variable cost of production will be $460 per lawn mower, and annual fixed costs will be $890,000 per year for each of the 7 years. Variable selling costs will be $40 per lawn mower and fixed selling costs will be $55,000 per year. In addition, the product development department estimates that $5.2 million of development costs will be necessary to design the lawn mower and the production process for it.

1. Compute the expected profit over the entire product life cycle of the proposed riding lawn mower.
2. Suppose Centeral expects pretax profits equal to 10% of sales on new products. Would the company undertake production and selling of the riding lawn mower?

3. Central Equipment uses a target costing approach to new products. What steps would management take to try to make a profitable product of the riding lawn mower?

CASES

5-62 Use of Capacity

St. Tropez S.A. manufactures several different styles of jewelry cases in southern France. Management estimates that during the second quarter of 20X1 the company will be operating at 80% of normal capacity. Because the company desires a higher utilization of plant capacity, it will consider a special order.

St. Tropez has received special-order inquiries from two companies. The first is from Lyon, which would like to market a jewelry case similar to one of St. Tropez's cases. The Lyon jewelry case would be marketed under Lyon's own label. Lyon has offered St. Tropez €67.5 per jewelry case for 20,000 cases to be shipped by July 1, 20X1. The cost data for the St. Tropez jewelry case, which would be similar to the specifications of the Lyon special order, are as follows:

Regular selling price per unit	€100
Costs per unit:	
Raw materials	€ 35
Direct labor, .5 hour at €60	30
Overhead, .25 machine hour at €40	10
Total cost per unit	€ 75

According to the specifications provided by Lyon, the special-order case requires less expensive raw materials, which will cost only €32.5 per case. Management has estimated that the remaining costs, labor time, and machine time will be the same as those for the St. Tropez jewelry case.

The second special order was submitted by the Avignon Co., for 7,500 jewelry cases at €85 per case. These cases would be marketed under the Avignon label and would have to be shipped by July 1, 20X1. The Avignon jewelry case is different from any jewelry case in the St. Tropez line. Its estimated per-unit costs are as follows:

Raw materials	€43
Direct labor, .5 hour at €60	30
Overhead, .5 machine hour at €40	20
Total costs	€93

In addition, St. Tropez will incur €15,000 in additional setup costs and will have to purchase a €20,000 special device to manufacture these cases; this device will be discarded once the special order is completed.

The St. Tropez manufacturing capabilities are limited by the total machine hours available. The plant capacity under normal operations is 90,000 machine hours per year, or 7,500 machine hours per month. The budgeted fixed overhead for 20X1 amounts to €2.16 million, or €24 per hour. All manufacturing overhead costs are applied to production on the basis of machine hours at €40 per hour.

St. Tropez will have the entire second quarter to work on the special orders. Management does not expect any repeat sales to be generated from either special order. Company practice precludes St. Tropez from subcontracting any portion of an order when special orders are not expected to generate repeat sales.

Should St. Tropez accept either special order? Justify your answer and show your calculations. (Hint: Distinguish between variable and fixed overhead.)

NIKE 10-K PROBLEM

5-63 Special Order

As discussed in Item 1 of **Nike**'s 10-K, one of the companies it owns is **Cole Haan**. Cole Haan makes a variety of fashion footwear, such as dress shoes. One of these products is a men's loafer. This shoe is in strong demand. Suppose sales on this loafer during the present year, 20X0, are expected to hit the 1,000,000 mark. Full plant capacity is 1,150,000 units, but the 1,000,000 unit mark is considered normal capacity. The following unit price and cost breakdown is applicable in 20X0:

		Per unit
Sales price		$145.00
Less: Manufacturing costs		
Materials		$ 49.00
Direct labor		22.00
Overhead:	Variable	14.00
	Fixed	16.00
Total manufacturing costs		$101.00
Gross margin		$ 44.00
Less selling and administrative expenses		
Selling:	Variable	$ 5.50
	Fixed	9.00
Administrative, fixed		12.00
Packaging, variable[*]		3.50
Total selling and administrative expenses		$ 30.00
Net profit before taxes		$ 14.00

[*]Two types of packaging are available: deluxe, $3.50 per unit; and standard, $2.00 per unit.

During March, the company received two special-order requests from Nordstrom and Macy's. These orders are not part of the budgeted 1,000,000 unit sales for 20X0, but there is sufficient capacity for possibly one order to be accepted. Orders received and their terms are as follows:

Order from Nordstrom: 75,000 loafers at $136.00 per unit, deluxe packaging

Order from Macy's: 90,000 loafers at $130.00 per unit, standard packaging
   Since these orders were made directly to Cole Haan, no variable selling costs will be incurred.

1. Analyze the profitability of each of these two special orders. Which special order should be accepted?
2. What other aspects need to be considered in addition to profitability?

EXCEL APPLICATION EXERCISE

5-64 Determining Whether to Accept a Special Order

Goal: Create an Excel spreadsheet to determine which special order to accept. Use the results to answer questions about your findings.

Scenario: The Ibunez Tool Company has been offered two different special orders: (1) the production of 40,000 plain circular saws or (2) the production of 20,000 professional circular saws. The company has enough excess capacity to accept either offer, but not both. The plain saw sells for $65 and has a variable cost of $50. The professional saw sells for $100 and has a variable cost of $75.

When you have completed your spreadsheet, answer the following questions:

1. What is the contribution margin and contribution-margin ratio per unit for the plain circular saw? For the professional circular saw?
2. What is the total contribution margin for the plain circular saw if the company fills this special order? For the professional circular saw special order?
3. What general conclusion can you draw from the data illustrated by the Excel problem?

Step-by-Step:
1. Open a new Excel spreadsheet.
2. In column A, create a bold-faced heading that contains the following:
   Row 1: Chapter 5 Decision Guideline
   Row 2: Ibunez Tool Company

Row 3: Special Order Analysis
Row 4: Today's Date

3. Merge and center the four heading rows across columns A–E.

4. Adjust column widths as follows:
Column A: 17
Column B: 15
Column C: 10
Column D: 15
Column E: 10

5. In row 7, create the following bold-faced column heading:
Column B: Products

6. Merge and center the Products heading across columns B–E.

7. In row 8, create the following bold-faced column headings:
Column B: Plain Circular Saw
Column D: Professional Circular Saw

8. Merge and center the Plain Circular Saw heading across columns B–C.

9. Merge and center the Professional Circular Saw heading across columns D–E.

10. In column A, create the following row headings:
Row 9: Selling price
Row 10: Variable cost
Row 11: Contribution margin
Skip four rows.
Row 16: Special order units:
Skip one row.
Row 18: Total contribution margin:

11. Merge the headings in rows 16–18 across columns A and B, then right-justify.

      Alignment tab: Horizontal: Right

12. Enter the selling price and variable cost for plain and professional saws in columns B and D, respectively.

13. In row 11, create formulas to calculate the contribution margin for each type of saw in columns B and D, respectively.

14. In row 11, create formulas to calculate the contribution-margin percent for each type of saw in columns C and E, respectively.

15. In row 16, enter the number of units requested in the special order for each type of saw in columns C and E, respectively.

16. In row 18, create formulas to calculate the total contribution margin for each type of saw in columns C and E, respectively.

17. Format all amounts in columns B and D as follows:

     Number tab: Category: Accounting ($ sign is left-justified)
                       Decimal places: 2
                       Symbol: $

18. Modify the format of the variable cost amounts to exclude the dollar ($) sign:

     Number tab: Symbol: None

19. Modify the format of the contribution-margin amounts to display a top border, using the default Line Style:

     Border tab: Icon: Top Border

20. Format the contribution-margin percent in columns C and E as follows:

     Number tab: Category: Percentage
                       Decimal places: 0
     Alignment tab: Horizontal: Center

21. Format the amount in row 16 as follows:

Number tab:	Category:	Number
	Decimal places:	0
	Use 1000 Separator (,):	Checked
Alignment tab:	Horizontal:	Center

22. Format total contribution-margin amounts as follows:

Number tab:	Category:	Accounting
	Decimal places:	0
	Symbol:	$

23. Save your work, and print a copy for your files.

COLLABORATIVE LEARNING EXERCISE

5-65 Understanding Pricing Decisions

Form teams of three to six students. Each team should contact and meet with a manager responsible for pricing in a company in your area. This might be a product manager or brand manager for a large company or a vice president of marketing or sales for a smaller company.

Explore with the manager how his or her company sets prices. Among the questions you might ask are the following:

- How do costs influence your prices? Do you set prices by adding a markup to costs? If so, what measure of costs do you use? How do you determine the appropriate markup?
- How do you adjust prices to meet market competition? How do you measure the effects of price on sales level?
- Do you use target costing? That is, do you find out what a product will sell for and then try to design the product and production process to make a desired profit on the product?
- What is your goal in setting prices? Do you try to maximize revenue, market penetration, contribution margin, gross margin, or some combination of these, or do you have other goals when setting prices?

After each team has conducted its interview, it would be desirable, if time permits, to get together as a class and share your findings. How many different pricing policies did the groups find? Can you explain why policies differ across companies? Are there characteristics of different industries or different management philosophies that explain the different pricing policies?

INTERNET EXERCISE

5-66 Marketing Decisions at Colgate-Palmolive

Managers need information of all types in order to make decisions. Many marketing decisions are strategic, such as setting pricing policies. Managers rely on multiple sources to help locate relevant information to support these decisions. Managers must know how to use the information that is available and what weight to assign to the information that is deemed to be useful.

A firm is not going to give us detailed information about its marketing strategy on its Web site. However, we can view a firm's Web site to look at some of the relevant information that managers might use to help make marketing decisions. Let's look at the **Colgate-Palmolive Company** to see what information on its site would be relevant for some marketing decisions.

1. Go to Colgate-Palmolive's home page at www.colgatepalmolive.com. Move your cursor to the heading "For Investors" at the top of the page. Click on "For Investors," then on "Financial Info," then "Annual Reports," and then on the "Message from the CEO" in the most recent annual report. In this section, Colgate shares its worldwide strategy. What types of pricing decisions that are discussed in this chapter are part of Colgate's strategy? What does this strategy reveal about the need for relevant information?
2. Many companies place a high priority on ethics. Examine the section "Living Our Values" under the "Our Company" heading back on the home page. Give two examples that show Colgate's commitment to ethical behavior.

3. One area that many companies identify as a key component to strategy is new product development. Locate where Colgate highlights its new products (you may want to use the search option on the Web site). Based on the information, what was a recent new product release? Is this a "new" product or is it simply a variation of an existing product?

4. Now, look at the products that the firm manufactures. What format is offered for learning about these products? Look at the fabric conditioner products. How many fabric conditioners does the firm offer? From looking at the information provided, can you tell what differentiates the products? Does the Web site provide any information on how or when to use the products? Would you want to make a decision about the "best" fabric conditioner for a specific type of laundry based on the information found on the Web site? Why or why not?

5. Let's look at the most recent annual report again. Is there evidence in the financial statements that Colgate is achieving its worldwide strategy? Is the company improving profitability?

Relevant Information for Decision Making with a Focus on Operational Decisions

LEARNING OBJECTIVES

When you have finished studying this chapter, you should be able to:

1. Use a differential analysis to examine income effects across alternatives and show that an opportunity-cost analysis yields identical results.

2. Decide whether to make or buy certain parts or products.

3. Choose whether to add or delete a product line using relevant information.

4. Compute the optimal product mix when production is constrained by a scarce resource.

5. Decide whether to process a joint product beyond the split-off point.

6. Decide whether to keep or replace equipment.

7. Identify irrelevant and misspecified costs.

8. Discuss how performance measures can affect decision making.

▶ NANTUCKET NECTARS

Starting a beverage business can be a complex maze of decisions. Tom First and Tom Scott should know. After graduating from college, they operated a two-person boat service business off Nantucket Island, provisioning and cleaning yachts during the summer. In 1989, they received the inspiration for a juice drink made with fresh peaches. After a bit of experimentation, the self-proclaimed "juice guys" began bottling and selling their nectar drink from their boat. That first summer, they sold 2,000 bottles at $1.00 each. Today, Nantucket Nectars, bought by Cadbury-Schweppes in 2002 and now owned by Dr Pepper Snapple Group, sells millions of cases each year. Product lines include Nantucket Squeezed Nectars, Freshly Blended Nantucket Nectars, Nantucket NectarFizz, 100% fruit juices, juice cocktails, carbonated juice drinks, and not-from-concentrate teas and lemonades.

Getting to this point, however, has been anything but smooth sailing. First and Scott's early attempts to sell juice to retailers failed; profits were nonexistent. They sold half the business to an equity partner for $500,000 to venture into distribution, but ended up losing $1 million the first year. Employees stole caseloads of merchandise from the warehouse, and there were product disappointments, such as Bayberry Tea. But the juice guys were quick learners. They got out of distribution, changed their marketing approach, and stopped the flow of red ink.

As the company grew, it tackled important operational decisions. For example, should it build and operate its own bottling facilities? What criteria should be used for developing new products? What's the best approach for tracking and analyzing the growing volume of production, distribution, and sales data?

After examining the cost of building and operating bottling plants, Nantucket Nectars chose to contract with existing beverage co-packers in Rhode Island, Nevada, Florida, Pennsylvania, and Maryland. This approach gave the company broader distribution options without the capital expenditure and overhead of multiple plants. Its managers scrutinized unit costs associated with new product ideas emerging from the test kitchen to be sure margins were on target, and they meticulously tracked every detail—from operational costs to pricing promotions—through an enterprise resource planning (ERP) information system from Oracle.

As with Nantucket Nectars, managers in other companies must make similar operational decisions. Should Toyota make the tires it mounts on its cars, or should it buy them from suppliers? Should General Mills sell the flour it mills, or should it use the flour to make more breakfast cereal? Should Air France add routes to use idle airplanes, or should it sell the planes? These decisions all require a good deal of accounting information. But what information will be relevant to each decision? In Chapter 5, we identified relevant information for pricing decisions. In this chapter, we examine relevance in the operational area. The basic framework for identifying relevant information remains the same for operations as it was for pricing. We are still looking only for future costs that differ among alternatives. However, we now expand our analysis by introducing the concepts of opportunity costs and differential costs. ■

When you relax with a bottle of Nantucket Nectars juice, you do not consider the various costs that go into producing, selling, and distributing the bottle. But these costs are very important to the managers at Nantucket Nectars.

© Business Wire/Getty Images

Analyzing Relevant Information: Focusing on the Future and Differential Attributes

Opportunity, Outlay, and Differential Costs and Analysis

Management decision making is a matter of comparing two or more alternative courses of action. Suppose a manager has only two alternatives to compare. The key to determining the financial difference between the alternatives is to identify the differential costs and revenues. **Differential cost** (**differential revenue**) is the difference in total cost (revenue) between two alternatives. For example, consider the decision about which of two machines to purchase. Both machines perform the same function. The differential cost is the difference in the price paid for the machines plus the difference in the costs of operating the machines. We call a decision process that compares the differential revenues and costs of alternatives a **differential analysis**.

When managers analyze the differential costs between the existing situation and a proposed alternative, they often refer to this as **incremental analysis**. They examine the incremental (additional) costs and benefits of the proposed alternative compared with the current situation. The **incremental costs** are additional costs or reduced revenues generated by the proposed alternative. **Incremental benefits** are the additional revenues or reduced costs generated by the proposed alternative. For instance, suppose Nantucket Nectars proposes to increase production of its NectarFizz juice drink from 1,000 bottles to 1,200 bottles per week. The incremental costs of the proposed alternative are the costs of producing the additional 200 bottles each week. The incremental benefits are the additional revenues generated by selling the extra 200 bottles.

When there are multiple alternative courses of action, managers often compare one particular action against the entire set of alternatives. Let's consider another example. Nantucket Nectars proposes introducing a new 100% juice drink, Papaya Mango, which requires the use of a machine that is currently sitting idle. Nantucket Nectars can sell the Papaya Mango produced over the remaining life of the machine for $500,000. In addition, the company will incur **outlay costs**—costs that require a future cash disbursement to purchase needed resources—of $400,000, producing a net financial benefit of $100,000.

Nantucket Nectars purchased the machine for $100,000 several years ago, but we know that the $100,000 paid for the machine is not relevant. Why? Because, as we learned from our discussion of relevant costs in Chapter 5, it is not a future cost nor does it differ across the alternatives. But what if the machine can be used for alternatives other than producing Papaya Mango? To decide whether to use the machine to produce Papaya Mango, the company needs to compare the benefit of using the machine for Papaya Mango against the other alternative uses of the machine. Suppose there are two alternative uses, 1) selling the machine for $50,000 and 2) using it to produce additional bottles of Original Peach juice, which would generate revenues less outlay costs of $60,000. Using an incremental approach, we compare the revenues and outlay costs of the proposed alternative, producing Papaya Mango, to those of the other alternative uses of the machine. In this case, the revenue less outlay costs for Papaya Mango is $100,000, for Original Peach is $60,000, and for selling the machine is $50,000. Thus, the result of the incremental analysis shows that producing Papaya Mango is $40,000 better than the next best alternative use of the machine.

Objective 1

Use a differential analysis to examine income effects across alternatives and show that an opportunity-cost analysis yields identical results.

differential cost
The difference in total cost between two alternatives.

differential revenue
The difference in total revenue between two alternatives.

differential analysis
A decision process that compares the differential revenues and costs of alternatives.

incremental analysis
An analysis of the incremental (additional) costs and benefits of a proposed alternative compared with the current situation.

incremental costs
The additional costs or reduced benefits generated by the proposed alternative in comparison with the current situation.

incremental benefits
The additional revenues or reduced costs generated by the proposed alternative in comparison with the current situation.

outlay cost
A cost that requires a future cash disbursement.

opportunity cost

For a resource that a company
already owns or that it has
already committed to purchase,
the maximum available benefit
forgone (or passed up) by using
such a resource for a particular
purpose.

If there are many alternative uses of the machine, incremental analysis can become cumber-some. In such a case, Nantucket Nectars could use an alternative approach using opportunity costs. Opportunity cost applies to a resource that a company already owns, so its use requires no additional cash disbursement. We define **opportunity cost** as the maximum available benefit forgone (or passed up) by using a resource a company already owns for a particular purpose instead of using it in the best alternative use.

In our example, there are only two alternative uses of the machine, selling it or using it to produce extra Original Peach. Using the machine to produce Papaya Mango requires Nantucket Nectars to forgo selling the machine for $50,000 and also to forgo using it for Original Peach and generating $60,000 of benefit. The best alternative use is producing Original Peach, so the opportunity cost of the machine is $60,000.

Using opportunity costs, we can compute the net financial benefit of producing Papaya Mango:

Revenues	$500,000
Costs:	
Outlay costs	400,000
Financial benefit before opportunity costs	$100,000
Opportunity cost of machine	60,000
Net financial benefit	$ 40,000

Nantucket Nectars will gain $40,000 more financial benefit using the machine to make Papaya Mango than it would gain using it for the next most profitable alternative. This is equivalent to the result using incremental analysis.

To further illustrate this equivalence, consider Maria Morales, a certified public accountant employed by a large accounting firm for a salary of $60,000 per year. She is considering an alternative use of her time, her most valuable resource. The alternative is to start an independent accounting practice. Maria's practice would have revenues of $200,000. This is $140,000 more than she would make as an employee of the large firm. However, she would also have to pay $120,000 to rent office space, lease equipment, buy advertising, and cover other out-of-pocket expenses.

An incremental analysis follows:

Assume Maria Opens Her Own Independent Practice	
Incremental benefits, $200,000 − $60,000 of increased revenues	$140,000
Incremental costs, $120,000 − $0 of additional costs	120,000
Incremental income effects per year	$ 20,000

If Maria opens her own practice, her income will be $20,000 higher than it is as an employee of the large firm.

Now let's take an opportunity-cost approach. We will look at the alternative of operating an independent practice, essentially comparing it to the alternative uses of Maria's time (which in this case is simply the alternative of working for the large firm). To do this we must consider another cost. Had Maria remained an employee, she would have made $60,000. By starting her own company, Maria will forgo this profit. Thus, the $60,000 is an opportunity cost of starting her own business:

		Alternative Chosen: Independent Practice
Revenue		$200,000
Expenses		
Outlay costs (operating expenses)	$120,000	
Opportunity cost of employee salary	60,000	180,000
Income effects per year		$ 20,000

Consider the two preceding tabulations. Each produces the correct key difference between alternatives, $20,000 per year. The first tabulation does not mention opportunity cost because we measured the differential economic impacts—differential revenues and differential costs—compared to the alternative. The second tabulation mentions opportunity cost because we included the $60,000 annual net economic impact of the excluded alternative as a cost of the chosen alternative. If we had failed to recognize opportunity cost in the second tabulation, we would have misstated the difference between the alternatives.

Why do we use opportunity costs when an incremental analysis produces the same result? When there is only one resource and one alternative opportunity to use that resource, the incremental analysis is more straightforward. However, suppose you were analyzing a project that uses five existing machines each with 10 alternative uses. An incremental analysis would require comparing the project with $10^5 = 100,000$ alternatives—every combination of alternative uses of the five machines. Using opportunity costs allows you to simplify the analysis. You just assess the 10 alternatives for each machine, pick the best one to use in determining each machine's opportunity cost, and add the five opportunity costs to the outlay costs of the project. The opportunity-cost approach is simpler than the incremental approach in such a situation.

This does not mean that estimating opportunity costs is easy. They depend on estimated revenues and costs for hypothetical alternatives—alternatives not taken. Furthermore, they depend on the alternatives that are available at a particular point in time. The same alternatives may not be available at a different time. For example, excess capacity in September does not mean that there will also be excess capacity in October. Finally, there is little historical information—sale or purchase prices—to help predict benefits for hypothetical alternatives.

We will next use the concepts in this section to analyze a variety of operational decisions. Just as we focused on relevant costs for pricing decisions in Chapter 5, we will focus on relevant costs for operational decisions in this chapter.

Making Managerial Decisions

Suppose you are a warehouse manager at Mattel, the toy company. Ace Hardware approaches you asking to rent warehouse space for January–April for storage of garden tools for the spring sales season. What is the likely opportunity cost to Mattel of the warehouse space? What if the request were for September–November?

Answer

At a toy company, excess warehouse space is a seasonal phenomenon. There is unlikely to be excess space late in the year as the holiday season approaches, but Mattel may have little use for the space in January–April. You might look for other temporary alternatives, ones that use the space for only a few months. If there are no such alternatives, the opportunity cost is close to zero. If other alternatives exist, the opportunity cost is the benefit that Mattel would receive from the next best alternative use. If the request came in September, the opportunity cost would likely be high because Mattel needs the space to accommodate its own toy inventory for holiday sales.

Make-or-Buy Decisions

Managers often must decide whether to produce a product or service within the firm or purchase it from an outside supplier. If they purchase products or services from an outside supplier, we often call it **outsourcing**. Managers apply relevant-cost analysis to a variety of outsourcing decisions such as the following:

- **Boeing** must decide whether to buy or make many of the tools used in assembling 787 airplanes.
- **Wells Fargo** must decide whether to operate its own call center or buy services from a call center in India.
- **Apple** must decide whether to develop its own Internet search software for a new computer or to buy it from a software vendor.

The Business First box on page 230 describes outsourcing and its growing popularity.

The Business First box on page 230 describes outsourcing and its growing popularity.

Objective 2

Decide whether to make or buy certain parts or products.

outsourcing
Purchasing products or services from an outside supplier.

Business First

An Example of Make or Buy: Outsourcing

Make-or-buy decisions (or outsourcing decisions) apply to services as well as to products. Companies are increasingly deciding to hire service firms to handle some of their internal operations. According to the Outsourcing Institute, outsourcing is "the strategic use of outside resources to perform activities traditionally handled by internal staff and resources."

Companies use outsourcing for many business processes within various value-chain functions. The most common business functions outsourced are within the value-chain functions of corporate support (e.g., administration, human resources, finance, and IT) and marketing (e.g., sales and call centers). Additionally, some companies outsource production processes and even research and development activities. For example, Eli Lilly has moved some of its chemistry lab work to China and is conducting more clinical trial activities overseas, primarily to reduce costs.

Although companies can outsource many processes, the Internet has driven much of the recent growth in outsourcing of computer applications. By the beginning of the twenty-first century, many companies realized that the huge investments necessitated by ERP systems may be unnecessary. They could purchase the required services over the Internet without investing in the systems' purchase and development costs. The formerly expensive process of communication using service providers had become essentially free via the Internet. A new group of computing service providers—called application service providers (ASPs)—arose to provide outsourcing opportunities for a variety of computing applications.

What are the key reasons for outsourcing? Over half of the companies in Outsourcing Institute's annual survey said they wanted to improve the company's focus and reduce operating costs. According to Todd Kertley, manager of IBM's outsourcing services, "Corporations increasingly want to focus on their core businesses, not technology." As the complexity of data processing and especially networking has grown, companies have found it harder and harder to keep current with the technology. Instead of investing huge sums in personnel and equipment and diverting attention from the value-added activities of their own businesses, many firms have found outsourcing financially attractive. Additionally, many companies are discovering that outsourcing aids corporate growth, making better use of skilled labor, and even job creation. Such "transformational outsourcing" exploits the enormous gains in efficiency, productivity, and revenues that accrue to firms from leveraging offshore talent.

The big stumbling block to outsourcing has been subjective factors, such as control. To make outsourcing attractive, the services must be reliable, be available when needed, and be flexible enough to adapt to changing conditions. Companies that have successful outsourcing arrangements have been careful to include the subjective factors in their decisions.

Outsourcing has become common—more than 75% of Fortune 500 companies outsource some aspect of their business support services. The McKinsey Global Institute estimates that companies have shifted abroad more than $18 billion in global IT work and over $11 billion in business process services.

Sources: Adapted from T. Kearney, "Why Outsourcing Is In," *Strategic Finance*, January 2000, pp. 34–38; J. Hechinger, "IBM to Take Over Operations of Auto-Parts Maker Visteon," *Wall Street Journal*, February 12, 2003; P. Engardio, M. Arndt, and D. Foust, "The Future of Outsourcing," *Business Week*, January 30, 2006; and the Outsourcing Institute (www.outsourcing.com).

Basic Make-or-Buy Decisions and Idle Facilities

A basic make-or-buy question is whether a company should make its own parts that it will use in its final products or buy the parts from vendors. Sometimes the answer to this question is based on qualitative factors. For example, some manufacturers always make parts because they want to control quality. Alternatively, some companies always purchase parts to protect long-run relationships with their suppliers. These companies may deliberately buy from vendors even during slack times to avoid difficulties in obtaining needed parts during boom times when there may be shortages of materials and workers, but no shortage of sales orders.

What quantitative factors are relevant to the decision of whether to make or buy? The answer, again, depends on the situation. A key factor is whether there are idle facilities. Many companies make parts when they cannot use their facilities to better advantage.

Assume that Nantucket Nectars reports the following costs:

Nantucket Nectars Company Cost of Making 12-Ounce Glass Bottles

	Total Cost for 1,000,000 Bottles	Cost per Bottle
Direct materials	$ 60,000	$.06
Direct labor	20,000	.02
Variable factory overhead	40,000	.04
Fixed factory overhead	80,000	.08
Total costs	$200,000	$.20

Another manufacturer offers to sell Nantucket Nectars the bottles for $.18. Should Nantucket Nectars make or buy the bottles?

Although the $.20/unit in-house cost seemingly indicates that the company should buy, the answer may be more complicated. The essential question is "What is the difference in expected future costs between the alternatives?" Suppose the $.08 fixed overhead per bottle consists of costs that will continue regardless of the decision, such as depreciation, property taxes, insurance, and foreman salaries for the plant. In that case, the entire $.08 becomes irrelevant.

Are the fixed costs always irrelevant? No. Suppose instead Nantucket Nectars will eliminate $50,000 of the fixed costs if the company buys the bottles instead of making them. For example, the company may be able to release a supervisor with a $50,000 salary. In that case, the fixed costs that the company will be able to avoid in the future are relevant.

For the moment, suppose the capacity now used to make bottles will become idle if the company purchases the bottles. Further, the $50,000 supervisor's salary is the only fixed cost that the company would eliminate. The relevant computations follow:

	Make		Buy	
	Total	Per Bottle	Total	Per Bottle
Purchase cost			$180,000	$.18
Direct materials	$ 60,000	$.06		
Direct labor	20,000	.02		
Variable factory overhead	40,000	.04		
Fixed factory overhead that can be avoided by not making (supervisor's salary)	50,000*	.05*		
Total relevant costs	$170,000	$.17	$180,000	$.18
Difference in favor of making	$ 10,000	$.01		

*Note that unavoidable fixed costs of $80,000 − $50,000 = $30,000 are irrelevant. Thus, the irrelevant costs per unit are $.08 − $.05 = $.03.

The key to optimal make-or-buy decisions is identifying and accurately measuring the additional costs for making (or the costs avoided by buying) a part or component. Companies with accurate cost accounting systems, such as ABC systems discussed in Chapter 4, are in a better position to perform make-or-buy analysis.

Make or Buy and the Use of Facilities

Make-or-buy decisions are rarely as simple as the one in our Nantucket Nectars example. As we said earlier, the use of facilities is a key to the make-or-buy decision. For simplicity, we assumed that the Nantucket Nectars facilities would remain idle if the company chose to buy the bottles. This implies the opportunity cost of the facilities is zero. In most cases, it is not optimal for companies to leave their facilities idle. Instead, they will often put idle facilities to some other use, and we must consider the financial outcomes of these uses when choosing to make or buy. The value received from the best of these alternative uses is an opportunity cost for the internal production of the parts or components.

Suppose Nantucket Nectars can use the released facilities in our example in some other manufacturing activity that generates additional contribution margin of $55,000, or can rent them out for $25,000. We now have four alternatives to consider. The following table is an incremental analysis that summarizes all the costs and revenues that differ among the four alternatives (amounts are in thousands):

	Make	Buy and Leave Facilities Idle	Buy and Rent Out Facilities	Buy and Use Facilities for Other Products
Rent revenue	$ ___	$ ___	$ 25	$ ___
Additional contribution margin from other products	___	___	___	55
Relevant cost of bottles	(170)	(180)	(180)	(180)
Net relevant costs	$(170)	$(180)	$(155)	$(125)

The final column indicates that buying the bottles and using the vacated facilities for the production of other products would yield the lowest net costs in this case, $170,000 − $125,000 = $45,000 less than the cost of making the bottles.

Alternatively, we can analyze this choice using opportunity costs. The opportunity cost of the facilities is $55,000 because that is the maximum benefit Nantucket Nectars could get if it did not use the facilities to make bottles. Add that to the outlay cost, and the total cost of making the bottles is $225,000. This is $45,000 higher than the $180,000 cost of purchasing the bottles.

Making Managerial Decisions

Suppose a company uses its facilities, on average, 80% of the time. However, because of seasonal changes in the demand for its product, the actual demand for the facilities varies from 60% in the off-season to over 100% in the peak season when it must outsource production of some parts. Under what circumstances would the company choose to take on work for other companies during the off-season? Why might it continue to outsource production of parts during the peak season—that is, why would the company choose not to expand its capacity?

Answer

During the off-season, the company would decide to take on work for other manufacturers (on a subcontract) if it is profitable. Such work may not be profitable enough to cover the cost of expanding the capacity of the facilities. The company will use facilities for these orders only when the opportunity cost of using the facilities is close to zero, that is, when there are no other more profitable uses for them. In contrast, during the peak season, the company meets the high volume by outsourcing the production of some parts. Again, the cost of purchased parts may be higher than the cost to make them in the company's own facilities if there were idle capacity, but purchasing the parts is less costly than expanding the facilities to produce them. Additionally, a company may increase production above demand (but below capacity) in the off-season in order to build inventory for the busy season.

Summary Problem for Your Review

PROBLEM

Exhibit 6-1 contains data for the Block Company for the year just ended. The company makes industrial power drills. Exhibit 6-1 shows the costs of the plastic housing separately from the costs of the electrical and mechanical components. Answer each of the following questions independently. (Requirement 1 reviews Chapter 5.)

	A	B	A + B
	Electrical and Mechanical Components*	Plastic Housing	Industrial Drills
Sales: 100,000 units, at $100			$10,000,000
Variable costs			
Direct materials	$4,400,000	$ 500,000	$ 4,900,000
Direct labor	400,000	300,000	700,000
Variable factory overhead	100,000	200,000	300,000
Other variable costs	100,000	—	100,000
Sales commissions, at 10% of sales	1,000,000	—	1,000,000
Total variable costs	$6,000,000	$1,000,000	$ 7,000,000
Contribution margin			$ 3,000,000
Total fixed costs	$2,220,000	$ 480,000	2,700,000
Operating income			$ 300,000

*Not including the costs of plastic housing (column B).

Exhibit 6-1
Block Company Cost of Industrial Drills

1. During the year, a prospective customer in an unrelated market offered $82,000 for 1,000 drills. The drills would be manufactured in addition to the 100,000 units sold. Block Company would pay the regular sales commission rate on the 1,000 drills. The president rejected the order because "it was below our costs of $97 per unit." What would operating income have been if Block Company had accepted the order?

2. A supplier offered to manufacture the year's supply of 100,000 plastic housings for $12.00 each. What would be the effect on operating income if the Block Company purchased rather than made the housings? Assume that Block Company would avoid $350,000 of the fixed costs assigned to housings if it purchases the housings.

3. Suppose that Block Company could purchase the housings for $13.00 each and use the vacated space for the manufacture of a deluxe version of its drill. Assume that it could make 20,000 deluxe units (and sell them for $130 each in addition to the sales of the 100,000 regular units) at a unit variable cost of $90, exclusive of housings and exclusive of the 10% sales commission. The company could also purchase the 20,000 extra plastic housings for $13.00 each. All the fixed costs pertaining to the plastic housings would continue because these costs relate primarily to the manufacturing facilities used. What would operating income have been if Block had bought the housings and made and sold the deluxe units?

SOLUTION

1. The costs of filling the special order follow:

Direct materials	$49,000
Direct labor	7,000
Variable factory overhead	3,000
Other variable costs	1,000
Sales commission at 10% of $82,000	8,200
Total variable costs	$68,200
Selling price	82,000
Contribution margin	$13,800

Operating income would have been $300,000 + $13,800 = $313,800 if Block Company had accepted the order. In a sense, the decision to reject the offer implies that the Block Company is willing to forego $13,800 in immediate gains (an opportunity cost) in order to preserve the long-run selling price structure.

2. Assuming that Block Company could have avoided $350,000 of the fixed costs by not making the housings and that the other fixed costs would have continued, we can summarize the incremental costs and benefits of buying the housings compared with making them as follows:

Incremental cost (Purchase cost of 100,000 × $12)	$1,200,000
Incremental benefits:	
Variable costs	$1,000,000
Avoidable fixed costs	350,000
Net incremental benefit	$ 150,000

If the facilities used for plastic housings became idle, the Block Company would prefer to buy the housings. Operating income would increase by $150,000.

3. The effect of purchasing the plastic housings and using the vacated facilities for the manufacture of a deluxe version of its drill follows:

Incremental Benefit:		
Sales increase, 20,000 units, at $130		$2,600,000
Variable costs exclusive of housings increase, 20,000 units, at $90	$1,800,000	
Plus: sales commission, 10% of $2,600,000	260,000	$2,060,000
Contribution margin on 20,000 units		$ 540,000
Incremental Cost:		
Housings: 120,000 rather than 100,000 would be needed; buy 120,000 at $13	$1,560,000	
Versus make 100,000 at $10 (only the variable costs are relevant)	1,000,000	
Incremental cost of outside purchase		560,000
Fixed costs, unchanged		—
Net incremental cost to buying		$ 20,000

Operating income would decline to $300,000 − $20,000 = $280,000. The deluxe units bring in a contribution margin of $540,000, but the additional costs of buying rather than making housings is $560,000, leading to a net disadvantage of $20,000.

Deletion or Addition of Products, Services, or Departments

Objective 3

Choose whether to add or delete a product line using relevant information.

Relevant information also plays an important role in decisions about adding or deleting products, services, or departments.

Avoidable and Unavoidable Costs

Often, existing businesses consider expanding or contracting their operations to improve profitability. Decisions to add or to drop products, or to add or drop departments use the same analysis: examining all the relevant costs and revenues. For example, consider a store that has three major departments: groceries, general merchandise, and drugs. Management is considering dropping the grocery department, which has consistently shown an operating loss. The following table reports the store's annual operating income (in thousands of dollars):

		Departments		
	Total	Groceries	General Merchandise	Drugs
Sales	$1,900	$1,000	$800	$100
Variable cost of goods sold and expenses*	1,420	800	560	60
Contribution margin	$ 480 (25%)	$ 200 (20%)	$240 (30%)	$ 40 (40%)
Fixed expenses (salaries, depreciation, insurance, property taxes, and so on):				
Avoidable	$ 265	$ 150	$100	$ 15
Unavoidable	180	60	100	20
Total fixed expenses	$ 445	$ 210	$200	$ 35
Operating income (loss)	$ 35	$ (10)	$ 40	$ 5

*Examples of variable expenses include product, paper shopping bags, and sales commissions.

Notice that we have divided the fixed expenses into two categories, avoidable and unavoidable. **Avoidable costs**—costs that will not continue if an ongoing operation is changed or deleted—are relevant. In our example, avoidable costs include department salaries and other costs that the store could eliminate by not operating the specific department. **Unavoidable costs**—costs that continue even if a company discontinues an operation—are not relevant in our example because a decision to delete the department does not affect them. Unavoidable costs include many **common costs**, which are those costs of facilities and services that are shared by users. For example, store depreciation, heating, air conditioning, and general management expenses are costs of shared resources used by all departments. For our example, assume first that we will consider only two alternatives, dropping or continuing the grocery department, which shows a loss of $10,000. Assume further that the decision will not affect the total assets invested in the store. The vacated space would be idle, and the unavoidable costs would continue. Which alternative would you recommend? An analysis (in thousands of dollars) follows:

avoidable costs
Costs that will not continue if an ongoing operation is changed or deleted.

unavoidable costs
Costs that will continue even if a company discontinues an operation.

common costs
Those costs of facilities and services that are shared by users.

	Store as a Whole		
Income Statements	Total Before Change (a)	Effect of Dropping Groceries (b)	Total After Change (a) − (b)
Sales	$1,900	$1,000	$ 900
Variable expenses	1,420	800	620
Contribution margin	$ 480	$ 200	$ 280
Avoidable fixed expenses	265	150	115
Profit contribution to common space and other unavoidable costs	$ 215	$ 50	$ 165
Common space and other unavoidable costs	180	—	180
Operating income (loss)	$ 35	$ 50	$ (15)

The preceding analysis shows that operating income would be worse, rather than better, if the store drops the groceries department and leaves the vacated facilities idle. In short, groceries bring in a contribution margin of $200,000, which is $50,000 more than the $150,000 fixed expenses the store would save by closing the grocery department. The grocery department showed a loss in the first income statement because of the unavoidable fixed costs charged (allocated) to it, and these costs will not be eliminated when the grocery department is dropped.

Most companies do not like having space left idle, so perhaps the preceding example was a bit too basic. Assume now that the store could use the space made available by dropping the groceries department to expand the general merchandise department. The space would be occupied by merchandise that would increase sales by $500,000, generate a 30% contribution-margin percentage, and have additional (avoidable) fixed costs of $70,000. The $80,000 increase in operating income of general merchandise more than offsets the $50,000 decline from eliminating groceries, providing an overall increase in operating income of $65,000 − $35,000 = $30,000. The analysis is as follows:

	Effects of Changes			
	Total Before Change (a)	Drop Groceries (b)	Expand General Merchandise (c)	Total After Changes (a) − (b) + (c)
(in thousands of dollars)				
Sales	$1,900	$1,000	$500	$1,400
Variable expenses	1,420	800	350	970
Contribution margin	$ 480	$ 200	$150	$ 430
Avoidable fixed expenses	265	150	70	185
Contribution to common space and other unavoidable costs	$ 215	$ 50	$ 80	$ 245
Common space and other unavoidable costs*	180	—	—	180
Operating income	$ 35	$ 50	$ 80	$ 65

*Includes the $60,000 of former grocery fixed costs, which were allocations of unavoidable common costs that will continue regardless of how the space is occupied.

This example illustrates that relevant costs are not always variable. The key to decision making is not relying on a hard and fast rule about what to include and what to ignore. Rather, you need to analyze all pertinent costs and revenues to determine what is and what is not relevant in the specific context. In this case, the relevant costs included the avoidable fixed costs.

It is also important to remember that nonfinancial information can influence decisions to add or delete products or departments. For example, when deciding to delete a product or to close a plant, there are ethical considerations. What happens to the employees in the area being discontinued? What about customers who might be relying on customer support in the future? What about the community in which a discontinued operation is located? Although the nonfinancial impacts of such considerations are hard to determine, they must be considered. This may be a situation where good ethics is good business, as a stable, committed workforce and a supportive community can be important assets to a company. Additionally, negative impacts on employees, customers, or communities could create future financial problems for the company that are much larger than short-term cost savings from discontinuing a product or plant.

Making Managerial Decisions

When managers face a decision about whether to add or delete a product, service, or department, it is useful to classify the associated fixed costs as avoidable or unavoidable. Indicate whether the following fixed costs are typically avoidable or unavoidable if a company deletes a product. Assume the company produces many products in a single plant.

1. Advertising costs for the product. The company places specific ads just for this product.
2. Salary of the plant manager.
3. Rent for the plant building.

4. Insurance costs on equipment used to produce the product. The company will sell the equipment if it discontinues the product.

Answer

Numbers 1 and 4 are avoidable fixed costs. The company is unlikely to change the salary of the plant manager if it discontinues only one product. Thus, it is unavoidable. The same is true for the plant rent. Hence, it is also an unavoidable cost.

Optimal Use of Limited Resources: Product-Mix Decisions

Objective 4

Compute the optimal product mix when production is constrained by a scarce resource.

limiting factor (scarce resource)

The item that restricts or constrains the production or sale of a product or service.

Suppose a plant makes more than one product and is operating at capacity. If demand for its products exceeds the amount the company can produce, managers must decide on the product mix to produce. The product-mix decision requires a focus on each product's contribution margin and its use of capacity. Managers should emphasize the product that makes the largest contribution per unit of the limiting factor. A **limiting factor** or **scarce resource** restricts or constrains the production or sale of a product or service. Examples of limiting factors include labor hours and machine hours that limit production (and hence sales) in manufacturing firms, and square feet of floor space or cubic meters of display space that limit sales in department stores.

Managers must use the contribution margin technique wisely. They sometimes mistakenly favor those products with the biggest contribution margin or gross margin per unit or per sales dollar, without regard to scarce resources. This could lead to an incorrect product-mix decision.

Consider two different athletic shoes produced by Nike, the Air Court tennis shoe and the Air Max running shoe. Assume that one factory is the only facility that produces these shoes, and Nike managers must decide how many shoes of each type to produce. Suppose machine time is the measure of capacity in this factory, and there is a maximum of 10,000 hours of machine time. The factory can produce 10 pairs of Air Court shoes or 5 pairs of Air Max shoes in 1 hour of machine time. Unit data follow:

	Air Court	Air Max
Selling price per pair	$80	$120
Variable costs per pair	60	84
Contribution margin per pair	$20	$ 36
Contribution margin ratio	25%	30%

Which is more profitable, the Air Court or Air Max? On which should Nike spend its resources? The correct answer is "It depends." Suppose the factory has excess capacity of 1,000 hours of machine time. Now a sports retailer approaches Nike and wants it to fill a special order for 1,000 pairs of shoes of either type. Which shoe would be most profitable to fill this order, the Air Court or the Air Max? Since there would still be an excess capacity of machine hours after filling the special order with either shoe, it would be better to produce and sell an Air Max pair contributing $36 than an Air Court pair contributing $20. In this case, Air Max shoes generate more profit per pair. Thus, if the limiting factor is demand—that is, pairs of shoes that Nike can sell—the more profitable product is the one with the higher contribution per unit.

Now suppose the demand for either shoe would exceed the factory's capacity. Production capacity is now the limiting factor because there is only one factory in which to make either the Air Max or the Air Court. In this case, the Air Court shoe is more profitable. Why? Because it generates $2,000,000 of contribution margin from the capacity that is available compared to $1,800,000 for Air Max:

	Air Court	Air Max
1. Pairs of shoes from 10,000 hours	100,000	50,000
2. Contribution margin per pair	$ 20	$ 36
3. Contribution margin from 10,000 hours of capacity, (1) × ((2)	$2,000,000	$1,800,000
Contribution margin per machine hour, (3) ÷ 10,000	$ 200	$ 180

Each machine hour used to produce Air Court shoes generates $200 of contribution, while an hour used to produce Air Max shoes generates only $180.

Now suppose that neither shoe alone has enough demand to fill the entire capacity, but the combined demand will more than fill the capacity. What our analysis tells us is the Air Court shoe is a better use of the production capacity than the Air Max shoe. Nike would want to make sure there are as many pairs of Air Court shoes available as customers demand, and only after satisfying this demand is it worth producing Air Max shoes using the remaining available capacity.

This analysis depends on the relative use of capacity by the two products. Suppose the factory can produce seven instead of five Air Max shoes per hour of machine time. With this change in assumptions, the Air Max becomes the more profitable use of the capacity. It would have a $252 contribution for each machine hour compared with Air Court's $200.

	Air Court	Air Max
Contribution from 10,000 machine hours	10,000 × 10 × $20 = $2,000,000	10,000 × 7 × $36 = $2,520,000
Contribution per machine hour	$2,000,000 ÷ 10,000 = $200	$2,520,000 ÷ 10,000 = $252

Air Max shoes have more contribution per unit of capacity—per hour or per 10,000 hours. Note that each of these financial measures shows that Air Max shoes are 26% more profitable than the Air Court. That is, ($252 − $200) ÷ $200 = 26%, and ($2,520,000 − $2,000,000) ÷ $2,000,000 = 26%.

This issue of optimizing the use of scarce resources is important in non-manufacturing companies as well. In retail stores, the limiting resource is often floor space. In such cases, companies focus either on products taking up less space or on using the space for shorter periods of time—greater **inventory turnover** (number of times the average inventory is sold per year). However, the product that is most profitable when one particular factor limits sales may be the least profitable if a different factor restricts sales. Consider an example of two department stores. The contribution margin percentage (contribution margin ÷ selling price) is an insufficient clue to profitability because, as we said, profits depend on the space occupied and the inventory turnover. Discount department stores, such as Wal-Mart, Target, and Kmart, have succeeded in using lower contribution margins (i.e., lower markups) than traditional department stores because they have been able to increase turnover and, thus, increase the contribution per unit of space. Exhibit 6-2 illustrates the same product, taking up the same amount of space, in each of two stores. The contribution margins per unit and per sales dollar are less in the discount

inventory turnover
The number of times the average inventory is sold per year.

Exhibit 6-2
Effect of Inventory
Turnover on Profit

	Regular Department Store	Discount Department Store
Retail price	$ 4.00	$ 3.50
Cost of merchandise and other variable costs	3.00	3.00
Contribution to profit per unit	$ 1.00 (25%)	$ .50 (14%)
Units sold per year	10,000	22,000
Total contribution to profit, assuming the same space allotment in both stores	$10,000	$11,000

store, but faster turnover makes the same product a more profitable use of space in the discount store. In general, retail companies seek faster inventory turnover. A survey of retail shoe stores showed that those with above-average financial performance had an inventory turnover of 2.6 times per year compared to an industry average of 2.0.

Joint Product Costs: Sell or Process Further Decisions

Objective 5

Decide whether to process a joint product beyond the split-off point.

joint products

Two or more manufactured products that (1) have relatively significant sales values and (2) are not separately identifiable as individual products until their split-off point.

split-off point

The juncture of manufacturing where the joint products become individually identifiable.

separable costs

Any cost beyond the split-off point.

joint costs

The costs of manufacturing joint products prior to the split-off point.

We now examine another operating decision for which relevant costs are important—decisions about whether to sell a product as is or to further process it. In this section, we will examine how joint product costs affect such decisions.

Consider ConAgra, which produces meat products with brand names such as Swift, Armour, and Butterball. ConAgra cannot kill a sirloin steak; it has to purchase and slaughter a steer, which supplies various cuts of dressed meat, hides, and trimmings. So how does ConAgra determine the proper allocation of the purchase cost paid for the steer to the various meat products and other products produced from a steer? When two or more manufactured products (1) have relatively significant sales values and (2) are not separately identifiable as individual products until their split-off point, we call them **joint products**. The **split-off point** is that juncture of manufacturing where the joint products become individually identifiable. Any costs beyond that stage are **separable costs** because they are not part of the joint process and the accounting system can exclusively identify them with individual products. We call the costs of manufacturing joint products prior to the split-off point **joint costs**. Further examples of joint products include chemicals, lumber, flour, and the products of petroleum refining.

To illustrate joint costs, suppose Dow Chemical Company produces two chemical products, X and Y, as a result of a particular joint process. The joint processing cost is $100,000. This includes raw material costs and the cost of processing before the joint products X and Y reach the split-off point. At the split-off point, Dow can sell X and Y to the petroleum industry, which uses them as ingredients for gasoline. The relationships follow:

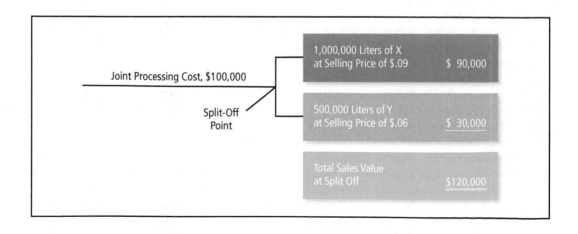

Alternatively, Dow can further process Y into a different product, YA, that it sells to the plastics industry as an ingredient for plastic sheeting. Let's see how Dow's managers develop relevant information to help them decide whether to sell joint products X and Y at the split-off point or to further process Y into YA.

Sell or Process Further

Suppose Dow can further process the 500,000 liters of Y into YA, but the additional processing cost would be $.08 per liter for manufacturing and distribution, a total of $40,000 for 500,000 liters. The net sales price of YA would be $.16 per liter, a total of $80,000.

Dow cannot process product X further and will sell it at the split-off point, but management is undecided about product Y. Should the company sell Y at the split-off point, or should it process Y into YA? To answer this question, we need to find the relevant items involved. Consider first the joint costs—those before the split-off point. They are past costs that cannot affect anything beyond the split-off point. They violate both attributes of relevancy; they are neither future costs nor differential across alternatives. Therefore they are irrelevant to the question of whether to sell or process further. Relevance requires that the analysis focus on the separable costs and revenues beyond split-off, as shown in Exhibit 6-3.

This analysis shows that it would be $10,000 more profitable to further process Y into YA than to sell Y at split-off. The rule is to extend processing on a joint product only if the additional revenue exceeds the additional costs.

Exhibit 6-4 illustrates another way to compare the alternatives of (1) selling Y at the split-off point and (2) processing Y into YA. It includes the joint costs, which are the same for each alternative and, therefore, do not affect the difference.

Because joint costs would not affect the decision (as Exhibit 6-4 demonstrates), we have not allocated the joint costs to products. However, no matter how we might allocate them, the total income effects for the firm would not change. We provide additional coverage of the allocation of joint costs and inventory valuation in Chapter 12.

	Sell at Split-Off as Y	Process Further and Sell as YA	Difference
Revenues	$30,000	$80,000	$50,000
Separable costs beyond split-off at $.08	—	40,000	40,000
Income effects	$30,000	$40,000	$10,000

Exhibit 6-3
Illustration of Sell or Process Further

	(1) Alternative One			(2) Alternative Two			(3)
	X	Y	Total	X	YA	Total	Differential Effects
Revenues	$90,000	$30,000	$120,000	$90,000	$80,000	$170,000	$50,000
Joint costs			$100,000			$100,000	—
Separable costs			—		40,000	40,000	40,000
Total costs			$100,000			$140,000	$40,000
Income effects			$ 20,000			$ 30,000	$10,000

Exhibit 6-4
Sell or Process Further Analysis—Firm as a Whole

Keeping or Replacing Equipment

depreciation

The periodic cost of equipment that a company spreads over the future periods in which the company will use the equipment.

book value (net book value)

The original cost of equipment less accumulated depreciation.

accumulated depreciation

The sum of all depreciation charged to past periods.

We next examine another common decision in business, the replacement of old equipment. One important aspect of such a situation is that the book value of the old equipment is not a relevant consideration in deciding whether to purchase a replacement. Why? Because it is a past cost, not a future cost. When a company purchases equipment, it spreads the cost via **depreciation** expense over the future periods in which it will use the equipment. The equipment's **book value**, or **net book value**, is the original cost less accumulated depreciation. **Accumulated depreciation** is the sum of all depreciation charged to past periods. For example, suppose a $10,000 machine with a 10-year life span has depreciation of $1,000 per year. At the end of 6 years, accumulated depreciation is $6 \times \$1,000 = \$6,000$, and the book value is $\$10,000 - \$6,000 = \$4,000$.

Consider the following data for a decision about whether to replace an old machine:

	Old Machine	Replacement Machine
Original cost	$10,000	$8,000
Useful life in years	10	4
Current age in years	6	0
Useful life remaining in years	4	4
Accumulated depreciation	$ 6,000	0
Book value	$ 4,000	Not acquired yet
Disposal value (in cash) now	$ 2,500	Not acquired yet
Disposal value in 4 years	0	0
Annual cash operating costs (maintenance, power, repairs, coolants, and so on)	$ 5,000	$3,000

sunk cost

A historical or past cost, that is, a cost that the company has already incurred and, therefore, is irrelevant to the decision-making process.

Let's prepare a comparative analysis of the two alternatives. Before proceeding, consider some important concepts. The most widely misunderstood facet of replacing equipment is the role of the book value of the old equipment in the decision. We often call the book value a **sunk cost**, which is really just another term for historical or past cost, a cost that the company has already incurred and, therefore, is irrelevant to the decision-making process. Nothing can change what has already happened. The Business First box on page 241 illustrates this concept.

The irrelevance of past costs for decisions does not mean that knowledge of past costs is useless. Often managers use past costs to help predict future costs. In addition, past costs affect future payments for income taxes (as explained in Chapter 11). However, the past cost itself is not relevant. The only relevant cost is the predicted future cost.

In deciding whether to replace or keep existing equipment, we must consider the relevance of four commonly encountered items:

1. Book value of old equipment: irrelevant because it is a past (historical) cost. Therefore, depreciation on old equipment is also irrelevant.
2. Disposal value of old equipment: relevant because it is an expected future inflow that usually differs across alternatives.
3. Gain or loss on disposal: This is the difference between book value and disposal value. It is therefore a meaningless combination of irrelevant and relevant items. The combination form, loss (or gain) on disposal, blurs the distinction between the irrelevant book value and the relevant disposal value. Consequently, it is best to think of each separately.
4. Cost of new equipment: relevant because it is an expected future outflow that will differ across alternatives. Therefore, the initial cost of new equipment (or its allocation in subsequent depreciation charges) is relevant.

Business First

Sunk Costs and Government Contracts

It is easy to agree that—in theory—managers should ignore sunk costs when making decisions. But in practice, sunk costs often influence important decisions, especially when a decision maker doesn't want to admit that a previous decision to invest funds was a bad decision.

Consider the governmental claims made during the famous Congressional debates regarding the termination of funding for the military's B-2 aircraft. As documented in the *St. Louis Post Dispatch*, Larry O. Welch, the air force chief of staff, claimed "the B-2 already is into production; cancel it and the $17 billion front end investment is lost." And Les Aspin, chairman of the House Armed Services Committee, stated "with $17 billion already invested in it, the B-2 is too costly to cancel."

The $17 billion already invested in the B-2 is a sunk cost. What matters are the future incremental costs and benefits—the costs necessary to complete production compared to the value of the completed B-2s. We want to avoid throwing good

money after bad—that is, if the value of the B-2 is not at least equal to the future investment in it, Congress should cancel funding regardless of the amount previously spent.

Failure to ignore sunk costs is not unique to the U.S. government. More than a decade ago, Motorola made critical decisions to ignore digital technology, and insisted that analog communications, in which it was heavily invested, was the wave of the future. Despite intense demands from wireless providers for digital cell phones, Motorola refused to even consider switching from analog to digital technology. It refused to acknowledge that its analog investments were a sunk cost. Motorola completely lost its dominance in the cell phone market, with its U.S. market share falling from 60% to 13% within 3 years.

Sources: Adapted from J. Berg, J. Dickhaut, and C. Kanodia, "The Role of Private Information in the Sunk Cost Phenomenon," unpublished paper, November 12, 1991; and W. Y. Davis, "Return the 'Sunk Costs are Sunk' Concept to Principles of Economics Textbooks," *Journal of Business and Economic Research*, Volume 3, Number 6, 2005.

Exhibit 6-5 shows the relevance of these items in our example. Book value of old equipment is irrelevant regardless of the decision-making technique we use. The "difference" column in Exhibit 6-5 shows that the $4,000 book value of the old equipment does not differ between alternatives. We should completely ignore it for decision-making purposes. The difference is merely one of timing. The amount written off is still $4,000, regardless of any available alternative. The $4,000 appears on the income statement either as a $4,000 deduction from the $2,500 cash proceeds received to obtain a $1,500 loss on disposal in the first year or as $1,000 of depreciation in each of 4 years. But how it appears is irrelevant to the replacement decision. In contrast, the $2,000 annual depreciation on the new equipment is relevant because the total $8,000 depreciation is a future cost that we can avoid by not replacing the equipment. The three relevant items—operating costs, disposal value, and acquisition cost—give replacement a net advantage of $2,500.

	Four Years Together		
	Keep	Replace	Difference
Cash operating costs	$20,000	$12,000	$8,000
Old equipment (book value)			
Periodic write-off as depreciation	4,000	—	—
or			
Lump-sum write-off		4,000*	
Disposal value	—	−2,500*	2,500
New machine			
Acquisition cost	—	8,000†	−8,000
Total costs	$24,000	$21,500	$2,500

The advantage of replacement is $2,500 for the 4 years together.

*In a formal income statement, these two items would be combined as "loss on disposal" of $4,000 − $2,500 = $1,500.

† In a formal income statement, written off as straight-line depreciation of $8,000 ÷ 4 = $2,000 for each of 4 years.

Exhibit 6-5
Cost Comparison—Replacement of Equipment Including Relevant and Irrelevant Items

Making Managerial Decisions

It is sometimes difficult to accept the proposition that past or sunk costs are irrelevant to decisions. Consider the ticket you have to a major football game in December. After getting the ticket, you learn that the game will be on TV, and you really prefer to watch the game in the comfort of your warm home. Does your decision about attending the game or watching it on TV depend on whether you were given the ticket for free or you paid $80 for it? What does this tell you about a manager's decision to replace a piece of equipment?

Answer

The amount paid, whether it be $0, $80, or $1,000, should make no difference to the decision. You have the ticket, and you have paid for it. That cannot be changed. If you really prefer to watch the game on TV, it may have been a bad decision to pay $80 for a ticket. But you cannot erase that bad decision. All you can do is choose the future action that has the most value to you. You should not suffer through a less pleasant experience just because you paid $80 for the ticket. Although the price you paid for the ticket is irrelevant, the price you could sell the ticket for now is relevant—this price is the opportunity cost of using the ticket yourself.

A manager must make the same analysis regarding the replacement of equipment. What the company spent for the old equipment is irrelevant. Keeping equipment that is no longer economical is just like using a ticket for an event that you would rather not attend. Additionally, the disposal value of the old equipment is relevant—this is the opportunity cost of keeping the equipment, corresponding to the opportunity cost of using the ticket rather than selling it to another fan.

Summary Problem for Your Review

PROBLEM

Exhibit 6-5 looks beyond 1 year. Examining the alternatives over the equipment's entire life ensures that peculiar nonrecurring items, such as loss on disposal, will not obstruct the long-run view vital to many managerial decisions. However, Exhibit 6-5 presents both relevant and irrelevant items. Prepare an analysis that concentrates on relevant items only.

SOLUTION

Exhibit 6-6 presents the analysis with relevant items only—the cash operating costs, the disposal value of the old equipment, and the acquisition cost of the new equipment. To demonstrate that the amount of the old equipment's book value will not affect the answer, suppose the book value of the old equipment is $500,000 rather than $4,000. Your final answer will not change. The cumulative advantage of replacement is still $2,500. (If you are in doubt, rework this example, using $500,000 as the book value.)

| | Four Years Together | | |
	Keep	Replace	Difference
Cash operating costs	$20,000	$12,000	$8,000
Disposal value of old machine	—	−2,500	2,500
New machine, acquisition cost	—	8,000	−8,000
Total relevant costs	$20,000	$17,500	$2,500

Exhibit 6-6
Cost Comparison—Replacement of Equipment, Relevant Items Only

Identify Irrelevant or Misspecified Costs

Objective 7

Identify irrelevant and misspecified costs.

The ability to recognize irrelevant or misspecified costs is sometimes just as important to decision makers as identifying relevant costs. How do we know that past costs, although sometimes good predictors of future costs, are irrelevant in decision making? Let's consider such past costs as obsolete inventory and see why they are irrelevant to decisions.

Suppose General Dynamics has 100 obsolete aircraft parts in its inventory. The original manufacturing cost of these parts was $100,000. General Dynamics can (1) re-machine the parts for $30,000 and then sell them for $50,000 or (2) sell them as scrap for $5,000. Which should it do? This is an unfortunate situation, yet the $100,000 past cost is irrelevant to the decision to re-machine or scrap. The only relevant factors are the expected future revenues and costs:

	Re-machine	Scrap	Difference
Expected future revenue	$ 50,000	$ 5,000	$45,000
Expected future costs	30,000	—	30,000
Relevant excess of revenue over costs	$ 20,000	$ 5,000	$15,000
Accumulated historical inventory cost*	100,000	100,000	—
Net overall loss on project	$(80,000)	$(95,000)	$15,000

*Irrelevant because it is unaffected by the decision.

As you can see from the fourth line of the preceding table, we can completely ignore the $100,000 historical cost and still arrive at the $15,000 difference, the key figure in the analysis that yields re-machining as the optimal decision.

In addition to past costs, some future costs may be irrelevant because they will be the same under all feasible alternatives. These, too, we may safely ignore for a particular decision. Top management salaries are examples of expected future costs that may be unaffected by the decision at hand.

Other irrelevant future costs include fixed costs that will be the same whether a company selects machine X or machine Y. However, it is incorrect to conclude that fixed costs are always irrelevant and variable costs are always relevant. Variable costs can be irrelevant, and fixed costs can be relevant. For instance, sales commissions are variable costs that are irrelevant to a decision on whether to produce a product in plant G or plant H. The rental cost of a warehouse is a fixed cost that is relevant if one alternative requires the warehouse while the other does not. In sum, future costs (both variable and fixed) are irrelevant whenever they do not differ among the alternatives at hand and are relevant whenever they do differ between the alternatives.

Finally, it is also critical in decision making to identify misspecified costs. The pricing illustration in Chapter 5 showed that managers should analyze unit costs with care in decision making. There are two major ways to go wrong: (1) including irrelevant costs, such as the $.03 allocation of unavoidable fixed costs in the Nantucket Nectars' make-or-buy example (pp. 226–227) that would result in a unit cost of $.20 instead of the relevant unit cost of $.17 and (2) comparing unit costs not computed on the same volume basis, as illustrated by the following example. Assume that a new $100,000 machine with a 5-year life span can produce 100,000 units a year at a variable cost of $1 per unit, as opposed to a variable cost per unit of $1.50 with an old machine. A sales representative claims that the new machine will reduce total cost by $.30 per unit after allowing $.20 per unit for depreciation on the new machine. Is the new machine a worthwhile acquisition?

If the customer's expected volume is 100,000 units, unit-cost comparisons are valid, provided that new depreciation is also considered. Assume that the disposal value of the old equipment is zero, so annual depreciation is $100,000 ÷ 5 years, which equals $20,000. Because depreciation is an allocation of historical cost, the depreciation on the old machine is irrelevant. In contrast, the depreciation on the new machine is relevant because the new machine entails a future cost that the customer can avoid by not acquiring it.

	Old Machine	New Machine
Units	100,000	100,000
Variable costs	$150,000	$100,000
Straight-line depreciation	—	20,000
Total relevant costs	$150,000	$120,000
Unit relevant costs	$ 1.50	$ 1.20

The preceding calculation shows that the sales representative is correct if the customer's expected volume is 100,000 units. However, sales personnel often boast about the low unit costs of using their new machines but may neglect to point out that the unit costs are based on outputs far in excess of the activity volume of their prospective customer. In this case, if the customer's expected volume is only 30,000 units per year, the unit costs change in favor of the old machine.

	Old Machine	New Machine
Units	30,000	30,000
Variable costs	$45,000	$30,000
Straight-line depreciation	—	20,000
Total relevant costs	$45,000	$50,000
Unit relevant costs	$ 1.50	$1.6667

Generally, be wary of unit fixed costs. When feasible, use total fixed cost in your analysis, not fixed cost per unit. Why? Because you need to calculate a new fixed cost per unit for every different volume of production—often a cumbersome task—and if you don't recalculate it, your costs will be misspecified.

Conflicts Between Decision Making and Performance Evaluation

Objective 8

Discuss how performance measures can affect decision making.

You should now know how to make good decisions based on relevant data. However, knowing how to make these decisions and actually making them are two different things. Managers might be tempted to make decisions they know are sub-optimal—not in the best interests of the company—if the performance measures in place will reward them for those decisions. To motivate managers to make firm-wide optimal decisions, methods of evaluating managers' performance should be consistent with the appropriate decision model for the company.

Let's look at an example of a conflict between the analysis for decision making and the method used to evaluate performance. Consider the replacement decision shown in Exhibit 6-6 on page 242, where there was a $2,500 advantage to replacing the machine rather than keeping it. To motivate managers to make the right choice, the method used to evaluate performance should be consistent with the decision model—that is, it should show better manager performance when a manager replaces rather than keeps the machine. Assume the firm uses accounting income to measure a manager's performance. The effect on accounting income in the first year after replacement compared with that in years 2, 3, and 4 follows:

	Year 1		Years 2, 3, and 4	
	Keep	Replace	Keep	Replace
Cash operating costs	$5,000	$3,000	$5,000	$3,000
Depreciation	1,000	2,000	1,000	2,000
Loss on disposal ($4,000 – $2,500)	—	1,500	—	—
Total cost	$6,000	$6,500	$6,000	$5,000

First-year costs will be $6,500 − $6,000 = $500 lower, making first-year income $500 higher, if the manager keeps the machine rather than replacing it. Because managers naturally want to make decisions that maximize the measure of their current performance, the manager may be inclined to keep the machine.

The conflict is especially severe if a company often transfers managers from one position to another. Why? Even though replacing the machine creates the $500 first-year decrease in income, over the long run this will be offset by a $1,000 annual increase in income in years 2 to 4. (Note that the net difference of $2,500 in favor of replacement over the 4 years together is the same as in Exhibit 6-6.) However, a manager who moves to a new position after the first year, bears the entire loss on disposal without reaping the benefits of lower operating costs in years 2 to 4, which creates a personal incentive for him to keep the machine.

The decision to replace a machine earlier than planned also reveals a possible error in the original decision to purchase the machine. The company bought the old machine 6 years ago for $10,000. Its expected life span was 10 years. However, if a better machine is now available, then the useful life of the old machine was really 6 years, not 10. This feedback on the actual life of the old machine has two possible effects, the first good and the second bad. First, managers might benefit by learning from the earlier mistake. If the manager overestimated the useful life of the old machine, the reliability of the predicted life for the new machine may be scrutinized. Feedback can help avoid repeating past mistakes. Second, the feedback on machine life creates incentives for a manager to make another mistake to cover up the earlier one. A "loss on disposal" could alert superiors to the incorrect economic-life prediction used in the earlier decision. By avoiding replacement, the manager avoids recognizing the loss on disposal and can spread the $4,000 remaining book value over the future as "depreciation," a more appealing term than "loss on disposal." The superiors may never find out about the incorrect prediction of economic life. Using accounting income for performance evaluation mixes the financial effects of various decisions, hiding both the earlier misestimation of useful life and the current failure to replace.

Conflicts between decision making and performance evaluation goals are widespread in practice. Unfortunately, there are no easy solutions. It is difficult to match performance evaluation and decision horizons, leading to conflicts like those in our equipment example. As a result, managers sometimes have incentives to focus on the short-term effects of decisions on their performance measures, rather than the long-term effects on the company.

Here and in Chapter 5 we introduced the important topics of relevant information and decision making. Our major focus was on how to determine and use relevant information when faced with various managerial decisions such as pricing, special orders, make or buy, adding or deleting a product line, and equipment replacement. We have emphasized the importance of understanding cost behavior in each of these decision situations. Now, we shift our emphasis from decision-making techniques to planning and control techniques. One of the most important planning techniques you will use as a manager is budgeting—the major topic in Chapters 7 and 8.

Highlights to Remember

1. **Use a differential analysis to examine income effects across alternatives and show that an opportunity-cost analysis yields identical results.** A differential analysis is a valuable tool for analyzing decisions; it focuses on the relevant items in the situation—differential revenues and differential costs. One should always consider opportunity costs when deciding on the use of limited resources. The opportunity cost of a course of action is the maximum profit forgone from other alternative actions. Decision makers may fail to consider opportunity costs because accountants do not report them in the financial accounting system.

2. **Decide whether to make or buy certain parts or products.** One of the most important production decisions is the make-or-buy decision. Should a company make its own parts or products or should it buy them from outside sources? Both qualitative and quantitative factors affect this decision. In applying relevant cost analysis to a make-or-buy situation, a key factor to consider is often the opportunity cost of facilities.

3. **Choose whether to add or delete a product line using relevant information.** Relevant information also plays an important role in decisions about adding or deleting products, services, or departments. Decisions on whether to delete a department or product line require analysis of the revenues forgone and the costs saved from the deletion.

4. **Compute the optimal product mix when production is constrained by a scarce resource.** When production is constrained by a limiting resource, the key to obtaining the maximum profit from a given capacity is to obtain the greatest possible contribution to profit per unit of the limiting or scarce resource.

5. **Decide whether to process a joint product beyond the split-off point.** Another typical production situation is deciding whether to process further a joint product or sell it at the split-off point. The relevant information for this decision includes the revenues and costs that differ beyond the split-off point. Joint costs that occur before split-off are irrelevant.

6. **Decide whether to keep or replace equipment.** In the decision to keep or replace equipment, the book value of old equipment is irrelevant. This sunk cost is a past or historical cost that a company has already incurred. Relevant costs normally include the disposal value of old equipment, the cost of new equipment, and the difference in the annual operating costs.

7. **Identify irrelevant and misspecified costs.** In certain production decisions, it is important to recognize and identify irrelevant costs. In the decision to dispose of obsolete inventory, the original cost of the inventory is irrelevant. In terms of misspecified costs, unit fixed costs can be misleading because of the differences in the assumed level of volume on which they are based. The more units a company makes, the lower the unit fixed cost will be. You can avoid being misled by unit costs by always using total fixed costs.

8. **Discuss how performance measures can affect decision making.** If companies evaluate managers using performance measures that are not in line with relevant decision criteria, there could be a conflict of interest. Managers often make decisions based on how the decision affects their performance measures. Thus, performance measures work best when they are consistent with the long-term good of the company.

Accounting Vocabulary

accumulated depreciation, p. 240
avoidable costs, p. 235
book value, p. 240
common costs, p. 235
depreciation, p. 240
differential analysis, p. 227
differential cost, p. 227
differential revenue, p. 227

incremental analysis, p. 227
incremental benefits, p. 227
incremental costs, p. 227
inventory turnover, p. 237
joint costs, p. 238
joint products, p. 238
limiting factor, p. 236
net book value, p. 240

opportunity cost, p. 228
outlay cost, p. 227
outsourcing, p. 229
scarce resource, p. 236
separable costs, p. 238
split-off point, p. 238
sunk cost, p. 240
unavoidable costs, p. 235

MyAccountingLab ## Fundamental Assignment Material

6-A1 Make or Buy

Vineyard Fruit Company sells premium-quality oranges and other citrus fruits by mail order. Protecting the fruit during shipping is important so the company has designed and produces shipping boxes. The annual cost to make 60,000 boxes is as follows:

Materials	$ 96,000
Labor	12,000
Indirect manufacturing costs	
Variable	9,600
Fixed	46,800
Total	$164,400

Therefore, the cost per box averages $2.74.

Suppose **Weyerhaeuser** submits a bid to supply Vineyard with boxes for $2.24 per box. Vineyard must give Weyerhaeuser the box design specifications, and the boxes will be made according to those specs.

1. How much, if any, would Vineyard save by buying the boxes from Weyerhaeuser?
2. What subjective factors should affect Vineyard's decision about whether to make or buy the boxes?

3. Suppose all the fixed costs represent depreciation on equipment that was purchased for $234,000 and is just about at the end of its 5-year life. New replacement equipment will cost $375,000 and is also expected to last 5 years. In this case, how much, if any, would Vineyard save by buying the boxes from Weyerhaeuser?

6-A2 Choice of Products

The Tipbox Tool Company has two products: a plain circular saw and a professional circular saw. The plain saw sells for $50 and has a variable cost of $35. The professional saw sells for $100 and has a variable cost of $60.

1. Compute contribution margins and contribution-margin ratios for plain and professional saws.
2. The demand is for more units than the company can produce. There are only 40,000 machine hours of manufacturing capacity available. Four plain saws can be produced in the same average time (1 hour) needed to produce one professional saw. Compute the total contribution margin for 40,000 hours for plain saws only and for professional saws only. Which product is the best use of machine hours?
3. Use two or three sentences to state the major lesson of this problem.

6-A3 Joint Products: Sell or Process Further

The Mussina Chemical Company produced three joint products at a joint cost of $117,000. These products were processed further and sold as follows:

Chemical Product	Sales	Additional Processing Costs
A	$230,000	$190,000
B	330,000	300,000
C	175,000	100,000

The company has had an opportunity to sell at split-off directly to other processors. If that alternative had been selected, sales would have been A, $54,000; B, $32,000; and C, $54,000.

The company expects to operate at the same level of production and sales in the forthcoming year.

1. Could the company increase operating income by altering its processing decisions? If so, what would be the expected overall operating income?
2. Which products should be processed further and which should be sold at split-off?

6-A4 Role of Old Equipment Replacement

On January 2, 2013, the T. W. McCann Company installed a brand new $108,000 special molding machine for producing a new product. The product and the machine have an expected life of 3 years. The machine's expected disposal value at the end of 3 years is zero.

On January 3, 2013, Joan Slater, a star salesperson for a machine tool manufacturer, tells Mr. McCann, "I wish I had known earlier of your purchase plans. I can supply you with a technically superior machine for $108,000. The machine you just purchased can be sold for $35,000. I guarantee that our machine will save $52,000 per year in cash operating costs, although it too will have no disposal value at the end of 3 years."

McCann examines some technical data. Although he has confidence in Slater's claims, McCann contends, "I'm locked in now. My alternatives are clear: (a) Disposal will result in a loss, (b) keeping and using the 'old' equipment avoids such a loss. I have brains enough to avoid a loss when my other alternative is recognizing a loss. We've got to use that equipment until we get our money out of it."

The annual operating costs of the old machine are expected to be $69,000, exclusive of depreciation. Sales, all in cash, will be $850,000 per year. Other annual cash expenses will be $740,000 regardless of this decision. Assume that the equipment in question is the company's only fixed asset.

Ignore income taxes and the time value of money.

1. Prepare statements of cash receipts and disbursements as they would appear in each of the next 3 years under both alternatives. What is the total cumulative increase or decrease in cash for the 3 years?
2. Prepare income statements as they would appear in each of the next 3 years under both alternatives. Assume straight-line depreciation. What is the cumulative increase or decrease in net income for the 3 years?

3. Assume that the cost of the "old" equipment was $800,000 rather than $108,000. Would the net difference computed in numbers 1 and 2 change? Explain.
4. As Joan Slater, reply to Mr. McCann's contentions.
5. What are the irrelevant items in each of your presentations for numbers 1 and 2? Why are they irrelevant?

6-B1 Make or Buy

Suppose a **BMW** executive in Germany is trying to decide whether the company should continue to manufacture an engine component or purchase it from Frankfurt Corporation for €50 each. Demand for the coming year is expected to be the same as for the current year, 200,000 units. Data for the current year follow:

Direct material	€ 5,000,000
Direct labor	1,900,000
Factory overhead, variable	1,100,000
Factory overhead, fixed	3,000,000
Total costs	€11,000,000

If BMW makes the components, the unit costs of direct material will increase by 10%.

If BMW buys the components, 30% of the fixed costs will be avoided. The other 70% will continue regardless of whether the components are manufactured or purchased. Assume that variable overhead varies with output volume.

1. Prepare a schedule that compares the make-or-buy alternatives. Show totals and amounts per unit. Compute the numerical difference between making and buying. Assume that the capacity now used to make the components will become idle if the components are purchased.
2. Assume also that the BMW capacity in question can be rented to a local electronics firm for €1,150,000 for the coming year. Prepare a schedule that compares the net relevant costs of the three alternatives: make, buy and leave capacity idle, buy and rent. Which is the most favorable alternative? By how much in total?

6-B2 Unit Costs and Capacity

Courcy Manufacturing Company produces two industrial solvents for which the following data have been tabulated. Fixed manufacturing cost is applied to products at a rate of $1.00 per machine hour.

Per Unit	XY-7	BD-4
Selling price	$6.45	$4.20
Variable manufacturing costs	2.70	1.70
Fixed manufacturing cost	.70	.20
Variable selling cost	1.80	1.75

The sales manager has had a $215,000 increase in her budget allotment for advertising and wants to apply the money on the most profitable product. The solvents are not substitutes for one another in the eyes of the company's customers.

1. How many machine hours does it take to produce one XY-7? To produce one BD-4? (Hint: Focus on applied fixed manufacturing cost.)
2. Suppose Courcy has only 140,000 machine hours that can be made available to produce XY-7 and BD-4. If the potential increase in sales units for either product resulting from advertising is far in excess of these production capabilities, which product should be produced and advertised, and what is the estimated increase in contribution margin earned?

6-B3 Dropping a Product Line

Hamleys Toy Store is on Regent Street in London. It has a magic department near the main door. Suppose that management is considering dropping the magic department, which has consistently shown an operating loss. The predicted income statements, in thousands of pounds (£), are (for ease of analysis, only three product lines are shown):

	Total	General Merchandise	Electronic Products	Magic Department
Sales	£6,000	£5,000	£400	£600
Variable expenses	4,090	3,500	200	390
Contribution margin	£1,910 (32%)	£1,500 (30%)	£200 (50%)	£210 (35%)
Fixed expenses (compensation, depreciation, property taxes, insurance, etc.)	1,100	750	50	300
Operating income (loss)	£ 810	£ 750	£150	£(90)

The £300,000 of magic department fixed expenses include the compensation of employees of £120,000. These employees will be released if the magic department is abandoned. All of the magic department's equipment is fully depreciated, so none of the £300,000 pertains to such items. Furthermore, disposal values of equipment will be exactly offset by the costs of removal and remodeling.

If the magic department is dropped, the manager will use the vacated space for either more general merchandise or more electronic products. The expansion of general merchandise would not entail hiring any additional salaried help, but more electronic products would require an additional person at an annual cost of £30,000. The manager thinks that sales of general merchandise would increase by £250,000, and electronic products by £200,000. The manager's modest predictions are partially based on the fact that she thinks the magic department has helped lure customers to the store and, thus, improved overall sales. If the magic department is closed, that lure would be gone.

Should the magic department be closed? Explain, showing computations.

6-B4 Sell or Process Further

ConAgra produces meat products with brand names such as Healthy Choice, Armour, and Butterball. Suppose one of the company's plants processes beef cattle into various products. For simplicity, assume that there are only three products: steak, hamburger, and hides, and that the average steer costs $700. The three products emerge from a process that costs $100 per steer to run, and output from one steer can be sold for the following net amounts:

Steak (100 pounds)	$ 400
Hamburger (500 pounds)	600
Hide (120 pounds)	100
Total	$1,100

Assume that each of these three products can be sold immediately or processed further in another ConAgra plant. The steak can be the main course in frozen dinners sold under the Healthy Choice label. The vegetables and desserts in the 400 dinners produced from the 100 pounds of steak would cost $110, and production, sales, and other costs for the 400 meals would total $330. Each meal would be sold wholesale for $2.10.

The hamburger could be made into frozen Salisbury steak patties sold under the Armour label. The only additional cost would be a $200 processing cost for the 500 pounds of hamburger. Frozen Salisbury steaks sell wholesale for $1.70 per pound.

The hide can be sold before or after tanning. The cost of tanning one hide is $80, and a tanned hide can be sold for $170.

1. Compute the total profit if all three products are sold at the split-off point.
2. Compute the total profit if all three products are processed further before being sold.
3. Which products should be sold at the split-off point? Which should be processed further?
4. Compute the total profit if your plan in number 3 is followed.

6-B5 Replacing Old Equipment

Consider the following data regarding Orange County's photocopying requirements.

	Old Equipment	Proposed Replacement Equipment
Useful life, in years	5	3
Current age, in years	2	0
Useful life remaining, in years	3	3
Original cost	$34,000	$14,700
Accumulated depreciation	13,600	0
Book value	20,400	Not acquired yet
Disposal value (in cash) now	3,600	Not acquired yet
Disposal value in 3 years	0	0
Annual cash operating costs for power, maintenance, toner, and supplies	17,000	11,000

The county administrator is trying to decide whether to replace the old equipment. Because of rapid changes in technology, she expects the replacement equipment to have only a 3-year useful life. Ignore the effects of taxes.

1. Prepare a schedule that compares both relevant and irrelevant items for the next 3 years. (Hint: See Exhibit 6-5, page 241.)
2. Prepare a schedule that compares all relevant items for the next 3 years. Which tabulation is clearer, this one or the one in requirement 1? (Hint: See Exhibit 6-6, page 242.)
3. Prepare a simple "shortcut" or direct analysis to support your choice of alternatives.

6-B6 Decision and Performance Models

Refer to the preceding problem.

1. Suppose the "decision model" favored by top management consisted of a comparison of a 3-year accumulation of cash under each alternative. As the manager of office operations, which alternative would you choose? Why?
2. Suppose the "performance evaluation model" emphasized the minimization of overall costs of photocopying operations for the first year. Which alternative would you choose?

MyAccountingLab ## Additional Assignment Material

QUESTIONS

6-1 Distinguish between an opportunity cost and an outlay cost.

6-2 "I had a chance to rent my summer home for 2 weeks for $800. But I chose to have it idle. I didn't want strangers living in my summer house." What term in this chapter describes the $800? Why?

6-3 "Accountants do not ordinarily record opportunity costs in the formal accounting records." Why?

6-4 Distinguish between an incremental cost and a differential cost.

6-5 "Incremental cost is the addition to costs from the manufacture of one unit." Do you agree? Explain.

6-6 "The differential costs or incremental costs of increasing production from 1,000 automobiles to 1,200 automobiles per week would be the additional costs of producing the additional 200 automobiles." If production were reduced from 1,200 to 1,000 automobiles per week, what would the decline in costs be called?

6-7 "Qualitative factors generally favor making over buying a component." Do you agree? Explain.

6-8 "Choices are often mislabeled as simply make or buy." Do you agree? Explain.

6-9 "The key to decisions to delete a product or department is identifying avoidable costs." Do you agree? Explain.

6-10 Give four examples of limiting or scarce factors.

6-11 What are joint products? Name several examples of joint products.

6-12 What is the split-off point, and why is it important in analyzing joint costs?

6-13 "No technique used to assign the joint cost to individual products should be used for management decisions regarding whether a product should be sold at the split-off point or processed further." Do you agree? Explain.

6-14 "Inventory that was purchased for $5,000 should not be sold for less than $5,000 because such a sale would result in a loss." Do you agree? Explain.

6-15 "Recovering sunk costs is a major objective when replacing equipment." Do you agree? Explain.

6-16 "Past costs are indeed relevant in most instances because they provide the point of departure for the entire decision process." Do you agree? Why?

6-17 Which of the following items are relevant to replacement decisions? Explain.
a. Book value of old equipment
b. Disposal value of old equipment
c. Cost of new equipment

6-18 "Some expected future costs may be irrelevant." Do you agree? Explain.

6-19 "Variable costs are irrelevant whenever they do not differ among the alternatives at hand." Do you agree? Explain.

6-20 There are two major reasons why unit costs should be analyzed with care in decision making. What are they?

6-21 "Machinery sales personnel sometimes erroneously brag about the low unit costs of using their machines." Identify one source of an error concerning the estimation of unit costs.

6-22 Give an example of a situation in which the performance evaluation model is not consistent with the decision model.

6-23 "Evaluating performance, decision by decision, is costly. Aggregate measures, such as the income statement, are frequently used." How might the wide use of income statements affect managers' decisions about buying equipment?

CRITICAL THINKING EXERCISES

6-24 Measurement of Opportunity Cost
"Accountants cannot measure opportunity cost. Only managers have the knowledge to measure it." Do you agree with this statement? Why or why not?

6-25 Outsourcing Decisions
Decisions on whether to outsource services such as payroll accounting and systems development are much like make-or-buy decisions. What cost factors should influence the decision on whether to outsource payroll functions?

6-26 Unitized Costs
Suppose you are a manager in a manufacturing company. Your accountant has just presented you with a very detailed cost analysis for a decision about whether to outsource or make a component of a product. You have to use this analysis in a meeting with other managers. Since the analysis is shown in totals and your colleagues prefer simple reports and unit costs, you divide the bottom-line amounts by the total units to be made or bought (outsourced) and present just these in a simple report. Your colleagues are pleased that your report is so easy to understand and simple to use. Then they begin to predict the total cost differences for several other possible numbers of units to be made or outsourced by simply multiplying the unit costs by the volume to be outsourced. Why should you feel uncomfortable?

6-27 Historical Costs and Inventory Decisions
Explain why it is sometimes best to sell inventory for less than the amount paid for it.

EXERCISES

6-28 Opportunity Costs
Emily Adessa is an attorney employed by a large law firm at a salary of $85,000 per year. She is considering whether to become a sole practitioner, which would probably generate annually $410,000 in operating revenues and $290,000 in operating expenses.

1. Present two tabulations of the annual income effects of these alternatives. The second tabulation should include the opportunity cost of Adessa's compensation as an employee.
2. Suppose Adessa prefers less risk and chooses to stay an employee. Show a tabulation of the income effects of rejecting the opportunity of independent practice.

6-29 Opportunity Cost of Home Ownership

Ernie McNaire has just made the final payment on his mortgage. He could continue to live in the home; cash expenses for repairs and maintenance (after any tax effects) would be $750 monthly. Alternatively, he could sell the home for $490,000 (net of taxes), invest the proceeds in 3% municipal tax-free bonds, and rent an apartment for $18,000 annually. The landlord would then pay for repairs and maintenance.

Prepare two analyses of McNaire's alternatives, one showing no explicit opportunity cost and the second showing the explicit opportunity cost of the decision to hold the present home.

6-30 Opportunity Cost at Nantucket Nectars

Suppose Nantucket Nectars has a machine for which it paid $160,000 several years ago and is currently not being used. It can use the machine to produce 12 oz. bottles of its juice cocktails or 12 oz. bottles of its 100% juices. The contribution margin from the additional sales of 100% juices would be $90,000. A third alternative is selling the machine for cash of $75,000. What is the opportunity cost of the machine when we analyze the alternative to produce 12 oz. bottles of juice cocktails?

6-31 Hospital Opportunity Cost

An administrator at Saint Jude Hospital is considering how to use some space made available when the outpatient clinic moved to a new building. She has narrowed her choices, as follows:

a. Use the space to expand laboratory testing. Expected future annual revenue would be $330,000; future costs would be $290,000.
b. Use the space to expand the eye clinic. Expected future annual revenue would be $500,000; future costs would be $480,000.
c. The gift shop is rented by an independent retailer who wants to expand into the vacated space. The retailer has offered $11,000 for the yearly rental of the space. All operating expenses will be borne by the retailer.

The administrator's planning horizon is unsettled. However, she has decided that the yearly data given will suffice for guiding her decision.

Tabulate the total relevant data regarding the decision alternatives. Omit the concept of opportunity cost in one tabulation, but use the concept in a second tabulation. As the administrator, which tabulation would you prefer if you could receive only one?

6-32 Make or Buy

Assume that a division of Bose makes an electronic component for its speakers. Its manufacturing process for the component is a highly automated part of a just-in-time production system. All labor is considered to be an overhead cost, and all overhead is regarded as fixed with respect to output volume. Production costs for 100,000 units of the component are as follows:

Direct materials		$400,000
Factory overhead		
Indirect labor	$80,000	
Supplies	30,000	
Allocated occupancy cost	40,000	150,000
Total cost		$550,000

A small, local company has offered to supply the components at a price of $4.20 each. If the division discontinued its production of the component, it would save two-thirds of the supplies cost and $30,000 of indirect-labor cost. All other overhead costs would continue.

The division manager recently attended a seminar on cost behavior and learned about fixed and variable costs. He wants to continue to make the component because the variable cost of $4.00 is below the $4.20 bid.

1. Compute the relevant cost of (a) making and (b) purchasing the component. Which alternative is less costly and by how much?
2. What qualitative factors might influence the decision about whether to make or to buy the component?

6-33 Make or Buy at Nantucket Nectars

Assume that Nantucket Nectars reports the following costs to make 17.5 oz. bottles for its juice cocktails:

Nantucket Nectars Company
Cost of Making 17.5-Ounce Bottles

	Total Cost for 1,000,000 Bottles	Cost per Bottle
Direct materials	$ 80,000	$.080
Direct labor	30,000	.030
Variable factory overhead	60,000	.060
Fixed factory overhead	85,000	.085
Total costs	$255,000	$.255

Another manufacturer offers to sell Nantucket Nectars the bottles for $.25. The capacity now used to make bottles will become idle if the company purchases the bottles. Further, one supervisor with a salary of $60,000, a fixed cost, would be eliminated if the bottles were purchased. Prepare a schedule that compares the costs to make and buy the 17.5 oz. bottles. Should Nantucket Nectars make or buy the bottles?

6-34 Make or Buy and the Use of Idle Facilities at Nantucket Nectars

Refer to the preceding exercise. Suppose Nantucket Nectars can use the released facilities in another manufacturing activity that makes a contribution to profits of $75,000 or can rent them out for $55,000. Prepare a schedule that compares the four alternative courses of action. Which alternative would yield the lowest net cost?

6-35 Profit per Unit of Space

1. Several successful chains of warehouse stores such as Costco and Sam's Club have merchandising policies that differ considerably from those of traditional department stores. Name some characteristics of these warehouse stores that have contributed to their success.
2. Food chains such as Safeway have typically regarded approximately 20% of selling price as an average target gross profit on canned goods and similar grocery items. What are the limitations of such an approach? Be specific.

6-36 Deletion of Product Line

St. Gallen American School is an international private elementary school. In addition to regular classes, after-school care is provided between 3:00 PM and 6:00 PM at CHF 10 per child per hour. Financial results for the after-school care for a representative month are as follows:

Revenue, 750 hours at CHF 10 per hour		CHF 7,500
Less		
Teacher salaries	CHF 5,300	
Supplies	1,200	
Depreciation	1,700	
Sanitary engineering	200	
Other fixed costs	400	8,800
Operating income (loss)		CHF (1,300)

The director of St. Gallen American School is considering discontinuing the after-school care services because it is not fair to the other students to subsidize the after-school care program. He thinks that eliminating the program will free up CHF 1,300 a month to support regular classes.

1. Compute the financial impact on St. Gallen American School from discontinuing the after-school care program.
2. List three qualitative factors that would influence your decision.

6-37 Sell or Process Further

An **Exxon** petrochemical factory produces two products, L and M, as a result of a particular joint process. Both products are sold to manufacturers as ingredients for assorted chemical products.

Product L sells at split-off for $.25 per gallon; M sells for $.30 per gallon. Data for April follow:

Joint processing cost	$1,600,000
Gallons produced and sold	
L	4,000,000
M	2,500,000

Suppose that in April the 2,500,000 gallons of M could have been processed further into Super M at an additional cost of $165,000. The Super M output would be sold for $.36 per gallon. Product L would be sold at split-off in any event.

Should M have been processed further in April and sold as Super M? Show your computations.

6-38 Joint Products, Multiple Choice

From a particular joint process, Demoulas company produces three products, A, B, and C. Each product may be sold at the point of split-off or processed further. Additional processing requires no special facilities, and production costs of further processing are entirely variable and traceable to the products involved. In 2012, all three products were processed beyond split-off. Joint production costs for the year were $100,000. Sales values and costs needed to evaluate Demoulas's 2012 production policy follow:

Product	Units Produced	Net Realizable Values (Sales Values) at Split-Off	Additional Costs and Sales Values if Processed Further	
			Sales Values	Added Costs
A	9,000	$33,000	$50,000	$ 18,000
B	5,000	44,000	50,000	13,000
C	6,000	28,000	35,000	6,000

Answer the following multiple-choice questions:

1. For units of C, the unit production cost most relevant to a sell-or-process-further decision is (a) $1, (b) $9, (c) $12, (d) $3.
2. To maximize profits, Demoulas should subject the following product(s) to additional processing: (a) C only, (b) B and C only (c) A, B, and C (d) A only.

6-39 Obsolete Inventory

The New York bookstore bought more "Jets Champs" calendars than it could sell. It was nearly June and 220 calendars remained in stock. The store paid $4.25 each for the calendars and normally sold them for $8.85. Since February, they had been on sale for $6.20, and 2 weeks ago the price was dropped to $4.95. Still, few calendars were being sold. The bookstore manager thought it was no longer worthwhile using shelf space for the calendars.

The proprietor of Old Orchard Collectibles offered to buy all 220 calendars for $88. He intended to store them until the 2013 football season was over and then sell them as novelty items.

The bookstore manager was not sure she wanted to sell for $.40 calendars that cost $4.25. The only alternative, however, was to scrap them because the publisher would not take them back.

1. Compute the difference in profit between accepting the $88 offer and scrapping the calendars.
2. Describe how the $4.25 × 220 = $935 paid for the calendars affects your decision.

6-40 Replacement of Old Equipment

Three years ago, the Oak Street TCBY bought a frozen yogurt machine for $11,200. A salesman has just suggested to the TCBY manager that she replace the machine with a new, $13,500 machine. The manager has gathered the following data:

	Old Machine	New Machine
Original cost	$11,200	$13,500
Useful life in years	8	5
Current age in years	3	0
Useful life remaining in years	5	5
Accumulated depreciation	$ 4,200	Not acquired yet
Book value	$ 7,000	Not acquired yet
Disposal value (in cash) now	$ 2,500	Not acquired yet
Disposal value in 5 years	0	0
Annual cash operating cost	$ 5,300	$ 2,700

1. Compute the difference in total costs over the next 5 years under both alternatives, that is, keeping the original machine or replacing it with the new machine. Ignore taxes.
2. Suppose the Oak Street TCBY manager replaces the original machine. Compute the "loss on disposal" of the original machine. How does this amount affect your computation in number 1? Explain.

6-41 Unit Costs

Brandon Company produces and sells a product that has variable costs of $8 per unit and fixed costs of $250,000 per year.

1. Compute the unit cost at a production and sales level of 10,000 units per year.
2. Compute the unit cost at a production and sales level of 20,000 units per year.
3. Which of these unit costs is most accurate? Explain.

6-42 Relevant Investment

Julia Rozzi had obtained a new truck with a list price, including options, of $27,000. The dealer had given her a "generous trade-in allowance" of $6,000 on her old truck that had a wholesale price of $3,200. Sales tax was $1,620.

The annual cash operating costs of the old truck were $5,250. The new truck was expected to reduce these costs by one-third, to $3,500 per year.

Compute the amount of the original investment in the new truck. Explain your reasoning.

6-43 Weak Division

Lake Forest Electronics Company paid $7 million in cash 4 years ago to acquire a company that manufactures CD-ROM drives. This company has been operated as a division of Lake Forest and has lost $500,000 each year since its acquisition.

The minimum desired return for this division is that, when a new product is fully developed, it should return a net profit of $500,000 per year for the foreseeable future.

Recently, the IBM Corporation offered to purchase the division from Lake Forest for $5 million. The president of Lake Forest commented, "I've got an investment of $9 million to recoup ($7 million plus losses of $500,000 for each of 4 years). I have finally got this situation turned around, so I oppose selling the division now."

Prepare a response to the president's remarks. Indicate how to make this decision. Be as specific as possible.

6-44 Opportunity Cost

Marnie McKay, MD, is a psychiatrist who is in heavy demand. Even though she has raised her fees considerably during the past 5 years, Dr. McKay still cannot accommodate all the patients who wish to see her.

McKay has conducted 7 hours of appointments a day, 6 days a week, for 46 weeks a year. Her fee averages $225 per hour.

Her variable costs are negligible and may be ignored for decision purposes. Ignore income taxes.

1. McKay is weary of working a 6-day week. She is considering taking every other Saturday off. What would be her annual income (a) if she worked every Saturday and (b) if she worked every other Saturday?
2. What would be her opportunity cost for the year of not working every other Saturday?
3. Assume that Dr. McKay has definitely decided to take every other Saturday off. She loves to repair her sports car by doing the work herself. If she works on her car during half a Saturday when she otherwise would not see patients, what is her opportunity cost?

PROBLEMS

6-45 Hotel Rooms and Opportunity Costs

The **Marriott Corporation** operates many hotels throughout the world. Suppose one of its Chicago hotels is facing difficult times because of the opening of several new competing hotels.

To accommodate its flight personnel, **American Airlines** has offered Marriott a contract for the coming year that provides a rate of $70 per night per room for a minimum of 50 rooms for 365 nights. This contract would assure Marriott of selling 50 rooms of space nightly, even if some of the rooms are vacant on some nights. Assume zero variable costs.

The Marriott manager has mixed feelings about the contract. On several peak nights during the year, the hotel could sell the same space for $150 per room.

1. Suppose the Marriott manager signs the contract. What is the opportunity cost of the 50 rooms on October 20, the night of a big convention of retailers when every nearby hotel room is occupied? What is the opportunity cost on December 28, when only 10 of these rooms would be expected to be rented at an average rate of $100?
2. If the year-round rate per room averaged $110, what percentage of occupancy of the 50 rooms in question would have to be rented to make Marriott indifferent about accepting the offer?

6-46 Extension of Preceding Problem

Assume the same facts as in the preceding problem. However, also assume that the variable costs per room, per day are $10.

1. Suppose the best estimate is a 62% general occupancy rate for the 50 rooms at an average $110 room rate for the next year. Should Marriott accept the contract?
2. What percentage of occupancy of the 50 rooms in question would make Marriott indifferent about accepting the offer?

6-47 Make or Buy

Dana Corporation, based in Toledo, Ohio, is a global manufacturer of highly engineered products that serve industrial, vehicle, construction, commercial, aerospace, and semiconductor markets. It frequently subcontracts work to other manufacturers, depending on whether Dana's facilities are fully occupied. Suppose Dana is about to make some final decisions regarding the use of its manufacturing facilities for the coming year.

The following are the costs of making part EC113, a key component of an emissions control system:

	Total Cost for 65,000 Units	Cost per Unit
Direct materials	$ 585,000	$ 9
Direct labor	715,000	11
Variable factory overhead	650,000	10
Fixed factory overhead	195,000	3
Total manufacturing costs	$2,145,000	$33

Another manufacturer has offered to sell the same part to Dana for $28 each. The fixed overhead consists of depreciation, property taxes, insurance, and supervisory salaries. All the fixed overhead would continue if Dana bought the component except that the cost of $130,000 pertaining to some supervisory and custodial personnel could be avoided.

1. Assume that the capacity now used to make parts will become idle if the parts are purchased. Should Dana buy or make the parts? Show computations.
2. Assume that the capacity now used to make parts will either (a) be rented to a nearby manufacturer for $25,000 for the year or (b) be used to make oil filters that will yield a profit contribution of $15,000. Should Dana buy or make part EC113? Show your computations.

6-48 Relevant-Cost Analysis

Following are the unit costs of making and selling a single product at a normal level of 5,000 units per month and a current unit selling price of $90:

Manufacturing costs	
Direct materials	$35
Direct labor	12
Variable overhead	8
Fixed overhead (total for the year, $300,000)	5
Selling and administrative expenses	
Variable	15
Fixed (total for the year, $480,000)	8

Consider each requirement separately. Label all computations, and present your solutions in a form that will be comprehensible to the company president.

1. This product is usually sold at a rate of 60,000 units per year. It is predicted that a rise in price to $98 will decrease volume by 10%. How much may advertising be increased under this plan without having annual operating income fall below the current level?
2. The company has received a proposal from an outside supplier to make and ship this item directly to the company's customers as sales orders are forwarded. Variable selling and administrative costs would fall 40%. If the supplier's proposal is accepted, the company will use its own plant to produce a new product. The new product would be sold through manufacturer's agents at a 10% commission based on a selling price of $40 each. The cost characteristics of this product, based on predicted yearly normal volume, are as follows.

	Per Unit
Direct materials	$ 6
Direct labor	12
Variable overhead	8
Fixed overhead	6
Manufacturing costs	$32
Selling and administrative expenses	
Variable (commission)	10% of selling price
Fixed	$ 2

What is the maximum price per unit that the company can afford to pay to the supplier for subcontracting production of the entire old product? Assume the following:

- Total fixed factory overhead and total fixed selling expenses will not change if the new product line is added.

- The supplier's proposal will not be considered unless the present annual net income can be maintained.
- Selling price of the old product will remain unchanged at $90.
- All $300,000 of fixed manufacturing overhead will be assigned to the new product.

6-49 Hotel Pricing and Use of Capacity

A growing corporation in a large city has offered a 200-room Holiday Inn a 1-year contract to rent 40 rooms at reduced rates of $50 per room instead of the regular rate of $86 per room. The corporation will sign the contract for 365-day occupancy because its visiting manufacturing and marketing personnel are virtually certain to use all the space each night.

Each room occupied has a variable cost of $12 per night (for cleaning, laundry, lost linens, and extra electricity).

The hotel manager expects an 85% occupancy rate for the year so she is reluctant to sign the contract. If the contract is signed, the occupancy rate on the remaining 160 rooms will be 95%.

1. Compute the total contribution margin for the year with and without the contract. Is the contract profitable to Holiday Inn?
2. Compute the lowest room rate that the hotel should accept on the contract so that the total contribution margin would be the same with or without the contract.

6-50 Special Air Fares

Denver-based Frontier Airlines provides service to 39 cities in the United States and Mexico. Frontier operates a fleet of 37 aircraft including sixteen 134-passenger Boeing 737-300 jets. The manager of operations of Frontier Airlines is trying to decide whether to adopt a new discount fare. Focus on one 134-seat 737 airplane now operating at a 56% load factor. That is, on average the airplane has $.56 \times 134 = 75$ passengers. The regular fares produce an average revenue of $.12 per passenger mile.

Suppose an average 40% fare discount (which is subject to restrictions regarding time of departure and length of stay) will produce three new additional passengers. Also suppose that three of the previously committed passengers accept the restrictions and switch to the discount fare from the regular fare.

1. Compute the total revenue per airplane-mile with and without the discount fares.
2. Suppose the maximum allowed allocation to new discount fares is 50 seats. These will be filled. As before, some previously committed passengers will accept the restrictions and switch to the discount fare from the regular fare. How many will have to switch so that the total revenue per mile will be the same either with or without the discount plan?

6-51 Choice of Products

Gulf Coast Fashions sells both designer and moderately priced women's wear in Tampa. Profits have been volatile. Top management is trying to decide which product line to drop. Accountants have reported the following data:

	Per Item	
	Designer	**Moderately Priced**
Average selling price	$240	$150
Average variable expenses	120	85
Average contribution margin	$120	$ 65
Average contribution-margin percentage	50%	43%

The store has 8,000 square feet of floor space. If moderately priced goods are sold exclusively, 400 items can be displayed. If designer goods are sold exclusively, only 300 items can be displayed. Moreover, the rate of sale (turnover) of the designer items will be two-thirds the rate of moderately priced goods.

1. Prepare an analysis to show which product to drop.
2. What other considerations might affect your decision in number 1?

6-52 Analysis of Unit Costs

Circuit Booster Company manufactures small appliances, such as electric can openers, toasters, food mixers, and irons. The peak manufacturing season is at hand, and the president is trying to decide whether to produce more of the company's standard line of can openers or its premium line that includes a built-in knife sharpener, a better finish, and a higher-quality motor. The unit data follow:

	Product	
	Standard	**Premium**
Selling price	$60	$70
Direct material	$ 9	$14
Direct labor	6	3
Variable factory overhead	6	8
Fixed factory overhead	14	21
Total cost of goods sold	$35	$46
Gross profit per unit	$25	$24

The sales outlook is very encouraging. The plant could operate at full capacity by producing either product or both products. Both the standard and the premium products are processed through the same departments. Selling and administrative costs will not be affected by this decision so they may be ignored.

Many of the parts are produced on automatic machinery. The factory overhead is allocated to products by developing separate rates per machine hour for variable and fixed overhead. For example, the total fixed overhead is divided by the total machine hours to get a rate per hour. Thus, the amount of overhead allocated to products is dependent on the number of machine hours used by the product. It takes 1 hour of machine time to produce one unit of the standard product.

Direct labor may not be proportionate with overhead because many workers operate two or more machines simultaneously.

Which product should be produced? If more than one should be produced, indicate the proportions of each. Show computations. Explain your answers briefly.

6-53 Use of Available Facilities

The Oahu Audio Company manufactures electronic subcomponents that can be sold as is or can be processed further into "plug-in" assemblies for a variety of intricate electronic equipment. The entire output of subcomponents can be sold at a market price of $2.20 per unit. The plug-in assemblies have been generating a sales price of $5.70 for 3 years, but the price has recently fallen to $5.30 on assorted orders.

Janet Oh, the vice president of marketing, has analyzed the markets and the costs. She thinks that production of plug-in assemblies should be dropped whenever the price falls below $4.70 per unit. However, at the current price of $5.30, the total available capacity should currently be devoted to producing plug-in assemblies. She has cited the data in Exhibit 6-7.

Exhibit 6-7
Oahu Audio Company
Product Profitability Data

Subcomponents		
Selling price, after deducting relevant selling costs		$2.20
Direct materials	$1.10	
Direct labor	.30	
Manufacturing overhead	.60	
Cost per unit		2.00
Operating profit		$ .20

Plug-In Assemblies		
Selling price, after deducting relevant selling costs		$5.30
Transferred-in variable cost for subcomponents	$1.40	
Additional direct materials	1.45	
Direct labor	.45	
Manufacturing overhead	1.20*	
Cost per unit		4.50
Operating profit		$ .80

*For additional processing to make and test plug-in assemblies.

Direct-materials and direct-labor costs are variable. The total overhead is fixed; it is allocated to units produced by predicting the total overhead for the coming year and dividing this total by the total hours of capacity available.

The total hours of capacity available are 600,000. It takes 1 hour to make 60 subcomponents and 2 hours of additional processing and testing to make 60 plug-in assemblies.

1. If the price of plug-in assemblies for the coming year is to be $5.30, should sales of subcomponents be dropped and all facilities devoted to the production of plug-in assemblies? Show your computations.
2. Prepare a report for the vice president of marketing to show the lowest possible price for plug-in assemblies that would be acceptable.
3. Suppose 40% of the manufacturing overhead is variable with respect to processing and testing time. Repeat numbers 1 and 2. Do your answers change? If so, how?

6-54 Joint Costs and Incremental Analysis

Jacque de Paris, a high-fashion women's dress manufacturer, is planning to market a new cocktail dress for the coming season. Jacque de Paris supplies retailers in Europe and the United States.

Four yards of material are required to lay out the dress pattern. Some material remains after cutting, which can be sold as remnants. The leftover material could also be used to manufacture a matching cape and handbag. However, if the leftover material is to be used for the cape and handbag, more care will be required in the cutting, which will increase the cutting costs.

The company expects to sell 1,000 dresses if no matching cape or handbag is available. Market research reveals that dress sales will be 15% higher if a matching cape and handbag are available. The market research indicates that the cape and handbag will not be sold individually, but only as accessories with the dress. The various combinations of dresses, capes, and handbags that are expected to be sold by retailers are as follows:

Percent of Total	
Complete sets of dress, cape, and handbag	72%
Dress and cape	10%
Dress and handbag	12%
Dress only	6%
Total	100%

The material used in the dress costs €90 a yard, or €360 for each dress. The cost of cutting the dress if the cape and handbag are not manufactured is estimated at €105 a dress, and the resulting remnants can be sold for €24 for each dress cut out. If the cape and handbag are to be manufactured, the cutting costs will be increased by €34 per dress. There will be no salable remnants if the capes and handbags are manufactured in the quantities estimated. The selling prices and the costs to complete the three items once they are cut are as follows:

	Selling Price per Unit	Unit Cost to Complete (Excludes Cost of Material and Cutting Operation)
Dress	€1,100	€600
Cape	120	70
Handbag	40	30

1. Calculate the incremental profit or loss to Jacque de Paris from manufacturing the capes and handbags in conjunction with the dresses.
2. Identify any non-quantitative factors that could influence the company's management in its decision to manufacture the capes and handbags that match the dress.

6-55 Joint Products: Sell or Process Further

Western, Corp., produces two products, cigars and chewing tobacco, from a joint process involving the processing of tobacco leaves. Joint costs are $60,000 for this process, and yield 2,000 pounds of cigars and 4,000 pounds of chewing tobacco. Cigars sell for $80 per pound, and chewing tobacco sells for $20 per pound. Cigars require $80,000 in separable costs, while chewing tobacco requires $50,000 in separable costs. Chewing tobacco can be processed further (for $30,000 in additional separable costs) into a mint-flavored premium chewing tobacco that would sell for $30 per pound.

1. Should Western process chewing tobacco into premium chewing tobacco?
2. What is the maximum amount that joint costs can increase before (a) it would not be better to process chewing tobacco further into premium chewing tobacco, and (b) it would be better to cease processing tobacco leaves to produce cigars and premium chewing tobacco?

6-56 Relevant Cost

Sunset Company's unit costs of manufacturing and selling a given item at the planned activity level of 20,000 units per month are as follows:

Manufacturing costs	
Direct materials	$4.30
Direct labor	.95
Variable overhead	1.10
Fixed overhead	1.05
Selling expenses	
Variable	2.90
Fixed	1.05

Ignore income taxes in all requirements. These four parts have no connection with each other.

1. Compute the planned annual operating income at a selling price of $19 per unit.
2. Compute the expected annual operating income if the volume can be increased by 12% when the selling price is reduced to $16. Assume that the implied cost behavior patterns are correct.
3. The company desires to seek an order for 6,800 units from a foreign customer. The variable selling expenses for the order will be 30% less than usual, but the fixed costs for obtaining the order will be $8,160. Domestic sales will not be affected. Compute the minimum break-even price per unit to be considered.
4. The company has an inventory of 7,000 units of this item left over from last year's model. These must be sold through regular channels at reduced prices. The inventory will be valueless unless sold this way. What unit cost is relevant for establishing the minimum selling price of these 7,000 units?

6-57 New Machine

A new $300,000 machine is expected to have a 5-year life and a terminal value of zero. It can produce 40,000 units a year at a variable cost of $4 per unit. The variable cost is $6.50 per unit with an old machine, which has a book value of $100,000. It is being depreciated on a straight-line basis at $20,000 per year. It too is expected to have a terminal value of zero. Its current disposal value is also zero because it is highly specialized equipment.

The salesperson of the new machine prepared the following comparison:

	New Machine	Old Machine
Units	40,000	40,000
Variable costs	$160,000	$260,000
Straight-line depreciation	60,000	20,000
Total cost	$220,000	$280,000
Unit cost	$ 5.50	$ 7.00

He said, "The new machine is obviously a worthwhile acquisition. You will save $1.50 for every unit you produce."

1. Do you agree with the salesperson's analysis? If not, how would you change it? Be specific. Ignore taxes.
2. Prepare an analysis of total and unit differential costs if the annual volume is 20,000 units.
3. At what annual volume would both the old and new machines have the same total relevant costs?

6-58 Conceptual Approach

A large automobile-parts plant was constructed 4 years ago in a Pennsylvania city served by two railroads. The PC Railroad purchased 40 specialized 60-foot freight cars as a direct result of the additional traffic generated by the new plant. The investment was based on an estimated useful life of 20 years.

Now the competing railroad has offered to service the plant with new 86-foot freight cars that would enable more efficient shipping operations at the plant. The automobile-parts company has threatened to switch carriers unless PC Railroad buys 10 new 86-foot freight cars.

The PC marketing management wants to buy the new cars, but PC operating management says, "The new investment is undesirable. It really consists of the new outlay plus the loss on the old freight cars. The old cars must be written down to a low salvage value if they cannot be used as originally intended."

Evaluate the comments. What is the correct conceptual approach to the quantitative analysis in this decision?

6-59 Book Value of Old Equipment

Consider the following data concerning the replacement of old equipment by new equipment:

	Old Equipment	Proposed New Equipment
Original cost	$30,400	$15,300
Useful life in years	8	3
Current age in years	5	0
Useful life remaining in years	3	3
Accumulated depreciation	$19,000	0
Book value	11,400	*
Disposal value (in cash) now	3,500	*
Annual cash operating costs (maintenance, power, repairs, lubricants, etc.)	$11,800	$ 6,200

*Not acquired yet.

1. Prepare a cost comparison of all relevant items for the next 3 years together. Ignore taxes.
2. Prepare a cost comparison that includes both relevant and irrelevant items. (See Exhibit 6-5, p. 241.)
3. Prepare a comparative statement of the total charges against revenue for the first year. Would the manager be inclined to buy the new equipment? Explain.

6-60 Decision and Performance Models

Refer to Problem 6-A4.

1. Suppose the "decision model" favored by top management consisted of a comparison of a 3-year accumulation of wealth under each alternative. Which alternative would you choose? Why? (Accumulation of wealth means cumulative increase in cash.)
2. Suppose the "performance evaluation model" emphasized the net income of a subunit, such as a division, each year rather than considering each project, one by one. Which alternative would you expect a manager to choose? Why?
3. Suppose the same quantitative data existed, but the "enterprise" was a city and the "machine" was a computer in the treasurer's department. Would your answers to the first two parts change? Why?

6-61 Review of Relevant Costs

Since the early 1960s, Neil Simon has been one of Broadway's most successful playwrights. The *New York Times* reported that Neil Simon planned to open his play, *London Suite*, off Broadway. Why? For financial reasons. Producer Emanuel Azenberg predicted the following costs before the play even opened:

	On Broadway	Off Broadway
Sets, costumes, lights	$ 357,000	$ 87,000
Loading in (building set, etc.)	175,000	8,000
Rehearsal salaries	102,000	63,000
Director and designer fees	126,000	61,000
Advertising	300,000	121,000
Administration	235,000	100,000
Total	$1,295,000	$440,000

Broadway ticket prices average $60, and theaters can seat about 1,000 persons per show. Off-Broadway prices average only $40, and the theaters seat only 500. Normally, plays run eight times a week, both on and off Broadway. Weekly operating expenses off Broadway average $102,000; they average an extra $150,000 on Broadway for a weekly total of $252,000.

1. Suppose 400 persons attended each show, whether on or off Broadway. Compare the weekly financial results from a Broadway production to one produced off Broadway.
2. Suppose attendance averaged 75% of capacity, whether on or off Broadway. Compare the weekly financial results from a Broadway production to one produced off Broadway.
3. Compute the attendance per show required just to cover weekly expenses (a) on Broadway and (b) off Broadway.
4. Suppose average attendance on Broadway was 600 per show and off Broadway was 400. Compute the total net profit for a 26-week run (a) on Broadway and (b) off Broadway. Be sure to include the pre-opening costs.
5. Repeat requirement 4 for a 100-week run.
6. Using attendance figures from numbers 4 and 5, compute (a) the number of weeks a Broadway production must run before it breaks even, and (b) the number of weeks an off-Broadway production must run before it breaks even.
7. Using attendance figures from numbers 4 and 5, determine how long a play must run before the profit from a Broadway production exceeds that from an off-Broadway production.
8. If you were Neil Simon, would you prefer *London Suite* to play on Broadway or off Broadway? Explain.

6-62 Make or Buy

Sunshine, Corp., estimates it will produce 20,000 units of a part that goes into its final product. It currently produces this part internally, but is considering outsourcing this activity. Current internal capacity permits for a maximum of 40,000 units of the part. The production manager has prepared the following information concerning the internal manufacture of 40,000 units of the part:

	Per unit
Direct materials	$ 7.00
Direct labor	9.00
Variable overhead	3.00
Fixed overhead	5.00
Total cost	$24.00

The fixed overhead of $5 per unit includes a $1.70 per unit allocation for salary paid to a supervisor to oversee production of the part. The fixed costs would not be reduced by outsourcing, except the supervisor would be terminated. Assume that if Sunshine outsources, its purchase price from the supplier is $18 per unit.

1. Should Sunshine outsource?
2. Assume Sunshine has received a special order for 12,000 units of the part from Express, Co. Express will pay Sunshine $28 per part, but will take the parts only if they have been manufactured by Sunshine. Thus, Express will engage in the special order only if Sunshine does not outsource any of its production. Should Sunshine accept the special order?

6-63 Make or Buy, Opportunity Costs, and Ethics

Agribiz Food Products produces a wide variety of food and related products. The company's tomato-canning operation relies partly on tomatoes grown on Agribiz's own farms and partly on tomatoes bought from other growers.

Agribiz's tomato farm is on the edge of Sharpestown, a fast-growing, medium-sized city. It produces 8 million pounds of tomatoes a year and employs 55 persons. The annual costs of tomatoes grown on this farm are as follows:

Variable production costs	$ 550,000
Fixed production costs	1,200,000
Shipping costs (all variable)	200,000
Total costs	$1,950,000

Fixed production costs include depreciation on machinery and equipment, but not on land because land should not be depreciated. Agribiz owns the land, which was purchased for $600,000 many years ago. A recent appraisal placed the value of the land at $18 million because it is a prime site for an industrial park and shopping center.

Agribiz could purchase all the tomatoes it needs on the market for $.25 per pound delivered to its factory. If it did this, it would sell the farmland and shut down the operations in Sharpestown. If the farm were sold, $300,000 of the annual fixed costs would be saved. Agribiz can invest excess cash and earn an annual rate of 10%.

1. How much does it cost Agribiz annually for the land used by the tomato farm?
2. How much would Agribiz save annually if it closed the tomato farm? Is this more or less than would be paid to purchase the tomatoes on the market?
3. What ethical issues are involved with the decision to shut down the tomato farm?

6-64 Irrelevance of Past Costs at Starbucks

Starbucks purchases and roasts high-quality, whole-bean coffees, its hallmark, and sells them along with other coffee-related products primarily through its company-operated retail stores.

Suppose that the quality-control manager at Starbucks discovered a 1,200-pound batch of roasted beans that did not meet the company's quality standards. Company policy would not allow such beans to be sold with the Starbucks name on them. However, they could be reprocessed, at which time they could be sold by Starbucks' retail stores, or they could be sold as is on the wholesale coffee bean market.

Assume that the beans were initially purchased for $800, and the total cost of roasting the batch was $2,520, including $420 of variable costs and $2,100 of fixed costs (primarily depreciation on the equipment).

The wholesale price at which Starbucks could sell the beans was $3.80 per pound. Purchasers would pay the shipping costs from the Starbucks plant to their individual warehouses.

If the beans were reprocessed, the processing cost would be $900 because the beans would not require as much processing as new beans. All $900 would be additional costs, that is, costs that would not be incurred without the reprocessing. The beans would be sold to the retail stores for $4.90 per pound, and Starbucks would have to pay an average of $.45 per pound to ship the beans to the stores.

1. Should Starbucks sell the beans on the market as is for $3.80 per pound, or should the company reprocess the beans and sell them through its own retail stores? Why?
2. Compute the amount of extra profit Starbucks earns from the alternative you selected in number 1 compared to what it would earn from the other alternative.
3. What cost numbers in the problem were irrelevant to your analysis? Explain why they were irrelevant.

CASES

6-65 Make or Buy

The Minnetonka Corporation, which produces and sells to wholesalers a highly successful line of water skis, has decided to diversify to stabilize sales throughout the year. The company is considering the production of cross-country skis.

After considerable research, a cross-country ski line has been developed. Because of the conservative nature of the company management, however, Minnetonka's president has decided to introduce only one type of the new skis for this coming winter. If the product is a success, further expansion in future years will be initiated.

The ski selected is a mass-market ski with a special binding. It will be sold to wholesalers for $80 per pair. Because of available capacity, no additional fixed charges will be incurred to produce the skis. A $125,000 fixed charge will be absorbed by the skis, however, to allocate a fair share of the company's present fixed costs to the new product.

Using the estimated sales and production of 10,000 pair of skis as the expected volume, the accounting department has developed the following costs per pair of skis and bindings:

Direct labor	$35
Direct materials	30
Total overhead	15
Total cost	$80

Minnetonka has approached a subcontractor to discuss the possibility of purchasing the bindings. The purchase price of the bindings from the subcontractor would be $5.25 per binding, or $10.50 per pair. If the Minnetonka Corporation accepts the purchase proposal, it is predicted that direct-labor and variable-overhead costs would be reduced by 10% and direct-materials costs would be reduced by 20%.

1. Should the Minnetonka Corporation make or buy the bindings? Show calculations to support your answer.
2. What would be the maximum purchase price acceptable to the Minnetonka Corporation for the bindings? Support your answer with an appropriate explanation.
3. Instead of sales of 10,000 pairs of skis, revised estimates show sales volume at 12,500 pairs. At this new volume, additional equipment, at an annual rental of $10,000, must be acquired to manufacture the bindings. This incremental cost would be the only additional fixed cost required, even if sales increased to 30,000 pairs. (The 30,000 level is the goal for the third year of production.) Under these circumstances, should the Minnetonka Corporation make or buy the bindings? Show calculations to support your answer.
4. The company has the option of making and buying at the same time. What would be your answer to number 3 if this alternative were considered? Show calculations to support your answer.
5. What nonquantifiable factors should the Minnetonka Corporation consider in determining whether it should make or buy the bindings?

6-66 Make or Buy

The Rohr Company's old equipment for making subassemblies is worn out. The company is considering two courses of action: (a) completely replacing the old equipment with new equipment or (b) buying subassemblies from a reliable outside supplier, who has quoted a unit price of $1 on a 7-year contract for a minimum of 50,000 units per year.

Production was 60,000 units in each of the past 2 years. Future needs for the next 7 years are not expected to fluctuate beyond 50,000 to 70,000 units per year. Cost records for the past 2 years reveal the following unit costs of manufacturing the subassembly:

Direct materials	$ .30
Direct labor	.35
Variable overhead	.10
Fixed overhead (including $.10 depreciation and $.10 for direct departmental fixed overhead)	.25
	$1.00

The new equipment will cost $188,000 cash, will last 7 years, and will have a disposal value of $20,000. The current disposal value of the old equipment is $10,000.

The sales representative for the new equipment has summarized her position as follows: The increase in machine speeds will reduce direct labor and variable overhead by $.35 per unit. Consider last year's experience of one of your major competitors with identical equipment. It produced 100,000 units under operating conditions very comparable to yours and showed the following unit costs.

Direct materials	$.30
Direct labor	.05
Variable overhead	.05
Fixed overhead, including depreciation of $.24	.40
Total	$.80

For purposes of this case, assume that any idle facilities cannot be put to alternative use. Also assume that $.05 of the old Rohr unit cost is allocated fixed overhead that will be unaffected by the decision.

1. The president asks you to compare the alternatives on a total-annual-cost basis and on a per-unit basis for annual needs of 60,000 units. Which alternative seems more attractive?
2. Would your answer to number 1 change if the needs were 50,000 units? 70,000 units? At what volume level would Rohr be indifferent between making and buying subassemblies? Show your computations.
3. What factors, other than the preceding ones, should the accountant bring to the attention of management to assist it in making its decision? Include the considerations that might be applied to the outside supplier.

6-67 Make or Buy

Levoy, Corp., estimates it will produce 25,000 units of an electronic sensor part that goes into one of its final products, called a Fluctotron. It currently produces this sensor internally but is considering outsourcing this activity. Current internal capacity permits the production of a maximum of 40,000 sensors. The production manager has prepared the following information concerning the internal manufacture of 40,000 sensors:

	Per Sensor
Direct materials	$15.00
Direct labor	8.00
Variable overhead	10.00
Fixed overhead	11.00
Total cost	$44.00

The fixed overhead of $11 per unit includes a $2 per unit allocation for salary paid to a supervisor to oversee production of sensors. The fixed costs would not be reduced by outsourcing, except the supervisor would be fired (the company would terminate his contract). Assume that if Levoy outsources, its purchase price from the outsourcer is $38 per unit.

1. Should Levoy outsource? Why or why not?
2. Assume that if Levoy outsourced, it would create sufficient excess capacity such that it would retain the supervisor and have him oversee production of a new optical reading product, called a Scanmeister. If each Scanmeister generates a contribution margin of $15 and the company produces 10,000 Scanmeisters, what is the maximum price Levoy would accept for outsourcing the sensors?

NIKE 10-K PROBLEM

6-68 Make or Buy

As described in Item 1 of Nike's 10-K, virtually all of its products are produced by independent contractors. Suppose that in one of those contracted production facilities where Nike golf clubs are produced, Nike estimates the need for 20,000 specialized head casings per year over the next 5 years for a custom driver club it manufactures. It can either make the casings internally or purchase them from an outside supplier for $29.75 per unit. If it makes the casings, it will have to purchase equipment costing $300,000 that has a 5-year life and no salvage value (assume straight line depreciation). The machine can produce up to 40,000 casings per year. The production manager thinks the company should purchase the casings based on the following information he has prepared concerning the internal manufacture of 20,000 casings per year:

	Per unit
Direct materials	$12.00
Direct labor	8.00
Variable overhead	4.50
Depreciation	3.00
Supervision	1.50
Rent	3.00
Total cost	$32.00

A supervisor would have to be hired and paid a salary of $30,000 to oversee production of the casings. The rent charge is based on the space utilized in the plant, but there is excess plant space available to manufacture the casings. Total rent on the plant is $250,000 per period.

1. If the casings are made internally, will the company be better off or worse off, and by how much?
2. If it is estimated that only 15,000 casings per year were required, should Nike make or buy them?

EXCEL APPLICATION EXERCISE

6-69 Identifying Relevant Revenue, Costs, and Income Effects

Goal: Create an Excel spreadsheet to assist with sell-or-process-further decisions by identifying the relevant revenue, costs, and income effects. Use the results to answer questions about your findings.

Scenario: Mussina Chemical Company has asked you to prepare an analysis to help it make decisions about whether to sell joint products at the split-off point or process them further. The background data for the analysis appears in the Fundamental Assignment Material 6-A3. Prepare the analysis report using a format similar to Exhibit 6-3 on page 239.

When you have completed your spreadsheet, answer the following questions:

1. How should the $117,000 be allocated to the three products?
2. Is the company currently making the right processing decisions? Explain.
3. If the company alters its processing decisions, what would be the expected combined operating income from the three products?

Step-by-Step:

1. Open a new Excel spreadsheet.
2. In column A, create a bold-faced heading that contains the following:
   Row 1: Chapter 6 Decision Guideline
   Row 2: Mussina Chemical Company
   Row 3: Sell-or-Process-Further Analysis
   Row 4: Today's Date
3. Merge and center the four heading rows across columns A–J.
4. In row 7, create the following bold-faced column headings:
   Column B: Chemical Product A
   Skip two columns.
   Column E: Chemical Product B
   Skip two columns.
   Column H: Chemical Product C
5. Merge and center the heading in row 7, column B across columns B–D.
   Merge and center the heading in row 7, column E across columns E–G.
   Merge and center the heading in row 7, column H across columns H–J.
6. In row 8, create the following center-justified column headings:
   Column B: Sell at Split-Off
   Column C: Process Further
   Column D: Difference
   Column E: Sell at Split-Off
   Column F: Process Further
   Column G: Difference
   Column H: Sell at Split-Off
   Column I: Process Further
   Column J: Difference
7. Change the format of the column headings in row 8 to permit the titles to be displayed on multiple lines within a single cell.

   Alignment tab: Wrap Text: Checked

8. In column A, create the following bold-faced row headings:
   Row 9: Revenues
   Row 10: Costs Beyond Split-Off
   Skip a row.
   Row 11: Income Effects
   Note: Adjust the width of column A to accommodate row headings.
9. Use the scenario data to fill in revenues and costs beyond split-off amounts for each of the products.

10. Use appropriate formulas to calculate the difference and income effects columns for each product as absolute values.
    5ABS(formula)
11. Format all amounts as follows:

Number:	Category:	Accounting
	Decimal places:	0
	Symbol:	$

12. Change the format of the costs beyond split-off amounts to not display a dollar symbol.
13. Change the format of the income effects amounts to display as bold.
14. Change the format of the revenues amounts to display a top border, using the default line style.

Border tab:	Icon:	Top Border

15. Change the format of the costs beyond split-off amounts to display a bottom border, using the default line style.

Border tab:	Icon:	Bottom Border

16. Change the format of row 7, column B to display an outline border, using the default line style.

Border tab:	Presets:	Outline

Repeat this step for column E.
Repeat this step for column H.

17. Save your work to disk, and print a copy for your files.

Note: Print your spreadsheet using landscape in order to ensure that all columns appear on one page.

COLLABORATIVE LEARNING EXERCISE

6-70 Outsourcing

A popular term for make-or-buy decisions is *outsourcing decisions*. There are many examples of outsourcing, from Nike's outsourcing of nearly all its production activities to small firms' outsourcing of their payroll activities. Especially popular outsourcing activities are warehousing and computer systems.

The purpose of this exercise is to share information on different types of outsourcing decisions. It can be done in small groups or as an entire class. Each student should pick an article from the literature that tells about a particular company's outsourcing decision. There are many such articles: A recent electronic search of the business literature turned up more than 4,000 articles. An easy way to find such an article is to search an electronic database of business literature. Magazines that have published outsourcing articles include *Fortune*, *Forbes*, *Business Week*, and *Strategic Finance*. Many business sections of newspapers also include such articles. The *Wall Street Journal* usually has a couple of articles on outsourcing each month.

1. List as many details about the outsourcing decision as you can. Include the type of activity that is being outsourced, the size of the outsourcing, and the type of company providing the outsourcing service.
2. Explain why the company decided to outsource the activity. If reasons are not given in the article, prepare a list of reasons that you think influenced the decision.
3. What disadvantages are there to outsourcing the activity?
4. Be prepared to make a 3- to 5-minute presentation to the rest of the group or to the class, covering your answers to numbers 1, 2, and 3.

INTERNET EXERCISE

6-71 Green Mountain Coffee Company

How do firms determine what type of information is useful for a given decision? Is it possible for firms to have too much information? While a look at a firm's Web site provides us with lots of information, not all of it is necessarily useful for a particular decision. Let's look at the **Green Mountain Coffee Company** and see what information on the site would be useful for some specific decisions.

1. Go to the home page of Green Mountain Coffee at www.greenmountaincoffee.com. What are the major topics on which a user can click to be taken to a page with more detailed information? Would you likely find the same type of information if you clicked on the links to any one of these? Why do you suppose Green Mountain Coffee chose those particular subtopics for its home page?

2. Where would you look on the site if you wanted to know more about Green Mountain Coffee's financial information? Locate the most recent annual report posted on this section of the Web site, and answer the following questions. Did the company make a profit for the year? What was the major expense that the firm encountered? Did the firm pay any dividends? If you were interested in an income-producing stock, would you want to invest in Green Mountain Coffee Roasters?

3. Which link would you want to use if you wanted to gain knowledge concerning the story of coffee? Click on this link now. This page has additional links about coffee. Which one(s) are likely to provide information to help you learn about the different coffees? Click on one of the links you just identified. What type of information about coffee differences does it provide? Did your link provide any information concerning prices as being a difference? Do you think that this would be a difference between coffees?

4. The site provides extensive information about social and environmental initiatives. What areas in particular does the firm highlight? Is this information useful in helping determine if the company's coffee products taste good? What about the quality of the product? Would this information be useful to a potential investor in Green Mountain Coffee's common stock?

Introduction to Budgets and Preparing the Master Budget

LEARNING OBJECTIVES

When you have finished studying this chapter, you should be able to:

1. Explain how budgets facilitate planning and coordination.

2. Anticipate possible human relations problems caused by budgets.

3. Explain potentially dysfunctional incentives in the budget process.

4. Explain the difficulties of sales forecasting.

5. Explain the major features and advantages of a master budget.

6. Follow the principal steps in preparing a master budget.

7. Prepare the operating budget and the supporting schedules.

8. Prepare the financial budget.

9. Use a spreadsheet to develop a budget (Appendix 7).

▶ RITZ-CARLTON

If you have ever traveled, you know that there is a big difference between staying in a cheap motel and staying in a five-star, world-class hotel. The cheap motel takes care of your basic needs, but the five-star hotel surrounds you in comfort and luxury, catering to your every whim. No one understands the difference better than the managers of the **Ritz-Carlton** chain of hotels. After all, the word *ritzy*, which means elegant and luxurious, is derived from the name of the Ritz Hotel. Thanks to fierce competition in the industry, though, Ritz-Carlton managers have their share of challenges in maintaining standards that keep their hotels successful.

What does it take to run a world-class hotel successfully? Good location, exquisite food, luxury, personalized service, and quality are all essential ingredients. But you might be surprised to learn that the budgeting process is also a key to success. According to Ralph Vick, former general manager of the Phoenix Ritz-Carlton, "Budgets are crucial to the ultimate financial success of our hotels." Why are budgets so important? Mainly because they serve as a road map to help managers understand, plan, and control operations. Ritz-Carlton wants to give its managers the best tools possible. As a result, the company takes the budgeting process very seriously.

At the Ritz-Carlton hotels, all employees, from the hotel manager, to the controller, to the newest housekeeper, are involved in the budgeting process. Working in teams, managers set budget targets for the expenses they can control. These target figures help not only in planning, but also in controlling and evaluating employee performance. Managers compare actual results with budgeted target figures, and they evaluate performance based on the differences. In addition to financial reports, Ritz-Carlton managers also use nonfinancial measures, such as quality and customer satisfaction, to evaluate and reward employees.

Planning is the key to good management. This statement is certainly true for Ritz-Carlton, and it is also true for other types of organizations—small, family-owned companies; large corporations; government agencies; and nonprofit organizations. All organizations need budgets to make the best and most profitable use of their resources. Budgeting can cover such diverse issues as how much time to spend inspecting a product and how much money the company will allot to research and development in the coming year. In this chapter, we look at the benefits (and costs) of budgets and illustrate the construction of a comprehensive, detailed budget. ■

© Holger Burmeister/Alamy

Budgets and the Organization

Many people associate the word *budget* primarily with limitations on spending. For example, management often gives each unit in an organization a spending budget and then expects them to stay within the limits prescribed by the budget. However, budgeting can play a much more important role than simply limiting spending. Budgeting moves planning to the forefront of the manager's mind. Well-managed organizations make budgeting an integral part of the formulation and execution of their strategy.

In Chapter 1, we defined a budget as a quantitative expression of a plan of action. Sometimes plans are informal, perhaps even unwritten, and informal plans sometimes work in a small organization. However, as an organization grows, seat-of-the-pants planning is not enough. Budgets impose the formal structure—a budgetary system—that is needed for all but the smallest organizations. There are numerous examples of seemingly healthy businesses that failed because managers did not bother to construct budgets that would have identified problems in advance or they failed to monitor and adjust budgets to changing conditions. While there will always be debate about the costs and benefits of budgeting, as indicated in the Business First box on page 272, the vast majority of managers continue to use budgeting as an effective cost-management tool.

A Ritz-Carlton hotel projects an image of quality. High quality is expensive so during the master budgeting process Ritz-Carlton managers must assess the planned expenditures for quality-enhancing features versus the added revenues these features will bring.

Objective 1

Explain how budgets facilitate planning and coordination.

Advantages of Budgeting

Budgeting is the process of formulating an organization's plans. We will discuss four major advantages of effective budgeting:

1. Budgeting compels managers to think ahead by formalizing their responsibilities for planning.
2. Budgeting provides an opportunity for managers to reevaluate existing activities and evaluate possible new activities.
3. Budgeting aids managers in communicating objectives and coordinating actions across the organization.
4. Budgeting provides benchmarks to evaluate subsequent performance.

Let's look more closely at each of these benefits.

FORMALIZATION OF PLANNING  Budgeting forces managers to devote time to planning. On a day-to-day basis, managers often move from extinguishing one business brush fire to another, leaving no time for thinking beyond the next day's problems. As a result, planning takes a backseat to, or is obliterated by, daily pressures. The budgeting process formalizes the need to anticipate and prepare for changing conditions.

To prepare a budget, a manager should set objectives and establish policies to aid their achievement. The objectives are the destination points, and budgets are the road maps guiding us to those destinations. In the absence of goals and objectives, results are difficult to interpret, managers do not foresee problems, and company operations lack direction.

EVALUATION OF ACTIVITIES Budgeting typically uses the current activities of the organization as a starting point for planning, but how managers use this starting point varies widely. At one extreme, in some organizations the budget process automatically assumes that activities for the new budget period will be the same as the activities for the previous period. At the other extreme,

Business First

Budgeting: Value Driver or Value Buster?

There is an ongoing debate about the costs and benefits of budgeting, focusing on four issues: (1) The budgeting process is time-consuming and expensive; (2) even the best-prepared budgets become inaccurate because marketplace change is frequent and unpredictable; (3) evaluating performance against a budget causes managers to bias their budgets, resulting in inaccurate planning; and (4) budget targets create incentives for individuals to take actions to meet targets even when the actions make the firm as a whole worse off.

Some studies suggest that the annual budgeting process can take up to 30% of management's time. For example, estimates place Ford Motor Company's cost of budgeting at $1.2 billion a year. Companies can justify such large budgeting costs only when there are corresponding large benefits. Companies that either fail to incorporate budgeting in their planning activities or react to changing economic conditions by ignoring the budget rather than adapting the budget to the changes will not reap some of the major benefits of budgeting. Consequently, these companies may find that large costs of budgeting are not justified.

Skeptical managers sometimes claim, "I face too many uncertainties and complications to make budgeting worthwhile for me." While it is true that budgeting is more difficult in uncertain or complicated environments, it is also true that these are the environments where the potential benefits are largest. When conditions are changing rapidly, a budget provides a framework for systematic response rather than chaotic reaction.

When managers anticipate that budget information will be used to set targets used in their subsequent performance evaluations, they have an incentive to provide budget information that is biased to make it easier to meet the targets. Biases severely limit the usefulness of budget information for planning and coordination. Moreover, widespread understanding and acceptance of built-in biases can create a pernicious "culture of lying" within the organization.

When managers realize that meeting budget targets affects their rewards, either explicitly through bonus plans or implicitly through promotion and recognition, they have incentives to take actions to meet the targets. This can be a positive motivation, but it can also lead to unethical behavior, such as "cooking the books" or putting pressure on employees to meet targets using whatever means possible. For example, the director of the Office of Federal Housing Enterprise Oversight (OFHEO)

denounced "an arrogant and unethical culture" at Fannie Mae, the giant mortgage finance company. An OFHEO report cited a corporate culture that allowed managers to disregard accounting standards when they got in the way of achieving earnings targets that were tied to bonuses. In other cases, managers have taken actions to ship faulty or incomplete products to meet budgeted sales targets, despite clear adverse effects on customer relations and the reputation of the firm.

Most companies that have experienced problems with their budgeting process are not abandoning traditional budgeting but instead are modifying their approach to budgeting. For example, some companies now separate planning budgets from control budgets, comparing actual performance to benchmarks based on performance of peers and best-in-class operations. Further, most managers still agree that budgeting, when correctly used, has significant value to management. More than 92% of the companies in a recent survey use budgets, and they rank budgeting among their top three cost-management tools.

Companies such as Allstate, Owens Corning, Sprint, Battelle, and Texaco are modifying their approach to budgeting by implementing new technologies. For example, Battelle's Pacific Northwest National Laboratory uses an intranet to reduce the time and expense of developing the annual budget. The new system enables support staff and managers to input their budget plans directly on this corporate intranet. In addition to decreasing the cost of budgeting, managers at Battelle report that the new system "results in higher quality and more accurate budgeting, reporting, and analysis." Many companies are tying their budgeting process more closely to their overall strategy and have expanded their performance measures beyond traditional financial measures to also consider nonfinancial measures, such as time to market for new products or services.

Sources: Adapted from R. Banham, "Better Budgets," *Journal of Accountancy*, February 2000, pp. 37–40; J. Hope and R. Fraser, "Who Needs Budgets?" *Harvard Business Review*, February 2003, pp. 108–115; P. Smith, C. Goranson, and M. Astley, "Intranet Budgeting," *Strategic Finance*, May 2003, pp. 30–33; T. Hatch and W. Stratton, "Scorecarding in North America: Who is Doing What?" Paper presented at the CAM-I/CMS 3rd quarter meeting, Portland, Oregon, September 10, 2002; M. Jensen, "Corporate Budgeting Is Broken, Let's Fix It," *Harvard Business Review*, November 2001, pp. 94–101; M. Jensen, "Paying People to Lie: the Truth About the Budgeting Process," *European Financial Management*, Vol. 9 No. 3, (2003), pp. 379–406; and "Fannie Mae Ex-Officials May Face Legal Action over Accounting," *Wall Street Journal*, May 24, 2006, p. A1.

zero-base budget
A budget that requires justification of expenditures for every activity, including continuing activities.

some organizations use a form of **zero-base budget**, which starts with the assumption that current activities will not automatically be continued. The term zero-base comes from the fundamental assumption that the budget for every activity starts at zero. The advantage of a zero-base system is that managers reevaluate all activities (including whether existing activities should be continued) in each new budget.

In practice, budgeting for most organizations falls somewhere between these two extremes. An effective budget process encourages managers to think carefully about whether to continue current activities and methods, whether there are opportunities to modify activities, and whether to add new activities to help the organization better achieve its goals in response to changing conditions. Used in this way, budgeting encourages managers to review whether a particular plan allocates resources optimally among the firm's various activities.

COMMUNICATION AND COORDINATION   The most effective budget processes facilitate communication both from the top down and from the bottom up. Top management communicates the strategic goals and objectives of the organization in its budgetary directives. Lower-level managers and employees contribute their own ideas and provide feedback on the goals and objectives. The result is two-way communication about opportunities and challenges that lie ahead.

Budgets also help managers coordinate activities across the organization. For example, a budget allows purchasing personnel to integrate their plans with production requirements, while production managers use the sales budget and delivery schedule to help them anticipate and plan for the employees and physical facilities they will need. Similarly, financial officers use the sales budget, purchasing requirements, and other planned expenditures to anticipate the company's need for cash. Thus, budgeting forces managers to communicate and coordinate their department's activities with those of other departments and the company as a whole.

PERFORMANCE EVALUATION   Budgeted performance goals generally provide a better basis for evaluating actual results than would a simple comparison with past performance. Relying only on historical results for judging current performance may allow inefficiencies in past performance to continue undetected. Changes in economic conditions, technology, personnel, competition, and other factors also limit the usefulness of comparisons with the past. For example, sales of $100 million this year, for a company that had sales of $80 million the previous year, may or may not indicate that company objectives have been met—perhaps conditions imply that the sales goal for this year should have been $110 million.

Making Managerial Decisions

Level 3 Communications is "a facilities-based provider of a broad range of communications services." The company has had losses for a number of years, which it attributes to a difficult competitive environment. For example, the 2011 annual report states, "Although the pricing for data services is currently relatively stable, the IP market is generally characterized by price compression and high unit growth rates depending upon the type of service. The Company experienced price compression in the high-speed IP market in 2011 and expects that aggressive pricing for its highspeed IP services will continue." The company has had a steady stream of large losses, $1,114 million in 2007, $318 million in 2008, $618 million in 2009, and $622 million in 2010.

Level 3's loss for 2011 was $756 million. Suppose the company budgeted to break even for 2011. Evaluate operating performance for 2011.

Answer

Level 3's performance in 2011 is consistent with what might be expected based on the losses that have occurred over the previous 4 years. However, if the company budgeted for break even in 2011, then performance is much worse than budgeted. This situation illustrates that a comparison to past results can provide a very different conclusion than a comparison to budget.

Potential Problems in Implementing Budgets

In this section, we discuss three problems that can limit, in some cases severely, the advantages of budgeting:

Objective 2

Anticipate possible human relations problems caused by budgets.

1. Low levels of participation in the budget process and lack of acceptance of responsibility for the final budget
2. Incentives to lie and cheat in the budget process
3. Difficulties in obtaining accurate sales forecasts

BUDGET PARTICIPATION AND ACCEPTANCE OF THE BUDGET   The advantages of budgeting are fully realized only when employees throughout the organization accept and take responsibility for the final budget. The main factors affecting budget acceptance are as follows:

1. The perceived attitude of top management.
2. The level of participation in the budget process.
3. The degree of alignment between the budget and other performance goals.

The attitude of top management will heavily influence lower-level managers' and employees' attitudes toward budgets. If top management does not use budgets effectively in controlling operations and adapting to change, others in the organization may come to view budgeting as irrelevant. Even with the support of top management, however, budgets—and the managers who implement them—can run into opposition.

Lower-level managers sometimes have negative attitudes toward budgets because they believe the primary purpose of the budget is to limit spending. These negative attitudes are reinforced when companies evaluate managerial performance by comparing actual expenditures against amounts budgeted without substantive input from the managers. Ensuring that managers at all levels participate in setting budgets is one way to reduce negative attitudes and improve the quality of planning decisions. Budgets created with the active participation of all affected employees—called **participative budgeting**—are generally more effective than budgets imposed on subordinates. For example, Ritz-Carlton's budgeting system involves all hotel employees and is thus a participative system. Employee "buy-in" to the budget is so important at Ritz-Carlton that self-directed employee teams at all levels of the company have the authority to change operations based on budgets as they see fit.

Misalignment between the performance goals stressed in budgets versus the performance measures the company uses to reward employees and managers can also limit the advantages of budgeting. For example, suppose a company rewards managers based on actual profit compared to budgeted profit and also on quality (defect rate) and timely delivery to customers (percent on time). Increased quality and more timely deliveries typically require higher costs, so the message conveyed by the budget system (minimize cost) may be misaligned with the incentives provided by the compensation system (maximize quality and timely delivery). Companies can manage the apparent misalignment by clearly specifying and communicating the tradeoff between costs and quality measures. This is particularly important for performance goals where the short-term impact on current performance relative to budget is negative but the long-term impact due to improved customer satisfaction is positive. We explore these issues in more detail in Chapter 9.

There is often too much concern with the mechanics of budgets and too little attention paid to the fact that the effectiveness of any budgeting system depends directly on whether the affected managers and employees understand and accept the budget. Management should seek to create an environment where there is a true two-way flow of information in the budget process so that lower level managers and employees perceive that their input has a real effect on budget outcomes. Top management must emphasize the importance of budgets in planning and communication and demonstrate how budgets can help each manager and employee achieve better results. Only then will the budgets become a positive aid in motivating employees at all levels to work toward goals, set objectives, measure results accurately, and direct attention to the areas that need investigation.

INCENTIVES TO LIE AND CHEAT Effective budgets provide targets for managers and motivate them to achieve the organization's objectives. However, misuse of budgets can lead to undesirable incentives—what Professor Michael Jensen calls incentives to lie and cheat. Not only do such incentives lead managers to make poor decisions, they undercut attempts to maintain high ethical standards in the organization.

Let's first consider lying. What incentives might cause managers to create biased budgets—essentially to lie about their plans? Managers may want to increase the resources allocated to their department—resources such as space, equipment, and personnel—and larger budgets may justify such allocations. Why do managers want more resources? Day-to-day managing is easier when the department has more resources to achieve its output targets. Further, it is common for managers of larger units with more resources to have higher pay, higher status, and greater prospects for promotion. Recognizing these incentives allows organizations to implement budgets in a way that minimizes bias. For example, when employees understand, accept, and participate in the budget process, they are less likely to introduce biased information. Also, decision makers can be aware of expected bias when they make decisions based on budget information.

When organizations use budgets as a target for performance evaluations, managers have additional incentives to lie. Managers have incentives to create **budgetary slack** or **budget padding**—that is, overstate their budgeted costs or understate their budgeted revenues to create a budget target that is easier to achieve. Budgetary slack also helps buffer managers from budget cuts imposed by higher-level management and provides protection against cost increases or revenue shortfalls due to unforeseen events.

participative budgeting
Budgets formulated with the active participation of all affected employees.

Objective 3

Explain potentially dysfunctional incentives in the budget process.

budgetary slack (budget padding)
Overstatement of budgeted cost or understatement of budgeted revenue to create a budget goal that is easier to achieve.

These incentives can lead to the following cycle that destroys the value of budget information: Lower-level managers bias their budgets to create budgetary slack. Knowing that lower-level managers face these incentives, upper-level managers correct for this bias in their inputs to the budget process. Lower-level managers, recognizing that upper-level managers are making this correction, then incorporate additional bias to compensate. Upper-level managers then introduce larger corrections to compensate for the increased bias. This cycle of increasing bias and increasing bias corrections causes increasing distortion in budget information. Inputs from both upper-level and lower-level managers become increasingly meaningless, and the budget process spirals out of control.

Now let's add one more complication—managerial bonuses based on making budget. Suppose a manager with a $100,000 annual salary will receive a bonus ranging from 80% to 120% of a target bonus of $50,000 if her division achieves between 80% and 120% of its budgeted profit target, as shown in Exhibit 7-1. In this example, representative of bonus plans commonly encountered in practice, there is a minimum level of division profit below which no bonus is paid (the bonus drops from a $40,000 bonus at 80% of budgeted profit to zero bonus at any profit level below 80% of budgeted profit) and a maximum level of division profit above which the maximum bonus is capped (above 120% of budgeted profit, the bonus is capped at $60,000).

We should first recognize that within the relevant range of 80%–120% of profits this system creates appropriate incentives to work harder, more efficiently, and more effectively to achieve desired results. But suppose, despite a manager's best efforts, it appears that reported profit will fall below 80% of the target profit in Exhibit 7-1. What inappropriate incentives does this bonus system provide for the manager? There are incentives to "cheat," to make results appear better than they actually are. The incentive to cheat is particularly strong when the division is in danger of falling just short of 80% of the profit target, so that a small increase in reported profit would lead to a large jump in the amount of the bonus.

An extreme form of cheating is to "cook the books," that is, report false profit numbers. The division manager may accomplish this by recording fictitious sales or omitting costs. For example, a few years ago **Enron** and other energy companies recorded questionable sales of energy contracts, and **WorldCom** increased reported income by treating expenses as capital investments. Such actions have serious ethical and legal consequences, but sometimes the pressure to meet profit targets has been great enough to motivate managers to go to such extremes.

Managers may instead choose less extreme actions to increase reported profits. They may increase current sales by offering customers discounts that cause them to accelerate purchases from future periods to the current period, or offer better credit terms that are costly to the company through increased financing costs or increased credit risk. Managers may cut discretionary expenditures, such as research and development (R&D) and advertising, trading future sales for current profits. These short-term actions allow managers to achieve their current bonus, but cheat the company and its shareholders whenever the actions are not in the company's best long-run interests.

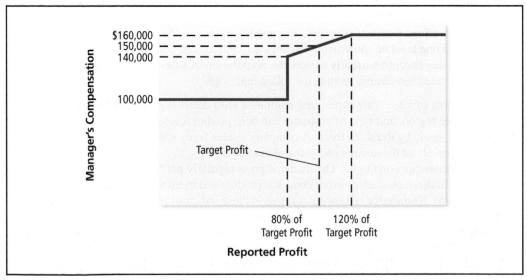

Exhibit 7-1
Bonus Payments Tied to Profit Levels

This compensation system can also create incentives to *decrease* profits when the manager sees actual profits exceeding 120% of the profit target in Exhibit 7-1 or when profits fall so far short of the 80% profit target that there is no hope of achieving a bonus. In these cases, managers may move current sales into the next year by encouraging customers to defer purchases until the next year, thus effectively transferring current income to the future. They might also speed up actual expenditures (for example, moving maintenance planned for future years into the current year) or accelerate recognition of expenses (for example, writing off costs of equipment that remains in use), taking as current period expenses some costs that rightly belong to future periods.

Why would managers take actions to decrease current reported profit? First, moving this year's sales into next year or moving next year's expenses into this year increases next year's income, ensuring a higher level of reported profit (and probably a higher bonus) next year. Second, by decreasing this year's income, the manager may avoid increasing performance expectations for the next year—and thus may avoid a higher budgeted profit target for next year.

To minimize the incentives to cheat, performance-linked payment plans should avoid "discontinuities" in payments. Note that in Exhibit 7-1 the manager's payment jumps up (that is, it is discontinuous) at 80% of the target profit level and the payment levels off (is discontinuous again) at the maximum bonus level. To minimize incentives to transfer income between periods, we can make bonuses and total payments increase continuously over the entire range of possible performance so that there is no point at which a small change in profit has a large effect on pay.

Perhaps the most serious concern raised by these inappropriate incentives for lying and cheating is that they foster cynicism about the budget process and create a culture of unethical behavior in the organization. When managers know that the budget and evaluation processes encourage employees to provide biased information and make questionable decisions, not only does information quality suffer, but a lack of trust begins to pervade the organization.

How can organizations avoid unwanted incentives in budgetary systems? The main way to avoid lying in preparing the budget is to reward good budget forecasts as well as good performance against the budget. It is also important to motivate managers to take personal responsibility for their budgets and motivate their superiors to take the budgeting process seriously.

Objective 4

Explain the difficulties of sales forecasting.

sales forecast

A prediction of sales under a given set of conditions.

sales budget

The sales forecast that is the result of decisions to create conditions that will generate a desired level of sales.

DIFFICULTIES OF OBTAINING ACCURATE SALES FORECASTS The third problem that limits the advantages of budgets is the difficulty of obtaining accurate sales forecasts. The sales budget is the foundation of budgeting. Why? Because the accuracy of all components of the budget depends on the accuracy of budgeted sales, as illustrated later in the chapter. At the **Ritz-Carlton** hotels, the process of developing the sales budget involves forecasting levels of room occupancy, group events, banquets, and other activities. Upper management initially sets the sales targets. Then, employee teams in each department provide their inputs. Once everyone agrees on a sales forecast, managers prepare monthly departmental budgets based on the sales forecast.

The sales budget is conceptually distinct from sales forecasts. A **sales forecast** is a prediction of sales under a given set of conditions. The **sales budget** is the specific sales forecast that is the result of decisions to create the conditions that will generate a desired level of sales. For example, you may have various forecasts of sales corresponding to various levels of advertising. The sales forecast for the one level of advertising you decide to implement becomes the sales budget.

The top sales executive usually directs the preparation of sales forecasts. Important factors considered by sales forecasters include the following:

1. Past patterns of sales: Past experience combined with detailed past sales by product line, geographic region, and type of customer can help predict future sales.
2. Estimates made by the sales force: A company's sales force is often the best source of information about the desires and plans of customers.
3. General economic conditions: The financial press regularly publishes predictions for many economic indicators, such as gross domestic product and industrial production indexes (local and foreign). Knowledge of how sales relate to these indicators can aid sales forecasting.
4. Competitors' actions: Sales depend on the strength and actions of competitors. To forecast sales, a company should consider the likely strategies and reactions of competitors, such as changes in their prices, product quality, or services.
5. Changes in the firm's prices: A company should consider the effects of planned price changes on customer demand (see Chapter 5). Normally, lower prices increase unit sales while higher prices decrease unit sales.

6. Changes in product mix: Changing the mix of products often can affect not only sales levels but also overall contribution margin. Identifying the most profitable products and devising methods to increase their sales is a key part of successful management.
7. Market research studies: Some companies hire marketing experts to gather information about market conditions and customer preferences. Such information is useful to managers making sales forecasts and product-mix decisions.
8. Advertising and sales promotion plans: Advertising and other promotional costs affect sales levels. A sales forecast should be based on anticipated effects of promotional activities.

Sales forecasting usually combines various techniques. In addition to the opinions of the sales staff, statistical analysis of correlations between sales and economic indicators (prepared by economists and members of the market research staff) provide valuable help. The opinions of line management also heavily influence the final sales forecasts. No matter how many technical experts a company uses in forecasting, the sales budget should ultimately be the responsibility of line management. Line managers who participate fully in setting the sales budget will be more committed to achieving the budget goals.

Governments and other nonprofit organizations face a similar problem in forecasting revenues from taxes, contributions, or other sources. For example, city revenues may depend on a variety of factors, such as property taxes, traffic fines, parking fees, license fees, and city income taxes. In turn, property taxes depend on the extent of new construction and general increases in real estate values. Thus, forecasting revenues for a government or nonprofit organization may require just as much sophistication as sales forecasts of a for-profit firm.

Types of Budgets

Businesses use several different types of budgets. The most forward-looking and least detailed budget is the **strategic plan**, which sets the overall goals and objectives of the organization. While the strategic plan does not deal with a specific time frame and does not produce forecasted financial statements, it provides the overall framework for the **long-range plan**. Long-range plans typically produce forecasted financial statements for 5- to 10-year periods. Decisions made during long-range planning include addition or deletion of product lines, design and location of new plants, acquisitions of buildings and equipment, and other long-term commitments. Companies coordinate their long-range plan with their **capital budget**, which details the planned expenditures for facilities, equipment, new products, and other long-term investments. Short-term plans and budgets guide day-to-day operations.

The **master budget** is a detailed and comprehensive analysis of the first year of the long-range plan. It quantifies targets for sales, purchases, production, distribution, and financing in the form of forecasted financial statements and supporting operating schedules. These schedules provide detailed information beyond what appears in the forecasted financial statements. Thus, the master budget includes forecasts of sales, expenses, balance sheets, and cash receipts and disbursements.

Many companies break their annual budgets into 4 quarterly or even 12 monthly budgets. A **continuous budget** or **rolling budget** is a master budget that simply adds a month (or quarter) in the future as the month (or quarter) just ended is dropped. Continuous budgets force managers to always think about the next full year, not just the remainder of the current fiscal year, so budgeting becomes an ongoing process instead of a once-a-year exercise.

Components of the Master Budget

The two major parts of a master budget are the operating budget and the financial budget. The **operating budget**—sometimes called the **profit plan**—focuses on the income statement and its supporting schedules or, in an organization with no sales revenues, on budgeted expenses and supporting schedules. In contrast, the **financial budget** focuses on the effects that the operating budget and other plans (such as capital expenditures and repayments of debt) will have on cash balances. The distinction between the operating budget and the financial budget is important because of the distinction between profitability and financial position. There are many examples of firms with strong profits where a weak cash position placed them in bankruptcy. There are also many examples of firms whose strong financial position allowed them to survive periods of temporary unprofitability.

---

strategic plan
A plan that sets the overall goals and objectives of the organization.

long-range plan
Forecasted financial statements for 5- to 10-year periods.

capital budget
A budget that details the planned expenditures for facilities, equipment, new products, and other long-term investments.

Objective 5

Explain the major features and advantages of a master budget.

master budget
An extensive analysis of the first year of the long-range plan. It summarizes the planned activities of all subunits of an organization.

continuous budget (rolling budget)
A common form of master budget that adds a month in the future as the month just ended is dropped.

operating budget (profit plan)
A major part of a master budget that focuses on the income statement and its supporting schedules.

financial budget
The part of a master budget that focuses on the effects that the operating budget and other plans (such as capital budgets and repayments of debt) have on cash balances.

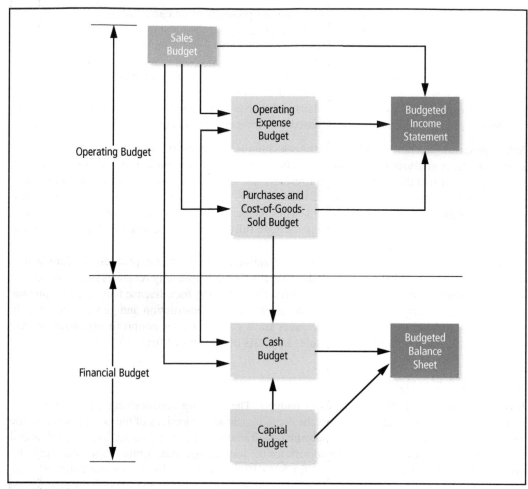

Exhibit 7-2
Preparation of the Master Budget for a Merchandising Company

The terms used to describe specific budget schedules vary from organization to organization. However, most master budgets share common elements. The usual master budget for a merchandising company has the following components as shown in Exhibit 7-2:

A. Operating budget
  1. Sales budget
  2. Operating expense budget
  3. Purchases and cost-of-goods-sold budget
  4. Budgeted income statement
B. Financial budget
  1. Cash budget
  2. Capital budget
  3. Budgeted balance sheet

Other companies add to or adapt these categories depending on the nature of their operations. For example, manufacturing companies add budgets for raw material, work-in-process, and finished good inventories, and budgets for each type of resource activity, such as labor, materials, and factory overhead. Similarly, a consulting company might adapt the operating expense budget to focus on its major cost—consultant salaries. In addition to the master budget, there are countless forms of special budgets and related reports. For example, a report might detail goals and objectives for improvements in quality or customer satisfaction during the budget period.

Preparing the Master Budget

Let's return to Exhibit 7-2 and trace the preparation of the master budget components. Although the process involves a large number of detailed calculations, always keep the big picture in mind. Remember that the master budgeting process provides an opportunity to review key decisions regarding all aspects of the company's value chain. Early drafts of the budget often lead to decisions that, in turn, lead to revisions in subsequent budget drafts. This cycle may be repeated several times before the budget is finalized.

The Cooking Hut

We illustrate the budgeting process using the Cooking Hut Company (CHC), a retailer of a wide variety of kitchen and dining room items, such as coffeemakers, silverware, and table linens. Although master budgets normally cover a full year, for the sake of brevity this illustration shows only the first 3 months of CHC's fiscal year, April–June. Exhibit 7-3 is the closing balance sheet for the previous fiscal year ending March 31, 20X1.

SALES BUDGET   Preparation of the master budget for the first 3 months of the new fiscal year requires a sales budget for 1 month beyond the 3 months because CHC bases its budgeted inventory purchases on the following month's sales. The sales budget for the next 4 months is as follows:

April	$50,000
May	$80,000
June	$60,000
July	$50,000

The master budget also requires information about actual sales in the previous month because CHC collects cash for the credit sales in the month following the sale. On average, 60% of sales are cash sales and the remaining 40% are credit sales. Sales in March were $40,000 and the $16,000 of accounts receivable on March 31 represents credit sales made in March (40% of $40,000). Uncollectible accounts are negligible and thus ignored. For simplicity's sake, we also ignore all local, state, and federal taxes for this illustration.

PLANNED INVENTORY LEVELS   Because deliveries from suppliers and customer demands are uncertain, at the end of each month CHC wants to have on hand a base inventory of $20,000 plus additional inventory equal to 80% of the expected cost of goods sold for the following month. The cost of goods sold averages 70% of sales. Therefore, the inventory on March 31 is $20,000 + (.8 × .7 × April sales of $50,000) = $20,000 + $28,000 = $48,000. On average, CHC

Exhibit 7-3
The Cooking Hut Company
Balance Sheet March 31, 20X1

Assets		
Current assets		
Cash	$10,000	
Accounts receivable, net (.4 × March sales of $40,000)	16,000	
Merchandise inventory, $20,000 +.8 × (.7 × April sales of $50,000)	48,000	
Unexpired insurance (for April–December 20X1)	1,800	$ 75,800
Plant assets		
Equipment, fixtures, and other	$37,000	
Accumulated depreciation	12,800	24,200
Total assets		$100,000
Liabilities and Owners' Equity		
Current liabilities		
Accounts payable (.5 × March purchases of $33,600)	$16,800	
Accrued wages and commissions payable ($1,250 + $3,000)	4,250	$ 21,050
Owners' equity		78,950
Total liabilities and owners' equity		$100,000

pays for 50% of each month's purchases during the month of purchase and 50% during the next month. Therefore, the accounts payable balance on March 31 is 50% of March purchases, or .5 × $33,600 = $16,800.

WAGES AND COMMISSIONS   CHC pays wages and commissions twice each month, with payments lagged half a month after they are earned. Each payment consists of two components: (i) one-half of monthly fixed wages of $2,500, and (ii) commissions equal to 15% of sales, which we assume are uniform throughout each month. To illustrate the wage and commission payments, the March 31 balance of accrued wages and commissions payable is (.5 × $2,500) + .5 × (.15 × $40,000) = $1,250 + $3,000 = $4,250. Because of the half-month lag, CHC will pay this $4,250 balance on April 15.

CAPITAL EXPENDITURES AND OPERATING EXPENDITURES   CHC's only planned capital expenditure is the purchase of new fixtures for $3,000 cash in April. CHC has monthly operating expenses as follows:

Miscellaneous expenses	5% of sales, paid as incurred
Rent	$2,000, paid as incurred
Insurance	$200 expiration per month
Depreciation, including new fixtures	$500 per month

CASH BALANCES   Because collections lag credit sales, CHC often struggles to come up with the cash to pay for purchases, employee wages, and other outlays. To meet cash needs, CHC uses short-term loans from local banks, paying them back when excess cash is available. CHC maintains a minimum $10,000 cash balance at the end of each month for operating purposes and can borrow or repay loans only in multiples of $1,000. Assume that borrowing occurs at the beginning and repayments occur at the end of the month. Also assume that interest of 1% per month is paid in cash at the end of each month.

Steps in Preparing the Master Budget

Objective 6

Follow the principal steps in preparing a master budget.

The principal steps in preparing the master budget are as follows:

Supporting Budgets and Schedules

1. Using the data given, prepare the following budgets and schedules for each of the months of the planning horizon:
    Schedule a. Sales budget
    Schedule b. Cash collections from customers
    Schedule c. Purchases and cost-of-goods-sold budget
    Schedule d. Cash disbursements for purchases
    Schedule e. Operating expense budget
    Schedule f. Cash disbursements for operating expenses

Operating Budget

2. Using the supporting budgets and schedules, prepare a budgeted income statement for the 3 months ending June 30, 20X1.

Financial Budget

3. Prepare the following budgets and forecasted financial statements:
    a. Capital budget
    b. Cash budget, including details of borrowings, repayments, and interest for each month of the planning horizon
    c. Budgeted balance sheet as of June 30, 20X1

Organizations with effective budget systems have specific guidelines for the steps and timing of budget preparation. Although the details differ, the guidelines invariably include the preceding steps. As we follow these steps to prepare CHC's master budget, be sure that you understand the source of each figure in each schedule and budget.

Step 1: Preparing Basic Data

STEP 1A: SALES BUDGET The sales budget is the starting point for budgeting because planned inventory levels, purchases, and operating expenses all depend on the expected level of sales. Schedule a includes information about actual March sales because March credit sales affect cash collections in April.

Objective 7

Prepare the operating budget and the supporting schedules.

Schedule a: Sales Budget

	March	April	May	June	April–June Total
Total Sales	$40,000	$50,000	$80,000	$60,000	$190,000

STEP 1B: CASH COLLECTIONS FROM CUSTOMERS Schedule b uses the sales budget to plan when CHC will collect cash. In turn, we will use Schedule b to prepare the cash budget in step 3. Cash collections from customers include the current month's cash sales plus collection of the previous month's credit sales.

Schedule b: Cash Collections from Customers

	April	May	June
Cash sales (60% of current month sales)	$30,000	$48,000	$36,000
Collection of last month's credit sales (40% of previous month sales)	16,000	20,000	32,000
Total collections	$46,000	$68,000	$68,000

STEP 1C: PURCHASES BUDGET The elements of the purchases budget are tied together by a simple intuitive identity that ignores minor complications such as returns and defects but relates the fundamental uses of inventory to the sources: Inventory is either sold or else carried over to the next period as ending inventory. Inventory comes from either beginning inventory or purchases. Therefore, cost of goods sold plus ending inventory equals beginning inventory plus purchases.

We budget cost of goods sold by multiplying the cost of merchandise sold percentage (70%) by budgeted sales. The total merchandise needed is the sum of budgeted cost of goods sold plus the desired ending inventory. Finally, we compute required purchases by subtracting beginning inventory from the total merchandise needed:

Schedule c: Purchases Budget

	March	April	May	June	April–June Total
Budgeted cost of goods sold[†]		$35,000	$ 56,000	$42,000	$133,000
Plus: Desired ending inventory**		64,800	53,600	48,000	
Total merchandise needed		$99,800	$109,600	$90,000	
Less: Beginning inventory		48,000‡	64,800	53,600	
Purchases	$33,600*	$51,800	$ 44,800	$36,400	

[†].7 × April sales of $50,000 = $35,000; .7 × May sales of $80,000 = $56,000; .7 × June sales of $60,000 = $42,000
** $20,000 + (.80 × next month cost of goods sold)
‡Ending inventory from March was $48,000 as shown in Exhibit 7-3.
*Purchases for March were ending inventory ($48,000 as shown in Exhibit 7-3) plus cost of goods sold (.7 × March sales of $40,000) less beginning inventory ($42,400 = $20,000 + [.8 × March cost of goods sold of $28,000]).

STEP 1D: DISBURSEMENTS FOR PURCHASES We use the purchases budget to develop Schedule d. In our example, disbursements are 50% of the current month's purchases and 50% of the previous month's purchases.

Schedule d: Cash Disbursements for Purchases

	April	May	June
50% of last month's purchases	$16,800	$25,900	$22,400
Plus 50% of this month's purchases	25,900	22,400	18,200
Disbursements for purchases	$42,700	$48,300	$40,600

STEP 1E: OPERATING EXPENSE BUDGET Month-to-month changes in sales volume and other cost-driver activities directly influence many operating expenses. Examples of expenses driven by sales volume include sales commissions and delivery expenses—these are included in miscellaneous expenses for CHC. Other expenses, such as rent, insurance, depreciation, and wages, are not influenced by sales (within appropriate relevant ranges), and we regard them as fixed. Schedule e summarizes operating expenses for CHC.

Schedule e: Operating Expense Budget

	March	April	May	June	April–June Total
Wages (fixed)	$2,500	$ 2,500	$ 2,500	$ 2,500	
Commissions (15% of current month's sales)	6,000	7,500	12,000	9,000	
Total wages and commissions	$8,500	$10,000	$14,500	$11,500	$36,000
Miscellaneous expenses (5% of current sales)		2,500	4,000	3,000	9,500
Rent (fixed)		2,000	2,000	2,000	6,000
Insurance (fixed)		200	200	200	600
Depreciation (fixed)		500	500	500	1,500
Total operating expenses		$15,200	$21,200	$17,200	$53,600

STEP 1F: DISBURSEMENTS FOR OPERATING EXPENSES Disbursements for operating expenses are based on the operating expense budget. Disbursements include 50% of last month's wages and commissions, 50% of this month's wages and commissions, and miscellaneous and rent expenses. There is no monthly cash disbursement for Insurance (which is paid annually at the beginning of the year) nor for depreciation (which does not involve any periodic cash disbursement). We will use the total of these disbursements for each month in preparing the cash budget.

Schedule f: Disbursements for Operating Expenses

	April	May	June
Wages and commissions			
50% of last month's expenses	$ 4,250	$ 5,000	$ 7,250
50% of this month's expenses	5,000	7,250	5,750
Total wages and commissions	$ 9,250	$12,250	$13,000
Miscellaneous expenses	2,500	4,000	3,000
Rent	2,000	2,000	2,000
Total disbursements	$13,750	$18,250	$18,000

Step 2: Preparing the Operating Budget

Steps 1a, 1c, and 1e, along with interest expense from the cash budget (which we will construct in step 2), provide information to construct the budgeted income statement in Exhibit 7-4. Budgeted income from operations is often a benchmark for judging management performance.

Exhibit 7-4

The Cooking Hut Company
Budgeted Income Statement for Three Months Ending June 30, 20X1

		Data	Source of Data
Sales		$190,000	Schedule a
Cost of goods sold		133,000	Schedule c
Gross margin		$ 57,000	
Operating expenses:			
Wages and commissions	$36,000		Schedule e
Rent	6,000		Schedule e
Miscellaneous	9,500		Schedule e
Insurance	600		Schedule e
Depreciation	1,500	53,600	Schedule e
Income from operations		$ 3,400	
Interest expense		410	Cash budget
Net income		$ 2,990	

Step 3: Preparation of Financial Budget

The second major part of the master budget is the financial budget, which consists of the capital budget, cash budget, and ending balance sheet.

Objective 8

Prepare the financial budget.

STEP 3A: CAPITAL BUDGET   In our illustration, the $3,000 planned purchase of new fixtures in April is the only item in the capital budget. More complex capital budgets are illustrated in Chapter 11.

STEP 3B: CASH BUDGET   The **cash budget** is a statement of planned cash receipts and disbursements. Cash budgets help management avoid either unnecessary idle cash or unnecessary cash deficiencies. The cash budget is heavily affected by the level of operations summarized in the budgeted income statement.

cash budget
A statement of planned cash receipts and disbursements.

The cash budget in Exhibit 7-5 has the following major sections, where the letters x, y, and z refer to the lines that summarize the effects of that section:

- The available cash balance (x) is the amount by which the beginning cash balance exceeds CHC's $10,000 minimum cash balance. Companies maintain a minimum cash balance to allow for fluctuations in the level of cash during the month—daily balances during the month typically fluctuate relative to the beginning and ending cash balances—and also to provide for unexpected cash needs.
- Net cash receipts and disbursements (y):
  1. Cash receipts depend on collections from customers' accounts receivable, cash sales, and on other operating cash income sources, such as interest received on notes receivable. Trace total collections from Schedule b to Exhibit 7-5.
  2. Disbursements for purchases depend on the credit terms extended by suppliers and the bill-paying habits of the buyer. Trace disbursements for merchandise from Schedule d to Exhibit 7-5.

	April	May	June
Beginning cash balance	$ 10,000	$ 10,410	$ 10,720
Minimum cash balance desired	10,000	10,000	10,000
Available cash balance (x)	$ 0	$ 410	$ 720
Cash receipts and disbursements			
Collections from customers (Schedule b*)	$ 46,000	$ 68,000	$ 68,000
Payments for merchandise (Schedule d)	(42,700)	(48,300)	(40,600)
Payments for operating expenses (Schedule f)	(13,750)	(18,250)	(18,000)
Purchase of new fixtures (Step 3a)	(3,000)		
Net cash receipts and disbursements (y)	$ (13,450)	$ 1,450	$ 9,400
Excess (deficiency) of cash before financing ($x + y$)	(13,450)	$ 1,860	$ 10,120
Borrowing (at beginning of month)	$ 14,000†		
Repayments (at end of month)		$ (1,000)	$ (9,000)
Interest payments (1% per month, end of month‡)	(140)	(140)	(130)
Total cash increase (decrease) from financing (z)	$ 13,860	$ (1,140)	$ (9,130)
Ending cash balance (beginning $+ y + z$)	$ 10,410	$ 10,720	$ 10,990

Exhibit 7-5

The Cooking Hut Company
Cash Budget for Three Months Ending June 30, 20X1

*Letters x, y, and z are keyed to the explanation in the text.
†Borrowing and repayment of principal are made in multiples of $1,000, at an interest rate of 1% per month.
‡Interest computations: $14,000 × .01 = $140; $14,000 × .01 = $140; $13,000 × .01 = $130.

3. Payroll depends on wages and commission terms and on payroll dates. Some costs and expenses depend on contractual terms for installment payments, mortgage payments, rents, leases, and miscellaneous items. Trace disbursements for operating expenses from Schedule f to Exhibit 7-5.

4. Other disbursements include outlays for fixed assets, long-term investments, dividends, and the like. An example is the $3,000 expenditure for new fixtures.

• The total cash increase (decrease) from financing (z) depends on the total available cash balance (x) and the net cash receipts and disbursements (y). If cash available plus net cash receipts less disbursements is negative, borrowing is necessary—Exhibit 7-5 shows that CHC will borrow $14,000 in April to cover the planned deficiency. If cash available plus net cash receipts less disbursements is sufficiently positive, CHC can repay loans—it repays $1,000 and $9,000 in May and June, respectively. This section of the cash budget also generally contains the outlays for interest expense. Trace the calculated interest expense, which in our example is the same as the cash interest payments for the 3 months, to Exhibit 7-4, which then will be complete.

• The ending cash balance is the beginning cash balance $+ y + z$. Financing, z, has either a positive (borrowing) or a negative (repayment) effect on the cash balance. The illustrative cash budget shows the pattern of short-term, "self-liquidating" financing. Seasonal peaks often result in heavy drains on cash—for merchandise purchases and operating expenses—before the company makes sales and collects cash from customers. The resulting loan is "self-liquidating"—that is, the company uses borrowed money to acquire merchandise for sale, and uses the proceeds from sales to repay the loan. This "working capital cycle" moves from cash to inventory to receivables and back to cash.

STEP 3C: BUDGETED BALANCE SHEET The final step in preparing the master budget is to construct the budgeted balance sheet (Exhibit 7-6) that projects each balance sheet item in accordance with the business plan as expressed in the previous schedules. Specifically, the

Exhibit 7-6

The Cooking Hut Company
Budgeted Balance Sheet
June 30, 20X1

Assets

Current Assets		
Cash (Exhibit 7-5)	$10,990	
Accounts receivable, net (.4 × June sales of $60,000)	24,000	
Inventory (Schedule c)	48,000	
Unexpired insurance (for July–December)	1,200	$ 84,190
Plant Assets		
Equipment, fixtures, and other ($37,000 + $3,000)	$40,000	
Accumulated Depreciation ($12,800 + $1,500)	(14,300)	25,700
Total assets		$109,890

Liabilities and Owners' Equity

Current liabilities		
Accounts payable (.5 × June purchases of $36,400)	$18,200	
Short-term bank loan	4,000	
Accrued wages and commissions payable (.5 × 11,500)	5,750	$ 27,950
Owners' equity (78,950 × 2,990 net income)		81,940
Total liabilities and owners' equity		$109,890

Note: March 31, 20X1 beginning balances are used for computations of unexpired insurance, plant assets, and owners' equity.

Business First

Business Plans and Budgets

Start-up companies in a variety of industries have mushroomed into multibillion-dollar companies. How do these companies get started? An essential component in securing initial funding for a start-up is the development of a business plan. The federal government's Small Business Administration recommends a business plan with three sections:

1. The Business—includes a description of the business, a marketing plan, an assessment of the competition, a list of operating procedures, and a roster of personnel
2. Financial Data—includes the following items:
   Loan applications
   Capital equipment and supply list
   Pro forma balance sheet
   Break-even analysis
   Pro forma income projections (income statements):
      Three-year summary
      Detail by month, first year
      Detail by quarters, second and third years
      Assumptions upon which projections were based
      Pro forma cash flow statements
3. Supporting Documents—includes a variety of legal documents and information about the principals involved, suppliers, customers, etc.

Financial data are an important part of a business plan, the centerpiece of which is the master budget. The budgeted income statement and budgeted cash flow statement are essential to predicting the future prospects of any business. They are especially critical to assessing the prospects of a new company that has little history to analyze.

The importance of a budget to a start-up company was emphasized by Jim Rowan, former senior vice president of SunAmerica, who left to form a new company, EncrypTix. He raised $36 million in investment funding to spin EncrypTix off from Stamps.com. The company focuses on Internet delivery and storage of tickets, coupons, and vouchers. Rowan stated, "The key thing for a start-up is to develop a budget and put it like a stake in the ground, so you can measure against it. It's not a ceiling, it's not carved in stone, but you have to have something that's a benchmark."

Budgeting is often not the most exciting task for entrepreneurs. However, lack of a credible budget is one of the main reasons venture capitalists cite when they refuse funding for a start-up. Further, a cash shortage is one of the main causes of failure among start-up companies. Anyone wanting to be an entrepreneur would be well-advised to study budgeting and learn how it can be a powerful tool both for managing the company and for promoting the company to potential investors.

Sources: Adapted from Small Business Administration, *The Business Plan: Roadmap to Success* (www.sba.gov/starting/indexbusplans.html); and K. Klein, "Budgeting Helps Secure Longevity," *Los Angeles Times*, August 2, 2000, p. C6.

beginning balances at March 31 would be increased or decreased in light of the expected cash receipts and cash disbursements in Exhibit 7-5 and in light of the effects of noncash items appearing on the income statement in Exhibit 7-4. For example, unexpired insurance is a noncash item that would decrease from its balance of $1,800 on March 31 to $1,200 on June 30.

Strategy and the Master Budget

The master budget is an important management tool for evaluating and revising strategy. For example, the initial formulation of the budgeted financial statements may prompt management to consider new sales strategies to generate more demand. Alternatively, management may explore the effects of various adjustments in the timing of cash receipts and disbursements. The large cash deficiency in April, for example, may lead to an emphasis on cash sales or an attempt to speed up collection of accounts receivable. In any event, the first draft of the master budget is rarely the final draft. As managers revise strategy, the budgeting process becomes an integral part of the management process itself—budgeting is planning and communicating. The Business First box above describes the important role of budgets in start-up companies.

Making Managerial Decisions

Some managers focus on the operating budget, while others are more concerned with the financial budget. How does the operating budget differ from the financial budget?

Answer

The operating budget focuses on the income statement, which uses accrual accounting. It measures revenues and expenses. Line operating managers usually prepare and use the operating budget. In contrast, the financial budget focuses primarily on cash flow. It measures the receipts and disbursements of cash. Financial managers, such as controllers and treasurers, focus on the financial budget. The operating budget is a better measure of long-run performance, but the financial budget is essential to plan for short-term cash needs and manage cash balances. A shortage of cash can get a company into financial trouble even when operating performance appears to be okay. Thus, both operating and financial budgets are important to an organization.

Summary Problem for Your Review

Be sure you understand every step of the CHC example before you tackle this review problem.

PROBLEM

The Country Store is a retail outlet for a variety of hardware and housewares. The owner is eager to prepare a budget and is especially concerned with her cash position. The company will have to borrow in order to finance purchases made in preparation for high expected sales during the busy last quarter of the year. When the company needs cash, borrowing occurs at the end of a month. When cash is available for repayments, the repayment occurs at the end of a month. The company pays interest in cash at the end of every month at a monthly rate of 1% on the amount outstanding during that month.

Review the structure of the example in the chapter and then prepare the Country Store's master budget for the months of October, November, and December. The owner has gathered the data shown in Exhibit 7-7 to prepare the simplified budget. In addition, she will purchase equipment in October for $19,750 cash and pay dividends of $4,000 in December.

Balance Sheet as of September 30, 20X1			Budgeted sales:	
Assets			September (actual)	$60,000
Cash		$ 9,000	October	70,000
Accounts receivable		48,000	November	85,000
Inventory		12,600	December	90,000
Plant and equipment (net)		200,000	January 20X2	50,000
Total assets		$269,600		
			Other data:	
Liabilities and stockholders' equity			Required minimum cash balance	$ 8,000
Interest payable		0	Sales mix, cash/credit	
Note payable		0	Cash sales	20%
Accounts payable		18,300	Credit sales (collected the following month)	80%
Capital stock		180,000	Gross profit rate	40%
Retained earnings		71,300	Loan interest rate (interest paid in cash monthly)	12%
Total liabilities and stockholders' equity		$269,600	Inventory paid for in	
			Month purchased	50%
Budgeted expenses (per month):			Month after purchase	50%
Salaries and wages		$ 7,500	Salaries and wages, freight-out, advertising,	
Freight out as a percent of sales		6%	and other expenses are paid in cash in the	
Advertising		$ 6,000	month incurred.	
Depreciation		$ 2,000		
Other expense as a percent of sales		4%		
Minimum inventory policy as a percent				
of next month's cost of goods sold		30%		

Exhibit 7-7
The Country Store
Budget Data

SOLUTION

Schedule a: Sales budget

	October	November	December	Total
Credit sales, 80%	$56,000	$68,000	$72,000	$196,000
Cash sales, 20%	14,000	17,000	18,000	49,000
Total sales	$70,000	$85,000	$90,000	$245,000

Schedule b: Cash collections from customers

	October	November	December	Total
Cash sales	$14,000	$17,000	$18,000	$ 49,000
Collections from prior month	48,000	56,000	68,000	172,000
Total collections	$62,000	$73,000	$86,000	$221,000

Schedule c: Purchases budget

	October	November	December	Total
Desired ending inventory	$15,300	$16,200	$ 9,000	$ 40,500
Plus cost of goods sold	42,000	51,000	54,000	147,000
Total needed	$57,300	$67,200	$63,000	$187,500
Less: Beginning inventory	12,600	15,300	16,200	44,100
Total purchases	$44,700	$51,900	$46,800	$143,400

Schedule d: Cash disbursements for purchases

	October	November	December	Total
For September*	$18,300			$ 18,300
For October	22,350	$22,350		44,700
For November		25,950	$25,950	51,900
For December			23,400	23,400
Total disbursements	$40,650	$48,300	$49,350	$138,300

*The amount payable on the September 30, 20X1, balance sheet.

Schedules e and f: Operating expenses and disbursements for expenses (except interest)

	October	November	December	Total
Cash expenses:				
Salaries and wages	$ 7,500	$ 7,500	$ 7,500	$22,500
Freight-out	4,200	5,100	5,400	14,700
Advertising	6,000	6,000	6,000	18,000
Other expenses	2,800	3,400	3,600	9,800
Total disbursements for expenses	$20,500	$22,000	$22,500	$65,000
Noncash expenses:				
Depreciation	2,000	2,000	2,000	6,000
Total expenses	$22,500	$24,000	$24,500	$71,000

The Country Store
Cash Budget for the Months of October–December, 20X1

	October	November	December
Beginning cash balance	$ 9,000	$ 8,000	$ 8,000
Minimum cash balance desired	8,000	8,000	8,000
Available cash balance	1,000	0	0
Cash receipts and disbursements:			
Collections from customers	62,000	73,000	86,000
Payments for merchandise	(40,650)	(48,300)	(49,350)
Operating expenses	(20,500)	(22,000)	(22,500)
Equipment purchases	(19,750)	0	0
Dividends	0	0	(4,000)
Interest*	0	(179)	(154)
Net cash receipts and disbursements	(18,900)	2,521	9,996
Excess (deficiency) of cash before financing	$ (17,900)	$ 2,521	$ 9,996
Financing:			
Borrowing†	$ 17,900	$ 0	$ 0
Repayments	0	(2,521)	(9,996)
Total cash from financing	17,900	(2,521)	(9,996)
Ending cash balance	$ 8,000	$ 8,000	$ 8,000

*Interest is paid on the loan amounts outstanding during the month. November: $(.01) \times (\$17,900) = \$179$; December: $(.01) \times (\$17,900 - \$2,521) = \$154$.

†Borrowings are at the end of the month in the amounts needed. Repayments also are made at the end of the month in the amount that excess cash permits.

The Country Store
Budgeted Income Statement for October–December, 20X1

	October	November	December	October–December Total
Sales	$70,000	$85,000	$90,000	$245,000
Cost of goods sold	42,000	51,000	54,000	147,000
Gross margin	28,000	34,000	36,000	98,000
Operating expenses				
Salaries and wages	7,500	7,500	7,500	22,500
Freight-out	4,200	5,100	5,400	14,700
Advertising	6,000	6,000	6,000	18,000
Other	2,800	3,400	3,600	9,800
Interest*	—	179	154	333
Depreciation	2,000	2,000	2,000	6,000
Total operating expense	$22,500	$24,179	$24,654	$ 71,333
Net operating income	$ 5,500	$ 9,821	$11,346	$ 26,667

*Interest expense is the monthly interest rate times the borrowed amount held for the month. November: $(.01) \times \$17,900 = \$179$; December: $(.01) \times \$15,379 = \$154$.

The Country Store
Budgeted Balance Sheets as of the Ends of October–December, 20X1

Assets	October	November	December*
Current assets			
Cash	$ 8,000	$ 8,000	$ 8,000
Accounts receivable	56,000	68,000	72,000
Inventory	15,300	16,200	9,000
Total current assets	79,300	92,200	89,000
Plant, less accumulated depreciation†	217,750	215,750	213,750
Total assets	$297,050	$307,950	$302,750
Liabilities and Stockholders' Equities			
Liabilities			
Accounts payable	$ 22,350	$ 25,950	$ 23,400
Notes payable	17,900	15,379	5,383
Total liabilities	40,250	41,329	28,783
Stockholders' equity			
Capital stock	180,000	180,000	180,000
Retained earnings	76,800	86,621	93,967
Total stockholders' equities	256,800	266,621	273,967
Total liabilities and stockholders' equities	$297,050	$307,950	$302,750

*The December 30, 20X1, balance sheet is the ending balance sheet for the quarter.

†October ending balance in Plant = beginning balance + equipment purchases − depreciation = $200,000 + $19,750 − $2,000 = $217,750.

Activity-Based Master Budgets

The budget process we have described thus far in this chapter can be called **functional budgeting** because the focus is on preparing budgets by function, such as production, selling, and administrative support. Organizations that have implemented activity-based cost accounting systems often use these systems as a vehicle to prepare an **activity-based budget (ABB)**—a budget that focuses on the budgeted cost of activities required to produce and sell products and services.

An activity-based budgetary system emphasizes the planning and control purpose of cost management. Our discussion of activity-based costing (ABC) in Chapter 4 focused on designing cost accounting and cost allocation systems that provided more accurate product and service costs. However, once a company has designed and implemented an ABC system, it can use the same framework for its budgetary system. Exhibit 7-8 highlights the main concepts and differences between ABC allocation of resource costs to activities and products, and ABB.

Just as in functional budgeting (see Exhibit 7-2), ABB begins with the forecasted demand for products or services—the sales budget. In functional budgeting, the next steps are to determine the ending-inventory budget, the material purchases budget, and the cost-of-goods-sold budget. In ABB, the focus is on estimating the demand for each activity's output as measured by its cost driver. Then, we use the rate at which activities consume resources to estimate or budget the resources needed. As we can see from comparing Exhibits 7-2 and 7-8, functional budgeting determines the resources needed directly from the predicted sales of products or services, while ABB uses the sales predictions to estimate the activities required, which in turn determines the resources needed. Because of the emphasis on activities and their consumption of resources, some managers believe that ABB is more useful for controlling waste and improving efficiency—a primary objective of budgeting.

functional budgeting
Budgeting process that focuses on preparing budgets for various functions, such as production, selling, and administrative support.

activity-based budget (ABB)
A budget that focuses on the budgeted cost of activities required to produce and sell products and services.

Exhibit 7-8
ABC and ABB Compared

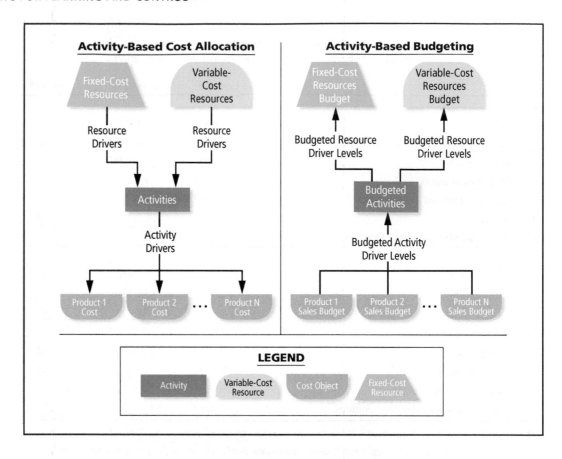

Most companies do not realize the full benefits of ABC until they also integrate it into their budgeting system. Often accountants "own" the costing system of a company, but the budgeting system "belongs" to managers. ABB requires managers to focus on managing activities as they prepare their budgets using the same framework used by the ABC system. For example, when **Dow Chemical** integrated its new ABC system with its budgeting process, it undertook a massive training effort for "controllers, accountants, work process subject matter experts, cost center owners, business manufacturing leaders, and site general managers." By creating budgets consistent with cost reports, Dow gained much greater benefit from its ABB system.

Government organizations such as the U.S. Small Business Administration (SBA) also use ABB. The SBA is one of the five largest federal credit agencies with over $50 billion in loans. An article published by the SBA touted its use of ABB:

> *Our goal is to clearly identify the activities that must be performed to produce critical outputs and then determine the level of resources that must be committed to successfully complete the activity. Once this is done, we can determine how various funding levels affect the outputs produced by the SBA. The ABB process provides SBA management the quality information necessary for sound decision making.*

Budgets as Financial Planning Models

financial planning model
A mathematical model of the master budget that can incorporate any set of assumptions about sales, costs, or product mix.

A well-made master budget that considers all aspects of the company (the entire value chain) provides the basis for an effective **financial planning model**, a mathematical model that can incorporate the effects of alternative assumptions about sales, costs, or product mix. Today, many large companies have developed large-scale financial planning models based on the master budget to predict how various decisions might affect the company. For example, a manager might want to predict the consequences of changing the mix of products offered for sale to emphasize several products with the highest prospects for growth. A financial planning model would provide operational and financial budgets under alternative assumptions about the product mix, sales levels, production constraints, quality levels, scheduling, and so on. Most importantly, managers can get answers to what-if questions, such as "What if sales are 10% below forecasts? What if material prices increase 8% instead of 4% as expected? What if the new union contract grants a 6% raise in consideration for productivity improvements?"

Using the master budget in this way is a step-by-step process in which managers revise their tentative plans as they exchange views on various aspects of expected activities. For instance, Dow Chemical's model uses 140 separate, constantly revised cost inputs that are based on several different cost drivers. By mathematically describing the relationships among all the operating and financial activities and among the other major internal and external factors that affect the results of management decisions, financial planning models allow managers to assess the predicted impacts of various alternatives before they make final decisions.

Financial planning models have shortened managers' reaction times dramatically. We can prepare in minutes (or even seconds) a revised plan for a large company that once took many accountants many days to prepare by hand. For example, Public Service Enterprise Group, a New Jersey utility company, can revise its total master budget several times a day, if necessary.

Spreadsheet software has put financial planning models within reach of even the smallest organizations. Appendix 7 illustrates how to use a spreadsheet model for planning. Ready access to powerful modeling, however, does not guarantee plausible or reliable results. Financial planning models are only as good as the assumptions and the inputs used to build and manipulate them—what computer specialists call GIGO (garbage in, garbage out). Nearly every CFO has a horror story to tell about following the bad advice generated from a financial planning model with accurate calculations but faulty assumptions or inputs.

Highlights to Remember

1. **Explain how budgets facilitate planning and coordination.** A budget expresses, in quantitative terms, an organization's objectives and possible steps for achieving them. Thus, a budget is a tool that helps managers in both their planning and control functions. Budgets provide a mechanism for communication between units and across levels of the organization. In an environment that encourages open communication of the opportunities and challenges facing the organization, the budget process allows managers to coordinate ongoing activities and plan for the future.

2. **Anticipate possible human relations problems caused by budgets.** The success of a budget depends heavily on employee reaction to it. Negative attitudes toward budgets often prevent realization of many of the potential benefits. Such attitudes are usually caused by managers who use budgets only to limit spending or to punish employees. Budgets generally are more useful when all affected parties participate in their preparation.

3. **Explain potentially dysfunctional incentives in the budget process.** When managers want to increase the resources allocated to their unit or when managers are evaluated based on performance relative to budgeted amounts, there are incentives to bias the information that goes into their budgets, making budget information less useful. When managers are compensated using typical bonus schemes, there may be pressure to report inflated results and incentives to make short-run decisions that are not in the best long-run interests of the organization. Not only do such incentives lead managers to make poor decisions, they undercut efforts to maintain high ethical standards in the organization.

4. **Explain the difficulties of sales forecasting.** Sales forecasting combines various techniques as well as opinions of sales staff and management. Sales forecasters must consider many factors, such as past patterns of sales, economic conditions, and competitors' actions. Sales forecasting is difficult because of its complexity and the rapid changes in the business environment in which most companies operate.

5. **Explain the major features and advantages of a master budget.** The two major parts of a master budget are the operating budget and the financial budget. Advantages of budgets include formalization of planning, providing a framework for judging performance, and aiding managers in communicating and coordinating their efforts.

6. **Follow the principal steps in preparing a master budget.** Master budgets typically cover relatively short periods—usually 1 month to 1 year. The steps involved in preparing the master budget vary across organizations but follow the general outline given on pages 281–285. Invariably, the first step is to forecast sales or service levels. The next step should be to forecast cost-driver activity levels, given expected sales and service. Using these forecasts and knowledge of cost behavior, collection patterns, and so on, managers can prepare the operating and financing budgets.

7. **Prepare the operating budget and the supporting schedules.** The operating budget includes the income statement for the budget period. Managers prepare it using the following supporting schedules: sales budget, purchases budget, and operating expense budget.

8. **Prepare the financial budget.** The second major part of the master budget is the financial budget. The financial budget consists of a cash budget, capital budget, and a budgeted balance sheet. Managers prepare the cash budget from the following supporting schedules: cash collections, disbursements for purchases, disbursements for operating expenses, and other disbursements.

Appendix 7: Use of Spreadsheet Models for Sensitivity Analysis

Spreadsheet software is a powerful and flexible tool for budgeting. An obvious advantage of a spreadsheet is that arithmetic errors are virtually nonexistent. More importantly, managers can use spreadsheets to make a mathematical model (a financial planning model) of the organization. At very low cost, they can apply this model with a variety of assumptions that reflect possible changes in expected sales, cost drivers, cost functions, and so on. The objective of this appendix is to illustrate how to use a spreadsheet model for sensitivity analysis.

Recall the chapter's Cooking Hut Company (CHC) example. Suppose CHC has prepared its master budget using spreadsheet software. To simplify making changes to the budget, we have placed the relevant forecasts and other budgeting details in Exhibit 7-9. Note that for simplification, we have included only the data necessary for the purchases budget. The full master budget would require a larger table that includes all the data given in the chapter.

Each cell of the spreadsheet is referenced by its column (a letter) and its row (a number). For example, the beginning inventory for the budget period is in "D4," which is shown as $48,000. By referencing the budget data's cell addresses, you can generate the purchases budget (Exhibit 7-11) within the same spreadsheet by entering formulas instead of numbers into the schedule. Consider Exhibit 7-10. Instead of retyping $48,000, April's beginning inventory in the purchases budget, in cell D17, type a formula with the cell address for the April beginning inventory from the preceding table, =D4 (the cell address preceded by an "=" sign—the common spreadsheet indicator for a formula). Likewise, all the cells of the purchases budget will contain formulas that include cell addresses instead of numbers. The total inventory needed in April (cell D16) is =D13 + D14, and budgeted purchases in April (cell D19) are =D16 – D17. We can compute the figures for May and June similarly within the respective columns. This approach gives the spreadsheet the most flexibility because you can change any number in the budget data in Exhibit 7-9 (for example, a sales forecast), and the software automatically recalculates the numbers in the entire purchases budget. Exhibit 7-10 shows the formulas used for the purchases budget. Exhibit 7-11 is the purchases budget displaying the numbers generated by the formulas in Exhibit 7-10 using the input data in Exhibit 7-9.

Exhibit 7-9

The Cooking Hut Company
Budget Data (Column and row labels are given by the spreadsheet.)

	A	B	C	D	E	F
1	Budgeted data					
2	Sales forecasts		Other information			
3						
4	March (actual)	$40,000	Beginning inventory	$48,000		
5	April	50,000	Desired ending inventory:			
			Base amount	$20,000		
6	May	80,000	Plus percent of next			
7	June	60,000	month's cost of			
8	July	50,000	goods sold	80%		
9			Cost of goods sold			
10			as percent of sales	70%		

	A	B	C	D	E	F
11	Schedule c					
12	Purchases budget			April	May	June
13	Desired ending inventory			= D5 + D8* (D10*B6)	= D5 + D8* (D10*B7)	= D5 + D8* (D10*B8)
14	Plus cost of goods sold			= D10*B5	= D10*B6	= D10*B7
15						
16	Total needed			= D13 + D14	= E13 + E14	= F13 + F14
17	Less beginning inventory			= D4	= D13	= E13
18						
19	Purchases			= D16 − D17	= E16 − E17	= F16 − F17

Exhibit 7-10
The Cooking Hut Company
Purchases Budget Formulas

Now, what if you want to know the effect on budgeted purchases if the sales forecast is revised upward by 10%? By changing the sales forecasts in spreadsheet Exhibit 7-9, you obtain a nearly instantaneous revision of the purchases budget. Exhibit 7-12 shows the revised budget based on these alternative sales forecasts. The revised sales forecasts are shown in red type and the revised purchases budget is shown in blue type. We can alter any piece of budget data in the table, and easily view or print out the effects on purchases. This sort of analysis, assessing the effects of varying one of the budget inputs, up or down, is an example of **sensitivity analysis**—the systematic varying of decision input assumptions to examine the effect on the decision. This is one of the most powerful uses of spreadsheets for financial planning models. Note that while you can vary more than one type of budget input at a time, it becomes more difficult to isolate the effects of individual changes once you start making multiple changes simultaneously.

sensitivity analysis
The systematic varying of decision input assumptions to examine the effect on a decision.

We can prepare every schedule, operating budget, and financial budget of the master budget on a spreadsheet, linking the various schedules using the appropriate cell addresses just as we linked the budget input data (Exhibit 7-9) to the purchases budget (Exhibits 7-10 and 7-11). As in the purchases budget, ideally all cells in the master budget are formulas, not numbers. That way, every budget input can be the subject of sensitivity analysis by simply changing the budget data in Exhibit 7-9.

Preparing the master budget on a spreadsheet is time-consuming the first time. However, once the spreadsheet is prepared, relatively little additional time is required to update the budget in subsequent periods, and the benefits from increased planning and sensitivity analysis capabilities are enormous. In order to obtain these benefits, it is essential for the master budget model to be well documented, with all assumptions described either within the spreadsheet or in a separate document that is readily available to subsequent users.

	A	B	C	D	E	F
11	Schedule c					
12	Purchases budget			April	May	June
13	Desired ending inventory			$64,800	$53,600	$48,000
14	Plus cost of goods sold			35,000	56,000	42,000
15						
16	Total needed			99,800	109,600	90,000
17	Less beginning inventory			48,000	64,800	53,600
18						
19	Purchases			$51,800	$44,800	$36,400

Exhibit 7-11
The Cooking Hut Company
Purchases Budget

	A	B	C	D	E	F
1	Budgeted data					
2	Sales forecasts		Other information			
3						
4	March (actual)	$40,000	Beginning inventory	$48,000		
5	April	55,000	Desired ending inventory:			
			Base amount	$20,000		
6	May	88,000	Plus percent of next			
7	June	66,000	month's cost of			
8	July	55,000	goods sold	80%		
9			Cost of goods sold			
10			as percent of sales	70%		
11	Schedule c					
12	Purchases budget			April	May	June
13	Desired ending inventory			$ 69,280	$ 56,960	$50,800
14	Plus cost of goods sold			38,500	61,600	46,200
15						
16	Total needed			107,780	118,560	97,000
17	Less beginning inventory			48,000	69,280	56,960
18						
19	Purchases			$ 59,780	$ 49,280	$40,040

Exhibit 7-12
The Cooking Hut Company
Purchases Budget

Accounting Vocabulary

activity-based budget (ABB), p. 289
budget padding, p. 274
budgetary slack, p. 274
capital budget, p. 277
cash budget, p. 283
continuous budget, p. 277

financial budget, p. 277
financial planning model, p. 290
functional budgeting, p. 289
long-range plan, p. 277
master budget, p. 277
operating budget, p. 277
participative budgeting, p. 274

profit plan, p. 277
rolling budget, p. 277
sales budget, p. 276
sales forecast, p. 276
sensitivity analysis, p. 293
strategic plan, p. 277
zero-base budget, p. 272

MyAccountingLab # Fundamental Assignment Material

Special note: Problems 7-A1 and Problems 7-B1 provide single-problem reviews of most of the chapter topics. Those readers who prefer to concentrate on the fundamentals in smaller chunks should consider any of the other problems.

7-AI Prepare Master Budget

You are the new manager of the local GreatBuy Electronics store. Top management of GreatBuy Electronics is convinced that management training should include the active participation of store managers in the budgeting process. You have been asked to prepare a complete master budget for your store for June, July, and August. All accounting is done centrally so you have no expert help on the premises. In addition, tomorrow the branch manager and the assistant controller will be here to examine your work; at that time, they will assist you in formulating the final budget document. The idea is to have you prepare the initial budget on your own so that you gain more confidence about accounting matters. You want to make a favorable impression on your superiors, so you gather the financial statement and sales data as of May 31, 20X8, on the top of the next page.

Credit sales are 70% of total sales. Seventy percent of each credit account is collected in the month following the sale and the remaining 30% is collected in the subsequent month. Assume that bad debts are negligible and can be ignored. The accounts receivable on May 31 are the result of the credit sales for April and May:

$$(.30 \times .70 \times \$130,000) + (1.0 \times .70 \times \$130,000) = \$118,300.$$

Cash	$ 6,600	Recent and Projected Sales	
Inventory	151,200	April	$130,000
Accounts receivable	118,300	May	130,000
Net furniture and fixtures	52,000	June	240,000
Total assets	$328,100	July	170,000
Accounts payable	$156,200	August	170,000
Owners' equity	171,900	September	120,000
Total liabilities and owners' equities	$328,100		

The policy is to acquire enough inventory each month to equal the following month's projected cost of goods sold. All purchases are paid for in the month following purchase.

The average gross profit on sales is 37%. Salaries, wages, and commissions average 24% of sales; all other variable expenses are 3% of sales. Fixed expenses for rent, property taxes, and miscellaneous payroll and other items are $9,000 monthly. Assume that these variable and fixed expenses require cash disbursements each month. Depreciation is $1,000 monthly.

In June, $5,000 is going to be disbursed for fixtures acquired and recorded in furniture and fixtures in May. The May 31 balance of accounts payable includes this amount.

Assume that a minimum cash balance of $4,000 is to be maintained. Also assume that all borrowings are effective at the beginning of the month and all repayments are made at the end of the month of repayment. Interest is compounded and added to the outstanding balance each month, but interest is paid only at the ends of months when principal is repaid. The interest rate is 9% per year; round interest computations and interest payments to the nearest dollar. Interest payments may be any dollar amount, but all borrowing and repayments of principal are made in multiples of $1,000.

1. Prepare a budgeted income statement for the coming June–August quarter, a cash budget for each of the 3 months, and a budgeted balance sheet for August 31, 20X8. All operations are evaluated on a before-income-tax basis, so income taxes may be ignored here.
2. Explain why there is a need for a bank loan and what operating sources supply cash for repaying the bank loan.

7-B1 Prepare Master Budget

Flying Fish Kite Company, a small Woy Woy, Australia, firm that sells kites on the Web, wants a master budget for the 3 months beginning January 1, 20X2. It desires an ending minimum cash balance of $15,000 each month. Sales are forecasted at an average wholesale selling price of $14 per kite. Merchandise costs average $5 per kite. All sales are on credit, payable within 30 days, but experience has shown that 40% of current sales are collected in the current month, 10% in the next month, and 50% in the month thereafter. Bad debts are negligible.

In January, Flying Fish Kite is beginning just-in-time (JIT) deliveries from suppliers, which means that purchases will equal expected sales. On January 1, purchases will cease until inventory decreases to $22,000, after which time purchases will equal sales. Purchases during any given month are paid in full during the following month.

Monthly operating expenses are as follows:

Wages and salaries	$80,000
Insurance expired	450
Depreciation	900
Miscellaneous	4,000
Rent	$500/month + 5% of quarterly sales over $50,000

Cash dividends of $2,400 are to be paid quarterly, beginning January 15, and are declared on the fifteenth of the previous month. All operating expenses are paid as incurred, except insurance, depreciation, and rent. Rent of $500 is paid at the beginning of each month, and the additional 5% of sales is settled quarterly on the tenth of the month following the end of the quarter. The next rent settlement date is January 10.

The company plans to buy some new fixtures for $4,000 cash in March.

Money can be borrowed and repaid in multiples of $2,000. Management wants to minimize borrowing and repay rapidly. Simple interest of 9% per annum is computed monthly but paid when the principal is repaid. Assume that borrowing occurs at the beginning, and repayments at the end, of the months in question. Compute interest to the nearest dollar.

Assets as of December 31, 20X1		Liabilities and Owners' Equities as of December 31, 20X1	
Cash	$ 30,000	Accounts payable	$151,500
Accounts receivable	180,600	(merchandise)	
Inventory*	153,000	Dividends payable	2,400
Unexpired insurance	5,400	Rent payable	27,950
Fixed assets, net	62,000	Owners' equity	249,150
	$431,000		$431,000

*November 30 inventory balance = $59,000.

Recent and forecasted sales:

October	$280,000	December	$161,000	February	$413,000	April	$280,000
November	168,000	January	378,000	March	273,000		

1. Prepare a master budget including a budgeted income statement, balance sheet, cash budget, and supporting schedules for the months January–March 20X2.
2. Explain why there is a need for a bank loan and what operating sources provide the cash for the repayment of the bank loan.

MyAccountingLab ## Additional Assignment Material

QUESTIONS

7-1 What are the major benefits of budgeting?

7-2 Is budgeting used primarily for scorekeeping, attention directing, or problem solving?

7-3 How do strategic planning, long-range planning, and budgeting differ?

7-4 "I oppose continuous budgets because they provide a moving target. Managers never know at what to aim." Discuss.

7-5 Why is it important to align performance goals of the company and the system used to evaluate and reward employees?

7-6 Explain the cycle of bias by lower-level managers and bias-adjustment by upper-level managers that can spiral out of control and result in meaningless budgets.

7-7 What are the incentives for inappropriate behaviors to *increase* reported profit when it appears that profits are likely to fall just short of a manager's bonus target?

7-8 Why is there an incentive for a manager to inappropriately *reduce* reported profit when it appears that profits are likely to be above the upper limit of a manager's bonus range?

7-9 Why is budgeted performance better than past performance as a basis for judging actual results?

7-10 "Budgets are okay in relatively certain environments. But everything changes so quickly in the electronics industry that budgeting is a waste of time." Comment on this statement.

7-11 "Budgeting is an unnecessary burden on many managers. It takes time away from important day-to-day problems." Do you agree? Explain.

7-12 Why is the sales forecast the starting point for budgeting?

7-13 What factors influence the sales forecast?

7-14 Differentiate between an operating budget and a financial budget.

7-15 Distinguish between operating expenses and disbursements for operating expenses.

7-16 What is the principal objective of a cash budget?

7-17 "Education and salesmanship are key features of budgeting." Explain.

7-18 What are the main differences between functional and activity-based budgets?

7-19 "Financial planning models guide managers through the budget process so that managers do not really need to understand budgeting." Do you agree? Explain.

7-20 Study Appendix 7. "I cannot be bothered with setting up my monthly budget on a spreadsheet. It just takes too long to be worth the effort." Comment.

7-21 Study Appendix 7. How do spreadsheets aid the application of sensitivity analysis?

CRITICAL THINKING EXERCISES

7-22 Budgets as Limitations on Spending
Many nonprofit organizations use budgets primarily to limit spending. Why does this limit the effectiveness of budgets?

7-23 Sales Personnel and Budgeting
The sales budget is the foundation of the entire master budget. How do sales personnel help formulate the budget? Compare the role of sales personnel to that of a central staff function, such as market research.

7-24 Master Budgets for Research and Development
The text focuses on budgets for organizations that have revenues and expenses. Suppose you were the manager of a research and development division of a biotech company that has no revenue. How would budgets be helpful to you?

7-25 Production Budgets and Performance Evaluation
The Akron plant of American Tire Company prepares an annual master budget each November for the following year. At the end of each year, it compares the actual costs incurred to the budgeted costs. How can American Tire get employees to accept the budget and strive to meet or beat the budgeted costs?

EXERCISES

7-26 Fill In the Blanks
Enter the word or phrase that best completes each sentence.

1. The financial budget process includes the following budgets:
   a. _____
   b. _____
   c. _____
2. The master budget process usually begins with the _____ budget.
3. A(n) _____ budget is a plan that is revised monthly or quarterly, dropping one period and adding another.
4. Strategic planning sets the _____.

7-27 Cash Budgeting
Blake and Anna Carlson are preparing a plan to submit to venture capitalists to fund their business, Music Masters. The company plans to spend $380,000 on equipment in the first quarter of 20X7. Salaries and other operating expenses (paid as incurred) will be $35,000 per month beginning in January 20X7 and will continue at that level thereafter. The company will receive its first revenues in January 20X8, with cash collections averaging $30,000 per month for all of 20X8. In January 20X9, cash collections are expected to increase to $100,000 per month and continue at that level thereafter.

   Assume that the company needs enough funding to cover all its cash needs until cash receipts start exceeding cash disbursements. How much venture capital funding should Blake and Anna seek?

7-28 Purchases and Cost of Goods Sold
Popeil Products, a wholesaler of fishing equipment, budgeted the following sales for the indicated months:

	June 20X8	July 20X8	August 20X8
Sales on account	$1,850,000	$1,920,000	$1,910,000
Cash sales	130,000	156,000	274,000
Total sales	$1,980,000	$2,076,000	$2,184,000

All merchandise is marked up to sell at its invoice cost plus 20%. Target merchandise inventories at the beginning of each month are 25% of that month's projected cost of goods sold.

1. Compute the budgeted cost of goods sold for the month of June 20X8.
2. Compute the budgeted merchandise purchases for July 20X8.

7-29 Purchases and Sales Budgets
All sales of Tracy's Jeans and Uniforms (TJU) are made on credit. Sales are billed twice monthly, on the fifth of the month for the last half of the prior month's sales and on the twentieth of the month for the first half of the current month's sales. For accounts paid within the first 10 days after the billing date, TJU gives customers a 2% discount; otherwise the full amount is due within 30 days of the

billing date, and customers that do not pay within the 10-day discount period generally wait the full 30 days before making payment. Based on past experience, the collection experience of accounts receivable is as follows:

Within the 10-day discount period	70%
At 30 days after billing	28%
Uncollectible	2%

Sales for May 20X8 were $790,000. The forecast sales for the next 4 months are as follows:

June	$810,000
July	990,000
August	940,000
September	660,000

TJU's average markup on its products is 40% of the sales price.

TJU purchases merchandise for resale to meet the current month's sales demand and to maintain a desired monthly ending inventory of 25% of the next month's cost of goods sold. All purchases are on credit. TJU pays for one-half of a month's purchases in the month of purchase and the other half in the month following the purchase.

All sales and purchases occur uniformly throughout the month.

1. How much cash can TJU plan to collect from accounts receivable collections during July 20X8?
2. Compute the budgeted dollar value of TJU inventory on May 31, 20X8.
3. How much merchandise should TJU plan to purchase during June 20X8?
4. How much should TJU budget in August 20X8 for cash payments for merchandise purchased?

7-30 Sales Budget

Suppose a lumber yard has the following data:

- Accounts receivable, May 31: (.2 × May sales of $360,000) = $72,000
- Monthly forecasted sales: June, $437,000; July, $441,000; August, $502,000; September, $531,000

Sales consist of 80% cash and 20% credit. All credit accounts are collected in the month following the sales. Uncollectible accounts are negligible and may be ignored.

Prepare a sales budget schedule and a cash collections budget schedule for June, July, and August.

7-31 Sales Budget

A Sendai clothing wholesaler was preparing its sales budget for the first quarter of 20X8. Forecast sales are as follows (All values are in thousands of yen).

January	¥203,000
February	¥227,000
March	¥248,000

Sales are 40% cash and 60% on credit. Fifty-five percent of the credit accounts are collected in the month of sale, 35% in the month following the sale, and 10% in the following month. No uncollectible accounts are anticipated. Accounts receivable at the beginning of 20X8 are ¥82,950 (10% of November credit sales of ¥150,000 and 45% of December credit sales of ¥151,000).

Prepare a schedule showing sales and cash collections for January, February, and March, 20X8.

7-32 Cash Collection Budget

Northwest Equipment offers a 3% discount to customers who pay cash at the time of sale and a 2% discount to customers who pay within the first 10 days of the month after sale. Past experience shows that cash collections from customers tend to occur in the following pattern:

Cash collected at time of sale	55%
Collected within cash discount period in first 10 days of month after sale	15
Collected after cash discount period in first month after month of sale	10
Collected after cash discount period in second month after month of sale	15
Never collected	5

Compute the total cash budgeted to be collected in March if sales forecasts are $370,000 for January, $420,000 for February, and $460,000 for March.

7-33 Purchases Budget

Green Lighting Supply plans inventory levels (at cost) at the end of each month as follows: May, $271,000; June, $226,000; July, $209,000; and August, $241,000.

Sales are expected to be June, $449,000; July, $359,000; and August, $306,000. Cost of goods sold is 65% of sales.

Purchases in April were $258,000 and in May they were $188,000. Payments for each month's purchases are made as follows: 15% during that month, 70% the next month, and the final 15% the next month.

Prepare budget schedules for June, July, and August for purchases and for disbursements for purchases.

7-34 Purchases Budget

Leimersheim GmbH has adopted the following policies regarding merchandise purchases and inventory. At the end of any month, the inventory should be €15,000 plus 90% of the cost of goods to be sold during the following month. The cost of merchandise sold averages 60% of sales. Purchase terms are generally net, 30 days. A given month's purchases are paid as follows: 20% during that month and 80% during the following month.

Purchases in May had been €150,000 and the inventory on May 31 was higher than planned at €230,000. The manager was upset because the inventory was too high. Sales are expected to be June, €300,000; July, €290,000; August, €340,000; and September, €400,000.

1. Compute the amount by which the inventory on May 31 exceeded the company's policies.
2. Prepare budget schedules for June, July, and August for purchases and for disbursements for purchases.

7-35 Cash Budget

Consider the budgeted income statement for Carlson Company for June 20X4 in Exhibit 7-13.

The cash balance, May 31, 20X4, is $15,000.

Sales proceeds are collected as follows: 80% the month of sale, 10% the second month, and 10% the third month.

Accounts receivable are $44,000 on May 31, 20X4, consisting of $20,000 from April sales and $24,000 from May sales.

Accounts payable on May 31, 20X4, are $145,000.

Carlson Company pays 25% of purchases during the month of purchase and the remainder during the following month.

All operating expenses requiring cash are paid during the month of recognition, except that insurance and property taxes are paid annually in December for the forthcoming year.

Prepare a cash budget for June. Confine your analysis to the given data. Ignore income taxes.

Exhibit 7-13

Carlson Company
Budgeted Income Statement for the Month Ended June 30, 20X4 (in thousands)

Sales		$290
Inventory, May 31	$ 50	
Purchases	192	
Available for sale	242	
Inventory, June 30	40	
Cost of goods sold		202
Gross margin		$ 88
Operating expenses		
Wages	$ 36	
Utilities	5	
Advertising	10	
Depreciation	1	
Office expenses	4	
Insurance and property taxes	3	59
Operating income		$ 29

PROBLEMS

7-36 Cash Budget

Daniel Merrill is the manager of an airport gift shop, Merrill News and Gifts. From the following data, Mr. Merrill wants a cash budget showing expected cash receipts and disbursements for the month of April, and the cash balance expected as of April 30, 20X7.

- Planned cash balance, March 31, 20X7: $100,000
- Customer receivables as of March 31: $530,000 total, $80,000 from February sales, $450,000 from March sales
- Accounts payable, March 31: $460,000
- Merchandise purchases for April: $450,000, 40% paid in month of purchase, 60% paid in next month
- Payrolls due in April: $90,000
- Other expenses for April, payable in April: $45,000
- Accrued taxes for April, payable in June: $7,500
- Bank note due April 10: $90,000 plus $7,200 interest
- Depreciation for April: $2,100
- Two-year insurance policy due April 14 for renewal: $1,500, to be paid in cash
- Sales for April: $1,000,000, half collected in month of sale, 40% in next month, 10% in third month

Prepare the cash budget for the month ending April 30, 20X7.

7-37 Cash Budget

Prepare a statement of estimated cash receipts and disbursements for October 20X7 for the Herbal Magic Company, which sells one product, herbal soap, by the case. On October 1, 20X7, part of the trial balance showed the following:

	DR	CR
Cash	$ 5,000	
Accounts receivable	15,620	
Allowance for bad debts		$2,100
Merchandise inventory	12,240	
Accounts payable, merchandise		7,280

The company pays for its purchases within 10 days of purchase, so assume that one-third of the purchases of any month are due and paid for in the following month.

The cost of the merchandise purchased is $12 per case. At the end of each month, it is desired to have an inventory equal in units to 60% of the following month's sales in units.

Sales terms include a 3% discount if payment is made by the end of the calendar month. Past experience indicates that 70% of sales will be collected during the month of the sale, 20% in the following calendar month, 5% in the next following calendar month, and the remaining 5% will be uncollectible. The company's fiscal year begins August 1.

Unit selling price	$ 22
August actual sales	$ 8,800
September actual sales	44,000
October estimated sales	37,400
November estimated sales	19,800
Total sales expected in the fiscal year	$528,000

Exclusive of bad debts, total budgeted selling and general administrative expenses for the fiscal year are estimated at $84,600, of which $27,000 is fixed expense (which includes a $12,900 annual depreciation charge). The Herbal Magic Company incurs these fixed expenses uniformly throughout the year. The balance of the selling and general administrative expenses varies with sales. Expenses are paid as incurred.

7-38 Budgeting at Intercontinental

Intercontinental has several hotels and resorts in the South Pacific. For one of these hotels, management expects occupancy rates to be 95% in December, January, and February; 85% in November, March, and April; and 70% the rest of the year. This hotel has 300 rooms and the average room rental is $250 per night. Of this, on average 10% is received as a deposit the month before the stay, 60% is received in the month of the stay, and 28% is collected the month after. The remaining 2% is never collected.

Most of the costs of running the hotel are fixed. The variable costs are only $30 per occupied room per night. Fixed salaries (including benefits) run $400,000 per month, depreciation is $350,000 a month, other fixed operating costs are $120,000 per month, and interest expense is $600,000 per month. Variable costs and salaries are paid in the month they are incurred, depreciation is recorded at the end of each quarter, other fixed operating costs are paid as incurred, and interest is paid semi-annually each June and December.

1. Prepare a monthly cash budget for this Intercontinental hotel for the entire year. For simplicity, assume that there are 30 days in each month.
2. How much would the hotel's annual profit increase if occupancy rates increased by 5% during the off-season (that is, from 70% to 75% in each of the months from May–October)?

7-39 Activity-Based Budgeting

A recent directive from Laura Jensen, CEO of Hermantown Manufacturing, had instructed each department to cut its costs by 15%. The traditional functional budget for the shipping and receiving department was as follows:

Salaries, four employees at $63,000	$252,000
Benefits at 10%	50,400
Depreciation, straight-line basis	114,000
Supplies	65,100
Overhead at 35% of above costs	168,525
Total	$650,025

Therefore, the shipping and receiving department needed to find $97,504 to cut.

Janice Starke, a recent MBA graduate, was asked to pare $97,504 from the shipping and receiving department's budget. As a first step, she recast the traditional budget into an activity-based budget.

Receiving, 620,000 pounds	$139,500
Shipping, 404,000 boxes	303,000
Handling, 11,200 moves	168,000
Record keeping, 65,000 transactions	39,525
Total	$650,025

1. What actions might Starke suggest to attain a $97,504 budget cut? Why would these be the best actions to pursue?
2. Which budget helped you most in answering number 1? Explain.

7-40 Budgeting, Behavior, and Ethics

Mathew Philp, president of North Idaho Mining, Ltd., has made budgets a major focus for managers. Making budgets was such an important goal that the only two managers who had missed their budgets in 20X7 (by 2% and 4%, respectively) had been summarily fired. This caused all managers to be wary when setting their 20X8 budgets.

The Red Mountain division of North Idaho Mining had the following results for 20X7:

Sales, 1.6 million pounds at $.95/pound	$1,520,000
Variable costs	880,000
Fixed costs, primarily depreciation	450,000
Pretax profit	$ 190,000

Molly Stark, general manager of Red Mountain, received a memo from Philp that contained the following:

We expect your profit for 20X8 to be at least $209,000. Prepare a budget showing how you plan to accomplish this.

Stark was concerned because the market had recently softened. Her market research staff forecast that sales would be at or below the 20X7 level, and prices would likely be between $.92 and $.94 per pound. Her manufacturing manager reported that most of the fixed costs were committed and there were few efficiencies to be gained in the variable costs. He indicated that perhaps a 2% savings in variable costs might be achievable but certainly no more.

1. Prepare a budget for Stark to submit to headquarters. What dilemmas does Stark face in preparing this budget?
2. What problems do you see in the budgeting process at North Idaho Mining?
3. Suppose Stark submitted a budget showing a $209,000 profit. It is now late in 20X8, and she has had a good year. Despite an industry-wide decline in sales, Red Mountain's sales matched last year's 1.6 million pounds, and the average price per pound was $.945, nearly at last year's level and well above that forecast. Variable costs were cut by 2% through extensive efforts. Still, profit projections were more than $9,000 below budget. Stark was concerned for her job so she approached the controller and requested that depreciation schedules be changed. By extending the lives of some equipment for 2 years, depreciation in 20X8 would be reduced by $15,000. Estimating the economic lives of equipment is difficult, and it would be hard to prove that the old lives were better than the new proposed lives. What should the controller do? What ethical issues does this proposal raise?

7-41 Spreadsheets and Sensitivity Analysis of Income Statement

Study Appendix 7. A Speedy-Mart Store in Northcenter Mall has the following budgeted sales, which are uniform throughout the month:

May	$450,000
June	375,000
July	330,000
August	420,000

Cost of goods sold averages 70% of sales, and merchandise is purchased and paid for essentially as needed. Employees earn fixed salaries of $22,000 monthly and commissions of 10% of the current month's sales, paid as earned. Other expenses are rent, $6,000, paid on the first of each month for that month's occupancy; miscellaneous expenses, 6% of sales, paid as incurred; insurance, $450 per month, from a 1-year policy that was paid for on January 2; and depreciation, $2,850 per month.

1. Using spreadsheet software, prepare a table of budget data for the Speedy-Mart Store.
2. Continue the spreadsheet in number 1 to prepare budget schedules for (a) disbursements for operating expenses and (b) operating income for June, July, and August.
3. Adjust the budget data appropriately for each of the following scenarios independently and recompute operating income using the spreadsheet:
   a. A sales promotion that will cost $30,000 in May could increase sales in each of the following 3 months by 5%.
   b. Eliminating the sales commissions and increasing employees' salaries to $52,500 per month could decrease sales thereafter by a net of 2%.

7-42 Spreadsheets and Sensitivity Analysis of Operating Expenses

Study Appendix 7. The high definition LCD division (HDLD) of Fisher Displays produces LCD TV displays. The displays are assembled from purchased components. The costs (value) added by HDLD are indirect costs, which include assembly labor, packaging, and shipping. HDLD produces two sizes of displays: 42 and 50″. Cost behavior of HDLD is as follows:

	Fixed Cost/Month	Variable Cost
Purchased components		
50″ Displays		$80 per component
42″ Displays		55 per component
Assembly labor	$40,000	16 per component
Packaging	8,000	4 per display
Shipping	5,000	2 per display

Both displays require three components per display. Therefore, the total cost of components for 50″ displays is $240 and for 42″ displays is $165. HDLD uses a 6-month continuous budget that is revised monthly. Sales forecasts reflect the expectation that unit sales of 42″ displays will be 25% higher than unit sales of 50″ displays. Sales forecasts for the next 8 months are as follows:

	50″ Displays	42″ Displays
October	3,200 units	4,000 units
November	2,400	3,000
December	5,600	7,000
January	3,200	4,000
February	3,200	4,000
March	2,400	3,000
April	2,400	3,000
May	2,800	3,500

Treat each of the following events in succession.

1. Use spreadsheet software to prepare a table of budgeting information and an operating expense budget for HDLD for October–March. Prepare a spreadsheet that can be revised easily for succeeding months in parts 2 and 3.
2. October's actual sales were 2,800 50″ displays and 3,600 42″displays. This outcome has caused HDLD to revise its sales forecasts downward by 10%. Revise the operating expense budget for November–April.
3. At the end of November, HDLD decides that the proportion of 50″ to 42″ displays is changing. Unit sales of 42″ displays are expected to be 50% higher than unit sales of 50″ displays sales. Expected sales of 50″ displays are unchanged from number 2. Revise the operating expense budget for December–May.

CASES

7-43 Comprehensive Cash Budgeting

Christine Morrison, treasurer of Salt Lake Light Opera (SLLO), was preparing a loan request to the South Utah National Bank in December 20X4. The loan was necessary to meet the cash needs of the SLLO for year 20X5. In a few short years, the SLLO had established itself as a premier opera company. In addition to its regular subscription series, it started a series for new composers and offered a very popular holiday production. The holiday production was the most financially successful of the SLLO's activities, providing a base to support innovative productions that were artistically important to the SLLO but did not usually succeed financially.

Exhibit 7-14
Salt Lake Light Opera
Balance Sheets as of December 31 (in thousands of dollars)

	20X2	20X3	20X4
Assets			
Cash	$2,688	$ 229	$ 208
Accounts receivable	2,942	3,372	4,440
Supplies inventory	700	700	500
Total current assets	$6,330	$4,301	$ 5,148
Plant and equipment	2,643	4,838	5,809
Total assets	$8,973	$9,139	$10,957
Liabilities and Equities			
Bank loan	$ 0	$ 0	$ 1,620*
Accounts payable	420	720	780
Accrued payroll expenses	472	583	646
Mortgage, current	250	250	250
Total current liabilities	$1,142	$1,553	$ 3,296
Other payables	270		
Mortgage payable, long-term	3,750	3,500	3,250
Net assets†	3,811	4,086	4,411
Total liabilities and equities	$8,973	$9,139	$10,957

*Includes $32,000 of accrued interest.
†The "Net assets" account for a nonprofit organization is similar to "Stockholders' equity" for a corporation.

Exhibit 7-15

Salt Lake Light Opera

Income Statements for the Year Ended December 31 (in thousands of dollars)

	20X2	20X3	20X4
Ticket sales	$3,303	$4,060	$5,263
Contributions	1,041	1,412	1,702
Grants and other revenues	1,202	1,361	1,874
Total revenues	$5,546	$6,833	$8,839
Expenses*			
Production	$4,071	$4,805	$6,307
Operations	271	332	473
Public relations and community development	1,082	1,421	1,734
Total expenses	$5,424	$6,558	$8,514
Excess of revenues over expenses	$ 122	$ 275	$ 325

*Expenses include depreciation of $355, $370, and $470 and general and administrative expenses of $1,549, $1,688, and $2,142 in the years 20X2, 20X3, and 20X4, respectively.

In total, the SLLO had done well financially, as shown in Exhibits 7-14 and 7-15. Its profitable operations had enabled it to build its own building and generally acquire a large number of assets. It had at least broken even every year since its incorporation, and management anticipates continued profitable operations. The Corporate Community for the Arts in Salt Lake and several private foundations had made many grants to the SLLO, and such grants are expected to continue. Most recently, the largest bank in town had agreed to sponsor the production of a new opera by a local composer. The SLLO's director of development, Harlan Wayne, expected such corporate sponsorships to increase in the future.

To provide facilities for the Opera's anticipated growth, SLLO began work on an addition to its building 2 years ago. The new facilities are intended primarily to support the experimental offerings that were becoming more numerous. The capital expansion was to be completed in 20X5; all that remained was acquisition and installation of lighting, sound equipment, and other new equipment to be purchased in 20X5.

SLLO had borrowed working capital from South Utah National Bank for the past several years. To qualify for the loans, the SLLO had to agree to the following:

1. Completely pay off the loan for 1 month during the course of the year.
2. Maintain cash and accounts receivable balances equal to (or greater than) 120% of the loan.
3. Maintain a compensating cash balance of $200,000 at all times.

In the past, the SLLO has had no problem meeting these requirements. However, in 20X4 the SLLO had been unable to reduce the loan to zero for an entire month. Although South Utah continued to extend the needed credit, the loan manager expressed concern over the situation. She asked for a quarterly cash budget to justify the financing needed for 20X5. Ms. Morrison began to assemble the data needed to prepare such a budget.

SLLO received revenue from three main sources: ticket sales, contributions, and grants. Ms. Morrison formed Exhibit 7-16 to calculate the accounts receivable balance for each of these sources for 20X5. She assumed that SLLO would continue its normal practices for collecting pledges and grant revenues.

	Ticket Sales		Contributions		Grants	
	Revenues	End of Quarter Receivables	Revenues	End of Quarter Receivables	Revenues	End of Quarter Receivables
First Quarter	$ 852	$2,795	$ 75	$ 794	$ 132	$ 1,027
Second Quarter	1,584	3,100	363	888	448	1,130
Third Quarter	2,617	3,407	1,203	1,083	1,296	1,240
Fourth Quarter	1,519	3,683	442	1,170	528	1,342

Exhibit 7-16

Salt Lake Light Opera

Estimated Quarterly Revenues and End of Quarter Receivables for the Year Ended December 31, 20X5 (in thousands of dollars)

Most expenses were constant from month to month. An exception was supplies, which were purchased twice a year in December and June. In 20X5, SLLO expects to purchase $200,000 of supplies in June and $700,000 in December on terms of net, 30 days. The supplies inventory at the end of December was expected to be $600,000. Depreciation expense of $500,000 was planned for 20X5, and other expenses were expected to run at a steady rate of $710,000 a month throughout the year, of which $700,000 was payroll costs. Salaries and wages were paid on the Monday of the first week following the end of the month. The remaining $10,000 of other expenses were paid as incurred.

The major portion of the new equipment to be installed in 20X5 was to be delivered in September; payments totaling $400,000 would be made in four equal monthly installments beginning in September. In addition, small equipment purchases are expected to run $20,000 per month throughout the year. They will be paid for on delivery.

In late 20X2, SLLO had borrowed $4 million (classified as a mortgage payable) from Farmers' Life Insurance Company. The SLLO is repaying the loan over 16 years, in equal principal payments in June and December of each year. Interest at 8% annually is also paid on the unpaid balance on each of these dates. Total interest payments for 20X5, according to Ms. Morrison's calculations, would be $275,000.

Interest on the working capital loan from South Utah National Bank was at an annual rate of 10%. Interest is accrued quarterly but paid annually; payment for 20X4's interest would be made on January 10, 20X5, and that for 20X5's interest would be made on January 10, 20X6. Working capital loans are taken out on the first day of the quarter that funds are needed, and they are repaid on the last day of the quarter when extra funds are generated. SLLO has tried to keep a minimum cash balance of $200,000 at all times, even if loan requirements do not require it.

1. Compute the cash inflows and outflows for each quarter of 20X5. What are SLLO's loan requirements each quarter?
2. Prepare a projected income statement and balance sheet for SLLO for 20X5.
3. What financing strategy would you recommend for SLLO?

7-44 Cash Budgeting for a Hospital
Highline Hospital provides a wide range of health services in its community. Highline's board of directors has authorized the following capital expenditures:

Intra-aortic balloon pump	$1,400,000
Computed tomography scanner	850,000
X-ray equipment	550,000
Laboratory equipment	1,200,000
Total	$4,000,000

The expenditures are planned for October 1, 20X7, and the board wishes to know the amount of borrowing, if any, necessary on that date. Rebecca Singer, hospital controller, has gathered the following information to be used in preparing an analysis of future cash flows.

Billings, made in the month of service, for 20X7 are shown next, with actual amounts for January–June and estimated amounts for July–December:

Month	Amount Billed
January	$5,300,000
February	5,300,000
March	5,400,000
April	5,400,000
May	5,700,000
June	6,000,000
July (estimated)	5,800,000
August (estimated)	6,200,000
September (estimated)	6,600,000
October (estimated)	6,800,000
November (estimated)	7,000,000
December (estimated)	6,600,000

Ninety percent of Highline billings are made to third parties, such as BlueCross, federal or state governments, and private insurance companies. The remaining 10% of the billings are made directly to patients. Historical patterns of billing collections are as follows:

	Third-Party Billings	Direct-Patient Billings
Month of service	20%	10%
Month following service	50	40
Second month following service	20	40
Uncollectible	10	10

Singer expects the same billing and collection patterns that have been experienced during the first 6 months of 20X7 to continue during the last 6 months of the year. The following schedule presents the purchases that have been made during the past 3 months and the planned purchases for the last 6 months of 20X7.

Month	Amount
April	$1,300,000
May	1,450,000
June	1,450,000
July	1,500,000
August	1,800,000
September	2,200,000
October	2,350,000
November	2,700,000
December	2,100,000

All purchases are made on account, and accounts payable are remitted in the month following the purchase.

- Salaries for each month during the remainder of 20X7 are expected to be $1,800,000 per month plus 20% of that month's billings. Salaries are paid in the month of service.
- Highline's monthly depreciation charges are $150,000.
- Highline incurs interest expenses of $180,000 per month and makes interest payments of $540,000 on the last day of each calendar quarter.
- Endowment fund income is expected to continue to total $210,000 per month.
- Highline has a cash balance of $350,000 on July 1, 20X7, and has a policy of maintaining a minimum end-of-month cash balance of 10% of the current month's purchases.
- Highline Hospital employs a calendar-year reporting period.

1. Prepare a schedule of budgeted cash receipts by month for the third quarter of 20X7.
2. Prepare a schedule of budgeted cash disbursements by month for the third quarter of 20X7.
3. Determine the amount of borrowing, if any, necessary on October 1, 20X7, to acquire the capital items totaling $4,000,000.

7-45 Comprehensive Budgeting for a University

Suppose you are the controller of Nebraska State University. The university president, Lisa Larsson, is preparing for her annual fund-raising campaign for 20X7–20X8. To set an appropriate target, she has asked you to prepare a budget for the academic year. You have collected the following data for the current year (20X6–20X7):

	Undergraduate Division	Graduate Division
Average salary of faculty member	$58,000	$58,000
Average faculty teaching load in semester credit-hours per year (eight undergraduate or six graduate courses)	24	18
Average number of students per class	30	20
Total enrollment (full-time and part-time students)	3,600	1,800
Average number of semester credit-hours carried each year per student	25	20
Full-time load, semester hours per year	30	24

For 20X7–20X8, all faculty and staff will receive a 6% salary increase. Undergraduate enrollment is expected to decline by 2%, but graduate enrollment is expected to increase by 5%.

- The 20X6–20X7 budget for operation and maintenance of facilities was $500,000, which includes $240,000 for salaries and wages. Experience so far this year indicates that the budget is accurate. Salaries and wages will increase by 6% and other operating costs will increase by $12,000 in 20X7–20X8.
- The 20X6–20X7 and 20X7–20X8 budgets for the remaining expenditures are as follows:

	20X6–20X7	20X7–20X8
General administrative	$500,000	$525,000
Library		
Acquisitions	150,000	155,000
Operations	190,000	200,000
Health services	48,000	50,000
Intramural athletics	56,000	60,000
Intercollegiate athletics	240,000	245,000
Insurance and retirement	520,000	560,000
Interest	75,000	75,000

- Tuition is $92 per credit hour. In addition, the state legislature provides $780 per full-time-equivalent student. (A full-time equivalent is 30 undergraduate hours or 24 graduate hours.) Full-tuition scholarships are given to 30 full-time undergraduates and 50 full-time graduate students.
- Revenues other than tuition and the legislative apportionment are as follows:

	20X6–20X7	20X7–20X8
Endowment income	$200,000	$210,000
Net income from auxiliary services	325,000	335,000
Intercollegiate athletic receipts	290,000	300,000

- The chemistry/physics classroom building needs remodeling during the 20X7–20X8 period. Projected cost is $575,000.

1. Prepare a schedule for 20X7–20X8 that shows, by division, (a) expected enrollment, (b) total credit hours, (c) full-time-equivalent enrollment, and (d) number of faculty members needed.
2. Calculate the budget for faculty salaries for 20X7–20X8 by division.
3. Calculate the budget for tuition revenue and legislative apportionment for 20X7–20X8 by division.
4. Prepare a schedule for President Larsson showing the amount that must be raised by the annual fund-raising campaign.

NIKE 10-K PROBLEM

7-46 Budgeting Assumptions at Nike
Examine Nike's 2011 10-K presented in Appendix C. Find the section of the 10-K titled "Results of Operations" showing a condensed income statement for fiscal years 2009, 2010, and 2011. Use the condensed income statement to calculate budgeted net income for fiscal 2012 under the following alternative sets of assumptions. Round amounts to the nearest million dollars.

1. Note that Nike's revenues increased by about 10% last year. Assume cost of sales is 55% of revenue, selling and administrative expense is 32% of revenue, and income tax expense is 25% of income before income taxes. Assume that all costs are variable.
   a. Calculate budgeted net income if revenue increases by 10%.
   b. Calculate budgeted net income if revenue decreases by 10%.

2. Now assume that selling and administrative expense is fixed at the dollar amount shown in the 2011 10-K, but continue to assume cost of sales is 55% of revenue and income tax expense is 25% of income before income taxes.
   a. Calculate budgeted net income if revenue increases by 10%.
   b. Calculate budgeted net income if revenue decreases by 10%.

3. Note that Nike's gross margin was about 45% in fiscal 2011 but was about 1% higher in 2010 and about 1% lower in 2009. Assume revenue for 2012 will be the same as in 2011, selling and administrative expense is a fixed cost equal to the dollar amount shown in the 2011 10-K, and income tax expense is 25% of income before income taxes.
   a. Calculate budgeted net income if the gross margin increases to 46%.
   b. Calculate budgeted net income if the gross margin decreases to 44%.

EXCEL APPLICATION EXERCISE

7-47 Preparing a Cash Budget to Assist Long-Range Planning

Goal: Create an Excel spreadsheet to prepare a cash budget to assist with long-range planning. Use the results to answer questions about your findings.

Scenario: Music Masters has asked you to prepare an analysis of its cash requirements until such time as its forecasted cash receipts begin to exceed its forecasted cash disbursements. The company will use your analysis to determine venture capital funding requests. Additional background information for your spreadsheet appears in Exercise 7-27 on page 297.

When you have completed your spreadsheet, answer the following questions:

1. Based on its stated objective of stopping venture capital funding when cash receipts begin to exceed cash disbursements, in what month/year should Music Masters no longer require venture capital funding? Why?
2. What is the total amount of expenditures Music Masters will incur before its cash receipts begin to exceed its cash disbursements? What is the total amount of venture capital funding that Music Masters should request?
3. Is the amount of venture capital funding that Music Masters should request equal to its total expenditures? If not, why are the amounts different?

Step-by-Step:

1. Open a new Excel spreadsheet.
2. In column A, create a bold-faced heading that contains the following:
   Row 1: Chapter 7 Decision Guideline
   Row 2: Music Masters
   Row 3: Cash Budget for Venture Capital Requirements
   Row 4: Today's Date
3. Merge and center the four heading rows across columns A–F.
4. In row 7, create the following bold-faced, center-justified column headings with a column width of 10.57:
   Column B: 20X7
   Column C: 20X8
   Column D: 20X9
   Column E: 20Y0
   Column F: Total
5. In column A, create the following row headings:
   Row 8: Equipment Purchase
   Row 9: Salaries and Other Operating Expenses
   Row 10: Revenues
   Row 11: Net Cash Requirements

   Note: Adjust column width as necessary.

6. Use data from Exercise 7-27 to enter the amounts for the yearly cash requirements for the three income/expense categories. Use formulas to calculate the appropriate yearly amounts within each category when necessary.

   Hint: Use different signs for the cash receipt (revenue) and cash disbursement (expense) amounts.

7. Use the SUM function to calculate totals for each column in row 11 and for each row in column F.

8. Format amounts in rows 8 and 11 as follows:

> **Number tab:**   Category:
>
> Decimal: 0
>
> Symbol: $

9. Format amounts in Rows 9 and 10 as follows:

> **Number tab:**   Category:
>
> Decimal: 0
>
> Symbol: None

10. Apply top and bottom borders to the amounts in row 11 by clicking the drop-down indicator on the Borders icon from the toolbar. Select the "Top and Double Bottom Border."
11. Save your work, and print a copy for your files.

COLLABORATIVE LEARNING EXERCISE

7-48 Personal Budgeting

Budgeting is useful to many different types of entities, including the individual. Consider an entity that you know well, the college or university student. Form a group of two to six students, and pool the information that you have about what it costs to spend a year as a full-time student.

Prepare a revenue and expense budget for an average prospective full-time student at your college or university. Identify possible sources of revenue and the amount to be received from each. Identify the costs a student is likely to incur during the year. To simplify your analysis, assume that cash disbursements are made immediately for all expenses so the budgeted income statement and cash budget are identical.

When all groups have completed their budgets, compare those budgets. What are the differences? What assumptions led to the differences?

INTERNET EXERCISES

7-49 Carnival Corporation

The budgeting process helps firms to identify sources of revenues and expenses as well as the timing of cash flows. While many parts of the budgeting process are confidential, there are some things that may be identifiable by someone outside the firm who would like to make some potential budget projections for the following year. Consider **Carnival Corporation**, the cruise ship firm. Go to the Carnival Web site at www.carnivalcorp.com.

1. Look at the list of Carnival Corporation's global brands. How many different brand lines operate under the corporation shell? What are they? Visit a couple of the links. Do the brands each offer exactly the same services? Why might the firm have different names for the cruise lines serving different areas?
2. The sales figure is one of the most important pieces of information the firm uses in beginning the planning process. Carnival's sales figure is made up primarily of two parts—the number of passenger cruise days and the price charged for each passenger cruise day. Go to "Investor Relations" and then "Financial Reports." From the list of Annual Reports, open Carnival's annual report (10-K) for the most recent year. Notice the total revenues for the year and then find information about passenger capacity. What is the occupancy percentage?
3. Find the information provided by management about the expected increase in passenger capacity during the coming years. Assuming revenue increases in proportion to passenger capacity, what would be the expected revenue for 2012? Should the firm expect an increase in costs associated with the increase in capacity? When budgeting for these costs, would the costs be proportional to the increase in revenues? Why or why not?
4. The other component in revenue is how much the passenger pays for the cruise. Select one of the cruise line links from the main page. Find the subsequent link that takes you to information about cruise prices. Are prices for the same length cruise always the same? Look at the fine print with respect to the cruise pricing. What does it tell about how the price is determined? Why might the capacity level of the cruise determine the price that is charged for the cruise?

Flexible Budgets and Variance Analysis

LEARNING OBJECTIVES

When you have finished studying this chapter, you should be able to:

1. Identify variances and label them as favorable or unfavorable.

2. Distinguish between flexible budgets and static budgets.

3. Use flexible-budget formulas to construct a flexible budget.

4. Compute and interpret static-budget variances, flexible-budget variances, and sales-activity variances.

5. Understand how the setting of standards affects the computation and interpretation of variances.

6. Compute and interpret price and quantity variances for materials and labor.

7. Compute variable overhead spending and efficiency variances.

8. Compute the fixed-overhead spending variance.

▶ MCDONALD'S

McDonald's is consistently ranked among the world's best-known brands in *BusinessWeek*'s annual ranking of global brands. You can eat a Big Mac under the Golden Arches in more than 115 countries.

With total sales of more than $65 billion, the challenge is to ensure that the taste of each Big Mac is the same at each of the more than 33,000 company-owned, franchised, or affiliated restaurants. How does McDonald's maintain cost and quality control? How does it ensure that each of the nearly 68 million customers it serves daily receives the same quality product? It uses standards, budgets, and variance analysis. For example, the standards for material are the same for hamburgers wherever they are sold—1 bun, 1 hamburger patty, 1 pickle slice, 1/8 tablespoon of dehydrated onion, 1/4 tablespoon mustard, and 1/2 ounce of ketchup. For each of these ingredients management determines variances—differences between the amount actually used and what should have been used given the number and types of sandwiches produced.

McDonald's managers budget sales for each hour during the day. Based on the sales budgeted, they construct a budget for each of the materials that make up their menu. They use the budget for planning (to make sure materials will be available when needed) and control (to evaluate the use of materials). McDonald's applies these planning and control concepts not just to material costs, but also to labor and overhead costs. Further, McDonald's uses budgets for planning and control of revenues, as well as costs. Understanding what went wrong and what went right helps managers plan and manage more effectively in future periods.

McDonald's also uses nonfinancial standards to meet its quality and service goals. Here are three examples: (1) The standard time for a drive-through customer is 310 seconds, from pulling up to the menu board to driving away; (2) employees must destroy cooked meat that is not used in a sandwich within

30 minutes; and (3) once employees make a sandwich and place it in the transfer bin, they must sell it within 10 minutes or throw it away.

This chapter focuses on flexible budgets and variances. Flexible budgets extend the budget developed in Chapter 7 for a single level of activity. Flexible budgets help managers plan and evaluate results for levels of activity other than the level originally planned. Variances are deviations of actual results from expected (or planned) results. Each variance should cause a manager to ask, "Why did results differ from the plan?" Variances are an important evaluation tool that directs management to areas that deserve attention and helps managers identify ways to improve future decisions and results. (For more background on how managers use variances, you might want to review the discussion of management by exception in Chapter 1, page 6.) ∎

© China Foto Press/ZUMA Press/Newscom

Using Budgets and Variances to Evaluate Results

To illustrate how companies use budgets and variances, consider the Dominion Company, a firm in Toronto that manufactures a wheeled, collapsible suitcase carrier popular with airline flight crews. Assume for simplicity that the company produces a single product, sales are equal to production, and inventory levels are zero. Exhibit 8-1 shows the actual results for sales volume of 7,000 units in June 20X1 in column (1); the budgeted amounts for sales volume of 9,000 units in column (2); and the variances, the differences between the first two columns, in column (3).

Using flexible budgets to analyze performance is important to individual McDonald's restaurants, such as this one in Asia, as well as to the company as a whole.

Favorable and Unfavorable Variances

Recall from Chapter 1 that variances are deviations from plans. In this chapter we focus on deviations of profits, revenues, and costs from budgeted amounts. We label profit, revenue, and cost variances as favorable or unfavorable depending on the direction of the effect on profitability. **Favorable profit variances** arise when actual profits exceed budgeted profits.

favorable profit variance
A variance that occurs when actual profit exceeds budgeted profit.

	Actual (1)	Budget @ 9,000 units (2)	Variances (3)
Units	7,000	9,000	2,000 U
Sales	$217,000	$279,000	$62,000 U
Variable costs			
Variable manufacturing costs	$151,270	$189,000	$37,730 F
Shipping costs (selling)	5,000	5,400	400 F
Administrative costs	2,000	1,800	200 U
Total variable costs	$158,270	$196,200	$37,930 F
Contribution margin	$ 58,730	$ 82,800	$24,070 U
Fixed expenses			
Fixed manufacturing costs	$ 37,300	$ 37,000	$ 300 U
Fixed selling and administrative costs	33,000	33,000	—
Total fixed costs	$ 70,300	$ 70,000	$ 300 U
Operating income (loss)	$(11,570)	$ 12,800	$24,370 U

U = Unfavorable cost variances occur when actual costs are more than budgeted costs. Unfavorable revenue (or profit) variances occur when actual revenues (or profits) are less than budgeted.

F = Favorable cost variances occur when actual costs are less than budgeted costs. Favorable revenue (or profit) variances occur when actual revenues (or profits) are more than budgeted.

Exhibit 8-1
Dominion Company
Performance Report Using a Static Budget for the Month Ended June 30, 20X1

unfavorable profit variance

A variance that occurs when actual profit falls below budgeted profit.

favorable revenue variance

A variance that occurs when actual revenue exceeds budgeted revenue.

unfavorable revenue variance

A variance that occurs when actual revenue falls below budgeted revenue.

unfavorable cost variance

A variance that occurs when actual costs exceed budgeted costs.

favorable cost variance

A variance that occurs when actual costs are less than budgeted costs.

Unfavorable profit variances arise when actual profits fall below budgeted profits. Because increases in revenues increase profits, revenue variances work in exactly the same way: Actual revenues that exceed budgeted revenues result in **favorable revenue variances**, and actual revenues that fall short of budgeted revenues result in **unfavorable revenue variances**. However, cost variances work in the opposite way because increases in costs decrease profitability: When actual costs exceed budgeted costs, we have **unfavorable cost variances**; when actual costs are less than budgeted costs, we have **favorable cost variances**. The following chart summarizes these relationships using the abbreviations that we will use for favorable (F) and unfavorable (U) variances.

Favorable (F) Versus Unfavorable (U) Variances

	Profits	Revenues	Costs
Actual > Expected	F	F	U
Actual < Expected	U	U	F

The favorable and unfavorable labels indicate only the directional relationships summarized in the chart above—they do not indicate that the explanation for the variance is necessarily good or bad. For example, spending less than budgeted for maintenance expenditures will create a favorable variance but may nonetheless have adverse effects, especially in later periods when the effects of too-low maintenance began to materialize. As another example, spending less than budgeted on research and development will create a favorable variance but might mean that research expenditures were lower than the optimal level. The important point is that the favorable and unfavorable labels do not, by themselves, indicate whether decisions were good or bad. Rather than basing evaluation of variances only on these labels, managers should determine the explanation for the direction of the relation between actual and expected results and then carefully evaluate the implications of the explanation.

Static Budgets Versus Flexible Budgets

Objective 2

Distinguish between flexible budgets and static budgets.

static budget

A budget that is prepared for only one expected level of activity.

Let's consider two ways to prepare a budget. A budget prepared for only one level of activity is a **static budget**. A budget that adjusts to different levels of activity is a **flexible budget** (sometimes called a **variable budget**). To illustrate these concepts, suppose Dominion Company expects to sell 9,000 units in 20X1. The static budget consists of the revenues, costs, and profits expected at a volume of 9,000 units. However, to prepare for the possibility that volume might be lower than 9,000 units, Dominion Company could prepare a flexible budget that predicts revenues, costs, and profits at lower volumes, say, volumes of 7,000 and 8,000 units. Flexible budgets show the revenues, costs, and profits expected at alternative volumes.

Flexible-Budget Formulas

Objective 3

Use flexible-budget formulas to construct a flexible budget.

To develop a flexible budget, managers use flexible-budget formulas that describe revenue and cost behavior with respect to appropriate cost drivers. The cost functions that we introduced in Chapter 2 and estimated in Chapter 3 are examples of flexible-budget formulas. Exhibit 8-2 shows a graphical version of the flexible-budget formula for Dominion Company based on a

Exhibit 8-2

Dominion Company

Graph of Flexible Budget of Costs

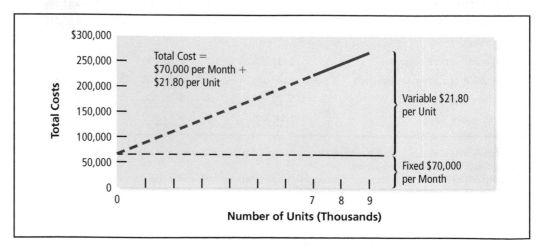

single cost driver, units of output. The solid line between 7,000 and 9,000 units indicates that the relevant range for these flexible-budget formulas is 7,000 to 9,000 units. Within this range, we expect fixed costs to be constant at $70,000 per month, the point where the line meets the vertical axis, and variable costs to be $21.80 per unit, the slope of the line. The dashed line below 7,000 units indicates that this portion of the flexible-budget line is outside the relevant range.

Exhibit 8-3 shows flexible budgets for output levels of 7,000, 8,000, and 9,000 units, respectively. The flexible budgets incorporate effects of changes in activity on each revenue and cost. Note that the static budget is just the flexible budget for the original planned level of activity. Thus, the amounts shown in the budget column in Exhibit 8-1 for sales of 9,000 unit, the static budget, are exactly the same as the amounts in the far right column of Exhibit 8-3, the flexible budget for sales of 9,000 units.

How does the master budget introduced in Chapter 7 relate to static and flexible budgets? The modifier "master" refers to the scope of the budget, not to whether it is static or flexible. Master budgets are comprehensive, encompassing all the components shown in Exhibit 7-2. Flexible budgets can also be comprehensive, although often they are more narrowly focused. The master budgets used in Chapter 7 were static master budgets that assumed one fixed level of volume. However, there is no reason that a company could not prepare a flexible master budget.

Activity-Based Flexible Budgets

Dominion Company's flexible budget in Exhibit 8-3 is based on a single cost driver—units of output. This is an appropriate approach when "units of output" is a plausible and reliable cost driver for all of a company's costs. But what if some of a company's costs are driven by activities such as order processing or setting up for production? A company that has an activity-based costing system with multiple cost drivers, such as the systems described in Chapter 4, will prepare an **activity-based flexible budget** by budgeting costs for each activity using the related cost driver.

Exhibit 8-4 shows an activity-based flexible budget for the Dominion Company. There are four activities: processing, setup, marketing, and administration. For each activity, costs depend on a different cost driver. For example, in Exhibit 8-4 we assume that setup costs are variable with respect to the "number of setups," whereas in Exhibit 8-3 we assumed that the $12,000 of setup costs included in the manufacturing costs of $37,000 are fixed with respect to "units of output." To see why setup costs might vary with respect to the number of setups but not with respect to the number of units, consider the example of setup supplies. Each time employees set up a production run, they use a batch of setup supplies. However, once the run is set up, production of additional units uses no additional setup supplies. Thus, the cost of supplies varies directly with the number of setups (at a cost of $500 per setup) but does not vary directly with the number of units produced.

Compare the traditional flexible budgets (Exhibit 8-3) and the activity-based flexible budgets (Exhibit 8-4). Note that assumptions about fixed and variable costs differ in the two exhibits. Because of differing assumptions about cost behavior, the calculated cost using a single cost driver differs from the calculated cost using multiple activity-based cost drivers.

flexible budget (variable budget)
A budget that adjusts to different levels of activity.

activity-based flexible budget
A budget based on budgeted costs for each activity using the related cost driver.

Exhibit 8-3
Dominion Company
Flexible Budgets

	Flexible-Budget Formula	Flexible Budgets for Various Levels of Sales/Production Activity		
Units		7,000	8,000	9,000
Sales	$ 31.00	$217,000	$248,000	$279,000
Variable costs				
Variable manufacturing costs	$ 21.00	$147,000	$168,000	$189,000
Shipping costs (selling)	.60	4,200	4,800	5,400
Administrative costs	.20	1,400	1,600	1,800
Total variable costs	$ 21.80	$152,600	$174,400	$196,200
Contribution margin	$ 9.20	$ 64,400	$ 73,600	$ 82,800
Fixed costs per month				
Fixed manufacturing costs	$37,000	$ 37,000	$ 37,000	$ 37,000
Fixed selling and administrative costs	33,000	33,000	33,000	33,000
Total fixed costs	$70,000	$ 70,000	$ 70,000	$ 70,000
Operating income (loss)		$ (5,600)	$ 3,600	$ 12,800

Exhibit 8-4

Dominion Company
*Activity-Based Flexible Budget for
the Month Ended June 30, 20X1*

	Budget Formula			
		Units		
Sales in units		7,000	8,000	9,000
Sales in dollars	$31.00/unit	$217,000	$248,000	$279,000
ACTIVITY				
Processing	Cost Driver: Number of Machine Hours (MH)			
Cost-driver level		14,000	16,000	18,000
Variable costs	$10.50/MH	$147,000	$168,000	$189,000
Fixed costs	$13,000	$ 13,000	$ 13,000	$ 13,000
Total costs of processing activity		$160,000	$181,000	$202,000
Setup	Cost Driver: Number of Setups			
Cost-driver level		20	22	24
Variable costs	$500/setup	$ 10,000	$ 11,000	$ 12,000
Fixed costs	$12,000	$ 12,000	$ 12,000	$ 12,000
Total costs of setup activity		$ 22,000	$ 23,000	$ 24,000
Marketing	Cost Driver: Number of Orders			
Cost-driver level		350	400	450
Variable costs	$12.00/order	$ 4,200	$ 4,800	$ 5,400
Fixed costs	$15,000	$ 15,000	$ 15,000	$ 15,000
Total costs of marketing activity		$ 19,200	$ 19,800	$ 20,400
Administration	Cost Driver: Number of Units			
Cost-driver level		7,000	8,000	9,000
Variable costs	$.20/unit	$ 1,400	$ 1,600	$ 1,800
Fixed costs	$18,000	$ 18,000	$ 18,000	$ 18,000
Total costs of administration activity		$ 19,400	$ 19,600	$ 19,800
Total costs		$220,600	$243,400	$266,200
Operating income (loss)		$ (3,600)	$ 4,600	$ 12,800

When should a company use a more sophisticated activity-based flexible budget with multiple cost drivers rather than a simple flexible budget with a single cost driver, such as units of output? When a significant portion of its costs vary with cost drivers other than units of output. For the remainder of this chapter, we return to a simpler flexible budget based on a single cost driver: units of output.

Static-Budget Variances and Flexible-Budget Variances

Objective 4

Compute and interpret static-budget variances, flexible-budget variances, and sales-activity variances.

How should we evaluate the performance of Dominion Company for June 20X1? We can examine variances, which compare actual amounts with budgeted amounts. However, we now have two candidates for "the" budgeted amount: The static budget for the original expected level of output or the flexible budget for the achieved level of output.

STATIC-BUDGET VARIANCE   Let's begin by comparing Dominion Company's actual results with the static budget for a projected sales volume of 9,000 units. Differences between actual results and the static budget for the original planned level of output are **static-budget variances**. Column 2 of Exhibit 8-1 is the static budget for projected sales of 9,000 units. Column 3 shows the static-budget variances. Exhibit 8-1 shows the difference between the actual operating loss of $11,570 and budgeted operating income of $12,800 is a $24,370 U static-budget income variance.

The static-budget variance shows the difference between actual results and the original budgeted amounts for sales of 9,000 units, but does not take into account that the actual level of sales was only

static-budget variance
The difference between actual results and the static budget for the original planned level of output.

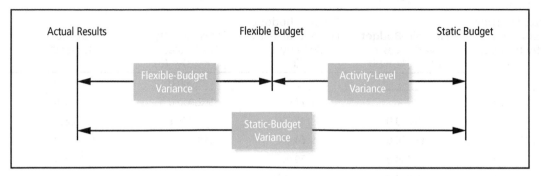

Exhibit 8-5
Relationship Between the Static-Budget Variance and the Flexible-Budget and Activity-Level Variances

7,000 units. When you produce only 7,000 units wouldn't you expect income to be lower than in the static budget for production of 9,000 units? Of course! Therefore, we introduce flexible-budget variances to compare actual results with budgeted results adjusted to reflect the actual volume achieved.

FLEXIBLE-BUDGET VARIANCE   Differences between actual results and the flexible budget for the actual level of output achieved are **flexible-budget variances**. Flexible budget variances reflect how actual results deviate from what was expected given the achieved level of activity. The flexible-budget approach says, "Give me any achieved activity level, and I'll provide a budget tailored to that particular level." For example, when Dominion's sales turn out to be 7,000 units instead of 9,000, the flexible budget shows what income to expect based on the achieved sales level of 7,000 units. Many companies routinely "flex" their budgets to provide a better benchmark for evaluating performance.

flexible-budget variance
The difference between actual results and the flexible budget for the actual level of output achieved.

Integrating Static-Budget, Flexible-Budget, and Sales-Activity Variances

We saw earlier that a static-budget variance is the difference between actual results and the original plan, the static budget. Exhibit 8-5 shows that the static-budget variance is the sum of (1) the difference between actual results and the flexible budget (the flexible-budget variance discussed previously), and (2) the difference between the flexible budget and the static budget— the **activity-level variance**. The activity-level variance describes the budgeted effect of operating at an actual level of activity that is different than the level of activity used to determine the static budget. Therefore, if the actual level of activity is the same as the level in the original, static budget, the activity-level variance will be zero. The flexible-budget variance is the difference between actual results and planned results in the flexible budget for the actual level of activity.

activity-level variances
The differences between the static budget amounts and the amounts in the flexible budget.

The division of static-budget variances into flexible-budget variances and activity-level variances is illustrated for Dominion Company in Exhibit 8-6. The activity-level variances here are **sales-activity variances** because sales is used as the measure of activity level. The flexible budget (column 3) for sales-activity of 7,000 units taken from Exhibit 8-3 (and simplified) provides an explanatory bridge between the static budget (column 5) for sales-activity of 9,000 units and the actual results (column 1). The bottom lines of Exhibit 8-6 summarize the income variances. Note that the sum of the activity-level variance and the flexible-budget variance equals the static-budget variance: $18,400 U + $5,970 U = $24,370 U.

sales-activity variances
The activity-level variances when sales is used as the cost driver.

Making Managerial Decisions

Consider a company that plans to sell 1,000 units for $3 per unit. Budgeted variable costs are $2 per unit, budgeted fixed costs are $700, and the static-budget profit is $300. Suppose the company actually sells 800 units and income is $110. Compute and interpret the static-budget income variance, the sales-activity income variance, and the flexible-budget income variance.

Answer
There is a $190 unfavorable static-budget income variance, the difference between static budgeted profit of $300 and the actual profit of $110. The static-budget variance is the

sum of two components: the sales-activity variance and the flexible-budget variance. The sales-activity income variance is the difference between the static-budgeted profit of $300 for planned production of 1,000 units versus the flexible-budgeted profit of $100 for production of 800 units, a $200 unfavorable variance that indicates the budgeted effect of failing to achieve the original planned level of sales. The flexible-budget income variance is the difference between the flexible-budgeted profit of $100 versus the actual profit of $110, a favorable variance of $10 that indicates that, given the achieved level of sales, the operation was efficient.

	Actual Results at Actual Activity Level* (1)	Flexible-Budget Variances † (2) = (1) − (3)	Flexible Budget For Actual Sales Activity ‡ (3)	Sales-Activity Variances (4) = (3) − (5)	Static Budget* (5)
Units	7,000	—	7,000	2,000 U	9,000
Sales	$ 217,000	—	$217,000	$62,000 U	$279,000
Variable costs	158,270	5,670 U	152,600	43,600 F	196,200
Contribution margin	$ 58,730	$5,670 U	$ 64,400	$18,400 U	$ 82,800
Fixed costs	70,300	300 U	70,000	—	70,000
Operating income	$ (11,570)	$5,970 U	$ (5,600)	$18,400 U	$ 12,800

Total flexible-budget variances
$5,970 U

Total sales-activity variances
$18,400 U

Total static budget variances, $24,370 U

U = Unfavorable. F = Favorable.
*Figures are from Exhibit 8-1.
†Figures are shown in more detail in Exhibit 8-7.
‡Figures are from the 7,000-unit column in Exhibit 8-3.

Exhibit 8-6
Dominion Company
Summary of Performance for the Month Ended June 30, 20X1

Revenue and Cost Variances

Because income is the sum of revenues less costs, we can describe any income variance as the sum of revenue and cost variances. For example, a static-budget income variance can be described as the sum of the static-budget revenue variance and the static-budget cost variances. Similarly, a flexible-budget income variance is the sum of the flexible-budget revenue variance and the flexible-budget cost variances, and an activity-level income variance is the sum of the activity-level revenue variance and the activity-level cost variances.

Sales-Activity Variances

For Dominion Company, we assume that the driver for variable costs in the flexible budget is unit sales volume, so the activity-level variances are sales-activity variances. Dominion Company's sales activity fell 2,000 units short of the planned level. The sales-activity variances (totaling $18,400 U) in the final three columns of Exhibit 8-6 measure the budgeted effect of falling short of the original sales objective. Falling short of the sales target by 2,000 units explains $18,400 of the income shortfall relative to the amount initially budgeted (a $5,600 flexible-budget loss instead of a $12,800 static-budget profit). Figure 8-6 also shows that we can express the sales-activity income variance as the sum of the sales-activity revenue variance and sales-activity cost variances:

Sales-activity income variance = Sales-activity revenue variance
+ Sales-activity variable-cost variance
+ Sales-activity fixed-cost variance
= $62,000 U + $43,600 F + $0
= $18,400 U

Alternatively, we can also derive this $18,400 sales-activity income variance as the shortfall of 2,000 units multiplied by the budgeted contribution margin of $9.20 per unit (from the first column of Exhibit 8-3):

Sales-activity income variance = (Actual units − Static budget units) × Budgeted contribution per unit
= (7,000 − 9,000) × $9.20
= $18,400 unfavorable

Who has responsibility for the sales-activity income variance? Marketing managers usually have the primary responsibility for reaching the sales level specified in the static budget. Many factors can cause variations in sales, including poor production quality and missed delivery schedules. Nevertheless, marketing managers are typically in the best position to explain why actual sales levels differed from plans.

Note that changes in unit prices or unit variable costs do not affect activity-level variances. Why? Only the unit sales volume affects the sales-activity variances because the flexible budget and the static budget use the same budgeted unit prices, unit variable costs, and total fixed costs. The static and flexible budgets differ only due to different assumed levels of activity. Also note that there can never be a sales-activity variance for fixed costs, as long as the budgeted activity levels remain within the relevant range. Why? Because for fixed costs, the total budgeted amounts are the same in the flexible budget and the static budget.

Flexible-Budget Variances

Exhibit 8-6 shows income variances as the sum of revenue and cost variances. The flexible-budget variances are shown in column (2), the difference between actual results in column (1) and the flexible-budget amounts for the actual sales activity in column (3). The flexible-budget income variance is as follows:

Flexible-budget income variance = Actual income − Flexible-budget income (at actual sales level)

$$= (-\$11,570) - (-\$5,600)$$
$$= \$5,970 \text{ U}$$

Column (2) of Exhibit 8-6 shows the $5,970 U flexible-budget income variance is the sum of three variances, the flexible-budget revenue variance (which in this example is $0 because there is no difference between the actual sales price and the flexible-budgeted sales price), a $5,670 U flexible-budget variable-cost variance, and a $300 U flexible-budget fixed-cost variance.

Note that Exhibit 8-1 showed a favorable total variable-cost static-budget variance, yet there is an unfavorable variable-cost flexible-budget variance in Exhibit 8-6. Why is this? Sales fell far short of the static-budget volume of 9,000 units. The favorable static-budget variance of $37,930 in Exhibit 8-1 occurs because actual variable costs to produce 7,000 units were lower than the budgeted costs to produce 9,000 units, the volume projected in the static budget. However, the variable-cost static-budget variance combines two effects, the expected effect of producing fewer units (measured by the activity-level variable-cost variance $43,600 F) and the difference between actual variable costs and the expected costs from the flexible budget for the achieved level of output (measured by the flexible-budget variable-cost variance $5,670 U).

Exhibit 8-7 provides flexible-budget cost variances in even more detail, showing flexible-budget variances for individual variable and fixed manufacturing costs. For example, the $5,670 U variable-cost flexible-budget variance in Exhibit 8-6 is the sum of eight individual variable-cost variances. These eight individual variances net to the overall variance of $5,670 U.

The last column of Exhibit 8-7 provides examples of some possible explanations for Dominion Company's variances. These explanations illustrate our earlier point that you should not assume that the "favorable" and "unfavorable" labels tell you everything you need to know. Instead, always ask questions and look for underlying explanations to be sure you understand why variances occurred and who is responsible. For example, the $400 U variance due to higher than budgeted cleanup costs does not indicate poor performance by the person responsible for cleaning—once the spill had occurred, the decision to clean up the spilled solvent was undoubtedly a good decision. Instead, this variance should be attributed to the person responsible for the spill. Similarly, it is not clear that the $800 U variance due to the use of airfreight is the responsibility of the shipping manager. Could the need for airfreight delivery have been avoided with additional planning and coordination by sales staff? Or by production? Evaluation of management's decisions and who is responsible depends on the answers to questions such as these.

	Actual Costs Incurred	Flexible Budget*	Flexible-Budget Variances†	Possible Explanation
Units	7,000	7,000	—	
Variable costs				
Direct materials	$ 69,920	$ 70,000	$ 80 F	Lower prices but higher usage
Direct labor	61,500	56,000	5,500 U	Higher wage rates and higher usage
Indirect labor	9,100	11,900	2,800 F	Decreased setup time
Idle time	3,550	2,800	750 U	Excessive machine breakdowns
Cleanup time	2,500	2,100	400 U	Cleanup of spilled solvent
Supplies	4,700	4,200	500 U	Higher prices and higher usage
Variable manufacturing costs	$151,270	$147,000	$4,270 U	
Shipping	5,000	4,200	800 U	Use of air freight to meet delivery
Administration	2,000	1,400	600 U	Excessive copying and long-distance calls
Total variable costs	$158,270	$152,600	$5,670 U	
Fixed costs				
Factory supervision	$ 14,700	$ 14,400	$ 300 U	Salary increase
Factory rent	5,000	5,000	—	
Equipment depreciation	15,000	15,000	—	
Other fixed factory costs	2,600	2,600	—	
Fixed manufacturing costs	$ 37,300	$ 37,000	$ 300 U	
Fixed selling and administrative costs	33,000	33,000	—	
Total fixed costs	$ 70,300	$ 70,000	$ 300 U	
Total variable and fixed costs	$228,570	$222,600	$5,970 U	

*From 7,000-unit column of Exhibit 8-3.
†This is a line-by-line breakout of the variances in column 2 of Exhibit 8-6.

Exhibit 8-7
Dominion Company
Cost-Control Performance Report for the Month Ended June 30, 20X1

The Role of Standards in Determining Variances

standard cost
A cost that should be achieved.

expected cost
The cost most likely to be attained.

currently attainable standards
Levels of performance that managers can achieve by realistic levels of effort.

perfection standards (ideal standards)
Expressions of the most efficient performance possible under the best conceivable conditions, using existing specifications and equipment.

Both static-budget variances and flexible-budget variances depend on the costs used in the budget formulas. Budget formula costs are **standard costs**—costs that should be achieved. However, standard costs are defined in different ways by different companies. Many companies set standard cost equal to **expected cost**, the cost that is most likely to be attained. However, other companies use a definition based on **currently attainable standards**—levels of performance that managers can achieve by realistic levels of effort, including allowances for normal defectives, spoilage, waste, and nonproductive time. However, depending on what is considered a "realistic" level of effort and what are "normal" allowances, currently attainable standards can range from easily attainable to extremely difficult to attain. The level at which standards are set will affect the variances generated and the incentives created.

Easily attainable standards will generally lead to favorable variances and, because employees can attain them with little effort, they may not provide much motivation. Extremely difficult-to-attain standards will generally lead to unfavorable variances and also may not motivate employees. The most difficult-to-attain standards are **perfection standards** (also called **ideal standards**). Perfection standards represent the most efficient performance possible under the best conceivable conditions, using existing specifications and equipment. Perfection standards make no provision for waste, spoilage, machine breakdowns, or other inefficiencies inherent in a normal system. Those who favor using perfection standards maintain that the generally unfavorable variances will constantly remind personnel of the need for continuous improvement in all phases of operations. Although concern for continuous improvement is widespread, perfection standards are not widely used because of their adverse effect on employee motivation. Employees tend to ignore goals that they know cannot be reached.

Business First

The Need to Adapt Standard Cost Approaches

Critics of standard costs and variance analysis maintain that predetermined standards do not work well in today's dynamic, fast-paced, just-in-time environment. Nonetheless, companies continue to use standards and to measure performance against them. Surveys in nine different countries have shown that between 56% and 92% of manufacturing companies use standard costs. Companies have apparently adapted the approach to fit their environment.

To apply standards in a dynamic environment, how should managers measure and report variances? First, they should continually evaluate their standards. If a company is in a state of continuous improvement, it must continually revise its standards. Second, standards and variances should measure key strategic variables. The concept of setting a benchmark, comparing actual results to the benchmark, and identifying causes for any differences is universal. We can apply it to many types of measures, such as production quantity or quality, as well as to costs. Finally, variances should not lead to affixing blame. Standards are plans, and things do not always go according to plan—often with no one being at fault.

One company that has adapted standard costs to meet its particular needs is the Brass Products Division (BPD) at **Parker Hannifin Corporation**, a $13 billion company that produces motion and control technologies and systems. BPD uses standard costs and variances to pinpoint problem areas that need attention if the division is to meet its goal of continuous improvement. Among the changes that have increased the value of the standard cost information are more timely product cost information, variances computed at more detailed levels, and regular meetings to help employees understand their impact on the variances.

Managers and accountants adapt the standard cost concept to fit the particular needs of a company. For example, BPD created three new variances: (1) The standard run quantity variance examines the effect of actual compared to optimal batch size for production runs; (2) the material substitution variance compares material costs to the costs of alternative materials; and (3) the method variance measures costs using actual machines compared to costs using alternative machines. All three variances use the concept of setting a standard and comparing actual results to the standard, but they do not apply the traditional standard cost-variance formulas.

Sources: Adapted from D. Johnsen and P. Sopariwala, "Standard Costing Is Alive and Well at Parker Brass," *Management Accounting Quarterly*, Winter 2000, pp. 12–20; C. B. Cheatham and L. R. Cheatham, "Redesigning Cost Systems: Is Standard Costing Obsolete?" *Accounting Horizons*, December 1996, pp. 23–31; C. Horngren, G. Foster, and S. Datar, *Cost Accounting: A Managerial Emphasis*, 12th ed. (Upper Saddle River, NJ: Prentice Hall, 2006), p. 229; and Parker Hannifin Corp., *Parker Hannifin 2012 Annual Report*.

Many companies set standards somewhere between easily-attained and extremely difficult-to-attain. The resulting variances reflect performance relative to an achievable standard so employees regard their attainment as probable if they apply normal effort and diligence. The major advantages of this approach to setting standards are as follows:

1. The resulting standards lead to variances that indicate a departure from what is normally expected and are more useful for management by exception. In contrast, perfection standards tend to lead to large unfavorable variances in every period because perfection is not attainable.
2. The standards represent what is expected under normal conditions, so companies can use the same standard costs for financial budgeting and inventory valuation. In contrast, they cannot use perfection standards for inventory valuation or financial budgeting because they know that the resulting standard costs are unrealistically low.
3. Reasonable standards have a desirable motivational impact on employees, especially when combined with incentives for continuous improvement. Employees accept the standards as reasonable performance goals.

What standards should a company use? Should a standard be so strict that the company rarely, if ever, meets it? Should the company attain the standard about 50% of the time? 90%? 20%? Individuals who have worked a lifetime setting and evaluating standards for budgeting disagree on this question, so there are no universal answers. As described in the Business First box above, companies are adapting standards to fit their particular needs.

Finding Explanations for Variances

When evaluating performance, managers distinguish between **effectiveness**—the degree to which an organization meets an objective—and **efficiency**—the degree to which an organization minimizes the resources used to achieve an objective. Performance may be effective, efficient, both, or neither.

effectiveness
The degree to which an organization meets an objective.

efficiency
The degree to which an organization minimizes the resources used to achieve an objective.

For example, Dominion Company set a static-budget objective of manufacturing and selling 9,000 units. It actually made and sold only 7,000 units. Was Dominion effective in meeting its sales objective? No. Performance was ineffective, as measured by the sales-activity variance. Was Dominion's performance efficient? Managers judge the degree of efficiency by comparing actual inputs used (such as the costs of direct materials and direct labor) to budgeted inputs for the level of output achieved (7,000 units). The less input used to produce a given output, the more efficient the operation. Dominion was inefficient because the actual cost of its inputs exceeded the cost expected for the actual level of output, as measured by the unfavorable flexible-budget variances.

A **McDonald's** restaurant could use a similar analysis to examine efficiency—the difference between actual costs and the flexible budget costs expected for the level of sales actually attained. Suppose the restaurant expects to sell 1 million Big Macs and prepares the static budget showing budgeted cost of $100,000 for buns at $.10 per bun. If the restaurant sells only 900,000 Big Macs and pays $94,000 for buns, the static-budget cost variance is $100,000 − $94,000 = $6,000 F. However, the static-budget variance doesn't adjust for the expected decrease in costs due to the decrease in sales volume. Buns for 900,000 Big Macs should cost only $90,000, the flexible budget expected cost for the achieved sales of 900,000 Big Macs. Therefore, the sales-activity cost variance is $100,000 − $90,000 = $10,000 F. The efficiency is measured by the flexible-budget cost variance of $94,000 − $90,000 = $4,000 U, which shows the inefficiency of spending $4,000 more for buns than expected given the lower actual sales level of 900,000 Big Macs.

Trade-Offs Among Variances

Because the various activities of an organization are interrelated, the level of performance in one area will often affect performance in other areas. Often there are trade-offs among costs. For example, McDonald's may generate favorable labor variances by hiring less-skilled and lower-paid employees, but this might also lead to more waste because substandard products need to be scrapped, resulting in unfavorable materials variances. As another example, **Ford** may experience unfavorable materials variances by purchasing higher-quality materials at a higher than planned price, but this may be more than offset by other favorable variances due to lower waste, fewer inspections, reduced labor time, and higher-quality products.

Because of the many interdependencies among activities, an "unfavorable" or "favorable" label should not lead a manager to jump to conclusions. By themselves, variances merely raise questions and provide clues to the causes of performance. Variances are attention directors, not problem solvers. Furthermore, because variances depend on standards as well as on actual results, the cause of unfavorable variances might be unrealistically high standards rather than poor execution by managers. One of the first questions a manager should consider when investigating a large variance is whether standards represented reasonable expectations.

When to Investigate Variances

When should management investigate a variance? For some critical items, any deviation may prompt a follow-up. However, for most items, managers recognize that, even if everything operates normally, variances are unlikely to be exactly zero. For these items, managers specify a range of "acceptable" variances based on economic analysis of how big a variance must be before investigation would be worth the effort. While the acceptable range is sometimes stated in percentage terms, it is important to also consider the dollar deviation from budget. For example, a 4% variance in a $1 million material cost may deserve more attention than a 20% variance in a $1,000 repair cost. Because knowing exactly when to investigate is difficult, many organizations have developed rules of thumb that incorporate both absolute and relative size measures such as "Investigate all variances exceeding either $5,000 or 15% of expected cost."

Comparisons with Prior Period's Results

Some organizations compare actual results with last year's results for the same period rather than using flexible-budget benchmarks. For example, an organization might compare March 2013's actual results to March 2012's actual results. However, simplistic comparisons with prior period results should always be used cautiously. In general, a carefully developed flexible budget provides a better benchmark than prior period results for evaluating performance. Why? First, using actual results from the prior year as a benchmark assumes that prior year values are what we aspire to achieve and don't contain any inefficiencies or substandard results. Second, many changes occur in the environment and in the organization, and these changes can make a comparison to the prior year invalid. Few organizations and environments are so stable that the only difference between now and a year ago is merely the passage of time. For example, the turmoil in the stock market in 2008 and 2009 led many financial institutions to make sweeping changes in operations. Comparisons of operating results in these years to previous years would not have been meaningful because the economic climate was so different. Even comparisons with the prior month's actual results may not be as useful as comparisons with an up-to-date flexible budget. Comparisons with previous years may be useful for analyzing trends in such key variables as sales volume, market share, and product mix, but they do not help answer questions such as Dominion Company's "Why did we have a loss of $11,570 in June, when we expected a profit of $12,800?"

Summary Problem for Your Review

PROBLEM

Refer to the data in Exhibits 8-1 and 8-3. Suppose actual production and sales were 8,500 units instead of 7,000 units; actual variable costs were $188,800; and actual fixed costs were $71,200. The selling price remained at $31 per unit.

1. Compute the static-budget income variance. What does this tell you about the efficiency of operations? The effectiveness of operations?

2. Compute the sales-activity income variance. Is the performance of the marketing function the sole explanation for this variance? Why?

3. Using a flexible budget at the actual activity level, compute the budgeted contribution margin, budgeted income, and flexible-budget income variance. What do you learn from this variance?

SOLUTION

1.   Actual operating income $= (8,500 \times \$31) - \$188,800 - \$71,200 = \$3,500$

Static-budget operating income $= \$12,800$ (from Exhibit 8-1)

Static-budget variance $= \$12,800 - \$3,500 = \$9,300$ U

Three factors affect the static-budget variance: sales activity, efficiency, and price changes. There is no way to tell from the static-budget variance alone how much of the $9,300 U was caused by each of these factors.

2. Sales-activity variance = Budgeted unit contribution margin $\times$ Difference between the actual unit sales and the static budget unit sales

$= \$9.20$ per unit CM $\times (8,500 - 9,000)$

$= \$4,600$ U

The sales-activity income variance quantifies the impact of the deviation from an original sales target while holding price and efficiency factors constant. This is a measure of the effectiveness of Dominion in meeting its sales objective. Management might attribute the failure to reach target sales to ineffectiveness of marketing personnel or to causes beyond the control of marketing personnel, such as material shortages, factory breakdowns, delivery problems, and so on.

3. The budget formulas in Exhibit 8-3 are the basis for the following answers:

Flexible-budget contribution margin $= \$9.20 \times 8,500 = \$78,200$

Flexible-budget operating income $= \$78,200 - \$70,000$ fixed costs $= \$8,200$

Actual operating income $= \$3,500$ (from number 1)

Flexible-budget income variance $= \$8,200 - \$3,500 = \$4,700$ U

The flexible-budget variance shows that the company spent $4,700 more to produce and sell the 8,500 units than it should have spent if operations had been efficient. Note that this $4,700 U flexible-budget variance plus the $4,600 U sales-activity variance total to the $9,300 U static-budget variance.

More Detailed Analysis of Flexible-Budget Variances

The remainder of this chapter explains how to further analyze flexible-budget variances by dividing them into component variances. Previously, we explained how to divide the static-budget variance into activity-level and flexible-budget variances. In this section, we describe how to divide the flexible-budget variance into price and quantity variances (for material or labor) and into spending and efficiency variances (for variable overhead).

We begin with material and labor variances. Exhibit 8-8 shows how price and quantity variances fit in the framework depicted in Exhibit 8-5 and specifically how the sum of price and quantity variances equals the flexible-budget variance. Exhibit 8-8 provides only a broad conceptual overview—actual calculations are illustrated in Exhibit 8-9 after we introduce some additional required information.

Variances for Direct Material and Direct Labor

Let's consider the components of the flexible-budget variances for the Dominion Company. As shown in Exhibit 8-7, the flexible-budget variances for material and labor are $80 F and $5,500 U, respectively:

	Actual Cost Incurred	Flexible Budget	Flexible-Budget Variance
Direct materials	$69,920	$70,000	$ 80 F
Direct labor	61,500	56,000	5,500 U

To further analyze the flexible-budget variances, we need more information. First, we need information about the standard prices and standard quantities used in the flexible budget formulas. Dominion Company's flexible budget is the amount that Dominion expected to incur based on standard quantities and standard prices for direct materials and direct labor to produce the output achieved, computed as follows:

$$\text{Flexible budget} = \text{Units of actual output achieved} \times \text{Standard input allowed per unit of output achieved} \times \text{Standard price per unit of input}$$

Note that the flexible budget is constructed for the level of actual output achieved. We will refer to the flexible budget for the actual output achieved as "standard cost allowed."

Let's assume the flexible-budget amounts in Exhibit 8-7 were based on $10 per unit of output for direct materials and $8 per unit of output for direct labor. Further assume these

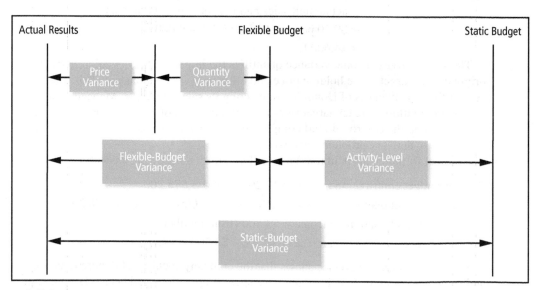

Exhibit 8-8

Relationship Between the Flexible-Budget Variance and the Price and Quantity Variances

amounts were the product of the standard quantities and the standard prices shown in the following table:

	Standards		
	Standard Quantity of Input Allowed per Unit of Output	Standard Price per Unit of Input	Flexible Budget Formula per Unit of Output
Direct materials	5 pounds	$2/pound	$10
Direct labor	$\frac{1}{2}$ hour	$16/hour	8

For the 7,000 units of output achieved by Dominion, these standards translate into the budgeted standard costs allowed shown in Exhibit 8-7:

Direct-materials cost allowed $= 7,000$ units $\times 5$ pounds $\times \$2.00$ per pound $= \$70,000$

Direct-labor cost allowed $= 7,000$ units $\times \frac{1}{2}$ hour $\times \$16.00$ per hour $= \$56,000$

We next introduce additional information about the actual quantities of material or labor used and the actual prices per unit of material or labor. Let's assume the following actual prices and quantities explain the actual direct material and direct labor costs shown in Exhibit 8-7:

- Direct materials: Dominion purchased and used 36,800 pounds of material at an actual unit price of $1.90 for a total actual cost of $36,800 \times \$1.90 = \$69,920$.
- Direct labor: Dominion used 3,750 hours of labor at an actual hourly price (rate) of $16.40, for a total cost of $3,750 \times \$16.40 = \$61,500$.

Computing Price and Quantity Variances

The flexible-budget variance (the difference between actual cost incurred and the flexible-budget cost) can be divided into 1) a quantity variance, attributable to the difference between actual quantity used and standard quantity allowed, and 2) a price variance, attributable to the difference between actual price per unit and standard price per unit. The **price variance** indicates whether the actual price paid was more or less than the standard price:

Price variance $=$ (Actual price $-$ Standard price) $\times$ Actual quantity used

The **quantity variance** indicates whether the actual quantity used was more or less than the standard quantity allowed for the output achieved:

Quantity variance $=$ (Actual quantity used $-$ Standard quantity allowed for actual output) $\times$ Standard price

Exhibit 8-9 shows the calculation of price and quantity variances for materials and labor for Dominion Company. Although the exhibit may seem complex at first, studying it will solidify your understanding of variance analysis.

Column A of Exhibit 8-9 contains the actual costs incurred based on the actual quantities used at actual prices. Column C is the flexible-budget amount based on standard input quantities allowed for the outputs achieved multiplied by standard prices. We insert column B, the actual input quantities used multiplied by standard prices, between A and C to separate price and quantity effects. The difference between columns A and B is the price variance, due to the difference between actual versus standard prices. The difference between columns B and C is the quantity variance, due to the difference between actual versus standard quantities.

The price and quantity variances corresponding to Dominion Company's flexible-budget variances for material and labor are as follows:

Materials price variance $=$ (Actual price $-$ Standard price) $\times$ Actual quantity

$= (\$1.90 - \$2.00)$ per pound $\times 36,800$ pounds

$= \$3,680$ Favorable

Labor price variance $=$ (Actual price $-$ Standard price) $\times$ Actual quantity

$= (\$16.40 - \$16.00)$ per hour $\times 3,750$ hours

$= \$1,500$ Unfavorable

Objective 6

Compute and interpret price and quantity variances for materials and labor.

price variance
The difference between actual input prices and standard input prices multiplied by the actual quantity of inputs used.

quantity variance
The difference between the actual quantity of inputs used and the standard quantity allowed for the good output achieved multiplied by the standard price of the input.

The quantity (or usage) variances are as follows:

$$\text{Materials quantity variance} = (\text{Actual quantity} - \text{Standard quantity}) \times \text{Standard price}$$
$$= [36,800 - (7,000 \times 5)] \text{ pounds} \times \$2.00 \text{ per pound}$$
$$= [36,800 - 35,000] \text{ pounds} \times \$2.00 \text{ per pounds}$$
$$= \$3,600 \text{ Unfavorable}$$

$$\text{Labor quantity variance} = (\text{Actual quantity} - \text{Standard quantity}) \times \text{Standard price}$$
$$= [3,750 - (7,000 \times 1/2)] \text{ hours} \times \$16.00 \text{ per hour}$$
$$= [3,750 - 3,500] \text{ hours} \times \$16.00 \text{ per hour}$$
$$= \$4,000 \text{ Unfavorable}$$

By definition, the sum of the direct-materials price and quantity variances equals the total direct-materials flexible-budget variance. Similarly, the sum of the direct-labor price and quantity variances equals the direct-labor flexible-budget variance.

$$\text{Materials flexible-budget variance} = \$3,680 \text{ Favorable} + \$3,600 \text{ Unfavorable}$$
$$= \$80 \text{ Favorable}$$

$$\text{Labor flexible-budget variance} = \$1,500 \text{ Unfavorable} + \$4,000 \text{ Unfavorable}$$
$$= \$5,500 \text{ Unfavorable}$$

Note that the flexible budget quantities used in computing price and quantity variance are quantities of inputs, which are related to, but different than, the quantity of output achieved. For Dominion Company, a single-product firm, standard inputs allowed is simply units of

Exhibit 8-9

General Approach to Analysis of Direct-Labor and Direct-Materials Variances

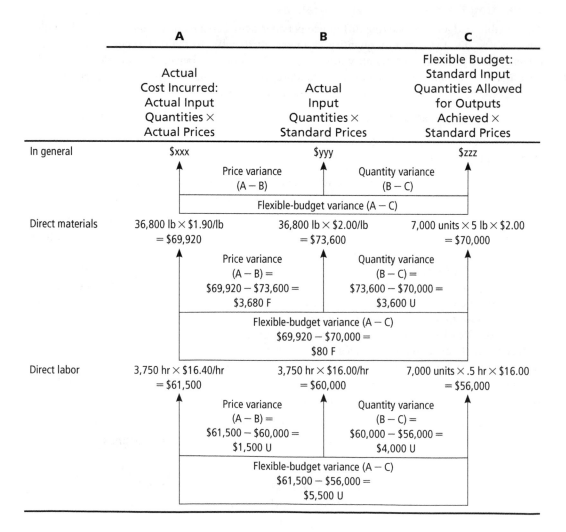

output multiplied by the standard quantity of input per unit. For more complex companies that manufacture a variety of products, there are standard inputs allowed for the output achieved for each product. For example, consider a furniture manufacturer that produced 12,000 chairs and 3,000 sofas. If each chair requires 1 standard labor hour and each sofa requires 2 standard labor hours, standard hours allowed for outputs achieved is $(12,000 \times 1) + (3,000 \times 2) = 18,000$. Standard hours allowed for output achieved is the result of translating disparate output units (chairs and sofas) into a common standard measure of activity (standard labor hours allowed for output achieved).

Exhibit 8-10 provides a graphical overview of the computation of price and quantity variances. Panels A and B show the simple cases where there is either a quantity or a price variance but not both, so there is no interaction between the price and quantity variances. In both panels, the flexible budget is the standard quantity allowed multiplied by the standard price—the rectangle shaded blue. The variances depend on the difference between standard and actual price and the difference between standard and actual quantity. In Panel A, the variance is the quantity used in excess of the standard quantity times the standard price—the rectangle shaded orange. In Panel B, the variance is the price paid in excess of the standard price times the standard quantity—the rectangle shaded purple.

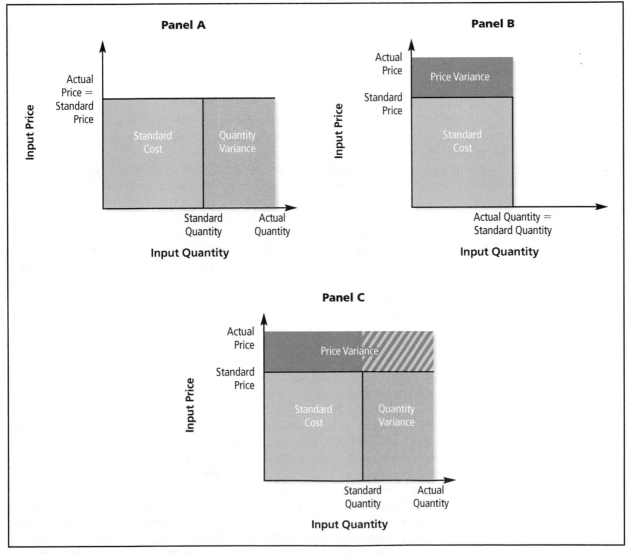

Exhibit 8-10
Graphical Representation of Quantity and Price Variances

Panel C illustrates the situation where both quantity and price variances exist. The interaction of the two variances is represented by the cross-hatched purple region. In concept, this joint effect could be defined to be a separate, third variance. In practice, most companies include this joint effect as part of the price variance, as in the calculations shown in Exhibit 8-9. This means the price variance is the result of multiplying the difference between actual and standard price by the total actual quantity used. This definition includes the joint effect represented by the purple cross-hatched area as part of the price variance. The quantity variance is then the difference between actual and standard quantity multiplied by the standard price.

You are likely to encounter various terms used for price and quantity variances in practice. For example, many companies call a price variance applied to labor a **rate variance**, and many refer to quantity variances as **usage** or **efficiency variances**. Moreover, you may encounter new variance definitions such as those created by the Brass Products Division in the Business First box on page 319 or in the Making Managerial Decisions section on page 315. Because there is so much variation in definitions and terminology, be sure to ask whatever questions are necessary to be sure that you understand the exact definition of any variance that you encounter.

rate variance
An alternative name for the price variance applied to labor.

usage variance (efficiency variance)
Alternative names for the quantity variance.

Interpreting Price and Quantity Variances

By dividing flexible-budget variances into price and quantity variances, we can better evaluate managers on variances that they can control. Consider an operating manager who has control over the quantity of materials used in the production process but little control over the price. In that case, the quantity variance will be more relevant than the price variance in evaluating the operating manager. Who has control over the price variance? The manager in charge of purchasing materials likely has some control over the price, and therefore is responsible for the price variance. However, even the purchasing manager may not have much control over price. Why? Because external market forces often are the primary influence on prices. Irrespective of whether any manager has control of price, it is useful to separate price and quantity variances whenever the quantity variance is important for evaluation. For example, the commodity prices of wheat, oats, corn, and rice may be outside the control of General Mills managers. By separating price variances from quantity variances, the breakfast cereal maker can focus on the quantity variance to assess whether managers used grain efficiently.

It is important to carefully consider the incentives created by price and quantity variances. Exclusive focus on material price variances can provide incentives that work against an organization's JIT and total quality management goals. For example, a purchasing manager focused only on creating a favorable material price variance may achieve a lower price by buying larger quantities or buying lower-quality material. However, the result could be excessive inventory handling and opportunity costs caused by large purchase quantities or increased manufacturing defects caused by lower-quality material. As another example, exclusive focus on labor price variances could motivate managers to use lower-cost (and lower-skilled) workers or to rush workers through critical tasks. In either case, the result could impair quality of products and services.

Companies that use variances primarily to fix blame often find that managers resort to cheating and subversion to beat the system. Lower-level operations managers usually have more information about their operations than higher-level managers. If supervisors use that information against them, lower-level managers might withhold or misstate valuable information for their own protection. For example, one manufacturing firm actually followed a policy of reducing the next period's departmental budget by the amount of the department's unfavorable variances in the current period. If a division had a $50,000 expense budget for labor and $52,000 of actual labor costs resulting in a $2,000 unfavorable labor variance, the following period's budget would be reduced to $48,000. This system led managers to cheat and to falsify reports to avoid unfavorable variances and avoid reductions in their budgets. We can criticize departmental managers' ethics in this situation, but the system design was also at fault.

Variances by themselves cannot provide the complete picture of why the company achieved or failed to achieve the budgeted results. For instance, one possible explanation for Dominion's set of variances is that a manager made a trade-off. Perhaps the manager purchased substandard-quality materials at a favorable price, saving $3,680 (the favorable materials price variance) knowing that the substandard material would lead to extra waste of materials (the $3,600 unfavorable material quantity variance). In this case, the material price variance more than offsets the material quantity variance, as indicated by the net materials flexible-budget variance of $80 favorable.

Of course, to fully understand the effect of the decision to purchase substandard materials, still more investigation and analysis might be required. For example, the material waste due to substandard materials might also have caused excess use of direct labor. Why? Perhaps Dominion used direct labor time working on units that ended up being defective, thus wasting that time. Suppose the labor wasted on the defective units was more than the $80 favorable materials flexible budget variance described in the previous paragraph. Then, the decision to purchase substandard material was not successful because the labor cost inefficiencies caused by using substandard materials exceeded the materials cost savings from the favorable price. The important point again is that variances are useful tools that provide clues and direct attention to problems, but variances are only the starting point of the search for answers to the complex question of why actual results differ from expectations.

Making Managerial Decisions

Managers can apply the concepts of variance analysis to construct new variance definitions to fit new situations. For example, consider a production plant that plans to produce 50 units per hour and work 8 hours per day for a total planned production of 400 units each day. On March 23, the plant produced just 276 units for a total unfavorable production variance of 124 units. Because of machine breakdowns, the plant operated for only 6 hours that day. Using a three-column framework like that used in Exhibit 8-9, define variances that separate how much of the 124 unit shortfall in production was caused by operating only 6 hours versus how much was caused by low production efficiency during the 6 hours of actual operation.

Answer

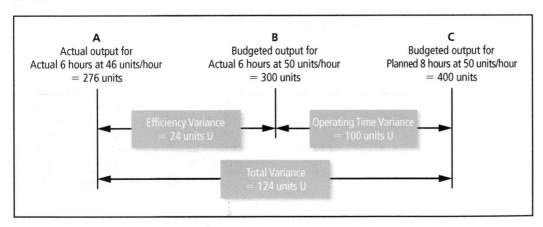

Column A shows actual production of 276 units over 6 actual operating hours equates to 46 units per hour. Column C shows standard production of 8 hours per day × 50 units per hour = 400 units per day. Column B shows standard production rates for actual operating hours, 6 hours of production × 50 units per hour = 300 units. The difference between columns B and C is the production shortfall caused by loss of 2 hours of operating time due to the machine breakdowns, 2 hours × 50 units per hour = 100 unit unfavorable variance. The difference between columns A and B is the shortfall caused by an actual rate of production (276 ÷ 6 = 46 units per hour) lower than the standard rate of 50 units per hour. This difference is the rate shortfall (4 units per hour) multiplied by the actual hours worked for the day (6 hours) = 24 unit unfavorable variance. The total variance, 100 units + 24 units = 124 units, is the difference between columns A and C.

Overhead Variances

The evaluation of overhead variances is different from the evaluation of direct materials and direct labor because overhead costs are generally indirect costs that companies allocate rather than trace to output. In this section, we outline the framework used to construct variable overhead variances and then briefly discuss variances for fixed overhead. (See Chapter 13 for more extensive discussion of fixed overhead variances.)

Objective 7

Compute variable overhead spending and efficiency variances.

Variable Overhead Variances

Companies allocate variable overhead to output based on some cost driver. For example, the variable-overhead cost driver for Dominion Company is direct-labor hours. The variable-overhead flexible-budget variance can be divided into two variances. When actual cost-driver activity differs from the standard amount allowed for the actual output achieved, we have a **variable-overhead efficiency variance**, calculated as follows:

variable-overhead efficiency variance
The difference between actual cost-driver activity and the standard amount allowed for the actual output achieved multiplied by the standard variable-overhead rate per cost-driver unit.

$$\text{Variable-overhead efficiency variance} = \left(\begin{array}{c} \text{Actual cost-} \\ \text{driver activity} \end{array} - \begin{array}{c} \text{Standard cost-driver} \\ \text{activity allowed} \end{array} \right) \times \begin{array}{c} \text{Standard variable-overhead} \\ \text{rate per cost-driver unit} \end{array}$$

The variable-overhead efficiency variance depends entirely on whether the quantity of the cost driver used is more or less than the quantity allowed for the actual output achieved. It measures how control of the cost driver activity affected variable overhead costs.

The **variable-overhead spending variance** arises when actual variable overhead costs differ from the amount predicted for the actual cost-driver activity:

variable-overhead spending variance
The difference between the actual variable overhead cost and the amount predicted for the actual level of cost-driver activity.

$$\text{Variable-overhead spending variance} = \begin{array}{c} \text{Actual variable} \\ \text{overhead} \end{array} - \left(\begin{array}{c} \text{Standard variable} \\ \text{overhead rate per} \\ \text{unit of cost-driver} \end{array} \times \begin{array}{c} \text{Actual cost-driver} \\ \text{activity used} \end{array} \right)$$

This variance combines price and quantity effects and tells us how the actual variable overhead cost compares to the predicted amount for the actual level of cost-driver activity.

Exhibit 8-11 illustrates the calculation of variable and fixed overhead variances for Dominion Company. The exhibit breaks the $500 unfavorable flexible-budget variable overhead variance for supplies into spending and efficiency variances. We compute the efficiency variance by multiplying the standard variable overhead rate times the difference between the quantity of the cost driver used and the quantity of the cost driver allowed for the output achieved. For Dominion Company, standards allow 1/2 hour of the cost driver direct labor for each unit of output, or 3,500 hours allowed for the 7,000 units of output achieved. Therefore, the flexible budget

Exhibit 8-11
General Approach to Analysis of Overhead Variances

	A	B	C
	Actual Overhead Costs Incurred	Predicted Overhead Based on Actual Driver Use × Standard Prices	Flexible Budget: Standard Driver Use Allowed for Output Achieved × Standard Prices
Variable Overhead: Supplies	$4,700 (given)	3,750 hr × $1.20/hr = $4,500	3,500 hr × $1.20/hr = $4,200

Spending variance (A − B)
$4,700 − $4,500 = $200 U

Efficiency variance (B − C)
$4,500 − $4,200 = $300 U

Flexible-budget variance (A − C)
$4,700 − $4,200 = $500 U

Fixed Overhead: Factory supervision	$14,700	$14,400	$14,400

Spending variance (A − B) =
$14,700 − $14,400 = $300 U

Never a variance (B − C) = 0
$14,400 − $14,400 = 0 by definition

Flexible-budget variance (A − C)
$14,700 − $14,400 = $300 U

amount of $4,200 for supplies in Exhibit 8-7 translates to $4,200 ÷ 3,500 hours = $1.20 per direct-labor hour allowed for output achieved. Because Dominion Company used 3,750 labor hours when the standard for production of 7,000 units is 1/2 hour/unit × 7,000 units = 3,500 standard hours allowed, it used an excess of 250 labor hours. Each labor hour drives $1.20 of variable overhead, so the excess labor hours drive 250 units × $1.20/unit = $300 of extra variable overhead costs.

$$
\begin{aligned}
\text{Variable-overhead efficiency} \atop \text{variance of supplies} &= \left(\begin{matrix} \text{Actual direct-} \\ \text{labor hours} \end{matrix} - \begin{matrix} \text{Standard direct-labor} \\ \text{hours allowed} \end{matrix} \right) \times \begin{matrix} \text{Standard variable-} \\ \text{overhead rates per hour} \end{matrix} \\
&= \left(\begin{matrix} \text{3,750 Actual} \\ \text{hours} \end{matrix} - \begin{matrix} \text{3,500 Standard} \\ \text{hours allowed} \end{matrix} \right) \times \quad \$1.20 \text{ per hour} \\
&= (250 \text{ excess hours}) \times \$1.20 \text{ per hour} \\
&= \$300 \text{ Unfavorable}
\end{aligned}
$$

This example illustrates a general principle: When actual cost-driver activity exceeds the activity allowed for the actual output achieved, variable-overhead efficiency variances are unfavorable and vice versa. In essence, the variable-overhead efficiency variance tells management how much variable overhead cost it wastes if the variance is unfavorable (or saves, if the variance is favorable) due to cost-driver activity.

The other component of the flexible-budget variance measures control of overhead spending given actual cost-driver activity. The variable-overhead spending variance is the difference between the actual variable overhead and the amount of variable overhead predicted when using 3,750 actual direct-labor hours:

$$
\begin{aligned}
\text{Variable-overhead spending} \atop \text{variance of supplies} &= \begin{matrix} \text{Actual variable} \\ \text{overhead} \end{matrix} - \left(\begin{matrix} \text{Standard variable} \\ \text{overhead rate} \end{matrix} \times \begin{matrix} \text{Actual direct-} \\ \text{labor hours used} \end{matrix} \right) \\
&= \$4,700 \quad - (\$1.20 \times 3,750) \\
&= \$4,700 \quad - \$4,500 \\
&= \$200 \text{ Unfavorable}
\end{aligned}
$$

Like other variances, a variable-overhead variance does not by itself identify the causes of results that differ from the static and flexible budgets. The distinction between efficiency and spending variances for variable overhead provides a springboard for more investigation, but the only way for management to discover why overhead performance did not agree with the budget is to investigate possible causes.

Fixed Overhead Variances

The framework for analysis of fixed overhead variances differs from the framework for variable cost variances. Consider factory supervision, a fixed cost, shown at the bottom of Exhibit 8-11. The flexible budget in column B based on actual use of the cost driver and the flexible budget in column C based on standard use of the cost driver are always the same. Why? Because fixed overhead does not vary with the level of use of the cost driver. Because there is no difference between columns B and C, the entire fixed overhead flexible-budget variance in Exhibit 8-11 is due to the difference between columns A and B. This difference between the actual fixed-overhead cost in column A and the budgeted cost in columns B and C is the **fixed-overhead spending variance**. For example, Dominion Company's factory supervision fixed-overhead spending variance is the flexible-budget variance of $14,700 − $14,400 = $300 unfavorable, the difference between the actual cost of factory supervision and the budgeted fixed amount.

In Chapter 13, you will encounter a second type of fixed-overhead variance, the production-volume variance. Because this second type of variance does not involve the control of costs, we consider only the fixed-overhead spending variance in this chapter.

Objective 8

Compute the fixed-overhead spending variance.

fixed-overhead spending variance

The difference between actual fixed overhead and budgeted fixed overhead.

Summary Problem for Your Review

PROBLEM

The following questions are based on standards for the Dominion Company in this chapter.

- Direct materials: standard, 5 pounds per unit at $2 per pound
- Direct labor: standard, 1/2 hour at $16 per hour

Earlier we computed variances based on actual results for production of 7,000 units. Suppose now we have actual results for production of 8,500 units:

- Direct materials: Dominion purchased and used 46,000 pounds at an actual unit price of $1.85 per pound, for an actual total cost of $85,100.
- Direct labor: Dominion used 4,125 hours of labor at an actual hourly rate of $16.80, for a total actual cost of $69,300.

1. Compute the flexible-budget variance and the price and quantity variances for direct labor and direct material.

2. In requirement 1, you should have computed a direct-materials price variance of $6,900 favorable. Is this a good outcome? Explain.

SOLUTION

1. The variances are as follows:

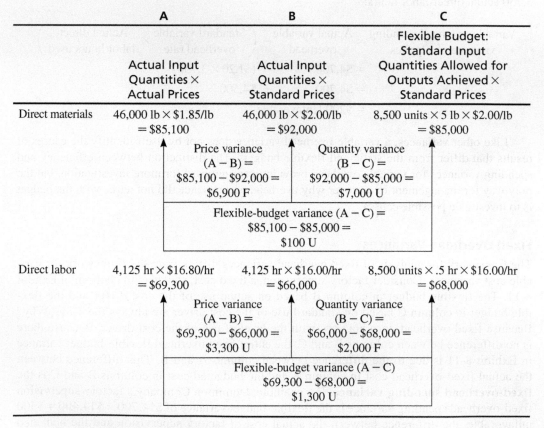

2. The favorable price variance may not be a good outcome. When prices are low, it may motivate Dominion Company managers to buy extra inventory in excess of its immediate needs, causing extra storage and handling costs. The favorable price variance may also mean that lower quality material has been purchased. The favorable materials price variance is a good outcome only if it exceeds any unfavorable material, labor, and overhead variances caused by the volume and quality of materials purchased.

Highlights to Remember

1. **Identify variances and label them as favorable or unfavorable.** Variances are differences between actual and budgeted results. When the direction of the difference corresponds to actual profit greater than budgeted, the variance is labeled as favorable. When the direction corresponds to actual profit less than budgeted, the variance is unfavorable.

2. **Distinguish between flexible budgets and static budgets.** Flexible budgets are geared to changing levels of cost-driver activity rather than to the single level of the static budget. Organizations tailor flexible budgets to particular levels of sales or cost-driver activity—before or after the fact. Flexible budgets tell how much revenue and cost to expect for any level of activity.

3. **Use flexible-budget formulas to construct a flexible budget.** Cost functions, or flexible-budget formulas, reflect fixed- and variable-cost behavior and allow managers to compute budgets for any volume of output achieved. We compute the flexible-budget amounts for variable costs by multiplying the variable cost per unit of output times the level of output. The flexible-budgeted fixed cost is a lump sum, independent of the level of output (within the relevant range).

4. **Compute and interpret static-budget variances, flexible-budget variances, and sales-activity variances.** Static-budget variances are differences between actual results and the budgeted amounts for the level of activity assumed in the static budget. Sales-activity variances are the budgeted effects of operating at the actual achieved level of activity rather than the level of activity assumed in the static budget. Flexible-budget variances are the deviations of actual results from the flexible budget amounts for the achieved level of activity.

5. **Understand how the setting of standards affects the computation and interpretation of variances.** Because variances are the difference between budgeted and actual amounts, they depend on the standards used to construct the budget. Most companies set standards that are neither too easy nor too hard to attain.

6. **Compute and interpret price and quantity variances for materials and labor.** Managers often find it useful to subdivide flexible-budget variances for variable inputs into price and quantity variances. Price variances (also referred to as rate variances) reflect the effects of changing input prices, holding inputs constant at actual input use. Quantity variances (also referred to as usage variances or efficiency variances) reflect the effects of different levels of input usage, holding prices constant at standard prices.

7. **Compute variable overhead spending and efficiency variances.** The variable-overhead spending variance is the difference between the actual variable overhead and the amount of variable overhead budgeted for the actual level of cost-driver activity. The variable-overhead efficiency variance is the difference between the actual cost-driver activity and the amount of cost-driver activity allowed for the actual output achieved, costed at the standard variable-overhead rate.

8. **Compute the fixed-overhead spending variance.** The fixed-overhead spending variance is the difference between the actual fixed overhead expenditures and the budgeted amount of fixed overhead.

Accounting Vocabulary

activity-based flexible budget, p. 313
activity-level variances, p. 315
currently attainable standards, p. 318
effectiveness, p. 319
efficiency, p. 319
efficiency variance, p. 326
expected cost, p. 318
favorable cost variance, p. 312
favorable profit variance, p. 311
favorable revenue variance, p. 312

fixed-overhead spending variance, p. 329
flexible budget, p. 313
flexible-budget variance, p. 315
ideal standards, p. 318
perfection standards, p. 318
price variance, p. 323
quantity variance, p. 323
rate variance, p. 326
sales-activity variances, p. 315
standard cost, p. 318
static budget, p. 312
static-budget variance, p. 314

unfavorable cost variance, p. 312
unfavorable profit variance, p. 312
unfavorable revenue variance, p. 312
usage variance, p. 326
variable budget, p. 313
variable-overhead efficiency variance, p. 328
variable-overhead spending variance, p. 328

MyAccountingLab **Fundamental Assignment Material**

8-A1 Flexible and Static Budgets

Walcker Transportation Company's general manager reports quarterly to the company president on the firm's operating performance. The company uses a budget based on detailed expectations for the forthcoming quarter. The general manager has just received the condensed quarterly performance report shown in Exhibit 8-12.

Although the general manager was upset about not obtaining enough revenue, she was happy that her cost performance was favorable; otherwise, her net income would be even worse.

The president was not satisfied with the performance report and remarked, "I can see some merit in comparing actual performance with budgeted performance because we can see whether actual revenue coincided with our best guess for budget purposes. But I can't see how this performance report helps me evaluate cost-control performance."

1. Prepare a columnar flexible budget for Walcker Transportation at revenue levels of $12,600,000, $13,000,000, and $13,400,000. Use the format of the last three columns of Exhibit 8-3, page 313. Assume that the prices and mix of products sold are equal to the budgeted prices and mix.
2. Write out the flexible budget formula for costs as a function of revenue.
3. Prepare a condensed table showing the static budget variance, the sales-activity variance, and the flexible-budget variance. Use the format of Exhibit 8-6, page 316.

8-A2 Activity Level Variances

The systems consulting department of Gullickson Golf Products designs systems for data collection, encoding, and reporting to fit the needs of other departments within the company. The cost driver for costs in the systems consulting department is the number of requests made to the department. The expected variable cost of handling a request was $500, and the number of requests expected for June 20X1 was 75. Gullickson budgeted its monthly fixed costs for the department (salaries, equipment depreciation, space costs) at $65,000.

The actual number of requests serviced by systems consulting in June 20X1 was 90, and the total costs incurred by the department was $124,000. Of that amount, $78,000 was for fixed costs.

Compute the static budget variances and the flexible-budget variances for variable and fixed costs for the systems consulting department for June 20X1.

Exhibit 8-12

Walcker Transportation
Operating Performance
Report

Second Quarter, 20X1

	Budget	Actual	Variance
Net revenue	$13,000,000	$12,700,000	$300,000 U
Variable Costs			
Fuel	$ 520,000	$ 516,000	$ 4,000 F
Repairs and maintenance	390,000	398,000	8,000 U
Supplies and miscellaneous	2,080,000	2,070,000	10,000 F
Variable payroll	8,060,000	7,940,000	120,000 F
Total variable costs*	$11,050,000	$10,924,000	$126,000 F
Fixed Costs			
Supervision	$ 160,000	$ 177,000	$ 17,000 U
Rent	200,000	200,000	—
Depreciation	460,000	460,000	—
Other fixed costs	170,000	163,000	7,000 F
Total fixed costs	990,000	1,000,000	$ 10,000 U
Total fixed and variable costs	$12,040,000	$11,924,000	$116,000 F
Operating income	$ 960,000	$ 776,000	$184,000 U

U = Unfavorable. F = Favorable.

*For purposes of this analysis, assume that all of these costs are totally variable with respect to sales revenue. In practice, many are mixed and would have to be subdivided into variable and fixed components before a meaningful analysis could be made. Also, assume that the prices and mix of services sold remain unchanged.

8-A3 Direct-Material and Direct-Labor Variances

Hill Fine Instruments manufactures trumpets, trombones, tubas, and other brass instruments. The following standards were developed for a line of trumpets:

	Standard Inputs Expected for Each Unit of Output Achieved	Standard Price per Unit of Input
Direct materials	5 pounds	$10 per pound
Direct labor	10 hours	$25 per hour

During April, Hill scheduled 550 trumpets for production. However, the company produced only 525.

Hill purchased and used 3,100 pounds of direct materials at a unit price of $9.00 per pound. It used 5,500 hours of direct labor at an actual rate of $26.00 per hour.

1. Compute the standard cost per trumpet for direct materials and direct labor.
2. Compute the price variances and quantity variances for direct materials and direct labor.
3. Based on these sketchy data, what clues for investigation are provided by the variances?

8-B1 Summary Performance Reports

Consider the following data for Robert Campbell Tax Services:

- Static budget data: sales, 3,500 clients at $350 each; variable costs, $300 per client; fixed costs, $150,000
- Actual results at actual prices: sales, 3,000 clients at $360 per client; variable costs, $920,000; fixed costs, $159,500

1. Prepare a summary performance report similar to Exhibit 8-6, page 316.
2. Fill in the blanks:

Static-budget income	$ —
Variances	
Sales-activity variances	$ —
Flexible-budget variances	— —
Actual income	$

8-B2 Material and Labor Variances

Consider the following data for Tripp Manufacturing:

	Direct Materials	Direct Labor
Actual price per unit of input (lb and hr)	$ 7.50	$ 12.00
Standard price per unit of input	$ 7.00	$ 14.00
Standard inputs allowed per unit of output	10	2
Actual units of input	116,000	29,000
Actual units of output (product)	14,400	14,400

1. Compute the price, quantity, and flexible-budget variances for direct materials and direct labor. Use U or F to indicate whether the variances are unfavorable or favorable.
2. Prepare a plausible explanation for the performance.

8-B3 Variable-Overhead Variances

You have been asked to prepare an analysis of the overhead costs in the order processing department of a mail-order company like **Eddie Bauer**. As an initial step, you prepare a summary of some events that bear on overhead for the most recent period. Variable overhead is applied based on hours of processing-clerk labor. The standard variable-overhead rate per order was $.06. The rate of 10 orders per hour is regarded as standard productivity per clerk. The total overhead incurred was $204,000, of which $138,000 was fixed. The fixed-overhead spending variance was $2,500 unfavorable. The variable-overhead flexible-budget variance was $6,000 unfavorable. The variable-overhead spending variance was $3,600 favorable.

Find the following:

1. Variable-overhead efficiency variance
2. Actual hours of input
3. Standard hours of input allowed for output achieved
4. Budgeted-fixed overhead

MyAccountingLab

Additional Assignment Material

QUESTIONS

8-1 Distinguish between favorable and unfavorable cost (and revenue) variances.

8-2 "The flex in the flexible budget relates solely to variable costs." Do you agree? Explain.

8-3 "We want a flexible budget because costs are difficult to predict. We need the flexibility to change budgeted costs as input prices change." Does a flexible budget serve this purpose? Explain.

8-4 Explain the role of understanding cost behavior and cost-driver activities for flexible budgeting.

8-5 "An activity-based flexible budget has a 'flex' for every activity." Do you agree? Explain.

8-6 "Effectiveness and efficiency go hand in hand. You can't have one without the other." Do you agree? Explain.

8-7 Differentiate between a static-budget variance and a flexible-budget variance.

8-8 "Managers should be rewarded for favorable variances and punished for unfavorable variances." Do you agree? Explain.

8-9 "A good control system places the blame for every unfavorable variance on someone in the organization. Without affixing blame, no one will take responsibility for cost control." Do you agree? Explain.

8-10 Who is usually responsible for sales-activity variances? Why?

8-11 Differentiate between perfection standards and currently attainable standards.

8-12 What are two possible approaches to setting "currently attainable standards"?

8-13 "A standard is one point in a band or range of acceptable outcomes." Evaluate this statement.

8-14 "Price variances should be computed even if prices are regarded as being outside of company control." Do you agree? Explain.

8-15 What are some common causes of unfavorable quantity variances?

8-16 "Failure to meet price standards is the responsibility of the purchasing officer." Do you agree? Explain.

8-17 "The variable-overhead efficiency variance is not really an overhead variance." Evaluate this statement.

8-18 Why do the techniques for controlling overhead differ from those for controlling direct materials?

CRITICAL THINKING EXERCISES

8-19 Interpretation of Favorable and Unfavorable Variances

A division budgeted an operating profit of $3,000 on sales of $8,000 and costs of $5,000. However, at the beginning of the period one of the division's machines broke down and could not be fixed until the end of the period. When the machine broke, the division manager determined that there were two feasible alternatives: First, production and sales could be cut back by 25%, reducing sales to $6,000 and costs to $4,000. (Note that costs are not reduced by 25% because some of the costs are fixed.) Second, a replacement machine could be obtained and installed, allowing sales to be maintained at $8,000 but increasing costs to $6,500. The division manager analyzed the alternatives and concluded that revenues less costs would be greater if sales were reduced ($6,000 less $4,000 = $2,000 operating profit) than if the replacement machine was obtained ($8,000 less $6,500 = $1,500 operating profit). The manager, therefore, chose not to replace the machine. However, because revenue was lower than planned by $2,000, there is an unfavorable revenue variance of $2,000. Comment on how the unfavorable revenue variance should be interpreted in evaluating the performance of the manager.

8-20 Marketing Responsibility for Sales-Activity Variances

Suppose a company budgeted an operating profit of $100 on sales of $1,000. Actual sales were $900. The marketing department claimed that because sales were down 10%, it was responsible for only 10% of $100 or $10 of any drop in profit. Any further shortfall must be someone else's responsibility. Comment on this claim.

8-21 Production Responsibility for Flexible-Budget Variances

Suppose a plant manager planned to produce 100 units of product at a total cost of $1,000. Instead, actual production was 10% higher at 110 units. When costs came in at less than a 10% increase in costs or $1,100, the plant manager claimed that she should get credit for a favorable variance equal to the amount by which the actual costs fell short of $1,100. Comment on this claim.

8-22 Responsibility of Purchasing Manager

A company's purchasing manager bought 5,000 pounds of material for $5.50 per pound instead of the budgeted $6.00 per pound, resulting in a favorable variance of $2,500. The company has a policy of rewarding employees with 20% of any cost savings they generate. Before awarding a $500 bonus to the purchasing manager, what other variances would you look at to determine the total effect of the purchasing decision? Explain.

8-23 Variable-Overhead Efficiency Variance

Birmingham Company had a $1,000 U variable-overhead efficiency variance. Neither the plant manager, who was responsible primarily for labor scheduling, nor the administrative manager, who was responsible for most support services, felt responsible for the variance. Who should be held responsible? Why?

EXERCISES

8-24 Flexible Budget

Coppins Sports Equipment Company made 44,000 basketballs in a given year. Its manufacturing costs were $294,800 variable and $9,100 fixed. Assume that no price changes will occur in the following year and that no changes in production methods are applicable. Compute the budgeted cost for producing 52,000 basketballs in the following year.

8-25 Basic Flexible Budget

The superintendent of police of Fargo is attempting to predict the costs of operating a fleet of police cars. Among the items of concern are fuel, $.22 per mile, and depreciation, $6,600 per car per year.

The manager is preparing a flexible budget for the coming year. Prepare the flexible-budget amounts for fuel and depreciation for each car at a level of 40,000, 50,000, and 60,000 miles.

8-26 Flexible Budget

Pohle Designs has a department that makes high-quality leather cases for iPads. Consider the following data for a recent month:

	Budget Formula per Unit	Various Levels of Output		
Units		10,000	11,000	12,000
Sales	$19	$?	$?	$?
Variable costs				
Direct materials	?	65,000	?	?
Hand labor	4.40	?	?	?
Fixed costs				
Depreciation		?	18,000	?
Salaries		?	?	33,000

Fill in the unknowns.

8-27 Basic Flexible Budget

The budgeted prices for materials and direct labor per unit of finished product are $8 and $7, respectively. The production manager is delighted about the following data:

	Static Budget	Actual Costs	Variance
Direct materials	$59,200	$49,900	$9,300 F
Direct labor	51,800	39,200	12,600 F

Is the manager's happiness justified? Prepare a report that might provide a more detailed explanation of why the static budget was not achieved. Good output was 5,300 units.

8-28 Activity-Level Variances

Materials-support costs for the Pittsburgh Steel Company (PSC) are variable costs that depend on the weight of material (plate steel, castings, etc.) moved. For the current budget period and based on scheduled production, PSC expected to move 750,000 pounds of material at a cost of $.25 per pound. Several orders were canceled by customers, and PSC moved only 650,000 pounds of material. Total materials support costs for the period were $177,000.

Compare actual support costs to the static-budget support costs by computing static budget, activity-level, and flexible-budget variances for materials-support costs.

8-29 Direct-Material Variances

Nakhon Custom Shirt Company uses a special fabric in the production of dress shirts. During August, Nakhon Custom Shirt purchased and used 4,100 square yards in the production of 3,700 shirts at a total cost of B2,812,600. (B stands for the Thai baht. There are roughly 30 bahts to a U.S. dollar.) The standard allows one yard at B680 per yard for each shirt.

Calculate the material price variance and the material quantity variance.

8-30 Labor Variances

Ellen Chenoweth, the manager of the city of St. Paul road maintenance shop, uses standards to judge performance. Because a clerk mistakenly discarded some labor records, however, Ellen has only partial data for April. She knows that the total direct-labor flexible-budget variance was $1,643 favorable. Moreover, a recent pay raise produced an unfavorable labor price variance for April of $1,157. The actual hours of input were 1,780 and the standard labor price was $20 per hour.

1. Find the actual labor rate per hour.
2. Determine the standard hours allowed for the output achieved.

8-31 Quantity Variances

Lindsey Toy Company produced 13,000 stuffed bears. The standard direct-material allowance is 1.5 kilograms per bear, at a cost per kilo of $3.20. Actually, 18,700 kilos of materials (input) were used to produce the 13,000 bears (output).

Similarly, the standard allowance for direct labor is 5.1 hours to produce one bear, and the standard hourly labor cost is $6. But 67,100 hours (input) were used to produce the 13,000 bears.

Compute the quantity variances for direct materials and direct labor.

8-32 Labor and Material Variances

Standard direct-labor rate	$ 15.00
Actual direct-labor rate	$ 11.50
Standard direct-labor hours	10,000
Direct-labor quantity variance—unfavorable	$ 9,000
Standard unit price of materials	$ 4.60
Actual quantity purchased and used	2,500
Standard quantity allowed for actual production	1,850
Materials purchase price variance—favorable	$ 500

1. Compute the actual hours worked, rounded to the nearest hour.
2. Compute the actual purchase price per unit of materials, rounded to the nearest penny.

8-33 Material and Labor Variances

Consider the following data:

	Direct Materials	Direct Labor
Costs incurred: actual inputs × actual prices incurred	$120,495	$101,255
Actual inputs × expected prices	127,155	96,250
Standard inputs allowed for actual outputs achieved × expected prices	130,200	92,500

Compute the price, quantity, and flexible-budget variances for direct materials and direct labor. Use U or F to indicate whether the variances are unfavorable or favorable.

PROBLEMS

8-34 National Park Service

The National Park Service prepared the following budget for one of its national parks for 20X1:

Revenue from fees	$5,000,000
Variable costs (miscellaneous)	500,000
Contribution margin	$4,500,000
Fixed costs (miscellaneous)	4,500,000
Income	$ 0

The fees were based on an average of 25,000 vehicle-admission days (vehicles multiplied by number of days in parks) per week for the 20-week season, multiplied by average entry and other fees of $10 per vehicle-admission day.

The season was booming for the first 4 weeks. During the fifth week, however, there were major forest fires. A large percentage of the park was scarred by the fires. As a result, the number of visitors to the park dropped sharply during the remainder of the season.

Total revenues fell $1.2 million short of the original budget. Variable costs fell as expected, and fixed costs were unaffected except for hiring extra firefighters at a cost of $300,000.

Prepare a columnar summary of performance, showing the original (static) budget, sales-activity variances, flexible budget, flexible-budget variances, and actual results.

8-35 Flexible and Static Budgets

Beta Gamma Sigma, the business honor society, recently held a dinner dance. The original (static) budget and actual results were as follows:

	Static Budget	Actual	Variance
Attendees	75	90	
Revenue	$2,625	$3,255	$630 F
Chicken dinners at $19.00	1,425	1,767	342 U
Beverages, $6 per person	450	466	16 U
Club rental, $75 plus 8% tax	81	81	0
Music, 3 hours at $250 per hour	750	875	125 U
Profit	$ (81)	$ 66	$147 F

1. Subdivide each variance into a sales-activity variance portion and a flexible-budget variance portion. Use the format of Exhibit 8-6, page 316.
2. Provide possible explanations for the variances.

8-36 Summary Explanation

Higgins Company produced 50,000 units, 10,000 more than budgeted. Production data are as follows. Except for physical units, all quantities are in dollars.

	Actual Results at Actual Prices	Flexible-Budget Variances	Flexible Budget	Sales-Activity Variances	Static Budget
Physical units	50,000	—	?	?	40,000
Sales	?	5,500 F	?	?	520,000
Variable costs	315,000	?	300,000	?	?
Contribution margin	?	?	?	?	?
Fixed costs	?	8,000 U	?	?	60,000
Income	?	?	?	?	?

1. Fill in the unknowns.
2. Give a brief summary explanation of why the original target income was not attained.

8-37 Explanation of Variance in Income

Damerow Credit Services produces reports for consumers about their credit ratings. The company's standard contribution margins average 70% of dollar sales, and average selling prices are $50 per report. Average productivity is four reports per hour. Some employees work for sales commissions and others for an hourly rate. The static budget for 20X1 had predicted processing 800,000 reports, but Damerow processed only 700,000 reports.

Fixed costs of rent, supervision, advertising, and other items were budgeted at $22 million, but the budget was exceeded by $600,000 because of extra advertising in an attempt to boost revenue. There were no variances from the average selling prices, but the actual commissions paid to preparers and the actual productivity per hour resulted in flexible-budget variances (i.e., total price and quantity variances) for variable costs of $900,000 unfavorable.

The president of Damerow was unhappy because the budgeted income of $6 million was not achieved. He said, "Sure, we had unfavorable variable-cost variances, but our income was down far more than that. Please explain why."

Explain why the budgeted income was not attained. Use a presentation similar to Exhibit 8-6, page 316. Enough data have been given to permit you to construct the complete exhibit by filling in the known items and then computing the unknowns. Complete your explanation by summarizing what happened, using no more than three sentences.

8-38 Activity and Flexible-Budget Variances at KFC

Suppose a chain of KFC franchises in Shanghai had budgeted sales for 2012 of RMB 7.8 million (where RMB stands for the Chinese unit of currency, officially the renminbi, also called the yuan). Cost of goods sold and other variable costs were expected to be 55% of sales. Budgeted annual fixed costs were RMB 2.1 million. A strong Chinese economy caused actual 2012 sales to rise to RMB 10 million and actual profits to increase to RMB 2,050,000. Fixed costs in 2012 were as budgeted. The franchisee was pleased with the increase in profit.

1. Compute the sales-activity variance and the flexible-budget variance for income for 2012. What can the franchisee learn from these variances?
2. Suppose that in 2013 the Chinese economy weakened, and the franchise's sales fell back to the RMB 7.8 million level. Given what happened in 2012, what do you expect to happen to profits in 2013?

8-39 Summary of Airline Performance

The performance (in thousands of dollars) of Sandpiper Airlines for the most recent year is shown in the following table:

	Actual Results at Actual Prices	Static Budget	Variance
Revenue	$?	$385,000	$?
Variable expenses	285,800	250,250*	35,550 U
Contribution margin	?	134,750	?
Fixed expenses	95,300	88,000	7,300 U
Income	$?	$ 46,750	$?

*Includes jet fuel of $55,000.

The static budget had been based on a budget of $.35 revenue per passenger mile. A passenger mile is one paying passenger flown one mile. An average airfare decrease of 6% had helped generate an increase in passenger miles flown that was 20% in excess of the static budget for the year.

The price per gallon of jet fuel rose above the price used to formulate the static budget. The average jet fuel price increase for the year was 20%.

1. Prepare a summary report similar to Exhibit 8-6, page 316, to help the president understand performance for the most recent year.
2. Assume that jet fuel costs are purely variable, and the quantity of fuel used was at the same level of efficiency as predicted in the static budget. What part of the flexible-budget variance for variable expenses is attributable to jet fuel expenses? Explain.

8-40 Hospital Costs and Explanation of Variances

The emergency room at Rochester General Hospital uses a flexible budget based on patients seen as the measure of activity. The hospital must maintain an adequate staff of attending and on-call physicians at all times, so patient activity does not affect physician scheduling. Nurse scheduling varies as volume changes, however. A standard of .5 nurse hours per patient visit was set. Hourly pay for nurses ranges from $9 to $18 per hour, and the average pay rate is $15 per hour. The hospital considers all materials to be supplies, a part of overhead; there are no direct materials. A statistical study showed that the cost of supplies and other variable overhead is more closely associated with nurse hours than with patient visits. The standard for supplies and other variable overhead is $10 per nurse hour.

The head physician of the emergency room unit, Brad Narr, is responsible for control of costs. During October the emergency room unit treated 4,000 patients. The budget and actual costs were as follows:

	Budget	Actual	Variance
Patient visits	3,800	4,000	200
Nurse hours	1,900	2,080	180
Nursing cost	$ 28,500	$ 33,180	$4,680
Supplies and other variable overhead	19,000	20,340	1,340
Fixed costs	92,600	92,600	0
Total cost	$140,100	$146,120	$6,020

1. Calculate price and quantity variances for nursing costs.
2. Calculate spending and efficiency variances for supplies and other variable overhead.
3. The hospital's chief administrator has asked Dr. Narr to explain the variances. Provide possible explanations.

8-41 Flexible Budgeting

For the convenience of its reporters and staff based in London, CNN operates a motor pool. The motor pool operated with 25 vehicles until February of this year, when it acquired an additional automobile. The motor pool furnishes petrol (gasoline), oil, and other supplies for the cars and hires one mechanic who does routine maintenance and minor repairs. Major repairs are done at a nearby commercial garage. A supervisor manages the operations.

Each year the supervisor prepares an operating budget, informing CNN management of the funds needed to operate the pool. Depreciation on the automobiles is recorded in the budget in order to determine the cost per mile.

The following schedule presents the annual budget approved by the news division. The actual costs for March are compared with one-twelfth of the annual budget.

CNN London Motor Pool				
Budget Report for March 20X1				
	Annual Budget	One-Month Budget	March Actual	Over (Under)
Petrol (gasoline)	£ 82,500	£ 6,875	£ 8,200	£1,325
Oil, minor repairs, parts, and supplies	30,000	2,500	2,540	40
Outside repairs	2,700	225	50	(175)
Insurance	4,800	400	416	16
Salaries and benefits	21,600	1,800	1,800	—
Depreciation	22,800	1,900	1,976	76
Total costs	£164,400	£13,700	£14,982	£1,282
Total kilometers	1,500,000	125,000	140,000	
Cost per kilometer	£ .1096	£ .1096	£ .1070	
Number of automobiles	25	25	26	

The annual budget was constructed based on the following assumptions:

1. 25 automobiles in the pool
2. 60,000 kilometers per year per automobile
3. 8 kilometers per liter of petrol for each automobile
4. £.44 per liter of petrol
5. £.02 per kilometer for oil, minor repairs, parts, and supplies
6. £108 per automobile in outside repairs

The supervisor is unhappy with the monthly report comparing budget and actual costs for March; she claims it presents her performance unfairly. Her previous employer used flexible budgeting to compare actual costs with budgeted amounts.

1. Employing flexible-budgeting techniques, prepare a report that shows budgeted amounts, actual costs, and monthly variation for March.
2. Explain briefly the basis of your budget figure for outside repairs.

8-42 Activity-Based Flexible Budget

Cost behavior analysis for the four activity centers in the billing department of Fargo Power Company is given next.

Activity Center	Traceable Costs		Cost-Driver Activity
	Variable	Fixed	
Account inquiry	$ 79,910	$156,380	3,300 labor hours
Correspondence	9,800	25,584	2,800 letters
Account billing	154,377	81,400	2,440,000 lines
Bill verification	10,797	78,050	20,000 accounts

The billing department constructs a flexible budget for each activity center based on the following ranges of cost-driver activity.

Activity Center	Cost Driver	Relevant Range	
Account inquiry	Labor hours	3,000	5,000
Correspondence	Letters	2,500	3,500
Account billing	Lines	2,000,000	3,000,000
Bill verification	Accounts	15,000	25,000

1. Develop flexible-budget formulas for each of the four activity centers.
2. Compute the budgeted total cost in each activity center for each of these levels of cost-driver activity: (a) the smallest activity in the relevant range, (b) the midpoint of the relevant range, and (c) the highest activity in the relevant range.
3. Determine the total cost function for the billing department.
4. The following table gives the actual results for the billing department. Prepare a cost-control performance report comparing the flexible budget to actual results for each activity center. Compute flexible-budget variances.

Activity Center	Actual Cost-Driver Level	Actual Cost
Account inquiry	4,300 labor hours	$235,400
Correspondence	3,200 letters	38,020
Account billing	2,950,000 lines	285,000
Bill verification	23,000 accounts	105,320

8-43 Straightforward Variance Analysis

Crescent Tool Works uses a standard cost system. The month's data regarding its iron castings follow:

- Materials purchased and used, 3,300 pounds
- Direct-labor costs incurred, 5,500 hours, $42,350
- Variable-overhead costs incurred, $4,620
- Finished units produced, 1,000
- Actual materials cost, $.97 per pound
- Standard variable-overhead rate, $.80 per direct-labor hour
- Standard direct-labor cost, $8 per hour
- Standard materials cost, $1 per pound
- Standard pounds of material in a finished unit, 3
- Standard direct-labor hours per finished unit, 5

Prepare schedules of all variances, using the formats of Exhibits 8-9 and 8-11 on pages 324 and 328.

8-44 Variance Analysis

The Lucerne Chocolate Company uses standard costs and a flexible budget to control its manufacture of fine chocolates. The purchasing agent is responsible for material price variances, and the production manager is responsible for all other variances. Operating data for the past week are summarized as follows:

1. Finished units produced: 2,900 boxes of chocolates.
2. Direct materials: Purchased and used, 3,400 pounds of chocolate at 17.3 Swiss francs (CHF) per pound; standard price is CHF 18 per pound. Standard allowed per box produced is 1 pound.
3. Direct labor: Actual costs, 3,925 hours at CHF 38.6, or CHF 151,505. Standard allowed per box produced is 1.25 hours. Standard price per direct-labor hour is CHF 38.
4. Variable manufacturing overhead: Actual costs, CHF 46,675. Budget formula is CHF 11 per standard direct-labor hour.

Compute the following:
1. a. Materials purchase-price variance
   b. Materials quantity variance
   c. Direct-labor price variance
   d. Direct-labor quantity variance
   e. Variable manufacturing-overhead spending variance
   f. Variable manufacturing-overhead efficiency variance
      (Hint: For format, see the solution to the Summary Problem for Your Review, page 330.)
2. a. What is the budget allowance for direct labor?
   b. Would it be any different if production were 3,900 boxes?

8-45 Similarity of Direct-Labor and Variable-Overhead Variances

The Koh Company has had great difficulty controlling costs in Singapore during the past 3 years. Last month, the company installed a standard-cost and flexible-budget system. A condensation of results for a department follows:

	Expected Cost per Standard Direct-Labor Hour	Flexible-Budget Variance
Lubricants	$ .60	$330 F
Other supplies	.30	225 U
Rework	.60	450 U
Other indirect labor	1.50	450 U
Total variable overhead	$3.00	$795 U

F = Favorable. U = Unfavorable.

The department had initially planned to manufacture 9,000 audio speaker assemblies in 6,000 standard direct-labor hours allowed. Material shortages and a heat wave resulted in the production of 8,100 units in 5,800 actual direct-labor hours. The standard wage rate is $5.25 per hour, which was $.15 higher than the actual average hourly rate.

1. Prepare a detailed performance report with two major sections: direct labor and variable overhead.
2. Prepare a summary analysis of price and quantity variances for direct labor and spending and efficiency variances for variable overhead.
3. Explain the similarities and differences between the direct-labor and variable-overhead variances. What are some of the likely causes of the overhead variances?

8-46 Material, Labor, and Overhead Variances

Poulsbo Kayak Company makes molded plastic kayaks. Standard costs for an entry-level whitewater kayak are as follows:

Direct materials, 60 lb at $5.50/lb	$330
Direct labor, 1.5 hr at $16/hr	24
Overhead, at $12 per kayak	12
Total	$366

The overhead rate assumes production of 450 kayaks per month. The overhead cost function is $2,808 + ($5.76 × number of kayaks).

During March, Poulsbo produced 430 kayaks and had the following actual results:

Direct materials purchased and used	27,000 pounds at $5.30/lb
Direct labor	670 hours at $15.90/hr
Actual overhead	$5,335

1. Compute material, labor, and overhead variances.
2. Interpret the variances.
3. Suppose the cost function for variable overhead was $3.84 per labor hour instead of $5.76 per kayak. Compute the variable-overhead efficiency variance and the total overhead spending variance. Would these variances lead you to a different interpretation of the overhead variances from the interpretation in requirement 2? Explain.

8-47 Automation and Direct Labor as Overhead

Kilgore Precision Machining (KPM) has a highly automated manufacturing process for producing a variety of auto parts. Through the use of computer-aided manufacturing and robotics, the company has reduced its labor costs to only 5% of total manufacturing costs. Consequently, the company does not account for labor as a separate item but instead accounts for labor as part of overhead.

Consider a part used in antilock braking systems. The static budget for producing 750 units in March 20X1 is as follows:

Direct materials	$18,000*
Overhead	
Supplies	1,875
Power	1,310
Rent and other building services	2,815
Factory labor	1,500
Depreciation	4,500
Total manufacturing costs	$30,000

*3 lb/unit * $8/lb * 750 units.

Supplies and power are variable, and the other overhead items are fixed costs.
Actual costs in March 20X1 for producing 900 units of the brake part were as follows:

Direct materials	$21,840*
Overhead	
Supplies	2,132
Power	1,612
Rent and other building services	2,775
Factory labor	1,618
Depreciation	4,500
Total manufacturing costs	$34,477

*KPM purchased and used 2,800 pounds of materials at $7.80 per pound.

1. Compute (a) the direct-materials price and quantity variances and (b) the flexible-budget variance for each overhead item.
2. Comment on the way KPM accounts for and controls factory labor.

8-48 Standard Material Allowances

Chesapeake Chemical Company supplies primarily industrial users. Your superior has asked you to develop a standard product cost for a new solution the company plans to introduce.

The new chemical solution is made by combining altium and bollium, boiling the mixture, adding credix, and bottling the resulting solution in 20-liter containers. The initial mix, which is 20 liters in volume, consists of 24 kilograms of altium and 19.2 liters of bollium. A 20% reduction in volume occurs during the boiling process. The solution is then cooled slightly before adding 10 kilograms of credix to each 20-liter container; the addition of credix does not affect the total liquid volume.

The purchase prices of the raw materials used in the manufacture of this new chemical solution are as follows:

Altium	$2.20 per kilogram
Bollium	$4.60 per liter
Credix	$3.20 per kilogram

Determine the standard quantity for each of the raw materials needed to produce 20 liters of Chesapeake Chemical Company's new chemical solution and the total standard materials cost of 20 liters of the new product.

8-49 Role of Defective Units and Nonproductive Time in Setting Standards

Haig McNamee owns and operates McNamee Machining, a subcontractor to several aerospace industry contractors. When Mr. McNamee wins a bid to produce a piece of equipment, he sets standard costs for the production of the item. He then compares actual manufacturing costs with the standards to judge the efficiency of production.

In April 20X1, McNamee won a bid to produce 15,000 units of a shielded component used in a navigation device. Specifications for the component were very tight, and Mr. McNamee expected that on average 1 out of every 6 finished components would fail his final inspection, even if employees exercise every care in production. There was no way to identify defective items before production was complete. Therefore, the company had to produce 18,000 units to get 15,000 good components. The company set standards to include an allowance for the expected number of defective items.

Each final component contained 3.2 pounds of direct materials, and the company expected normal scrap from production to average an additional .4 pounds per unit. It expected the direct material to cost $11.40 per pound plus $.80 per pound for shipping and handling.

Machining of the components required close attention by skilled machinists. Each component required 4 hours of machining time. McNamee paid the machinists $20 per hour, and they worked 40-hour weeks. Of the 40 hours, employees spent an average of 32 hours directly on production. The other 8 hours consisted of time for breaks and waiting time when machines were broken down or there was no work to be done. Nevertheless, the company considered all payments to machinists to be direct labor, whether or not they represented time spent directly on production. In addition to the basic wage rate, McNamee paid fringe benefits averaging $6 per hour and payroll taxes of 10% of the basic wages.

Determine the standard cost of direct materials and direct labor for each good unit of output.

8-50 Review of Major Points in This Chapter

The following questions are based on the Dominion Company data contained in Exhibit 8-1 (page 311) and in the table showing Dominion's direct material and direct labor price and quantity standards on page 318.

1. Suppose actual production and sales were 8,000 units instead of 7,000 units. (a) Compute the sales-activity variance. Is the performance of the marketing function the sole explanation for this variance? Why? (b) Using a flexible budget, compute the budgeted contribution margin, the budgeted income, budgeted direct material, and budgeted direct labor.
2. Suppose the following were the actual results for the production of 8,000 units.
    Direct materials: 42,000 pounds were used at an actual unit price of $1.86, for a total actual cost of $78,120.
    Direct labor: 4,140 hours were used at an actual hourly rate of $16.40, for a total actual cost of $67,896.
    Compute the flexible-budget variance and the price and quantity variances for direct materials and direct labor. Present your answers in the form shown in Exhibit 8-9, page 324.
3. Evaluate Dominion Company's performance based on the variances you calculated in numbers 1 and 2.

8-51 Review Problem on Standards and Flexible Budgets; Answers Are Provided

The Des Moines Leather Company makes a variety of leather goods. It uses standard costs and a flexible budget to aid planning and control. Budgeted variable overhead at a 45,000-direct-labor-hour level is $81,000.

During April, the company had a favorable variable-overhead efficiency variance of $2,970. Material purchases were $241,900. Actual direct-labor costs incurred were $422,100. The direct-labor quantity variance was $15,300 unfavorable. The actual average wage rate was $.60 lower than the standard average wage rate.

The company uses a variable-overhead rate of 20% of standard direct-labor cost for flexible-budgeting purposes. Actual variable overhead for the month was $92,250.

Compute the following amounts; use U or F to indicate whether variances are unfavorable or favorable.

1. Standard direct-labor cost per hour
2. Actual direct-labor hours worked
3. Total direct-labor price variance
4. Total flexible budget for direct-labor costs
5. Total direct-labor flexible-budget variance
6. Variable-overhead spending variance in total

8-51 Answers to Problem 8-51

1. $9. The variable-overhead rate is $1.80, obtained by dividing $81,000 by 45,000 hours. Therefore, the direct-labor rate must be $1.80 ÷ .20 = $9.
2. 50,250 hours. Actual costs, $422,100 ÷ ($9 − $.60) = 50,250 hours.
3. $30,150 F. 50,250 actual hours × $.60 = $30,150.
4. $436,950. Quantity variance was $15,300 U. Therefore, excess hours must have been $15,300 ÷ $9 = 1,700. Consequently, standard hours allowed must be 50,250 − 1,700 = 48,550. Flexible budget = 48,550 × $9 = $436,950.
5. $14,850 F. $436,950 − $422,100 = $14,850 F; or $30,150 F − $15,300 U = $14,850 F.
6. $7,830 U. Flexible budget = 48,550 × 1.80 = $87,390. Total variance = $92,250 − $87,390 = $4,860 U. Spending variance = Total variance − Efficiency variance = $4,860 + $2,970 = $7,830 U. Check: $92,250 − (.20 × $422,100) = $7,830.

CASES

8-52 Activity and Flexible-Budget Variances

Several years ago, Methodist Hospital initiated its substance abuse program, which focused on counseling current and potential substance abusers. The program was funded by a grant from the state department of health that paid $76 per visit for counseling. Pat Leizinger, CFO of Methodist Hospital, was concerned about the substance abuse program. It had never broken even and, thus, was subsidized by the other patients in the hospital. Mr. Leizinger was preparing the hospital's budget for 20X8, and he did not like the substance abuse program's financial situation. The results for 20X7 are shown below:

Revenues ($76 per visit; 17,000 visits)	$1,292,000
Cost of services:	
Supplies	$ 114,750
Physician salaries	204,000
Nurse salaries	153,000
Overhead	676,200
Total direct cost of services	1,147,950
General and administrative expenses	194,250
Total expenses	1,342,200
Net loss	$ (50,200)

Substance Abuse Program
20X7 Results

A recent cost analysis had determined the following facts about the behavior of costs in the substance abuse program:

a. Supplies and physician and nurse salaries were totally variable with respect to number of visits within the range of 15,000–30,000.
b. Variable overhead was equal to 20% of labor costs in 20X7; the remainder of the overhead was fixed.
c. $181,500 of the general and administrative cost was fixed; the remainder varied with number of visits.
d. Costs in 20X8 are expected to behave the same as those in 20X7, except that variable-overhead costs will be 21% of labor costs in 20X8 compared to only 20% of labor costs in 20X7. (Fixed overhead costs will remain the same in 20X8 as in 20X7.)

Leizinger had been pressuring the director of the substance abuse program, Jody Lee, for the last couple of years to try to get her costs under control. Ms. Lee responded that it was a very important program for the community. Besides, the program was so close to breaking even that all it needed was a little more time and the results would be better. She predicted 18,000 visits in 20X8, an increase of nearly 6%, which would certainly make the financial picture brighter.

Leizinger agreed on the importance of the program, but he also said that pressures were building from others in Methodist Hospital to eliminate programs that were a drain on the hospital's resources. Thus, he believed that if the substance abuse program was not at least at a break-even point in 20X8, the program would be in jeopardy. He doesn't believe that even the increase of 1,000 visits would be enough to break even.

1. Compute the cost function for the substance abuse program for use in budgeting for 20X8. That is, compute the variable cost per visit and the total annual fixed cost based on the cost analysis that Leizinger conducted.
2. Compute the budgeted profit (loss) for 20X8, assuming that there will be 18,000 visits at $76 each and the costs behave as expected.
3. Suppose that Methodist Hospital accepted the budget for the substance abuse program that you computed in number 2. At the end of 20X8, the actual loss for the program was $15,500 and the actual number of visits was 18,400. Explain the difference between the amount of loss you budgeted in number 2 and the actual loss of $15,500 in as much detail as you can, given the information you have. Based on this, give a one-sentence answer to each of the following questions:
   a. What was the financial impact of the extra 400 visits?
   b. How well did the substance abuse program control its costs in 20X8?

8-53 Activity-Based Costing and Flexible Budgeting

A new printing department provides printing services to the other departments of Farmers & Mechanics Insurance Company (FMIC). Before the establishment of the in-house printing department, the departments contracted with external printers for their printing work. FMIC's printing policy is to charge departments for the variable printing costs on the basis of number of pages printed. The company recovers fixed costs in pricing of external jobs.

The first year's budget for the printing department was based on the department's expected total costs divided by the planned number of pages to be printed.

Most external government accounts and all internal jobs were expected to use only single-color printing. External commercial accounts use primarily four-color printing. FMIC estimated its variable costs based on the typical mix of single-color versus four-color printing and the average variable cost of printing a four-color page that is one-fourth graphics and three-fourths text. The expected annual costs for each division were as follows:

Department	Planned Pages Printed	Budgeted Charges	Estimated Cost per Page
Government accounts	120,000	$ 90,000	
Commercial accounts	250,000	300,000	
Internal departments	50,000	30,000	
Total	420,000	$420,000	$1

After the first month of operations, the printing department announced that its variable cost estimate of $1 per page was too low. The first month's actual costs were $51,000 to print 40,000 pages.

Government accounts	9,000 pages
Commercial accounts	27,500
Central administration	3,500

Two reasons were cited for higher-than-expected costs: All departments were using more printing services than planned, and government and internal jobs were using more four-color printing and more graphics than anticipated in the original variable cost projections. The printing department also argued that it would have to purchase additional four-color printing equipment if demand for four-color printing continued to grow.

1. Compare the printing department actual results, static budget, and flexible budget for the month just completed.
2. Discuss possible reasons why the printing department static budget was inaccurate.
3. An ABC study completed by a consultant indicated that printing costs are driven by number of pages (at $.35 per page), and use of colors (at $1 extra per page for color).
    a. Discuss the likely effects of using the ABC results for budgeting and control of printing department use.
    b. Discuss the assumptions regarding cost behavior implied in the ABC study results.
    c. All commercial accounts during the first month (27,500 pages) used four colors per page. Compare the cost of commercial accounts under the old and the proposed ABC system.

8-54 Analyzing Performance

Hopkins Community Hospital operates an outpatient clinic in a town several miles from the main hospital. For several years the clinic has struggled just to break even. The clinic's financial budget for 20X7 is shown below:

20X7 Budget

	Total		Per Patient
Revenues (4,000 patients at $180 each)		$ 720,000	$180
Cost of services			
Physicians	$240,000		
Nurses and technicians	180,000		
Supplies	60,000		
Overhead	252,000	732,000	183
Net loss		$ (12,000)	$ (3)

On the average, billings for each patient-visit are expected to be $180. Costs in 20X7 are expected to average $183 per patient-visit, as follows:

Physician time	$ 60
Nurse and technician time	45
Supplies	15
Overhead	63
Total	$183

The clinic is generally staffed by one physician who must be present whether or not there is a patient to see. Currently, about 10% of the physician's time is idle. The clinic employs nurses and technicians to meet the actual workload necessitated by patient appointments. Their cost averages $30 per hour, and usage varies proportionately with the number of patient-visits. Supplies cost is also variable with respect to patient-visits. Fixed overhead in 20X7 was expected to be $180,000; the remaining $72,000 of overhead varies with respect to patient visits. Included in the fixed overhead was $30,000 of hospital-wide administrative costs that the hospital allocates to the clinic and $37,500 of depreciation on the clinic's property and equipment.

Cindy Ryden, controller of Hopkins Community Hospital, reported the actual loss of $20,200 in 20X7 shown next. This represented the fifth straight year of losses. She does not feel it is right for patients in the main hospital to subsidize those using the clinic. Therefore, she suggested that unless the situation could be changed, the clinic should be closed. Brett Johnson, administrative vice president of the hospital, charged with oversight of the clinic, disagreed: "We provide a valuable service to the community with the clinic. Even if we are losing money, it is worthwhile to keep it open."

At the end of 20X7, the clinic's actual results for the year were as follows:

		Total
Revenues (3,800 patients at $180)		$ 684,000
Cost of services		
Physicians	$231,000	
Nurses and technicians (5,800 hours)	182,700	
Supplies	58,500	
Overhead	232,000	704,200
Net loss		$ (20,200)

1. Would Hopkins Community Hospital have saved money in 20X7 if the outpatient clinic was closed? Explain.
2. Explain the difference between the budgeted loss of $12,000 and the actual loss of $20,200 (that is, the static-budget variance of $8,200) in as much detail as possible. From the analysis of the 20X7 results, what actions would you suggest to avoid a loss in 20X8?

8-55 Complete Variance Analysis

Gates Video Games manufactures video game machines. Market saturation and technological innovations have caused pricing pressures that have resulted in declining profits. To stem the slide in profits until the company can introduce new products, top management has turned its attention to both manufacturing economies and increased production. To realize these objectives, management developed an incentive program to reward production managers who contribute to an increase in the number of units produced and achieve cost reductions. In addition, the company instituted a JIT purchasing program so that it purchases raw materials on an as-needed basis.

The production managers have responded to the pressure to improve manufacturing performance in several ways that have resulted in an increase over normal production levels. The video game machines put together by the assembly group require parts from both the printed circuit boards (PCB) and the reading heads (RH) departments. To attain increased production levels, the PCB and RH departments started rejecting parts from suppliers that previously would have been tested and modified to meet manufacturing standards. Preventive maintenance on machines used in the production of these parts has been postponed with only emergency repair work being performed to keep production lines moving. The maintenance staff is concerned that there will be serious breakdowns and unsafe operating conditions.

The more aggressive assembly group production supervisors have pressured maintenance personnel to attend to their machines at the expense of other groups. This has resulted in machine downtime in the PCB and RH departments which, when coupled with demands for accelerated parts delivery by the assembly department, has led to more frequent parts rejections and increased friction among departments. Gates Video Games operates under a standard-costing system. The standard costs at a production level of 24,000 units per year are in part A of Exhibit 8-13.

Exhibit 8-13
Gates Video Games

	Standard Cost per Unit		
	Quantity	**Cost**	**Total**
A. Standard Cost Report			
Direct materials:			
Housing unit	1 unit	$ 20	$ 20
Printed circuit boards (PCB)	2 boards	15	30
Reading heads (RH)	4 heads	10	40
Direct labor:			
Assembly department	2.0 hours	8	$ 16
PCB department	1.0 hour	9	9
RH department	1.5 hours	10	15
Overhead:			
Variable	4.5 hours	$ 2	$ 9
Fixed	4.5 hours	4	18
Total manufacturing cost per unit			$157
Selling and administrative:			
Fixed		$ 12	$ 12
Total standard cost per unit			$169
B. Income Statement for May			
Revenues (2,200 units)		$440,000	
Variable costs:			
Direct materials	220,400		
Direct labor	93,460		
Variable overhead	18,800		
Fixed costs:			
Overhead	37,600		
Selling and administrative	22,000		
Total costs		392,260	
Income before taxes		$ 47,740	
C. Usage Report for May			
Cost Item	**Actual Quantity**	**Actual Cost**	
Direct materials:			
Housing units	2,200 units	$ 44,000	
Printed circuit boards	4,700 boards	75,200	
Reading heads	9,200 heads	101,200	
Direct labor:			
Assembly department	3,900 hours	31,200	
PCB department	2,400 hours	23,760	
RH department	3,500 hours	38,500	
Overhead:			
Variable		18,800	
Fixed		37,600	
Total manufacturing costs		$370,260	

Gates Video Games prepares monthly income statements based on actual expenses. Part B of Exhibit 8-13 shows the statement for May, when production and sales both reached 2,200 units. The budgeted sales price was $200 per unit, and budgeted (normal) production and sales were 24,000 units per year. Top management was surprised by the low profit in spite of increased sales for May. The original budget had called for income before taxes of $62,000, and with the added sales, the president had expected at least $68,200 of income ($6,200 more income; 200 extra units × $31 per unit).

The president called on Michelle Barber, director of cost management, to report on the reasons for the shortfall in income. After a thorough review of the data, Barber prepared the report in part C of Exhibit 8-13.

1. Prepare a budgeted income statement in contribution margin format for Gates Video Games showing why the company expected income before taxes to be $62,000.
2. Assume that you have been given Michelle Barber's task. Prepare a complete analysis explaining the reason for the difference between the original projected income before taxes of $62,000 and the actual of $47,740. Compute all the variances that are helpful in explaining this difference, and explain what you learn from the variances.

NIKE 10-K PROBLEM

8-56 Performance Standards

Examine Nike's income statement shown in condensed form as "Results of Operations" for fiscal years 2009, 2010, and 2011 in Appendix C. Suppose that Nike used results for 2010 to set standards for 2011. Assume that cost of sales is a variable cost and that selling and administrative costs are fixed costs and that income is simply revenue − cost of sales − selling and administrative costs. Prepare a static budget based on the assumption that sales and cost of sales (variable costs) will grow by 10%. Prepare a flexible budget based on the sales level achieved for 2011. Using the actual results for 2011, determine the static-budget variances, the sales-activity variances, and the flexible-budget variances for sales, cost of sales, selling and administrative costs, and income.

EXCEL APPLICATION EXERCISE

8-57 Flexible-Budget and Sales-Activity Variances

Goal: Create an Excel spreadsheet to prepare a summary performance report that identifies flexible-budget and sales-activity variances. Use the results to answer questions about your findings.
Scenario: David Campbell Tax Services has asked you to prepare a summary performance report identifying its flexible-budget and sales-activity variances. The background data for the summary performance report appears in the Fundamental Assignment Material 8-B1. Prepare the summary performance report using a format similar to Exhibit 8-6.
   When you have completed your spreadsheet, answer the following questions:

1. What caused the flexible-budget variance for sales?
2. What was the change in actual income compared to the income calculated in the static budget?
3. Can the amount in question 2 be explained by the flexible-budget and sales-activity variances? Explain.

Step-by-Step:

1. Open a new Excel spreadsheet.
2. In column A, create a bold-faced heading that contains the following:
   Row 1: Chapter 8 Decision Guideline
   Row 2: Campbell Tax Services
   Row 3: Summary Performance Report
   Row 4: Today's Date
3. Merge and center the four heading rows across columns A–H.
4. In column A, create the following row headings:
   Row 8: Clients
   Skip a row.
   Row 10: Sales
   Row 11: Variable Costs
   Row 12: Contribution Margin
   Row 13: Fixed Costs
   Skip a row.
   Row 15: Operating Income
5. Change the format of Contribution margin (row 12) and Operating income (row 15) to boldfaced headings.
   Note: Adjust width of column A to accommodate row headings.
6. In row 7, create the following bold-faced, center-justified column headings:
   Column B: Actual Results at Actual Activity
   Column C: Flexible-Budget Variances

Skip a column.
Column E: Flexible Budget at Actual Activity
Column F: Sales-Activity Variances
Skip a column.
Column H: Static Budget

7. Change the format of the column headings in row 7 to permit the titles to be displayed on multiple lines within a single cell.

Alignment tab:	Wrap Text:	Checked

Note: Adjust column widths so that headings use only two lines. Adjust row height to ensure that row is same height as adjusted headings.

8. Change format of the column width of columns D and G to a size of 2.

9. Use the scenario data to fill in client and fixed cost amounts for actual, flexible-budget, and static-budget columns as well as variable costs for the actual column.

10. Calculate variable costs for flexible-budget and static budget columns. Use appropriate formulas to calculate sales, contribution margin, and operating income amounts for actual, flexible-budget, and static-budget columns.

11. Use appropriate formulas to calculate flexible-budget variances as actual − flexible budget and sales-activity variances as flexible budget − static budget and display as absolute values.
= ABS(*variance formula*)

12. To indicate whether variances are favorable (F) or unfavorable (U), use one of the following formula templates:
For sales, margin and income variances and for client variances,
= IF(*variance formula* > 0,"F",IF(*variance formula* < 0,"U","—"))
For clients, variable and fixed cost variances,
= IF(*variance formula* < 0,"F",IF(*variance formula* > 0,"U","—"))

(Hint: Go to the "Help" text and type "copy formulas" in the search area to obtain instructions for copying formulas from one cell to another. If done correctly, you should have to type in each of the formula templates only once.)

13. Format all amounts as follows:

Number:	Category:	
	Decimal places:	0
	Symbol:	None
	Negative numbers:	Red with parentheses

14. Change the format of the amounts for sales, contribution margin, and operating income to display a dollar symbol.

15. Change the format of the operating income amounts for actual, flexible budget, and static budget to display as bold.

16. Change the format of the row headings for contribution margin and operating income to display as indented.

Alignment tab:	Horizontal:	Left (Indent)
	Indent:	1

Note: Adjust width of column A to accommodate row headings.

17. Save your work, and print a copy for your files.

Note: Print your spreadsheet using landscape format in order to ensure that all columns appear on one page.

COLLABORATIVE LEARNING EXERCISE

8-58 Setting Standards

Form groups of two to six persons each. The groups should each select a simple product or service. Be creative, but do not pick a product or service that is too complex. For those having difficulty choosing a product or service, some possibilities are as follows:

- One dozen chocolate-chip cookies
- A 10-mile taxi ride
- One copy of a 100-page course syllabus
- A machine-knit wool sweater
- A hand-knit wool sweater
- One hour of lawn mowing and fertilizing
- A hammer

1. Each student should individually estimate the direct materials and direct labor inputs needed to produce the product or service. For each type of direct material and direct labor, determine the standard quantity and standard price. Also, identify the overhead support needed, and determine the standard overhead cost of the product or service. The result should be a total standard cost for the product or service.

2. Each group should compare the estimates of its members. Where estimates differ, determine why there were differences. Did assumptions differ? Did some members have more knowledge about the product or service than others? Form a group estimate of the standard cost of the product or service.

3. After the group has agreed on a standard cost, discuss the process used to arrive at the cost. What assumptions did the group make? Is the standard cost an "ideal" standard or a "currently attainable" standard? Note how widely standard costs can vary depending on assumptions and knowledge of the production process.

INTERNET EXERCISE

8-59 Flexible Budgets at Hershey Food Corporation

This chapter focused on flexible budgets and variance analysis. While the information used to determine both of these is generally for internal purposes only and not available to an outsider, it is possible to look at what information a firm reports and, based on that information, to make some judgments about what occurred.

1. Look at the Hershey Company home page at www.hersheys.com. Who is Hershey's home page directed to? What are the most prominent items on the page? Where do you find financial information?

2. Click on "Corporate Information," then on "Investors," and then "Financial Reports." Examine Hershey's income statement from its most recent 10-K in "SEC Filings." Prepare a static budget for income before income taxes based on the assumption that net sales and variable costs are expected to increase by 4% for the next fiscal year. Assume that cost of sales is the only variable cost and that all other costs are fixed costs. (The assumption that all other costs—including items such as realignment and impairment charges, gains on sales of businesses, and other such one-time charges—are fixed costs, is a simplification. A more realistic assumption might be that these are nonrecurring costs.)

3. Now, suppose that selling prices were exactly as budgeted in question 2, but sales and variable costs actually increased by 6% and fixed costs increased by 1%. Determine the static-budget variance, the sales-activity variance, and the flexible-budget variance for operating income.

Management Control Systems and Responsibility Accounting

LEARNING OBJECTIVES

When you have finished studying this chapter, you should be able to:

1. Describe the relationship of management control systems to organizational goals.

2. Explain the importance of evaluating performance and describe how it impacts motivation, goal congruence, and employee effort.

3. Develop performance measures and use them to monitor the achievements of an organization.

4. Use responsibility accounting to define an organizational subunit as a cost center, a profit center, or an investment center.

5. Prepare segment income statements for evaluating profit and investment centers using the contribution margin and controllable-cost concepts.

6. Measure performance against nonfinancial performance measures such as quality, cycle time, and productivity.

7. Use a balanced scorecard to integrate financial and nonfinancial measures of performance.

8. Describe the difficulties of management control in service and nonprofit organizations.

► HEALTH NET

It's 2:30 AM. You don't feel well. Should you call your doctor? Go to the emergency room? Is what you're feeling really something to worry about? What you need is good quality health care and you need it now, not tomorrow morning, and you do not want to worry about its cost. Sound familiar? This is a dilemma that we have all faced at some time. One health-care organization that has a solution is Health Net, one of the largest managed health-care organizations in the United States. With approximately 7,500 employees and 2011 revenues of about $12 billion, it provides coverage to 5.6 million health plan members.

Health-care organizations must compete just as any other business, offering high-quality health care at an affordable cost. To maintain its competitive advantage, Health Net undertook a major information systems development program called "fourth generation medical management." According to Dr. Malik Hasan, former chairman and CEO, Health Net created this new management control system "because the greatest opportunity for increasing overall quality and decreasing the cost of health care lies in managing patient care by seamlessly linking the entire health care delivery system electronically." The system "gives physicians and health care providers instant, user-friendly electronic access to comprehensive information about a patient's medical history and the best clinical treatments recommended."

The result? A fast and preapproved referral to the best clinical resource, whether it be a specialist, the emergency room or urgent care center, your regular physician, or safe self-care. In other words, a satisfied customer! And as a bonus, costs are reduced. As Medical Director John Danaher, MD, explains, "Paper charting and duplicative lab and radiology tests are eliminated."

This chapter builds on concepts developed in previous chapters to explore how managers blend the individual tools of management accounting to help achieve organizational goals. Tools such as activity-based costing, relevant costing, budgeting, and variance analysis are useful by themselves. They are most useful, however, when they are parts of an integrated system—a comprehensive plan to coordinate and evaluate all the activities of the organization's value chain. Just as in the case of Health Net, managers of most organizations today realize that long-run success requires a focus on cost, quality, and service—the three components of the competitive edge. This chapter considers how the management control system helps managers achieve such a focus. As you will see, no single management control system is inherently superior to another. The "best" system for any organization is the one that most consistently leads to actions that meet the organization's goals and objectives. ∎

© Stockbroker/Alamy

Management Control Systems

A **management control system** is an integrated set of techniques for gathering and using information to make planning and control decisions, for motivating employee behavior, and for evaluating performance. A well-designed management control system supports and coordinates the decision-making process and motivates individuals throughout the organization to act in concert. It also facilitates forecasting and budgeting. An effective management control system should

- clearly define and communicate the organization's goals,
- ensure that managers and employees understand the specific actions required to achieve organizational goals,
- communicate results of actions across the organization, and
- motivate managers and employees to achieve the organization's goals.

Exhibit 9-1 describes elements of the planning and control processes. As we pointed out in Chapter 1, planning and control are so strongly interrelated that it is somewhat artificial to separate them in practice. To the extent we can separate them, planning includes defining goals (A) and establishing and carrying out plans to achieve the goals (B). Control includes measuring and reporting results (C) and performance evaluation (D). The clockwise ordering of the elements represents the order that managers would naturally follow when designing and evaluating the management control system. However, once an organization has implemented the control system, it continues to adapt and revise the interrelated elements through feedback and learning. For example, the organization may revise the measures used to monitor and report in C to better fit with the goals in A. Similarly, it might realign the performance evaluation system in D to better fit with the specific plans and objectives in B. We will refer to Exhibit 9-1 often as we consider the design and operation of management control systems.

Management Control Systems and Organizational Goals

The first and most basic component in a management control system is the organization's goals. Top managers set organization-wide goals, performance measures, and targets. These goals provide a long-term framework around which an organization will form its comprehensive plan for positioning itself in the market. Goals address the question in Exhibit 9-1, "What do we want to achieve?" However, goals without performance measures do not motivate managers.

A basic adage of management control is that "you get what you measure." Because measures of performance set direction and motivate managers' decisions, every performance measure should be consistent with organizational goals. Otherwise, managers who achieve high performance measures may not create value for the company and its owners. An ideal management control system should include at least one performance measure related to every goal. The book *Cracking the Value Code* states this succinctly when it says that we tend to "value what we measure but we do not always measure what we value."

Doctors and managers at Health Net use a state-of-the-art medical management system and management control system to offer high-quality health care at an affordable price.

management control system
An integrated set of techniques for gathering and using information to make planning and control decisions, for motivating employee behavior, and for evaluating performance.

Objective 1

Describe the relationship of management control systems to organizational goals.

Exhibit 9-1
The Management Control System

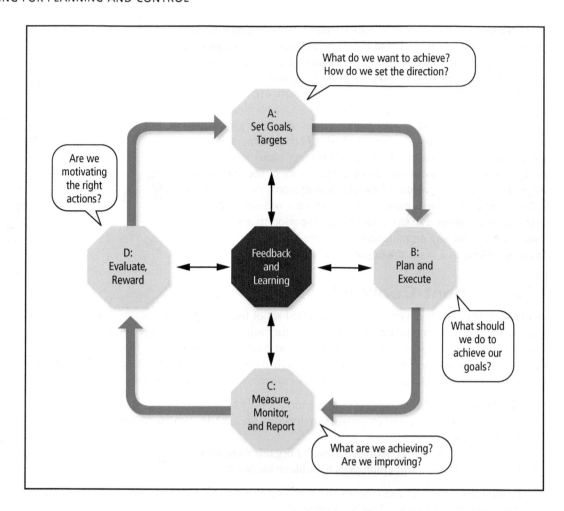

To illustrate, suppose a hotel such as Arizona-based Scottsdale Luxury Suites has the following organizational goals and related performance measures:

Organizational Goals	Performance Measures
Exceed guest expectations	• Customer satisfaction index • Number of repeat stays
Maximize revenue yield	• Occupancy rate • Average room rate • Income before fixed costs
Focus on innovation	• New products/services implemented per year • Number of employee suggestions

The company sets quantifiable targets for each of the measures. For example, the target for occupancy rate might be "at least 70%." Note that every goal has at least one performance measure, and every measure is related to at least one goal.

Exhibit 9-2 illustrates how managers set goals and objectives and develop related performance measures for the organization. Performance measures become more specific as we move to lower levels of the organization. For example, higher-level managers work with subordinates within each business unit to select specific short-term actions (or activities) that managers can carry out, along with observable performance measures. One approach to selecting these actions and measures is for top managers to identify **key success factors**—characteristics or attributes that managers must achieve in order to drive the organization toward its goals. For example, at Scottsdale Luxury Suites, a key success factor for the goal to exceed guest expectations might be timeliness. This key success factor suggests that Scottsdale Luxury Suites should consider

key success factors

Characteristics or attributes that managers must achieve in order to drive the organization toward its goals.

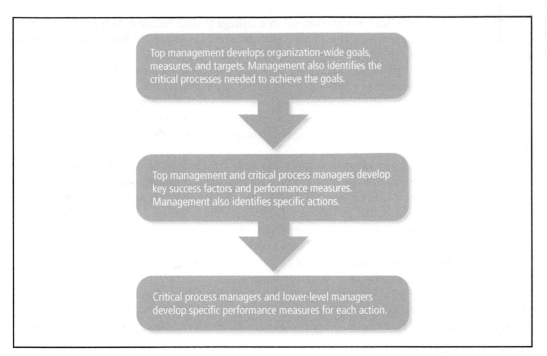

Exhibit 9-2
Translating Goals and Objectives into Performance Measures

specific actions, such as implementing an express check-in system. In addition, it should measure timeliness by using performance measures, such as time to check in, time to check out, and response time to guest requests (for example, number of rings before someone at the front desk answers the telephone).

Balancing various goals is an important part of designing a management control system. Managers often face trade-offs. For example, a manager may meet a goal of increased customer satisfaction by establishing a more generous policy for accepting returned merchandise. However, this policy will also impose additional costs that decrease short-term profitability. Choosing the best trade-off between short-term profitability and long-term customer satisfaction is often difficult, especially when the long-term benefits of increased customer satisfaction are hard to predict.

Designing Management Control Systems

To design a management control system that meets the organization's needs, managers must identify what motivates employees, develop performance measures based on these motivations, and establish a monitoring and reporting structure for these measures. Let's look at each of these.

Motivating Employees

An important goal of the management control system is to motivate employees to work in the best interests of the organization. A good management control system fosters both goal congruence and managerial effort. A system fosters **goal congruence** when employees, responding to the incentives created by the control system, make decisions that help meet the overall goals of the organization. To be effective, goal congruence must be accompanied by **managerial effort**— exertion toward a goal or objective—including not only working harder or faster but also working smarter. It includes all conscious actions (such as supervising, planning, and analysis) that result in more efficiency and effectiveness.

As we saw in Exhibit 9-1, the challenge of management control system design is to induce (or at least not discourage) employee decisions that achieve organizational goals. For example, an organization may identify continuous improvement in employee efficiency and effectiveness as one of its goals. Employees, however, might perceive that continuous improvements will result in tighter standards, faster pace of work, and loss of jobs. Even though they may agree with management that continuous improvements are competitively necessary, management should not expect them to exert effort for continuous improvements unless rewards are in place to make this effort in their own best interests.

Objective 2

Explain the importance of evaluating performance and describe how it impacts motivation, goal congruence, and employee effort.

goal congruence
A condition where employees, responding to the incentives created by the control system, make decisions that help meet the overall goals of the organization.

managerial effort
Exertion toward a goal or objective, including all conscious actions (such as supervising, planning, and thinking) that result in more efficiency and effectiveness.

As another example, students may enroll in a college course because their goal is to learn about management accounting. The faculty and the students share the same goal, but goal congruence is not enough. Faculty also introduce a grading system to reward student effort. Grading is a form of performance evaluation, similar to organizations using management control reports for raises, promotions, and other forms of rewards. Performance evaluation improves effort because most individuals tend to perform better when performance reports lead directly to personal rewards. Thus, manufacturers that set quality improvements as critical organizational goals, such as **Allen-Bradley** and **Corning**, put quality targets into the bonus plans of top managers and factory workers.

motivation
The drive that creates effort and action toward a goal.

Motivation—the drive that creates effort and action toward a goal—is key to management control. Yet employees differ widely in their motivations. This makes the system designer's task complex and ill-structured. Each system must fit the specific organizational environment and behavioral characteristics of the employees. The system designer must align individuals' self-interests with the goals of the organization. Thus, the designer must predict the motivational impact of a particular system—how it will cause people to respond—and compare it to the motivational impact of other potential systems. Designing performance measures is not a back-office accounting task. It requires direction from top management and the direct involvement of those affected. Stephen Kaufman, former chairman of the board of **Arrow Electronics** put it this way: "It's very difficult to define the right metric and anticipate exactly how your people will react to it. Your best chance of knowing whether it will have the intended effect is to talk to the people directly involved."

All management control tools, such as budgets and variances, should constructively influence behavior. These tools are most effective when managers use them positively to encourage employees to improve performance, rather than negatively to punish, place blame, or find fault. Used negatively, these tools pose a threat to employees, who will resist the use of such techniques. Critics have pointed to **Enron**'s management control system as a major cause of the company's problems. Employees were heavily rewarded for good performance. More importantly, the employees who were ranked lowest at each evaluation were fired. This created intense competition, which at first seemed to create exceptional performance levels for the company. Later, it became clear that the pressure for good performance caused some employees to use unethical methods to increase their performance measures, which eventually led to the demise of the company.

Developing Performance Measures

Objective 3

Develop performance measures and use them to monitor the achievements of an organization.

For most organizations, an effective management control system requires multiple performance measures, including both financial and nonfinancial measures, where the measures have the following characteristics:

1. Reflect key actions and activities that relate to the goals of the organization
2. Affected by actions of managers and employees
3. Readily understood by employees
4. Reasonably objective and easily measured
5. Used consistently and regularly in evaluating and rewarding managers and employees
6. Balance long-term and short-term concerns

Sometimes accountants and managers focus too much on financial measures—such as operating budgets, profit targets, or required return on investment—because the accounting system readily produces such measures. Further, it is often difficult to construct performance measures for nonfinancial goals such as customer satisfaction, improvements in quality, environmental stewardship, social responsibility, and organizational learning, which many companies list as key goals. However, well-designed management control systems develop and report both financial and nonfinancial measures of performance because "You can't manage something you can't measure."

Nonfinancial measures often motivate employees toward achieving important performance goals. For example, **AT&T Universal Card Services**, which received the prestigious Baldrige National Quality Award (presented by the U.S. Department of Commerce), used 18 performance measures for its customer inquiries process. These measures include average speed of

Business First

Performance Measures in Practice

An organization's performance measures depend on its goals and objectives. For example, a software company and an auto manufacturer have different goals and objectives and therefore have different performance measures. The measures also must span a variety of key success factors for the organization. Performance measures too focused on one aspect of performance may foster neglect of other important factors.

Let's look at a classic management control system, the one developed by General Electric in the 1950s. The system focused on eight "key result areas," as GE called them:

Financial Key Result Areas
1. Profitability
2. Productivity
3. Market position

Nonfinancial Key Result Areas
4. Product leadership
5. Personnel development
6. Employee attitudes
7. Public responsibility
8. Balance between short-run and long-range goals

Measures in each of these eight areas are just as relevant today as in the 1950s. These are clearly long-run strategic goals. Measures might change as an organization adapts the means of achieving the goals, but the basic framework of a management control system does not need to change as management fads come and go.

A more recent example is Southwest Airlines. The mission of Southwest Airlines is "dedication to the highest quality of customer service delivered with a sense of warmth, friendliness, individual pride, and company spirit." Yet, until recently, the company focused mainly on financial measures in evaluating managers. Recently, Southwest introduced nonfinancial measures into the mix, including the following:

- Load factor (percentage of seats occupied)
- Utilization factors on aircraft and personnel
- On-time performance
- Available seat miles
- Denied boarding rate
- Lost bag reports per 10,000 passengers
- Flight cancellation rate
- Employee head count
- Customer complaints per 10,000 passengers

By including nonfinancial measures, Southwest focuses managers' attention on the key success factors that relate most closely to Southwest's mission and goals.

Sources: David Solomons, *Divisional Performance: Measurement and Control* (Homewood, IL: Irwin, 1965); and Southwest Airlines Web site (www.southwest.com).

---

answer, abandon rate, and application processing time (3 days compared to the industry average of 34 days).

Financial measures often are lagging indicators that arrive too late to help prevent problems and ensure the organization's health. The effects of poor nonfinancial performance (for example, lack of organizational learning and low customer satisfaction) may not show up in the financial measures until the company has lost considerable ground. Many companies now stress management of the activities that drive revenues and costs, rather than waiting to explain the revenues or costs themselves. Superior financial performance usually follows from superior nonfinancial performance. Examples of both financial and nonfinancial measures are in the accompanying Business First box.

Monitoring and Reporting Results

Notice that Exhibit 9-1 has feedback and learning at the center of the management control system. Organization-wide learning is fundamental to gaining and maintaining financial strength. Some management experts have said that the only sustainable competitive advantage is the rate at which a company's managers learn. Harley-Davidson, a company with 2011 sales of about $5.3 billion, emphasizes learning for operational excellence—eliminating waste, improving quality, and helping drive customer satisfaction.

Once a company has superior intellectual capital, how can it best maintain its leadership? Exhibit 9-3 shows how organizational learning leads to financial strength. Measures such as training time, employee turnover, and staff satisfaction scores on employee surveys monitor organizational learning. The result of learning is continuous process improvement. Measures such as lead time, number of defects (quality), and activity costs can assess improvement. Customers will value improved response time, higher quality, and lower prices and will increase their demand for products and services. Increased demand, combined with lower costs to make and deliver products and services, results in improved product profitability and earnings.

Exhibit 9-3

The Components of a
Successful Organization and
Measures of Achievement

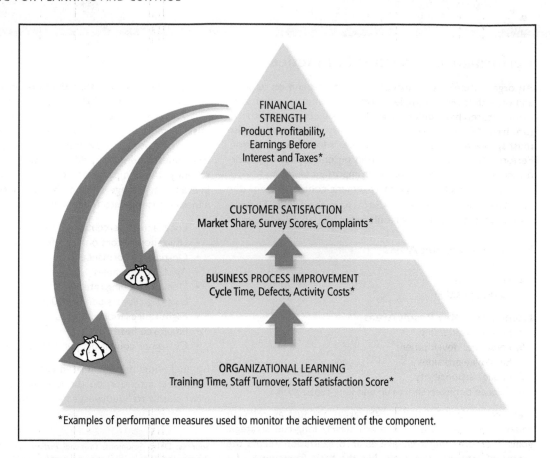

Successful organizations continuously repeat this cycle, where learning leads to process improvements, which lead to increased customer satisfaction, which leads to improved financial strength, which provides the financial resources required to begin a new cycle of learning and process improvements.

There are no guarantees that each of the components automatically follows from success at the previous component. If efforts are not coordinated throughout the value chain, the cause-effect links can be broken. For example, new and improved products or services may fail if marketing and distribution techniques do not place them at the location desired by the customer. As another example, development of a great Web site does no good if customers never visit the site. The point is that improvement in business processes must be coordinated across all parts of the value chain.

Another message from Exhibit 9-3 is that a key driver of enterprise performance is the culture within the company that fosters continual learning and growth at all levels of management. It is not sufficient to use money to train managers without making sure that the resulting learning translates into improved processes, products, and services. This requires a culture of learning that motivates managers to translate learning into growth.

General Electric provides a good example of the application of the enterprise learning culture. With sales of nearly $150 billion, GE has demonstrated a remarkable ability to generate formidable profits with products ranging from aircraft engines to medical imaging to business and consumer financing. GE employs more than 300,000 people worldwide. In 2012, GE was fifteenth on *Fortune* magazine's "Most Admired Company in America," and has consistently been at or near the top of the list throughout the last decade. Many of the company's divisions dominate their markets.

Just before he retired, former CEO John Welch attributed GE's success to

> . . . .*a General Electric culture that values the contributions of every individual, thrives on learning, thirsts for the better idea, and has the flexibility and speed to put the better idea into action every day. We are a learning company, a company that studies its own successes and failures and those of others—a company that has the self-confidence and the resources to take big swings and pursue numerous opportunities based on winning ideas*

and insights, regardless of their source. That appetite for learning, and the ability to act quickly on that learning, will provide GE with what we believe is an insurmountable and sustainable competitive advantage.

Exactly what did John Welch mean by the "ability to act quickly on that learning"? According to Welch, GE "opened [its] culture up to ideas from everyone, everywhere, killed NIH (Not Invented Here) thinking, decimated the bureaucracy, and made boundaryless behavior a reflexive and natural part of our culture, thereby creating the learning culture." His successor, Jeff Immelt, points out another important part of the GE learning culture—openness to dropping old management approaches in favor of new and better techniques: "Most people inside GE learn from the past but have a healthy disrespect for history. They have an ability to live in the moment and not be burdened by the past, which is extremely important."

Weighing Costs and Benefits

The designer of a management control system must always weigh the costs and benefits of various alternatives. Benefits and costs of management control systems are often difficult to measure, and both may become apparent only after implementation. For example, the director of accounting policy of Citicorp stated that, after using a very detailed management control system for several years, the system proved to be too costly to administer relative to the perceived benefits. Accordingly, Citicorp returned to a simpler, less costly—though less detailed—management control system. In contrast, Home Depot added detail in the form of additional metrics to its management control system. When employees asked then-CEO Bob Nardelli why they should use the new metrics, he compared the metrics to gauges in a car: "Why do you need a gas gauge? Why do you need a speedometer?" He believed the metrics were worth the cost because they help top management know what is occurring throughout the company.

Summary Problem for Your Review

PROBLEM

The Blue Harbor Inn is developing performance measures for each of its major goals. Top management established an organization-wide goal to "exceed guest expectations." Among the key success factors are timeliness of customer service and quality of personalized service. Patty Bowen, vice president of sales, is the manager responsible for the actions required to meet the goal of exceeding guest expectations. She has already identified one action (objective) for the coming year—upgrade customer service department capabilities.

1. Identify several possible performance measures for the quality-of-personalized-service key success factor.
2. Recommend several specific actions or activities associated with upgrading customer service department capabilities that would drive Luxury Suites toward its goal of exceeding customer expectations.

SOLUTION

1. Performance measures for the quality of personalized service might include the number of changes to registration, rating on the "friendly, knowledgeable staff" question on the guest survey, number of complaints, percentage of return guests, and percentage of customers with completed customer profile (which profiles the special needs of customers).
2. Specific actions or activities might include training employees, implementing a call checklist (list of services and options available to the guest) and monitoring compliance with the list, developing a customer satisfaction survey, and reengineering the guest registration and reservation processes.

Controllability and Measurement of Financial Performance

controllable cost

Any cost that a manager's decisions and actions can influence.

uncontrollable cost

Any cost that the management of a responsibility center cannot affect within a given time span.

Management control systems often distinguish between controllable and uncontrollable events and between controllable and uncontrollable costs. These terms refer to relative rather than absolute controllability—no cost is completely under the control of a manager. A **controllable cost** is one that a manager's decisions and actions can influence to a reasonable extent. An **uncontrollable cost** is any cost that management cannot reasonably affect within a given time span. For example, Dow Chemical is likely to consider the cost of the crude oil used to make various chemicals as uncontrollable by the manager of a chemical factory because the manager cannot control the market price of crude oil. On the other hand, Dow Chemical is likely to consider labor costs as controllable by the factory manager even though there are some aspects of labor costs that are not controlled by the manager, such as the effects of union contracts on pay rates and labor usage.

The distinction between controllable and uncontrollable costs is used in evaluating the performance of a manager. Costs that are completely uncontrollable provide no insight into a manager's decisions and actions because, by definition, manager actions will not affect uncontrollable costs. In contrast, controllable costs provide evidence about costs that are affected by the manager's decisions.

Identifying Responsibility Centers

Objective 4

Use responsibility accounting to define an organizational subunit as a cost center, a profit center, or an investment center.

responsibility center

A set of activities and resources assigned to a manager, a group of managers, or other employees.

Designers of management control systems identify the responsibilities of each manager by establishing responsibility centers based on what a manager can control. A **responsibility center** is a set of activities and resources assigned to a manager, a group of managers, or other employees. A set of machines and machining activities, for example, may be a responsibility center for a production supervisor. The full production department may be a responsibility center for the department head. Finally, the entire organization may be a responsibility center for the president. In some organizations, groups of employees share management responsibility to create wide "ownership" of management decisions, to allow creative decision making, and to prevent one person's concern (or lack of concern) over risk from dominating decisions.

responsibility accounting

Identifying what parts of the organization have primary responsibility for each action, developing performance measures and targets, and designing reports of these measures by responsibility center.

An effective management control system gives each manager responsibility for a group of activities and actions and then, as Exhibit 9-1 shows, monitors and reports on (1) the results of the activities and (2) the manager's influence on those results. Such a system has intrinsic appeal for most top managers (because it helps them delegate decision making and frees them to focus on more strategic issues) and lower-level managers (who value the decision-making autonomy they inherit). Thus, system designers apply **responsibility accounting** to identify what parts of the organization have primary responsibility for each action, develop performance measures and targets, and design reports of these measures by responsibility center. Responsibility centers usually have multiple goals and actions that the management control system monitors. We classify responsibility centers as cost centers, profit centers, or investment centers based on their managers' primary financial responsibilities.

cost center

A responsibility center in which managers are responsible for costs only.

COST, PROFIT, AND INVESTMENT CENTERS   In a **cost center**, managers are responsible for costs only. A cost center may encompass an entire department, or a department may contain several cost centers. For example, although one manager may supervise an assembly department, the department may contain several assembly lines and each assembly line may be considered a separate cost center. Likewise, within each line, each separate machine may be its own cost center. The determination of the number of cost centers depends on cost-benefit considerations—do the benefits (for planning, control, and evaluation) of smaller, more numerous cost centers exceed the higher costs of reporting?

profit center

A responsibility center in which managers are responsible for revenues as well as costs—that is, profitability.

In a **profit center** managers are responsible for controlling revenues as well as costs—that is, profitability. Despite the name, a profit center can exist in nonprofit organizations (though it might not be referred to as such) when a responsibility center receives revenues for its services. For example, the Western Area Power Authority (WAPA) is charged with recovering its costs of operations through sales of power to electric utilities in the western United States. Therefore, WAPA is a profit center responsible for both revenues and costs, though its objective is not to maximize profits but rather to break even.

An **investment center** adds responsibility for investment to profit-center responsibilities. Investment-center success depends on both income and invested capital, measured by relating income generated to the value of the capital employed.

Systems designers must understand operating processes and cost behavior to help identify responsibility for controllable costs. For example, by isolating activities and related cost drivers, activity-based costing (see Chapter 4) can help to point out controllable costs. Procter & Gamble credited its activity-based management control system with identifying controllable costs in one of its detergent divisions, which led to major strategic changes.

Responsibility center managers are often able to explain their center's uncontrollable costs, even in situations where they are not held responsible for these uncontrollable costs. For example, an importer of grapes from Chile to the United States suffered a sudden loss of sales several years ago after a few grapes were found to contain poisonous cyanide. Because the tampering was beyond the import manager's control, the manager was responsible for efficiency (the flexible-budget variance [see Chapter 8]) but not for the effects of activity volume (the sales-activity variance). Even though he was not held responsible for the sales-activity variance, the manager was in the best position to provide an explanation for the variance because he had the best information about the reasons for the decline in sales.

Contribution Margin

Many organizations combine the contribution approach to measuring income with responsibility accounting—that is, they report by cost behavior as well as by degrees of controllability. Exhibit 9-4 is an organization chart showing selected units of a retail grocery company like Safeway, Kroger, or SuperValu. Exhibit 9-5 illustrates the contribution approach to measuring financial performance of the various units shown on the organization chart. **Segments** are responsibility centers for which a company develops separate measures of revenues and costs. Exhibit 9-5 provides perspective on how a management-control system report can stress cost behavior, controllability, manager performance, and responsibility center performance simultaneously.

Line (a) in Exhibit 9-5 shows the contribution margin, sales revenues less variable expenses. The contribution margin ratio, defined as the ratio of contribution margin to sales, is especially helpful for predicting the impact on income of short-run changes in sales volume. Managers may quickly calculate expected changes in income by multiplying the contribution margin ratio by the expected change in dollar sales. For example, the contribution margin ratio for meats in the West Division is $180 \div $900 = .20$. A $1,000 increase in sales of meats in the West Division should produce a $200 increase in contribution margin and income ($.20 \times $1,000 = 200) if there are no changes in selling prices, variable operating expenses per unit, fixed costs, or mix of sales.

investment center
A responsibility center where managers are responsible for investment as well as profits.

segments
Responsibility centers for which a company develops separate measures of revenues and costs.

Exhibit 9-4
Retail Grocery Company Organization Chart

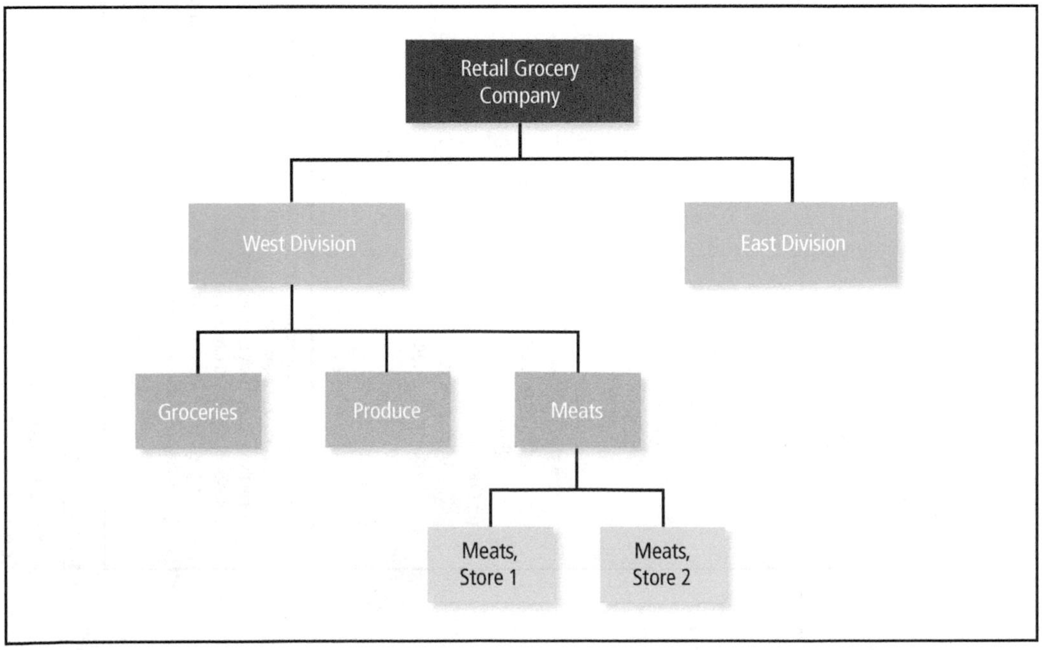

	Company as a Whole	Company Breakdown into Two Divisions		Breakdown of West Division Only				Breakdown of West Division, Meats Only		
		East Division	West Division	Not Allocated†	Groceries	Produce	Meats	Not Allocated†	Store 1	Store 2
Net sales	$4,000	$1,500	$2,500	—	$1,300	$300	$900	—	$600	$300
Variable costs										
Cost of merchandise sold	$3,000	$1,100	$1,900	—	$1,000	$230	$670	—	$450	$220
Variable operating costs‡	260	100	160	—	100	10	50	—	35	15
Total variable costs	$3,260	$1,200	$2,060	—	$1,100	$240	$720	—	$485	$235
(a) Contribution margin	$ 740	$ 300	$ 440	—	$ 200	$ 60	$180	—	$115	$ 65
Less: Fixed costs controllable by segment managers§	260	100	160	$ 20	40	10	90	$ 30	35	25
(b) Contribution controllable by segment managers	$ 480	$ 200	$ 280	$(20)	$ 160	$ 50	$ 90	$(30)	$ 80	$ 40
Less: Fixed costs controllable by others¶	200	90	110	20	40	10	40	10	22	8
(c) Contribution by segments	$ 280	$ 110	$ 170	$(40)	$ 120	$ 40	$ 50	$(40)	$ 58	$ 32
Less: Unallocated costs‖	100									
(d) Income before income taxes	$ 180									

*Three different types of segments are illustrated here: divisions, product lines, and stores. As you read across, note that the focus becomes narrower; from East and West divisions to West Division only, to meats in West Division only.

†Only those costs clearly identifiable to a product line or store should be allocated.

‡Principally wages and payroll-related costs.

§Examples are certain advertising, sales promotions, salespersons' salaries, management consulting, training, and supervision costs.

¶Examples are depreciation, property taxes, insurance, and perhaps the segment manager's salary.

‖These costs are not clearly or practically allocable to any segment except by some highly questionable allocation base.

Exhibit 9-5
Retail Grocery Store
Contribution Approach: Model Income Statement by Segments (thousands of dollars)

Contribution Controllable by Segment Managers

Designers of management control systems distinguish between the segment as an economic investment and the manager as a decision maker. For instance, an extended period of drought coupled with an aging population may adversely affect the desirability of continued economic investment in a ski resort, but the resort manager may nonetheless be doing an excellent job under these adverse circumstances.

Objective 5

Prepare segment income statements for evaluating profit and investment centers using the contribution margin and controllable-cost concepts.

Exhibit 9-5 separates costs by controllability. The manager of meats at Store 1 may have influence over some local advertising but not other advertising, some fixed salaries but not other salaries, and so forth. Moreover, the meat manager at both the division and store levels may have zero influence over store depreciation or the president's salary. Managers on all levels help explain the total segment contribution, but they are responsible only for the controllable contribution. Note that we deduct the fixed costs controllable by the segment managers from the contribution margin to obtain the contribution controllable by segment managers. These controllable costs are usually discretionary fixed costs such as local advertising and some salaries.

As we move to the right in Exhibit 9-5, we see allocations of only part of the fixed costs to lower levels in the organization. For example, consider the line with fixed costs controllable by segment managers. Of the $160,000 fixed costs that the West Division manager controls, groceries, produce, and meat departments control only $140,000. We do not allocate the remaining $20,000 of West Division fixed costs because they are not controllable farther down in the organization chart. That is, the West Division manager controls all $160,000 of fixed costs, but subordinates (grocery, produce, and meat managers) control only $140,000. Similarly, the meats manager controls $90,000 of fixed costs, but subordinates at stores 1 and 2 control only $35,000 and $25,000, respectively.

Contribution by Segments

The contribution by segments, line (c) in Exhibit 9-5, is an attempt to approximate the financial performance of the segment, as distinguished from the financial performance of its manager, which we measure in line (b). The "fixed costs controllable by others" typically include committed costs (such as depreciation and property taxes) and discretionary costs (such as the segment manager's salary). Although the segment manager does not control these costs, they are necessary for the operation of the segment.

Unallocated Costs

Exhibit 9-5 shows "unallocated costs" immediately before line (d). These costs might include central corporate costs, such as the costs of top management and some corporate-level services (for example, legal and taxation). When an organization cannot find a persuasive cause-and-effect or activity-based justification for allocating such costs, it generally should not allocate them to segments.

Summary

The correct classification of costs as illustrated in Exhibit 9-5 is sometimes ambiguous. Determining controllability is a problem when a company allocates service department costs to other departments. Should a store manager bear a part of the division headquarters' costs? If so, how much and on what basis? How much, if any, store depreciation or lease expenses should we deduct in computing the controllable contribution? There are no universally correct answers to these questions. Each organization makes choices that balance costs and benefits. (This differs from the situation in external accounting systems, where tax or financial reporting regulations usually specify the required classification of costs.)

Because of the subjectivity involved in classification of costs, measures of financial performance such as those illustrated in Exhibit 9-5 are subjective. The calculation of the contribution margin near the top of the report tends to be the most objective, because managers can usually objectively identify and assign variable costs. As you read downward in the report, the allocations become increasingly subjective, and the resulting measures of contributions become more subject to dispute. Nonetheless, many organizations find that allocation of costs to units makes managers more aware of the costs of the entire organization and leads to better organizational cost control.

Making Managerial Decisions

Managers should try to distinguish between controllable and uncontrollable costs when designing segment financial reports. For each of the following costs of a suburban **Wal-Mart** store, indicate whether it is a variable cost, fixed cost controllable by segment managers, fixed cost controllable by someone other than the segment manager, or a cost the company normally does not allocate:

> Property taxes
> Supervision of local sales staff
> Depreciation of store
> Cost of goods sold
> Local store advertising
> Corporate-level advertising
> Corporate-level public relations
> Temporary sales labor

Answer

Variable costs are generally controllable by the store manager. Cost of goods sold and temporary sales labor are examples.

Fixed costs controllable by the segment (store) manager include local store advertising and supervision of the local sales staff. The store manager usually decides the appropriate level for these costs.

Fixed costs controllable by those other than the store manager include property taxes and depreciation of the store. These costs relate directly to the store, but the store manager cannot change them.

Unallocated costs include corporate-level advertising and public relations. These costs have a tenuous link to the store.

Summary Problem for Your Review

PROBLEM

The Book & Game Company has two bookstores: Auntie's and Merlin's. Each store has managers who have a great deal of decision authority over their store. Advertising, market research, acquisition of books, legal services, and other staff functions, however, are handled by a central office. The Book & Game Company's current accounting system allocates all costs to the stores. Results for 20X1 were as follows:

Item	Total Company	Auntie's	Merlin's
Sales revenue	$ 700,000	$ 350,000	$ 350,000
Cost of merchandise sold	450,000	225,000	225,000
Gross margin	250,000	125,000	125,000
Operating expenses			
Salaries and wages	63,000	30,000	33,000
Supplies	45,000	22,500	22,500
Rent and utilities	60,000	40,000	20,000
Depreciation	15,000	7,000	8,000
Allocated staff costs	60,000	30,000	30,000
Total operating expenses	243,000	129,500	113,500
Operating income (loss)	$ 7,000	$ (4,500)	$ 11,500

Each bookstore manager makes decisions that affect salaries and wages, supplies, and depreciation. In contrast, rent and utilities are beyond the managers' control because the managers did not choose the location or the size of the store.

Supplies are variable costs. Variable salaries and wages are equal to 8% of the cost of merchandise sold; the remainder of salaries and wages is a fixed cost. Rent, utilities, and depreciation also are fixed costs. Staff costs represent the cost of activities performed by the central office. Events at the individual bookstores do not affect staff costs; nevertheless, Book & Game Company allocates staff costs as a proportion of sales revenue.

1. Using the contribution approach, prepare a performance report that distinguishes the performance of each bookstore from that of the bookstore manager.
2. Evaluate the financial performance of each bookstore.
3. Evaluate the financial performance of each manager.

SOLUTION

1. See Exhibit 9-6.
2. We can evaluate the financial performances of the bookstores (that is, segments of the company) using the line "contribution by bookstore." Merlin's has a substantially higher contribution, despite equal levels of sales revenues in the two stores. The major reason for this advantage is that Merlin's pays less for rent and utilities.
3. We can evaluate the financial performance of the managers using the line "contribution controllable by managers." By this measure, the performance of Auntie's manager is better than that of Merlin's. The contribution margin is the same for each store, but Merlin's manager paid $4,000 more in controllable fixed costs than did Auntie's manager. Note that the additional fixed costs could be beneficial in the long run. What is missing from each of these segment reports is the year's master budget and a flexible budget, which would be the best benchmark for evaluating both bookstores and bookstore managers.

Item	Total Company	Auntie's	Merlin's
Sales revenue	$700,000	$350,000	$350,000
Variable costs			
Cost of merchandise sold	450,000	225,000	225,000
Salaries and wages—variable portion	36,000	18,000	18,000
Supplies	45,000	22,500	22,500
Total variable costs	531,000	265,500	265,500
Contribution margin by bookstore	169,000	84,500	84,500
Less: Fixed costs controllable by bookstore managers			
Salaries and wages—fixed portion	27,000	12,000	15,000
Depreciation	15,000	7,000	8,000
Total controllable fixed costs	42,000	19,000	23,000
Contribution controllable by managers	127,000	65,500	61,500
Less: Fixed costs controllable by others			
Rent and utilities	60,000	40,000	20,000
Contribution by bookstore	67,000	$ 25,500	$ 41,500
Unallocated staff costs	60,000		
Operating income	$ 7,000		

Exhibit 9-6
The Book & Game Company
Performance Report

Measurement of Nonfinancial Performance

In recent years, many organizations have developed a new awareness of the importance of controlling aspects of nonfinancial performance. For example, sales organizations follow up on customers to ensure their satisfaction, and manufacturers track manufacturing defects and product performance. We first examine individual examples of nonfinancial performance measures such as quality, cycle time, and productivity. Then, we discuss the balanced scorecard, a popular approach that integrates financial and nonfinancial performance measures tied to the organization's fundamental strategy.

Objective 6

Measure performance against nonfinancial performance measures such as quality, cycle time, and productivity.

Control of Quality

Many companies use performance metrics that measure the quality of their products or services. **Quality control** is the effort to ensure that products and services perform to customer requirements. Customer needs define quality. For example, customers judge the quality of an automobile

quality control
The effort to ensure that products and services perform to customer requirements.

relative to their needs for reliability, performance, styling, safety, image, and other attributes. Defining quality in terms of customer requirements is only half the battle. There remains the problem of reaching and maintaining the desired level of quality.

The traditional approach to controlling quality in the United States was to inspect products after completing them and reject or rework those that failed the inspections. Because testing is expensive, companies often inspected only a sample of products. They judged the process to be in control as long as the number of defective products did not exceed an acceptable quality level. This meant that some defective products could still make their way to customers. When a company does not discover defects until the product reaches the customer, it is costly to repair products already in use by a customer or to win back a dissatisfied customer. IBM's former CEO John Akers was quoted in the *Wall Street Journal* as saying, "I am sick and tired of visiting plants to hear nothing but great things about quality and cycle time—and then to visit customers who tell me of problems."

cost of quality report
A report that displays the financial impact of quality.

A **cost of quality report** displays the financial impact of quality. The quality cost report shown in Exhibit 9-7 measures four categories of quality costs:

1. Prevention—costs incurred to prevent the production of defective products or delivery of substandard services including engineering analyses to improve product design for better manufacturing, improvements in production processes, increased quality of material inputs, and programs to train personnel
2. Appraisal—costs incurred to identify defective products or services including inspection and testing
3. Internal failure—costs of defective components and final products or services that are scrapped or reworked; also costs of delays caused by defective products or services
4. External failure—costs caused by delivery of defective products or services to customers, such as field repairs, returns, and warranty expenses

Exhibit 9-7 shows that internal or external failures caused most of the costs incurred by Eastside Manufacturing Company. These costs almost certainly are understated, however, because they omit opportunity costs of internal delays and lost sales. For example, quality problems in American-built automobiles in the 1980s caused sales to drop for many years. The opportunity cost of these lost future sales were much more significant than the immediate tangible costs measured in any quality cost report.

In recent years, more U.S. companies have moved away from the traditional approach to achieve quality by "inspecting it in." Many companies have discovered that it is more cost effective to prevent defects rather than inspect and correct them. The resources consumed to detect defective products do not add value. Further, if the company must scrap the defective product, it wastes the resources that were consumed to produce it. Even when the company can correct the product defects, it wastes the resources required for rework.

total quality management (TQM)
An approach to quality that focuses on prevention of defects and on customer satisfaction.

Many companies have adopted an approach first espoused by an American, W. Edwards Deming, and embraced by Japanese companies decades ago: **total quality management (TQM)**. Following the old adage "an ounce of prevention is worth a pound of cure," it focuses on prevention of defects and on achievement of customer satisfaction. The TQM approach builds on the assumption that an organization minimizes the cost of quality when it achieves high quality levels. TQM is the application of quality principles to all of the organization's endeavors to satisfy customers. TQM has significant implications for organization goals, structure, and management control systems.

quality-control chart
The statistical plot of measures of various product quality dimensions or attributes.

To implement TQM, an organization trains employees to prepare, interpret, and act on quality-control charts, such as that shown in Exhibit 9-8. The **quality-control chart** is a statistical plot of measures of various product quality dimensions or attributes. This plot helps detect process deviations and identify excessive variation in product dimensions or attributes that process or design engineers should address. The chart in Exhibit 9-8 shows that, except for a brief period near the end of April, the Eastside Manufacturing Company generally is not meeting its defects objective of .6% defects. Managers looking at this chart would know that they should take corrective action.

The most recent trend in quality control is Six Sigma, defined in Chapter 1 as a data-driven approach to eliminating defects and improving quality. The name Six Sigma comes from the idea of an extremely low defect rate of fewer than 3.4 defects per million (far lower than the objective

Month			Quality Cost Area	Year to Date		
Actual	Plan	Variance		Actual	Plan	Variance
			1. Prevention Cost			
3	2	1	A. Quality—administration	5	4	1
16	18	(2)	B. Quality—engineering	37	38	(1)
7	6	1	C. Quality—planning by others	14	12	2
5	7	(2)	D. Supplier assurance	13	14	(1)
31	33	(2)	Total prevention cost	69	68	1
5.5%	6.1%		Percentage of total quality cost	6.2%	6.3%	
			2. Appraisal cost			
31	26	5	A. Inspection	55	52	3
12	14	(2)	B. Test	24	28	(4)
7	6	1	C. Inspection & test of purchased materials	15	12	3
11	11	0	D. Product quality audits	23	22	1
3	2	1	E. Maintenance of inspection & test equipment	4	4	0
2	2	0	F. Materials consumed in inspection & testing	5	4	1
66	61	5	Total appraisal cost	126	122	4
11.8%	11.3%		Percentage of total quality cost	11.4%	11.3%	
			3. Internal failure cost			
144	140	4	A. Scrap & rework—manufacturing	295	280	15
55	53	2	B. Scrap & rework—engineering	103	106	(3)
28	30	(2)	C. Scrap & rework—supplier	55	60	(5)
21	22	(1)	D. Failure investigation	44	44	0
248	245	3	Total internal failure cost	497	490	7
44.3%	45.4%		Percentage of total quality cost	44.9%	45.3%	
345	339	6	Total internal quality cost (1 + 2 + 3)	692	680	12
61.6%	62.8%		Percentage of total quality cost	62.6%	62.8%	
			4. External failure quality cost			
75	66	9	A. Warranty expense—manufacturing	141	132	9
41	40	1	B. Warranty expense—engineering	84	80	4
35	35	0	C. Warranty expense—sales	69	70	(1)
46	40	6	D. Field warranty cost	83	80	3
18	20	(2)	E. Failure investigation	37	40	(3)
215	201	14	Total external failure cost	414	402	12
38.4%	37.2%		Percentage of total quality cost	37.4%	37.2%	
560	540	20	Total quality cost	1,106	1,082	24
9,872	9,800		Total product cost	20,170	19,600	
5.7%	5.5%		Total quality cost as percentage of total production cost	5.5%	5.5%	

*Adapted from Allen H. Seed III, *Adapting Management Accounting Practice to an Advanced Manufacturing Environment* (Montvale, NJ: National Association of Accountants, 1988), Table 5-2, p. 76.

Exhibit 9-7
Eastside Manufacturing Company
Quality Cost Report (thousands of dollars)*

of less than 6 defects per thousand in the Eastside Manufacturing example). However, the Six Sigma approach has broadened into a general approach to defining, measuring, analyzing, and improving a production process to minimize errors. The focus is on measuring how many defects a company has in its process because, once a company measures the defects, it can take steps to eliminate them. Developed by Motorola, Six Sigma is making large impacts at companies such as General Electric, Dow Chemical, and 3M. At Dow, each Six Sigma project has created an average of $500,000 in savings.

Control of Cycle Time

Reducing cycle time is a key to improving quality. **Cycle time**, or **throughput time**, is the time it takes to complete a product or service. It is a summary measure of efficiency and effectiveness and is also an important cost driver. You may find it surprising that faster cycle times often lead to higher quality and lower defect rates. A faster cycle time requires smooth-running processes and high quality. It also creates increased flexibility and brings products or services to customers more quickly, which increases customer satisfaction.

cycle time (throughput time)
The time taken to complete a product or service.

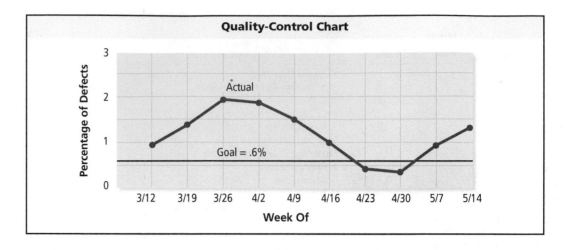

One way to measure cycle time is to attach an identifier such as a bar code or RFID (radio-frequency identification) tag to each component or product and use a scanner to read the code at the end of each stage of completion. Cycle time for each stage is the time between readings of the identifier tag. Tagging also permits effective tracking of materials and products for inventories, scheduling, and delivery.

Exhibit 9-9 is a sample cycle-time report showing that Eastside Manufacturing Company is meeting its cycle-time objectives at two of its five production process stages. This report is similar to the flexible budget reports of Chapter 8, but note that the variances here are measured in units of time, rather than in dollars of revenue or cost. Explanations for the variances in the right column indicate that poor-quality materials and poor design led to extensive rework and retesting.

Control of Productivity

productivity
A measure of outputs divided by inputs.

More than half the companies in the United States measure and manage productivity as part of the effort to improve their competitiveness. **Productivity** is a measure of outputs divided by inputs. The fewer inputs needed to produce a given output, the more productive the organization. This simple definition, however, raises difficult measurement questions. How should the company measure outputs and inputs? Specific management control issues usually determine the most appropriate measures. Labor-intensive organizations, especially service organizations, focus on increasing the productivity of labor, so labor-based measures are appropriate. Highly automated companies focus on machine use and productivity of capital investments, so capacity-based measures, such as the percentage of time machines are available, may be most important to them. Manufacturing companies, in general, monitor the efficient use of materials. For them, measures of material yield (a ratio of material outputs over material inputs) may be useful indicators of productivity.

Exhibit 9-10 shows 12 examples of productivity measures. As you can see from these examples, measures vary widely according to the type of resource that management wishes

Process Stage	Actual Cycle Time*	Standard Cycle Time	Variance	Explanation
Materials processing	2.1	2.5	0.4 F	
Circuit board assembly	44.7	28.8	15.9 U	Poor-quality materials caused rework
Power unit assembly	59.6	36.2	23.4 U	Engineering change required rebuilding all power units
Product assembly	14.6	14.7	0.1 F	
Functional and environmental test	53.3	32.0	21.3 U	Software failure in test procedures required retesting

F = Favorable. U = Unfavorable.
*Average time per stage over the week.

Exhibit 9-10
Measures of Productivity

Resource	Possible Outputs (Numerator)		Possible Inputs (Denominator)
Labor	Standard direct-labor hours allowed for good output	÷	Actual direct-labor hours used
	Sales revenue	÷	Number of employees
	Sales revenue	÷	Direct-labor costs
	Bank deposit/loan activity (by a bank)	÷	Number of employees
	Service calls	÷	Number of employees
	Customer orders	÷	Number of employees
Materials	Weight of output	÷	Weight of input
	Number of good units	÷	Total number of units
Equipment, capital, physical capacity	Time (e.g., hours) used	÷	Time available for use
	Time available for use	÷	Time (e.g., 24 hours per day)
	Expected machine hours for good output	÷	Actual machine hours
	Sales revenue	÷	Direct-labor cost

to use efficiently. In all cases, a measure of the resource that management wishes to control is in the denominator (the input) and a measure of the objective of using the resource is in the numerator (the output).

Choice of Productivity Measures

Which productivity measures should a company choose to manage? The choice determines the incentives created by the management control system. For example, if top management evaluates subordinates' performance based on direct-labor productivity, lower-level managers will focus on improving that specific measure.

The challenge in choosing productivity measures is to avoid motivating decisions that improve one dimension of performance but hurt another dimension. For example, measuring and rewarding productivity per machine would provide incentives for longer production runs. However, longer production runs might result in excessive inventory handling and holding costs. As another example, measuring labor productivity might motivate workers to produce more units per hour. However, spending less time on each unit produced may cause a higher rate of product defects.

Use of a single measure of productivity is unlikely to result in overall improvements in performance. The choice of performance measures requires anticipating the trade-offs that employees will make. Many organizations implement management controls for all of the most important activities, including nonfinancial measures such as quality and customer satisfaction, and use multiple measures to monitor the actual benefits of improvements in these activities.

Productivity Measures Over Time

Be careful when comparing productivity measures over time. Changes in the process or in the rate of inflation can make results misleading. For example, consider labor productivity at Adobe Systems. One measure of productivity is sales revenue per employee.

	2001	2011	Percent Change
Total revenue (millions)	$ 1,230	$ 4,216	243%
Employees	÷ 3,043	÷ 9,925	226%
Revenue per employee (unadjusted for inflation)	$404,206	$424,786	5%

By this measure, Adobe appears to have achieved a 5% increase in the productivity of labor because the number of employees grew more slowly than total revenue. However, total revenue has not been adjusted for the effects of inflation. Because of inflation, each 2001 dollar was equivalent to 1.27 dollars in 2011. Therefore, Adobe's 2001 sales revenue, expressed in 2011

Business First

Balanced Scorecard Hall of Fame

Robert Kaplan and David Norton created the balanced scorecard (BSC) in 1992. The Balanced Scorecard Hall of Fame honors organizations that have achieved execution excellence through the use of the BSC. To be selected for the Hall of Fame, a company must apply one or more of the following five principles to create a strategy-focused organization: "mobilize change through executive leadership; translate the strategy into operational terms; align the organization around its strategy; make strategy everyone's job; and make strategy a continual process." By the end of 2011, the Balanced Scorecard Collaborative had recognized a total of 167 Hall of Fame organizations. Past inductees include Army and Air Force Exchange Service (AAFES), the City of Corpus Christi, BMW Financial Services, and Wendy's International.

AAFES is a $9.9 billion global retailer with 43,000 employees serving military customers in 3,100 stores in 30 countries. AAFES adopted the BSC to prepare the organization to meet growing and diverse demands of its increasingly mobile customers. The BSC helps create alignment, drive accountability, optimize resource allocation, and link strategy to operations. In 4 years revenue increased by 11%, dividends 19%, employee satisfaction 16%, and customer satisfaction 17%. Inventory was reduced by about $108 million. Michael Howard, AAFES chief operating officer, observed the following: "The BSC has given us the ability to look beyond traditional financial measures to drive long-term sustainability that focuses on employee optimization. The BSC aligns corporate resources and energies to drive performance that ensure AAFES continues to provide a valued benefit to the military market."

The City of Corpus Christi is the largest coastal city in Texas and the nation's sixth largest port. The city employs about 3,000, serving a population of 305,000. The city adopted the BSC to clarify and communicate its strategy; align departments, divisions, and employees; and make more timely and better informed decisions that impact citizens' lives. Constituent satisfaction increased 16%, workforce retention was up, and citizen/customer wait time down. The city's bond rating improved, fueled in part by the BSC management system. Angel R. Escobar, interim city manager commented, "Now, with the BSC, we know what we are great at and what we need to improve upon...our monthly BSC meetings unify departmental directors to collectively focus on and discuss solutions to real issues."

BMW Financial Services was established in 1993 to support the sales and marketing efforts of BMW North America. The company has more than $24 billion in managed assets and offers customers flexible lease and retail financing options. BMW Financial Services adopted the BSC in 1998 and has seen remarkable growth in annual sales and number of customer accounts. The company uses the scorecard to link objectives, initiatives, and metrics to its strategy and communicate these links throughout the company.

Wendy's International is one of the world's largest restaurant operating and franchising companies, with about 6,600 restaurants and 2011 revenue of $2.4 billion. The company implemented the BSC to get a better handle on intangible assets, such as intellectual capital and customer focus. CEO Jack Schuessler lauded the BSC's success in "establishing targets and measuring our progress in key dimensions ranging from employee retention at the restaurant level, to restaurant evaluation scores, to business processes, to total revenue growth. They are all vitally important, not just the financial measures." The BSC provides a framework for balancing financial and nonfinancial measures.

The BSC has helped these and other award-winning organizations in many different ways. It has gained wide acceptance and successful implementation in many companies since its introduction more than 15 years ago.

Sources: AAFES Web site (www.shopmyexchange.com); City of Corpus Christi Web site (cctexaswww.cctexas); BMW of North America Web site (www.bmwusa.com); *The Wendy's Company 2011 Annual Report*; Palladium Group Web site (www.thepalladiumgroup.com).

---

dollars (so we can compare it with 2011 sales revenue), is $1,230 \times 1.27 = \$1,562$. The adjusted 2001 sales revenue per employee is as follows:

	2001 (adjusted)	2011	Percent Change
Total revenue (millions)	$ 1,562	$ 4,216	170%
Employees	÷ 3,043	÷ 9,925	226%
Revenue per employee (adjusted for inflation)	$513,309	$424,786	−17%

Adjusting for the effects of inflation reveals that Adobe's labor productivity has actually decreased by 17% rather than increased by 5%.

The Balanced Scorecard

Objective 7

Use a balanced scorecard to integrate financial and nonfinancial measures of performance.

A **balanced scorecard (BSC)** is a system that strikes a balance between financial and nonfinancial measures in the performance measurement process, links performance to rewards, and gives explicit recognition to the link between performance measurement and organizational goals and objectives. The balanced scorecard focuses management attention on measures that drive an organization to achieve its goals. About 50% of the 1,000 largest U.S. firms use some version of the

Exhibit 9-11
Performance Indicators for
Philips Electronics' Balanced
Scorecard

Financial	Processes
Economic profit realized	Percentage reduction in process cycle time
Income from operations	Number of engineering changes
Working capital	Capacity utilization
Operational cash flow	Order response time
Inventory turns	Process capability
Customers	**Competence**
Rank in customer survey	Leadership competence
Market share	Percentage of patent-protected turnover
Repeat order rate	Training days per employee
Complaints	Quality improvement team participation
Brand index	

Exhibit 9-11
Performance Indicators for
Philips Electronics' Balanced
Scorecard

balanced scorecard, including **Microsoft**, **American Express**, **ExxonMobil**, **Allstate**, and **Apple Computer**. Government and nonprofit agencies, such as the U.S. Department of Transportation and the United Way of America, also use the balanced scorecard. We describe some of the more successful organizations that use the balanced scorecard in the Business First box on page 370.

The balanced scorecard helps line managers understand the relationship between nonfinancial measures and organizational goals. The balanced scorecard identifies performance measures from each of the four components of the successful organization shown in Exhibit 9-3 on page 358. Links between the measures and organizational objectives help managers throughout the organization understand how their actions support the organization's goals.

What does a balanced scorecard look like? The classic balanced scorecard developed by Robert Kaplan and David Norton includes **key performance indicators**—measures that drive the organization to meet its goals—grouped into four categories: (1) financial, (2) customers, (3) internal business processes, and (4) innovation and learning. Some companies use other terminology and some include additional categories—the most common are additional categories for employees or other stakeholders.

All balanced scorecards develop performance measures for each objective within each category. For example, **Philips Electronics** uses the categories and performance indicators in Exhibit 9-11. Most companies that use a balanced scorecard specify the categories that each business segment will use but allow the segments to choose the relevant performance measures for each category. For example, every Microsoft division has measures for financial, customer, internal processes, and learning perspectives, but the Latin American division has different measures in each category than does the Seattle headquarters. The balanced scorecard should not be a straightjacket; rather it is a flexible framework for motivating and measuring performance.

balanced scorecard (BSC)
A performance measurement and reporting system that strikes a balance between financial and nonfinancial measures, links performance to rewards, and gives explicit recognition to the link between performance measurement and organizational goals and objectives.

key performance indicators
Measures that drive the organization to achieve its goals.

Making Managerial Decisions

The balanced scorecard emphasizes the connections between performance measures and financial and nonfinancial goals. Indicate where each of the following goals of **Whirlpool** fits with the four components of a successful organization shown in Exhibit 9-3 on page 358, and explain how these components relate to one another:

    People commitment
    Total quality
    Customer satisfaction
    Financial performance
    Growth and innovation

Answer

The components listed in Exhibit 9-3 depict the causal links from organizational learning to business process improvement,

to customer satisfaction, and finally to financial strength. The five goals set by top managers at Whirlpool suggest the following links among the goals:

If Whirlpool makes a solid commitment to its people and invests in growth and innovation, the company will make progress in organizational learning. This will lead to business process improvements that decrease costs, increase efficiency, and increase the total quality of its products, which will then lead to increased customer satisfaction. The ultimate result of satisfied customers is improved financial performance. Sustainable financial strength should allow Whirlpool to repeat the cycle and continue to invest in both organizational learning and internal business processes.

Management Control Systems in Service, Government, and Nonprofit Organizations

Objective 8

Describe the difficulties of management control in service and nonprofit organizations.

Many service organizations face substantial difficulty implementing management control systems. Why? Because the outputs of service organizations are difficult to measure. For example, what is a good measure of output for a bank's call center (where service representatives answer customers' questions)? Number of calls or total time spent on calls? The measure "number of calls" might motivate many short calls that do not provide thorough answers to customers. The measure "total time spent on calls" might motivate long, time-wasting calls. It is often difficult to know the quality, or sometimes even the quantity, of the service provided until long after the organization delivers the service. When quality and quantity of output are hard to measure, developing timely measures of input/output relationships is nearly impossible.

The keys to successful management control in any organization are proper training and motivation of employees to achieve the organization's strategic objectives, accompanied by consistent monitoring of measures chosen to fit with these objectives. These keys are equally important in service-oriented organizations. **MBNA America**, a large issuer of bank credit cards, works hard to measure the amount and quality of its service. It identifies customer retention as its most important key success factor. MBNA trains its customer representatives carefully. Each day it measures and reports performance on 14 objectives consistent with customer retention, and it rewards every employee based on those 14 objectives. Measures include answering every call by the second ring, keeping the computer up 100% of the time, and processing credit-line requests within 1 hour. Employees earn bonuses as high as 20% of their annual salaries by meeting those objectives.

Government and nonprofit organizations face additional difficulties. When for-profit organizations confront conflicting goals, the appropriate trade-off is determined by the net effect on the financial "bottom line." When government and nonprofit organizations face conflicting goals as to when, where, and to whom they will provide services, the relevant trade-offs are often unclear. Because they have no precisely defined objective function that specifies how to make these trade-offs, it is difficult to determine the "right" incentives to be incorporated in the management control system.

Further, the design of management control systems in nonprofit organizations is complicated by the fact that many people in these organizations seek primarily nonmonetary rewards. For example, volunteers in the **Peace Corps** receive little pay but derive much satisfaction from helping to improve conditions in underdeveloped countries. **AmeriCorps** volunteers have similar objectives domestically. Thus, monetary incentives are generally less effective in nonprofit organizations.

In summary, management control systems in nonprofit organizations probably will never be as highly developed as are those in profit-seeking firms because of the following:

1. Organizational goals and objectives are less clear. Moreover, there are often multiple goals and objectives, requiring difficult trade-offs.
2. Professionals (for example, teachers, attorneys, physicians, scientists, economists) tend to dominate nonprofit organizations. Because of their perceived professional status, they are often less receptive to the installation of formal control systems.
3. Measurements are more difficult because
   a. there is no profit measure, and
   b. there are heavy amounts of discretionary fixed costs, which make the relationships of inputs to outputs difficult to specify and measure.
4. There is less competitive pressure from other organizations or "owners" to improve management control systems. As a result, many cities in the United States are "privatizing" some essential services, such as sanitation, by contracting with private firms.
5. The role of budgeting, instead of being a rigorous planning process, is often more a matter of playing bargaining games with sources of funding to get the largest possible authorization.
6. Motivations and incentives of employees may differ from those in for-profit organizations.

Making Managerial Decisions

Study Exhibit 9-3 again. Use the same four general components, but rearrange them to reflect a framework that might help managers of a successful governmental or nonprofit organization.

Answer

For governmental and nonprofit organizations, the ultimate objective is not to focus on financial results but to deliver the maximum benefits to customers (or citizens) based on an available pool of financial resources. Thus, the causal relationships might be as follows:

Organizational learning → process improvements in delivering programs → improved fiscal or financial strength → greater program benefits for citizens or clients

Future of Management Control Systems

As organizations mature and as environments change, managers expand and refine their management control tools. The management control techniques that were satisfactory 10 or 20 years ago are not adequate for many organizations today.

A changing environment often means that organizations adjust their goals or key success factors. New goals require different benchmarks for evaluating performance. The management control system must evolve, too, or the organization may not manage its resources effectively or efficiently. A summary of management control principles that will always be important and can guide the redesign of systems follows:

1. Always expect that individuals will be pulled in the direction of their own self-interest. You may be pleasantly surprised that some individuals will act selflessly, but management control systems should be designed to take advantage of more typical human behavior. Also, be aware that managers in different cultures may perceive self-interest differently.
2. Design incentives so that individuals who pursue their own self-interest also achieve the organization's objectives. Because there are usually multiple objectives, multiple incentives are appropriate. Do not underestimate the difficulty of balancing multiple incentives.
3. Evaluate actual performance relative to planned performance. Where appropriate, revise planned performance to reflect actual output achieved. You can apply the concept of flexible budgeting to many goals and actions, both financial and nonfinancial.
4. Consider nonfinancial performance to be an important determinant of long-term success. In the short run, a manager may be able to generate good financial performance while neglecting nonfinancial performance, but it is not likely over the long haul.
5. Array performance measures across the entire value chain of the company to ensure that the management control system incorporates all activities that are critical to the long-run success of the company.
6. Periodically review the success of the management control system. Is the organization achieving its overall goals? Do the actions motivated by the management control system lead to goal achievement? Do individuals understand the management control system and effectively use the information it provides?
7. Learn from the management control successes (and failures) of competitors around the world. Despite cultural differences, human behavior is remarkably similar. Managers can learn from successful applications of new technology and management controls by reading books or attending courses that describe management control systems at other companies.

Highlights to Remember

1. **Describe the relationship of management control systems to organizational goals.** The starting point for designing and evaluating a management control system is the identification of organizational goals as specified by top management.

2. **Explain the importance of evaluating performance and describe how it impacts motivation, goal congruence, and employee effort.** The way an organization measures and evaluates performance affects individuals' behavior. The more that it ties rewards to performance measures, the more incentive there is to improve the measures. Poorly designed measures may actually work against the organization's goals.

3. **Develop performance measures and use them to monitor the achievements of an organization.** A well-designed management control system measures both financial and nonfinancial performance. Superior nonfinancial performance usually leads to superior financial performance in time. The performance measures should tell managers how well they are meeting the organization's goals.

4. **Use responsibility accounting to define an organizational subunit as a cost center, a profit center, or an investment center.** Responsibility accounting assigns revenue and cost objectives to the management of the subunit that has the greatest influence over them. Cost centers focus on costs only, profit centers on both revenues and costs, and investment centers on profits relative to the amount invested.

5. **Prepare segment income statements for evaluating profit and investment centers using the contribution margin and controllable-cost concepts.** The contribution approach to measuring a segment's income aids performance evaluation by separating a segment's costs into those controllable by the segment management and those beyond management's control. It allows separate evaluation of a segment as an economic investment and the performance of the segment's manager.

6. **Measure performance against nonfinancial performance measures such as quality, cycle time, and productivity.** Measuring performance in areas such as quality, cycle time, and productivity causes employees to direct attention to those areas. Achieving goals in these nonfinancial measures can help meet long-run financial objectives.

7. **Use a balanced scorecard to integrate financial and nonfinancial measures of performance.** The balanced scorecard helps managers monitor actions that are designed to meet the various goals of the organization. It integrates key performance indicators that measure how well the organization is meeting its goals.

8. **Describe the difficulties of management control in service and nonprofit organizations.** Management control in service and nonprofit organizations is difficult because of a number of factors, including a relative lack of clearly observable outcomes and, for many nonprofit organizations, the lack of a clearly defined objective function.

Accounting Vocabulary

balanced scorecard (BSC), p. 371
controllable cost, p. 360
cost center, p. 360
cost of quality report, p. 366
cycle time, p. 367
goal congruence, p. 355
investment center, p. 361
key performance indicators, p. 371

key success factor, p. 354
management control system, p. 353
managerial effort, p. 355
motivation, p. 356
productivity, p. 368
profit center, p. 360
quality control, p. 365
quality-control chart, p. 366

responsibility accounting, p. 360
responsibility center, p. 360
segments, p. 361
throughput time, p. 367
total quality management (TQM), p. 366
uncontrollable cost, p. 360

Fundamental Assignment Material

9-A1 Responsibility of Purchasing Agent

Excel Electronics Company, a privately held enterprise, has a subcontract from a large aerospace company in Chicago. Although Excel was a low bidder, the aerospace company was reluctant to award the business to the company because it was a newcomer to this kind of activity. Consequently, Excel assured the aerospace company of its financial strength by submitting its audited financial statements. Moreover, Excel agreed to a pay a penalty of $5,000 per day for each day of late delivery for whatever cause.

Amy Greer, the Excel purchasing agent, is responsible for acquiring materials and parts in time to meet production schedules. She placed an order with an Excel supplier for a critical manufactured component. The supplier, who had a reliable record for meeting schedules, gave Greer an acceptable delivery date. Greer checked up several times and was assured that the component would arrive at Excel on schedule.

On the date specified by the supplier for shipment to Excel, Greer was informed that the component had been damaged during final inspection. It was delivered 10 days late. Greer had allowed 4 extra days for possible delays, but Excel was 6 days late in delivering to the aerospace company and so had to pay a penalty of $30,000.

What department should bear the penalty? Why?

9-A2 Contribution Approach to Responsibility Accounting

Joe Albright owns and operates a small chain of convenience stores in Waterloo and Cedar Rapids. The company has five stores including a downtown store and a Sumner store in the Waterloo division, and a downtown store, a Solon store, and an airport store in the Cedar Rapids division. There is also a separate administrative staff that provides market research, personnel, and accounting and finance services.

The company had the following financial results for 20X1 (in thousands):

Sales revenue	$8,000
Cost of merchandise sold	3,500
Gross margin	4,500
Operating expenses	2,200
Income before income taxes	$2,300

The following data about 20X1 operations were also available:

1. All five stores used the same pricing formula; therefore, all had the same gross margin percentage.
2. Sales were largest in the two downtown stores, with 30% of the total sales volume in each. The Solon and airport stores each provided 15% of total sales volume, and the Sumner store provided 10%.
3. Variable operating costs at the stores were 10% of revenue for the downtown stores. The other stores had lower variable and higher fixed costs. Their variable operating costs were only 5% of sales revenue.
4. The fixed costs over which the store managers had control were $125,000 in each of the downtown stores, $180,000 at Solon and airport, and $40,000 at Sumner.
5. The remaining $910,000 of operating costs consisted of
   a. $210,000 controllable by the Cedar Rapids division manager but not by individual stores,
   b. $100,000 controllable by the Waterloo division manager but not by individual stores, and
   c. $600,000 controllable by the administrative staff.
6. Of the $600,000 spent by the administrative staff, $350,000 directly supported the Cedar Rapids division, with 20% for the downtown store, 30% for each of the Solon and airport stores, and 20% for Cedar Rapids operations in general. Another $140,000 supported the Waterloo division, 50% for the downtown store, 25% for the Sumner store, and 25% supporting Waterloo operations in general. The other $110,000 was for general corporate expenses.

Prepare an income statement by segments using the contribution approach to responsibility accounting. Use the format of Exhibit 9-4, page 361. Column headings should be as follows:

Company as a whole	Breakdown into Two Divisions		Breakdown of Waterloo Division			Breakdown of Cedar Rapids Division			
	Waterloo	Cedar Rapids	Not allocated	Downtown	Sumner	Not allocated	Downtown	Solon	Airport

9-A3 Comparison of Productivity

Forsythe and Sorteberg are manufacturing companies. Comparative data for 20X1 and 20X7 are as follows:

		Forsythe	Sorteberg
Sales revenue	20X1	$4,720,000,000	$7,997,000,000
	20X7	$6,500,000,000	$9,007,000,000
Number of employees	20X1	53,600	77,900
	20X7	57,800	78,200

Assume that inflation has totaled 18% during these 6 years so that each 20X1 dollar is equivalent to 1.18 dollars in 20X7, due to inflation.

1. Compute 20X1 and 20X7 productivity measures in terms of revenue per employee for Forsythe and Sorteberg.
2. Compare the change in productivity between 20X1 and 20X7 for Forsythe with that for Sorteberg.

9-B1 Responsibility Accounting

The Kephart Company produces precision machine parts. Kephart uses a standard cost system, calculates standard cost variances for each department, and reports them to department managers. Managers use the information to improve their operations. Superiors use the same information to evaluate managers' performance.

Liz Elder was recently appointed manager of the assembly department of the company. She has complained that the system as designed is disadvantageous to her department. Included among the variances charged to the departments is one for rejected units. The inspection occurs at the end of the assembly department. The inspectors attempt to identify the cause of the rejection so that the department where the error occurred can be charged with it. Not all errors can be easily identified with a department, however. The nonidentified units are totaled and apportioned to the departments according to the number of identified errors. The variance for rejected units in each department is a combination of the errors caused by the department plus a portion of the unidentified causes of rejects.

1. Is Elder's complaint valid? Explain the reason(s) for your answer.
2. What would you recommend that the company do to solve its problem with Elder and her complaint?

9-B2 Divisional Contribution, Performance, and Segment Margins

The president of Reading Railroad wants to obtain an overview of the company's operations, particularly with respect to comparing freight and passenger business. He has heard about "contribution" approaches to cost allocations that emphasize cost behavior patterns and contribution margins, contributions controllable by segment managers, and contributions by segments. The president has hired you as a consultant to help him. He has given you the following information.

Total revenue in 20X3 was $80 million, of which $72 million was freight traffic and $8 million was passenger traffic. Forty percent of the passenger revenue was generated by division 1, 50% by division 2, and 10% by division 3.

Total variable costs were $40 million, of which $36 million was caused by freight traffic. Of the $4 million allocable to passenger traffic, $2.1, $1.6, and $.3 million could be allocated to divisions 1, 2, and 3, respectively.

Total separable discretionary fixed costs were $8 million, of which $7.6 million applied to freight traffic. For the remaining $400,000 applicable to passenger traffic, $80,000 could not be allocated to specific divisions, while $200,000, $100,000, and $20,000, were allocable to divisions 1, 2, and 3, respectively.

Total separable committed costs, which were not regarded as being controllable by segment managers, were $25 million, of which 80% was allocable to freight traffic. Of the 20% traceable to passenger traffic, divisions 1, 2, and 3 should be allocated $3 million, $700,000, and $300,000, respectively; the balance was unallocable to a specific division.

The common fixed costs not clearly allocable to any part of the company amounted to $800,000.

1. The president asks you to prepare statements, dividing the data for the company as a whole between the freight and passenger traffic and then subdividing the passenger traffic into three divisions.
2. Some competing railroads actively promote a series of one-day sightseeing tours on summer weekends. Most often, these tours are timed so that the cars with the tourists are hitched on with regularly scheduled passenger trains. What costs are relevant for making decisions to run such

tours? Other railroads, facing the same general cost structure, refuse to conduct such sightseeing tours. Why?

3. Suppose that the railroad has petitioned government authorities for permission to drop division 1. What would be the effect on overall company net income for 20X4, assuming that the figures are accurate and that 20X4 operations are expected to be in all respects a duplication of 20X3 operations?

9-B3 Balanced Scorecard for a Law Firm

Young, Martinez, and Cheung (YMC) is a law firm in Chicago. The firm has had a very loose and relaxed management style that has served it well in the past. However, more aggressive law firms have been winning new clients faster than YMC has. Thus, the managing partner, Jerry Martinez, recently attended an ABA seminar on performance measurement in law firms, where he learned about the balanced scorecard. He thought it might be a good tool for YMC, one that would allow the firm to keep its culture yet still more aggressively seek new clients.

Martinez identified the following strategic objectives that fit with the firm's core values and provide a framework for assessing progress toward the firm's goals:

Financial

    a. Steadily increase the firm's revenues and profits.

Customer

    a. Understand the firm's customers and their needs.

    b. Value customer service over self-interest.

Internal Business Process

    a. Encourage knowledge sharing among the legal staff.

    b. Communicate with each other openly, honestly, and often.

    c. Empower staff to make decisions that benefit clients.

Organizational Learning

    a. Maintain an open and collaborative environment that attracts and retains the best legal staff.

    b. Seek staff diversity.

1. Develop at least one measure for each of the strategic objectives listed.
2. Explain how YMC can use this balanced scorecard to evaluate staff performance.
3. Should staff compensation be tied to the scorecard performance measures? Why or why not?

Additional Assignment Material

MyAccountingLab

QUESTIONS

9-1 What is a management control system?

9-2 What are the purposes of a management control system?

9-3 What are the major components of a management control system?

9-4 What is a key success factor?

9-5 "Goals are useless without performance measures." Do you agree? Explain.

9-6 "There are corporate goals other than to improve profit." Name three.

9-7 How does management determine its key success factors?

9-8 Give three examples of how managers may improve short-run performance to the detriment of long-run results.

9-9 Name three kinds of responsibility centers.

9-10 How do profit centers and investment centers differ?

9-11 List five characteristics of a good performance measure.

9-12 List four nonfinancial measures of performance that managers find useful.

9-13 "Performance evaluation seeks to achieve goal congruence and managerial effort." Explain what is meant by this statement.

9-14 "Managers of profit centers should be held responsible for the center's entire profit. They are responsible for profit even if they cannot control all factors affecting it." Discuss.

9-15 "Variable costs are controllable and fixed costs are uncontrollable." Do you agree? Explain.

9-16 "The contribution margin is the best measure of short-run performance." Do you agree? Explain.

9-17 Give four examples of segments.

9-18 "Always try to distinguish between the performance of a segment and its manager." Why?

9-19 "The contribution margin approach to performance evaluation is flawed because focusing on only the contribution margin ignores important aspects of performance." Do you agree? Explain.

9-20 What is a balanced scorecard and why are more companies using one?

9-21 What are key performance indicators?

9-22 There are four categories of cost in the quality cost report; explain them.

9-23 Why are companies increasing their quality control emphasis on the prevention of defects?

9-24 "Nonfinancial measures of performance can be controlled just like financial measures." Do you agree? Explain.

9-25 Identify three measures of labor productivity, (a) one using all physical measures, (b) one

using all financial measures, and (c) one that mixes physical and financial measures.

9-26 Discuss the difficulties of comparing productivity measures over time.

9-27 "Control systems in nonprofit organizations will never be as highly developed as in profit-seeking organizations." Do you agree? Explain.

CRITICAL THINKING EXERCISES

9-28 Management Control Systems and Innovation

The president of a fast-growing, high-technology firm remarked, "Developing budgets and comparing performance with the budgets may be fine for some firms. But we want to encourage innovation and entrepreneurship. Budgets go with bureaucracy, not innovation." Do you agree? How can a management control system encourage innovation and entrepreneurship?

9-29 Municipal Responsibility Accounting

After barely avoiding bankruptcy, New York City established one of the most sophisticated budgeting and reporting systems of any municipality. The Integrated Financial Management System (IFMS) "clearly identifies managers in line agencies and correlates allocations and expenditures with organizational structure. . . . In addition, managers have more time to take corrective measures when variances between budgeted and actual expenditures start to develop." (*FE—The Magazine for Financial Executives*, 1, no. 8, p. 26.)

Discuss how a responsibility accounting system such as IFMS can help manage a municipality such as New York City.

9-30 Control Systems and Customer Service Function of the Value Chain

Companies increasingly use nonfinancial measures to supplement financial measures of performance. One of the most important areas of nonfinancial performance is customer service. The last decade has brought an increased focus on the customer, and this focus is reflected in many companies' management control systems, where companies use "customer-value metrics." That is, they develop measures that monitor how well the company is meeting its customers' interests. What customer-value metrics might a company such as Volvo, the Swedish automobile company, use in its management control system?

9-31 Control Systems and the Production Function of the Value Chain

In recent years, many organizations have focused on the value of controlling nonfinancial performance as a key to improved productivity. In particular, to gain and maintain a competitive edge, companies focus on quality and cycle time. Discuss how quality, cycle time, and productivity are related.

9-32 Key Performance Indicators

Research on performance management suggests that organizations can compete most effectively by identifying and monitoring those elements that are most closely linked to organizational success. A key performance indicator can be thought of as a measure that drives organizational success. For each of the following companies or organizations, identify two possible key performance indicators.

1. Delta Airlines
2. Wal-Mart
3. Hewlett Packard
4. New York Department of Motor Vehicles

EXERCISES

9-33 Responsibility for Stable Employment Policy

The Mid-Atlantic Metal Fabricating Company has been manufacturing machine tools for a number of years and has had an industry-wide reputation for doing high-quality work. The company has been faced with fluctuations in demand over the years. It has been company policy to lay off welders as soon as there was insufficient work to keep them busy and to rehire them when demand warranted. Because of this lay-off policy, the company now has poor labor relations and finds it difficult to hire good welders. Consequently, the quality of the products has been declining steadily.

The plant manager has proposed that welders, who earn $20 per hour, be retained during slow periods to do menial plant maintenance work that is normally performed by workers earning $14 per hour in the plant maintenance department.

You, as controller, must decide the most appropriate accounting procedure to handle the wages of the welders doing plant maintenance work. What department(s) should be charged with this work, and at what rate? Discuss the implications of your plan.

9-34 Salesclerk's Compensation Plan

You are the manager of a department store in Tokyo. Sales are subject to month-to-month variations, depending on the individual salesclerk's efforts and other factors. A new salary-plus-bonus plan has been in effect for 4 months, and you are reviewing a sales performance report. The plan provides for a base salary of ¥50,000 per month, a ¥68,000 bonus each month if the salesclerk meets the monthly sales quota, and an additional commission of 5% of all sales over the monthly quota. Each month, the quota is reset at approximately 3% above the previous month's sales to motivate clerks to continually increase sales. The monthly quotas and actual amounts for the first 4 months of the plan are shown in the following sales report (in thousands):

		Salesclerk A	Salesclerk B	Salesclerk C
January	Quota	¥4,500	¥1,500	¥7,500
	Actual	1,500	1,500	9,000
February	Quota	¥1,545	¥1,545	¥9,270
	Actual	3,000	1,545	3,000
March	Quota	¥3,090	¥1,590	¥3,090
	Actual	5,250	750	9,000
April	Quota	¥5,400	¥ 775	¥9,270
	Actual	1,500	780	4,050

1. Compute the compensation for each salesclerk for each month.
2. Evaluate the compensation plan. Be specific. What changes would you recommend?

9-35 Common Measures on a Balanced Scorecard

Listed next are common performance measures appearing on balanced scorecards. Indicate whether the listed measure is primarily associated with the financial, customer, internal process, or learning and growth perspective. (Note that some measures might reasonably be associated with more than one perspective.)

- Return on sales
- Retention of target customers
- Net cash flow
- Training hours
- Employee turnover rate
- Materials handling cost per unit
- Market share
- Product-development cycle time
- Revenue growth in segments
- Occupational injuries and illness
- Day's sales in inventory
- Average cost per invoice

9-36 Goals and Objectives at Health Net

Health Net provides health care to more than 5.6 million members. As a managed health-care organization, the company strives to provide high-quality health care at a reasonable cost. Many stakeholders have an interest in Health Net's operations, including doctors and other medical personnel, patients, insurance companies, government regulators, and the general public.

Prepare a goal and one measure for assessing achievement of that goal for each of the following key areas:

Customer satisfaction
Efficient use of lab tests
Usage of physician time
Maintenance of state-of-the-art facilities
Overall financial performance

9-37 Performance Evaluation

Daniel Merrill & Co. is a stock brokerage firm that evaluates its employees on sales activity generated. Recently, the firm also began evaluating its stockbrokers on the number of new accounts generated.

Discuss how these two performance measures are consistent and how they may conflict. Do you believe that these measures are appropriate for the long-term goal of profitability?

9-38 Simple Controllable Costs

Shortline Espresso is a gourmet dessert restaurant in Seattle. Margie McMahon, the sole proprietor, expanded to a second location in Bellingham 3 years ago. Recently, McMahon decided to enroll in a PhD program and retire from active management of the individual restaurants but continues to oversee the entire company. She hired a manager for each restaurant. In 20X3, each had sales of $1,200,000. The Bellingham restaurant is still pricing lower than the Seattle restaurant to establish a customer base. Variable expenses run 70% of sales for the Seattle restaurant and 75% of sales for the Bellingham restaurant.

Each manager is responsible for the rent and some other fixed costs for his or her restaurant. These costs amounted to $110,000 for the Seattle restaurant and $75,000 for the one in Bellingham. The difference is primarily due to lower rent in Bellingham. In addition, several costs, such as advertising, legal services, accounting, and personnel services, were centralized. The managers had no control of these expenses, but some of them directly benefited the individual restaurants. Of the $345,000 cost in this category, $100,000 related to Seattle and $185,000 to Bellingham, where most of the additional cost in Bellingham is due to the cost of extra advertising to build up its customer base. The remaining $60,000 was general corporate overhead.

1. Prepare income statements for each restaurant and for the company as a whole. Use a format that allows easy assessment of each manager's performance and each restaurant's economic performance.
2. Using only the information given in this exercise, do the following:
    a. Evaluate each restaurant as an economic investment.
    b. Evaluate each manager.

9-39 Quality Theories Compared

Examine the following two graphs. Compare the total quality management approach to the traditional theory of quality. Which theory do you believe represents the current realities of today's global competitive environment? Explain.

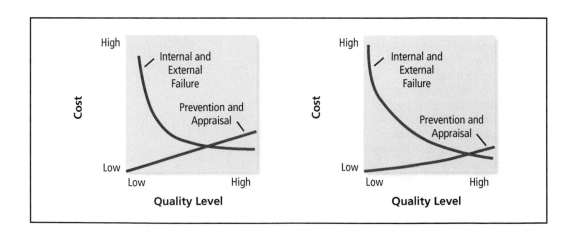

9-40 Quality-Control Chart

San Angelo Manufacturing Company was concerned about a growing number of defective units being produced. At one time, the company had the percentage of defective units down to less than five per thousand, but recently rates of defects have been near, or even above, 1%. The company decided to graph its defects for the last 8 weeks (40 working days), beginning Monday, September 1 through Friday, October 24. The graph is shown in Exhibit 9-12.

1. Identify two important trends evident in the quality-control chart.
2. What might management of San Angelo do to deal with each trend?

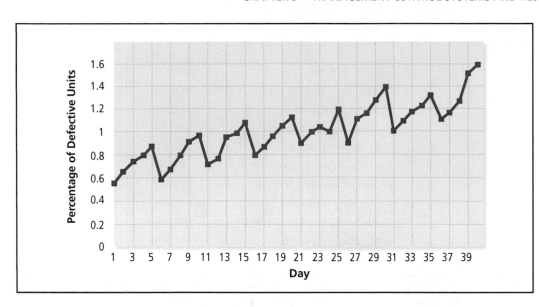

Exhibit 9-12
San Angelo Manufacturing Company
Quality-Control Chart for September 1 Through October 24

9-41 Cycle-Time Reporting

The Pierre plant of Global Electronics produces computers. The plant monitors its cycle time closely to prevent schedule delays and excessive costs. The standard cycle time for the manufacture of printed circuit boards for one of its computers is 26 hours. Consider the following cycle-time data from the past 6 weeks of circuit board production:

Week	Units Completed	Total Cycle Time
1	564	14,108 hours
2	544	14,592
3	553	15,152
4	571	16,598
5	547	17,104
6	552	16,673

Analyze circuit board cycle time performance in light of the 26-hour objective.

PROBLEMS

9-42 Multiple Goals and Profitability

The following multiple goals were identified by **General Electric**:

Profitability
Market position
Productivity
Product leadership
Personnel development
Employee attitudes
Public responsibility
Balance between short-range and long-range goals

General Electric is a huge, highly decentralized corporation. At the time it developed these goals, GE had approximately 170 responsibility centers called departments, but that is a deceptive term. In most other companies, these departments would be called divisions. For example, some GE departments had sales of more than $500 million.

Each department manager's performance was evaluated annually in relation to the specified multiple goals. A special measurements group was set up to devise ways of quantifying accomplishments in each of the areas. In this way, the evaluation of performance would become more objective as the various measures were developed and improved.

1. How would you measure performance in each of these areas? Be specific.
2. Can the other goals be encompassed as ingredients of a formal measure of profitability? In other words, can profitability per se be defined to include the other goals?

9-43 Responsibility Accounting, Profit Centers, and Contribution Approach

Richfield Honda had the following data for the year's operations:

Sales of vehicles	$3,100,000
Sales of parts and service	500,000
Cost of vehicle sales	2,480,000
Parts and service materials	100,000
Parts and service labor	200,000
Parts and service overhead	40,000
General dealership overhead	180,000
Advertising of vehicles	100,000
Sales commissions, vehicles	155,000
Sales salaries, vehicles	88,000

The president of the dealership has long regarded the markup on material and labor for the parts and service activity as the amount that is supposed to cover all parts and service overhead plus some general overhead of the dealership. In other words, the parts and service department is viewed as a cost-recovery operation, while the sales of vehicles is viewed as the income-producing activity.

1. Prepare a departmentalized operating statement that harmonizes with the views of the president.
2. Prepare an alternative operating statement that would reflect a different view of the dealership operations. Assume that $30,000 and $89,000 of the $180,000 general overhead can be allocated with confidence to the parts and service department and to sales of vehicles, respectively. The remaining $61,000 cannot be allocated except in some highly arbitrary manner.
3. Comment on the relative merits of numbers 1 and 2.

9-44 Incentives in Planned Economies

Often government-owned companies in planned economies reward managers based on nonfinancial measures. For example, the government might give managers a bonus for exceeding a 5-year-planned target for production quantities. A problem with this method is that managers tend to predict low volumes so that officials will set the targets low. This makes it easier for the managers to meet the targets, but it severely hinders planning because managers do not provide accurate information about production possibilities.

The former Soviet Union developed an alternative performance measurement and reward system. Suppose F is the forecast of production, A is actual production, and X, Y, and Z are positive constants set by top officials, with X, Y, $Z > 0$. The following performance measure was designed to motivate both high production and accurate forecasts.

$$\text{performance measure} = (Y \times F) + [X \times (A - F)] \text{ if } F \le A$$
$$(Y \times F) - [Z \times (F - A)] \text{ if } F > A$$

Assume that Cuba adopted this measure at a time when Soviet influence was great. Consider the Havana Television Manufacturing Company (HTMC). During 19X3, the factory manager, Che Chavez, had to predict the number of TVs that HTMC could produce during the next year. He was confident that at least 700,000 TVs could be produced in 19X4, and most likely they could produce 800,000 TVs. With good luck, they might even produce 900,000. Government officials told him that the new performance evaluation measure would be used, and that $X = .50$, $Y = .80$, and $Z = 1.00$ for 19X4 and 19X5.

1. Suppose Chavez predicted production of 800,000 TVs and HTMC actually produced 800,000. Calculate the performance measure.
2. Suppose again that HTMC produced 800,000 TVs. Calculate the performance measure if Chavez had been conservative and predicted only 700,000 TVs. Also calculate the performance measure if he had predicted 900,000 TVs.
3. Now suppose it is November 19X4, and it is clear that HTMC cannot achieve the 800,000 target. Does the performance measure motivate continued efforts to increase production? Suppose it is clear that HTMC will easily meet the 800,000 target. Will the system motivate continued efforts to increase production?

9-45 Balanced Scorecard

Indianapolis Pharmaceuticals Company (IPC) recently revised its performance evaluation system. The company identified four major goals and several objectives required to meet each goal. Kris Nordmark, controller of IPC, suggested that a balanced scorecard be used to report on progress toward meeting the objectives. At a recent meeting, she told the managers of IPC that listing the objectives was only the first step in installing a new performance measurement system. Each objective has to be accompanied by one or more measures to monitor progress toward achieving the objectives. She asked the help of the managers in identifying appropriate measures.

The goals and objectives determined by the top management of IPC are as follows:

1. Maintain strong financial health.
   a. Keep sufficient cash balances to assure financial survival.
   b. Achieve consistent growth in sales and income.
   c. Provide excellent returns to shareholders.
2. Provide excellent service to customers.
   a. Provide products that meet the needs of customers.
   b. Meet customer needs on a timely basis.
   c. Meet customer quality requirements.
   d. Be the preferred supplier to customers.
3. Be among the industry leaders in product and process innovations.
   a. Bring new products to market before competition.
   b. Lead competition in production process innovation.
4. Develop and maintain efficient, state-of-the-art production processes.
   a. Excel in manufacturing efficiency.
   b. Meet or beat product introduction schedules.

Propose at least one measure of performance for each of the objectives of IPC.

9-46 Quality Cost Report

The manufacturing division of Red Lake Enterprises makes a variety of home furnishings. The company prepares monthly reports on quality costs. In early 20X7, Red Lake's president asked you, the controller, to compare quality costs in 20X6 to those in 20X4. He wanted to see only total annual numbers for 20X6 compared with 20X4. You have prepared the report shown in Exhibit 9-13.

1. For each of the four quality cost areas, explain what types of costs are included and how those costs have changed between 20X4 and 20X6.
2. Assess overall quality performance in 20X6 compared with 20X4. What do you suppose has caused the changes observed in quality costs?

9-47 Six Sigma, Mean, and Variance

A major objective of Six Sigma quality-control programs is to better meet customers' needs. One place companies have applied Six Sigma is to order delivery times. They have directed efforts at reducing both the mean (average) time to delivery and the variance or standard deviation (dispersion) of the delivery times. Customers want to get their products sooner, as reflected in the mean. But they also want assurance that the product will arrive when promised. This requires delivery schedules to have little random variance.

Quality Cost Area	20X4 Cost	20X6 Cost
1. Prevention cost	45	107
Percentage of total quality cost	3.3%	12.4%
2. Appraisal cost	124	132
Percentage of total quality cost	9.1%	15.2%
3. Internal failure cost	503	368
Percentage of total quality cost	36.9%	42.5%
Total internal quality cost (1 + 2 + 3)	672	607
Percentage of total quality cost	49.3%	70.1%
4. External failure cost	691	259
Percentage of total quality cost	50.7%	29.9%
Total quality cost	1,363	866
Total product cost	22,168	23,462

Exhibit 9-13
Red Lake Enterprises
Quality Cost Report (thousands of dollars)

Consider the following experience with the implementation of Six Sigma at a major manufacturing company:

Order Delivery Times (Days)	
Before Six Sigma	**After Six Sigma**
28	16
10	21
13	12
7	7
24	16
21	4
22	5
24	16
28	11
43	2

Compute the mean and standard deviation of order-delivery time before and after implementation of Six Sigma. From a customer's perspective, how would you view the results of this application of Six Sigma?

9-48 Productivity

In early 20X1, SpaceTel Communications, a U.S.-based international telephone communications company, purchased the controlling interest in Sofia Telecom, Ltd. (STL) in Bulgaria. A key productivity measure monitored by SpaceTel is the number of customer telephone lines per employee. Consider the following data for SpaceTel:

	20X1 without STL	20X1 with STL	20X0
Customer lines	15,370,000	21,460,000	14,787,000
Employees	72,500	116,000	69,750
Lines per employee	212	185	212

1. What are SpaceTel's 20X0 productivity and 20X1 productivity without STL?
2. What are STL's 20X1 productivity and SpaceTel's 20X1 productivity with STL?
3. What difficulties do you foresee if SpaceTel brings STL's productivity in line?

9-49 Productivity Measurement

Morrison's Laundry had the following results in 20X1 and 20X3:

	20X1	20X3
Pounds of laundry processed	1,420,000 pounds	1,505,000 pounds
Sales revenue	$690,000	$1,024,000
Direct-labor hours worked	44,500 hours	46,450 hours
Direct-labor cost	$318,000	$400,000

The laundry used the same facilities in 20X3 as in 20X1. During the past 3 years, however, the company put more effort into training its employees. The manager of Morrison's was curious about whether the training had increased labor productivity.

1. Compute a measure of labor productivity for 20X3 based entirely on physical measures. Do the same for 20X1. That is, from the data given, choose measures of physical output and physical input, and use them to compare the physical productivity of labor in 20X3 with that in 20X1.
2. Compute a measure of labor productivity for 20X3 based entirely on financial measures. Do the same for 20X1. That is, from the data given, choose measures of financial output and financial input, and use them to compare the financial productivity of labor in 20X3 with that in 20X1.

3. Suppose the following productivity measure was used:

$$\text{Productivity} = \frac{\text{sales revenue}}{\text{direct-labor hours worked}}$$

Because of inflation, each 20X1 dollar is equivalent to 1.13 dollars in 20X3. Compute appropriate productivity numbers for comparing 20X3 productivity with 20X1 productivity.

CASES

9-50 Trade-Offs Among Objectives

Computer Data Services (CDS) performs routine and custom information systems services for many companies in a large midwestern metropolitan area. CDS has built a reputation for high-quality customer service and job security for its employees. Quality service and customer satisfaction have been CDS's primary subgoals—retaining a skilled and motivated workforce has been an important factor in achieving those goals. In the past, temporary downturns in business did not mean layoffs of employees, though some employees were required to perform other than their usual tasks. In anticipation of growth in business, CDS leased new equipment that, beginning in August, added $10,000 per month in operating costs. Three months ago, however, a new competitor began offering the same services to CDS customers at prices averaging 19% lower than those of CDS. Rico Estrada, the company founder and president, believes that a significant price reduction is necessary to maintain the company's market share and avoid financial ruin, but he is puzzled about how to achieve it without compromising quality, service, and the goodwill of his workforce.

CDS has a productivity objective of 20 accounts per employee. Estrada does not think that he can increase this productivity and still maintain both quality and flexibility to customer needs. CDS also monitors average cost per account and the number of customer satisfaction adjustments (resolutions of complaints). The average billing markup rate is 25% of cost. Consider the following data from the past 6 months:

	June	July	August	September	October	November
Number of accounts	797	803	869	784	723	680
Number of employees	40	41	44	43	43	41
Average cost per account	$ 153	$ 153	$ 158	$ 173	$ 187	$ 191
Average salary per employee	$3,000	$3,000	$3,000	$3,000	$3,000	$3,000

1. Discuss the trade-offs facing Rico Estrada.
2. Can you suggest solutions to his trade-off dilemma?

9-51 Six Sigma

The chapter mentions four companies that use Six Sigma for measuring and controlling quality: Motorola, General Electric, 3M, and Dow Chemical. Go to the Web site for each of these companies and find what each says about its Six Sigma efforts.

9-52 Review of Chapters 1–9

William Whitebear, general manager of the Kamloops Division of Canada Enterprises, is preparing for a management meeting. His divisional controller provided the following information:

1. The master budget for the fiscal year ended June 30, 20X4, follows:

Sales (50,000 units of A and 70,000 units of B)	$870,000
Manufacturing cost of goods sold	740,000
Manufacturing margin	$130,000
Selling and administrative expenses	120,000
Operating income	$ 10,000

2. The standard variable manufacturing cost per unit follows:

	Product A		Product B	
Direct materials	10 pieces at $.25	$2.50	5 pounds at $.30	$1.50
Direct labor	1 hour at $3.00	3.00	.3 hour at $2.50	.75
Variable overhead	1 hour at $2.00	2.00	.3 hour at $2.50	.75
Total		$7.50		$3.00

3. All budgeted selling and administrative expenses are common, fixed expenses; 60% are discretionary expenses.

4. The actual income statement for the fiscal year ended June 30, 20X4, follows:

Sales (53,000 units of A and 64,000 units of B)	$861,000
Manufacturing cost of goods sold	749,200
Manufacturing margin	$111,800
Selling and administrative expenses	116,000
Operating income	$ (4,200)

5. The budgeted sales prices for products A and B were $9 and $6, respectively. Actual sales prices equaled budgeted sales prices.

6. The schedule of the actual variable manufacturing cost of goods sold by product follows (actual quantities in parentheses):

Product A:	Materials	$134,500	(538,000 pieces)
	Labor	156,350	(53,000 hours)
	Overhead	108,650	(53,000 hours)
Product B:	Materials	102,400	(320,000 pounds)
	Labor	50,000	(20,000 hours)
	Overhead	50,000	(20,000 hours)
Total		$601,900	

7. Products A and B are manufactured in separate facilities. Of the budgeted fixed manufacturing cost, $130,000 is separable as follows: $45,000 to product A and $85,000 to product B. Ten percent of these separate costs are discretionary. All other budgeted fixed manufacturing expenses, separable and common, are committed.

8. There are no beginning or ending inventories.

During the upcoming management meeting, it is quite likely that some of the information from the controller will be discussed. In anticipation you set out to prepare answers to possible questions.

1. Determine the firm's budgeted break-even point in dollars, overall contribution-margin ratio, and contribution margins per unit by product. Assume no change in product mix.
2. Considering products A and B as segments of the firm, find the budgeted "contribution by segments" for each.
3. It is decided to allocate the budgeted selling and administrative expenses to the segments (in number 2) as follows: committed costs on the basis of budgeted unit sales mix and discretionary costs on the basis of actual unit sales mix. What are the final expense allocations? Briefly appraise the allocation method.
4. How would you respond to a proposal to base commissions to salespersons on the sales (revenue) value of orders received? Assume all salespersons have the opportunity to sell both products.
5. Determine the firm's actual "contribution margin" and "contribution controllable by segment managers" for the fiscal year ended June 30, 20X4. Assume no variances in committed fixed costs.
6. Determine the "sales-activity variance" for each product for the fiscal year ended June 30, 20X4.
7. Determine and identify all variances in variable manufacturing costs by product for the fiscal year ended June 30, 20X4.

NIKE 10-K PROBLEM

9-53 **Strategy at Nike**

Find "Item 7 Management's Discussion and Analysis of Financial Condition and Results of Operations" near the beginning of the **Nike** 10-K report in Appendix C.

1. Outline Nike's strategy to convert revenue growth to shareholder value in five key areas.
2. What are four long-term financial goals?
3. How well have these financial goals been met?
4. List some nonfinancial goals that Nike might use in a BSC.

EXCEL APPLICATION EXERCISE

9-54 **Wages for New Salary-Plus-Bonus Plan**

Goal: Create an Excel spreadsheet to calculate the impact on employee wages of a new salary-plus-bonus plan established to motivate salesclerks to increase sales. Use the results to answer questions about your findings.

Scenario: As the department store manager, you must determine if the new plan is the best way to motivate salesclerks and meet the objective of increasing sales. The background data for the compensation plan appear in Exercise 9-34. Use only data for salesclerk A and salesclerk B to prepare your spreadsheet.

When you have completed your spreadsheet, answer the following questions:

1. Which salesclerk has the highest average total salary over the four-month period?
2. What part of the compensation plan had the most impact on the salesclerks' salaries? The least impact?
3. Do you see any problems with this compensation plan? Explain.

Step-by-Step:

1. Open a new Excel spreadsheet.
2. In column A, create a bold-faced heading that contains the following:
   Row 1: Chapter 9 Decision Guideline
   Row 2: Tokyo Department Store
   Row 3: Salary-Plus-Bonus Plan Analysis
   Row 4: Today's Date
3. Merge and center the four heading rows across columns A–H.
4. In column A, create the following row headings:
   Row 7: Salesclerk A
   Row 8: Month
   Row 9: January
   Row 10: February
   Row 11: March
   Row 12: April
   Skip three rows.
   Row 16: Salesclerk B
   Row 17: Month
   Row 18: January
   Row 19: February
   Row 20: March
   Row 21: April
5. Change the format of salesclerk names (rows 7, 16) to bold-faced, underlined headings.
6. Change the format of month (rows 8, 17) to bold-faced headings.
7. In rows 8 and 17, create the following bold-faced, right-justified column headings:
   Column B: Quota
   Column C: Sales
   Column D: Over Quota
   Column E: Base Salary
   Column F: Quota Bonus
   Column G: Commission
   Column H: Total Salary

Note: Adjust column widths as necessary.

8. In column G, create the following right-justified cell headings:
   Row 14: Average:
   Row 23: Average:

9. Use the scenario data to fill in quota, sales, and base salary amounts from January–April for each salesclerk.

10. Use the appropriate IF statements to calculate over quota and quota bonus amounts when the salesclerks' sales met or exceeded their respective quotas (negative commissions should not be calculated).

$$= \text{IF (formula} > 0,\text{formula},0)$$
For Over Quota only.

$$= \text{IF (formula} < 0,0,68000) \quad \text{OR} \quad = \text{IF (formula} > 0,68000,0)$$
For Quota Bonus only.

Hint: Go to the "Help" text and type "copy formulas" in the search area to obtain instructions for copying formulas from one cell to another. If done correctly, you should have to type in each of the formulas only once.

11. Use appropriate formulas to calculate commission and total salary amounts for each month, as well as an average amount for the January–April period for each salesclerk.

12. Format all amounts as follows:

Number tab:	Category:	Currency
	Decimal places:	0
	Symbol:	None
	Negative numbers:	Black with parentheses

13. To format specific amounts to display with a yen symbol, do the following:
    a. In an empty cell, hold down the Alt key and enter 0165 from the numeric keypad. When you stop holding the Alt key down, a yen sign will be displayed.

    Note: If your keyboard does not have a numeric keypad, use the shift and NumLk keys to activate the imbedded numeric keypad. Then, follow the instructions in part a. Use the shift and NumLk keys to turn the feature off.

    b. Highlight the yen character you have just created, select Edit, Cut. This will paste the yen sign to the clipboard. To see the clipboard, select View, Toolbars, Clipboard.
    c. Select the average amount for salesclerk A and open the Format, Cells. . . . dialog box.
    d. Select the custom category on the number tab. Scroll down toward the bottom of the type list and highlight the type shown next.

    Type: ($*#, ##0); ($*#, ##0); ($*" − "); (@)

    Change the data between the quotation marks in the third grouping from "−" to "0."
    Paste the yen sign over EACH occurrence of the dollar sign.

    Hint: Highlight the $ sign; press "Ctrl" and "V." This will paste the yen sign from the clipboard over the $ sign that has been highlighted in the Type field.

    e. Click the OK button.
    f. Utilize the custom format, which should now be at the bottom of the type list, to print the yen sign for all January amounts for both clerks and the average amount for salesclerk B.

14. Save your work, and print a copy for your files.

    Note: Print your spreadsheet using landscape in order to ensure that all columns appear on one page.

COLLABORATIVE LEARNING EXERCISE

9-55 Goals, Objectives, and Performance Measures

There is increasing pressure on colleges and universities to develop measures of accountability. The objective is to specify goals and objectives and to develop performance measures to assess the achievement of those goals and objectives.

Form a group of four to six students to be a consulting team to the accounting department at your college or university. (If you are not using this book as part of a course in an accounting department, select any department at your college or university.) Based on your collective knowledge of the department, its mission, and its activities, formulate a statement of goals for the department. From that statement, develop several specific objectives, each of which can be measured. Then, develop at least one measure of performance for each objective.

An optional second step in this exercise is to meet with a faculty member from the department, and ask him or her to critique your objectives and performance measures. To the department member, do the objectives make sense? Are the proposed measures feasible, and will they correctly measure attainment of the objectives? Will they provide proper incentives to the faculty? If the department has created objectives and performance measures, compare them to those your group developed.

INTERNET EXERCISE

9-56 Management Control System at Procter & Gamble

Setting up management control systems and determining measurement methods and who should be responsible for particular revenues, costs, and information can be a large task. The structure of the organization plays a part in how well a particular measure is likely to work. Ensuring that the goals of the organization are in concert with the management control system is also an important factor. It is not possible to evaluate a company's management control system from an Internet site. What we can do, however, is to use a site as an example and apply some of the concepts of the chapter to measures and tools that would be possibilities for a firm.

1. A well-known and well-established company with worldwide acceptance is **Procter & Gamble (P&G)**. Log on to the company's Web site at www.pg.com. Locate the most recent annual report by following the links under the "Investor/Shareholder Relations" tab to "Financial Reporting." Examine the "Letter to Shareholders" section of the annual report. What does P&G consider to be the most important factors that drive their growth strategy? How does P&G ensure that managers meet the company's objectives?

2. The company has numerous products, and the Web site divides them into different categories and brands to help customers find relevant product information. Click on "Brands and Innovation." What are the major categories of brands listed on the Web site? Click on the "Household Care" category. What are some of the brands in this category that you are familiar with? How could a system be set up to help measure the success of the firm's goal to build brands in the "Household Care" category? What would be three possible financial measures? What about three nonfinancial measures?

Management Control in Decentralized Organizations

LEARNING OBJECTIVES

When you have finished studying this chapter, you should be able to:

1. Define *decentralization* and identify its expected benefits and costs.

2. Distinguish between responsibility centers and decentralization.

3. Explain how the linking of rewards to responsibility-center performance metrics affects incentives and risk.

4. Compute return on investment (ROI), economic profit, and economic value added (EVA).

5. Compare the incentives created by income, ROI, and economic profit (or EVA) performance measures.

6. Define *transfer prices* and identify their purpose.

7. State the general rule for transfer pricing and use it to assess alternative transfer prices based on total costs, variable costs, or market prices.

8. Identify the factors affecting multinational transfer prices.

9. Explain how controllability and management by objectives (MBO) aid the implementation of management control systems.

▶ **NIKE**

In a little more than 30 years, Nike has become the largest sports and fitness company in the world. It has grown from a small Beaverton, Oregon, company into a global giant with a presence in many different sports. For example, in the world of soccer, Nike was only a minor factor 10 years ago. Now Nike has placed itself at the center of attention for soccer fans worldwide. Nike has endorsement arrangements with the Italian and French national teams, as well as Manchester United, FC Barcelona, Inter Milan, and PSV Eindhoven. Further, its visibility continues to grow. Nike was the official sponsor and supplier for Chinese athletes for the 2008 Beijing Olympic Games.

From 1986 to 2011, Nike's revenues increased from $1 billion to almost $21 billion. During this same period, the percentage of non-U.S. revenues increased from 25% to 57%. Nike now has more stores outside the United States than inside. While footwear still accounts for more than half of Nike's sales, apparel sales now account for nearly one-third. A sampling of endorsements (promotional contracts with famous sports teams, individuals, and organizations) in addition to the soccer teams previously listed gives another perspective on the company's global presence. Tennis stars Roger Federer, Rafael Nadal, Maria Sharapova, Serena Williams; basketball stars Kobe Bryant, LeBron James, and Kevin Durant; and golf's Trevor Immelman, Anthony Kim, and Paul Casey all have endorsement deals with Nike. Watch almost any sports event on television, and you are likely to see the Nike "swoosh" logo.

Nike made a conscious decision to go global—a process that has generated substantial financial rewards. What are some of the keys to success when a company like Nike decides to significantly expand its operations abroad? To manage and coordinate widely dispersed operations, Nike needs information. Increasing sophistication of communications—Internet, e-mail, and worldwide cellular phone coverage—means that geographical separation no longer implies lack of access to information. While communications technology can help Nike and others get information quickly, the information they receive is determined by their management control system.

© Interfoto/Alamy

This chapter focuses on the role of management control systems in decentralized organizations such as Nike. We discuss how companies use performance metrics to motivate managers of separate units, including various ways of measuring performance to encourage actions by managers that are in the company's best interests. Finally, we address the special problems created when one segment of an organization charges another for providing goods or services. ■

Centralization Versus Decentralization

As organizations grow and undertake more diverse and complex activities, they face decisions about how much decision-making authority to delegate to lower levels of the organization. Concentration of decision-making authority only at the highest levels of the organization is **centralization**. Delegation of decision-making authority to lower levels is **decentralization**. Note that centralization or decentralization is a matter of degree, depicted as a choice along the continuum shown in Exhibit 10-1. The lower in the organization that authority is delegated, the greater the decentralization.

Nike has delegated a great deal of decision-making authority to the local-market level. For example, local Nike managers in Germany made the decision to sign an endorsement contract with world-champion racecar driver Michael Schumacher. According to CEO Philip Knight, "[Previously] it would have taken a move from within the company headquarters to strike such a deal. . . . But this time it was a decision made in country." The local German manager knew that Schumacher was extremely relevant to the German market and that this would be a "profit driven, culturally significant, and brand enhancing move." Knight credits this move toward decentralization for Nike's rapid increase in international sales: "It is a great example of what we are trying to do: Make decisions on the ground in faraway places."

The best choice along the continuum between centralization and decentralization is seldom obvious. In fact, organizations and industries seem to cycle from increasing decentralization to increasing centralization, and back again. For example, a decade or so ago most airlines, such as South China Airlines, Iberia Airlines, and Air France, decentralized. In contrast, at the same time, Sabena, Belgium's state-owned airline until its bankruptcy in 2001, undertook a centralization effort. In the insurance industry, Aetna decentralized at the same time AXA Equitable was centralizing. Let's take a look at some of the factors companies consider as they choose their position along the centralization/decentralization continuum.

Nike is a globally decentralized company. Customers throughout the world recognize its "swoosh" trademark. Achieving the appropriate balance between autonomy at the local level and efficiencies at the corporate level is a challenge when designing Nike's management control system.

Objective 1

Define *decentralization* and identify its expected benefits and costs.

centralization
Concentration of decision-making authority only at the highest levels of an organization.

decentralization
The delegation of decision-making authority to lower levels of the organization. The lower in the organization that authority is delegated, the greater the decentralization.

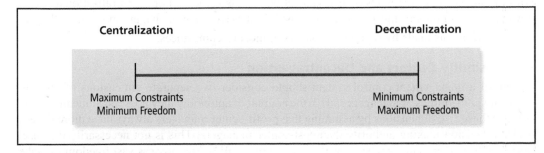

Centralization	Decentralization
Maximum Constraints Minimum Freedom	Minimum Constraints Maximum Freedom

Exhibit 10-1
Centralization Versus Decentralization

Costs and Benefits of Decentralization

Most organizations realize benefits from some level of decentralization. Managers of lower-level units (which we will refer to as "local" managers), often have the best information concerning local conditions and, therefore, are able to make faster and better decisions on local issues than higher-level managers (which we will refer to as "central" managers). By delegating decision-making authority to local managers, central managers free up time to deal with larger issues and fundamental strategy. In addition, decentralization gives local managers an opportunity to develop their decision-making ability and other management skills, ensuring that the organization develops future leaders. Finally, local managers who are given more authority often have greater motivation and job satisfaction.

Decentralization also has its costs. Local managers may make decisions that are not in the organization's best interests. Why? Either because they act to improve their own segment's performance at the expense of the organization or because they do not fully understand the effects of their decisions on other segments and the organization as a whole. In a decentralized organization, innovative ideas to improve performance are less likely to be shared across units. Local managers in decentralized organizations also tend to duplicate services that might be less expensive if centralized (e.g., accounting, advertising, and personnel). Furthermore, costs of accumulating and processing information frequently rise under decentralization because top management needs additional accounting reports to learn about and evaluate decentralized units and their managers. Finally, managers in decentralized units may waste time negotiating with other units about goods or services that are being transferred between units. You can see some of the costs and benefits of decentralization in the Business First box on page 393.

Decentralization is more popular in profit-seeking organizations (where accountants can more easily measure outputs and inputs) than in nonprofit organizations (where it is more difficult to find reliable performance measures, so granting managers freedom is more risky). Central management can give local managers more freedom when it can more easily measure the results of their decisions and thereby hold local managers accountable for the results. In a profit-seeking firm, poor decisions become apparent from the inadequate profit generated.

Middle Ground

The optimal choice along the centralization/decentralization continuum is likely to differ from one company to the next. For every Nike that finds the benefits of increased decentralization exceeding the costs, another company finds the costs exceeding the benefits. In fact, the optimal choice for one part of the organization may differ from the optimal choice for another part. For example, many companies decentralize much of the controller's problem-solving and attention-directing functions and handle them at lower levels. In contrast, they generally centralize income tax planning and mass scorekeeping functions such as accounting for payroll.

Decentralization is more successful when an organization's segments are relatively independent of one another—that is, when the decisions of a manager in one segment will not affect other segments. When segments do much internal buying or selling, much buying from the same outside suppliers, or much selling to the same outside markets, they are candidates for more centralization.

In Chapter 9, we stressed that managers should consider cost-benefit tests, goal congruence, and managerial effort when designing a management control system. If management has decided in favor of heavy decentralization, then **segment autonomy**—the delegation of decision-making power to managers of segments of an organization—is also crucial. For decentralization to work, however, this autonomy must be real, not just "lip service." Top managers must be willing to abide by decisions made by segment managers in most circumstances.

segment autonomy
The delegation of decision-making power to managers of segments in an organization.

Responsibility Centers and Decentralization

Objective 2

Distinguish between responsibility centers and decentralization.

Design of a management control system should consider two separate dimensions of control: (1) the responsibilities of managers and (2) the amount of autonomy they possess. Some managers confuse these two dimensions by assuming that profit-center managers always have more decentralized decision-making authority than cost-center managers. This is not necessarily the case. Some profit-center managers, such as those at General Electric, possess vast freedom to make decisions concerning labor contracts, supplier choices, equipment purchases, personnel decisions, and so on. In contrast, profit-center managers at other companies need top-management

Business First

Benefits and Costs of Decentralization

Many companies believe that decentralization is important to their success, including PepsiCo, DuPont, and Procter & Gamble. But one company stands out from the others in its efforts to decentralize: Johnson & Johnson. Johnson & Johnson (with 2011 sales of $65 billion, 118,000 employees, and more than 250 companies operating in 60 countries) is the maker of products such as Tylenol, Listerine, Johnson's Baby Powder, Neutrogena, and Neosporin. The company has a long history of decentralization, beginning in the 1930s. Its 2011 annual report states ". . . the Company views its principle of decentralized management as an asset and fundamental to the success of a broadly based business. It also fosters an entrepreneurial spirit, combining the extensive resources of a large organization with the ability to anticipate and react quickly to local market changes and challenges."

Under the company's management structure, each of its operating companies functions autonomously. One benefit is that decisions are made by executives who are closer to the marketplace. One disadvantage is the additional expense because many of the operating companies duplicate many overhead costs. Although ultimately accountable to executives at Johnson & Johnson headquarters in New Brunswick, New Jersey, some segment presidents see their bosses as few as four times a year. Bill Weldon, Johnson & Johnson chairman of the board and former CEO, extols the virtues of decentralization: "Johnson & Johnson has maintained a significant and well-established presence in these markets for decades, utilizing our decentralized operating model to stay close to patients, consumers and health care providers with local market insights, products, and strategies." He believes the structure has been essential to its strategy of developing executives from within because young managers can be given responsibility for running whole companies. "This allows people to be entrepreneurial," he said, "and to grow."

BusinessWeek summarized Weldon's approach as follows: "[Johnson & Johnson's] success has hinged on its unique culture and structure.... Each of its far-flung units operates pretty much as an independent enterprise. Businesses set their own strategies; they have their own finance and human resources departments, for example. While this degree of decentralization makes for relatively high overhead costs, no chief executive, Weldon included, has thought that too high a price to pay."

As you can see, decentralization has benefits and costs. Some companies have vacillated between decentralization and centralization, sometimes believing that the benefits of centralizing common activities dominate the benefits of decentralization, while at other times seeking the decision-making advantages of decentralization. In contrast, Johnson & Johnson has continued its policy of decentralization in good times and bad, through a long succession of top management leadership. The company has a long-term credo that mandates decentralization. It would take a brave (or foolhardy) leader to change Johnson & Johnson's philosophy of decentralization.

Sources: Adapted from *Johnson & Johnson 2011 Annual Report*; M. Petersen, "From the Ranks, Unassumingly," *New York Times*, February 24, 2002, Section 3, page 2; and A. Barrett, "Staying on Top," *BusinessWeek*, May 5, 2003.

approval for almost all the decisions just mentioned. Similarly, cost centers may be more heavily decentralized than profit centers. The fundamental question in deciding between using a cost center or a profit center for a given segment is not whether heavy decentralization exists. Instead, the fundamental question is, for whatever level of decentralization that exists, "Will a profit center or a cost center better solve the problems of goal congruence and management effort?"

The management control system should be designed to achieve the best possible alignment between local manager decisions and the actions central management seeks. For example, a plant may seem to be a "natural" cost center because the plant manager has no influence over decisions concerning the marketing of its products. Nevertheless, some companies insist on evaluating a plant manager by the plant's profitability. Why? Because they believe this broader evaluation base will positively affect the plant manager's behavior. Instead of being concerned solely with running an efficient cost center, the system motivates the plant manager to consider quality control more carefully and react to customers' special requests more sympathetically. In designing accounting control systems, top managers must consider the system's impact on behavior desired by the organization.

Performance Metrics and Management Control

A major factor in designing decentralized management control systems is how the system's performance metrics affect managers' incentives. **Incentives** are the rewards, both implicit and explicit, for managerial effort and actions. A **performance metric** is a specific measure of management accomplishment. Organizations should choose performance metrics that improve the alignment of manager incentives with organizational objectives. The organization wants managers to use decision-making autonomy to meet the company's objectives, not to pursue

Objective 3

Explain how the linking of rewards to responsibility-center performance metrics affects incentives and risk.

incentives
Rewards, both implicit and explicit, for managerial effort and actions.

performance metric
A specific measure of management accomplishment.

agency theory
A theory that deals with relationships where one party (the principal) delegates decision-making authority to another party (the agent).

other goals. For example, Nike executives wanted the company's manager of German operations to sign auto-racer Michael Schumacher to a contract only if it would create additional profits for Nike, not to provide an entree for the manager into the inner circles of auto racing.

Agency Theory, Performance, and Rewards

Agency theory provides a model to analyze relationships where one party (the principal) delegates decision-making authority to another party (the agent). Agency theory is useful to analyze situations where there is imperfect alignment between the principal's and agent's 1) information and 2) objectives. As discussed earlier, it is common for local managers to have better information about their units than do higher-level central managers. Because the local managers have different information than central managers, they make different decisions. Similarly, as discussed in Chapter 9, it is common for the objectives of local managers to differ from central organizational objectives. Agency theory provides a framework to analyze these differences in designing a management control system.

Exhibit 10-2 shows how the design of a management control system affects the actions of managers. Managers have beliefs about how alternative action choices will lead to outcomes for their unit, and the management control system specifies how outcomes translate into unit performance metrics and into both explicit and implicit rewards. Managers' preferences motivate them to select actions that generate outcomes measured and rewarded by a company's management control system. The manager's understanding of how the control system links outcomes, performance metrics, and rewards influences the manager's choice of actions. Thus, the right metrics and rewards motivate actions that are in the company's best interests.

The links between outcomes and performance metrics and rewards are critical features of the management control system. While the importance of explicit links is clear, implicit links may also be important. For example, the management control system might include an explicit link that specifies the amount of bonus that will be paid for different levels of profit, but there may be an additional implicit link between performance and promotions. Similarly, it is important to recognize that rewards may be monetary or nonmonetary. Examples of monetary rewards include pay raises and bonuses. Examples of nonmonetary rewards include praise, better offices, and other perquisites. Thus, while we often focus on explicit monetary rewards, remember that implicit and nonmonetary rewards associated with outcomes and metrics play important roles in the management control system.

One important rule for performance measurement is clear: *You get what you measure.* Managers focus on areas where an organization measures managerial performance, even when the management control system does not include explicit rewards tied to the measures. Therefore, it is important to choose accounting measures that provide objective and easy-to-understand evaluations of performance, where managers believe there is a clear connection between their action choices and the performance metric.

Agency Theory and Risk

Ideally, companies should reward managers based on their individual performance, but often an organization cannot directly measure a manager's performance. For example, a company may not be able to separate the manager's effect on responsibility-center results from the effect of other factors beyond a manager's control. The greater the influence of noncontrollable factors

Exhibit 10-2
Design of a Management Control System

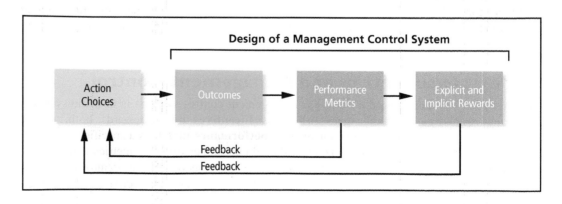

on responsibility-center results, the more problems there are in using the results to measure and reward a manager's performance.

Consider a particular Niketown store. Suppose its profits increased dramatically. The following factors all contributed to the increase in profits:

- A lengthy strike by employees of a competitor resulted in many customers switching to Nike.
- The store implemented a new cost management system resulting in a significant reduction in the costs of handling merchandise.
- Overall population growth in the store's region has been much higher than in other Niketown locations.
- Labor costs in the region have not increased as much as in most Niketown locations.
- Employee turnover is lower than the system average. Employees cite their excellent relationship with fellow employees and management as the reason for their high level of job satisfaction.

From the factors listed, it is likely that a significant portion of the store's profit increase was due to factors the store manager could not control (the competitor's strike, population growth, and regional labor costs). Nonetheless, it is also likely that a portion of the profit increase was due to factors the manager could control (adopting the cost-management system and creating a productive working environment for all employees). How should Nike evaluate the performance of the store manager? Should it measure the manager's performance by comparing profit across other Niketown stores? What other measures could Nike use?

An ideal performance metric would measure and reward the manager for controllable factors and neither reward nor punish the manager for uncontrollable factors. Although this ideal is hard to achieve, agency theory can guide the design of a system to link performance metrics and rewards. When an organization hires a manager, the employment contract details performance metrics and how they will affect rewards. However, not all rewards are explicitly specified. For example, a company can reward a manager with a promotion, but the contract will probably not explicitly specify the requirements for promotion.

According to agency theory, employment contracts must balance three factors:

1. Incentive: The more a manager's reward depends on a performance metric, the more incentive the manager has to take actions that maximize that measure. Top management should define the performance metric to promote goal congruence and base enough reward on it to achieve managerial effort.
2. Risk: The more uncontrollable factors affect a manager's reward, the more risk the manager bears. People generally avoid risk, so a company must pay managers more if it expects them to bear more risk. Creating incentive by linking rewards to responsibility-center results, which is generally desirable, has the undesirable side effect of imposing risk on managers if noncontrollable factors affect some part of the center's results.
3. Cost of measuring performance: The incentive versus risk trade-off is not necessary if a manager's controllable performance can be perfectly measured. Why? Because managers completely control their own performance, perfect measurement of controllable performance would eliminate risk to the manager. With perfect performance measurement, a manager could be paid a fixed amount if he or she performs as agreed, and nothing otherwise. But perfectly measuring controllable performance is usually inordinately expensive if not outright impossible. The cost-benefit criterion therefore leads companies to rely on imperfect but low-cost measures. Unfortunately, these measures frequently confound the manager's controllable performance with uncontrollable factors.

Consider the example of a promoter hired by a group of investors to promote and administer an outdoor concert. Suppose the investors offer the promoter a contract with part guaranteed pay and part bonus based on total attendance. A larger bonus portion compared with the guaranteed portion creates more incentive, but it also creates more risk for the promoter. For example, what happens if it rains? The promoter could do an outstanding job promoting the concert but the weather might keep fans away. To compensate the promoter for added risk, the expected total payment to the promoter will have to be higher for a contract where a higher portion of the total payment is based on attendance. The investors must decide on the optimal trade-off between the benefit from the added incentive created by a larger bonus and the extra total payment necessary to compensate for the added risk. Note that these contracting issues would not arise if the investors could directly measure the promoter's effort and judgment, rather than basing the bonus on attendance at the concert, a low-cost and readily-available measure that unfortunately is also influenced by factors outside the control of the promoter.

Measures of Segment Performance

Objective 4

Compute return on investment (ROI), economic profit, and economic value added (EVA).

It is hard to find a company that does not include some measure of profitability among its segment performance metrics. For example, companies that use performance measurement systems such as the balanced scorecard (discussed in Chapter 9) almost always include a profitability measure among their multiple metrics. The trouble is that there are many ways to measure profitability, and it is not clear which is the best measure. Is it income? Is it income before or after interest and taxes? Is it an absolute amount? A percentage? If a percentage, is it a percentage of revenue or of investment? In this section, we consider how alternative profitability measures affect managers' incentives.

Income Measures

Measures of income are readily available from the financial reporting system at any level of the organization for which a company can identify revenues and expenses, such as a subsidiary, a division, or a business unit. Moreover, accountants can easily customize income measures to exclude factors that the company considers to be outside the control of the manager. For example, earnings before interest and taxes (EBIT) excludes the effects of interest and taxes, while earnings before interest, taxes, depreciation, and amortization (EBITDA) also excludes the effects of depreciation and amortization.

However, income measures can create incentives to focus too narrowly on income without considering the resources required to generate income. For example, suppose a manager is considering an investment that will generate $1,000 of income. If the manager is evaluated only on income, the incentive is to make this investment, whether the required investment is $5,000 or $500,000. Thus, performance evaluation based on income measures can lead managers to focus only on income and ignore the investment required to generate that income.

Similarly, income measures can provide misleading performance comparisons. Suppose a company has two divisions, A, with operating income of $200,000, and B, with operating income of $150,000. Further suppose the investment in division A is $20 million while the investment in division B is $1 million. The operating income measure obviously provides an incomplete comparison of the performance of the two divisions. Although division A is generating slightly higher operating income than division B, division A requires a far larger investment. Division B is generating much higher income relative to the resources used to generate the income—$150,000 of income using $1 million of investment is far better performance than $200,000 of income using $20 million of investment.

Return on Investment (ROI)

return on investment (ROI)
A measure of income divided by the investment required to obtain that income.

A more comprehensive measure of profitability that takes into account the investment required to generate income is the **return on investment (ROI)**. ROI is income divided by the investment required to generate that income. For a given amount of investment (and holding risk constant), the investor wants the maximum income.

ROI facilitates the comparison of a unit's performance with other segments within the company or with similar units outside the company. Why? Because, unlike income alone, ROI takes into account the investment required to generate the income. Further, ROI is a return per unit of investment and does not depend on the size of the segments being compared. In the preceding example, division A has a much lower ROI than division B:

$$ROI = \frac{income}{investment}$$

$$ROI \text{ division A} = \frac{\$200,000}{\$20,000,000} = 1\%$$

$$ROI \text{ division B} = \frac{\$150,000}{\$1,000,000} = 15\%$$

	ROI	Income / Invested Capital	=	Income / Revenue	×	Revenue / Invested Capital
Present Outlook	20%	$\dfrac{16}{80}$	=	$\dfrac{16}{100}$	×	$\dfrac{100}{80}$
Alternative: 1. Increase return on sales by reducing expenses relative to sales.	25%	$\dfrac{20}{80}$	=	$\dfrac{20}{100}$	×	$\dfrac{100}{80}$
Alternative: 2. Increase capital turnover by decreasing investment.	25%	$\dfrac{16}{64}$	=	$\dfrac{16}{100}$	×	$\dfrac{100}{64}$

Exhibit 10-3
Return on Investment as the Product of Return on Sales and Capital Turnover

Every dollar invested in division B is generating income of $.15, compared to the $.01 generated by every dollar invested in division A.

ROI as the Product of Return on Sales and Investment Turnover

As shown in the following equations, we can write ROI as the product of two items: **return on sales** (income divided by revenue) and **capital turnover** (revenue divided by invested capital).

$$\text{return on investment} = \frac{\text{income}}{\text{invested capital}}$$

$$= \frac{\text{income}}{\text{revenue}} \times \frac{\text{revenue}}{\text{invested capital}}$$

$$= \text{return on sales} \times \text{capital turnover}$$

return on sales
Income divided by revenue.

capital turnover
Revenue divided by invested capital.

This expression shows that increasing either return on sales or capital turnover will increase ROI. Exhibit 10-3 shows an example where either of two alternatives could increase ROI to 25% from its current value of 20%. Alternative 1 improves return on sales by decreasing expenses relative to sales without increasing investment. Alternative 2 increases capital turnover by decreasing investment without reducing sales. Increasing capital turnover by decreasing investment means using fewer assets, such as cash, receivables, inventories, or equipment, for each dollar of revenue generated.

Increasing turnover is one of the advantages of implementing the just-in-time (JIT) philosophy (see Chapter 1). Many companies implementing JIT purchasing and production systems are able to lower inventory levels while maintaining the return on sales, resulting in dramatic improvements in ROI.

Measuring Investment

To understand what an ROI measure implies for a particular company, you must first determine how the company defines its components: income and investment. We discussed alternative definitions of segment income in Chapter 9, pages 360–363, so we will not repeat them here. In this section, we discuss alternative definitions of investment.

Definitions of Investment

Consider the following balance sheet:

Current assets	$ 400,000	Current liabilities	$ 200,000
Property, plant, and equipment, net	900,000	Long-term liabilities	400,000
		Stockholders' equity	700,000
Total assets	$1,300,000	Total liabilities and stockholders' equity	$1,300,000

Possible definitions of investment in this example are as follows:

1. Stockholders' equity: This definition considers only the investment by the stockholders, $700,000.
2. Stockholders' equity and long-term liabilities, $700,000 + $400,000 = $1,100,000. This definition encompasses not only the investment by stockholders but also the investment by debt investors. The combination of stockholders' equity and long-term liabilities is sometimes described as long-term invested capital. Note that because of the accounting identity total assets = short-term liabilities + long-term liabilities + stockholders' equity, this can alternatively be computed as total assets less short-term liabilities, $1,300,000 – $200,000 = $1,100,000.
3. Stockholders' equity, long-term liabilities, and current liabilities, $1,300,000: This definition encompasses all sources of financing for the firm. Because of the accounting identity, this is also equal to total assets.

Each of these alternative measures of investment paired with a measure of income yields a specific ROI measure. For example, net income divided by the first measure, investment by stockholders, is return on equity (ROE) while net income divided by the third measure, total assets, is return on assets (ROA).

For measuring segment performance, firms usually rely on ROA because it is impossible to measure investment by stockholders separately for segments. Further, ROA focuses on how well the division manager is using assets without regard to how they were financed.

Valuation of Assets

gross book value
The original cost of an asset before deducting accumulated depreciation.

net book value
The original cost of an asset less any accumulated depreciation.

When firms use ROA measures, two additional issues arise related to the valuation of total assets. First, companies could value assets contained in the investment base at either **gross book value** (the original cost of an asset) or **net book value** (the original cost of an asset less any accumulated depreciation). Second, they could value assets at either historical cost or some version of current cost. Practice is overwhelmingly in favor of using net book value based on historical costs, which are measures consistent with the numbers reported in the financial statements. However, the following three sections explain when gross book value or current cost might provide a better measure of performance to achieve desired incentives, and how to decide whether to measure assets at beginning-of-the-period values, end-of-the-period values, or at the average value duing the period.

HISTORICAL OR CURRENT COST? Most companies favor historical cost over any measure of current cost such as replacement cost or liquidation values. Yet, critics maintain that historical cost provides a faulty basis for decision making and performance evaluation. Historical costs may be far from what a company might pay to purchase the asset today or the amount it could get from selling it—the values relevant to decisions affecting the asset. Despite these criticisms, managers have been slow to depart from historical cost.

Why is historical cost so widely used? Some critics would say that sheer ignorance is the explanation. But a more persuasive answer comes from cost-benefit analysis. Accounting systems are costly. Companies must keep historical records for many legal purposes, so historical records are already in place. A company spends no additional money evaluating performance based on historical costs. Many top managers believe that improvements in collective operating decisions that would result from using current cost are not large enough to warrant the added expense.

PLANT AND EQUIPMENT: GROSS OR NET? In valuing assets, we need to distinguish between net and gross book values. Most companies use net book value in calculating their investment base. However, a significant minority uses gross book value. The proponents of gross book value maintain that it facilitates comparisons between years and between plants or divisions. Under gross values, performance evaluations depend only on what assets are in use, not on the depreciation assumptions or how old the assets are.

Consider an example of a $600,000 piece of equipment with a 3-year life and no residual value.

Year	Operating Income Before Depreciation	Depreciation	Operating Income	Average Net Book Value*	Net BV Rate of Return	Gross Book Value	Gross BV Rate of Return
1	$260,000	$200,000	$60,000	$500,000	12%	$600,000	10%
2	260,000	200,000	60,000	300,000	20	600,000	10
3	260,000	200,000	60,000	100,000	60	600,000	10

*($600,000 + $400,000) ÷ 2; ($400,000 + $200,000) ÷ 2; and so on.

Notice that operating income does not change in the example, yet the rate of return on net book value increases as the equipment ages. In contrast, the rate of return on gross book value is unchanged. Proponents of using gross book value for performance evaluation maintain that a performance metric should not improve simply because assets are getting older. On the other hand, advocates maintain that using net book value is less confusing because it is consistent with the assets shown on the conventional balance sheet and with net income computations.

When choosing between net and gross book value, companies should focus on the effect on managers' incentives. Managers evaluated using gross book value will tend to replace assets sooner than will managers in firms using net book value. Consider a division of Nike that has a 4-year-old machine with an original cost of $1,000 and net book value of $200. The division can replace the machine with a new one that also costs $1,000. The choice of net or gross book value does not affect net income. However, if Nike uses the net book value for measuring the investment base, replacement will increase the investment base from $200 to $1,000. In contrast, if Nike uses gross book value, the base is $1,000 irrespective of whether the asset is replaced. In summary, to maximize ROI, managers in firms using net book value have incentives to keep old assets with their low book value because the lower book value implies a lower measured investment. Managers in firms using gross book value have less incentive to keep old assets. Therefore, using gross book value will motivate managers to use more state-of-the-art production technology.

ASSET VALUES: BEGINNING, ENDING, OR AVERAGE?   If investment does not change throughout the year, it will not matter whether we measure assets at the beginning, the end, or average for the year. However, if investment changes throughout the year, we should measure invested capital as an average for the period. Why? Because income is a flow of resources over a period of time, and we should measure the effect of the flow on the average amount invested. The most accurate measures of average investment take into account the amount invested month-by-month, or even day-by-day. However, a simple average of the beginning and ending balances often provides nearly the same result without going to the trouble required to produce greater accuracy. Suppose division B had $800,000 of investment at the beginning of the year and the flow of income gradually increased it to $1,200,000 by the end of the year. The average of the beginning and ending investment amounts is ($800,000 + $1,200,000) ÷ 2 = $1,000,000.

SUMMARY   There are no universally correct answers with respect to such controversial issues as historical values versus current values, or gross versus net asset values, or beginning versus average versus ending values. Each organization must design its management control system to achieve the best possible decision making, taking into account the cost-benefit trade-off. This approach is not concerned with "truth" or "perfection" by itself. Instead, the design should ask questions such as the following: Will improvements in the system be worth the added cost? Will a different system achieve better goal congruence and managerial effort? Or, will our existing imperfect system provide about the same set of decisions at lower cost?

Incentives from ROI

Although evaluation based on ROI causes managers to consider both income and investment in their decisions, it still may not align the incentives for the manager with the goals of the firm. ROI-based performance evaluation may provide inappropriate incentives for managers to reject profitable investment opportunities or accept unprofitable investment opportunities. Consider a company with two divisions A and B, where currently division A has an

ROI of 5% and division B has an ROI of 15%. Suppose that the target return on investments is 10%—the corporate goal is to make investments where the return is 10% or more and reject investments where the return is less than 10%. If the company evaluates division managers based on ROI, their incentives will not be aligned with this corporate goal. For example, the division A manager has an incentive to adopt any investment that increases the division A return above its current value of 5%, including investments with returns between 5% and 10%, below the corporate target of 10%. Similarly, the division B manager has an incentive to reject any investment that decreases the division B return below its current value of 15%, including investments with returns between 10% and 15%, which are above the corporate target of 10%. The following sections explain how this issue is addressed by performance measures such as economic profit.

Economic Profit and Economic Value Added (EVA)

economic profit (residual income)

After-tax operating income less a capital charge.

net operating profit after-tax (NOPAT)

Income before interest expense but after tax.

capital charge

Company's cost of capital × average invested capital.

cost of capital

The cost of long-term liabilities and stockholders' equity weighted by their relative size.

Economic profit, also called **residual income**, is defined as net operating profit after-tax (NOPAT) less a capital charge. **Net operating profit after-tax (NOPAT)** is income before interest expense but after tax. The **capital charge** is the company's weighted-average cost of capital multiplied by the average invested capital, where the **cost of capital** is the after-tax cost of long-term liabilities and stockholders' equity weighted by their relative size. For example, a division with net operating profit after-tax of $250,000, average invested capital for the year of $1,000,000, and after-tax cost of capital of 10% has economic profit of $150,000:

Divisional net operating profit after-tax	$250,000
Minus charge for average invested capital (.10 × $1,000,000)	100,000
Equals economic profit (or residual income)	$150,000

Economic profit tells you the amount by which after-tax operating income exceeds the cost of the capital employed to generate that income. In the example, divisional income exceeds the cost of capital by $150,000.

Suppose a corporation has a goal to earn a return on investment greater than the cost of capital. Economic profit aligns incentives for individual managers with this corporate goal. Investments that earn a return in excess of the cost of capital will have positive economic profit while investments that earn a return below the cost of capital will have negative economic profit. Therefore, managers evaluated based on economic profit have incentives to make an investment if, and only if, its return exceeds the corporate cost of capital.

There are different ways to calculate measures of economic profit, depending on exactly how a company chooses to define the terms used. One popular variant developed and marketed by the consulting firm Stern Stewart & Co. is **economic value added (EVA)**. In formula form, Stern Stewart defines EVA as

economic value added (EVA)

Adjusted after-tax operating income minus the weighted-average cost of capital multiplied by the adjusted average invested capital.

EVA = adjusted NOPAT − (weighted-average cost of capital × adjusted average invested capital)

Stern Stewart's EVA measure incorporates adjustments to NOPAT and to invested capital. These adjustments are designed to convert after-tax operating income into a closer approximation of cash income and invested capital into a closer approximation of the cash invested in the economic resources the company uses to create value. Examples of these adjustments include the following:

- Use taxes paid rather than tax expense.
- Capitalize (rather than expense) research and development costs as an asset.
- Use FIFO for inventory valuation (thus companies using LIFO must add back the LIFO reserve to invested capital and add the increase or deduct the decrease in the LIFO reserve to after-tax operating income).
- If a company deducts interest expense in computing operating income, it must add back after-tax interest expense to find NOPAT.

Year	EP Operating Income	EVA Operating Income	EP Average Capital†	EVA Average Capital†	EP Capital Charge at 10%‡	EVA Capital Charge at 10%§	Economic Profit	Economic Value Added
Year 1	$ 8	8 + 4 − 1 = $11*	$42	$42	$ 4.2	$ 4.2	$ 3.8	$ 6.8
Year 2	12	12 − 1 = 11	50	53	5.0	5.3	7.0	5.7
Year 3	12	12 − 1 = 11	62	64	6.2	6.4	5.8	4.6
Year 4	12	12 − 1 = 11	74	75	7.4	7.5	4.6	3.5
Total	$44	$44			$22.8	$23.4	$21.2	$20.6

†Income flows are assumed to occur at the end of each year so average capital for each year is equal to beginning capital. Beginning capital in year 1 is $42. In subsequent years, beginning capital increases by the corresponding income from the previous year. For example, year 2 EP beginning capital is $42 + 8 = 50 and year 2 EVA beginning capital is $42 + 11 = 53.
‡10% × EP average capital.
§10% × EVA average capital.
*Accounting operating income + R&D expense − R&D amortization = $8 + $4 − $1 = $11.

All amounts in this Exhibit are in millions of dollars.

Exhibit 10-4
Comparison of Economic Profit (EP) and Economic Value Added (EVA)

Exhibit 10-4 compares economic profit and EVA for an example where EVA incorporates an adjustment for research and development (R&D). Assume a division of Nike starts with invested capital of $42 (all amounts in this example are in millions of dollars) and ends each year with invested capital equal to beginning invested capital plus the income for the year. Further, to simplify the average capital calculations, assume that income flows do not increase invested capital during the year but instead are added to capital at the very end of the year. Under this assumption, average capital is simply the beginning capital. Finally, assume the division's operating income before accounting for R&D is $12 each year and that Nike's cost of capital is 10%. For simplicity, we ignore income taxes in our example, but remember that EVA uses after-tax numbers.

Suppose the division spent $4 during year 1 for R&D of a new shoe with a product life cycle of 4 years and there are no subsequent expenditures for R&D. Economic profit calculated according to U.S. financial reporting rules would show an expense equal to the entire $4 of R&D in the first year, and no subsequent expense for R&D, resulting in income after R&D for the 4 years of $8, $12, $12, and $12. Invested capital would grow by corresponding amounts from $42 at the beginning of year 1 to $50, $62, $74, and finally to $86 at the end of year 4. In contrast, EVA companies look upon R&D as a capital investment. For purposes of calculating EVA, Nike's division capitalizes R&D expenditures and expenses the $4 total cost as $1 of expense each year of the product's 4-year life cycle, resulting in income after R&D of $11, $11, $11, and $11. Invested capital would grow from $42 to $53, $64, $75, and $86 at the end of year 4. Thus, total operating income across the 4 years is $44 for either economic profit or EVA, and invested capital amounts at the beginning and at the end of the four-year example are the same under either economic profit or EVA. However, the timing of the recognition of income and the corresponding timing of the increases in capital during the four years of the example differ between EP and EVA, and therefore the capital charge differs between EP and EVA.

Economic profit over the 4 years is $21.2, or $44 less a capital charge of $22.8. EVA reflects the fact that capital is adjusted upward by $3 at the beginning of the second year ($4 investment in R&D less the $1 amortized in year 1) to reflect the capitalized investment in R&D and then declines by $1 per year as the company amortizes the remaining R&D. These adjustments in EVA imply a larger capital charge of $.3 in the second year, $.2 in the third year, and $.1 in the fourth year, so over the 4 years EVA deducts an additional $.6 capital charge for the capital invested in R&D and EVA = $44 − $23.4 = $20.6. After learning about present value in Chapter 11, you will also be able to show that although total EP and total EVA differ, the present value of the streams of EP and EVA discounted at the cost of capital are the same.

Stern Stewart has identified more than 160 different adjustments such as the adjustment illustrated for R&D but usually recommends only a few for a specific client. Many companies using economic profit for performance evaluation develop their own set of adjustments to income and capital, but all companies use the basic concept of net operating profit after-tax less a capital charge.

Economic profit and EVA have received much attention recently as scores of companies are adopting them as financial performance metrics. AT&T, Coca-Cola, CSX, FMC, and Quaker Oats claim that using EVA motivated managers to make decisions that increased shareholder value. Because EVA explicitly recognizes the cost of the capital deployed, it helps managers in these companies make better capital allocation decisions. Further, some investment companies, such as Manhattan-based broker-dealer **Matrix USA**, use economic profit to rate stocks for their investment clients.

Many companies are convinced that EVA has played a large role in their success. James M. Cornelius, chairman of **Guidant Corporation**—a medical device company, owned by Boston Scientific, that is focused on cardiovascular disease—paid tribute to EVA on Stern Stewart's Web site:

> *From day one at Guidant, we linked management bonuses to EVA performance targets. . . . If a target acquisition isn't EVA positive here, we don't do it. We pay EVA performance bonuses to Guidant technologists who develop new products within specified time frames, and we are seeing product innovation here that we've never seen before. All of our employees . . . are performing at levels we've never before experienced. I'm convinced these results are largely because of EVA. [Employees] keep looking for ways to improve our business because at the end of the day a significant share of their annual cash bonuses are tied to EVA improvement. . . . All that they have accomplished couldn't have been done without EVA.*

Siemens Corporation, Europe's largest electronics and electrical engineering firm and Stern Stewart's first EVA client in Europe, reported in its annual report that "Siemens focuses on EVA as the yardstick by which we measure the success of our efforts. The EVA performance standard encourages our people to be efficient, productive and proactive in thinking about our customers and their customers. These attributes translate into profitable growth and higher returns." Examples of actions taken by Siemens to improve EVA include the sale of **Siecor**, the fiber-optic cable business, to **Corning**, and the sale of its retail and banking business. As stated by Siemens, "Divesting selected businesses has generated funds for more strategic investments."

Making Managerial Decisions

One company that improved its EVA performance dramatically over the past two decades is **IBM**. In 1993, its EVA was a negative $13 billion. By 2000, the company improved its EVA to $2.2 billion. Like most companies, the economic downturn in the early 2000s hurt its EVA, dropping it into the negative range by 2002. By 2005, IBM again had a positive EVA at just under $1 billion, and it remained positive through 2010.

Compute the EVA for IBM for 2011 using the following data (in billions of dollars) without any of the specific adjustments recommended by Stern Stewart. As a manager, how would you explain the past history of EVA and the current EVA to investors?

	2011
Net operating profit after tax	$ 16.3
Invested capital	74
Cost of capital (assumed)	10%

Answer

Amounts are in billions as follows:

$$\text{EVA} = \text{Net operating profit after tax} - \text{cost-of-capital percentage} \times \text{capital invested}$$
$$= \$16.3 - .10 \times \$74$$
$$= \$16.3 - \$7.4 = \$8.9 \text{ Billion}$$

The improvement from 1993 to 2000 was dramatic as IBM moved from large negative EVA to positive EVA of $2.2 billion. The company continued to show strong improvements as EVA rose to $8.9 billion by 2011.

Incentives from Income, ROI, or Economic Profit

Objective 5

Compare the incentives created by income, ROI, and economic profit (or EVA) performance measures.

We have already discussed the main advantage of ROI relative to income measures—ROI provides incentives for segment managers to take into account the cost of resources used to generate income. But why do some companies prefer economic profit (or EVA) to ROI? After all, both take into account the cost of resources used to generate income. As explained

	Without Project		With Project	
	Division X	Division Y	Division X	Division Y
Net after-tax operating income	$ 200,000	$ 40,000	$ 275,000	$ 96,000
Invested capital	$1,000,000	$800,000	$1,500,000	$1,600,000
ROI (net operating income ÷ invested capital)	20%	5%	18.3%	6%
Capital charge (10% × invested capital)	$ 100,000	$ 80,000	$ 150,000	$ 160,000
Economic profit (net operating income – capital charge)	$ 100,000	$ (40,000)	$ 125,000	$ (64,000)

Exhibit 10-5
ROI and Economic Profit for Divisions X and Y

on p. 396, ROI can motivate segment managers to make investment decisions that are not in the best interests of the company as a whole. In contrast, when a company uses economic profit (or EVA) as a performance metric, managers have incentive to invest only in projects earning more than the cost of capital because only those projects increase the division's economic profit.

Consider two divisions of a company, division X with operating income of $200,000 and division Y with operating income of $40,000. Division X has average invested capital of $1 million and division Y has average invested capital of $800,000. Assume that the company's cost of capital is 10%, and, for simplicity, ignore taxes. Suppose each division is considering a new proposed project. Division X is considering Project A that will earn 15% annually on a $500,000 investment, or $75,000 a year. Division Y is considering Project B that will earn 7% annually on an $800,000 investment, or $56,000 a year. Exhibit 10-5 shows ROI and economic profit with and without the project for the two divisions.

Suppose performance evaluation is based on ROI. Would the manager of division X invest in Project A? No. Even though Project A earns a return of 15% (which is above the 10% cost of capital), it would decrease ROI for division X from 20% to 18.3%. Would the manager of division Y invest in Project B? Yes. Even though Project B earns a return of 7% (below the 10% cost of capital), it would increase ROI for division Y from 5% to 6%. In general, the ROI profitability metric provides an incentive for divisions to invest in new projects that earn a return in excess of their current return, rather than an incentive to invest in new projects with a return in excess of the cost of capital. Thus, performance evaluation based on ROI leads division X to reject a project with a 15% return and division Y to accept a project with a 7% return.

Now suppose performance evaluation is based on economic profit. For division X, investing in Project A would change economic profit from $100,000 to $125,000. This $25,000 increase in economic profit is the $75,000 annual return from the new project less the $50,000 annual cost of capital for the new project. In contrast to the decision under ROI, the manager of division X would accept Project A. For division Y, investing in Project B would change economic profit from $–40,000 to $–64,000. This $24,000 decrease is the $56,000 annual return from the new project less the $80,000 annual cost of capital for the new project. Thus, the manager of division Y would reject Project B. Evaluation based on economic profit motivates both managers to invest only in projects that earn a return in excess of the cost of capital, whereas evaluation based on ROI leads both managers to incorrect decisions— division A rejecting a desirable project and division B accepting an undesirable one. In general, use of economic profit or EVA will promote goal congruence and lead to better decisions than using ROI.

Despite the success of economic profit and EVA, many companies still use ROI. Why? Perhaps because it is simpler to compute, more readily understandable by managers, and easier to compare across divisions. Furthermore, in some cases, top management minimizes the dysfunctional incentives from ROI by emphasizing that managers should compare project ROI to the cost of capital, rather than to their existing ROI. Remember that companies try to choose a profitability measure to use in performance evaluation that aligns managers' incentives with organizational goals without being overly complex or too expensive to apply.

Summary Problem for Your Review

PROBLEM

Suppose a division of Google has assets of $2,000,000, invested capital of $1,800,000, and net operating income of $600,000. Ignore taxes.

1. What is the division's ROI?
2. If the weighted-average cost of capital is 14%, what is the EVA?
3. Suppose management uses ROI as a performance metric. What effects on management behavior do you expect?
4. Suppose management uses economic profit as a performance metric. What effects on management behavior do you expect?

SOLUTION

1. ROI = $600,000 ÷ $1,800,000 = 33%.
2. EVA = $600,000 − .14 ($1,800,000) = $600,000 − $252,000 = $348,000.
3. If the company uses ROI, the division manager has an incentive to reject new projects that do not earn an ROI of at least 33%, the division's current ROI. From the viewpoint of the organization as a whole, this is undesirable if the cost of capital is only 14%. If a division is enjoying a high ROI, it is less likely to expand if top management evaluates performance using ROI than if it evaluates performance using EVA.
4. If the company uses EVA, the manager is inclined to accept all projects whose expected rate of return exceeds the weighted-average cost of capital. The manager is more likely to expand the division because his or her goal is to maximize a dollar amount rather than a rate.

Transfer Pricing

Objective 6

Define *transfer prices* and identify their purpose.

When all the segments of a decentralized organization are independent of one another, segment managers can focus only on their own segments because what is best for their segment is generally best for the organization as a whole. In contrast, when segments interact, such as buying or selling in the same markets, there is a possibility that what helps one segment hurts another segment badly enough to have a negative net effect on the entire organization. For example, two Nike sales divisions may compete for the same customer by cutting prices, thereby reducing the company's overall margin on sales to the customer. The more customers (and suppliers) two segments have in common, the more a company should consider combining the two segments into one to minimize dysfunctional incentives for one segment to gain at the expense of the other.

Other potential interactions between segment and organizational interests occur when one segment sells products or services to another segment of the same organization for a price called the **transfer price**. For example, when one segment produces a component and sells it to another segment that then incorporates the component in a final product, a transfer price is required. Transfer prices also apply to services, such as when a product manager buys advertising services from the marketing support segment. The transfer price for the component or service is revenue to the producing segment and a cost to the acquiring segment. Thus, transfer prices allocate profit among segments—a change in the transfer price increases the computed profit for one segment and decreases the profit for the other segment—without affecting profit for the firm as a whole.

transfer price
The price at which one segment of an organization sells products or services to another segment of the same organization.

Transfer pricing policies are especially important in decentralized companies where top management believes that segment autonomy has important benefits. In such companies, segment managers decide how many products or services will be transferred from one segment to another. Delegating these decisions to segment managers creates benefits when the segment managers, being "closer to the action," have better information than top management about the items being transferred. The challenge to such companies is to design a transfer pricing policy that motivates segment managers to transfer the quantity of products and services that both maximizes the segment's profitability metric and is also in the best interests of the company as a whole. There is seldom a perfect transfer pricing policy, so decentralization inevitably leads to some dysfunctional transfer decisions. But companies that adhere to a decentralization philosophy believe that the benefits of decentralization and the preservation of segment autonomy exceed the costs of occasional dysfunctional decisions.

When there is little information advantage at the segment level, companies generally centralize decisions and have top management dictate the quantity and price of products and services transferred between segments. This ensures that segment managers cannot make a decision to transfer an amount of a product or service that is not in the company's best interests.

Purposes of Transfer Pricing

What does a decentralized company want from its transfer pricing system? Ideally, it wants to ensure that managers who make decisions to improve their segment's performance also increase the performance of the company as a whole. Therefore, a company wants profitability metrics that reward the segment manager for decisions that increase the profitability of the entire company. For example, transfer prices should guide managers to make the best possible decisions regarding whether to buy or sell products and services inside or outside the total organization. Decisions by the buying and selling segment managers, acting without top-management intervention, should be the best decisions for their segment and for the entire organization. In other words, decisions that increase a segment's profitability metric should lead to increased profitability for the company as a whole.

Organizations use a variety of transfer prices. They use cost-based prices for some transfers, market-based prices for other transfers, and negotiated prices for others. Therefore, do not expect to find a single, universally applicable answer to the problem of transfer pricing. There is no perfect transfer-pricing system. Almost every manager in a decentralized organization has had experience with transfer-pricing systems that seem less than ideal. For example, a manager at Weyerhaeuser, a large wood-products firm, called transfer pricing his firm's most troublesome management control issue.

A General Rule for Transfer Pricing

Although no single rule always meets the goals of transfer pricing, a general rule can provide guidance:

Objective 7

$$\text{transfer price} = \text{outlay cost} + \text{opportunity cost}$$

State the general rule for transfer pricing and use it to assess transfer prices based on total costs, variable costs, and market prices.

As described earlier on page 404, outlay costs require a cash disbursement. They are essentially the additional amount the producing segment must pay to produce the product or service. Opportunity cost is the contribution to profit that the producing segment forgoes by transferring the item internally. For example, if capacity constraints prevent a segment from producing enough to meet both external demand and internal demand from the other segment, the opportunity cost is the contribution margin the producing segment could have received from selling in the external market rather than transferring internally.

Why does this rule provide incentives for segment decisions that also maximize profitability for the firm as a whole? Consider the following example of two hypothetical Nike divisions. The fabric division (the producing division) is considering transferring the fabric required for a golf shirt to the sportswear division (the buying division), as shown in Exhibit 10-6.

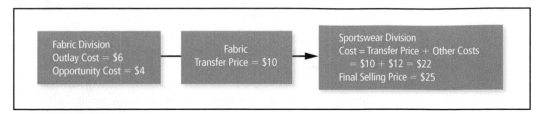

Exhibit 10-6
Transfer Pricing Example

Suppose the fabric division's $4 opportunity cost arises because it can get $10 by selling the fabric to a buyer outside the company. Thus, the foregone contribution by not selling to the outside buyer is $10 − $6 = $4. At any transfer price less than $10, the producing division is better off selling the fabrics to the outside buyer rather than transferring it. Thus, the minimum transfer price the fabric division would accept is $6 + $4 = $10.

Now consider how much the item is worth to the sportswear division. For the fabric to be profitable to the sportswear division, it must be able to sell the final product for more than the transfer price plus the other costs it must incur to finish and sell the product. Because it can sell the golf shirt for $25 and its other costs are $12, the maximum price the sportswear division would be willing to pay is $25 − $12 = $13. At any higher price, the sportswear division would choose not to produce the shirt at all. But there is a second constraint: The sportswear division will not pay more to the fabric division than it would have to pay an outside supplier. Thus, the largest transfer price acceptable to the sportswear division is the lesser of (1) $13 or (2) the cost charged by an outside supplier.

Now consider the transfer decision from the company's point of view. Transfer is desirable whenever (1) the total cost to the company for producing the fabric internally ($10, including opportunity cost, as determined by the fabric division) is less than its value to the company ($13 as determined by the sportswear division), and (2) the fabric division's costs (again including opportunity costs) are less than the price the sportswear division would have to pay to an outside supplier. The first criterion guarantees that the company does not decide to produce a product where the total cost to produce exceeds the final selling price to the end user. The second guarantees that it does not pay more to produce the fabric internally than it would have to pay to buy it in the marketplace. The only transfer price that will always meet these criteria is $10, the fabric division's outlay cost plus opportunity cost. Why? Any price between $10 and $13 meets the first criterion. However, only $10 meets the second because any transfer price above $10 opens the possibility that the sportswear division will buy the fabric externally when the company would be better off producing and transferring it from the fabric division.

Exhibit 10-7 summarizes the division's decision and the effect on Nike as a whole when an outside supplier offers the fabric at either greater than $10 or less than $10. At a $10 transfer price, regardless of what price outside suppliers offer, the division managers, acting independently, make the decision that is most profitable for the company as a whole. Any other transfer price creates a possibility of a manager making the decision that is best for his or her segment but not for the company as a whole. The fabric division would reject the transfer at less than $10 regardless of how much profit it creates for the sportswear division. The sportswear division would reject the transfer whenever the transfer price is greater than the price from alternative sources.

Note that any transfer price greater than the $10 price specified by the general rule runs the risk of the sportswear division purchasing outside the company even when the internal cost is lower. For example, with a transfer price of $12 and an outside purchase cost of $11, the sportswear division would pay $11 to the outside supplier when the company could have spent only $10 (including opportunity cost) to produce the fabric in the fabric division.

This general rule doesn't always provide a unique transfer price. For example, suppose there is no outside supplier for the fabric (but continue to assume there is an outside customer that will buy from the producing division for $10). Then the general rule tells us only that the transfer

Exhibit 10-7

Effects of a $10 Transfer Price on Decisions

Outside Supplier Price	Best Decision for Division	Best Decision for Company
Less than $10	Do not transfer—buying division rejects transfer because buying internally will reduce its profits	Do not transfer—buy from outside supplier because it is cheaper for the company as a whole
Greater than $10	If value to buying division is greater than $10: Transfer at $10—both divisions benefit	Transfer—cost of internal production is less than cost of buying externally
	If value to buying division is less than $10: Do not transfer—buying division rejects transfer	Do not transfer—value of the fabric to the company is less than its cost

price must be greater than $10 (the outlay cost plus opportunity cost for the producing division) and less than $13 (the final selling price minus the outlay costs for the sportswear division). Thus, the rule does not specify a specific price within this range. As another example, suppose that when selling the fabric to the outside buyer, there is a $.75 shipping and handling cost that is saved if the fabric is transferred internally. The general rule does not tell us how to allocate the $.75 savings between the two divisions.

Because transfer-pricing systems have multiple goals, there is no universally optimal transfer price. Nonetheless, the general rule provides a good benchmark by which to judge transfer-pricing systems. We analyze the following transfer-pricing systems, the most popular systems in practice, by examining how close the transfer price comes to the benchmark of outlay cost plus opportunity cost:

1. Market-based transfer prices
2. Cost-based transfer prices
   a. Variable cost
   b. Full cost (possibly plus profit)
3. Negotiated transfer prices

In addressing these transfer-pricing systems, we will assume that a company has multiple divisions that transfer items to one another, and that the company wants to preserve segment autonomy in a decentralized operation.

Market-Based Transfer Prices

When there is a ready market for an item or service transferred from one segment to another, transfer pricing policies are straightforward. The common maxim is "if a market price exists, use it." The more competitive the market, the better the maxim applies.

If there is a competitive market for the product or service being transferred internally, using the market price as a transfer price will generally lead to goal congruence. Why? Because the market price equals the variable cost plus opportunity cost.

$$\text{transfer price} = \text{variable cost} + \text{opportunity cost}$$
$$= \text{variable cost} + (\text{market price} - \text{variable cost})$$
$$= \text{market price} + \text{variable cost} - \text{variable cost}$$
$$= \text{market price}$$

If the selling division avoids some marketing and delivery costs when selling internally, many companies deduct these costs from the market price when computing the transfer price. That is, the transfer price is the net amount the selling division would receive selling the item on the market after deducting marketing and delivery costs.

To illustrate market-based transfer prices, reconsider the two hypothetical divisions of Nike. The fabric division makes fabrics it sells directly to external customers as well as to other Nike divisions, such as the sportswear division. The fabric division makes a particular fabric for an outlay cost of $6 and can sell it to external customers for $10. The sportswear division can buy that same fabric on the market for $10 and use it to make a golf shirt, spending an extra $12 in production costs. The golf shirt sells for $25. Should the sportswear division obtain the fabric from the fabric division of Nike or purchase it from an external supplier?

Assume for the moment that the fabric division can sell its entire production to external customers without incurring any marketing or shipping costs. The manager of the fabric division will not sell the fabric for less than $10. Why? Because he or she can sell it on the market for $10, so any price less than $10 will reduce the manager's division's profit. Furthermore, the sportswear division manager will refuse to pay a transfer price greater than $10 for the fabric for each golf shirt. Why? Because if the transfer price is greater than $10, he or she will purchase the fabric from the external supplier for the lower price of $10 in order to maximize his or her division's profit. The only transfer price that allows both managers to maximize their division's profit is $10, the market price. If the managers had autonomy to make decisions, at any transfer price other than $10 one of the managers would decline the internal transfer of the fabric.

Now suppose the fabric division incurs a $.75 per square yard marketing and shipping cost that it can avoid by transferring the fabric to the sportswear division instead of marketing it to outside customers. Most companies would then use a transfer price of $9.25, often called a "market-price-minus" transfer price. The fabric division would get the same net amount from the transfer ($9.25 with no marketing or shipping costs) as from an external sale ($10 less $.75 marketing and shipping costs), whereas the sportswear division saves $.75 per shirt. The fabric division will produce and transfer the fabric only if the transfer price is at least $9.25, and the sportswear division will buy the fabric internally only if it costs less than $10 and is worth at least $9.25 to the division. These criteria drive a decision to transfer only if it is in Nike's overall best interests.

While market-based transfer prices generally provide the correct incentives, market prices are not always available. Therefore, we next discuss some other systems commonly used in the absence of market-based prices.

Transfers at Cost

When market prices don't exist, most companies resort to cost-based transfer prices. In fact, about half the major companies in the world use a cost-based transfer-pricing system. However, there are many possible definitions of cost. Some companies use only variable cost, others use full cost, and still others use full cost plus a profit markup. Some use standard costs, and some use actual costs. Cost-based transfer prices are easy to understand and use, but they can easily lead to **dysfunctional decisions**—decisions in conflict with the company's goals. The key to successful cost-based transfer prices is to minimize such dysfunctional decisions. Let's examine some of these cost-based transfer-pricing systems.

dysfunctional decision
Any decision that is in conflict with organizational goals.

TRANSFERS AT VARIABLE COST Companies that transfer items at variable cost implicitly assume that the selling division has no opportunity cost. Why? Because the outlay cost is generally about equal to variable cost: transfer price = outlay (variable) cost + $0. Therefore, a variable-cost transfer-pricing system is most appropriate when the selling division forgoes no opportunities when it transfers the item internally, for example when there is plenty of excess capacity in the selling division.

Variable-cost transfer prices cause dysfunctional decisions when the selling segment has significant opportunity costs. In our fabric division–sportswear division example, there are two ways this could happen. First, if there are positive opportunity costs, the fabric division manager would turn down any transfer, preferring to pursue the alternative opportunities, perhaps selling the fabric on the open market or using facilities to make a different, more profitable, fabric. This would be dysfunctional if the sportswear division could make more profit from its golf shirt than the fabric division makes from pursuing its alternative opportunities. Second, realizing the lack of incentive for the fabric division to transfer the fabric, top management might insist that the fabric division produce and transfer the fabric. This would be against the company's interests if the fabric division passes up opportunities that yield more profit than the sportswear division's golf shirt. In addition, this policy violates segment autonomy.

TRANSFERS AT FULL COST OR FULL COST PLUS PROFIT Full-cost transfer prices include not only variable cost but also an allocation of fixed costs. In addition, some companies also add a markup for profit. This implicitly assumes the allocated fixed costs (and, if included, the profit markup) is a good approximation of the opportunity cost. In cases of constrained capacity, where the selling division cannot satisfy all internal and external demand for its products, the opportunity cost is positive. As explained in the previous section, when the opportunity cost is positive, variable-cost transfer prices are problematic. While there is no guarantee that adding an allocation of fixed cost is a good approximation of the opportunity cost, it may be a better approximation than assuming a zero opportunity cost. Some companies believe that using activity-based costing improves cost-based transfer prices, as described in the Business First box on page 411.

Dysfunctional decisions arise with full-cost transfer prices when the selling segment has opportunity costs that differ significantly from the allocation of fixed costs and profit. In our example, suppose the fabric division has excess capacity so that opportunity cost is zero. Nevertheless, it has large fixed costs so that the full cost of the transferred fabric includes $8 of fixed cost in addition to the $6 variable cost. At a transfer price of $14, and assuming an external supplier either doesn't exist or would also charge at least $14, the sportswear division would refuse the transfer unless it could sell the golf shirt for at least $14 + $12 = $26. Therefore, because the shirt sells for $25, the sportswear division would decide not to produce it.

But this decision costs Nike a contribution margin of $25 − ($6 + $12) = $7. The decision not to produce the shirt is dysfunctional—that is, it conflicts with Nike's goal of generating additional profit.

Cost-based transfer prices can create problems when a company uses actual cost rather than standard cost as a transfer price. Because the buying division will not know its actual cost in advance, it will not be able to accurately plan its costs. More importantly, a transfer price based on actual costs merely passes cost inefficiencies in the selling division along to the buying division. Therefore, the selling division lacks incentive to control its costs. Thus, we recommend using budgeted or standard costs instead of actual costs for cost-based transfer prices.

Finally, cost-based transfer prices can undercut segment autonomy and sometimes lead to conflicts between segment and organizational goals. Suppose managers believe it is best for the company to transfer an item internally rather than purchasing it externally but also believe that the transfer price is unfair to their segment. They may either do what they think top management wants but resent its negative effect on their segment, or they may do what is best for their segment, ignoring its negative impact on the organization as a whole. Neither alternative is desirable.

Supporters point out that cost-based transfer prices are easy to understand and inexpensive to implement. However, any cost-based transfer price can lead to dysfunctional decisions. Companies transferring goods or services in the absence of market prices must decide whether the effects of dysfunctional decisions are great enough to abandon cost-based transfer prices. One alternative is to give up decentralized decision making—essentially have top management dictate whether to transfer items internally or purchase them from external suppliers—but this also sacrifices the benefits of decentralization. Another alternative is negotiated transfer prices, which we discuss next.

Making Managerial Decisions

Consider the following data concerning a subassembly that Willamette Manufacturing Company produces in its fabricating division and uses in products assembled in its assembly division.

Fabricating Division	
Variable cost of subassembly	$35
Excess capacity (in units)	1,000
Assembly Division	
Market price for buying the subassembly from external sources	$50
Number of units needed	900

If you were the manager of the fabricating division, what is the lowest transfer price you would accept for the subassembly? If you were the manager of the assembly division, what is the most you would be willing to pay for the subassembly? Is there a transfer price that would motivate production and transfer of the subassembly? If so, what is the price?

Answer

The fabricating division has excess capacity, so its manager would be willing to accept any price above the variable cost of $35. The assembly division can buy the subassembly for $50 on the external market, so its manager would be willing to pay no more than $50 to buy it from the fabricating division. The transfer would take place at some price between $35 and $50.

Negotiated Transfer Prices

Companies heavily committed to segment autonomy often allow managers to negotiate transfer prices. The managers may consider both costs and market prices in their negotiations, though they are not required to do so. Supporters of negotiated transfer prices maintain that the managers involved have the best knowledge of what the company will gain or lose by producing and transferring the product or service, so open negotiation allows the managers to make optimal decisions. Critics of negotiated prices focus on the time and effort spent negotiating, an activity that adds nothing directly to the profits of the company.

Let's look at how our fabric division and sportswear division managers might approach a negotiation of a transfer price. The sportswear division manager might look at the selling price of the golf shirt, $25, less the additional cost the division incurs in making it, $12, and decide to purchase fabric at any transfer price less than $25 − $12 = $13. The sportswear division will add to its profit by making and selling the shirt if the transfer price is below $13. At a transfer price above $13, the sportswear division will choose to not make and sell the shirt, assuming there is no other supplier of fabric at a price below $13.

Similarly, the fabric division manager will look at what it costs to produce and transfer the fabric. If there is excess capacity and thus no opportunity cost, any transfer price above $6 will increase the fabric division's profit. Negotiation will result in a transfer if the maximum transfer price the sportswear division is willing to pay is greater than the minimum transfer price the fabric division is willing to accept. The fabric division manager is willing to accept any price above $6 and the sportswear division manager will pay up to $13. The exact transfer price will depend on the negotiating ability and power of the two division managers.

Now suppose there is no excess capacity in the fabric division and an outside customer is willing to pay $10 for the fabric. Transferring the fabric internally causes the division to give up a contribution of $4 as well as paying variable costs of $6, so the minimum transfer price acceptable to the fabric division is now $10. A transfer will take place at a price between $10 and $13.

If the opportunity cost had been more than $7, a transfer would not occur. Why? Because the fabric division's minimum price of $6 variable costs plus opportunity cost would now be greater than $13 and the sportswear division's maximum price would be just $13. This decision is exactly what Nike would prefer. When the fabric division's opportunity cost is less than $7, the golf shirt is more profitable than the fabric division's other business, and the transfer should occur. When the fabric division's opportunity cost is greater than $7, the additional contribution from the fabric division's other business will be greater than the sportswear division's contribution on the shirt, and the transfer should not occur. Therefore, the manager's decisions are congruent with the company's best interests.

What should top management of a decentralized organization do if it sees segment managers making dysfunctional decisions through their negotiations? As usual, the answer is, "It depends." Top management can step in and force the "correct" decision, but doing so undermines segment managers' autonomy and the overall notion of decentralization. It also assumes top management has the information necessary to determine the correct decision. Most important, frequent intervention results in recentralization. Indeed, if more centralization is desired, the organization might want to reorganize by combining segments.

Top managers who wish to encourage decentralization will often make sure that both producing and purchasing division managers understand all the facts and then allow the managers to negotiate a transfer price. Even when top managers suspect that the segments might make a dysfunctional decision, they may swallow hard and accept the segment manager's judgment as a cost of decentralization. (Repeated dysfunctional decision making may be a reason to change the organizational design or to change managers.)

Well-trained and informed segment managers who understand opportunity costs and the behavior of fixed and variable costs will often make better decisions than will top managers. The producing division manager knows best the various uses of its capacity, and the purchasing division manager knows best what profit can be made on the items to be transferred. In addition, negotiation allows segments to respond flexibly to changing market conditions when setting transfer prices. One transfer price may be appropriate in a time of idle capacity and another when demand increases and operations approach full capacity.

Multinational Transfer Pricing

Objective 8

Identify the factors affecting multinational transfer prices.

So far, we have focused on how transfer-pricing policies affect the motivation of managers. However, in multinational companies, other factors may dominate. For example, multinational companies use transfer prices to minimize worldwide income taxes, import duties, and tariffs. For example, Nike might prefer to make its profits in Singapore, where the marginal corporate tax rate is less than half the rate in the United States.

Suppose a division in a high-income-tax-rate country produces a component for another division in a low-income-tax-rate country. By setting a low transfer price, the company can recognize most of the profit from the production in the low-income-tax-rate country, thereby minimizing taxes. Likewise, items produced by divisions in a low-income-tax-rate country and transferred to a division in a high-income-tax-rate country should have a high transfer price to minimize taxes.

Sometimes import duties offset income tax effects. Most countries base import duties on the price paid for an item, whether bought from an outside company or transferred from another division. Therefore, low transfer prices generally lead to low import duties.

Business First

Activity-Based Costing and Transfer Pricing

Teva Pharmaceutical Industries Ltd. is a global health-care company specializing in pharmaceuticals. It is headquartered in Israel and had 2011 sales of $18.3 billion. Teva entered the lucrative generic drug market in the mid-1980s. Each of the marketing divisions purchases generic drugs from the manufacturing division. As part of its strategy, the company decentralized its pharmaceutical business into cost and profit centers. Prior to decentralization, each marketing division was a revenue center. With the new organizational structure, management had to decide how to measure marketing division costs because profits were now the key financial performance metric.

A key cost to the marketing divisions is the transfer price paid for drugs purchased from the manufacturing division. Management considered several alternative bases for the company's transfer prices. Market price was not a feasible basis for transfer pricing because there was no competitive market. Negotiated prices were rejected because management believed the resulting debates over the proper price would be lengthy and disruptive. Teva adopted variable cost (raw material and packaging costs) transfer pricing for a short time but eventually rejected it because it did not lead to congruent decisions—managers did not differentiate products using many scarce resources from those using few. Further, when a local source for the drug did exist, the market price was always above the variable-cost transfer price. Thus, managers in Teva's manufacturing division had little incentive to keep costs low.

Management also rejected traditional full cost that did not capture the actual cost structure of the manufacturing division. Specifically, the traditional full-cost system undercosted

the low-volume products and overcosted the large-volume products. The system traced only raw materials directly to products. It divided the remaining manufacturing costs into two cost pools and allocated them based on labor hours and machine hours. One problem with the traditional system was its inability to capture and correctly allocate the non-value-added cost of setup activity. Management did not know the size of the errors in product cost, but the lack of confidence in the traditional cost system led to rejection of full cost as the transfer-pricing base.

Then Teva's management adopted an activity-based-costing (ABC) system to improve the accuracy of its product costs. The ABC system has five activity centers and related cost pools: receiving, manufacturing, packaging, quality assurance, and shipping. Because of the dramatic increase in costing accuracy, management was able to adopt full activity-based cost as the transfer price.

Teva's managers are pleased with their transfer-pricing system. The benefits include increased confidence that the costs being transferred are closely aligned with the actual short- and long-run costs being incurred, increased communication between divisions, and an increased awareness of the costs of low-volume products and the costs of capacity required to support these products. They believe their activity-based costs are the best approximation to outlay cost plus opportunity costs because the allocation of the fixed costs is a good measure of the value (opportunity cost) of the resources being consumed.

Sources: Adapted from Robert Kaplan, Dan Weiss, and Eyal Desheh, "Transfer Pricing with ABC," *Management Accounting*, May, 1997, pp. 20–28; and Teva Pharmaceutical Industries Ltd. *2011 Annual Report.*

Tax authorities also recognize the incentive to set transfer prices to minimize taxes and import duties. Therefore, most countries have restrictions on allowable transfer prices. U.S. multinationals must follow an Internal Revenue Code rule specifying that transfers be priced at "arm's-length" market values, or at the price one division would pay another if they were independent companies. Even with this rule, companies have some latitude in deciding an appropriate "arm's-length" price.

Consider a high-end running shoe produced by an Irish Nike division with a 12% income tax rate and transferred to a division in Germany with a 40% rate. In addition, suppose Germany imposes an import duty equal to 20% of the price of the item and that Nike cannot deduct this import duty for tax purposes. Suppose the full unit cost of a pair of the shoes (translated to U.S. dollars) is $100, and the variable cost is $60. If tax authorities allow either variable- or full-cost transfer prices, which should Nike choose? By transferring at $100 rather than at $60, the company gains $3.20 per unit:

Effect of Transferring at $100 Instead of at $60	
Income of the Irish division is $40 higher; therefore, it pays 12% × $40 more income taxes	$(4.80)
Income of the German division is $40 lower; therefore, it pays 40% × $40 less income taxes	16.00
Import duty is paid by the German division on an additional $100 − $60 = $40; therefore, it pays 20% × $40 more duty	(8.00)
Net savings from transferring at $100 instead of $60	$ 3.20

Companies may also use transfer prices to avoid the financial restrictions imposed by some governments. For example, a country might restrict the amount of dividends paid to foreign owners. It may be easier for a company to get cash from a foreign division as payment for items transferred than as cash dividends.

In summary, transfer pricing becomes even more complex in a multinational company. Multinational companies try to achieve more objectives through transfer-pricing policies, and the objectives sometimes conflict with one another.

Summary Problem for Your Review

PROBLEM

Reconsider **Nike**'s fabric division and sportswear division described earlier on page 390. In addition to the data there, suppose the fabric division has annual fixed manufacturing costs of $800,000 and expected annual production of enough fabric to make 100,000 golf shirts. The "fully-allocated cost" of the material for one golf shirt is as follows:

Variable costs	$ 6.00
Fixed costs, $800,000 ÷ 100,000 shirts	8.00
Fully allocated cost of the material for one golf shirt	$14.00

Assume that the fabric division has idle capacity. The sportswear division is considering whether to buy enough fabric for 10,000 golf shirts. It will sell each shirt for $25. The additional processing and selling costs in the sportswear division to produce and sell one shirt are $12. If Nike bases its transfer prices on fully-allocated cost, would the sportswear division manager buy? Explain. Would the company as a whole benefit if the sportswear division manager decided to buy? Explain.

SOLUTION

The sportswear division manager would not buy. The fully-allocated cost-based transfer price of $14 would make the acquisition of the fabric unattractive to the sportswear division:

Sportswear Division:		
Sales price of final product		$25
Deduct costs		
Transfer price paid to the fabric division (fully-allocated cost)	$14	
Additional processing and selling costs	12	
Total costs to the sportswear division		26
Contribution to profit of the sportswear division		$ (1)
Company as a whole:		
Sales price of final product		$25
Deduct variable costs and opportunity costs		
Fabric department	$ 6	
Sportswear department	12	
Total variable and opportunity costs		18
Contribution to company as a whole		$ 7

The company as a whole would benefit by $70,000 (10,000 shirts × $7) if the fabric division produces and transfers the fabric.

The major lesson here is that transfer prices based on fully-allocated costs may induce the wrong decisions when there is idle capacity in the supplier division. Working in his or her own best interests, the sportswear division manager has no incentive to buy from the fabric division.

Keys to Successful Management Control Systems

Objective 9

Explain how controllability and management by objectives (MBO) aid the implementation of management control systems.

Like management in general, management control systems are more art than science. A company such as Nike will certainly include many subjective factors as well as more objective measures of profitability in its performance-evaluation system. Intelligent use of the available information is as important as generating the information itself. Next, we briefly explore three factors that help managers interpret and use management control information.

Focus on Controllability

As Chapter 9 explained (see Exhibit 9-5, page 362), companies should distinguish between the performance of the division manager and the performance of the division as an investment by the corporation. Top management should evaluate segment managers on the basis of their controllable performance. However, management should base decisions such as increasing or decreasing investment in a division on the economic viability of the division, not on the performance of its managers.

This distinction helps to clarify some vexing difficulties. For example, top management may use an investment base to gauge the economic performance of a retail store, but judge the store's manager by focusing on income and ignoring any investment allocations. The aim is to evaluate the manager on controllable factors, but controllability depends on what decisions managers can make. In a highly decentralized company such as Johnson & Johnson or General Electric, for instance, managers can influence investments in assets and can exercise judgment regarding the appropriate amount of short-term credit and some long-term credit. Investment decisions that managers do not influence should not affect their performance evaluations.

Management by Objectives and Setting Expectations

Management by objectives (MBO) describes the joint formulation by managers and their superiors of a set of goals and plans for achieving the goals for a forthcoming period. For our purposes here, the terms *goals* and *objectives* are synonymous. The plans often take the form of a responsibility accounting budget (together with supplementary goals, such as levels of management training and safety that managers may not incorporate into the accounting budget). The company then evaluates a manager's performance in relation to these agreed-on budgeted objectives. It is important that managers' expectations be consistent with those of their superiors.

management by objectives (MBO)
The joint formulation by managers and their superiors of a set of goals and plans for achieving the goals for a forthcoming period.

An MBO approach tends to reduce complaints about lack of controllability because managers first agree on a reasonable budget. That is, a particular manager and his or her superior negotiate a budget for a particular period and a particular set of expected outside and inside influences. For example, by evaluating results compared to expectations, a manager may more readily accept an assignment to a less successful segment. Why? Because a manager can reasonably expect to meet goals that recognize that the segment is economically struggling. Thus, an MBO system is preferable to a system that emphasizes absolute profitability for its own sake. Unless evaluation focuses on meeting reasonable expectations, able managers will be reluctant to accept responsibility for segments that are in economic trouble. Whether using MBO or not, skillful budgeting and intelligent performance evaluation will go a long way toward overcoming the common lament, "I'm being held responsible for items beyond my control."

MBO is also especially useful in nonprofit organizations where financial goals may be less important than nonfinancial goals. Managers can set objectives that fit well with overall organizational objectives. The accompanying Business First box on page 414 illustrates how an academic institution can use decentralization to further the university's financial and nonfinancial objectives.

Budgets, Performance Targets, and Ethics

Organizations can minimize many of the troublesome motivational effects of performance evaluation systems by the astute use of budgets. We cannot overemphasize the desirability of tailoring budgets to a particular manager. For example, either an ROI or an economic profit system can promote goal congruence and managerial effort if top management gets everybody to focus on what is currently attainable in the forthcoming budget period.

Business First

Decentralization in Academia

Corporations are not the only types of organizations that decentralize. Many nonprofit organizations, such as universities, hospitals, and churches, also decentralize by delegating decision-making authority to segments of the organization. It is important for each segment to set objectives consistent with the overall organizational goals.

An example of such an organization is Harvard University. Using a philosophy of "every tub on its own bottom," Harvard is divided into 11 academic units: (1) Faculty of Arts and Sciences, which includes Harvard College, Graduate School of Arts and Sciences, and Division of Continuing Education; (2) Business School; (3) Design School; (4) Divinity School; (5) Graduate School of Education; (6) John F. Kennedy School of Government; (7) Law School; (8) Medical School; (9) Dental School; (10) School of Public Health; and (11) Radcliffe Institute for Advanced Study. At the head of each unit is a dean appointed by the president. The dean is directly responsible for his or her unit's finances and organization. In essence, each unit functions like a division of a decentralized corporation. Although the units have a great deal of independence, they must still set financial and nonfinancial objectives that are consistent with Harvard's goals, and their accomplishments will be measured against their objectives.

Because each unit at Harvard is responsible for its own revenues and expenses, many of the issues are similar to those of a for-profit corporation. The governing board that is responsible for the day-to-day operations at Harvard—called the Harvard Corporation and known formally as the President and Fellows of Harvard College—is a seven-member board headed by the president. To effectively manage the university, the board needs information from the units, but it intentionally does not directly make decisions for the units—that is left to the deans. Only when reports indicate that something is awry does the board intervene.

To the extent that the units are independent of one another, decentralization works well. But, just as in a for-profit organization, difficulties can arise when there are real or potential interactions among units. For example, how is tuition divided among units when students admitted to one unit take classes in another? This is a classic transfer-pricing problem. Or what about two units (for example the Law School and the Business School) competing for a particular faculty member. How is the good of the entire university reflected in such hiring decisions? Or how does the university encourage cross-functional programs and research involving more than one unit? Or how does the university choose whether to invest scarce funds into the Dental School or the Divinity School? These are all issues that arise from decentralization.

Like any organization, Harvard must balance overall organizational objectives versus the advantages of local decision making and superior motivation of divisional authority. While Harvard is an example of decentralization, other universities favor a more centralized approach.

Source: "Harvard at a Glance" (http://www.harvard.edu/Harvard-glance.html).

Using budgets as performance targets also has its dangers. On pages 274–276 of Chapter 7 we pointed out how misuse of budgets for performance evaluation can lead to lying and cheating. Companies that make meeting a budget too important when evaluating managers may motivate unethical behavior. Top management at companies such as WorldCom gave "making the numbers" such a high priority that when it became clear that a segment would not meet its goals, managers fabricated the accounting reports. At Enron, the consequences of poor performance evaluations were so great that managers played bookkeeping games and allegedly manipulated electricity prices to make their performance look better. The lesson is that "astute" use of budgets is good, but using budgets to put unreasonable pressure on managers can undermine the ethics of an organization.

As we said earlier in the chapter, "You get what you measure." It is important to use measures that are consistent with organizational goals. Yet, measurement is only part of the management control system. Managers should also think hard about how they use the measures to achieve the organization's objectives. Even good measures can lead to dysfunctional decisions when managers misuse them. A management control system is only as good as the managers who use it.

Highlights to Remember

1. **Define *decentralization* and identify its expected benefits and costs.** As companies grow, the ability of managers to effectively plan and control becomes more difficult because top managers are further removed from day-to-day operations. One approach to effective planning and control in large companies is to decentralize decision making. This means that top management gives mid- and lower-level managers the authority to make decisions that impact the subunit's performance. The more that decision-making authority is delegated, the greater the decentralization. Often, the subunit manager is most knowledgeable of the factors that management should consider in the decision-making process.

2. **Distinguish between responsibility centers and decentralization.** Top management must design the management control system so that it motivates managers to act in the best interests of the company. This is done through the choice of responsibility centers and the appropriate performance metrics and rewards. The degree of decentralization does not depend upon the type of responsibility center chosen. For example, a cost-center manager in one company may have more decision-making authority than does a profit-center manager in a highly centralized company.

3. **Explain how the linking of rewards to responsibility-center performance metrics affects incentives and risk.** It is generally a good idea to link managers' rewards to responsibility-center results to promote goal congruence. However, linking rewards to results creates risk for the manager. The greater the influence of uncontrollable factors on a manager's reward, the more risk the manager bears.

4. **Compute return on investment (ROI), economic profit, and economic value added (EVA).** It is typical to measure the results of investment centers using a set of performance metrics that include financial measures, such as return on investment (ROI), economic profit, or economic value added (EVA). ROI is any income measure divided by the dollar amount invested and is expressed as a percentage. Economic profit, or economic value added, is operating income less a capital charge based on the capital invested. It is an absolute dollar amount.

5. **Compare the incentives created by income, ROI, and economic profit (or EVA) performance measures.** Income performance measures create incentives to make decisions that increase income, without regard to the resources required. ROI creates incentives to adopt any and all projects with returns greater than existing ROI, rather than with returns greater than the cost of capital. EVA directly incorporates the cost of capital and provides incentives to adopt those projects with returns greater than the cost of capital.

6. **Define *transfer prices* and identify their purpose.** In large companies with many different segments, one segment often provides products or services to another segment. Deciding on the amount the selling division should charge the buying division for these transfers (the transfer price) is difficult. Companies use various types of transfer pricing policies. The overall purpose of transfer prices is to motivate managers to act in the best interests of the company, not just their segment.

7. **State the general rule for transfer pricing and use it to assess alternative transfer prices based on total costs, variable costs, or market prices.** As a general rule, transfer prices should approximate the outlay cost plus opportunity cost of the producing segment. Each type of transfer price has its own advantages and disadvantages. Each has a situation where it works best, and each can lead to dysfunctional decisions in some instances. When a competitive market exists for the product or service, transfer prices based on market prices usually lead to goal congruence and optimal decisions. When idle capacity exists in the segment providing the product or service, transfer prices based on variable cost usually lead to goal congruence. Cost-based transfer prices should usually be based on planned, rather than actual, costs. If a company uses actual costs, there is little incentive for the selling segment manager to minimize costs and the receiving segment manager does not know the cost in advance, which makes cost planning difficult.

8. **Identify the factors affecting multinational transfer prices.** Multinational organizations often use transfer prices as a means of minimizing worldwide income taxes, import duties, and tariffs.

9. **Explain how controllability and management by objectives (MBO) aid the implementation of management control systems.** Regardless of what measures a management control system uses, measures used to evaluate managers should focus on only the controllable aspects of performance. MBO can focus attention on performance compared to expectations, which is better than evaluations based on absolute profitability. Misuse of budgets and performance metrics can motivate managers to violate ethical standards.

Accounting Vocabulary

agency theory, p. 394
capital charge, p. 400
capital turnover, p. 397
centralization, p. 391
cost of capital, p. 400
decentralization, p. 391
dysfunctional
　decisions, p. 408
economic profit, p. 400

economic value added
　(EVA), p. 400
gross book value, p. 398
incentives, p. 394
management by objectives
　(MBO), p. 413
net book value, p. 398
net operating profit after-tax
　(NOPAT) , p. 400

performance metric, p. 394
residual income, p. 400
return on investment
　(ROI), p. 396
return on sales, p. 397
segment autonomy, p. 392
transfer price, p. 404

MyAccountingLab **Fundamental Assignment Material**

10-A1 ROI and Economic Profit Calculations

Consider the following data (in thousands):

	Division		
	Hubert	**Duane**	**Louis**
Average invested capital	$2,000	$ 600	$1,800
Revenue	3,600	1,200	9,000
Income	180	84	216

1. For each division, compute the return on sales, the capital turnover, and the return on investment (ROI).
2. Which division is the best performer if evaluation is based on ROI? Explain.
3. Suppose each division is assessed a cost of capital of 10% on invested capital. Compute the economic profit for each division. Which division is the best performer based on economic profit? Explain.

10-A2 Transfer-Pricing Dispute

Zurich Équipement, SA, a Swiss transportation equipment manufacturer, is heavily decentralized. Each division head has full authority on all decisions regarding sales to internal or external customers. The Lucerne division has always acquired a certain equipment component from the Geneva division. The Geneva division recently acquired specialized equipment that is used primarily to make this component. The Geneva division has informed the Lucerne division that its fixed costs have increased by CHF 25 per unit because of the depreciation charges on the new equipment, so the unit price will be increased to CHF 325. However, the Lucerne division's management has now decided to purchase the component from outside suppliers at a price of CHF 300.

The Geneva division has supplied the following production cost data for this component:

Annual production of component (all for sale to Lucerne division)	3,000 units
Geneva's variable costs per unit	CHF 280
Geneva's fixed costs per unit	CHF 40

1. Suppose there are no alternative uses of the Geneva facilities and that fixed costs will continue if Geneva no longer produces the component for Lucerne. Will the company as a whole benefit if the Lucerne division buys from the outside suppliers for CHF 300 per unit? Show computations to support your answer.
2. Suppose there is an alternative use for the Geneva facilities. If the Geneva facilities are used to produce the component for the Lucerne division, the Geneva division will give up a contribution of CHF 85,000 from this alternative use. Should the Lucerne division purchase from outsiders at CHF 300 per unit?

3. Suppose that there are no alternative uses for Geneva's internal facilities and that the outsiders' selling price drops by CHF 50 to CHF 250. Should the Lucerne division purchase from outsiders?

4. As the president, how would you respond if the Geneva division manager requests that you require the Lucerne division to purchase the component from Geneva? Would your response differ depending on the specific situations described in numbers 1–3? Why?

10-A3 Transfer Pricing

Refer to problem 10-A2, number 1 only. Suppose the Geneva division could modify the component at an additional variable cost of CHF 25 per unit and sell the 3,000 units to other customers for CHF 330. Then, would the entire company benefit if the Lucerne division purchased the 3,000 components from outsiders at CHF 300 per unit?

10-A4 Rate of Return and Transfer Pricing

Consider the following data regarding budgeted operations for 20X7 of the Austin division of Texas Products:

Average total assets	
Receivables	$ 220,000
Inventories	290,000
Plant and equipment, net	450,000
Total	$ 960,000
Fixed overhead	$ 300,000
Variable costs	$.72 per unit
Desired rate of return on average total assets	20%
Expected volume	150,000 units

1. a. What average unit sales price does the Austin division need to obtain its desired rate of return on average total assets?
   b. What would be the expected capital turnover?
   c. What would be the return on sales?

2. a. If the selling price is as previously computed, what rate of return will the division earn on total assets if sales volume is 170,000 units?
   b. If sales volume is 130,000 units?

3. Assume that the Austin division plans to sell 45,000 units to the Galveston division of Texas Products and that it can sell only 105,000 units to outside customers at the price computed in requirement 1a. The Galveston division manager has balked at a tentative transfer price of $4. She has offered $2.25, claiming that she can manufacture the units herself for that price. The Austin division manager has examined his own data. He had decided that he could eliminate $60,000 of inventories, $90,000 of plant and equipment, and $22,500 of fixed overhead if he did not sell to the Galveston division and sold only 105,000 units to outside customers. Should the Austin division manager sell for $2.25? Show computations to support your answer.

10-B1 ROI or Economic Profit

Melbourne Co. is a large integrated Australian conglomerate with shipping, metals, and mining operations throughout Asia. Melbourne is just starting a new manufacturing division and the newly appointed general manager plans to submit a proposed capital budget for 20X8 for inclusion in the company-wide budget.

The division manager has for consideration the following projects, all of which require an outlay of capital. All projects have equal risk.

Project	Investment Required	Income
1	$4,800,000	$1,200,000
2	1,900,000	627,000
3	1,400,000	182,000
4	950,000	152,000
5	650,000	136,500
6	300,000	90,000

The division manager must decide which of the projects to take. The company has a cost of capital of 20%. An amount of $12 million is available to the division for investment purposes.

1. What will be the total investment, total return, return on capital invested, and economic profit of the rational division manager if
   a. the company has a rule that managers should accept all projects promising a return on investment of at least 15%?
   b. the company evaluates division managers on the return on capital invested (assume this is a new division so that invested capital will consist only of capital invested in new projects adopted by the manager)?
   c. the division manager is expected to maximize economic profit computed using the 20% cost of capital?
2. Which of the three approaches will induce the most effective investment policy for the company as a whole? Explain.

10-B2 Computing EVA

A company that uses EVA reported the following results for 20X4 and 20X5 (in millions):

	20X4	20X5
Pretax operating income	$6,105	$6,100
Cash taxes	1,686	1,620

Average adjusted invested capital was $16,125 million in 20X4 and $18,110 million in 20X5, and the cost of capital was 14% in both 20X4 and 20X5.

1. Compute the company's EVA for 20X4 and 20X5.
2. Compare the company's performance in creating value for its shareholders in 20X5 with that in 20X4.

10-B3 Transfer Pricing

Spartan Enterprises runs a chain of drive-in ice cream stands in Lansing during the summer season. Managers of all stands are told to act as if they owned the stand and are judged on their profit performance. Spartan Enterprises has rented an ice cream machine for the summer for $3,600 to supply its stands with ice cream. Spartan is not allowed to sell ice cream to other dealers because it cannot obtain a dairy license. The manager of the ice cream machine charges the stands $4 per gallon. Operating figures for the machine for the summer are as follows:

Sales to the stands (16,000 gallons at $4)		$64,000
Variable costs, at $2.00 per gallon	$32,000	
Fixed costs		
Rental of machine	3,600	
Other fixed costs	10,000	45,600
Operating margin		$18,400

The manager of the Okemos Drive-In, one of the Spartan drive-ins, is seeking permission to sign a contract to buy ice cream from an outside supplier at $3.35 a gallon. The Okemos Drive-In uses 4,000 gallons of ice cream during the summer. Elizabeth Chuk, controller of Spartan, refers this request to you. You determine that the other fixed costs of operating the machine will decrease by $900 if the Okemos Drive-In purchases from an outside supplier. Chuk wants an analysis of the request in terms of overall company objectives and an explanation of your conclusion. What is the appropriate transfer price?

10-B4 Rate of Return and Transfer Pricing

The Sendai division of Shusei Toy Company manufactures units of the game Shogi and sells them in the Japanese market for ¥7,350 each. The following data are from the Sendai division's 20X8 budget:

Variable cost	¥ 4,900 per unit
Fixed overhead	¥ 5,700,000
Total assets	¥16,000,000

Shusei has instructed the Sendai division to budget a rate of return on total assets (before taxes) of 24%.

1. Suppose the Sendai division expects to sell 3,350 games during 20X8.
    a. What rate of return will be earned on total assets?
    b. What would be the expected capital turnover?
    c. What would be the return on sales?
2. The Sendai division is considering adjustments in the budget to reach the desired 24% rate of return on total assets.
    a. How many units must be sold to obtain the desired return if no other part of the budget is changed?
    b. Suppose sales cannot be increased beyond 3,350 units. How much must total assets be reduced to obtain the desired return? Assume that for every ¥1,000 decrease in total assets, fixed costs decrease by ¥100.
3. Assume that only 2,950 units can be sold in the Japanese market. However, another 1,200 units can be sold to the European marketing division of Shusei. The Sendai manager has offered to sell the 1,200 units for ¥6,450 each. The European marketing division manager has countered with an offer to pay ¥6,150 per unit, claiming that she can subcontract production to an Italian producer at a cost equivalent to ¥6,150. The Sendai manager knows that if his production falls to 2,950 units, he could eliminate some assets, reducing total assets to ¥11 million and annual fixed overhead to ¥5.4 million. Should the Sendai manager sell for ¥6,150 per unit? Support your answer with the relevant computations. Ignore the effects of income taxes and import duties.

Additional Assignment Material

MyAccountingLab

QUESTIONS

10-1 "Decentralization has benefits and costs." Name three of each.

10-2 Sophisticated accounting and communications systems aid decentralization. Explain how they accomplish this.

10-3 Why is decentralization more popular in profit-seeking organizations than in nonprofit organizations?

10-4 "The essence of decentralization is the use of profit centers." Do you agree? Explain.

10-5 What kinds of organizations find decentralization to be preferable to centralization?

10-6 According to agency theory, employment contracts balance what three factors?

10-7 What is the major benefit of the ROI technique for measuring performance?

10-8 What two major items affect ROI?

10-9 How does economic profit differ from net income?

10-10 Define *economic value added (EVA)* and describe three ways a company can improve its EVA.

10-11 Division A's ROI is 20%, and B's is 10%. The company pays each division manager a bonus based on his or her division's ROI. Discuss whether each division manager would accept or reject a proposed project with a rate of return of 15%. Would either of them make a different decision if the company evaluated managers using economic profit with a capital charge of 11%? Explain.

10-12 Give three possible definitions of invested capital that we can use in measuring ROI or economic profit.

10-13 "Managers who use a historical-cost accounting system look backward at what something cost yesterday, instead of forward to what it will cost tomorrow." Do you agree? Why?

10-14 Ross Company uses net book value as a measure of invested capital when computing ROI. A division manager has suggested that the company change to using gross book value instead. What difference in motivation of division managers might result from such a change? Do you suppose most of the assets in the division of the manager proposing the change are relatively new or old? Why?

10-15 Why do companies need transfer-pricing systems?

10-16 Describe two problems that can arise when using actual full cost as a transfer price.

10-17 How does the presence or absence of idle capacity affect the optimal transfer-pricing policy?

10-18 "We use variable-cost transfer prices to ensure that we make no dysfunctional decisions." Discuss.

10-19 What is the major advantage of negotiated transfer prices? What is the major disadvantage?

10-20 Discuss two factors that affect multinational transfer prices but have little effect on purely domestic transfers.

10-21 Describe management by objectives (MBO).

10-22 How can performance measurement lead to unethical behavior by managers?

CRITICAL THINKING EXERCISES

10-23 Decentralization
Many companies implement organizational changes to centralize or decentralize operations only to follow with later changes in the opposite direction. Why might a company that at one time decentralizes decide later to centralize?

10-24 Comparing Financial Measures of Performance
"Both ROI and economic profit use profit and invested capital to measure performance. Therefore it really doesn't matter which we use." Do you agree? Explain.

10-25 Performance Metrics and Ethics
"Financial performance metrics cause managers to ignore ethics and focus just on meeting their profit targets. After all, look at what happened at Enron, Global Crossing, WorldCom, Tyco, HealthSouth, and several other companies." Evaluate this quote. Can financial performance metrics be compatible with ethical behavior?

10-26 Transfer Pricing and Organizational Behavior
The principle reason for transfer-pricing systems is to communicate data that will lead to goal-congruent decisions by managers of different business units. When managers take actions that conflict with organizational goals, dysfunctional behavior exists. Why does top management sometimes accept a division manager's judgments, even if the division manager appears to behave in a dysfunctional manner?

EXERCISES

10-27 Simple ROI Calculation
You are given the following data:

Sales	$227,500,000
Invested capital	$ 65,000,000
Net income	$ 9,100,000

Compute the following:

1. Turnover of capital
2. Return on sales
3. Return on investment (ROI)

10-28 Simple ROI Calculation
Fill in the blanks:

	Division		
	A	B	C
Return on sales	6%	4%	__%
Capital turnover	3	__	5
Rate of return on invested capital	__%	18%	20%

10-29 Simple ROI and Economic Profit Calculations

Consider the following data:

	Division		
	X	**Y**	**Z**
Invested capital	$1,050,000	$ _____	$1,200,000
Income	$ _____	$ 142,800	$ 210,000
Revenue	$2,310,000	$2,856,000	$ _____
Return on sales	3%	_____ %	_____ %
Capital turnover	_____	_____	3.5
Rate of return on invested capital	_____ %	10.5%	_____ %

1. Prepare a similar tabular presentation, filling in all blanks.
2. Suppose each division is assessed a capital charge based on a cost of capital of 10% of invested capital. Compute the economic profit for each division.
3. Which division is the best performer? Explain.

10-30 EVA

Lohmann Corporation is a major supplier to makers of outdoor power equipment. According to the company's annual report, "management subscribes to the premise that the value of our company is enhanced if the capital invested in its operations yields a cash return that is greater than that expected by the providers of capital."

The following data are from Lohmann's annual report that incorporate EVA adjustments to operating profit and average invested capital (amounts in thousands):

	20X1	20X2
Adjusted before tax operating profit	$ 78,000	$ 80,000
Cash taxes	20,500	22,600
Adjusted average invested capital	650,000	600,000
Cost of capital	9.4%	9.4%

1. Compute the EVA for Lohmann for 20X1 and 20X2.
2. Did Lohmann's overall performance improve from 20X1 to 20X2? Explain.

10-31 Comparison of Asset and Equity Bases

Hope Company has assets of $3 million and long-term, 12% debt of $1,240,000. Crosby Company has assets of $3 million and no long-term debt. The annual operating income (before interest) of both companies is $690,000. Ignore taxes.

1. Compute the rate of return on
   a. assets, and
   b. stockholders' equity.
2. Evaluate the relative merits of each base for appraising operating management.

10-32 Finding Unknowns

Consider the following data:

	Division		
	J	**K**	**L**
Income	$450,000	$ _____	$ _____
Revenue	$ _____	$ _____	$ _____
Invested capital	$ _____	$5,000,000	$20,000,000
Return on sales	5%	9%	_____ %
Capital turnover	6	_____	2
Rate of return on invested capital	_____ %	27%	16%
Cost of capital	7%	14%	_____ %
Economic profit	$ _____	$ _____	$ 200,000

1. Prepare a similar tabular presentation, filling in all blanks.
2. Which division is the best performer? Explain.

10-33 Gross Versus Net Asset Value

The Alexandria division of Atkinson Company just purchased an asset for $120,000. The asset has a 3-year life. Atkinson's top management evaluates Lisa LaVilla, manager of the Alexandria division, based on ROI for this asset. She can choose to measure the asset using either gross asset value or net asset value. Her operating income before depreciation each year is $100,000.

1. What is the Alexandria division's ROI for each of the 3 years using the gross asset value?
2. What is the Alexandria division's ROI for each of the 3 years using the net asset value?
3. If LaVilla expects Atkinson to transfer her to a different division in about a year, which asset valuation policy would she prefer?

10-34 Variable Cost as a Transfer Price

A chair's variable cost is $52 and its market value as a piece of unfinished furniture is $65 at a transfer point from the assembly division to the finishing division. The finishing division's variable cost of sanding and finishing the chair is $26, and the selling price of the chair after sanding and finishing is $83.

1. Prepare a tabulation of the contribution margin per unit for the finishing division's performance and overall company performance under the two alternatives of (a) selling to outsiders at the transfer point and (b) sanding and finishing the chair and then selling to outsiders.
2. As finishing division manager, which alternative would you choose? Explain.

10-35 Maximum and Minimum Transfer Price

Sherwin Company makes bicycles. Various divisions make components and transfer them to the Dayton division for assembly into final products. The Dayton division can also buy components from external suppliers. The Toledo division makes the wheels, and it also sells wheels to external customers. All divisions are profit centers, and managers are free to negotiate transfer prices. Prices and costs for the Toledo and Dayton divisions are as follows:

Toledo Division	
Sales price to external customers	$ 14
Internal transfer price	?
Costs	
Variable costs per wheel	$ 10
Total fixed costs	$320,000
Budgeted production	64,000 wheels*

*Includes production for transfer to Dayton

Dayton Division	
Sales price to external customers	$ 170
Costs	
Wheels, per bicycle	?
Other components, per bicycle	$ 85
Other variable costs, per bicycle	$ 45
Total fixed costs	$640,000
Budgeted production	16,000 bicycles

Fixed costs in both divisions will be unaffected by the transfer of wheels from Toledo to Dayton.

1. Compute the maximum transfer price per wheel the Dayton division would be willing to pay to buy wheels from the Toledo division.

2. Compute the minimum transfer price per wheel at which the Toledo division would be willing to produce and sell wheels to the Dayton division. Assume that Toledo has excess capacity.

10-36 Multinational Transfer Prices

Princeton International has production and marketing divisions throughout the world. It produces one particular product in Ireland, where the income tax rate is 24%, and transfers it to a marketing division in Japan, where the income tax rate is 45%. Assume that Japan places an import tax of 13% on the product and that import duties are not deductible for income tax purposes.

The variable cost of the product is £500 and the full cost is £800. Suppose the company can legally select a transfer price anywhere between the variable and full cost.

1. What transfer price should Princeton International use to minimize taxes? Explain why this is the tax-minimizing transfer price.
2. Compute the amount of taxes saved by using the transfer price in requirement 1 instead of the transfer price that would result in the highest taxes.

PROBLEMS

10-37 Agency Theory

The Tamura International Trading Company plans to hire a manager for its division in Mexico City. Tamura International's president and vice president of personnel are trying to decide on an appropriate incentive employment contract. The manager will operate far from the Tokyo corporate headquarters, so evaluation by personal observation will be limited. The president insists that a large incentive to produce profits is necessary; he favors a salary of ¥150,000 and a bonus of 10% of the profits above ¥1,200,000. If operations proceed as expected, profits will be ¥4,600,000, and the manager will receive ¥490,000. But both profits and compensation might be more or less than planned.

The vice president of personnel responds that ¥490,000 is more than most of Tamura International's division managers make. She is sure that the company can hire a competent manager for a guaranteed salary of ¥400,000. She argued, "Why pay ¥490,000 when we can probably hire the same person for ¥400,000?"

1. What factors would affect Tamura International's choice of employment contract? Include a discussion of the pros and cons of each proposed contract.
2. Why is the expected compensation more with the bonus plan than with the straight salary?

10-38 Margins and Turnover

Accountants often express ROI as the product of two components—capital turnover and return on sales. You are considering investing in one of three companies, all in the same industry, and are given the following information:

	Company		
	Adam	Basil	Collin
Sales	$8,500,000	$ 1,500,000	$29,000,000
Income	$ 765,000	$ 180,000	$ 180,000
Capital	$3,200,000	$12,000,000	$12,000,000

1. Why would you desire the breakdown of return on investment into return on sales and turnover on capital?
2. Compute the return on sales, turnover on capital, and ROI for the three companies, and comment on the relative performance of the companies as thoroughly as the data permit.
3. Notice that Basil and Collin have the same income and capital but vastly different levels of sales. Discuss the types of strategies that Basil and Collin might be employing.

10-39 ROI by Business Segment

ViaMedia does business in three different business segments: (1) entertainment, (2) publishing/information, and (3) consumer/commercial finance. Results for a recent year were as follows (in millions):

	Revenues	Operating Income	Total Assets
Entertainment	$1,050	$210	$1,000
Publishing/Information	$ 700	$140	$1,400
Consumer/Commercial Finance	$1,060	$265	$ 848

1. Compute the following for each business segment:
   a. Return on sales
   b. Capital turnover
   c. ROI
2. Comment on the differences in ROI among the business segments. Include reasons for the differences.

10-40 EVA Versus Economic Profit

The primary difference between the EVA and economic profit measures is the increased focus on cash flow by EVA. For example, economic profit generally uses the provision for income taxes from the income statement while EVA uses cash taxes paid. EVA companies typically make several adjustments (from 5 to 15 adjustments for the typical EVA company) to both operating income from the income statement and invested capital from the balance sheet. Common examples include adjustments for R&D, LIFO, and warranty costs.

The following data were taken from the 20X3 annual report of Burton Company (thousands of dollars):

Income from operations	$ 267,400
Provision for income taxes	57,455
Net EVA adjustments added to income from operations	5,398
Additional capital employed from EVA adjustments	234,159
Ending total shareholders' equity	845,632
Cash taxes	64,800
Ending total current liabilities	340,125
Ending total assets	1,834,456
Beginning total shareholders' equity	841,589
Beginning total current liabilities	471,859
Beginning total assets	1,889,321
Management's estimate of the cost-of-capital	11.3%

Prepare a schedule that calculates and compares EVA to economic profit for Burton Company.

10-41 EVA

The Jeske Company had the following financial results for two recent fiscal years (in millions):

	Year 2	Year 1
Revenues	$4,463	$4,510
Operating expenses	3,569	3,615
Cash income taxes	292	255
Average invested capital (total assets less current liabilities)	$2,854	$2,689

1. Suppose that Jeske's cost of capital is 11.5%. Compute the company's EVA for years 1 and 2. Assume definitions of after-tax operating income and invested capital as reported in Jeske's annual reports without adjustments advocated by Stern Stewart or others.
2. Discuss the change in EVA between years 1 and 2.

10-42 EVA and Cost of Capital

The Holt Company uses EVA to evaluate top management performance. In 20X8, Holt had net operating income of $8,210 million, income taxes of $1,395 million, and average noncurrent liabilities plus stockholders' equity of $27,555 million. The company's capital is about 55% long-term debt and 45% equity. Assume that the after-tax cost of debt is 10% and the cost of equity is 12%.

1. Compute Holt's EVA. Assume definitions of after-tax operating income and invested capital as reported in Holt's annual reports without adjustments advocated by Stern Stewart.
2. Explain what EVA tells you about the performance of the top management of Holt in 20X8.

10-43 Evaluation of Divisional Performance

As the CEO of Middling Hardware Company, you examined the following measures of the performance of three divisions (in thousands of dollars):

	Average Net Assets Based On		Operating Income Based On*	
Division	Historical Cost	Replacement Cost	Historical Cost	Replacement Cost
Tools	$15,000	$16,000	$2,600	$2,500
Appliances	44,000	55,000	6,750	6,150
Lighting	27,000	48,000	5,000	3,900

*The differences in operating income between historical and replacement cost are attributable to the differences in depreciation expenses.

1. Calculate for each division the rate of return on net assets and the economic profit based on historical cost and on replacement cost. For purposes of calculating economic profit, use 10% as the cost of capital.
2. Rank the performance of each division under each of the four different measures computed in number 1.
3. What do these measures indicate about the performance of the divisions? Of the division managers? Which measure do you prefer? Why?

10-44 Use of Gross or Net Book Value of Fixed Assets

Assume that a machine shop acquires $520,000 of fixed assets with a useful life of 4 years and no residual value. The shop uses straight-line depreciation. The company judges the shop manager based on income in relation to these fixed assets. Annual net income, after deducting depreciation, is $20,000.

Assume that sales, and all expenses except depreciation, are on a cash basis. Dividends equal net income. Thus, cash in the amount of the depreciation charge will accumulate each year. The plant manager's performance is judged in relation to fixed assets because all current assets, including cash, are considered under central-company control. Assume (unrealistically) that any cash accumulated remains idle. Ignore taxes.

1. Prepare a comparative tabulation of the plant's rate of return and the company's overall rate of return based on
   a. gross (i.e., original cost) assets.
   b. net book value of assets.
2. Evaluate the relative merits of gross assets and net book value of assets as investment bases.

10-45 Role of Economic Value and Replacement Value

(This problem requires understanding of the concept of present values. See Appendix B.)

"To me, economic value is the only justifiable basis for measuring plant assets for purposes of evaluating performance. By economic value, I mean the present value of expected future services. Still, we do not even do this on acquisition of new assets—that is, we may compute a positive net present value, using discounted cash flow; but we record the asset at no more than its cost. In this way, the excess present value is not shown in the initial balance sheet. Moreover, the use of replacement costs in subsequent years is also unlikely to result in showing economic values. The replacement cost will probably be less than the economic value at any given instant of an asset's life.

"Market values are totally unappealing to me because they represent a second-best alternative value—that is, they ordinarily represent the maximum amount obtainable from an alternative that has been rejected. Obviously, if the market value exceeds the economic value of the assets in use, they should be sold. However, in most instances, the opposite is true; market values of individual assets are far below their economic value in use.

"The obtaining and recording of total present values of individual assets based on discounted-cash-flow techniques is an infeasible alternative. I, therefore, conclude that replacement cost (less accumulated depreciation) of similar assets producing similar services is the best practical approximation of the economic value of the assets in use. Of course, it is more appropriate for the evaluation of the division's performance than the division manager's performance."

Critically evaluate these comments. Please do not wander; concentrate on the issues described by the quotation.

10-46 Profit Centers and Transfer Pricing in an Automobile Dealership

A large automobile dealership in Chicago is installing a responsibility accounting system and three profit centers: parts and service, new vehicles, and used vehicles. Top management has told the three department managers to run their shops as if they were in business for themselves. However, there are interdepartmental dealings. For example,

a. the parts and service department prepares new cars for final delivery and repairs used cars prior to resale.

b. the used-car department's major source of inventory has been cars traded in as partial payment for new cars.

The owner of the dealership has asked you to draft a company policy statement on transfer pricing, together with specific rules to be applied to the examples cited. He has told you that clarity is of paramount importance because he will rely on your statement for settling transfer-pricing disputes.

10-47 Transfer Pricing

The shocks and struts division of Transnational Motors Company produces strut assemblies for automobiles. It has been the sole supplier of strut assemblies to the automotive division and charges $48 per unit, the current market price for very large wholesale lots. The shocks and struts division also sells to outside retail outlets, at $61 per unit. Normally, outside sales amount to 30% of a total sales volume of 1 million strut assemblies per year. Typical combined annual data for the division follow:

Sales	$51,900,000	
Variable costs, at $38.50 per strut assembly		$38,500,000
Fixed costs		4,200,000
Total costs	$42,700,000	
Gross margin	$ 9,200,000	

Flint Auto Parts Company, an entirely separate entity, has offered the automotive division comparable strut assemblies at a firm price of $42.70 per unit. The shocks and struts division of Transnational Motors claims that it cannot possibly match this price because it could not earn any margin at the price Flint is offering.

1. Assume that you are the manager of the automotive division of Transnational Motors. Comment on the shocks and struts division's claim. Assume that normal outside volume cannot be increased.

2. Now assume the shocks and struts division believes that it can increase outside sales by 700,000 strut assemblies per year by increasing fixed costs by $2.5 million and variable costs by $4.50 per unit while reducing the selling price to $58. Assume that maximum capacity is 1 million strut assemblies per year. Should the division reject intracompany business and concentrate solely on outside sales?

10-48 Transfer-Pricing Concession

You are the divisional controller of the U.S. division of Samtech Electronics. Your division is operating at capacity. The Australian division has asked the U.S. division to supply a sound system (chip and speaker), which it will use in a new model Game Box that it is introducing. The U.S. division currently sells identical sound systems to outside customers at $11.00 each.

The Australian division has offered to pay $7.00 for each sound system. The total cost of the Game Box is as follows:

Purchased parts from outside vendors	$28.10
Sound system from U.S. division	7.00
Other variable costs	17.50
Fixed overhead	10.00
Total	$62.60

The Australian division is operating at 50% of capacity, and this Game Box is an important new product introduction to increase its use of capacity. Based on a target-costing approach, the Australian division management has decided that paying more than $7.00 for the sound system would make production of the Game Box infeasible because the predicted selling price for the Game Box is only $62.00.

Samtech Electronics evaluates divisional managers on the basis of pretax ROI and dollar profits compared to the budget. Ignore taxes and tariffs.

1. As divisional controller of the U.S. division, would you recommend supplying the sound system to the Australian division for $7.00 each? Why or why not?
2. Would it be to the short-run economic advantage of Samtech Electronics for the U.S. division to supply the sound system to the Australian division? Explain your answer.
3. Discuss the organizational and behavioral difficulties, if any, inherent in this situation. As the U.S. division controller, what would you advise the Samtech Electronics president to do in this situation?

10-49 Transfer Prices and Idle Capacity

The Eugene division of Union Furniture purchases lumber, which it uses to fabricate tables, chairs, and other wood furniture. It purchases most of the lumber from Shasta Mill, also a division of Union Furniture. Both the Eugene division and Shasta Mill are profit centers.

The Eugene division proposes to produce a new Shaker-style chair that will sell for $95. The manager is exploring the possibility of purchasing the required lumber from Shasta Mill. Production of 800 chairs is planned, using capacity in the Eugene division that is currently idle.

The Eugene division can purchase the lumber needed for one chair from an outside supplier for $72. Union Furniture has a policy that internal transfers are priced at fully allocated cost.

Assume the following costs for the production of one chair and the lumber required for the chair:

Shasta Mill—Lumber Cost		Eugene Division—Chair Cost		
Variable cost	$48	Variable costs		
Allocated fixed cost	22	Lumber from Shasta Mill		$70
Fully allocated cost	$70	Eugene division variable costs		
		Manufacturing	$23	
		Selling	6	29
		Total variable cost		$99

1. Assume that the Shasta Mill has idle capacity and, therefore, would incur no additional fixed costs to produce the required lumber. Would the Eugene division manager buy the lumber for the chair from the Shasta Mill given the existing transfer-pricing policy? Why or why not? Would the company as a whole benefit if the manager decides to buy from the Shasta Mill? Explain.
2. Assume that there is no idle capacity at the Shasta Mill and the lumber required for one chair can be sold to outside customers for $72. Would the company as a whole benefit if the Eugene manager buys from Shasta? Explain.

10-50 Transfer-Pricing Principles

A law firm, Arno Legal Services, is decentralized with 25 offices around the state of California. The headquarters is based in San Francisco. Another operating division is located in San Jose, 50 miles away. A subsidiary printing operation, ArnoPrint, is located in the headquarters building. Top management has indicated the desirability of the San Jose office using ArnoPrint for printing reports. All charges are eventually billed to the client, but Arno Legal Services was concerned about keeping such charges competitive.

ArnoPrint charges San Jose the following:

Photographing page for offset printing (a setup cost)	$.200
Printing cost per page	.02

At this rate, ArnoPrint sales have a 50% contribution margin to fixed overhead.

Outside bids for 250 copies of a 180-page report needed immediately have been as follows:

Print 4U	$942.00
Jiffy Press	918.25
Kustom Print	923.50

These three printers are located within a 5-mile radius of Arno Legal Services' San Jose office and can have the reports ready in 2 days. A messenger would have to be sent to drop off the original and pick up the copies. The messenger usually goes to headquarters, but in the past, special trips have been required to deliver the original or pick up the copies. It takes 3–4 days to get the copies from ArnoPrint (because of the extra scheduling difficulties in delivery and pickup).

Quality control at ArnoPrint is poor. Reports received in the past have contained wrinkled pages, have occasionally been mis-collated, or have had pages deleted altogether. (In one instance, an intra-company memorandum including the San Jose Office's financial performance statistics was inserted in a report prepared for an outside client. Fortunately, the San Jose office detected the error before the report was distributed to the client.) The degree of quality control in the three outside print shops is unknown.

(Although the differences in costs may seem immaterial in this case, regard the numbers as significant for purposes of focusing on the key issues.)

1. If you were the decision maker at the San Jose office of Arno Legal Services, to which print shop would you give the business? Is this an optimal economic decision from the entire organization's viewpoint?
2. What would be the ideal transfer price in this case, if based only on economic considerations?
3. Time is an important factor in maintaining client goodwill. There is potential return business from this client. Given this perspective, what might be the optimal decision for the company?
4. Comment on the wisdom of top management in indicating that ArnoPrint should be used.

10-51 Negotiated Transfer Prices

The Lighting division of Ibex Office Furniture needs 1,200 units of a leaded-glass lamp shade from the fabricating division. The company has a policy of negotiated transfer prices. The fabricating division has enough excess capacity to produce 2,000 units of the lamp shade. Its variable cost of production is $23. The market price of the lamp shade to external customers is $39.

What is the natural bargaining range for a transfer price between the two divisions? Explain why no price below your range would be acceptable. Also explain why no price above your range would be acceptable.

10-52 Transfer Prices and Minority Shareholders

This chapter discussed transferring profits between divisions of a multinational company. Another situation where transfer prices have a similar effect is when a parent company transfers items to or from a subsidiary when there are minority shareholders in the subsidiary. Consider the Michelin Group and its Polish subsidiary, Stomil Olsztyn, of which Michelin owns 70%. Michelin buys tires from Stomil Olsztyn at a transfer price. Since Michelin owns a majority of Stomil Olsztyn, it controls the transfer-pricing policy. The holders of the other 30% of Stomil Olsztyn claim that Michelin sets the transfer prices too low, thereby reducing the profits of Stomil Olsztyn. They maintain that Stomil Olsztyn would be more profitable if it were allowed to sell its tires on the market rather than transfer them to Michelin. In reply, Michelin managers maintain that Stomil Olsztyn is more profitable than other members of the Michelin Group, and, therefore, the transfer prices must be fair.

Discuss the incentives for Michelin to transfer tires at a low price from Stomil Olsztyn to its Michelin parent. What transfer price do the minority shareholders in Stomil Olsztyn favor? Use an example of a tire that Stomil Olsztyn produces at a variable cost of €20 that is transferred to Michelin for €25. How should Michelin and Stomil Olsztyn establish a fair transfer price?

10-53 Multinational Transfer Prices

Minnesota Medical Instruments produces a variety of medical products at its plant in Minneapolis. The company has sales divisions worldwide. One of these sales divisions is located in Stockholm, Sweden. Assume that the U.S. income tax rate is 30%, the Swedish rate is 65%, and a 5% import duty is imposed on medical supplies brought into Sweden.

One product produced in Minneapolis and shipped to Sweden is a heart defibrillator. The variable cost of production is $200 per unit, and the fully allocated cost is $350 per unit.

1. Suppose the Swedish and U.S. governments allow either the variable or fully allocated cost to be used as a transfer price. Which price should Minnesota Medical Instruments choose to minimize the total of income taxes and import duties? Compute the amount the company saves if it uses your suggested transfer price instead of the alternative. Assume import duties are not deductible for tax purposes.
2. Suppose the Swedish parliament passed a law decreasing the income tax rate to 40% and increasing the duty on heart monitors to 15%. Repeat number 1, using these new facts.

10-54 Review of Major Points in This Chapter

The Canadian Instruments Company uses the decentralized form of organizational structure and considers each of its divisions as an investment center. The Toronto division is currently selling 15,000 air filters annually, although it has sufficient productive capacity to produce 21,000 units per year. Variable manufacturing costs amount to $21 per unit, while the total fixed costs amount to $90,000. These 15,000 air filters are sold to outside customers at $40 per unit.

The Montreal division, also a part of Canadian Instruments, has indicated that it would like to buy 1,500 air filters from the Toronto division, but at a price of $37 per unit. This is the price the Montreal division is currently paying an outside supplier.

1. Compute the effect on the operating income of the company as a whole if the Montreal division purchases the 1,500 air filters from the Toronto division.
2. What is the minimum price that the Toronto division should be willing to accept for these 1,500 air filters?
3. What is the maximum price that the Montreal division should be willing to pay for these 1,500 air filters?
4. Suppose instead that the Toronto division is currently producing and selling 21,000 air filters annually to outside customers. What is the effect on the overall Canadian Instruments Company operating income if the Toronto division is required by top management to sell 1,500 air filters to the Montreal division at (a) $21 per unit and (b) $37 per unit?
5. For this question only, assume that the Toronto division is currently earning an annual operating income of $36,000, and the division's average invested capital is $300,000. The division manager has an opportunity to invest in a proposal that will require an additional investment of $20,000 and will increase annual operating income by $2,000. (a) Should the division manager accept this proposal if the Canadian Instruments Company uses ROI in evaluating the performance of its divisional managers? (b) If the company uses economic profit? (Assume a cost of capital of 7%.)

CASES

10-55 Profit Centers and Central Services

Star Manufacturing, manufacturer of Starlite brand small appliances, has a process engineering department (PED). The department's major task has been to help the production departments improve their operating methods and processes.

For several years, Star Manufacturing has charged the cost of consulting services to the production departments based on a signed agreement between the managers involved. The agreement specifies the scope of the project, the predicted savings, and the number of consulting hours required. The charge to the production departments is based on the costs to the engineering department of the services rendered. For example, senior engineer hours cost more per hour than junior engineer hours. An overhead cost is included. The agreement is really a "fixed-price" contract. That is, the production manager knows the total cost of the project in advance. A recent survey revealed that production managers have a high level of confidence in the engineers.

The PED department manager oversees the work of about 40 engineers and 10 technicians. She reports to the engineering manager, who reports to the vice president of manufacturing. The PED manager has the freedom to increase or decrease the number of engineers under her supervision. The PED manager's performance evaluation is based on many factors including the annual incremental savings to the company in excess of the costs of operating the PED department.

The production departments are profit centers. Their goods are transferred to subsequent departments, such as a sales department or sales division, at prices that approximate market prices for similar products.

Top management is seriously considering a "no-charge" plan. That is, production departments would receive engineering services at absolutely no cost. Proponents of the new plan maintain that it would motivate the production managers to take better advantage of engineering talent. In all other respects, the new system would be unchanged from the present system.

1. Compare the present and proposed plans. What are their strong and weak points? In particular, will the PED manager tend to hire the "optimal" amount of engineering talent?
2. Which plan do you favor? Why?

10-56 Management by Objectives

Roger Ravenhill is the CEO of Haida Company. Ravenhill has a financial management background and is known throughout the organization as a "no-nonsense" executive. When Ravenhill became CEO, he emphasized cost reduction and savings and introduced a comprehensive cost control and budget system. The company goals and budget plans were established by Ravenhill and given to his subordinates for implementation. Some of the company's key executives were dismissed or demoted for failing to meet projected budget plans. Under the leadership of Roger Ravenhill, Haida has once again become financially stable and profitable after several years of poor performance.

Recently, Ravenhill has become concerned with the human side of the organization and has become interested in the management technique referred to as "management by objectives" (MBO). If there are enough positive benefits of MBO, he plans to implement the system throughout the company. However, he realizes that he does not fully understand MBO because he does not understand how it differs from the current system of establishing firm objectives and budget plans.

1. Briefly explain what MBO entails and identify its advantages and disadvantages.
2. Does Roger Ravenhill's management style incorporate the human-value premises and goals of MBO? Explain your answer.

NIKE 10-K PROBLEM

10-57 ROI and Economic Profit

Examine Nike's segments as defined in Note 18 to its financial statements in the 10-K report in Appendix C. We will use the segment information from the first six segments listed to calculate approximations to ROI and economic profit. For purposes of this problem, define segment income as segment EBIT and define segment assets as the sum of the assets shown in note 18, namely receivables, inventory, and property plant and equipment. Therefore, pretax and pre-interest ROA is EBIT divided by segment assets and an approximation to economic profit is EBIT minus a charge for the cost of capital to finance segment assets.

Using these definitions, determine ROA and economic profit for each segment in 2010 and 2011 using EBIT from Note 18 in the 10-K and the information on segment assets in the following table. Assume that Nike's cost of capital is 10%. Use your results to evaluate the performance of each segment. Which segment management seems to be doing the best job? What subjective factors would you consider, in addition to ROA and economic profit, in assessing segment performance?

Ending Accounts Receivable, Inventories, and Property, Plant, and Equipment		
Segment	2011	2010
North America	$2,433	$1,941
Western Europe	1,272	1,031
Central and Eastern Europe	448	384
Greater China	471	379
Japan	595	568
Emerging Markets	953	683
Nike Total (includes corporate assets not in segments)	$7,968	$6,623

EXCEL APPLICATION EXERCISE

10-58 Return on Investment and Economic Profit

Goal: Create an Excel spreadsheet to calculate performance of divisional segments using the ROI and economic profit methods. Use the results to answer questions about your findings.

Scenario: The company has asked you to calculate ROI and economic profit for three divisions. The background data for your analysis appears in Fundamental Assignment Material 10-A1. Use an interest rate of 10% when calculating the capital charge.

When you have completed your spreadsheet, answer the following questions:

1. Which division has the best performance using the ROI method? Using the economic profit method?
2. Which division has the worst performance under both methods?
3. Which method would you suggest for evaluating the manager of each division?

Step-by-Step:

1. Open a new Excel spreadsheet.
2. In column A, create a bold-faced heading that contains the following:
   Row 1: Chapter 10 Decision Guideline
   Row 2: Divisions Hubert, Duane, and Louis
   Row 3: Measures of Profitability
   Row 4: Today's Date
3. Merge and center the four heading rows across columns A–I.
4. In row 7, create the following center-justified column headings:
   Column A: Division
   Column B: Invested Capital
   Column C: Revenue
   Column D: Income
   Column E: Capital Charge
   Column F: Economic Profit
   Column G: Return on Investment
   Column H: Return on Sales
   Column I: Capital Turnover
5. Change the format of Economic Profit and Return on Investment to bold-faced headings.
6. Change the format of the column headings in row 7 to permit the titles to be displayed on multiple lines within a single cell.

Alignment tab:	Wrap Text:	Checked

Note: Adjust column widths so the headings only use two lines.

Adjust row height to insure that row is the same height as adjusted headings.

7. In column A, create the following center-justified row headings:
   Row 8: Hubert
   Skip a row.
   Row 10: Duane
   Skip a row.
   Row 12: Louis
8. Use the scenario data to fill in invested capital, revenue, and income amounts for each division.
9. Use the scenario data and appropriate formulas to calculate capital charge amounts for each division.
10. Use the appropriate formulas from this chapter to calculate economic profit, ROI, return on sales, and capital turnover amounts for each division.
11. Format amounts in columns B, C, D, E, and F for division A as follows:

Number tab:	Category:	Currency
	Decimal places:	0
	Symbol:	$
	Negative numbers:	Black with parentheses

12. Format amounts in columns B, C, D, E, and F for divisions B and C as follows:

Number tab:	Category:	Currency
	Decimal places:	0
	Symbol:	None
	Negative numbers:	Black with parentheses

13. Format amounts in columns G and H to display as percentages without decimal places.

Number tab:	Category:	Percentage
	Decimal places:	0

14. Format the capital turnover amounts to display two decimal places, followed by the word **times**.

Number tab:	Category:	Custom

From the Type list, highlight the type shown next:

	Type:	0.00

Change the data in the Type field from 0.00 to the following:

	Type:	0.00 "times"

Click the OK button.

15. Save your work, and print a copy for your files.

Note: Print your spreadsheet using landscape in order to ensure that all columns appear on one page.

COLLABORATIVE LEARNING EXERCISE

10-59 ROI

Form groups of three to six students. Each student should select a company. Coordinate the selection of companies so that each group has companies from a wide variety of industries. For example, a good mix of industries for a group of five students would be a retail company, a basic manufacturing company, a computer software company, a bank, and an electric utility company.

1. Each student should find the latest annual report for his or her company. (If you cannot find the company's home page, try www.sec.gov, and search the Security and Exchange Commission's Edgar files for the company's 10-K report, which will contain its financial statements.) Compute the following:
   a. Return on sales
   b. Capital turnover
   c. ROI
2. As a group, compare these performance metrics for the chosen companies. Why do they differ across companies? What characteristic of the company and its industry might explain the differences in the measures?

INTERNET EXERCISE

10-60 Decentralization at Marriott International

Decentralization of an organization can occur for many reasons. It may be that the organization is involved in multiple activities that are not closely related to each other, such as construction and auto sales. In other cases, the decision may be due to the structure of the firm's ownership and how it chooses to manage its image. Let's look at a firm that falls under this category—Marriott International.

1. Go to Marriott International's Web site at www.marriott.com. Does the home page emphasize corporate information or promotional information?
2. How has Marriott decentralized its businesses? Click on "Explore Our Brands" near the bottom of the page to find a list of Marriott's divisions. Do you suppose the divisions are cost centers, profit centers, or investment centers?

3. Go to the most recent annual report by clicking on "About Marriott," "Investors," "Financial Information," and finally click on "Financial Reports & Proxy" to find the most recent annual report. Locate the information on business segments in the Notes to Financial Statements. How many segments does Marriott identify? What are these segments? What information does the firm report with respect to each of the different segments?

4. Marriott provides both income and assets for each of the segments. Calculate the return on average total assets for the past year for each of the segments.

5. What was the return on average total assets for the corporation as a whole for the past year? Given the different kinds of business segments the company has, do you think that operating return on average total assets would be a good measure for evaluating the individual segments? What factors might influence your answer?

6. Is Marriott likely to have any transfer prices? If Marriott has transfers, how do you suppose the company determines its transfer prices?

11 Capital Budgeting

LEARNING OBJECTIVES

When you have finished studying this chapter, you should be able to:

1. Describe capital-budgeting decisions and use the net-present-value (NPV) method to make such decisions.

2. Use sensitivity analysis to evaluate the effect of changes in predictions on investment decisions.

3. Calculate the NPV difference between two projects using both the total project and differential approaches.

4. Identify relevant cash flows for NPV analyses.

5. Compute the after-tax net present values of projects.

6. Explain the after-tax effect on cash received from the disposal of assets.

7. Use the payback model and the accounting rate-of-return model and compare them with the NPV model.

8. Reconcile the conflict between using an NPV model for making decisions and using accounting income for evaluating the related performance.

9. Compute the impact of inflation on a capital-budgeting project (Appendix 11).

▶ TOYOTA MOTOR CORPORATION

Toyota Motor Corporation was founded in 1937 by Japanese entrepreneur, Kiichiro Toyoda, to produce and sell Toyoda autos. Almost immediately the name was changed to Toyota because (according to Wikipedia) "it took eight brush strokes (a fortuitous number) to write in Japanese, was visually simpler (leaving off two ticks at the end), and sounded better with two 't's." In 1957 Toyota entered the U.S. market with a car called the Toyopet Crown. Unfortunately, U.S. consumers associated these cars with toys and pets, so Toyota quickly dropped the Toyopet name. Nevertheless, the company continued selling Toyotas in the United States. In 1963 Toyota built its first car outside of Japan (in Australia) and in 1982 began producing cars in the United States. In 2008, Toyota became the largest automobile company in the world, replacing General Motors. It has production or assembly plants in more than 25 countries.

Toyota was instrumental in developing lean manufacturing and just-in-time production. Its management philosophy focuses on four areas: 1) long-term thinking, 2) a process for problem-solving, 3) growth and development of employees, and 4) organizational learning. This has led to a variety of awards for quality, from the Deming Prize for Total Quality Management in 1965 to recent J.D. Power awards for automobile quality. This reputation for quality was instrumental in Toyota's worldwide growth.

Toyota invested heavily in U.S. manufacturing facilities, especially those for full-size pickup trucks and sports-utility vehicles. With the economic downturn beginning in 2008, Toyota found itself with excess manufacturing capacity. The company moved quickly to shut down two factories for several months each and to switch production in another from the Highlander SUV to the Prius. Every forward-looking company must make long-term investment decisions based on uncertain predictions. Despite using the best information available at the time the decision is made, some predictions subsequently turn out to be incorrect. Consequently, some investment decisions do not turn out well, as illustrated by some of Toyota's investments in production facilities. This chapter focuses on investment decisions, which are critical to the long-term success of most organizations. ■

© EPA European Pressphoto Agency B.V./Alamy

Capital Budgeting for Programs or Projects

The Toyota Prius was the first mass-produced hybrid vehicle.

Major corporations such as Toyota are not the only companies that face decisions about capital investment and expansion. Every company makes decisions about when and how to spend money on major projects. This chapter concentrates on investment decisions for programs or projects that affect financial results over a period longer than just the current year. Such decisions typically require commitment of relatively large amounts of resources—called capital outlays—in anticipation of future benefits that are often uncertain. The term **capital budgeting** describes the long-term planning for long-term investment decisions such as (1) investment in new equipment, (2) replacement of assets, (3) expansion of facilities, (4) investment in employee training programs, or (5) expenditures to improve process efficiency and reduce future costs. We discuss a number of specific investment examples in this chapter, but it is important to remember that capital-budgeting concepts apply to a wide variety of decisions.

capital budgeting
The long-term planning for investment commitments with returns spread over time, typically over multiple years.

Capital budgeting has three phases: (1) identifying potential investments, (2) choosing which investments to make (which includes gathering data to aid the decision), and (3) follow-up monitoring, or "post-audit," of the investments. The cost-management system often provides information to help managers assess the future cash flows needed as inputs to capital-budgeting models. In addition, accountants provide post-audit information to assess the success of projects. Let's take a look at how some capital-budgeting models work.

Discounted-Cash-Flow Models

The most widely used capital-budgeting models are **discounted-cash-flow (DCF) models**. These models focus on a project's cash inflows and outflows while taking into account the time value of money. The value of a dollar today is greater than the value of a dollar to be received in the future. Therefore, investors expect to be repaid more than the original amount invested, and the excess of the amount repaid over the original amount is interest. On the investor side of the transaction, this interest is income, while on the borrower's side of the transaction, this interest is expense. More than 85% of the large industrial firms in the United States evaluate investment decisions using the DCF model, which explicitly incorporates the time value of money.

discounted-cash-flow (DCF) models
Capital-budgeting models that focus on cash inflows and outflows while taking into account the time value of money.

Major Aspects of DCF

As the name suggests, DCF models focus on cash flows rather than on net income. These models convert future cash flows into the corresponding **present values**, the value today of a future cash flow. Companies invest cash today because they expect to receive a larger amount of cash in future periods. DCF models compare today's cash outflows with the predicted future cash inflows and outflows by converting all cash flows into present values based on the theory of compound interest. If your knowledge of compound interest and time value of money is a little rusty, be sure to read Appendix B, pages A5–A10, before you continue with the rest of the discussion of DCF methods.

present value (PV)
The value today of a future cash flow.

Net Present Value (NPV)

net-present-value (NPV) method
A discounted-cash-flow approach to capital budgeting that computes the present value of all expected future cash flows using a required rate of return.

required rate of return (hurdle rate, discount rate)
The minimum acceptable rate of return, based on the firm's cost of capital.

We will focus on the most widely-used version of DCF, the **net-present-value (NPV) method**. The NPV method computes the present value of all cash flows using an interest rate called the **required rate of return**. This rate, also called the **hurdle rate** or **discount rate**, depends on the risk of a proposed project—the higher the risk, the higher the rate. It is often based on the cost of capital—what the firm pays to acquire more capital. This rate is applied to the cash flows for a project, which can be classified into one of three categories: 1) the net initial cash flow, the cash outflow for acquisition of assets less any offsetting cash inflows from disposal of existing assets; 2) periodic cash flows during the life of the project; and 3) net cash flow at termination of the project.

Using the required rate, managers sum the present values of all expected future cash flows associated with the project and subtract the initial investment. This total is the project's **net present value** (**NPV**). A positive NPV means that the present value of the project's future cash flows exceeds the investment, so the project should be undertaken. Conversely, a negative NPV means the investment exceeds the present value (PV) of the future cash flows, so the project should not be undertaken.

Objective 1

Describe capital-budgeting decisions and use the net-present-value (NPV) method to make such decisions.

net present value
The sum of the present values of all expected cash flows.

Applying the NPV Method

To illustrate how DCF models work, we will use the following example throughout the rest of this section: Managers at Toyota's Tupelo, Mississippi, plant are contemplating the purchase of new, more efficient auto painting equipment that they expect will increase efficiency and produce operating savings. The cash flows associated with this investment consist of 1) an initial investment outflow of $5,827 at time zero for the acquisition cost, followed by 2) annual cash savings (equivalent to a cash inflow) of $2,000 at the end of each year for the 4-year life of the equipment, and 3) no net cash flow at termination of the project. The required rate of return is 10% per year.

To apply the NPV method, you can use the following three steps, which we illustrate in Exhibit 11-1.

1. *Identify the amount and timing of relevant expected cash inflows and outflows:* The right-hand side of Exhibit 11-1 sketches these cash flows, with outflows shown in parentheses. Sketches like this one can help you visualize costs and cost relationships over time.

	Present Value of $1, Discounted at 10%	Total Present Value	Sketch of Cash Flows at End of Year				
			0	1	2	3	4
Approach 1: Discounting Each Year's Cash Flows Separately*							
Cash flows							
Annual savings	.9091	$1,818		$2,000			
	.8264	1,653			$2,000		
	.7513	1,503				$2,000	
	.6830	1,366					$2,000
Present value of future inflows		$6,340					
Initial outlay	1.0000	(5,827)	$(5,827)				
Net present value		$ 513					
Approach 2: Using Annuity Table†							
Annual savings	3.1699	$6,340		$2,000	$2,000	$2,000	$2,000
Initial outlay	1.0000	(5,827)	$(5,827)				
Net present value		$ 513					

*Present values from Table B-1, Appendix B, page A6.

†Present value of annuity from Table B-2, Appendix B, page A9. (Incidentally, calculators or computers may give slightly different answers than do the tables because of rounding differences.)

Exhibit 11-1

Net-Present-Value Method
Initial investment, $5,827. Useful life, 4 years. Annual cash inflow from operations, $2,000. Required rate of return, 10%. Cash outflows are in parentheses, while cash inflows are not. Total present values are rounded to the nearest dollar.

2. *Find the present value of each expected cash inflow or outflow:* Examine Table B-1 in Appendix B on page A6. Find the PV factor for each year's cash flow from the correct row and column of the table. Multiply each expected cash inflow or outflow by the appropriate PV factor. For example, the present value of the $2,000 cash savings that will occur 2 years hence is $2,000 × .8264 = $1,653. As another example, the initial acquisition cost outflow of $5,827 at time zero has a present value of $5,827.

3. *Sum the individual present values:* The sum is the project's NPV. Accept a project whose NPV is positive, and reject a project whose NPV is negative.

The present value of the initial cash investment is $5,827, the present value of the four annual cash inflows is $6,340, and there are no cash flows at termination. Thus, the net present value of all the cash flows is $6,340 − $5,827 = $513. Because the net present value is positive, Toyota's managers should accept the investment.

Choice of the Correct Table

Exhibit 11-1 also shows another way to calculate the NPV, shown as approach 2. The basic steps are the same as for approach 1. The only difference is that approach 2 uses Table B-2 in Appendix B (see page A9) to find the present value of the four annual amounts. Table B-2 is an annuity table that provides discount factors for computing the PV of a series of equal cash flows at equal intervals. Because the four annual cash flows in our example are all equal, you can use Table B-2 to make one PV computation instead of using Table B-1 to make four individual computations. Table B-2 merely sums up the pertinent PV factors of Table B-1. Therefore, the annuity factor for 4 years at 10% is[1]

$$.9091 + .8264 + .7513 + .6830 = 3.1698$$

Beware of using the wrong table. Use Table B-1 for discounting individual amounts and Table B-2 for a series of equal amounts spread evenly in time. Instead of using Tables B-1 and B-2, you can use the PV function on a handheld calculator or in a spreadsheet program. When you use a calculator or spreadsheet, you still need to be sure to choose the proper function to discount a single amount or to discount a series of equal amounts. While you are initially learning the NPV method, we encourage you to use the tables and explicitly draw out all the cash flows. This will help you better understand the process of PV computation. Once you are comfortable with the method, you can take advantage of the speed and convenience of calculators and spreadsheets.

Making Managerial Decisions

For major capital investments, managers usually prepare a detailed NPV analysis. For smaller items, sometimes they make a quick calculation or use intuition. Suppose you are in charge of a company's mail room. An employee has suggested the purchase of a $12,000 letter sorting machine. She says that it will save 1 hour per day for 250 working days a year for an employee making a total of $12 per hour. She indicates that the $12,000 expenditure will save $15,000 over the machine's 5-year life. Should you approve the purchase?

Answers

The employee's calculation of the $15,000 total savings is correct:

1 hour × 250 days × $12/hour × 5 years = $15,000

However, her calculation ignores the time value of money. The $12,000 must be paid immediately, and the $15,000 of savings is spread over the next 5 years at $3,000 per year. You know that the present value of the savings is less than the $15,000 total, but the exact amount depends on the required

rate of return. Therefore, you must know the required rate before you can answer the question.

Suppose the required rate is 10%. Using Table B-1, the NPV is negative, $(627.90):

.9091 × $3,000 + .8264 × $3,000 + .7513 × $3,000 + .6830 × $3,000 + .6209 × $3,000 − $12,000 = $2,727.30 + $2,479.20 + $2,253.90 + $2,049.00 + $1,862.70 = $11,372.10 − 12,000 = $(627.90).

Using Table B-2, the NPV is 3.7908 × $3,000 − $12,000 = $11,372.40 − $12,000 = $(627.60), which differs from the Table B-1 result by $.30 due to rounding error. With a 10% required rate, the NPV is negative and the investment should not be accepted.

Now, suppose instead the required rate is 5%. The lower discount rate increases the present value of the annual cost savings and the NPV becomes positive. Using Table B-2, 4.3295 × $3,000 − $12,000 = $12,988.50 − $12,000 = $988.50. With this change in the required rate of return, the investment should be accepted.

---

[1]Rounding error causes a .0001 difference between the Table B-2 factor and the summation of Table B-1 factors. See Appendix B for further discussion of the effect of rounding error.

Effect of Required Rate

We have just seen that a decrease in the required rate of return can change the NPV from negative to positive. In general, the higher the required rate of return, the lower the PV of each future cash inflow. Why? Because the higher the rate of return, the more it costs you to wait for the cash rather than having it available today. Thus, higher required rates lead to lower NPVs.

For example, at a rate of 16%, the NPV of the project in Exhibit 11-1 would be −$231. That is, $2,000 × 2.7982 = $5,596, which is $231 less than the investment of $5,827, instead of the +$513 computed with a 10% rate. (PV factor 2.7982 is taken from Table B-2 in Appendix B on page A9.) When the required rate of return is 16% rather than 10%, the project should be rejected.

Assumptions of the NPV Model

We make two major assumptions when using the NPV model. First, we assume a world of certainty. That is, we act as if the predicted cash inflows and outflows are certain to occur at the times specified. Second, we assume perfect capital markets. That is, if we need to get extra cash or invest excess cash at any time, we can borrow or lend money at the same interest rate, which is our required rate of return. In a world that meets these assumptions, no model could possibly be better than the NPV model.

Unfortunately, the real world has neither certainty nor perfect capital markets. Nevertheless, the NPV model is usually preferred to other models because the assumptions of most other models are even less realistic. The NPV model is not perfect, but it generally meets our cost-benefit criterion. That is, the benefit of better decisions based on NPV is greater than the cost of applying it. More sophisticated models often do not improve decisions enough to be worth their cost.

Review of Decision Rules

Be sure that you understand why the NPV method works, not just how to apply it. The decision maker in our example cannot directly compare an immediate outflow of $5,827 with a series of four future inflows of $2,000 each because of the time value of money. The NPV model adds together the net monetary units (such as dollars, euros, or yen) after converting them to their present value at time zero. The required rate of return measures the cost of using money.

Internal Rate of Return (IRR) Model

internal rate of return (IRR) model
A capital-budgeting model that determines the interest rate, the IRR, at which the NPV equals zero.

Another popular DCF model is the **internal rate of return (IRR) model**. This model determines the interest rate at which the NPV equals zero. The rate that makes the NPV = 0 is called the IRR. For Toyota's painting equipment, we know that a rate of 10% yields a positive NPV (as shown in Exhibit 11-1) while a rate of 16% yields a negative NPV (as discussed in the Effect of Required Rate section). Therefore, we know that the IRR, the rate that yields a NPV=0, is somewhere between 10% and 16%. The following graph plots the relationship between NPV and required rate of return for our example:

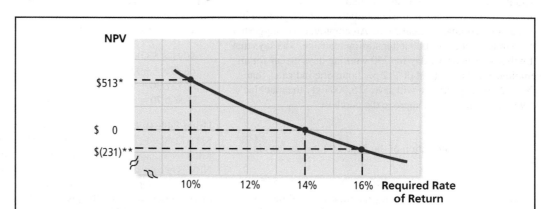

*($2,000 × 3.1699) − $5,827 = $513
**($2,000 × 2.7982) − $5,827 = $(231)

The IRR for our example can be found by trying values between 10% and 16%, converging on the return that yields a present value of zero. Most spreadsheets and many financial calculators include functions that solve for the IRR. As shown in the graph, the IRR for the painting equipment example is 14%. To confirm that this is the IRR, compute the NPV at a rate of 14%:

Outflow in today's dollars	$(5,827)
Inflows equivalent in today's dollars at 14%	5,827*
Net present value	$ 0

*$2,000 × 2.9137 from Table B-2 = $5,827.

The calculation confirms that at a required rate of return of 14%, the NPV is zero, and at this rate the decision maker is indifferent between having $5,827 now or having a stream of four annual inflows of $2,000 each.

Finance textbooks provide descriptions of the IRR method, and we will not go into details here. However, in most cases the IRR method gives equivalent decisions to the NPV method. In general, we find the following:

If IRR > required rate of return, then NPV > 0 and we should accept the project.

If IRR < required rate of return, then NPV < 0 and we should reject the project.

Because of the equivalence of NPV and IRR models for most investment proposals, we use only the NPV model for all the illustrations in this chapter.

Real Options

Whereas the IRR model is generally just an alternative formulation that yields decisions equivalent to the NPV model, the use of real options is an improvement on NPV. A **real options model** recognizes the value of contingent investments—that is, investments that a company can adjust as it learns more about their potential for success. For example, a project that a company can implement in stages, where investment in one stage occurs only if the previous stage was successful, has an advantage over an "all or nothing" project, one where the entire investment must take place up front.

The real options framework has some non-intuitive implications. For example, suppose that a project can either be implemented all at once or implemented in stages at greater cost. Despite the higher cost, staging the project might nonetheless be a preferred alternative if the company gains enough information in the early stages to make better decisions in the later stages. A real options model recognizes the value of such staging. Like the IRR model, we will leave the details of real options to the finance textbooks. However, real options models are an important innovation, and these models are becoming increasingly popular.

real options model
A capital-budgeting model that recognizes the value of contingent investments—that is, investments that a company can adjust as it learns more about its potential for success.

Sensitivity Analysis and Risk Assessment in DCF Models

The NPV model finds the present value of a set of predicted cash flows, but because the future is uncertain, actual cash inflows may differ from what was predicted. Managers often use sensitivity analysis to deal with this uncertainty. Sensitivity analysis determines what would occur if actual cash inflows and outflows differ from what was predicted. The analysis addresses what-if questions such as *What will happen to the NPV if my predictions of useful life or periodic cash flows or cash flows at termination change?*

Sensitivity analysis allows managers to find immediate answers about the effects of possible future events. It also helps managers evaluate prediction risk by showing how sensitive the decision is to changes in predictions. If only a small change in predicted cash flows would change the NPV for a project from positive NPV to negative, the project is subject to high prediction risk. The best way to understand sensitivity analysis is to see it in action, so let's apply sensitivity analysis to our example.

The Toyota managers know that the annual cash savings in Exhibit 11-1 could fall below the predicted level of $2,000. Suppose the managers want to know how far the annual cash savings could drop before the NPV becomes negative? The managers find the value of annual cash inflows that result in NPV = 0:

$$NPV = 0$$
$$(3.1699 \times \text{cash flow}) - \$5,827 = 0$$
$$\text{cash flow} = \$5,827 \div 3.1699$$
$$= \$1,838$$

Objective 2

Use sensitivity analysis to evaluate the effect of changes in predictions on investment decisions.

This sensitivity analysis shows that if the annual cash savings fall below $1,838, the NPV falls below zero, and the managers would reject the project. Therefore, annual cash savings can drop only $2,000 − $1,838 = $162, or 8.1% below the predicted amount, before the managers would change their decision.

Sensitivity analysis can become complicated very quickly, and manual calculations can be complex and tedious. Fortunately, there is a good deal of sensitivity analysis software available that does the calculations, thus, permitting managers and accountants to focus on interpreting the results of the analysis.

The NPV Comparison of Two Projects

Objective 3

Calculate the NPV difference between two projects using both the total project and differential approaches.

So far we have seen how to use the NPV method to evaluate a single project. In practice, managers rarely look at only one project or option at a time. Instead, managers compare several options to see which is the best or most profitable. We will now see how to use NPV to compare two or more alternatives.

Total Project Versus Differential Approach

Two common methods for comparing alternatives are (1) the total project approach and (2) the differential approach.

total project approach
A method for comparing alternatives that computes the total impact on cash flows for each alternative and then converts these total cash flows to their present values.

The **total project approach** computes the total impact on cash flows for each alternative and then converts these total cash flows to their present values. The alternative with the largest NPV of total cash flows is best. The total project approach is the most popular approach, and it can be used with any number of alternatives.

The **differential approach** computes the differences in cash flows between alternatives and then converts these differences to their present values. We cannot use this method to compare more than two alternatives.

differential approach
A method for comparing alternatives that computes the differences in cash flows between alternatives and then converts these differences in cash flows to their present values.

Let's compare the differential and total project approaches. Consider a motor that drives one of the assembly lines at **Toyota**'s San Antonio plant. Assume that Toyota purchased the motor 3 years ago for $56,000. It has a remaining useful life of 5 years but will require a major overhaul at the end of two more years at a cost of $10,000. Its disposal value now is $20,000. Its predicted disposal value in 5 years is $8,000, assuming that the company does the scheduled $10,000 major overhaul. The predicted cash-operating costs of this motor are $40,000 annually. A sales representative has offered a substitute motor for $51,000. The new motor will reduce annual cash-operating costs by $10,000, will not require any overhauls, will have a useful life of 5 years, and will have a disposal value of $3,000. If the required rate of return is 14%, what should Toyota do to minimize long-run costs: keep the old machine or replace it with the new one? (Try to solve this problem yourself before examining the solution that follows.)

Regardless of the approach used, perhaps the hardest part of making capital-budgeting decisions is predicting the relevant cash flows accurately and completely. Seeing which events will cause money to flow either in or out can be complex, especially when there are many sources of cash flows. However, you cannot compare alternatives if you do not know their cash flows, so the first step for either the total project or differential approach is to estimate the relevant cash flows. Exhibit 11-2 sketches these cash flows for each approach.

Total Project Approach: For the total project approach we list the cash flows for each project, replace or keep, separately. We then determine the NPV of the cash flows for each individual project and choose the project with the largest positive NPV or smallest negative NPV. Exhibit 11-2 shows that the NPV of replacing the motor, −132,435, is better than the − $140,864 NPV of keeping the old motor. The advantage is $140,864 − $132,435 = $8,429. Most cash flows are negative because these are the costs of operating the motor. The alternative with the lowest cost—the smallest negative NPV—is the most desirable.

Differential Approach: For the differential approach, we first list the difference in cash flow for each year. In other words, assume implementation of one of the projects as a baseline and perform a differential analysis as discussed in Chapter 6. Suppose we use keeping the old machine as the baseline. Then we subtract the cash flows for keeping from the cash flows for replacement. This isolates the advantages (cash inflows or cost savings) and disadvantages (cash outflows) of replacement compared to the baseline, keeping the machine. (Remember that cash inflows are positive numbers, while cash outflows are negative.) Next, calculate the NPV of the differential cash flows.

Sketch of After-Tax Cash
Flows at End of Year

	Present Value Discount Factor, at 14%	Total Present Value	0	1	2	3	4	5
I. Total Project Approach								
A. Replace								
Recurring cash operating costs, using an annuity table*	3.4331	$(102,993)		$(30,000)	$(30,000)	$(30,000)	$(30,000)	$(30,000)
Disposal value, end of year 5	.5194	1,558						$ 3,000
Initial required investment	1.0000	(31,000)	$(31,000)					
NPV of net cash flows		$(132,435)						
B. Keep								
Recurring cash operating costs, using an annuity table*	3.4331	$(137,324)		$(40,000)	$(40,000)	$(40,000)	$(40,000)	$(40,000)
Overhaul, end of year 2	.7695	(7,695)			$(10,000)			
Disposal value, end of year 5	.5194	4,155						$ 8,000
NPV of net cash flows		$(140,864)						
Difference in NPV between the alternatives		$ 8,429						
II. Differential Approach								
A–B. Analysis confined to differences								
Recurring cash operating savings, using an annuity table*	3.4331	$ 34,331		$ 10,000	$ 10,000	$ 10,000	$ 10,000	$ 10,000
Overhaul avoided, end of year 2	.7695	7,695			$ 10,000			
Difference in disposal values, end of year 5	.5194	(2,597)						$ (5,000)
Incremental initial investment	1.0000	(31,000)	$(31,000)					
Difference in NPV between alternatives		$ 8,429						

*Table B-2, Appendix B.

Exhibit 11-2

Total Project Versus Differential Approach to Net Present Value

If the NPV is positive, choose the replacement alternative; if it is negative, choose the baseline alternative to keep the motor. Whereas the total project approach computed the difference in the NPVs of the two projects, the differential method computes the NPV of the difference in cash flows of the two projects. Both give the same total difference, an $8,429 advantage to replacement.

Exhibit 11-2 illustrates that both methods produce the same answer as long as you are considering only two alternatives. However, to compare more than two alternatives, you should use the total project approach.

Summary Problem for Your Review

PROBLEM

Review the example shown in Exhibit 11-2, page 441. Conduct three independent sensitivity analyses:

1. Compute the difference in the NPV of the alternatives if the required rate of return were 20% instead of 14%.
2. Compute the difference in the NPV of the alternatives if predicted cash operating costs of the new motor were $35,000 annually instead of $30,000, using the 14% discount rate.
3. By how much may the annual cash operating savings fall short of the $10,000 predicted amount before the difference in NPV between the alternatives reaches zero? Use the original discount rate of 14%.

SOLUTION

1. You can use either the total project approach or the differential approach. The differential approach shows the following:

	Present Value
Recurring cash operating savings, using an annuity table (Table B-2, p. A9): 2.9906 × $10,000 =	$ 29,906
Overhaul avoided: .6944 × $10,000 =	6,944
Difference in disposal values: .4019 × $5,000 =	(2,010)
Incremental initial investment	(31,000)
Difference in NPV between the alternatives	$ 3,840

With a 20% required rate of return, replacement is still the preferred alternative. However, the difference in NPV is reduced from the $8,429 shown in Exhibit 11-2 to $3,840.

2.

Difference in NPV value in Exhibit 11-2	$ 8,429
Present value of additional $5,000 annual operating costs 3.4331 × $5,000	(17,166)
Difference in NPV between the alternatives	$ (8,737)

With $5,000 less in annual savings, the new motor yields a negative difference in the NPV between the alternatives, and therefore is not desirable.

3. Let X = annual cash operating savings and find the value of X so that the difference in NPV between the two alternatives = 0. Then,

$$0 = 3.4331(X) + \$7,695 - \$2,597 - \$31,000$$
$$3.4331(X) = \$25,902$$
$$X = \$7,545$$

(Note that the $7,695, $2,597, and $31,000 are shown at the bottom of Exhibit 11-2.)

If the annual savings fall from $10,000 to $7,545, a decrease of $2,455 or almost 25%, the NPV will fall to zero.

An alternative way to obtain the same answer would be to divide the NPV of $8,429 (see bottom of Exhibit 11-2) by 3.4331, obtaining $2,455, the amount of the annual difference in savings that will eliminate the $8,429 of NPV.

Relevant Cash Flows

Predicting cash flows is often the hardest part of capital budgeting. We organize the discussion of predicting cash flows into three project phases: (1) cash flows at project initiation, (2) cash flows at project termination, and (3) periodic cash flows between project initiation and termination.

Objective 4

Identify relevant cash flows for NPV analyses.

Predicting Relevant Cash Flows

INITIAL CASH INFLOWS AND OUTFLOWS   These cash flows include both outflows for the purchase and installation of new equipment and other assets (such as additional investments in working capital) required by the project and cash inflows or outflows from disposal of any items that are replaced. For example, in Exhibit 11-2, we subtracted the $20,000 cash inflow from selling the old motor that was being replaced from the $51,000 cash outflow to purchase the new motor, resulting in the initial net cash outflow of $31,000. As another example, if instead of selling the old motor the company had to pay to dismantle it, the net cash outflow at project initiation would be $51,000 plus the cost of dismantling the old motor.

CASH INFLOWS AND OUTFLOWS AT TERMINATION   At project termination, assets may have cash disposal values that represent a cash inflow. In other cases, there may be costs at termination to dispose of an asset that represent a cash outflow.

OPERATING CASH FLOWS DURING THE LIFE OF THE PROJECT   The major purpose of most investments is to affect periodic cash inflows and outflows during the life of the project. Many of these effects are difficult to measure, and three points deserve special mention:

1. The only relevant cash flows are those that will differ among alternatives, and it is frequently difficult to identify exactly which costs will differ. Fixed overhead will often be the same under all the available alternatives. If so, you can safely ignore it.
2. We treat a reduction in a cash outflow (a cash savings) the same as a cash inflow—both signify increases in value. Similarly, we treat a reduction in a cash inflow the same as a cash outflow—both signify decreases in value.
3. Remember that you are predicting cash inflows and outflows, not revenues and expenses. When there are differences between accrual basis revenues and expenses versus the corresponding cash inflows and cash outflows, the DCF model requires you to use the cash flow. For example, we might record a $10,000 sale on credit as accrual revenue in one period but if the related cash inflow comes in a later period, the $10,000 cash inflow will be recognized in the DCF model in the later period. In this chapter, we generally assume that cash inflows are equivalent to accrual revenues and that cash outflows are equivalent to accrual expenses, except in two major areas—depreciation and gains or losses on disposal of assets.

There is no cash outflow corresponding to depreciation expense in NPV calculations. Why not? Because depreciation expense is not a cash flow. Depreciation is an accrual expense that allocates the cost of a long-lived asset across the periods during which the asset is used. It is easy to confuse depreciation and cash flows because they are related to a common set of facts. Suppose a company acquires a machine for $54,000 that will be used for 5 years and then sold for $4,000. For NPV purposes, the relevant cash flows are a $54,000 cash outflow at acquisition and a $4,000 cash inflow at disposal. For financial reporting purposes, depreciation expense is the $54,000 acquisition cost less the $4,000 disposal value, a total of $50,000 spread across the 5-year life of the asset. For NPV purposes, it is incorrect to account for the acquisition and disposal cash flows and then also deduct depreciation over the asset's life as cash outflows—this would be like counting the net of the acquisition cost and disposal value twice.

The accrual gain or loss on disposal of an asset being replaced is another potential source of confusion. The gain or loss calculated by comparing the disposal value of the asset with its depreciated book value is not the cash flow. Rather, the cash flow is the disposal value. For example, suppose the asset in the previous example was purchased to replace an asset with a book value of $5,000. If the actual cash disposal value of the asset being replaced is $6,000, there is a gain on disposal of $1,000. Is the relevant initial cash flow from disposal of the replaced asset the $1,000 gain, the $5,000 book value, or the $6,000 selling price? It is the $6,000 selling price, the cash inflow from selling the asset that is being replaced.

Business First

Does DCF Apply to Technology Investments?

Although DCF models are widely used, some have criticized them for leading to overly cautious investment decisions in information technology (IT). The critics maintain that the benefits of IT investments are difficult to quantify and such investments lead to unforeseen opportunities. By ignoring some of the potential benefits and opportunities, companies pass up desirable IT investments.

The economic shakeout in 2001 and 2002 identified the winners and losers—and there were plenty of both. Winners (identified by *BusinessWeek*) included Expedia, Amazon, eBay, Yahoo!, and Dell. Losers, at least in the short run, included Hewlett-Packard, Barnes & Noble, AOL Time Warner, drkoop.com, and many startups. What differentiated winners from losers? Partly it was how they evaluated capital investment decisions. Some were overly cautious in employing technology. But others forgot the basic economics of investment analysis. Instead of focusing on cash flows and DCF analysis, companies touted their revenue per dollar of investment or, even worse, Web site hits per dollar of investment. They forgot that only positive net cash flows generate value. Increasing revenues are worse than worthless if related expenses grow faster so that net cash flows are negative. No one becomes rich because of an increasing number of visits to their Web site if the visits do not translate into cash flows.

How did the winners approach capital-budgeting decisions? First, they identified ways that technology solutions could generate cash—either new inflows or savings of outflows. Their analysis showed whether technology investments would become profitable and how profitable they would be. Second, the companies did not try to protect existing business while simultaneously pursuing new technology. If new technology served customers better than existing technology, companies lagging in technology would lose them anyway. And finally, they used DCF analysis. They realized that dollars in the future are worth less than those today, so they needed large future profits to justify investments that would not pay off in the short term.

In the aftermath of the technology crash, many companies focused on how to correctly apply DCF to technology investments. Microsoft developed guides to its software that showed how to apply DCF to investments in technology and developed blogs to allow managers to share experiences applying DCF methods.

Companies also used new developments in finance and accounting to aid in the application of DCF analyses. For example, Scott Gamster of Grant Thornton's Performance Management Practice suggested using activity-based costing (ABC) to better estimate future cash flows. Analyses that focused primarily on how technology reduced direct costs ignored potentially large savings in indirect costs. Because an ABC system focuses on indirect costs, it can help identify other cost impacts of new technology systems. The attention to activities helps managers better assess the various impacts of new systems.

Many firms also began to apply real options theory to value technology investments. For example, the Yankee 24, a shared electronic banking network in New England that subsequently merged with NYCE Payments Network, applied real options theory to the decision on timing the deployment of point-of-sale debit services. The method explicitly recognized the future opportunities created by a current investment decision, and it used the complete range of possible outcomes to determine the investment's value.

Criticisms of using DCF for investment decisions were primarily criticisms of incorrect or incomplete applications of it. The criticisms have led to a better understanding of how to apply DCF to technology investments and to refinements in DCF analysis that are especially useful to investments in technology.

Sources: Adapted from S. Gamster, "Using Activity Based Management to Justify ERP Implementations," *Journal of Cost Management*, September/October 1999, pp. 24–33; M. Benaroch and R. J. Kauffman, "A Case for Using Real Options Pricing Analysis to Evaluate Information Technology Project Investments," *Information Systems Research*, March 1999, pp. 70–76; "The E-Business Surprise," *BusinessWeek*, May 12, 2003, pp. 60–68; Microsoft Dynamics, "Using ROI analysis to prioritize technology purchases," March 7, 2007, http://community.dynamics.com/blogs/articles/archive/2007/03/07/using-roi-analysis-to-prioritize-technology-purchases.aspx.

Cash Flows for Investments in Technology

Many capital-budgeting decisions compare a potential investment in improved technology versus the alternative of retaining the existing technology. For example, consider investment in a highly automated production system to replace a traditional system. Cash flows predicted for the automated system should be compared with those predicted for continuation of the existing system into the future. However, it is important to note that the current cash flows for the existing system may not be the expected future cash flows from the existing system. Why? Because the competitive environment is changing. If competitors invest in automated systems, continuing with an existing system that produces lower quality or less reliable output may cause a decline in sales and cash inflows.

Suppose a company currently has a $10,000 net cash inflow annually using a traditional system. Investing in an automated system will increase the net cash inflow to $12,000. Failure to switch to the automated system will result in lower quality output and cause net cash inflows to fall to $8,000. The relevant annual cash flow during the life of the investment is a net cash inflow of $12,000 − $8,000 = $4,000, not $12,000 − $10,000 = $2,000. Similar situations arise in many technology investments such as those described in the Business First box above.

Income Tax Effects

For companies that are subject to income taxes, another type of cash flow enters into capital-budgeting decisions: income taxes. (Tax-exempt organizations such as churches, schools, or governmental units do not pay income taxes and therefore do not have tax-related cash flows.) Income taxes paid by companies are cash outflows. Savings of income taxes that would have been paid are equivalent to cash inflows.

The basic role of tax-related cash flows in capital budgeting does not differ from that of any other cash outflow. However, income taxes modify the cash flows of projects for taxable entities by making the government a profit-sharing partner. For example, if the annual cash inflow from a project is $1 million, a 40% tax rate shrinks the net inflow to $600,000. Why? Because the company would have to pay 40% × $1 million = $400,000 of the inflow in taxes, leaving just $600,000 net inflow for the company. The cash flow before considering the effect of income taxes is called the pretax cash flow (in this example, $1 million), and the amount after the effect of taxes is the **after-tax cash flow** ($600,000). All of our previous examples in the chapter have ignored the effect of taxes so the cash flows discussed have been pretax cash flows.

Corporations in the United States pay both federal and state taxes on their income. Federal income tax rates rise as income rises. The current federal tax rate on ordinary corporate taxable income below $50,000 is 15%. Rates then increase until companies with taxable income over $335,000 pay between 34% and 38% on additional income. State tax rates vary widely from state to state. Therefore, the total tax rate a company has to pay, federal rates plus state rates, also varies widely.

In capital budgeting, the relevant tax rate is the **marginal income tax rate**, the tax rate paid on incremental cash flows from a project. Suppose a corporation pays income taxes of 15% on the first $50,000 of pretax income and 30% on pretax income over $50,000. What is the company's marginal income tax rate when it initially has $75,000 of pretax income? The marginal rate is 30%, because the company will pay 30% of any incremental income in taxes. In contrast, the company's average income tax rate is only 20% (that is, 15% × $50,000 + 30% × $25,000 = $15,000 of taxes on $75,000 of pretax income). The marginal tax rate generally depends on both the initial amount of income and the amount of incremental income. Suppose the initial pretax income had been $40,000 in our example. Then the marginal tax rate on incremental income up to $10,000 would be 15% but incremental income beyond $10,000 would increase the marginal rate to 30%. When we assess tax effects of capital-budgeting decisions in the examples that follow, we always assume a single marginal tax rate applies to all incremental cash flows for a project.

Effects of Depreciation Deductions

Organizations that pay income taxes generally keep two sets of books—one set that follows the rules for financial reporting and one set that follows the tax rules. This practice is not illegal or immoral—it is necessary. Tax reporting rules are designed to achieve certain social goals. These rules are in many instances different from the financial reporting rules designed to best measure an organization's financial results and position.

Managers have an obligation to stockholders to minimize taxes to the extent permitted by law. Minimization of taxes permitted by law is called tax avoidance. In contrast, reduction of taxes by illegally recording fictitious deductions or failing to report income is called tax evasion. Managers who avoid taxes get bonuses; those who evade taxes often land in jail. Because the line between tax evasion and tax avoidance is sometimes gray, it is important to act both legally and ethically when trying to minimize taxes.

One item that usually differs between tax reporting and financial reporting is depreciation. Recall that depreciation spreads the cost of an asset over its useful life. U.S. tax laws allow **accelerated depreciation**, which charges a larger proportion of an asset's cost to the earlier years and less to later years. In contrast, an asset's depreciation for financial reporting purposes is often the same each year, called straight-line depreciation. For example, a $10,000 asset depreciated over a 5-year useful life results in straight-line depreciation of $10,000 ÷ 5 = $2,000 each year. In contrast, accelerated depreciation provides more than $2,000 of depreciation per year in the early years and less than $2,000 in the later years. In addition, U.S. tax laws generally permit companies to spread the cost of an asset over a **recovery period**—the number of years over which a company can depreciate an asset for tax purposes—that is shorter than the assets' useful life that the company uses to calculate depreciation for financial reporting purposes.

Objective 5

Compute the after-tax net present values of projects.

after-tax cash flow
The cash flow after the effect of income taxes, generally the pretax cash flow multiplied by (1 – marginal tax rate).

marginal income tax rate
The tax rate paid on incremental taxable income.

accelerated depreciation
A pattern of depreciation that charges a larger proportion of an asset's cost to the earlier years and less to later years.

recovery period
The number of years over which a company can depreciate an asset for tax purposes.

Annual Income Statement Effects		
(S)	Sales	$130,000
(E)	Less: Expenses, excluding depreciation	$ 70,000
(D)	Depreciation (straight-line)	25,000
	Total expenses	$ 95,000
	Income before taxes	$ 35,000
(T)	Income taxes at 40%	14,000
(I)	Net income	$ 21,000
	Total after-tax effect on cash is	
	either S − E − T = $130,000 − $70,000 − $14,000 = $46,000	
	or I + D = $21,000 + $25,000 = $46,000	

Annual Cash Flow Effects		
	Cash effects of operations:	
(S − E)	Pretax cash inflow from operations: $130,000 − $70,000	$ 60,000
	Multiplied by (1 − tax rate)	× .60
	After-tax cash inflow from operations	$ 36,000
	Cash effects of depreciation tax deduction:	
(D)	Depreciation tax deduction: $125,000 ÷ 5	$ 25,000
	Multiplied by tax rate	× .40
	Tax savings due to depreciation	10,000
	Total after-tax effect on cash	$ 46,000

Exhibit 11-3

Toyota Machine

Basic Analysis of Income Statement, Income Taxes, and Cash Flows

Exhibit 11-3 shows the interrelationship of income before taxes, income taxes, and depreciation for a hypothetical asset owned by Toyota. Assume that Toyota's U.S. operation purchases for $125,000 cash a machine that produces replacement parts used in Lexus exhaust systems. The machine has a 5-year recovery period and also a 5-year useful life. Management expects the value of the machine at the end of its useful life to be zero. Toyota uses straight-line depreciation for both financial reporting and tax purposes, resulting in annual depreciation of $25,000. Using the machine produces annual sales revenue of $130,000 and expenses (excluding depreciation) of $70,000. For this example, and the remaining examples in this chapter, we assume that revenues equal cash inflows and that all expenses other than depreciation equal cash outflows. We also assume a marginal tax rate of 40% applies to all incremental cash flows and that the income tax flows occur at the same time as the related pretax cash flows. Here, we assume that both the net ($130,000 − $70,000) = $60,000 pretax cash inflow from the machine and the related tax payments occur at the end of each year during the 5-year life of the machine.

The bottom part of Exhibit 11-3 shows the three components of the after-tax cash flow: cash inflow from operations, income taxes on the inflows from operations, and income-tax savings from depreciation. Consider first the cash inflow from operations and the related tax effect. Each additional $1 of net cash inflow from operations also results in a cash outflow for income tax payments of $.40, leaving a net cash inflow of $.60. Thus, the after-tax effect of the $60,000 pretax net cash inflow from operations is an after-tax inflow of ($60,000 − (.4 × $60,000) = $60,000 × .6 = $36,000.

The cash flow effect of the depreciation tax deduction is a decrease in the cash outflow for income taxes, equivalent to a cash inflow. We compute the tax savings due to the depreciation tax deduction by multiplying the depreciation of $25,000 by the tax rate, or $25,000 × .40 = $10,000. The depreciation deduction reduces taxes, and thereby increases cash flows, by $10,000 annually.

Exhibit 11-4 analyzes the entire set of cash flows for Toyota's machine. The initial $125,000 investment buys two 5-year streams of cash: (1) net after-tax cash flows from operations of $36,000 annually plus (2) annual savings of $10,000 of income tax outflows due to the depreciation tax deduction over the recovery period. The after-tax NPV for the investment in this asset is $40,821, so Toyota management should accept it.

	12% Discount Factors, from Appropriate Tables	Total Present Value at 12%	Sketch of After-Tax Cash Flows at End of Year					
			0	1	2	3	4	5
Cash effects of operations, excluding depreciation, $60,000 × (1 − .4)	3.6048	$ 129,773		36,000	36,000	36,000	36,000	36,000
Cash effects of straight-line depreciation: savings of income taxes, $25,000 × .4	3.6048	36,048		10,000	10,000	10,000	10,000	10,000
Total after-tax effect on cash		165,821						
Investment	1.0000	(125,000)	(125,000)					
Net present value of the investment		$ 40,821						

Exhibit 11-4

Impact of Income Taxes on Capital-Budgeting Analysis

Assume: original cost of equipment, $125,000; 5-year recovery period with straight-line depreciation assumed for simplicity; 5-year useful life; zero terminal disposal value; pretax annual net cash inflow from operations, $60,000; income tax rate, 40%; required after-tax rate of return, 12%. All items are in dollars except discount factors. The after-tax cash flows are from Exhibit 11-3.

Summary Problem for Your Review

PROBLEM

Consider Toyota's purchase of the $125,000 machine analyzed in Exhibits 11-3 and 11-4. Suppose the machine had a useful life of 6 years, but the recovery period remains 5 years. What is the net present value of the investment?

SOLUTION

The present value of the tax savings will not change because only the recovery period, not the useful life, affects the depreciation deductions. The tax law specifies recovery periods for various types of depreciable assets. The economic useful life of the asset may be different than the recovery period permitted by tax law. Thus, a longer useful life for an asset increases the present value of the operating cash flows but does not change the PV of the tax savings.

There will be one extra year of operating savings in year 6. The present value of the additional operating savings in year 6 is $36,000 × .5066 = $18,238. Therefore, the net present value is $59,059:

Original NPV (from Exhibit 11-4)	$40,821
Added PV of savings in year 6	18,238
NPV	$59,059

Timing of Depreciation Tax Deductions and Cash Flow Effects

The value of the depreciation tax deduction depends not only on the amount of the reduction in cash payments for income taxes but also on the timing of the reduction. A $1 reduction now is worth more than a $1 reduction several years from now. To illustrate the importance of timing, reconsider the facts in Exhibit 11-4. Suppose that Toyota could deduct the entire initial investment immediately rather than spreading the cost over the 5-year life of the machine.

The immediate tax deduction of $125,000 would be the same as the total tax deduction of 5 × $25,000 = $125,000 in Exhibit 11-4, and the total reduction in tax payments would be 40% × $125,000 = $50,000 in both cases. However, because the tax savings occur sooner, the present value of the immediate $125,000 deduction is $50,000 compared to only $36,048 when the deduction is spread over 5 years. As the following calculations show, when the entire $125,000 is deductible immediately the NPV will rise from $40,821 to $54,773:

	Present Values	
	As in Exhibit 11-4	Complete Write-Off Immediately
Cash effects of operations	$ 129,773	$ 129,773
Cash effects of depreciation	36,048	50,000
Total after-tax effect on cash	165,821	179,773
Investment	(125,000)	(125,000)
Net present value	$ 40,821	$ 54,773

In general, the earlier you can take a depreciation deductions, the greater the PV of the income tax savings. Therefore, a shorter recovery period and a depreciation method that takes more of the depreciation sooner during the recovery period will increase the PV of the tax deduction.

Modified Accelerated Cost Recovery System (MACRS)

modified accelerated cost recovery system (MACRS)
The method companies use to depreciate most assets under U.S. income tax laws.

Depreciation methods that take more depreciation sooner are called accelerated depreciation methods. The example discussed in Exhibits 11-3 and 11-4 assumed that Toyota used straight-line depreciation for tax purposes. However, under U.S. income tax laws, companies depreciate most assets using the **modified accelerated cost recovery system (MACRS)**. This system specifies a recovery period and an accelerated depreciation schedule for all types of assets. The MACRS system places each asset in one of the eight classes shown in Exhibit 11-5.

Exhibit 11-5

Examples of Assets in Modified Accelerated Cost Recovery System (MACRS) Classes

3-year	Special tools for several specific industries, tractor units for over-the-road
5-year	Automobiles, trucks, research equipment, computers, machinery and equipment in selected industries
7-year	Office furniture, railroad tracks, machinery and equipment in a majority of industries
10-year	Water transportation equipment, machinery and equipment in selected industries
15-year	Most land improvements, machinery and equipment in selected industries
20-year	Farm buildings, electricity generation and distribution equipment
27.5-year	Residential rental property
31.5-year	Nonresidential real property

Exhibit 11-6

Selected MACRS Depreciation Schedules

Tax Year	3-Year Property	5-Year Property	7-Year Property	10-Year Property
1	33.33%	20.00%	14.29%	10.00%
2	44.45	32.00	24.49	18.00
3	14.81	19.20	17.49	14.40
4	7.41	11.52	12.49	11.52
5		11.52	8.93	9.22
6		5.76	8.92	7.37
7			8.93	6.55
8			4.46	6.55
9				6.56
10				6.55
11				3.28

Exhibit 11-6 presents MACRS depreciation schedules for recovery periods of 3, 5, 7, and 10 years. Note that each schedule extends 1 year beyond the recovery period because MACRS assumes one half-year of depreciation in the first year and one half-year in the final year. For example, a 3-year MACRS depreciation schedule has one half-year of depreciation in years 1 and 4 and a full year of depreciation in years 2 and 3. We can apply MACRS depreciation to the example in Exhibit 11-4 as follows, assuming that the machine that Toyota purchased is a 5-year MACRS asset:

Year	Tax Rate (1)	PV Factor at 12% (2)	Depreciation (3)	PV of Tax Savings (1) × (2) × (3)
1	.40	0.8929	$125,000 × .2000 = $25,000	$ 8,929
2	.40	0.7972	125,000 × .3200 = 40,000	12,755
3	.40	0.7118	125,000 × .1920 = 24,000	6,833
4	.40	0.6355	125,000 × .1152 = 14,400	3,660
5	.40	0.5674	125,000 × .1152 = 14,400	3,268
6	.40	0.5066	125,000 × .0576 = 7,200	1,459
				$36,904

How much did Toyota gain by using MACRS instead of straight-line depreciation? The $36,904 present value of tax savings is $856 higher with MACRS than the $36,048 present value achieved with straight-line depreciation (see Exhibit 11-4 on page 447).

Present Value of MACRS Depreciation Tax Deduction

The present value of the tax savings from depreciation is often referred to as the **depreciation tax shield**. As explained earlier, the value of a depreciation deduction depends on timing. Because MACRS specifies the timing of deductions for each recovery period, we can easily compute the present value of the depreciation tax shield for any recovery period.

Exhibit 11-7 provides present values for the depreciation deductions from $1 of investment using MACRS schedules for 3-, 5-, 7-, and 10-year recovery periods for a variety of interest

depreciation tax shield
The tax savings due to depreciation deductions, generally the present value of the product of the tax rate and the depreciation deduction.

Discount Rate	3-year	5-year	7-year	10-year
3%	0.9439	0.9215	0.9002	0.8698
4%	0.9264	0.8975	0.8704	0.8324
5%	0.9095	0.8746	0.8422	0.7975
6%	0.8931	0.8526	0.8155	0.7649
7%	0.8772	0.8315	0.7902	0.7344
8%	0.8617	0.8113	0.7661	0.7059
9%	0.8468	0.7919	0.7432	0.6792
10%	0.8322	0.7733	0.7214	0.6541
12%	0.8044	0.7381	0.6810	0.6084
14%	0.7782	0.7055	0.6441	0.5678
15%	0.7657	0.6902	0.6270	0.5492
16%	0.7535	0.6753	0.6106	0.5317
18%	0.7300	0.6473	0.5798	0.4993
20%	0.7079	0.6211	0.5517	0.4702
22%	0.6868	0.5968	0.5257	0.4439
24%	0.6669	0.5740	0.5019	0.4201
25%	0.6573	0.5631	0.4906	0.4090
26%	0.6479	0.5526	0.4798	0.3985
28%	0.6299	0.5327	0.4594	0.3787
30%	0.6128	0.5139	0.4404	0.3606
40%	0.5381	0.4352	0.3632	0.2896

Exhibit 11-7
Present Value of MACRS Depreciation Deductions for $1 Investment

rates. To see how these present values are derived, consider a company with a 5-year asset and a 12% required rate of return. The PV of $1 of MACRS depreciation is as follows:

Year	Depreciation* (1)	PV Factor at 12% (2)	PV of Depreciation (1) × (2)
1	$0.2000	0.8929	$0.1786
2	0.3200	0.7972	0.2551
3	0.1920	0.7118	0.1367
4	0.1152	0.6355	0.0732
5	0.1152	0.5674	0.0654
6	0.0576	0.5066	0.0292
Total Depreciation	$1.0000		
Present Value of $1 depreciation, shown in Exhibit 11-7			$0.7381

*From the 5-Year Property column of Exhibit 11-6.

You can find the PV of the depreciation tax shield from an investment in three steps:

1. Find the factor for the present value of the depreciation tax deductions from Exhibit 11-7 for the appropriate recovery period and required rate of return.
2. Multiply the factor by the amount of the investment to find the PV of the total tax deductions.
3. Multiply the PV of the total tax deductions by the marginal tax rate to find the PV of the total tax savings.

Consider Toyota's investment of $125,000 in a machine with a 5-year MACRS recovery period. A 12% after-tax required rate of return and a 40% tax rate produce a tax savings with a present value of .7381 × $125,000 × .40 = $36,905. (This differs by $1 from the $36,904 calculated earlier due only to the cumulative effect of rounding in the earlier calculation.)

Making Managerial Decisions

Why do managers prefer accelerated depreciation for tax purposes? Consider an investment of $100,000 in an asset with a 10-year economic life and a 10-year MACRS recovery period. The asset has no salvage value at the end of 10 years. The tax rate is 40%, and the required rate of return is 10%. What is the PV of the depreciation tax savings using straight-line (SL) depreciation? What is the PV of the depreciation tax savings using MACRS depreciation? Which depreciation method would you prefer if you were managing the company?

Answers

Straight-line depreciation = $10,000 per year, so tax savings with SL is .40 × $10,000 = $4,000 per year. The present value of the SL tax savings is $4,000 × 6.1446 = $24,578.40.

The PV of MACRS depreciation tax savings using Exhibit 11-7 is .6541 × $100,000 × .40 = $26,164.00. Although the total tax savings is $40,000 regardless of the depreciation method, the tax savings occur earlier under the MACRS accelerated depreciation schedule, which creates a greater PV by $26,164.00 – $24,578.40 = $1,585.60. By choosing MACRS rather than straight-line depreciation, the manager saves $1,585.60 for the company.

Tax Effects of Gains or Losses on Disposal at Termination

Objective 6

Explain the after-tax effect on cash received from the disposal of assets.

The disposal of equipment for cash can also affect income taxes. Suppose Toyota sells its $125,000 machine at the end of year 3 after taking 3 years of straight-line depreciation. If Toyota sells it for its net book value, $125,000 – (3 × $25,000) = $50,000, there is no taxable gain and therefore no effect on tax payments. If Toyota receives more than $50,000, there is a gain and an additional tax payment. If the company receives less than $50,000, there is a loss and a tax savings. The following table shows the effects on cash flow for sales prices of $70,000 and $20,000:

(a)	Cash proceeds of sale	$70,000	$ 20,000
	Book value: [$125,000 – (3 × $25,000)]	50,000	50,000
	Gain (loss)	$20,000	$(30,000)
	Effect on income taxes at 40%:		
(b)	Tax savings, an inflow effect: .40 × loss		$ 12,000
(c)	Tax paid, an outflow: .40 × gain	$ (8,000)	
	Net cash inflow from sale:		
	(a) plus (b)		$ 32,000
	(a) minus (c)	$62,000	

Exhibit 11-8
Cash Flow Effects of
Disposal of Equipment

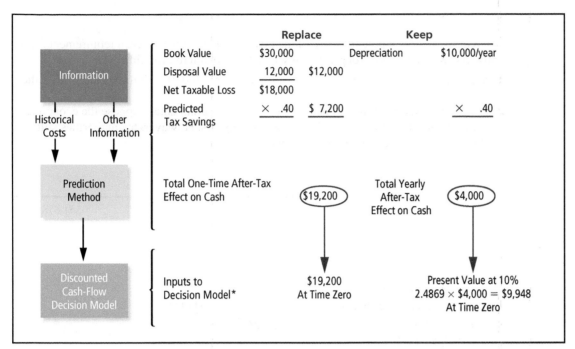

*There will be other related inputs to the replacement decision—for example, the cost of the new equipment, the tax effect of
depreciation on the new equipment, and the differences in future annual cash flows from operations.

A second tax effect occurs when a company disposes of an asset before the end of its recovery
period. In addition to taxable gains or losses, disposal eliminates future tax depreciation on the asset.

Suppose General Electric replaces some old copying equipment with a book value of $30,000,
an expected terminal disposal value of zero, a current disposal value of $12,000, and 3 years
remaining in its recovery period. For simplicity, assume that General Electric uses straight-line
depreciation, amounting to $10,000 of depreciation per year. The tax rate is 40% and the required
rate of return is 10%.

Exhibit 11-8 shows the cash flow effects due only to disposal of the old copying equipment.
(That is, Exhibit 11-8 does not show the cost, annual cash flow effects, nor the depreciation tax
savings related to the new copying equipment.) The cash inflow from disposal of the old copying
equipment is $19,200, the disposal value plus the tax savings resulting from the tax loss on dis-
posal. This immediate cash inflow is partially offset by the loss of future tax deductions of $10,000
per year for the next 3 years, which have a present value of 2.4869 × ($10,000 × 40%) = $9,948.
The net cash inflow due to disposal of the old equipment is ($19,200 − $9,948) = $9,252.

Summary Problem for Your Review

PROBLEM

Consider the investment opportunity in Exhibit 11-4, page 447: original cost of machine,
$125,000; 5-year useful life; zero terminal salvage value; pretax annual cash inflow from
operations, $60,000; income tax rate, 40%; required after-tax rate of return, 12%. Assume the
equipment is a 5-year MACRS asset for tax purposes. The NPV is as follows:

	Present Values (PV)
Cash effects of operations,*$60,000 × (1 − .40) × 3.6048	$129,773
Cash effects of depreciation on income tax savings using MACRS, $125,000 × .7381[†] × .40	36,905
Total after-tax effect on cash	$166,678
Investment	125,000
NPV	$ 41,678

*See Exhibit 11-4, page 447, for details.
[†]Factor .7381 is from Exhibit 11-7, page 449.

For each requirement, compute the NPV of the investment but consider each requirement independently. Assume the original depreciation schedule is not altered for either requirement.

1. Suppose Toyota ends up selling the equipment for $20,000 cash immediately after the end of year 5.
2. Ignore the assumption in number 1. Return to the original data. Suppose the economic life of the machine turns out to be 8 years, not 5 years. However, tax authorities still allow MACRS cost recovery over 5 years.

SOLUTION

1.

NPV as given		$41,678
Cash proceeds of sale	$20,000	
Book value	0	
Taxable gain	$20,000	
Income taxes at 40%	8,000	
Total after-tax effect on cash	$12,000	
PV of $12,000 to be received in 5 years at 12%, $12,000 × .5674		6,809
NPV of investment		$48,487

2.

NPV as given		$41,678
Add the PV of $36,000 per year for 8 years		
Discount factor of 4.9676* × $36,000 =	$178,834	
Deduct the PV of $36,000 per year for 5 years	129,773	
Increase in PV		49,061
NPV		$90,739

*Factor 4.9676 is from Table B-2.

The investment becomes more attractive with the increased economic life because there are operating savings for an additional three years and no reduction in the tax savings from depreciation.

Objective 7

Use the payback model and the accounting rate-of-return model and compare them with the NPV model.

Other Models for Analyzing Long-Range Decisions

Although most companies use DCF models to make major capital-budgeting decisions, some companies still use simpler models, either in place of or in addition to the NPV model. We will examine two such models, the payback and accounting rate-of-return models.

Payback Model

payback period (payback time)

The time it will take to recoup, in the form of cash inflows from operations, the initial dollars invested in a project.

Payback time or **payback period** is the time it will take to recoup, in the form of undiscounted cash inflows from operations, the initial dollars invested in a project. Assume that Toyota spends $12,000 for a forklift that has an estimated useful life of 4 years. Toyota expects the new forklift to reduce cash outflows by $4,000 each year. The payback period is 3 years, calculated as follows:

$$\text{payback time} = \frac{\text{initial incremental amount invested}}{\text{equal annual incremental cash inflow from operations}}$$

$$P = \frac{I}{O} = \frac{\$12,000}{\$4,000} = 3 \text{ years}$$

We can use this formula for payback time only when there are equal annual cash inflows from operations. When annual cash inflows are not equal, we must add up each year's net cash inflows until the point in time where the cumulative cash flows add up to the amount of the initial investment.

Assume the following cash flow pattern for the forklift:

End of Year	0	1	2	3	4
Investment	($12,000)				
Cash inflows		$4,000	$6,000	$5,000	$5,000

The calculation of the payback period is as follows:

Year	Initial Investment	Net Cash Inflows Each Year	Net Cash Inflows Cumulative
0	$12,000	—	—
1	—	$4,000	$ 4,000
2	—	6,000	10,000
2+	—	2,000	12,000

In this case, the payback time is slightly beyond the second year. Interpolation within the third year reveals that an additional 4/10 of a year is needed to recoup the final $2,000, making the payback period 2.4 years:

$$2 \text{ years} + \left(\frac{\$2,000}{\$5,000} \times 1 \text{ year} \right) = 2.4 \text{ years}$$

The major weakness of the payback model is that it merely measures how many years it takes to recover the original investment. The payback model ignores elements of timing and duration of cash flows that the DCF models recognize. For example, consider two investment projects with the same 3-year payback period and the same total cash flows for their 4-year lives. However, suppose most of the Project B cash flows occur in the first year of the 3-year payback period while most of the Project A cash flows occur in the third year. The payback periods for these two projects are identical, yet project B is superior because the cash flows arrive earlier. As another example, suppose Project C has the same cash flows over the first 4 years as Project A but the Project A cash flows stop after 4 years while the Project C cash flows continue for a total of 10 years. The payback period for these two projects is identical, yet project C is superior because the cash flows continue for a much longer period of time. The payback model measures only how quickly a company will recoup its investment dollars but ignores the time value of money and ignores cash flows beyond the payback period.

Despite its conceptual weaknesses, the payback model may be useful in certain circumstances. In some situations, managers use the payback model rather than DCF because of greater uncertainty about projections of cash flows further into the future. Suppose a company faces rapid technological changes so that cash flows beyond the first few years are extremely uncertain. In such a situation, managers may decide to base their decisions on the payback period because it emphasizes how quickly projects recoup their investment and ignores the highly uncertain cash flows farther into the future. In other situations, managers use the payback model because of cash constraints. We noted earlier that the DCF model assumes that additional funds can be borrowed at the required rate of return. Some firms, such as early-stage startups, may not be able to easily borrow additional funds, so managers may use the payback model because it focuses on how quickly the firm can recover its cash investments.

Accounting Rate-of-Return Model

The **accounting rate-of-return (ARR) model** expresses a project's return as the increase in expected average annual operating income divided by the initial required investment.

$$\text{accounting rate-of-return (ARR)} = \frac{\text{increase in expected average annual operating income}}{\text{initial required investment}}$$

accounting rate-of-return (ARR) model
A non-DCF capital-budgeting model expressed as the increase in expected average annual operating income divided by the initial required investment.

If operating income is the same as cash flow except for the effect of depreciation expense, then operating income = cash flow − depreciation, and the ARR becomes

$$ARR = \frac{\text{average annual incremental net cash inflow from operations}}{\text{initial required investment}} - \text{average incremental annual depreciation}$$

ARR computations dovetail most closely with conventional accounting models of calculating income and required investment, and they show the effect of an investment on an organization's financial statements.

To see how ARR works, assume the same facts as in Exhibit 11-1: Investment is $5,827, useful life is 4 years, estimated disposal value is zero, and expected annual cash inflow from operations is $2,000. Annual depreciation is $5,827 ÷ 4 = $1,456.75, rounded to $1,457. Substitute these values in the accounting rate-of-return equation:

$$ARR = \frac{(\$2,000 - \$1,457)}{\$5,827} = 9.3\%$$

Some companies use the "average" investment (often assumed to be the average book value over the useful life) instead of original investment in the denominator. The investment committed to the project would decline at a rate of $1,456.75 per year from $5,827 to zero; hence, the average investment would be the beginning balance plus the ending balance ($5,827 + 0) divided by 2, or $2,913.50. Therefore, the ARR using the average investment is

$$ARR = \frac{(\$2,000 - \$1,457)}{\$2,913.50} = 18.6\%$$

The accounting rate-of-return model has significant limitations. Like the payback model, the ARR model ignores important aspects of the timing and duration of cash flows. For example, consider two projects that require the same initial required investment and have the same average increase in operating income over the life of the projects, where most of the savings for Project B occur in the early years while most of the savings for Project A occur in later years. The ARRs for these two projects are identical, even though project B provides returns earlier. As another example, suppose Project C has the same ARR over a 10-year life as Project A has over a 4-year life. Although these two projects have identical ARRs, the return for project C continues for a much longer period of time.

Despite some obvious limitations, some firms still use the ARR and payback models in certain situations. The Business First box on page 455 describes the increasing use of DCF models as well as the continued use of alternative models, including the payback and accounting rate of return models.

Performance Evaluation

Potential Conflict

Objective 8

Reconcile the conflict between using an NPV model for making decisions and using accounting income for evaluating the related performance.

Many managers who are evaluated on the basis of accounting income or an ARR model are reluctant to accept DCF models as the best way to make capital-budgeting decisions. To illustrate, consider the potential conflict that might arise in the example of Exhibit 11-1. Recall that the NPV was $513 based on a 10% required rate of return, an investment of $5,827, cash savings of $2,000 for each of 4 years, and no terminal disposal value. Using ARR where accounting income is computed with straight-line depreciation, the evaluation of performance for years 1–4 would be as follows:

	Year 1	Year 2	Year 3	Year 4
Cash-operating savings	$2,000	$2,000	$2,000	$2,000
Straight-line depreciation, $5,827 ÷ 4	1,457	1,457	1,457	1,457*
Effect on operating income	543	543	543	543
Book value at beginning of year	5,827	4,370	2,913	1,456
ARR	9.3%	12.4%	18.6%	37.3%

*Total depreciation of 4 × $1,457 = $5,828 differs from $5,827 because of rounding error. Also, the ARR is based on the book value at the beginning of the year as a proxy for the investment.

Business First

Who Uses What Capital Budgeting Model?

Companies are increasingly using formal capital-budgeting models, and most use more than one model. Of the 1,000 largest U.S. companies, more than 95% use a DCF model for their large investment decisions, although about half of them use such methods only for investments over $500,000. The NPV model is the most popular DCF method, with many also using IRR. However, use of the payback model remains strong, with more than half of the companies using it for at least some decisions.

There is a clear relationship between size and capital-budgeting methods. The larger the company and the larger the investment, the more likely is the use of DCF methods. Smaller companies use the payback method more often. Companies that have high financial leverage and young, highly-educated CFOs are more likely to use DCF methods. Fast-growing companies use the payback method more than similar-sized, low-growth companies, due at least in part to constraints on the ability of fast-growing companies to raise additional capital.

DCF methods have also made inroads into nonprofit companies. For example, hospitals make huge capital investment decisions. A few years ago the payback model was the dominant capital budgeting model used, but recent studies show that DCF models are used as often as payback. Further, large, multihospital systems generally use DCF methods.

More companies in the United States use DCF methods than in other countries, but the usage is nearly as high in the United Kingdom, Australia, and the Netherlands. Even in China, nearly 90% of the large companies use DCF methods. However, in China the dominant DCF method is IRR and a larger percentage of companies continue to use the payback method for some investments. As companies become more sophisticated and more dependent on capital markets, they tend to progress from payback to IRR and then to NPV.

Companies are also using more sophisticated techniques to analyze capital investment decisions. The most popular is sensitivity analysis. However, the use of real options is growing quickly. In 2002 a quarter of large U.S. companies already used real options, as did a third of Australian firms in 2008. Within the next few years it is likely that half of the large companies in the developed world will use capital budgeting models based on real options for at least some of their major investments.

Sources: G. Truong, G. Partington, and M. Peat, "Cost-of-Capital Estimation and Capital-Budgeting Practices in Australia," *Australian Journal of Management*, June 2008, pp. 95–121; C. Kocher, "Hospital Capital Budgeting Practices and Their Relation to Key Hospital Characteristics: A Survey of U.S. Manager Practices," *Journal of Global Business Issues*, July 1, 2007, pp. 21–30 ; J. Graham and C. Harvey, "How Do CFOs Make Capital Budgeting and Capital Structure Decisions?" *Journal of Applied Corporate Finance*, Spring 2002, pp. 8–23; P. Ryan and G. Ryan, "Capital Budgeting Practices of the Fortune 1000: How Have Things Changed?" *Journal of Business and Management*, Winter 2002, pp. 355–364; and N. Hermes, P. Smid, and L. Yao, "Capital Budgeting Practices: A Comparative Study of The Netherlands and China," November 2005, available at SSRN: http://ssrn.com/abstract=881754.

Many managers would be reluctant to replace equipment, despite the positive NPV, if superiors evaluated their performance by accounting rate of return. They might be especially reluctant if they are likely to transfer to a new position (or retire) within the first year or two. Why? This accrual accounting system understates the return in early years, especially in year 1 when the return is below the required rate, and a manager who transfers will not be around to reap the benefits of the later overstatement of returns.

As Chapter 6 indicated, managers are especially reluctant to replace assets if a heavy book loss on old equipment would appear in year 1's income statement—even though such a loss is irrelevant in a properly constructed decision model. Thus, performance evaluation based on typical accounting measures can lead to rejection of major, long-term projects where a large portion of the benefit does not appear in income immediately, such as investments in technologically advanced production systems. This pattern may help explain why many U.S. firms seem to be excessively short-term oriented.

Reconciliation of Conflict

The best way to reconcile the potential conflict between capital budgeting and performance evaluation is to use DCF for both capital-budgeting decisions and performance evaluation. Companies that use EVA for performance evaluation, as described in Chapter 10, page 400, avoid some of the conflict. Although EVA has the weakness of relying on accrual accounting measures rather than cash flows, it is conceptually linked to the NPV method. Both EVA and NPV recognize that a firm creates value only when investment projects cover their cost of capital.

Another way to address this issue is to conduct a follow-up evaluation of capital-budgeting decisions, often called a **post-audit**. Most large companies (76% in a recent survey) post-audit at least some capital-budgeting decisions. The purposes of a post-audit include the following:

post-audit
A follow-up evaluation of capital-budgeting decisions.

1. Seeing that investment expenditures are proceeding on time and within budget
2. Comparing actual cash flows with those originally predicted, in order to motivate and reward careful and honest predictions

3. Providing information for improving future predictions of cash flows
4. Evaluating the continuation of the project

By focusing the post-audit on actual versus predicted cash flows, we can make the evaluation consistent with the decision process. However, post-auditing of all capital-budgeting decisions is costly. Most accounting systems are best at evaluating operating performances of products, departments, divisions, territories, and so on, year by year. In contrast, capital-budgeting decisions frequently deal with individual projects, not the collection of projects that are usually being managed at the same time by division or department managers. Therefore, most companies audit only selected capital-budgeting decisions.

The conflicts between the longstanding, pervasive accrual accounting model and various formal decision models create some of the most serious unsolved problems in the design of management control systems. Top management cannot expect goal congruence if it favors the use of one type of model for decisions and the use of another type for performance evaluation.

Highlights to Remember

1. **Describe capital-budgeting decisions and use the net-present-value (NPV) method to make such decisions.** Capital budgeting is long-term planning for investments where returns are spread over multiple years. The net-present-value (NPV) model aids this planning process by computing the present value (PV) of all expected future cash flows using a required rate of return. A company should accept projects with an NPV greater than zero.

2. **Use sensitivity analysis to evaluate the effect of changes in predictions on investment decisions.** Managers use sensitivity analysis to assess the effects of changes in predicted cash flows and other variables used in investment decisions.

3. **Calculate the NPV difference between two projects using both the total project and differential approaches.** The total project approach compares the NPVs of the total cash flows from each project, while the differential approach computes the NPV of the difference in cash flows between two projects. Both produce the same results when there are two alternatives. When there are more than two alternatives, you should use the total project approach.

4. **Identify relevant cash flows for NPV analyses.** Predicting cash flows is the hardest part of capital budgeting. Managers should consider three categories of cash flows: initial cash inflows and outflows at time zero, including additional required investments in working capital, future disposal values, and operating cash flows.

5. **Compute the after-tax net present values of projects.** Income taxes can have a significant effect on the desirability of an investment. Additional taxes are cash outflows, and tax savings are cash inflows. Accelerated depreciation speeds up a company's tax savings. In most cases, companies should take depreciation deductions as early as legally permitted.

6. **Explain the after-tax effect on cash received from the disposal of assets.** When companies sell assets for more than the tax book value, the gain generates additional taxes. When they sell assets for less than the tax book value, the loss generates tax savings.

7. **Use the payback model and the accounting rate-of-return model and compare them with the NPV model.** The payback model is simple to apply, but it does not measure profitability. The accounting rate-of-return model uses accounting measures of income and investment, but it ignores the time value of money. Both models have significant limitations relative to the NPV model.

8. **Reconcile the conflict between using an NPV model for making decisions and using accounting income for evaluating the related performance.** NPV is a summary measure of all the cash flows from a project. Accounting income is a one-period measure. A positive NPV project can have low (or even negative) accounting income in the first year. Managers may be reluctant to invest in such a project, despite its positive value to the company, especially if they expect to transfer to a new position before they can benefit from the positive returns that come later.

Appendix 11: Capital Budgeting and Inflation

Capital-budgeting decision makers should also consider the effects of inflation on their cash-flow predictions. **Inflation** is the decline in the general purchasing power of the monetary unit. For example, a dollar today will buy only a fraction of what it did in the late-1980s. At a 5% annual inflation rate, average prices rise more than 60% over 10 years and 165% over 20 years. The United States had double-digit inflation rates in the late 1970s, and some countries, such as Brazil and Argentina, have had triple-digit annual inflation rates (that is, average prices more than doubling each year). In the last decade, inflation rates in the United States have been low—generally around 3%—but it is possible that rates in the future might increase. If a company expects significant inflation over the life of a project, it should specifically and consistently recognize inflation in its capital-budgeting decisions.

Objective 9

Compute the impact of inflation on a capital-budgeting project.

inflation
The decline in the general purchasing power of the monetary unit.

Watch for Consistency

The key to appropriate consideration of inflation in capital budgeting is consistent treatment of the required rate of return and the predicted cash inflows and outflows. We can achieve such consistency by either 1) including an element for inflation in both the required rate and in the cash-flow predictions, or 2) excluding the effects of inflation in both the required rate and in the cash-flow predictions. We limit our discussion to the first approach, which is both simple and widely-used.

Many firms base their required rate of return on market interest rates, also called **nominal rates**, that include an inflation element. For example, consider three possible components of a 12% nominal rate:

nominal rate
Interest rate that includes an inflation element.

(a)	Risk-free element—the "pure" rate of interest	3%
(b)	Business-risk element—the "risk" premium that is demanded for taking larger risks	5
(a) + (b)	Often called the "real rate"	8%
(c)	Inflation element—the premium demanded because of expected deterioration of the general purchasing power of the monetary unit	4
(a) + (b) + (c)	Often called the "nominal rate"	12%

In this example, 4 percentage points out of the 12 percentage-point return compensate an investor for receiving future payments in inflated dollars, that is, in dollars with less purchasing power than those invested. Therefore, basing the required rate of return on quoted market rates automatically includes an inflation element in the rate. Companies that base their required rate of return on market rates should also adjust their cash-flow predictions for anticipated inflation. For example, suppose a company expects to sell 1,000 units of a product in each of the next 2 years. Assume this year's price is $50, and inflation causes next year's price to be $52.50. This year's predicted cash inflow is 1,000 × $50 = $50,000, and next year's inflation-adjusted cash inflow is 1,000 × $52.50 = $52,500. Inflation-adjusted cash flows are the inflows and outflows expected after adjusting prices to reflect anticipated inflation.

Consider another illustration: purchase cost of equipment, $200,000; useful life, 5 years; zero terminal salvage value; pretax operating cash savings per year, $83,333 (in 20X0 dollars); income tax rate, 40%. For simplicity, we assume ordinary straight-line depreciation of $200,000 ÷ 5 = $40,000 per year. The after-tax required rate, based on quoted market rates, is 25%. It includes an inflation factor of 10%.

Exhibit 11-9 displays correct and incorrect ways to analyze the effects of inflation. The key words are *internal consistency*. The correct analysis (1) uses a required rate that includes an element attributable to inflation and (2) explicitly adjusts the predicted operating cash flows for the effects of inflation. Note that the correct analysis favors the purchase of the equipment, but the incorrect analysis does not.

The incorrect analysis in Exhibit 11-9 is incorrect because it is internally inconsistent. The predicted cash inflows exclude adjustments for inflation. Instead, they are stated in 20X0 dollars. However, the discount rate includes an element attributable to inflation. An analytical mistake like this might lead to an unwise refusal to purchase.

458

Sketch of Relevant Cash Flows (at End of Year)

Description		At 25%							
		PV Factor	Present Value	0	1	2	3	4	5
Correct analysis (Be sure the discount rate includes an element attributable to inflation and adjust the predicted cash flows for inflationary effects.)									
Cash operating inflows:									
Pretax inflow in 20X0 dollars	$83,333								
Income tax effect at 40%	33,333								
After-tax effect on cash	$50,000								
		.8000	$ 44,000		$55,000*				
		.6400	38,720			$60,500			
		.5120	34,074				$66,550		
		.4096	29,985					$73,205	
		.3277	26,388						$80,526
Subtotal			$173,167						
Annual depreciation $200,000 ÷ 5 = $40,000									
Cash effect of depreciation Savings in income taxes at 40% = $40,000 × .40 = $16,000		2.6893	43,029		$16,000†	$16,000	$16,000	$16,000	$16,000
Investment in equipment		1.0000	(200,000)	($200,000)					
Net present value			$ 16,196						
Incorrect analysis (The error is to include an inflation element in the discount rate as shown, but not adjust the operating cash inflows.)									
Cash operating inflows after taxes		2.6893	$134,465		$50,000	$50,000	$50,000	$50,000	$50,000
Tax effect of depreciation		2.6893	43,029		16,000	16,000	16,000	16,000	16,000
Investment in equipment		1.0000	(200,000)	($200,000)					
Net present value			$ (22,506)						

*Each year is adjusted for anticipated inflation: $50,000 × 1.10 = $55,000 , $50,000 × 1.10² = $60,500, $50,000 × 1.10³ = $66,550, and so on.

†Inflation will not affect the annual savings in income taxes from depreciation. Why? Because the income tax deduction must be based on original cost of the asset in 20X0 dollars.

Exhibit 11-9

Inflation and Capital Budgeting

Role of Depreciation

While internally consistent analysis using nominal interest rates must adjust cash flows for inflation, you will notice that the correct analysis in Exhibit 11-9 shows that we did not adjust the tax effects of depreciation for inflation. Why? Because the depreciation deductions under U.S. income tax laws are based on the original dollars invested, not the inflation-adjusted amount of the investment.

Critics of U.S. income tax laws emphasize that such laws discourage capital investment by not allowing companies to adjust depreciation deductions for inflationary effects. For instance, the NPV in Exhibit 11-9 would be larger if depreciation for tax purposes were based on the inflation-adjusted value of the $200,000 investment. As shown in Exhibit 11-9, the unadjusted depreciation of $40,000 per year generates a $16,000 savings in 20X1 dollars, then $16,000 in 20X2 dollars, and so forth. If tax depreciation were based on the inflation-adjusted value of the investment which grows by 10% to $220,000 during the second year, the tax depreciation would grow to $220,000 ÷ 5 = $44,000 in the second year, generating a tax savings of $44,000 × 40% = $17,600. When the inflation-adjusted value of the investment grows by another 10% to $242,000 during the third year, the inflation-adjusted depreciation would grow to $242,000 ÷ 5 = $48,400, generating a tax savings of $48,400 × 40% = $19,360. On the other hand, defenders of existing U.S. tax laws point out that tax laws encourage capital investment in many other ways. The most prominent example is provision for accelerated depreciation over lives that are much shorter than the economic lives of the assets.

Summary Problems for Your Review

PROBLEM

Examine the correct analysis in Exhibit 11-9. Suppose the cash-operating inflows persisted for an extra year. Compute the PV of the inflow for the sixth year. Ignore depreciation.

SOLUTION

The cash operating inflow would be $50,000 × 1.10^6, or $80,526 × 1.10, or $88,579. Its PV would be $88,579 × .2621, the factor from Table B-1 of Appendix B (period 6 row, 25% column), or $23,217.

PROBLEM

Examine the MACRS depreciation schedule in Exhibit 11-7 on page 449. Assume an anticipated inflation rate of 7%. How would you change the PVs of depreciation to accommodate the inflation rate?

SOLUTION

The computations on page 449 would not change. Inflation does not affect the tax effects of depreciation. Income tax laws in the United States permit a deduction based on the original dollars invested, nothing more.

Accounting Vocabulary

accelerated depreciation, p. 445
accounting rate-of-return (ARR) model, p. 453
after-tax cash flow, p. 445
capital budgeting, p. 435
depreciation tax shield, p. 449
differential approach, p. 440
discount rate, p. 436
discounted-cash-flow (DCF) models, p. 435

hurdle rate, p. 436
inflation, p. 457
internal rate of return (IRR) model, p. 438
marginal income tax rate, p. 445
modified accelerated cost recovery system (MACRS), p. 448
net present value, p. 436

net-present-value (NPV) method, p. 436
nominal rate, p. 457
payback period, p. 452
payback time, p. 452
post-audit, p. 455
present value (PV), p. 435
real options model, p. 439
recovery period, p. 445
required rate of return, p. 436
total project approach, p. 440

Fundamental Assignment Material

Special note: In all assignment materials that include taxes, assume—unless directed otherwise—that (1) all income tax cash flows occur simultaneously with the pretax cash flows, and (2) the companies in question will have enough taxable income from other sources to use all income tax benefits from the situations described.

11-A1 Exercises in Compound Interest: Answers Supplied

Use the appropriate interest table from Appendix B (see page A6 or A9) to complete the following exercises. The answers appear at the end of the assignment material for this chapter, page 479.

1. It is your sixtieth birthday. You plan to work 5 more years before retiring, at which point you and your spouse want to take $25,000 for a round-the-world tour. What lump sum do you have to invest now to accumulate the $25,000? Assume that your required rate of return is
   a. 5%, compounded annually.
   b. 10%, compounded annually.
   c. 20%, compounded annually.

2. You want to spend $2,000 on a vacation at the end of each of the next 5 years. What lump sum do you have to invest now to take the five vacations? Assume that your required rate of return is
   a. 5%, compounded annually.
   b. 10%, compounded annually.
   c. 20%, compounded annually.

3. At age 60, you find that your employer is moving to another location. You receive termination pay of $100,000. You have some savings and wonder whether to retire now.
   a. If you invest the $100,000 now at 5%, compounded annually, how much money can you withdraw from your account each year so that at the end of 5 years there will be a zero balance?
   b. Answer part a, assuming that you invest it at 10%.

4. Two NBA basketball players, LeBron and Kobe, signed 5-year, $60-million contracts. At 16%, compounded annually, which of the following contracts is more desirable in terms of present values? Show computations to support your answer.

Annual Cash Inflows (in thousands)

Year	LeBron	Kobe
1	$20,000	$ 4,000
2	16,000	8,000
3	12,000	12,000
4	8,000	16,000
5	4,000	20,000
	$60,000	$60,000

11-A2 NPV for Investment Decisions

A manager of the engineering department of Manchester University is contemplating acquiring 120 computers. The computers will cost £240,000 cash, have zero terminal salvage value, and a useful life of 3 years. Annual cash savings from operations will be £110,000. The required rate of return is 14%. There are no taxes.

1. Compute the NPV.
2. Should the engineering department acquire the computers? Explain.

11-A3 Taxes, Straight-Line Depreciation, and Present Values

A manager of Cascade Mutual Funds is contemplating acquiring servers to operate its website. The servers will cost $660,000 cash and will have zero terminal salvage value. The recovery period and useful life are both 3 years. Annual pretax cash savings from operations will be $300,000. The income tax rate is 40%, and the required after-tax rate of return is 12%.

1. Compute the NPV, assuming straight-line depreciation of $220,000 yearly for tax purposes. Should Cascade acquire the computers? Explain.
2. Suppose the computers will be fully depreciated at the end of year 3 but can be sold for $90,000 cash. Compute the NPV. Should Cascade acquire the computers? Explain.
3. Ignore number 2. Suppose the required after-tax rate of return is 8% instead of 12%. Should Cascade acquire the computers? Show computations.

11-A4 MACRS and Present Values

Managers of Northwest Forge are considering whether to buy some equipment for the company's Fargo plant. The equipment will cost $2 million cash and will have a 10-year useful life and zero terminal salvage value. Annual pretax cash savings from operations will be $420,000. The income tax rate is 45%, and the required after-tax rate of return is 14%.

1. Compute the NPV, using a 7-year recovery period and MACRS depreciation for tax purposes. Should the company acquire the equipment?
2. Suppose the economic life of the equipment is 15 years, which means that there will be $420,000 additional annual cash savings from operations in each of the years from 11 to 15. Assume that a 7-year recovery period and MACRS depreciation is used. Should the company acquire the equipment? Show computations.

11-A5 Gains or Losses on Disposal

On January 1, 20X1, Melbourne Company sold an asset with a book value of $250,000 for cash.

Assume two selling prices: $305,000 and $230,000. For each selling price, prepare a tabulation of the gain or loss, the effect on income taxes, and the total after-tax effect on cash. The applicable income tax rate is 25%.

11-B1 Exercises in Compound Interest

Use the appropriate table to compute the following:

1. You have always dreamed of taking a safari in Africa. What lump sum do you have to invest today to have the $22,000 needed for the trip in 5 years? Assume that you can invest the money at
   a. 6%, compounded annually.
   b. 10%, compounded annually.
   c. 14%, compounded annually.
2. You are considering partial retirement. To do so you need to use part of your savings to supplement your income for the next 4 years. Suppose you need an extra $50,000 per year. What lump sum do you have to invest now to supplement your income for 4 years? Assume that your required rate of return is
   a. 6%, compounded annually.
   b. 10%, compounded annually.
   c. 14%, compounded annually.
3. You just won a lump sum of $6,000,000 in a state lottery. You have decided to invest the winnings and withdraw an equal amount each year for 20 years. How much can you withdraw each year and have a zero balance left at the end of 20 years if you invest at
   a. 4%, compounded annually?
   b. 8%, compounded annually?
4. An NHL hockey player is offered the choice of two 4-year salary contracts, contract X for $2.85 million and contract Y for $2.72 million:

	Contract X	Contract Y
End of year 1	$ 250,000	$ 550,000
End of year 2	750,000	820,000
End of year 3	850,000	650,000
End of year 4	1,000,000	700,000
Total	$2,850,000	$2,720,000

Which contract has the higher PV at 16% compounded annually? Show computations to support your answer.

11-B2 NPV for Investment Decisions

The head of the oncology department of FH Research Center is considering the purchase of some new equipment. The cost is $420,000, the economic life is 5 years, and there is no terminal disposal value. Annual cash inflows from operations would increase by $140,000, and the required rate of return is 14%. There are no taxes.

1. Compute the NPV.
2. Should the research center acquire the equipment? Explain.

11-B3 Taxes, Straight-Line Depreciation, and NPV

The president of Big Fish Games, an online gaming company, is considering the purchase of some equipment used for the development of new games. The cost is $400,000, the economic life and the recovery period are both 5 years, and there is no terminal disposal value. Annual pretax cash inflows from operations would increase by $130,000, giving a total 5-year pretax savings of $650,000. The income tax rate is 40%, and the required after-tax rate of return is 14%.

1. Compute the NPV, assuming straight-line depreciation of $80,000 yearly for tax purposes. Should Big Fish Games acquire the equipment?
2. Suppose the asset will be fully depreciated at the end of year 5 but is sold for $25,000 cash. Should Big Fish Games acquire the equipment? Show computations.
3. Ignore number 2. Suppose the required after-tax rate of return is 10% instead of 14%. Should Big Fish Games acquire the equipment? Show computations.

11-B4 MACRS and Present Values

The general manager of a New Mexico mining company has a chance to purchase a new drill at a total cost of $300,000. The recovery period is 5 years. Additional annual pretax cash inflow from operations is $75,000, the economic life of the drill is 5 years, there is no salvage value, the income tax rate is 45%, and the after-tax required rate of return is 10%.

1. Compute the NPV, assuming MACRS depreciation for tax purposes. Should the company acquire the drill?
2. Suppose the economic life of the drill is 6 years, which means that there will be a $75,000 cash inflow from operations in the sixth year. The recovery period is still 5 years. Should the company acquire the drill? Show computations.

11-B5 Income Taxes and Disposal of Assets

Assume that the combined federal and state income tax rate for Kafka Company is 30%.

1. The book value of an old machine is $40,000. Kafka sold the machine for $35,000 cash. What is the effect of this decision on after-tax cash flows?
2. The book value of an old machine is $40,000. Kafka sold the machine for $85,000 cash. What is the effect of this decision on after-tax cash flows?

MyAccountingLab # Additional Assignment Material

QUESTIONS

11-1 Capital budgeting has three phases: (a) identification of potential investments, (b) selection of investments, and (c) post-audit of investments. What is the accountant's role in each phase?

11-2 Why is discounted cash flow a superior method for capital budgeting?

11-3 "The higher the required rate of return, the higher the price that a company will be willing to pay for cost-saving equipment." Do you agree? Explain.

11-4 "The DCF model assumes certainty and perfect capital markets. Thus, it is impractical to use it in most real-world situations." Do you agree? Explain.

11-5 "Double-counting of costs occurs if depreciation is separately considered in DCF analysis." Do you agree? Explain.

11-6 Does the IRR model make significantly different decisions than does the NPV model? Why or why not?

11-7 What does the real options model recognize that the NPV and IRR models do not?

11-8 "We can't use sensitivity analysis because our cash-flow predictions are too inaccurate." Comment.

11-9 Why should the differential approach to alternatives always lead to the same decision as the total project approach?

11-10 "The NPV model should not be used for investment decisions about advanced technology, such as computer-integrated manufacturing systems." Do you agree? Explain.

11-11 Distinguish between average and marginal tax rates.

11-12 "Congress should pass a law forbidding corporations to keep two sets of books." Do you agree? Explain.

11-13 Distinguish between tax avoidance and tax evasion.

11-14 "Companies that try to avoid taxes are unethical." Do you agree? Discuss.

11-15 Explain why accelerated depreciation methods are superior to straight-line methods for income tax purposes.

11-16 "An investment in equipment really buys two streams of cash." Do you agree? Explain.

11-17 Why should companies take tax deductions sooner rather than later?

11-18 "The MACRS half-year convention causes assets to be depreciated beyond the lives specified in the MACRS recovery schedules." Do you agree? Explain.

11-19 "When there are income taxes, depreciation is a cash outlay." Do you agree? Explain.

11-20 "If DCF approaches are superior to the payback and the accounting rate-of-return methods, why should we bother to learn the others? All it does is confuse things." Answer this contention.

11-21 What is the basic flaw in the pay-back model?

11-22 Explain how a conflict can arise between capital-budgeting decision models and performance evaluation methods.

11-23 Study Appendix 11. What are the three components of market (nominal) interest rates?

11-24 Study Appendix 11. Describe how internal consistency is achieved when considering inflation in a capital-budgeting model.

CRITICAL THINKING EXERCISES

11-25 Investment in R&D
"It is impossible to use DCF methods for evaluating investments in R&D. There are no cost savings to measure, and we don't even know what products might come out of our R&D activities." This is a quote from an R&D manager who was asked to justify investment in a major research project based on its expected NPV. Do you agree with her statement? Explain.

11-26 Business Valuation and NPV
When a company elects to invest in a project with a positive NPV, what will generally happen to the value of the company? What will happen to this value when the company invests in a negative NPV project?

11-27 Replacement of Production Facilities
A manufacturing company recently considered replacing one of its forming machines with a newer, faster, more accurate model. What cash flows would this decision be likely to affect? List both cash flows that would be easy to quantify and those for which measurement would be difficult.

11-28 Capital Budgeting, Taxes, and Ethics
The U.S. tax law is complex. Sometimes the line between tax avoidance and tax evasion is not clear. Discuss the legal and ethical implications of the following two capital investment decisions:

a. A company invested in an asset that it expects to grow rather than decline in value. Nevertheless, the tax law allows the company to deduct depreciation on the asset. Therefore, the company depreciated the asset for tax purposes using an accelerated MACRS schedule.

b. There are often tax advantages to investments "offshore." For example, in Bermuda there are no taxes on profits, dividends, or income, and there is no capital gains tax, no withholding tax, and no sales tax. A U.S. company decided to invest in a manufacturing plant in Bermuda and use transfer prices to move as much of the company's profits as possible to the Bermuda plant.

EXERCISES

11-29 Exercise in Compound Interest
Serena Madison wishes to purchase a $820,000 house. She has accumulated a $180,000 down payment, but she wishes to borrow $640,000 on a 15-year mortgage. For simplicity, assume annual mortgage payments occur at the end of each year and there are no loan fees.

1. What are Madison's annual payments if her interest rate is (a) 4%, (b) 8%, and (c) 12%, compounded annually?
2. Repeat number 1 for a 10-year mortgage.
3. Suppose Madison had to choose between a 15-year and a 10-year mortgage, either one at a 8% interest rate. Compute the total payments and total interest paid on (a) a 15-year mortgage and (b) a 10-year mortgage.

11-30 Exercise in Compound Interest
Suppose **Pfizer** wishes to borrow money from **Bank of America**. They agree on an annual rate of 4%.

1. Suppose Pfizer agrees to repay $750 million at the end of 10 years. How much will Bank of America lend Pfizer?
2. Suppose Pfizer agrees to repay a total of $750 million at a rate of $75 million at the end of each of the next 10 years. How much will Bank of America lend Pfizer?

11-31 Exercise in Compound Interest

Suppose you are a loan officer for a bank. A start-up company has qualified for a loan. You are pondering various proposals for repayment:

1. Lump sum of $250,000 five years hence. How much will you lend if your required rate of return is (a) 8%, compounded annually, and (b) 12%, compounded annually?
2. Repeat number 1, but assume that the interest rates are compounded semiannually.
3. Suppose the loan is to be paid in full by equal payments of $50,000 at the end of each of the next 5 years. How much will you lend if your required rate of return is (a) 8%, compounded annually, and (b) 12%, compounded annually?

11-32 Basic Relationships in Interest Tables

1. Suppose you borrow $300,000 now at 10% interest, compounded annually. You will repay the borrowed amount plus interest in a lump sum at the end of 4 years. How much must you repay? Use Table B-1 (page A6) and the basic equation PV = future amount × conversion factor.
2. Assume the same facts as previously except that you will repay the loan in equal installments at the end of each of the 4 years. How much must you repay each year? Use Table B-2 (page A-9) and the basic equation: PV = future annual amounts × conversion factor.

11-33 PV and Sports Salaries

Because of a salary cap, **NBA** teams are not allowed to exceed a certain annual limit in total player salaries. Suppose the Minnesota Timberwolves had scheduled salaries exactly equal to their cap of $90 million for 2012. Kim Jenner, a star player, was scheduled to receive $15 million in 2012. To free up money to pay a prize rookie, Jenner agreed on July 1, 2012, to defer $8 million of his salary for 2 years, by which time the salary cap will have been increased. His contract called for salary payments of $15 million in 2012, $19 million in 2013, and $21 million in 2014, all on July 1 of the respective year. Now, he will receive $7 million in 2012, still $19 million in 2013, and $29 million in 2014. Jenner's required rate of return is 10%.

Did the deferral of salary cost Jenner anything? If so, how much? Compute the PV of the sacrifice as of July 1, 2012. Explain.

11-34 Simple NPV

Rajgopal Company expects to receive $600 at the end of each of the next 3 years and an additional $3,500 at the end of the third year. Therefore, the total payments will be $5,300. What is the NPV of the payments at an interest rate of 4%?

11-35 NPV Relationships

Fill in the blanks.

	Number of Years			
	7	18	18	28
Amount of annual cash inflow*	$8,000	$	$ 30,000	$16,000
Required initial investment	$	$70,000	$ 50,000	$29,000
Required rate of return	10%	18%	$	20%
NPV	$ 980	($10,009)	$231,157	$

*To be received at the end of each year.

11-36 New Equipment

The Montevideo Office Equipment Company has offered to sell some new packaging equipment to the Cortez Company. The list price is $65,000, but Montevideo has agreed to allow a trade-in allowance of $21,000 on some old equipment. The old equipment was carried at a book value of $21,300 and could be sold outright for $20,000 cash. Cash-operating savings are expected to be $22,000 annually for the next 8 years. The required rate of return is 14%. The old equipment has a remaining useful life of 8 years. Both the old and the new equipment will have zero disposal values 8 years from now.

Should Cortez buy the new equipment? Show your computations, using the NPV method. Ignore income taxes.

11-37 Present Values of Cash Inflows

City View Restaurant is about to open at a new location. Operating plans indicate the following expected cash flows:

		Outflows	Inflows
Initial investment now		$235,000	$ —
End of year:	1	$150,000	200,000
	2	$200,000	250,000
	3	$250,000	300,000
	4	$300,000	450,000
	5	$350,000	500,000

1. Compute the NPV for all these cash flows. This should be a single amount. Use a discount rate of 14%.
2. Suppose the required rate was 12%. Without further calculations, determine whether the NPV is positive or negative. Explain.

11-38 Effect of Required Rate

Blanchard Company has an opportunity to invest $15,000 in a new automated lathe that will reduce annual operating costs by $2,300 per year and will have an economic life of 12 years.

1. Suppose Blanchard Company has a required rate of return of 10%. Compute the NPV of the investment and recommend to Blanchard Company whether it should purchase the lathe.
2. Suppose Blanchard Company has a required rate of return of 12%. Compute the NPV of the investment and recommend to Blanchard Company whether it should purchase the lathe.
3. How does the required rate of return affect the NPV of a potential investment?

11-39 NPV and IRR

Czick Company is considering an investment in a machine that costs $36,048 and would result in cash savings of $10,000 per year for 5 years. The company's cost of capital is 10%.

1. Compute the project's NPV at 10%, 12%, and 14%.
2. Compute the project's IRR.
3. Suppose the company uses the NPV model. Would it accept the project? Why or why not?
4. Suppose the company uses the IRR model. Would it accept the project? Why or why not?

11-40 Sensitivity Analysis

Mack and Myer, LLP, a law firm, is considering the replacement of its old accounting system with new software that should save $10,000 per year in net cash operating costs. The old system has zero disposal value, but it could be used for the next 5 years. The estimated useful life of the new software is 5 years with zero salvage value, and it will cost $40,000. The required rate of return is 14%.

1. What is the payback period?
2. Compute the NPV.
3. Management is unsure about the useful life. What would be the NPV if the useful life were (a) 3 years instead of 5 or (b) 10 years instead of 5?
4. Suppose the life will be 5 years, but the savings will be $8,000 per year instead of $10,000. What would be the NPV?
5. Suppose the annual savings will be $9,000 for 4 years. What would be the NPV?

11-41 NPV and Sensitivity Analysis

Chippewa County Jail currently has its laundry done by a local cleaner at an annual cost of $46,000. It is considering a purchase of washers, dryers, and presses at a total installed cost of $52,000 so that inmates can do the laundry. The county expects savings of $15,000 per year, and it expects the machines to last 5 years. The required rate of return is 10%.

Answer each part separately.

1. Compute the NPV of the investment in laundry facilities.
2. a. Suppose the machines last only 4 years. Compute the NPV.
   b. Suppose the machines last 7 years. Compute the NPV.

CHAPTER 11

3. a. Suppose the annual savings are only $12,000. Compute the NPV.
   b. Suppose the annual savings are $18,000. Compute the NPV.

4. a. Compute the most optimistic estimate of NPV, combining the best outcomes in numbers 2 and 3.
   b. Compute the most pessimistic estimate of NPV, combining the worst outcomes in numbers 2 and 3.

5. Accept the expected life estimate of 5 years. What is the minimum annual savings that would justify the investment in the laundry facilities?

11-42 Depreciation, Income Taxes, Cash Flows

Fill in the unknowns (in thousands of dollars):

(S)	Sales	750
(E)	Expenses excluding depreciation	275
(D)	Depreciation	200
	Total expenses	475
	Income before income taxes	?
(T)	Income taxes at 36%	?
(I)	Net income	?
	Cash effects of operations	
	Cash inflow from operations, before tax	?
	Cash inflow from operations, after tax	?
	Tax savings due to depreciation	?
	Total after-tax effect on cash	?

11-43 After-Tax Effect on Cash

The 20X9 income statement of United Cable Company included the following:

Sales		$1,700,000
Less: Expenses, excluding depreciation	$350,000	
Depreciation	425,000	
Total expenses		$ 775,000
Income before taxes		$ 925,000
Income taxes (37%)		342,250
Net income		$ 582,750

Compute the total after-tax effect on cash. Use the format of the second part of Exhibit 11-3, page 446, "Annual Cash Flow Effects."

11-44 MACRS Depreciation

In 20X8, Tebow Athletic Shoe Company acquired the following assets and immediately placed them into service.

1. Special tools (a 3-year-MACRS asset) that cost $55,000 on February 1.
2. A desktop computer that cost $3,500 on December 15.
3. Special calibration equipment that was used in running-shoe research and cost $16,000 on July 7.
4. A set of file cabinets that cost $9,500, purchased on March 1.

Compute the depreciation for tax purposes, under the prescribed MACRS method, in 20X8 and 20X9. Round amounts to the nearest whole dollar.

11-45 Present Value of MACRS Depreciation

Compute the PV of the MACRS tax savings for each of the following five assets:

	Asset Cost	Recovery Period	Discount Rate	Tax Rate
(a)	$220,000	7-year	18%	33%
(b)	$640,000	7-year	12%	33%
(c)	$ 40,000	10-year	8%	29%
(d)	$950,000	10-year	5%	45%
(e)	$420,000	3-year	14%	25%

11-46 NPV, ARR, and Payback

Snuffy's Drive-In is considering a proposal to invest in a speaker system that would allow its employees to service drive-through customers. The cost of the system (including installation of special windows and driveway modifications) is $28,000. Brad Board, manager of Snuffy's, expects the drive-through operations to increase annual sales by $14,000, with a 25% contribution margin ratio. Assume that the system has an economic life of 10 years, at which time it will have no disposal value. The required rate of return is 10%. Ignore taxes.

1. Compute the payback period. Is this a good measure of profitability?
2. Compute the NPV. Should Brad Board accept the proposal? Why or why not?
3. Using the ARR model, compute the rate of return on the initial investment.

11-47 Weaknesses of the Payback Model

Stallone Company is considering two possible investments, each of which requires an initial investment of $36,000. Investment A will provide a cash flow of $4,000 at the end of each year for 20 years. Investment B will provide a cash flow of $4,500 at the end of each year for 8 years.

1. Determine the payback period for each investment. Which investment is most desirable using the payback method?
2. Compute the NPV of each investment using a required rate of return of 8%. Which investment is most desirable using the NPV method?
3. Explain why the payback method does not lead to an optimal decision for the Stallone Company.

11-48 Comparison of Capital-Budgeting Techniques

The City of Industry parks department is considering the purchase of a new, more efficient pool heater for its Campbell Swimming Pool at a cost of $28,000. It should save $7,000 in cash operating costs per year. Its estimated useful life is 10 years, and it will have zero disposal value. Ignore taxes.

1. What is the payback time?
2. Compute the NPV if the required rate of return is 10%. Should the department buy the heater? Why?
3. Using the ARR model, compute the rate of return on the initial investment.

11-49 Inflation and Capital Budgeting

Study Appendix 11. The head of the corporate tax division of a major public relations firm has proposed investing $290,000 in personal computers for the staff. The useful life and recovery period for the computers are both 5 years. The firm uses MACRS depreciation. There is no terminal salvage value. Labor savings of $140,000 per year (in year-zero dollars) are expected from the purchase. The income tax rate is 35%, and the after-tax required rate of return is 25%, which includes a 5% element attributable to inflation.

1. Compute the NPV of the computers. Use the nominal required rate of return and adjust the cash flows for inflation. (For example, year 1 cash flow = 1.05 × year 0 cash flow.)
2. Compute the NPV of the computers using the nominal required rate of return without adjusting the cash flows for inflation.
3. Compare your answers in numbers 1 and 2. Which is correct? Would using the incorrect analysis generally lead to overinvestment or underinvestment? Explain.

11-50 Sensitivity of Capital Budgeting to Inflation

Study Appendix 11. Enrique Mendoza, the president of a Mexican wholesale company, is considering whether to invest 420,000 pesos in new semiautomatic loading equipment that will last 5 years, have zero scrap value, and generate cash operating savings in labor usage of 150,000 pesos annually, using 20X0 prices and wage rates. It is December 31, 20X0.

   The required rate of return is 18% per year.

1. Compute the NPV of the project. Use 150,000 pesos as the savings for each of the 5 years. Assume a 40% tax rate and, for simplicity, assume ordinary straight-line depreciation of 420,000 pesos ÷ 5 = 84,000 pesos annually for tax purposes.
2. Mendoza is wondering if the model in number 1 provides a correct analysis of the effects of inflation. He maintains that the 18% rate embodies an element attributable to anticipated inflation. For purposes of this analysis, he assumes that the existing rate of inflation, 10% annually, will persist over the next 5 years. Repeat number 1, adjusting the cash operating savings upward by using the 10% inflation rate.
3. Which analysis, the one in number 1 or 2, is correct? Why?

PROBLEMS

11-51 Replacement of Office Equipment

Midwestern University is considering replacing some **Xerox** copiers with faster copiers purchased from **Brother**. The administration is very concerned about the rising costs of operations during the last decade.

To convert to Brother, two operators would have to be retrained. Required training and remodeling would cost $3,500. Midwestern's three Xerox machines were purchased for $8,000 each, 5 years ago. Their expected life was 15 years. Their resale value now is $1,750 each and will be zero in 10 more years. The total cost of the new Brother equipment will be $60,000; it will have zero disposal value in 10 years.

The three Xerox operators are paid $12 an hour each. They usually work a 40-hour week. Machine breakdowns occur monthly on each machine, resulting in repair costs of $75 per month and overtime of 6 hours, at time-and-one-half, per machine per month, to complete the normal monthly workload. Toner, supplies, and so on, cost $50 a month for each Xerox copier.

The Brother system will require only two regular operators, on a regular work week of 40 hours each, to do the same work. Rates are $14 an hour, and no overtime is expected. Toner, supplies, and so on, will cost a total of $4,500 annually. Maintenance and repairs are fully serviced by Brother for $600 annually. (Assume a 52-week year.)

1. Using DCF techniques, compute the PV of all relevant cash flows, under both alternatives, for the 10-year period discounted at 14%. As a nonprofit university, Midwestern does not pay income taxes.
2. Should Midwestern keep the Xerox copiers or replace them if the decision is based solely on the given data?
3. What other considerations might affect the decision?

11-52 Replacement Decision for Railway Equipment

Suppose the **Burlington Northern Railway** is considering replacement of a power jack tamper, used for maintenance of track, with a new automatic raising device that can be attached to a production tamper.

The present power jack tamper cost $35,000 seven years ago and had an estimated life of 15 years. Two years from now, the machine will require a major overhaul estimated to cost $6,500. It can be disposed of now via an outright cash sale for $5,500. There will be no value at the end of another 8 years.

The automatic raising attachment has a delivered selling price of $45,000 and an estimated life of 17 years. Because of anticipated future developments in combined maintenance machines, Burlington Northern management predicts that the company will dispose of the machine at the end of the eighth year to take advantage of newly developed machines. Estimated sales value at the end of 8 years is $6,500.

Tests have shown that the automatic raising machine will produce a more uniform surface on the track than does the power jack tamper now in use. The new equipment will eliminate one laborer whose annual compensation, including fringe benefits, is $36,000.

Track maintenance work is seasonal, and the equipment normally works from May 1 to October 31 each year. Machine operators and laborers are transferred to other work after October 31, at the same rate of pay.

The salesman claims that the annual normal maintenance of the new machine will run about $900 per year. Because the automatic raising machine is more complicated than the manually operated machine, it will probably require a thorough overhaul at the end of the third year, at an estimated cost of $5,500.

Records show the annual normal maintenance of the power jack tamper to be $1,500. Fuel consumption of the two machines is equal. Should Burlington Northern keep or replace the power jack tamper? The company requires a 14% rate of return. Compute PV. Ignore income taxes.

11-53 Discounted Cash Flow, Uneven Revenue Stream, Relevant Costs

Mildred Driver, the owner of a nine-hole golf course on the outskirts of a large city, is considering a proposal that the course be illuminated and operated at night. Ms. Driver purchased the course early last year for $480,000. Her receipts from operations during the 28-week season were $135,000. Total disbursements for the year, for all purposes, were $84,000.

The required investment in lighting this course is estimated at $90,000. The system will require 300 lamps of 1,000 watts each. Electricity costs $.08 per kilowatt-hour. The expected average hours of operation per night is 5. Because of occasional bad weather and the probable curtailment of night operation at the beginning and end of the season, it is estimated that there will be only 130 nights of operation per year. Labor for keeping the course open at night will cost $75 per night. Lightbulb cost is estimated at $1,500 per year; other maintenance and repairs, per year, will amount to 4% of the initial cost of the lighting system. Annual property taxes on this equipment will be about 1.7% of its initial cost. It is estimated that the average revenue, per night of operation, will be $420 for the first 2 years.

Considering the probability of competition from the illumination of other golf courses, Ms. Driver decides that she will not make the investment unless she can make at least 10% per annum on her investment. Because of anticipated competition, revenue is expected to drop to $300 per night for years 3–5. It is estimated that the lighting equipment will have a salvage value of $35,000 at the end of the 5-year period.

Using DCF techniques, determine whether Ms. Driver should install the lighting system.

11-54 Investment in Machine

The Soho Ale Company has an old brewing machine with a net disposal value of £12,000 now and £4,000 five years from now. A new brewing machine is offered for £57,000 cash or £45,000 with a trade-in. The new machine will result in an annual operating cash outflow of £40,000 as compared with the old machine's annual outflow of £50,000. The disposal value of the new machine 5 years hence will be £2,000.

The required rate of return is 20%. The company uses DCF techniques to guide these decisions.

Should Soho Ale acquire the new brewing machine? Show your calculations. Company procedures require the computing of the PV of each alternative. The most desirable alternative is the one with the least cost. Assume that the PV of £1 at 20% for 5 years is £.40; the PV of an annuity of £1 at 20% for 5 years is £3.

11-55 Replacement Decision

The **Metropolitan Transit Authority (MTA)** has included a cafeteria car on the passenger train it operates. Yearly operations of the cafeteria car have shown a consistent loss, which is expected to persist, as follows:

Revenue (in cash)		$200,000
Expenses for food, supplies, etc. (in cash)	$100,000	
Salaries	110,000	210,000
Net loss (ignore depreciation on the dining car itself)		$(10,000)

The Auto-Vend Company has offered to sell automatic vending machines to MTA for $22,000, less a $3,000 trade-in allowance on old equipment (which is carried at $3,000 book value, and which can be sold outright for $3,000 cash) now used in the cafeteria-car operation. The useful life of the vending equipment is estimated at 10 years, with zero scrap value. Experience elsewhere has led executives to predict that the equipment will serve 50% more food than the dining car, but prices will be 50% less, so the new revenue will probably be $150,000. The variety and mix of food sold are expected to be the same as for the cafeteria car. A catering company will completely service and supply food and beverages for the machines, paying 10% of revenue to MTA and bearing all costs of food, repairs, and so on. All dining-car employees will be discharged immediately. Their termination pay will total $35,000. However, an attendant who has some general knowledge of vending machines will be needed for one shift per day. The annual cost to MTA for the attendant will be $13,000.

For political and other reasons, the railroad will definitely not abandon its food service. The old equipment will have zero scrap value at the end of 10 years.

Using the preceding data, compute the following. Label computations. Ignore income taxes.

1. Use the NPV method to analyze the incremental investment. Assume a required rate of return of 10%. For this problem, assume that the PV of $1 at 10% to be received at the end of 10 years is $.400 and that the PV of an annuity of $1 at 10% for 10 years is $6.000.
2. What would be the minimum amount of annual revenue that MTA would have to receive from the catering company to justify making the investment? Show computations.

11-56 Minimization of Transportation Costs Without Income Taxes

Green Lighting Company produces industrial and residential lighting fixtures at its manufacturing facility located in Scottsdale, Arizona. The company currently ships products to an eastern warehouse via common carriers at a rate of $.27 per pound of fixtures. The warehouse is located in Atlanta, 1,900 miles from Scottsdale.

Alexis Azra, the treasurer of Green Lighting, is considering whether to purchase a truck for transporting products to the eastern warehouse. The following data on the truck are available:

Purchase price	$75,000
Useful life	4 years
Salvage value after 4 years	0
Capacity of truck	7,000 lb
Cash costs of operating truck	$.95 per mile

Azra feels that an investment in this truck is particularly attractive because of her successful negotiation with Jetson to back-haul Jetson's products from Atlanta to Scottsdale on every return trip from the warehouse. Jetson has agreed to pay Green Lighting $2,300 per load of Jetson's products hauled from Atlanta to Scottsdale up to and including 100 loads per year.

Green Lighting's marketing manager has estimated that the company will ship 385,000 pounds of fixtures to the eastern warehouse each year for the next 4 years. The truck will be fully loaded on each round trip.

Ignore income taxes.

1. Assume that Green Lighting requires a rate of return of 18%. Should it purchase the truck? Show computations to support your answer.
2. What is the minimum number of trips that Jetson must guarantee to make the deal acceptable to Green Lighting, based on the preceding numbers alone?
3. What qualitative factors might influence your decision? Be specific.

11-57 Straight-Line Depreciation, MACRS Depreciation, and Immediate Write-Off

Mr. Hiramatsu bought a new $50,000 freezer for his grocery store on January 2, 2013. The freezer has a 5-year economic life and recovery period, Mr. Hiramatsu's required rate of return is 12%, and his tax rate is 40%.

1. Suppose Mr. Hiramatsu uses straight-line depreciation for tax purposes. Compute the PV of the tax savings from depreciation. Assume that Mr. Hiramatsu takes a full year of depreciation at the end of 2013.
2. Suppose Mr. Hiramatsu uses MACRS depreciation for tax purposes. Compute the PV of the tax savings from depreciation.
3. Suppose Mr. Hiramatsu was allowed to immediately deduct the entire cost of the freezer for tax purposes. Compute the PV of the tax savings from depreciation.
4. Which of the three methods of deducting the cost of the freezer would Mr. Hiramatsu prefer if all three were allowable for tax purposes? Why?

11-58 MACRS, Residual Value

The Donald Company estimates that it can save $20,000 per year in annual operating cash costs for the next 3 years if it buys a special-purpose machine at a cost of $46,000. Residual value is expected to be $6,000, although no residual value is being provided for in using MACRS depreciation (3-year recovery period) for tax purposes. The company will sell the equipment at the end of the third year. The required rate of return is 16%. Assume the income tax rate is 30%.

Using the NPV method, show whether the investment is desirable.

11-59 Purchase of Equipment, MACRS

The Scranton Clinic, a for-profit medical facility, is planning to spend $35,000 for modernized MRI equipment. It will replace equipment that has zero book value and no salvage value, although the old equipment would have lasted another 10 years.

The new equipment will save $6,000 in cash operating costs for each of the next 10 years, at which time the clinic will sell it for $8,500. A major overhaul costing $9,000 will occur at the end of the seventh year; the old equipment would require no such overhaul. The entire cost of the overhaul is deductible for tax purposes in the seventh year. The equipment has a 3-year recovery period. The clinic uses MACRS depreciation for tax purposes.

The required rate of return is 8%. The applicable income tax rate is 44%.

Compute the after-tax NPV. Is the new equipment a desirable investment?

11-60 MACRS and Low-Income Housing

Aaron Hersch is a real estate developer who specializes in residential apartments. A complex of 20 run-down apartments has recently come on the market for $332,500. Hersch predicts that after remodeling, the 12 one-bedroom units will rent for $380 per month and the 8 two-bedroom apartments for

$440. He budgets 15% of the rental fees for repairs and maintenance. It should be 30 years before the apartments need remodeling again, if the work is done well. Remodeling costs are $15,000 per apartment. Both purchase price and remodeling costs qualify as 27.5-year MACRS property.

Assume that the MACRS schedule uses the straight-line method. It divides the total cost recovery amount by 27.5 and assigns a full year of depreciation to year 1 and a half year to year 28.

Hersch does not believe he will keep the apartment complex for its entire 30-year life. Most likely he will sell it just after the end of the tenth year. His predicted sales price is $980,000.

Hersch's required rate of return is 10%, and his tax rate is 38%.

Should Hersch buy the apartment complex? What is the after-tax NPV? Ignore tax complications, such as capital gains.

11-61 PV of After-Tax Cash Flows, Payback, and ARR

Suppose that Mitsubishi Chemical Corporation is planning to buy new equipment to expand its production of a popular solvent. Estimated data are as follows (monetary amounts are in thousands of Japanese yen):

Cash cost of new equipment now	¥400,000
Estimated life in years	10
Terminal salvage value	¥ 50,000
Incremental revenues per year	¥330,000
Incremental expenses per year other than depreciation	¥165,000

Assume a 60% flat rate for income taxes. The company receives all revenues and pays all expenses other than depreciation in cash. Use a 14% discount rate. Assume that the company uses ordinary straight-line depreciation based on a 10-year recovery period for tax purposes. Also assume that the company depreciates the original cost less the terminal salvage value.

Compute the following:

1. Depreciation expense per year
2. Anticipated net income per year
3. Annual net cash flow
4. Payback period
5. ARR on initial investment
6. NPV

11-62 Investment Justification Analysis and Graphs

Consider a new video game developed by Dynamic Gaming, Inc. (DGI). DGI's development team was formed at the end of 2009 and has been working on the development of the game for several years. After spending $175,000 on the development, the team has reached the point in 2013 where it must make a decision on whether to proceed with production of the game. Production of the game will require an initial investment in facilities of $199,500 at the end of 2013. The project has an expected life cycle of 7 years (end of 2013 through 2020). Predicted cash flows for the game are as follows (assuming that all cash flows occur at the end of the year):

End of Year	Cash Inflow	Cash Outflow
2013	$ 0	$199,500
2014	100,000	100,000
2015	220,000	180,000
2016	340,000	260,000
2017	460,000	320,000
2018	470,000	280,000
2019	410,000	200,000
2020	150,000	120,000

DGI's applicable tax rate is 40%, and DGI uses straight-line depreciation over the asset's expected life for tax purposes. The salvage value of the facilities will be zero in 7 years. DGI uses two criteria to evaluate potential investments: payback time and NPV. It wants a payback period of 3 years or less and an NPV greater than zero. DGI has a cost of capital of 18%.

1. Prepare a table that shows the after-tax annual net cash flows, cumulative net cash flow, and cumulative discounted net cash flow each year.
2. Would DGI invest in production of the game if it uses the payback period?
3. Would DGI invest in production of the game if it uses the NPV model?
4. Would you recommend that DGI invest in this project? Explain.

11-63 Fixed and Current Assets; Evaluation of Performance

Museum Clinic has been under pressure to keep costs down. The clinic administrator has been managing various revenue-producing centers to maximize contributions to the recovery of the operating costs of the clinic as a whole. The administrator has been considering whether to buy a special-purpose CAT scan machine for $251,000. Its unique characteristics would generate additional cash operating income of $50,000 per year for the clinic as a whole.

The clinic expects the machine to have a useful life of 8 years and a terminal salvage value of $35,000. The machine is delicate. It requires a constant inventory of various supplies and spare parts. When the clinic uses some of these items, it instantly replaces them so it maintains an investment of $7,000 at all times. However, the clinic fully recovers this investment at the end of the useful life of the machine.

1. Compute NPV if the required rate of return is 10%.
2. Compute the ARR on (a) the initial investment and (b) the "average" investment. Assume straight-line depreciation.
3. Why might the administrator be reluctant to base her decision on the DCF model?

11-64 Investment Before and After Taxes

Deer Valley Lodge, a ski area near Salt Lake City, has plans to eventually add five new chairlifts. Suppose that one of the lifts costs $2.2 million, and preparing the slope and installing the lift costs another $1.48 million. The lift will allow 300 additional skiers on the slopes, but there are only 40 days a year when the lodge needs the extra capacity. (Assume that Deer Valley will sell all 300 lift tickets on those 40 days.) Running the new lift will cost $500 a day for the entire 200 days the lodge is open. Assume that lift tickets at Deer Valley cost $65 a day and added cash expenses for each skier-day are $9. The new lift has an economic life of 20 years.

1. Assume that the before-tax required rate of return for Deer Valley is 14%. Compute the before-tax NPV of the new lift and advise the managers of Deer Valley about whether adding the lift will be a profitable investment.
2. Assume that the after-tax required rate of return for Deer Valley is 8%, the income tax rate is 40%, and the MACRS recovery period is 10 years. Compute the after-tax NPV of the new lift and advise the managers of Deer Valley about whether adding the lift will be a profitable investment.
3. What subjective factors would affect the investment decision?

11-65 After-Tax NPV

Berradi Corp. is considering the purchase of a new stamping machine to manufacture its product. The following information is available:

New Machine	
Purchase cost new	$85,000
Annual increase in cash revenues	60,000
Annual increase in cash operating costs	42,000
Salvage value—10 years from now	5,000

If Berradi purchases the new machine, it will use it for 10 years and then trade it in on another machine. The company computes depreciation on a straight-line basis, for both taxes and financial reporting purposes. Assume Berradi currently has an old stamping machine with a book value of $30,000 that it can currently dispose of for $8,000 if it buys the new machine. Assume Berradi's cost of capital is 14%, and its tax rate is 30%.

Should the new machine be purchased based on the NPV method?

11-66 Minimization of Transportation Costs After Taxes, Inflation

Study Appendix 11. (This problem is similar to Problem 11-56, but the numbers are different and it includes taxes and inflation elements.) The Green Lighting Company produces industrial and residential lighting fixtures at its manufacturing facility in Scottsdale. The company currently ships products to an eastern warehouse via common carriers at a rate of $.26 per pound of fixtures (expressed in year-zero dollars). The warehouse is located in Cleveland, 2,500 miles from Scottsdale. The rate will increase with inflation.

Alexis Azra, the treasurer of Green Lighting, is currently considering whether to purchase a truck for transporting products to the eastern warehouse. The following data on the truck are available:

Purchase price	$50,000
Useful life	5 years
Salvage value after 5 years	0
Capacity of truck	10,000 lb
Cash costs of operating truck	$.90 per mile

Azra feels that an investment in this truck is particularly attractive because of her successful negotiation with Jetson to back-haul Jetson's products from Cleveland to Scottsdale on every return trip from the warehouse. Jetson has agreed to pay Green Lighting $2,400 per load of Jetson's products hauled from Cleveland to Scottsdale for as many loads as Green Lighting can accommodate, up to and including 100 loads per year over the next 5 years.

Green Lighting's marketing manager has estimated that the company will ship 500,000 pounds of fixtures to the eastern warehouse each year for the next 5 years. The truck will be fully loaded on each round trip.

Make the following assumptions:

a. Green Lighting requires a 20% after-tax rate of return, which includes a 10% element attributable to inflation.
b. A 40% tax rate.
c. MACRS depreciation based on 5-year cost recovery period.
d. An inflation rate of 10%.

1. Should Green Lighting purchase the truck? Show computations to support your answer.
2. What qualitative factors might influence your decision? Be specific.

11-67 Inflation and Nonprofit Institution

Study Appendix 11. MLK Elementary School is considering the purchase of a photocopying machine for $7,000 on December 31, 20X0. The machine will have a useful life of 5 years and no residual value. The cash operating savings are expected to be $2,000 annually, measured in 20X0 dollars.

The required rate is 14%, which includes an element attributable to anticipated inflation of 6%. (Remember that the school district pays no income taxes.)

Use the 14% required rate for numbers 1 and 2:

1. Compute the NPV of the project without adjusting the cash operating savings for inflation.
2. Repeat number 1, adjusting the cash operating savings upward in accordance with the 6% inflation rate.
3. Compare your results in numbers 1 and 2. What generalization seems applicable about the analysis of inflation in capital budgeting?

CASES

11-68 Investment in CAD/CAM

Aswega AS is an Estonian manufacturer of electromagnetic flowmeters, heatmeters, and calibration equipment located in Tallinn. Suppose that it is considering the installation of a computer-aided design/computer-aided manufacturing (CAD/CAM) system. The current proposal calls for implementation of only the CAD portion of the system. The manager in charge of production design and planning has estimated that the CAD portion of CAD/CAM could do the work of five designers, who are each paid EEK 520,000 per year (52 weeks × 40 hours × EEK 250 per hour), where EEK is the symbol for the Estonian kroon.

Aswega can purchase the CAD/CAM system for EEK 2.8 million. (It cannot purchase the CAD portion separately.) The annual out-of-pocket costs of running the CAD portion of the system are EEK 1.8 million. The company expects to use the system for 8 years. The company's required rate of return is 12%. Ignore income taxes.

1. Compute the NPV of the investment in the CAD/CAM system. Should Aswega purchase the system? Explain.
2. Suppose the manager was not certain about her predictions of savings and economic life. Possibly the company will replace only four designers, but if everything works out well, it may replace as many as six. If better systems become available, the company may use the CAD/CAM system for

only 5 years, but it might last as long as 10 years. Prepare pessimistic, most likely, and optimistic predictions of NPV. Would this analysis make you more confident or less confident in your decision in number 1? Explain.

3. What subjective factors might influence your decision?

11-69 Investment in Technology

Nashville Tool Company is considering installation of a CIM system as part of its implementation of a JIT philosophy. Gretchen Torres, company president, is convinced that the new system is necessary, but she needs the numbers to convince the board of directors. This is a major move for the company, and approval at board level is required.

Maria, Gretchen's daughter, has been assigned the task of justifying the investment. She is a business school graduate and understands the use of NPV for capital-budgeting decisions. To identify relevant costs, she developed the following information.

Nashville Tool Company produces a variety of small automobile components and sells them to auto manufacturers. It has a 40% market share, with the following condensed results expected for 2011:

Sales		$12,000,000
Cost of goods sold		
Variable	$4,000,000	
Fixed	4,300,000	8,300,000
Selling and administrative expenses		
Variable	$2,000,000	
Fixed	400,000	2,400,000
Operating income		$ 1,300,000

Installation of the CIM system will cost $6 million, and the company expects the system to have a useful life of 6 years with no salvage value. Installation will occur at the beginning of 2012. In 2012, the training costs for personnel will exceed any cost savings by $400,000. In years 2013–2017, variable cost of goods sold will decrease by 35%, an annual savings of $1.4 million. There will be no savings in fixed cost of goods sold—it will increase by the amount of the straight-line depreciation on the new system. Selling and administrative expenses will not be affected. The required rate of return is 12%. Assume that all cash flows occur at the end of the year the revenue or expense is recognized, except the initial investment, which occurs at the beginning of 2012. Ignore income taxes.

1. Suppose that Maria assumes that production and sales would continue for the next 6 years as they are expected in 2011 in the absence of investment in the CIM. Compute the NPV of investing in the CIM.

2. Now suppose Maria predicts that it will be difficult to compete without installing the CIM. She has undertaken market research that estimates a drop in market share of three percentage points a year starting in 2012 in the absence of investment in the CIM (i.e., market share will be 37% in 2012, 34% in 2013, 31% in 2014, etc.). Her study also showed that the total market sales level will stay the same, and she does not expect market prices to change. Compute the NPV of investing in the CIM.

3. Prepare a memo from Maria to the board of directors of Nashville Tool Company. In the memo, explain why the analysis in number 2 is appropriate and why analyses such as that in number 1 cause companies to underinvest in high-technology projects. Include an explanation of qualitative factors that are not included in the NPV calculation.

11-70 Investment in Quality

The Sydney Manufacturing Company produces a single model of a high-quality DVD player that it sells to Australian manufacturers of sound systems. It sells each DVD player for $210, resulting in a contribution margin of $70 before considering any costs of inspection, correction of product defects, or refunds to customers.

On January 1, 2014, top management at Sydney is contemplating a change in its quality control system. Currently, the company spends $30,000 annually on quality control inspections for the 50,000 DVD players it produces and ships each year. In producing those DVD players, the company produces an average of 2,000 defective units. The inspection process identifies 1,500 of these, and the company spends an average of $85 on each to correct the defects. The company ships the other 500 defective players to customers. When a customer discovers a defective DVD player, Sydney Manufacturing refunds the $210 purchase price.

Many of Sydney's customers build the DVD players into home-entertainment units. As more of these customers change to JIT inventory systems and automated production processes, the receipt of defective goods poses greater and greater problems for them. Sometimes a defective DVD player causes them to delay their whole production line while they replace the DVD player. Companies competing with Sydney recognize this situation, and most have already begun extensive quality control programs. If Sydney does not improve quality, sales volume is expected to fall by 5,000 DVD players a year, beginning after 2014:

	Predicted Sales Volume in Units Without Quality Control Program	Predicted Sales Volume in Units with Quality Control Program
2014	50,000	50,000
2015	45,000	50,000
2016	40,000	50,000
2017	35,000	50,000

The proposed quality control program has two elements. First, Sydney would spend $950,000 immediately to train workers to recognize and correct defects at the time they occur. This is expected to cut the number of defective DVD players produced from 2,000 to 500 without incurring additional manufacturing costs. Second, an earlier inspection point would replace the current inspection. This would require purchase of an X-ray machine at a cost of $250,000 plus additional annual operating costs of $60,000 more than the current inspection costs. Early detection of defects would reduce the average amount spent to correct defects from $85 to $50, and only 50 defective DVD players would be shipped to customers. To compete, Sydney would refund one-and-one-half times the purchase price ($315) for defective DVD players delivered to customers.

Top management at Sydney has decided that a 4-year planning period is sufficient for analyzing this decision. The required rate of return is 20%. For simplicity, assume that under the current quality control system, if the volume of production decreases, the number of defective DVD players produced remains at 2,000. Also assume that all annual cash flows occur at the end of the relevant year. Should Sydney undertake the new quality control program? Explain using the NPV model. Ignore income taxes.

11-71 Make or Buy and Replacement of Equipment

International Hoists is one of the largest producers of hoists of all types. An especially complex part of a particular auto hoist needs special tools that are not useful for other products. The company purchased these tools on July 1, 20X0, for $2,000,000.

It is now July 1, 20X4. The manager of the auto hoists division, David Lee, is contemplating three alternatives. First, he could continue to produce the ship using the current tools; they will last another 5 years, at which time they would have zero terminal value. Second, he could sell the tools for $400,000 and purchase the parts from an outside supplier for $110 each. Third, he could replace the tools with new, more efficient tools costing $1,800,000.

Lee expects to produce 8,000 units of this particular hoist each of the next 5 years. Manufacturing costs for the hoist have been as follows, and no change in costs is expected:

Direct materials	$ 38
Direct labor	37
Variable overhead	17
Fixed overhead*	45
Total unit cost	$137

*Depreciation accounts for two-thirds of the fixed overhead. The balance is for other fixed overhead costs of the factory that require cash outlays, 60% of which would be saved if production of the parts were eliminated.

The outside supplier offered the $110 price on a 5-year contract as a once-only offer. It is unlikely it would make such a low price available later. International Hoists would also have to guarantee to purchase at least 7,000 parts for each of the next 5 years.

The new tools that are available would last for 5 years with a disposal value of $500,000 at the end of 5 years. The old tools are a 5-year MACRS property, the new tools are a 3-year MACRS property, and both use the current MACRS schedules. International Hoists uses straight-line depreciation for book purposes and MACRS for tax purposes. The sales representative selling the new tools stated, "The new tools will allow direct labor and variable overhead to be reduced by $21 per unit." Lee thinks this estimate is accurate. However, he also knows that a higher quality of materials would be necessary with the new tools. He predicts the following costs with the new tools:

Direct materials	$ 40
Direct labor	25
Variable overhead	8
Fixed overhead	60*
Total unit cost	$133

*The increase in fixed overhead is caused by depreciation on the new tools.

The company has a 40% marginal tax rate and requires a 12% after-tax rate of return.

1. Calculate the NPV of each of the three alternatives. Recognize the tax implications. Which alternative should Lee select?
2. What are some factors besides the NPV that should influence Lee's selection?

NIKE 10-K PROBLEM

11-72 Nike Capital Budgeting with NPV

Examine Nike's financial statements and notes 1 and 3 to those statements in Appendix C.

1. What method of depreciation does Nike use in reporting to shareholders? Do you think it uses the same method for tax purposes? If not, what method do you suppose they use for tax reporting? Why?
2. What is the original cost of the machinery and equipment currently used by Nike? If Nike generally invests about $400 million per year in machinery and equipment, what is the average useful life of its machinery and equipment?
3. Nike's Statement of Cash Flows shows that the company invested $432 million in property, plant, and equipment during fiscal 2011. Assume that these assets have a useful life of 5 years and that Nike requires a 14% pretax rate of return. Compute the minimum average annual pretax net cash inflow that would justify this investment.
4. Using the $432 million of investment and the net cash flow you computed in requirement 3 (and assuming zero residual value), determine the investment's a) payback period and b) accounting rate of return on average investment.

EXCEL APPLICATION EXERCISE

11-73 Net Present Value and Payback Period for a Purchase Decision

Goal: Create a spreadsheet to compute the NPV and payback period to assist with a purchase decision. Use the results to answer questions about your findings.

Scenario: Amazon.com is planning to purchase a new bar-coding machine for one of its warehouses. You have been asked to prepare a simple analysis to determine whether Amazon should purchase the machine. The bar-coding machine costs $60,000. It has a 5-year economic life and an estimated residual value of $10,000. The estimated annual net cash flow from the machine is $16,000. Amazon.com's required rate of return is 16%.

When you have completed your spreadsheet, answer the following questions:

1. What is the machine's NPV?
2. What is the machine's payback period?
3. Should Amazon.com purchase the machine? Why or why not?

Step-by-Step:

1. Open a new Excel spreadsheet.
2. In column A, create bold-faced headings that contain the following:
   Row 1: Chapter 11 Decision Guideline
   Row 2: Amazon.com
   Row 3: Analysis for Purchase of Bar-Coding Machine
   Row 4: Today's Date
3. Merge and center the four heading rows across columns A–H.

4. In row 7, create the following bold-faced headings:
   Column A: Cash Outflow
   Column B: Calculations
   Column D: Annualized Cash Flows

5. Center the heading in column A, row 7 and then shade the heading as follows:

          Patterns tab: Color: Lightest gray (above white)

   Note: Adjust column width as necessary.

6. Merge and center the heading in column B, row 7 across columns B–C.

7. Merge and center the heading in column D, row 7 across columns D–H and shade the heading as follows:

          Patterns tab: Color: Lightest gray (above white)

8. In row 8, create the following bold-faced, center-justified column headings:
   Column A: Investment
   Column B: Net Present Value
   Column C: Payback Period
   Column D: Year 1
   Column E: Year 2
   Column F: Year 3
   Column G: Year 4
   Column H: Year 5

   Note: Adjust the width of columns B and C as necessary.

9. Use the scenario data to fill in the investment and annualized cash flows for each of the 5 years.

   Note: The amount in the Investment column should be entered as a negative amount because it represents cash outflow. Be sure to include the machine's residual value in the appropriate column when entering the Annualized Cash Flows data.

10. Use the NPV function to calculate the NPV of the machine in column B, row 9.
    Click Insert on the tool bar and select Function. Then do the following:

        Function category: Financial

        Function name: NPV

    Complete the fill-in form that appears with the appropriate data from the scenario.

    Hint: Go to "Help" and search the topic "NPV." Review the help text that appears. Carefully read the examples given and their associated formulas. Use the formula that matches the scenario data for the problem.

11. Enter a formula to calculate the payback period in column C, row 9. Ensure a positive result by using the absolute value function in your payback formula. (The formula can be found in the chapter.)

12. Modify the format of the payback period result by clicking in the cell containing the results. At the end of the formula that appears in the formula bar, type the following: & "years".
    Right justify the result.

13. Format row 9, columns A–B and columns D–H as follows:

        Number tab: Category: Currency
        Decimal places: 2
        Symbol: $
        Negative numbers: Red with parentheses

14. Save your work, and print a copy for your files.

    Note: Print your spreadsheet using landscape to ensure that all columns appear on one page.

COLLABORATIVE LEARNING EXERCISE

11-74 Capital Budgeting, Sensitivity Analysis, and Ethics

Abrielle Rossi had recently been appointed controller of the soup division of a major food company. The division manager, Asim Sharma, was known as a hard-driving, intelligent, uncompromising manager. He had been very successful and was rumored to be on the fast track to corporate top management, maybe even in line for the company presidency. One of Abrielle's first assignments was to prepare the financial analysis for a new soup, Delhi Chicken. This product was especially important to Sharma because he was convinced that it would be a success and thereby a springboard for his ascent to top management.

Rossi discussed the product with the food lab that had designed it, with the market research department that had tested it, and with the finance people who would have to fund its introduction. After putting together all the information, she developed the following optimistic and pessimistic sales projections:

	Optimistic	Pessimistic
Year 1	$ 1,600,000	$ 800,000
Year 2	3,600,000	1,200,000
Year 3	5,000,000	1,000,000
Year 4	8,000,000	800,000
Year 5	10,000,000	400,000

The optimistic predictions assume a successful introduction of a popular product. The pessimistic predictions assume that the product is introduced but does not gain wide acceptance and is terminated after 5 years. Rossi thinks the most likely results are halfway between the optimistic and pessimistic predictions.

Rossi learned from finance that this type of product introduction requires a predicted pretax rate of return of 16% before top management will authorize funds for its introduction. She also determined that the contribution margin should be about 50% on the product but could be as low as 42% or as high as 58%. Initial investment would include $3.5 million for production facilities and $2.5 million for advertising and other product introduction expenses. The production facilities would have a value of $1.2 million after 5 years.

Based on her preliminary analysis, Rossi recommended to Sharma that the product not be launched. Sharma was not pleased with the recommendation. He claimed that Rossi was much too pessimistic and asked her to redo her numbers so that he could justify the product to top management.

Rossi carried out further analysis, but her predictions came out no different. She became even more convinced that her projections were accurate. Yet, she was certain that if she returned to Sharma with numbers that did not support introduction of the product, she would incur his wrath. And he could be right—that is, there is so much uncertainty in the forecasts that she could easily come up with believable numbers that would support going forward with the product. She would not believe them, but she believed she could convince top management that they were accurate.

The entire class could role-play this scenario or it could be done in teams of three to six persons. Here, it is acted out by a team.

Choose one member of the team to be Abrielle Rossi and one to be Asim Sharma.

1. With the help of the entire team except the person chosen to be Sharma, Rossi should prepare the capital-budgeting analysis used for her first meeting with Sharma.
2. Next, Rossi should meet again with Sharma. They should try to agree on the analysis to take forward to top management. As they discuss the issues and try to come to an agreement, the remaining team members should record all the ethical judgments each discussant makes.
3. After Rossi and Sharma have completed their role-playing assignment, the entire team should assess the ethical judgments made by each and recommend an appropriate position for Rossi to take in this situation.

INTERNET EXERCISE

11-75 Capital Budgeting at Carnival Corporation

Many companies strive to continue to grow and develop. Some companies grow through the expansion of existing operations and increased utilization of existing assets. Others grow through the acquisition of firms within their industry or by purchasing a firm that opens up new direction for them. No matter which method a company selects, capital budgeting is an important part of a systematic expansion plan. Consider the expansion activities of Carnival Corporation, the cruise ship company.

1. Go to Carnival Corporation's home page at www.carnivalcorp.com. What cruise lines does Carnival own or have an interest in? Now go to the page "Corporate Information." How many ships does Carnival currently operate? What type of plans does the firm list for future expansion? What does this information indicate about the intent of the firm?
2. As we can see, the firm has looked ahead to buying new ships. To get additional information, click on the link to "Investor Relations" and then "Financial Reports." Select the most recent annual report and open it. Go to the section on Highlights near the beginning of the report. Looking at passengers carried and passenger capacity, examine how capacity available and capacity used have changed over the past 5 years.
3. Now examine the CEO's letter. What does the letter tell the investor about new investment during the current year and investment plans for the future?
4. Let's look at the Statement of Cash Flows to see if we can determine where the firm got the cash to pay for the new ships. Based on your review of the cash flow statement, how much money did

the firm invest in new property and equipment? Did Carnival generate the cash to pay for this investment from operations or from financing activities?

Solutions to Exercises in Compound Interest, Problem 11-A1

The general approach to these exercises centers on one fundamental question: Which of the two basic tables am I dealing with? No calculations should be made until after this question is answered with assurance. If you made any errors, it is possible that you used the wrong table.

1. From Table B-1, Appendix B, page A6:

   a. $19,587.50
   b. $15,522.50
   c. $10,047.50

   The $25,000 is an amount of future worth. You want the PV of that amount:

   $$PV = \$25,000 \times \frac{1}{[(1+i)^n]}$$

   The conversion factor, $1/(1+i)^n$, is on line 5 of Table B-1. Substituting,

   $$PV = \$25,000(.7835) = \$19,587.50$$
   $$PV = \$25,000(.6209) = \$15,522.50$$
   $$PV = \$25,000(.4019) = \$10,047.50$$

   Note that the higher the interest rate, the lower the PV.

2. From Table B-2, Appendix B, page A9:

   a. $8,659.00
   b. $7,581.60
   c. $5,981.20

   The $2,000 withdrawal is a uniform annual amount, an annuity. You need to find the PV of an annuity for 5 years:

   $$PV_A = \text{annual withdrawal} \times F, \text{where F is the conversion factor.}$$

   Substituting:

   $$PV_A = \$2,000(4.3295) = \$8,659.00$$
   $$PV_A = \$2,000(3.7908) = \$7,581.60$$
   $$PV_A = \$2,000(2.9906) = \$5,981.20$$

3. From Table B-2:

   a. $23,097.36
   b. $26,379.66

   You have $100,000, the PV of your contemplated annuity. You must find the annuity that will just exhaust the invested principal in 5 years:

   $$PV_A = \text{annual withdrawal} \times F$$
   $$\$100,000 = \text{annual withdrawal} \times 4.3295$$
   $$\text{annual withrawal} = \$100,000 \div 4.3295$$
   $$= \$23,097.36$$
   $$\$100,000 = \text{annual withdrawal} \times 3.7908$$
   $$\text{annual withdrawal} = \$100,000 \div 3.7908$$
   $$= \$26,379.66$$

4. Amounts are in thousands. From Table B-1: LeBron's contract is preferable; its PV exceeds that of Kobe's contract by $43,143 − $35,441 = $7,702. Note that the nearer dollars are more valuable than the distant dollars.

Year	Present Value at 16% from Table B-1	Present Value of LeBron's Contract	Present Value of Kobe's Contract
1	.8621	$17,242	$ 3,448
2	.7432	11,891	5,946
3	.6407	7,688	7,688
4	.5523	4,418	8,837
5	.4761	1,904	9,522
		$43,143	$35,441

Cost Allocation

LEARNING OBJECTIVES

When you have finished studying this chapter, you should be able to:

1. Describe the general framework for cost allocation.

2. Allocate the variable and fixed costs of service departments to other organizational units.

3. Use the direct and step-down methods to allocate service department costs to user departments.

4. Allocate costs from producing departments to products or services using the traditional and ABC approaches.

5. Allocate costs associated with customer actions to customers.

6. Allocate the central corporate costs of an organization.

7. Allocate joint costs to products using the physical-units and relative-sales-value methods.

► L.A. DARLING

Recall the last time you shopped in one of the following stores—**Wal-Mart**, **Kmart**, **Dollar General**, **Best Buy**, **Walgreens**, or **Payless ShoeSource**. Do you remember anything about the store fixtures? Chances are, the answer is no. Store fixtures such as shelving, counters, garment racks, and displays are an important part of the merchandising programs of retail stores, but not many people are aware of them when shopping. An industry leader in store fixtures is **L.A. Darling Company**, which designs and manufactures metal, wood, and wire display systems for retail stores worldwide. Darling is one of 125 business units that operate independently within the **Marmon Group**, which itself is part of **Berkshire Hathaway**. According to Ray Watson, former controller of Darling, "One of the advantages Darling offers companies is its large production capacity." But while this gives the company a competitive advantage, accounting for capacity costs, most of which are fixed manufacturing overhead, is a real challenge.

Should Darling allocate these fixed overhead costs to individual products or services when assessing their profitability? When estimating a customer's profitability? When evaluating a manager's performance? These are important questions for managers as well as for accountants.

Many managerial decisions require information about product or customer profitability. For example, a sales manager at L.A. Darling knows that large customers such as Wal-Mart require different kinds and amounts of Darling's resources than small specialty stores. The mix of products that Wal-Mart orders from Darling is vastly different from products ordered by specialty stores, as are the costs of ordering, shipping, and customer service. Fortunately, improvements in computer technology and cost-allocation techniques enable better measurements of both product and customer profitability.

Cost allocations also can affect the evaluation of managers. Darling evaluates managers based partly on the income of the organizational segment they manage. Therefore, both accountants and managers are concerned with how the allocations affect segment income.

Just as is the case for Darling, cost allocation is of strategic importance to most businesses. For example, many faculty use a university's computer systems for both teaching and performing government-funded research. How much of the computer systems' costs should the university assign to the research projects? Or consider the cost to a law firm of preparing a particular case. What is the total cost of the effort, including various support costs including the cost of renting the law firm's offices and the cost of its law library? Finally, suppose a company uses a machine to make two different product lines. How much of the cost of the machine should the company assign to each product line? These are all problems of cost allocation, the subject of this chapter. ■

© Ian Dagnall/Alamy

A General Framework for Cost Allocation

As described in Chapter 4, cost-allocation methods are an important part of a company's cost accounting system—the techniques it uses to determine the cost of a product, service, customer, or other cost object. Why? Because less than half of most companies' operating costs can be traced directly to products and services. The rest of a company's costs must either be allocated using a cost-allocation base or left unallocated.

Because the profitability of their products, services, or customers is important to most organizations, we focus on how companies assign direct costs and indirect (allocated) costs to these cost objects. For external financial reporting purposes, companies must assign all production costs (and no other costs) to products. However, for internal management purposes, they can assign to products whatever costs are useful for management's decisions. For management purposes, companies trace or allocate many of the costs in their value-chain functions to products or customers. The following graph shows the percent of costs of several value-chain functions that companies trace or allocate to products or customers:

L.A. Darling is not a household name, but everyone has seen the company's products. L.A. Darling makes displays for many of the best known retail stores such as this Walmart Supercenter in Haines City, Florida.

Objective 1

Describe the general framework for cost allocation.

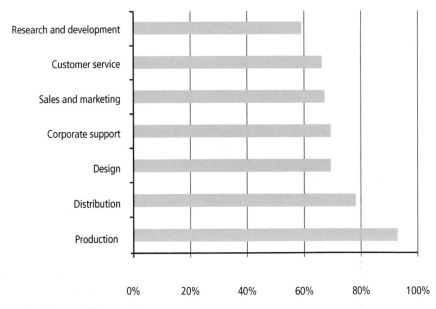

After developing a general framework for allocation, we will take a careful look at the development and use of allocation systems. We will use the framework in Exhibit 12-1 to show how cost allocation fits into the overall cost accounting system. Each of the arrows in Exhibit 12-1 represents an assignment of some costs to a cost objective. We show four types of cost objectives—service departments, producing departments, products/services, and customers. The cost accounting system first accumulates costs and assigns them to organizational units. We will call each unit a department. There are two types of departments: (1) **producing departments**, where employees work on the organization's products or services, and (2) **service departments**, which exist only to support other departments or customers. Examples of service departments are personnel departments, laundry departments in hospitals, technical support centers, and facility management departments. We can trace the *direct* costs to each department, shown by the arrows labeled 1. In contrast, we have to *allocate* the *indirect* costs, such as rent for facilities used by more than one department. We label these allocations as 2 in Exhibit 12-1.

producing departments
Departments where employees work on the organization's products or services.

service departments
Units that exist only to support other departments or customers.

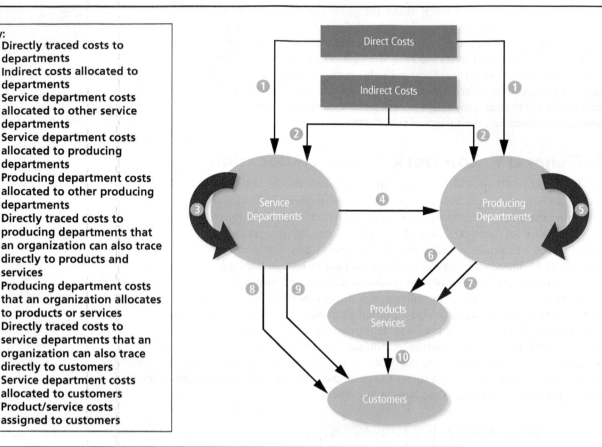

Key:
1. Directly traced costs to departments
2. Indirect costs allocated to departments
3. Service department costs allocated to other service departments
4. Service department costs allocated to producing departments
5. Producing department costs allocated to other producing departments
6. Directly traced costs to producing departments that an organization can also trace directly to products and services
7. Producing department costs that an organization allocates to products or services
8. Directly traced costs to service departments that an organization can also trace directly to customers
9. Service department costs allocated to customers
10. Product/service costs assigned to customers

Exhibit 12-1
Framework for Cost Accounting Systems

After assigning resource costs 1 and 2 to producing and service departments, we examine service departments that provide services to other service departments. An example is personnel services provided to employees in the facilities maintenance department. Arrow 3 represents the allocation of these costs. After making assignments 1, 2, and 3, managers can evaluate the performance of each service department.

Many companies next develop allocation methods to assign service department costs to the producing departments. Why? Because managers want to know total costs of production, both costs within the producing-department and the cost of using resources from service departments. We show these assignments as 4 in Exhibit 12-1. Notice that direct service department costs—labeled as 1—become indirect costs to the producing department when they are part of allocation 4. For example, the salaries of human resources personnel are a direct departmental cost for the human resources department. However, when we allocate these costs, along with all other human resource department costs, to producing departments, they become indirect to the producing department.

Sometimes, producing departments transfer items to other producing departments as well as producing products or services. For example, a producing department may process a chemical resulting in several finished products and several products that need further processing in another department. We transfer the costs of products that need further processing to other producing departments—labeled as 5 in Exhibit 12-1.

At this point, we have accumulated all service department and producing department costs into the producing departments. The next step is to assign costs to products or services. There are significant producing department costs that are directly traceable to products and services. We indicate these costs as 6; examples are direct materials and direct labor. The other producing department costs are allocated to products and services, labeled as 7 in Exhibit 12-1. Again, because we have changed the cost objectives, some costs that were directly traceable to the producing departments will be indirect when the cost objective is the various products or services; examples include salaries of production supervisors, supplies, and most equipment costs.

Some service department activities support customers rather than the production process; examples include order processing and customer service activities. Therefore, many companies assign the costs of such services to customers rather than to the producing departments. We can trace some of these costs directly to customers—labeled 8 in Exhibit 12-1. Examples are sales commissions and dedicated customer support, such as presales negotiations. We then allocate the other customer-related services, such as order processing—arrow 9 in Exhibit 12-1. The last step shown in Exhibit 12-1 is to assign the cost of products or services to customers who purchase them. After this last assignment, a company can determine customer profitability by subtracting costs 8, 9, and 10 from customer revenue.

Why is it important to directly trace and allocate customer-related service department costs to customers (8 and 9 in Exhibit 12-1) rather than assigning them first to producing departments and then to customers? If we assigned these costs to producing departments and then to products, the allocation to products would be based on production-related output measures that may have little relationship to the cause of customer-service costs. This would cause cost distortions to both the product and customer cost objectives. We discuss this in detail later in the chapter.

Most of the direct and indirect costs for each department will be traced or allocated to the department's outputs, although some costs may remain unallocated if there is no logical basis for allocating them. Allocating indirect costs requires accountants to identify and measure a department's output (to which it will allocate costs) and determine an appropriate cost-allocation base. For example, the pediatrics department of a medical clinic might allocate its indirect costs to patients based on physician time per patient. Or a manufacturing firm might allocate its indirect assembly costs to units assembled based on machine hours used. Or the tax department of a CPA firm might allocate indirect costs to clients based on professional hours spent.

As indicated in Chapter 4, when selecting a cost-allocation base, we try to use cost drivers that have a logical cause-and-effect relationship to costs being allocated. For example, a logical cost-allocation base for allocating building rent costs to departments is the square feet that each department occupies. Other logical cost-allocation bases include cubic feet for allocating depreciation of heating and air conditioning equipment and total direct cost for allocating general administrative expense. Some individual indirect costs are important enough that we allocate them individually. For example, we would allocate the cost of professional labor for a law firm to departments, jobs, and projects using labor hours used. Other costs are not important enough to justify being allocated individually. We group these costs together into a cost pool, and allocate the pool of costs to cost objectives using a single cost-allocation base. For example, building rent, utilities cost, and janitorial services may be in the same cost pool because a company allocates all of them on the basis of square footage of space occupied. Similarly, a university could pool all the operating costs of its registrar's office and allocate them to individual colleges on the basis of the number of students in each college.

The next section looks in detail at allocation of service department costs, and the following sections focus on allocation to products or services and to customers.

Allocation of Service Department Costs

In our general framework shown in Exhibit 12-1, we label service department allocations as 3, 4, and 9. Before discussing methods of allocation, we give some general guidelines that managers should consider when designing allocation systems.

Objective 2

Allocate the variable and fixed costs of service departments to other organizational units.

General Guidelines

Following are three general guidelines for allocating service department costs:

1. Allocate variable- and fixed-cost pools separately. Each service department can contain multiple cost pools if more than one cost driver causes the department's costs. At a minimum, there should be a variable-cost pool and a fixed-cost pool. The variable- and fixed cost pools should be based on the fixed and variable cost specifications in a department's flexible budget.

2. Establish the cost-allocation procedure in advance of rendering the service rather than after the fact. This approach establishes the "rules of the game" so that all departments can plan appropriately.
3. Evaluate performance using flexible budgets for each service (staff) department, just as for each production or operating (line) department. Managers should evaluate the performance of a service department by comparing actual costs with a budget, regardless of how the company allocates costs.

Consider an example of a service department—the computer department of a university—that serves two major users, the School of Business and the School of Engineering. Suppose there are two major reasons for allocating computer costs to the two schools: (1) predicting economic effects of the use of the computer, and (2) motivating the individuals in the two schools to use computer services most effectively. How should the university allocate the costs of the computer department (salaries, depreciation, energy, materials, and so on) to the two schools?

We begin by analyzing the costs of the computer department in detail. The primary activity performed is computer processing. The university acquired the computer mainframe on a 5-year noncancelable lease. Resources consumed include processing time, operator time, energy, materials, and building space. Suppose the computer department's flexible budget for the forthcoming year is $100,000 monthly fixed cost plus $200 variable cost per hour of computer time used.

Variable-Cost and Fixed-Cost Pools

Guideline 1 requires the separation of fixed and variable costs. Costs in the variable-cost pool include energy, operator labor costs, and materials. The cost-allocation base for variable-cost pools should be a measure of activity within the departments that causes the variable costs—that is, the cost driver of the variable costs. In our university example, there is only one such cost driver, actual hours of computer time used, so we put all variable costs into one cost pool. The cause-and-effect relationship is clear—the larger the number of hours of computer time used, the higher the total variable costs. Therefore, the university should allocate variable costs as follows:

Cost-allocation rate per hour × actual hours of computer time used

Costs in the fixed-cost pool include the lease payment on the computers, salaries of managers and supervisors, and building occupancy costs (depreciation, insurance, and so on). These fixed costs do not change with short-term fluctuations in the actual hours of computer time used. Rather, they all depend on the initial decision about the capacity of computer services the university required. Therefore, the best cost-allocation base is the predicted level of usage of computer hours, a prediction made when the university decided how large a computer operation it needed. This results in the following lump-sum allocation each month:

Percentage of predicted usage × monthly fixed cost

Budgeted Cost-Allocation Rates

To satisfy guideline 2, companies should determine in advance the cost-allocation rate per hour for variable costs and the monthly lump-sum fixed cost, based on the flexible budget. In this example, the budgeted variable cost-allocation rate is $200 per hour, the flexible budget for variable costs, which we can determine by dividing the total budgeted costs of energy, operators, and materials by the total budgeted hours of computer time. The budgeted monthly fixed cost is the lump-sum flexible-budget amount, $100,000. Neither the budgeted cost-allocation rate per hour nor the budgeted fixed cost is affected by actual results. Exhibit 12-2 shows the cost-allocation system for the computer department.

The use of budgeted cost rates rather than actual cost rates for allocating costs of service departments protects the user departments from inefficiencies in the service departments. If an organization were to allocate *actual* total service department cost, it would hold user department managers responsible for costs beyond their control and provide less incentive for service departments to be efficient. Both effects are undesirable.

Consider the allocation of variable costs to the Engineering School when it uses 500 hours of computer time. Suppose inefficiencies in the computer department caused the variable costs of providing those 500 hours of service to be $120,000 instead of the 500 hours × $200 = $100,000 budgeted. A good cost-allocation scheme would allocate only the $100,000 to the Engineering School and would let the $20,000 remain as an unallocated unfavorable budget variance of the

Exhibit 12-2
Allocation of Variable- and
Fixed-Cost Pools

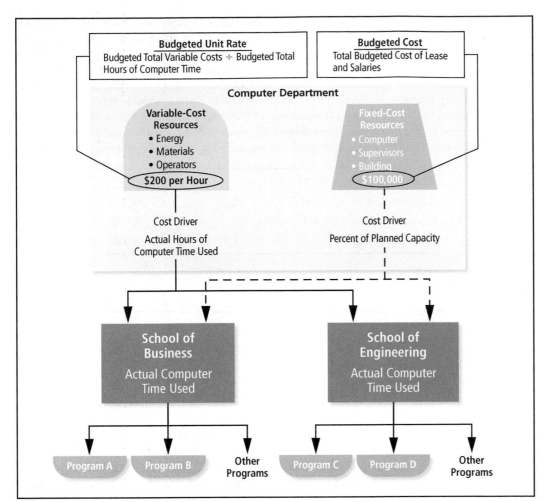

computer department. This allocation method holds computer department managers responsible for the $20,000 variance, as specified in guideline 3. It also may reduce the resentment of user managers. User department managers sometimes complain more vigorously about uncertainty over allocations and the poor cost control in a service department than about the choice of a cost-allocation base (such as direct-labor dollars or number of employees). Such complaints are less likely if the service department managers have budget responsibility and the user departments are protected from short-run price fluctuations and inefficiencies.

Allocating the budgeted fixed costs is similar. Costs that differ from the flexible-budget fixed cost of $100,000 per month are the responsibility of the computer department managers and should not be allocated to the user departments.

Allocating Fixed Costs Based on Capacity Available

Let's consider further the allocation of fixed costs based on predicted usage. This means that the allocation will be based on the long-run capacity available to the user, regardless of actual usage from month to month. The reasoning is that long-range planning regarding the expected required overall level of service, not short-run fluctuations in actual usage, affects the level of fixed costs.

Suppose the deans had originally predicted the long-run average monthly usage by the School of Business at 210 hours, and by the School of Engineering at 490 hours, a total of 700 hours. These estimates resulted in a set of committed fixed costs that remain largely uncontrollable over many years. We should allocate the fixed-cost pool as follows:

	Business	Engineering
Fixed costs per month		
210/700, or 30% of $100,000	$30,000	
490/700, or 70% of $100,000		$70,000

A major strength of using capacity available rather than capacity used when allocating budgeted fixed costs is that actual usage by user departments does not affect the short-run allocations to other user departments. Such a budgeted lump-sum approach is more likely to have the desired motivational effects with respect to the ordering of services in both the short run and the long run.

In practice, companies often inappropriately allocate fixed-cost pools on the basis of capacity used, not capacity available. Suppose for two successive months the computer department's actual fixed costs were exactly the $100,000 budgeted. The university allocated these costs based on actual hours used by the consuming departments. Compare the costs borne by the two schools in the first month when business uses 210 hours and engineering 490 hours, as originally predicted.

Total fixed costs incurred, $100,000	
Business: 210/700 × $100,000 =	$ 30,000
Engineering: 490/700 × $100,000 =	70,000
Total cost allocated	$100,000

What happens if business uses only 110 hours during the following month, and engineering still uses 490 hours?

Total fixed costs incurred, $100,000	
Business: 110/600 × $100,000 =	$ 18,333
Engineering: 490/600 × $100,000 =	81,667
Total cost allocated	$100,000

Engineering's usage was unchanged, but it must bear an additional cost of ($81,667 − $70,000) = $11,667, an increase of 17%. Its short-run costs depend on what other consumers have used, not solely on its own actions. This phenomenon is caused by a faulty allocation method for the fixed portion of total costs, a method in which one department's usage affects the allocation to other departments. We can avoid this weakness by using a predetermined lump-sum allocation of fixed costs based on budgeted usage, but this approach is not without problems itself. If a company allocates fixed costs on the basis of long-range plans, there is a natural tendency on the part of managers to underestimate their planned usage and thus obtain a smaller fraction of the cost allocation. Top management can counteract these tendencies by monitoring predictions and by following up and using feedback to keep future predictions more honest.

In some organizations, there are even definite rewards for managers who make accurate predictions. Moreover, some cost-allocation methods provide for penalties for underpredictions. For example, suppose a manager predicts usage of 210 hours and then demands 300 hours. The manager either doesn't get the hours or pays a higher rate for every hour beyond 210 in such systems.

Allocating Service Department Costs to Producing Departments

Recall from Exhibit 12-1 on page 482 that assignment type 4 is allocating service department costs to producing departments. We now explore methods commonly used for this type of allocation. Suppose one of L.A. Darling's display facilities assembles parts into custom and standard displays that Darling sells to Wal-Mart, Target, and Walgreens. The facility has two producing departments, processing and assembly. There are also two service departments, facilities management (rent, power, insurance, janitorial services, and some corporate resources such as administration and engineering) and human resources. In this section of the chapter, we treat the processing and assembly departments as cost objectives to which we allocate service department costs. Normally there would be at least two cost pools in each service department, one for variable costs and one for fixed costs. However, for simplicity we will assume that all costs are variable. We would allocate fixed costs in a similar manner but with different cost-allocation bases.

Let's assume that a single plausible and reliable cost driver serves as a cost-allocation base for the costs of each service department and that all resource costs vary in proportion to this cost driver. Managers have determined that the cost driver for facilities management costs is the square footage occupied and the cost driver for human resources costs is the number of employees.

Exhibit 12-3
L.A. Darling's Processing
Facility: Service Department
Allocation

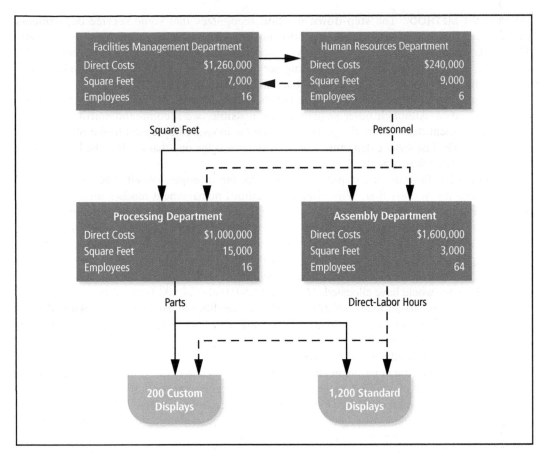

Exhibit 12-3 shows the costs for a recent month when the company produced 200 custom and 1,200 standard displays. It also shows the square footage occupied and number of employees for each department. Note that facilities management provides services for the human resources department in addition to providing services for the producing departments and that human resources aids employees in facilities management as well as those in production departments.

There are two popular methods for allocating service department costs to producing departments in such cases: the direct method and the step-down method.

DIRECT METHOD   The **direct method** ignores other service departments when allocating any given service department's costs to the producing departments. For example, the direct method ignores the services that facilities management provides for human resources and the services that human resources provides to facilities management.

Consider facilities management costs. The direct method allocates these costs to the processing and assembly departments based on the relative square footage occupied by each of the two departments.

- Total square footage in producing departments = 15,000 + 3,000 = 18,000
- Facilities management cost allocated to processing department = (15,000 ÷ 18,000) × $1,260,000 = $1,050,000
- Facilities management cost allocated to assembly department = (3,000 ÷ 18,000) × $1,260,000 = $210,000

Likewise, the direct method allocates human resources department costs to the producing departments on the basis of the relative number of employees in the producing departments.

- Total employees in producing departments = 16 + 64 = 80
- Human resources costs allocated to processing department = (16 ÷ 80) × $240,000 = $48,000
- Human resources costs allocated to assembly department = (64 ÷ 80) × $240,000 = $192,000

Objective 3

Use the direct and step-down methods to allocate service department costs to user departments.

direct method
A method for allocating service department costs that ignores other service departments when allocating any given service department's costs to the operating departments.

step-down method
A method for allocating service department costs that recognizes that some service departments support the activities in other service departments as well as those in operating departments.

STEP-DOWN METHOD   The **step-down method** recognizes that some service departments support the activities in other service departments as well as those in producing departments. This method allocates the costs of one service department at a time, assigning the costs to the producing departments and to the remaining service departments. Once we have allocated a department's costs, we never allocate costs back to the department in a later step.[1]

To apply the step-down method, we need to choose the sequence in which to allocate service department costs. Although other sequences are possible, we recommend starting with the service department that renders the greatest service (as measured by costs) to the other service departments. The last service department in the sequence is the one that renders the least service to the other service departments.

Exhibit 12-4 illustrates the step-down method for our example. We allocate facilities management department costs first. Why? Because facilities management renders more support to human resources than human resources provides to facilities management. How should we determine which of the two service departments provides more service to the other? We can carry out step 1 of the step-down method with facilities management costs allocated first, and then repeat it assuming we allocate personnel costs first. With facilities management costs allocated first, we allocate $420,000 to human resources, as shown in Exhibit 12-4. If we had allocated human resources first, we would have allocated $(16 \div 96) \times \$240,000 = \$40,000$ to facilities management. Because $40,000 is smaller than $420,000, we allocate facilities management first. After allocating facilities management costs, we do not allocate any costs back to facilities management, even though human resources provides services to facilities management.

The next step is to allocate human resources cost. The $660,000 of human resources costs allocated to the producing departments includes the $420,000 allocated to human resources from facilities management in addition to the $240,000 of direct human resources department costs. Notice that we ignored services provided by a service department to itself. Even though there are six employees in human resources and facilities maintenance occupies 7,000 square feet of space, these numbers do not affect the service department cost allocations.

Now examine the last column of Exhibit 12-4. Before allocation, the four departments incurred costs of $4,100,000. In step 1, we deducted $1,260,000 from facilities management and added it to the other three departments. There was no net effect on the total cost. In step 2, we deducted $660,000 from human resources and added it to the remaining two departments. Again, total cost was unaffected. After allocation, all $4,100,000 remains, but it is all in the processing and assembly departments. Nothing is left in facilities management or human resources.

	Facilities Management	Human Resources	Processing	Assembly	Total
Direct department costs before allocation	$ 1,260,000	$ 240,000	$1,000,000	$1,600,000	$4,100,000
Step 1 Facilities Management	$(1,260,000)	$(9 \div 27) \times$ $1,260,000 = $ 420,000	$(15 \div 27) \times$ $1,260,000 = $ 700,000	$(3 \div 27) \times$ $1,260,000 = $ 140,000	
Step 2 Human Resources		$ (660,000)	$(16 \div 80) \times$ $ 660,000 = $ 132,000	$(64 \div 80) \times$ $ 660,000 = $ 528,000	
Total cost after allocation	$ 0	$ 0	$1,832,000	$2,268,000	$4,100,000

Exhibit 12-4
Step-Down Allocation

---

[1]There is another method of allocation that allocates costs both forward and backward, called reciprocal allocation, which requires the solution of simultaneous linear equations. This method is discussed in advanced managerial accounting texts but is beyond the scope of this book.

COMPARISON OF THE METHODS   Compare the costs of the producing departments under direct and step-down methods, as shown in Exhibit 12-5. Note that the method of allocation can significantly affect the costs. Processing appears to be a more expensive operation to a manager using the direct method than it does to one using the step-down method. Conversely, assembly seems more expensive to a manager using the step-down method.

Which method is better? Generally, the step-down method. Why? Because it recognizes the effects of the most significant support provided by service departments to other service departments. The greatest virtue of the direct method is its simplicity. If the two methods do not produce significantly different results, many companies elect to use the direct method because it is easier for managers to apply and understand.

COSTS NOT RELATED TO COST DRIVERS   Our example illustrating direct and step-down allocation methods assigned all costs using a single cost driver as a cost-allocation base. For example, we assumed that we could use square footage occupied to allocate all facilities-management costs. But what if some of the costs in facilities management do not vary proportionately to the cost-driver square footage? Some may vary with another cost driver. For example, heating costs may vary with cubic footage rather than square footage, and power costs may vary with megawatt hours used. Other costs—supervisors' salaries, for example—may be fixed over large ranges of cost-driver activity and therefore require predicted capacity as a cost-allocation base. For still other costs it may be nearly impossible to identify an appropriate cost-allocation base.

We suggest two alternatives for situations where costs are not related to a single cost driver:

1. Identify multiple cost pools, each with its own cost-allocation base. Divide facilities-management costs into two or more cost pools and use a different cost-allocation base to allocate the costs in each pool via the direct or step-down method. For cost pools with costs that vary with the cost-allocation base, the allocation is straightforward—the use of more units of the cost-allocation base result in the allocation of more cost. Fixed cost pools are more complex. A company may allocate fixed costs on the basis of a long-term cause-effect relationship. While supervisors' salaries may not change immediately if the department changes the amount of square footage it uses, growth in the size of the department may eventually lead to the need for more supervisors. Remember to use the budgeted amount of the cost-allocation base, not the actual amount used, to allocate these fixed costs. That is, we might use budgeted square footage for allocating supervisors' salaries. A fixed-cost pool that does not have a plausible or reliable long-term cost driver might remain unallocated.
2. Allocate all costs by the direct or step-down method using the same cost-allocation base. In our example, we might choose square footage as the cost-allocation base. In this simplified alternative, we implicitly assume that, in the long run, square footage causes all facilities management costs—even if we cannot easily identify a short-term causal relationship. In other words, the need for more square footage may not cause an immediate increase in all facilities management costs, but management may believe that all costs are related to square footage because both costs and the amount of space used change as the size of the department changes.

	Processing		Assembly	
	Direct	**Step-Down***	**Direct**	**Step-Down***
Direct costs	$1,000,000	$1,000,000	$1,600,000	$1,600,000
Allocated from				
facilities management	1,050,000	700,000	210,000	140,000
Allocated from personnel	48,000	132,000	192,000	528,000
Total costs	$2,098,000	$1,832,000	$2,002,000	$2,268,000

*From <Exhibit 12-4>.

Exhibit 12-5
Direct Versus Step-Down Method

Making Managerial Decisions

Suppose you are on a cross-functional team that is discussing how to allocate the costs of a purchasing department. One team member suggested that "number of purchase orders issued" is the best cost driver to use as a cost-allocation base. However, a scatter graph of total costs versus number of purchase orders issued shows the following:

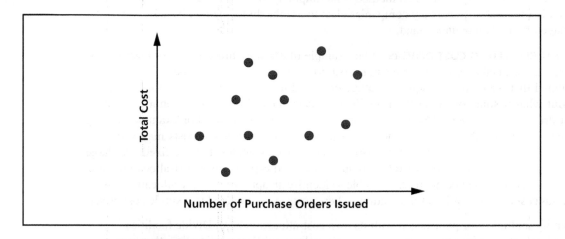

Because the data clearly indicate that the single cost driver "number of purchase orders issued" is not a reliable measure of the work done in the department, the team investigated further. It discovered that a significant amount of work of the purchasing department was certifying new vendors in addition to issuing purchase orders. What alternative method of allocation would you recommend?

Answer

Because a large percentage of the work of the purchasing department is not related to the single cost driver "number of purchase orders," the team should use a second cost pool with another cost-allocation base, such as "number of new vendors."

Allocation of Costs to Product or Service Cost Objects

cost application
The allocation of total departmental costs to the revenue-producing products or services.

After the allocation of service department costs, we have all costs except unallocated costs residing in the producing departments. All that remains is to allocate the costs in the producing departments to the product or service cost objects. Examples of such cost objects are products such as automobiles, furniture, and newspapers, and services such as bank accounts, patient visits, and student credit hours. Some accountants use the term **cost application** for the allocation of departmental costs to the revenue-producing products or services.

A Traditional Approach

The traditional approach to cost allocation has the following four steps:

1. Divide the costs in each producing department, including both the direct department costs and all the costs allocated to it, into two categories: (1) the direct costs that you can physically trace to the product or service cost objectives and (2) the remainder, the indirect costs, which must be allocated.
2. Trace the direct costs to the appropriate products or services. Note that some costs that are direct to the department will be indirect to the product or service cost objectives—for example, depreciation on the department's equipment.
3. Select cost pools and related cost-allocation bases in each production department, and assign all the indirect departmental costs to the appropriate cost pool. For example, you might assign a portion of the indirect departmental costs on the basis of direct-labor hours, another portion on the basis of machine hours, and the remainder on the basis of number of parts. Be sure to use separate cost pools for fixed and variable costs.

4. Allocate (apply) the costs in each cost pool to the products or services in proportion to their usage of the related cost-allocation base. Apply variable costs on the basis of the actual amount of the cost-allocation base. Apply fixed costs on the basis of the budgeted amount of the cost-allocation base.

Consider our example of the **L.A. Darling** display facility. Exhibit 12-6 shows the process map for the facility assuming that the facility uses the step-down method for allocating service department costs. We now shift our focus from the two operating departments as cost objectives to the two types of displays—the products manufactured by the L.A. Darling display facility.

The first step is to determine the operating department costs that we can directly trace to displays. Of the $1,832,000 total costs in the processing department, we can trace the $800,000 cost of parts to custom and standard displays, as shown in Exhibit 12-6. Similarly, of the $2,268,000 total costs in the assembly department, we can directly trace the wages for direct labor, $50,000 to custom and $150,000 to standard displays. The remaining costs in the producing departments are indirect costs with respect to the displays, and we will assume they represent fixed-cost resources. You may wonder why there are no direct-labor costs in the processing department. It is because this is a machine intensive department with only indirect labor maintaining the machines.

In step 2, we trace the direct costs to the two display types as shown in Exhibit 12-6. Compare the processing department costs in Exhibits 12-3 and 12-6. How did $1,000,000 in direct processing department costs in Exhibit 12-3 decrease to only $800,000 direct costs in Exhibit 12-6?

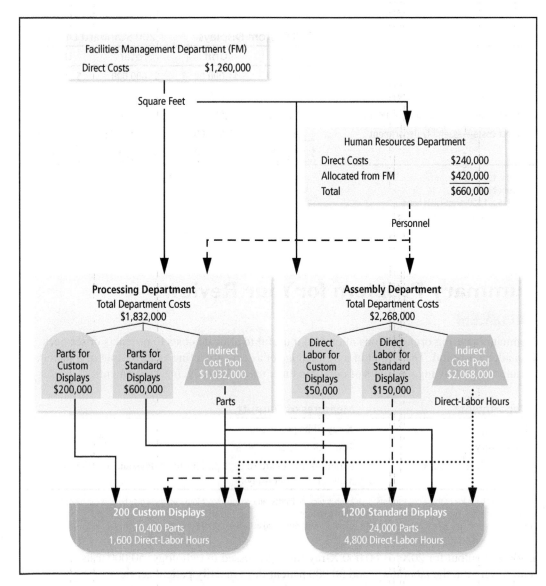

Exhibit 12-6

L.A. Darling Display Facility: Allocation to Cost Objects Using Traditional Approach and Step-Down Allocation Method

The answer lies in our change in cost objectives. We are assuming that $200,000 represents costs such as depreciation on department equipment and costs of supervisors that are wholly in support of the department—a single cost object—and do not need to be allocated. When we changed the cost objective to the two displays, these resources became shared. Since we could find no economically feasible way to trace their use directly, we need to allocate their costs or leave them unallocated. In this case, we will allocate all of the indirect costs.

Next, in step 3, we select cost pools and related cost-allocation bases for the indirect costs of each department. We assign the remaining $1,032,000 of indirect costs in the processing department to one fixed-cost pool with budgeted number of parts as the cost-allocation base. Similarly, we assign all the remaining $2,068,000 indirect costs in the assembly department to one fixed-cost pool with budgeted direct-labor hours as the cost-allocation base.

Therefore, we allocate indirect departmental costs to the displays as follows:

$$\text{Processing: } \$1,032,000 \div (10,400 + 24,000) \text{ parts} = \$30.00 \text{ per part}$$
$$\text{Assembly: } \$2,068,000 \div (1,600 + 4,800) \text{ direct-labor hours}$$
$$= \$323.125 \text{ per direct-labor hour}$$

The total and unit costs of making 200 custom and 1,200 standard displays are shown in Exhibit 12-7.

Exhibit 12-7
Total and Unit Costs for Custom and Standard Displays

	200 Custom Displays		1,200 Standard Displays	
	Total	Unit	Total	Unit
Parts	$ 200,000	$1,000.00	$ 600,000	$ 500.00
Direct labor	50,000	250.00	150,000	125.00
Indirect costs—processing department	312,000*	1,560.00	720,000†	600.00
Indirect costs—assembly department	517,000‡	2,585.00	1,551,000§	1,292.50
	$1,079,000	$5,395.00	$3,021,000	$2,517.50

*$30.00 × 10,400 parts
†$30.00 × 24,000 parts
‡$323.125 × 1,600 direct-labor hours
§$323.125 × 4,800 direct-labor hours

Summary Problem for Your Review

PROBLEM

Nonmanufacturing organizations often find it useful to allocate costs to products or services. Consider a hospital. The output of a hospital is not as easy to define as the output of a factory. Assume the following measures of output in three revenue-producing departments:

Department*	Measures of Output†
Radiology	X-ray films processed
Laboratory	Tests administered
Daily patient services	Patient-days of care (e.g., 1 patient for 2 days and 1 patient for 3 days is 5 patient-days)

*There would be many of these departments, such as obstetrics, pediatrics, and orthopedics. Moreover, there may be both inpatient and outpatient care; for simplicity, we do not distinguish between them.
†These become the "product" cost objectives, the various revenue-producing activities of a hospital.

Budgeted output for 20X1 is 60,000 X-ray films processed in radiology, 50,000 tests administered in the laboratory, and 30,000 patient-days in daily patient services.

In addition to the revenue-producing departments, the hospital has three service departments: administrative and fiscal services, plant operations and maintenance, and laundry. (Real hospitals have more than three revenue-producing departments and more than three service departments. This problem is simplified to keep the data manageable.)

The hospital management has decided that the cost-allocation base for administrative and fiscal services costs is the direct department costs of the other departments. The cost-allocation base for plant operations and maintenance is square feet occupied, and for laundry is pounds of laundry. The pertinent budget data for 20X1 are as follows:

	Direct Department Costs	Square Feet Occupied	Pounds of Laundry
Administrative and fiscal services	$1,000,000	1,000	—
Plant operations and maintenance	800,000	2,000	—
Laundry	200,000	5,000	—
Radiology	1,000,000	12,000	80,000
Laboratory	400,000	3,000	20,000
Daily patient services	1,600,000	80,000	300,000
Total	$5,000,000	103,000	400,000

1. Allocate service department costs using the direct method.
2. Allocate service department costs using the step-down method. Allocate administrative and fiscal services first, plant operations and maintenance second, and laundry third.
3. Compute the cost per unit of output in each of the revenue-producing departments using (a) the costs determined using the direct method for allocating service department costs and (b) the costs determined using the step-down method for allocating service department costs.

SOLUTION

1. Exhibit 12-8 shows the solutions to all three problems. We present the direct method first. Note that we did not allocate service department costs to another service department. Therefore, we base allocations on the relative amounts of the cost-allocation base in the revenue-producing department only. For example, in allocating plant operations and maintenance, we ignore square footage occupied by the service departments. The cost-allocation base is the 95,000 square feet occupied by the revenue-producing departments.

   Note that the total cost of the revenue-producing departments after allocation, $1,474,386 + $568,596 + $2,957,018 = $5,000,000, is equal to the total of the direct department costs in all six departments before allocation.
2. The lower half of Exhibit 12-8 shows the step-down method. First, we allocate the costs of administrative and fiscal services to all five other departments. Because we do not allocate a department's own costs to itself, the cost-allocation base consists of the $4,000,000 direct department costs in the five departments excluding administrative and fiscal services. Second, we allocate plant operations and maintenance on the basis of square feet occupied. We allocate no cost to the department itself or back to administrative and fiscal services. Therefore, the square footage used for allocation is the 100,000 square feet occupied by the other four departments.

   Third, we allocate laundry. We would not allocate cost back to the first two departments, even if they had used laundry services.

   As in the direct method, note that the total costs of the revenue-producing departments after allocation, $1,430,000 + $545,000 + $3,025,000 = $5,000,000, equals the total of the direct department costs before allocation.

Allocation Base	Administrative and Fiscal Services	Plant Operations and Maintenance	Laundry	Radiology	Laboratory	Daily Patient Services
	Accumulated Costs	Sq. Footage	Pounds			
1. Direct method:						
Direct departmental costs before allocation	$ 1,000,000	$ 800,000	$ 200,000	$1,000,000	$400,000	$1,600,000
Administrative and fiscal services	(1,000,000)			333,333*	133,333	533,334
Plant operations and maintenance		(800,000)		101,053†	25,263	673,684
Laundry			(200,000)	40,000‡	10,000	150,000
Total costs after allocation				$1,474,386	$568,596	$2,957,018
3a. Product output in films, tests, and patient-days, respectively				60,000	50,000	30,000
Cost per unit of output				$24.573	$ 11.372	$ 98.567
2. Step-down method:						
Direct departmental costs before allocation	$ 1,000,000	$ 800,000	$ 200,000	$1,000,000	$400,000	$1,600,000
Administrative and fiscal services	(1,000,000)	200,000§	50,000	250,000	100,000	400,000
Plant operations and maintenance		(1,000,000)	50,000¶	120,000	30,000	800,000
Laundry			(300,000)	60,000#	15,000	225,000
Total costs after allocation				$1,430,000	$545,000	$3,025,000
3b. Product output in films, tests, and patient-days, respectively				60,000	50,000	30,000
Cost per unit of output				$23.833	$ 10.900	$ 100.833

*$1,000,000 ÷ (1,000,000 + 400,000 + 1,600,000) = $.33, 1/3 × 1,000,000 = $333,333; and so on.

†$800,000 ÷ (12,000 + 3,000 + 80,000) = $8.4210526; $8.4210526 × 12,000 sq. ft. = $101,053; and so on.

‡$200,000 × (80,000 + 20,000 + 300,000) = $.50; $.50 × 80,000 = $40,000; and so on.

§$1,000,000 ÷ (800,000 + 200,000 + 1,000,000 + 400,000 +1,600,000) = $.25; .25 × 800,000 = $200,000; and so on.

¶$1,000,000 × (5,000 + 12,000 + 3,000 + 80,000) = $10.00; $10.00 × 5,000 sq. ft. = $50,000; and so on.

#$300,000 ÷ (80,000 + 20,000 + 300,000) = $.75; $.75 × 80,000 = $60,000; and so on.

Exhibit 12-8

Allocation of Hospital Service Department Costs: Direct and Step-Down Methods

3. The per-unit costs are shown in lines 3a and 3b in Exhibit 12-8. Compare the unit costs derived from the direct method with those of the step-down method. In many instances, the product costs may not differ enough to warrant investing in a cost-allocation method that is any fancier than the direct method. But sometimes even small differences may be significant to a government agency or anybody paying for a large volume of services based on costs. For example, in Exhibit 12-8 the "cost" of an "average" laboratory test is either $11.37 or $10.90. This may be significant for the fiscal committee of the hospital's board of trustees, who must decide on hospital prices. Thus, cost allocation often helps answer the vital question, "Who should pay for what, and how much?"

An ABC Approach

The traditional approach to cost allocation focuses on accumulating and reporting costs by department. Many companies have started using an alternative approach, activity-based costing, as described in Chapter 4. It focuses on activities rather than departments. Let's examine how the same facility of **L.A. Darling** might apply ABC to determine the costs of custom and standard displays.

Assume that management decides to apply ABC only to the production activities; the company will continue to allocate the service department costs using traditional costing using the step-down method. First, we replace the production departments with the production activities—in this case three activities: design activity, processing activity, and assembly activity. Then we allocate facilities management department costs to the human resources department and to each production activity. Then, we allocate the human resources department costs, both the direct department costs and the costs allocated from facilities management, to the activities. Finally, we allocate the costs of each activity to the custom and standard displays using a two-stage ABC system. This ABC approach uses the three-step procedure that follows and is illustrated in Exhibit 12-9, a process map for the ABC costing system.

STEP 1: DETERMINE THE KEY COMPONENTS OF THE SYSTEM AND THE RELATIONSHIP AMONG THEM. The costing objective is to determine the costs of custom and standard displays—the final cost objects for L.A. Darling shown at the bottom of Exhibit 12-9. We focus on the production-related activities. If the company allocates costs from other value-chain activities, the process would be similar.

Production-related costs flow into the final cost objects in two ways: 1) direct costs (parts and direct labor) are traced to the cost objectives, and 2) indirect costs are allocated via the three production activities (design, processing, and assembly). Accounting for the direct costs does not differ from a traditional system. Both systems physically trace such costs to the cost objectives.

Now let's consider the indirect costs. The key is to identify the production activities and an appropriate cost-allocation base for each. Often production departments will have multiple activities. However, in this case, management decided that the processing and assembly department each have a single activity. Therefore, the first two activities are processing and assembly, and the cost-allocation bases are machine hours and direct-labor hours. In addition, management decided that part of the facilities management department, the design of products and processes, is a third production activity with number of distinct parts as an appropriate cost-allocation base. Exhibit 12-9 shows these activities in the rectangles in the middle of the page.

Once we have identified the activities, we next determine the resources used by the activities. In this case there are three resources: 1) engineers and CAD equipment used only in the design activity; 2) machines, tools, machinists, and supplies used in both processing and assembly activities; and 3) supervision and equipment, also used in both processing and assembly activities.

In addition to resources, the activities require support from the service departments. The structure of the service department component of the cost-allocation system is unchanged—we still have two service departments that use the step-down method. However, the cost of engineers and CAD equipment has been removed from the facilities management department, so the costs to be allocated from that service department are smaller.

Exhibit 12-9

L.A. Darling Display Facility: Allocation to Final Cost Objectives Using the ABC Approach

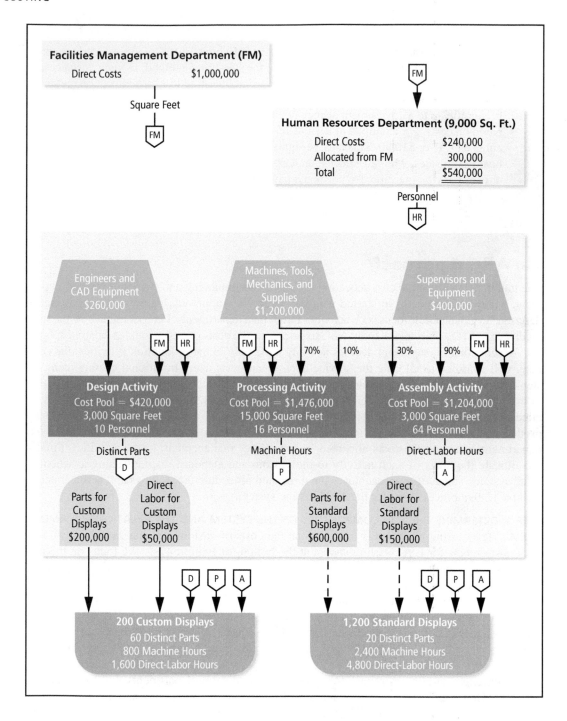

STEP 2: COLLECT RELEVANT DATA CONCERNING COSTS AND THE PHYSICAL FLOW OF COST-ALLOCATION BASE UNITS AMONG RESOURCES AND ACTIVITIES. Using the process map as a guide, accountants collected the required cost and operational data from the accounting system and by interviews with relevant personnel. The data collected, shown in Exhibit 12-9, include the following: 1) costs for each service department, resource, and direct cost, 2) cost-allocation base amounts for each cost pool, 3) allocation percentages for shared resources and service departments. Note that the total costs of the facilities management department is only $1,000,000 instead of the $1,260,000 used under the traditional approach. The difference is the cost of engineers and CAD equipment that management now treats as a production activity. From the data collected, we can compute the total indirect cost of each activity as shown in Exhibit 12-10.

Activity	Design	Processing	Assembly
Service department allocations:			
Facilities maintenance[1]	$100,000	$ 500,000	$ 100,000
Human resources[2]	60,000	96,000	384,000
Resource allocations:			
Engineers and CAD[3]	260,000	—	—
Machines, tools, mechanics, and supplies[4]	—	840,000	360,000
Supervision and equipment[5]	—	40,000	360,000
Total indirect activity costs	$420,000	$1,476,000	$1,204,000

Exhibit 12-10
L.A. Darling Display Facility: Computation of Indirect Activity Costs

[1] $1,000,000 \times [3,000 \div (9,000 + 3,000 + 15,000 + 3,000)] = \$100,000$, etc.
[2] ($240,000 + $300,000) $\times [10 \div (10 + 16 + 64)] = \$60,000$, etc.
[3] Total cost of engineers and CAD is assigned to design.
[4] $1,200,000 \times 70\% = \$840,000$, etc.
[5] $400,000 \times 10\% = \$40,000$, etc.

STEP 3: CALCULATE AND INTERPRET THE NEW ABC INFORMATION. Exhibit 12-11 shows the last step of allocating the costs of activities to the custom and standard displays. For each activity, the exhibit shows the cost pool of indirect costs from Exhibit 12-9, allocates these costs to the displays via the appropriate cost-allocation bases, and then adds the direct costs.

Now that we have completed the three steps, let's compare the cost per unit figures using the traditional and ABC approaches:

	Allocated Cost	
	Custom Displays	Standard Displays
Traditional approach	$5,395.00	$2,517.50
ABC approach	$6,175.00	$2,387.50

The ABC cost of standard displays is ($6,175 − $5,395) ÷ $5,395 = 14.5% higher than the costs measured by the traditional system, and the ABC cost of custom displays is ($2,517.50 − $2,387.50) ÷ $2,517.50 = 5.2% lower. If managers believe that the ABC system is more accurate, the traditional system leads them to overestimate the profitability of the custom displays and to underestimate the profitability of the standard displays.

A company that switched from traditional to ABC costing is Dow Chemical. The Business First box on page 498 explains how Dow used ABC to help implement a new business strategy.

Activity/Resource (Cost Driver)	Cost Pool	Physical Flow of Cost Driver	Cost per Driver Unit	Custom Displays		Standard Displays	
				Flow	Cost	Flow	Cost
Design (distinct parts)	$ 420,000	80	$5,250.000	60	$ 315,000	20	$ 105,000
Processing (machine hours)	1,476,000	3,200	461.250	800	369,000	2,400	1,107,000
Assembly (direct-labor hours)	1,204,000	6,400	188.125	1,600	301,000	4,800	903,000
Parts					200,000		600,000
Direct labor					50,000		150,000
Total direct and allocated cost					$1,235,000		$2,865,000
Units					÷ 200		÷ 1,200
Display cost per unit					$ 6,175.00		$ 2,387.50

Exhibit 12-11
L.A. Darling Display Facility: Allocation to Final Cost Objects Using the ABC Approach

Business First

Companies Use ABC to Improve the Allocation of Service Costs and Lower the Costs to Serve Customers

Dow Chemical believes that its ABC allocation system is the foundation of its cost-management system. Dow, with annual revenues of more than $60 billion, is the largest chemical company in the United States and number two worldwide. The company has three major business segments: plastics, chemicals, and agricultural products. Dow switched from a traditional allocation system to ABC as part of a major shift in its total strategy. It sold its pharmaceutical, energy, and consumer products businesses and set a goal to be the number one company in chemicals, plastics, and agroscience. Dow believed that, to accomplish its goal, it needed to improve the quality and accuracy of its costing system, including the costs of internal services such as those provided by the human resources and maintenance departments.

Service providers, such as human resources and maintenance, identified the major activities performed, determined the appropriate cost-allocation base for each activity, and computed costs for each activity and service provided to using departments. The focus on activities has led to a better understanding of costs by everyone and better cost control. Another advantage of the ABC system is improved resource planning and utilization. By focusing on activities and their related

cost-allocation bases, Dow's maintenance department managers can more effectively plan maintenance resource needs and availability. Overall, since the company integrated ABC into its cost management system, it has realized significant benefits.

Another company that used ABC to improve its allocation system is Kemps LLC, a manufacturer of dairy products such as milk, yogurt, and ice cream. Kemps' customers range from small convenience stores to large retailers such as Target. When Kemp changed its strategy to focus more on being a low-total-cost provider, it recognized the need to measure and manage the costs to serve its diverse customer base. Using an ABC system it was able to identify customers who had a high cost to serve and thus were unprofitable. Many of these customers ordered in low quantities or made frequent returns. By implementing a menu-based pricing strategy where Kemps charged higher prices for low-volume orders and offered discounts for lowering product returns, Kemps realized significant cost savings.

Sources: J. Damitio, G. Hayes, and P. Kintzele, "Integrating ABC and ABM at Dow Chemical," *Management Accounting Quarterly*, Winter 2000, pp. 22–26; R. Kaplan and S. Anderson, "Time-Driven Activity-Based Costing," *Harvard Business Review*, November 2004, pp. 131–138; and *Dow Chemical Company, 2011 Annual Report*.

Allocation of Costs to Customer Cost Objects to Determine Customer Profitability

Objective 5

Allocate costs associated with customer actions to customers.

So far, we have seen how to accumulate costs and trace or allocate them to products or services—numbers 1–7 in Exhibit 12-1. This enables the calculation of gross profit for products or services. Many managers recognize that to achieve overall profitability goals, it is necessary to have both profitable products or services and profitable customers. We now consider how organizations measure and manage customer profitability.

As shown in Exhibit 12-1 on p. 482, customer profitability depends on more than the gross margin of the products or services purchased. Customer profitability also depends on the costs incurred to fulfill customer orders and to provide other customer services such as order changes, returns, and expedited scheduling or delivery. Exhibit 12-12 shows how these two factors determine profitability.

Exhibit 12-12

Customer Profitability as a Function of Customer Gross Margin and Cost to Serve

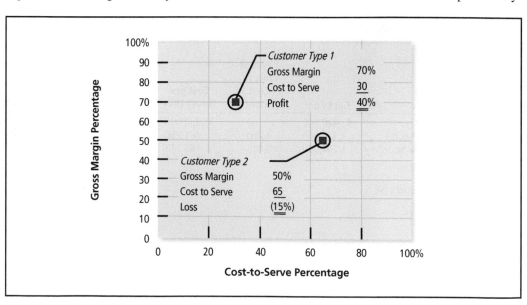

Consider customer type 1. This customer buys a mix of products that have high gross margins yielding a high gross margin percentage, about 70%. Customer type 1 has a low cost-to-serve percentage (cost to serve ÷ sales revenue), about 30%. As a result, customer type 1 will have a high level of profitability, 70% − 30% = 40%. On the other hand, customer type 2 buys products with a lower gross margin and is very costly to serve resulting in a loss to the company of 50% − 65% = −15%. Most of this difference reflects the 35% higher cost to serve. The following list is a profile of low and high cost-to-serve customers.

Low Cost to Serve	High Cost to Serve
Large order quantity	Small order quantity
Few order changes	Many order changes
Little pre- and post-sales support	Large amounts of pre- and post-sales support
Regular scheduling	Expedited scheduling
Standard delivery	Special delivery requirements
Few returns	Frequent returns

Measuring and Managing Customer Profitability

In the general framework for cost allocation, we stated that it is often important to directly trace or allocate costs associated with customer actions to customers rather than assigning them first to producing departments and then to customers. This is because if we assigned these costs to producing departments and then to products, the allocation to customers would be based on production-related cost-allocation bases that may have little relationship to the cause of customer-service costs. Such allocations can lead to cost distortions and resulting erroneous customer-profitability measures. Let's consider an example that illustrates this important concept.

Cedar City Distributors (CCD) is a distributor of athletic apparel and sports gear. CCD distributes many products to retail outlets but classifies products into just two product groups—apparel and sports gear.

- Apparel items arrive at CCD in prepackaged cases and CCD ships them to customers in these cases. Examples include shirts, shorts, socks, and hats.
- CCD receives sports gear in bulk shipments and then unpacks the products and repacks them to meet small order quantities for specific gear. Examples include tennis rackets and balls, baseball bats and gloves, and golf clubs and bags.

CCD has two types of customers:

1. Small stores: stores that order low volumes (an average of 10 cases per order), the majority being apparel
2. Large stores: stores that order large volumes of both apparel and sports gear

CCD's management has set a strategic goal to improve both product and customer profitability. A related and necessary subgoal that supports this strategy is to identify profitable products and customers using an accurate cost-accounting system.

SIMPLE COST ACCOUNTING SYSTEM CCD currently uses a simple cost accounting system to calculate both product and customer profitability. The only direct costs are the purchase costs of apparel and sports gear products. CCD allocates indirect costs to the product groups using a single indirect cost pool for all indirect costs with "actual pounds of product" as the cost-allocation base. Although it is preferable to allocate variable and fixed costs separately, each with its own cost-allocation base, it is not unusual for companies to use a simpler system that combines all indirect costs in a department into one cost pool. If most indirect costs are variable and vary with changes in the cost-allocation base, this is a reasonable simplification. We will see later if it is reasonable for CCD.

Product Data

	Apparel	Sports Gear
Annual demand in cases	1,400	1,000
Average purchase cost per case	$80	$140
Average weight per purchased case	15 pounds	25 pounds
Average sales price per case	$570	$830

Customer Data

	Small Stores	Large Stores
Apparel demand in cases	600	800
Sports gear demand in cases	200	800
Total annual demand in cases	800	1,600
Orders	80	35

Indirect Cost Data

A single indirect cost pool consists of resources needed to perform receiving, storing, picking, packing, shipping, order processing, and customer service activities. The annual cost of these resources is $690,000. The cost-allocation base used to allocate this pool to the two product groups is pounds of product sold.

Exhibit 12-13
Operating Data for Cedar City Distributors

Cost and operating data accumulated for the most recent year are shown in Exhibit 12-13. To determine the profitability of a customer under this simple system, we first calculate the profit margin per case for each product. Then, we use the product mix ordered by each customer to calculate profitability. Exhibit 12-14 shows how to calculate the profit margin per case and the profit margin percentage of both products. Based on the profit-margin percentage, apparel products are more profitable than sports gear. Since small stores' product mix is 75% apparel compared to only 50% for large stores, we expect small store customers to have

	Output Measure or Cost-Allocation Base	Revenue or Cost per Unit	Apparel		Sports Gear	
			Amount of Output or Cost-Allocation Base	Total Revenue or Cost	Amount of Output or Cost-Allocation Base	Total Revenue or Cost
Apparel revenue	Cases	$570.00	1,400	$798,000		
Sports gear revenue	Cases	$830.00			1,000	$830,000
Apparel purchase cost	Cases	$ 80.00	1,400	112,000		
Sports gear purchase cost	Cases	$140.00			1,000	140,000
Indirect cost pool, $690,000	Pounds	$ 15.00*	21,000**	315,000	25,000	375,000
Total cost				427,000		515,000
Profit margin				$371,000		$315,000
Profit margin per case				$ 265.00		$ 315.00
Profit margin percentage				46.5%†		38.0%‡

*$690,000 ÷ (15 lb per case × 1,400 cases) + (25 lb per case × 1,000 cases)
**15 lb per case × 1,400 cases
†$371,000 ÷ $798,000
‡$315,000 ÷ $830,000

Exhibit 12-14
Profit Margin Per Case of Apparel and Sports Gear

	Small Stores			Large Stores		
	Cases	Profit Margin Per Case	Total Profit Margin	Cases	Profit Margin Per Case	Total Profit Margin
Apparel	600	$265.00	$159,000	800	$265.00	$212,000
Sports Gear	200	315.00	63,000	800	315.00	252,000
			$222,000			$464,000
Total Profit Margin Percentage			43.7%*			41.4%†

*$222,000 ÷ (600 cases × $570 per case + 200 cases × $830 per case) = $222,000 ÷ ($342,000 + $166,000) = $222,000 ÷ $508,000 = .437
†$464,000 ÷ (800 cases × $570 per case + 800 cases × $830 per case) = $464,000 ÷ ($456,000 + $664,000) = $464,000 ÷ $1,120,000 = .414

Exhibit 12-15
Customer Profitability at Cedar City Distributors

a larger profit margin percentage. We verify this in Exhibit 12-15, which shows customer profitability. Note that customer profitability is based solely on the product mix ordered by a particular customer.

Our analysis indicates that a strategy to increase CCD's overall profitability would involve an emphasis on apparel products and small stores. However, in setting this strategy, CCD's management relied on the accuracy of the costs. CCD's simple cost-accounting system may accurately allocate indirect costs if the single cost-allocation base, pounds of product sold, is a plausible and reliable cost driver for all resources in the indirect cost pool. Let's see if that is the case.

REFINED COST ACCOUNTING SYSTEM We look again at Exhibit 12-13 and ask, "Is it plausible that all the activities and associated indirect resources included in the indirect cost pool are related solely to the weight of purchased product?" Might "number of customer orders" be a more plausible cost-allocation base for some items, like the order processing and customer service activities and related resources?

Let's assume that "number of orders" was indeed a better cost-allocation base for the order processing and customer service activities. The cost of the resources used by these two activities is $276,000 out of the total indirect cost pool of $690,000. CCD should exclude these costs from the computation of product profit margin. Instead, it should set up an additional cost pool and allocate these costs to customer types. (Note, this is shown as allocation type "9" in Exhibit 12-1 on page 482.)

The partial process map in Exhibit 12-16 shows how we can refine CCD's simple allocation system. The exhibit does not contain revenue and direct product costs because they will not change. It shows only the $690,000 of indirect costs, separated into two cost pools. One cost pool is the $276,000 cost of resources used for processing customer orders and providing customer services. We will examine how to allocate this cost shortly. The other cost pool is the $690,000 − $276,000 = $414,000 associated with resources used for receiving, unpacking, storing, packing, and shipping that remains in the original indirect cost pool. The allocation of this $414,000 does not change and is still based on pounds of product.

In our refined system, we allocate the $276,000 to the customer cost objectives on the basis of number of orders, an allocation base that represents the cause of the costs much better than does pounds of product. An analysis of the allocation percentages in Exhibit 12-16 reveals how customer profitability will change under the refined allocation system. Consider the allocations of the $276,000 to large stores under both systems. In the old system, large stores receive (32,000 lb ÷ 46,000 lb) × $276,000 = $192,000 because shipments to large stores weigh 32,000 pounds out of total shipments of 46,000 pounds. In the refined allocation system, the allocation of the $276,000 is based on the proportion of orders by large stores. Large stores make only 35 out of 115 orders, so the allocation is (35 ÷ 115) × $276,000 = $84,000. The refined cost-accounting system allocates $192,000 − $84,000 = $108,000 less indirect, customer-related costs to large stores and, correspondingly, $108,000 more cost to small stores.

Exhibit 12-16
Cedar City Distributors'
Refined Cost-Allocation
System

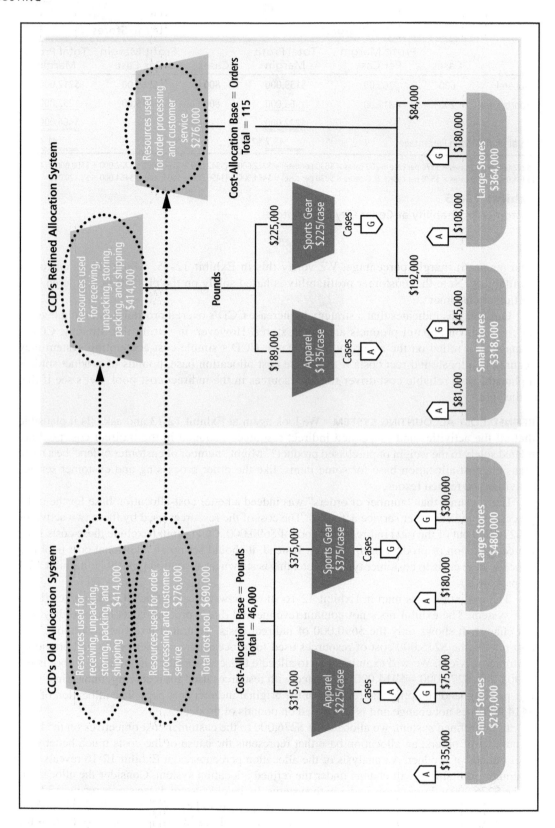

The refined cost-allocation system significantly changes the profitability measures of small and large stores. Exhibit 12-17 shows the calculation of product gross margin, customer gross margin, customer cost to serve, and customer profitability.

Contrary to the results based on the simple, existing cost-accounting system (Exhibit 12-14), the refined system shows that large stores are the most profitable customers. Exhibit 12-18 is based on Exhibit 12-17 and depicts both the customer product gross margin and cost to serve. It is easy to see why large stores are the major source of profit for CCD. The cost to serve is low and the product mix yields a substantial gross margin. This example demonstrates why it is important for accountants to carefully choose and measure cost-allocation bases. The refined system gives managers at CCD more insight into operations, and they have a tool to measure and manage customer profitability.

Product Profitability Measures

	Output Measure or Cost-Allocation Base	Revenue or Cost per Unit of Cost-Allocation Base	Apparel		Sports Gear	
			Amount of Output or Cost-Allocation Base	Total Revenue or Cost	Amount of Output or Cost-Allocation Base	Total Revenue or Cost
Apparel revenue	Cases	$570.00	1,400	$798,000		
Sports gear revenue	Cases	830.00			1,000	$830,000
Apparel purchase cost	Cases	80.00	1,400	112,000		
Sports gear purchase cost	Cases	140.00			1,000	140,000
Indirect cost pool, $414,000	Pounds	9.00*	21,000	189,000	25,000	225,000
Total cost				301,000		365,000
Product gross margin				$497,000		$465,000
Product gross margin per case				$ 355.00		$ 465.00
Product gross margin percentage				62.3%		56.0%

Customer Profitability Measures

	Small Stores			Large Stores		
	Amount of Output or Cost-Allocation Base	Margin or Cost Per Unit of Cost-Allocation Base	Total Margin or Cost	Amount of Output or Cost-Allocation Base	Margin or Cost Per Unit	Total Margin or Cost
Apparel product gross margin	600 Cases	$355.00	$213,000	800 Cases	$355.00	284,000
Sports gear product gross margin	200 Cases	465.00	93,000	800 Cases	465.00	372,000
Gross margin for product mix			306,000			656,000
Cost to serve, $2,400 per order§	80 Orders	2,400	192,000	35 Orders	2,400	84,000
Customer profit margin			$114,000			$572,000
Customer gross margin percentage			60.2%[†]			58.6%[‡]
Cost to service percentage			37.8%			7.5%
Customer profit margin percentage			22.4%[¶]			51.1%[#]

*$414,000 ÷ (15 lb per case × 1,400 cases + 25 lb per case × 1,000 cases)
[†]$306,000 ÷ (600 cases × $570 per case + 200 cases × $830 per case)
[‡]$656,000 ÷ (800 cases × $570 per case + 800 cases × $830 per case)
§$276,000 ÷ (80 orders + 35 orders)
[¶]60.2% − 37.8% or $114,000 ÷ (600 cases × $570 per case + 200 cases × $830 per case)
[#]58.6% − 7.5% or $572,000 ÷ (800 cases × $570 per case + 800 cases × $830 per case)

Exhibit 12-17
Product and Customer Profitability Measures Based on CCD's Refined Cost-Allocation System

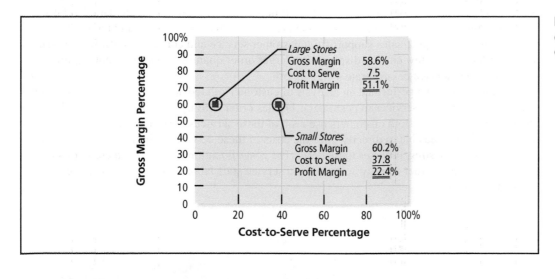

Exhibit 12-18
Customer Profitability at Cedar City Distributors

Making Managerial Decisions

Louder Is Better Company makes two speaker models— standard (S) and deluxe (D). The following diagrams show how ABC and traditional allocation systems allocate overhead costs to the deluxe model. The production department has overhead costs of $36,000. Why does the cost allocated to the deluxe type speakers by the ABC system differ from that in the traditional system?

Answer

In the traditional system, the deluxe product receives only 25% of the overhead costs because it uses only 25% of the machine hours. But in the ABC system, it receives 72% of the overhead because it uses 63% of the parts and 83% of the setups.

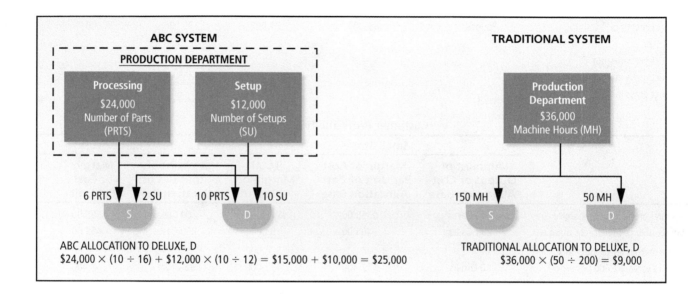

Summary Problem for Your Review

PROBLEM

Consider our example of **L.A. Darling**'s display facility. Exhibits 12-9, 12-10, and 12-11 on pages 496 and 497 show how the company used the ABC approach to determine the cost of goods sold for custom and standard displays. Suppose that management wants to know the profitability of its major customers. Assume that two major customers are Southwest Hardware Stores (SHS) and **Target Corporation**. SHS orders a mix of custom and standard displays. It also has unique service requirements, orders relatively small order sizes, and requires substantial pre- and post-sales support from customer service and corporate staff. In contrast, Target orders only a few custom displays, has larger order quantities, and does not require much customer service or corporate staff support.

Accountants have performed an analysis of customer-related activities and concluded that two activities provide services to customers: 1) sales order activity and 2) customer service and corporate support. Both customers use each of these services to some extent, and it is not economically feasible to directly trace the costs of these services to individual customers. Therefore, L.A. Darling allocates these costs. The cost-allocation bases chosen are number of orders for the sales order activity cost pool and service staff labor hours for the customer and corporate support cost pool.

To determine the profitability of the two customers, the company has collected the following data:

- Average price of a custom display $12,000
- Average price of a standard display $ 8,500
- Number of custom displays ordered by SHS   180
- Number of custom displays ordered by Target   20
- Number of standard displays ordered by SHS   220
- Number of standard displays ordered by Target   980
- Cost to serve activity analysis data:
  - Total sales order activity cost pool $3,000,000
  - Total customer and corporate support cost pool $1,150,000
- Amount of each cost-allocation base used by each customer:

Cost-Allocation Base	SHS	Target
Orders	40	20
Hours	6,400	3,600

1. Calculate the gross margin percentage and cost-to-serve percentage for Southwest Hardware Stores and Target.
2. Construct a graph similar to Exhibit 12-18 that depicts customer profitability for Southwest Hardware Stores and Target.
3. Suggest a strategy for profit improvement for both customers.

SOLUTION

1. Exhibit 12-19 shows the calculation of customer gross margin and customer cost to serve.
2. Exhibit 12-20 depicts the profitability of SHS and Target.
3. You can use Exhibit 12-20 as a guide for setting strategy for profit improvement. Target is generating much more profit for the company than is SHS. L.A. Darling managers should protect customers such as Target from possible competitor actions, perhaps offering discounts to ensure continued business. In addition, the sales department manager should profile this type of customer to make it easier for salespersons to identify profitable new business. SHS is very expensive to serve because of its small order quantities and extensive pre- and post-sales support. Possible actions that would improve its profitability include charging for corporate support, reviewing internal processes within L.A. Darling's customer service and corporate support function to improve efficiencies, and increasing prices for custom displays.

			SHS		Target	
	Cost-Allocation Base	Revenue or Cost per Unit of Cost-Allocation Base	Amount of Cost-Allocation Base	Revenue/ Cost	Amount of Cost-Allocation Base	Revenue/ Cost
Revenue—Custom	Displays	$12,000.00	180	$2,160,000	20	$ 240,000
Revenue—Standard	Displays	8,500.00	220	1,870,000	980	8,330,000
Total Revenue				4,030,000		8,570,000
Cost of goods sold—Custom	Displays	6,175.00*	180	1,111,500	20	123,500
Cost of goods sold—Standard	Displays	2,387.50*	220	525,250	980	2,339,750
Total cost of goods sold				1,636,750		2,463,250
Gross margin				2,393,250		6,106,750
Cost to serve:						
Sales order activity	Orders	50,000.00†	40	2,000,000	20	1,000,000
Customer service and corporate support	Hours	115.00‡	6,400	736,000	3,600	414,000
Total cost to serve				2,736,000		1,414,000
Contribution to unallocated corporate overhead				$ (342,750)		$4,692,750
Gross margin percentage				59.4%		71.3%
Cost-to-serve percentage				67.9%		16.5%
Customer profit margin percentage				(8.5)%		54.8%

*From Exhibit 12-11
†$3,000,000 ÷ (40 orders + 20 orders)
‡$1,150,000 ÷ (6,400 hours + 3,600 hours)

Exhibit 12-19
Contribution to Unallocated Corporate Overhead at L.A. Darling Display Facility

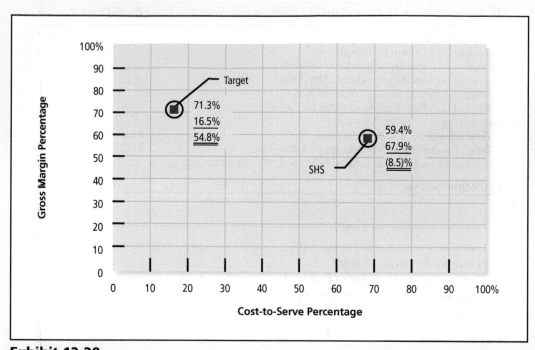

Exhibit 12-20
L.A. Darling Display Facility: Customer Profitability Using the ABC Approach

This concludes our discussion of service department allocation. We will next consider two specific types of cost allocations: (1) allocation of central corporate costs such as public relations and legal costs, and (2) allocation of joint and by-product costs.

Allocation of Central Corporate Support Costs

Many managers believe it is desirable to fully allocate all of an organization's costs, including central corporate support costs, to the revenue-producing (operating) parts of the organization. Such allocations are not necessary from a financial accounting viewpoint and usually not useful as management information. For this reason, we do not consider central costs to be part of the value chain in this text, and we generally recommend that companies not allocate these costs. However, if a company chooses to allocate central support costs, it is important to allocate them in a way that managers accept as "fair." It is often difficult to find a good measure of the usage of central services, but some companies find measures that managers believe are fair, such as usage, either actual or estimated. Consider the experience of J. C. Penney Company as reported in *BusinessWeek*:

> *The controller's office wanted subsidiaries such as Thrift Drug Co. and the insurance operations to base their share of corporate personnel, legal, and auditing costs on their revenues. The subsidiaries contended that they maintained their own personnel and legal departments, and should be assessed far less.... The subcommittee addressed the issue by asking the corporate departments to approximate the time (a measure of usage) and costs involved in servicing the subsidiaries. The final allocation plan, based on these studies, cost the divisions less than they were initially assessed but more than they had wanted to pay. Nonetheless, the plan was implemented easily.*

It is often difficult to find a cause and effect relationship between a cost-allocation base and costs such as the president's salary and related expenses, public relations, legal services, income tax planning, company-wide advertising, and basic research. As a result, some companies use cost-allocation bases such as the revenue of each division, the cost of goods sold by each division, the total assets of each division, or the total costs of each division (before allocation of the central costs) to allocate central costs, even though these bases are not necessarily the cost drivers.

Although the foregoing cost-allocation bases may not reflect a cause-and-effect relationship, they may represent an "ability to bear" philosophy of cost allocation. For example, a company might allocate the costs of company-wide advertising, such as the sponsorship of a program on a PBS station, to all products and divisions on the basis of the revenues in each. But such discretionary costs are determined by management policies, not by sales results. Although 60% of the companies in a large survey use sales revenue as a cost-allocation base for some cost-allocation purposes, sales revenue is seldom truly a cost driver in the sense of being an activity that causes the costs.

Use of Budgeted Sales for Allocation

If management feels it must allocate the costs of central services based on sales, even though the costs do not vary in proportion to sales, it should use budgeted sales rather than actual sales as an allocation base. This method has the advantage that the fortunes of other departments will not affect the costs allocated to a given department. However, it also has the disadvantage of providing an incentive for the department to under-predict their own sales. For example, suppose **L.A. Darling Company** budgets central advertising as 10% of forecasted sales in two countries—Mexico and Canada. The forecasted sales are $500,000 in both Mexico and Canada so the total advertising budget, a fixed cost, is $100,000. Actual sales in Mexico and Canada are $300,000 and $600,000, respectively. How does the company allocate the $100,000 advertising budget if it uses forecasted sales compared to actual sales?

Allocation of $100,000 Central Advertising Budget

	Mexico	Canada
Forecast sales	$500,000	$500,000
Allocation based on forecast sales	50,000	50,000
Actual sales	300,000	600,000
Allocation based on actual sales	33,333	67,667

The preferred allocation is based on forecast sales. Why? Because it indicates a low ratio of sales to advertising in Mexico—it directs attention to a potential problem. In contrast, allocation based on actual sales soaks the Canadian operations with more advertising cost because of the achieved results and relieves Mexican operations despite its lower success. This is another example of the confusion that can arise when cost allocations to one company unit depend on the activity of other units.

Allocation of Joint Costs and By-Product Costs

Joint costs and by-product costs create especially difficult cost-allocation problems. By definition, such costs relate to more than one product, and we cannot separately identify them with an individual product. Let's examine these special cases, starting with joint costs.

Objective 7

Allocate joint costs to products using the physical-units and relative-sales-value methods.

Joint Costs

So far, we have assumed that we could identify cost-allocation bases with an individual product. For example, if we are allocating activity costs to products or services on the basis of machine hours, we have assumed that we can measure the amount of machine time consumed in making each product. However, sometimes we add inputs to the production process before we can separately identify individual products (i.e., before the split-off point). Recall from Chapter 6 (page 238) that we call such costs joint costs. Joint costs include all inputs of material, labor, and overhead costs that are incurred before the split-off point.

Suppose a department has more than one product and some costs are joint costs. How should we allocate such joint costs to the products? Companies routinely allocate joint product costs to products for purposes of inventory valuation and income determination, so we illustrate two methods of allocation. *However, it is important to remember that allocation of joint costs should not affect decisions about the individual products, such as selling a joint product or processing it further.*

Consider the example of joint product costs that we used in Chapter 6. A department in **Dow Chemical Company** produces two chemicals, X and Y. The joint cost is $100,000, and production is 1,000,000 liters of X and 500,000 liters of Y. X sells for $.09 per liter and Y for $.06 per liter.

We want to find a method to allocate some part of the $100,000 joint cost to the inventory of X and the rest to the inventory of Y. There are two conventional ways of allocating joint costs to products: physical units and relative sales values.

If a company uses the *physical units method*, it would allocate the joint costs as follows, using liters as the physical units:

	Liters	Weighting	Allocation of Joint Costs	Sales Value at Split-Off Point
X	1,000,000	$(10 \div 15) \times \$100,000$	$ 66,667	$ 90,000
Y	500,000	$(5 \div 15) \times \$100,000$	33,333	30,000
	1,500,000		$100,000	$120,000

Because two-thirds of the liters produced are chemical X, we allocate two-thirds of the joint cost to X. Likewise, one-third of the liters are chemical Y, so we allocate one-third of the cost to Y.

The physical-units method requires a common physical unit for measuring the output of each product. For example, board feet is a common unit for allocating the cost of logs to a variety of products in the lumber industry. However, sometimes a common physical unit is lacking. Consider the production of meat and hides from butchering a steer. You might use pounds as a common denominator, but pounds is not a good measure of the output of hides. As an alternative, many companies use the *relative-sales-value method* for allocating joint costs. The following allocation results from applying the relative-sales-value method to the Dow Chemical department:

	Relative Sales Value at Split-Off Point	Weighting	Allocation of Joint Costs
X	$ 90,000	$(90 \div 120) \times \$100,000$	$ 75,000
Y	30,000	$(30 \div 120) \times \$100,000$	25,000
	$120,000		$100,000

The weighting is based on the sales values of the individual products. Because the sales value of X at the split-off point is $90,000 and total sales value at the split-off point is $120,000, we allocate $90 \div 120$ of the joint cost to X.

This method might eliminate one problem, but it creates another. Note how the allocation of a cost to a particular product, such as Y, depends not only on the sales value of Y but also on the sales value of X. For example, suppose you were the product manager for Y. You planned to sell your 500,000 liters for $30,000, achieving a profit of $30,000 − $25,000 = $5,000. Everything went as expected except that the price of X fell to $.07 per liter for revenue of $70,000 rather than $90,000. Instead of $30 \div 120$ of the joint cost, Y received $30 \div 100 \times \$100,000 = \$30,000$ and had a profit of $0. Despite the fact that Y operations were exactly as planned, the cost-allocation method caused the profit on Y to be $5,000 below plan.

We can also use the relative-sales-value method when we cannot sell one or more of the joint products at the split-off point. To apply the method, we approximate the sales value at split-off as follows:

$$\text{sales value at split-off} = \text{final sales value} - \text{separable costs}$$

For example, suppose the 500,000 liters of Y requires $20,000 of processing beyond the split-off point, after which we can sell it for $.10 per liter. The sales value at split-off would be $(\$.10 \times 500,000) - \$20,000 = \$50,000 - \$20,000 = \$30,000$.

Avoid Using Allocated Joint Costs for Individual Product Decisions

We want to reemphasize the point made at the beginning of our discussion of joint costs: *Allocation of joint costs should not affect decisions about the individual products, such as selling a joint product or processing it further.* For example, the physical units approach showed that the $33,333 joint cost of producing Y exceeds its $30,000 sales value at the split-off point. This might seem to indicate that the company should not produce Y. However, because we can only produce the two products jointly, decisions about the products must be made jointly, not individually. Thus, a decision to produce Y must be a decision to produce X and Y—the production decision must be viewed as a joint decision. Because total revenue of $120,000 exceeds the total joint cost of $100,000, we should produce both. The allocation showing that one of the joint products is "unprofitable" is not relevant for this joint decision.

By-Product Costs

By-products are similar to joint products. A **by-product** is a product that, like a joint product, is not individually identifiable until manufacturing reaches a split-off point. By-products differ from joint products because they have relatively insignificant total sales values in comparison with the other products emerging at split-off. In contrast, joint products have relatively significant total sales values at split-off in comparison with the other jointly produced items. Examples of by-products are glycerine from soap making and mill ends of cloth and carpets.

by-product
A product that, like a joint product, is not individually identifiable until manufacturing reaches a split-off point, but has relatively insignificant total sales value.

If we account for an item as a by-product, we allocate only separable costs to it. We allocate all joint costs to the main products. We deduct any revenues from by-products, less their separable costs, from the cost of the main products.

Consider a lumber company that sells sawdust generated in the production of lumber to companies making particle board. Suppose the company regards the sawdust as a by-product. In 20X1, sales of sawdust totaled $30,000, and the cost of loading and shipping the sawdust (i.e., costs incurred beyond the split-off point) was $20,000. The inventory cost of the sawdust would consist of only the $20,000 separable cost. The company would allocate none of the joint cost of producing lumber and sawdust to the sawdust. It would deduct the difference between the revenue and separable cost, $30,000 − $20,000 = $10,000, from the cost of the lumber produced.

Highlights to Remember

1. **Describe the general framework for cost allocation.** Companies assign direct and indirect costs to various cost objects, including service departments, producing departments, products, and customers. All organizations allocate indirect costs to producing departments and to the products or services delivered to customers. These allocations often include the costs of service departments. Some organizations carry cost allocation one more step—to customers.

2. **Allocate the variable and fixed costs of service departments to other organizational units.** Companies should use separate cost pools for variable and fixed costs when allocating service department costs. They should allocate variable costs using budgeted cost rates times the actual cost-driver level. They should allocate fixed costs using budgeted percent of capacity available times the total budgeted fixed costs.

3. **Use the direct and step-down methods to allocate service department costs to user departments.** When service departments support other service departments in addition to producing departments, they can use either the direct or step-down method for allocation. The direct method ignores other service departments when allocating costs. The step-down method recognizes other service departments' use of services.

4. **Allocate costs from producing departments to products or services using the traditional and ABC approaches.** When a company's products or services are the final cost object, it should integrate its service department allocation with the allocation system used to determine the cost of products and services. A traditional system traces the direct costs in each department to its products or services and allocates indirect costs using a cost-allocation base. The ABC approach uses three steps to assign costs to products or services: 1) Determine the key components and the relationship among them, 2) collect relevant data, and 3) calculate and interpret ABC information. The ABC approach provides more accurate estimates of product or service costs than the traditional approach but is more costly to maintain.

5. **Allocate costs associated with customer actions to customers.** Customer profitability is a function of product mix and the cost to serve. Activities that can drive up the costs to serve customers include small order quantities, pre-sales support, order changes, returns, special delivery requirements, and post-sales support.

6. **Allocate the central corporate costs of an organization.** Central costs include public relations, top corporate management overhead, legal, data processing, controller's department, and company-wide planning. Often, it is best to allocate only those central costs of an organization for which measures of usage by departments are available.

7. **Allocate joint costs to products using the physical-units and relative-sales-value methods.** Companies often allocate joint costs to products for inventory valuation and income determination using the physical-units or relative-sales-value method. However, such allocations should not affect decisions.

Accounting Vocabulary

by-product, p. 509   producing departments, p. 481
cost application, p. 490   service departments, p. 481
direct method, p. 487   step-down method, p. 488

MyAccountingLab # Fundamental Assignment Material

12-A1 Direct and Step-Down Methods of Allocation; General Framework for Allocation

Swarez Tool and Die has three service departments:

	Budgeted Department Costs
Cafeteria, revenue of $100,000 less expenses of $250,000	$ 150,000
Engineering	1,600,000
General factory administration	950,000

Cost-allocation bases are budgeted as follows:

Production Departments	Employees	Engineering Hours Worked for Production Departments	Total Labor Hours
Machining	120	50,000	300,000
Assembly	540	20,000	720,000
Finishing and painting	60	10,000	120,000

1. Swarez allocates all service department costs directly to the production departments without allocation to other service departments. Show how much of the budgeted costs of each service department are allocated to each production department. Choose the most logical cost-allocation base for each service department. To plan your work, examine number 2 before undertaking this question.

2. The company has decided to use the step-down method of cost allocation. General factory administration would be allocated first, then cafeteria, then engineering. Cafeteria employees work 36,000 labor hours per year. There were 60 engineering employees with 120,000 total labor hours. Recompute the results in number 1, using the step-down method. Show your computations. Compare the results in numbers 1 and 2. Which method of allocation do you favor? Why?

3. Refer to Exhibit 12-1 on page 482. For each type of cost assignment made in number 2 using the step-down method, indicate the assignment type from Exhibit 12-1.

12-A2 Customer Profitability

The following table gives sales, product cost, and cost-to-serve data for a company that makes three product lines: A, B, and C. The company has two customer types.

	Product A	Product B	Product C
Sales	$5,000	$6,000	$25,000
Cost of sales	4,500	4,800	15,000

	Customer Type 1	Customer Type 2	Total
Product A Sales	$ 500	$ 4,500	$ 5,000
Product B Sales	1,000	5,000	6,000
Product C Sales	13,000	12,000	25,000
Manager Visits	4	16	20

The cost to serve all customers is $12,000 and is allocated to customer types based on the number of manager visits to customer locations for pre- and post-sales support.

1. Determine the gross profit margin percentage of sales for each product. Which product is the most profitable?
2. Determine the gross profit margin and the gross profit margin percentage of sales for each customer type.
3. Determine the cost-to-serve percentage of sales for each customer type.
4. Determine the operating income and operating income percentage of sales for each customer type.
5. Which customer is the most profitable based the following profitability measures:
   a. Gross margin
   b. Gross margin percentage of sales
   c. Operating income
   d. Operating income percentage of sales

12-A3 Joint Products

Mesabi Metals buys raw ore on the open market and processes it into two products, A and B. The ore costs $11 per pound, and the process separating it into A and B has a cost of $4 per pound. During 20X1, Mesabi plans to produce 200,000 pounds of A and 800,000 pounds of B from 1,000,000 pounds of ore. A sells for $30 a pound and B for $15 a pound. The company allocated joint costs to the individual products for inventory valuation purposes.

1. Allocate all the joint costs to A and B using the physical-units method.
2. Allocate all the joint costs to A and B using the relative-sales-value method.
3. Suppose Mesabi cannot sell product B in the form in which it emerges from the joint process. Instead, it must be processed further at a fixed cost of $200,000 plus a variable cost of $1 per pound. Then, it can be sold for $18.75 a pound. Allocate all the joint costs to A and B using the relative-sales-value method.

12-B1 Allocation of Service Department Costs; General Framework for Allocation

Texas Building Services provides cleaning services for a variety of clients. The company has two producing departments, residential and commercial, and two service departments, personnel and administrative. The company has decided to allocate all service department costs to the producing departments, personnel on the basis of number of employees and administrative costs on the basis of direct department costs. The budget for 20X2 shows the following:

	Personnel	Administrative	Residential	Commercial
Direct department costs	$70,000	$100,000	$ 240,000	$ 400,000
Number of employees	3	5	12	18
Direct-labor hours			24,000	36,000
Square feet cleaned			4,500,000	9,970,000

1. Allocate service department costs using the direct method.
2. Allocate service department costs using the step-down method. Personnel costs should be allocated first.
3. Suppose the company prices by the hour in the residential department and by the square foot cleaned in the commercial department. Using the results of the step-down allocations in number 2,
   a. compute the cost of providing one direct-labor hour of service in the residential department.
   b. compute the cost of cleaning one square foot of space in the commercial department.
4. Refer to Exhibit 12-1 on page 482. For each type of cost assignment made in number 2 using the step-down method, indicate the assignment type from Exhibit 12-1.

12-B2 Customer Profitability

Blakely Company makes three product lines and has two customer types. The following table gives sales, product cost, and cost-to-serve data for Blakely:

	Product		
	Alpha	**Beta**	**Gamma**
Sales	$4,000	$8,000	$20,000
Cost of goods sold	2,000	2,000	14,000

	Customer Type 1	**Customer Type 2**	**Total**
Product Alpha Sales	$2,000	$ 2,000	$ 4,000
Product Beta Sales	5,000	3,000	8,000
Product Gamma Sales	1,000	19,000	20,000
Manager Visits	6	4	10

The cost to serve all customers is $10,000 and is allocated to customer types based on the number of manager visits to customer locations for pre- and post-sales support.

1. Determine the gross profit margin percentage of sales for each product. Which product is the most profitable?
2. Determine the gross profit margin and the gross profit margin percentage of sales for each customer type.
3. Determine the cost-to-serve percentage of sales for each customer type.
4. Determine the operating income and operating income percentage of sales for each customer type.
5. Which customer is the most profitable based the following profitability measures:
   a. Gross margin
   b. Gross margin percentage of sales
   c. Operating income
   d. Operating income percentage of sales

12-B3 Joint Products

St. Paul Milling buys oats at $.80 per pound and produces SPM Oat Flour, SPM Oat Flakes, and SPM Oat Bran. The process of separating the oats into oat flour and oat bran costs $.40 per pound. The oat flour can be sold for $1.50 per pound, the oat bran for $2.00 per pound. Each pound of oats has .2 pounds of oat bran and .8 pounds of oat flour. A pound of oat flour can be made into oat flakes for a fixed cost of $240,000 plus a variable cost of $.60 per pound. St. Paul Milling plans to process 1 million pounds of oats in 20X0, at a purchase price of $800,000.

1. Allocate all the joint costs to oat flour and oat bran using the physical-units method.
2. Allocate all the joint costs to oat flour and oat bran using the relative-sales-value method.
3. Suppose there were no market for oat flour. Instead, it must be made into oat flakes to be sold. Oat flakes sell for $2.90 per pound. Allocate the joint cost to oat bran and oat flakes using the relative-sales-value method.

Additional Assignment Material

QUESTIONS

12-1 Why is the cost-allocation method used by an organization an important part of its cost accounting system?

12-2 What are the 10 types of cost assignments?

12-3 What types of costs would a company leave unallocated?

12-4 List three guidelines for the allocation of service department costs.

12-5 Explain how a direct department cost can become an indirect cost.

12-6 Why should budgeted cost rates, rather than actual cost rates, be used for allocating the variable costs of service departments?

12-7 "We used a lump-sum allocation method for fixed costs a few years ago, but we gave it up because managers always predicted usage below what they actually used." Is this a common problem? How might it be prevented?

12-8 "A cost pool for a particular resource is either a variable cost pool or a fixed cost pool. There should be no mixed-cost pools." Do you agree? Explain.

12-9 Briefly describe the two popular methods for allocating service department costs.

12-10 What does the direct method of allocating service department costs ignore? Why do companies use the direct method despite this weakness?

12-11 "The step-down method allocates more costs to the producing departments than does the direct method." Do you agree? Explain.

12-12 Name the four steps for allocating costs to product or service cost objectives by the traditional approach.

12-13 How are costs of various overhead resources allocated to products, services, or customers in an ABC system?

12-14 Give four examples of activities and related cost-allocation bases that can be used in an ABC system to allocate costs to products, services, or customers.

12-15 Name the three steps used to allocate producing department activity cost pools using the ABC approach.

12-16 Suppose Snoqualmie Company has two plants—the Salem plant and the Youngstown plant. The Youngstown plant produces only three components that are very similar in material and production requirements. The Salem plant makes a wide variety of parts. Which type of costing system would you recommend for each plant (traditional or ABC)? Explain.

12-17 When determining customer profitability, why is it important to directly trace and allocate customer-related service department costs to customers rather than assigning them first to producing departments and then to customers?

12-18 Why is it necessary to know the profitability of customers? If all the products of a company are profitable, shouldn't its customers also be profitable? Explain.

12-19 List several factors that determine whether a customer has a low or high cost to serve.

12-20 What problem might arise when central corporate costs are allocated based on actual sales?

12-21 "The more the better!" was a comment made by the CEO of a major company when asked about allocation of sales, general, and administrative costs to products. Do you agree? Explain.

12-22 Chapter 6 explained that joint costs should not be allocated to individual products for decision purposes. For what purposes are such costs allocated to products?

12-23 Briefly explain each of the two conventional ways of allocating joint costs of products.

12-24 What are by-products and how do we account for them?

CRITICAL THINKING EXERCISES

12-25 Allocation and Cost Behavior

There are three general guidelines to use when allocating service department (support) costs. One of these guidelines deals with the cost behavior of support costs. Why do many companies allocate fixed support costs separately from variable support costs?

12-26 Allocation and the Sales Function

Confusion can arise when cost allocations to one consuming department depend on the activity of another consuming department. "A commonly misused basis for allocation of central support costs is actual dollar sales." Explain.

12-27 Allocation and Marketing

Many companies are allocating more nonproduction costs because of the increasing magnitude of these value-chain costs. One value-chain function that is receiving more attention is marketing. How should national advertising costs be allocated to territories?

EXERCISES

12-28 Allocation of Computer Costs

Review the section Allocation of Service Department Costs, pages 483–490, especially the example of the use of the computer by the university. Recall that the budget formula was $100,000 fixed cost monthly plus $200 per hour of computer time used. Based on long-run predicted usage, the fixed costs were allocated on a lump-sum basis, 30% to business and 70% to engineering.

1. Show the total allocation if business used 210 hours and engineering used 400 hours in a given month. Assume that the actual costs coincided exactly with the budgeted amount for total usage of 610 hours.
2. Assume the same facts as in number 1 except that the fixed costs were allocated on the basis of actual hours of usage. Show the total allocation of costs to each school. As the dean of the School of Business, would you prefer this method or the method in number 1? Explain.

12-29 Fixed- and Variable-Cost Pools

The city of Lancaster signed a lease for a photocopy machine at $3,000 per month and $.02 per copy. Operating costs for toner, paper, operator salary, and so on are all variable at $.03 per copy. Departments had projected a need for 100,000 copies a month. The city planning department predicted its usage at 36,000 copies a month. It made 42,000 copies in August.

1. Suppose one predetermined rate per copy was used to allocate all photocopy costs. What rate would be used and how much cost would be allocated to the city planning department in August?
2. Suppose fixed- and variable-cost pools were allocated separately. Specify how each pool should be allocated. Compute the cost allocated to the city planning department in August.
3. Which method, the one in number 1 or the one in number 2, do you prefer? Explain.

12-30 Sales-Based Allocations

Roberto's Markets, Inc., has three grocery stores in the metropolitan Atlanta area. The company allocates central costs using sales as the cost-allocation base. The following are budgeted and actual sales during November:

	Bellevue	Richfield	Hightower
Budgeted sales	$600,000	$1,000,000	$400,000
Actual sales	600,000	700,000	500,000

Central costs of $360,000 are to be allocated in November.

1. Compute the central costs allocated to each store with budgeted sales as the cost-allocation base.
2. Compute the central costs allocated to each store with actual sales as the cost-allocation base.
3. What advantages are there to using budgeted rather than actual sales for allocating the central costs?

12-31 Direct and Step-Down Allocations, Activity-Based Allocation

M&O Partners provides consulting services for a variety of clients. The company has two producing divisions, one for retail companies and one for industrial companies, and two service departments, personnel and administrative. Until now the company has not allocated service department costs. However, M&O has decided to allocate these costs to the producing departments using an activity-based allocation system. The retail division has Activity 1 and Activity 2 and the industrial division has Activity 3, Activity 4, and Activity 5. The company has decided to allocate personnel costs on the basis of number of employees and administrative costs on the basis of the direct costs of the activities in each division. However, administrative services are provided only to activities 2 and 3, so no administrative costs are allocated to activities 1, 4, and 5. Data for the activities follow:

	Number of Personnel	Direct costs
Personnel	2	$ 92,000
Administrative	5	170,000
Retail:		
Activity 1	3	60,000
Activity 2	12	240,000
Industrial:		
Activity 3	18	400,000
Activity 4	0	90,000
Activity 5	8	110,000

1. Determine the costs allocated to the retail and industrial divisions using the direct method.
2. Determine the costs allocated to the retail and industrial divisions using the step-down method. The personnel department costs should be allocated first.

12-32 Direct and Step-Down Allocations

Longworth Manufacturing has two producing departments, machining and assembly, and two service departments, personnel and custodial. The company's budget for April 20X1 is as follows:

	Service Departments		Production Departments	
	Personnel	Custodial	Machining	Assembly
Direct department costs	$45,000	$70,000	$600,000	$800,000
Square feet	2,000	1,000	10,000	25,000
Number of employees	15	30	200	250

Longworth allocates personnel costs on the basis of number of employees and custodial costs on the basis of square feet.

1. Allocate personnel and custodial costs to the producing departments using the direct method.
2. Allocate personnel and custodial costs to the producing departments using the step-down method. Allocate personnel costs first.

12-33 Customer Profitability; Strategy

The following table gives the sales, product cost, and cost-to-serve data for a merchandising store. The store has four types of merchandise and three types of customers.

Product A		Product B		Product C		Product D	
Sales	$32,000	Sales	$88,000	Sales	$280,000	Sales	$143,000
Cost of sales	20,000	Cost of sales	70,400	Cost of sales	224,000	Cost of sales	81,000

	Customer Type 1	Customer Type 2	Customer Type 3	Total Units Sold
Product A units	200	2,200	500	2,900
Product B units	100	1,200	3,000	4,300
Product C units	50	400	5,000	5,450
Product D units	400	800	400	1,600
Total units sold	750	4,600	8,900	14,250

The costs to serve all customers is $140,000 and is allocated to customer types based on the number of units sold.

1. Determine the gross profit margin percentage of sales for each product. Which product is the most profitable?
2. Determine the gross profit margin percentage of sales for each customer type.
3. Determine the cost-to-serve percentage of sales for each customer type.

4. Which customer is the most profitable?
5. Prepare a chart similar to Exhibit 12-18 on p. 503 that shows the customer gross margin percentage and cost-to-serve percentage for the three customers. Recommend a strategy for profit improvement for each customer.

12-34 Joint Costs

Zephyr Chemical Company's production process for two of its solvents can be diagrammed as follows:

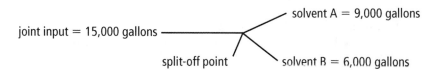

The cost of the joint input, including processing costs before the split-off point, is $100,000. Solvent A can be sold at split-off for $10 per gallon and solvent B for $15 per gallon.

1. Allocate the $100,000 joint cost to solvents A and B by the physical-units method.
2. Allocate the $100,000 joint cost to solvents A and B by the relative-sales-value method.

12-35 Joint Costs

The output of one of Montero Chemical Company's production processes is two solvents, Rexon and Texon. The two products cannot be separated until $500,000 of processing costs have been incurred. At that point there are 15,000 gallons of Rexon that can be sold for $25 per gallon and 5,000 gallons of Texon that can be sold for $50 per gallon.

1. Allocate the $500,000 joint cost to Rexon and Texon by the physical-units method.
2. Allocate the $500,000 joint cost to Rexon and Texon by the relative-sales-value method.

12-36 By-Product Costing

Yakima Vineyards buys grapes from local orchards and presses them to produce grape juice for wine making. The pulp that remains after pressing is sold to farmers as livestock food. This livestock food is accounted for as a by-product.

During the 20X1 fiscal year, the company paid $1 million to purchase 4 million pounds of grapes. After processing, 1 million pounds of pulp remained. Yakima spent $40,000 to package and ship the pulp, which was sold for $50,000.

1. How much of the joint cost of the grapes is allocated to the pulp?
2. Compute the total inventory cost (and therefore the cost of goods sold) for the pulp.
3. Assume that $130,000 was spent to press the grapes and $150,000 was spent to filter, pasteurize, pack, and ship the juice to wineries in the Puget Sound area. Compute the total cost of the grape juice produced.

PROBLEMS

12-37 General Framework for Allocation, Service Departments, ABC, Customer Profitability, and Process Maps

Consider one of **L.A. Darling**'s manufacturing facilities. Suppose this facility assembles parts for displays to be sold to **Wal-Mart**, **Kmart**, and **Walgreens**. There are three departments—assembly, power, and maintenance. The assembly department uses an ABC system. The general cost of occupancy is allocated to the maintenance department and the assembly department based on the space occupied. Power department costs are allocated based on megawatt hours used. The assembly process produces three different types of displays with diverse demands on various activities and resources. Display type X consists of simple parts that are produced in high volume. Display type Y has parts that are of medium volume and complexity. Display type Z consists of complex parts that are produced in small lots.

Management implemented ABC in this facility using the three-step procedure outlined on pages 495–497. The first steps have been completed, and the results are depicted in the process map shown in Exhibit 12-21.

1. Refer to Exhibit 12-1 on page 482. For each type of cost assignment listed in Exhibit 12-1, give an example from L.A. Darling. If no example exists, note as such.
2. What allocation method for service department costs does this facility use? Explain.

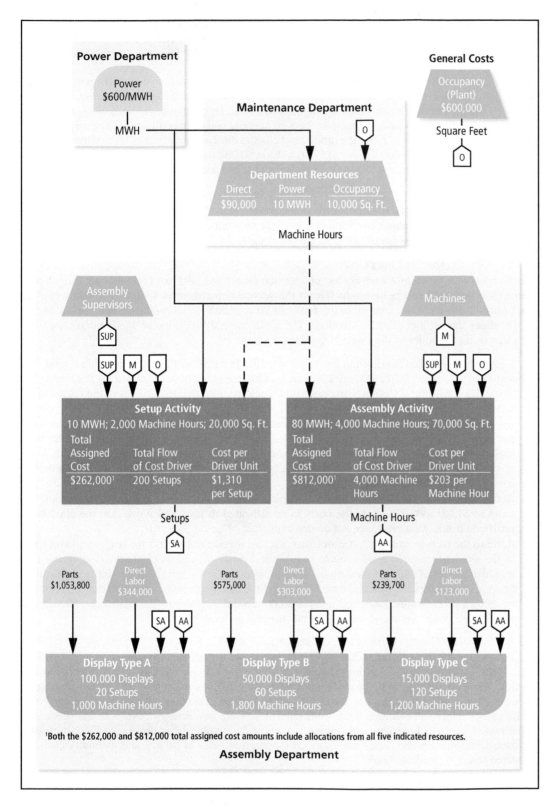

Power Department

Power
$600/MWH

MWH

Maintenance Department

O

General Costs

Occupancy
(Plant)
$600,000

Square Feet

O

Department Resources		
Direct	Power	Occupancy
$90,000	10 MWH	10,000 Sq. Ft.

Machine Hours

Assembly
Supervisors

SUP

SUP M O

Machines

M

SUP M O

Setup Activity
10 MWH; 2,000 Machine Hours; 20,000 Sq. Ft.

Total Assigned Cost	Total Flow of Cost Driver	Cost per Driver Unit
$262,000[1]	200 Setups	$1,310 per Setup

Assembly Activity
80 MWH; 4,000 Machine Hours; 70,000 Sq. Ft.

Total Assigned Cost	Total Flow of Cost Driver	Cost per Driver Unit
$812,000[1]	4,000 Machine Hours	$203 per Machine Hour

Setups

SA

Machine Hours

AA

Parts
$1,053,800

Direct
Labor
$344,000

Parts
$575,000

Direct
Labor
$303,000

Parts
$239,700

Direct
Labor
$123,000

SA AA

SA AA

SA AA

Display Type A
100,000 Displays
20 Setups
1,000 Machine Hours

Display Type B
50,000 Displays
60 Setups
1,800 Machine Hours

Display Type C
15,000 Displays
120 Setups
1,200 Machine Hours

[1]Both the $262,000 and $812,000 total assigned cost amounts include allocations from all five indicated resources.

Assembly Department

3. Calculate the allocations of service department and general costs to the assembly department activities.
4. Calculate the activity-based cost of each display type.

12-38 **Allocation of Automobile Costs**

The motor pool of a major city provides automobiles for the use of various city departments. Currently, the motor pool has 50 autos. A recent study showed that it costs $4,800 of annual fixed cost per automobile plus $.30 per mile variable cost to own, operate, and maintain autos like those provided by the motor pool.

Each month, accountants allocate the costs of the motor pool to the user departments on the basis of miles driven. On average, each auto is driven 24,000 miles annually (that is, 2,000 miles monthly), although wide month-to-month variations occur. In April 20X1, the 50 autos were driven a total of 50,000 miles. The motor pool's total costs for April were $45,000.

The chief planner for the city always seemed concerned about her auto costs. She was especially upset in April when she was charged $13,500 for the 15,000 miles driven in the department's five autos. This is the normal monthly mileage in the department. Her memo to the head of the motor pool stated, "I can certainly get autos at less than the $.90 per mile you charged in April." The response was, "I am under instructions to allocate the motor pool costs to the user departments. Your department was responsible for 30% of the April usage (15,000 miles ÷ 50,000 miles) so I allocated 30% of the motor pool's April costs to you (.30 × $45,000 = $13,500). That just seems fair."

1. Calculate the city's average annual cost per mile for owning, maintaining, and operating an auto.
2. Explain why the allocated cost in April ($.90 per mile) exceeds the average in number 1.
3. Describe any undesirable behavioral effects of the cost-allocation method used.
4. How would you improve the cost-allocation method?

12-39 Allocation of Costs

The Sommerville Trucking Company has one service department and two regional operating departments. The budgeted cost behavior pattern of the service department is $750,000 monthly in fixed costs plus $.80 per 1,000 ton-miles in the East and West regions. (Ton-miles are the number of tons carried times the number of miles traveled.) The actual monthly costs of the service department are allocated using ton-miles as the single cost-allocation base.

1. Sommerville handled 500 million ton-miles of traffic in April, half in each operating region. The actual costs of the service department were exactly equal to those predicted by the budget for 500 million ton-miles. Compute the costs that would be allocated to each operating region on an actual ton-miles basis.
2. Suppose the East region was plagued by strikes, so that the amount of freight handled was much lower than originally anticipated. East handled only 150 million ton-miles of traffic. The West region handled 250 million ton-miles. The actual costs were exactly as budgeted for this lower level of activity. Compute the costs that would be allocated to East and West on an actual ton-mile basis. Note that the total costs will be lower.
3. Refer to the facts in number 1. Various inefficiencies caused the service department to incur total costs of $1,250,000. Compute the costs to be allocated to East and West. Are the allocations justified? If not, what improvement do you suggest?
4. Refer to the facts in number 2. Assume that assorted investment outlays for equipment and space in the service department were made to provide a basic maximum capacity to serve the East region at a level of 360 million ton-miles and the West region at a level of 240 million ton-miles. Suppose fixed costs are allocated on the basis of this capacity to serve. Variable costs are allocated by using a predetermined standard rate per 1,000 ton-miles. Compute the costs to be allocated to each region. What are the advantages of this method over other methods?

12-40 Service Department Allocation and ABC, Product Costing

Garden Enclosures, Inc., makes metal gates. The company has three product lines—standard, deluxe, and custom gates. Garden Enclosures integrates its service department allocation system with its ABC system. There are two service departments—power and facilities management. Garden Enclosures allocates its two service department costs to the processing department using the direct method based on megawatt hours and machine hours consumed. There are two activity centers in the processing department—setup/maintenance and assembly. Parts and assembly labor are traced directly to each product. Setup/maintenance costs are allocated based on number of setups, and assembly costs are allocated based on machine hours.

Data for a recent reporting period follow:

	Product Line		
	Standard	**Deluxe**	**Custom**
Units produced and sold	100,000	10,000	1,000
Sales price per unit	$ 20	$ 50	$ 250
Total parts costs	$1,003,800	$115,080	$15,980
Total direct-labor costs	$ 298,000	$ 72,000	$68,000
Setups	20	12	8
Machine hours in assembly	1,000	400	100

			Activity Centers' Use of Driver Unit	
Resource/Department	Total Cost	Driver Unit	Setup/ Maintenance	Assembly
Assembly supervisors	$ 90,000	%	3%	97%
Assembly machines	$247,000	Machine hours	400	1,500
Facilities management department	$ 95,000	Machine hours	400	1,500
Power department	$ 54,000	Megawatt hours	10	80

Prepare a schedule that calculates the gross profit available to cover other value-chain costs for each product and Garden Enclosures as a whole company.

12-41 Service Department Allocation and ABC; Customer Profitability

(This problem should not be assigned unless Problem 12-40 is also assigned.) Refer to Problem 12-40. Garden Enclosures has two types of customers. Customer type 1 purchases mostly standard displays. Customer type 2 purchases all three product lines but is the only customer type that purchases custom displays. Data regarding the product mix for each customer follows:

	Units Sold by Product Line			
	Standard	Deluxe	Custom	Total
Customer type 1	75,000	5,000	0	80,000
Customer type 2	25,000	5,000	1,000	31,000
Total	100,000	10,000	1,000	111,000

Prepare a schedule that calculates the gross profit available to cover other value-chain costs for each customer type.

12-42 Customer Profitability at a Distributor

Twin Cities Sports (TCS) is a distributor of sports footwear and equipment. TCS distributes many products to retail accounts but classifies products into just two product groups—footwear and equipment.

- Footwear items arrive at TCS in cases and are shipped to customers in these cases.
- TCS receives equipment in bulk shipments. TCS must unpack these products and then repack them to meet small order quantities for specific equipment. Examples include weight-training equipment and golf clubs and bags.

TCS has two types of customers:

1. Specialty stores: stores that order low volumes, the majority being footwear
2. Department stores: stores that order large volumes of both footwear and equipment

TCS's management has set a strategic goal to improve both product and customer profitability. A related subgoal that supports this strategy is to identify profitable products and customers using an accurate cost-accounting system.

TCS currently uses a simple cost-accounting system to calculate both product and customer profitability. The only direct costs are the purchase costs of footwear and equipment products. TCS allocates indirect costs to the product groups using a single indirect cost pool for all indirect costs with "pounds of product" as the cost-allocation base. Cost and operating data accumulated for the most recent year are in Exhibit 12-22.

1. Prepare a schedule that shows the gross margin of each product group.
2. Prepare a schedule that shows the gross margin of each customer type.
3. Based on your answers to numbers 1 and 2, recommend a strategy to improve customer profitability.

Exhibit 12-22

Operating Data for
Twin Cities Sports

Product Data

	Footwear	Equipment
Annual demand in cases	2,800	2,000
Average purchase cost per case	$ 70	$120
Average weight per purchased case	18.75 pounds	31.25 pounds
Average sales price per case	$460	$800

Customer Data

Stores	Specialty Stores	Department
Footwear demand in cases	1,200	1,600
Equipment demand in cases	400	1,600
Total annual demand in cases	1,600	3,200
Orders	160	70

Other Data

A single cost pool consists of resources needed to perform receiving, storing, picking, packing, shipping, order processing, and customer service activities. The annual cost of these resources is $1,380,000. The cost-allocation base used to allocate this pool to the two product groups is pounds of product sold.

12-43 Customer Profitability and Allocation of Costs to Serve

(This problem is a continuation of Problem 12-42 and should be assigned only if 12-42 is also assigned.)

Based on a study of operations at TCS, it was determined that "number of orders" was a better cost-allocation base for the order processing and customer service activities. The cost of the resources used by these two activities is $552,000 out of the total indirect cost pool of $1,380,000. TCS now wants to refine its costing system by allocating order processing and customer service activities to customers rather than to products.

1. Prepare a schedule that shows product gross margin for each of the products made by TCS.
2. Prepare a schedule that shows customer product gross margin, customer cost to serve, and customer profitability.
3. Prepare a chart that shows customer product gross margin percentage versus customer cost-to-serve percentage for each of the customer types. Based on this chart, recommend a strategy that can be used to improve customer profitability for each customer type.
4. Compare customer profitability results determined by this refined costing system to the results obtained in Problem 12-42. Explain any significant differences.

12-44 Medical Equipment

Winston Medical Clinic proposed the acquisition of some expensive X-ray equipment to be used for unusual cases. The equipment would be shared by the Orthopedic Department and the Rehabilitation Department. The depreciation and related fixed costs of operating the equipment were predicted at $14,000 per month. The variable costs were predicted at $30 per patient procedure.

Clinic management asked each department to predict its usage of the equipment over its expected useful life of 5 years. The Orthopedic Department predicted an average usage of 75 X-rays per month, while the Rehabilitation Department predicted 50 X-rays. Management regarded this information as critical to the size and degree of sophistication that would be justified. That is, if the number of X-rays exceeded a certain quantity per month, a different configuration of space, equipment, and personnel would be required that would mean higher fixed costs per month.

1. Suppose fixed costs are allocated on the basis of the hospitals' predicted average use per month. Variable costs are allocated on the basis of $30 per X-ray, the budgeted variable-cost rate for the current fiscal year. In October, the Orthopedic Department had 50 X-rays and the Rehabilitation Department had 50 X-rays. Compute the total costs allocated to each department.
2. Suppose the manager of the equipment had various operating inefficiencies so that the total October costs were $18,500. Would you change your answers in number 1? Why?
3. A traditional method of cost allocation does not use the method in number 1. Instead, an allocation rate depends on the actual costs and actual volume encountered. The actual costs are totaled for the month and divided by the actual number of X-rays during the month. Suppose the actual costs agreed exactly with the budget for a total of 100 actual X-rays in October. Compute the total costs allocated to the Orthopedic Department and to the Rehabilitation Department. Compare the

results with those in number 1. What is the major weakness in this traditional method? What are some of its possible behavioral effects?

4. Describe any undesirable behavioral effects of the method described in number 1. How would you counteract any tendencies toward deliberate false predictions of long-run usage?

12-45 Direct Method for Service Department Allocation

Kazuo Piano Company has two producing departments, traditional pianos and electronic pianos. In addition, there are two service departments, building services and materials receiving and handling. The company purchases a variety of component parts from which the departments assemble pianos for sale in domestic and international markets.

The electronic pianos division is highly automated. The manufacturing costs depend primarily on the number of subcomponents in each piano. In contrast, the traditional pianos division relies primarily on a large labor force to hand-assemble pianos. Its costs depend on direct-labor hours.

The costs of building services depend primarily on the square footage occupied. The costs of materials receiving and handling depend primarily on the total number of components handled.

Pianos M1 and M2 are produced in the traditional pianos department, and E1 and E2 are produced in the electronic pianos department. Data about these products follow:

	Direct-Materials Cost	Number of Components	Direct-Labor Hours
M1	$740	110	3.0
M2	860	90	6.0
E1	630	100	1.5
E2	910	200	1.0

Budget figures for 20X7 include the following:

	Building Service	Materials Receiving and Handling	Traditional Pianos	Electronic Pianos
Direct department costs (excluding direct materials cost)	$1,500,000	$1,200,000	$6,800,000	$5,480,000
Square footage occupied		5,000	50,000	25,000
Number of final pianos produced			8,000	10,000
Average number of components per piano			100	160
Direct-labor hours			30,000	8,000

1. Allocate the costs of the service departments using the direct method.
2. Using the results of number 1, compute the cost per direct-labor hour in the traditional pianos department and the cost per component in the electronic pianos department.
3. Using the results of number 2, compute the cost per unit of product for pianos M1, M2, E1, and E2.

12-46 Step-Down Method for Service Department Allocation

Refer to the data in Problem 12-45.

1. Allocate the costs of the service departments using the step-down method.
2. Using the results of number 1, compute the cost per direct-labor hour in the traditional pianos department and the cost per component in the electronic pianos department.
3. Using the results of number 2, compute the cost per unit of product for pianos M1, M2, E1, and E2.

12-47 ABC Allocations; Process Map; What If Analysis

Tokuga Company makes printed circuit boards in a suburb of Tokyo. The production process is automated with computer-controlled robotic machines assembling each circuit board from a supply of parts and then soldering the parts to the board. Materials-handling and quality-assurance activities use a combination of labor and equipment. Although a few resources that are used are variable with respect to changes in the demand of boards, these costs are not material compared to the fixed-cost resources that are used.

Tokuga makes three types of circuit boards, models 1, 2, and 3. Steps 1 and 2 of the design process for an ABC system have been completed. Exhibit 12-23 shows the process-based map of Tokuga's operations.

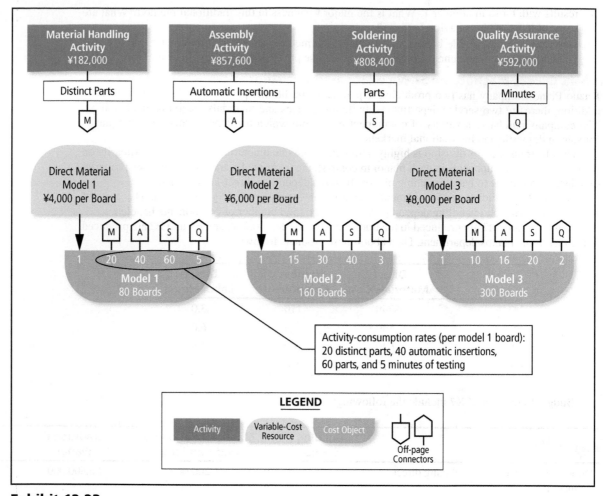

Exhibit 12-23
Tokuga Company's Two-Stage ABC System

1. Compute the cost of production for each of the three types of circuit boards and the cost per circuit board for each type.
2. What if the design of model 1 could be simplified so that it required only 8 distinct parts (instead of 20) and took only 3 minutes of testing time (instead of five). Compute the cost of model 1 circuit boards and the cost per circuit board. Will the costs per circuit board for models 2 and 3 change? You do not need to compute the costs per circuit board for models 2 and 3, only note whether the costs will increase, decrease, remain unchanged, or cannot be determined. Explain.

12-48 Activity-Based Allocations

Memphis Wholesale Distributors uses an ABC system to determine the cost of handling its products. One important activity is receiving shipments in the warehouse. Three resources support that activity: (1) recording and record keeping, (2) labor, and (3) inspection.

Recording and record keeping is a variable cost driven by number of shipments received. The cost per shipment is $20.

Labor is driven by pounds of merchandise received. Because labor is hired in shifts, it is fixed for large ranges of volume. Currently, labor costs are running $32,200 per month for handling 460,000 pounds. This same cost would apply to all volumes between 300,000 pounds and 550,000 pounds.

Finally, inspection is a variable cost driven by the number of boxes received. Inspection costs are $3.75 per box.

One product distributed by Memphis Wholesale Distributors is cans of soup. There is a wide variety of soups so many different shipments are handled in the warehouse. In July, the warehouse received 500 shipments, consisting of 4,000 boxes weighing a total of 80,000 pounds.

1. Compute the cost of receiving soup shipments during July.
2. Management is considering elimination of brands of soup that have small sales levels. This would reduce the warehouse volume to 200 shipments, consisting of 3,000 boxes weighing a total of 60,000 pounds. Compute the amount of savings from eliminating the small-sales-level brands.

3. Suppose receiving costs were estimated on a per-pound basis. What was the total receiving cost per pound of soup received in July? If management had used this cost to estimate the effect of eliminating the 20,000 pounds of soup, what mistake might be made?

12-49 Allocation of Central Costs

The Cheeta Bus Company allocates all central corporate overhead costs to its divisions. Some costs, such as specified internal auditing and legal costs, are identified on the basis of time spent. However, other costs are harder to allocate so the revenue achieved by each division is used as an allocation base. Examples of such costs are executive salaries, travel, secretarial, utilities, rent, depreciation, donations, corporate planning, and general marketing costs.

Allocations on the basis of revenue for 20X1 are as follows (in millions):

Division	Revenue	Allocated Costs
Northeast	$120	$ 6
Mid-Atlantic	240	12
Southeast	240	12
Total	$600	$30

In 20X2, Northeast's revenue remained unchanged. However, Southeast's revenue increased to $260 million because of unusually large imports. The latter are troublesome to forecast because of variations in world markets. Mid-Atlantic had expected a sharp rise in revenue, but severe competitive conditions resulted in a decline to $220 million. The total central corporate overhead cost allocated on the basis of revenue was again $30 million, despite rises in many other costs. The president was pleased that central costs did not rise for the year.

1. Compute the allocations of costs to each division for 20X2.
2. How would each division manager probably feel about the cost allocation in 20X2 as compared with 20X1? What are the weaknesses of using revenue as a basis for cost allocation?
3. Suppose the budgeted revenues for 20X2 were $120, $240, and $280, respectively, and the budgeted revenues were used as a cost-allocation base for allocation. Compute the allocations of costs to each division for 20X2. Do you prefer this method to the one used in number 1? Why?
4. Many accountants and managers oppose allocating any central costs. Why?

12-50 Joint Costs and Decisions

A chemical company has a batch process that takes 1,000 gallons of a raw material and transforms it into 80 pounds of X1 and 400 pounds of X2. Although the joint costs of their production are $2,400, both products are worthless at their split-off point. Additional separable costs of $700 are necessary to give X1 a sales value of $2,000 as product A. Similarly, additional separable costs of $400 are necessary to give X2 a sales value of $2,000 as product B.

You are in charge of the batch process and the marketing of both products. (Show your computations for each answer.)

1. a. Assuming that you believe in assigning joint costs on a physical basis, allocate the total profit of $500 per batch to products A and B.
   b. Would you stop processing one of the products? Why?
2. a. Assuming that you believe in assigning joint costs on a net-realizable-value (relative-sales-value) basis, allocate the total operating profit of $500 per batch to products A and B. If there is no market for X1 and X2 at their split-off point, a net realizable value is usually imputed by taking the ultimate sales values at the point of sale and working backward to obtain approximated "synthetic" relative sales values at the split-off point. These synthetic values are then used as weights for allocating the joint costs to the products.
   b. You have internal product-profitability reports in which joint costs are assigned on a net-realizable-value basis. Your chief engineer says that, after seeing these reports, he has developed a method of obtaining more of product B and correspondingly less of product A from each batch, without changing the per-pound cost factors. Would you approve this new method? Why? What would the overall operating profit be if 40 pounds more of B were produced and 40 pounds less of A?

CASES

12-51 Customer Profitability

Distribution Solutions, Inc., (DSI) is a regional distributor providing logistical support for merchandisers over a tristate area. Its distribution centers have been profitable until recently. DSI provides logistics solutions in industries such as fashion apparel, electronics, housewares, building materials, automotive tools, and beverages. Its locations are convenient to major ports and transportation hubs. DSI has an outstanding reputation for customer service.

Profit margins have declined over the past several years due mostly to a weak regional economy and competition from larger merchandisers such as **Home Depot**, **Lowe's**, and **Wal-Mart** who use logistic services of larger national distributors. Thus, the market share of merchandisers has declined along with their need for logistics support from DSI.

DSI orders supplies from a variety of manufacturers. All goods processed through the warehouse are stored on pallets and are handled by forklifts driven by forklift operators, who are assisted by warehouse labor. Processing of product consists of unloading at the receiving area (receiving activity), moving to the warehouse storage (put away activity), moving/shifting within the warehouse (warehousing activity), removal from racks (picking activity), and repacking (repacking activity). Customer-specific processing consists of order taking, customer service, order changes, returns, scheduling (regular or expedited), and shipping.

Prices at DSI are set using a cost-plus formula based on the average cost per case delivered during the previous year. Two markups are used. The first markup covers the cost of warehousing and distribution. The second markup covers the costs of general and selling expenses and an allowance for profit. Currently (2013) this price is $7.25 per case. However, with the various discounts and promotions, this year's actual price averages $4.75 per case for all products.

DSI has six distinct product groups:

1. Regular products are prepackaged arriving and leaving in cases.
2. Fragile products are prepackaged but require care in handling.
3. Bulk products arrive in loose lots in crates or cases and are repackaged in smaller boxes, polybags, or small cartons before packing in cases.
4. High-security products must be locked in high-security area.
5. Short shelf-life products are dated products.
6. Singles are received in bundles and will be unbundled and hand-stacked for storage.

Traditionally, the regular prepackaged product has generated both high margins and high volume. Fragile pre-packaged product has high margin but low volume. Bulk products and singles have poor margins but have been part of DSI's offerings because of customer demands for a full-line distributor. As DSI focused on increasing sales, mega stores and local small stores have increased their purchases of bulk products and singles. Until now, no premium has been charged for these products.

DSI has for many years classified its customer base into various types. Prior to 2008, almost all its customers were mega stores or large local stores. Since 2008, local small store and specialty store business has been aggressively pursued. The customer types can be described as follows:

- Mega stores (CT1): a few very large stores that order large volumes of all product types (7,680,000 cases annually)
- Local small stores (CT2): many stores that order low volumes of all products for each store (6,000,000 cases annually)
- Local large stores (CT3): many stores that order large volumes of only regular, fragile, and bulk products (14,400,000 cases annually)
- Specialty stores (CT4): a few stores that order low volumes of only regular, high-security, and short shelf-life products (600,000 cases annually)

Over the past several months, Paul Doxey, controller, working closely with Jane Stratford, chief marketing officer, and a cross-functional implementation team have been developing the ABC system to include all costs as well as customer profitability. A study has been conducted to determine the key drivers of work associated with the various customer types. These drivers include order frequency, order size, pallets ordered, customer-specific service, and order changes.

Key activities associated with serving customers include the following:

- Shipping
- Parcel delivery
- Truck delivery
- Customer support
- Regular scheduling
- Expedited scheduling
- Order processing
- Order changes
- Corporate support

The implementation team headed by Paul Doxey has completed the activity analysis interviews, prepared a process map, collected data, and validated the new model both operationally and financially. The new process map is shown in Exhibit 12-24. In order to link the product and customer

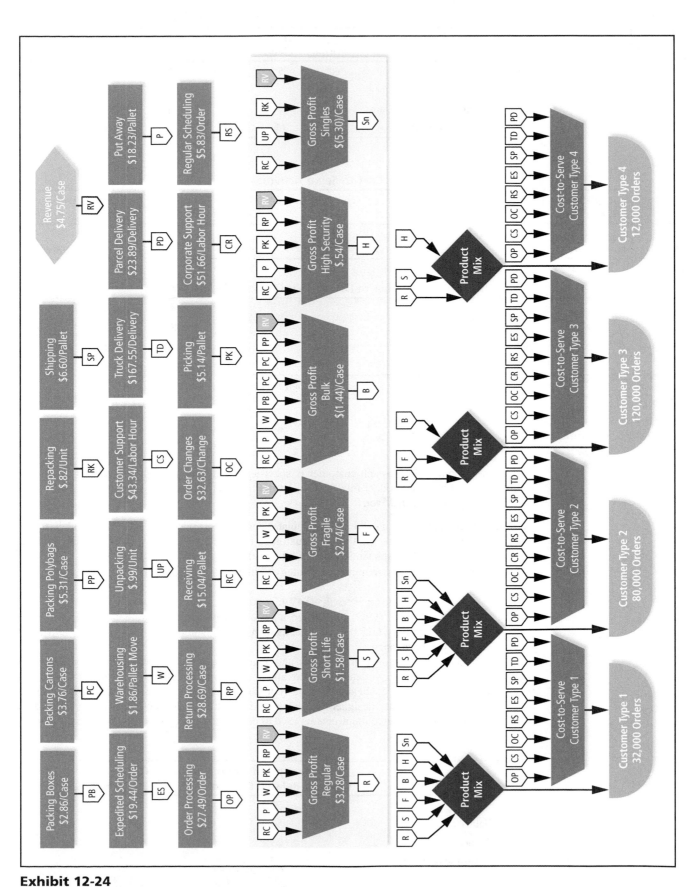

Exhibit 12-24
Distribution Solutions, Inc.
Process Map for Product/Customer Profitability

Exhibit 12-25

Distribution Solutions, Inc.
Product Mix Data for Product/
Customer Profitability Model

			Product Mix (%)			
	Regular	Short Lived	Fragile	Bulk	High Security	Singles
Customer Type 1 Mega Stores	60%	5%	5%	20%	5%	5%
Customer Type 2 Local Small Stores	50	5	5	30	8	2
Customer Type 3 Local Large Stores	80	—	10	10	—	—
Customer Type 4 Specialty Stores	10	20	—	—	70	—

				Cost-to-Serve Activities					
	Order Processing	Customer Support	Order Changes	Corporate Support	Scheduling— Regular	Scheduling— Expedited	Shipping	Delivery— Truck	Delivery— Parcel
Cost Driver	Orders	Labor Hours	Number of Changes	Labor Hours	Orders	Orders	Pallets	Deliveries	Deliveries
Cost per Driver Unit	$27.49	$43.34	$32.63	$51.66	$5.83	$19.44	$6.60	$167.55	$23.89
				Number of Driver Units (Thousands)					
CT1	32	18.7	3.2	0	29	3	416	25.6*	1.6*
CT2	80	100.0	8.0	20	72	8	640	68.0	8.0
CT3	120	70.0	2.4	80	108	12	840	90.0	6.0
CT4	12	30.0	1.2	0	10	2	60	4.8	2.4

*The sum of deliveries (25.6 + 1.6 = 27.2 on average) is less than the number of orders (29 + 3) because a few customers picked up their order at the distribution center.

Exhibit 12-26

Distribution Solutions, Inc.
Cost Driver Data by Customer Type and Cost-to-Serve Activity

models the product mix for each customer is specified giving the gross profit for each customer. Exhibit 12-25 shows the product mix for each of the four customer types. Exhibit 12-26 shows the cost-to-serve data for each driver.

1. Using Excel, construct an exhibit that calculates customer gross margin percentage and customer cost-to-serve percentage for the four customer types. Plot these points along with one for customer type 2 on a graph similar to Exhibit 12-20 on page 506.
2. For each customer type, recommend a strategy to improve profitability.

12-52 Allocation of Data Processing Costs

The Gibraltar Insurance Co. (GIC) established a systems department to implement and operate its own data processing systems. GIC believed that its own system would be more cost-effective than the service bureau it had been using.

GIC's three departments—claims, records, and finance—have different requirements with respect to hardware and other capacity-related resources and operating resources. The system was designed to recognize these differing needs. In addition, the system was designed to meet GIC's long-term capacity needs. The excess capacity designed into the system would be sold to outside users until needed by GIC. The estimated resource requirements used to design and implement the system are shown in the following schedule:

	Hardware and Other Capacity-Related Resources	Operating Resources
Records	25%	60%
Claims	50	15
Finance	20	20
Expansion (outside use)	5	5
Total	100%	100%

GIC currently sells the equivalent of its expansion capacity to a few outside clients.

At the time the system became operational, management decided to redistribute total expenses of the systems department to the user departments based on actual computer time used. The actual costs for the first quarter of the current fiscal year were distributed to the user departments as follows:

Department	Percentage Utilization	Amount
Records	60%	$330,000
Claims	15	82,500
Finance	20	110,000
Outside	5	27,500
Total	100%	$550,000

The three user departments have complained about the cost-distribution method since the systems department was established. The records department's monthly costs have been as much as three times the costs experienced with the service bureau. The finance department is concerned about the costs distributed to the outside user category because these allocated costs form the basis for the fees billed to the outside clients.

Mostafa Al Rashed, GIC's controller, decided to review the cost-allocation method. The additional information he gathered for his review is reported in Tables 1, 2, and 3 in Exhibit 12-27.

TABLE 1 Systems Department Costs and Activity Levels

| | Annual Budget | | First Quarter | | | |
| | | | Budget | | Actual | |
	Hours	Dollars	Hours	Dollars	Hours	Dollars
Hardware and other capacity-related costs	—	$ 600,000	—	$150,000	—	$155,000
Software development	18,750	562,500	4,725	141,750	4,250	130,000
Operations						
Computer related	3,750	750,000	945	189,000	920	187,000
Input/output related	30,000	300,000	7,560	75,600	7,900	78,000
Total		$2,212,500		$556,350		$550,000

TABLE 2 Historical Usage

| | Hardware and other capacity needs | Software development | | Operations | | | |
| | | | | Computer | | Input/output | |
		Range	Average	Range	Average	Range	Average
Records	25%	0%–30%	15%	55%–65%	60%	10%–30%	15%
Claims	50	15–60	40	10–25	15	60–80	75
Finance	20	25–75	40	10–25	20	3–10	5
Outside	5	0–25	5	3–8	5	3–10	5
	100%		100%		100%		100%

TABLE 3 Usage of Systems Department's Services First Quarter (in hours)

| | Software Development | Operations | |
		Computer Related	Input/Output
Records	450	540	1,540
Claims	1,800	194	5,540
Finance	1,600	126	410
Outside	400	60	410
Total	4,250	920	7,900

Exhibit 12-27
Data for Gibraltar Insurance Co.

Al Rashed has concluded that the method of cost allocation should be changed. He believes that the hardware and capacity-related costs should be allocated to the user departments in proportion to the planned long-term needs. Any difference between actual and budgeted hardware costs would not be allocated to the departments, but would remain with the systems department.

The costs for software development and operations would be charged to the user departments based on actual hours used. A predetermined hourly rate based on the annual budget data would be used. The hourly rates that would be used for the current fiscal year are as follows:

Function	Hourly Rate
Software development operations	$ 30
Computer related	200
Input/output related	10

Al Rashed plans to use first-quarter activity and cost data to illustrate his recommendations. The recommendations will be presented to the systems department and the user departments for their comments and reactions. He then expects to present his recommendations to management for approval.

1. Calculate the amount of data-processing costs that would be included in the claims department's first-quarter budget according to the method Al Rashed has recommended.
2. Prepare a schedule to show how the actual first-quarter costs of the systems department would be charged to the users if GIC adopts Al Rashed's recommended method.
3. Explain whether Al Rashed's recommended system for charging costs to the user departments will
   a. improve cost control in the systems department.
   b. improve planning and cost control in the user departments.

NIKE 10-K PROBLEM

12-53 Allocation of Corporate Expenses
Footnote 18 to Nike's 2011 financial statements in Appendix C shows net corporate expenses of $771 million as well as revenues and earnings before interest and taxes by geographical areas. Suppose that Nike wants to allocate its net corporate expenses to the following six geographic regions on the basis of the revenues of the regions: North America, Western Europe, Central & Eastern Europe, Greater China, Japan, and Emerging Markets. Compute the earnings before interest and taxes for each region after the allocation. Comment on the desirability of this allocation.

EXCEL APPLICATION EXERCISE

12-54 Allocating Costs Using Direct and Step-Down Methods
Goal: Create an Excel spreadsheet to allocate costs using the direct method and the step-down method. Use the results to answer questions about your findings.

Scenario: Texas Building Services has asked you to help it determine the best method for allocating costs from its service departments to its producing departments. Additional background information for your spreadsheet appears in Fundamental Assignment Material 12-B1. Exhibit 12-4 on page 488 illustrates the types of calculations that are used for allocating costs using the step-down method.

When you have completed your spreadsheet, answer the following questions:

1. What are the total costs for the residential department using the direct method?
   What are the total costs for the commercial department using the direct method?
2. What are the total costs for the residential department using the step-down method?
3. What are the total costs for the commercial department using the step-down method?
4. Which method would you recommend that Dallas Cleaning use to allocate its service departments' costs to its producing departments? Why?

Step-by-Step:

1. Open a new Excel spreadsheet.
2. In column A, create a bold-faced heading that contains the following:
   Row 1: Chapter 12 Decision Guideline
   Row 2: Texas Building Services
   Row 3: Cost Allocations from Service Departments to Producing Departments
   Row 4: Today's Date
3. Merge and center the four heading rows across columns A–H.
4. In row 7, create the following bold-faced, center-justified column headings:
   Column B: Personnel
   Column C: Administrative
   Column D: Residential
   Column E: Commercial
   Column F: Total Res/Comm
   Column G: Total Admin/Res/Comm
   Column H: Grand Total
5. Change the format of the column headings in row 7 to permit the titles to be displayed on multiple lines within a single cell.

   Alignment tab: Wrap Text: Checked

   Note: Adjust column widths so that headings use only two lines.

   Adjust row height to ensure that row is same height as adjusted headings.

6. In column A, create the following row headings:
   Row 8: Direct Department Costs
   Row 9: Number of Employees
   Skip two rows.

   Note: Adjust the width of column A to 27.14.

7. In column A, create the following bold-faced, underlined row heading:
   Row 12: Direct Method:
8. In column A, create the following row headings:
   Row 13: Direct Department Costs
   Row 14: Personnel Allocation
   Row 15: Administrative Allocation
   Row 16: Total Costs
   Skip two rows.
9. In column A, create the following bold-faced, underlined row heading:
   Row 19: Step-Down Method:
10. In column A, create the following row headings:
    Row 20: Direct Department Costs
    Row 21: Step 1—Personnel Allocation
    Row 22: Step 2—Administrative Allocation
    Row 23: Total Costs
11. Use data from Fundamental Assignment 12-B1 to enter the amounts in columns B–E for rows 8, 9, 13, and 20.
12. Use the appropriate calculations to do the totals in row 8 for columns F and H.
    Use the appropriate calculations to do the totals in row 9 for columns F and G.
13. Use the appropriate formulas to allocate the costs from the service departments to the producing departments using each of the methods.
14. Use the appropriate calculations to do the totals in columns B–E and in column H, rows 16 and 23.

15. Format amounts in columns B–H, rows 8, 13, 16, 20, and 23 as follows:

Number tab:	Category:	Accounting
	Decimal:	0
	Symbol:	$

16. Format the amount in columns B–E, rows 14, 15, 21, and 22 as follows:

Number tab:	Category:	Accounting
	Decimal:	0
	Symbol:	None

17. Change the format of the total costs amounts in columns B–E, rows 16 and 23, to display a top border, using the default line style.

Border tab:	Icon:	Top Border

18. Change the format of the amounts in row 9, columns B–G to center justified.
19. Save your work, and print a copy for your files.

Note: Print your spreadsheet using landscape in order to ensure that all columns appear on one page.

COLLABORATIVE LEARNING EXERCISE

12-55 Library Research on ABC and Customer Profitability

Form groups of three to five people each. Each member of the group should pick one of the following industries:

- Manufacturing
- Insurance
- Health care
- Government
- Service

Each person should explore the Internet for an example of a company that implemented ABC and ABM with a focus on determining customer profitability. Prepare and give a briefing for your group. Do this by completing the following:

1. Describe the company and its business.
2. What was the scope of the ABC/ABM project?
3. What were the goals for the ABC/ABM project?
4. Summarize the results of the project.

After each person has briefed the group on his or her company, discuss within your group the commonalities between the ABC/ABM applications.

INTERNET EXERCISE

12-56 Cost Allocation at Sears Holdings Corporation

Allocating indirect costs can be a challenging task. Almost all firms have some type of cost centers (departments), whether it is the administration overseeing the corporation as a whole or the accounting department processing billing and invoicing customers. Deciding what to do with the costs generated by these cost centers can be difficult. Let's take a look at Sears Holdings Corporation.

1. Go to the home page for Sears Holdings at www.searsholdings.com. How many companies are listed under the umbrella of Sears Holdings Corporation? What are these companies? How many stores do the companies operate? How many of them are located in the area where you are located? If one or more is not located in your area, have you heard of it before?
2. Locate Sears Holdings' most recent annual report by clicking on "Investors" at Sears Holdings' home page and then on the most recent annual report. Look at the "Notes to Consolidated Financial Statements." Did the firm provide any information on segment revenues? What are its

operating segments? What is the sum the operating incomes of the segments for the current year? Now, look at the income statement for the current year. What is the firm-wide operating income for the year? Is the firm-wide operating income different from the sum of the segment operating incomes? What does this tell you about what portion of company-wide operating costs are allocated to segments? What percent of the total selling and administrative costs are allocated to each segment?

3. If Sears Holdings allocates the selling and administrative costs to the major segments based on total segment revenue, what percent of selling and administrative expenses is allocated to each segment? What would be the allocation if the company used the total assets as the allocation basis? Do these differ from the actual allocation bases that are implied by the segment selling and administrative expenses?

CHAPTER 12

Accounting for Overhead Costs

LEARNING OBJECTIVES

When you have finished studying this chapter, you should be able to:

1. Compute budgeted factory-overhead rates and apply factory overhead to production.

2. Determine and use appropriate cost-allocation bases for overhead application to products and services.

3. Use normalized variable- and fixed-overhead application rates and explain the disposition of overhead variances.

4. Compare variable- and absorption-costing systems.

5. Construct an income statement using the variable-costing approach.

6. Construct an income statement using the absorption-costing approach.

7. Distinguish between product-costing and planning-and-control purposes in accounting for variable and fixed costs.

8. Compute the production-volume variance and show how it should appear in the income statement.

9. Reconcile variable- and absorption-costing operating income and explain why a company might prefer to use a variable-costing approach.

▶ **DELL**

Dell is the world's leading direct-sale marketer of made-to-order computer systems. Dell does not manufacture computer components (e.g., circuit boards, hard drives), but instead assembles them into computers on a made-to-order basis.

Dell pioneered the "direct business model"—selling directly to end users instead of using a network of dealers, which avoids the dealer markup and gives Dell a competitive price advantage. Customers can design their own computer systems to specifications they desire, choosing from among a full complement of options. Before ordering, customers can receive advice and price quotes for a wide variety of computer configurations.

Once an order is taken, Dell assembles it in a manufacturing work cell called a "mod." There is a separate mod for each of Dell's lines of business (e.g., Vostro Desktop PCs, OptiPlex Desktops for networked environments, Inspiron and XPS Notebooks, PowerEdge network servers, and Precision workstation products). Rapid response to customer orders is key to maintaining Dell's competitive edge.

Dell takes orders over the phone or over the Internet. Dell had revenues in excess of $62 billion for the year ended February 3, 2012, and derived a large portion of these revenues from the company's Web site, www.dell.com. Customers may review, configure, and price systems within Dell's entire product line. Dell's Web site also offers personalized system-support pages and technical services. Customers of all kinds prefer Dell's direct business model, and the Internet affords Dell a perfect way to implement this model. They like the immediacy, convenience, savings, and personal touches the Internet-direct customer experience provides.

Why are managers at a profitable company like Dell interested in knowing as much as possible about the cost of their individual product lines? With strong profits being reported over the years, is there a clear need for costs for other management purposes? The answer is yes. Most of the reason why Dell's profitability has been strong is the strategic and operational decisions its managers make. These decisions are based on detailed cost information. For example, Dell's cost accounting systems supply product costs to managers for evaluating pricing policy and product lines. Dell managers need to know the cost of each kind of computer being produced to set prices, to determine marketing and production strategies for various models, and to evaluate production operations. At the same time, product costs appear as cost of goods sold in income statements and as finished-goods inventory values in balance sheets. Although it would be possible to have two product-costing systems, one for management decision making and one for financial reporting, seldom do the benefits of using two completely separate systems exceed the costs. Therefore, both decision-making and financial-reporting needs influence the design of a company's product-costing system.

© AFP Photos/Newscom

Dell sells computers directly to customers around the world.

In Chapter 4, you learned about three types of costs in a manufacturing company: direct materials, direct labor, and factory overhead (or indirect manufacturing) costs. You also learned that for many organizations, indirect costs account for as much as 40% of total operating costs. Thus, this is an important area of concern for managers. In this chapter, we focus on overhead. ■

Accounting for Factory Overhead

Years ago, direct materials and direct labor were the largest costs for most companies. Today, automated companies such as Dell have lower direct labor costs but much larger overhead costs. Thus, methods for assigning overhead costs to products are an important part of accurately measuring product costs.

How to Apply Factory Overhead to Products

Managers need to know product costs in order to make ongoing decisions, such as which products or services to emphasize or deemphasize and how to price each product or service. Ideally, managers would know all costs precisely, including overhead, when they make these decisions. Because accountants directly trace direct materials and direct labor costs to products and services, these costs are available immediately on completion of production, and they are known precisely. In contrast, because it is not economically feasible to know all of the indirect manufacturing costs immediately, accountants must estimate them. For this reason, accountants use budgeted (predetermined) overhead rates to apply overhead to jobs. As a result, estimates of total product cost are immediately available. Besides this product costing benefit, budgeted overhead rates also provide planning and control benefits to the firm, as these rates (1) require managers to develop cost forecasts and (2) determine estimated costs that they can compare to actual costs. When overhead costs are large, it is important to have an accurate system for factory overhead accounting.

Dell has increased the accuracy of its product cost information by converting some of its factory-overhead costs from indirect to direct costs. How did the company do this? By dedicating assembly labor and factory equipment to specific product lines. Work cells (mods) do the assembly and software loading for specific product lines. This makes it easier to trace some of the equipment costs to products. Nevertheless, significant overhead costs remain to be allocated. So let's consider how companies such as Dell allocate these overhead costs to products and services.

Budgeted Overhead Application Rates

The following steps summarize how to account for factory overhead:

1. Select one or more cost-allocation bases for applying overhead costs to products or services. In this chapter, we often use the term *apply* instead of *allocate* when assigning overhead costs to a product or service. However, the concept is essentially the same—determining the amount of each cost pool to assign to each cost object. Examples of cost-allocation bases include direct-labor hours, direct-labor costs, machine hours, and

Compute budgeted factory-overhead rates and apply factory overhead to production.

production setups. The cost-allocation base should be a measure of the amount of overhead resources—a cost or a group of costs such as machinery cost, set-up costs, or energy cost—used by each product. The cost-allocation base(s) should be the most plausible and reliable measure(s) available of the cause-and-effect relationships between overhead costs and production volume.

2. Prepare a factory-overhead budget for the planning period, ordinarily a year. The two key items are (a) budgeted overhead and (b) budgeted volume of the cost-allocation base. There will be a set of budgeted overhead costs and an associated budgeted cost-allocation base level for each overhead cost pool.[1] In businesses with simple production systems, there may be just one set.

budgeted factory-overhead rate

The budgeted total overhead for each cost pool divided by the budgeted cost-allocation base level.

3. Compute the **budgeted factory-overhead rate**(s) by dividing the budgeted total overhead for each cost pool by the budgeted cost-allocation base level.

4. Obtain actual cost-allocation base data (such as direct-labor hours or machine hours) used for each product.

5. Apply the budgeted overhead to the products or services by multiplying the budgeted rate(s) in step 3 times the actual cost-allocation base data from step 4.

6. At the end of the year, account for any differences between the amount of overhead actually incurred and overhead applied to products.

Illustration of Overhead Application

Now that you know the steps in accounting for factory overhead, let's examine how they work in a realistic example. Consider the Enriquez Machine Parts Company.[2] Its manufacturing-overhead budget for 20X0 follows:

	Machining	Assembly
Indirect labor	$ 75,600	$ 36,800
Supplies	8,400	2,400
Utilities	20,000	7,000
Repairs	10,000	3,000
Factory rent	10,000	6,800
Supervision	42,600	35,400
Depreciation on equipment	104,000	9,400
Insurance, property taxes, etc.	7,200	2,400
Total	$277,800	$103,200

Enriquez selected a single cost-allocation base in each department, machine hours in machining and direct-labor cost in assembly, for applying overhead. As Enriquez works on a product, it applies the factory overhead to the product using a budgeted overhead rate, computed as follows:

$$\text{budgeted overhead application rate} = \frac{\text{total budgeted factory overhead}}{\text{total budgeted amount of cost driver}}$$

The overhead rates for the two departments are as follows:

	Year 20X0	
	Machining	Assembly
Budgeted manufacturing overhead	$277,800	$103,200
Budgeted machine hours	69,450	
Budgeted direct-labor cost		$206,400
Budgeted overhead rate per machine hour: $277,800 ÷ 69,450 =	$ 4	
Budgeted overhead rate per direct labor dollar: $103,200 ÷ $206,400 =		50%

---

[1]Cost pools were defined in Chapter 4, page 128, as a group of individual costs that a company allocates to activities or cost objects using a single cost driver.

[2]The Enriquez Machine Parts Company example used here and in the Chapter 14 discussion of job-order-costing are the same, with all data completely compatible.

Note that the overhead rates are budgeted; they are estimates. Accountants at Enriquez then use these budgeted rates to apply overhead based on actual events. That is, the total overhead applied to a particular product is the result of multiplying the budgeted overhead rates by the actual machine hours or labor cost used by that product. Thus, we would apply $44 of overhead to a product that uses 6 machine hours in machining and incurs direct-labor cost of $40 in assembly:

Machining: 6 actual machine hours × $4 per machine hour	$24
Assembly: $40 of direct-labor cost × 50%	20
Total overhead	$44

Suppose Enriquez had used 70,000 machine hours in machining and incurred $190,000 of direct-labor cost in assembly during the year. It would have applied a total of $375,000 of overhead to the products produced:

Machining: 70,000 actual machine hours × $4	$280,000
Assembly: $190,000 actual direct-labor cost × 50%	95,000
Total factory overhead applied	$375,000

This $375,000 is an estimate of Enriquez's overhead for the year, and it will become part of the cost of goods sold expense on Enriquez's income statement when the units produced are subsequently sold. If the actual overhead costs differ from $375,000, the company will usually charge the difference to expense in the period of production. For example, if Enriquez's actual overhead in 20X0 was $392,000, it would add $392,000 − $375,000 = $17,000 additional expense to cost of goods sold on the income statement in 20X0.

This completes our six steps. Next let's go back to step 1 and explore how a company might choose appropriate cost-allocation bases.

Choice of Cost-Allocation Bases

As you have seen several times in this text, no single cost-allocation base is appropriate in all situations. The accountant's goal is to find the cost-allocation base that best links cause and effect. In the Enriquez machining department, use of machines causes most overhead cost, such as depreciation and repairs. Therefore, machine hours represent the most appropriate cost-allocation base for applying overhead costs. Thus, Enriquez must keep track of the machine hours used for each product, creating an added data collection cost. That is, it must accumulate machine hours in addition to direct-materials costs and direct-labor costs for each product.

In contrast, direct labor is the principal cost-allocation base in the Enriquez assembly department because employees assemble parts by hand. Suppose the company records the time each worker spends on each product (or batch of products). Then, Enriquez simply applies the 50% overhead rate to the cost of direct labor already recorded. No additional data are needed.

If the hourly labor rates for workers differ greatly for individuals performing identical tasks, Enriquez might use the hours of labor, rather than the dollars spent for labor, as a base. Otherwise, Enriquez would apply more overhead to a product when a $10-per-hour worker works an hour than when an $8-per-hour worker works an hour, even though each employee uses the same facilities and generally consumes the same overhead support. However, sometimes direct-labor cost is the best overhead cost-allocation base even if wage rates vary within a department. For example, higher-skilled (and consequently higher-paid) labor may use more costly equipment and have more indirect labor support than low-skilled (lower-paid) workers. Moreover, many factory-overhead costs include expensive labor fringe benefits such as pensions and payroll taxes. Direct-labor cost rather than direct-labor hours often drive such fringe-benefit costs.

If a department identifies more than one cost-allocation base for overhead costs, it should accumulate a separate cost pool for each cost-allocation base and put each overhead cost into the appropriate cost pool. In practice, such a system is too costly for many organizations. Instead, these organizations select a few cost-allocation bases (often only one) to serve as a basis for allocating overhead costs. We often use the 80–20 rule in these situations—20% of the cost-allocation bases drive 80% of the overhead costs. For example, suppose a company identifies 10 separate overhead pools with 10 different cost-allocation bases. Often, it can accurately apply approximately 80% of the total overhead cost with only two allocation bases. It may be too costly to devise separate cost pools for the other 20%, so it arbitrarily assigns those costs to the two main cost pools.

Objective 2

Determine and use appropriate cost-allocation bases for overhead application to products and services.

Consider Dell. As we mentioned earlier, Dell has converted many of its overhead costs into direct costs. However, two important costs that it cannot directly trace (that is, that remain indirect costs) are facilities and engineering. Facilities costs include occupancy costs such as depreciation, insurance, and taxes on the factory. Dell applies these costs using the cost-allocation base "square footage used by each line of business (assembly line)." Dell incurs large product and process engineering costs as part of the design phase of the company's value chain. It applies these costs to lines of business using a "complexity" cost-allocation base such as number of distinct parts in the motherboard. Server computer products, for example, require much more engineering time and effort due to the number of distinct parts in the motherboard (complexity of the product) compared to laptops or PCs. Thus, server products receive a much greater allocation of engineering costs than laptops or PCs.

Another example is Harley-Davidson, which changed from using direct labor as a cost-allocation base to using process hours, as described in the Business First box on page 537.

Problems of Overhead Application

Normalized Overhead Rates

Objective 3

Use normalized variable- and fixed-overhead application rates and explain the disposition of overhead variances.

normal costing system

The cost system in which the cost of the manufactured product is composed of actual direct material, actual direct labor, and normal applied overhead.

The Enriquez illustration demonstrated what we call the normal costing approach. Why the term *normal*? Because we use an annual average overhead rate consistently throughout the year for product costing, without altering it from day to day and from month to month. The resultant "normal" product costs include an average or normalized chunk of overhead. Hence, in a **normal costing system** the cost of the manufactured product is composed of actual direct material, actual direct labor, and normal applied overhead.

A department's applied overhead will rarely equal the actual overhead incurred. Managers can analyze this variance between applied and incurred cost. The most common—and important—contributor to these variances is operating at a different level of volume than the level used as a denominator in calculating the budgeted overhead rate (for instance, using 100,000 budgeted direct-labor hours as the denominator and then actually working only 80,000 hours). Other frequent causes include poor forecasting, inefficient use of overhead items, price changes in individual overhead items, erratic behavior of individual overhead items (e.g., repairs made only during slack time), and calendar variations (e.g., 20 workdays in one month, 22 in the next).

Companies generally prefer to use an annual budgeted factory-overhead rate regardless of the month-to-month peculiarities of specific overhead costs. Such an approach is more defensible than, for example, applying the actual overhead for each month. Why? Because a normal product cost is more useful for decisions, and more representative for inventory-costing purposes, than an "actual" product cost that is distorted by month-to-month fluctuations in production volume and by the erratic behavior of many overhead costs. For example, the employees of a gypsum plant using an "actual" product cost system had the privilege of buying company-made items "at cost." Employees joked about the benefits of buying "at cost" during high-volume months, when unit costs were lower because volume was higher, as the following table illustrates:

	Actual Overhead			Direct-Labor	Actual Overhead Application
	Variable	Fixed	Total	Hours	Rate per Direct-Labor Hour*
Peak-volume month	$60,000	$40,000	$100,000	100,000	$1.00
Low-volume month	30,000	40,000	70,000	50,000	1.40

*Divide total overhead by direct-labor hours. Note that the presence of fixed overhead causes the fluctuation in unit overhead costs from $1.00 to $1.40. The variable component is $.60 an hour in both months, but the fixed component is $.40 in the peak-volume month ($40,000 ÷ 100,000) and $.80 in the low-volume month ($40,000 ÷ 50,000).

Disposition of Underapplied or Overapplied Overhead

The last of the six steps on page 534 dealt with differences between actual and applied overhead. Let's look in more detail at options for accounting for such differences. Recall that Enriquez applied $375,000 to the products produced during the period. This amount is part of the cost of goods sold expense for those units that were sold and is included in ending inventory for those units that remain unsold at the end of 20X0. However, Enriquez actually incurred $392,000 of overhead costs. The difference is a $17,000 variance (the amount of actual cost not yet applied

Business First

Overhead Allocation at Harley-Davidson

Milwaukee-based Harley-Davidson, the motorcycle manufacturer, recently celebrated its one hundredth birthday. As happy as everyone at Harley-Davidson is today, it is a bit surprising to some how far the company has come over the past several decades. From near collapse, Harley-Davidson turned its business around during the 1980s and 1990s, and in 1999 captured the number one market position from Honda for the first time in three decades. Harley-Davidson (2011 sales of $5.3 billion) is the only major U.S.-based motorcycle producer. One of the keys to the company's return to competitiveness was the adoption of a JIT philosophy. It is not unusual for a company to discover that a change in an important component of operations requires a corresponding change in the company's accounting system. The main focus of the old accounting system was direct labor, which not only made up a part of product cost itself but also functioned as an all-purpose base for allocating overhead. However, direct labor was only 10% of total product cost. It certainly did not generate a majority of overhead costs. Although Harley-Davidson's production process had changed, the accounting system remained static.

The JIT system served to emphasize that detailed information on direct-labor costs was not useful to managers. It was costly to have each direct laborer record the time spent on each product or part and then enter the information from these time cards into the accounting system. For example, if each of 500 direct laborers works on 20 products per day, the system must record 10,000 entries per day, which equates to 200,000 entries per month. The time spent by direct laborers to record the time, by clerks to enter the data into the system, and by accountants to check the data's accuracy, is enormous—all to produce product cost information that was used for financial reporting but was useless to managers.

The JIT system forced manufacturing managers to focus on satisfying customers and minimizing non-value-added activities. Gradually, accountants began to focus on the same objectives. Accounting's customers were the managers who used the accounting information, and effort devoted to activities that did not help managers was deemed counterproductive (non-value-added). Therefore, eliminating the costly, time-consuming recording of detailed labor costs became a priority. Harley-Davidson eliminated direct labor as a direct cost, and consequently could not use it for overhead application. After considering process hours, flow-through time, materials value, and individual cost per unit as possible cost-allocation bases for applying overhead, the company selected process hours. Direct labor and overhead were combined to form conversion costs, which accountants applied to products on the basis of total process hours. This did not result in costs significantly different from the old system, but the new system was much simpler and less costly. The company traced only direct material directly to the product. It applied conversion costs at completion of production based on a simple measure of process time.

Accounting systems should generate benefits greater than their costs. More sophisticated systems are not necessarily better systems. Harley-Davidson's main objective in changing its accounting system was simplification—elimination of unnecessary tasks and streamlining others. These changes resulted in a revitalized accounting system.

Sources: Adapted from W.T. Turk, "Management Accounting Revitalized: The Harley-Davidson Experience," in B.J. Brinker, Ed., *Emerging Practices in Cost Management* (Boston: Warren, Gorham & Lamont, 1990), pp. 155–166; K. Barron, "Hog Wild," *Forbes*, May 15, 2000; and *Harley-Davidson 2011 Annual Report*.

---

to product), which we call **underapplied overhead** because the amount applied is less than the amount incurred. The opposite, **overapplied overhead**, occurs when the amount applied exceeds the amount incurred. At the end of a given period, the company needs to produce its financial statements, which require production costs based on the actual costs incurred. To yield this result, it must dispose of any under- or overapplied overhead. Accountants use one of two methods to perform this adjustment: 1) A simple but imprecise approach disposes of the entire amount as a write-off to cost of goods sold, or 2) a better but more complex approach is **proration**, which means apportioning over- or underapplied overhead to cost of goods sold, work-in-process inventory, and finished-goods inventory in proportion to the ending balances of each account.

IMMEDIATE WRITE-OFF The immediate write-off method regards the $17,000 underapplied overhead as a reduction in current income by adding it to cost of goods sold. By the same logic, we would deduct any overapplied overhead from cost of goods sold.

The reasoning behind this method is that the company has probably sold most of the goods produced during the period, so that prorating part of the variance to inventory accounts would not produce a materially different result. Another justification is that, if extra overhead costs result from inefficiencies in the current period, they should not be included as part of ending inventory costs because they do not represent assets. Because of its simplicity, the immediate write-off method is most commonly used.

underapplied overhead
The difference between actual and applied overhead when the amount applied is less than the amount incurred.

overapplied overhead
The difference between actual and applied overhead when the amount applied exceeds the amount incurred.

proration
To assign underapplied overhead or overapplied overhead to cost of goods sold, work-in-process inventory, and finished-goods inventory in proportion to the ending balances of each account.

PRORATION AMONG INVENTORIES If the objective is to obtain as accurate an application of actual costs as possible, theoretically we should recompute all the overhead costs of the individual products using the actual, rather than the budgeted, rates. This approach is rarely feasible, so proration apportions over- or underapplied overhead among work-in-process (WIP), finished goods (FG), and cost of goods sold because these are the accounts where the applied factory overhead resides at the end of the period. While prorating over- or underapplied overhead means to assign it in proportion to the magnitude of applied factory overhead in the ending balances of these accounts, a more practical approach is to prorate on the basis of the ending balances in each of the three accounts. Assume that the ending balances for Enriquez are WIP, $155,000; Finished Goods, $32,000; and Cost of Goods Sold, $2,480,000 (a total of $2,667,000). The results of proration follow:

	(1) Unadjusted Balance, End of 20X0	(2) Proration of Underapplied Overhead		(3) Adjusted Balance, End of 20X0
WIP	$ 155,000	$(155,000 \div 2,667) \times \$17,000 =$	$ 988	$ 155,988
Finished goods	32,000	$(32 \div 2,667) \times 17,000 =$	204	32,204
Cost of goods sold	2,480,000	$(2,480 \div 2,667) \times 17,000 =$	15,808	2,495,808
Total	$2,667,000		$17,000	$2,684,000

The amounts prorated to inventories are not significant, so proration is probably not cost beneficial here. In actual practice, companies generally prorate overhead variances only when it would materially affect inventory valuations and net income. For simplicity, we will assume for the rest of this chapter that companies immediately write off any over- or underapplied overhead.

The Use of Variable and Fixed Application Rates

The cost of a product or service is the sum of direct costs and allocated costs. As we have seen, overhead application is the most troublesome aspect of product costing. The presence of fixed costs is a major reason for the costing difficulties. Many companies make no distinction between variable- and fixed-cost behaviors in the design of their accounting systems. For instance, the machining department at Enriquez Machine Parts Company developed the following rate that includes both variable and fixed costs:

$$\text{budgeted overhead application rate} = \frac{\text{budgeted total overhead}}{\text{budgeted machine hours}}$$

$$= \frac{\$277,800}{69,450}$$

$$= \$4 \text{ per machine hour}$$

Some companies, though, do distinguish between variable overhead and fixed overhead for product costing as well as for control purposes. Suppose the machining department at Enriquez had made this distinction. Managers determined that rent, supervision, depreciation, and insurance were fixed costs and indirect labor, supplies, utilities, and repairs were variable costs. The department developed two rates:

$$\text{budgeted variable-overhead application rate} = \frac{\text{budgeted total variable overhead}}{\text{budgeted machine hours}}$$

$$= \frac{\$114,000}{69,450}$$

$$= \$1.64 \text{ per machine hour}$$

$$\text{budgeted fixed-overhead application rate} = \frac{\text{budgeted total fixed overhead}}{\text{budgeted machine hours}}$$

$$= \frac{\$163,800}{69,450}$$

$$= \$2.36 \text{ per machine hour}$$

Some companies use such rates for product costing. However, it is more important to make distinctions between variable- and fixed-overhead application rates for control purposes. Why? Because the explanations for over- or underapplied overhead are usually quite different for variable and fixed costs.

After the following summary problem, we will turn our attention to some other issues arising from differences between fixed and variable overhead.

Summary Problem for Your Review

PROBLEM

Review the Enriquez illustration. Suppose Enriquez had sales in 20X0 of $5,000,000. There were no beginning or ending inventories. That is, Enriquez sold everything it produced in 20X0. The company used the budgeted factory-overhead rates on page 534. Production in 20X0 required 85,000 machine hours in machining and $260,000 direct-labor cost in assembly. The materials used in 20X0 cost $2,400,000, and the total direct-labor cost was $490,000. Actual factory-overhead cost was $455,000. Prepare an income statement for 20X0 through the gross profit line. Include a separate line for the immediate write-off method for overapplied or underapplied overhead.

SOLUTION

See Exhibit 13-1. You can compute the overhead component of cost of goods sold as follows:

Machining: 85,000 machine hours × $4 per machine hour	$340,000
Assembly: $260,000 direct-labor cost × 50% of direct-labor dollars	130,000
Total overhead	$470,000

Overapplied overhead is $470,000 − $455,000 = $15,000.

Sales		$ 5,000,000
Cost of goods sold:		
Direct materials	$2,400,000	
Direct labor	490,000	
Factory overhead	470,000	
Total		(3,360,000)
Overapplied overhead		15,000
Gross profit		$ 1,655,000

Exhibit 13-1
Enriquez Machine Parts Company
Income Statement, 20X0

Variable Versus Absorption Costing

Accounting for Fixed-Manufacturing Overhead

We compare two major methods of product costing in this section: variable costing (the contribution approach) and absorption costing (the functional, full-costing, or financial-reporting approach). You encountered these methods already in Chapter 5, but here we will provide more details. They differ in only one major respect: Fixed manufacturing overhead is excluded from the cost of products under variable costing but is included in the cost of products under absorption costing.

As Exhibit 13-2 shows, a variable-costing system charges fixed manufacturing overhead (fixed factory overhead) as a period cost that is an immediate expense on the income statement— not as a product cost that is added to inventory and charged against sales as cost of goods sold

Objective 4

Compare variable- and absorption-costing systems.

Exhibit 13-2
Comparison of Flow of Costs

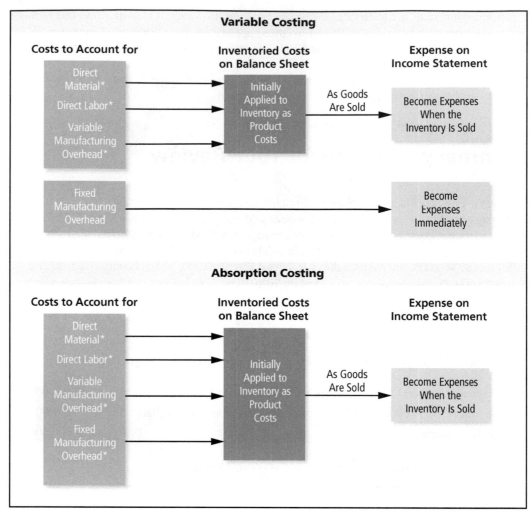

*As goods are manufactured, the costs are "applied" to inventory, usually via the use of unit costs.

when the company sells the inventory. Note that the only difference between variable- and absorption-costing net incomes is the accounting for fixed manufacturing overhead.[3]

Absorption costing is more widely used than variable costing. Why? Because variable costing is not allowed for either external-reporting or tax purposes. An example of how one company uses variable costing is shown in the Business First box on page 541.

Nonetheless, the growing use of the contribution approach in performance measurement and cost analysis has led to increasing use of variable costing for internal-reporting purposes. Over half the major firms in the United States use variable costing for some internal reporting, and nearly a quarter use it as the primary internal format. For example, the Muncie, Indiana, plant of **BorgWarner** changed its product-line performance reporting from an absorption-costing approach to variable costing. Why? Because management believes variable costing links manufacturing performance more closely with measures of that performance by removing the impact of changing inventory levels from financial results.

Until the last decade or two, use of variable costing for internal reporting was expensive. It requires a company to process information two ways, one for external reporting and one for internal reporting. The increasing use and decreasing cost of computers has reduced the added cost of a variable-costing system. Most managers no longer face the question of whether to invest in a separate variable-costing system. Rather, they simply choose a variable-costing or absorption-costing format for reports. Many well-designed accounting systems used today can produce either format.

---

[3]Variable costing is sometimes called direct costing. However, variable costing is a more descriptive term, so we will use it exclusively in this text.

Business First

Variable Costing at Nortel Networks

Nortel Networks was at one time a Canada-based "global leader in telephone, data, wireless, and wireline solutions for the Internet," with revenues of $10.4 billion in 2008. In 2009 the company filed for bankruptcy and began to sell its assets, which is ongoing as of 2012. In the 1990s, while still known as Northern Telecom, Nortel gradually came to understand that its standard absorption costing income statement did not provide the information that managers needed. The company also realized the information needed for a more meaningful income statement was in the accounting system, but the traditional reported income statement did not present the information in the most useful way. Therefore, Nortel's accountants adopted a "variable costing" approach to the income statement.

Statutory and regulatory reporting requirements did not allow Northern Telecom to completely abandon absorption costing. The company's solution left the top line—revenue—and the bottom line—earnings before tax—unchanged. But everything in between was reported differently, in the following format:

Revenue
> Product cost

Product margin
> Manufacturing/operational costs

Inventory provisions
> New product introduction

Selling and marketing
> Direct margin

Administrative cost
> Other operating (income) expense

Operating profit
> Corporate assessments
> Other nonoperating (income) expense

Earnings before balance sheet adjustments
> Balance sheet adjustment

Earnings before tax

This format represents an extreme application of variable costing. Only direct-materials costs are considered product costs. All other costs, including direct labor and variable overhead, are period costs that are charged to expense when incurred, not added to inventory. For example, direct labor is part of manufacturing costs. The amount charged in any period is the amount actually incurred during that period, regardless of whether the labor is related to goods sold or those still in inventory. Managers used four measures of "profit": product margin (to measure the value added), direct margin (to measure results of product production and sales), operating profit (to measure total results of operations), and earnings before balance sheet adjustments (to measure the effect on company-wide profits).

The main difference between the old absorption-costing system and the new system is that the new system expenses all costs except materials costs, whereas the old system capitalized all production costs. Reconciling the two systems was an accounting problem, unrelated to operating the business. Therefore, a final line was added to the income statement to provide a reconciliation—balance sheet adjustment. This represents the difference between the absorption and variable costing statements, but it can be ignored by managers.

Nortel's efforts illustrate two important points. First, it is possible to adapt accounting methods to meet the specific needs of managers. Second, companies often do not have to choose between absorption and variable costing—either format can be produced by the same basic accounting system.

Sources: From P. Sharman, "Time to Re-examine the P&L," *CMA Magazine*, September 1991, pp. 22–25; Nortel Networks 2011 10-K.

Facts for Illustration

To see exactly how these two product costing systems work, we will use a hypothetical division of Dell—let's call it the Desk PC division—as an illustration. The division makes a variety of desktop computers, but for simplicity we will consider all the computers to be identical. The division had the following standard costs for the production of computers:

Basic Production Data at Standard Cost	
Direct materials	$205
Direct labor	75
Variable manufacturing overhead	20
Standard variable costs per computer	$300

The annual budget for fixed manufacturing overhead is $1,500,000. Expected (or budgeted) production is 15,000 computers per year, and the sales price is $500 per computer. For simplicity, we will assume that number of computers produced is the single cost-allocation base for the $20 per computer variable-manufacturing overhead. Also, we will assume that annual budgeted fixed selling and administrative expenses are $650,000 and the only variable selling and administrative cost is a sales commission of 5% of dollar sales. Actual product quantities are as follows:

	20X0	20X1
In units (computers)		
Opening inventory	—	3,000
Production	17,000	14,000
Sales	14,000	16,000
Ending inventory	3,000	1,000

There are no variances from the standard variable manufacturing or selling and administrative costs, the actual fixed manufacturing overhead incurred is exactly $1,500,000 each year, and the actual fixed selling and administrative cost is $650,000 each year.

Based on this information, we can

1. prepare income statements for 20X0 and 20X1 under variable costing,
2. prepare income statements for 20X0 and 20X1 under absorption costing, and
3. show a reconciliation of the difference in operating income for 20X0, 20X1, and the two years as a whole.

Variable-Costing Method

Objective 5

Construct an income statement using the variable-costing approach.

We begin by preparing income statements under variable costing. The variable-costing statement shown in Exhibit 13-3 has a familiar contribution-approach format, the same format introduced in Chapter 5. The only new characteristic of Exhibit 13-3 is the presence of a detailed calculation of cost of goods sold, which is affected by changes in the beginning and ending inventories. In contrast, the income statements in earlier chapters assumed that there were no changes in the beginning and ending inventories.

We account for the costs of the product by applying all variable manufacturing costs to the goods produced at a rate of $300 per computer. This values inventories at standard variable costs. We do not apply any fixed manufacturing costs to products; instead we regard them as expenses in the period they are incurred.

	20X0		20X1	
Sales, 14,000 and 16,000 computers, respectively		$7,000,000		$8,000,000
Variable expenses:				
Variable manufacturing cost of goods sold				
Opening inventory, at standard variable costs of $300	$—		$ 900,000	
Add: variable cost of goods manufactured at standard, 17,000 and 14,000 computers, respectively	5,100,000		4,200,000	
Available for sale, 17,000 computers in each year	$5,100,000		$5,100,000	
Deduct: ending inventory, at standard variable cost of $300	900,000*		300,000†	
Variable manufacturing cost of goods sold	$4,200,000		$4,800,000	
Variable selling expenses, at 5% of dollar sales	350,000		400,000	
Total variable expenses		4,550,000		5,200,000
Contribution margin		$2,450,000		$2,800,000
Fixed expenses:				
Fixed factory overhead	$1,500,000		$1,500,000	
Fixed selling and administrative expenses	650,000		650,000	
Total fixed expenses		2,150,000		2,150,000
Operating income, variable costing		$ 300,000		$ 650,000

*3,000 computers at $300 = $900,000.
†1,000 computers at $300 = $300,000.

Exhibit 13-3
Desk PC Division: Comparative Income Statements Using Variable Costing
Years 20X0 and 20X1

Before reading on, be sure to trace the facts from our Desktop PC division example to the presentation in Exhibit 13-3, step-by-step. Note that we deduct both variable cost of goods sold and variable selling and administrative expenses in computing the contribution margin. However, variable selling and administrative expenses are not inventoriable. Why? They are not incurred in production and so are not considered to be product costs. Only the level of sales, not changes in inventory, affect them.

Absorption-Costing Method

Exhibit 13-4 shows the standard absorption-costing framework. As you can see, it differs from the variable-costing format in three ways.

First, the unit product cost used for computing cost of goods sold is $400, not $300. Why? Because we add fixed manufacturing overhead of $100 to the $300 variable manufacturing cost. The $100 of fixed manufacturing overhead applied to each unit is the **fixed-overhead rate**. We determine this rate by dividing the budgeted fixed overhead by the expected cost-allocation base activity. The expected cost-allocation base activity selected to determine the fixed-overhead rate is labeled the **denominator level**. In this case the denominator level is the expected volume of production for the budget period:

$$\text{fixed-overhead rate} = \frac{\text{budgeted fixed manufacturing overhead}}{\text{expected volume of production}}$$

$$= \frac{\$1,500,000}{15,000 \text{ units}}$$

$$= \$100$$

Second, fixed factory overhead does not appear as a separate line in an absorption-costing income statement. Instead, the fixed factory overhead appears in two places: as part of the cost of goods sold and as a **production-volume variance**.[4] A production-volume variance (which we explain further in the next section) appears whenever actual production deviates from the expected volume of production used in computing the fixed overhead rate:

production-volume variance = (actual volume − expected volume) × fixed-overhead rate

Objective 6

Construct an income statement using the absorption-costing approach.

fixed-overhead rate
The amount of fixed manufacturing overhead applied to each unit of production. It is determined by dividing the budgeted fixed overhead by the expected cost-allocation base activity for the budget period.

Denominator level
The expected cost-allocation base activity selected to determine the fixed-overhead rate.

production-volume variance
A variance that appears whenever actual production deviates from the expected volume of production used in computing the fixed overhead rate. It is calculated as (actual volume − expected volume) × fixed-overhead rate.

	20X0		20X1	
Sales		$7,000,000		$8,000,000
Cost of goods sold:				
Opening inventory, at standard absorption cost of $400*	$ —		$1,200,000	
Cost of goods manufactured at standard of $400	6,800,000		5,600,000	
Available for sale	6,800,000		6,800,000	
Deduct: ending inventory at standard absorption cost of $400	1,200,000		400,000	
Cost of goods sold, at standard		5,600,000		6,400,000
Gross profit at standard		1,400,000		1,600,000
Production-volume variance[†]		200,000 F		100,000 U
Gross margin or gross profit, at "actual"		1,600,000		1,500,000
Selling and administrative expenses		1,000,000		1,050,000
Operating income		$ 600,000		$ 450,000

Exhibit 13-4
Desk PC Division: Comparative Income Statements Using Absorption Costing
Years 20X0 and 20X1

*Variable cost	$300
Fixed cost ($1,500,000 ÷ 15,000)	100
Standard absorption cost	$400

[†]Computation of production-volume variance based on expected volume of production of 15,000 computers:

20X0	$200,000 F	(17,000 − 15,000) × $100
20X1	100,000 U	(14,000 − 15,000) × $100
Two years together	$100,000 F	(31,000 − 30,000) × $100

U = Unfavorable, F = Favorable

---

[4]In general, this will be a cost-driver activity variance. In our example, production volume is the only cost driver, so it can be called a production-volume variance.

For example, the production-volume variance for 20X1 is $(14,000 - 15,000) \times \$100 = -\$100,000$, an underapplied overhead. At \$100 per computer, Dell applies only \$1,400,000 of fixed overhead to production while actual overhead is exactly equal to its budget of \$1,500,000. Assuming it uses the immediate write-off approach, Dell must add the \$100,000 to the 20X1 cost of goods sold.

Finally, the format for an absorption-costing income statement separates costs into the major categories of manufacturing and nonmanufacturing. In contrast, a variable-costing income statement separates costs into the major categories of fixed and variable. In an absorption-costing statement, revenue less manufacturing cost (both fixed and variable) is gross profit or gross margin. In a variable-costing statement, revenue less all variable costs (both manufacturing and nonmanufacturing) is the contribution margin. We illustrate this difference by a condensed comparison of 20X1 income statements:

Variable Costing		Absorption Costing	
Revenue	$8,000,000	Revenue	$8,000,000
All variable costs	5,200,000	All manufacturing costs*	6,500,000
Contribution margin	2,800,000	Gross margin	1,500,000
All fixed costs	2,150,000	All nonmanufacturing costs	1,050,000
Operating income	$ 650,000	Operating income	$ 450,000

*Standard absorption cost of goods sold $(16,000 \times \$400)$ plus the production-volume variance (\$100,000 U).

Making Managerial Decisions

When making decisions, it is important for managers to distinguish between gross margin and contribution margin. List the ways in which these two margins differ.

Answer
Among the differences are the following:
- Gross margin appears in an absorption-costing income statement; contribution margin is in a variable-costing income statement.
- Gross margin is revenue less manufacturing cost; contribution margin is revenue less all variable costs.

- Gross margin is based on a categorization of costs by function (manufacturing versus non-manufacturing); contribution margin is based on a categorization of costs by cost behavior pattern (variable versus fixed).
- Gross margin is required for external financial reporting; contribution margin is most useful for short-term management decisions and other settings where the variable versus fixed cost distinction is relevant.

Fixed Overhead and Absorption Costs of Product

Objective 7

Distinguish between product-costing and planning-and-control purposes in accounting for variable and fixed costs.

The differences between variable- and absorption-costing formats arise because the two formats treat fixed manufacturing overhead differently. In this and subsequent sections, we explore how to account for manufacturing overhead in an absorption-costing system. We do not further examine this issue under variable costing because its treatment of fixed manufacturing overhead is straightforward—we simply deduct the total amount of actual fixed factory overhead on the current-period income statement.

Variable and Fixed Unit Costs

Continuing our example of the Desktop PC division, we begin by comparing (1) the manufacturing overhead costs in the flexible budget used for departmental budgeting and control purposes with (2) the manufacturing overhead costs applied to products under an absorption-costing system. To stress the basic assumptions behind absorption costing, we will also split manufacturing overhead into variable and fixed components.

Consider the following graphs of variable-overhead costs:

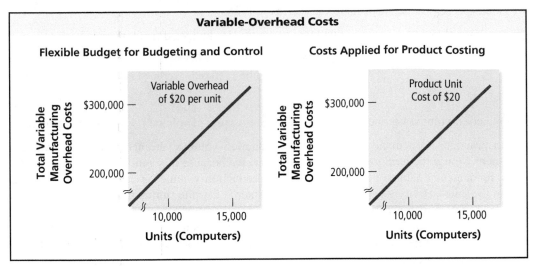

Note that the two graphs are identical. The expected variable-overhead costs from the flexible budget are the same as the variable-overhead costs applied to the products. Both budgeted and applied variable overhead are $20 per computer. Each time we produce 1,000 additional computers, we expect to incur an additional $20,000 of variable overhead, and we add $20,000 of variable-overhead cost to the inventory account for computers. The variable costs used for budgeting and control are the same as those used for product costing.

In contrast, the graph for applied fixed-overhead costs differs from that for the flexible budget:

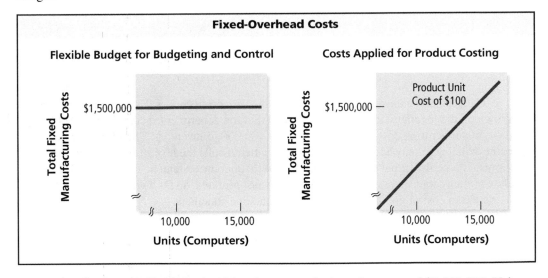

The flexible budget for fixed overhead is a lump-sum budgeted amount of $1,500,000. Volume does not affect it. In contrast, the applied fixed cost depends on actual volume and the predicted volume (denominator level) used to set the budgeted rate for fixed factory overhead.

$$\text{Fixed cost applied} = \text{actual volume} \times \text{fixed-overhead rate}$$

$$= \text{units produced} \times \$100$$

Suppose actual volume equals the expected volume of 15,000 computers. Applied fixed overhead would be 15,000 computers × $100 per computer = $1,500,000, the same as the flexible-budget amount. However, if actual volume differs from expected volume, the costs used for budgeting and control differ from those used for product costing. For budgeting and control purposes, managers use the true cost behavior pattern for fixed costs. In contrast, as the graphs indicate, the absorption product-costing approach applies these fixed costs as though they had a variable-cost behavior pattern. The difference between applied and budgeted fixed overhead is the production-volume variance.

Objective 8

Compute the production-volume variance and show how it should appear in the income statement.

Nature of Production-Volume Variance

We calculate the production-volume variance as follows:

$$\text{production-volume variance} = \text{applied fixed overhead} - \text{budgeted fixed overhead}$$
$$= (\text{actual volume} \times \text{fixed-overhead rate})$$
$$- (\text{expected volume} \times \text{fixed-overhead rate})$$

or

$$\text{production-volume variance} = (\text{actual volume} - \text{expected volume}) \times \text{fixed-overhead rate}$$

volume variance

A common name for the production-volume variance.

In practice, accountants often call the production-volume variance simply the **volume variance**. We use the term *production-volume variance* because it is a more precise description of the fundamental nature of the variance. Using production-volume variance also distinguishes it from the sales-activity variance described in Chapter 8. Despite similar nomenclature, they are completely different concepts.

A production-volume variance arises when the actual production volume achieved does not coincide with the expected volume of production used as a denominator for computing the fixed-overhead rate for product-costing purposes:

1. When expected production volume and actual production volume are identical, there is no production-volume variance.
2. When actual volume is less than expected volume, the production-volume variance is unfavorable because usage of facilities is less than expected and fixed overhead is underapplied. It is measured in Exhibit 13-4 for 20X1 as follows:

$$\text{production-volume variance} = (\text{actual volume} - \text{expected volume}) \times \text{budgeted fixed-overhead rate}$$
$$= (14,000 \text{ units} - 15,000 \text{ units}) \times \$100$$
$$= -\$100,000 \text{ or } \$100,000 \text{ U}$$

or

$$\text{production-volume variance} = \text{budget minus applied}$$
$$= \$1,500,000 - \$1,400,000 = \$100,000 \text{ U}$$

The $100,000 unfavorable production-volume variance increases the manufacturing costs shown on the income statement. Why? Recall that the department incurred $1,500,000 of fixed manufacturing cost, but applied only $1,400,000 to inventory. Therefore, the department will charge only $1,400,000 as expense when it sells the inventory. But eventually it must charge the actual cost of $1,500,000 to the income statement as expense. Recall for simplicity that we assumed any variance is not prorated, so **Dell** writes off the extra $100,000 to cost of goods sold in the current income statement.

3. When actual volume exceeds expected volume, as was the case in 20X0, the production-volume variance is favorable because use of facilities is better than expected, and fixed overhead is overapplied.

$$\text{production-volume variance} = (17,000 \text{ units} - 15,000 \text{ units}) \times \$100 = \$200,000 \text{ F}$$

In this case, the department will charge $1,700,000 through inventory. Because the department incurs actual costs of only $1,500,000, future expenses will be overstated by $200,000. Therefore, we reduce current period expenses by the $200,000 favorable variance.

The production-volume variance is the conventional measure of the cost of departing from the level of activity originally used to set the fixed-overhead rate. Most companies consider production-volume variances to be beyond immediate control, although sometimes a manager responsible for volume has to do some explaining or investigating. Sometimes, idle facilities caused by disappointing total sales, poor production scheduling, unusual machine breakdowns, shortages of skilled workers, strikes, storms, and the like are responsible for the failure to reach the expected volume.

There is no production-volume variance for variable overhead. Why? The concept of production-volume variance arises for fixed overhead because of the conflict between accounting for control (by flexible budgets) and accounting for product costing (by application rates), and there is no such conflict for variable-overhead costs as they are incurred in direct proportion to volume. Unlike variable costs, fixed costs are simply not divisible. Rather, they come in large lump sums and are related to the provision of large amounts of production or sales capability, not to the production or sale of a single unit of product.

Making Managerial Decisions

Some accountants claim that the production-volume variance is a good measure of how well a company uses its capacity: Favorable (unfavorable) variances imply effective (ineffective) use of capacity. As a manager, why would you want to be careful not to fall into that trap?

Answer

The production volume variance tells you one thing and only one thing—whether actual production was above or below the predicted volume used in setting the fixed overhead rate. Suppose a manager can avoid an unfavorable production-volume variance by lowering the product's selling price to increase sales volume enough to use up the idle capacity. However, if the result is a decline in total contribution margin, this would not be an effective use of the capacity. Similarly, a favorable production-volume variance is not desirable if it occurs because management forces excess production through the facility, despite quality declines or other inefficiencies caused by overburdened production facilities.

Reconciliation of Variable Costing and Absorption Costing

We can easily reconcile the operating incomes shown in Exhibits 13-3 and 13-4. The difference in income equals the difference in the total amount of fixed manufacturing overhead charged as an expense during a given year. Examine Exhibit 13-5. The total fixed manufacturing overhead incurred ($1,500,000 in 20X1) is always recognized as an expense on a variable-costing income statement. Under absorption costing, fixed manufacturing overhead appears in two places on the income statement: cost of goods sold and production-volume variance.

Objective 9

Reconcile variable- and absorption-costing operating income and explain why a company might prefer to use a variable-costing approach.

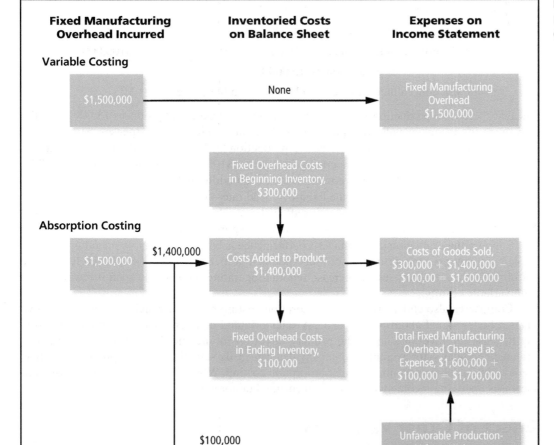

Exhibit 13-5
Flow of Fixed Manufacturing Overhead Costs During 20X1

Under absorption costing, the beginning inventory includes $300,000 of fixed costs incurred before 20X1. During 20X1, accountants added $1,400,000 of fixed manufacturing overhead to inventory, and $100,000 remained in the ending inventory of 20X1 (1,000 units in ending inventory times the $100 fixed factory overhead rate applied to them). Thus, the fixed manufacturing overhead included in cost of goods sold for 20X1 was $300,000 + $1,400,000 − $100,000 = $1,600,000. In addition, the production-volume variance is $100,000, unfavorable. The total fixed manufacturing overhead charged as 20X1 expenses under absorption costing is $1,700,000, or $200,000 more than the $1,500,000 charged under variable costing. Therefore, 20X1 variable-costing income is higher by $200,000.

We can quickly explain the difference in variable-costing and absorption-costing operating income by multiplying the fixed-overhead product-costing rate by the change in the total units in the beginning and ending inventories. Consider 20X1: The change in inventory was 2,000 units, so the difference in net income would be 2,000 units × $100 = $200,000.

Remember that it is the relationship between sales and production that determines the difference between variable-costing and absorption-costing income. Whenever units sold are greater than units produced—that is when inventories decrease—variable-costing income is greater than absorption-costing income. Whenever units produced are greater than units sold—that is when inventories increase—absorption-costing income is greater than variable-costing income.

Why Use Variable Costing?

Why do many companies use variable costing for internal statements? One reason is that production volume affects absorption-costing income but has no effect on variable-costing income. Consider the 20X1 absorption-costing statement in Exhibit 13-4, which shows operating income of $450,000. Suppose a manager decides to produce 1,000 additional units in December 20X1 even though they will remain unsold. Will this affect operating income? First, note that the gross profit will not change because both revenue and goods sold are based on units sold, not on production volume. However, the production-volume variance will change:

$$\text{If production} = 14,000 \text{ units}$$
$$\text{Production-volume variance} = (15,000 - 14,000) \times \$100 = \$100,000 \text{ U}$$
$$\text{If production} = 15,000 \text{ U}$$
$$\text{Production-volume variance} = (15,000 - 15,000) \times \$100 = \$0$$

Because there is no production-volume variance when the department produces 15,000 units, the new operating income equals gross profit less selling and administrative expenses, $1,600,000 − $1,050,000 = $550,000. Therefore, increasing production by 1,000 units without any increase in sales increases absorption-costing operating income by $100,000, from $450,000 to $550,000. The general rule under absorption costing is that each additional unit produced will increase operating income by the amount of the fixed-overhead rate—in this case, by $100 per unit.

How will such an increase in production affect the variable-costing statement in Exhibit 13-3? Nothing will change. Production does not affect operating income under variable costing.

Suppose the evaluation of a manager's performance is based primarily on operating income. If the company uses the absorption-costing approach, a manager might be tempted to produce additional unneeded units just to increase reported operating income. No such incentive exists with variable costing.

Companies also choose variable or absorption costing based on which system they believe gives a better signal about performance. A sales-oriented company may prefer variable costing because the level of sales is the primary effect on its income. In contrast, a production-oriented company—for example, a company that can easily sell all the units it produces (such as a gold mining company)—might prefer absorption costing. Why? Because additional production increases operating income with absorption costing but not with variable costing.

Effect of Other Variances

So far, our example has deliberately ignored the possibility of any variance except the production-volume variance, which appears only on an absorption-costing statement. All other variances appear on both variable- and absorption-costing income statements. In this section, we will consider these other variances that you encountered in Chapter 8.

Flexible-Budget Variances

Returning again to the Desktop PC division, we will assume some additional facts for 20X1 (the second of the 2 years covered by our example):

Flexible-budget variances	
Direct materials	None
Direct labor	$ 170,000 U
Variable factory overhead	$ 30,000 U
Fixed factory overhead	$ 70,000 U
Supporting data (used to compute the preceding variances as shown in Appendix 13):	
Standard direct-labor hours allowed for 14,000 units of output produced	87,500
Standard direct-labor rate per hour	$ 12.00
Actual direct-labor hours of inputs	100,000
Actual direct-labor rate per hour	$ 12.20
Variable manufacturing overhead actually incurred	$ 310,000
Fixed manufacturing overhead actually incurred	$1,570,000

As Chapter 8 explained, flexible-budget variances may arise for both variable overhead and fixed overhead. Consider the following:

	Actual Amounts	Flexible Budget Amounts at 14,000 Units	Flexible Budget Variances
Variable factory overhead	$ 310,000	$ 280,000	$30,000 U
Fixed factory overhead	1,570,000	1,500,000	70,000 U

Exhibit 13-6 shows the relationship between the fixed-overhead flexible-budget variance and the production-volume variance. The difference between the actual fixed overhead and that applied to products is the underapplied (or overapplied) overhead. Because the actual fixed overhead of $1,570,000 exceeds the $1,400,000 applied, fixed overhead is underapplied by $170,000, which means that the variance is unfavorable. The $170,000 underapplied fixed overhead has two components: (1) a production-volume variance of $100,000 U and (2) a fixed-overhead flexible-budget variance (also called the fixed-overhead spending variance) of $70,000 U.

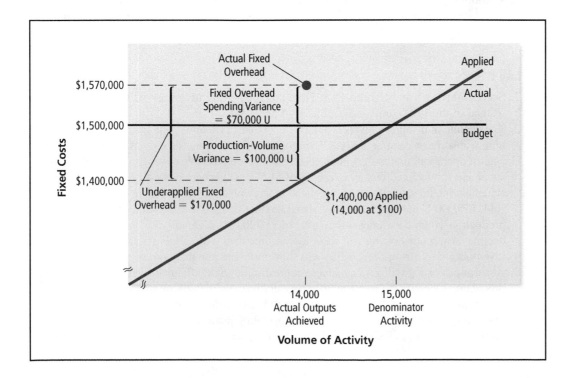

Exhibit 13-6
Fixed-Overhead Variances for 20X1
Data are from Exhibit 13-4

Exhibit 13-7 contains the income statement under absorption costing that incorporates these new facts. These new variances decrease income by $270,000 because, like the production-volume variance, they are all unfavorable variances that are charged against income in 20X1. If any cost variances were favorable, they would increase operating income.

Exhibit 13-7

Absorption Costing Modification of Exhibit 13-4 for 20X1
(additional facts are in text)

Sales, 16,000 at $500		$8,000,000
Opening inventory at standard, 3,000 at $400	$1,200,000	
Cost of goods manufactured at standard, 14,000 at $400	5,600,000	
Available for sale, 17,000 at $400	$6,800,000	
Deduct ending inventory at standard, 1,000 at $400	400,000	
Cost of goods sold at standard, 16,000 at $400		6,400,000
Gross profit at standard		$1,600,000
Flexible-budget variances, both unfavorable		
Variable manufacturing costs ($170,000 + $30,000)	$ 200,000	
Fixed factory overhead	70,000	
Production-volume variance (arises only because of		
fixed overhead), unfavorable	100,000	
Total variances		370,000
Gross profit at "actual"		$1,230,000
Selling and administrative expenses		1,050,000
Operating income		$ 180,000

Summary Problem for Your Review

PROBLEM

1. Reconsider Exhibits 13-3 and 13-4 on pages 542 and 543. Suppose production in 20X1 was 14,500 units instead of 14,000 units, but sales remained at 16,000 units. Assume that the net variances for all variable manufacturing costs were $200,000, unfavorable. Regard these variances as adjustments to the standard cost of goods sold for the year. Also assume that actual fixed costs were $1,570,000. Prepare income statements for 20X1 under variable costing and under absorption costing.

2. Explain why operating income was different under variable costing from what it was under absorption costing. Show your calculations.

3. Without regard to number 1, would variable costing or absorption costing give a manager more flexibility in influencing short-run operating income through production-scheduling decisions? Why?

SOLUTION

1. See Exhibit 13-8 and Exhibit 13-9. Note that the ending inventory will be 1,500 units instead of the 1,000 units in Exhibits 13-3 and 13-4.

2. The decline in inventory levels is 3,000 – 1,500, or 1,500 units. The fixed-overhead rate per unit in absorption costing is $100. Therefore, $150,000 more fixed overhead was charged against operations under absorption costing than under variable costing. The variable-costing statement shows fixed factory overhead of $1,570,000, whereas the absorption-costing statement includes fixed factory overhead in three places: $1,600,000 in cost of goods sold, $70,000 U in fixed factory-overhead flexible-budget variance, and $50,000 U as a production-volume variance—for a total of $1,720,000. Generally, (1) when inventories decline, absorption costing will show less income than will variable costing; (2) when inventories rise, absorption costing will show more income than variable costing.

3. Absorption costing will give a manager more discretion in influencing operating income via production scheduling. Operating income will fluctuate in harmony with changes in net sales under variable costing, but both production and sales influence it under absorption costing. For example, compare the variable costing operating income in Exhibits 13-3 and 13-8. As the second note to Exhibit 13-8 indicates, all variances except the production-volume

Sales		$8,000,000
Opening inventory, at variable		
standard cost of $300	$ 900,000	
Add: Variable cost of goods manufactured	4,350,000	
Available for sale	$5,250,000	
Deduct: Ending inventory, at variable		
standard cost of $300	450,000	
Variable cost of goods sold, at standard		$4,800,000
Net flexible-budget variances for		
all variable costs, unfavorable		200,000
Variable cost of goods sold, at actual		$5,000,000
Variable selling expenses, at 5% of dollar sales		400,000
Total variable costs charged against sales		5,400,000
Contribution margin		$2,600,000
Fixed factory overhead	$1,570,000*	
Fixed selling and administrative expenses	650,000	
Total fixed expenses		2,220,000
Operating income		$ 380,000†

*This could be shown in two lines, $1,500,000 budget plus $70,000 variance.
†The difference between this and the $650,000 operating income in Exhibit 13-3 occurs because of the $200,000 unfavorable variable-cost variances and the $70,000 unfavorable fixed-cost flexible-budget variance.

Exhibit 13-8
Desk PC Division
Income Statement (variable costing), Year 20X1

Sales			$8,000,000
Opening inventory, at standard cost of $400		$1,200,000	
Cost of goods manufactured, at standard		5,800,000	
Available for sale		$7,000,000	
Deduct: Ending inventory, at standard		600,000	
Cost of goods sold, at standard		$6,400,000	
Net flexible-budget variances for all variable			
manufacturing costs, unfavorable	$200,000		
Fixed factory overhead flexible-budget			
variance, unfavorable	70,000		
Production-volume variance, unfavorable	50,000*		
Total variances		320,000	
Cost of goods sold, at "actual"			6,720,000†
Gross profit, at "actual"			$1,280,000
Selling and administrative expenses			
Variable		400,000	
Fixed		650,000	1,050,000
Operating income			$ 230,000‡

*Production-volume variance is $100 × (15,000 expected volume − 14,500 actual production).
†This format differs slightly from Exhibit 13-7. The difference is deliberate; it illustrates that the formats of income statements are not rigid.
‡Compare this result with the $180,000 operating income in Exhibit 13-7. The only difference is traceable to the production of 14,500 units instead of 14,000 units, resulting in an unfavorable production-volume variance of $50,000 instead of $100,000.

Exhibit 13-9
Desk PC Division
Income Statement (absorption costing), Year 20X1

variance affect operating income under variable costing, reducing income by $200,000 + $70,000 = $270,000, from $650,000 to $380,000. However, none of these variances, and thus none of the differences in operating income, is a result of production scheduling decisions, so the increase in units produced has no effect on operating income.

On the other hand, compare the operating income of Exhibits 13-4 and 13-9. As the third note to Exhibit 13-9 explains, production scheduling and sales influence operating income. Without the increase in production, operating income would have decreased by the same $270,000 as under variable costing, from $450,000 to $180,000. However, production was 14,500 rather than 14,000 units. So $50,000 of fixed overhead became a part of ending inventory (an asset) instead of part of the production-volume variance (an expense)—that is, the production-volume variance is $50,000 lower, which increases income by $50,000 to $230,000. Each additional unit produced adds $100 to inventory instead of to expense, thus increasing operating income by $100.

Highlights to Remember

1. **Compute budgeted factory-overhead rates and apply factory overhead to production.** Accountants usually apply indirect manufacturing costs (factory overhead) to products using budgeted overhead rates. They compute the rates by dividing total budgeted overhead by a measure of cost-allocation base activity such as expected machine hours.

2. **Determine and use appropriate cost-allocation bases for overhead application to products and services.** There should be a strong cause-and-effect relationship between cost-allocation bases and the overhead costs that are applied using these bases.

3. **Use normalized variable- and fixed-overhead application rates and explain the disposition of overhead variances.** Budgeted overhead rates are usually annual averages. The resulting product costs arc normal costs, consisting of actual direct materials, actual direct labor, and applied overhead using the budgeted rates. Normal product costs are often more useful than actual costs for decision-making and inventory-costing purposes. Variances under a normal costing system are either prorated or written-off to cost of goods sold.

4. **Compare variable- and absorption-costing systems.** Two major methods of product costing are variable (contribution approach) and absorption costing. They differ in how they account for fixed manufacturing overhead. Variable costing cannot be used for financial reporting or tax purposes, but it is used internally by many companies.

5. **Construct an income statement using the variable-costing approach.** The variable-costing method emphasizes the effects of cost behavior on income. This method excludes fixed manufacturing overhead from the cost of products and expenses it immediately.

6. **Construct an income statement using the absorption-costing approach.** The absorption or traditional approach ignores cost behavior distinctions. As a result, all costs incurred in the production of goods become part of the inventory cost. Thus, we add fixed manufacturing overhead to inventory and it appears on the income statement only when the company sells the goods.

7. **Distinguish between product-costing and planning-and-control purposes in accounting for variable and fixed costs.** Variable-overhead costs are the same for product-costing and planning-and-control purposes. In contrast, fixed costs are a lump sum for planning-and-control purposes but are unitized and therefore vary with production volume for product-costing purposes.

8. **Compute the production-volume variance and show how it should appear in the income statement.** Whenever a company employs the absorption method and the actual production volume does not equal the budgeted volume (denominator level) that it used for computing the fixed-overhead rate, a production-volume variance arises. When the actual production volume is less than budgeted, the variance is unfavorable; when actual volume exceeds budgeted volume, the variance is favorable. The amount of the variance is equal to the fixed-overhead rate times the difference between the budgeted and actual volume. Companies usually dispose of this variance by adjusting the current-period income. Favorable variances increase current-period income and unfavorable variances reduce current-period income.

9. **Reconcile variable- and absorption-costing operating income and explain why a company might prefer to use a variable-costing approach.** Whenever sales volume exceeds production volume, variable-costing operating income exceeds absorption-costing operating income; when production exceeds sales, absorption-costing operating has the greater operating income. Companies that use operating income to measure results may prefer variable costing. This is because changes in production volume affect absorption-costing income but not variable-costing income. A company that wants to focus managers' energies on sales would prefer to use variable costing, since the level of sales is the primary driver of variable-costing income.

Appendix 13: Comparisons of Production-Volume Variance with Other Variances

The only new variance introduced in this chapter is the production-volume variance, which arises because companies using absorption costing apply fixed overhead to units produced using a fixed-overhead rate. Let's examine this variance in perspective by using the approach originally demonstrated in Exhibit 8-11 of Chapter 8 (p. 328). The results of the approach appear in Exhibit 13-10, which deserves your careful study, particularly the two footnotes. Please examine the exhibit before reading on.

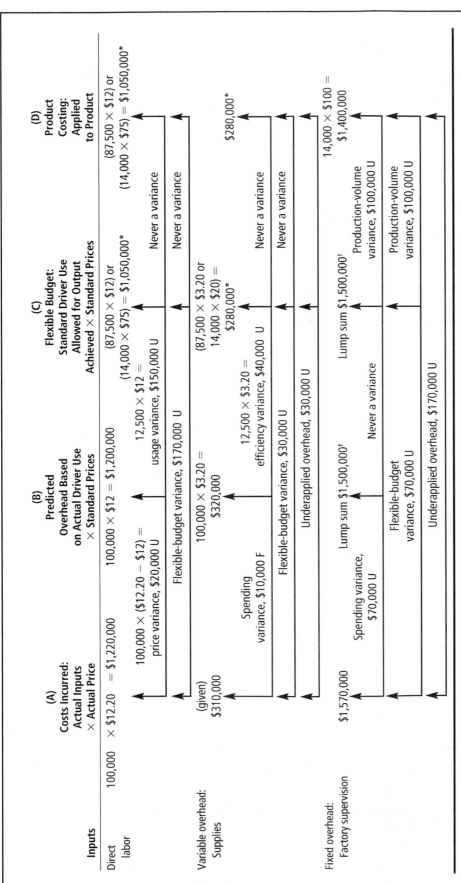

Inputs	(A) Costs Incurred: Actual Inputs × Actual Price	(B) Predicted Overhead Based on Actual Driver Use × Standard Prices	(C) Flexible Budget: Standard Driver Use Allowed for Output Achieved × Standard Prices	(D) Product Costing: Applied to Product
Direct labor	100,000 × $12.20 = $1,220,000	100,000 × $12 = $1,200,000	(87,500 × $12) or (14,000 × $75) = $1,050,000*	(87,500 × $12) or (14,000 × $75) = $1,050,000*
	100,000 × ($12.20 − $12) = price variance, $20,000 U	12,500 × $12 = usage variance, $150,000 U	Never a variance	Never a variance
	Flexible-budget variance, $170,000 U			
Variable overhead: Supplies	(given) $310,000	100,000 × $3.20 = $320,000	(87,500 × $3.20 or 14,000 × $20) = $280,000*	$280,000*
	Spending variance, $10,000 F	12,500 × $3.20 = efficiency variance, $40,000 U	Never a variance	Never a variance
	Flexible-budget variance, $30,000 U			
	Underapplied overhead, $30,000 U			
Fixed overhead: Factory supervision	$1,570,000	Lump sum $1,500,000†	Lump sum $1,500,000†	14,000 × $100 = $1,400,000
	Spending variance, $70,000 U	Never a variance	Production-volume variance, $100,000 U	Production-volume variance, $100,000 U
	Flexible-budget variance, $70,000 U			
	Underapplied overhead, $170,000 U			

U = Unfavorable, F = Favorable.

*Note especially that the flexible budget for variable costs rises and falls in direct proportion to production. Note also that the control-budget purpose and the product-costing purpose harmonize completely. The total costs in the flexible budget will always agree with the standard-variable costs applied to the product because they are based on standard costs per unit multiplied by units produced.

†In contrast with variable costs, the flexible-budget total for fixed costs will always be the same regardless of the units produced. However, the control-budget purpose and the product-costing purpose conflict; whenever actual production differs from expected production, the standard costs applied to the product will differ from the flexible budget. This difference is the production-volume variance. In this case, the production-volume variance may be computed by multiplying the $100 rate times the difference between the 15,000 expected volume and the 14,000 units of output achieved.

Exhibit 13-10

Analysis of Variances
(data are from text for 20X1)

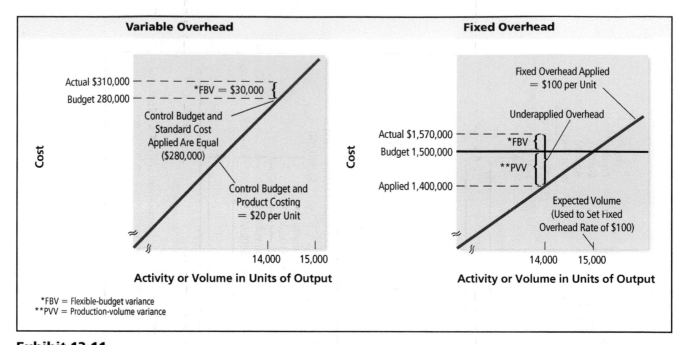

*FBV = Flexible-budget variance
**PVV = Production-volume variance

Exhibit 13-11
Comparison of Control and Product-Costing Purposes, Variable Overhead, and Fixed Overhead (not to scale)

Exhibit 13-11 graphically compares the variable- and fixed-overhead costs analyzed in Exhibit 13-10. Note how the control-budget line and the product-costing line (the applied line) are superimposed in the graph for variable overhead but differ in the graph for fixed overhead.

Underapplied or overapplied overhead is always the difference between the actual overhead incurred and the overhead applied. An analysis may then be made:

$$\text{underapplied overhead} = \left(\begin{array}{c}\text{flexible-budget}\\ \text{variance}\end{array}\right) + \left(\begin{array}{c}\text{production-volume}\\ \text{variance}\end{array}\right)$$

for variable overhead = $30,000 + 0 = $30,000
for fixed overhead = $70,000 + $100,000 = $170,000

Accounting Vocabulary

budgeted factory-overhead rate, p. 534
denominator level, p. 543
fixed-overhead rate, p. 543

normal costing system, p. 536
overapplied overhead, p. 537
production-volume variance, p. 543

proration, p. 537
underapplied overhead, p. 537
volume variance, p. 546

MyAccountingLab Fundamental Assignment Material

13-A1 Accounting for Overhead; Budgeted Rates

Kevin Aeronautics Company uses a budgeted overhead rate in applying overhead to products on a machine-hour basis for department A and on a direct-labor hour basis for department B. At the beginning of 20X0, the company's management made the following budget predictions:

	Department A	Department B
Direct-labor cost	$1,540,000	$1,230,000
Factory overhead	$1,936,000	$1,020,600
Direct-labor hours	88,000	126,000
Machine hours	352,000	18,000

Cost records of recent months show the following accumulations for product M89:

	Department A	Department B
Material placed in production	$12,500	$19,529
Direct-labor cost	$10,600	$ 9,600
Direct-labor hours	880	1,260
Machine hours	3,520	130

1. What is the budgeted overhead rate that should be applied in department A? In department B?
2. What is the total overhead cost of product M89?
3. If 105 units of product M89 are produced, what is its unit cost?
4. At the end of 20X0, actual results for the year's operations were as follows:

	Department A	Department B
Actual overhead costs incurred	$1,390,000	$1,230,000
Actual direct-labor hours	83,000	117,000
Actual machine hours	304,000	22,000

Find the underapplied or overapplied overhead for each department and for the factory as a whole.

13-A2 Disposition of Overhead

Gammaro Precision Tooling applies factory overhead using machine hours and number of component parts as cost-allocation bases. In 20X0, actual factory overhead incurred was $119,000 and applied factory overhead was $126,000. Before disposition of underapplied or overapplied factory overhead, the cost of goods sold was $505,000, gross profit was $55,000, and ending inventories were as follows:

Direct materials	$ 20,000
WIP	72,000
Finished goods	99,000
Total inventories	$191,000

1. Was factory overhead overapplied or underapplied? By how much?
2. Assume that Gammaro writes off overapplied or underapplied factory overhead as an adjustment to cost of goods sold. Compute adjusted gross profit.
3. Assume that Gammaro prorates overapplied or underapplied factory overhead based on end-of-the-year unadjusted balances. Compute adjusted gross profit.
4. Assume that actual factory overhead was $128,000 instead of $119,000, and that Gammaro writes off overapplied or underapplied factory overhead as an adjustment to cost of goods sold. Compute adjusted gross profit.

13-A3 Comparison of Variable Costing and Absorption Costing

Consider the following information pertaining to a year's operation of Blair Company:

Units produced	2,500
Units sold	2,100
Direct labor	$4,000
Direct materials used	$3,000
Selling and administrative expenses (all fixed)	$ 900
Fixed manufacturing overhead	$5,000
Variable manufacturing overhead	$2,500
All beginning inventories	$ 0
Gross margin (gross profit)	$2,200
Direct-materials inventory, end	$ 400
Work-in-process inventory, end	$ 0

1. What is the ending finished-goods inventory cost under variable costing?
2. What is the ending finished-goods inventory cost under absorption costing?
3. Would operating income be higher or lower under variable costing? By how much? Why? (Answer: $800 lower, but explain why.)

13-A4 Comparison of Absorption and Variable Costing

Examine Hoffman Company's simplified income statement based on variable costing. Assume that the budgeted volume for absorption costing in 20X0 and 20X1 was 1,470 units and that total fixed costs were identical in 20X0 and 20X1. There is no beginning or ending work in process.

Income Statement Year Ended December 31, 20X1		
Sales, 1,250 units at $15		$18,750
Deduct variable costs		
Beginning inventory, 80 units at $9	$ 720	
Variable manufacturing cost of goods manufactured, 1,220 units at $9	10,980	
Variable manufacturing cost of goods available for sale	$11,700	
Ending inventory, 50 units at $9	450	
Variable manufacturing cost of goods sold	$11,250	
Variable selling and administrative expenses	450	
Total variable costs		11,700
Contribution margin		$ 7,050
Deduct fixed costs		
Fixed factory overhead at budget	$ 5,145	
Fixed selling and administrative expenses	300	
Total fixed costs		5,445
Operating income		$ 1,605

1. Prepare an income statement based on absorption costing. Assume that actual fixed costs were equal to budgeted fixed costs.
2. Explain the difference in operating income between absorption costing and variable costing. Be specific.

13-B1 Disposition of Overhead

Richie Manufacturing had underapplied overhead of $42,000 in 20X0. Before adjusting for overapplied or underapplied overhead, the ending inventories for direct materials, WIP, and finished goods were $71,000, $161,000, and $138,000, respectively. Unadjusted cost of goods sold was $276,000.

1. Assume that the $42,000 was written off solely as an adjustment to cost of goods sold. Compute the adjusted cost of goods sold.
2. Management has decided to prorate the $42,000 to the appropriate accounts (using the unadjusted ending balances) instead of writing it off solely as an adjustment of cost of goods sold. Would gross profit be higher or lower than in requirement 1? By how much?

13-B2 Application of Overhead Using Budgeted Rates

The Eaton Clinic computes a cost of treating each patient. It allocates costs to departments and then applies departmental overhead costs to individual patients using a different budgeted overhead rate in each department. Consider the following predicted 20X0 data for two of Eaton's departments:

	Pharmacy	Medical Records
Department overhead cost	$216,000	$246,400
Number of prescriptions filled	80,000	
Number of patient visits		44,000

The cost-allocation base for overhead in the pharmacy is number of prescriptions filled; in medical records it is number of patient visits.

In June 20X0, Zack Pierce paid one visit to the clinic and had five prescriptions filled at the pharmacy.

1. Compute departmental overhead rates for the two departments.
2. Compute the overhead costs applied to the patient Zack Pierce in June 20X0.

3. At the end of 20X0, actual overhead costs were as follows:

Pharmacy	$240,000
Medical records	$305,000

The pharmacy filled 82,000 prescriptions, and the clinic had 65,000 patient visits during 20X0. Compute the overapplied or underapplied overhead in each department.

13-B3 Comparison of Variable Costing and Absorption Costing
Consider the following information pertaining to a year's operations of Hartford Manufacturing:

Units sold	1,600
Units produced	2,300
Direct labor	$4,400
Direct materials used	3,900
Fixed manufacturing overhead	3,000
Variable manufacturing overhead	400
Selling and administrative expenses (all fixed)	850
Beginning inventories	0
Contribution margin	5,500
Direct-material inventory, end	850

There are no work-in-process inventories.

1. What is the ending finished-goods inventory cost under absorption costing?
2. What is the ending finished-goods inventory cost under variable costing?

13-B4 Extension of Chapter Illustration
Reconsider Exhibits 13-3 and 13-4, pages 542 and 543. Suppose that in 20X1 production was 15,500 computers instead of 14,000 computers, and sales were 15,000 computers. Also assume that the net variances for all variable manufacturing costs were $18,000, unfavorable. Also assume that actual fixed manufacturing costs were $1,560,000.

1. Prepare income statements for 20X1 under variable costing and under absorption costing. Use a format similar to Exhibits 13-8 and 13-9, on page 551.
2. Explain why operating income was different under variable costing and absorption costing. Show your calculations.

Additional Assignment Material   MyAccountingLab

QUESTIONS

13-1 Suppose a company uses machine hours as a cost-allocation base for factory overhead. How does the company compute a budgeted overhead application rate? How does it compute the amounts of factory overhead applied to a particular job?

13-2 "Each department must choose one cost-allocation base to be used for cost application." Do you agree? Explain.

13-3 "Sometimes direct-labor cost is the best cost-allocation base for overhead application even if wage rates vary within a department." Do you agree? Explain.

13-4 Identify four cost-allocation bases that a manufacturing company might use to apply factory overhead costs to jobs.

13-5 Is the comparison of actual overhead costs to budgeted overhead costs part of the product-costing process or part of the control process? Explain.

13-6 What are some reasons for differences between the amounts of incurred and applied overhead?

13-7 "Under actual overhead application, unit costs soar as volume increases, and vice versa." Do you agree? Explain.

13-8 Define *normal costing*.

13-9 What is the best theoretical method of allocating underapplied or overapplied overhead, assuming that the objective is to obtain as accurate a cost application as possible?

13-10 There are two different methods for computing proration. Compare the two approaches.

13-11 Compare variable and absorption costing regarding the treatment of fixed manufacturing costs.

13-12 Compare variable and absorption costing regarding the treatment of production-volume variance.

13-13 In the United States, more than half of the major companies use variable costing for at least some internal-reporting purposes. These companies must make adjustments to these reports for external-reporting purposes. Explain.

13-14 "With variable costing, only direct materials and direct labor are inventoried." Do you agree? Why?

13-15 "Absorption costing regards more categories of costs as product costs." Explain. Be specific.

13-16 "An increasing number of companies are using variable costing in their corporate annual reports." Do you agree? Explain.

13-17 Why is variable costing used only for internal reporting and not for external financial reporting or tax purposes?

13-18 "Variable costing is consistent with cost-volume-profit analysis." Explain.

13-19 Compare the contribution margin with the gross margin.

13-20 How is fixed overhead applied to products?

13-21 Name the three ways that an absorption-costing format differs from a variable-costing format.

13-22 "The flexible budget for budgeting and control differs from the costs applied for product costing." What type of cost is being described? Explain.

13-23 "In a standard absorption-costing system, the amount of fixed manufacturing overhead applied to the products rarely equals the budgeted fixed manufacturing overhead." Do you agree? Explain.

13-24 "The dollar amount of the production-volume variance depends on what expected volume of production was chosen to determine the fixed-overhead rate." Explain.

13-25 Why is there no production-volume variance for direct labor?

13-26 "An unfavorable production-volume variance means that fixed manufacturing costs have not been well controlled." Do you agree? Explain.

13-27 "The fixed cost per unit is directly affected by the expected volume selected as the denominator." Do you agree? Explain.

13-28 "Absorption-costing income exceeds variable-costing income when the number of units sold exceeds the number of units produced." Do you agree? Explain.

13-29 Suppose a manager is paid a bonus only if standard absorption-costing operating income exceeds the budget. If operating income through November is slightly below budget, what might the manager do in December to increase his or her chance of getting the bonus?

13-30 Why are companies with small levels of inventory generally unconcerned with the choice of variable or absorption costing?

13-31 "Overhead variances arise only with absorption-costing systems." Do you agree? Explain.

CRITICAL THINKING EXERCISES

13-32 Relationship Between Cost-Allocation Bases and Factory Overhead
"There should be a strong relationship between the factory overhead incurred and the cost-allocation base chosen for its application." Why?

13-33 Cost Application in Service Firms
"Service firms trace only direct-labor costs to jobs. All other costs are applied as a percentage of direct-labor cost." Do you agree? Explain.

13-34 Accounting for Fixed Costs
Applying fixed costs to products seems to cause all kinds of problems. Why do companies continue to use accounting systems that assign fixed costs to products on a per unit basis?

13-35 Marketing Decisions and Absorption Costing
Product pricing and promotion decisions should usually be based on their effect on contribution margin, not on gross margin. Explain how using an absorption costing format for the income statement can provide misleading information on the effect of pricing and promotion decisions.

13-36 Evaluating Production Using the Production-Volume Variance
The sales-volume variance (see Chapter 8) highlights the effect on income of sales exceeding or falling short of sales targets. Does the production-volume variance provide parallel information for evaluating the effect of exceeding or falling short of production targets? Explain.

13-37 Absorption Costing and the Value Chain
Many costs on a product's value chain, such as R&D and product design costs, are considered period costs and are not assigned to units of product. An absorption-costing system could be expanded to apply such costs to the products. What would be the advantages and disadvantages of doing so? Would this help managers make better decisions?

EXERCISES

13-38 Discovery of Unknowns

The Monachino Manufacturing Company has the following budgeted overhead cost and other data for its machining department for the month of December:

Budgeted Data:	
Indirect labor and supplies	$69,000
Factory rent	$22,000
Supervision	$88,000
Depreciation on equipment	$21,000
Cost-allocation base for overhead application	Machine hours
Budgeted overhead application rate	$4 per machine hour
Other Data:	
Actual machine hours during December	62,000
Actual overhead cost incurred during December	$260,000

Compute the total budgeted machine hours, total applied overhead cost, and indicate how any difference between the actual overhead cost incurred and applied overhead would be treated on Monachino's income statement for the month of December.

13-39 Discovery of Unknowns

The Lawson Manufacturing Company has the following budgeted overhead cost and other data for its assembly department for the month of April:

Budgeted Data:	
Indirect labor and supplies	$170,000
Factory rent	$ 52,000
Supervision	$ 67,000
Depreciation on equipment	$216,000
Cost-allocation base for overhead application	Direct-labor hours
Total budgeted direct-labor hours	50,000
Other Data:	
Total applied overhead costs for April	$616,100
Actual overhead cost incurred during April	$577,000

Compute the budgeted factory overhead rate, actual direct-labor hours, and indicate how the difference between the actual overhead cost incurred and applied overhead would be treated on Lawson's income statement for the month of April.

13-40 Relationship Among Overhead Items

Fill in the unknowns:

	Case 1	Case 2
a. Budgeted factory overhead	$646,000	$415,000
b. Cost-allocation base, budgeted direct-labor cost	425,000	?
c. Budgeted factory-overhead rate	?	125%
d. Direct-labor cost incurred	555,000	?
e. Factory overhead incurred	850,000	420,000
f. Factory overhead applied	?	?
g. Underapplied (overapplied) factory overhead	?	30,000

13-41 Underapplied and Overapplied Overhead

San Antonio Welding Company applies factory overhead at a rate of $8.20 per direct-labor hour. Selected data for 20X0 operations are as follows (in thousands):

	Case 1	Case 2
Direct-labor hours	25	35
Direct-labor cost	$224	$250
Indirect-labor cost	29	43
Sales commissions	22	10
Depreciation, manufacturing equipment	16	33
Direct-materials cost	228	247
Factory fuel costs	36	49
Depreciation, finished-goods warehouse	8	19
Cost of goods sold	415	505
All other factory costs	137	207

Compute for both cases

1. factory overhead applied.
2. total factory overhead incurred.
3. amount of underapplied or overapplied factory overhead.

13-42 Disposition of Year-End Underapplied Overhead

Tammy's Cosmetics uses a normal costing system and has the following balances at the end of its first year's operations.

WIP inventory	$231,000
Finished-goods inventory	198,000
Cost of goods sold	396,000
Actual factory overhead	416,000
Factory overhead applied	456,000

Compute cost of goods sold for two different ways to dispose of the year-end overhead balances. By how much would gross profit differ?

13-43 Simple Comparison of Variable and Absorption Costing

Kerwin Company began business on January 1, 20X1, with assets of $153,000 cash and equities of $153,000 capital stock. In 20X1, it manufactured some inventory at a cost of $56,000 cash, including $19,000 for factory rent and other fixed factory overhead. In 20X2, it manufactured nothing and sold half of its inventory for $44,000 cash. In 20X3 it manufactured nothing and sold the remaining half for another $44,000 cash. It had no fixed expenses in 20X2 or 20X3.

There are no other transactions of any kind. Ignore income taxes.

Prepare an ending balance sheet plus an income statement for 20X1, 20X2, and 20X3 under (1) absorption costing and (2) variable costing (direct costing). Explain the differences in net income between absorption and variable costing.

13-44 Comparisons over Four Years

The Garrard Corporation began business on January 1, 20X0, to produce and sell a single product. Reported operating income figures under both absorption and variable costing for the first 4 years of operation are as follows:

Year	Absorption Costing	Variable Costing
20X0	$75,000	$70,000
20X1	65,000	65,000
20X2	60,000	45,000
20X3	40,000	60,000

Standard production costs per unit, sales prices, application (absorption) rates, and expected volume levels were the same in each year. There were no flexible-budget variances for any type of cost. All nonmanufacturing expenses were fixed, and there were no nonmanufacturing cost variances in any year.

1. In what year(s) did "units produced" equal "units sold"?
2. In what year(s) did "units produced" exceed "units sold"?
3. What is the dollar amount of the December 31, 20X3, finished-goods inventory? (Give absorption-costing value.)
4. What is the difference between "units produced" and "units sold" in 20X3 if you know that the absorption-costing fixed-manufacturing overhead application rate is $4 per unit? (Give answer in units.)

13-45 Variable and Absorption Costing

Kwan Manufacturing Company data for 20X0 follow:

Sales: 11,000 units at $19 each	
Actual production	15,500 units
Expected volume of production	15,000 units
Manufacturing costs incurred	
Variable	$124,000
Fixed	54,000
Nonmanufacturing costs incurred	
Variable	$ 11,000
Fixed	17,800

1. Determine operating income for 20X0, assuming the firm uses the variable-costing approach to product costing. (Do not prepare a statement.)
2. Assume that there is no January 1, 20X0, inventory; no variances are allocated to inventory; and the firm uses a "full absorption" approach to product costing. Compute (a) the cost assigned to December 31, 20X0, inventory, and (b) operating income for the year ended December 31, 20X0. (Do not prepare a statement.)

13-46 Computation of Production-Volume Variance

Kagawa Manufacturing Company budgeted its 20X0 variable overhead at ¥13,800,000 and its fixed overhead at ¥24,192,000. Expected 20X0 volume was 5,600 units. Actual costs for production of 5,700 units during 20X0 were as follows:

Variable overhead	¥14,400,000
Fixed overhead	27,250,000
Total overhead	¥41,650,000

Compute the production-volume variance. Be sure to label it favorable or unfavorable.

13-47 Reconciliation of Variable-Costing and Absorption-Costing Operating Income

Blackstone Tools produced 12,000 electric drills during 20X0. Expected production was only 10,500 drills. The company's fixed-overhead rate is $7 per drill. Absorption-costing operating income for the year is $18,000, based on sales of 11,000 drills.

1. Compute the following:
   a. Budgeted fixed overhead
   b. Production-volume variance
   c. Variable-costing operating income
2. Reconcile absorption-costing operating income and variable-costing operating income. Include the amount of the difference between the two and an explanation for the difference.

13-48 Overhead Variances

Study Appendix 13. Consider the following data for the Hamlin Company:

	Factory Overhead	
	Fixed	**Variable**
Actual incurred	$12,800	$14,400
Budget for standard hours allowed for output achieved	12,000	10,200
Applied	11,800	10,200
Budget for actual hours of input	12,000	10,800

From the preceding information, fill in the following blanks. Be sure to mark your variances F for favorable and U for unfavorable.

a. Flexible-budget variance $_____ Fixed $_____
                                    Variable $_____

b. Production-volume variance $_____ Fixed $_____
                                    Variable $_____

c. Spending variance $_____ Fixed $_____
                              Variable $_____

d. Efficiency variance $_____ Fixed $_____
                                Variable $_____

13-49 Variances

Study Appendix 13. Consider the following data regarding factory overhead:

	Variable	Fixed
Budget for actual hours of input	$45,000	$70,000
Applied	41,000	64,800
Budget for standard hours allowed for actual output achieved	?	?
Actual incurred	48,100	66,500

Using the preceding data, fill in the following blanks with the variance amounts. Use F for favorable or U for unfavorable for each variance.

	Total Overhead	Variable	Fixed
1. Spending Variance	_____	_____	_____
2. Efficiency Variance	_____	_____	_____
3. Production-Volume Variance	_____	_____	_____
4. Flexible-budget variance	_____	_____	_____
5. Underapplied Overhead	_____	_____	_____

PROBLEMS

13-50 Choice of Cost-Allocation Base at Enriquez Machine Parts Company

Refer to the chapter discussion of Enriquez Machine Parts Company beginning on page 534. Suppose Enriquez decided to use only one overhead cost pool for both departments with machine hours as the single cost-allocation base.

1. Compute the budgeted overhead application rate for the factory using the budgeted data on page 534.
2. If Enriquez used 70,000 machine hours during 20X0, what was the total factory overhead applied to products?
3. The applied factory overhead based on separate application rates for the machining and assembly departments was $375,000. Explain why this amount is different than the applied amount from requirement 2.

13-51 Choice of Cost-Allocation Base at Enriquez Machine Parts Company

Refer to the chapter discussion of Enriquez Machine Parts Company beginning on page 534. Suppose Enriquez decided to use only one overhead cost pool for both departments with direct labor cost as the single cost-allocation base.

1. Compute the budgeted overhead application rate for the factory using the budgeted data on page 534.
2. If Enriquez incurred $190,000 of direct labor cost during 20X0, what was the total factory overhead applied to products?
3. The applied factory overhead based on separate application rates for the machining and assembly departments was $375,000. Explain why this amount is different than the applied amount from requirement 2.

13-52 Choice of Cost-Allocation Bases in Accounting Firm

Brenda McCoy, the managing partner of McCoy, Brennan, and Cable, a public accounting firm, is considering the desirability of tracing more costs to jobs than just direct labor. In this way, the firm will be able to justify billings to clients.

Last year's costs were as follows:

Direct-professional labor	$ 5,000,000
Overhead	10,000,000
Total costs	$15,000,000

The following costs were included in overhead:

Computer time	$ 750,000
Secretarial cost	700,000
Photocopying	250,000
Fringe benefits to direct labor	800,000
Phone call time with clients (estimated but not tabulated)	500,000
Total	$3,000,000

The firm's data processing techniques now make it feasible to document and trace these costs to individual jobs.

As an experiment, in December Brenda McCoy arranged to trace these costs to six audit engagements. Two job records showed the following:

	Engagement	
	Eagledale Company	First Valley Bank
Direct-professional labor	$15,000	$15,000
Fringe benefits to direct labor	3,000	3,000
Phone call time with clients	1,500	500
Computer time	3,000	700
Secretarial costs	2,000	1,500
Photocopying	500	300
Total direct costs	$25,000	$21,000

1. Compute the overhead application rate based on last year's costs.
2. Suppose last year's costs were reclassified so that $3 million would be regarded as direct costs instead of overhead. Compute the overhead application rate as a percentage of direct labor and as a percentage of total direct costs.
3. Using the three rates computed in numbers 1 and 2, compute the total costs of engagements for Eagledale Company and First Valley Bank.
4. Suppose that client billing was based on a 30% markup of total job costs. Compute the billings that would be forthcoming in number 3.
5. Which method of costing and overhead application do you favor? Explain.

13-53 Allocated Costs and Public Services

The Napa County (California) grand jury charged the city of St. Helena with overbilling customers for water and sewer services. The city allocated "administrative overhead" to the water and sewer department's budget. These costs were then added to the "jobs"—that is, to the accounts of the customers of the water and sewer department. The grand jury called the $76,581.20 allocated to the department in the last year "merely a ruse" to generate funds to cover city expenses that were unrelated to water and sewer services, resulting in "bloated water bills" for local customers.

The city finance director explained that the overhead allocation was the way in which the city bills the water and sewer department for time that other departments spend on water and sewer issues. Mayor John Brown concluded that "it was very clear to me that they [the grand jury] didn't know what they were talking about."

1. Was the overhead charge to the water and sewer department a legitimate cost to be covered by water and sewer bills? Explain your reasoning to the citizens of St. Helena.
2. Assume that at least part of the overhead charge is a legitimate cost of the water and sewer department. Suggest possible changes in the accounting system that would provide a more accurate measure of the cost of services provided to the water and sewer department by other departments.

13-54 Overhead Accounting for Control and for Product Costing

The pickle department of a major food manufacturer has an overhead rate of $5 per direct-labor hour, based on expected variable overhead of $150,000 per year, expected fixed overhead of $350,000 per year, and expected direct-labor hours of 100,000 per year.

Data for the year's operations follow:

	Direct-Labor Hours Used	Overhead Costs Incurred*
First 6 months	52,000	$264,000
Last 6 months	42,000	239,000

*Fixed costs incurred were exactly equal to budgeted amounts throughout the year.

1. What is the underapplied or overapplied overhead for each 6-month period? Label your answer as underapplied or overapplied.
2. Explain briefly (no more than 50 words for each part) the probable causes for the underapplied or overapplied overhead. Focus on variable and fixed costs separately. Give the exact figures attributable to the causes you cite.

13-55 Comparison of Variable Costing and Absorption Costing

Simple numbers are used in this problem to highlight the concepts covered in the chapter.

Assume that the Perth Woolen Company produces a rug that sells for $20. Perth uses a standard cost system. Total standard variable costs of production are $8 per rug, fixed manufacturing costs are $150,000 per year, and selling and administrative expenses are $30,000 per year, all fixed. Expected production volume is 25,000 rugs per year.

1. For each of the following nine combinations of actual sales and production (in thousands of units) for 20X0, prepare condensed income statements under variable costing and under absorption costing.

	(1)	(2)	(3)	(4)	(5)	(6)	(7)	(8)	(9)
Sales units	15	20	25	20	25	30	25	30	35
Production units	20	20	20	25	25	25	30	30	30

Use the following formats:

Variable Costing		Absorption Costing	
Revenue	$ aa	Revenue	$ aa
Cost of goods sold	(bb)	Cost of goods sold	(uu)
Contribution margin	$ cc	Gross profit at standard	$ vv
Fixed manufacturing costs	(dd)	Favorable (unfavorable)	
Fixed selling and administrative expenses	(ee)	production-volume variance	ww
		Gross profit at "actual"	$ xx
		Selling and administrative expenses	(yy)
Operating income	$ ff	Operating income	$ zz

2. a. In which of the nine combinations is variable-costing income greater than absorption-costing income? In which is it lower? The same?
   b. In which of the nine combinations is the production-volume variance unfavorable? Favorable?
   c. How much profit is added by selling one more unit under variable costing? Under absorption costing?
   d. How much profit is added by producing one more unit under variable costing? Under absorption costing?
   e. Suppose sales, rather than production, is the critical factor in determining the success of Perth Woolen Company. Which format, variable costing or absorption costing, provides the better measure of performance?

13-56 All-Fixed Costs

The New York Company has built a massive water-desalting factory next to an ocean. The factory is completely automated. It has its own source of power, light, heat, and so on. The salt water costs nothing. All producing and other operating costs are fixed; they do not vary with output because the volume is governed by adjusting a few dials on a control panel. The employees have flat annual salaries.

The desalted water is not sold to household consumers. It has a special taste that appeals to local breweries, distilleries, and soft-drink manufacturers. The price, $.66 per gallon, is expected to remain unchanged for quite some time.

The following are data regarding the first 2 years of operations:

	In Gallons		Costs (All Fixed)	
	Sales	**Production**	**Manufacturing**	**Other**
20X0	1,700,000	3,400,000	$748,000	$225,000
20X1	1,700,000	0	748,000	225,000

Orders can be processed in 4 hours so management decided, in early 20X1, to gear production strictly to sales.

1. Prepare three-column income statements for 20X0, for 20X1, and for the 2 years together using (a) variable costing and (b) absorption costing.
2. What is the break-even point under (a) variable costing and (b) absorption costing?
3. What inventory costs would be carried on the balance sheets on December 31, 20X0 and 20X1, under each method?
4. Comment on your answers in numbers 1 and 2. Which costing method appears more useful?

13-57 Semifixed Costs

The Plymouth Company differs from the New York Company (described in Problem 13-56) in only one respect: It has both variable and fixed manufacturing costs. Its variable costs are $.14 per gallon, and its fixed manufacturing costs are $510,000 per year.

1. Using the same data as in the preceding problem, except for the change in production-cost behavior, prepare three-column income statements for 20X0, for 20X1, and for the 2 years together using (a) variable costing and (b) absorption costing.
2. What inventory costs would be carried on the balance sheets on December 31, 20X0 and 20X1, under each method?

13-58 Absorption and Variable Costing

The Twin Lakes Company had the following actual data for 20X0 and 20X1:

	20X0	20X1
Units of finished goods		
Opening inventory	—	3,600
Production	17,200	13,600
Sales	13,600	15,600
Ending inventory	3,600	1,600

The basic production data at standard unit costs for the 2 years were as follows:

Direct materials	$16
Direct labor	20
Variable factory overhead	4
Standard variable costs per unit	$40

Fixed factory overhead was budgeted at $146,000 per year. The expected volume of production was 14,600 units so the fixed overhead rate was $146,000 ÷ 14,600 = $10 per unit.

Budgeted sales price was $79 per unit. Selling and administrative expenses were budgeted at variable, $11 per unit sold, and fixed, $83,000 per year.

Assume that there were absolutely no variances from any standard variable costs or budgeted selling prices or budgeted fixed costs in 20X0.

There were no beginning or ending inventories of work in process.

1. For 20X0, prepare income statements based on standard variable (direct) costing and standard absorption costing. (The next problem deals with 20X1.)
2. Explain why operating income differs between variable costing and absorption costing. Be specific.

13-59 Absorption and Variable Costing

Assume the same facts as in the preceding problem. In addition, consider the following actual data for 20X1:

Direct materials	$ 262,000
Direct labor	171,000
Variable factory overhead	38,000
Fixed factory overhead	143,500
Selling and administrative costs	
Variable	165,100
Fixed	83,000
Sales	1,252,400

1. For 20X1, prepare income statements based on standard variable (direct) costing and standard absorption costing.
2. Explain why operating income differs between variable costing and absorption costing. Be specific.

13-60 Fundamentals of Overhead Variances

The Durant Company is installing an absorption standard-cost system and a flexible-overhead budget. Standard costs have recently been developed for its only product and are as follows:

Direct materials, 3 pounds at $20	$60
Direct labor, 2 hours at $14	28
Variable overhead, 2 hours at $5	10
Fixed overhead	?
Standard cost per unit of finished product	$?

Expected production activity is expressed as 7,500 standard direct-labor hours per month. Fixed overhead is expected to be $60,000 per month. The predetermined fixed-overhead rate for product costing is not changed from month to month.

1. Calculate the proper fixed-overhead rate per standard direct-labor hour and per unit.
2. Graph the following for expected production activity from 0 to 10,000 hours:
   a. Budgeted variable overhead
   b. Variable overhead applied to product
3. Graph the following for expected production activity from 0 to 10,000 hours:
   a. Budgeted fixed overhead
   b. Fixed overhead applied to product

4. Assume that 6,000 standard direct-labor hours are allowed for the output achieved during a given month. Actual variable overhead of $31,000 was incurred; actual fixed overhead amounted to $62,000. Calculate the following:
   a. Fixed-overhead flexible-budget variance
   b. Fixed-overhead production-volume variance
   c. Variable-overhead flexible-budget variance
5. Assume that 7,800 standard direct-labor hours are allowed for the output achieved during a given month. Actual overhead incurred amounted to $99,700, $62,000 of which was fixed. Calculate the following:
   a. Fixed-overhead flexible-budget variance
   b. Fixed-overhead production-volume variance
   c. Variable-overhead flexible-budget variance

13-61 Production-Volume Variance at L.A. Darling Company

Review the Chapter 12 opening vignette on L.A. Darling Company (page 507). L.A. Darling receives about $6 billion of revenue each year from designing, manufacturing, and installing store fixtures in retail stores. Accounting for fixed manufacturing overhead is a challenge for the company. Suppose a manufacturing division of the company has the following budgeted costs for production of 800,000 shelving units in 2012:

Direct materials	$160,000,000
Direct labor	24,000,000
Other variable manufacturing costs	20,000,000
Fixed manufacturing costs	100,000,000
Total manufacturing cost	$304,000,000

During 2012, this division of L.A. Darling produced 850,000 of the shelving units and sold 820,000 of them for $450 million. Assume that L.A. Darling does not allocate selling or administrative costs to the individual products.

1. Compute the following budgeted unit costs for 2012:

Variable manufacturing costs per unit	?
Fixed manufacturing costs per unit	?
Total manufacturing costs per unit	?

2. Compute the production-volume variance for 2012. Be sure to label it favorable or unfavorable.
3. Compute the 2012 profit from the production and sales of the shelving using absorption costing. Ignore selling and administrative costs.
4. Compute the 2012 profit from the production and sales of the shelving using variable costing. Ignore selling and administrative costs.
5. Which measure of profit, absorption-costing profit or variable-costing profit, is a better measure of performance during 2012? Explain.

13-62 Fixed Overhead and Practical Capacity

The expected activity of the paper-making plant of Conroy Paper Company was 58,400 machine hours per month. Practical capacity was 73,000 machine hours per month. The standard machine hours allowed for the actual output achieved in January were 61,000. The budgeted fixed-factory-overhead items were as follows:

Depreciation, equipment	$339,000
Depreciation, factory building	66,000
Supervision	51,000
Indirect labor	232,000
Insurance	20,000
Property taxes	22,000
Total	$730,000

Because of unanticipated scheduling difficulties and the need for more indirect labor, the actual fixed factory overhead was $757,000.

1. Using practical capacity as the base for applying fixed factory overhead, prepare a summary analysis of fixed-overhead variances for January.
2. Using expected activity as the base for applying fixed factory overhead, prepare a summary analysis of fixed-overhead variances for January.
3. Explain why some of your variances in numbers 1 and 2 are the same and why some differ.

13-63 Selection of Expected Volume

Heidi Brooke is a consultant to Colorado Paper Products Company. She is helping one of the company's divisions to install a standard cost system for 20X0. For product-costing purposes, the system must apply fixed factory costs to products manufactured. She has decided that the fixed-overhead rate should be based on machine hours, but she is uncertain about the appropriate volume to use in the denominator. Colorado Paper has grown rapidly; the division has added production capacity approximately every 4 years. The last addition was completed in early 20X0, and the total capacity is now 3,000,000 machine hours per year. Brooke predicts the following operating levels (in machine hours) through 20X4:

Year	Capacity Used
20X0	2,200,000 hours
20X1	2,500,000 hours
20X2	2,850,000 hours
20X3	3,000,000 hours
20X4	3,100,000 hours

The current plan is to add another 500,000 machine hours of capacity in 20X4.

Brooke has identified three alternatives for the application base:
a. Predicted volume for the year in question
b. Average volume over the 4 years of the current production setup
c. Practical (or full) capacity

1. Suppose annual fixed factory overhead is expected to be $36,000,000 through 20X3. For simplicity, assume no inflation. Calculate the fixed-overhead rates (to the nearest cent) for 20X1, 20X2, and 20X3, using each of the three alternative application bases.
2. Provide a brief description of the effect of using each method of computing the application base.
3. Which method do you prefer? Why?

13-64 Analysis of Operating Results

Leeds Tool Company produces and sells a variety of machine-tooled products. The company employs a standard cost accounting system for record-keeping purposes.

At the beginning of 20X0, the president of Leeds Tool presented the budget to the company's board of directors. The board accepted a target 20X0 profit of £16,800 and agreed to pay the president a bonus if profits exceeded the target. The president has been confident that the year's profit would exceed the budget target, since the monthly sales reports that he has been receiving have shown that sales for the year will exceed budget by 10%. The president is both disturbed and confused when the controller presents an adjusted forecast as of November 30, 20X0, indicating that profit will be 14% under budget:

Leeds Tool Company		
Forecasts of Operating Results		
		Forecasts as of
	1/1/X0	**11/30/X0**
Sales	£156,000	£171,600
Cost of sales at standard	108,000*	118,800
Gross margin at standard	£ 48,000	£ 52,800
Over- (under-) absorbed fixed manufacturing overhead	0	(6,000)
Actual gross margin	£ 48,000	£ 46,800
Selling expenses	£ 11,200	£ 12,320
Administrative expenses	20,000	20,000
Total operating expenses	£ 31,200	£ 32,320
Earnings before tax	£ 16,800	£ 14,480

*Includes fixed manufacturing overhead of £30,000.

There have been no sales price changes or product-mix shifts since the January 1, 20X0, forecast. The only cost variance on the income statement is the underapplied manufacturing overhead. This arose because the company produced only 16,000 standard machine hours (budgeted machine hours were 20,000) during 20X0, as a result of a shortage of raw materials while its principal supplier was closed by a strike. Fortunately, Leeds Tool's finished-goods inventory was large enough to fill all sales orders received.

1. Analyze and explain why the profit has declined despite increased sales and good control over costs. Show computations.
2. What plan, if any, could Leeds Tool adopt during December to improve its reported profit at year-end? Explain your answer.
3. Illustrate and explain how Leeds Tool could adopt an alternative internal cost-reporting procedure that would avoid the confusing effect of the present procedure. Show the revised forecasts under your alternative.
4. Would the alternative procedure described in number 3 be acceptable to the board of directors for financial-reporting purposes? Explain.

13-65 Standard Absorption and Standard Variable Costing

Schlosser Company has the following results for a certain year. All variances are written off as additions to (or deductions from) the standard cost of goods sold. Find the unknowns, designated by letters.

Sales: 150,000 units, at $20	$3,000,000
Net variance for standard variable manufacturing costs	$ 33,000 unfavorable
Variable standard cost of goods manufactured	$ 11 per unit
Variable selling and administrative expenses	$ 3 per unit
Fixed selling and administrative expenses	$ 650,000
Fixed manufacturing overhead	$ 165,000
Maximum capacity per year	190,000 units
Expected production volume for year	150,000 units
Beginning inventory of finished goods	15,000 units
Ending inventory of finished goods	10,000 units
Beginning inventory: Variable-costing basis	a
Contribution margin	b
Operating income: Variable-costing basis	c
Beginning inventory: Absorption-costing basis	d
Gross margin	e
Operating income: Absorption-costing basis	f

13-66 Disposition of Variances

In January 20X0, Georgia Garden Equipment Company started a division for making grass clippers. Management hoped that these grass clippers were significantly better than most competitors in the market. During 20X0, it produced 97,500 grass clippers. Financial results were as follows:

- Sales: 78,000 units at $20
- Direct labor at standard: 97,500 × $9 = $877,500
- Direct-labor variances: $33,000 U
- Direct materials at standard: 97,500 × $4 = $390,000
- Direct-material variances: $11,500 U
- Overhead incurred at standard: 97,500 × $2 = $195,000
- Overhead variances: $2,500 F

Georgia uses an absorption-costing system and allows divisions to choose one of two methods of accounting for variances:

a. Direct charge to income
b. Proration to the production of the period; method b requires variances to be spread equally over the units produced during the period

1. Calculate the division's operating income (a) using method a and (b) using method b. Assume no selling and administrative expenses.
2. Calculate ending inventory value (a) using method a and (b) using method b. Note that there was no beginning inventory.
3. What is the major argument in support of each method?

13-67 Straightforward Problem on Standard Cost System

Study Appendix 13. The Winnipeg Chemical Company uses flexible budgets and a standard cost system.

- Direct-labor costs incurred, 12,000 hours, $150,000
- Variable-overhead costs incurred, $37,000
- Fixed-overhead flexible-budget variance, $1,600, favorable
- Finished units produced, 1,800
- Fixed-overhead costs incurred, $38,000
- Variable overhead applied at $3 per hour
- Standard direct-labor cost, $13 per hour
- Denominator production per month, 2,000 units
- Standard direct-labor hours per finished unit, 6

Prepare an analysis of all variances (similar to Exhibit 13-10, p. 553).

13-68 Straightforward Problem on Standard Cost System

Study Appendix 13. The München Company uses a standard cost system. The month's data regarding its single product follow (where € is the symbol for the euro, the currency of most countries of the European Union):

- Fixed-overhead costs incurred, €6,300
- Variable overhead applied at €11 per hour
- Standard direct-labor cost, €44 per hour
- Denominator production per month, 220 units
- Standard direct-labor hours per finished unit, 5
- Direct-labor costs incurred, 1,000 hours, €42,500
- Variable-overhead costs incurred, €10,400
- Fixed-overhead flexible-budget variance, €300, favorable
- Finished units produced, 180

Prepare an analysis of all variances (similar to Exhibit 13-10, p. 553).

CASES

13-69 Multiple Overhead Rates and Activity-Based Costing

A division of **Hewlett-Packard** assembles and tests printed circuit (PC) boards. The division has many different products. Some are high volume; others are low volume. For years, manufacturing overhead was applied to products using a single overhead rate based on direct-labor dollars. However, direct labor has shrunk to 6% of total manufacturing costs.

Managers decided to refine the division's product-costing system. Abolishing the direct-labor category, they included all manufacturing labor as a part of factory overhead. They also identified several activities and the appropriate cost-allocation base for each. The cost-allocation base for the first activity, the start station, was the number of raw PC boards. The application rate was computed as follows:

$$\text{application rate for start station activity} = \frac{\text{budgeted total factory overhead at the activity}}{\text{budgeted raw PC boards for the year}}$$

$$= \frac{\$150,000}{125,000}$$

$$= \$1.20$$

Each time a raw PC board passes through the start station activity, $1.20 is added to the cost of the board. The product cost is the sum of costs directly traced to the board plus the indirect costs (factory overhead) accumulated at each of the manufacturing activities undergone.

Using assumed numbers, consider the following data regarding PC board 37:

Direct materials	$55.00
Factory overhead applied	?
Total manufacturing product cost	?

The activities involved in the production of PC board 37 and the related cost-allocation bases were as follows:

Activity	Cost-Allocation Base	Factory-Overhead Costs Applied for Each Activity
1. Start station	Number of raw PC boards	$1 \times \$1.20 = \$1.20$
2. Axial insertion	Number of axial insertions	$39 \times\ \ .07 =\ \ \ ?$
3. Dip insertion	Number of dip insertions	$? \times\ \ .20 =\ \ 5.60$
4. Manual insertion	Number of manual insertions	$15 \times\ \ \ ? =\ \ 6.00$
5. Wave solder	Number of boards soldered	$1 \times\ 3.20 =\ \ 3.20$
6. Backload	Number of backload insertions	$8 \times\ \ .60 =\ \ 4.80$
7. Test	Standard time board is in test activity	$.15 \times 80.00 =\ \ \ ?$
8. Defect analysis	Standard time for defect analysis and repair	$.05 \times\ \ \ ? =\ \underline{\ 4.50}$
Total		$\underline{\underline{\$\ \ ?}}$

1. Fill in the numbers where there are question marks.
2. How is direct labor identified with products under this product-costing system?
3. Why would managers favor this multiple-overhead rate, ABC system instead of the older system?

13-70 Inventory Measures, Production Scheduling, and Evaluating Divisional Performance

The Calais Company stresses competition between the heads of its various divisions, and it rewards stellar performance with year-end bonuses that vary between 5% and 10% of division net operating income (before considering the bonus or income taxes). The divisional managers have great discretion in setting production schedules.

The Brittany division produces and sells a product for which there is a long-standing demand but which can have marked seasonal and year-to-year fluctuations. On November 30, 20X0, Veronique Giraud, the Brittany division manager, is preparing a production schedule for December. The following data are available for January 1 through November 30 (€ is the symbol for euro, the currency for most countries of the European Union):

Beginning inventory, January 1, in units	10,000
Sales price, per unit	€ 400
Total fixed costs incurred for manufacturing	€ 9,350,000
Total fixed costs: Other (not inventoriable)	€10,200,000
Total variable costs for manufacturing	€18,150,000
Total other variable costs (fluctuate with units sold)	€ 4,000,000
Units produced	110,000
Units sold	100,000
Variances	None

Production in October and November was 10,000 units each month. Practical capacity is 12,000 units per month. Maximum available storage space for inventory is 25,000 units. The sales outlook for December–February is 6,000 units monthly. To retain a core of key employees, monthly production cannot be scheduled at less than 4,000 units without special permission from the president. Inventory is never to be less than 10,000 units.

The denominator used for applying fixed factory overhead is regarded as 120,000 units annually. The company uses a standard absorption-costing system. All variances are disposed of at year-end as an adjustment to standard cost of goods sold.

1. Given the restrictions as stated, and assuming that Giraud wants to maximize the company's net income for 20X0, answer the following:
   a. How many units should be scheduled for production in December?
   b. What net operating income will be reported in 20X0 as a whole, assuming that the implied cost-behavior patterns will continue in December as they did throughout the year to date? Show your computations.
   c. If December production is scheduled at 4,000 units, what would reported net income be?
2. Assume that standard variable costing is used rather than standard absorption costing.
   a. What would net income for 20X0 be, assuming that the December production schedule is the one in part a of number 1?
   b. What would net income for 20X0 be, assuming that December production was 4,000 units?
   c. Reconcile the net incomes in this requirement with those in number 1.

3. From the viewpoint of the long-run interests of the company as a whole, what production schedule should the division manager set? Explain fully. Include in your explanation a comparison of the motivating influence of absorption and variable costing in this situation.

4. Assume standard absorption costing. Giraud wants to maximize her after-income tax performance over the long run. Given the data at the beginning of the problem, assume that income tax rates will be halved in 20X1. Assume also that year-end write-offs of variances are acceptable for income tax purposes. How many units should be scheduled for production in December? Why?

13-71 Performance Evaluation

A division of Iowa/Illinois Corn Company produces seed corn for farmers throughout the Midwest. Jens Jensen became president in 20X0. He is concerned with the ability of his division manager to control costs. To aid his evaluation, Jensen set up a standard cost system.

Standard costs were based on 20X0 costs in several categories. Each 20X0 cost was divided by 1,520,000 cwt—the volume of 20X0 production—to determine a standard for 20X1 (cwt means hundredweight, or 100 pounds):

	20X0 Cost (thousands)	20X1 Standard (per hundredweight)
Direct materials	$1,824	$1.20
Direct labor	836	.55
Variable overhead	1,596	1.05
Fixed overhead	2,432	1.60
Total	$6,688	$4.40

At the end of 20X1, Jensen compared actual results with the standards he established. Production was 1,360,000 cwt, and variances were as follows:

	Actual	Standard	Variance
Direct materials	$1,802	$1,632	$170 U
Direct labor	735	748	13 F
Variable overhead	1,422	1,428	6 F
Fixed overhead	2,412	2,176	236 U
Total	$6,371	$5,984	$387 U

Jensen was not surprised by the unfavorable variance in direct materials. After all, corn prices in 20X1 averaged 10% above those in 20X0. But he was disturbed by the lack of control of fixed overhead. He called in the production manager and demanded an explanation.

1. Prepare an explanation for the large unfavorable fixed-overhead variance.
2. Discuss the appropriateness of using one year's costs as the next year's standards.

13-72 Converting an Income Statement from Absorption Costing to Variable Costing

Holden Corp. has the following income statement under standard absorption costing:

Sales	$1,000,000
Cost of goods sold:	
Beginning inventory	$ 0
Production	$ 975,000
Ending inventory	$ 225,000
Cost of goods sold:	$ 750,000
Less adjustment for variances	$ 95,000
Adjusted cost of goods sold	$ 655,000
Gross profit	$ 345,000
Selling and administrative expenses	
Variable selling and administrative	$ 30,000
Fixed selling and administrative	$ 170,000
Net income	$ 145,000

During the period Holden produced 130,000 units and sold 100,000 units. There was no beginning or ending WIP inventory. Budgeted fixed factory overhead was $150,000, actual fixed factory overhead was $90,000, and denominator level was 100,000 units. Holden does not prorate variances.

Present a variable costing income statement. Be sure to list the amount of any variance in an adjustment for variances.

13-73 Converting an Income Statement from Variable Costing to Absorption Costing

Moseley Corp. currently uses variable costing in its accounting system, with the following selected results (assume there were no variances):

Contribution margin	$300,000
Variable selling and administrative	$100,000
Fixed selling and administrative	$ 60,000
Net income	$150,000

During the period Moseley produced 160,000 units and sold 80,000 units. Selling price is $10/unit. There was no beginning or ending WIP inventory, and no beginning FG inventory. Moseley is considering a standard absorption costing system. It estimates that if it had used such a system this year, it would have budgeted fixed factory overhead at $100,000, and would have selected a denominator level of 200,000 units. The company also estimates that there would have still been no variances related to direct materials, direct labor, and variable factory overhead.

Present a standard absorption costing income statement with proration. Be sure to present the adjustment for variances amount on the income statement.

NIKE 10-K PROBLEM

13-74 Overhead Costs at Umbro

Read **Nike**'s 10-K Item 1 description of its business. Although Nike does not manufacture the products it sells, its subsidiaries do some manufacturing. For example, Nike's subsidiary, **Umbro**, headquartered in Cheadle, England, manufactures and distributes soccer equipment and clothing.

1. What kinds of sports gear does Umbro make? Consider the Umbro plant that makes soccer clothing. List five variable-cost resources and five fixed-cost resources that are part of the plant's overhead.
2. Suppose that Umbro uses a dedicated production line to make only soccer shoes. What are some resources that are normally part of overhead that would be directly traceable to the soccer-shoe cost object?

EXCEL APPLICATION EXERCISE

13-75 Computing Budgeted Factory Overhead

Goal: Create an Excel spreadsheet to compute budgeted factory overhead rates and apply factory overhead to production. Use the results to answer questions about your findings.

Scenario: Kevin Aeronautics Company has asked you to determine its budgeted factory overhead rates. It would also like you to apply the appropriate factory overhead amounts to actual production and determine any variances. Additional background information for your spreadsheet appears in Fundamental Assignment Material 13-A1. (Ignore data in the Fundamental Assignment Material for product M89.)

When you have completed your spreadsheet, answer the following questions:

1. What was the budgeted factory overhead rate for department A? Department B?
2. What overhead amount was distributed to department A? Was the overhead over- or underapplied? By what amount?
3. What overhead amount was distributed to department B? Was the overhead over- or underapplied? By what amount?

Step-by-Step:
1. Open a new Excel spreadsheet.
2. In column A, create a bold-faced heading that contains the following:
   Row 1: Chapter 13 Decision Guideline
   Row 2: Kevin Aeronautics Company
   Row 3: Overhead Applications Using Budgeted Rates
   Row 4: Today's Date

3. Merge and center the four heading rows across columns A–G.
4. In row 7, create the following column headings:
   Column B: 20X0 Budget
   Column D: 20X0 Actual
   Column F: Variances
5. Merge and center the 20X0 Budget heading across columns B–C.
6. Merge and center the 20X0 Actual heading across columns D–E.
7. Merge and center the Variances heading across columns F–G.
8. In row 8, create the following center-justified column headings:
   Columns B, D, and F: Dept. A
   Columns C, E, and G: Dept. B
9. In column A, create the following row headings:
   Row 9: Factory Overhead
   Row 10: Direct-Labor Hours
   Row 11: Machine Hours
   Skip a row.
   Row 13: Overhead Rate
   Row 14: Distributed Overhead
   Row 15: Over/(Under) Applied

   Note: Recommended column widths: column A = 18, columns B–G = 12.

10. Use data from Fundamental Assignment Material 13-A1 to enter the amounts for the department A and B 20X0 budget predictions and 20X0 actual results.
11. Use the appropriate formulas to calculate the following amounts:

20X0 budgeted overhead rates for depts. A and B	Row 13, columns B and C
20X0 distributed overhead for depts. A and B	Row 14, columns D and E
20X0 over/under applied overhead	Row 15, columns D and E
Flexible budget variances for depts. A and B	Row 9, columns F and G
Activity budget variance for dept. B	Row 10, column G
Activity budget variance for dept. A	Row 11, column F
Total variances for depts. A and B	Row 15, columns F and G

12. Format amounts in rows 10 and 11 as follows:

    Number tab:
Category:	Accounting
Decimal:	0
Symbol:	None

13. Format amounts in rows 9, 14, and 15 as follows:

    Number tab:
Category:	Accounting
Decimal:	0
Symbol:	$

14. Format amounts in row 13 as follows:

    Number tab:
Category:	Accounting
Decimal:	2
Symbol:	$

15. Modify the format of the total variances in row 15, columns F and G to display a top border using the default Line Style.

    Border tab:
Icon:	Top Border

16. Save your work, and print a copy for your files.

    Note: Print your spreadsheet using landscape in order to ensure that all columns appear on one page.

COLLABORATIVE LEARNING EXERCISE

13-76 Accounting for Overhead

Form groups of four to six persons. Each group should identify a cost accountant at a local company to interview. The interviewee could be the top financial officer of a small company, but a division controller or cost analyst might be more appropriate for a large company. The essential factor is that the person chosen understands how overhead costs are allocated to products or services in the company.

Set up an interview with the cost accountant, and explore the following issues. Be prepared with follow-up questions if your question receives a superficial answer. Your goal should be to get as much operational detail as possible about the procedures used for allocating overhead costs at the company. If the company is large, you may want to focus on one department, one product line, or some other subdivision of the company.

The issues to explore are as follows:

1. What types of costs are included in overhead? How large is overhead compared with direct materials and labor costs?
2. What types of overhead cost pools exist? Are there different pools by department? By activity? By cost-allocation base? By fixed or variable cost? Be prepared to explain what you mean by these terms because terminology varies widely.
3. How is overhead applied to final products or services? What cost-allocation bases are used?

After the interview, draw a diagram of the cost application system in as much detail as possible. Be prepared to share this with the entire class, using it to explain the overhead cost application system at the company your group studied.

INTERNET EXERCISE

13-77 Dell

Published income statements use the absorption-costing basis—after all, that is the method that is acceptable for use under GAAP. But the absorption-costing statement might not really provide the information that management needs to make future decisions because it does not separate fixed from variable costs. This exercise focuses on extracting contribution information from published absorption-costing financial statements of Dell Computer. As a manufacturer of computers, Dell has become a well-known, household name.

1. Go to the home page for Dell at www.dell.com. Take a look at one of the computers for home being offered. Once you've arrived at the product page, what type of information do you find about the computer? What information is available about prices? Is it possible that the model could have more than one price? Why or why not?
2. Look at the most recent 10-K report for Dell by following links to Investor Relations, Financial Reporting, and 10-K filings. Go to the section, "Management's Discussion and Analysis of Financial Condition and Results of Operations." What was the total revenue for Dell? What is the change in the average selling price for desktop PCs? Why do you think this change occurred?
3. Look at the most recent Consolidated Statement of Operations. What were the cost of goods sold and the selling, administrative, and engineering expenses for the current year? Refer to the cash flow statement for the current year. How much was the depreciation and amortization for the current year? Assume that $3 billion of operating expense in addition to the depreciation and amortization are all the fixed expenses. Compute the average variable cost of goods sold percentage. Compute the average contribution margin percentage. What would be the break-even sales dollars under this scenario? Does this seem reasonable, given the current operating income reported by the firm?

Job-Order Costing and Process-Costing Systems

LEARNING OBJECTIVES

When you have finished studying this chapter, you should be able to:

1. Distinguish between job-order costing and process costing.

2. Prepare summary journal entries for the typical transactions of a job-order costing system.

3. Use an ABC system in a job-order environment.

4. Show how service organizations use job-order costing.

5. Explain the basic ideas underlying process costing and how they differ from job-order costing.

6. Compute output in terms of equivalent units.

7. Compute costs and prepare journal entries for the principal transactions in a process-costing system.

8. Demonstrate how the presence of beginning inventories affects the computation of unit costs under the weighted-average method.

9. Understand the concept of transferred-in costs in a process-costing system with sequential processes.

10. Use backflush costing with a JIT production system.

▶ **JELLY BELLY**

Here is a trivia question: Name the favorite candy of former President Ronald Reagan, the candy featured in the hit Harry Potter series (with flavors like dirt, grass, and vomit), and the first candy to travel into outer space. The answer is jelly beans. And one of the most famous brands is Jelly Belly Candy. As noted by the authors of this text, this candy often shows up on the desks of students taking long, difficult management-accounting exams.

Jelly Belly is the world's number one gourmet jelly bean. The Jelly Belly Candy Company makes candy corn and more than 100 mouthwatering candies, including such delights as chocolates, gummies, sour candies, and confections for all the seasons. To make a Jelly Belly jelly bean in either of its two factories, several processes are required. A hot kettle of gooey mix is flavored and colored with ingredients such as real peanut butter, peach puree, or milk chocolate. Then, 1,260 tiny beans are placed in a tray, cooled, and coated with corn starch and sugar before a shell is added. The final processes include polishing, printing the Jelly Belly name on each piece, and packaging.

How do Jelly Belly's accountants, affectionately called bean counters, determine the cost of each of these processing steps? How is the cost of flavoring transferred to the sugar-coating process and then to the process that adds a shell? Finally, how are all these processing costs combined to determine the cost of the hundreds of products that are sold worldwide? The answers to these questions enable management to determine the profit of each of the products sold and to set prices. To answer such questions, the accountants at Jelly Belly have developed a process-costing system with capabilities that are carefully tailored to meet the decision-making needs of management. ■

© Jeff Greenberg/Alamy

Jelly Belly produces a fun experience as well as candy, as is evident at this Jelly Belly Candy Store.

Distinction Between Job-Order Costing and Process Costing

The two most common systems of product costing are job-order costing and process costing. **Job-order costing** (or simply **job costing**) allocates costs to heterogeneous products that are readily identified by individual units or batches, each of which requires differential (sometimes custom) amounts of materials, labor, and overhead. Industries that commonly use job-order methods include construction, printing, aircraft, furniture, special-purpose machinery, and any manufacturer of tailor-made or unique goods.

Process costing averages costs over large numbers of homogeneous or nearly identical products. It is most often found in such industries as chemicals, oil, plastics, rubber, lumber, food processing, glass, mining, cement, and meatpacking. These industries mass produce homogeneous units that usually pass in continuous fashion through a series of uniform production steps called operations or processes.

The distinction between the job-cost and the process-cost methods centers largely on how they measure, aggregate, and apply product costs. Job costing applies costs to specific jobs, which may consist of either a single physical unit (such as a custom sofa) or a few like units (such as a dozen tables) in a distinct batch or job lot. In contrast, process costing deals with great masses of identical units and computes broad averages of unit costs.

The most important point is that product costing is an averaging process. The unit cost used for inventory purposes is the result of taking some accumulated cost of production (e.g., the sum of production-related activity costs) and dividing it by some measure of production. The basic distinction between job-order costing and process costing is the breadth of the denominator: In job-order costing, the denominator is small (e.g., 1 painting, 100 advertising circulars, 1 special packaging machine, or 1 highway bridge); however, in process costing, the denominator is large (e.g., thousands of pounds, gallons, or board feet).

Job costing and process costing are extremes along a continuum of potential costing systems. Each company designs its own accounting system to fit its underlying production activities. Some companies use **hybrid costing systems**, which are blends of ideas from both job costing and process costing.

Illustration of Job Costing

Job costing is best learned by example. But first we examine the basic records used in a job-cost system. The centerpiece of a job-costing system is the **job-cost record** (also called a **job-cost sheet** or **job order**), shown in Exhibit 14-1. The job-cost record contains all costs for a particular product, service, or batch of products. A file of job-cost records for partially completed jobs provides supporting details for the Work-in-Process Inventory account, often simply called Work in Process (WIP). A file of completed job-cost records comprises the Finished-Goods Inventory account.

As Exhibit 14-1 shows, the job-cost record summarizes information contained on source documents, such as materials requisitions and labor time tickets. **Materials requisitions** are records of materials used in particular jobs. **Labor time tickets** (or **time cards**) record the time a particular direct laborer spends on each job.

Today, job-cost records and other source documents are likely to be computer files, not paper records. With online data entry, bar coding, and optical scanning, much of the information needed for such records enters the computer without ever being written on paper. Nevertheless, whether records are on paper or in computer files, the accounting system must collect and maintain the same basic information.

As each job begins, we create its own job-cost record. As units are worked on, we make entries on the job-cost record. We accumulate three classes of costs on the job-cost record as units pass through the departments: Materials requisitions are the source of direct-materials

Objective 1

Distinguish between job-order costing and process costing.

job-order costing (job costing)
The method of allocating costs to heterogeneous products that are readily identified by individual units or batches, each of which requires differential (sometimes custom) amounts of materials, labor, and overhead.

process costing
The method of allocating costs to homogeneous products by averaging costs over large numbers of nearly identical products.

hybrid costing systems
An accounting system that is a blend of ideas from both job costing and process costing.

job-cost record (job-cost sheet, job order)
A document that shows all costs for a particular product, service, or batch of products.

materials requisitions
Records of materials used in particular jobs.

labor time tickets (time cards)
The record of the time a particular direct laborer spends on each job.

Exhibit 14-1

Completed Job-Cost Record and Sample Source Documents*

*Note that 7 of the 8 hours and $105 of the $120 in time ticket 7Z4 belong to job no. 963.

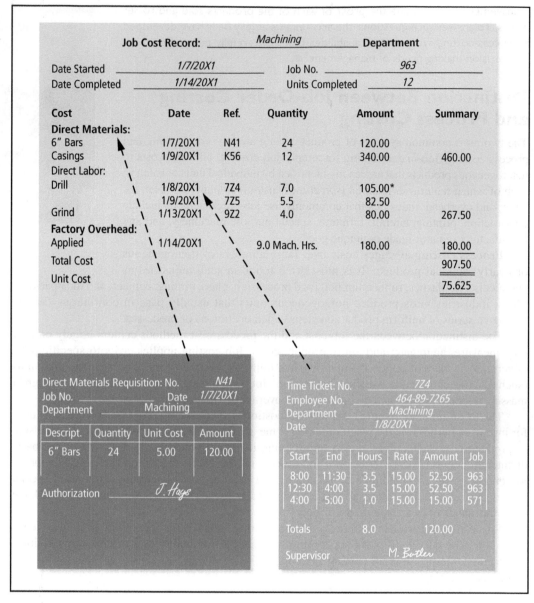

costs, time tickets provide direct-labor costs, and budgeted overhead rates (a separate rate for each overhead cost pool) are used to apply factory overhead to products. (The computation of these budgeted rates will be described later in this chapter.)

Basic Records of Enriquez Machine Parts Company

To illustrate the functioning of a job-order costing system, we will use the records and journal entries of the Enriquez Machine Parts Company. The following is a summary of pertinent transactions for the year 20X1:

		Machining	Assembly	Total
1.	Direct materials purchased on account	—	—	$1,900,000
2.	Direct materials requisitioned for manufacturing	$1,000,000	$890,000	1,890,000
3.	Direct-labor costs incurred	200,000	190,000	390,000
4a.	Factory overhead incurred	290,000	102,000	392,000
4b.	Factory overhead applied*	280,000	95,000	375,000
5.	Cost of goods completed and transferred to finished-goods inventory	—	—	2,500,000
6a.	Sales on account	—	—	4,000,000
6b.	Cost of goods sold	—	—	2,480,000

*We explain the nature of factory overhead applied in Chapter 13, pages 533–534.

On December 31, 20X0, the firm had the following inventories:

Direct materials (12 types)	$110,000
Work in process	—
Finished goods (unsold units from two jobs)	12,000

Exhibit 14-2 is an overview of the general flow of costs through the Enriquez Machine Parts Company's job-order costing system.[1] The exhibit summarizes the effects of transactions on the key manufacturing accounts in the firm's books. As you proceed through the following transaction-by-transaction summary analysis, keep checking each explanation against the overview in Exhibit 14-2 (companies usually make entries as transactions occur but to obtain a sweeping overview, our illustration uses summary entries for the entire 20X1 year). Essentially, we bring into WIP the costs of direct material used, direct labor, and factory overhead applied. In turn, we transfer the costs of completed goods from WIP to Finished Goods. As the company sells goods, its costs become expense in the form of Cost of Goods Sold.

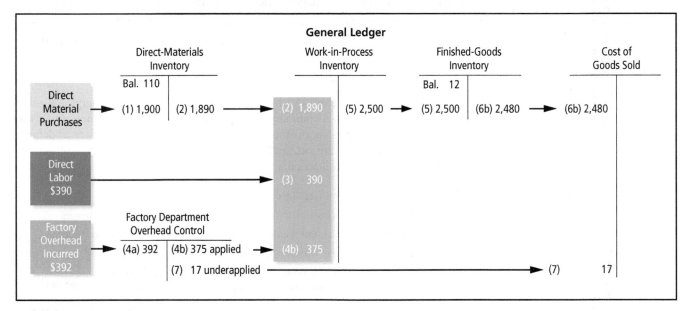

Exhibit 14-2
Job-Order Costing, General Flow of Costs (thousands)

---

[1]Exhibit 14-2 and the following explanation of transactions assume knowledge of basic accounting procedures. We will use the T-account format for a company's accounts. Entries on the left of the *T* are debits and those on the right are credits. Asset T-accounts, such as the inventory accounts, show increases on the left (debit) side and decreases on the right (credit) side of the *T*:

Inventory	
Beginning Balance	Decreases
Increases	
Ending Balance	

We record transactions affecting the accounts as journal entries. We show debit (left-side) entries flush with the left margin, we indent credit (right-side) entries, and often we include an explanation. For example, we would show a $10,000 transfer from Direct-Materials Inventory to WIP Inventory as follows:

WIP inventory 10,000
    Direct-materials inventory 10,000
To increase WIP inventory and decrease
    Direct-materials inventory by $10,000.

Objective 2

Prepare summary journal entries for the typical transactions of a job-costing system.

Applying Direct Materials and Direct Labor Costs

The first three transactions in Exhibit 14-2 trace direct materials and direct labor costs to WIP. The entries are straightforward.

1.   Transaction: Direct materials purchased, $1,900,000 on account

    Analysis: The asset Direct-materials inventory is increased. The liability Accounts payable is increased.

    Journal Entry: Direct-materials inventory 1,900,000

                      Accounts payable 1,900,000

2.   Transaction: Direct materials requisitioned, $1,890,000

    Analysis: The asset WIP inventory is increased. The asset Direct-materials inventory is decreased.

    Journal Entry: WIP inventory 1,890,000

                      Direct-materials inventory 1,890,000

3.   Transaction: Direct-labor cost incurred, $390,000

    Analysis: The asset WIP inventory is increased. The liability Accrued payroll is increased.

    Journal Entry: WIP inventory 390,000

                      Accrued payroll..390,000

Applying Factory Overhead Costs

Transactions 4a and 4b deal with factory overhead costs. In transaction 4a we charge the actual factory overhead costs as a debit to a summary account called Factory Department Overhead Control, which we temporarily regard as an asset. Each department will have a variety of detailed overhead accounts to help control overhead, but for our purposes we summarize them all into the Factory Department Overhead Control account.

4a.   Transaction: Actual factory overhead incurred, $392,000

    Analysis: The temporary account Factory department overhead control is increased. Assorted asset accounts are decreased and/or liability accounts increased.

    Journal Entry: Factory department overhead control 392,000

                      Cash, Accounts payable, and various other balance sheet accounts 392,000

In transaction 4b we apply factory overhead costs to jobs by debiting (increasing) WIP Inventory and crediting (decreasing) Factory Department Overhead Control.[2] While accountants directly trace actual direct materials and direct labor costs to products (as in transactions 2 and 3), they apply factory overhead costs to WIP via budgeted (predetermined) overhead rates. As described in Chapter 13 (pp. 533–534), to compute the budgeted overhead rates we need the following for each department: 1) cost-allocation base, 2) budgeted overhead costs, and 3) budgeted amount of each cost-allocation base. Enriquez allocates overhead based on machine hours in machining and direct-labor cost in assembly, resulting in the following overhead rates:

	Machining	Assembly
Budgeted manufacturing overhead	$277,800	$103,200
Budgeted machine hours	69,450	
Budgeted direct-labor cost		$206,400
Budgeted overhead rate per machine hour: $277,800 ÷ 69,450	$ 4	
Budgeted overhead rate per direct-labor dollar: $103,200 ÷ $206,400		50%

[2]Refer to pages 533–539 in Chapter 13 for an expanded discussion of the application of overhead. For our example here, we use the same overhead cost scenario and values for Enriquez Machine Parts Company found on pages 534–535 in Chapter 13.

Using these rates, the applied overhead for 20X1 is $375,000:

Machining: Actual machine hours of 70,000 × $4	$280,000
Assembly: Actual direct-labor cost of $190,000 × 50%	95,000
Total factory overhead applied	$375,000

The summary journal entry for this application follows:

4b.   Transaction: Factory overhead applied, $95,000 + $280,000 = $375,000

      Analysis: The asset WIP inventory is increased. The asset Factory department overhead control is decreased.

      Journal Entry: WIP inventory 375,000

            Factory department overhead control...375,000

Finished Goods, Sales, and Cost of Goods Sold

Transactions 5, 6a, and 6b recognize the completion of production and the eventual sale of the goods. When Enriquez completes a particular job, it transfers the costs assigned to that job to Finished-Goods Inventory, and when it sells the job those same costs become expenses on the income statement in the form of Cost of Goods Sold.

5.   Transaction: Cost of goods manufactured, $2,500,000

      Analysis: The asset Finished-goods inventory is increased. The asset WIP inventory is decreased.

      Journal Entry: Finished-goods inventory......................................2,500,000

            WIP inventory 2,500,000

6a.   Transaction: Sales on account, $4,000,000

      Analysis: The asset Accounts receivable is increased. The revenue account Sales is increased.

      Journal Entry: Accounts receivable 4,000,000

            Sales 4,000,000

6b.   Transaction: Cost of goods sold, $2,480,000

      Analysis: The expense Cost of goods sold is increased. The asset Finished-goods inventory is decreased.

      Journal Entry: Cost of goods sold..2,480,000

            Finished-goods inventory..2,480,000

Finally, transaction 7 in Exhibit 14-2 deals with differences between actual and applied overhead. In 20X1, Enriquez applied $375,000 of overhead to its products but actually incurred $392,000 of overhead costs. We call this difference underapplied overhead because the amount applied is less than the amount incurred. The opposite, overapplied overhead, occurs when the amount applied exceeds the amount incurred. As discussed more fully on pages 536–538 of Chapter 13, the Enriquez Company disposes of under- or overapplied overhead by some method at year-end. We will assume it uses the immediate write-off method, so it adds the $17,000 of underapplied overhead to cost of goods sold:

7.   Transaction: Underapplied overhead, $17,000

      Analysis: Cost of goods sold is increased and Factory department overhead control is decreased.

      Journal Entry: Cost of goods sold...17,000

            Factory department overhead control................................17,000

These seven transactions have accounted for all direct materials, direct labor, and factory overhead costs incurred during 20X1. As shown in Exhibit 14-2, all these costs flowed through WIP and ended up in either Direct-Materials Inventory, WIP Inventory, Finished-Goods Inventory, or Cost of Goods Sold.

Making Managerial Decisions

Suppose you are a manager of a manufacturing department. Confirm your understanding of product costing in a job-order environment by indicating the transactions that occurred for each of the following journal entries. Which of these transactions records actual costs versus cost estimates?

1. WIP inventory............... XXX
    Accrued payroll..........................XXX
2. WIP inventory............... XXX
    Factory department
    overhead control XXX
3. Cost of goods sold.......... XXX
    Finished goods XXX

Answer

The first entry records the actual cost of direct labor that the accounting system traces to the specific job being costed. We make the second entry to record the application of factory overhead. This is an estimate of the costs of indirect resources used in producing the job. The last entry records the cost of goods sold when the company sells the job. The cost in this transfer from finished-goods inventory to cost of goods sold is a mix of actual costs (direct material and direct labor) and estimated costs (applied factory overhead).

Activity-Based Costing/Management in a Job-Costing Environment

Regardless of the nature of its production system, firms will inevitably have resources they share among different products. The costs of these resources are part of the overhead the company must account for in its system. In many cases, the magnitude of overhead is large enough to justify a significant investment in a costing system that provides accurate cost information. Whether companies use this cost information for planning and control or product costing, often the benefits of more accurate costs exceed the costs of installing and maintaining the cost system. As we have seen, ABC usually increases costing accuracy because it focuses on the cause-and-effect relationships between work performed (activities) and the consumption of resources (costs).

Illustration of ABC in a Job-Order Environment

Objective 3

Use an ABC system in a job-order environment.

We illustrate an ABC system in a job-order environment by considering Dell. Recall that Dell was the subject of the introduction to Chapter 13, page 532. Several years ago, Dell adopted an ABC job-order costing system. What motivated Dell to adopt ABC? Company managers cite two reasons: (1) the aggressive cost-reduction targets set by top management and (2) the need to understand product-line profitability. As is the case with any business, understanding profitability means understanding the cost structure of the entire business. One of the key advantages of an ABC system is its focus on understanding how work (activity) is related to the consumption of resources (costs). Therefore, an ABC system was a logical choice for Dell, and once managers improved their understanding of the company's cost structure, cost reduction through ABM (activity-based management) was much easier.

Like most companies that implement ABC, Dell began developing its ABC system by focusing on the most critical (core) processes across the value chain. These were the design and production processes. After it put the initial system in place, Dell added the remaining phases of the value chain. Exhibit 14-3 shows the functions (or core processes) that add value to the company's products and how Dell assigns the costs of these functions to an individual job under the current ABC system.

To understand product-line profitability, Dell managers identified key activities for the R&D, product design, production, marketing, distribution, and customer service phases. Then, they used appropriate cost drivers to allocate activity costs to the produced product lines. While each of the phases shown in Exhibit 14-3 is important, we will focus on the product design and production phases. Product design is one of Dell's most important value-adding functions, providing a defect-free computer product that is easy to manufacture and reliable to use. Engineering costs (primarily salaries and CAD equipment depreciation) account for most of the design costs. These costs are indirect and, thus, Dell must allocate them to product lines using a cost-allocation base.

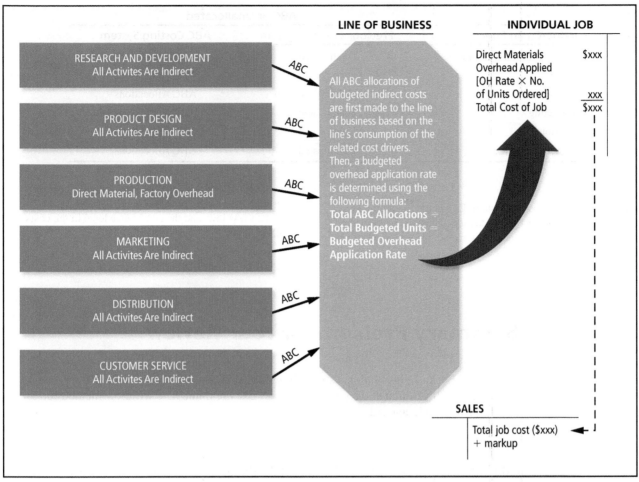

Exhibit 14-3
Dell Computer Corporation's Value Chain and ABC System

The production costs include direct materials and factory overhead. Factory overhead consists of six activity centers and related cost pools (including a direct-labor cost pool where appropriate): receiving, preparation, assembly, testing, packaging, and shipping. Facility costs (plant depreciation, insurance, taxes) are considered part of the production function and are allocated to each activity center based on the square feet occupied by the center.

Dell divided the total annual budgeted indirect cost allocated to a product line by the total budgeted units produced to find a budgeted overhead rate. It then used this rate, which is adjusted periodically to reflect changes in the budget, to cost individual jobs.

Dell now breaks down each activity center into value added and non-value added activities, with the intent of targeting non-value added activities for cost reduction programs. An example of a non-value-added activity is the preparation activity in the production function.

Making Managerial Decisions

Refer to Exhibit 14-3. One of the primary purposes of an ABC system is to increase the accuracy of product costs so managers can make better cost-based decisions. Assume that you are a manager at **Dell** and that you have to determine prices for computers by adding a markup to the cost accumulated by the costing system. For example, if the accumulated total job cost is $800, a markup sufficient to "cover" all unallocated costs and provide a reasonable profit is added to the cost in determining the price. Using the table at the top of page 584, determine whether the percentage markup under the ABC system is higher or lower than under the previous system. Which system gives you a higher degree of confidence that the price for a computer is adequate to cover all costs and provide a reasonable profit? Why?

	ABC or Unallocated	
Value-Chain Function	Previous Costing System	ABC Costing System
Research and development	Unallocated	ABC Allocations
Design	Unallocated	ABC Allocations
Production	Traditional Allocation	ABC Allocations
Marketing	Unallocated	ABC Allocations
Distribution	Unallocated	ABC Allocations
Customer service	Unallocated	ABC Allocations

Answer

Under the previous costing system, Dell determined prices by marking up only the cost of production. Thus, the markup was relatively high so that the company would cover all the unallocated costs and also achieve a reasonable profit, and managers had a low level of confidence in this cost system. The ABC system provided estimates of all value-chain costs, so the size of the markup was low, and the confidence level in the costs provided was high.

Summary Problem for Your Review

PROBLEM

Review the Enriquez illustration, especially Exhibit 14-2 on page 579. Prepare an income statement for 20X1 through the gross profit line. Use the immediate write-off method for overapplied or underapplied overhead.

SOLUTION

Exhibit 14-4 recapitulates the final impact of the Enriquez illustration on the financial statements. Note how the immediate write-off means that we add $17,000 to cost of goods sold. As you study Exhibit 14-4, trace the three major elements of cost (direct materials, direct labor, and factory overhead) through the accounts.

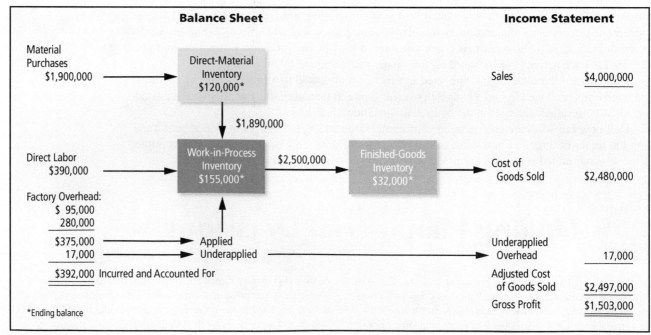

Exhibit 14-4
Relation of Costs to Financial Statements

Job Costing in Service and Nonprofit Organizations

This chapter has initially concentrated on applying costs to manufactured products. However, the job-costing approach is used in nonmanufacturing situations, too. For example, universities have research "projects," airlines have repair and overhaul "jobs," and public accountants have audit "engagements." In such situations, the focus shifts from the costs of products to the costs of services, projects, or programs.

Objective 4

Show how service organizations use job-order costing.

Service and nonprofit organizations do not usually call their "product" a "job order." Instead, they may call it a program or a class of service. A "program" is an identifiable group of activities that frequently provides services rather than goods. Examples include a safety program, an education program, or a family counseling program. Accountants can trace costs or revenues to individual hospital patients, individual social welfare cases, and individual university research projects. However, internal departments in service organizations often work simultaneously on many programs, so the "job-order" costing challenge is to "apply" the diverse department costs to the various programs. Only then can managers best allocate limited resources among competing programs.

In service industries—such as repairing, consulting, legal, and accounting services—each customer order is a different job with a special account or order number. Accountants can trace just costs, just revenues, or both to jobs. For example, automobile repair shops typically have a repair order for each car worked on, with space for allocating materials and labor costs. Customers see only a copy showing the retail prices of the materials, parts, and labor billed to their orders. Meanwhile, accountants trace the actual parts and labor costs of each order to a duplicate copy of the repair order, providing a measure of profit for each job. To record these actual costs, auto mechanics enter their starting and stopping times on time tickets for each new order.

Budgets and Control of Engagements

In many service organizations and some manufacturing operations, job orders provide not only product/service costing, but also planning and control benefits. For example, a public accounting firm might have a condensed budget for 20X1 as follows:

Revenue	$10,000,000	100%
Direct labor (for professional hours charged to engagements)	2,500,000	25%
Contribution to overhead and operating income	$ 7,500,000	75%
Overhead (all other costs)	6,500,000	65%
Operating income	$ 1,000,000	10%

In this illustration,

$$\text{budgeted overhead rate} = \frac{\text{budgeted overhead}}{\text{budgeted direct labor}}$$

$$= \frac{\$6,500,000}{\$2,500,000}$$

$$= 260\%$$

To prepare a budget for each engagement, the partner in charge of the audit predicts the expected number of direct-professional hours. Direct-professional hours are those that partners, managers, and staff auditors work to complete the engagement. The budgeted direct-labor cost is the pertinent hourly labor costs multiplied by the budgeted hours. Accounting firms charge partners' time to the engagement at much higher rates than subordinates' time.

How do such firms apply overhead? Accounting firms usually use either direct-labor cost or direct-labor hours as the cost driver for overhead application. In our example, the firm uses direct-labor cost. The budgeted total cost of an engagement is the direct-labor cost plus applied overhead, 260% of direct-labor cost in this illustration, plus any other direct costs.

This practice implies that partners require proportionately more overhead support for each of their hours charged. For example, 1 hour of partner work that has a direct-labor cost of $200 would result in a projected overhead support cost of $520. If this work can be done by a staff person whose charge rate is only $50, the estimated overhead is only $130.

The engagement partner uses a budget for a specific audit job that includes detailed scope and procedures. For instance, the budget for auditing cash or receivables on the engagement would specify the exact work to be done, and the necessary hours of partner time, manager time, and staff time. The partner monitors progress by comparing the hours logged to date with the original budget, and with the estimated hours remaining on the engagement. If the firm quoted a fixed audit fee, the profitability of an engagement depends on whether it can accomplish the audit within the time allocated in the budget.

Accuracy of Costs of Engagements

Managers of service firms, such as auditing and consulting firms, frequently use budgeted costs of engagements as guides to pricing and for allocating effort to customized services or particular customers. Hence, the accuracy of projected costs of various engagements may affect pricing and operational decisions.

Suppose the accounting firm's policy for price quotes for engagements is 200% of total estimated professional costs, plus reimbursement of travel costs. The firm projects costs and sets the price on an auditing engagement as follows:

	Projected Cost	Price
Direct-professional labor	$ 50,000	$100,000
Applied overhead, 260% of direct-professional labor	130,000	260,000
Total professional costs excluding travel costs	$180,000	360,000
Travel costs	14,000	14,000
Total projected costs of engagement	$194,000	$374,000

Note that costs reimbursed by the client—such as travel costs—do not add to overhead costs and so are not subject to any markups in the setting of fees. Once the client accepts the offer, the firm needs to monitor the assignment of work as well as the overhead incurred to insure control of costs.

Process Costing Basics

In this mine, owned and operated by **Nally & Gibson Georgetown**, limestone rock is mined from a quarry, and transported by a conveyor system to plant areas. Nally & Gibson uses a process-costing system to determine the costs of mining, crushing, transporting, processing, and storing limestone.

© JG Photography/Alamy

As indicated on page 577, an alternative to job costing is process costing. Before we examine the procedures of process costing, let's examine a real application. **Nally & Gibson Georgetown** is a leading producer of limestone products used for industrial and commercial purposes. Limestone is used in highways, high school track beds, concrete sidewalks, buildings, soil enhancement products, residential homes, and about a million other places (yes, even in some toothpastes).

The making of limestone products is an excellent example of a process costing system. A single raw material—limestone rock—is subjected to several processes that result in finished limestone products. The basic production processes that convert limestone rock into usable limestone are easy to understand and are reasonably simple. Basically, the limestone rock is mined from Nally & Gibson's quarry and mine in Georgetown, Kentucky, and transported to the processing facility. There it passes through several stages of crushing and grinding, depending on how fine the limestone needs to be for the finished product. The ease and homogeneous nature of these processes might make you think the cost accounting system used to track product costs should also be fairly simple and unimportant to the success of the company. However, accurate and timely cost information is critical for both product costing and decision-making purposes at Nally & Gibson.

For example, the accurate allocation of the costs of mining and transporting limestone and subsequently crushing the limestone for various products is essential to the success of the company. The company's cost accounting system accumulates the costs of these processes and then calculates an average cost per ton of product using a process-costing system. According to company president Frank Hamilton Jr., "If Nally & Gibson did not keep a handle on costs, we would not be here."

One of Nally & Gibson's costs is transporting quarried rock from the mine to plants. Using trucks that have to travel up to a mile into the mine and then up a steep grade is expensive and hazardous. The solution to this transportation problem was provided by **Process Machinery, Inc**, a full-service equipment dealer servicing Kentucky, Indiana, and Ohio. Process Machinery designed, constructed, and installed a 3,000-foot conveyor system used by Nally & Gibson. Interestingly, the accounting system used by Process Machinery to account for this job is an excellent example of a job-order system, as they produced a customer-specific product that required a unique combination of resources.

The result—Nally & Gibson increased its production by up to 50% with increased safety and at a reduced cost. We can see from this example that the cost accounting system a company uses depends on the nature of its products and services. The cost information needed by managers determines the type of cost accounting system. Process Machinery's managers need costs for specific products that have unique features. Nally & Gibson's managers, whose product is crushed limestone, have much different cost-information needs as dictated by their production process.

Companies like **Jelly Belly** and Nally & Gibson that produce large quantities of a generic or homogeneous product in a continuous process, do not use the job-costing techniques we discussed previously. Why? Because a method called process costing fits their production process better and so is a more efficient costing system for such companies.

Why doesn't Nally & Gibson use a job-cost system to assign costs to its products? The primary reason is that its manufacturing process does not produce discrete jobs. The company does not wait for a specific customer order before producing the product. The company makes a forecast of the demand for the product, and produces to meet this expected demand. Second, it is costly (and difficult) to trace costs to a specific truckload of limestone, while the benefit from improving accuracy is negligible. So the cost-benefit criterion clearly dictates that the company determines unit costs using much larger quantities—for example, a whole month's production.

As we noted early in this chapter, all product costing uses averaging to determine costs per unit of production. Sometimes those averages apply to a relatively small number of units, such as a particular printing job produced in a job-order production system. Other times, the averages might be extremely broad, based on generic products from a continual-process production system, such as limestone road-fill. Process-costing systems apply costs to homogeneous products that a company mass produces in continuous fashion through a series of production processes. Examples include chemicals, flour, glass, toothpaste, paper, and potato chips as well as computer chips. These processes usually occur in separate departments, although a single department sometimes contains more than one process.

Process Costing Compared with Job Costing

It is easiest to understand process costing if you compare it with something you already know: job costing. Exhibit 14-5 shows the major differences between job-order costing and process costing. Job-order costing has one WIP for each job. In contrast, process costing requires one WIP account for each process. As goods move from process to process, accountants transfer their costs accordingly.

Objective 5

Explain the basic ideas underlying process costing and how they differ from job-order costing.

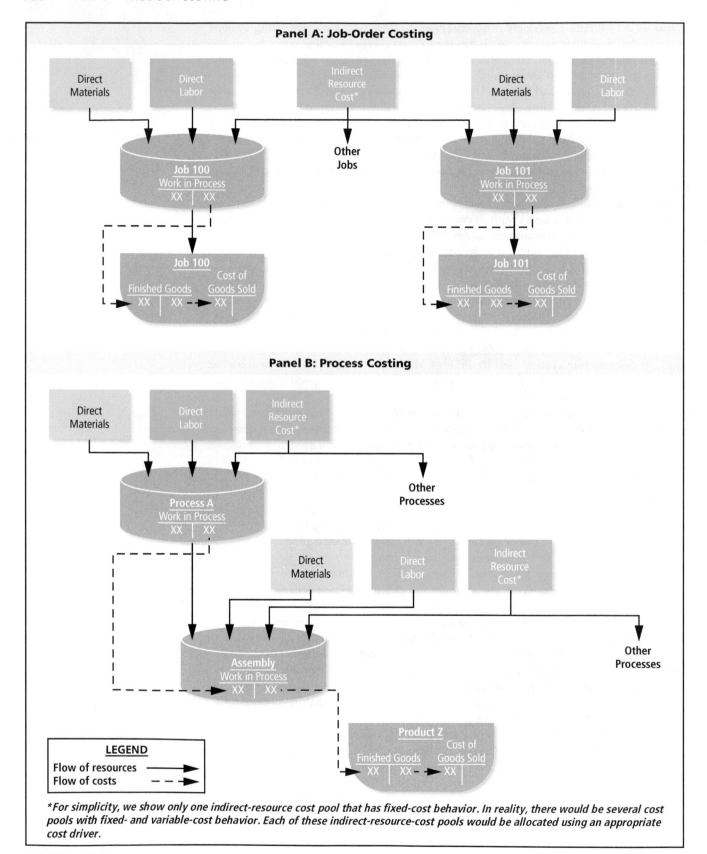

For simplicity, we show only one indirect-resource cost pool that has fixed-cost behavior. In reality, there would be several cost pools with fixed- and variable-cost behavior. Each of these indirect-resource-cost pools would be allocated using an appropriate cost driver.

Exhibit 14-5
Comparison of Job-Order and Process Costing

Consider Nally & Gibson's process-costing system. The company's production system has four core processes as shown in Exhibit 14-6. The company first extracts limestone rock from surface quarries or from mines. It then transports the rock to the plant by rail or truck. At the plant, machines crush the rock and screen it to various sizes demanded by customers. The crushed limestone is then stocked in large piles of inventory for shipment. Each process requires resources. The direct-materials resource is the limestone rock itself. All four processes use direct labor and overhead resources.

The process-costing approach does not distinguish between individual units of product. Instead, it accumulates costs for a period and divides them by quantities produced during that period to get broad, average unit costs. We can apply process costing to nonmanufacturing activities as well as to manufacturing activities. For example, we can divide the costs of giving state automobile driver's license tests by the number of tests given, and we can divide the cost of a post office sorting department by the number of items sorted.

To get a rough feel for process costing, consider Magenta Midget Frozen Vegetables. This company quick-cooks tiny carrots, beans, and other vegetables before freezing them. It has only two processes: cooking and freezing. As the following T-accounts show, the costs of cooked vegetables (in millions of dollars) are transferred from the cooking department to the freezing department:

Work in Process—Cooking

Direct materials	14	Transfer cost of goods completed to freezing department	23
Direct labor	4		
Factory overhead	8		
	26		
Ending inventory	3		

Work in Process—Freezing

Cost transferred in from cooking	23	Transfer cost of goods completed to finished goods	21
Direct labor	1		
Factory overhead	2		
	26		
Ending inventory	5		

We determine the amount of cost to be transferred from cooking to freezing by dividing the accumulated costs in the cooking department by the pounds of vegetables processed. We then multiply the resulting cost per pound by the pounds of vegetables physically transferred to the freezing department.

The journal entries for process-costing systems are similar to those for the job-order costing system. That is, we account for direct materials, direct labor, and factory overhead as before. However, now there is more than a single WIP account for all units being manufactured. There is one WIP account for each processing department, WIP—Cooking and WIP—Freezing, in our example. The Magenta Midget data are recorded as follows:

1. Work in process—cooking.. 14
        Direct-materials inventory 14
    To record direct materials used.

2. Work in process—cooking.. 4
        Accrued payroll..4
    To record direct labor incurred in cooking.

3. Work in process—cooking..8
        Factory overhead..8
    To record factory overhead applied to product in cooking.

Exhibit 14-6
Process Costing at Nally &
Gibson

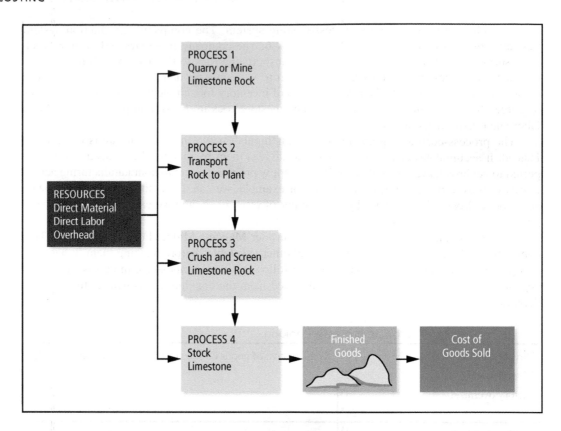

4. Work in process—freezing...23

      Work in process—cooking... 23

      To transfer goods from the cooking process to the freezing process; 3 million remains in cooking.

5. Work in process—freezing...1

      Accrued payroll.. 1

      To record direct labor incurred in freezing.

6. Work in process—freezing...2

      Factory overhead.. 2

      To record factory overhead applied to product in freezing.

7. Finished goods 21

      Work in process—freezing...21

      To transfer goods from the freezing process to finished goods; 5 million remains in freezing.

Process manufacturing systems vary in design. The design shown in panel B of Exhibit 14-5 (as well as Exhibit 14-6) is sequential—units pass from process to process until the product is finished. You will find many other designs in practice—each tailored to meet specific production requirements. For example, a firm may operate two processes at the same time to produce different parts of a finished product. Whatever the specific layout, the basic principles of process costing are the same. The central product-costing problem is how each department should calculate unit cost, which is then used to compute the cost of goods transferred out and the cost of goods remaining in the department. If the same amount of work were done on each unit transferred out and on each unit in ending inventory, the cost allocation process would be easy. We could simply divide total costs by total units. Then, we would use this unit cost to calculate the total cost of units transferred out and the remaining cost of unfinished units. However, this is not possible because units in ending inventory cannot be complete, which makes them different from the completed units transferred out. Thus, the product-costing system must distinguish between the costs of fully completed units that a department transfers out and the costs of partially completed units that still remain in ending inventory. Let's now see how process costing systems accomplish this.

Application of Process Costing

To help you better understand our discussion of process costing, we will use the example of Oakville Wooden Toys. The company buys wood as a direct material for its forming department, which processes only one type of toy, marionettes. It inserts all the wood into this department at the beginning of the process. After forming, the company transfers the marionettes to the finishing department where workers hand shape them and add strings, paint, and clothing.

The forming department had no beginning inventory and completely manufactured 25,000 identical units during April, leaving no ending inventory. Its costs that month were as follows:

Direct materials		$ 75,000
Conversion costs		
Direct labor	$15,000	
Factory overhead	40,000	55,000
Costs to account for		$130,000

Since there is no ending inventory, the unit cost of goods completed is simply $130,000 ÷ 25,000 = $5.20. An itemization would show the following:

Direct materials, $75,000 ÷ 25,000	$3.00
Conversion costs, $55,000 ÷ 25,000	2.20
Unit cost of a whole completed marionette	$5.20

But what if not all 25,000 marionettes were completed during April? For example, assume that 5,000 were still in process at the end of April—only 20,000 were started and fully completed. All units—both those transferred out and those still in inventory—have obviously received all the necessary direct materials. However, only the units transferred out have received the full amount of conversion resources. Oakville determined that the 5,000 marionettes that remain in process have received, on average, only 40% of conversion resources. How should the forming department calculate the cost of goods transferred out and the cost of goods remaining in the ending WIP inventory? The answer lies in the following five key steps, which we describe in the next two sections:

- Step 1: Summarize the flow of physical units.
- Step 2: Calculate output in terms of equivalent units.
- Step 3: Summarize the total costs to account for, which are the costs applied to WIP.
- Step 4: Calculate cost per equivalent unit.
- Step 5: Apply costs to units completed and to units in the ending WIP.

As we work through each of these five steps, keep in mind that each step provides managers with data that are useful for product costing and operational control purposes.

Physical Units and Equivalent Units (Steps 1 and 2)

Step 1, as the first column in Exhibit 14-7 shows, tracks the physical units of production. How should we measure the output—the results of the department's work? This tracking tells us we have a total of 25,000 physical units to account for, but not all these units count the same in the forming department's output. Why not? Because only 20,000 units were fully completed and transferred out. The remaining 5,000 units are only partially complete, and we cannot assign partially completed units the same cost as the completed output. As a result, we have to state output not in terms of physical units but in terms of a different unit measure called an "equivalent unit."

Equivalent units are the number of completed (whole) units that the department could have produced from the resources required for the partially completed units. For example, four units that are each one-half completed represent two equivalent units. Similarly, if each unit had been one-fourth completed, the four together would represent one equivalent unit. So, we determine equivalent units of partially completed units by multiplying physical units by the percent of completion. This equivalent unit measure correctly equates the completed physical units that are transferred out with the partially completed physical units in ending inventory.

Objective 6

Compute output in terms of equivalent units.

equivalent units
The number of completed (whole) units that could have been produced from the resources required for the partially completed units.

Exhibit 14-7

Forming Department Output
in Equivalent Units
Month Ended April 30, 20X0

	(Step 1)	(Step 2) Equivalent Units	
Flow of Production	Physical Units	Direct Materials	Conversion
Started and completed	20,000	20,000	20,000
Work in process, ending inventory	5,000	5,000	2,000*
Units accounted for	25,000		
Work done to date		25,000	22,000*

*5,000 physical units × .40 degree of completion of conversion costs.

In our example, as step 2 in Exhibit 14-7 shows, we measure the output as 25,000 equivalent units of direct-materials cost but only 22,000 equivalent units of conversion costs. Why? Because direct materials had been fully added to all 25,000 units. In contrast, only 40% of the conversion costs were applied to the 5,000 partially completed units, which would have been sufficient to complete only 2,000 equivalent units in addition to the 20,000 units that were actually completed.

To compute equivalent units, you need to estimate how much of a given resource was applied to units in process, which is not always an easy task. Some estimates are easier to make than others. For example, estimating the amount of direct materials used is fairly easy. However, how do you measure how much energy, maintenance labor, or supervision was incurred for a given unit? Conversion costs can involve a number of these hard-to-measure resources, which leaves you estimating both how much total effort it takes to complete a unit and how much of that effort has already been put into the units in process. Coming up with accurate estimates is further complicated in industries such as textiles, where there is a great deal of work in process at all times. To simplify estimation, some companies may decide that all unfinished work in process must be deemed either one-third, one-half, or two-thirds complete. In other cases where continuous processing leaves roughly the same amount in process at the end of every month, accountants ignore work in process altogether and assign all monthly production costs to units completed and transferred out.

Measures in equivalent units are not confined to manufacturing situations. Such measures are a popular way of expressing workloads in terms of a common denominator. For example, radiology departments measure their output in terms of weighted units. Various X-ray procedures are ranked in terms of the time, supplies, and related costs devoted to each procedure. A simple chest X-ray may receive a weight of one. But a skull X-ray may receive a weight of three because it uses three times more resources (for example, technicians' time) than a procedure with a weight of one.

Calculation of Product Costs (Steps 3 to 5)

Objective 7

Compute costs and prepare journal entries for the principal transactions in a process-costing system.

Exhibit 14-8 is a production-cost report. It shows steps 3–5 of process costing. Step 3 summarizes the total costs to account for (that is, the total costs incurred and applied to WIP—Forming). Step 4 obtains unit costs by dividing the two categories of total costs by the appropriate measures of equivalent units. The unit cost of a completed unit—materials cost plus conversion costs per equivalent unit—is $3.00 + $2.50 = $5.50. Why is the unit cost $5.50 instead of the $5.20 calculated on page 591? Because the $55,000 conversion cost is spread over 22,000 units instead of 25,000 units. Step 5 then uses these unit costs to apply costs to products. The 20,000 finished units are complete in terms of both direct materials and conversion costs. Thus, we can multiply the full unit cost times the number of completed units to determine their costs, which is 20,000 units times $5.50, or $110,000. The 5,000 physical units in ending work-in-process inventory are fully completed in terms of direct materials. Therefore, the direct materials applied to ending work in process are 5,000 equivalent units times $3.00, or $15,000. In contrast, the 5,000 physical units are 40% completed in terms of conversion costs. Therefore, the conversion costs applied to work in process are 2,000 equivalent units (40% of 5,000 physical units) times $2.50, or $5,000. Thus, the total cost of the ending inventory is $20,000.

		Total Costs	Details	
			Direct Materials	Conversion Costs
(Step 3)	Costs to account for	$130,000	$75,000	$55,000
(Step 4)	Divide by equivalent units		÷ 25,000	÷ 22,000
	Unit costs	$ 5.50	$ 3.00	$ 2.50
(Step 5)	Application of costs			
	To units completed and transferred to the finishing department, 20,000 units at $5.50	$110,000		
	To units not completed and still in process, April 30, 5,000 units			
	Direct materials	$ 15,000	5,000 × $3.00	
	Conversion costs	5,000		2,000 × $2.50
	Work in process, April 30	$ 20,000		
	Total costs accounted for	$130,000		

Exhibit 14-8
Forming Department Production Cost Report
Month Ended April 30, 20X0

Journal entries for the data in our illustration would appear as follows:

1. Work in process—forming 75,000
        Direct-materials inventory 75,000
    Materials added to production in forming for April.

2. Work in process—forming 15,000
        Accrued payroll 15,000
    Direct labor incurred in forming for April.

3. Work in process—forming 40,000
        Factory overhead 40,000
    Factory overhead applied in forming for April.

4. Work in process—finishing................................... 110,000
        Work in process—forming 110,000
    Cost of goods completed and transferred from forming to assembly in April.

The $130,000 added to the Work in Process—Forming account less the $110,000 transferred out leaves an ending balance of $20,000:

Work in Process—Forming

1. Direct materials	$75,000	4. Transferred out to finishing	$110,000
2. Direct labor	15,000		
3. Factory overhead	40,000		
Costs to account for	130,000		
Bal. April 30	$20,000		

Summary Problem for Your Review

PROBLEM

Consider **Nally & Gibson**'s plant operations in Georgetown. The plant processes limestone rock that is quarried in a nearby mine. Exhibit 14-6 (page 590) shows the various processing steps. Process 3 is crushing and screening the rock. To produce the crushed limestone, the company starts with limestone rocks from its quarry in Georgetown, Kentucky, and puts the rocks through a crushing process. Suppose that during May, the company quarried and transported to its processing plant 288 tons of rock from its quarry, and at the end of the month 15 tons remained in process, on average 20% complete. The cost of rocks from the quarry for the last 5 months has been $120 per ton, so the cost of the limestone rock put into Process 3 is $120/ton times 288 tons, or $34,560. Labor and overhead costs during May in the rock crushing process were $35,880. Assume there was no work in process at the beginning of May.

1. Compute the cost of crushed rock processed and transferred out in May.
2. Compute the cost of the work-in-process inventory at the end of May.

SOLUTION

Flow of Production	(Step 1) Physical Units (Tons)	(Step 2) Equivalent Units in Tons	
		Direct Materials	Conversion
Started and completed	273	273	273
Ending work in process	15	15*	3*
Units accounted for	288		
Work done to date		288	276

*$15 \times 100\% = 15; 15 \times 20\% = 3.$

		Details	
	Total Costs	Limestone Rock	Conversion Costs
(Step 3) Costs to account for	$70,440	$34,560	$35,880
(Step 4) Divide by equivalent units		÷ 288	÷ 276
Unit costs	$250.00*	$120.00	$130.00
(Step 5) Application of costs			
To units completed and transferred, 273 tons at $250.00	$68,250		
To ending work in process, 15 tons			
Direct materials	$ 1,800	15 × $120.00	
Conversion costs	390		3 × $130.00
Work in process, ending inventory	$ 2,190		
Total costs accounted for	$70,440		

*Cost per ton ($250) = limestone rock costs ($120) + conversion costs ($130).

Effects of Beginning Inventories: Weighted-Average Method

Objective 8

Demonstrate how the presence of beginning inventories affects the computation of unit costs under the weighted-average method.

So far, our example has been very straightforward because all units were started during the period. In other words, there were no units in beginning inventory. The presence of units in beginning inventory actually complicates matters a great deal.

There are several ways to deal with beginning inventories, but we will describe only the most popular alternative, the weighted-average method. We will explore this method using the following data from our Oakville example for the month of May. Recall that the ending WIP inventory for April in the forming department was 5,000 units. These units become the beginning inventory for May.

Units

    Work in process, April 30: 5,000 units; 100% completed for materials,
       but only 40% completed for conversion costs

    Units started in May: 26,000

    Units completed in May: 24,000

    Work in process, May 31: 7,000 units; 100% completed for materials, but
       only 60% completed for conversion costs

Costs

Work in process, April 30		
Direct materials	$15,000	
Conversion costs	5,000	$ 20,000
Direct materials added during May		84,200
Conversion costs added during May		62,680
Total costs to account for		$166,880*

*Note that the $166,880 total costs to account for include the $20,000 of beginning inventory in addition to the $146,880 added during May.

The **weighted-average (WA) process-costing method** determines total costs by adding together the cost of (1) all work done in the current period and (2) the work done in the preceding period on the current period's beginning inventory of work in process. Then, you divide this total cost by the total equivalent units of work done to date, whether that work was done in the current or previous period.

Why do we use the term *weighted average* to describe this method? Primarily because the unit costs used for applying costs to products are based on the total cost incurred to date, regardless of whether the department incurred those costs in the current period or in the prior period. If costs of materials, labor, or overhead change across periods, essentially the weighted-average method reweights these comingled costs to determine a revised unit cost.

Exhibit 14-9 shows the first two steps in this process-costing method: computation of physical units and equivalent units. The computation of equivalent units ignores where the 31,000 units to account for came from: either beginning work in process or those started in May. Exhibit 14-10 presents a production-cost report, summarizing steps 3–5 regarding computations of unit product costs and the resulting cost allocations to inventory accounts.

weighted-average (WA) process-costing method
A process-costing method that determines total cost by adding together the cost of (1) all work done in the current period and (2) the work done in the preceding period on the current period's beginning inventory of work in process, and divides the total by the equivalent units of work done to date.

Transferred-In Costs

Many companies that use process costing have sequential production processes. For example, Oakville Wooden Toys transfers the items completed in its forming department to the finishing department. The finishing department would label the costs of the items it receives from the

Objective 9

Understand the concept of transferred-in costs in a process-costing system with sequential processes.

	(Step 1)	(Step 2) Equivalent Units	
	Physical	Direct	
Flow of Production	**Units**	**Materials**	**Conversion**
Work in process, April 30	5,000 (40%)*		
Started in May	26,000		
To account for	31,000		
Completed and transferred out			
during current period	24,000	24,000	24,000
Work in process, May 31	7,000 (60%)*	7,000	4,200†
Units accounted for	31,000		
Work done to date		31,000	28,200

*Degrees of completion for conversion costs at the dates of inventories.
†.60 × 7,000 = 4,200.

Exhibit 14-9
Forming Department Output in Equivalent Units, Weighted-Average Method
Month Ended May 31, 20X0

Business First

Process Costing at a Snack Peanut Company

Americans consume more than 300 million pounds of snack peanuts each year. The leading producer of snack peanuts is Planters Specialty Products Company, an operating unit of Kraft Foods. Planters markets regular-roast, dry-roast, salted, and unsalted peanuts in the United States. Processing a peanut snack food involves several activities. Most snack peanuts are blanched (removing the skins) before roasting. Peanuts can be oil-roasted or dry-roasted before being packaged and shipped.

The major activities in the processing of peanuts are shown below. This system not only tracks transferred-in costs between operating departments, such as the "blanching and fry-ing department" and the "packing and shipping department," it also tracks these costs for support (services) departments, such as receiving, moving, and storing activities within the overall process costing sequence. This is because Planters incorpo-rates ABC concepts within its process costing environment, designing a system that focuses on tracking and reporting costs by key activities within the system, regardless of traditional operating versus support department classifications.

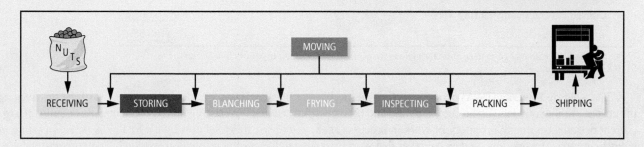

transferred-in costs

In process costing, costs incurred in a previous department for items that have been received by a subsequent department.

forming department as **transferred-in costs**—costs incurred in a previous department for items that have been received by a subsequent department. They are similar but not identical to addi-tional direct-materials costs incurred in the finishing department. Because transferred-in costs are a combination of all types of costs (direct-materials and conversion costs) incurred in previ-ous departments, they should not be called a direct-materials cost in the finishing department.

We account for transferred-in costs just as we would account for a direct material that is 100% added at the beginning of the finishing department, with one exception: We keep transferred-in costs separate from the direct materials added in the department as they truly are distinct categories of cost in a department. Therefore, Exhibit 14-10 would be modified to include

Exhibit 14-10
Forming Department
Production-Cost Report,
Weighted-Average Method
Month Ended May 31, 20X0

		Totals	Details — Direct Materials	Details — Conversion Costs
(Step 3)	Work in process, April 30	$ 20,000	$15,000	$ 5,000
	Costs added currently	146,880	84,200	62,680
	Total costs to account for	$166,880	$99,200	$67,680
(Step 4)	Divisor, equivalent units for work done to date*		÷31,000	÷28,200
	Unit costs (weighted averages)	$ 5.60	$ 3.20	$ 2.40
(Step 5)	Application of costs			
	Completed and transferred, 24,000 units × $5.60	$134,400		
	Work in process, May 31, 7,000 units			
	Direct materials	$ 22,400	7,000 × $3.20	
	Conversion costs	10,080		4,200* × $2.40
	Total work in process	$ 32,480		
	Total costs accounted for	$166,880		

*Equivalent units of work done. For more details, see Exhibit 14-9.

three columns of costs instead of two: transferred-in costs, direct-materials costs, and conversion costs. The total unit cost will be the sum of all three types of unit costs. For an interesting look at how one major snack food company designed its costing system with numerous transferred-in costs, see the Business First box on page 596.

Summary Problem for Your Review

PROBLEM

Consider the cooking department of **Middleton Foods**, a British food-processing company. Compute the cost of work completed and the cost of the ending inventory of work in process using the weighted-average method.

Units		
Beginning work in process: 5,000 units; 100% completed for materials, 40% completed for conversion costs		
Started during month: 28,000 units		
Completed during month: 31,000 units		
Ending work in process: 2,000 units; 100% completed for materials, 50% for conversion costs		
Costs		
Beginning work in process		
Direct materials	£8,060	
Conversion costs	1,300	£ 9,360
Direct materials added in current month		41,440
Conversion costs added in current month		14,700
Total costs to account for		£65,500

SOLUTION

Flow of Production	(Step 1) Physical Units	(Step 2) Equivalent Units	
		Material	Conversion
Completed and transferred out	31,000	31,000	31,000
Ending work in process	2,000	2,000*	1,000*
Equivalent units	33,000	33,000	32,000

*2,000 × 100% = 2,000; 2,000 × 50% = 1,000.

Weighted-Average Method	Total Cost	Direct Materials	Conversion Costs
Beginning work in process	£ 9,360	£ 8,060	£ 1,300
Costs added currently	56,140	41,440	14,700
Total costs to account for	£65,500	£49,500	£16,000
Equivalent units, weighted-average		÷33,000	÷32,000
Unit costs, weighted-average	£ 2.00	£ 1.50	£ 0.50
Transferred out, 31,000 × £2.00	£62,000		
Ending work in process			
Direct materials	£ 3,000	2,000 × £1.50	
Conversion cost	500		1,000 × £.50
Total work in process	£ 3,500		
Total costs accounted for	£65,500		

Costing in a JIT System: Backflush Costing

Objective 10

Use backflush costing with a JIT production system.

Tracking costs through various stages of inventory—raw material, work-in-process inventory for each process (or department), and finished-goods inventory—makes accounting systems complex. If there were no inventories, we could charge all costs directly to cost of goods sold, and accounting systems would be much simpler. Organizations using JIT production systems usually have very small inventories, or no inventories at all. For them, a traditional accounting system that traces costs through several different types of inventories may be of limited value. One such company is American Gypsum Company. The company manufactures gypsum wallboard for commercial and residential use. Like many companies that use the JIT production system, American Gypsum has very low inventory levels and uses **backflush costing**, an accounting system that applies costs to products only when the production is complete. How does backflush costing work? As we shall see, it is a fairly simple costing system.

backflush costing

An accounting system that applies costs to products only when the production is complete.

Principles of Backflush Costing

Backflush costing has only two categories of costs: materials and conversion costs. Its unique feature is an absence of a WIP account. Accountants enter actual material costs into a materials inventory account, and they enter actual labor and overhead costs into a conversion costs account. They then transfer costs from these two temporary accounts directly into finished-goods inventories. Some backflush systems even eliminate the finished-goods inventory accounts and transfer costs directly to cost of goods sold, especially if the company does not have a finished-goods inventory but rather sells products before producing them so that it can ship them immediately upon completion. Backflush systems assume that the company completes production so soon after the application of conversion activities that balances in the conversion costs accounts remain near zero because it transfers costs out almost immediately after initially recording them.

Example of Backflush Costing

Speaker Technology, Inc., (STI) produces speakers for automobile stereo systems. STI recently introduced a JIT production system and backflush costing. Consider the July production for speaker model AX27. The standard material cost per unit of AX27 is $14, and the standard unit conversion cost is $21. During July, STI purchased materials for $5,600, incurred conversion costs of $8,400 (which included all labor costs and manufacturing overhead), and produced and sold 400 units of AX27.

Backflush costing is accomplished in three steps:

1. Record actual materials and conversion costs. For simplicity, we initially assume that actual materials and conversion costs are identical to standard costs. As a company purchases materials, backflush systems add their cost to the Materials Inventory account:

   Materials inventory 5,600
       Accounts payable (or Cash) 5,600
   To record actual material purchases.

   Similarly, we add direct labor and manufacturing overhead costs to the Conversion Costs account when the company incurs them:

   Conversion costs 8,400
       Accrued wages and other accounts 8,400
   To record actual conversion costs incurred.

2. Apply costs to completed units. When production is complete, we transfer the costs from Materials Inventory and Conversion Costs accounts to Finished-Goods Inventory, based on the number of units completed and the standard cost of each unit:

   Finished-goods inventory(400 × $35)......................................14,000
       Materials inventory 5,600
       Conversion costs 8,400
   To record costs of completed production.

Because of short production cycle times, there is little lag between additions to the Conversion Costs account and transfers to Finished-Goods Inventory. The Conversion Costs account, therefore, remains near zero.

3. Record cost of goods sold during the period. We transfer the standard cost of the items sold from Finished-Goods Inventory to Cost of Goods Sold:

Cost of goods sold	14,000	
Finished-goods inventory		14,000

To record cost of 400 units sold at $35 per unit.

Suppose the company immediately delivers completed units to customers so that finished-goods inventories are negligible. We can combine steps 2 and 3 to eliminate the Finished-Goods Inventory account:

Cost of goods sold	14,000	
Material inventory		5,600
Conversion costs		8,400

What if actual costs added to the Conversion Costs account do not equal the standard amounts that are transferred to Finished-Goods Inventory? We treat the variances like overapplied or underapplied overhead. Backflush systems assume that account balances for conversion costs are approximately zero at all times. Thus, we charge any remaining balance in the account at the end of an accounting period to Cost of Goods Sold. Suppose actual conversion costs for July are $8,600 and the amount transferred to finished goods (that is, applied to the product) is $8,400. We would write off the $200 balance in the Conversion Costs account to Cost of Goods Sold at the end of the month:

Cost of goods sold	200	
Conversion costs		200

To recognize underapplied conversion costs.

Summary Problem for Your Review

PROBLEM

The most extreme (and simplest) version of backflush costing makes product costing entries at only one point, when the production of a unit is completed. Suppose STI had no Materials Inventory account (in addition to no WIP Inventory account). It purchases materials only when it needs them for production. Therefore, STI enters both materials and conversion costs directly into its Finished-Goods Inventory account.

Prepare journal entries (without explanations) and T-accounts for July's production of 400 units. As given earlier, materials purchases totaled $5,600, and conversion costs were $8,400. Why might a company use this extreme type of backflush costing?

SOLUTION

In one step, material and conversion costs are applied to finished-goods inventories:

Finished-Goods Inventories	14,000	
Accounts Payable		5,600
Wages Payable and Other Accounts		8,400

Finished-Goods Inventories		Accounts Payable, Wages Payable, and Other Accounts	
Materials 5,600			5,600
Conversion costs 8,400			8,400

This example shows that backflush costing is simple and inexpensive. Backflush costing provides reasonably accurate product costs if (1) materials inventories are low (most likely because of JIT delivery schedules), and (2) production cycle times are short, so that at any time a company has incurred only inconsequential amounts of materials costs and conversion costs for products that have yet to be completed.

Highlights to Remember

1. **Distinguish between job-order costing and process costing.** Product costing is an averaging process. Job-order costing involves narrow averages and unique units or a small batch of similar units. Process costing deals with broad averages and large volumes of homogeneous units.

2. **Prepare summary journal entries for the typical transactions of a job-costing system.** The focus of journal entries in a job-order costing system is on inventory accounts. The WIP Inventory account receives central attention. Direct materials used, direct labor, and factory overhead applied are accumulated in WIP. In turn, the cost of completed goods is transferred from WIP to Finished Goods.

3. **Use an ABC system in a job-order environment.** ABC can be used for any type of business that has significant levels of shared resources. In a job-order system, ABC helps managers understand the cost structure of the business on a job-by-job basis. Overhead costs are assigned to activity centers and then to jobs based on appropriate cost drivers. ABM uses ABC information and the increased understanding of the organization's cost structure to control and reduce overhead costs.

4. **Show how service organizations use job-order costing.** The job-costing approach is used in nonmanufacturing as well as manufacturing environments. Examples include costs of services such as auto repair, consulting, and auditing. For example, the job order is a key tool for planning and controlling an audit engagement by a public accounting firm.

5. **Explain the basic ideas underlying process costing and how they differ from job-order costing.** Process costing is used for inventory costing when there is continuous mass production of homogeneous units. Process-cost systems accumulate costs by department (or process); each department has its own WIP account. Job-order cost systems differ because costs are accumulated and tracked by the individual job order.

6. **Compute output in terms of equivalent units.** The key concept in process costing is that of equivalent units, the number of fully completed units that could have been produced from the resources required for the partially completed units.

7. **Compute costs and prepare journal entries for the principal transactions in a process-costing system.** There are five basic steps to process costing:
   1. Summarize the flow of physical units.
   2. Calculate output in terms of equivalent units.
   3. Summarize the total costs to account for.
   4. Calculate unit costs (step 3 ÷ step 2).
   5. Apply costs to units completed and to units in the ending work in process.

   Steps 3 and 5 provide the data for journal entries. These entries all involve the WIP accounts for the various departments (processes) producing products.

8. **Demonstrate how the presence of beginning inventories affects the computation of unit costs under the weighted-average method.** Process costing is complicated by the presence of beginning inventories. The weighted-average method calculates a unit cost that includes the work done and costs incurred in previous periods on the current period's beginning inventory with work done and costs incurred in the current period.

9. **Understand the concept of transferred-in costs in a process-costing system with sequential processes.** Transferred-in costs are costs incurred in a previous department for items that have been received by a subsequent department. Although we consider transferred-in costs as a separate cost category, we treat them as if they were direct materials that are 100% added at the beginning of the subsequent department.

10. **Use backflush costing with a JIT production system.** Many companies with JIT production systems use backflush costing. Such systems have no WIP Inventory account and apply costs to products only after the production process is complete.

Accounting Vocabulary

backflush costing, p. 598	job-cost sheet, p. 577	process costing, p. 577
equivalent units, p. 591	job order, p. 577	time cards, p. 577
hybrid costing systems, p. 577	job-order costing, p. 577	transferred-in costs, p. 596
job costing, p. 577	labor time tickets, p. 577	weighted-average (WA) process-
job-cost record, p. 577	materials requisitions, p. 577	costing method, p. 595

Fundamental Assignment Material

MyAccountingLab

14-A1 Job-Order Costing, Basic Journal Entries

The following data (in thousands) summarize the factory operations of the Jonas Manufacturing Company for the year 20X1, its first year in business:

a.	Direct materials purchased for cash	$350
b.	Direct materials issued and used	210
c.	Labor used directly on production	150
d1.	Indirect labor	130
d2.	Depreciation of plant and equipment	40
d3.	Miscellaneous factory overhead (ordinarily would be detailed)	70
e.	Overhead applied: 180% of direct labor cost	?
f.	Cost of production completed	575
g.	Cost of goods sold	415

1. Prepare summary journal entries. Omit explanations. For purposes of this problem, combine the items in part d as "overhead incurred."
2. Show the T-accounts for all inventories, Cost of Goods Sold, and Factory Department Overhead Control. Compute the ending balances of the inventories. Do not adjust for underapplied or over-applied factory overhead.

14-A2 Basic Process Costing

iCell produces cellular phones in large quantities. For simplicity, assume that the company has two departments, assembly and testing. The manufacturing costs in the assembly department during February were as follows:

Direct materials added		$ 73,600
Conversion costs		
Direct labor	$59,000	
Factory overhead	54,400	113,400
Assembly costs to account for		$187,000

There was no beginning inventory of work in process. Suppose work on 23,000 phones was begun in the assembly department during February, but only 20,000 phones were fully completed. All the parts had been made or placed in process, but only a third of the conversion costs had been completed for each of the phones still in process.

1. Compute the equivalent units and unit costs for February.
2. Compute the costs of units completed and transferred to the testing department. Also compute the cost of the ending work in process. (For journal entries, see problem 14-34.)

14-A3 Weighted-Average Process-Costing Method

The Magnatto Company manufactures electric drills. Material is introduced at the beginning of the process in the assembly department. Conversion costs are applied uniformly throughout the process. As the process is completed, goods are immediately transferred to the finishing department.

Data for the assembly department for the month of July 20X1 follow:

Work in process, June 30: $175,500 (consisting of $138,000 materials and $37,500 conversion costs); 100% completed for direct materials, but only 25% completed for conversion costs	10,000 units
Units started during July	80,000 units
Units completed during July	70,000 units
Work in process, July 31: 100% completed for direct materials, but only 50% completed for conversion costs	20,000 units
Direct materials added during July	$852,000
Conversion costs added during July	$634,500

1. Compute the total cost of goods transferred out of the assembly department during July.
2. Compute the total costs of the ending work in process. Prepare a production-cost report or a similar orderly tabulation of your work. Assume weighted-average product costing. (For journal entries, see Exercise 14-38.)

14-A4 Backflush Costing

The Temp makes electronic thermostats for homes and offices. The Orlando division makes one product, Autotherm, which has a standard cost of $33, consisting of $22 of materials and $11 of conversion costs. In January, actual purchases of materials totaled $235,000, labor payroll costs were $24,000, and manufacturing overhead was $76,000. Completed output was 10,000 units.

The Orlando division uses a backflush-costing system that records costs in materials inventory and conversion costs accounts and applies costs to products at the time production is completed. There were no finished-goods inventories on January 1 and 30 units on January 31.

1. Prepare journal entries (without explanations) to record January's costs for the Orlando division. Include the purchase of materials, incurrence of labor and manufacturing overhead costs, application of product costs, and recognition of cost of goods sold.
2. Prepare the journal entry to recognize overapplied or underapplied conversion costs at the end of January.

14-B1 Job-Order Costing, Basic Journal Entries

Consider the following data for Birmingham Printing Company (in thousands):

Inventories, December 31, 2011	
Direct materials	£ 12
Work in process	20
Finished goods	130

Summarized transactions for 2012 are as follows:

a.	Purchases of direct materials	£ 74
b.	Direct materials used	52
c.	Direct labor	200
d.	Factory overhead incurred	156
e.	Factory overhead applied, 80% of direct labor cost	?
f.	Cost of goods completed and transferred to finished goods	417
g.	Cost of goods sold	532
h.	Sales on account	742

1. Prepare summary journal entries for 2012 transactions. Omit explanations.
2. Show the T-accounts for all inventories, Cost of Goods Sold, and Factory Department Overhead Control. Compute the ending balances of the inventories. Do not adjust for underapplied or overapplied factory overhead.

14-B2 Basic Process Costing

Parenzo Company produces digital watches in large quantities. The manufacturing costs of the assembly department were as follows:

Direct materials added		$2,394,000
Conversion costs		
Direct labor	$561,000	
Factory overhead	870,000	1,431,000
Assembly costs to account for		$3,825,000

For simplicity, assume that this is a two-department company: assembly and finishing. There was no beginning work in process.

Suppose 570,000 units were started in the assembly department. There were 287,000 units completed and transferred to the finishing department. The 283,000 units in ending work in process were fully completed regarding direct materials but one-quarter completed regarding conversion costs.

1. Compute the equivalent units and unit costs in the assembly department.
2. Compute the costs of units completed and transferred to the finishing department. Also compute the cost of the ending work in process in the assembly department. (For journal entries, see Exercise 14-35.)

14-B3 Weighted-Average Process-Costing Method

The Shamrock Paint Company uses a process-costing system. Materials are added at the beginning of a particular process, and conversion costs are incurred uniformly. Work in process at the beginning of the month is 30% complete, while at the end it is 25% complete. One gallon of material makes one gallon of product. Data follow:

Beginning inventory	900 gal
Direct materials added	9,200 gal
Ending inventory	2,400 gal
Conversion costs incurred	$39,800
Cost of direct materials added	$82,950
Conversion costs, beginning inventory	$ 1,700
Cost of direct materials, beginning inventory	$ 2,900

Use the weighted-average method. Prepare a schedule of output in equivalent units and a schedule of application of costs to products. Show the cost of goods completed and cost of ending work in process. (For journal entries, see Exercise 14-37.)

14-B4 Backflush Costing

Remote Components recently installed a backflush-costing system. One department makes 4-inch speakers with a standard cost as follows:

Materials	$ 9.40
Conversion costs	4.70
Total	$14.10

Speakers are scheduled for production only after orders are received, and products are shipped to customers immediately on completion. Therefore, no finished-goods inventories are kept, and product costs are applied directly to cost of goods sold.

In October, 2,200 speakers were produced and shipped to customers. Materials were purchased at a cost of $23,980, and actual conversion costs (labor plus manufacturing overhead) of $10,490 were recorded.

1. Prepare journal entries to record October's costs for the production of 4-inch speakers.
2. Prepare a journal entry to recognize underapplied or overapplied conversion costs.

Additional Assignment Material

QUESTIONS

14-1 "There are different product costs for different purposes." Name at least two purposes.

14-2 Distinguish between job costing and process costing.

14-3 Describe the supporting details for work in process in a job-cost system.

14-4 What types of source documents provide information for job-cost records?

14-5 State three examples of service industries that use the job-costing approach.

14-6 "Law firms use job-costing to cost engagements. Thus, the markup required to cover overhead costs is not as great as in companies that use a process-costing system." Do you agree? Explain.

14-7 Give three examples of industries where process-costing systems are probably used.

14-8 Give three examples of nonprofit organizations where process-costing systems are probably used.

14-9 "There are five key steps in process-cost accounting." What are they?

14-10 Identify the major distinction between the first two and the final three steps of the five major steps in accounting for process costs.

14-11 Suppose a university has 10,000 full-time students and 5,000 half-time students. Using the concept of equivalent units, compute the number of "full-time equivalent" students.

14-12 Present an equation that describes the physical flow in process costing when there are beginning inventories in work in process.

14-13 How are transferred-in costs similar to direct materials costs? How are they different?

14-14 Explain what happens in a backflush-costing system when the amount of actual conversion cost in a period exceeds the amount applied to the products completed during that period.

CRITICAL THINKING EXERCISES

14-15 Purposes of Accumulating Job Costs
"Job costs are accumulated for purposes of inventory valuation and income determination." State two other purposes.

14-16 Job-Order Compared to Process Costing
"The basic distinction between job-order costing and process costing is the breadth of the denominator." Explain.

14-17 Cost Allocation in Service Firms
"Service firms trace only direct-labor costs to jobs. All other costs are applied as a percentage of direct-labor cost." Do you agree? Explain.

14-18 Purpose of Product Costing in a Process Production Environment
All product costing uses averages to determine costs per unit of product produced. In job-order production systems, the averages are based on a relatively small number of units. In a process production environment, the number of units is much larger. Once the average unit cost is determined, what is the central product-costing problem in process costing?

14-19 Process Costing in a JIT Environment
Companies using JIT production systems usually have very small inventories or no inventories at all. As a result, a traditional accounting system may be inappropriate. Many of these companies have adopted backflush-costing systems. Do backflush-costing systems work only for companies using a JIT production system? Explain.

EXERCISES

14-20 Job Costing in Business Sectors
Job costing systems are used in all business sectors. For each example listed, indicate whether the company is in the manufacturing, merchandising, or service sector:

a. Audit engagements by Ernst & Young
b. Advertising new products by Target
c. Assembly of desktop computers by Dell
d. Consulting engagement by McKensey & Co.

14-21 Direct Materials
For each of the following independent cases, fill in the blanks (in millions of dollars):

	1	2	3	4
Direct-materials inventory, December 31, 20X0	7	15	6	—
Purchased	10	7	—	7
Used	10	—	10	6
Direct-materials inventory, December 31, 20X1	—	13	11	4

14-22 Use of WIP Inventory Account
April production resulted in the following activity in a key account of Loopit Casting Company (in thousands):

WIP Inventory	
April 1 balance	9
Direct materials used	47
Direct labor charged to jobs	30
Factory overhead applied to jobs	27

Job Orders A13 and A37, with total costs of $35,000 and $40,000, respectively, were completed in April.

1. Journalize the completed production for April.
2. Compute the balance in WIP Inventory, April 30, after recording the completed production.
3. Journalize the credit sale of Job A13 for $49,000.

14-23 Job-Cost Record
Central State University uses job-cost records for various research projects. A major reason for such records is to justify requests for reimbursement of costs on projects sponsored by the federal government.

Consider the following summarized data regarding a cancer research project in the Medical School:

- September 5 — Direct materials, various medical supplies, $675
- September 7 — Direct materials, various chemicals, $1,525
- September 5–12 — Direct labor, research associates, 125 hours
- September 7–12 — Direct labor, research assistants, 205 hours

Research associates receive $42 per hour, while assistants receive $18. The overhead rate is 60% of direct-labor cost.

Sketch a job-cost (project-cost) record. Post all the data to the project-cost record. Compute the total cost of the project through September 12.

14-24 Analysis of Job-Cost Data

Job-cost records for Peter Construction contained the following data:

		Dates		
Job No.	Started	Finished	Sold	Total Cost of Job at May 31
1	April 19	June 14	June 15	$8,400
2	April 26	June 22	June 25	4,800
3	May 2	May 6	June 8	9,200
4	May 9	May 29	June 5	8,600
5	May 14	May 14	May 16	6,700

Compute Peter's (1) WIP Inventory at May 31, (2) Finished-Goods Inventory at May 31, and (3) Cost of Goods Sold for May.

14-25 Analysis of Job-Cost Data

The Cabrillo Construction Company constructs houses on speculation. That is, the houses are started before any buyer is known. Even if the buyer agrees to purchase a house under construction, no sales are recorded until the house is completed and accepted for delivery. The job-cost records contained the following (in thousands):

		Dates		Total Cost of Job at September 30	Total Construction Cost Added in October
Job No.	Started	Finished	Sold		
43	4/26	9/7	9/8	$180	
51	5/17	9/14	9/17	170	
52	5/20	9/30	10/4	150	
53	5/28	10/14	10/18	200	$50
61	6/3	10/20	11/24	115	20
62	6/9	10/21	10/27	180	25
71	7/7	11/6	11/22	118	36
81	8/7	11/24	12/24	106	48

1. Compute Cabrillo's cost of (a) construction-in-process inventory at September 30 and October 31, (b) finished-houses inventory at September 30 and October 31, and (c) cost of houses sold for September and October.
2. Prepare summary journal entries for the transfer of completed houses from construction in process to finished houses for September and October.
3. Record the cash sale (price = $345,000) and the cost of the house sold for Job 53.

14-26 Discovery of Unknowns

Enos Chemicals has the following balances (in millions) on December 31, 20X1:

Factory overhead applied	$960
Cost of goods sold	975
Factory overhead incurred	950
Direct-materials inventory	55
Finished-goods inventory	95
WIP inventory	988

The cost of goods completed was $970. The cost of direct materials requisitioned for production during 20X1 was $328. The cost of direct materials purchased was $225. Factory overhead was applied to production at a rate of 160% of direct-labor cost.

Compute the beginning inventory balances of direct materials, WIP, and finished goods. Make these computations before considering any possible adjustments for overapplied or underapplied overhead.

14-27 Discovery of Unknowns
The Brody Manufacturing Company has the following balances (in millions) as of December 31, 20X1:

WIP inventory	$ 18
Finished-goods inventory	180
Direct-materials inventory	74
Factory overhead incurred	192
Factory overhead applied at 150% of direct-labor cost	174
Cost of goods sold	592

The cost of direct materials purchased during 20X1 was $299. The cost of direct materials requisitioned for production during 20X1 was $242. The cost of goods completed was $630, all in millions.

Before considering any year-end adjustments for overapplied or underapplied overhead, compute the beginning inventory balances of direct materials, WIP, and finished goods.

14-28 Relationships Among Overhead Items
Fill in the unknowns:

	Case A	Case B	Case C
Budgeted factory overhead	$3,600,000	$?	$1,500,000
Budgeted cost drivers			
Direct-labor cost	$2,000,000		
Direct-labor hours		450,000	
Machine hours			250,000
Overhead application rate	?	$ 5	?

14-29 Process Costing in Business Sectors
Process-costing systems are used in all business sectors. For each example listed, indicate whether the company is in the manufacturing or service sector.

a. Beverage bottling at Coca-Cola
b. Postal delivery of mail by the U.S. Post Office
c. Limestone production at Nally & Gibson
d. Processing a life insurance application by State Farm

14-30 Process Map and Process Costing
Refer to Exhibit 14-5, panel B, on page 588. Identify an example of (1) a transferred-in cost, (2) a variable-cost resource, (3) a direct fixed-cost resource, and (4) an indirect resource cost for the process-costing system.

14-31 Equivalent Units
Confirm your understanding of the equivalent units concept by computing the equivalent units for material, direct labor, and overhead for the following hypothetical case at Nally & Gibson (refer to Exhibit 14-6, page 590).

In Process 3—crush and screen limestone rock—400 tons of limestone rock were transported to the plant during March. There was no beginning inventory of rock. During March, 320 tons were crushed, screened, and stocked. At the end of March, 80 tons of rock were 40% crushed and screened. Direct labor and overhead are incurred evenly during the crushing and screening process.

14-32 Basic Process Costing

A department of Jamestown Textiles produces cotton fabric. All direct materials are introduced at the start of the process. Conversion costs are incurred uniformly throughout the process.

In April, there was no beginning inventory. Units started, completed, and transferred were 675,000. Units in process on April 30 were 249,000. Each unit in ending work in process was 35% converted. Costs incurred during April were direct materials at $4,158,000 and conversion costs at $1,905,375.

1. Compute the total work done in equivalent units and the unit cost for April.
2. Compute the cost of units completed and transferred. Also, compute the cost of units in ending work in process.

14-33 Uneven Flow

One department of Dallas Instruments Company manufactures basic handheld calculators. Several materials are added at various stages of the process. The outer front shell and the carrying case, which represent 10% of the total materials cost, are added at the final step of the assembly process. All other materials are considered to be "in process" by the time the calculator reaches a 50% stage of completion.

During 20X0, 74,000 calculators were started in production. At year-end, 6,000 calculators were in various stages of completion, but all of them were beyond the 50% stage and, on the average, they were regarded as being 70% completed.

The following costs were incurred during the year: direct materials, $205,520; conversion costs, $397,100. There was no beginning WIP inventory.

1. Prepare a schedule of physical units and equivalent units.
2. Tabulate the unit costs, cost of goods completed, and cost of ending work in process.

14-34 Journal Entries

Refer to the data in problem 14-A2. Prepare summary journal entries for the use of direct materials, direct labor, and factory overhead applied. Also prepare a journal entry for the transfer of goods completed and transferred. Show the postings to the WIP account.

14-35 Journal Entries

Refer to the data in problem 14-B2. Prepare summary journal entries for the use of direct materials, direct labor, and factory overhead applied. Also prepare a journal entry for the transfer of goods completed and transferred. Show the posting to the WIP—Assembly Department account.

14-36 Compute Equivalent Units

Consider the following data for 20X1:

	Physical Units
Started in 20X1	70,000
Completed in 20X1	115,000
Ending inventory, work in process	35,000
Beginning inventory, work in process	80,000

The beginning inventory was 95% complete regarding direct materials and 90% complete regarding conversion costs. The ending inventory was 25% complete regarding direct materials and 15% complete regarding conversion costs.

Prepare a schedule of equivalent units for the work done to date.

14-37 Journal Entries

Refer to the data in problem 14-B3. Prepare summary journal entries for the use of direct materials and conversion costs. Also, prepare a journal entry for the transfer of goods completed, assuming that the goods are transferred to another department.

14-38 Journal Entries

Refer to the data in problem 14-A3. Prepare summary journal entries for the use of direct materials and conversion costs. Also, prepare a journal entry for the transfer of the goods completed and transferred from the assembly department to the finishing department.

PROBLEMS

14-39 Job Costing at Dell Computer

Dell's manufacturing process at its Austin, Texas, facility consists of assembly, functional testing, and quality control of the company's computer systems. The company's build-to-order manufacturing process is designed to allow the company to quickly produce customized computer systems. For example, the company contracts with various suppliers to manufacture unconfigured base Latitude notebook computers, and then Dell customizes these systems for shipment to customers. Quality control is maintained through the testing of components, parts, and subassemblies at various stages in the manufacturing process.

Describe how Dell might set up a job-costing system to determine the costs of its computers. What is a "job" to Dell? How might the costs of components, assembly, testing, and quality control be allocated to each "job"?

14-40 Relationships of Manufacturing Costs

Selected data concerning the past fiscal year's operations of the Woodson Manufacturing Company are as follows (in thousands):

	Inventories		
	Beginning	**Ending**	
Raw materials	$ 70	$ 90	
WIP	75	35	
Finished goods	100	120	
Other data:			
Raw materials used			$468
Total manufacturing costs charged to production during the year (includes raw materials, direct labor, and factory overhead applied at a rate of 80% of direct-labor cost)			864
Selling and general expenses			50

Answer each of the following items:

1. Compute the cost of raw materials purchased during the year.
2. Compute the direct-labor costs charged to production during the year.
3. Compute the cost of goods available for sale during the year.
4. Compute the cost of goods sold during the year.

14-41 Relationship of Subsidiary and General Ledgers, Journal Entries

The following summarized data are available on three job-cost records of Red Lake Manufacturing Company, a producer of packaging equipment:

	Job 412		Job 413		Job 414
	April	**May**	**April**	**May**	**May**
Direct materials	$9,000	$2,500	$12,000	—	$13,000
Direct labor	4,000	1,500	5,000	2,500	2,000
Factory overhead applied	8,000	?	10,000	?	?

The company's fiscal year ends on May 31. Factory overhead is applied as a percentage of direct-labor costs. The balances in selected accounts on April 30 were as follows: direct-materials inventory, $19,000; finished-goods inventory, $18,000.

Job 412 was completed during May and transferred to finished goods. Job 413 was still in process at the end of May, as was Job 414, which had started May 24. These were the only jobs worked on during April and May.

Job 412 was sold, along with other finished goods, by May 30. The total cost of goods sold during May was $33,000. The balance in Cost of Goods Sold for sales through April 30 was $450,000.

1. Prepare a schedule showing the balance of the WIP Inventory for April 30. This schedule should show the total costs of each job record. Taken together, the job-cost records are the subsidiary ledger supporting the general ledger balance of work in process.
2. What is the overhead application rate?
3. Prepare summary general journal entries for all costs added to WIP during May. Also prepare entries for all costs transferred from WIP to Finished Goods and from Finished Goods to Cost of Goods Sold. Post to the appropriate T-accounts.
4. Prepare a schedule showing the balance of the WIP Inventory, May 31.

14-42 **Job Costing in a Consulting Firm**

Tanner Engineering Consultants is a firm of professional civil engineers. It mostly does surveying jobs for the heavy construction industry throughout Texas. The firm obtains its jobs by giving fixed-price quotations, so profitability depends on the ability to predict the time required for the various subtasks on the job. (This situation is similar to that in the auditing profession, where times are budgeted for such audit steps as reconciling cash and confirming accounts receivable.)

A client may be served by various professional staff members who hold positions in the hierarchy from partners to managers to senior engineers to assistants. In addition, there are secretaries and other employees.

Tanner Engineering has the following budget for 20X1:

Compensation of professional staff	$3,000,000
Other costs	937,500
Total budgeted costs	$3,937,500

Each professional staff member must submit a weekly time report, which is used for charging hours to a client job-order record. The time report has seven columns, one for each day of the week. Its rows are as follows:

- Chargeable hours
    Client Job #156
    Client Job #183
    etc.
- Nonchargeable hours
    Attending seminar on new equipment
    Unassigned time
    etc.

In turn, these time reports are used for charging hours and costs to the client job-order records. The managing partner regards these job records as absolutely essential for measuring the profitability of various jobs and for providing an "experience base for improving predictions on future jobs."

1. This firm applies overhead to jobs at a budgeted percentage of the professional compensation charged directly to the job ("direct labor"). For all categories of professional personnel, chargeable hours average 75% of available hours. Nonchargeable hours are regarded as additional overhead. What is the overhead rate as a percentage of "direct labor," the chargeable professional compensation cost?
2. A senior engineer works 48 weeks per year, 40 hours per week. His compensation is $99,840. He has worked on two jobs during the past week, devoting 24 hours to Job 156 and 16 hours to Job 183. How much cost should be charged to Job 156 because of his work there?

14-43 **Weighted-Average Process Costing at Nally & Gibson**

Nally & Gibson produces crushed limestone, among other products, used in highway construction. To produce the crushed limestone, the company starts with limestone rocks from its quarry in Georgetown, Kentucky, and puts the rocks through a crushing process. Suppose that on May 1, Nally & Gibson has 24 tons of rock (75% complete) in the crushing process. The cost of that beginning WIP inventory was $6,000. During May, the company added 288 tons of rock from its quarry, and at the end of the month 15 tons remained in process, on average one-third complete. The cost of rocks from the quarry for the last 5 months has been $120 per ton. Labor and overhead cost during May in the rock-crushing process were $40,670. Nally & Gibson uses weighted-average process costing.

1. Compute the cost per ton of crushed rock for production in May.
2. Compute the cost of the WIP inventory at the end of May.
3. Suppose the flexible budget for labor and overhead was $16,000 plus $80 per ton. Evaluate the control of overhead and labor costs during May.

14-44 **Process and ABC**

Consider the potato chip production process at a company such as Frito-Lay. Frito-Lay uses a continuous flow technology that is suited for high volumes of product. At the Plano, Texas, facility, between 10,000 and 10,500 pounds of potato chips are produced each hour. The plant operates 24 hours a day.

It takes 30 minutes to completely produce a bag of potato chips from the raw potato to the packed end product.

1. What product and process characteristics of potato chips dictate the cost accounting system used? Describe the costing system best suited to Frito-Lay.
2. What product and process characteristics dictate the use of an ABC system? What implications does this have for Frito-Lay?
3. When beginning inventories are present, product costing becomes more complicated. Estimate the relative magnitude of beginning inventories at Frito-Lay compared to total production. What implication does this have for the costing system?

14-45 Nonprofit Basic Process Costing

The IRS must process millions of income tax returns yearly. When the taxpayer sends in a return, documents such as withholding statements and checks are matched against the data submitted. Then, various other inspections of the data are conducted. Some returns are more complicated than others so the expected time allowed to process a return is geared to an "average" return.

Some work-measurement experts have been closely monitoring the processing at a particular branch. They are seeking ways to improve productivity.

Suppose 8 million returns were received on April 15. On April 22, the work-measurement teams discovered that all supplies (punched cards, inspection check-sheets, and so on) had been affixed to the returns, but 20% of the returns still had to undergo a final inspection. The other returns were fully completed.

1. Suppose the final inspection represents 5% of the overall processing time in this process. Compute the total work done in terms of equivalent units.
2. The materials and supplies consumed were $400,000. For these calculations, materials and supplies are regarded just like direct materials. The conversion costs were $4,910,400. Compute the unit costs of materials and supplies and of conversion.
3. Compute the cost of the tax returns not yet completely processed.

14-46 Two Materials, Basic Process Costing

The following data pertain to the blending department at Pennsylvania Chemicals for April:

Units		
	Work in process, March 31	0
	Units started	50,000
	Completed and transferred to finishing department	40,000
Costs		
	Materials	
	Plastic compound	$450,000
	Softening compound	$ 60,000
	Conversion costs	$220,000

The plastic compound is introduced at the start of the process, while the softening compound is added when the product reaches an 80% stage of completion. Conversion costs are incurred uniformly throughout the process.

The ending work in process is 40% completed for conversion costs. None of the units in process reached the 80% stage of completion.

1. Compute the equivalent units and unit costs for April.
2. Compute the total cost of units completed and transferred to finished goods. Also compute the cost of the ending work in process.

14-47 Materials and Cartons in Basic Process Costing

A Manchester, England, company manufactures and sells small portable digital voice recorders. Business is booming. Several materials are added at various stages in the assembly department. Costs are accounted for on a process-cost basis. The end of the process involves conducting a final inspection and adding a cardboard carton.

The final inspection requires 5% of the total processing time. All units inspected during the period successfully passed inspection. All materials, besides the carton, are added by the time the recorders reach an 80% stage of completion of conversion.

There were no beginning inventories. During 20X1, 150,000 recorders were started in production. At the end of the year, which was not a busy time, 5,000 recorders were in various stages of completion. All the ending units in work in process were at the 95% stage. They awaited final inspection before being placed in cartons.

Total direct materials consumed in production, except for cartons, cost £2,250,000. Cartons used cost £319,000. Total conversion costs were £1,198,000.

1. Present a schedule of physical units, equivalent units, and unit costs of direct materials, cartons, and conversion costs.
2. Present a summary of the cost of goods completed and the cost of ending work in process.

14-48 Weighted-Average Process Costing with Transferred-in-Costs

Given the second process in a two-process manufacturer for January, 20X1:

Inventory in process, January 1, 50% completed	10,000 units
Completed and transferred out of process in January	40,000 units
Started into process in January	50,000 units
Inventory in process, January 31, 30% completed	???
Direct-material costs, January 1 inventory	$ 40,000
Direct-material costs, current costs	$120,000
Conversion costs, January 1 inventory	$ 30,000
Conversion costs, current costs	$246,000
Transferred-in costs, January 1 inventory	$ 50,000
Transferred-in costs, current costs	$250,000

Conversion costs are incurred uniformly during the process, while direct material is added when units are 40% complete.

1. Assuming Weighted average, what is the dollar valuation of the units transferred out for the month?

14-49 Backflush Costing

Sawtooth Meter manufactures a variety of measuring instruments. One product is an altimeter used by hikers and mountain climbers. Sawtooth adopted a JIT viewpoint with an automated, computer-controlled, robotic production system. The company schedules production only after an order is received, materials and parts arrive just as they are needed, the production cycle time for altimeters is less than one day, and completed units are packaged and shipped as part of the production cycle.

Sawtooth's backflush-costing system has only three accounts related to production of altimeters: materials and parts inventory, conversion costs, and finished-goods inventory. At the beginning of April (as at the beginning of every month), each of the three accounts had a balance of zero. Following are the April transactions related to the production of altimeters:

Materials and parts purchased	$273,800
Conversion costs incurred	$ 89,600
Altimeters produced	12,800 units

The budgeted (or standard) cost for one altimeter is $21 for materials and parts and $7 for conversion costs.

1. Prepare summary journal entries for the production of altimeters in April.
2. Compute the cost of goods sold for April. Explain any assumptions you make.
3. Suppose the actual conversion costs incurred during April were $90,600 instead of $89,600, and all other facts were as given. Prepare the additional journal entry that would be required at the end of April. Explain why the entry was necessary.

14-50 Review of Chapters 13 and 14

Pasadena Co. uses normal absorption costing. Factory overhead is applied to production at a budgeted rate based on direct labor cost. At the end of the period, there are two unfinished jobs. Additional information is available as follows:

Direct materials used = $90,000
Direct labor = $130,000
Beginning balance of work in process = $120,000
Cost of goods manufactured = $220,000
Finished goods beginning inventory = $70,000
Finished goods ending inventory = $130,000
Factory overhead is overapplied by $80,000
Actual factory overhead = $141,000

Determine the following:

1. The cost of goods sold before disposition of overapplied overhead
2. Ending balance in WIP
3. Budgeted rate for applying factory overhead
4. Assuming the overapplied factory overhead is not prorated, what is adjusted cost of goods sold?

14-51 Review of Chapters 13 and 14

Clark Co. uses normal absorption job-order costing. Factory overhead is applied to production at a budgeted rate of 300% of prime costs (direct materials plus direct labor). Clark Co.'s policy is to not prorate any over- or underapplied overhead amounts. All inventory amounts listed next are after disposition of any over- or under- applied overhead:

Direct labor = $100,000
Beginning balance of stores (direct materials) = $20,000
Ending balance of stores = $20,000
Purchased $50,000 of direct materials during period
Beginning balance of work in process = $300,000
Ending balance of work in process = $300,000
Cost of goods sold = $350,000
Finished goods beg. inventory = $100,000
Finished goods ending inventory = $200,000

Determine the following:

1. Direct materials used
2. Factory overhead applied
3. Cost of goods manufactured
4. Actual factory overhead for the period

NIKE 10-K PROBLEM

14-52 ABC and Distribution Centers

Read **Nike**'s 10-K in Appendix C. Item 1 describes its business, especially in the United States. A simplified description of Nike's supply chain follows:

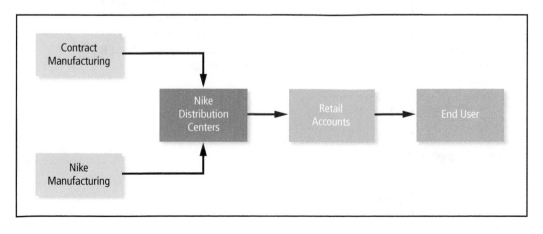

1. What kind of production system and associated costing system would you expect at the contract manufacturers? Nike distribution centers? How many distribution centers does Nike operate in the United States? Where are they located? How many retail accounts are in the United States?

2. Suppose Nike is implementing an ABC system to improve its accounting for overhead costs at its Memphis facility. Some of the activities performed at a Nike distribution center are listed below, along with a resource used by each activity. Because each of the resources is also used by more than one activity, its cost must be allocated. For each of the activities-resource pairs, suggest a plausible cost-allocation base that could be used to allocate the resource cost to the activities.

Activities	Resource Used
Receiving, put away apparel, picking products to fill an order, loading pallets onto trucks for shipment	Forklift
Receiving, put away apparel, repacking in boxes, repacking in cartons, shipping	Occupancy costs
Supplies ordering, customer order processing, invoicing and payment for parcel deliveries	Variable computer costs

EXCEL APPLICATION EXERCISE

14-53 Value of Units Produced

Goal: Create an Excel spreadsheet to compute the value of units produced using the weighted-average process-costing method. Use the results to answer questions about your findings.

Scenario: The Magnatto Company has asked you to compute costs for the electric drills produced in its assembly department during the month of July. You will need to use the weighted-average process-costing method to determine costs for beginning work in process, completed units, and ending work in process. Additional background information for your spreadsheet appears in Fundamental Assignment Material 14-A3.

When you have completed your spreadsheet, answer the following questions:

1. At the end of July, what is the value of the 20,000 units remaining in the WIP ending inventory?
2. What were the materials, conversion, and total cost of goods amounts for the units transferred to the finishing department during the month of July?
3. What are the materials and conversion cost per unit amounts for the accumulated units and costs in July?

Step-by-Step:

1. Open a new Excel spreadsheet.
2. In column A, create a bold-faced heading that contains the following:
   Row 1: Chapter 14 Decision Guideline
   Row 2: Magnatto Company
   Row 3: Weighted-Average Process Costing for July, 20X1
   Row 4: Today's Date
3. Merge and center the four heading rows across columns A–K.
4. In row 7, create the following column headings justified as indicated:
   Column B: Number   Center-justify
   Column C: Percent Complete   Merge and center across columns C and D
   Column E: Equivalent Units   Merge and center across columns E and F
   Column G: Cost of Goods   Merge and center across columns G–I
   Column J: Cost per Unit   Merge and center across columns J and K
5. In row 8, create the following center-justified column headings:
   Column B: of Units
   Columns C, E, G, and J: Materials
   Columns D, F, H, and K: Conversion
   Column I: Total
6. In column A, create the following row headings:
   Row 9: Beginning WIP
   Skip a row.
   Row 11: Units started
   Row 12: Less: Ending units
   Row 13: Units started and completed in July

Row 14: Beginning units completed
Skip a row.
Row 16: Accumulated units and costs in July
Skip a row.
Row 18: Value of transferred units

Note: Recommended column widths:

Column A = 28
Column B = 7
Columns C, E, and J = 8
Columns D, F, G, H, and K = 9
Column I = 11

7. Format columns C and D as follows:

Number tab:	Category:	Percentage
	Decimal places:	0

8. Use data from Fundamental Assignment Material 14-A3 to enter the following amounts:

Beginning WIP:	units, percent complete, cost of goods
Units started:	units
Less: Ending units:	units, percent complete
Accumulated units and costs in July:	cost of goods for materials and conversion
Value of transferred units:	units

9. Calculate the following amounts:

Units started and completed in July:	units, percent complete
Beginning units completed:	units, percent complete

10. In the sequence listed, use formulas to calculate the following amounts:

Equivalent units for:	Beginning WIP
	Less: Ending units
	Units started and completed in July
	Beginning units completed
	Accumulated units and costs in July
Cost per unit for:	Beginning WIP
	Accumulated units and costs in July
Materials cost of goods for:	Less: Ending units
	Units started and completed in July
	Beginning units completed
	Value of transferred units
Conversion cost of goods for:	Less: Ending units
	Units started and completed in July
	Beginning units completed
	Value of transferred units
Total cost of goods for:	Less: Ending units
	Units started and completed in July
	Beginning units completed
	Accumulated units and costs in July
	Value of transferred units
Cost per unit for:	Value of transferred units

11. Format columns B, E, F, G, H, and I as follows:

Number tab:	Category:	Number
	Decimal places:	0
	Use 1000 Separator (,):	Checked
	Negative numbers:	Red with parentheses

12. Format columns J and K as follows:

Number tab:	Category:	Currency
	Decimal places:	2
	Symbol:	$
	Negative numbers:	Red with parentheses

13. Format the cost of goods rows 9, 12, 16, and 18 as follows:

Number tab:	Category:	Accounting
	Decimal places:	0
	Symbol:	$

14. Modify the format of column B, rows 13 and 18; and row 16, columns E–I to display a top border using the default Line Style.

Border tab:	Icon:	Top Border

15. Modify the format of row 7, columns C, D, G, H, and I; and row 8, columns E, F, J, and K to display with a light gray fill.

Patterns tab:	Color:	Lightest Grey (above white)

16. Save your work, and print a copy for your files.

   Note: Print your spreadsheet using landscape in order to ensure that all columns appear on one page.

COLLABORATIVE LEARNING EXERCISE

14-54 Job and Process Costing

Form into groups of three to six students. For each of the following production processes, assess whether a job-cost or process-cost system is most likely to be used to determine the cost of the product or service. Also, explain why you think that system is most logical. (This can be done by individuals, but it is a much richer experience when done as a group, because the knowledge and judgment of several students interact to produce a much better analysis than a single student can produce.)

   a. Producing Cheerios by General Mills
   b. Processing an application for life insurance by Prudential
   c. Producing a couch by Ethan Allen
   d. Building a bridge by Kiewit Construction Co.
   e. Producing gasoline by Chevron
   f. Printing 200 copies of a 140-page course packet by FedEx Office
   g. Producing a superferry by Vigor Industrial

INTERNET EXERCISE

14-55 Process Costing at a Variety of Companies

Process costing assigns costs by measuring overall production costs and averaging them based on total production in units over a period of time, usually a month. The resulting average unit costs are then used to determine inventory cost and the cost of goods sold. Let's look at some companies and see if any of them might be candidates for using a process-costing system.

1. Log on to the **Lands' End** Web site at www.landsend.com. Click on "About Us" on the bottom of the page. What type of firm is Lands' End? What is its main activity? Do you think that the firm would be a good candidate for using a process-costing system? Why or why not?

2. Log on to **La-Z-Boy**'s Web site at www.lazboy.com. Click on "About La-Z-Boy." What type of firm is La-Z-Boy? What is its main activity? Do you think that the firm would be a good candidate for using a process-costing system? Why or why not?

3. Log on to **Tasty Baking Company**'s Web site at www.tastykake.com. What type of firm is Tasty Baking Company? What is its main activity? Do you think that the firm would be a good candidate for using a process-costing system? Why or why not?

15

Basic Accounting: Concepts, Techniques, and Conventions

LEARNING OBJECTIVES

When you have finished studying this chapter, you should be able to:

1. Read and interpret basic financial statements.

2. Analyze typical business transactions using the balance sheet equation.

3. Distinguish between the accrual basis of accounting and the cash basis of accounting.

4. Make adjustments to the accounts under accrual accounting.

5. Explain the nature of dividends and retained earnings.

6. Select relevant items from a set of data and assemble them into a balance sheet and an income statement.

7. Distinguish between the reporting of corporate owners' equity and the reporting of owners' equity for partnerships and sole proprietorships.

8. Explain the role of auditors in financial reporting and how accounting standards are set.

9. Identify how the measurement principles of recognition, matching and cost recovery, and stable monetary unit affect financial reporting.

10. Define continuity, relevance, faithful representation, materiality, conservatism, and cost-benefit (Appendix 15 A).

11. Use T-accounts, debits, and credits to record transactions (Appendix 15 B).

► GENERAL MILLS

Chances are you have eaten Big-G cereals from General Mills, such as Wheaties or Cheerios. Or perhaps you have baked with Betty Crocker flour or Bisquick, or snacked on Bugles, Yoplait yogurt, or Häagen-Dazs ice cream. General Mills sells nearly $17 billion of these and other food products throughout the world each year. General Mills' customers want foods that are convenient, tasty, and affordable. Managers at General Mills take pride in developing and marketing food products that meet these customer demands. Just as important to the managers is whether the company is making a profit. How can the company's managers see how much profit General Mills is making? The same way you can—by reading the company's financial statements.

Financial statements are generated by a company's financial accounting system. General Mills, like all well-managed companies, has a financial accounting system that not only generates company-wide financial statements but also provides detailed information about the financial results of each product. General Mills holds managers responsible for meeting their segment's profit targets. In his 2011 letter to shareholders, Ken Powell, chairman and CEO, indicated that the company expects each segment's operating profit to grow in the "mid-single digits" annually.

Suppose you want to buy General Mills stock instead of its food products. Then you too would be interested in the company's financial performance. You would want to know the company's financial position and its prospects to judge whether it is wise to invest in General Mills stock. The company's financial statements can be a great help in making this judgment, but only if you know a bit about accounting. Accounting is the language of business. Its special vocabulary conveys the financial story of an organization. To understand corporate annual reports, you must learn this language—the words and ideas used by accountants and other managers when discussing financial matters.

This chapter explores the essence of profit-making activities and how accountants portray them in financial statements. We leave the more technical topics for the chapter appendices. As you examine what accountants do, you will also learn many of the relevant concepts and principles of accounting. Although the focus will be on profit-seeking organizations, the main ideas also apply to nonprofit organizations. ■

© ZUMA Press/Alamy

The Need for Accounting

Accountants record the financial history of a company. You can use accounting information to assess the past financial performance of a company and to help predict its future performance. In addition to businesses, all kinds of organizations—government agencies, nonprofit organizations, and others—rely on accounting to gauge their progress.

The accounting process begins by recording an organization's transactions. A **transaction** is any event that affects the financial position of an organization and requires recording. Many concepts, conventions, and rules determine what events a company records as accounting transactions and how accountants measure the financial impact of each transaction. As you learn about these concepts, conventions, and rules, you will also learn about **financial statements**, which are summaries of recorded accounting transactions.

Managers, investors, and other interest groups often want the answers to two important questions about an organization: How well did the organization perform for a given period? Where does the organization stand financially at a given point? Accountants answer these questions with three major financial statements: The income statement and statement of cash flows summarize two different aspects of performance over a period of time, and the balance sheet shows the financial position at a point in time. This chapter discusses the income statement and balance sheet. Chapter 16 introduces the statement of cash flows.

Financial Statements—Balance Sheet and Income Statement

An efficient way to learn about accounting is to study a specific illustration. Suppose King Hardware Company began business as a **corporation**—a business organized as a separate legal entity and owned by its stockholders. The company's first transaction occurred on February 28, 20X1, when its stockholders invested a total of $100,000 cash. The following additional transactions occurred during March:

1. Acquisition of inventory for $75,000 cash.
2. Acquisition of inventory for $35,000 on open account. A purchase on open account allows the buyer to pay cash after the date of purchase, often in 30 days. Amounts owed to vendors for purchases on open accounts are **accounts payable**.
3. Merchandise carried in inventory at a cost of $100,000 was sold for $130,000. King Hardware received $10,000 in cash and recorded accounts receivable of $120,000. **Accounts receivable** are amounts due from customers for sales charged to an account instead of being paid for in cash.
4. Cash collections of a portion of accounts receivable from item 4, $15,000.
5. Cash payments of a portion of accounts payable from item 3, $20,000.
6. On March 1, King Hardware paid $3,000 cash for store rent for March, April, and May. Rent is $1,000 per month, payable quarterly in advance, beginning March 1.

General Mills cereals — from heart-healthy Cheerios to kids' favorites Cocoa Puffs and Trix — are popular throughout the world.

transaction
Any event that affects the financial position of an organization and requires recording.

financial statements
Summarized reports of accounting transactions.

Objective 1

Read and interpret basic financial statements.

corporation
A business organized as a separate legal entity and owned by its stockholders.

accounts payable
Amounts owed to vendors for purchases on open accounts.

accounts receivable
Amounts due from customers for sales charged to an account instead of being paid for in cash.

The Balance Sheet

balance sheet (statement of financial position)
A snapshot of the financial status of an organization at a point in time.

King Hardware's **balance sheet** (also called a **statement of financial position**)—a snapshot of the financial status of an organization at a specific point in time—after the first transaction, investment by stockholders, follows:

King Hardware
Balance Sheet (Statement of Financial Position) as of February 28, 20X1

Assets		Liabilities and Stockholders' Equity	
Cash	$100,000	Paid-in capital	$100,000

assets
Economic resources that a company owns and expects to provide future benefits.

liabilities
The entity's economic obligations to nonowners.

owners' equity
The excess of the assets over the liabilities.

account
Each item in a financial statement.

stockholders' equity
The owners' equity of a corporation.

The balance sheet has two sections—(1) assets and (2) liabilities plus owners' (stockholders') equity. **Assets** are economic resources that a company owns and expects to provide future benefits. **Liabilities** are the entity's economic obligations to nonowners. **Owners' equity** is the excess of the assets over the liabilities. You can think of the two sections of the balance sheet as the two sides of an equation:

$$\text{Assets} = \text{Liabilities} + \text{Owners' Equity}$$

Liabilities and owners' equity are essentially claims on the assets by creditors and owners, respectively. A company typically has multiple assets, liabilities, and owners' equity items—a large company may have thousands, or even millions, of individual assets and liabilities. The accounting process aggregates and summarizes results reported on the balance sheet. Each separate asset, liability, or owners' equity item shown on a balance sheet is an **account**—the term used for any item in a financial statement.

Because the stockholders own a corporation, we call the owners' equity of a corporation **stockholders' equity**. In turn, the stockholders' equity has two major components, (1) **paid-in capital**, the ownership claim arising from funds paid in by the owners, and (2) **retained earnings** (or **retained income**), the ownership claim arising from reinvestment of previous profits:

$$\text{assets} = \text{liabilities} + \text{stockholders' equity}$$
$$= \text{liabilities} + (\text{paid-in capital} + \text{retained earnings})$$

Objective 2

Analyze typical business transactions using the balance sheet equation.

paid-in capital
The ownership claim arising from funds paid in by the owners.

retained earnings (retained income)
The ownership claim arising from the reinvestment of previous profits.

Now let's examine how King Hardware's March transactions affect the balance sheet. The balance sheet equation, shown in Exhibit 15-1, summarizes the cumulative effect of all these transactions (including the initial investment). Note that most of the transactions are summaries of a larger set of underlying transactions. For example, the sales did not all occur in a single sales transaction. Similarly, there were multiple purchases of inventory, collections from customers, or disbursements to suppliers. Consider sales of Cheerios by General Mills. It sells millions of boxes of Cheerios and other products during a year in thousands of transactions. Accountants record each transaction in the accounting system and then add together all the sales amounts to find the total sales to report in the financial statements.

You can see in Exhibit 15-1 that King Hardware's transaction 1, the initial investment by owners, increases assets and increases stockholders' equity. That is, cash increases and so does paid-in capital—the claim arising from the owners' total initial investment in the corporation. The balance sheet after this first transaction, shown at the top of this page, contains only two accounts.

Transaction 2, the purchase of inventory for cash, is an exchange of one asset for another. This transaction changes the balances in individual assets, increasing one asset (inventory) and decreasing another asset (cash), but does not change total assets or claims on those assets. Transaction 3, the purchase of inventory on account, adds an asset (inventory) and a liability (accounts payable), increasing total assets and total liabilities and stockholders' equity to $135,000. After the first three transactions, the balance sheet now includes four accounts, cash, inventory, accounts payable, and paid-in capital:

King Hardware
Balance Sheet after Transactions 1, 2, and 3

Assets		Liabilities and Stockholders' Equity	
Cash	$ 25,000	Account payable	$ 35,000
Inventory	110,000	Paid-in capital	100,000
Total assets	$135,000	Total liabilities and stockholders' equity	$135,000

Assets = Liabilities + Stockholders' Equity

Transactions	Cash	+	Accounts Receivable	+	Inventory	+	Prepaid Rent	=	Accounts Payable	+	Paid-in Capital	+	Retained Earnings
1. Initial investment	+ 100,000							=			+ 100,000		
2. Acquire inventory for cash	− 75,000				+ 75,000			=					
3. Acquire inventory for credit					+ 35,000			=	+ 35,000				
4a. Sales on credit and for cash	+ 10,000		+ 120,000					=					+ 130,000 (revenue)
4b. Cost of inventory sold					− 100,000			=					− 100,000 (expense)
5. Collect from customers	+ 15,000		− 15,000					=					
6. Pay accounts of suppliers	− 20,000							=	− 20,000				
7a. Pay rent in advance	− 3,000						+ 3,000	=					
7b. Recognize expiration of rental services							− 1,000	=					− 1,000 (expense)
Balance, 3/31/X1	+ 27,000		+ 105,000		+ 10,000		+ 2,000	=	+ 15,000		+ 100,000		+ 29,000
	144,000										144,000		

Exhibit 15-1

King Hardware Co.
Analysis of Transactions (in dollars) for March 20X1

Transaction 4 is the sale of $100,000 of inventory for $130,000. This is our first example of a transaction that reflects the fundamental purpose of providing a good or service that has a value to the purchaser ($130,000) greater than the cost of providing the good or service ($100,000). In this transaction, two things happen simultaneously—the company acquires new assets, Cash and Accounts Receivable (4a), in exchange for Inventory (4b). The assets Cash and Accounts Receivable and the Retained Earnings portion of Stockholders' Equity increase by the selling price, $130,000. (Notice that the $10,000 increase in Cash plus the $120,000 increase in Accounts Receivable equals the $130,000 increase in stockholders' equity.) The asset Inventory and the Retained Earnings portion of Stockholders' Equity decrease by the cost of the items sold, $100,000. The $30,000 net increase in retained earnings represents stockholders' claims arising from the profitable sale. Transaction 4a is also our first example of a **compound entry**, a transaction that affects more than two accounts.

Transaction 5, cash collection of accounts receivable, is another example of an event that affects individual asset accounts but has no impact on liabilities or stockholders' equity. Collections are merely the transformation of one asset (Accounts Receivable) into another (Cash). Transaction 6, cash payment of accounts payable, affects assets and liabilities only. In general, collections from customers and payments to suppliers have no direct impact on stockholders' equity.

In transaction 7, the company pays cash for rent to acquire the right to use store facilities for the next 3 months. On March 1, we create the asset Prepaid Rent (7a), a measure of the future benefit from the right to use these facilities. Assets include legal rights to receive goods and services such as the future use of facilities as well as items you can see or touch such as cash or inventory. Transaction 7b recognizes that King Hardware received one-third of the 3 months of rental services during March. Because the company has "used up" $1,000 of the asset Prepaid Rent during March, we reduce both the asset and stockholders' equity by $1,000.

The balance sheet for King Hardware at the end of March follows:

compound entry
A transaction that affects more than two accounts.

revenue
Increases in ownership claims arising from the delivery of goods or services.

King Hardware Co.
Balance Sheet as of March 31, 20X1

Assets		Liabilities and Stockholders' Equity		
Cash	$ 27,000	Liabilities: Accounts payable		$ 15,000
Accounts receivable	105,000	Stockholders' equity		
Inventory	10,000	Paid-in capital	$100,000	
Prepaid rent	2,000	Retained earnings	29,000	129,000
Total	$144,000	Total		$144,000

recognize
To formally record in the accounting records during the current period.

Revenues, Expenses, and the Income Statement

expenses
Decreases in ownership claims arising from delivering goods or services or using up assets.

Let's review transaction 4 in more detail. Recall that this transaction has two phases, (a) and (b). Transaction 4a illustrates the recognition of revenue. **Revenues** are increases in ownership claims arising from the delivery of goods or services. We **recognize** revenue by formally recording it in the accounting records during the current period. We do this only after it meets two tests. First, the company must earn the revenues. That is, it must deliver the goods or render the services to customers. Second, the revenue must be realized or realizable. If the company collects payment, it has realized the revenue. If it has not collected payment but is reasonably sure that it will collect the receivable, the revenue is realizable.

income (net income, profits, earnings)
The excess of revenues over expenses.

Transaction 4b illustrates the incurrence of an expense. **Expenses** are decreases in ownership claims arising from delivering goods or services or using up assets. The expense in this case is cost of goods sold, the amount paid for the items sold to the customer.

Transactions 4a and 4b also illustrate the fundamental meaning of **income** (also called **net income**, **profits**, or **earnings**), which is the excess of revenues over expenses. As the Retained Earnings column in Exhibit 15-1 shows, increases in revenues increase stockholders' equity. In contrast, increases in expenses decrease stockholders' equity.

income statement
A statement that summarizes a company's revenues and expenses. It measures the performance of an organization by matching its accomplishments (revenue from customers) and its efforts (cost of goods sold and other expenses).

A company's **income statement** summarizes its revenues and expenses. It measures the performance of an organization by matching its accomplishments (revenue from customers, often called **sales revenue** or simply **sales**) and its efforts (cost of goods sold and other expenses) for a span of time, often a month, a quarter, or a year.

sales revenue (sales)
Revenue from customers.

The income statement is the major link between balance sheets:

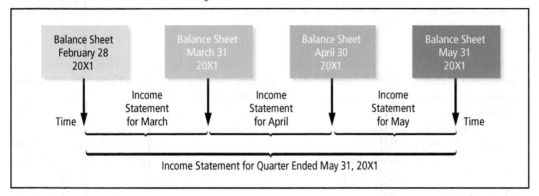

Notice that each balance sheet is a snapshot at a point in time. In contrast, each income statement summarizes events during a period that cause changes in the stockholders' equity (specifically retained earnings) section of the balance sheet. Examine the changes in retained earnings in Exhibit 15-1. The revenues and expenses during March explain why retained earnings changed from $0 at the beginning of the month to $29,000 at the end of the month. The revenues increase stockholders' equity, and expenses decrease stockholders' equity.

The following King Hardware income statement summarizes the company's revenues and expenses for the month of March:

King Hardware Co.
Income Statement for the Month Ended March 31, 20X1

Revenues (sales)		$130,000
Expenses		
Cost of goods sold	$100,000	
Rent	1,000	
Total expenses		101,000
Net income		$ 29,000

Real income statements and balance sheets use the same formats as those for King Hardware, though they usually contain more details. Consider General Mills. Simplified versions of its balance sheet and income statement follow (in millions):

General Mills, Inc.
Balance Sheet May 29, 2011

Assets		Liabilities and Stockholders' Equity	
Cash	$ 620	Liabilities	$12,063
Accounts receivable	1,162	Stockholders' equity	6,612
Other assets	16,893		
Total assets	$18,675	Total liabilities and stockholders' equity	$18,675

General Mills, Inc.
Income Statement for the Year Ended May 29, 2011

Sales	$14,880
Expenses	13,076
Net income	$ 1,804

The income statement shows that General Mills' stockholders' equity (retained earnings) increased by $1,804 million because of profitable operations in the year ended May 29, 2011. This $1,804 million is included in the $6,612 million of stockholders' equity on the May 29, 2011, balance sheet.

The Analytical Power of the Balance Sheet Equation

The balance sheet equation highlights the link between the income statement and balance sheet. Indeed, the entire accounting system is based on the simple balance sheet equation,

$$\text{Assets (A)} = \text{liabilities (L)} + \text{stockholders' equity (SE)} \qquad (1)$$

SE equals the original ownership claims plus the increase in ownership claims from profitable operations. That is, SE equals the claim arising from paid-in capital plus the claim arising from retained earnings. Therefore,

$$A = L + \text{paid-in capital} + \text{retained earnings} \qquad (2)$$

For most companies, the major changes in retained earnings come from revenues and expenses—revenues increase retained earnings and expenses decrease them. Revenue and expense accounts are nothing more than current period changes in retained earnings. They are temporary retained earnings accounts that are reset to zero at the start of each new period. They summarize the revenues and expenses that occurred during the current period, summarizing the reasons for the changes in retained earnings. After a company adds the revenues less expenses for the current period to the balance in retained earnings, it resets revenue and expense accounts to zero so that it can use them to accumulate the revenues and expenses for the next period.

Notice in Exhibit 15-1 that, for each transaction, the equation is always in balance. How do we keep it in balance? If a transaction affects items on only one side of the equation, the total amount added equals the total amount subtracted on that side. If the transaction affects items on both sides, then we add or subtract equal amounts on each side.

The striking feature of the balance sheet equation is its universal applicability. Every transaction, no matter how simple or complex, can be analyzed via the equation. The top technical partners in the world's largest professional accounting firms, when confronted with the most intricate transactions of multinational companies, inevitably discuss and analyze transactions in terms of the balance sheet equation.

Accrual Basis and Cash Basis

Objective 3

Distinguish between the accrual basis of accounting and the cash basis of accounting.

accrual basis

A process of accounting that recognizes the impact of transactions on the financial statements in the time periods when revenues and expenses occur instead of when the company pays or receives cash.

There are two approaches to accounting: the cash basis and the accrual basis. You may not realize it, but you are probably already familiar with the cash basis. We keep our checkbooks on the cash basis. We simply record the receipts and payments of cash. Many small nonprofit organizations use the cash basis of accounting.

In contrast, corporations and many other large organizations measure income and financial position using the accrual basis of accounting. The **accrual basis** recognizes the impact of transactions on the financial statements in the periods when revenues and expenses occur instead of when the company receives or pays cash. That is, a company records revenue when it meets the criteria for recognition, and it records expenses when it uses resources to generate revenue—not necessarily when cash changes hands.

Transaction 4a in Exhibit 15-1, on page 621, shows an example of the accrual basis. King Hardware recognizes revenue when it makes sales on credit, not when it receives cash. Similarly, transactions 4b and 7b (for cost of goods sold and rent) show that King Hardware records expenses as it expends efforts or uses services to obtain the revenue, regardless of when it pays out the cash. Most users of financial statements believe that the accrual basis provides the best framework for relating accomplishments (revenues) with efforts (expenses). That is, they believe that revenue less expenses is a better measure of a company's performance during a period than is cash receipts less cash payments. Why do they believe this? Companies conduct more than 95% of all business on a credit basis, so cash receipts and payments are not the critical transactions for recognizing accomplishments and efforts. The accrual basis evolved to provide a more complete and timely, and therefore more accurate, report of the financial impact of various events.

cash basis

A process of accounting where revenue and expense recognition occur when the company receives and pays out cash.

If King Hardware used the **cash basis** of accounting instead of the accrual basis, revenue and expense recognition would occur when the company receives and pays out cash. In March, King Hardware would show $25,000 of revenue, the amount of cash collected from customers. Similarly, cost of goods sold would be the $20,000 cash payment for the purchase of inventory, and rent expense would be the $3,000 cash payment for rent rather than the $1,000 rent applicable to March. Consider the rent example for King Hardware. Under the cash basis, March must bear expenses for the entire quarter's rent of $3,000, merely because the cash outflow occurs then. Most accountants maintain that it is nonsense to say that March's rent expense was $3,000 while rent expense for April and May was zero. In contrast, the accrual basis better measures performance by assigning one-third of the total 3-month rental expenses to each of the 3 months that benefits from the use of the facilities. This method makes the economic performance of each month comparable to that of other months.

The major deficiency of the cash basis of accounting is that it fails to properly match efforts and accomplishments (expenses and revenues) to measure performance. Moreover, it omits key assets (such as accounts receivable and prepaid rent) and key liabilities (such as accounts payable) from balance sheets that measure financial position.

Nonprofit Organizations

The examples in this chapter focus on profit-seeking organizations, but nonprofit organizations, such as government agencies and charitable organizations, also use balance sheets and income statements. For many years, most nonprofit organizations used cash-basis rather than accrual accounting. However, that is changing quickly. As these organizations face more pressure to develop accurate measures of performance, they are increasingly using accrual accounting.

The basic concepts of assets, liabilities, revenues, and expenses apply to all organizations, whatever their goals and wherever they are located. However, organizations that do not seek profits do not measure income. Further, because they have no owners, there is no owners' equity. Nevertheless, they have parallels to income statements and balance sheets. For example, balance sheets of nonprofit organizations show a category of "net assets" instead of "owners' equity" to measure the difference between assets and liabilities. Instead of an income statement, nonprofit organizations have a "statement of activities" that reports changes in net assets.

Adjustments to the Accounts

Earlier, we defined a transaction as any economic event that an accountant should record. Under accrual accounting, accountants record both **explicit transactions**—day-to-day routine events, such as credit sales, credit purchases, cash received on account, and cash payments on account—and **implicit transactions**—events that day-to-day recording procedures temporarily ignore, such as expiration of prepaid rent or accrual of interest due to the passage of time. Explicit transactions are easy to identify because they record market transactions, exchanges of goods and services between the entity and another party. They are generally supported by **source documents**, clear evidence of transactions, such as sales slips and purchase invoices.

In contrast, accountants need a way to ensure that they record all implicit transactions. At the end of each accounting period accountants systematically make **adjustments** (or **adjusting entries**) to account for implicit transactions such as unpaid wages, prepaid rent, interest owed, and the like. We classify the principal adjustments into four types, each of which we will discuss in detail:

1. Expiration of Unexpired Costs
2. Recognition (Earning) of Unearned Revenues
3. Accrual of Unrecorded Expenses
4. Accrual of Unrecorded Revenues

These adjustments are an essential part of accrual accounting. They provide a more complete and timely measure of efforts, accomplishments, and financial position.

Adjustment Type I: Expiration of Unexpired Costs

You can view assets other than cash and receivables as bundles of economic services awaiting future use—prepaid or stored costs that the accounting system carries forward to future periods. The values of assets frequently decline (and eventually disappear) because of the passage of time. We illustrated this first type of adjustment in Exhibit 15-1 by recognizing the rent expense in transaction 7b. Rather than immediately charging these costs as expenses, we charge them as expenses in future periods when the company uses the services:

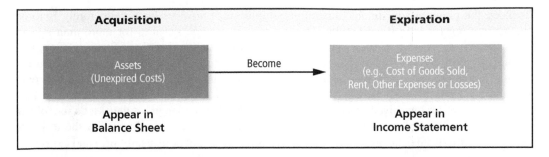

explicit transactions
Transactions that record day-to-day routine events—such as credit sales, credit purchases, cash received on account, and cash disbursed on account—that are supported by source documents.

implicit transactions
Transactions that record events that day-to-day recording procedures temporarily ignore, such as expiration of prepaid rent or accrual of interest due to the passage of time.

source documents
Clear evidence of transactions, such as sales slips and purchase invoices.

adjustments (adjusting entries)
Entries that record implicit transactions such as unpaid wages, prepaid rent, interest owed, and the like.

Objective 4

Make adjustments to the accounts under accrual accounting.

unexpired cost

Any asset that managers expect to become an expense in future periods, for example, inventory and prepaid rent.

When a company uses the services represented by a particular cost, we say the cost expires. Therefore, an **unexpired cost** is any asset that managers expect to become an expense in future periods. Examples in our King Hardware illustration are inventory and prepaid rent. Other examples are equipment and various prepaid expenses, such as prepaid insurance and prepaid property taxes. When accountants say they are "writing off" an asset, they mean they are recording the decline in asset value as an expense.

The analysis of the inventory and rent transactions in Exhibit 15-1 maintains this distinction between acquisition and expiration. The unexpired costs of inventory and prepaid rent are assets until the company uses them up, at which time they become expenses.

Timing of Asset Expiration

Sometimes companies acquire and use resources almost simultaneously. Examples are advertising services and sales salaries and commissions. Conceptually, we can view these costs, at least momentarily, as assets on acquisition before we write them off as expenses. For example, suppose an eighth transaction in Exhibit 15-1 was newspaper advertising acquired for $1,000 cash. We can analyze the transaction in two phases:

| | Assets | | | = | Liabilities | + | Stockholders' Equity | |
| | Cash + | Other Assets + | Unexpired Advertising | = | | | Paid-in Capital | Retained Earnings |
Transaction				=				
8a. Acquire advertising services	−1,000		+1,000	=				
8b. Use advertising services			−1,000	=				−1,000 (expense)

In concept, the benefit of the newspaper ad is to increase sales, and this benefit expires over a period of days or weeks after the ad runs. However, when the benefit expires quickly, accountants often do not bother to take two steps to record an asset, Unexpired Advertising, and then write it off. Instead, they take a shortcut and record the expense immediately:

Transaction	Cash + Other Assets	=	Liabilities + Paid-in Capital + Retained Earnings
8. Acquire and use advertising services	−1,000	=	−1,000 (expense)

Making the entry in two steps instead of one is cumbersome from a practical bookkeeping viewpoint. But it is useful to think about how accounting entries relate to what managers actually do. Managers acquire goods and services, not expenses per se. These goods and services become expenses as managers use them to obtain revenue.

When does an asset expire and become an expense? Sometimes this question is hard to answer. For example, some accountants prefer to record as assets the amounts spent for research and development (R&D) and write them off (charge as an expense) in some systematic manner over a period of years. Why? Because they maintain that money spent for R&D creates future benefits and, thus, qualifies as an asset. But the regulators of financial accounting in the United States have ruled that all such costs have vague future benefits that are difficult to measure reliably. Thus, financial reporting rules in the United States require companies to write off R&D costs as expenses immediately. You will not find R&D costs listed as assets in U.S. balance sheets. Outside the United States, international financial accounting standards allow companies to differentiate between research costs—which they immediately expense—and development costs—which they are allowed to record as assets and write off to expense in future periods if the development costs meet some specific criteria.

long-lived assets

Assets that will provide services for more than a year.

Depreciation

To keep the expense-adjustment illustration simple, until now we have deliberately ignored the accounting for **long-lived assets**—assets that will provide services for more than a year. Equipment is an example of a long-lived asset that is essentially a bundle of future services that a company will use over a series of years. The cost of equipment becomes an expense on the income statement via depreciation, which is the cost of equipment that a company spreads over the future periods in which the company will be able to use the equipment.

useful life

The number of years the company expects to use an asset.

residual value

The predicted sales value of a long-lived asset at the end of its useful life.

To account for long-lived assets, accountants (1) predict the length of the asset's **useful life** (that is, the number of years the company expects to use the asset), (2) predict the ultimate **residual value** (that is, the predicted value of the asset at the end of its useful life) and (3) spread the cost of the asset less the residual value to the years of its useful life in some systematic way. This process of systematically spreading the equipment cost across the years of its useful life is called depreciation for physical assets—such as buildings, equipment, furniture, and fixtures— that the entity owns. (Land is not subject to depreciation. Why? Because we do not use up land.) The same process is called depletion when it is applied to natural resources and amortization when it is applied to intangible (non-physical) assets.

The most popular depreciation method for financial reporting is the **straight-line method**, which depreciates an asset by the same amount each year. Suppose King Hardware had acquired some store equipment for $14,000 on March 1. The predicted life of the equipment is 10 years, and the estimated residual value is $2,000:

straight-line method
A method that depreciates an asset by the same amount each year.

$$\text{straight-line depreciation per year} = \frac{\text{original cost} - \text{estimated residual value}}{\text{years of useful life}}$$

$$= \frac{\$14,000 - \$2,000}{10}$$

$$= \$1,200 \text{ per year, or } \$100 \text{ per month}$$

Depreciation illustrates the essence of the general concept of expense. The purchase and use of a resource (that is, a good or service, such as inventories, rent, or equipment) ordinarily consists of two basic steps: (1) the acquisition of the asset (transactions 2, 3, and 7a) and (2) the expiration of the asset as an expense (transactions 4b and 7b). When we use an asset, whether immediately or in some future period, we say part of the asset expires, and we decrease the value of the asset and decrease owners' equity by the same amount.

Summary Problem for Your Review

PROBLEM

We analyzed the King Hardware transactions for March in Exhibit 15-1 on page 621. The balance sheet showed the following balances as of March 31, 20X1:

	Assets	Liabilities and Stockholders' Equity
Cash	$ 27,000	
Accounts receivable	105,000	
Inventory	10,000	
Prepaid rent	2,000	
Accounts payable		$ 15,000
Paid-in capital		100,000
Retained earnings		29,000
	$144,000	$144,000

Here is a summary of the transactions that occurred during the next month, April:

1. Cash collections of accounts receivable, $88,000.
2. Cash payments of accounts payable, $24,000.
3. Acquisitions of inventory on open account, $80,000.
4. Merchandise carried in inventory at a cost of $70,000 was sold on open account for $85,000.
5. Adjustment for recognition of rent expense for April.

Using the accrual basis of accounting, prepare an analysis of transactions, employing the equation approach demonstrated in Exhibit 15-1.

SOLUTION

The answer is in the top half of Exhibit 15-2 ending with transaction 5. We will explain transactions 6–9 in the following sections.

Transaction	Cash	+	Accounts Receivable	+	Inventory	+	Prepaid Rent	=	Accounts Payable	+	Accrued Wages Payable	+	Unearned Revenue*	+	Paid-in Capital	+	Retained Earnings
	Assets								Liabilities					+	Stockholders' Equity		
Bal. 3/31/X1	+ 27,000		+ 105,000		+ 10,000		+ 2,000	=	+ 15,000						+ 100,000		+ 29,000
1.	+ 88,000		− 88,000					=									
2.	− 24,000							=	− 24,000								
3.					+ 80,000			=	+ 80,000								
4a.			+ 85,000					=									+ 85,000 (revenue)
4b.					− 70,000			=									− 70,000 (expense)
5.							− 1,000	=									− 1,000 (expense)
6.	+ 3,000							=					+ 3,000*				
7.	− 6,000							=									− 6,000 (expense)
8.								=			+ 600						− 600 (expense)
9.	− 18,000							=									− 18,000 (dividend)
4/30/X1	+ 70,000		+ 102,000		+ 20,000		+ 1,000	=	+ 71,000		+ 600		+ 3,000		+ 100,000		+ 18,400
			193,000										193,000				

*Some accountants would call this account "Customer Deposits," "Advances from Customers," "Deferred Sales Revenue," or "Unrealized Sales Revenue."

Exhibit 15-2
King Hardware Co.
Analysis of Transactions (in dollars) for April 20X1

Adjustment Type II: Recognition (Earning) of Unearned Revenues

Now let's examine a second type of adjustment. Consider the following transaction for King Hardware in April:

6. Some customers paid $3,000 cash in advance for merchandise that they ordered but that King Hardware did not expect to deliver until mid-May.

See transaction 6 in Exhibit 15-2. We call this $3,000 **unearned revenue** or **deferred revenue**. Why? Because King Hardware collected cash from customers and recorded the amount received before the company earned it by delivering the merchandise. Unearned revenue is a liability because King Hardware is obligated to deliver the merchandise ordered or to refund the money if it does not deliver the merchandise. Some companies call this account *advances from customers* or *customer deposits*. Advance collections of rent and magazine subscriptions are other examples.

Sometimes it is easier to see how accountants analyze transactions by visualizing the financial positions of both parties to a contract. For instance, consider the rent transaction of March 1. You are already familiar with the King Hardware analysis. The $1,000 monthly entries for King Hardware are examples of the first type of adjustments, the expiration of unexpired costs. Compare this financial impact on King Hardware with the impact on the landlord who receives the rental payment:

> **unearned revenue (deferred revenue)**
> Collections from customers that companies receive and record before they earn the revenue.

	Owner of Property (Landlord, Lessor)			King Hardware (Tenant, Lessee)			
	A =	L	+ SE	A	= L	+	SE
	Cash	Unearned Rent Revenue	Rent Revenue	Cash	Prepaid Rent		Rent Expense
a. Explicit transaction (advanced payment of 3 months' rent)	+3,000 =	+3,000		−3,000	+3,000	=	
b. March adjustment (for 1 month's rent)	=	−1,000	+1,000		−1,000	=	−1,000
c. April adjustment (for 1 month's rent)	=	−1,000	+1,000		−1,000	=	−1,000
d. May adjustment (for 1 month's rent)	=	−1,000	+1,000		−1,000	=	−1,000

From the viewpoint of the owner of the rental property, the first transaction recognizes unearned revenue. This is a liability because the owner is obligated to deliver the rental services (or to refund the money if it does not deliver the services).

As you can see from the preceding table, adjustments for the expiration of unexpired costs (Type I) and adjustments for the recognition of unearned revenues (Type II) are mirror images of each other. If one party to a contract has a prepaid expense, the other has unearned revenue. We can make a similar analysis for a 3-year magazine subscription. The buyer recognizes a prepaid expense (asset) and uses adjustments of Type I to spread the initial cost to expense over the 3-year life of the services. In turn, the magazine publisher must initially recognize its liability, unearned subscription revenue. It then changes the unearned revenue to earned revenue (i.e., increases rent revenue and decreases unearned revenue) when the company delivers magazines throughout the life of the subscription—adjustment Type II.

Adjustment Type III: Accrual of Unrecorded Expenses

> **accrue**
> To accumulate a receivable or payable during a given period, even though no explicit transaction occurs.

Let's proceed now to the third type of adjustment: accrual of unrecorded expenses. To **accrue** something means to accumulate and record a receivable or payable during a given period even though no explicit transaction occurs. Examples of **accrued expenses**—expenses reported on the income statement before a company pays for them with cash—are the wages of employees

> **accrued expenses**
> Expenses reported on the income statement before a company pays for them with cash.

for partial payroll periods and the interest that accumulates on borrowed money before the interest payment is made. The liability corresponding to such expenses, such as wages payable or interest payable, grows as time passes—it is accruing (or accumulating). Computerized accounting systems can make daily or even "real-time" recordings in the accounts for many accruals. However, such frequent entries are often costly and unnecessary. Instead, accountants usually make adjustments to bring each expense and corresponding liability account up to date only periodically, such as at the end of a period for which they are preparing formal financial statements.

Accounting for Payment of Wages

Consider the following two transactions relating to wages paid by King Hardware to its employees:

7. King Hardware paid employees $1,500 each Friday in April, for total wages of $6,000. (For simplicity, we ignored wages in March.) King Hardware recognizes these payments for employee services by increasing Wages Expense and decreasing Cash.
8. King Hardware incurred 2 days of wages totaling $600 near the end of April, but it did not pay the employees until after April 30. Accordingly, the accountant increased Wages Expense and increased a liability, Accrued Wages Payable.

Most companies pay their employees at predetermined times. For example, the University of Washington pays employees on the tenth and twenty-fifth of each month for the half-month period ending 10 days earlier. King Hardware pays its employees each Friday for services rendered during that week. Here is a sample calendar for April:

The cumulative total wages paid on the Fridays during April were $6,000. King Hardware accounts for wages expense using the shortcut procedure described earlier for goods and services that a company routinely consumes in the period of their purchase. Transaction 7 in Exhibit 15-2 (and summarized next) shows King Hardware's entry for April's wages through April 26:

		Assets (A)	=	Liabilities (L)	+	Stockholders' Equity (SE)
		Cash	=			Wages Expense
7.	Routine entry for explicit transactions	−6,000	=			−6,000

Accounting for Accrual of Wages

King Hardware's wages of $1,500 per week are $300 per day for a 5-day work week. At the end of April, in addition to the $6,000 already paid and recorded, King Hardware owes $600 for the time employees worked during the last 2 days of April but will not pay the employees for these services until the next regular weekly payday, May 3. Thus, to bring the financial statements up to date through April 30, an accrual is necessary to record wages owed but not yet recorded. Periodic adjustments ensure that the financial statements apply accrual accounting to measure revenues, expenses, assets, and liabilities on a timely basis. King Hardware accounts for this implicit transaction with entry 8:

	A	=	L	+	SE
			Accrued Wages Payable		Wages Expense
8. Adjustment for the accrual of unrecorded wages		=	+600		−600

Accrued expenses, such as accrued wages payable, arise when payment follows the rendering of services. Other examples of accrued expenses include sales commissions, property taxes, income taxes, and interest on borrowed money. In all of these, the payment generally comes after the company recognizes the expense. Consider interest expense, which is an amount paid for the use of money. It is similar to the rent you pay for the use of buildings or automobiles. The interest accumulates (accrues) as time unfolds, regardless of when the company actually pays the interest in cash. So when General Mills showed interest expense of $346 million on its 2011 income statement, it means that it accrued $346 million of interest that year, not necessarily that it paid $346 million in cash.

Adjustment Type IV: Accrual of Unrecorded Revenues

The final type of adjustment, the recognition of **accrued revenues**—revenues that a company has earned but has not yet received in cash—does not appear in Exhibit 15-2. It is the mirror image of the accrual of unrecorded expenses. Suppose Security State Bank lends $50,000 in cash to King Hardware on a 3-month promissory note with interest at 1% per month payable at the end of the 3 months. The following tabulation shows the effect of the adjustment for interest at the end of the first month (.01 × $50,000 = $500) on both King Hardware (the accrual of unrecorded expenses, adjustment type III covered in the previous section) and Security State Bank (the accrual of unrecorded revenues, the subject of this section):

accrued revenues
Revenues that a company has earned but has not yet received in cash.

Security State Bank (Lender)				King Hardware Co. (Borrower)			
A	=	L	+	SE	A	=	L	+	SE
Accrued Interest Receivable				Interest Revenue		Accrued Interest Payable			Interest Expense
+500	=			+500		=	+500		−500

No cash changes hands at the end of the first month, but King Hardware records interest expense and Security State Bank records interest revenue.

This completes our discussion of the four types of accruals. We summarize these in Exhibit 15-3, which shows accruals of expenses or revenues in the columns and the timing of the accrual compared to the cash flows in the rows.

	Expense	Revenue
Payment precedes recognition of expense or revenue	I Expiration of unexpired costs. Illustration: The write-off of prepaid rent as rent expense (Exhibit 15-2, entry 5)	II Recognition (earning) of unearned revenues. Illustration: The mirror image of Type I, whereby the landlord recognizes rent revenue and decreases unearned rent revenue (rent collected in advance)
Recognition of expense or revenue precedes payments	III Accrual of unrecorded expenses. Illustration: Wage expense for wages earned by employees but not yet paid (Exhibit 15-2, entry 8)	IV Accrual of unrecorded revenues. Illustration: Interest revenue earned but not yet collected by a financial institution

Exhibit 15-3
Four Major Types of Accounting Adjustments Before Preparation of Financial Statements

Making Managerial Decisions

The manager of the DVD division of a large electronics firm complained, "I don't understand all this accrual stuff. Why can't you just measure my performance based on cash in and cash out?" Provide a brief answer to this question.

Answer

Accrual accounting more accurately matches accomplishment with effort. When you buy a machine that will last 5 years, do you think the entire cost of the machine should be charged against your performance at the time of purchase? Or when you sell a carton of DVD players on credit to a long-standing customer who is virtually certain to pay, should your credit for the sale await eventual collection of the cash? Accrual accounting gives you credit for accomplishments when you achieve them and charges for the expenses associated with those accomplishments. Thus, it provides a much better measure of performance than does "cash in and cash out."

Dividends and Retained Earnings

Objective 5

Explain the nature of dividends and retained earnings.

We have now covered all the entries in Exhibit 15-2 that show how revenues increase and expenses decrease the retained earnings portion of stockholders' equity. Now, let's look at transaction 9, which shows another type of transaction that decreases retained earnings—payment of dividends:

9. Cash dividends of $18,000 were declared by the board of directors and disbursed to stockholders on April 29.

Dividends Are Not Expenses

cash dividends (dividends)

Distributions of cash to stockholders that reduce retained earnings.

Cash dividends (often called simply **dividends**) are distributions of cash to stockholders. Dividends reduce retained earnings, but they are not expenses like rent and wages. Companies do not deduct them from revenues when measuring income because dividends do not help to generate sales or conduct operations. Cash dividends simply distribute assets (cash) to the owners of those assets (stockholders). They reduce both assets (cash) and owners' claims on those assets (retained earnings).

A company's board of directors decides when to pay dividends and how much to pay. The amount of cash dividends declared by the board of directors of a company depends on many factors. A company's cash position and future needs for cash to pay debts or to purchase additional assets are usually more important than the balance in retained earnings. A company with a large retained earnings balance but little cash will find it difficult to pay dividends. Many companies try to maintain a stable dividend policy, paying dividends consistently even if they encounter a few years of little or no net income. For example, General Mills has paid shareholder dividends, uninterrupted and without reduction, for 112 consecutive years.

Nature of Retained Earnings

Let's examine the retained earnings account in more detail. On page 620 we explained that you can think of the entire right-hand side of the balance sheet equation as claims against the total assets. The liabilities are the claims of creditors. The stockholders' equity represents the claims of owners arising out of their initial investment (paid-in capital) and subsequent profitable operations (retained earnings). On August 12, 2012, General Mills had retained earnings of $10.3 billion, nearly seven times its paid-in capital of $1.3 billion. As a company grows, the Retained Earnings account can soar if the company does not pay large dividends. Retained Earnings is frequently the largest stockholders' equity account, especially for older companies. For example, General Electric had retained earnings of $142 billion on September 30, 2012, compared to paid-in capital of less than $1 billion. In contrast, Amgen, a biotech company that had huge investments before it began generating any profits, had paid-in capital of $28 billion and a retained deficit (negative retained earnings) of $9 billion.

Some users of financial statements have the mistaken impression that retained earnings represents a pot of cash awaiting distribution to stockholders. Rather, retained earnings (and also paid-in capital) is a general claim against, or undivided interest in, total assets, not a specific claim against cash or against any other particular asset. Do not confuse the assets themselves with the claims of stockholders against the assets.

We can illustrate this for King Hardware by looking at cash and retained earnings at three points in time (from the top line and bottom line of Exhibit 15-1 on page 621, and the bottom line of Exhibit 15-2 on page 628):

	Cash	Retained Earnings
February 28, 20X1	$100,000	$ 0
March 31, 20X1	27,000	29,000
April 30, 20X1	70,000	18,400

On February 28, King Hardware had $100,000 in cash (all from investments by stockholders) and no retained earnings because King Hardware had not yet begun operations and, thus, had generated no profits or losses. By March 31, cash had fallen by $73,000 to $27,000, primarily because the company had used cash to buy inventories. Meanwhile, retained earnings increased by $29,000 because of profitable operations. Finally, during April, cash increased by $43,000 (mainly because King Hardware began to collect its accounts receivable), while retained earnings fell by $10,600, mainly because King Hardware paid more dividends than it earned in net income. You can see that cash can increase while retained earnings decreases, and vice versa. It is clear that there is no direct relationship between retained earnings and available cash.

Preparing Financial Statements

We will use the data from the balance sheet equation in Exhibit 15-2 (p. 628) to prepare King Hardware's April financial statements. The balance sheet and income statement, shown in Exhibits 15-4 and 15-5, are similar to those illustrated earlier. The balance sheet uses the totals at the bottom of Exhibit 15-2, and the income statement uses the revenue and expense entries in the retained earnings column.

Objective 6

Select relevant items from a set of data and assemble them into a balance sheet and an income statement.

Assets		Liabilities and Stockholders' Equity		
Cash	$ 70,000	Liabilities		
Accounts receivable	102,000	Accounts payable	$ 71,000	
Inventory	20,000	Accrued wages payable	600	
Prepaid rent	1,000	Unearned revenue	3,000	$ 74,600
		Stockholders' equity		
		Paid-in capital	$100,000	
		Retained earnings	18,400	118,400
Total assets	$193,000	Total liabilities and stockholders' equity		$193,000

Exhibit 15-4
King Hardware Company
Balance Sheet as of April 30, 20X1

Sales		$85,000
Cost of goods sold		70,000
Gross profit		$15,000
Operating expenses		
Rent	$1,000	
Wages	6,600	7,600
Net income		$ 7,400

Exhibit 15-5
King Hardware Company
Income Statement for the Month Ended April 30, 20X1

Exhibit 15-6
King Hardware Company
*Changes in Retained Earnings for
the Month Ended April 30, 20X1*

Retained earnings, March 31, 20X1	$29,000
Net income for April	7,400
Total	$36,400
Dividends	18,000
Retained earnings, April 30, 20X1	$18,400

**statement of
stockholders' equity**

A statement that shows the
changes in each stockholders'
equity account during the period.

Exhibit 15-6 shows the linkage between the balance sheet and income statement. It lists the items affecting retained earnings during April. It starts with the beginning balance, adds net income for the period, and deducts cash dividends, to arrive at the ending balance. This explanation of changes in retained earnings is often included as part of a **statement of stockholders' equity**, which shows the changes in each individual stockholders' equity account (including retained earnings) during the period. Accountants call the income statement in Exhibit 15-5 a "multiple-step" statement because it includes a subtotal for gross profit. As described in Chapter 2 on page 58, gross profit (sometimes called gross margin) is the excess of sales over the cost of the inventory that was sold. A "single-step" statement would merely list all the expenses, including cost of goods sold, and deduct the total from sales. More complex multiple-step income statements may have additional subtotals.

Sole Proprietorships and Partnerships

Objective 7

Distinguish between the reporting
of corporate owners' equity and
the reporting of owners' equity
for partnerships and sole
proprietorships.

sole proprietorship

A business entity with a
single owner.

partnership

An organization that joins
two or more individuals
together as co-owners.

To this point, the discussion has focused on the accounting for a corporation. However, the basic accounting concepts also apply to a **sole proprietorship**—a business entity with a single owner—or a **partnership**—an organization that joins two or more individuals together as co-owners. Accounting for assets, liabilities, revenues, and expenses is identical for all forms of businesses. The basic concepts relating to owners' equity are also identical, except that financial statements for proprietorships and partnerships rarely make distinctions between paid-in capital and retained earnings. Let's compare the owners' equity section of King Hardware as of April 30 to similar presentations for a sole proprietorship owned by Alice Walsh or a partnership owned equally by Susan Zingler and John Martin:

Owners' Equity for a Corporation		
Stockholders' equity		
Capital stock (paid-in capital)	$100,000	
Retained earnings	18,400	
Total stockholders' equity		$118,400

Owners' Equity for a Sole Proprietorship	
Alice Walsh, capital	$118,400

Owners' Equity for a Partnership	
Susan Zingler, capital	$ 59,200
John Martin, capital	59,200
Total partners' equity	$118,400

This example shows that, unlike corporations, sole proprietorships and partnerships do not distinguish between paid-in capital (i.e., amounts invested by owners) and retained earnings. Instead, they typically accumulate a single amount for each owner's original investment, subsequent investments, share of net income, and withdrawals.

net worth

A synonym for owners' equity.

Some accountants call owners' equity **net worth**. This is unfortunate because naïve users of financial statements might interpret this as meaning that owners' equity is a measure of the market value of the business to an outside buyer. It is not. The market value of a business depends on future profit projections that may have little relationship to the existing assets, liabilities, or stockholders' equity of the entity as measured by its accounting records. For example, General Mills' shareholders' equity (or net worth) in June 2011, was just over $6.6 billion, while its market value was approximately $37 billion.

Making Managerial Decisions

When entrepreneurs start a company, they must decide whether the company will be a sole proprietorship, a partnership, or a corporation. As the accountant for such a start-up company, explain how the accounting system would differ for each of the three types of organizational structures.

Answer

Most important aspects of the accounting system are the same for all three types of organizational structures. The only difference will be in the owners' equity section. For a sole proprietorship, there is only one owners' equity account. A partnership has one owners' equity account for each partner. This requires the accountant to attribute all increases or decreases in owners' equity to a particular partner. For example, income will be split among the partners according to a predetermined formula. Finally, a corporation divides owners' equity into paid-in capital and retained earnings to distinguish resources contributed by the owners from those generated by profitable operations.

Generally Accepted Accounting Principles

Accounting is commonly misunderstood as being a precise discipline that produces exact measurements of a company's financial position and performance. As a result, many individuals regard accountants as little more than mechanical tabulators who grind out financial reports after processing an imposing amount of detail in accordance with stringent predetermined rules. Although accountants take methodical steps with masses of data, their rules of measurement allow much room for judgment—accounting is more an art than a science. These judgments are guided by a set of principles on which there is general agreement, not on rules that can be "proved." These principles and procedures that together make up accepted accounting practice at any given time—generally accepted accounting principles (GAAP)—were introduced in Chapter 1 on page 8.

Objective 8

Explain the role of auditors in financial reporting and how accounting standards are set.

Auditor's Independent Opinion

To ensure that companies abide by GAAP, the financial statements of publicly held corporations are subject to an independent audit. An **audit** is an examination or in-depth inspection of financial statements and companies' records made by an independent registered public accounting firm in accordance with auditing standards approved by the Public Company Accounting Oversight Board (PCAOB) in the United States. The PCAOB is a part of the **Securities and Exchange Commission (SEC)**, a government agency that regulates U.S. financial markets, including financial reporting. After auditing a company's financial statements, an accounting firm issues an **independent opinion**—the accountant's assurance that management's financial statements are in conformity with GAAP. The audit opinion typically includes the following key phrasing found in General Mills' 2012 annual report:

> *In our opinion, the consolidated financial statements referred to above present fairly, in all material respects, the financial position of General Mills, Inc. and subsidiaries as of May 27, 2012 and May 29, 2011, and the results of their operations and their cash flows for each of the fiscal years in the three-year period ended May 27, 2012, in conformity with U. S. generally accepted accounting principles.*

Audit opinions are not infallible guarantees of financial truth. Why? Financial statements may seem precise because their numbers all add up. However, they are the result of a complex measurement process that rests on a large number of assumptions and conventions. Further, it is impossible for auditors to examine every bit of data that goes into the financial statements.

audit
An "examination" or in-depth inspection of financial statements and companies' records made in accordance with auditing standards.

Securities and Exchange Commission (SEC)
A government agency that regulates the financial markets in the United States, including financial reporting.

independent opinion
The accountant's assurance that management's financial statements are in conformity with GAAP.

Although audits are not perfect, financial statement users rely on them as being honest and impartial assessments of the financial statements. However, in the last decade the shareholders of several companies, including Enron, WorldCom, Washington Mutual, Fannie Mae, and Tyco, accused auditors of being either negligent or deceitful (and sometimes both). These companies experienced financial troubles after receiving a "clean bill of health" from their auditors. In response to the scandals in the early 2000s, the U.S. Congress passed the Sarbanes-Oxley Act (SOX) as described in Chapter 1, p. 8. SOX required independent audits of companies' internal control systems—the policies that protect and ensure efficient use of a company's assets. One function of internal controls is to make sure that a company's financial records and reports are accurate. Management must file a statement attesting to the quality of its internal control system, and auditors examine both the system and management's statement about it. Then they issue an opinion, such as the following one about General Mills:

We also have audited General Mills, Inc.'s internal control over financial reporting as of May 27, 2012, based on criteria established in Internal Control—Integrated Framework issued by the Committee of Sponsoring Organizations of the Treadway Commission (COSO). . . We conducted our audits in accordance with the standards of the Public Company Accounting Oversight Board (United States). . . . [I]n our opinion, General Mills, Inc. maintained, in all material respects, effective internal control over financial reporting as of May 27, 2012.

Accounting Standard Setters

Financial Accounting Standards Board (FASB)
The body that sets GAAP in the United States.

International Accounting Standards Board (IASB)
The group that establishes international GAAP.

Auditors and the investing public rely on GAAP determined by the **Financial Accounting Standards Board (FASB)** in the United States and the **International Accounting Standards Board (IASB)** in much of the rest of the world. The FASB, consisting of 7 full-time members plus a staff of more than 60 members, is an independent creation of the private sector. Its mission is to "establish and improve standards of financial accounting and reporting for the guidance and education of the public, including issuers, auditors, and users of financial information." The IASB is a similar independent organization whose pronouncements, called International Financial Reporting Standards (IFRS) as discussed in Chapter 1 on page 8, define GAAP in the European Union and more than 100 other countries. In 2008 the SEC started accepting financial statements based on IFRS for non-U.S. companies whose stock is traded in U.S. capital markets. It also defined a "road-map" for eventual adoption of international standards by U.S. companies as well. The FASB and IASB are currently working on converging their separate standards into one set of world-wide standards.

The SEC has the ultimate responsibility for specifying GAAP for U.S. companies with publicly traded stock. However, the SEC has informally delegated much rule-making power to the FASB. If and when the pending move to international standards occurs, such power will also be delegated to the IASB. This public sector–private sector relationship may be sketched as follows:

Business First

Corporate Citizenship Awards

The media have criticized many businesses recently for their greed and lack of ethics. While some companies deserve such criticism, many more go out of their way to prove their integrity and good citizenship through their dealings with customers, suppliers, employees, and the community. To recognize some of these activities, for the last 12 years *Corporate Responsibility Magazine* has annually named the 100 best corporate citizens of the year. Three companies have made the list all 12 years: Intel, Cisco Systems, and Starbucks. In 2011 the top 10 companies were Johnson Controls Inc., Campbell Soup Co., International Business Machines Corp., Bristol-Meyers Squibb Co., Mattel, Inc., 3M Co., Accenture, Kimberly-Clark Corp., Hewlett-Packard Co., and Nike Inc. What these companies have in common with those included on past lists is a commitment to social responsibility, including an assessment of concern for stakeholders in seven areas: environment, climate change, human rights, philanthropy, employee relations, finance, and governance.

CRO also maintains that good corporate social policies can lead to improved financial performance. According to an analysis of the 2009 "100 Best," companies on the list outperformed the companies not on the list by 26% in the last 3 years. Especially in the recession of 2008–2009, which was caused partly by falling trust in businesses and their leaders, companies found it important to make transparent their commitment to social responsibility. This was made clear by Richard Clark, CEO of Merck: "We've really stepped back and made sure that we are more transparent about our business. I think we have always done good things, but I don't know we have always communicated them internally or externally the best way we should. It's even more important today because we are operating in a very difficult environment, and our reputation is being challenged. We need to go the extra mile now so our stakeholders can see what we do and regain their trust." Sandra Leung, senior vice president of Bristol Myers-Squibb explained why corporate social responsibility can lead to a more productive workforce: "People like working at a place that has a vision and has respect for the environment as well as sustainability. They have respect for a company where they know their concerns will be not only heard but addressed."

Corporate social responsibility cannot rescue a failing company. But it can be an important competitive advantage, as Dan Henkle, senior vice president of social responsibility of Gap, said: "Making our company a good corporate citizen and increasingly transparent is a competitive imperative. It's that simple."

Sources: LaMotta, Lisa, "The 100 Best Corporate Citizens," Forbes.com (March 6, 2009); and *Corporate Responsibility Magazine* Web site (http://thecro.com/files/100Best2011_List_revised.pdf).

The FASB and IASB issue pronouncements on accounting issues that govern the preparation of financial statements. However, both Congress and the SEC can overrule the standard setters if they disagree with a particular accounting standard. Such disagreements are rare because setting accounting standards usually involves a long due process that includes many discussions among the affected parties: public regulators (Congress and SEC in the United States, the European Commission and others abroad), private regulators (FASB and IASB), companies, the public accounting profession, representatives of investors, and other interested groups. In the United States, Congress and the SEC generally make their opinions known long before the FASB or IASB approves standards.

Ethics

Regardless of what the accounting standards say, they do no good if accountants fail to follow them. A hallmark of the accounting profession has been its ethics and integrity. Most accountants and auditors are highly ethical and truthfully report their financial results in accordance with GAAP. The media have feasted on a few recent allegations of untruthful reporting in companies such as Washington Mutual, AIG, and Freddie Mac, but these are the exceptions. The Business First box above highlights some of the companies that have outstanding records for corporate citizenship.

Confidence in financial information is important to the smooth functioning of the world's capital markets, and confidence in financial statements depends on the competence and integrity of accountants and auditors. The leading professional organization of accountants in the United States, the American Institute of CPAs (AICPA), has a code of professional conduct that specifies the ethical obligations of accountants. The accounting problems in recent years have just highlighted the importance of accurate financial information and, therefore, the importance of recognizing and adhering to these ethical standards.

Three Measurement Principles

GAAP in the United States is based on a conceptual framework that the FASB first established in the 1970s and is currently revising in a joint effort with the IASB. Among the most important concepts are three broad measurement or valuation principles that underlie accrual accounting: recognition (when to record revenue), matching and cost recovery (when to record expense), and the stable monetary unit (what unit of measure to use).

Recognition

recognition
The principle that specifies when a company should record revenue in the accounting records.

The first principle, **recognition**, introduced on page 622, specifies when a company should record revenue in the accounting records.[1] We indicated that companies recognize revenue when it is both earned and realized or realizable. Consequently, most companies recognize revenue when they deliver goods or services to customers. However, in some industries revenue recognition is not so straightforward. Suppose Oracle sells some software to a client and promises to help until the installation is complete. When has Oracle earned the revenue? At the point of sale? At the time the installation is complete? Or some time between? This might be further complicated if the customer is a small start-up company that may run out of cash before it is able to pay for the software. How certain must Oracle be that it will receive payment before it can recognize the revenue? These are judgment issues, and Oracle's accountants together with its auditor will decide when earning and realization are sufficiently complete to recognize the revenue.

Matching and Cost Recovery

matching
The linking of revenues (as measured by the selling prices of goods and services delivered) with the expenses incurred to generate them (as measured by the cost of goods and services used).

The timing of revenue recognition is important because it leads to the recording of expenses through the concept of **matching**—the linking of revenues (as measured by the selling prices of goods and services delivered) with the expenses incurred to generate them (as measured by the cost of goods and services used).

Accountants apply matching as follows:

1. Identify the revenue recognized during the period.
2. Record expenses that relate directly to the recognized revenue, such as sales commissions or costs of goods sold.
3. Record expenses that are costs of operations during a specific time period that have no measurable benefit for a future period and, thus, must be linked to the current period's revenues. Examples are administrative salaries, wages of janitors, and costs of supplies used.

cost recovery
A concept in which companies carry forward as assets such items as inventories, prepayments, and equipment because they expect to recover the costs of these assets in the form of cash inflows (or reduced cash outflows) in future periods.

The heart of recognizing expense is the **cost recovery** concept. That is, companies carry forward as assets such items as inventories, prepayments, and equipment. Why? Because companies expect to recover the costs of these assets in the form of cash inflows (or reduced cash outflows) in future periods. At the end of each period, accountants examine evidence to assure themselves that they should not write off these assets—these unexpired costs—as an expense of the current period. For instance, in our chapter example, King Hardware carried forward the asset Prepaid Rent of $2,000 on March 31 because the accountant is virtually certain that it represents a future benefit. Why? Because King is planning to use the rented facilities in April and May and without the prepayment, King would have to pay $2,000 for rent in April and May. So the presence of the prepayment is a benefit in the sense that it reduces future cash outflows by $2,000.

Stable Monetary Unit

The monetary unit (for example, the dollar in the United States, the yen in Japan, or the euro in the European Union) is the principal means for measuring assets, liabilities, and stockholders' equity. It is the common denominator for quantifying the effects of a wide variety of transactions.

Such measurement assumes that the monetary unit—the dollar, for example—is an unchanging yardstick. Yet, we all know that a 2010 dollar does not have the same purchasing power as a 2000 or 1990 dollar. Therefore, users of accounting statements that include dollars from different years must recognize the limitations of the basic measurement unit.

---

[1]At the time this book went to press the FASB and IASB were jointly working on a project to change how revenue is recognized. If the boards adopt the proposal, it will emphasize the earning of revenue and minimize the effect of realization. However, for most transactions in this textbook, the new standard will not affect when companies recognize revenue.

Some accountants have criticized the FASB and IASB for not making explicit and formal adjustments to remedy the defects of the measuring unit. Supporters of the status quo maintain that price-level adjustments would lessen objectivity and would be confusing to users. They claim that critics have exaggerated the price-level problem and that the adjustments would not significantly affect the vast bulk of corporate statements. Why? Because many accounts, such as cash, receivables, and payables, are already in current or nearly current dollars, and inflation rates have been low in recent years.

On the other hand, although inflation rates in developed countries have recently run only 1%–4%, those in some developing countries have been 10%–20%, enough to have a large effect, especially on long-lived assets. In addition, companies in countries with hyperinflation have felt the need to inflation-adjust their accounting numbers for them to make any sense at all. However, even low inflation rates can create large changes in value when the inflation persists over a long time period. The most troublesome aspect of adjusting accounting numbers for inflation, however, is how to interpret the results after we measure them. Investors and managers in the United States are accustomed to the conventional statements. The intelligent interpretation of statements adjusted for changes in the price level would require extensive changes in the habits of users, and, therefore, price-level adjustment faces widespread opposition. Rather than explicitly adjusting values for inflation, most users prefer to live with an "elastic" measuring stick.

The body of GAAP contains more than the measurement conventions just discussed. We introduce some other major concepts, including going concern, objectivity, materiality, and cost benefit, in Appendix 15A. In Chapter 16, we will look in more detail at the income statement and balance sheet and introduce the third major financial statement, the statement of cash flows.

Summary Problem for Your Review

PROBLEM

Suppose a friend approaches you after learning that you have taken an accounting course. She makes the following remarks regarding financial statements. Do you agree or disagree? Explain fully.

1. "If I purchase 100 shares of the outstanding common stock of General Mills, I invest my money directly in that corporation. General Mills must record that transaction."
2. "Sales revenue is the cash coming in from customers and the various expenses show the cash going out for goods and services. The difference is net income."
3. Consider the following 2011 accounts of Nike (in millions):

Paid-in capital	$3,947
Retained earnings	5,801
Other	95
Total stockholders' equity	$9,843

A shareholder commented, "Why can't Nike pay higher wages and dividends? It can use its nearly $6 billion of retained earnings to do so."

4. "If Nike were sold to another company, the Nike shareholders would receive $9,843 billion, the total shareholders' equity."

SOLUTION

1. Money is invested directly in a corporation only upon original issuance of the stock by the corporation. For example, a corporation might issue 100,000 shares of stock at $80 per share, bringing in $8 million to the corporation. This is a transaction between the corporation and the stockholders. It affects the corporate financial position:

Cash	$8,000,000	Stockholders' equity	$8,000,000

In turn, an original stockholder (A) may later sell 100 shares of that stock to another individual (B) for $92 per share. This is a private transaction; no cash comes to the corporation. The corporation records the fact that B now owns the 100 shares originally owned by A, but the corporate financial position is unchanged. Accounting focuses on the business entity; the private dealings of the owners have no direct effect on the financial position of the entity and hence are unrecorded (except for detailed records of the owners' identities).

2. Cash receipts and disbursements are not the fundamental basis for the accounting recognition of revenues and expenses. If a company delivers goods or renders services to a customer, a receivable is generally sufficient justification for recognizing revenue. Similarly, if a company uses up goods or services, an obligation in the form of a payable is justification for recognizing expense. This approach to the measurement of net income is the accrual basis. Companies recognize revenue as they earn and realize it. They recognize expenses or losses when they use goods or services in obtaining revenue (or when they can no longer justify carrying forward such goods or services as an asset because they have no potential future benefit). Companies deduct the expenses and losses from the revenue, and the result of this matching process is net income, the net increase in stockholders' equity from the conduct of operations.

3. Retained earnings is not cash. It is a stockholders' equity account that represents the accumulated increase in ownership claims because of profitable operations less the decrease from payment of cash dividends. The erroneous linking of retained earnings and cash is a common misinterpretation. As a general rule, there is no direct relationship between the individual items on the two sides of the balance sheet. For example, Nike had less than $2 billion of cash when its retained earnings were nearly $6 billion. **IBM** has an even larger difference between cash and retained earnings, with a recent $11 billion cash balance when its retained earnings were more than $100 billion. Similarly, General Mills had retained earnings of $10,290 million, which was nearly 7 times larger than its cash balance of $1,508 million.

4. Stockholders' equity is not a market value. It is the difference between assets and liabilities measured at historical cost expressed in an unchanging monetary unit. Intervening changes in markets and general price levels in inflationary times may mean that financial statements list assets at amounts far below their market values.

Market values for publicly traded companies are determined by daily trading conducted in the financial marketplaces, such as the New York Stock Exchange. Numerous factors affect these values, including the expectations of (a) price appreciation and (b) cash flows in the form of dividends. The focus is on the future; investors examine the present and the past only as clues to what may be forthcoming. Therefore, the present stockholders' equity is usually of only incidental concern. For example, stockholders' equity for Nike in 2012 was slightly more than $10 per share, while the company's market price per common share was more than $100.

Highlights to Remember

1. **Read and interpret basic financial statements.** This chapter introduces two basic financial statements: the balance sheet (or statement of financial position) and income statement. Their main elements are assets, liabilities, owners' equity, revenues, and expenses. Income statement and balance sheets are linked because the revenues and expenses appearing on an income statements are components of stockholders' equity on the balance sheet. Revenues increase stockholders' equity, and expenses decrease stockholders' equity.

2. **Analyze typical business transactions using the balance sheet equation.** The balance sheet equation provides a framework for recording accounting transactions: assets = liabilities + owners' equity.

3. **Distinguish between the accrual basis of accounting and the cash basis of accounting.** The accrual basis is the heart of accounting. Under accrual accounting, companies recognize revenues as they earn and realize them, and they record expenses as they use resources, not necessarily when they receive or pay cash. Do not confuse expense with the term *cash payment*, or revenue with the term *cash receipt*.

4. **Make adjustments to the accounts under accrual accounting.** At the end of each account-ing period, companies make adjustments so that they can present financial statements on an accrual basis. The major adjustments are for (a) expiration of unexpired costs, (b) recognition (earning) of unearned revenues, (c) accrual of unrecorded expenses, and (d) accrual of unrecorded revenues.

5. **Explain the nature of dividends and retained earnings.** Dividends are not expenses; they are distributions of assets that reduce ownership claims. Similarly, retained earnings is not cash; it is a claim against total assets.

6. **Select relevant items from a set of data and assemble them into a balance sheet and an income statement.** After a company records transactions and makes adjustments, it can compile the data into financial statements. The balances in the accounts comprise the balance sheet. The changes in the retained earnings account form the basis for the income statement. Therefore, the changes in retained earnings link the income statement with the balance sheet.

7. **Distinguish between the reporting of corporate owners' equity and the reporting of owners' equity for partnerships and sole proprietorships.** Entities can be organized as corporations, partnerships, or sole proprietorships. The type of organization does not affect most accounting entries. Only the owners' equity section will differ among organizational types.

8. **Explain the role of auditors in financial reporting and how accounting standards are set.** Auditors examine companies' records and financial statements to ensure they comply with GAAP. Accounting standards are set in the United States by the Financial Accounting Standards Board (FASB) and in most other countries by the International Accounting Standards Board (IASB).

9. **Identify how the measurement principles of recognition, matching and cost recovery, and stable monetary unit affect financial reporting.** Three major conven-tions that affect accounting are recognition, matching and cost recovery, and stable monetary unit. Recognition determines when companies record revenues in the income statement, matching and cost recovery specify when to record expenses, and stable monetary units justify use of a unit of currency (the dollar in the United States) to measure accounting transactions.

Appendix 15A: Additional Accounting Concepts

This appendix describes several concepts that are prominent parts of the body of GAAP: continuity or going concern, relevance and faithful representation, materiality, conservatism, and cost-benefit.

Objective 10

Define continuity, relevance, faithful representation, materiality, conservatism, and cost-benefit.

The Continuity or Going Concern Convention

The **continuity** or **going concern convention** is the assumption that an organization will continue to exist and operate. This notion implies that a company will use existing resources, such as plant assets, to fulfill the general purposes of a continuing entity rather than sell them in tomorrow's real estate or equipment markets. It also implies that the company will pay existing liabilities at maturity in an orderly manner.

continuity convention (going concern convention)
The assumption that an organization will continue to exist and operate.

Suppose some old specialized equipment has a net book value (defined on p. 240 as original cost less accumulated depreciation) of $10,000, a replacement cost of $12,000, and a realizable value of $7,000 on the used-equipment market. Accountants often cite the continuity conven-tion as the justification for adhering to net book value, $10,000 in this example, as the primary basis for valuing assets such as inventories, land, buildings, and equipment. Some critics of these accounting practices believe that such valuations are not as informative as their replacement cost ($12,000) or their realizable values on sale ($7,000). Defenders of using $10,000 as an appropri-ate asset valuation argue that a going concern will generally use the asset as originally intended. Therefore, the net book value (the acquisition cost less depreciation) is the preferable basis for accountability and evaluation of performance. Hence, other values are not germane because the company is using, not replacing or disposing of, the asset.

The opposite view to this going concern or continuity convention is an immediate-liquidation assumption, whereby a company values all items on a balance sheet at the amounts appropriate if it

relevance
The capability of information to make a difference to the decision maker.

predictive value
A quality of information that allows it to help users form their expectations about the future.

confirmatory value
A quality of information that allows it to confirm or change existing expectations.

faithful representation
A quality of information that ensures that it captures the economic substance of the transactions, events, or circumstances it describes. It requires information to be complete, neutral, and free from material errors.

comparability
A characteristic of information produced when all companies use similar concepts and measurements and use them consistently.

consistency
Using the same accounting policies and procedures from period to period.

verifiability
A characteristic of information that can be checked to ensure it is correct.

Timeliness
The quality that information must reach decision makers while it can still influence their decisions.

understandable
A criterion that requires accountants to present information clearly and concisely.

materiality
The accounting convention that justifies the omission of insignificant information when its omission or misstatement would not mislead a user of the financial statements.

conservatism convention
Selecting the method of measurement that yields the gloomiest immediate results.

were to sell its assets and pay off its liabilities in piecemeal fashion within a few days or months. A company would use this liquidation approach to valuation only when it is in severe financial trouble.

Relevance and Faithful Representation

Relevance and faithful representation are the two main qualities that make accounting information useful for decision making. **Relevance** refers to whether the information makes a difference to a decision maker. If information has no impact on a decision, it is not relevant to that decision. The two things that can make information relevant are predictive value and confirmatory value. Information has **predictive value** if users of financial statements can use the information to help them form their expectations about the future. Information has **confirmatory value** if it can either confirm or change existing expectations.

Users of financial statements want assurance that management has accurately and truthfully reported its financial results. Consequently, in addition to relevance, accountants want information to exhibit **faithful representation**—that is, it should truly capture the economic substance of the transactions, events, or circumstances it describes. Faithful representation requires information to be complete, neutral, and free from material errors. Information is complete if it contains all the information necessary to faithfully represent an economic phenomenon. It is neutral if it is unbiased—that is, the information is not slanted to influence behavior in a particular direction. Finally, information should be free from material errors, which means that estimates are based on appropriate inputs, which in turn are based on the best information available.

Four characteristics can enhance both relevance and faithful representation. The first such characteristic is **comparability**—requiring all companies to use similar concepts and measurements and to use them consistently. Comparability requires **consistency**, using the same accounting policies and procedures from period to period. The second enhancing characteristic is **verifiability**, which means that information can be checked to ensure it is correct. That is, knowledgeable and independent observers would agree that the information presented has been appropriately measured. **Timeliness** is obviously desirable. Information must reach decision makers while it can still influence their decisions. Finally, information should be **understandable**, which requires accountants to present information clearly and concisely.

Materiality

Because accounting is a practical art, accountants often temper their reports by applying judgments about **materiality**. A financial statement item is material if its omission or misstatement would be likely to mislead a user of the financial statements. Items with a sufficiently small value are immaterial. For example, accountants write off as expenses many small outlays that they should theoretically record as assets. Why? Because they are small enough to be immaterial. For example, many corporations have a rule that requires the immediate write-off to expense of all outlays under a specified minimum of, for example, $100, regardless of the useful life of the asset acquired. In such a case, a company might acquire coat hangers that will last many years but never add them to its balance sheet as assets. Why? The resulting $100 understatement of assets and stockholders' equity would be too trivial to affect any user decisions. The cost of recording and annually depreciating a $100 asset is greater than the benefit of more accurate financial statements.

When is an item material? There will probably never be a definitive answer. What is trivial to IBM may be material to a two-person start-up company. A working rule is that an item is material if its proper accounting would probably affect the decision of a knowledgeable user. In sum, although materiality is an important convention, it is difficult to use anything other than prudent judgment to tell whether an item is material.

Conservatism Convention

Conservatism is a hallmark of accounting. The **conservatism convention** means selecting the method of measurement that yields the gloomiest immediate results. This attitude affects such working rules as "Anticipate no gains, but provide for all possible losses," and "If in doubt, write it off."

Accountants have traditionally regarded the historical costs of acquiring an asset as the ceiling for its valuation. Asset values may be increased (written up) only when the asset is sold or exchanged, but the asset value may be reduced (written down) without an exchange. For example, companies write down inventories (and recognize a loss) when replacement costs decline, but they never write them up when replacement costs increase.

Critics maintain that conservatism is inherently inconsistent. If replacement market prices are sufficiently objective and verifiable to justify write-downs, why aren't they just as valid for write-ups? Furthermore, the critics maintain that conservatism is not a fundamental concept. Accounting reports should try to present the most accurate picture feasible—neither too high nor too low. Accountants defend their attitude by saying that erring in the direction of conservatism would usually have less severe economic consequences than erring in the direction of overstating assets and net income.

In a way, conservatism is a double-edged sword. Conservatism that leads to understating net income in one period subsequently creates an overstatement of net income in a future period. For example, suppose a company writes down inventory from $100 to $80. The company's operating income falls by $20 in the period of the write-down, but it increases by $20 in the period it sells the inventory.

Cost-Benefit

Accounting systems vary in complexity from the minimum crude records kept to satisfy government authorities to the sophisticated budgeting and feedback systems that are at the heart of management planning and control. Recent innovations include huge, multimillion dollar enterprise resource planning (ERP) systems. As companies change their accounting systems, the potential benefits should exceed the additional costs. Often, the benefits are difficult to measure, but the **cost-benefit criterion** at least implicitly underlies the decisions about the design of accounting systems. Sometimes, the reluctance to adopt suggestions for new ways of measuring financial position and performance is because of inertia. More often, it is because the apparent benefits do not exceed the costs of gathering and interpreting the information. Some companies, such as Hershey Foods, have found out too late that huge investments in accounting systems such as ERP sometimes do not deliver the benefits promised.

Appendix 15B: Using Ledger Accounts

This chapter focused on the balance sheet equation, the general framework used by accountants to record economic transactions. This appendix focuses on some of the main techniques that accountants use to record the transactions illustrated in the chapter.

The Account

To begin, consider how the accountant would record the King Hardware transactions that you encountered in the chapter. Exhibit 15-1 (p. 621) showed their effects on the elements of the balance sheet equation:

	A		=	L	+	SE
	Cash	Inventory		Accounts Payable		Paid-in Capital
1. Initial investment by owners	+100,000		=			+100,000
2. Acquire inventory for cash	−75,000	+75,000	=			
3. Acquire inventory on credit		+35,000	=	+35,000		

This balance-sheet-equation approach emphasizes the concepts, but it can become unwieldy if many transactions occur. Changes in the balance sheet equation can occur many times daily. In large retail businesses, such as Target, Costco, and Macy's, thousands of repetitive transactions occur hourly. In practice, accountants use **ledger accounts** to keep track of how these transactions affect each particular asset, liability, revenue, expense, and so forth. We use simplified versions of ledger accounts called **T-accounts**. We call them T-accounts because they take the form of the capital letter *T*. Increases in the account go on one side of the vertical line of the T-account, and decreases go on the other side. Asset accounts have positive balances on the left side of the T-account. Entries on the left side increase the asset accounts and entries on the right side decrease them. Liabilities and stockholders' equity accounts have positive balances on the

cost-benefit criterion
An approach that implicitly underlies the decisions about the design of accounting systems. As companies change their accounting systems, the potential benefits should exceed the costs of gathering and interpreting the information.

Objective 11

Use T-accounts, debits, and credits to record transactions.

ledger accounts
A method of keeping track of how transactions affect each particular asset, liability, revenue, and expense.

T-accounts
Simplified versions of ledger accounts that take the form of the capital letter *T*.

right-side. We increase them by recording entries on the right side and decrease them by recording entries on the left side. The following T-accounts illustrate the preceding transactions:

Assets			=	Liabilities + Stockholders' Equity		
Cash				**Accounts Payable**		
Increases		Decreases		Decreases	Increases	
(1)	100,000	(2) 75,000			(3)	35,000
Bal.	25,000					
Inventory				**Paid-in Capital**		
Increases		Decreases		Decreases	Increases	
(2)	75,000				(1)	100,000
(3)	35,000					
Bal.	110,000					

double-entry system
A method of record keeping in which each transaction affects at least two accounts.

We made the T-account entries using a **double-entry system**, whereby each transaction affects at least two accounts. Each T-account is similar to a column in the balance sheet equation. To keep assets equal to liabilities plus stockholders' equity, the amount of the left-side entries to the T-accounts must always equal the amount of the right-side entries.

Each T-account summarizes the changes in a particular asset, liability, or stockholders' equity. We key each transaction in some way, such as by the numbering in parentheses used in this illustration or by date or both. This keying facilitates the rechecking (auditing) process by helping accountants trace transactions to their original sources. You can compute the balance of any account by totaling each side of the account and deducting the smaller total amount from the larger. Accounts exist to keep an up-to-date summary of the changes in specific assets, liabilities, and stockholders' equity. Accountants can prepare a balance sheet at any time if they keep the accounts up to date. The accounts contain all the necessary information. For example, the balance sheet for King Hardware after the first three transactions is as follows:

Assets		Liabilities and Stockholders' Equity	
Cash	$ 25,000	Liabilities	
Inventory	110,000	Accounts payable	$ 35,000
		Stockholders' equity	
		Paid-in capital	100,000
Total assets	$135,000	Total liabilities and stockholders' equity	$135,000

General Ledger

general ledger
A collection of the group of accounts that supports the items shown in the major financial statements.

We show King Hardware's general ledger in Exhibit 15-7. A **general ledger** is a collection of the group of accounts that supports the items shown in the major financial statements.[2] Exhibit 15-7 is merely a recasting of the facts that we analyzed in Exhibit 15-1. Study Exhibit 15-7 by comparing its analysis of each transaction against its corresponding analysis in Exhibit 15-1 on page 621.

Debits and Credits

debit
An entry on the left side of an account.

credit
An entry on the right side of an account.

When placing transaction amounts in the appropriate accounts, accountants often use the technical terms debit and credit. **Debit** means one thing and one thing only—"left side of an account." **Credit** means one thing and one thing only—"right side of an account." Neither debit nor credit has a connotation of "good" or "bad." In our everyday conversation, we sometimes use the words *debit* and *credit* in a general sense that may completely diverge from their technical accounting uses. When you study accounting, forget these general uses of the words. Merely think right-side or left-side entries to T-accounts and whether the right side or left side increases or decreases the type of account you are analyzing.

---

[2] The general ledger is usually supported by various subsidiary ledgers that provide details for accounts in the general ledger. For instance, an accounts receivable subsidiary ledger would contain a separate account for each credit customer. For example, the accounts receivable balance of $1,162 million that appears in the General Mills 2011 balance sheet is a single account in the company's general ledger. However, that single balance is the sum of the detailed individual accounts receivable balances of thousands of credit customers.

Assets
(increases on left, decreases on right)

Liabilities and Stockholders' Equity
(decreases on left, increases on right)

Cash

(1)	100,000	(2)	75,000
(4a)	10,000	(6)	20,000
(5)	15,000	(7a)	3,000
3/31 Bal.	17,000		

Accounts Payable

(6)	20,000	(3)	35,000
		3/31 Bal.	15,000

Paid-in Capital

		(1)	100,000
		3/31 Bal.	100,000

Accounts Receivable

(4a)	120,000	(5)	15,000
3/31 Bal.	105,000		

Inventory

(2)	75,000	(4b)	100,000
(3)	35,000		
3/31 Bal.	10,000		

Retained Earnings

		3/31 Bal.	29,000*

Sales

		(4a)	130,000

Prepaid Rent

(7a)	3,000	(7b)	1,000
3/31 Bal.	2,000		

*Expense and Revenue Accounts

Cost of Goods Sold

(4b)	100,000	

Rent Expense

(7b)	1,000	

Exhibit 15-7
General Ledger of King Hardware Co.

For example, an accountant making an entry for transaction 4b would say "debit (or charge) Cost of Goods Sold $100,000 and credit Inventory $100,000." This is an abbreviated way of saying, "Place $100,000 on the left (debit) side of the Cost of Goods Sold T-account and place $100,000 on the right (credit) side of the Inventory T-account." Note that the total dollar amounts of the debits (entries on the left side of the account[s] affected) will always equal the total dollar amount of credits (entries on the right side of the account[s] affected) because the accounting equation must always stay in balance.

You can use *debit* and *credit* as verbs, adjectives, or nouns. The instruction "debit $1,000 to cash" uses *debit* as a verb, meaning that you should place $1,000 on the left side of the cash account. When you say "make a debit to cash," *debit* is a noun. In the statement "cash has a debit balance of $12,000," *debit* is an adjective that indicates that the balance is on the left (rather than right) side of the account.

Assets generally have left-side (debit) balances. Why do expenses also carry debit balances? Expense accounts are places to temporarily record reductions in stockholders' equity. Because stockholders' equity normally has a right-side balance, we place entries on the left side to decrease the account.

The following table summarizes the following rules: (1) debits are on the left, (2) credits are on the right, (3) debits increase and credits decrease assets, and (4) credits increase and debits decrease liabilities and stockholders' equities.

Assets		=	Liabilities		+	Stockholders' Equity	
Increase	Decrease		Decrease	Increase		Decrease	Increase
+	–		–	+		–	+
debit	credit		debit	credit		debit	credit
left	right		left	right		left	right

Because revenues increase stockholders' equity, we record them as credits. Because expenses decrease stockholders' equity, we record them as debits.

Accounting Vocabulary

This chapter and its appendices introduce more new terms than any other, so be sure that you understand them thoroughly.

account, p. 620
accounts payable, p. 619
accounts receivable, p. 619
accrual basis, p. 624
accrue, p. 629
accrued expenses, p. 629
accrued revenues, p. 631
adjusting entries, p. 625
adjustments, p. 625
assets, p. 620
audit, p. 635
balance sheet, p. 620
cash basis, p. 624
cash dividends, p. 632
comparability, p. 642
compound entry, p. 622
confirmatory value, p. 642
conservatism convention, p. 642
consistency, p. 642
continuity convention, p. 641
corporation, p. 619
cost recovery, p. 638
cost-benefit criterion, p. 643
credit, p. 644

debit, p. 644
deferred revenue, p. 629
dividends, p. 632
double-entry system, p. 644
earnings, p. 622
expenses, p. 622
explicit transactions, p. 625
faithful representation, p. 642
Financial Accounting Standards
    Board (FASB), p. 636
financial statements, p. 619
general ledger, p. 644
going concern
    convention, p. 641
implicit transactions, p. 625
income, p. 622
income statement, p. 622
independent opinion, p. 635
International Accounting
    Standards Board
    (IASB), p. 636
ledger accounts, p. 643
liabilities, p. 620
long-lived assets, p. 626

matching, p. 638
materiality, p. 642
net income, p. 622
net worth, p. 634
owners' equity, p. 620
paid-in capital, p. 620
partnership, p. 634
predictive value, p. 642
profits, p. 622
recognition, p. 638
recognize, p. 622
relevance, p. 642
residual value, p. 626
retained earnings, p. 620
retained income, p. 620
revenue, p. 622
sales, p. 622
sales revenue, p. 622
Securities and Exchange
    Commission (SEC), p. 635
sole proprietorship, p. 634
source documents, p. 625
statement of financial
    position, p. 620

statement of stockholders'	T-accounts, p. 643	unearned revenue, p. 629
equity, p. 634	timeliness, p. 642	unexpired cost, p. 626
stockholders' equity, p. 620	transaction, p. 619	useful life, p. 626
straight-line method, p. 627	understandable, p. 642	verifiability, p. 642

Assignment Material

The assignment material for each remaining chapter is divided as follows:

- Fundamental Assignment Material
    General Exercises and Problems
    Understanding Published Financial Reports
- Additional Assignment Material
    Questions
    Critical Thinking Exercises
    General Exercises and Problems
    Understanding Published Financial Reports
    Nike 10-K Problem
- Excel Application Exercise
- Collaborative Learning Exercise
- Internet Exercise

The general exercises and problems subgroups focus on concepts and procedures that are applicable to a wide variety of specific settings. Many instructors believe that these "traditional" types of exercises and problems have proved their educational value over many years of use in introductory textbooks. The understanding published financial reports subgroups focus on real-life situations. They have the same basic aims as the general exercises and problems subgroups. Indeed, some instructors may confine their assignments to the understanding published financial reports subgroups. The distinctive characteristic of the latter subgroups is the use of actual companies and news events to enhance the student's interest in accounting. Many students and instructors get more satisfaction out of a course that frequently uses actual situations as a means of learning accounting methods and concepts.

Fundamental Assignment Material   MyAccountingLab

GENERAL EXERCISES AND PROBLEMS

15-A1 Balance Sheet Equation

For each of the following independent cases, compute the amounts (in thousands) for the items indicated by letters, and show your supporting computations:

	Case		
	1	2	3
Revenues	$140	$ K	$300
Expenses	120	170	270
Dividends declared	0	5	Q
Additional investment by stockholders	0	30	35
Net income	E	20	P
Retained earnings			
Beginning of year	40	55	90
End of year	D	J	110
Paid-in capital			
Beginning of year	25	10	N
End of year	C	H	85
Total assets			
Beginning of year	80	F	L
End of year	90	275	M
Total liabilities			
Beginning of year	A	90	105
End of year	B	G	95

15-A2 Analysis of Transactions; Preparation of Statements

The Montha Company was incorporated on April 1, 20X1. Montha had 10 holders of common stock. Chenda Montha, who was the president and CEO, held 51% of the shares. The company rented space in chain discount stores and specialized in selling running shoes. Montha's first location was a store in Centerville Mall.

The following events occurred during April:

a. The company was incorporated. Common stockholders invested $150,000 cash.
b. Purchased merchandise inventory for cash, $35,000.
c. Purchased merchandise inventory on open account, $25,000.
d. Merchandise carried in inventory at a cost of $40,000 was sold for $110,000, $35,000 for cash and $75,000 on open account. Montha carries and will collect these accounts receivable.
e. Collection of a portion of the preceding accounts receivable, $20,000.
f. Payments of a portion of accounts payable, $18,000. See transaction c.
g. Special display equipment and fixtures were acquired on April 1 for $36,000. Their expected useful life was 36 months with no terminal scrap value. Straight-line depreciation was adopted. This equipment was removable. Montha paid $12,000 as a down payment and signed a promissory note for $24,000.
h. On April 1, Montha signed a rental agreement with Centerville Mall. The agreement called for rent of $2,000 per month, payable quarterly in advance. Therefore, Montha paid $6,000 cash on April 1.
i. The rental agreement also called for a payment of 10% of all sales. This payment was in addition to the flat $2,000 per month. In this way, Centerville Mall would share in any success of the venture and be compensated for general services such as cleaning and utilities. This payment was to be made in cash on the last day of each month as soon as the sales for the month were tabulated. Therefore, Montha made the payment on April 30.
j. Wages, salaries, and sales commissions were all paid in cash for all earnings by employees. The amount was $49,000.
k. Depreciation expense for April was recognized. See transaction g.
l. The expiration of an appropriate amount of prepaid rental services was recognized. See transaction h.

1. Prepare an analysis of Montha Company's transactions, employing the equation approach demonstrated in Exhibit 15-1. Two additional columns will be needed, one for Equipment and Fixtures and one for Note Payable. Show all amounts in thousands.
2. Prepare a balance sheet as of April 30, 20X1, and an income statement for the month of April. Ignore income taxes.
3. Given these sparse facts, analyze Montha's performance for April and its financial position as of April 30, 20X1.

15-A3 Cash Basis Versus Accrual Basis

Refer to the preceding problem. If Montha Company measured income on the cash basis, what revenue would be reported for April? Which basis (accrual or cash) provides a better measure of revenue? Why?

UNDERSTANDING PUBLISHED FINANCIAL REPORTS

15-B1 Balance Sheet Equation

Nordstrom operates 207 fashion specialty retail stores in 28 states. The company's actual data (slightly simplified) follow for its fiscal year ended January 29, 2011 (in millions of dollars):

Assets, beginning of period	$6,579
Assets, end of period	E
Liabilities, beginning of period	A
Liabilities, end of period	5,441
Paid-in capital, beginning of period	1,066
Paid-in capital, end of period	D
Retained earnings, beginning of period	506
Retained earnings, end of period	C
Revenues	9,700
Costs and expenses	B
Net income	613
Dividends	266
Additional investments by stockholders	102

Find the unknowns (in millions), showing computations to support your answers.

15-B2 Analysis of Transactions; Preparation of Statements

The Volvo Group, headquartered in Gothenburg, Sweden, is one of the world's leading manufacturers of trucks, buses, and construction equipment, in addition to autos. Volvo's actual condensed balance sheet data for January 1, 2012, follows (in millions of Swedish kroner, SEK):

Assets		Liabilities and Stockholders' Equity	
Cash and cash equivalents	SEK 30,379	Accounts payable	SEK 56,546
Receivables	81,472	Other liabilities	211,017
Inventories	44,599		
Property, plant, and equipment	53,657	Stockholders' equity	85,681
Other assets	143,137		
Total	SEK 353,244	Total	SEK 353,244

Suppose the following summarizes some major transactions of the truck division of Volvo during January, 2012 (in millions):

a. Sold trucks for cash of SEK 190 and on open account of SEK 460 for a grand total of SEK 650. Volvo carried the trucks in inventory for SEK 390.
b. Acquired inventory on account, SEK 500.
c. Collected receivables, SEK 300.
d. On January 2, used SEK 250 cash to prepay some rent and insurance for 2012.
e. Payments on accounts payable (for inventories), SEK 450.
f. Paid selling and administrative expenses in cash, SEK 110.
g. A total of SEK 90 of prepaid expenses for rent and insurance expired in January 2012.
h. Recognized depreciation expense of SEK 20 for January.

1. Prepare an analysis of these truck transactions on the balance sheet of Volvo, employing the equation approach demonstrated in Exhibit 15-1 on page 621. Show all amounts in millions of SEK. (For simplicity, only a few major transactions are illustrated here.)
2. Prepare an income statement for these transactions for the month ended January 31, 2012, and a balance sheet as of January 31, 2012, that incorporates these transactions. Ignore income taxes.

15-B3 Cash Basis Versus Accrual Basis

Refer to the preceding problem. If Volvo measured income on the cash basis, what revenue would the company report for January from the transactions listed? Which basis (accrual or cash) provides a better measure of revenue? Why?

Additional Assignment Material

QUESTIONS

15-1 What types of questions are answered by the income statement and balance sheet?
15-2 Define *assets* and *liabilities*.
15-3 How are the income statement and balance sheet related?
15-4 Criticize the following statement: "Net income is the difference in the ownership capital account balances at two points in time."
15-5 Distinguish between the accrual basis and the cash basis of accounting.
15-6 How do adjusting entries differ from routine entries?
15-7 Explain why some accountants want to record research expenditures as an asset on acquisition.
15-8 Why is it better to refer to the costs, rather than values, of assets such as plant or inventories?
15-9 "Depreciation is cost allocation, not valuation." Do you agree? Explain.

15-10 What types of companies would you expect to have unearned revenues (or deferred revenues) on their balance sheets?
15-11 What is meant by an account labeled "Accrued wages?" Would it be on an income statement or a balance sheet?
15-12 Criticize the following statement: "As a stockholder, I have a right to more dividends. You have millions stashed away in retained earnings. It's about time that you let the true owners get their hands on that pot of gold."
15-13 Criticize the following statement: "Dividends are distributions of profits."
15-14 "I don't need to know accounting principles because my business is a sole proprietorship." Comment on this statement.
15-15 Explain the relationship between the FASB and the SEC in the United States.

15-16 "The FASB sets standards in the United States, so there is little need to learn International Financial Reporting Standards (IFRS)." Do you agree? Explain.

15-17 Why are ethics and integrity important to accountants?

15-18 When do accountants recognize revenue? Why is this so important in an accrual accounting system?

15-19 What is the major criticism of the dollar (or euro or yen or any other monetary unit) as the principal accounting measure?

15-20 Study Appendix 15A. What does the accountant mean by going concern?

15-21 Study Appendix 15A. What does the accountant mean by relevance? By faithful representation?

15-22 Study Appendix 15A. What is the role of cost-benefit (economic feasibility) in the development of accounting principles?

15-23 Study Appendix 15B. Describe the role of debits and credits in a double-entry bookkeeping system.

CRITICAL THINKING EXERCISES

15-24 Accounting Valuation of Fixed Assets

Consider two types of assets held by Weyerhaeuser Company: 1) timber-growing land purchased in 1912 when the company was known as Weyerhaeuser Timber Company and 2) machinery purchased and installed at its paper processing plant in Saskatchewan, Canada, in 2012. How close do you suppose the December 31, 2013, balance sheet value of each asset is to the market value of the asset at that date?

15-25 Marketing, the Income Statement, and the Balance Sheet

The marketing manager of a major electronics company said, "The balance sheet isn't of much use to me. It is so static. But the income statement is a primary tool for managing my dynamic business." Why would a marketing manager find the income statement more useful than the balance sheet?

15-26 Revenue Recognition and Evaluation of Sales Staff

Revenue on an accrual-accounting basis must be both earned and realized (or realizable) before accountants recognize it in the income statement. Companies recognize revenue in cash-basis accounting only when they have received the cash. Is an accrual-basis or cash-basis recognition of revenue more relevant for evaluating the performance of a sales staff? Why?

15-27 Relationship Between the Balance Sheet and the Income Statement

Suppose a company has no transactions with its owners during 20X0. That is, paid-in capital remains unchanged, and retained earnings increases by the entire amount of the net income. During 20X0 the company's net income is $50,000. At the beginning of the year, the company's balance sheet equation was as follows:

$$\text{assets} = \text{liabilities} + \text{stockholders' equity}$$

$$\$450,000 = \$200,000 + \$250,000$$

What do you know about the balance sheet equation at the end of 20X0?

15-28 Concepts of Relevance and Faithful Representation

The FASB and IASB both state that relevance and faithful representation are crucial concepts for financial reporting. Why are these concepts so important?

GENERAL EXERCISES AND PROBLEMS

15-29 True or False

Use T or F to indicate whether each of the following statements is true or false. Change each false statement into one that is true.

1. A large cash balance is the best evidence of previous profitable operations.
2. Accounts receivable should be classified as a liability.
3. Machinery used in the business should be recorded at replacement cost.
4. It is not possible to determine changes in the condition of a business from a single balance sheet.
5. From a single balance sheet, you can find stockholders' equity for a period of time but not for a specific day.
6. Retained earnings is just one part of stockholders' equity.

15-30 Simple Balance Sheet

Fill in the missing numbers from the following simple balance sheet for Cabo Company:

Assets		Liabilities and Stockholders' Equity	
Cash	$?	Accounts payable	$ 10,000
Accounts receivable	15,000	Long-term debt	?
Plant and equipment	75,000	Stockholders' equity	$ 45,000
Total assets	$100,000	Total Liabilities and stockholders' equity	$?

15-31 Nature of Retained Earnings

This is an exercise on the relationships among assets, liabilities, and ownership equities.

1. Prepare an opening balance sheet of

Cash	$1,000	Paid-in capital	$1,000

2. Purchase inventory for $500 cash. Prepare a balance sheet. A heading is unnecessary in this and subsequent requirements.
3. Sell the entire inventory for $850 cash. Prepare a balance sheet. Where is the retained earnings in terms of relationships within the balance sheet? That is, what is the meaning of the retained earnings? Explain in your own words.
4. Buy inventory for $400 cash and equipment for $750 cash. Prepare a balance sheet. Where is the retained earnings in terms of relationships within the balance sheet? That is, what is the meaning of the retained earnings? Explain in your own words.
5. Buy inventory for $350 on open account. Prepare a balance sheet. Where is the retained earnings and account payable in terms of the relationships within the balance sheet? That is, what is the meaning of the account payable and the retained earnings? Explain in your own words.

15-32 Income Statement

Here is a proposed income statement of a children's clothing store:

Kids 2 Klad
Statement of Profit and Loss, December 31, 20X1

Revenues:		
Sales	$1,300,000	
Increase in market value of land and building	50,000	
Cash received from loan	200,000	$1,550,000
Deduct expenses:		
Advertising	$ 100,000	
Sales commissions	60,000	
Utilities	20,000	
Wages	150,000	
Dividends	200,000	
Cost of clothes purchased	800,000	1,330,000
Net profit		$ 220,000

List and describe any shortcomings of this statement.

15-33 Income Statement, Balance Sheet, and Dividends

LaPlace Company had retained earnings of $56,780 at the beginning of 2013. During the year the company had total revenues of $530,000, total expenses (including taxes) of $495,000, bought property and equipment for $340,000, and paid cash dividends of $12,000. Compute LaPlace Company's retained earnings at the end of 2013.

15-34 Customer and Airline

Suppose Macy's decided to hold a managers' meeting in Honolulu in February. To take advantage of special fares, Macy's purchased airline tickets in advance from Delta Airlines at a total cost of $55,000. Macy's acquired the tickets on December 1 for cash. Using the balance-sheet-equation format, analyze the impact of the December payment and the February travel on the financial position of both Macy's and Delta.

15-35 Tenant and Landlord

Madison Hardware, a franchise of Ace Hardware Corporation, pays quarterly rent of $15,000 to Baldwin Commercial Real Estate at the beginning of each quarter for its location in Baldwin Mall. Using the balance-sheet-equation format, analyze the effects of the following on the tenant's and the landlord's financial position:

1. Madison Hardware pays $15,000 rent on July 1.
2. Adjustment for July.
3. Adjustment for August.
4. Adjustment for September.

15-36 Adjustments

1. Steinberg Company sells annual subscriptions to its investment-advice magazine for €50. Suppose it sold 5,000 subscriptions in December, 2012, for magazines to be delivered quarterly in 2013. How would Steinberg Company show this on its December 31, 2012, balance sheet? How would it affect the company's 2012 income statement? How would it affect the income statement for the first 6 months of 2013?
2. Steinberg Company pays its salaried personnel monthly on the fifth day of the following month. That is, it pays January's salaries on February 5. The company's total salaries for 2012 were €240,000, spread evenly over the 12 months. How will this affect the December 31, 2012, balance sheet? When will the December salaries (which are paid on January 5) be charged as expenses on the income statement?

15-37 Find Unknowns

The following data pertain to Andaman Tours, a travel company in Thailand where the currency is the baht (B). Total assets at January 1, 20X0, were B80,000, and at December 31, 20X0, they were B125,000. During 20X0, sales were B265,000, cash dividends were B16,000, and operating expenses (exclusive of costs of goods sold) were B50,000. Total liabilities at December 31, 20X0, were B45,000, and at January 1, 20X0, they were B30,000. There was no additional capital paid in during 20X0. Calculate the following items. (These need not be computed in any particular order.)

1. Stockholders' equity, for January 1, 20X0
2. Net income for 20X0
3. Cost of goods sold for 20X0

15-38 Balance Sheet Equation; Solving for Unknowns

Compute the unknowns (X, Y, Z, A, and B) in each of the individual cases, columns 1–7, in Exhibit 15-8. Each column is independent of the others.

15-39 Fundamental Transaction Analysis and Preparation of Statements

Three former RIM employees decided to go into business for themselves and open a store near an office park to sell wireless equipment to young professionals. Their first products were cell phones, PDAs, netbook and notebook computers, and computer accessories. The business was incorporated as Connectivity Plus. The following transactions occurred during April:

a. On April 1, 20X1, each of the three invested $12,000 in cash in exchange for 1,000 shares of stock each.
b. The corporation quickly acquired $40,000 in inventory, half of which had to be paid for in cash. The other half was acquired on open accounts that were payable after 30 days.
c. A store was rented for $500 monthly. A lease was signed for one year on April 1. The first 2 months' rent was paid in advance. Monthly payments were to be made on the second of each month.
d. Advertising during April was purchased on open account for $3,000 from a newspaper owned by one of the stockholders. Additional advertising services of $6,000 were acquired for cash.
e. Sales were $62,000. Merchandise was sold for twice its purchase cost. Sales of $52,000 were on open account, and the remaining $10,000 were for cash.
f. Wages and salaries incurred in April amounted to $11,000, of which $4,000 was paid in cash.

Given	1	2	3	4	5	6	7
Assets at beginning of period		$ 9,000				B	$ 8,200
Assets at end of period		11,000					9,900
Liabilities at beginning of period		6,000				$12,000	4,000
Liabilities at end of period		Y					6,000
Stockholders' equity at beginning of period	$9,000	X				A	X
Stockholders' equity at end of period	X	5,000				10,000	Y
Sales			$16,000		X	14,000	20,000
Inventory at beginning of period			6,000	$ 8,000		Z	
Inventory at end of period			7,000	6,000		7,000	
Purchase of inventory			10,000	12,000		6,000	
Gross profit			Y		$3,000	6,000	A
Cost of goods sold*			X	X	4,500	X	B
Other expenses			4,000			4,000	4,700
Net profit	4,000	Z	Z			Y	Z
Dividends	2,000	0				1,500	400
Additional investments by stockholders						5,000	0

*Note that cost of goods sold = beginning inventory + purchases − ending inventory.

Exhibit 15-8
Data for Exercise 15-38

g. Miscellaneous services paid for in cash were $2,510.
h. On April 1, fixtures and equipment were purchased for $6,000 with a down payment of $1,000 plus a $5,000 note payable in one year.
i. See transaction h and make the April 30 adjustment for interest expense accrued at 9.6%. (The interest is not due until the note matures.)
j. See transaction h and make the April 30 adjustment for depreciation expense on a straight-line basis. The estimated life of the fixtures and equipment is 10 years with no expected residual value. Straight-line depreciation here would be $6,000 ÷ 10 years = $600 per year, or $50 per month.
k. Cash dividends of $6,000 were declared and disbursed to stockholders on April 29.

1. Using the accrual basis of accounting, prepare an analysis of transactions, employing the equation approach demonstrated in Exhibit 15-1 on page 621. Use the following headings: Cash, Accounts Receivable, Inventory, Prepaid Rent, Fixtures and Equipment, Accounts Payable, Notes Payable, Accrued Wages Payable, Accrued Interest Payable, Paid-in Capital, and Retained Earnings.
2. Prepare a balance sheet and a multiple-step income statement. Also show the components of the change in retained earnings.
3. What advice would you give the owners based on the information compiled in the financial statements?

15-40 Measurement of Income for Tax and Other Purposes

The following are the summarized transactions of dentist Frieda Rivera, DDS for 20X1, her first year in practice:

a. Acquired equipment and furniture for $84,000. Its expected useful life is 6 years. Dr. Rivera will use straight-line depreciation, assuming zero terminal disposal value.

b. Fees collected, $79,000. These fees included $2,000 paid in advance by some patients on December 31, 20X1.

c. Rent is paid at the rate of $500 monthly, payable quarterly on the twenty-fifth of March, June, September, and December for the following quarter. Total disbursements during 20X1 for rent were $7,500 including an initial payment on January 1.

d. Fees billed but uncollected, December 31, 20X1, $20,000.

e. Utilities expense paid in cash, $700. Additional utility bills unpaid at December 31, 20X1, $100.

f. Salary expense for dental assistant and secretary, $16,000 paid in cash. In addition, $1,000 was earned but unpaid on December 31, 20X1.

Dr. Rivera may elect either the cash basis or the accrual basis of measuring income for income tax purposes, provided that she uses it consistently in subsequent years. Under either alternative, the original cost of the equipment and furniture must be written off over its 6-year useful life rather than being regarded as a lump-sum expense in the first year.

1. Prepare income statements for the year on both the cash and accrual bases, using one column for each basis.

2. Which basis do you prefer as a measure of Dr. Rivera's performance? Why? What do you think is the justification for the government's allowing the use of the cash basis for income tax purposes?

15-41 Debits and Credits

Study Appendix 15B. Determine for the following transactions whether the account named in parentheses is to be debited or credited:

1. Paid rent in advance (Prepaid Expenses), $1,200
2. Bought merchandise on open account (Accounts Payable), $5,000
3. Borrowed money from First National Bank (Notes Payable), $12,000
4. Sold merchandise (Merchandise Inventory), $1,000
5. Paid O'Brien Associates $3,000 owed them (Accounts Payable)
6. Paid dividends (Cash), $500
7. Delivered merchandise to customers (Merchandise Inventory), $3,000
8. Received cash from customers on accounts due (Accounts Receivable), $2,000

15-42 True or False

Study Appendix 15B. Use T or F to indicate whether each of the following statements is true or false. For each false statement, explain why it is false.

1. Purchase of inventory on account should be credited to Inventory and debited to Accounts Payable.
2. Increases in asset accounts must always be entered on the right.
3. Increases in stockholders' equity should always be entered as credits.
4. Decreases in liability accounts should be recorded on the right.
5. Debit entries must always be recorded on the left. Credit entries can be recorded either on the right or on the left.
6. Money borrowed from the bank should be credited to Cash and debited to Notes Payable.
7. Decreases in accounts must be shown on the credit side.
8. Both increases in liabilities and decreases in assets should be entered on the right.
9. Asset credits should be entered on the right and liability credits on the left.
10. Payments on mortgages should be debited to Cash and credited to Mortgages Payable. Mortgages are liabilities.

15-43 Use of T-Accounts

Study Appendix 15B. The Eastside Tennis Club had the following transactions during June:

a. Collected $600 of dues that had been billed in May.
b. Sold an old computer for $150 cash and a promise to pay $200 in one month. The balance sheet value of the computer was $350.
c. Bought a postage meter on credit for $210.
d. Received the $200 promised in transaction b.

1. Set up T-accounts for the following accounts:
   Cash
   Dues Receivable
   Accounts Receivable
   Equipment
   Accounts Payable
2. Make entries for each of the four transactions into the T-accounts. Label each entry a, b, c, or d.

15-44 Use of T-Accounts
Study Appendix 15B. Refer to problem 15-A2. Make entries for April in T-accounts. Key your entries and check to see that the ending balances agree with the financial statements.

15-45 Use of T-Accounts
Study Appendix 15B. Refer to problem 15-39. Use T-accounts to present an analysis of April transactions. Key your entries and check to see that the ending balances agree with the financial statements.

UNDERSTANDING PUBLISHED FINANCIAL REPORTS

15-46 Balance Sheet Effects
JPMorgan Chase & Co., one of the largest financial institutions in the United States with total assets of nearly $2,266 billion, showed the following items (among others) on its balance sheet at January 1, 2012 (in millions):

Cash (an asset)	$ 59,602
Total deposits (a liability)	$1,127,806

1. Suppose you deposited $5,000 in the bank. How would your deposit affect each of the bank's assets, liabilities, and stockholders' equities? How much would your deposit affect each of your personal assets, liabilities, and owners' equities? Be specific.
2. Suppose JPMorgan Chase makes a $950,000 loan to Evergreen Hospital for remodeling purposes. How would this loan affect each of the bank's assets, liabilities, and stockholders' equities? Be specific.
3. Suppose you borrowed $20,000 from JPMorgan Chase on a personal loan. How would such a transaction affect your personal assets, liabilities, and owners' equities?

15-47 Preparation of Balance Sheet for Costco
Costco Wholesale Corporation operates more than 590 membership warehouses and employs more than, 164,000 people. Its annual report included the following items at August 28, 2011 (in millions of dollars):

Accrued liabilities	$ 2,093
Cash and cash equivalents	4,009
Total stockholders' equity	b
Total liabilities	c
Long-term debt	1,253
Total revenues	88,915
Accounts receivable	965
Common stock	4,518
Inventories	a
Accounts payable	6,544
Property, net of accumulated depreciation	12,432
Retained earnings	7,111
Other assets	2,717
Other liabilities	4,298
Other stockholders' equity	944
Total assets	26,761

Prepare a condensed balance sheet including amounts for the following:

a. Inventory
b. Total stockholders' equity
c. Total liabilities

15-48 Net Income and Retained Earnings

Google Inc. is a well-known Internet company. The following data are from its financial statement for the year ended December 31, 2011 (in millions):

Google, Inc.

Retained earnings, end of year	$37,605	Dividends paid	$?
Revenues	37,905	Retained earnings, beginning of year	27,868
Net interest income	584	Operating costs and expenses	26,163
Provision for income taxes	2,589	Cash	9,983

1. Prepare Google's income statement for the year. The final three lines of the income statement were labeled as income before taxes, provision for income taxes, and net income.
2. Compute the change in retained earnings, and use that to determine the amount of dividends paid.
3. Comment briefly on the relative size of the cash dividend.

15-49 Earnings Statement, Retained Earnings

Dell, Inc. is a global information technology company headquartered in Round Rock, Texas. The following is a reproduction of the terms and amounts in the financial statements contained in the company's annual report for the fiscal year ended February 3, 2012 (in millions):

Net revenue	$62,071	Retained earnings at	
Cash	13,852	beginning of year	$24,744
Interest and other expenses	191	Cost of products and services	48,260
Income tax provision	748	Retained earnings at end of year	28,236
Accounts payable	11,656		
Research, development and engineering expenses	856	Selling and administrative expenses	8,524

Choose the relevant data and prepare the income statement for the fiscal year. The final three lines of the income statement should be labeled earnings before income taxes, income tax provision, and net income. Also, using the retained earnings account, compute the amount of cash dividends paid during the fiscal year ending February 3, 2012.

15-50 Sole Proprietorship and Corporation

Makaw Company is a sole proprietorship with the following simplified balance sheet:

Assets		Liabilities and Owner's Equity	
Cash	$ 30,000	Accounts payable	$ 15,000
Accounts receivable	25,000	Other liabilities	35,000
Equipment	145,000	Makaw, capital	150,000
Total assets	$200,000	Total liabilities and owners' equity	$200,000

Tom Makaw decided to incorporate his company on May 31, 20X1, by selling 5,000 shares of stock for $10 each and keeping 10,000 shares for himself. Prepare a balance sheet for the new corporation.

NIKE 10-K PROBLEM

15-51 Interpreting the Income Statement and Balance Sheet

Turn to Nike's income statement and balance sheet in Appendix C. Answer the following questions using the two statements:

1. Compute Nike's percentage increase in revenues and in total assets in fiscal 2011. Which increased more?
2. Illustrate the balance sheet equation, using total assets, total liabilities, and shareholders' equity from Nike's May 31, 2011, balance sheet.

3. Nike's retained earnings decreased from \$6,095 million to \$5,801 million during fiscal 2011. A decrease of \$1,858 was due to transactions not discussed in this chapter. Explain the remainder of the change in retained earnings.

4. Did Nike's net income grow by a larger percentage in fiscal 2011 or fiscal 2010?

EXCEL APPLICATION EXERCISE

15-52 Monthly Transactions Using the Balance Sheet Equation

Goal: Create an Excel spreadsheet to analyze the monthly transactions of a company using the balance sheet equation. Use the results to answer questions about your findings.

Scenario: Montha Company has asked you to prepare a transaction analysis report to help the company analyze what transpired during its first month of operation. The company would like you to record the transactions and calculate the appropriate totals using the balance sheet equation. The background data for your analysis appears in Fundamental Assignment Material 15-A2 on page 648. Prepare the transaction analysis using a format similar to Exhibit 15-1 on page 621.

When you have completed your spreadsheet, answer the following questions:

1. What are the total Assets of the firm at the end of April, 20X1?
2. Did the Stockholders' Equity increase or decrease during the month of April, 20X1? What caused the change?
3. Discuss what occurred in the Cash account and its implications.

Step-by-Step:

1. Open a new Excel spreadsheet.
2. In column A, create a bold-faced heading that contains the following:
   Row 1: Chapter 15 Decision Guideline
   Row 2: Montha Company
   Row 3: Transaction Analysis (in Dollars) for April 20X1
   Row 4: Today's Date
3. Merge and center the four heading rows across columns A–L.
4. In row 7, create the following bold-faced column headings:
   Column B: Assets
   Column H: Liabilities
   Column J: Stockholders' Equity
5. Merge and center the Assets heading across columns B–G.
6. Merge and center the Liabilities heading across columns H–I.
7. Merge and center the Stockholders' Equity heading across columns J–L.
8. Create a border around each of the headings created in row 7.
   Border tab: Presets: Outline
9. In row 8, create the following center-justified column headings:
   Column B: Cash
   Column C: A/R
   Column D: Inven.
   Column E: Ppd. Rent
   Column F: Equip.
   Column G: Acc. Dep.
   Column H: A/P
   Column I: N/P
   Column J: PIC
   Column K: Revenue
   Column L: Expense
10. Create a border around each of the column headings created in row 8.
    Border tab: Presets: Outline
11. In column A, create the following row headings:
    Row 9: Transactions:
    Row 10: a. Incorporation
    Row 11: b. Inven. for cash
    Row 12: c. Inven. for credit
    Row 13: d1. Merch. sold
    Row 14: d2. COGS

Row 15: e. Collect A/R
Row 16: f. Payment of A/P
Row 17: g. Equip. purchased
Row 18: h. Prepaid rent
Row 19: i. Add'l. rental fees
Row 20: j. Wage expense
Row 21: k. Depreciation exp.
Row 22: l. Rent expense
Skip a row.
Row 24: Balance, 4/30/X1
Skip two rows.
Row 27: Totals

Note: Adjust width of row A to accommodate row headings.

12. Use the data from Fundamental Assignment Material 15-A2 and enter the amounts for transactions a–h and j in the appropriate columns.
13. Use formulas to compute the adjusting entries needed for transactions i, k, and l.
14. Use formulas to calculate the totals in each of the columns for row 24, Balance, 4/30/X1.
15. Use formulas to generate totals for Assets, Liabilities, and Stockholders' Equity in row 27.
Print the total for Assets in column B.
Merge and center the total across columns B–G.
Print the total for Liabilities in column H.
Merge and center the total across columns H–I.
Print the total for Stockholders' Equity in column J.
Merge and center the total across columns J–L.
Change the format of the three total amounts to display as bold-faced.
16. Format all amounts in rows 10–22 as follows:
Number tab: Category: Currency
Decimal places: 0
Symbol: None
Negative numbers: Black with parentheses
17. Format amounts on row 24 as follows:
Number tab: Category: Accounting
Decimal places: 0
Symbol: $
18. Format amounts on row 27 as follows:
Number tab: Category: Currency
Decimal places: 0
Symbol: $
Negative numbers: Black with parentheses
19. Modify the Page Setup by selecting File, Page Setup.
Page tab: Orientation: Landscape
Sheet tab: Gridlines: Checked
20. Save your work, and print a copy for your files.

COLLABORATIVE LEARNING EXERCISE

15-53 Implicit Transactions
Form groups of from three to six "players." Each group should have a die and paper (or board) with four columns labeled as follows:

1. Expiration of unexpired costs
2. Realization of unearned revenues
3. Accrual of unrecorded expenses
4. Accrual of unrecorded revenues

The players should select an order in which they wish to play. Then, the first player rolls the die. If he or she rolls a 5 or 6, the die passes to the next player. If he or she rolls a 1, 2, 3, or 4, he or she must, within 20 seconds, name an example of a transaction that fits in the corresponding category; for example, if a 2 is rolled, the player must give an example of realization of unearned revenues.

Each time a correct example is given, the player receives one point. If someone doubts the correctness of a given example, he or she can challenge it. If the remaining players unanimously agree that the example is incorrect, the challenger gets a point and the player giving the example does not get a point for the example and is out of the game. If the remaining players do not unanimously agree that the answer is incorrect, the challenger loses a point and the player giving the example gets a point for a correct example. If a player fails to give an example within the time limit or gives an incorrect example, he or she is out of the game (except for voting when an example is challenged), and the remaining players continue until everyone has failed to give a correct example within the time limit. Each correct answer should be listed under the appropriate column. The player with the most points is the group winner. When all groups have finished a round of play, a second level of play can begin. All the groups should get together and list all the examples for each of the four categories by group. Discussion can establish the correctness of each entry; the faculty member or an appointed discussion leader will be the final arbitrator of the correctness of each entry. Each group gets one point for each correct example and loses one point for each incorrect entry. The group with the most points is the overall winner.

INTERNET EXERCISE

15-54 McDonald's Financial Statements

Go to www.mcdonalds.com to find the **McDonald's** home page. Click on the "Corporate Info" heading under "Our Story." Then select the "Investors" heading. Finally click on "Annual Reports" and select the most recent report.

Answer the following questions:

1. First open the balance sheet. Name two items on the McDonald's balance sheet that most likely represent unexpired (prepaid) costs. Name two items that most likely represent accruals of unrecorded expenses.
2. Has McDonald's grown in the past year? What did you look at to determine this?
3. Now look at McDonald's income statement. Did the company's sales (revenues) grow during the past year? By how much? Did its income increase or decrease? By how much? Do the sales and income changes bode well or poorly for McDonald's future?
4. Which financial statements provide evidence that McDonald's is a corporation, not a sole proprietorship or partnership?
5. Where can you find evidence in the McDonald's annual report that the financial statements were prepared using GAAP?

Understanding Corporate Annual Reports: Basic Financial Statements

LEARNING OBJECTIVES

When you have finished studying this chapter, you should be able to:

1. Recognize and define the main types of assets in the balance sheet of a corporation.

2. Recognize and define the main types of liabilities in the balance sheet of a corporation.

3. Recognize and define the main elements of the stockholders' equity section of the balance sheet of a corporation.

4. Recognize and define the principal elements in the income statement of a corporation.

5. Recognize and define the elements that cause changes in stockholders' equity accounts.

6. Explain the purposes of the cash flow statement, identify activities that affect cash, and classify the activities as operating, investing, or financing activities.

7. Assess financing and investing activities using the statement of cash flows.

8. Use both the direct method and the indirect method to explain cash flows from operating activities.

9. Explain the role of depreciation in the statement of cash flows.

10. Describe and assess the effects of the four major methods of accounting for inventories (Appendix 16A).

► NIKE

"Just do it!" Competitive athletes, armchair athletes, and nonathletes around the world recognize Nike's slogan and its "swoosh" logo. In just over two decades, the company grew from a small shoe company to a major producer of athletic footwear and other leisure wear with annual sales of more than $24 billion. The "Just do it!" slogan also would have been apt for early investors in Nike. A dollar invested in Nike stock in 1987 was worth nearly $95 by 2012. But is Nike stock a good investment now? Prospective investors look to the company's financial statements to help answer that question. Let's look at the kind of information that Nike includes in its financial statements.

Each year, Nike issues an annual report summarizing the 12 months ended on May 31. Like most companies, Nike uses its annual report partly as a promotion piece. For example, the 2011 annual report is filled with pictures of athletes, many of whom have endorsed Nike products. But, for investors, the most important part of Nike's annual report is the financial section, which contains four basic financial statements, footnotes to those statements, and reports by management and auditors. You can examine the financial statements to learn about Nike's financial position at the beginning and end of the year. You can also glean information about its performance during the year. Yet, investors want to know about the future, not just about the past. Accountants do not predict the future. However, the history recorded in the financial statements gives a baseline for investors to evaluate past performance and make judgments about how likely it is that future performance will be similar to that in the past. This chapter focuses on what you can learn from financial statements such as those of Nike. It extends our discussion of balance sheets and income statements from the preceding chapter and introduces two other major financial statements, the statement of cash flows and the statement of changes in stockholders' equity.

A common misunderstanding is that accounting is a precise discipline that produces exact measurements of a company's financial position and performance. Although accountants do take methodical steps with masses of data, their rules of measurement require judgment. Both U.S. GAAP and international standards (IFRS) allow much room for judgment. Managers and accountants who exercise this judgment have a major effect on a company's financial statements. To understand financial statements fully, you must recognize the judgmental decisions that go into their construction. Questionable accounting judgments in the last decade by companies such as Enron, WorldCom, Tyco, HealthSouth, AIG, and Freddie Mac in the United States and Parmalat, ComROAD AG, and Royal Ahold in Europe have illustrated just how important accountants' decisions are to users of financial statements. ■

© Lou-Foto/Alamy

Nike's "swoosh" is recognized throughout the world.

Classified Balance Sheet

Exhibit 16-1 shows the 2011 and 2010 classified balance sheets for Nike. We will examine the five main sections of Nike's balance sheet: current assets, noncurrent assets, current liabilities, noncurrent liabilities, and shareholders' equity. By understanding what items Nike and other companies include in each of these categories, you will be able to better interpret the company's financial position. Be sure to locate each of these items in the exhibit as you read the description of the item in the following pages.

Objective 1

Recognize and define the main types of assets in the balance sheet of a corporation.

Current Assets

Current assets include cash and all other assets that a company reasonably expects to convert to cash or sell or consume within one year or during the normal operating cycle, if longer than a year. A company's **operating cycle** is the time span during which it spends cash to acquire goods and services that it uses to produce its outputs, which in turn it sells to customers, who in turn pay for their purchases with cash. The following diagram illustrates what Nike's operating cycle might look like (dollar amounts are hypothetical):

current assets
Cash and all other assets that a company reasonably expects to convert to cash or sell or consume within one year or during the normal operating cycle, if longer than a year.

operating cycle
The time span during which a company spends cash to acquire goods and services that it uses to produce the organization's output, which it in turn sells to customers, who in turn pay for their purchases with cash.

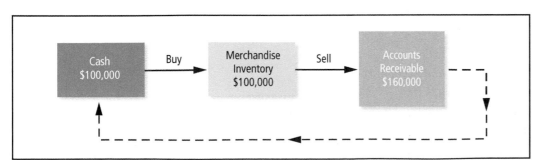

The box for Accounts Receivable (amounts customers owe to the business) is larger than the other two boxes because the objective of a business is to sell goods at a price higher than their acquisition cost. The total amount of profit a firm earns during a particular period depends on how much its selling prices exceed its costs, including both costs of producing or purchasing the goods to be sold and additional costs incurred during the period. The time span represented by the cycle might be as short as a few days (for a grocery store chain such as Albertsons or Kroger) or many years (for a timber company such as Georgia-Pacific or Weyerhaeuser).

As Exhibit 16-1 shows, Nike's current assets include cash and cash equivalents, short-term investments, accounts receivable, inventories, deferred income taxes, and prepaid expenses and other current assets. Cash consists primarily of balances in checking and other deposit accounts.

Exhibit 16-1

Nike, Inc.

Balance Sheet (in millions)

	May 31	
	2011	**2010**
ASSETS		
Current Assets		
Cash and equivalents	$ 1,955	$ 3,079
Short-term investments	2,583	2,067
Accounts receivable, less allowance for doubtful accounts of $74 and $74, respectively	3,138	2,650
Inventories	2,715	2,041
Deferred income taxes	312	249
Prepaid expenses and other current assets	594	873
Total current assets	11,297	10,959
Noncurrent Assets		
Property, plant, and equipment		
At cost	4,906	4,390
Less: Accumulated depreciation	2,791	2,458
Net property, plant, and equipment	2,115	1,932
Identifiable intangible assets, net	487	467
Goodwill	205	188
Deferred income taxes and other assets	894	873
Total noncurrent assets	3,701	3,460
Total assets	$14,998	$14,419
LIABILITIES AND SHAREHOLDERS' EQUITY		
Current Liabilities		
Current portion of long-term debt	$ 200	$ 7
Notes payable	187	139
Accounts payable	1,469	1,255
Accrued liabilities	1,985	1,904
Income taxes payable	117	59
Total current liabilities	3,958	3,364
Noncurrent Liabilities		
Long-term debt	276	446
Deferred income taxes and other liabilities	921	855
Total noncurrent liabilities	1,197	1,301
Total liabilities	5,155	4,665
Shareholders' Equity		
Redeemable preferred stock	*	*
Common stock at stated value:		
Class A convertible—90 and 90 shares outstanding	*	*
Class B—378 and 394 shares outstanding	3	3
Capital in excess of stated value	3,944	3,441
Retained earnings	5,801	6,095
Accumulated other comprehensive income	95	215
Total shareholders' equity	9,843	9,754
Total liabilities and shareholders' equity	$14,998	$14,419

* Less than $0.5 million.

Cash equivalents are investments that a company can easily convert into cash with little delay, such as money market funds and Treasury bills. They represent an investment of excess cash that a company does not immediately need. The balance sheet shows these securities at their market value. At May 31, 2011, the end of Nike's fiscal year, Nike had $1,955 million in cash and cash equivalents. A **fiscal year** is the year established for accounting purposes for the preparation of annual reports. Nike's fiscal year is June 1 through May 31.

Short-term investments are temporary investments in marketable securities. Companies often invest cash, which otherwise would be idle, in short-term investments, such as the stocks or bonds of other companies or debt securities issued by governments. Nike had $2,583 million in short-term investments on May 31, 2011.

Accounts receivable is the total amount owed to the company by its customers. Accountants often classify all accounts receivable as current assets, even though they may not fully collect them within one year. However, Nike divides accounts receivable into current and noncurrent portions depending on whether they are due within the next year. It includes the noncurrent portion in "other assets." Because some customers ultimately will not pay their bill, we reduce the total receivables by an allowance or provision for "doubtful accounts" or "bad debts." Gross accounts receivable less the allowance or provision is the net amount the company expects to collect. On May 31, 2011, Nike had gross accounts receivable due within the next year of $3,212 million and $74 million for doubtful accounts, resulting in a net asset of $3,138 million.

Inventories for wholesalers and retailers consist of merchandise held for sale. Manufacturing companies generally have three inventory accounts: raw materials, goods in the process of being manufactured, and finished products. Accountants regard all inventories as current assets. Companies state inventories at their cost or market price (defined as replacement cost by U.S. GAAP and net realizable value by IFRS), whichever is lower. Cost of manufactured products normally includes raw material cost plus the costs of converting it into a finished product (direct labor and manufacturing overhead). Under IFRS, companies can choose among three alternative methods to account for inventories: FIFO (first-in, first-out), weighted-average cost, or specific identification. U.S. companies have an added alternative, LIFO (last-in, first-out). Appendix 16A describes all four methods. Nike uses FIFO for some of its inventories and weighted-average cost for others. Its 2011 inventories stood at $2,715 million.

Nike reports $312 million of *deferred income tax* assets. These arise because the rules for financial reporting to the public differ from the rules for reporting to tax authorities. We will not discuss these assets further—just consider them as expected reductions of future income taxes that arise because of past transactions. You can read more about deferred taxes in Appendix 16B.

Prepaid expenses are advance payments to suppliers. They are usually small in relation to other assets. Examples are payments in advance for rent or for insurance premiums. They belong in current assets because, if they were not present, the company would need more cash to conduct current operations.

Other current assets are miscellaneous current assets that do not fit into the listed categories. In 2011, Nike shows $594 million of prepaid expenses and other current assets, which is just over 5% of total current assets.

Noncurrent Assets: Property, Plant, and Equipment

Property, plant, and equipment are examples of **fixed assets** or **tangible assets**—physical items that a person can see and touch. Companies usually provide details about property, plant, and equipment in a footnote to the financial statements, such as the one for Nike shown in Exhibit 16-2. Footnotes are an integral part of financial statements. They contain explanations for the summary figures that appear in the statements.

Companies typically show land as a separate asset and carry it indefinitely at its original cost. They also initially record buildings and machinery and equipment at cost: the invoice amount, plus freight and installation, less cash discounts. However, unlike land, the recorded values of buildings, machinery, and equipment gradually decline through depreciation (see Chapter 15, pp. 626–627).

The purpose of depreciation is to allocate the asset's original cost to the particular periods that benefit from the use of the asset. The value that appears on the balance sheet is the original cost less the accumulated depreciation (the sum of all depreciation to date on the asset), which we call the net book value. The net book value is simply the result of the allocation process. It is not necessarily a good approximation to other common concepts of value, such as replacement cost or resale value.

cash equivalents
Short-term investments that a company can easily convert into cash with little delay.

fiscal year
The year established for accounting purposes for the preparation of annual reports.

short-term investments
Temporary investments in marketable securities.

fixed assets (tangible assets)
Physical items that a person can see and touch, such as property, plant, and equipment.

Exhibit 16-2

Nike, Inc.
Footnote 3 to the 2011 Financial Statements

	Property, Plant, and Equipment (millions)	
	2011	2010
Land	$ 237	$ 223
Buildings	1,124	952
Machinery and equipment	2,487	2,217
Leasehold improvements	931	821
Construction-in-process	127	177
	4,906	4,390
Less: Accumulated depreciation	2,791	2,458
Net property, plant, and equipment	$2,115	$1,932

The amount of depreciation charged as expense each year depends on three factors:

1. The depreciable amount, which is the difference between the total acquisition cost and the estimated residual value. The residual value is the amount a company expects to receive when selling the asset at the end of its economic life.
2. The estimate of the asset's useful life. This estimate often depends more on technological changes and economic obsolescence than on physical wear and tear. Thus, the useful life is usually less than the physical life.
3. The depreciation method. There are three general methods of depreciation: straight-line, accelerated, and activity-based. The straight-line method allocates the same cost to each year of an asset's useful life. Accelerated methods allocate more of the cost to the early years and less to the later years.[1] The activity-based methods allocate cost based on either input activity (such as hours of machine time used) or output activity (such as units of production).

Which method is best? It depends on the firm's goals, the asset involved, and the type of financial statement being prepared. The straight-line method is most popular. More than 90% of all firms use it for at least some assets when preparing financial statements for reporting to the public. They believe that it best matches the cost of an asset with the benefits from its use. In contrast, most U.S. firms use accelerated depreciation when preparing financial statements for tax reporting to the IRS. Why? Because it is the most beneficial method allowed under U.S. tax laws.

Suppose a business spends $42,000 to buy equipment with an estimated useful life of 4 years and an estimated residual value of $2,000. If we use the straight-line method of depreciation, the annual depreciation expense in each of the 4 years would be as follows:

$$\frac{\text{original cost} - \text{estimated residual value}}{\text{years of useful life}}$$

$$= \frac{(\$42,000 - \$2,000)}{4}$$

$$= \$10,000 \text{ per year}$$

Exhibit 16-3 shows how we would measure the net book value that appears on the balance sheet at the end of each year. In Exhibits 16-1 and 16-2, the original cost of fixed assets on Nike's 2011 balance sheet is $4,906 million. There is accumulated depreciation of $2,791 million, the portion of the original cost of the asset that Nike has already charged as depreciation expense. Therefore, the net book value of Nike's property, plant, and equipment at May 31, 2011, is $4,906 million − $2,791 million = $2,115 million.

Leasehold improvements are investments made by a lessee (tenant) in items such as painting, decorating, fixtures, and air-conditioning equipment that it cannot remove from the premises when a lease expires. Companies write off the costs of leasehold improvements in the same manner as depreciation, but we call their periodic write-off amortization rather than depreciation. Nike's leasehold improvements of $931 million are 19% of the original cost of its total property, plant, and equipment.

---

[1] Accelerated depreciation is described in Chapter 11. However, knowledge of accelerated depreciation methods is not necessary for understanding this chapter.

Exhibit 16-3
Straight-Line Depreciation
(figures assumed)

	Balances at End of Year			
	1	2	3	4
Plant and equipment (at original acquisition cost)	$42,000	$42,000	$42,000	$42,000
Less: Accumulated depreciation (the portion of original cost that has already been charged to operations as depreciation expense)	10,000	20,000	30,000	40,000
Net book value (the portion of original cost not yet charged as expense)	$32,000	$22,000	$12,000	$ 2,000

Nike shows construction in progress separately from other assets because the assets are not yet ready for use. The balance of $127 million represents construction costs for buildings, machinery, or equipment that is not yet completed. Nike does not depreciate the assets until they are ready for use.

Long-term investments are also noncurrent assets. They include long-term holdings of securities of other firms. We discuss the accounting for such investments in Chapter 17. Nike does not show any long-term investments on its balance sheet.

Intangible Assets

We can physically observe tangible assets such as buildings or equipment. In contrast, **intangible assets** are a class of long-lived assets that are not physical in nature. They are rights to expected future benefits. Examples are franchises, patents, trademarks, and copyrights. In Exhibit 16-1, Nike shows identifiable intangible assets of $487 million at May 31, 2011.

Sometimes it is hard to determine whether amounts spent for items such as research and development (R&D) are ordinary expenses or should be capitalized as intangible assets. To **capitalize** an amount means to record it as an asset rather than as an expense. The FASB and IASB have given explicit guidance on R&D. Research costs should be charged immediately to expense. The authorities admit that research costs may generate long-term benefits, but the general high degree of uncertainty about the extent and measurement of future benefits has led to conservative accounting—immediately charging research costs as an expense. U.S. GAAP requires companies to expense immediately most development costs also. However, companies reporting under IFRS can capitalize development costs if they can demonstrate the technological and economic feasibility of a project.

Companies divide their intangible assets into two categories, (1) those with definite lives and (2) those with indefinite lives. They spread the costs of definite-lived intangibles over the life of the asset using a method identical to straight-line depreciation—except they call it amortization rather than depreciation. Companies do not depreciate or amortize indefinite-lived intangibles. However, they must annually apply an impairment test to assure that the asset has kept its value. (The specific methods of checking for impairment differ under U.S. GAAP and IFRS, and they are beyond the scope of this text.) If the intangible has lost value, a company must reduce its balance-sheet value by the amount of the decrease and charge that same amount as an impairment expense on the income statement. Nike has three types of definite-lived intangible assets shown in footnote 4 to its financial statements, patents ($56 million), trademarks ($19 million), and other ($25 million). The only indefinite-lived identifiable intangible is trademarks ($387 million).

Another intangible asset, discussed in more detail in the next chapter, is **goodwill**, the excess of the cost of an acquired company over the sum of the fair market values of its identifiable individual assets less its liabilities. For example, Nike acquired Umbro, a United Kingdom–based soccer equipment company, for $576 million in 2008. It could assign only $233 million to various identifiable assets, such as receivables, plant, and patents, less liabilities assumed by Nike. It recorded the remaining $343 million as goodwill. This $343 million represents a value that Nike saw in Umbro beyond its recorded assets less liabilities. Accountants record it as an asset only because Nike was willing to pay $343 million more than the identifiable value of the assets less liabilities it acquired. The same value may have existed when Umbro was an independent company, but it did not appear on Umbro's balance sheet. This illustrates how an exchange

intangible assets
Long-lived assets that are not physical in nature. Examples are goodwill, franchises, patents, trademarks, and copyrights.

capitalize
To record an amount as an asset rather than as an expense.

goodwill
The excess of the cost of an acquired company over the sum of the fair market values of its identifiable individual assets less its liabilities.

transaction is a basic concept of accounting. Even though many owners, like those of Umbro, could obtain a premium price if they sold their companies, we never record such goodwill. The only goodwill you will find on a balance sheet arises from an actual acquisition when a purchaser pays more than the amount assigned to individual assets less liabilities.

Goodwill remains on a company's books until management determines that its value is impaired. In 2009 Nike performed an impairment test on Umbro and determined that the value of its goodwill in Umbro had fallen to $144 million. Therefore, Nike reduced the value of its goodwill on its balance sheet by $343 million − $144 million = $199 million and charged $199 million as an impairment expense on its income statement. Nike recognized no further impairment, and the $144 million goodwill from the Umbro purchase remained on its books at May 31, 2011.

Liabilities

Objective 2

Recognize and define the main types of liabilities in the balance sheet of a corporation.

current liabilities

An organization's debts that fall due within the coming year or within the normal operating cycle if longer than a year.

working capital

Current assets less current liabilities.

noncurrent liabilities (long-term liabilities)

An organization's debts that fall due beyond one year.

debentures

Formal certificates of indebtedness that are accompanied by a promise to pay interest at a specified annual rate.

Assets are only part of the picture of any organization's financial health. Its liabilities, both current and noncurrent, are equally important.

Current liabilities are an organization's debts that fall due within the coming year or within the normal operating cycle if longer than a year. Turn again to Exhibit 16-1 on page 662. The first current liability is the *current portion of long-term debt*, which shows the payments due within the next year on bonds and other long-term debt. *Notes payable* are short-term debts backed by formal promissory notes held by a bank or business creditors. *Accounts payable* are amounts owed to suppliers who extended credit for purchases on open account. *Accrued liabilities* (also called *accrued expenses payable*) are amounts owed for wages, salaries, interest, and similar items. The accountant recognizes expenses as they occur—regardless of when a company pays for them in cash. *Income taxes payable* is a special accrued liability of enough magnitude to warrant a separate classification.

This concludes Nike's current liabilities, which total $3,958 million. However, some other companies also list unearned revenue, also called deferred revenue, among their current liabilities. Such revenue occurs when a company receives cash before delivering the related goods or services. For example, on January 1, 2012, Time Warner Inc., publisher of 21 magazines in the United States and another 70 worldwide (including *Time*, *People*, and *Sports Illustrated*) had $1,084 million in deferred revenue because it was obligated to send magazines to subscribers with prepaid subscriptions.

Now that you understand both current assets and current liabilities, we can introduce the term **working capital**—current assets less current liabilities. Investors watch working capital carefully to assess whether a company has enough current assets to pay current liabilities as they come due. Nike's working capital on May 31, 2011, was $11,297 million − $3,958 million = $7,339 million.

Noncurrent liabilities, also called **long-term liabilities**, are an organization's debts that fall due beyond one year. Exhibit 16-1 shows Nike's noncurrent liabilities for 2011 as $1,197 million, making its total liabilities $5,155 million. Nike has two identified noncurrent liabilities, long-term debt (which we will discuss in more depth) and deferred income taxes. Deferred income tax liabilities are a counterpart to the deferred tax assets discussed earlier. Deferred tax liabilities are expected *increases* in future income taxes that arise because of past transactions. They arise because the financial statements used for reporting to shareholders differ legitimately from those used for reporting to the income tax authorities. Appendix 16B provides more details about deferred taxes.

Exhibit 16-4 is a footnote from Nike's financial statements that provides details about its long-term debts. Note the next-to-last line in this exhibit, "Less: Current maturities." In this line, Nike subtracts the $200 million of payments due in the next year from long-term debt because it has already included the $200 million in current liabilities. Nike shows the remaining $276 million as "Long-term debt" in Exhibit 16-1.

Long-term debt may be secured or unsecured. Secured debt provides debt holders with first claim on specified assets. Mortgage bonds are an example of secured debt. If the company is unable to meet its regular obligations on the bonds, it may sell the specified assets and use the proceeds to pay off the firm's obligations to its bondholders, in which case secured debt holders have first claim to these proceeds.

Unsecured debt consists of **debentures** (bonds, notes, or loans), which are formal certificates of indebtedness accompanied by a promise to pay interest at a specified annual rate. Unsecured

Exhibit 16-4
Nike, Inc.
Footnote 8 to the 2011 Financial Statements

	May 31	
Long-term debt includes the following (in millions)	2011	2010
5.66% Corporate bond, payable July 23, 2012	$ 26	$ 27
5.4% Corporate bond, payable August 7, 2012	16	16
4.7% Corporate bond, payable October 1, 2013	50	50
5.15% Corporate bond, payable October 15, 2015	114	112
4.3% Japanese Yen note, payable June 26, 2011	130	116
1.52% Japanese Yen note, payable February 14, 2012	62	55
2.6% Japanese Yen note, maturing August 20, 2001, through November 20, 2020	54	53
2.0% Japanese Yen note, maturing August 20, 2001, through November 20, 2020	24	24
Subtotal	476	453
Less: Current maturities	200	7
Total	$276	$446

debt holders are creditors who have a general claim against total assets rather than a specific claim against particular assets. Most of Nike's long-term debt is unsecured. Holders of **subordinated** bonds or debentures are junior to the other creditors in exercising claims against assets.

subordinated
A creditor claim that is junior to the other creditors in exercising claims against assets.

To increase the appeal of their bonds, many companies issue debt that holders can convert into common stock. Convertibility allows bondholders to participate in a company's success without the risk of holding common stock. Suppose Nike issued convertible bonds for $1,000 when its stock price was $88, with a provision that investors can convert each bond into 10 common shares. If the stock price increases by 50% to $132 a share, the bondholder could exchange the $1,000 bond for 10 shares worth $10 \times \$132 = \$1,320$. If the stock price falls (or does not increase beyond $100 a share), the bondholder can keep the bond and receive $1,000 at maturity.

Consider the following example of how a corporation distributes resources when bankruptcy forces it to liquidate. **Liquidation** means converting assets to cash and using the cash to pay off outside claims. The company had a single asset, a building, that it sold for $120,000 cash:

liquidation
Converting assets to cash and using the cash to pay off outside claims.

Assets		Liabilities and Stockholders' Equity	
Cash	$120,000	Accounts payable	$ 60,000
		First-mortgage bonds payable	80,000
		Subordinated debentures payable	40,000
		Total liabilities	$180,000
		Stockholders' equity (negative)	(60,000)
Total assets	$120,000	Total liabilities and stockholders' equity	$120,000

The company would pay the mortgage (secured) bondholders in full ($80,000). It would pay trade creditors, such as suppliers, the remaining $40,000 for their $60,000 claim ($.67 on the dollar). The remaining claimants (the subordinated debenture holders and the stockholders) would get nothing. If the debentures were unsubordinated, the company would use the $40,000 of cash remaining after paying $80,000 to the mortgage holders to settle the $100,000 claims of the unsecured creditors proportionately as follows:

To trade creditors	$6/10 \times \$40,000 =$	$24,000
To debenture holders	$4/10 \times \$40,000 =$	16,000
Total cash distributed		$40,000

Stockholders' Equity

The final element of a balance sheet is stockholders' equity (called shareholders' equity by Nike), the total residual interest in the business. As we saw in Chapter 15, it is the excess of total assets over total liabilities. The main elements of stockholders' equity arise from two sources: (1) contributed or paid-in capital and (2) retained income and other comprehensive income.

Objective 3

Recognize and define the main elements of the stockholders' equity section of the balance sheet of a corporation.

common stock

Stock that has no predetermined rate of dividends and is the last to obtain a share in the assets when the corporation liquidates. It usually confers voting power to elect the board of directors of the corporation.

limited liability

A provision that a company's creditors cannot seek payment from stockholders as individuals if the corporation itself cannot pay its debts.

preferred stock

Stock that typically has some priority over other shares in the payment of dividends or the distribution of assets upon liquidation.

par value (stated value)

The value often printed on the face of stock certificates.

Paid-in capital typically comes from owners who invest in the business in exchange for shares of stock that specify their ownership interest. Holders of stock are stockholders or shareholders. There are two major classes of capital stock: common stock and preferred stock. Some companies have several categories of each, all with a variety of different attributes.

All corporations have **common stock**. Such stock has no predetermined rate of dividends and is the last to obtain a share in the assets when the corporation liquidates. Common stockholders usually elect the board of directors of the corporation. Common stock is the riskiest investment in a corporation, being unattractive in dire times because common stockholders can lose their entire investment but attractive in prosperous times because there is no limit to the common stockholder's potential participation in earnings. The corporate form of ownership provides one additional benefit to common shareholders—**limited liability**. This means that a company's creditors cannot seek payment from stockholders as individuals if the corporation itself cannot pay its debts.

Exhibit 16-1 shows that Nike has a small amount of preferred stock, in addition to common stock. About 40% of the major companies in the United States issue **preferred stock**. It typically has some priority over other shares in the payment of dividends or the distribution of assets on liquidation. For example, Nike pays an annual dividend of $.10 per preferred share on its 300,000 preferred shares, or $30,000 in total. Nike must pay these dividends in full before it pays dividends to any other classes of stock. Preferred shareholders in Nike, like preferred shareholders in most other corporations, have no voting privileges.

The face of a stock certificate often shows the **par** or **stated value**. For preferred stock, par is a basis for determining the amount of dividends or interest. Many preferred stocks have $100 par values. That is, a 9%, $100-par preferred stock would carry a $9 annual dividend. In contrast, par value has no practical importance for common stock. If a company were to issue stock for a price below par value, shareholders could be held liable for the difference between the issue price and par value if, upon liquidation, the company had insufficient resources to pay its creditors. However, as a practical matter, companies do not issue shares for less than par value. Instead, they set par or stated value at a nominal amount in relation to the market value of the stock on issuance (for example, stock issued for $70 might have a par value of $1).

Capital in excess of stated (or par) value is the difference between the amount a company receives when issuing new shares and the stated or par value of the shares issued. Suppose Nike had issued all its outstanding class A and B common shares for cash. The cumulative balance sheet effect at May 31, 2011, would be as follows (in millions):

Cash	$3,947	Common stock, at stated value	$ 3
		Capital in excess of stated value	3,944
		Total paid-in capital	$3,947

Retained earnings, also called *retained income*, is the balance in stockholders' equity due to the cumulative effect over the life of the corporation of all profits or losses generated less amounts distributed to shareholders (see Chapter 15). Retained earnings is the dominant item of stockholders' equity for most companies. For instance, as of May 31, 2011, Nike had shareholders' equity of $9,843 million of which $5,801 million or 59% was retained earnings.

Another element of stockholders' equity is *accumulated other comprehensive income.*

other comprehensive income

A few special types of gains and losses that do not appear on the income statement and thus do not become part of retained earnings.

treasury stock

A corporation's own stock that it has issued and subsequently repurchased but has not permanently retired.

Other comprehensive income consists of a few special types of gains and losses that do not appear on the income statement and thus do not become part of retained earnings. The specific gains and losses are beyond the scope of this text. While you will find accumulated other comprehensive income on most balance sheets, it is generally quite small. Nike's balance on May 31, 2011, was only $95 million, or 1% of the total shareholders' equity.

Many companies have **treasury stock**, which is a corporation's own stock that the company issued and subsequently repurchased but has not permanently retired. They hold it temporarily "in the treasury" to be distributed later, possibly as a part of an employee stock purchase plan or as an executive bonus or for use in acquiring another company. Such a repurchase is a decrease in ownership claims. Therefore, it should appear on a balance sheet as a deduction from total stockholders' equity. A company does not pay cash dividends on shares held in the treasury. Companies distribute dividends only to the outstanding shares (those in the hands of stockholders). Nike had no treasury stock in 2011. In contrast, McDonald's Corporation had more than $28 billion of treasury stock on January 1, 2012 (in millions):

Shareholders' equity before deducting treasury stock	$42,661
Treasury stock	(28,271)
Total shareholders' equity	$ 14,390

Summary Problems for Your Review

PROBLEM

"The book value of plant assets is the amount that a company would have to spend today to replace the assets." Do you agree? Explain.

SOLUTION

No. Net book value of the plant assets is the result of deducting accumulated depreciation from original cost. This process does not attempt to capture all the technological and economic events that may affect replacement value. Consequently, there is little likelihood that net book value will approximate replacement cost.

PROBLEM

Suppose that on December 31, 2012, Time Warner sells 3-year subscriptions to *Time Magazine* for a total of $150,000 cash.

It regards this sum as unearned revenue. Show the balances in unearned revenue at December 31, 2012, 2013, 2014, and 2015. How much revenue would Time Warner earn from the subscriptions in each of 2013, 2014, and 2015?

SOLUTION

The balance in unearned revenue would decline at the rate of $50,000 yearly as shown in the following table. Time Warner would recognize $50,000 as earned revenue in each of 2013, 2014, and 2015.

	December 31			
	2012	2013	2014	2015
Unearned revenue	$150,000	$100,000	$50,000	$0

Income Statement

Most investors are vitally concerned about a company's ability to produce long-run earnings and dividends. In this regard, income statements are more important than balance sheets. (Other names for the income statement include statement of earnings, statement of profit and loss, and P&L statement.) Income statements first list revenues, the total sales value of products delivered and services rendered to customers. From revenues they deduct expenses to get net income. We next examine how the format of the income statement can help users judge a company's performance.

Objective 4

Recognize and define the principal elements in the income statement of a corporation.

Operating Performance

An income statement can take one of two major forms: single-step or multiple-step. A single-step statement merely lists all expenses without drawing subtotals. It provides an overall measure of performance, but it does not allow direct assessment of performance in specific areas. In contrast, a multiple-step statement contains one or more subtotals. By dividing expenses into categories, we can more easily evaluate a company's performance in different dimensions.

Exhibit 16-5

Nike, Inc.

Statement of Income (millions except per share data)

	Year Ended May 31	
	2011	2010
Revenues	$20,862	$19,014
Cost of sales	11,354	10,214
Gross margin	$ 9,508	$ 8,800
Demand creation expense	2,448	2,356
Operating overhead expense	4,245	3,970
Total selling and administrative expense	$ 6,693	$ 6,326
Income from operations	$ 2,815	$ 2,474
Other expense (income)		
Interest expense, net	$ 4	$ 6
Other income, net	(33)	(49)
Total other expense (income)	$ (29)	$ (43)
Income before income taxes	$ 2,844	$ 2,517
Income taxes	711	610
Net income	$ 2,133	$ 1,907
Basic earnings per common share*	$ 4.48	$ 3.93

*Computation of earnings per share:

	2011	2010
Net income	$2,133,000,000	$1,907,000,000
Divided by average common shares outstanding	475,500,000	485,500,000
Earnings per share	$ 4.48*	$ 3.93

*Although ($2,133 million ÷ 475.5 million) = $4.49, if there were no rounding error in the $2,133 million and 475.5 million, this would be $4.48.

Exhibit 16-5 illustrates the two most common subtotals used to assess operating performance: *gross margin* (or *gross profit*) and *income from operations* (or *operating income* or *operating profit*). Gross margin is sales less cost of goods sold. It measures the amount by which sales prices exceed merchandise costs. A shrinking gross margin can indicate increasing competition in the market for the company's goods or services.

If you try to compare gross margins for two companies, you should be aware that a company's inventory method affects its gross profit. Why? Because the method that determines the value of inventory also determines the cost of goods sold. Appendix 16A provides additional discussion and examples to explain why understanding inventory methods is important to interpreting differences in gross margin.

Operating income (or *loss*) summarizes the results of the basic operating activities of the company—the day-to-day activities that generate sales revenue. Income statements often group depreciation expense, selling expenses, and administrative expenses as "operating expenses" and deduct them from the gross margin to obtain operating income. Nike shows two operating expenses, demand creation expense (more often called marketing expense) and operating overhead expense. (Note that cost of goods sold is also an operating expense. Why? Because we also deduct it from sales revenue to obtain "operating income.") In 2011, Nike had a gross margin of $9,508 million and operating income of $2,815 million. This summarizes Nike's success in producing and selling its products.

Financial Management

Managers are responsible for financial management as well as operating management. Financial management focuses on where to get cash and how to use cash for the benefit of the organization. That is, financial management attempts to answer questions such as the following: How much cash should we hold in our checking accounts? Should we pay a dividend? Should we borrow money or issue common stock? The best managers are superb at both operating and financial

Making Managerial Decisions

Suppose that you are a regional manager for **Wal-Mart** who is analyzing the performance of a **Sam's Club** warehouse in Texas. The income statement includes the following (in millions):

	2012	2011
Total revenue	$140.2	$140.0
Cost of revenue	125.1	122.5
Gross profit	15.1	17.5
Operating expenses	13.3	13.6
Operating income	1.8	3.9

What has caused the operating income to fall by $2.1 million in 2012?

Answer

Although revenue increased in 2012 by $.2 million, cost of revenue climbed by $2.6 million, causing the gross profit to fall by $2.4 million. This means that there must have been pressure on prices in 2012 and the warehouse was not able to maintain the markup it achieved in 2011. This decrease in gross profit was offset by a $.3 million decrease in operating expenses, so that total operating income was $2.1 million less in 2012 than in 2011. The warehouse manager was able to control operating expenses but was not able to maintain the warehouse's gross profit.

management. However, many managers are better operating managers than financial managers, or vice versa.

Because financial decisions and operating decisions have their own distinct effect on income, it is useful to separate the two effects in the income statement. Financing decisions affect primarily interest income and expense, so we present them as separate items after operating income. This approach facilitates comparisons of operating income between years and between companies. Some companies make heavy use of debt, which causes high interest expense, whereas other companies incur little debt and interest expense. Nike's debt is quite small, so its interest expense was only $4 million larger than its interest income. Other nonoperating items might also include income or loss on investments and gains or losses from foreign exchange transactions or from disposals of fixed assets. For Nike these totaled $33 million of nonoperating income.

The final expense on most income statements is income tax expense. Income statements usually deduct income taxes as a separate item placed immediately before net income. Nike's 2011 income statement in Exhibit 16-5 shows income taxes of $711 million.

The amount left after deducting all operating and nonoperating expenses from revenue is net income, sometimes called *net earnings* or *net profits* or simply the "bottom line." Nike's 2011 net income was $2,133 million.

Income statements conclude with the disclosure of earnings per share (EPS). Most companies report two EPS numbers: basic EPS and diluted EPS. Diluted EPS includes the potential effect of issuing additional common shares to holders of convertible securities or options. We focus only on basic EPS. Exhibit 16-5 illustrates basic **earnings per share** (EPS) as the net income divided by the average number of common shares outstanding during the year. Nike's basic EPS was $4.48 per share in 2011.

earnings per share (EPS)
Net income divided by the average number of common shares outstanding during the year.

Statement of Changes in Stockholders' Equity

To explain the changes in the stockholders' equity accounts, companies prepare a *statement of stockholders' equity* (or *statement of changes in stockholders' equity*), which shows the changes in each of the stockholders' equity accounts. Nike's statement is in Exhibit 16-6. The statement shows the four main stockholders' equity accounts: Common Stock, Capital in Excess of Stated Value, Accumulated Other Comprehensive Income, and Retained Earnings. We will focus on the changes in retained earnings. As the last column in Exhibit 16-6 demonstrates, net income increases retained earnings, and dividends reduce retained earnings. Note especially that dividends are not expenses; companies do not deduct them in computing net income, as explained in Chapter 15 on page 632 . Nike also reduced retained earnings by buying back some of its common shares, essentially giving some shareholders cash in exchange for their equity claims.

Objective 5

Recognize and define the elements that cause changes in stockholders' equity accounts.

Exhibit 16-6

Nike, Inc.
Statement of Stockholders'
Equity for the Year Ended May
31, 2011 (millions of dollars)

	Common Stock	Capital in Excess of Stated Value	Accumulated Other Comprehensive Income	Retained Earnings
Balance, May 31, 2010	$3	$3,441	$215	$6,095
Net income (Exhibit 16-5)				2,133
Dividends on common stock				(569)
Repurchase of common stock		(14)		(1,857)
Stock options exercised		368		
Issuance of shares to employees		49		
Stock-based compensation		105		
Other comprehensive income			(120)	
Other		(5)		(1)
Balance, May 31, 2011	$3	$3,944	$ 95	$5,801

Summary Problem for Your Review

PROBLEM

The Felski Company had the following items on its December 31, 20X1, balance sheet and 20X1 income statement:

Revenues	$830,000
Inventories	19,000
Notes payable	90,000
Long-term debt, excluding current portion	81,000
Goodwill, patents, and trademarks	70,000
Interest income	19,000
Accounts receivable, net	38,000
Provision for income taxes	55,000
Other long-term assets	78,000
Interest expense	45,000
Deferred income tax liability—long-term	36,000
Cash and equivalents	80,000
Retained earnings	?
Income taxes payable	8,000
Cost of sales	490,000
Additional paid-in capital	35,000
Prepaid expenses	48,000
Common stock (120,000 shares outstanding)	120,000
Property, plant, and equipment, at cost	680,000
Accounts payable	81,000
Current portion of long-term debt	12,000
Less: Accumulated depreciation	260,000
Selling and administrative expenses	190,000

Prepare in proper form the December 31, 20X1, balance sheet and the 20X1 income statement for Felski Company. Include the proper amount for retained earnings.

SOLUTION

See Exhibit 16-7 for the balance sheet and Exhibit 16-8 for the income statement. To determine the amount of retained earnings, begin by computing total liabilities and shareholders' equity = total assets = $753,000.

Exhibit 16-7
Felski Company
Balance Sheet, December 31, 20X1

ASSETS:

Current assets:	
Cash and equivalents	$ 80,000
Accounts receivable, net	38,000
Inventories	19,000
Prepaid expenses	48,000
Total current assets	185,000
Noncurrent assets:	
Property, plant, and equipment, at cost	680,000
Less: Accumulated depreciation	260,000
Property, plant, and equipment, net	420,000
Goodwill, patents, and trademarks	70,000
Other long-term assets	78,000
Total noncurrent assets	568,000
Total assets	$753,000

LIABILITIES AND SHAREHOLDERS' EQUITY:

Current liabilities:	
Notes payable	$ 90,000
Accounts payable	81,000
Income taxes payable	8,000
Current portion of long-term debt	12,000
Total current liabilities	191,000
Noncurrent liabilities:	
Long-term debt, excluding current portion	81,000
Deferred income tax liability	36,000
Total noncurrent liabilities	117,000
Total liabilities	308,000
Shareholders' equity:	
Common stock (120,000 shares @ $1.00)	120,000
Additional paid-in capital	35,000
Retained earnings	290,000
Total shareholders' equity	445,000
Total liabilities and shareholders' equity	$753,000

Exhibit 16-8
Felski Company
Income Statement for the Year Ended December 31, 20X1

Revenues	$830,000
Cost of sales	490,000
Gross profit	$340,000
Selling and administrative expenses	190,000
Income from operations	$150,000
Other income (expense):	
Interest expense	$ (45,000)
Interest income	19,000
Total other income (expense)	$ (26,000)
Income before income taxes	$124,000
Provision for income taxes	55,000
Net income	$ 69,000
Earnings per share ($69,000 ÷ 120,000)	$ 0.58

Then,

Total shareholders' equity = total liabilities and shareholders' equity − total liabilities

$$= \$753,000 - \$308,000$$
$$= \$445,000$$

Retained earnings = shareholders' equity − common stock − additional paid-in capital

$$= \$445,000 - \$120,000 - \$35,000$$
$$= \$290,000$$

Statement of Cash Flows

statement of cash flows
A statement that reports the cash receipts and cash payments of an organization during a particular period.

Another required statement, the statement of cash flows, has important information to help decision makers assess a company's generation and use of cash. The **statement of cash flows** reports the cash receipts and cash payments of an organization during a particular period. The statement has the following purposes:

- It shows the relationship of net income to changes in cash balances. Cash balances can decline despite positive net income and vice versa.
- It reports past cash flows as an aid in
  a. predicting future cash flows.
  b. evaluating management's generation and use of cash.
  c. determining a company's ability to pay interest and dividends and to pay debts when they are due.

Basic Concepts

Recall that balance sheets show the status of an entity at a point in time. In contrast, statements of cash flows and income statements cover periods of time. They explain why the balance sheet items have changed. The accompanying diagram depicts this linkage, where the arrows represent the flow of events that affect a company's balance sheet during the year:

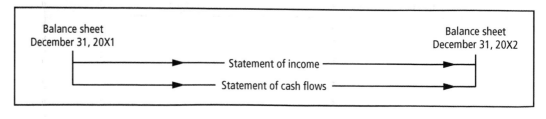

The income statement summarizes events that contribute to changes in retained earnings. The statement of cash flows summarizes events that explain changes in cash—where cash came from during a period and where it was spent.

The statement of cash flows explains changes in cash and cash equivalents, both of which a company can use almost immediately to meet obligations. Recall from page 663 that cash equivalents are highly liquid short-term investments that a company can easily convert into cash with little delay. Hereafter, when we refer to cash, we mean both cash and cash equivalents.

Typical Activities Affecting Cash

The fundamental approach to the statement of cash flows includes two steps: (1) List the activities that increased cash (cash inflows) and those that decreased cash (cash outflows), and (2) place each cash inflow and outflow into one of three categories according to the type of activity that caused it: operating activities, investing activities, and financing activities.

Following are examples of activities frequently found in statements of cash flows:

Objective 6

Explain the purposes of the cash flow statement, identify activities that affect cash, and classify the activities as operating, investing, or financing activities.

Operating Activities

Cash Inflows:	*Cash Outflows:*
Collections from customers	Cash payments to suppliers
Receipt of cash interest or dividends	Cash payments to employees
Other operating receipts	Interest paid
	Taxes paid
	Other operating cash payments

Investing Activities

Cash Inflows:	*Cash Outflows:*
Sale of property, plant, and equipment	Purchase of property, plant, and equipment
Sale of securities that are not cash equivalents	Purchase of securities that are not cash equivalents
Receipt of loan principal repayments	Lending cash

Financing Activities

Cash Inflows:	*Cash Outflows:*
Borrowing cash from creditors	Repayment of amounts borrowed
Issuing equity securities	Repurchase of equity shares (including the purchase of treasury stock)
	Payment of dividends

Let's look briefly at each of the three categories. **Cash flows from operating activities** are generally the effects of transactions that affect the income statement. **Cash flows from investing activities** include (1) lending and collecting principle repayments on loans and (2) acquiring and selling long-term assets. **Cash flows from financing activities** include obtaining cash from creditors and owners, repaying creditors or buying back stock from owners, and paying cash dividends.

Perhaps the most troublesome classifications are the receipts and payments of interest and the receipts of dividends. Standard setters in the United States decided to include these items with cash flows from operating activities, even though they are a result of investment and financing activities. Why? Mainly because they affect the computation of income. In contrast, payments of cash dividends are financing activities because they do not affect income.

Most companies reporting under IFRS use the same method as those reporting under U.S. GAAP. However, companies using IFRS have the option to classify dividend or interest payments as either operating or financing activities and interest or dividend receipts as either operating or investing activities.

cash flows from operating activities
The section in the statement of cash flows that lists the cash-flow effects of transactions that affect the income statement.

cash flows from investing activities
The section in the statement of cash flows that lists the cash-flow effects of (1) lending and collecting on loans and (2) acquiring and selling long-term assets.

cash flows from financing activities
The section in the statement of cash flows that lists the cash-flow effects of obtaining cash from creditors and owners, repaying creditors or buying back stock from owners, and paying cash dividends.

Focus of a Statement of Cash Flows

To see the basic ideas underlying the statement of cash flows, we first consider a simple hypothetical company, the Michael Foster Company, and later we will look at **Nike**'s statement of cash flows. Exhibit 16-9 shows Foster Company's summary transactions for 20X2, Exhibit 16-10 shows its 20X2 income statement, and Exhibit 16-11 shows condensed balance sheets for 20X1 and 20X2. Because the statement of cash flows explains the causes for the change in cash, our first step is to compute the amount of the change (which represents the net effect we need to explain):

Cash, December 31, 20X1	$25,000
Cash, December 31, 20X2	16,000
Net decrease in cash	$ 9,000

Exhibit 16-12 illustrates a statement of cash flows that explains this $9,000 decrease in cash. Let's look at each of the three sections of this cash flow statement.

Cash Flows from Financing Activities

Objective 7

Assess financing and investing activities using the statement of cash flows.

Although most companies list operating activities as the first section of the cash flow statement, it is easier to understand the cash flows from financing activities, so we will begin with that section. It shows cash flows to and from providers of capital. The easiest way to determine cash flows from financing activities is to examine changes in the cash account in the balance sheet equation and identify those associated with financing activities.

Foster Company had three such transactions in 20X2, as shown in Exhibit 16-9:

Transaction 9, issue long-term debt, $120,000

Transaction 10, issue common stock, $98,000

Transaction 11, pay dividends, $19,000

The first two of these transactions are cash inflows, and the last is a cash outflow. Notice that we put cash outflows in parentheses. Therefore, Foster's net cash inflow from financing activities totals $199,000:

Foster Company

Cash Flows from Financing Activities, 20X2	
Proceeds from issuance of long-term debt	$120,000
Proceeds from issuance of common stock	98,000
Payment of dividends	(19,000)
Net cash provided by financing activities	$199,000

A general rule for financing activities is as follows:

- Increases in cash (cash inflows) stem from increases in liabilities or paid-in capital.
- Decreases in cash (cash outflows) stem from decreases in liabilities or paid-in capital or payment of dividends.

The following is a list of some financing activities and their effect on cash:

Type of Transaction	Increase (+) or Decrease (−) in Cash
Increase long-term or short-term debt	+
Reduce long-term or short-term debt	−
Sell common or preferred shares	+
Repurchase common shares	−
Pay dividends	−
Convert debt to common stock	No effect

Liabilities and Stockholders' Equity

	Assets					=	Liabilities			Stockholders' Equity	
Transaction	Cash	Accounts Receivable	Inventories	Fixed Assets, Gross	Accumulated Depreciation	=	Accounts Payable	Wages and Salaries Payable	Long-Term Debt	Paid-In Capital	Retained Earnings
Balance, 12/31/X1	+ 25	+ 25	+ 60	+ 330	– 110	=	+ 6	+ 4	+ 5	+ 210	+ 105
1a. Purchase inventory on account			+ 140			=	+ 140				
1b. Payments to suppliers	– 72					=	– 72				
2a. Sales on credit		+ 200				=					+ 200
2b. Cash collections from customers	+ 180	– 180				=					
2c. Cost of goods sold			– 100			=					– 100
3a. Wages and salaries expense						=		+ 36			– 36
3b. Payments to employees	– 15					=		– 15			
4. Depreciation expense					– 17	=					– 17
5. Interest expense—paid-in capital	– 4					=					– 4
6. Income tax expense—paid-in capital	– 20					=					– 20
7. Purchase of fixed assets for cash	– 287			+ 287		=					
8. Sales of fixed assets*	+ 10			– 36	+ 26	=					
9. Issue long-term debt for cash	+ 120					=			+ 120		
10. Issue common stock for cash	+ 98					=				+ 98	
11. Pay cash dividends	– 19					=					– 19
Balance, 12/31/X2	+ 16	+ 45	+ 100	+ 581	– 101	=	+ 74	+ 25	+ 125	+ 308	+ 109

*Foster Company sold assets with a gross book value of $36,000 and accumulated depreciation of $26,000, receiving cash of $10,000.

Exhibit 16-9

Foster Company *Summarized Transactions, 20X2 (in thousands of dollars)*

Exhibit 16-10
Foster Company
Statement of Income for the
Year Ended December 31, 20X2
(in thousands)

Sales		$200
Costs and expenses		
Cost of goods sold	$100	
Wages and salaries	36	
Depreciation	17	
Interest	4	
Total costs and expenses		157
Income before income taxes		43
Income taxes		20
Net income		$ 23

Assets				Liabilities and Stockholders' Equity			
	20X2	20X1	Increase (Decrease)		20X2	20X1	Increase (Decrease)
Current assets				Current liabilities			
Cash	$ 16	$ 25	$ (9)	Accounts payable	$ 74	$ 6	$ 68
Accounts receivable	45	25	20	Wages and salaries			
Inventories	100	60	40	payable	25	4	21
Total current assets	161	110	51	Total current liabilities	99	10	89
Fixed assets, gross	581	330	251	Long-term debt	125	5	120
Less accum. depreciation	(101)	(110)	9	Stockholders' equity	417	315	102
Net fixed assets	480	220	260	Total liabilities and			
Total assets	$641	$330	$311	stockholders' equity	$641	$330	$311

Exhibit 16-11
Foster Company
Balance Sheets as of December 31 (in thousands)

Exhibit 16-12
Foster Company
Statement of Cash Flows for
the Year Ended December 31,
20X2 (in thousands)

Cash Flows from Operating Activities		
Cash collections from customers		$180
Cash payments		
To suppliers	$72	
To employees	15	
For interest	4	
For taxes	20	
Total cash payments		(111)
Net cash provided by operating activities		$ 69

Cash Flows from Investing Activities		
Purchases of fixed assets	$(287)	
Proceeds from sale of fixed assets	10	
Net cash used in investing activities		(277)

Cash Flows from Financing Activities		
Proceeds from issue of long-term debt	$120	
Proceeds from issue of common stock	98	
Dividends paid	(19)	
Net cash provided by financing activities		199
Net decrease in cash		$ (9)
Cash, December 31, 20X1		25
Cash, December 31, 20X2		$ 16

Cash Flows from Investing Activities

Another part of the cash flow statement, cash flows from investing activities, lists cash flows from the purchase or sale of plant, property, equipment, and other long-lived assets. It is usually the second section in the statement. To determine the cash flows from investing activities, you need to look at transactions that increase or decrease long-lived assets, loans made by the company, or securities it owns that are not cash equivalents. Foster Company has only one such asset, fixed assets, and its related accumulated depreciation account. There were two cash transactions relating to fixed assets during 20X2:

Transaction 7, purchase fixed assets for cash, $287,000

Transaction 8, sale of fixed assets for cash, $10,000

The first of these transactions is a cash outflow, and the second is a cash inflow. The investing activities section of Foster's cash flow statement is as follows:

Foster Company	
Cash Flows from Investing Activities, 20X2	
Purchase of fixed assets	$(287,000)
Proceeds from sale of fixed assets	10,000
Net cash used by investing activities	$(277,000)

Because there is a net cash outflow, investing activities used cash during January. This contrasts with financing activities, which provided cash.

The general rule for investing activities is as follows:

- Increases in cash (cash inflows) stem from sales of long-lived assets, collection of loans, and sales of investments.
- Decreases in cash (cash outflows) stem from purchases of long-lived assets, loans made to others, and purchases of investments.

Following are examples of investing activities and their effects on cash:

Type of Transaction	Increase (+) or Decrease (−) in Cash
Purchase fixed assets for cash	−
Purchase fixed assets by issuing debt	No effect
Sell fixed assets for cash	+
Purchase securities that are not cash equivalents	−
Sell securities that are not cash equivalents	+
Make a loan	−
Collect a loan	+

Noncash Investing and Financing Activities

Sometimes financing or investing activities do not affect cash but are similar to transactions that have a cash-flow effect. Companies must list such activities in a separate schedule accompanying the statement of cash flows. In our example, Foster Company did not have any noncash investing or financing activities. However, suppose Foster's purchase of fixed assets was not for cash but was financed as follows:

A. Foster acquired $150,000 of the fixed assets by issuing common stock.
B. Foster acquired the other $137,000 of fixed assets by signing a note payable for $137,000.

Foster could have taken the $150,000 and $137,000 in cash and then used that cash to buy fixed assets, but it never actually received the cash. Thus, there is no entry to the statement of cash flows. However, because of the similarities between this noncash transaction and the purchase for cash, readers of statements of cash flows want to be informed of such noncash activities.

Companies must report such items in a schedule of noncash investing and financing activities. If Foster Company had acquired the store equipment for common stock and a note payable, the purchase of fixed assets for $287,000 shown earlier would not appear in the investing section of the statement of cash flows. Instead, Foster Company's schedule for these hypothetical transactions would be as follows:

Foster Company	
Schedule of noncash investing and financing activities, 20X2	
Common stock issued to acquire store equipment	$150,000
Note payable for acquisition of store equipment	$137,000

Cash Flow from Operating Activities

Objective 8

Use both the direct method and the indirect method to explain cash flows from operating activities.

Analyzing the results of financing and investing activities informs investors about management's ability to make financial and investment decisions. However, users of financial statements are even more concerned with assessing management's operating decisions. They focus on the first major section of cash flow statements, cash flows from operating activities (or cash flows from operations). This section shows the cash effects of transactions that affect the income statement.

Approaches to Calculating the Cash Flow from Operating Activities

direct method for operating cash flows

A method for computing cash flows from operating activities that subtracts operating cash disbursements from cash collections to arrive at cash flows from operations.

indirect method for operating cash flows

A method for computing cash flows from operating activities that adjusts the previously calculated accrual net income from the income statement to reflect only cash receipts and cash disbursements.

We can use either of two approaches to compute cash flows from operating activities (or cash flow from operations). The **direct method for operating cash flows** subtracts operating cash disbursements from operating cash collections to arrive at cash flows from operations. The **indirect method for operating cash flows** adjusts the previously-calculated accrual net income from the income statement to reflect only operating cash receipts and cash disbursements. Both methods show the same total amount of cash provided by (or used for) operating activities. The only difference is the format and individual components of the statement.

The IASB and FASB prefer the direct method because it is a straightforward listing of cash inflows and cash outflows and is easier for investors to understand. The boards have a joint proposal that would mandate use of the direct method, and it may be approved in the near future. However, today almost all companies use the indirect method, which links cash flows directly with net income, emphasizing how income and cash flows differ. We will discuss the direct method first because you will probably find it easier to understand. However, it is essential to understand also the indirect method that most companies use.

Consider first the types of cash flows that accountants classify as operating activities. Exhibit 16-13 lists many such activities. These cash flows are associated with revenues and expenses on the income statement. Notice that recording revenues from the sales of goods or services on account does not increase cash immediately. Instead, the increase in cash occurs when a company collects its accounts receivable.

The cash effects of expenses are similar. Sometimes—depreciation is an example—the cash outflow precedes the recording of the expense on the income statement. For example, Foster Company paid $287,000 in cash for its fixed assets and recorded the purchase as an investing cash outflow. The company then records depreciation expenses as it uses the equipment, long after the cash payment. Thus, depreciation is never a cash flow.

Other times the cash outflow follows the recording of the expense. For example, most companies pay salaries and wages after employees have earned them. Suppose that Foster Company pays salaries and wages on the tenth day of each month for the amount earned the previous month. Then, the accrual of the expense would occur one month, and the related cash outflow would come the following month. The expense appears in the first month's income statement, but the cash outflow appears in the second month's statement of cash flows.

Now let's examine the two formats used for showing the cash flow effects of operations.

Type of Transaction	Increase (+) or Decrease (−) in Cash
Operating activities	
Sales of goods and services for cash	+
Sales of goods and services on credit	No effect
Collection of accounts receivable	+
Receive dividends or interest	+
Recognize cost of goods sold	No effect
Purchase inventory for cash	−
Purchase inventory on credit	No effect
Pay accounts payable	−
Accrue operating expenses	No effect
Pay operating expenses	−
Accrue taxes	No effect
Pay taxes	−
Accrue interest	No effect
Pay interest	−
Prepay expenses for cash	−
Record the using up of prepaid expenses	No effect
Charge depreciation	No effect

Cash Flow from Operations—The Direct Method

The direct method consists of a listing of cash receipts (inflows) and cash disbursements (outflows). The easiest way to construct the statement of cash flows from operations using the direct method is to examine the cash column of the balance sheet equation. The following entries from Exhibit 16-9 affect cash and are not financing or investing activities:

Transaction	Cash Effect
(1b) Payments to suppliers	−72,000
(2b) Collections from customers	+180,000
(3b) Payments to employees	−15,000
(5) Interest expense and payment	−4,000
(6) Income tax expense and payment	−20,000

Therefore, the direct-method cash flow statement is as follows:

Foster Company	
Cash Flows from Operating Activities, 20X2	
Cash collections from customers	$180,000
Cash payments:	
To suppliers	(72,000)
To employees	(15,000)
For interest	(4,000)
For taxes	(20,000)
Net cash provided by operating activities	$ 69,000

This completes the statement of cash flows in Exhibit 16-12. We can see that operations generated $69,000 of cash, and Foster Company raised an additional $199,000 from financing activities, for a total of $268,000. However, because the company used $277,000 for investing, cash still declined $9,000 over the year.

Cash Flow from Operations—The Indirect Method

Most income statement items have a parallel item in the statement of cash flows. Each sale eventually results in cash inflows; each expense entails cash outflows at some time. When the cash inflow from a sale or the cash outflow for an expense occurs in one accounting period and we record the sales revenue or expense in another, net income can differ from the cash flows from operations. The indirect method reconciles these differences by starting with net income (which is revenues less expenses) and then listing all the adjustments necessary to turn net income into cash flows from operating activities. We can construct the indirect method cash flow statement for Foster Company from 20X2's income statement and the beginning and ending balance sheets in Exhibits 16-10 and 16-11, respectively. Exhibit 16-14 illustrates the indirect method, and we will next explain the entries in this exhibit.

If Foster's sales were all for cash and it paid all expenses in cash as incurred, the cash flows from operating activities would be identical to the net income. Thus, you can think of the first line of Exhibit 16-14, net income, as the cash flow from operating activities when revenues equal cash inflows and expenses equal cash outflows. The subsequent adjustments recognize the differences 1) between revenues and cash inflows and 2) between expenses and cash outflows.

The first adjustment is to add the depreciation expense to net income. We do this because we deducted depreciation of $17,000 when computing the net income of $23,000, but depreciation does not cause an operating cash outflow. Depreciation represents an expense for which there is never an operating cash flow. The related cash flow was an investing outflow when Foster purchased the equipment.

The remaining adjustments represent situations where net income and cash flows from operations differ only because of timing. That is, the timing of revenues or expenses differs from that of the related operating cash inflow or outflow.

Consider the sales revenue of $200,000 shown on the income statement. If all sales were for cash, the associated cash flows would occur at the time of sale, and the cash inflow would equal the sales revenue. However, Foster's sales are all on account. Thus, the sale initially increases accounts receivable, and the cash inflow occurs when Foster collects the receivables. You can compute the amount of cash collections from the income statement and balance sheet data in one of two ways. First, you can compute the total collections Foster could possibly collect during the year, which is the accounts receivable balance at the beginning of the year plus the sales during the year. From this, you subtract the amount that Foster has not yet collected at the end of the year, the ending accounts receivable. This gives collections in 20X2 of $180,000:

Beginning accounts receivable	$ 25,000
+ Sales	200,000
Potential collections	$225,000
− Ending accounts receivable	(45,000)
Cash collections from customers	$180,000

Alternatively, you can start with the sales for the year. If accounts receivable had remained unchanged, cash collections would equal sales. If accounts receivable increased, collections fell short of the sales, causing net income to be higher than cash flows from operations. If accounts receivable decreased, then collections exceeded sales, causing net income to be lower than cash

Net income	$23,000
Adjustments to reconcile net income to net cash provided (used) by operating activities:	
Depreciation	17,000
Net increase in accounts receivable	(20,000)
Net increase in inventories	(40,000)
Net increase in accounts payable	68,000
Net increase in wages and salaries payable	21,000
Net cash provided by operating activities	$69,000

Exhibit 16-14
Foster Company
Cash Flows from Operating Activities—Indirect Method

flows from operations. In 20X2, Foster's accounts receivables increased from $25,000 to $45,000 so cash collections were only $180,000:

Sales	$200,000
Decrease (increase) in accounts receivable[*]	(20,000)
Cash collections from customers	$180,000

[*] The format "decrease (increase)" means that decreases are positive amounts and increases are negative amounts.

Because Foster's accounts receivable increased in 20X2, we need to deduct the $20,000 from net income to get cash provided by operating activities. Entry 1 in Exhibit 16-15 shows this adjustment.

Just as we adjusted sales to compute cash collections from customers, we can adjust the cost of goods sold from the income statement to compute cash outflow for payments to suppliers. To do this, we look at one income statement account, cost of goods sold, and two balance sheet accounts, inventory and accounts payable. We adjust cost of goods sold to get cash payments to suppliers in two steps: Cost of Goods Sold → Purchases → Payments to Suppliers.

These two steps yield the following:

Step 1:	
Ending inventory, December 31, 20X2	$100,000
+ Cost of goods sold in 20X2	100,000
Inventory to account for	$200,000
− Beginning inventory, December 31, 20X1	(60,000)
Inventory purchased in 20X2	$140,000
Step 2:	
Inventory purchased in 20X2	$140,000
+ Beginning accounts payable, December 31, 20X1	6,000
Total amount to be paid	$146,000
− Ending accounts payable, December 31, 20X2	(74,000)
Amount paid in cash during 20X2	$ 72,000

In step 1, we compute the amount of inventory purchased in 20X2, independent of whether we purchase the inventory for cash or credit. The calculation requires taking the amount of

Net Income		Adjustments		Cash Provided by Operating Activities	
1) Sales revenues	$200,000	Increase in accounts receivable	$(20,000)	Cash collections from customers	$180,000
2) Cost of goods sold	(100,000)	Increase in inventories	(40,000)	Cash payments to suppliers	(72,000)
		Increase in accounts payable	68,000		
3) Wages and salaries expense	(36,000)	Increase in wages and salaries payable	21,000	Cash payments to employees	(15,000)
4) Interest	(4,000)	None		Cash payments for interest	(4,000)
5) Income taxes	(20,000)	None		Cash payments for income taxes	(20,000)
6) Depreciation	(17,000)	Depreciation	17,000		
Net income	$ 23,000	Total adjustments	$ 46,000	Net cash provided by (used for) operating activities	$ 69,000

Exhibit 16-15
Foster Company
Comparison of Net Income and Cash Provided by Operating Activities

inventory used in 20X2 (that is, the cost of goods sold), plus the amount of inventory left at the end of the year, less the amount that was already in inventory at the beginning of the year.

If Foster had bought all its inventory for cash, we could stop at this point. Its cash outflow to suppliers would be equal to the amount purchased, $140,000. However, because Foster purchased inventory on credit, we must take step 2. If Foster had paid off all its accounts payable by the end of the year, it would have paid an amount equal to the beginning accounts payable plus the purchases in 20X2, a total of $146,000. But $74,000 remained payable at the end of 20X2, meaning that of the $146,000 of potential payments, Foster paid only $146,000 − $74,000 = $72,000 in 20X2.

From these two steps, we can determine the two adjustments to net income needed to adjust it to a cash outflow number:

Cost of goods sold in 20X2	$100,000
Increase (decrease) in inventory during 20X2	40,000
Decrease (increase) in trade accounts payable during 20X2	(68,000)
Payments to suppliers during 20X2	$ 72,000

This gives us the two adjustments to net income required to compute cash provided by operating activities. Exhibit 16-15 shows this in entry 2. First, remember that we subtract cost of goods sold in computing net income just as we subtract the cash payments to suppliers in determining cash provided by operating activities. Any adjustment showing a cash outflow greater than the cost of goods sold will lead to cash provided by operations that is less than net income. Because the increase in inventory caused the cash outflow to exceed the cost of goods sold by $40,000, net income will be $40,000 more than cash provided by operations. In contrast, the increase in accounts payable caused the cash outflow to fall short of cost of goods sold by $68,000, which results in net income that is $68,000 less than cash provided by operations.

Before considering the other adjustments in Exhibit 16-15, let's create a general approach to adjustments. Then we can apply the approach to wages and salaries.

- Adjust for revenues and expenses not requiring cash
  Add back depreciation and other noncash expenses
- Adjust for changes in noncash assets and liabilities relating to operating activities
  Add decreases in assets
  Deduct increases in assets
  Add increases in liabilities
  Deduct decreases in liabilities

Adjustments discussed so far have included adding back the $17,000 of depreciation (entry 6 in Exhibit 16-15), deducting the $20,000 increase in accounts receivable (an asset), deducting the $40,000 increase in inventory (an asset), and adding the $68,000 increase in accounts payable (a liability). Take time now to verify that each of these adjustments is consistent with the rules in the general approach.

Now let's consider the wages and salaries expense. Notice that Wages and Salaries Payable, a liability account, increased from $4,000 at the beginning of the year to $25,000 at the end of the year. Thus, we need to add a $21,000 adjustment for wages and salaries, as shown in entry 3 of Exhibit 16-15. This $21,000 is the result of charging $36,000 for wages and salaries in the income statement but paying only $15,000 in cash. This means that Foster's expense exceeded the cash outflow by $21,000, as shown in the adjustment we made in Exhibit 16-14 that added $21,000 to net income when computing net cash provided by operating activities.

Finally, Foster pays both interest expense and taxes in cash when incurred. Thus, they require no adjustments—the cash flow equals the expense, as shown in entries 4 and 5.

To summarize, look at the bottom line of Exhibit 16-15. The comparison of net income to cash flows from operating activities begins with the net income of $23,000 from the first column, adds the adjustments of $46,000 in the middle column, and ends with the $69,000 net cash provided by operating activities in the right-hand column. Exhibit 16-14 shows this same information in the proper indirect-method format that gives the details of all $46,000 of adjustments.

Making Managerial Decisions

Managers often want quick approximations of the financial statement effects of their decisions. Suppose we have a simple company that sells only on a cash basis and pays all expenses except depreciation in cash. In a recent month, the company had sales of $100,000 and expenses of $85,000, of which $20,000 was depreciation. Therefore, it had net income of $15,000. Prepare two statements of cash flows from operating activities, one using the direct method and one using the indirect method. Describe the basic difference between the two methods.

Answer

The direct method shows differences between income and cash flow by adjusting the individual items on the income statement to a cash basis. In this example, sales revenue of $100,000 is already the same as the cash collected from customers of $100,000. Then, we adjust the income statement expense of $85,000 by the $20,000 of depreciation to get cash expenses of $65,000.

Direct Method

Cash collections from customers	$100,000
Cash expenses	65,000
Cash provided by operating activities	$ 35,000

In contrast, the indirect method starts with the net income, revenues less expenses, of $15,000. Then, we must list the adjustments needed to convert this to cash from operations. In this example, the list contains only one adjustment, depreciation.

Indirect Method

Net income	$15,000
Add: Depreciation	20,000
Cash provided by operating activities	$35,000

Reconciliation Statement

When a company uses the direct method for reporting cash flows from operating activities, users of the financial statements would miss information that relates net income to operating cash flows. Thus, direct-method statements must also include a supplementary schedule reconciling net income to net cash provided by operations. Such a supplementary statement is essentially an indirect-method cash flow statement. In essence, companies that choose to use the direct method must also report using the indirect method. In contrast, those using the indirect method never explicitly report the information on a direct-method statement. The supplementary statement included with direct-method cash flow statements would be identical to the body of Exhibit 16-14, but we would label it "Reconciliation of Net Income to Net Cash Provided by Operating Activities."

Interpreting the Cash Flow Statement

Let's look back on what we learned from Foster Company's cash flow statement. For growing companies, cash often declines. Why? Because growing companies usually need cash for investment in various business assets required for expansion, including investment in accounts receivable and inventories. Notice that Foster Company's total assets nearly doubled between 20X1 and 20X2, so we should not be surprised at the decrease in cash.

The statement in Exhibit 16-12 on page 678 gives a direct picture of where Foster's cash came from and where it went. Operations generated $69,000 of cash, investing activities used $277,000, and the company raised $199,000 from financing activities. The excess of cash outflows over cash inflows reduced cash in total by $9,000. Without the statement of cash flows, the readers of the annual report would have to conduct their own analyses of the beginning and ending balance sheets, the income statement, and the changes in retained income to get a grasp of the impact of financial management decisions.

Many analysts focus on **free cash flow**—cash flows from operations less capital expenditures. This is the cash flow left over after undertaking the firm's operations and making the investments necessary to ensure its continued operation. Some also subtract dividends, assuming they are necessary to keep shareholders happy. A company that cannot generate enough cash from operations to cover its investments must raise more capital, either by selling assets or by issuing debt or equity. If investment supports growth, this situation may be acceptable. If the investment is merely to maintain the status quo, the company is probably in trouble.

free cash flow
Cash flows from operations less capital expenditures.

Foster Company has a large negative free cash flow, $69,000 − $287,000 = −$218,000, meaning that it cannot maintain its current plans without raising substantial capital, which it did during 20X2.

The Foster Company illustration demonstrates how a firm may simultaneously (1) have a significant amount of net income, as computed by accountants on the accrual basis, and yet (2) have a decline in cash that could become severe. Indeed, many growing businesses are desperate for cash even though reported net income zooms upward. For example, in the years leading up to Enron's bankruptcy, it had annual net income between $500,000 million and $1 billion, but it used much more cash for investment activities than it generated from operations—an average of about $2 billion a year more. Examining its free cash flow might have provided a warning to investors of bad things to come.

Role of Depreciation

Objective 9

Explain the role of depreciation in the statement of cash flows.

Readers of indirect-method statements of cash flows sometimes misunderstand the reason for adding depreciation to net income when computing cash flows from operating activities. Depreciation is an allocation of historical cost to expense. Therefore, depreciation expense does not entail a current outflow of cash. Consider again the comparison of Foster Company's net income and cash flows in Exhibit 16-15 on page 683. Why do we add the $17,000 of depreciation to net income to compute cash flow? We do so because we had earlier subtracted depreciation in calculating net income. Thus, adding back depreciation merely cancels its earlier deduction. Unfortunately, use of the indirect method may at first glance create an erroneous impression that we add depreciation because it, by itself, is a source of cash. If that were really true, a corporation could double or triple its bookkeeping entry for depreciation expense when it needs cash! Of course, this is not correct. What would happen? Reported income would decline, but cash provided by operations would not change. Suppose we doubled Foster Company's depreciation:

	With Depreciation of $17,000	With Depreciation of $34,000
Sales	$200,000	$200,000
Cash expenses (all expenses except depreciation)[*]	(160,000)	(160,000)
Depreciation	(17,000)	(34,000)
Net income	$ 23,000	$ 6,000
Nondepreciation adjustments[†]	29,000	29,000
Add depreciation	17,000	34,000
Net cash provided by operating activities	$ 69,000	$ 69,000

[*]$100,000 + $36,000 + $4,000 + $20,000 = $160,000.
[†]$(20,000) + $(40,000) + $68,000 + $21,000 = $29,000.

The doubling would affect depreciation and net income, but it would not affect cash provided by operations, which would still amount to $69,000.

Statement of Cash Flows for Nike

Exhibit 16-16 contains the 2011 statement of cash flows for **Nike**. Most corporations use this general format for their statement of cash flows. Like Nike, they use the indirect method to report the cash flows from operating activities.

We have discussed most of the items in Exhibit 16-16 earlier in the chapter, but two deserve mention here. First, Nike deducts deferred income taxes from net income. Nike paid more taxes to the government than it charged on its income statement so cash flow is less than net income. Second, stock-based compensation is compensation expense that was not paid in cash so, like depreciation, Nike adds it back to net income.

Cash provided (used) by operations:	
Net income	$2,133
Income charges not affecting cash	
Depreciation	335
Deferred income taxes	(76)
Stock-based compensation	105
Amortization and other	23
Changes in certain working capital components:	
Increase in accounts receivable	(273)
Increase in inventories	(551)
Increase in prepaid expenses and other current assets	(35)
Increase in accounts payable, accrued liabilities, and income taxes payable	151
Cash provided by operations	1,812

Cash provided (used) by investing activities:	
Purchases of short-term investments	(7,616)
Maturities of short-term investments	4,313
Sales of short-term investments	2,766
Additions to property, plant, and equipment	(432)
Disposals of property, plant, and equipment	1
Increase in other assets, net of other liabilities	(30)
Settlement of net investment hedges	(23)
Cash used by investing activities	(1,021)

Cash provided (used) by financing activities:	
Reductions in long-term debt, including current portion	(8)
Increase in notes payable	41
Proceeds from exercise of stock options and other stock issuances	345
Excess tax benefits from share-based payment arrangements	64
Repurchase of common stock	(1,859)
Dividends—common and preferred	(555)
Cash used by financing activities	(1,972)
Other*	57
Net decrease in cash and equivalents	(1,124)
Cash and equivalents, beginning of year	3,079
Cash and equivalents, end of year	$1,955

Exhibit 16-16
Nike, Inc.
Statement of Cash Flows for the Year Ended May 31, 2011 (millions)

*This is the effect of exchange rate changes, which is beyond the scope of our discussion.

Annual Reports

This completes our overview of financial statements. You have learned about the four main statements: the balance sheet, the income statement, the statement of cash flows, and the statement of changes in stockholders' equity. Companies include all four reports in their **annual report**, which management prepares for the company's shareholders. (See the Business First box on page 688 for more about annual reports.) In addition to the financial statements, annual reports generally contain a letter to shareholders from the chairman and/or CEO, discussions of financial results, and other information that management thinks is important to shareholders. U.S. companies also include the financial statements in another more-detailed report, the 10-K, that they submit to the SEC. You can access 10-K reports through the SEC's EDGAR database (http://www.sec.gov/edgar.shtml).

annual report
A report prepared by management for the company's shareholders.

Business First

The Changing Face of Annual Reports

Until the last decade, annual reports were generally glossy documents produced by companies about 3 months or more after year-end. In addition to including the major financial statements and their footnotes, annual reports also contained much other information about the company. However, the Internet has changed the way investors get information about a company. Today, much information is available more quickly on the Web than on paper. Nearly all publicly-held companies include their basic financial statements on their Web sites, usually in a section labeled "Investors" or "Investor Relations." You might also find them under the category "SEC Filings." If so, look for a filing called "10-K." The 10-K contains a great deal of information, and the basic financial statements will be under "Item 8."

Some financial statements will be in PDF or HTML files that you can read but you cannot easily navigate. An example is Honda Motor Company, Ltd. (http://world. honda.com/investors/library/annual_report/). However, an increasing number of companies are making financial statements available in an interactive format; see Microsoft, for example (http://www.microsoft.com/investor/reports/ ar11/financial_review/index.html). With this format you can go to any section of the annual report with a click of your mouse.

There is also a worldwide competition for the best annual reports. In 2011 the League of American Communications Professionals announced its latest winners of the best annual reports in a variety of categories, including

Best Overall	Vossloh AG (Germany)
Best Financials	Duefol AG (Germany)
Best Report Narrative	US Department of State (United States)
Most Creative	RTL Group (Germany)
Most Engaging	PT Andaro Energy Tbk (Indonesia)
Best Letter to Shareholders	Garanti Emeklilik (Turkey)

Some executives use their annual report to educate investors. The best example is Warren Buffett, chairman and CEO of Berkshire Hathaway, who always includes a long letter explaining his philosophies as well as his company's performance. His letter to shareholders in the 2011 annual report is 20 pages long (http://www.berkshirehathaway. com/2011ar/2011ar.pdf) and includes a section explaining the "irrational reaction of many investors to changes in stock prices."

Annual reports have been a key source of information for investors for years. Because the Internet allows them to be more timely and to contain more in-depth information, today they are more important than ever.

Sources: LACP 2010 Vision Awards Annual Reports Competition, http://www. lacp.com/2010vision/competition.htm; Honda Motor Company, 2011 Annual report; Microsoft, 2011 Annual Report; Berkshire Hathaway, 2011 Annual Report.

Summary Problem for Your Review

PROBLEM

The Buretta Company has prepared the data in Exhibit 16-17. In December 20X1, Buretta paid $54 million cash for a new building acquired to accommodate an expansion of operations. This was financed partly by a new issue of long-term debt for $40 million cash. During 20X1, the company also sold fixed assets for $5 million cash, which was equal to its book value. All sales and purchases of merchandise were on credit.

Because the net income of $4 million was the highest in the company's history, Mr. Buretta, the chairman of the board, was perplexed by the company's extremely low cash balance.

1. Prepare a statement of cash flows. Ignore income taxes. You may wish to use Exhibit 16-12, page 678, as a guide. Use the direct method for reporting cash flows from operating activities.
2. Prepare a supporting schedule that reconciles net income to net cash provided by operating activities.
3. What is revealed by the statement of cash flows? Will it help Mr. Buretta understand what has happened? Why?

Exhibit 16-17
Buretta Co. Financial Statements

Income Statement and Changes in Retained Earnings for the Year Ended December 31, 20X1 (millions)

Sales		$100
Less cost of goods sold		
Inventory, December 31, 20X0	$ 15	
Purchases	104	
Cost of goods available for sale	$119	
Inventory, December 31, 20X1	46	73
Gross profit		$ 27
Less other expenses		
General expenses	$ 8	
Depreciation	8	
Property taxes	4	
Interest expense	3	23
Net income		$ 4
Retained earnings, December 31, 20X0		7
Total		$ 11
Dividends		1
Retained earnings, December 31, 20X1		$ 10

Balance Sheets as of December 31 (millions)

Assets	20X1	20X0	Increase (Decrease)
Cash	$ 1	$20	$(19)
Accounts receivable	20	5	15
Inventory	46	15	31
Prepaid general expenses	4	2	2
Fixed assets, net	91	50	41
	$162	$92	$ 70

Liabilities and Stockholders' Equity			
Accounts payable for merchandise	$ 39	$14	$ 25
Accrued property tax payable	3	1	2
Long-term debt	40	—	40
Capital stock	70	70	—
Retained earnings	10	7	3
	$162	$92	$ 70

SOLUTION

1. See Exhibit 16-18. We can explain cash flows from operating activities as follows (in millions):

Sales	$100
Less increase in accounts receivable	(15)
Cash collections from customers	$ 85
Cost of goods sold	$ 73
Plus increase in inventory	31
Purchases	$104
Less increase in accounts payable	(25)
Cash paid to suppliers	$ 79
General expenses	$ 8
Plus increase in prepaid general expenses	2
Cash payment for general expenses	$ 10
Property taxes	$ 4
Less increase in accrued property tax payable	(2)
Cash paid for property taxes	$ 2
Cash paid for interest	$ 3

Exhibit 16-18

Buretta Company
Statement of Cash Flows for the Year Ended December 31, 20X1 (in millions)

Cash Flows from Operating Activities		
Cash collections from customers		$ 85
Cash payments		
Cash paid to suppliers	$(79)	
General expenses	(10)	
Interest paid	(3)	
Property taxes	(2)	(94)
Net cash provided by operating activities		$ (9)
Cash Flows from Investing Activities		
Purchases of fixed assets (building)	$(54)	
Proceeds from sale of fixed assets	5	
Net cash used by investing activities		(49)
Cash Flows from Financing Activities		
Long-term debt issued	$ 40	
Dividends paid	(1)	
Net cash provided by financing activities		39
Net decrease in cash		$ (19)
Cash balance, December 31, 20X0		20
Cash balance, December 31, 20X1		$ 1

2. Exhibit 16-19 reconciles net income to net cash provided by operating activities.

3. The statement of cash flows shows where cash has come from and where it has gone. Operations used $9 million of cash. Why? Exhibit 16-19 shows that large increases in accounts receivable ($15 million) and inventory ($31 million), plus a $2 million increase in prepaid expenses, used $48 million of cash. In contrast, Buretta generated only $39 million (i.e., $4 + $8 + $25 + $2 million). Exhibit 16-18 explains the $9 million use of cash slightly differently. It shows directly the $85 million of cash receipts and $94 million in disbursements. Investing activities also consumed cash because Buretta invested $54 million in a building, and it received only $5 million from sales of fixed assets. Financing activities generated $39 million cash, which was $19 million less than the $58 million used by operating and investing activities.

Mr. Buretta should no longer be puzzled. The statement of cash flows shows clearly that cash payments exceeded receipts by $19 million. However, he may still be concerned about the depletion of cash. Either Buretta Company must change operations so that it does not require so much cash, or it must curtail investment, or it must raise more long-term debt or ownership equity. Otherwise, Buretta Company will soon run out of cash.

Exhibit 16-19

Buretta Company
Reconciliation of Net Income to Net Cash Provided by Operating Activities for the Year Ended December 31, 20X1 (millions)

Net income (from income statement)	$ 4
Adjustments to reconcile net income to net cash provided by operating activities	
Add: depreciation, which was deducted in the computation of net income but does not decrease cash	8
Deduct: Increase in accounts receivable	(15)
Deduct: Increase in inventory	(31)
Deduct: Increase in prepaid general expenses	(2)
Add: Increase in accounts payable	25
Add: Increase in accrued property tax payable	2
Net cash provided by operating activities	$ (9)

Highlights to Remember

1. **Recognize and define the main types of assets in the balance sheet of a corporation.** Assets are divided into current and noncurrent categories. Common current assets are cash, accounts receivable, inventories, and prepaid expenses. The largest noncurrent asset is generally property, plant, and equipment. The amount shown for property, plant, and equipment is its acquisition cost minus accumulated depreciation.

2. **Recognize and define the main types of liabilities in the balance sheet of a corporation.** Liabilities are divided into current liabilities and long-term liabilities. Current liabilities include notes payable and accounts payable. Long-term debt in the form of debentures or mortgages is the most common noncurrent liability.

3. **Recognize and define the main elements of the stockholders' equity section of the balance sheet of a corporation.** Stockholders' equity contains paid-in capital, accumulated other comprehensive income, and retained earnings. Paid-in capital is often divided into a par value amount and an amount in excess of par value.

4. **Recognize and define the principal elements in the income statement of a corporation.** Income statements contain revenues and expenses. Multistep income statements have some of the following subtotals: gross margin (gross profit), operating income, and income before income taxes.

5. **Recognize and define the elements that cause changes in stockholders' equity accounts.** The statement of changes in stockholders' equity includes analysis of changes in all stockholders' equity accounts. For large profitable companies, retained earnings may be by far the largest component of stockholders' equity. Net income increases retained earnings and losses and dividends decrease them.

6. **Explain the purposes of the cash flow statement, identify activities that affect cash, and classify the activities as operating, investing, or financing activities.** The statement of cash flows lists cash inflows and cash outflows in one of three categories. Operating cash flows include collections from customers and payments to suppliers, employees, the government, and others. Investing cash flows include purchases and sales of fixed assets. Financing cash flows include borrowings and repayment of borrowings, sales of shares of stock, and payment of dividends.

7. **Assess financing and investing activities using the statement of cash flows.** Financing activities include cash flows to and from providers of capital. Investing activities include cash flows from the purchase or sale of plant, property, equipment, and other long-lived assets.

8. **Use both the direct method and the indirect method to explain cash flows from operating activities.** In the direct method, cash flows from operating activities include all cash receipts from customers and all cash payments to suppliers, employees, the government, and others for activities supporting operations. The indirect method begins with net income, adds depreciation and other noncash expenses, adds (subtracts) decreases (increases) in operating current assets, and adds (subtracts) increases (decreases) in operating current liabilities.

9. **Explain the role of depreciation in the statement of cash flows.** Depreciation is not a cash inflow. When using an indirect method cash flow statement, we add it to net income to get cash flow from operating activities only to offset the fact that we deducted it in computing net income.

Appendix 16A: Accounting for Inventory

A company's inventory method affects its income statement as well as its balance sheet. This appendix focuses on how choices in accounting for inventory can significantly affect a company's reported net income.

Each period, accountants divide the costs of merchandise acquired between cost of goods sold and cost of items remaining in ending inventory using one of several inventory methods. If unit prices and costs did not fluctuate, all inventory methods would show identical results. But prices change, and these changes raise central issues regarding cost of goods sold (income measurement) and inventories (asset measurement).

Let's explore inventory accounting using a simple example. Consider a new vendor of a cola drink at the fairgrounds. He began the week with no inventory. He bought one can of cola on Monday for 30 cents, a second can on Tuesday for 40 cents, and a third can on Wednesday for 56 cents. He then sold one can on Thursday for 90 cents. What is his gross margin? What is his ending inventory?

Four Major Inventory Methods

Objective 10

Describe and assess the effects of the four major methods of accounting for inventories.

In choosing an inventory method, it is important to recognize the link between the cost of goods sold and the valuation of ending inventory. The cola vendor began his business, acquired three cans of cola during the week, and had a total cost of goods available for sale of $1.26. At the end of the period, he must allocate this $1.26 either to cans sold or to cans in ending inventory. This example illustrates an important principle to remember as you study various inventory methods: By assigning a value to ending inventory, an inventory method also implicitly assigns a value to cost of goods sold, which equals the cost of goods available for sale less the value of the ending inventory.

U.S. GAAP accepts four principal inventory methods: specific identification; weighted average; first-in, first-out (FIFO); and last-in, last-out (LIFO). International standards are similar but do not permit LIFO. Exhibit 16-20 provides a quick glimpse into the nature of these four methods and applies them to our example of the cola vendor. As you can see, the choice of an inventory method can significantly affect gross margin and hence net income. (It can also affect ending inventory valuation for balance sheet purposes.)

Specific Identification

specific identification

An inventory method that recognizes the actual cost paid for the specific physical item sold.

The **specific identification** method (column 1) recognizes the actual cost paid for the specific physical item sold. Gross profit depends on which can the vendor sells. As Exhibit 16-20 shows, cost of goods sold could be either 30, 40, or 56 cents. Therefore, gross profit for operations of Monday–Thursday could be 60 cents, 50 cents, or 34 cents, depending on the particular can handed to the customer. By reaching for the "Monday" can instead of the "Wednesday" can, the vendor makes a gross profit of 60 cents instead of 34 cents.

Specific identification, which uses physical observation or the labeling of items in stock with individual numbers or codes, is easy and economically justifiable for relatively expensive, low-volume merchandise, such as custom artwork, diamond jewelry, and automobiles. It is especially appropriate when each product is unique. However, many organizations have large amounts of physically identical products. While bar-code and scanning technology could allow use of the specific identification method, it is often not worth the effort. In addition, because the specific item handed to the customer affects the cost of goods sold, the specific identification method permits managers to manipulate income and inventory values when filling a sales order by selecting a particular item from several physically equivalent items with different historical costs.

| | (1) Specific Identification | | | (2) | (3) | (4) |
	(1A)	(1B)	(1C)	FIFO	LIFO	Weighted Average
Income statement for the period Monday–Thursday						
Sales (1 unit at 90)	90	90	90	90	90	90
Deduct cost of goods sold*						
1 30-cent (Monday) unit	30			30		
1 40-cent (Tuesday) unit		40				
1 56-cent (Wednesday) unit			56		56	
1 weighted-average unit [(30 + 40 + 56) ÷ 3 = 42]						42
Gross profit for Monday–Thursday	60	50	34	60	34	48
Ending inventory, Thursday, 2 units:						
[(30 + 40 + 56) − cost of goods sold]	96	86	70	96	70	84

*The cost of goods sold can also be computed as follows, using FIFO cost of goods sold as an example:

Beginning inventory	0
+ Purchases	126
= Cost of goods available for sale	126
− Ending inventory	96
= Cost of goods sold	30

Exhibit 16-20

Comparison of Inventory Methods for Cola Vendor (all monetary amounts are in cents)

First-In, First-Out (FIFO) Method

The **first-in, first-out (FIFO)** method (column 2) assumes that a company sells or uses up first the stock acquired earliest. Thus, FIFO assumes that the vendor sells the "Monday" can before the "Tuesday" or "Wednesday" cans regardless of the actual can delivered to the customer. By using the latest costs to measure the ending inventory, FIFO tends to provide inventory valuations that closely approximate the actual market value of the inventory at the balance sheet date. In addition, in periods of rising prices, FIFO leads to higher gross profit (60 cents in Exhibit 16-20). Why? Because older, lower costs become the cost of goods sold expense (and the newer, higher costs remain in ending inventory). Higher reported incomes may favorably affect investor attitudes toward the company. Similarly, higher reported incomes may lead to higher salaries, higher bonuses, or higher status for the management of the company. Unlike specific identification, FIFO dictates the order in which acquisition costs will become cost of goods sold. Therefore, managers cannot affect income by choosing to sell one item rather than another, identical one.

first-in, first-out (FIFO)
An inventory method that assumes that a company sells or uses up first the stock acquired earliest.

Last-In, First-Out (LIFO) Method

The **last-in, first-out (LIFO)** method (column 3) assumes that a company sells or uses up first the stock acquired most recently. That is, whereas FIFO associates the most recent costs with inventories, LIFO treats the most recent costs as cost of goods sold. Thus, LIFO assumes that the vendor sells the "Wednesday" can first, regardless of the actual can delivered. Many accountants believe that LIFO provides a more realistic income number because net income measured using LIFO matches current sales prices with more current acquisition costs.

last-in, first-out (LIFO)
An inventory method that assumes that a company sells or uses up the stock acquired most recently first.

In contrast, LIFO inventory values on the balance sheet are less realistic because they are older costs. In a period of rising prices and constant or growing inventories, LIFO yields lower net income than the other inventory methods (34 cents in Exhibit 16-20) because it charges recent higher costs as cost of goods sold. Why is lower net income such an important feature of LIFO? Because when a company reports lower income to the tax authorities, it pays lower taxes. In the United States, the IRS accepts LIFO for income tax purposes but requires companies that use LIFO for tax purposes to use it also for financial reporting purposes. Therefore, it is not surprising that almost two-thirds of U.S. corporations use LIFO for at least some of their inventories.

A disadvantage of LIFO is that it permits management to influence income by the timing of purchases of inventory items. Consider our cola vendor. Suppose acquisition prices increase from 56 cents on Wednesday to 68 cents on Thursday, the day of the sale of the one unit. How does the acquisition of one more unit on Thursday affect net income? Under LIFO, cost of goods sold would change from 56 cents to 68 cents (the cost of the last unit purchased, the one bought on Thursday), and profit would fall by 12 cents. In contrast, a FIFO valuation of the cost of goods sold and gross profit would be unchanged:

	LIFO		FIFO	
	Without Thursday Purchase	With Thursday Purchase	Without Thursday Purchase	With Thursday Purchase
(Amounts are in cents)				
Sales	90	90	90	90
Cost of goods sold	56	68	30	30
Gross profit	34	22	60	60
Ending inventory (cents)				
(30 + 40)	70			
(30 + 40 + 56)		126		
(40 + 56)			96	
(40 + 56 + 68)				164

LIFO layers (LIFO increments)
Separately identifiable additions to a LIFO inventory.

Another disadvantage of LIFO is that income can soar when a company reduces its inventories. Under LIFO, inventory consists of **LIFO layers** (or **LIFO increments**), which are separately identifiable additions to inventory. For example, on Wednesday our cola vendor had three LIFO layers:

- Layer 1: 30-cent unit purchased on Monday
- Layer 2: 40-cent unit purchased on Tuesday
- Layer 3: 56-cent unit purchased on Wednesday

As a company grows, the LIFO layers tend to pile on one another as the years go by. Thus, many LIFO companies show inventories that have ancient layers (going back more than 50 years in some instances). The reported LIFO value may, therefore, be far below what FIFO values might otherwise show.

When a company reduces its inventory, old LIFO layers become the cost of goods sold. These old values may be much below current replacement values, leading to overstatement of income. In other words, in times of rising prices the LIFO method gives lower net income because it uses the most recent values for the cost of goods sold. But when a company reduces its inventories, LIFO can lead to just the opposite effect. Cost of goods sold includes old values, and net income is higher under LIFO than under other methods.

Suppose our cola vendor worked the fair for 20 years and never had less than one can of cola in inventory. By the end of the 20 years, he could buy a can of cola for $3 and sell it for $4. Now, he decides to get out of the cola business and sells his last can for $4. What would be his profit on that last can under LIFO? It would be $4 − $.30 = $3.70. Why? Because the original cost of the Monday can would finally become the cost of goods sold. Under FIFO, profit would be only $4 − $3 = $1 because the cost of goods sold would be the cost of a recently purchased can of cola.

Weighted-Average Cost

weighted-average cost
An inventory method that assigns the same unit cost to each unit available for sale.

The **weighted-average cost** method assigns the same unit cost to each unit available for sale during the period. The unit cost is the cost of all units available for sale divided by the number of units available, as shown in Exhibit 16-20. The weighted-average method usually produces a gross profit somewhere between that obtained under FIFO and that under LIFO (48 cents as compared with 60 cents and 34 cents in Exhibit 16-20).

To better understand the term *weighted average*, assume that our cola vendor bought two cans rather than one on Monday at 30 cents each. To get the weighted average, we must consider not only the price paid, but also the number of units purchased:

$$\text{weighted average} = \text{cost of goods available for sale} \div \text{units available for sale}$$
$$\text{weighted average} = [(2 \times 30 \text{ cents}) + (1 \times 40 \text{ cents}) + (1 \times 56 \text{ cents})] \div 4$$
$$= 156 \text{ cents} \div 4 = 39 \text{ cents}$$

Inventory Methods and Physical Flow of Inventories

Which inventory method should a company use? One way to choose an inventory method is to match the cost flow with the physical flow of inventory units. Consider four different ways that our cola vendor might physically store and sell his cola. (1) Let someone (either the seller or the purchaser) choose a specific can from the inventory available at the time of sale. This physical flow is consistent with a specific-identification cost flow. (2) The vendor could put each new can acquired into the top of a cooler. As each customer arrives, the vendor sells the top can. This is consistent with a LIFO cost flow. (3) The vendor might place each new can at the back of the cooler to chill and sell the oldest, coldest can at the front of the cooler first. This is consistent with FIFO. (4) Finally, if the vendor just mixes the cans together and chooses randomly the can to sell, all cans have an equal likelihood of being chosen so all should have the same cost—the average-cost method.

Even if it is possible to match the cost flow with the physical flow, the accounting profession has concluded that the physical flow of units should not determine the choice of the inventory method. U.S. companies may choose any of the four methods (and companies reporting under IFRS may choose among three methods, excluding LIFO) to record the cost of goods sold, but they must apply the method consistently. That is, they cannot change the choice of method from period to period.

Now suppose the vendor sells the remaining two cans of inventory on Friday. Exhibit 16-21 shows the results. Note that cumulative gross profit over the life of the vendor's business would

| | (1) Specific Identification | | | (2) | (3) | (4) |
	(1A)	(1B)	(1C)	FIFO	LIFO	Weighted Average
Sales, 2 units at 90 on Friday	180	180	180	180	180	180
Cost of goods sold (Thursday ending inventory from Exhibit 16-20)	96	86	70	96	70	84
Gross profit, Friday only	84	94	110	84	110	96
Gross profit, Monday–Thursday (from Exhibit 16-20)	60	50	34	60	34	48
Gross profit, Monday through Friday (3 cans sold)	144	144	144	144	144	144

Exhibit 16-21
Income Statements for Friday Only and for Monday–Friday for Cola Vendor (all monetary amounts are in cents)

be the same $1.44 under any of the inventory methods. The inventory method affects only how the total profit is divided among the accounting periods. Nevertheless, to evaluate performance over a particular period, we must understand how the inventory method affects a company's financial statements for that period.

Lower-of-Cost-or-Market (LCM) Method

Regardless of the inventory method used, accountants must decrease the inventory value if the inventory's market price drops below its acquisition cost. As a general rule, the acquisition cost provides a ceiling for the valuation of all assets; companies can decrease inventory values below cost when prices fall, but they cannot increase values above cost when prices rise.

Inventory accounting uses the **lower-of-cost-or-market (LCM)** method, whereby accountants compare the current market price of inventory with its cost (derived by specific identification, FIFO, LIFO, or weighted average) and select the lower of the two as the inventory value. Market generally means the current replacement cost under U.S. GAAP or net realizable value under IFRS.

Consider the following facts. A company has 100 units in its ending FIFO inventory on December 31, 20X0, at $7.90 per unit. Its tentative gross profit for 20X0 is $990:

lower-of-cost-or-market (LCM)
An inventory method in which accountants compare the current market price of inventory with its cost (derived by specific identification, FIFO, LIFO, or weighted average) and select the lower of the two as the inventory value.

Sales		$2,180
Cost of goods available for sale	$1,980	
Ending inventory, at cost of 100 units	790	
Cost of goods sold		1,190
Gross profit		$ 990

However, market prices during the final week of December suddenly declined to $4 per unit. An inventory write-down of $790 − (100 × $4) = $390 is in order. Therefore, reported income for 20X0 would be $990 − $390 = $600. The theory states that of the $790 cost, $390 expired during 20X0 because we cannot justify carrying the cost forward to the future as an asset.

Now suppose the market price rises to $8 per unit in January 20X1. U.S. GAAP does not permit restoration of the December write-down. The $4 cost as of December 31 is the "new cost" of the inventory. In contrast, IFRS allow companies to increase inventory values up to the original acquisition cost, $7.90 per unit, but not above that.

Summary Problem for Your Review

PROBLEM

Refer to Exhibit 16-20, page 692. Suppose the vendor sold two cans on Thursday for 90 cents each. All other data are unchanged.

1. Compute (a) the gross profit for Monday–Wednesday, (b) the gross profit for Thursday, and (c) the ending inventory on Thursday under FIFO and under LIFO.

2. Assume the same facts as in number 1, except that the vendor purchased one additional can of cola on Thursday for 65 cents. Compute Thursday's gross profit under FIFO and under LIFO.

SOLUTION

All amounts are in cents.

1. a. The vendor would recognize no gross profit on Monday–Wednesday because there were no sales.

   b.

	FIFO		LIFO
Sales	180		180
Cost of goods sold			
Beginning inventory (from Exhibit 16-20)	126		126
Purchases	0		0
Cost of goods available for sale	126		126
Ending inventory	56		30
Cost of goods sold		70	96
Gross profit, Thursday		110	84

   c. The ending inventory on Thursday was one Wednesday unit at 56 cents under FIFO and one Monday unit at 30 cents under LIFO.

2. Note how the late purchase affects LIFO gross profit but not FIFO gross profit:

	FIFO		LIFO
Sales	180		180
Cost of goods sold			
Beginning inventory (from Exhibit 16-20)	126		126
Purchases	65		65
Cost of goods available for sale	191		191
Ending inventory*	121		70
Cost of goods sold		70	121
Gross profit, Thursday		110	59

*Wednesday and Thursday units for FIFO (56 cents + 65 cents) and Monday and Tuesday units for LIFO (30 cents + 40 cents).

Appendix 16B: Shareholder Reporting, Income Tax Reporting, and Deferred Taxes

Reports to stockholders must abide by generally accepted accounting principles (GAAP). In contrast, reports to income tax authorities must abide by the income tax rules and regulations. Tax regulations are the same as GAAP in many respects, but in others they diverge. Therefore, there is nothing immoral or unethical about "keeping two sets of books." In fact, it is necessary.

Keep in mind that the income tax laws are patchworks that governments often design to give taxpayers special incentives, such as incentives for making investments. For example, tax authorities in some countries have permitted taxpayers to write off the full cost of new equipment as expense in the year acquired. Although tax authorities may permit (or even require) such a total write-off, GAAP does not permit it for shareholder reporting purposes.

Depreciation causes the largest differences between tax and shareholder reporting. Most companies use straight-line depreciation for reporting to shareholders. Why? Managers believe that it best matches expenses with revenues. But companies use accelerated depreciation for tax reporting where it is allowed because it postpones (or defers) tax payments. Governments often provide this deferral opportunity to motivate companies to increase the amount they invest.

For reporting to shareholders, accountants must match income tax expense with the revenues and expenses that cause the taxes. When revenues and expenses on the statement to tax authorities differ from the revenues and expenses on the shareholders' report, deferred taxes can arise. Most often, deferred taxes arise when tax expenses exceed book expenses. The result is a deferred tax liability.

Consider a simple example. The total depreciation on a company's only asset over a 2-year period, 20X0–20X1, was $20,000. Revenue was $100,000 each year, expenses (other than depreciation) were $80,000, and the income tax rate was 40%. For tax purposes, the company charged the entire $20,000 of depreciation as an expense in 20X0; for shareholder reporting, it charged $10,000 each year.

Exhibit 16-22 illustrates tax deferral. Total operating income over the 2 years was $20,000, and total taxes were $8,000. According to tax law, all $20,000 of operating income and $8,000 of taxes applied to 20X1. In contrast, for financial reporting, the company recognized half of the operating income each year, so it should recognize half of the taxes each year. Although $4,000 of taxes was related to 20X0 revenues and expenses, the payment was postponed (deferred) to 20X1. The 20X0 financial reporting income statement included a $4,000 expense for deferred taxes, and the obligation for future payment of the tax is a liability on the 20X0 balance sheet. In 20X1, $4,000 of tax expense was again related to the revenues and expenses of the period. However, the tax payment was $8,000. The payment covers the $4,000 expense for 20X1 and pays off the $4,000 of taxes deferred from 20X0.

	20X0	20X1	Total
Income statement for tax purposes			
Revenue	$100,000	$100,000	$200,000
Expenses, except depreciation	80,000	80,000	160,000
Depreciation	20,000	0	20,000
Operating income			
(or taxable income)	$ 0	$ 20,000	$ 20,000
Taxes payable at 40%	0	8,000	8,000
Net income	$ 0	$ 12,000	$ 12,000
Income statement for			
shareholder reporting			
Revenue	$100,000	$100,000	$200,000
Expenses, except depreciation	80,000	80,000	160,000
Depreciation	10,000	10,000	20,000
Operating income	$ 10,000	$ 10,000	$ 20,000
Less income taxes			
Paid or payable almost			
immediately	0	8,000	8,000
Deferred	4,000	(4,000)	0
Net income	$ 6,000	$ 6,000	$ 12,000

	December 31	
	20X0	20X1
Balance sheet effect		
Liability: Deferred income taxes	$4,000	$0

Exhibit 16-22
Illustration of Deferred Taxes

Accounting Vocabulary

annual report, p. 687	first-in, first-out (FIFO), p. 693	operating cycle, p. 661
capitalize, p. 665	fiscal year, p. 663	other comprehensive income,
cash equivalents, p. 663	fixed assets, p. 663	p. 668
cash flows from financing	free cash flow, p. 685	par value, p. 668
activities, p. 675	goodwill, p. 665	preferred stock, p. 668
cash flows from investing	indirect method for operating	short-term investments,
activities, p. 675	cash flows, p. 680	p. 663
cash flows from operating	intangible assets, p. 665	specific identification, p. 692
activities, p. 675	last-in, first-out (LIFO), p. 693	stated value, p. 668
common stock, p. 668	LIFO increments, p. 694	statement of cash flows,
current assets, p. 661	LIFO layers, p. 694	p. 674
current liabilities, p. 666	limited liability, p. 668	subordinated, p. 667
debentures, p. 666	liquidation, p. 667	tangible assets, p. 663
direct method for operating	long-term liabilities, p. 666	treasury stock, p. 668
cash flows, p. 680	lower-of-cost-or-market	weighted-average cost, p. 694
earnings per share (EPS),	(LCM), p. 695	working capital, p. 666
p. 671	noncurrent liabilities, p. 666	

MyAccountingLab ## Fundamental Assignment Material

GENERAL EXERCISES AND PROBLEMS

16-A1 Balance Sheet and Income Statement

The Reigle Company had the following items on its December 31, 20X0, balance sheet and 20X0 income statement (in dollars except for number of shares outstanding):

Cash and equivalents	$ 60,000
Revenues	790,000
Notes payable	51,000
Long-term debt, excluding current portion	210,000
Accounts receivable, net	48,000
Provision for income taxes	60,000
Other long-term assets	110,000
Interest expense	55,000
Deferred income tax liability–long-term	44,000
Retained earnings	204,000
Income taxes payable	37,000
Cost of sales	470,000
Inventories	36,000
Prepaid expenses	15,000
Common stock (50,000 shares outstanding)	25,000
Property, plant, and equipment, at cost	580,000
Accounts payable	43,000
Interest income	15,000
Goodwill, patents, and trademarks	75,000
Current portion of long-term debt	16,000
Less: Accumulated depreciation	170,000
Selling and administrative expenses	150,000
Additional paid-in capital	?

Prepare in proper form the December 31, 20X0, balance sheet and the 20X0 income statement for Reigle Company. Include the proper amount for additional paid-in capital.

16-A2 Statement of Cash Flows, Direct Method

Ridgewood Antiques had a cash balance on December 31, 20X0, of $50,000. Its net income for 20X1 was $361,000. Its 20X1 transactions affecting income or cash were (in thousands):

1. Sales of $1,600, all on credit. Cash collections from customers, $1,270.
2. The cost of items sold, $850. Purchases of inventory totaled $900; inventory and accounts payable were affected accordingly.
3. Cash payments on trade accounts payable, $725.
4. Salaries and wages: accrued, $190; paid in cash, $180.
5. Depreciation, $48.
6. Interest expense, all paid in cash, $11.
7. Other expenses, all paid in cash, $100.
8. Income taxes accrued, $40; income taxes paid in cash, $35.
9. Bought plant and facilities for $235 cash.
10. Issued debt for $110 cash.
11. Paid cash dividends of $39.

Prepare a statement of cash flows using the direct method for reporting cash flows from operating activities. Omit supporting schedules.

16-A3 Reconciliation of Net Income and Net Cash Provided by Operating Activities

Refer to Problem 16-A2 Prepare a supporting schedule that reconciles net income to net cash provided by operating activities for Ridgewood Antiques.

16-A4 Depreciation and Cash Flows

Manitoba Snowmobiles, Inc. had sales of $695,000, all received in cash. Total operating expenses were $600,000. All except depreciation were paid in cash. Depreciation of $80,000 was included in the $600,000 of operating expenses. Ignore income taxes.

1. Compute net income and net cash provided by operating activities.
2. Assume that depreciation is tripled. Compute net income and net cash provided by operating activities.

UNDERSTANDING PUBLISHED FINANCIAL REPORTS

16-B1 Classified Balance Sheet

Intel, the world's largest microprocessor chip company, lists the following balance sheet items for January 1, 2012 (in millions):

Property, plant, and equipment, at cost	$58,073
Short-term investments	5,181
Common stock and capital in excess of par value	17,036
Cash and cash equivalents	5,065
Other accrued liabilities	2,814
Accounts receivable	3,650
Other current assets	7,880
Accumulated depreciation	(34,446)
Accounts payable	?
Identified intangible assets	6,267
Inventories	4,096
Deferred income	1,929
Accrued advertising liability	1,134
Other assets	4,648
Other long-term liabilities	3,479
Accumulated other comprehensive income (loss)	(781)
Goodwill	9,254
Accrued compensation and benefits	2,948
Long-term investments	1,451
Long-term deferred liabilities	2,617
Short-term debt	247
Long-term debt	7,084
Retained earnings	29,656

Prepare a balance sheet in proper form for Intel. Include the proper amount for accounts payable.

16-B2 Preparation of Statement of Cash Flows

Walgreen Co., the largest drugstore chain in the United States, had the following items in its financial statements for the year ended August 31, 2011 (in millions):

Net sales	$72,184
Net earnings	2,714
Additions to property and equipment	(1,213)
Depreciation and amortization	1,086
Proceeds from sale of business	442
Cash dividends paid	(647)
Other noncash expenses	53
Increases in other current liabilities	112
Business acquisitions, net of cash received	(630)
Increases in inventories	(592)
Increases in trade accounts payable	384
Increases in other current assets	(24)
Stock repurchases	(2,028)
Other cash provided by financing activities	15
Other cash used for investing activities	(203)
Proceeds related to employee stock plans	235
Increases in accrued expenses and other liabilities	218
Increases in accounts receivable	(243)
Repayments on long-term debt	(17)
Retained earnings	18,877
Stock compensation expense	135
Deferred income taxes	132
Gain on sale of business	(434)
Increases in income taxes payable	102
Proceeds from sale of assets	79
Total assets	27,454
Cash and cash equivalents at beginning of year	?
Cash and cash equivalents at end of year	1,556
Net decrease in cash and cash equivalents	(324)

Select the items from this list that would appear in Walgreens' statement of cash flows and prepare the statement in proper form. Fill in the appropriate amount for cash and cash equivalents at the beginning of the period. Use the indirect method for reporting cash flows from operating activities. (Note: Deferred income taxes, stock compensation expense, and gain on sale of business are noncash expenses, and proceeds related to employee stock plans is a financing activity.)

16-B3 Cash Provided by Operations

Target Corporation had net earnings of $2,929 million in the fiscal year ending January 28, 2012. Additional information follows (in millions):

	Year Ended January 28, 2012	
Depreciation and amortization	$ 2,131	
Bad debt expense	$ 154	
Non-cash losses	$ 22	
Other noncash charges affecting earnings	$ 90	
Cost of sales	$47,860	
Deferred income taxes	$ 371	
Changes in noncash working capital accounts:		
Accounts receivable	$ 187	Increase
Inventory	$ 322	Increase
Other assets	$ 107	Increase
Accrued liabilities	$ 218	Increase
Accounts payable	$ 232	Increase
Other liabilities	$ 97	Decrease

Compute the net cash provided by operating activities. Explain why the net cash provided by operating activities is greater than the net income. (Note that both the bad debt expense and deferred income taxes are noncash expenses.)

Additional Assignment Material

MyAccountingLab

QUESTIONS

16-1 "The operating cycle for a company is one year." Do you agree? Why?

16-2 Why should short-term prepaid expenses be classified as current assets?

16-3 Enumerate the items most commonly classified as current assets.

16-4 "Accumulated depreciation is a sum of cash being accumulated for the replacement of fixed assets." Do you agree? Explain.

16-5 Criticize the following: "Depreciation is the loss in value of a fixed asset over a given span of time."

16-6 What factors influence the estimate of useful life in depreciation accounting?

16-7 "To capitalize an amount spent means that it will not be charged as an expense." Do you agree? Explain.

16-8 "Goodwill may have nothing to do with the personality of the manager or employees." Do you agree? Explain.

16-9 "Working capital helps tell potential investors whether a company has enough current assets to pay current liabilities as they become due." Do you agree? Explain.

16-10 What is a subordinated debenture?

16-11 "Common shareholders have limited liability." Explain.

16-12 What is the role of the par value of stocks or bonds?

16-13 What is other comprehensive income? Where do you find it on the balance sheet? Is it usually large or small in amount?

16-14 "Treasury stock is negative stockholders' equity." Do you agree? Explain.

16-15 What advantages does a multiple-step income statement have over a single-step statement?

16-16 Name the three items that most often cause changes in retained earnings as shown in the statement of changes in stockholders' equity.

16-17 What are the purposes of a statement of cash flows?

16-18 What three types of activities are summarized in the statement of cash flows?

16-19 Name four major operating activities included in a statement of cash flows.

16-20 Name three major investing activities included in a statement of cash flows.

16-21 Name three major financing activities included in a statement of cash flows.

16-22 Where does interest received or paid appear on the statement of cash flows? Explain.

16-23 "Borrowing cash or repayment of borrowings are investing activities because companies borrow when they need cash for investments." Comment on this quote.

16-24 The Lawrence Company sold fixed assets for cash of $8,000. The assets had a book value of $5,000. How should this be reported in the investing activities section of a statement of cash flows?

16-25 Why are noncash investing and financing activities listed on a separate schedule accompanying the statement of cash flows?

16-26 What are the two major ways of computing net cash provided by operating activities? How do they differ?

16-27 The indirect method for reporting cash flows from operating activities can create an erroneous impression about noncash expenses (such as depreciation). What is the impression and why is it erroneous?

16-28 Why is there usually a difference between the cash collections from customers and sales revenue in a period's financial statements?

16-29 Why do analysts focus on free cash flow rather than just on cash flow from operating activities?

16-30 "Depreciation is an integral part of a statement of cash flows." Do you agree? Explain.

16-31 An investor's newsletter had the following item: "The company expects increased cash flow in 2011 because depreciation charges will be substantially greater than they were in 2010." Comment.

16-32 Study Appendix 16A. Name and briefly describe each of the four inventory methods that are generally accepted in the United States.

16-33 Study Appendix 16A. Suppose prices are rising and inventories are increasing. Which of the four generally accepted inventory methods will usually result in the highest net income? Explain.

16-34 Study Appendix 16A. "Purchases of inventory at the end of a fiscal period can have a direct effect on income under LIFO." Do you agree? Explain.

16-35 Study Appendix 16A. "In applying the lower-of-cost-or-market method to inventories, inventory values are written down when replacement cost falls. If the replacement cost then increases, inventory values are written up, but not to an amount greater than the original cost." Do you agree? Explain.

16-36 Study Appendix 16B. "The presence of a deferred tax liability on the balance sheet means that cumulative tax payments have exceeded the cumulative tax expense charged on financial reports to shareholders." Do you agree? Explain.

CRITICAL THINKING EXERCISES

16-37 Production Facilities and Depreciation

A manager complained about the amount of depreciation charged on the plant for which she was responsible: "The market value of my plant just continues to increase, yet I am hit with large depreciation charges on my income statement and the value of my plant and equipment on the balance sheet goes down each year. This doesn't seem fair." Comment on this statement, focusing on the relation of asset values on the balance sheet to market values of the assets.

16-38 R&D and the Recognition of Intangible Assets

Under the current rules of both U.S. GAAP and IFRS, companies must charge research expenditures directly to expense. Some accountants believe that companies should be allowed to recognize some such costs as assets. Suppose you were a manager of a research department of a pharmaceutical company. Which method of accounting for research expenditures would be most consistent with the information you use for decision making? Explain.

16-39 Using the Income Statement to Evaluate Sales Success

The net income of a company is the result of many factors. Sometimes managers want to measure the performance of one part of the organization separate from the effects of other parts. How might a company evaluate the success of its sales efforts using a classified income statement? Assume that the sales department is responsible for pricing and, thus, influences both the total amount sold and the margin on the items sold.

16-40 Capital Investment and the Statement of Cash Flows

Growing companies often need capital to purchase or build additional facilities. There are many potential sources of such capital. Describe how an investor might use the statement of cash flows to learn how a company financed its capital expansion.

16-41 Purchasing Operations and LIFO Versus FIFO

Study Appendix 16A. Suppose that the evaluation of the purchasing officer for a refinery is based on the gross margin on the oil products produced and sold during the year. During the year, the price of a barrel of oil has increased from $50 to $70. All the inventory of oil at the beginning of the year is valued at $50 or less. On the last day of the year, the purchasing agent is contemplating the purchase of additional oil at $70 per barrel. Is the agent more likely to purchase additional oil if the company uses the FIFO or the LIFO method for its inventories? Explain.

GENERAL EXERCISES AND PROBLEMS

16-42 Meaning of Book Value

Twenty years ago Sigurdsen Corp. purchased an office building in Oslo for 12 million Norwegian kroner (Kr), 4 million of which was attributable to land. Sigurdsen has fully paid off the mortgage. The current balance sheet follows (in millions):

Cash		Kr 3.0	Stockholders' equity	Kr 8.3
Land		4.0		
Building at cost	Kr 8.0			
Accumulated depreciation	6.7			
Book value		1.3		
Total assets		Kr 8.3		

The company is about to borrow Kr 18 million on a first mortgage to modernize and expand the building. This amounts to 60% of the Kr 30 million appraised value of the combined land and building before the modernization and expansion. Prepare a balance sheet after Sigurdsen Corp. obtains the loan and expands and modernizes the building, but before it charges any further depreciation. Comment on the usefulness of the balance sheet.

16-43 Balance Sheet and Income Statement

The fiscal year for Hokkaido Company ends on May 31. Results for the year ended May 31, 20X1, included the following (in millions of Japanese yen except for number of shares outstanding):

Cash and cash equivalents	¥ 45,000
Cost of goods sold	195,000
Inventories	29,000
Other current assets	6,000
Fixed assets, net	217,000
Net sales	422,000
Receivables	22,000
Debentures	77,000
Research and development expenses	42,000
Administrative and general expenses	65,000
Other income (expenses), net	(12,000)
Capital construction fund*	28,000
Selling and distribution expenses	41,000
Other current liabilities	9,000
Treasury stock	(13,000)
Long-term investments	?
Accounts payable	24,000
Mortgage bonds payable	84,000
Deferred income tax liability	12,000
Redeemable preferred stock	15,000
Common stock, at par (50,000 shares outstanding)	5,000
Paid-in capital in excess of par	102,000
Income tax expense	51,000
Accrued expenses payable	20,000
Retained income	48,000
Intangible assets	21,000

*A noncurrent asset

Prepare in proper form the balance sheet as of May 31, 20X1, and the income statement for the year ended May 31, 20X1. Include the proper amount for long-term investments.

16-44 Simple Changes in Retained Earnings and Total Stockholders' Equity

Sydney Company had retained earnings of $56,000 and total stockholders' equity of $75,000 at the beginning of 20X1. During 20X1 the company had net income of $21,000, declared and paid cash dividends of $8,000, and had other comprehensive income of $4,000. Sydney Company neither issued nor bought back shares in 20X1. Compute the retained earnings and total stockholders' equity at the end of 20X1.

16-45 Cash Received from Customers

Sales for Harlem Tool & Die during 20X1 were $600,000, 75% of them on credit and 25% for cash. During the year, accounts receivable increased from $56,000 to $67,000, an increase of $11,000. What amount of cash did Harlem receive from customers during 20X1?

16-46 Cash Paid to Suppliers

Cost of goods sold for Harlem Tool & Die during 20X1 was $400,000. Beginning inventory was $64,000 and ending inventory was $89,000. Beginning trade accounts payable were $13,000, and ending trade accounts payable were $41,000. What amount of cash did Harlem pay to suppliers?

16-47 Cash Paid to Employees

Harlem Tool & Die reported wage and salary expenses of $155,000 on its 20X1 income statement. It reported cash paid to employees of $136,000 on its statement of cash flows. The beginning balance of accrued wages and salaries payable was $8,000. What was the ending balance in accrued wages and salaries payable? Ignore payroll taxes.

16-48 Simple Cash Flows from Operating Activities

Hoogendoorn and Associates provides consulting services in Amsterdam. In 20X0, net income was € 230,000 on revenues of € 510,000 and expenses of € 280,000 (€ stands for euro, the European currency). The only noncash expense was depreciation of € 50,000. The company has no inventory.

Accounts receivable increased by € 17,000 during 20X0, and accounts payable and salaries payable were unchanged.

Prepare a statement of cash flows from operating activities. Use the direct method. Omit supporting schedules.

16-49 Net Income and Cash Flow

Refer to Problem 16-48 Prepare a schedule that reconciles net income to net cash provided by operating activities.

16-50 Net Loss and Cash Flows from Operating Activities

The Halifax Company had a net loss of $25,000 in 20X2. The following information is available:

Depreciation	$19,000
Decrease in accounts receivable	4,000
Increase in inventory	3,000
Increase in accounts payable	18,000
Increase in salaries and wages payable	5,000

Present a schedule that reconciles net income (loss) to net cash provided by operating activities.

16-51 Preparation of a Statement of Cash Flows

Denali Ale Company is a microbrewery in Anchorage. By the end of 20X1, the company's cash balance had dropped to $12,000, despite net income of $239,000 in 20X1. Its transactions affecting income or cash in 20X1 were as follows (in thousands):

1. Sales were $3,003, all on credit. Cash collections from customers were $2,890.
2. The cost of items sold was $2,096.
3. Inventory increased by $56.
4. Cash payments on trade accounts payable were $2,130.
5. Payments to employees were $305; accrued wages payable decreased by $24.
6. Other operating expenses, all paid in cash, were $105.
7. Interest expense, all paid in cash, was $26.
8. Income tax expense was $105; cash payments for income taxes were $107.
9. Depreciation was $151.
10. A warehouse was acquired for $540 cash.
11. Equipment was sold for $37 cash; original cost was $196, accumulated depreciation was $159.
12. Received $28 for issue of common stock.
13. Retired long-term debt for $21 cash.
14. Paid cash dividends of $89.

Prepare a statement of cash flows using the direct method for reporting cash flows from operating activities. Omit supporting schedules.

16-52 Reconciliation of Net Income and Net Cash Provided by Operating Activities

Refer to Problem 16-51. Prepare a supporting schedule to the statement of cash flows that reconciles net income to net cash provided by operating activities.

16-53 Depreciation and Cash Flows

The following condensed income statement and reconciliation schedule are from the annual report of Alpha Biotech, Inc. (in millions):

Sales	$203
Expenses	169
Net income	$ 34

Reconciliation Schedule of Net Income to Net Cash Provided by Operating Activities	
Net income	$ 34
Add noncash expenses	
Depreciation	17
Deduct net increase in noncash	
operating working capital	(15)
Net cash provided by operating activities	$ 36

A shareholder has suggested that the company switch from straight-line to accelerated depreciation on its annual report to shareholders. He maintains that this will increase the cash flow provided by operating activities. According to his calculations, using accelerated methods would increase depreciation to $27 million, an increase of $10 million; net cash flow from operating activities would then be $46 million.

1. Suppose Alpha Biotech adopts the accelerated depreciation method proposed. Compute net income and net cash flow from operating activities. Ignore income taxes.
2. Use your answer to number 1 to prepare a response to the shareholder.

16-54 Cash Flows; Indirect Method

The O'Toole Company has the following balance sheet data (in millions):

	December 31				December 31		
	20X2	20X1	Change		20X2	20X1	Change
Current assets				Current liabilities (detailed)	$101	$ 24	$ 77
Cash	$ 12	$ 25	$ (13)				
Receivables, net	65	30	35	Long-term debt	120	—	120
Inventories	100	50	50	Stockholders' equity	231	181	50
Total current assets	$177	$105	$ 72				
Plant assets							
(net of accumulated depreciation)	275	100	175				
				Total liabilities and			
Total assets	$452	$205	$ 247	stockholders' equity	$452	$205	$247

Net income for 20X2 was $60 million. Net cash inflow from operating activities was $72 million. Cash dividends paid were $10 million. Depreciation was $20 million. Fixed assets were purchased for $195 million, $120 million of which was financed via the issuance of long-term debt, the balance outright for cash. Sean O'Toole, Jr., the president and majority stockholder of O'Toole Company, was a superb operating executive. He was imaginative and aggressive in marketing and ingenious and creative in production. But he had little patience with financial matters. After examining the most recent balance sheet and income statement, he muttered, "We've enjoyed 10 years of steady growth; 20X2 was our most profitable ever. Despite such profitability, we're in the worst cash position in our history. Just look at those current liabilities in relation to our available cash! This whole picture of the more you make, the poorer you get, just does not make sense. These statements must be cockeyed."

1. Prepare a statement of cash flows using the indirect method, which includes a schedule reconciling net income to net cash provided by operating activities in the body of the statement.
2. Using the statement of cash flows and other information, write a short memorandum to Mr. O'Toole, explaining why there is such a squeeze on cash.

16-55 Preparation of Statement of Cash Flows

South African Imports Company has assembled the (a) balance sheet and (b) income statement and change in retained earnings for 20X1 shown in Exhibit 16-23. On December 30, 20X1, South African Imports paid R103 million in cash to acquire a new warehouse to expand operations. (R stands for rand, the South African currency.) This was partly financed by an issue of long-term debt for R 50 million cash. The company sold plant assets for their book value of R 6 million during 20X1. Because net income was R 26 million, the highest in the company's history, Julie Botha, the CEO, was distressed by the company's extremely low cash balance.

1. Prepare a statement of cash flows using the direct method for reporting cash flows from operating activities. You may wish to use Exhibit 16-12 on page 678 as a guide.
2. Prepare a schedule that reconciles net income to net cash provided by operating activities.
3. What is revealed by the statement of cash flows? Does it help you reduce Ms. Botha's distress? Why? Briefly explain to Ms. Botha why cash has decreased even though net income was R 26 million.

Balance Sheet December 31, 20X1 (in millions)

	20X1	20X0	Change
Assets			
Cash	R 5	R 25	R(20)
Accounts receivable	55	28	27
Inventory	72	50	22
Prepaid general expenses	4	3	1
Plant assets, net	207	150	57
	R343	R256	R 87
Liabilities and shareholders' equity			
Accounts payable for merchandise	R 74	R 60	R 14
Accrued tax payable	3	2	1
Long-term debt	50	—	50
Capital stock	100	100	—
Retained earnings	116	94	22
	R343	R256	R 87

Income Statement and Change in Retained Earnings for the Year Ended December 31, 20X1 (in millions)

Sales		R315
Less cost of goods sold		
Inventory, December 31, 20X0	R 50	
Purchases	210	
Cost of goods available for sale	R260	
Inventory, December 31, 20X1	72	188
Gross profit		R127
Less other expenses		
General expense	R 51	
Depreciation	40	
Taxes	10	101
Net income		R 26
Dividends		4
Net income of the period retained		R 22
Retained earnings, December 31, 20X0		94
Retained earnings, December 31, 20X1		R116

Exhibit 16-23
South African Imports Co.
Financial Statements

16-56 LIFO and FIFO
Study Appendix 16A. The inventory of the West Virginia Coal Company on June 30 shows 500 tons at $62 per ton. A physical inventory on July 31 shows a total of 600 tons on hand. Revenue from sales of coal for July totals $105,000. The following purchases were made during July: July 5, 1,000 tons at $64 per ton; July 15, 250 tons at $66 per ton; July 25, 300 tons at $69 per ton.

1. Compute the inventory value as of July 31, using (a) FIFO and (b) LIFO.
2. Compute the gross profit using each method.

16-57 Lower of Cost or Market—U.S. GAAP
Study Appendix 16A. Hamlin Toy Company prepared financial statements using U.S. GAAP. It uses cost or market, whichever is lower, for its inventories.

There were no sales or purchases during the periods indicated, although selling prices generally fluctuated in the same directions as replacement costs. What amount for merchandise inventories would you show on the quarterly balance sheet on the dates listed next?

	Invoice Cost	Replacement Cost
March 31, 20X1	$200,000	$170,000
June 30, 20X1	200,000	180,000
September 30, 20X1	200,000	205,000
December 31, 20X1	200,000	150,000

16-58 Lower of Cost or Market—IFRS

Study Appendix 16A. Hamlin Toy Company prepares financial statements using IFRS. It uses cost or market, whichever is lower, for its inventories. There were no sales or purchases during the periods indicated. What amount for merchandise inventories would you show on the quarterly balance sheet on the dates listed next?

	Invoice Cost	Realizable Value
March 31, 20X1	$200,000	$170,000
June 30, 20X1	200,000	180,000
September 30, 20X1	200,000	205,000
December 31, 20X1	200,000	150,000

16-59 LIFO, FIFO, and Cash Effects

Study Appendix 16A. Kalitzki Implements Company had sales revenue of $710,000 in 20X2. Pertinent data for its only product in 20X2 included the following:

Inventory, December 31, 20X1	15,000 units at $12	$180,000
February purchases	20,000 units at $14	280,000
August purchases	34,000 units at $16	544,000
Sales for the year	30,000 units	

1. Prepare a statement of gross margin for 20X2. Use two columns, one assuming LIFO and one assuming FIFO.
2. Assume that Kalitzki is reporting to the tax authorities and has a 45% income tax rate. Suppose all transactions are for cash. Which inventory method results in more cash for Kalitzki? By how much?

16-60 LIFO and FIFO; Prices Rising and Falling

Study Appendix 16A. The Omaha Fertilizer Company had inventory on December 31, 20X0, of 20,000 bags at $10 = $200,000. Purchases during 20X1 were 30,000 bags. Sales were 28,000 bags for sales revenue of $17 per bag. Prepare a four-column comparative statement of gross margin for 20X1:

1. Assume that purchases were at $12 per unit. Assume FIFO and then LIFO (columns 1 and 2).
2. Assume that purchases were at $8 per unit. Assume FIFO and LIFO (columns 3 and 4).
3. Assume Omaha Fertilizer is reporting for tax purposes and has an income tax rate of 35%. Suppose all transactions are for cash.
   a. Which inventory method in number 1 results in more cash for Omaha Fertilizer Company? By how much?
   b. Which inventory method in number 2 results in more cash for Omaha Fertilizer Company? By how much?

UNDERSTANDING PUBLISHED FINANCIAL REPORTS

16-61 Various Intangible Assets

Consider the following:

1. a. Dow Chemical Company's annual report indicated that R&D expenditures were $1,646 million during 2011. How did this amount affect income before income taxes, which was $3,601 million? Dow reports using U.S. GAAP.
   b. Suppose the entire $1,646 million arose from outlays for patents acquired from various outside parties on December 30, 2011. What would be the operating income for 2011?

c. How would the Dow balance sheet, December 31, 2011, be affected by your treatment of R&D in a?

d. Suppose Dow used IFRS and identified $500 million of the $1,646 million of R&D costs as development costs for which the technical and economic feasibility has been demonstrated. How would your answer to part a change?

2. Suppose that on December 30, 2012, Verizon acquired new patents on some communications equipment for $20 million. Technology changes quickly. The equipment's useful life is expected to be 4 years rather than the 17-year life of the patent. What will be the amortization for 2013?

3. Philip Morris purchased Kraft several years ago for approximately $13 billion. Of the $13 billion purchase price, only about $2 billion could be assigned to identifiable individual assets. What was the total amount of goodwill from the purchase recorded on the Philip Morris balance sheet? How should Philip Morris account for the goodwill in the years after the acquisition?

16-62 Various Liabilities

For each of the following items, indicate how the financial statements will be affected. Identify the affected accounts specifically.

1. Whirlpool Corporation sells electric appliances, including washing machines. On January 1, 2012, Whirlpool had a liability of $191 million for future warranty claims. Suppose that experience in recent years has indicated that warranty costs for washing machines average 3.2% of sales, and sales of washing machines for January 2012 were $1,000 million. During January Whirlpool paid $30 million to service warranties on previously sold washing machines.

2. In Iowa customers buying soft drinks pay a 5¢ deposit on each bottle or can purchased. (Many other states and countries have similar laws.) The bottler/distributor then pays 5¢ plus a 1¢ handling fee for each returned bottle or can. About 86% of the bottles and cans are redeemed. Suppose PepsiCo sold 1.96 million bottles of soda in August and paid $101,000 for bottles returned.

3. Wells Fargo received a $4,000 savings deposit on April 1. On June 30, it recognized interest thereon at an annual rate of 3%. On July 1, the depositor closed her account with the bank.

4. Suppose The Contemporary Theater Company sold for $320,000 cash a "season's series" of tickets in advance of December 31 for four performances, each to be held in successive months beginning in January.
(a) What is the effect on the balance sheet, December 31? (b) What is the effect on the balance sheet, January 31?

16-63 Exercises in Assets, Liabilities, and Stockholders' Equity

Hewlett-Packard (HP) is a leading direct marketer of computers and peripherals. The company made a profit of $7,074 million on sales of more than $127 billion in the year ended October 31, 2011.

1. On October 31, 2010, the end of HP's fiscal year, it had accounts receivable totaling $19,006 million on its books and, after subtracting estimated uncollectible accounts of $525 million, the company reported net accounts receivable of $18,481 million on its balance sheet. In fiscal 2011, accounts receivable before subtracting estimated uncollectibles decreased by $312 million and estimated uncollectible accounts decreased by $55 million. What amount was reported for net accounts receivable on HP's October 31, 2011, balance sheet?

2. HP began the 2011 fiscal year with approximately $2,447 million in its liabilities for warranties account. The company paid $2,653 million during the year to settle warranty claims, and it accrued warranty expenses of $2,657 million. What was the liability for warranties shown on HP's October 31, 2011, balance sheet?

3. Retained earnings at the end of fiscal 2010 were $32,695 million on HP's balance sheet. During fiscal 2011 HP's net income was $7,074 million and HP paid dividends of $834 million. In addition, repurchases of stock and other items decreased HP's retained earnings by $3,669 million. What was the balance in retained earnings in HP's October 31, 2011, balance sheet?

16-64 Classified Income Statement and Balance Sheet

In Exhibit 16-24 are all the items in the income statement and balance sheet for Microsoft Corporation for the quarter ending March 31, 2012. All items on the statements are listed, but no totals or subtotals are shown. Recast the income statement and balance sheet to show as many meaningful totals and subtotals as the data allow. All dollar amounts are in millions.

Microsoft Corporation Income Statement

Revenue	$17,407
Cost of revenue	3,952
Research and development	2,517
Sales and marketing	3,414
General and administrative	1,150
Other income (expense)	(11)
Provision for income taxes	1,255

Microsoft Corporation Balance Sheet

Cash and cash equivalents	$ 6,388
Short-term investments	53,141
Accounts receivable, net of allowance for doubtful accounts of $322	10,961
Inventories	1,412
Deferred income taxes	2,350
Other current assets	2,608
Property and equipment, net of accumulated depreciation of $10,952	8,225
Equity and other investments	9,068
Goodwill	19,698
Intangible assets	2,756
Other long-term assets	1,403
Accounts payable	3,790
Accrued compensation	3,272
Income taxes	958
Short-term unearned revenue	13,929
Securities lending payable	1,210
Other current liabilities	3,011
Long-term debt	11,938
Long-term unearned revenue	1,262
Deferred income taxes	1,456
Other long-term liabilities	8,525
Common stock and paid-in capital—shares authorized 24,000; outstanding 8,400	65,273
Retained earnings	3,386

Exhibit 16-24
Microsoft Corporation
*Financial Statements
for the 3 Months Ended March
31, 2012*

CHAPTER 16

16-65 Classified Balance Sheet—Britain

J. Sainsbury plc operates Sainsbury's Supermarkets, Britain's longest-standing major food retailing chain with 934 stores throughout the United Kingdom and sales of nearly £21 billion in 2011. The company's classified balance sheet for March 19, 2011, is in Exhibit 16-25.

Suppose J. Sainsbury plc used the format adopted by most U.S. companies for its balance sheet. How would the format of its balance sheet differ from that shown?

16-66 Gain on Airplane Crash

Several years ago, a Delta Airlines 727 crashed in Dallas. The crash resulted in a gain of $.11 per share of Delta. How could this happen? Consider the accounting for airplanes. Airlines insure their airplanes at market value, $6.5 million for Delta's 727. However, the planes' book values are often much less because of large accumulated depreciation amounts. The book value of Delta's 727 was only $962,000.

Exhibit 16-25

J. Sainsbury plc
Balance Sheet
March 19, 2011
(in millions of pounds)

Non-current assets	
Property, plant, and equipment	£ 8,784
Intangible assets	151
Investments in joint ventures	502
Available-for-sale financial assets	176
Other receivables	36
Retirement benefit asset	29
	9,678
Current assets	
Inventories	812
Trade and other receivables	343
Derivative financial instruments	52
Cash and cash equivalents	501
	1,708
Non-current assets held for sale	13
	1,721
Total assets	11,399
Current liabilities	
Trade and other payables	(2,597)
Short-term borrowings	(74)
Derivative financial instruments	(59)
Taxes payable	(201)
Provisions	(11)
	(2,942)
Net current liabilities	(1,221)
Non-current liabilities	
Other payables	(120)
Long-term borrowings	(2,339)
Deferred income tax liability	(172)
Provisions	(62)
Retirement benefit obligations	(340)
	(3,033)
Net assets	£ 5,424
Equity	
Called up share capital	£ 535
Share premium account	1,048
Capital redemption reserve	680
Other reserves	(213)
Retained earnings	3,374
Total equity	£ 5,424

1. Suppose Delta received the insurance payment and immediately purchased another 727 for $6.5 million. Compute the effect of the crash on pretax income. Also compute the effect on Delta's total assets.

2. Do you think a casualty loss should generate a reported gain? Why?

16-67 Identification of Operating, Investing, and Financing Activities

The items listed below were found on the 2011 statement of cash flows of Chevron Corporation, a company engaged in the exploration, production, refining, and distribution of petroleum products. For each item, indicate which section of the statement should contain the item—the operating, investing, or financing section. Does Chevron use the direct or indirect method for reporting cash flows from operating activities?

a. Capital expenditures
b. Proceeds from issuances of long-term debt
c. Net income
d. Net (increase) decrease in operating working capital
e. Cash dividends—common stock
f. Acquisition of Atlas Energy
g. Proceeds from asset sales
h. Net borrowings (payments) of short-term obligations
i. Depreciation, depletion, and amortization
j. Repayments of long-term debt and other financing obligations

16-68 Interest Expense

J. M. Smucker Company has many brands including Smucker's, Jif, Pillsbury, Hungry Jack, and Crisco. In fiscal 2011, the company reported interest expense of $69,594,000 on its income statement. Footnote K showed a cash payment for interest of $62,075,000. Suppose that accrued interest, a current liability on the balance sheet, was $8,105,000 at the beginning of fiscal 2011.

1. Describe how the transactions relating to interest would be shown in the body of the statement of cash flows if J. M. Smucker Company used the direct method for reporting cash flows from operating activities. Be specific, including amounts shown.
2. Describe how J. M. Smucker would show the transactions relating to interest on a supplementary schedule that reconciles net income and net cash provided by operating activities.

16-69 Indirect and Direct Cash Flows from Operations

Costco Wholesale Corporation operates more than 600 warehouse stores in the United States and abroad. The following items were in a slightly simplified version of the company's statement of cash flows for the fiscal year ending August 28, 2011 (in millions):

Increase in merchandise inventories	$ 642
Net income	1,542
Depreciation and amortization	855
Other noncash expenses	269
Increase in payables	804
Increase in other operating liabilities, net	451
Increase in receivables	81

The company's income statement showed (in millions):

Total revenues	$88,915
Cost of merchandise	77,739
Operating expenses	8,737
Operating income	2,439
Other expenses, net	56
Income before income taxes	2,383
Income tax	841
Net income	$ 1,542

1. Prepare a statement of cash flows from operating activities using the indirect method.
2. Prepare a statement of cash flows from operating activities using the direct method. Assume that all other expenses and income taxes were paid in cash, all operating liabilities relate to operating expenses, and that all depreciation and other noncash expenses are included in operating expenses.

16-70 Statement of Cash Flows, Direct and Indirect Methods

Nordstrom, the Seattle-based department store, had the following income statement for the year ended January 28, 2012 (in millions):

Total revenues		$10,877
Costs and expenses		
Cost of sales	$6,592	
Selling, general, and administrative	3,036	
Interest	130	
Total costs and expenses		9,758
Earnings before income taxes		$ 1,119
Income taxes		436
Net earnings		$ 683

The company's net cash provided by operating activities (slightly modified), prepared using the indirect method, was as follows:

Net earnings	$ 683
Adjustments to reconcile net earnings to net cash provided by operating activities	
Depreciation and amortization expenses	371
Other noncash expenses	117
Changes in	
Accounts receivable	(98)
Merchandise inventories	(137)
Accounts payable	54
Accrued salaries, wages, and related benefits	6
Income taxes payable	(12)
Other liabilities	193
Net cash provided by operating activities	$1,177

Prepare a statement showing the net cash provided by operating activities using the direct method. Assume that depreciation and amortization expenses, other noncash expenses, accrued salaries, wages, and related benefits, and other liabilities relate to selling, general, and administrative expenses.

16-71 Comparison of Inventory Methods

Study Appendix 16A. **Unisys Corporation** is a producer of computer-based information systems. The following actual data and descriptions are from the company's 2011 annual report as of December 31 (in millions):

	2011	2010
Inventories	$64.8	$88.9

A footnote states that "Inventories are valued at the lower of cost or market. Cost is determined principally on the first-in, first-out method."

The income statement for 2011 included the following (in millions):

Total revenues	$3,853.8
Cost of revenue	2,866.8

Suppose a division of Unisys had the accompanying data regarding computer parts that it acquires and resells to customers for maintaining equipment:

	Units	Total
Inventory (December 31, 2011)	100	$ 800
Purchase (February 20, 2012)	200	2,000
Sales (March 17, 2012)	150	2,250
Purchase (April 25, 2012)	140	1,820
Sales (June 27, 2012)	160	2,400

1. For these computer parts only, prepare a tabulation of the cost-of-goods-sold section of the income statement for the 6 months ended June 30, 2012. Support your computations. Round totals to the nearest dollar. Show your tabulation for four different inventory methods: (a) FIFO, (b) LIFO, (c) weighted-average, and (d) specific identification.
   For part d, assume that the purchase of February 20 was identified with the sale of March 17. Also assume that the purchase of April 25 was identified with the sale of June 27; the additional units sold were identified with the beginning inventory.
2. By how much would income taxes differ if Unisys used (a) LIFO instead of FIFO for this inventory item? (b) weighted average instead of FIFO? Assume a 40% tax rate.

16-72 Effects of Late Purchases

Study Appendix 16A. Refer to the preceding problem. Suppose Unisys acquired 60 extra units at $15 each on June 29, 2012, a total of $900. How would gross margin and income taxes be affected under FIFO? (That is, compare FIFO results before and after the purchase of 60 extra units.) Under LIFO? (That is, compare LIFO results before and after the purchase of 60 extra units.) Show computations and explain.

16-73 LIFO and FIFO at Home Depot

Study Appendix 16A. Home Depot, one of the five largest retailers in the United States, uses the FIFO inventory method. On January 29, 2012, the company reported merchandise inventory of $10.3 billion. At the beginning of the fiscal year, the inventory amount was $10.6 billion. Cost of merchandise sold for fiscal 2012 (the year ended January, 2012) was $46.1 billion, and operating income was $6.7 billion. During the year, Home Depot purchased merchandise for $45.8 billion. Suppose Home Depot had changed to LIFO on the first day of fiscal 2012, using the current inventory amount ($10.6 billion) as the first LIFO layer. Assume that its LIFO inventory on February 1, 2012, was $9.8 billion instead of the FIFO value of $10.3 billion.

1. Compute Home Depot's cost of merchandise sold and operating income for the year ended February 1, 2012, assuming that the switch to LIFO had been made at the beginning of fiscal 2012.
2. How would the switch to LIFO have affected Home Depot's fiscal 2012 income taxes, assuming a 40% tax rate? Assume that Home Depot switches to LIFO for both financial reporting and tax purposes.
3. Were the prices Home Depot paid for merchandise inventory rising or falling during fiscal 2012? How do you know?

16-74 Effect of LIFO

Study Appendix 16A. General Mills, producer of Wheaties, Cheerios, Gold Medal Flour, and many other food products, reported fiscal 2011 income before taxes of $2,428 million. Part of footnote 2 to the financial statements stated the following:

All inventories in the United States other than grain and certain organic products are valued at the lower of cost, using the last-in first-out (LIFO) method, or market.

Inventories valued at the lower of LIFO cost or market are as follows (in millions):

	May 29, 2011	May 30, 2010
Inventories	$1,609	$1,344

If LIFO inventories were valued at the lower of FIFO cost or market, the inventories would have been $168 million and $142 million higher than those reported for fiscal 2011 and 2010, respectively.

Suppose the FIFO method had always been used for all inventories. Calculate General Mills' operating income for fiscal 2011. By how much would the cumulative operating income for all years through 2011 differ from that reported? Would it be more or less than that reported?

NIKE 10-K PROBLEM

16-75 Using Financial Statements

Use the Nike 10-K report in Appendix C to answer the following questions.

1. What is Nike's principal business activity? What percentage of its sales are in the United States?
2. How much did Nike's gross margin and gross margin as a percentage of revenue increase (decrease) in fiscal 2011 compared with fiscal 2010?
3. Compare Nike's working capital in fiscal 2010 with that in fiscal 2011?
4. Nike had a decrease in cash of $1,124 million in fiscal 2011. What were the major causes or this decrease in cash?
5. Did Nike's board declare any cash dividends in fiscal 2011? If so, how much? On what financial statement did you find this?

EXCEL APPLICATION EXERCISE

16-76 Analyzing Differences Between Inventory Valuation Methods

Goal: Create an Excel spreadsheet to analyze differences between inventory valuation methods during inflationary and deflationary economies. Use the results to answer questions about your findings.

Scenario: The Omaha Fertilizer Company has asked you to compute its cost of goods sold and ending inventories for 20X1 using both FIFO and LIFO inventory valuation methods. Your computations will include scenarios for both rising and declining purchase prices. The company has a beginning inventory balance on January 1, 20X1, of 20,000 bags purchased at $10 per bag. For Scenario 1, assume that the company purchased 30,000 bags of fertilizer at $12 per bag in 20X1. For Scenario 2, assume that the company purchased 30,000 bags of fertilizer at $8 per bag in 20X1. The company sold 28,000 bags of fertilizer at $17 per bag during 20X1.

Note: This scenario is based on data in General Exercises and Problems 16-60. It requires study of Appendix 16A.

When you have completed your spreadsheet, answer the following questions:

1. In scenario 1, which assumes rising prices, which method's ending inventory most accurately reflects current replacement cost? Why?
2. In scenario 2, which assumes declining prices, which method's ending inventory most accurately reflects current replacement cost? Why?
3. Does LIFO always show the highest cost of goods sold (COGS)? Explain.

Step-by-Step:

1. Open a new Excel spreadsheet.
2. In column A, create a bold-faced heading that contains the following:
   Row 1: Chapter 16 Decision Guideline
   Row 2: Omaha Fertilizer Company
   Row 3: Inventory Valuation Analysis
   Row 4: Today's Date
3. Merge and center the four heading rows across columns A–F.
4. In row 7, create the following column headings:
   Column B: Beginning Inventory
   Column C: Inventory Purchases
   Column D: Available Inventory
   Column E: COGS
   Column F: Ending Inventory
5. Change the format of the column headings in row 7 to permit the titles to be displayed on multiple lines within a single cell.

       Alignment tab: Wrap text: Checked

6. Change the format of the column headings in row 7 to display as bold-faced.

Note: Adjust column widths so that headings only use two lines.

Adjust row height to ensure that row is same height as adjusted headings.

7. Change the format of each column heading in row 7 to be center justified.
8. In row 8, create the following bold-faced row heading:
   Column A: Scenario #1 ($12 per bag):

Note: Adjust the column width as necessary.

9. In row 9, create the following right-justified row heading:
   Column A: FIFO
10. Use formulas to calculate the amounts for columns B–F in row 9.

   Note: Formulas for COGS and Ending Inventory (columns E and F, respectively) will need a multistep formula if they are composed of items that do not all have the same inventory/purchase price. An example of the multistep formula needed in this situation would be $= (a \times b) + (c \times d)$

See Exhibit 16-20 for examples on how to calculate COGS and Ending Inventory.

11. Skip a row.
12. In row 11, create the following right-justified row heading:
    Column A: LIFO
13. Use formulas to calculate the amounts for columns B–F in row 11.
14. Skip two rows.
15. In row 14, create the following bold-faced row heading:
    Column A: Scenario #2 ($8 per bag):
16. In row 15, create the following right-justified row heading:
    Column A: FIFO
17. Use formulas to calculate the amounts for columns B–F in row 15.
18. Skip a row.
19. In row 17, create the following right-justified row heading:
    Column A: LIFO
20. Use formulas to calculate the amounts for columns B–F in row 17.
21. Format all amounts in rows 9, 11, 15, and 17 as follows:

Number tab:	Category:	Currency
	Decimal places:	0
	Symbol:	$
	Negative numbers:	Black with parentheses

22. Accentuate the COGS and Ending Inventory columns by applying cell-shading to columns E and F for rows 7–17.

Patterns tab:	Color:	Lightest gray

23. Save your work and print a copy for your files.

COLLABORATIVE LEARNING EXERCISE

16-77 Income Statement and Balance Sheet Accounts
Form teams of two persons each. Each person should make a list of 10 account names, with approximately half being income statement accounts and half being balance sheet accounts. Give the list to the other member of the team, who is to identify the financial statement (*I* for income statement or *B* for balance sheet) on which it belongs. If there are errors or disagreements in classification, discuss the account and come to an agreement about which financial statement it belongs to.

INTERNET EXERCISE

16-78 Lowe's Companies Financial Statements
Go to http://lowes.com to locate financial information for Lowe's Companies. You can follow the link at the bottom of the page to "Investor Relations," to "Investor Documents," to "SEC Filings" and finally to the most recent 10-K. Answer the following questions about the company:

1. Examine Lowe's income statement. What does the company call this statement? Does it use the single-step or multiple-step format? What subtitles does Lowe's use in its income statement? What was Lowe's net income in the most recent year? Was this more or less income than the company had in the preceding year?
2. Now look at Lowe's balance sheet. What is the company's largest current asset? What is its largest current liability? What is the balance in its property account? What was the original cost of the property and the accumulated depreciation? (See the notes to the financial statements.)
3. What is the largest component of Lowe's stockholders' equity? What proportion of total stockholders' equity does it represent? What does this imply about Lowe's profitability in the past?
4. Examine Lowe's statement of cash flows. Is the company's cash flow from operating activities more or less than its net earnings? Why? Did cash increase or decrease during the year? By how much?
5. Compare Lowe's depreciation and amortization to its cash used for acquiring fixed assets. Which is larger? What does this tell you?

17 Understanding and Analyzing Consolidated Financial Statements

LEARNING OBJECTIVES

When you have finished studying this chapter, you should be able to:

1. Contrast accounting for investments using the equity method and the market-value method.

2. Explain the basic ideas and methods used to prepare consolidated financial statements.

3. Describe how goodwill arises and how to account for it.

4. Use financial statement analysis to evaluate an organization's performance.

5. Explain and use a variety of popular financial ratios.

6. Identify the major implications that efficient stock markets have for accounting.

▶ BERKSHIRE HATHAWAY

In 1960 Warren Buffett, then 30 years old, asked 10 friends to invest $10,000 each in an investment partnership. That partnership eventually became Berkshire Hathaway, and today each $10,000 investment is worth more than $50 million. Berkshire has provided investors with an average annual return of 19.8% between 1965 and 2011. Buffett was named by *Forbes* magazine as the second richest person in the United States in 2012 with a fortune worth $46 billion. Known as the "Oracle of Omaha," Buffett is revered for his investment savvy. Berkshire Hathaway's annual meeting, where Buffett spends hours presenting his investment philosophy (and often his life philosophy), regularly attracts nearly 30,000 participants.

Berkshire Hathaway Inc. is a holding company located in Omaha, Nebraska. It owns all or part of more than 75 companies, including 100% ownership of companies as diverse as Burlington Northern Santa Fe, MidAmerican Energy, GEICO Insurance, Dairy Queen, and Fruit of the Loom. These companies are separate entities, each with its own financial records. However, authorities require Berkshire to combine their financial records when preparing its financial statements for the public.

Berkshire is not the only company that has to combine the financial records of its subsidiaries. Pick up the annual report of almost any major company, and you will find **consolidated financial statements**. This term means that the company has combined the books of two or more separate legal entities into one set of financial statements. Berkshire Hathaway's annual report states that its "Consolidated Financial Statements include the accounts of Berkshire consolidated with the accounts of all subsidiaries and affiliates in which we hold a controlling financial interest."

The consolidated Berkshire statements in the company's annual report combine the financial results of multiple companies making millions of transactions in many different currencies throughout the world. Consolidated financial statements show all these transactions as if they were made by a single company, rather than multiple separate companies.

Berkshire also has smaller investments in companies in which it does not hold a controlling financial interest, such as Coca Cola, Procter & Gamble, and American Express. It lists these on its balance sheet at market values, as explained in this chapter.

consolidated financial statements

Financial statements that combine the books of two or more separate legal entities into one set of financial statements.

This chapter contains two parts. You can study either part or both, depending on your specific interest. Part One shows how to account for the investments one company makes in another, such as Berkshire's investment in its subsidiaries and affiliates, with a focus on consolidated financial statements. Part Two covers the analysis of consolidated financial statements, focusing on the financial statements of **Nike**, which are included in Appendix C at the end of the book. ■

© Nicholas Kamm/Newscom

Warren Buffett, Chairman and CEO of Berkshire Hathaway, shares his philosophy of business and life at the company's annual meeting each May in Omaha, Nebraska.

Part One: Intercorporate Investments Including Consolidations

Firms often invest in the equity securities of another company. The investing company may be simply investing excess cash, or it may be seeking some degree of control over the investee. The way we account for these investments depends on management's reasons for making the investment.

The following sections will describe three methods of accounting for intercorporate investments: (1) market-value method, (2) equity method, and (3) consolidation. Accountants require investors without significant influence over the decisions of an investee firm to account for the investment using the market-value method. Investors that have significant influence but not control use the equity method. Investors that have control use the consolidation approach. The primary indicator of whether an investor has significant influence or control is the percentage ownership of the investee firm, although other evidence beyond percentage ownership can override this primary indicator. Accountants assume an investor that holds less than 20% of another company cannot significantly influence the decisions of the investee and therefore this investor uses the market-value method. They assume that investors with between 20% and 50% ownership have the ability to exert significant influence on, but do not control, the investee. These investors use the equity method. Finally, companies with an interest in excess of 50% have control and use the consolidation approach. For example, during 2005 **General Motors** purchased additional shares of GM Daewoo, increasing its ownership from 44.6% to 50.9%. Therefore, General Motors had to change its accounting for GM Daewoo from the equity method to consolidation.

Market-Value and Equity Methods

Companies that hold less than 50% of the common stock of another company generally use either the market-value method or the equity method. Let's look at each.

Market-Value Method

An investment in less than 20% of the common stock of another company normally requires use of the market-value method. An investor using the **market-value method** shows the investment on its balance sheet at market value (also called *fair value*). Companies often call such investments "marketable securities" in the financial statements.

The effect of such securities on the income statement depends on whether management classifies them as trading securities or available-for-sale securities. **Trading securities** are investments the investor company intends to sell in the near future. **Available-for-sale securities** are investments that the investor company does not intend to sell in the near future.

Trading securities and available-for-sale securities provide returns to the investor in two ways: (1) dividend revenue and (2) changes in market value. The investor company records dividend revenue on its income statement when received for both types of investments. It also accounts for changes in market value for both types of investments by increasing or decreasing the value of the asset. However, on the owners' equity side, the investor company accounts for changes in market value differently for trading securities than for available-for-sale securities.

As you can see from Exhibit 17-1, the only difference between trading securities and available-for-sale securities is how the change in market value gets incorporated into stockholders' equity. For trading securities, price increases and decreases are included in net income and therefore become part of retained earnings. For available-for-sale securities, price increases and decreases affect a different component of stockholders' equity, other comprehensive income or loss.

market-value method
The method of accounting for investments in equity securities that shows the investment on the balance sheet at market value.

trading securities
Investments "held for current resale," that is, investments that the investor company intends to sell in the near future.

available-for-sale securities
Investments that the investor company does not intend to sell in the near future.

Exhibit 17-1
Summary of Trading and
Available-for-Sale Securities

Income Statement Effects	Balance Sheet Effects
Trading Securities:	Trading Securities:
Net income includes:	Asset: Investment shown at current market value
Dividend revenue	Stockholders' equity:
Change in market value (add increases and deduct decreases)	Retained earnings increased by the amount of net income (which *includes* increases and decreases in market value)
Available-for-Sale Securities:	Available-for-Sale Securities:
Net income includes:	Asset: Investment shown at current market value
Dividend revenue	Stockholders' equity:
	Retained earnings increased by the amount of net income (which *excludes* increases and decreases in market value)
	Comprehensive income includes the change in market value (add increases and deduct decreases)

Equity Method

Now consider investing companies that have the power to exert significant influence on investees. Usually this means that they hold 20% to 50% of the common shares of the investee. These companies must use the **equity method**, which adjusts the acquisition cost of an investment for the investor's share of earnings or losses of the investee after the date of investment and for dividends received. Investors increase both income and the carrying amount of the investment by their share of the investee's earnings, and they decrease the carrying amount of the investment for dividends received.

equity method
A method of accounting for an investment by adjusting the acquisition cost of the investment for the investor's share of earnings or losses of the investee after the date of investment and for dividends received.

Let's compare the market value and equity methods. Suppose Berkshire Hathaway acquires 40% of the voting stock of Springfield Auto Interiors (SAI) for $80 million. In year 1, SAI has a net income of $30 million and pays cash dividends of $10 million. Berkshire's 40% shares of income and dividends would be $12 million and $4 million, respectively. At the end of the year, the market value of Berkshire's investment is $91 million. For illustrative purposes, suppose that Berkshire could use either the market-value or equity method. (In reality, Berkshire must use the equity method because 40% ownership indicates significant influence.) The following balance sheet equation shows how Berkshire would record the transactions under each of the methods (in millions):

	Equity Method				Market-Value Method			
	Assets		=	Liab. & Stk. Eq.	Assets		=	Liab. & Stk. Eq.
	Cash	Investments		Liab. Stk. Eq.	Cash	Investments		Liab. Stk. Eq.
1. Acquisition	−80	+80	=		−80	+80	=	
2. Net income of SAI		+12	=	+12	No entry and no effect			
3. Dividends from SAI	+ 4	− 4	=		+ 4		=	+ 4
4. Increase in SAI market value Effects for the year	No entry and no effect					+11		+11
	−76	+88	=	+12	−76	+91	=	+15

The investment account will have a net increase of $8 million for the year. The dividend will increase the cash account by $4 million.

The investment account will increase by the $11 million increase in market value. The dividend will increase the cash account by $4 million.

If accounting rules allowed Berkshire to account for this investment using the *market-value method*, Berkshire would recognize income when SAI declares the $4 million dividend. In addition, at the end of the accounting period, Berkshire would determine the market price of the shares and increase income (if it is a trading security) or other comprehensive income (if it is an available-for-sale security) for the $11 million increase in market value. If Berkshire classified the investment as a trading security, the $11 million would be part of retained earnings (because net income becomes part of retained earnings). If Berkshire classified the investment as an available-for-sale security, the $11 million would be in the other comprehensive income account. Either way it would be part of stockholders' equity.

Under the *equity method*, Berkshire would recognize income as SAI earns it rather than when SAI pays dividends or when market values change. The recorded value of Berkshire's investment in SAI grows by its $12 million share of SAI's net income, and Berkshire's income increases by that same $12 million. The $4 million of dividends SAI pays to Berkshire increases Berkshire's cash and decreases the amount of its investment in SAI by $4 million. The dividends do not affect Berkshire's net income.

Making Managerial Decisions

Berkshire Hathaway owns 13.0% of **American Express Company**. As part of its decision on how much of American Express to own, Warren Buffett probably considered the effect of being below or above 20% ownership. Suppose Buffett was considering whether to either retain 13.0% ownership or increase it to 21%. Berkshire plans to hold the stock indefinitely. What difference would it make if Berkshire continues to own 13.0% of the stock rather than increasing its ownership to 21%?

Answer

The accounting for the investment would be different under these two options. If Berkshire continues to own just 13.0% (or any percentage less than 20%), it uses the market-value method. Because Berkshire plans to hold the stock indefinitely, it classifies the stock as an available-for-sale investment and includes changes in market value in other comprehensive income. This means that Berkshire's balance sheet includes the market value of the investment as an asset and changes in the market value as other comprehensive income, and its income statement includes only the dividends received from American Express.

In contrast, if Berkshire increases its ownership to 21% (or any percentage of 20% or more, but less than 50%), it will use the equity method. The investment account on the balance sheet will grow with the net income of American Express less dividends received. The balance sheet amount will not fluctuate with market values. In addition, Berkshire's income statement will include its portion of American Express's net income, regardless of dividend payments or changes in market prices.

If Berkshire expects American Express to have increasing earnings but to pay few dividends, Berkshire would recognize more income from the investment under the equity method. Further, wide swings in the market value of American Express will not affect Berkshire's books under the equity method. However, because of this, Berkshire's books would get no immediate benefit from large increases in the American Express's market value.

The choice of the amount of investment can have a significant impact on Berkshire's future financial statements. Depending on what Berkshire wants to accomplish, it might prefer either the market-value or the equity method, which in turn affects Berkshire's decision about the percentage of American Express that it wants to acquire.

Consolidated Financial Statements

Objective 2

Now let's consider a company that has effective control over another company. Usually this means that it owns more than 50% of the company's stock. We call the controlling company a **parent company** and the controlled company a **subsidiary**. Although parent and subsidiary companies typically are separate legal entities, in many regards they function as one unit.

Explain the basic ideas and methods used to prepare consolidated financial statements.

Why have subsidiaries? Why isn't every company a single legal entity? Subsidiaries often limit risk, save income taxes, help conform to government regulations, and allow the parent to do business in a foreign country. For example, when Berkshire purchases a company, it buys the stock of the company, not the individual assets and liabilities, and Berkshire's risk is limited to the amount of their investment. As another example, there are often tax advantages in acquiring the capital stock of a going concern rather than buying its individual assets.

parent company
A company that has effective control over another company. Usually this means owning more than 50% of the company's stock.

The parent–subsidiary relationship requires special accounting treatment. Parent companies issue consolidated financial statements that combine the financial statements of the parent company with those of its subsidiaries. That is, we account for the parent and subsidiary companies as if they were a single entity. Why? Because consolidated statements give investors a more accurate picture of the whole organization's health. Let's look at the issues that arise when consolidating financial statements.

subsidiary
A company controlled by a parent company that generally owns more than 50% of its stock.

The Acquisition

When consolidating parent and subsidiary financial statements, accountants must avoid double-counting of assets, liabilities, and stockholders' equities. Accomplishing this is a complex process in real companies, but we can see the basic principles in a simple example. Suppose company P (parent) acquired 100% of the common stock of S (subsidiary) for $210 million cash at the beginning of the year.[1] The following table analyzes the balance sheet accounts of both companies, and the last line is a consolidated balance sheet for P after accounting for its acquisition of S. (Investment in S appears in the first column because it is a focal point in this chapter, not because it comes first in actual balance sheets.) Figures in this and subsequent tables are in millions of dollars:

	Assets		=	Liabilities	+	Stockholders' Equity
	Investment in S	+ Cash and Other Assets	=	Accounts Payable, Etc.	+	Stockholders' Equity
P's accounts, January 1						
Before acquisition		650	=	200	+	450
Acquisition of S	+210	−210	=			
S's accounts, January 1	—	400	=	190	+	210
Totals before eliminating entries	210	840	=	390	+	660
Intercompany eliminations for a consolidated balance sheet	−210		=			−210
Consolidated, January 1	0	+ 840	=	390	+	450

Note that P purchases the common stock of S by paying the $210 million to the former owners of S as private investors, not to S itself. That is, P's purchase of stock in S does not affect S's books. S does not disappear, but it lives on as a separate legal entity but with a different owner. Each legal entity has its individual set of books.

The consolidated entity does not keep a separate set of books. Rather, it relies on the accounting records of P and S. The consolidated statement combines all assets and liabilities of both the parent and the subsidiary but eliminates instances of double counting:

Entity	Types of Records
P	Parent books
+ S	Subsidiary books
= Preliminary consolidated report	No separate books for the consolidated entity, but periodically P and S assets and liabilities are added together via work sheets
− E	"Eliminating entries" to remove double-counting
= Consolidated report to investors	

Look again at the example in the preceding table. The Investment in S account on P's books is the evidence of P's ownership interest in all the assets and liabilities of S. The consolidated statements cannot show both the evidence of ownership interest from P's books *and* the detailed underlying assets and liabilities from S's books. That would be double-counting the assets and liabilities. Similarly, the Stockholders' Equity accounts on P's books record the total ownership interest of P's shareholders, including their ownership of S, while the Stockholders' Equity accounts on S's books also record the ownership interest of P's shareholders in S (remember that P is the sole shareholder of S). We make eliminating entries in two places to avoid double-counting: we subtract (1) the Investment in S on P's books and (2) the Stockholders' Equity on S's books. In summary, if the $210 million elimination of the reciprocal accounts did not occur, there would be double-counting in the consolidated balance sheet.

Recognizing Income after Acquisition

Now let's look at how we combine the income of a parent and its subsidiary. A parent company carries its investment in subsidiaries, such as this investment in S, on its balance sheet by the equity method, described earlier in this chapter. Suppose S has a net income of $50 million for the year. If P were reporting alone, it would account for the net income of its subsidiary

---

[1] In this example, the purchase price equals the stockholders' equity of the acquired company. On pages 725–726, we discuss the preparation of consolidated statements in situations in which these two amounts differ.

by increasing its Investment in S account and its Stockholders' Equity account (in the form of Retained Earnings) by its share (100%) of the $50 million income. P's parent-company-only income statement for the year is in the first column below (numbers in millions):

	P	S	Consolidated
Sales	$900	$300	$1,200
Expenses	800	250	1,050
Operating income	$100	$ 50	$ 150
Pro rata share (100%) of subsidiary net income	50	—	
Net income	$150	$ 50	

P's statement shows its own sales and expenses plus its share of S's net income (as the equity method requires). The consolidated statement (the last column) adds together all the revenues and expenses of the parent (first column) and the subsidiary (second column).

Reflect on the changes in P's accounts, S's accounts, and the consolidated accounts in the following table (in millions of dollars):

	Assets			=	Liabilities	+	Stockholders' Equity
	Investment in S	+	Cash and Other Assets	=	Accounts Payable, Etc.	+	Stockholders' Equity
P's accounts							
Beginning of year	210	+	440	=	200	+	450
Operating income			+100	=			+100*
Share of S income	+ 50			=			+ 50*
End of year	260	+	540	=	200	+	600
S's accounts							
Beginning of year			400	=	190	+	210
Net income			+ 50	=			+ 50*
End of year	—		450	=	190	+	260
Totals before eliminating entries	260		990	=	390	+	860
Intercompany eliminations	−260			=			−260
Consolidated, end of year	0	+	990	=	390	+	600

*Changes in the retained earnings portion of stockholders' equity.

Note that consolidated statements summarize the individual accounts of two or more separate legal entities, eliminating double-counting.[2] The income statement for P shows a $150 million net income; for S, a $50 million net income; for P and S consolidated, a $150 million net income. The consolidated net income will always be the same as P's net income. Why? Because P has already recognized its share of S's income in its own income statement.

Noncontrolling Interests

In the preceding example, P owned 100% of S. What happens when a parent holds less than 100% (but more than 50%) of the stock of a subsidiary? In such a case, a consolidated balance sheet includes an account on the equities side called noncontrolling interests in subsidiaries, or simply **noncontrolling interests**. The account summarizes the outside stockholders' interest, as opposed to the parent's interest, in a subsidiary corporation. It arises because the consolidated balance sheet

noncontrolling interests
An account that summarizes the outside stockholders' interest, as opposed to the parent's interest, in a subsidiary corporation.

---

[2]Another example of double-counting is sales by P to S or by S to P. For the sake of simplicity, our example does not include any sales between P and S. However, remember that we need to avoid double-counting in situations where there are sales among consolidated companies. For example, suppose P bought an item for $1,000 and sold it to S for $1,200. P recognized revenue of $1,200, cost of goods sold of $1,000, and income of $200. S recorded an inventory item of $1,200. From a consolidated point of view, the item has not yet been sold to an external party but has only been transferred within the consolidated entity. Therefore, after adding together the individual accounts of P and S, the company must deduct $1,200 from revenue, $1,000 from cost of goods sold, and $200 from inventory. This eliminates the $200 of income that P recognized and reduces inventory to the original $1,000 that P paid for the item.

includes 100% of the assets and liabilities of a subsidiary even when the parent owns less than 100%. Suppose the parent owns 90% of the subsidiary's stock, and outsiders to the consolidated group own the other 10%. The Noncontrolling Interests account is a measure of the outside stockholders' interest. The diagram that follows provides an overview of the role of the noncontrolling interests account in the consolidated statements. The consolidated balance sheet includes all the subsidiary's assets and liabilities, item by item. However, because of the outsiders' interests, P does not have an ownership claim on all the assets and liabilities listed. The Noncontrolling Interests account, in effect, summarizes the outside stockholders' ownership interest and the remainder, after deducting noncontrolling interests, is P's total ownership interest:

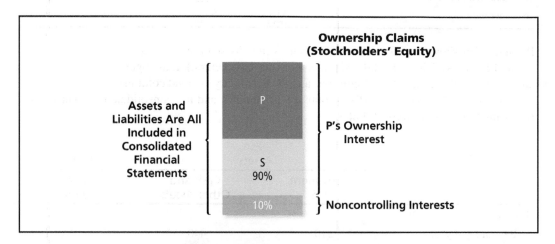

The next table continues the basic assumptions of the previous example but now assumes P bought 90% of the stock of S for a cost of 0.90 × $210, or $189 million. This leaves a 10% noncontrolling interest with a value of 0.10 × $210, or $21 million, which represents the value of the interest that has not been purchased by, and is not owned by, P.

	Assets		=	Liabilities	+	Stockholders' Equity		
	Investment in S	+ Cash and Other Assets	=	Accounts Payable, Etc.	+	Noncontrolling Interest	+	P's Stockholders' Equity
P's accounts, January 1								
Before acquisition		650	=	200			+	450
Acquisition of 90% of S	+189	−189	=					
S's accounts, January 1	−	400	=	190			+	210
Totals before eliminating entries	189	+ 861	=	390			+	660
Intercompany eliminations	−189		=			+21		−210
Consolidated, January 1	0	+ 861	=	390	+	21	+	450

Again, suppose S has a net income of $50 million for the year. P and S follow the same basic procedures in preparing their separate financial statements, regardless of whether P owns 100% or 90% of S. However, the presence of the 10% noncontrolling interest changes the consolidated income statement as follows:

	P	S	Consolidated
Sales	$900	$300	$1,200
Expenses	800	250	1,050
Operating income	$100	$50	$ 150
Pro rata share (90%) of subsidiary net income	45	—	
Net income	$145	$ 50	
Noncontrolling interest (10%) in subsidiaries' net income			5
Net income to consolidated entity			$ 145

The noncontrolling interest also changes the consolidated balance sheets at the end of the year, as follows:

	Assets		=	Liabilities	+	Stockholders' Equity		
	Investment in S	+	Cash and Other Assets =	Accounts Payable, Etc.	+	Noncontrolling Interest	+	P's Stockholders' Equity
P's accounts								
Beginning of year, before acquisition			650 =	200			+	450
Acquisition	189		−189 =					
Operating income			+100 =					+100
Share of S income	+ 45		____ =	____				+ 45
End of year	234	+	561 =	200			+	595
S's accounts								
Beginning of year			400 =	190			+	210
Net income			+ 50 =					+ 50
End of year		+	450 =	190			+	260
Total before eliminating entries	234	+	1,011 =	390			+	855
Intercompany eliminations	−234		=			+26*		−260
Consolidated, end of year	0	+	1,011 =	390	+	26	+	595

*Beginning noncontrolling interest plus noncontrolling interest in net income: $21 + (0.10 \times 50) = 21 + 5 = 26$.

Notice that the entry to consolidate the statements eliminates $260 million of stockholders' equity (on S's books) and $234 million of investment in S (on P's books). The $26 million difference is the noncontrolling interest (on consolidated statements), which includes the original $21 million at acquisition and the noncontrolling shareholders' $5 million interest in S's net income. The $26 million represents the interest of those shareholders who own the 10% of the subsidiary's stockholders' equity.

Income statements and balance sheets would show the noncontrolling interests as follows, where we include only the pertinent part of each statement:

Company P Consolidated Income Statement

Net income before noncontrolling interests	$150
Noncontrolling interests	5
Net income attributable to Company P stockholders	$145

Company P Consolidated Balance Sheet

Shareholders' equity:	
Total Company P stockholders' equity	$595
Noncontrolling interests	26
Total stockholders' equity	$621

Perspective on Consolidated Statements

To get a clear idea of how investments in other companies affect income statements and balance sheets, consider Exhibits 17-2 and 17-3, the 2011 balance sheet and income statement of Starbucks Company. We have simplified the statements and highlighted the items of interest by showing them in italics. However, we have used Starbucks' terminology for all the items we will discuss in this section.

Exhibit 17-2
Starbucks Corporation
Consolidated Balance Sheet
October 2, 2011 (in millions)

Cash and cash equivalents		$ 1,148.1
Short-term investments—available-for-sale securities		*855.0*
Short-term investments—trading securities		*47.6*
Accounts receivable, net		386.5
Inventories		965.8
Other current assets		391.9
Total current assets		3,794.9
Long-term investments—available-for-sale securities		*107.0*
Equity method investments		*334.4*
Property, plant and equipment, net		2,355.0
Other assets		769.1
TOTAL ASSETS		$ 7,360.4
Total liabilities		2,973.1
Shareholders' equity:		
Paid-in capital	41.2	
Retained earnings	4,297.4	
Accumulated other comprehensive income*	*46.3*	
Total shareholders' equity		4,384.9
Noncontrolling interests		*2.4*
Total equity		4,387.3
TOTAL LIABILITIES AND EQUITY		$ 7,360.4

*Includes unrealized gain on available-for-sale securities.

Exhibit 17-3
Starbucks Company
*Consolidated Income
Statement Year Ended
October 2, 2011 (in millions)*

Net revenues	$11,700.4
Cost of sales including occupancy costs	(4,949.3)
Other operating expenses	(5,226.5)
Gain on sale of properties	30.2
Income from equity investees	*173.7*
Operating income	1,728.5
Interest income and other, net	82.6
Earnings before income taxes	1,811.1
Income taxes	(563.1)
Net earnings including noncontrolling interests	1,248.0
Net earnings attributable to noncontrolling interests	*(2.3)*
Net earnings attributable to Starbucks	$ 1,245.7

First look at the headings of both exhibits. Starbucks highlights the fact that the statements are consolidated. This means that the accounts listed include both Starbucks' parent company amounts and those of its subsidiaries. Starbucks has added the assets, liabilities, revenues, and expenses of these subsidiaries to their own and eliminated double counting to produce the consolidated statements.

Now look at the balance sheet (Exhibit 17-2). Starbucks shows four assets related to investments in other companies: "Short-term investments—available-for-sale securities," "Short-term investments—trading securities," "Long-term investments—available-for-sale securities," and "Equity method investments." Starbucks has short-term trading securities and both short-term and long-term available-for-sale securities. These are all securities over which Starbucks has no influence or control. The equity method investments account means that Starbucks owns between 20% and 50% of some companies. These companies are primarily international companies such as **Starbucks Coffee Korea Co., Ltd.**, **Shanghai President Coffee Co.**, and **Starbucks Coffee Japan, Ltd.** The $334.4 million shown is the original price Starbucks paid for these affiliates plus Starbucks's proportional interest in their net income since acquisition less dividends paid to Starbucks.

Starbucks's liabilities and stockholders' equity includes two items to discuss: "Accumulated other comprehensive income" and "Noncontrolling interests." The accumulated other comprehensive income contains Starbucks's net unrealized gain (or loss) on its available-for-sale securities as well as other items. The net unrealized gain arose because of increases in the market value of the securities since Starbucks purchased them.

Noncontrolling interests is the part of the equity in consolidated subsidiaries—subsidiaries over which Starbucks has control—that Starbucks does not own. It belongs to shareholders who own a noncontrolling (or minority) interest in the subsidiaries' stock. Starbucks consolidates all the subsidiaries' assets and liabilities, but a proportion of those assets and liabilities does not belong to the shareholders of Starbucks. The total stockholders' equity includes the equity of the Starbucks shareholders and the noncontrolling interests of the minority or noncontrolling shareholders.

Next, we will examine the income statement (Exhibit 17-3). As part of its revenues, Starbucks has a line for "Income from equity investees." This is Starbucks's portion of the net income of companies that are not consolidated but accounted for by the equity method. Another item is "Net earnings attributable to noncontrolling interests"—the portion of Starbucks's income from consolidated investments that belongs to noncontrolling shareholders. Starbucks includes the entire revenues and expenses of consolidated subsidiaries in its income statement, but then subtracts out $2.3 million, the income from these subsidiaries that belongs to the noncontrolling shareholders.

Exhibit 17-4 summarizes all the relationships depicted in Exhibits 17-2 and 17-3 Take a few moments to review all three exhibits. In particular, note that noncontrolling interests arise only when a parent company consolidates its statements with those of subsidiaries. Why? Because consolidated balance sheets and income statements aggregate 100% of the detailed assets, liabilities, sales, and expenses of the subsidiary companies. Thus, if Starbucks did not recognize the amount owned by noncontrolling investors, the financial statements would overstate the stockholders' equity and net income belonging to Starbucks' shareholders. In contrast, noncontrolling interests do not arise in connection with the accounting for equity-method investments. Why? Because we record investments in these companies on a pro rata basis only—the consolidated statements do not include all the assets, liabilities, revenues, and expenses of the equity investees but instead include a single balance sheet line, equity-method investments, and a single income statement line, income from equity investees, both reflecting only the portion owned by the parent.

Accounting for Goodwill

Objective 3

Describe how goodwill arises and how to account for it.

Now we will consider one more complication that arises when a company purchases more than 50% of another company. Our previous example of companies P and S assumed (1) the acquisition cost of S by P was equal to the amount of the stockholders' equity, or the book value, of S, and (2) the book value was equal to the sum of the fair-market value of the assets and liabilities acquired. In actual acquisitions, the total purchase price paid by P often exceeds the book values of the net assets acquired. In addition, the purchase price also often exceeds the sum of

Percentage of Ownership	Type of Accounting	Balance Sheet Effects	Income Statement Effects
100%	Consolidation	Individual assets, individual liabilities added together	Individual revenues, individual expenses added together
Greater than 50% and less than 100%	Consolidation	Same as 100% ownership, but recognition given to noncontrolling interest in stockholders' equity section	Same as 100% ownership, but recognition given to noncontrolling interest near bottom of statement when consolidated income is computed
20% to and including 50%	Equity method	Investment carried at cost plus pro rata share of subsidiary earnings less dividends received	Equity in earnings of affiliated or associated companies shown on one line as addition to income

Exhibit 17-4
Summary of Equity Method and Consolidations

the fair-market values (current values) of the identifiable individual assets less the liabilities. For example, when **Philip Morris** paid $13 billion for **Kraft** several years ago, it assigned only $2 billion to identifiable individual assets. It assigned the remainder to goodwill. Recall from Chapter 16 that goodwill is the excess of the cost of an acquired company over the sum of the fair (market) values of identifiable assets less liabilities.

Companies record goodwill as an asset only when one company purchases another and pays more than the sum of the fair values of the assets and liabilities acquired. A purchaser may be willing to pay more than the sum of the fair values because the acquired company is able to generate abnormally high earnings. For example, a purchaser may be willing to pay extra because it expects excess earnings from

1. potential efficiencies gained by combination, rearrangement, or elimination of duplicate facilities and administration,
2. excellent general management skills present in the purchased company,
3. a unique product line, and/or
4. an established brand name and reputation.

To see the impact of goodwill on the consolidated statements, refer to our example where P acquired a 100% interest in S for $210 million. Suppose P paid $40 million more, or a total of $250 million cash. For simplicity, assume that the fair values of the individual assets and liabilities of S are equal to their book values. The balance sheets immediately after the acquisition are as follows:

	Assets				=	Liabilities	+	Stockholders' Equity
	Investment in S	+	Goodwill	+	Cash and Other Assets =	Accounts Payable, Etc.	+	Stockholders' Equity
P's accounts								
Before acquisition					650 =	200	+	450
Acquisition	+250				−250 =			
S's accounts					400 =	190	+	210
Totals before eliminating entries	250	+			800 =	390	+	660
Intercompany eliminations	−250	+	40		=			−210
Consolidated	0	+	40*	+	800 =	390	+	450

*The $40 million "goodwill" would appear in the consolidated balance sheet as a separate intangible asset account.

What if the book values of the individual assets of S are not equal to their fair values? The usual procedures are as follows:

1. S continues as a going concern and keeps its accounts on the same basis as before.
2. P records its investment at its acquisition cost (the agreed purchase price).
3. For consolidated reporting purposes, we first assign part of the excess of the acquisition cost over the book value of S to the individual assets, item by item, to adjust each to its fair value at the time of the acquisition.
4. Assign the remaining excess of the acquisition cost over the fair value of the assets less liabilities to goodwill.

Suppose the fair value of S's equipment exceeded its book value by $30 million in our example. With this change, the balance sheets immediately after acquisition would be the same as previously, with only two exceptions. The additional $30 million would appear in the consolidated balance sheet as an integral part of the equipment account (part of Other Assets in the example), and the goodwill that had previously been $40 million would now be only $10 million. Because the consolidated statement would show S's equipment at $30 million higher than the carrying amount on S's books, the depreciation expense on the consolidated income statement would be higher. For instance, if the equipment had 5 years of useful life remaining, the straight-line depreciation would be $30 million ÷ 5 = $6 million higher per year for the next 5 years.

As in the preceding tabulation, the $10 million "goodwill" appears in the consolidated balance sheet as a separate intangible asset account. Goodwill balances remain on the balance sheet until management judges that its value is impaired—that is, until it is evident that the advantages that created the goodwill are no longer present.

Summary Problem for Your Review

PROBLEM

1. Review the section on noncontrolling interests, pages 721–723. Suppose P purchases 60% of the stock of S for a cost of .60 × $210, or $126 million cash. Assume that the assets, liabilities, and shareholders' equity of S are unchanged from the amounts given in the example on noncontrolling interests. Also, return to our original assumption that the fair value of the net assets of S and the book value of the net assets of S are both equal to $210 million, which is also equal to the value of the total firm implied by the $126 million price for 60% of the firm.

    The total assets of P consist of this $126 million investment plus $524 million of other assets, a total of $650 million. The assets, liabilities, and shareholders' equity of S are unchanged from the amounts given in the example on noncontrolling interests. Prepare an analysis showing what amounts would appear in a consolidated balance sheet immediately after the acquisition.

2. Suppose S has a net income of $50 million for the year, and P has an operating income of $100 million. Other details are described in the example on pages 722–723. Prepare an analysis showing what amounts would appear in a consolidated income statement and year-end balance sheet.

SOLUTION

1.

	Assets		=	Liabilities	+			Stockholders' Equity
	Investment in S	+	Cash and Other Assets =	Accounts Payable, Etc.	+	Noncontrolling Interest	+	Stockholders' Equity
P's accounts, January 1:								
Before acquisition		650	=	200			+	450
Acquisition of 60% of S	+126	−126	=					
S's accounts, January 1	—	400	=	190			+	210
Totals before eliminating entries	126	+ 924	=	390			+	660
Intercompany eliminations	−126		=			+84	+	−210
Consolidated, January 1	0	+ 924	=	390	+	84	+	450

2.

	P	S	Consolidated
Sales	$900	$300	$1,200
Expenses	800	250	1,050
Operating income	$100	$ 50	$ 150
Pro rata share (60%) of unconsolidated subsidiary net income	30	—	
Net income	$130	$ 50	
Noncontrolling interest (40%) in consolidated subsidiary net income			20
Net income to consolidated entity			$ 130

	Assets		=	Liabilities			+	Stockholders' Equity
	Investment in S	+ Cash and Other Assets	=	Accounts Payable, Etc.	+ Noncontrolling Interest		+	Stockholders' Equity
P's accounts								
Beginning of year, before acquisition		650	=	200			+	450
Acquisition	126	− 126	=					
Operating income		+ 100						+100
Share of S income	+ 30		=					+ 30
End of year	156	+ 624	=	200			+	580
S's accounts								
Beginning of year		400	=	190			+	210
Net income		+ 50	=					+ 50
End of year		450	=	190			+	260
Totals before eliminating entries	156	+ 1,074	=	390			+	840
Intercompany eliminations	−156	—	=	—	+104*			−260
Consolidated, end of year	0	+ 1,074	=	390	+	104	+	580

*84 beginning of year + (0.40 × 50) = 84 + 20 = 104.

Part Two: Analysis of Financial Statements

For financial statements to be useful, managers and investors need to be able to analyze and interpret the statements. Careful analysis of financial statements can help decision makers evaluate an organization's past performance and predict its future performance. Such evaluations help managers, investors, and others make intelligent, informed financial decisions. We use the 2010 and 2011 financial statements of Nike in Exhibits 17-5 and 17-6 to focus on financial statement analysis.

Many decisions are based on comparisons of financial statements. For example, investors use them to decide whether to buy, sell, or hold common stock. Managers and the financial community (such as bank officers and stockholders) use them to help evaluate the operating and financial outlook for an organization. Budgets or pro forma statements—carefully formulated expressions of predicted results—are helpful to extenders of credit, who want assurance of being paid in full and on time. For example, a set of budgeted financial statements is one of the first things a banker will request from an entrepreneur proposing a new business. Even well-established companies usually need to provide pro forma statements to assure creditors that the company will pay back the amounts borrowed. Let's look at some ways that users analyze financial statements.

May 31 ASSETS	2011	2010
Current assets		
Cash and equivalents	$ 1,955	$ 3,079
Short-term investments	2,583	2,067
Accounts receivable, less allowance for doubtful accounts of $74 and $74	3,138	2,650
Inventories	2,715	2,041
Deferred income taxes	312	249
Prepaid expenses and other current assets	594	873
Total current assets	11,297	10,959
Noncurrent assets		
Property, plant, and equipment		
At cost	4,906	4,390
Less: accumulated depreciation	2,791	2,458
Net property, plant, and equipment	2,115	1,932
Identifiable intangible assets, net	487	467
Goodwill	205	188
Deferred income taxes and other assets	894	873
Total noncurrent assets	3,701	3,460
Total assets	$14,998	$14,419
LIABILITIES AND SHAREHOLDERS' EQUITY		
Current liabilities		
Current portion of long-term debt	$ 200	$ 7
Notes payable	187	139
Accounts payable	1,469	1,255
Accrued liabilities	1,985	1,904
Income taxes payable	117	59
Total current liabilities	3,958	3,364
Noncurrent liabilities		
Long-term debt	276	446
Deferred income taxes and other liabilities	921	855
Total noncurrent liabilities	1,197	1,301
Total liabilities	5,155	4,665
Shareholders' equity		
Common stock at stated value:		
Class A convertible—90 and 90 shares outstanding	–	–
Class B—378 and 394 shares outstanding	3	3
Capital in excess of stated value	3,944	3,441
Accumulated other comprehensive income	95	215
Retained earnings	5,801	6,095
Total shareholders' equity	9,843	9,754
Total liabilities and shareholders' equity	$14,998	$14,419

Exhibit 17-5
Nike, Inc.
Balance Sheet (in millions)

Exhibit 17-6

Nike, Inc.

Statement of Income (in millions except per share data)

	Year Ended May 31	
	2011	2010
Revenues	$20,862	$19,014
Cost of sales*	11,354	10,214
Gross margin	9,508	8,800
Demand creation expense	2,448	2,356
Operating overhead expense	4,245	3,970
Total selling and administrative expense	6,693	6,326
Income from operations	2,815	2,474
Interest expense, net	4	6
Other (income), net	(33)	(49)
Income before income taxes	2,844	2,517
Income taxes	711	610
Net income	$ 2,133	$ 1,907
Basic earnings per common share†	$ 4.48	$ 3.93
Diluted earnings per common share	$ 4.39	$ 3.86
Dividends declared per common share‡	$ 1.20	$ 1.06

*Also called cost of goods sold.

†Average shares outstanding for computation of basic EPS are approximately 475.5 million in 2011 and 485.5 million in 2010.

‡Publicly held companies must show earnings per share on the face of the income statement, but it is not necessary to show dividends per share.

Component Percentages

component percentages

Analysis and presentation of financial statements in percentage form to aid comparability, frequently used when companies differ in size.

common-size statements

Financial statements expressed in component percentages.

When comparing companies that differ in size, analysts often apply percentage relationships, called **component percentages**, to income statements and balance sheets (see Exhibit 17-7). We call the resulting statements **common-size statements**. For example, it is difficult to compare Nike's $11,297 million of current assets with the $1,050 million of Columbia Sportswear Company, a smaller Oregon-based designer and manufacturer of active outdoor apparel. It's much easier to compare Nike's 75% current asset percentage (shown in Exhibit 17-7) with Columbia Sportswear's $1,050 million ÷ $1,383 million = 76%.

Balance sheet percentages are usually based on total assets = 100%. Note in Exhibit 17-7 that Nike's current asset percentage decreased slightly in 2011 while the current liabilities percentage increased. Other note-worthy changes in percentages were the slight increase in property, plant, and equipment and the decrease in stockholders' equity.

Income statement amounts are expressed as percentages of sales so that, by definition, sales = 100%. Nike's gross margin rate of 46% and net income percentage of 10% both show significant profitability. However, averages for these items vary greatly by industry. Comparison with other similar firms or industry averages is necessary to interpret the rates fully. Changes between one year and the next can also reveal important information. Nike's gross margin percentage did not change between 2010 and 2011, reflecting stable profit margins.

management's discussion and analysis (MD&A)

A section of annual reports and 10-K filings that concentrates on explaining the major changes in the income statement, changes in liquidity and capital resources, and the impact of inflation from one year to the next.

Corporate annual reports to the public and 10-K filings with the SEC must contain a section called **management's discussion and analysis** (or **MD&A**). This section explains the major changes in the income statement, changes in liquidity and capital resources, and the impact of inflation. The focus is on a comparison with the prior year or years. For example, Nike's annual report had several pages of detailed discussions, including the following relating to some of the issues just discussed:

Income before income taxes increased 13% for fiscal 2011 primarily as a result of the increase in revenues and leverage on selling and administrative expense, which more than offset a decrease in gross margin percentage. For fiscal 2011, our consolidated gross margin percentage was 70 basis points [0.7 percentage points] lower than the prior year. The primary factors contributing to this decrease were . . . [1] Higher input costs across most businesses, [2] Increased transportation costs, . . . and [3] A lower mix of licensee revenue as distribution for certain markets within our Other Businesses transitioned from licensees to operating units . . . Our effective tax rate for fiscal 2011 was 80 basis points higher than the effective rate for fiscal 2010 due primarily to the change in geographic mix of earnings.

	For the Year Ended May 31				
Statement of Income		2011		2010	
Revenues	$ 20,862*	100%	$19,014	100%
Cost of sales	11,354	54	10,214	54
Gross margin	$ 9,508	46%	$ 8,800	46%
Total selling and administrative expense	$ 6,693	32%	$ 6,326	33%
Operating income	$ 2,815	14%	$ 2,474	13%
Interest income, net	4	0%	6	0%
Other (expense) income, net	(33)	−0	(49)	−0
Income before income taxes	$ 2,844	14%	$ 2,517	13%
Income taxes	711	3	610	3
Net income	$ 2,133	10%**	$ 1,907	10%
Balance sheet				
Current assets	$11,297	75%	$10,959	76%
Plant, property, and equipment, net	2,115	14	1,932	13
Other assets	1,586	11	1,528	11
Total assets	$14,998	100%	$14,419	100%
Current liabilities	$ 3,958	27%	$ 3,364	24%
Total noncurrent liabilities	1,197	10	1,301	10
Shareholders' equity	9,843	63	9,754	66
Total liabilities and shareholders' equity	$14,998	100%	$14,419	100%

*Note the use of dollar signs in columns of numbers. Frequently, companies use them at the top and bottom only and not for every subtotal.
**Percentages do not add up because of rounding errors.

Exhibit 17-7
Nike, Inc.
Common-Size Statements
(in millions, except percentages)

Uses of Ratios

Comparing component percentages across time or to those of other companies is one way of analyzing financial statements, but another way is to use ratios. To illustrate how useful ratios can be, we calculate some ratios for Nike in Exhibit 17-8.

Data for computing ratios are available from many sources. One is the 10-K report that each company files annually with the Securities and Exchange Commission (SEC). The SEC makes these available online in its EDGAR database (www.sec.gov/edgar.shtml). The SEC now requires all companies to report using XBRL (see Chapter 1, p. 16), which makes comparisons across companies easier. XBRL and other technology allow analysts to use an expanded set of information about companies, as indicated in the Business First box on p. 733.

Comparisons

Evaluations of financial ratios require comparisons. There are three main types of comparisons: (1) **time-series comparisons** with a company's own historical ratios, (2) **benchmark comparisons** with general rules of thumb, and (3) **cross-sectional comparisons** with ratios of similar companies or with industry averages or "best-practices" ratios for the same period.

First let's consider time-series comparisons. Because analysts rely heavily on the trend of a company's ratios, annual reports typically contain a table of comparative statistics for 5 or 10 years. For example, consider the trends in three of Nike's profitability ratios:

	2007	2008	2009	2010	2011
Return on sales	9.1%	10.1%	7.8%	10.0%	10.2%
Return on stockholders' equity	22.4%	25.4%	18.0%	20.7%	21.8%
Earnings per share	$2.96	$3.80	$3.07	$3.93	$4.48

Objective 5

Explain and use a variety of popular financial ratios.

time-series comparisons
Comparison of a company's financial ratios with its own historical ratios.

benchmark comparisons
Comparison of a company's financial ratios with general rules of thumb.

cross-sectional comparisons
Comparisons of a company's financial ratios with ratios of similar companies, with industry averages, or "best-practices" ratios for the same period.

Typical Name of Ratio	Numerator	Denominator	Appropriate Nike Numbers Applied to May 31 of Year	
			2011	2010
Short-term ratios				
Current ratio	Current assets	Current liabilities	$11,297 \div 3,958 = 2.9$	$10,959 \div 3,364 = 3.3$
Average collection period in days	Average accounts receivable† × 365	Sales on account	$[1/2(3,138 + 2,650) \times 365] \div 20,862 = 51$ days*	$[1/2(2,650 + 2,884) \times 365] \div 19,014 = 53$ days
Debt-to-equity ratio				
Total debt to equity	Total liabilities	Stockholders' equity	$5,155 \div 9,843 = 52.4\%$	$4,665 \div 9,754 = 47.8\%$
Profitability ratios				
Gross profit rate or percentage	Gross profit or gross margin	Sales	$9,508 \div 20,862 = 45.6\%$	$8,800 \div 19,014 = 46.3\%$
Return on sales	Net income	Sales	$2,133 \div 20,862 = 10.2\%$	$1,907 \div 19,014 = 10.0\%$
Return on stockholders' equity	Net income	Average stockholders' equity†	$2,133 \div 1/2(9,843 + 9,754) = 21.8\%$	$1,907 \div 1/2(9,754 + 8,693) = 20.7\%$
Basic earnings per share	Net income less dividends on preferred stock, if any	Average common shares outstanding	$2,133 \div 475.5 = \$4.48^{**}$	$1,907 \div 485.5 = \$3.93$
Price earnings	Market price per share of common stock‡	Earnings per share	$84 \div 4.48 = 18.8$	$72 \div 3.93 = 18.3$
Dividend ratios				
Dividend yield	Dividends per common share‡	Market price per common share	$1.20 \div 84 = 1.4\%$	$1.06 \div 72 = 1.5\%$
Dividend payout	Dividends per common share	Earnings per share	$1.20 \div 4.48 = 26.8\%$	$1.06 \div 3.93 = 27.0\%$

*This may be easier to see as follows:

Average receivables = 1/2 (3,138 + 2,650) = 2,894

Average receivables as a percentage of annual sales = 2,894 ÷ 20,862 = 13.87%

Average collection period = 13.87% × 365 days = 51 days

†Relevant 2009 amounts: accounts receivable, $2,884 million; stockholders' equity, $8,693 million

**Nike reported this as $4.48, which differs from 2,133 ÷ 475.5 = 4.48 because of rounding errors in the 2,133 and 475.5.

‡Market price: May 31, 2011, $84; May 31, 2010, $72.

Exhibit 17-8

Some Typical Financial Ratios

Business First

Technology Changes Financial Statement Analysis

The key to financial analysis is the availability of data. Companies can accumulate, categorize, and summarize basic financial data in many ways. In the past, investors and analysts had access only to the summary data in quarterly and annual financial statements. Analysts then used the methods discussed in this chapter, along with many others, to try to predict the future financial performance of a company. Enter technology. By making more data available on a more timely basis and making mathematical analysis easier and faster, technology is enabling investors and analysts to obtain and analyze more information about a company than ever before.

Many companies, for example Microsoft, are making interactive annual reports available online. Instead of paging through a long document to find what they need, users can find any section of the annual report with a single click of the mouse. The SEC also has a table of contents on their 10-K filings to allow quick access to any particular section of a company's 10-K. It also has a quick-reference interactive data section for annual and quarterly financial filings.

The SEC's ability to provide its interactive data section came about when it required eXtensible Business Reporting Language (XBRL) for company filings. Under the leadership of the AICPA, a group of technology firms and consultants formed XBRL International to create a common XML-based computer language for the reporting of business information. Today, a consortium of more than 650 companies, organizations, and government agencies supports XBRL International's efforts. According to Sunir Kapoor, CEO of UBmatrix, "XBRL is the common language of financial information exchange, much as English has become the worldwide language of business." The SEC requires firms to report using XBRL, and it is also used by the FDIC and the central banks of the European Union, among others. According to former SEC Chairman Christopher Cox, XBRL "represent[s] a quantum leap over existing disclosure technologies."

XBRL provides "an XML-based framework that the global business information supply chain will use to create, exchange, and analyze financial reporting information including, but not limited to, regulatory filings such as annual and quarterly financial statements, general ledger information, and audit schedules." Instead of treating financial information as a block of text—as in a standard Internet page or a printed document—XBRL "provides an identifying tag for each individual item of data. This tag is computer readable. For example, company net profit has its own unique tag." XBRL is the language of the future for exchanging financial information. It has the potential to make vast sums of data available in an easily accessible format.

Sources: XBRL International Web site (www.xbrl.org); and C. Babcock, "SEC Requires XBRL Financial Reporting By Large Public Firms," *Information Week*, May 14, 2008 (www.informationweek.com/news/management/compliance/showArticle.jhtml?articleID=207800147).

Except for 2009, which reflects the effects of the recession of 2008–2009, each year return on sales has been near 10% and return on stockholders' equity has exceeded 20%. In addition, earnings per share increased every year, except 2009.

The second type of comparison uses benchmarks. One type of benchmark is a general consensus on appropriate levels for ratios, or rules of thumb. For instance, the most quoted rule-of-thumb is a current ratio of 2 to 1. Others are described in *Key Business Ratios* by Dun & Bradstreet (D&B), a financial services firm. For example,

Total debt to equity. In general, total liabilities shouldn't exceed net worth [equity] (100%) since in such cases creditors have more at stake than owners.

Return on equity. Generally, a relationship of at least 10% is regarded as a desirable objective.

Many analysts prefer to use the third type of comparison, examining ratios of similar companies, industry averages, or "best-practices" ratios, often identified by industry associations or other professional organizations. Analysts often look to D&B, which informs its subscribers of the credit-worthiness of thousands of individual companies. D&B regularly compiles and publishes statistics on many ratios of the companies it monitors in a book called *Industry Norms and Key Business Ratios*. Using these data, we can compare each ratio in Exhibit 17-8 with industry statistics. For example, some of the D&B ratios for 60 Sporting and Recreational Goods companies showed the following:

	Current Ratio (times)	Collection Period (days)	Total Debt to Equity (percent)	Return on Sales (percent)	Return on Stockholders' Equity (percent)
84 companies					
Upper quartile*	3.6	15	36.2	3.5	23.5
Median	2.4	26	63.0	2.0	8.9
Lower quartile	1.6	44	155.5	0.5	2.7
Nike†	2.9	51	52.4	10.2	21.8

*The individual ratios are ranked from best to worst. The figure ranked in the middle of the distribution is the median. The figure ranked halfway between the median and the highest ranked figure is the upper quartile. Similarly, the figure ranked halfway between the median and the worst is the lower quartile.

†Ratios are from Exhibit 17-8 for 2011. Please consult that exhibit for an explanation of the components of each ratio.

Our illustration focuses on one company and 1 or 2 years. This is sufficient as a start, but analysts also examine other firms in the industry, industry averages, and a series of years to get a better perspective. Above all, recognize that a ratio by itself is of limited use. There must be a standard for comparison—a history, a similar entity, an industry average, a benchmark, or a budget.

Discussion of Specific Ratios

Consider again the ratios in Exhibit 17-8. First is the current ratio. Other things being equal, the higher the current ratio, the more assurance short-term creditors have about being paid in full and on time. Nike's current ratio of 2.9 is down from the 3.3 in 2010, but it is still well into the top half in the industry.

Nike's average collection period of 51 days places it in the lower quartile of sporting and recreational goods firms. A long collection period might indicate acceptance of poor credit risks or lax collection efforts.

The third column of the D&B tabulation shows the total debt-to-equity ratio. Both creditors and shareholders watch this ratio to judge the risk of insolvency and stability of profits. Typically, companies with heavy debt in relationship to ownership capital are in greater danger of suffering net losses or even bankruptcy when business conditions sour. Why? Because revenues and many expenses decline during economic downturns, but interest expenses and maturity dates do not change. Nike's ratio of 52.4% is below the industry median of 63.0%. It reflects low levels of risk or uncertainty concerning the company's ability to pay its debts on time.

Investors find profitability ratios especially helpful. Examine the gross profit rate and the return on sales. Nike's gross profit rate decreased from 46.3% in 2010 to 45.6% in 2011, yet its return on sales increased from 10.0% to 10.2%. These are both measures of operating success. D&B does not report gross profit rates, but Nike's return on sales is high enough to put the firm high in the top quartile of sporting and athletic goods companies.

More important to shareholders is the rate of return on their invested capital, a measure of overall accomplishment. Nike's 2011 rate of 21.8% is higher than the 20.7% of 2010. It is near the top quartile for the industry.

The final four ratios in Exhibit 17-8 are based on earnings and dividends. The first, earnings per share of common stock (EPS), is perhaps the most widely used of all ratios. Companies must present basic EPS on the face of the income statement. Most companies calculate it as in Exhibit 17-8: net income less dividends on preferred stock divided by average common shares outstanding. Companies holding securities that can be exchanged for or converted to common shares also report a diluted EPS; its calculations are more complex and are beyond the scope of this discussion. Nike's 2011 EPS is $4.48, up 14% over 2010.

Exhibit 17-8 shows three other ratios, price earnings (P/E), dividend yield, and dividend payout. These ratios are especially useful to investors. They use the P/E ratio to help determine if the market price of a share of stock is reasonable based on the company's earnings. Nike's 2011 P/E ratio of 18.8 is higher than its 2010 ratio of 18.3 but still below Nike's historical average. Fast growing companies tend to have high P/E ratios, and, since Nike's P/E is above average, investors apparently believe that Nike's above-average growth will continue into the future. The dividend yield gives the percentage return an investor receives in dividends on investments in a company's stock. If dividends do not change, Nike shareholders who buy the stock at the May 31, 2011, market price of $84 will receive annual dividends equal to 1.4% of their investment. Nike's payout ratio shows that for each $1 of earnings, Nike returns nearly $.27 to shareholders. This means that it retains more than 73% of its profits for reinvestment in the business.

Operating Performance Ratios

In addition to the more focused ratios just cited, investors often look at the rate of return on invested capital as an important measure of overall accomplishment:

$$\text{rate of return on invested capital} = \frac{\text{income}}{\text{invested capital}} \tag{1}$$

On the surface, this measure is straightforward, but its ingredients may differ according to the purpose it is to serve. What is invested capital, the denominator of the ratio? What income figure is appropriate? The measurement of operating performance (how profitably managers employ assets) can be separated from the influence of management's financial decisions (i.e., how they obtain and finance assets). The best measure of operating performance is pretax operating rate of return on average total assets:

$$\text{pretax operating rate of return on average total assets} = \frac{\text{operating income}}{\text{average total assets}} \tag{2}$$

For Nike, this ratio is $2,815 \div [1/2 \times (\$14,998 + \$14,419)] = 19.14\%$

We can express the right-hand side of equation (2) as the product of two important ratios:

$$\frac{\text{operating income}}{\text{average total assets}} = \frac{\text{operating income}}{\text{sales}} \times \frac{\text{sales}}{\text{average total assets}} \tag{3}$$

The right-hand terms in equation (3) are the operating return on sales and total asset turnover, respectively. Therefore, we can show Nike's operating performance as

$$\frac{\text{pretax operating rate}}{\text{of return on average total assets}} = \frac{\text{operating return}}{\text{on sales}} \times \frac{\text{total asset}}{\text{turnover}} \tag{4}$$

$$= (\$2,815 \div \$20,862) \times [\$20,862 \div (1/2)$$

$$\times (\$14,998 + \$14,419)]$$

$$= 13.493\% \times 1.4184 = 19.14\%$$

By studying equation (4), you will see that there are two basic factors in profit making: operating margin percentages and asset turnover. An improvement in either will, by itself, increase the rate of return on total assets.

Efficient Markets and Investor Decisions

How investors use accounting information, such as ratios, depends on whether they believe stock markets are efficient. An **efficient capital market** is one in which market prices fully reflect all information available to the public. Therefore, searching for underpriced securities in such a market would be fruitless unless an investor has information that is not generally available. If real-world markets are indeed efficient, a relatively inactive portfolio approach would be an appropriate investment strategy for most investors. The hallmarks of the approach are risk control, high diversification, and low turnover of securities. The role of accounting information would mainly be to help investors identify the different degrees of risk among various stocks so they can maintain desired levels of risk and diversification.

Objective 6

Identify the major implications that efficient stock markets have for accounting.

efficient capital market
A market in which market prices fully reflect all information available to the public.

Making Managerial Decisions

Which is better, an investment in Costco, an operator of membership warehouse stores, or one in Nordstrom, operator of upscale clothing stores? How might one use financial ratios to better understand the different ways that Costco and Nordstrom create value for investors? Would you expect Costco and Nordstrom to have different pretax operating rate of return on average total assets? Would you expect them to have different operating return on sales and total asset turnover?

Answers

Investors have many different alternative investments. If either Costco or Nordstrom offered lower returns to investors, they would not find many people willing to invest. (This assumes that the riskiness of investing in the two companies is about the same.) However, even if the two companies seek the same total return on assets, they pursue this return quite differently. For example, in fiscal 2011 Costco had a high total asset turnover and a low operating return on sales, while Nordstrom had the opposite (dollar amounts are in millions):

Costco: Operating return on sales = $2,439 \div $87,048 = 2.80\%$

Total asset turnover = $87,048 \div [1/2 \times ($26,761 + $23,815)]$
$$= 3.44$$

Return on assets = $2.80\% \times 3.44 = 9.6\%$

Nordstrom: Operating return on sales = $1,118 \div $9,310$
$$= 12.0\%$$

Total asset turnover = $9,310 \div [1/2 \times ($7,462 + $6,579)] = 1.33$
Return on assets = $12.0\% \times 1.33 = 16.0\%$

In 2011, Nordstrom had a higher return on assets than Costco. Nordstrom had a lower total asset turnover, but it more than made up for it with a much higher operating return on sales.

Research has shown that financial ratios and other data, such as reported earnings, help predict such economic phenomena as financial failure or earnings growth. To make these predictions, analysts use many ratios simultaneously rather than one at a time. Above all, the research shows that accounting reports are only one source of information and that in the aggregate the market is not fooled by companies that choose the least-conservative accounting policies. In sum, the market as a whole generally sees through any attempts by companies to gain favor through the choice of accounting policies that tend to boost immediate income. Thus, there is evidence that the stock markets may indeed be reasonably "efficient," at least in their reflection of most accounting data. This does not mean that there are no irrational swings in stock prices, only that exploiting accounting data for an advantage in the market is difficult.

Suppose you are the CEO of a company with reported earnings of $4 per share and a stock price of $40. You are contemplating changing your method of depreciation for investor–reporting purposes from accelerated to straight line. Your competitors use straight line. You think your company's stock price unjustifiably suffers in comparison with other companies in the same industry.

If you adopt straight-line depreciation, your company's reported earnings will be $5 instead of $4 per share. Would the stock price rise accordingly from $40 to $50? No, the research on these issues indicates that the stock price would remain at $40 (all other things equal). Because the information on the depreciation method is publicly available, investors have already adjusted for the difference between your company and competitors.

It is important to recognize that the market is efficient only with respect to information that is already publicly available. Therefore, accounting issues that deal with the disclosure of new information are more important than those that simply change the format for reporting already available data.

Be aware also that accounting statements are not the only source of financial information about companies. Some alternative sources are the following: company press releases (e.g., capital expenditure announcements), trade association publications (e.g., reports with industry statistics), brokerage house analyses (e.g., company or industry studies), and government economic reports (e.g., gross national product and unemployment figures). For accounting reports to be useful, they must have some advantage over alternative sources in disclosing new information. Financial statement information may be more directly related to the item of interest, and it may be more reliable, less costly, or more timely than information from alternative sources.

In the end, investors have two basic choices: (1) trust their investment decisions to experts, such as investment advisers or mutual fund portfolio managers, or (2) carefully analyze information from a variety of sources, including companies' financial statements, and make their own investment decisions. Those who try the latter will soon learn that they cannot undertake intelligent analysis without understanding how to analyze financial statements, including appreciation of the assumptions and limitations of the statements.

Summary Problem for Your Review

PROBLEM

Examine Exhibits 17-5 and 17-6, pages 729 and 730. Assume some new data in place of certain old data for the May 31, 2011, balance sheet (in millions):

	Old Data	New Data
Accounts receivable	$ 3,138	$ 3,638
Total current assets	11,297	11,797
Capital in excess of stated value	3,944	4,144
Total stockholders' equity	9,843	10,043

Compute the following ratios applicable to May 31, 2011, or to the fiscal year 2011, as appropriate: current ratio, average collection period, and return on stockholders' equity. Compare this new set of ratios with the old set of ratios. Are the new ratios more desirable? Explain.

SOLUTION

All the ratios would be affected.

$$\text{current ratio} = \frac{\text{current assets}}{\text{current liabilities}}$$

$$= \$11,797 \div \$3,958 = 3.0 \text{ instead of } 2.9$$

$$\text{average collection period} = \frac{\text{average accounts receivable} \times 365}{\text{sales on account}}$$

$$= [1/2 \times (\$3,638 + \$2,650) \times 365] \div \$20,862$$

$$= 55 \text{ days instead of } 51 \text{ days}$$

$$\text{return on stockholders' equity} = \frac{\text{net income}}{\text{average stockholders' equity}}$$

$$= \$2,133 \div [1/2 \times (10,043 + 9,754)]$$

$$= 21.5\% \text{ instead of } 21.8\%$$

The new set of ratios has good news and bad news. The good news is that the company appears to be slightly more liquid (a current ratio of 3.0 instead of 2.9). The bad news is that the average collection period (55 days compared with 51) and the rate of return on stockholders' equity (21.5% compared with 21.8%) are less attractive.

Highlights to Remember

1. **Contrast accounting for investments using the equity method and the market-value method.** Companies often invest in the equity securities of another company. If they have neither control nor influence over the other company, which generally means owning less than 20% of the company, they use the market-value method to account for the investment. Under the market-value method, the balance sheet shows the current market value of the securities. If a company expects to sell the securities shortly, it calls them trading securities, and changes in market value are part of income. If there is no intention to sell the securities in the near future, they are available-for-sale securities, and the company places changes in market value in a separate account in stockholders' equity called other comprehensive income. If a company has influence but not control over another company, which generally means owning between 20% and 50% of the company, it uses the equity method to account for the investment. Under the equity method the balance sheet shows the investment at the acquisition cost adjusted for dividends received and the investor's share of earnings or losses of the investee after the date of investment. The income statement includes a pro rata share of the investee's net income.

2. **Explain the basic ideas and methods used to prepare consolidated financial statements.** When a parent company owns more than 50% of another company, the owned company is a subsidiary and the companies must prepare consolidated financial statements. Each company continues to keep its own books, but the consolidated statements prepared for reporting to the public combine their assets and liabilities and eliminate double-counting. If the parent owns less than 100% of a subsidiary, the statements will show a noncontrolling interest.

3. **Describe how goodwill arises and how to account for it.** If a parent pays more than the fair-market value of the net assets when acquiring a subsidiary, it must record the difference as goodwill. Goodwill is an intangible asset that remains on the company's books until its value is impaired.

4. **Use financial statement analysis to evaluate an organization's performance.** Decision makers use financial statement analysis to evaluate past performance and predict future performance. Budgets or pro forma statement are especially useful. To compare companies that differ in size, analysts use component percentages. Much analysis is contained in the management's discussion and analysis (MD&A) section of annual reports and 10-K filings.

5. **Explain and use a variety of popular financial ratios.** Financial ratios aid the intelligent analysis of financial statements. Analysts prepare a variety of ratios and compare them with the company's own historical ratios, with general rules of thumb and with ratios of other companies or industry averages. They use short-term ratios, debt-to-equity ratios, profitability ratios, and dividend ratios. An especially important ratio for assessing operating performance is the rate of return on invested capital.

6. **Identify the major implications that efficient stock markets have for accounting.** Financial statements are only one among many sources of information used by investors. Evidence indicates that stock prices fully reflect most publicly available information, including accounting numbers. The format of the information apparently does not fool investors. Therefore, accounting regulators should focus on disclosure issues more than format.

Accounting Vocabulary

For various financial ratios, see Exhibit 17-8, page 732. Also become familiar with the following terms.

available-for-sale securities, p. 717	cross-sectional comparisons, p. 731	noncontrolling interests, p. 721
benchmark comparisons, p. 731	efficient capital market, p. 735	parent company, p. 719
common-size statements, p. 730	equity method, p. 718	subsidiary, p. 719
component percentages, p. 730	management's discussion and analysis (MD&A), p. 730	time-series comparisons, p. 731
consolidated financial statements, p. 716	market-value method, p. 717	trading securities, p. 717

MyAccountingLab # Fundamental Assignment Material

Special Note: Problems relating to Part One of the chapter are presented first in each subgrouping of the assignment material.

GENERAL EXERCISES AND PROBLEMS

17-A1 Market-Value or Equity Method

Star Electronics, Inc., acquired 25% of the voting stock of Mobile Media for $75 million cash. In year 1, Mobile Media had a net income of $48 million and paid a cash dividend of $28 million. The investment had a market value of $81 million at the end of the year.

1. Using the equity method, show the effects of the three transactions—acquisition and Mobile Media's net income and cash dividend—on the accounts of Star Electronics. Use the balance-sheet-equation format.

2. Assume that Star Electronics could use the market-value method for this investment and that it classified the investment as an available-for-sale security. Show the effects of the three transactions on the accounts of Star Electronics. Use the balance-sheet-equation format.

17-A2 Consolidated Financial Statements

Suppose Poseidon Publishing Company acquired all the common shares of Neptune Book Company for $80 million cash at the start of the year. Immediately before the business combination, each company had the following condensed balance sheet accounts (in millions):

	Poseidon	Neptune
Cash and other assets	$350	$100
Accounts payable, etc.	$110	$ 20
Stockholders' equity	240	80
Total equities	$350	$100

1. Prepare a tabulation of the consolidated balance sheet accounts immediately after the acquisition. Use the balance-sheet-equation format.
2. Suppose Poseidon and Neptune have the following results for the year:

	Poseidon	Neptune
Sales	$330	$110
Expenses	245	90

Prepare income statements for the year for Poseidon, Neptune, and the consolidated entity. Assume that neither Poseidon nor Neptune sells items to the other.

3. Present the effects of the operations for the year on Poseidon's accounts and on Neptune's accounts, using the balance sheet equation. Also tabulate the consolidated balance sheet accounts at the end of the year. Assume that liabilities are unchanged.
4. Suppose Neptune paid a cash dividend of $10 million. What accounts in requirement 3 would this affect and by how much?

17-A3 Noncontrolling Interests

This modifies and extends the preceding problem. However, this problem is self-contained because all the facts are reproduced here. Poseidon Publishing Company acquired 80% of the common shares of Neptune Book Company for $64 million cash at the start of the year. Immediately before the business combination each company had the following condensed balance sheet accounts (in millions):

	Poseidon	Neptune
Cash and other assets	$350	$100
Accounts payable, etc.	$110	$ 20
Stockholders' equity	240	80
Total equities	$350	$100

1. Prepare a tabulation of the consolidated balance sheet accounts immediately after the acquisition. Use the balance sheet equation format.
2. Suppose Poseidon and Neptune have the following results for the year:

	Poseidon	Neptune
Sales	$330	$110
Expenses	245	90

Prepare income statements for the year for Poseidon, Neptune, and the consolidated entity.

3. Using the balance-sheet-equation format, present the effects of the operations for the year on Poseidon's accounts and Neptune's accounts. Also tabulate consolidated balance sheet accounts at the end of the year. Assume that liabilities are unchanged.
4. Suppose Neptune paid a cash dividend of $10 million. What accounts in number 3 would be affected and by how much?

17-A4 Goodwill and Consolidation

This modifies and extends Problem 17-A2. However, this problem is self-contained because all the facts are reproduced. Poseidon Publishing Company acquired all the common shares of Neptune Book Company for $105 million cash at the start of the year. Immediately before the business combination, each company had the following condensed balance sheet accounts (in millions):

	Poseidon	Neptune
Cash and other assets	$350	$100
Accounts payable, etc.	$110	$ 20
Stockholders' equity	240	80
Total equities	$350	$100

Assume that the fair values of Neptune's individual assets and liabilities were equal to their book values.

1. Prepare a tabulation of the consolidated balance sheet accounts immediately after the acquisition. Use the balance-sheet-equation format.
2. Suppose the book values of Neptune's individual assets are equal to their fair-market values except for equipment. The net book value of equipment is $15 million and its fair-market value is $27 million. The equipment has a remaining useful life of 4 years. Straight-line depreciation is used.
   a. Describe how the consolidated balance sheet accounts immediately after the acquisition would differ from those in number 1. Be specific as to accounts and amounts.
   b. By how much will consolidated income differ in comparison with the consolidated income that would be reported when the entire excess of purchase cost over book value of net assets was assigned to goodwill? Assume no impairment of goodwill.

17-A5 Rate-of-Return Computations

1. Wellington Woolens Company reported a 6% operating margin on sales, a 12% pretax operating return on total assets, and $500 million of average total assets. Compute the (a) operating income, (b) total sales, and (c) total asset turnover.
2. Osaka Electronics Corporation reported ¥200 million of sales, ¥20 million of operating income, and a total asset turnover of four times. (¥ is Japanese yen.) Compute the (a) total assets, (b) operating return on sales, and (c) pretax operating return on total assets.

UNDERSTANDING PUBLISHED FINANCIAL REPORTS

17-B1 Equity and Market-Value Methods

Suppose Google acquired one-third of the common shares of Chang Web Design for $50 million cash. In year 1, Chang had a net income of $30 million and paid cash dividends of $9 million. At the end of the year, the market value of the investment had fallen to $39 million. Prepare a tabulation that compares the equity method and the market-value method of accounting for Google's investment in Chang. Show the effects on the balance sheet equation under each method. (Assume that under the market-value method this investment is a trading security.) What is the year-end balance in the Investment in Chang account under the equity method? Under the market-value method? Which method should Google use for reporting its investment in Chang?

17-B2 Consolidated Financial Statements

Consider the actual purchase several years ago of boat maker Bayliner by Brunswick Corporation, modified slightly to simplify the numbers. The purchase price was $400 million for a 100% interest. Assume that the book value and the fair-market value of Bayliner's net assets were $400 million. The balance sheet accounts immediately after the transaction were approximately (in millions):

	Brunswick	Bayliner
Investment in Bayliner	$ 400	$ —
Cash and other assets	1,000	600
Total assets	$1,400	$600
Liabilities	$ 800	$200
Stockholders' equity	600	400
Total equities	$1,400	$600

1. Using the balance-sheet-equation format, prepare a tabulation of the consolidated balance sheet accounts immediately after the acquisition.
2. Suppose Bayliner had sales of $500 million and expenses of $350 million for the year, and Brunswick had sales of $1,800 million and expenses of $1,400 million. Prepare income statements for Brunswick, for Bayliner, and for the consolidated company. Assume that neither Brunswick nor Bayliner sold items to the other.
3. Using the balance sheet equation, present the effects of the operations for the year on the accounts of Bayliner and Brunswick. Also tabulate the consolidated balance sheet accounts at the end of the year. Assume that liabilities are unchanged.
4. Suppose Bayliner paid a cash dividend of $12 million. What accounts in number 3 would be affected and by how much?

17-B3 Investment in Equity Securities: Equity Method and Market-Value Method

Berkshire Hathaway, the Omaha company run by Warren Buffett, owns 13.0% of the stock of American Express Company. In 2011, American Express reported a net income of $4,935 million and declared cash dividends on common stock of $855 million. For parts 1 and 2 assume Berkshire Hathaway accounted for its investment in American Express using the equity method (even though this is not allowed for investments of less than 20%).

1. Compute the amount of income Berkshire Hathaway would recognize in 2011 from its investment in American Express.
2. Suppose Berkshire Hathaway had a balance of $6,200 million in its "Investment in American Express" account at the beginning of 2011. Compute the balance in the account at the end of 2011.
3. Because its investment in American Express is less than 20%, Berkshire Hathaway actually used the market-value method to account for its investment in American Express and classified this investment as an available-for-sale security. The market value of Berkshire Hathaway's investment in American Express securities was $6,404 million at the end of 2010 and $7,151 million at the end of 2011.
   a. Compute the amount of income recognized by Berkshire Hathaway in 2011 from its investment in American Express.
   b. Under the market-value method, Berkshire Hathaway had a balance of $6,404 million in its Investment in American Express account at the beginning of 2011. Compute the balance in the account at the end of 2011.
   c. Explain how Berkshire Hathaway would account for the $747 million increase in market value.
4. Indicate briefly how the following three classes of investments should be accounted for: (a) greater than 50% interest, (b) 20% through 50% interest, and (c) less than 20% interest.

17-B4 Income Ratios and Asset Turnover

Burberry plc, the British luxury fashion house that manufactures clothing, fragrance, and fashion accessories, had net income of £206.3 million on sales of £1,501.3 million in 2011. (£ is the British currency, the pound.) The company's operating statistics for 2011 included the following:

Operating return on sales	13.741%
Operating return on average total assets	16.610%
Total asset turnover	1.209
Return on shareholders' equity	30.855%

1. Compute the following 2011 amounts for Burberry:
   a. Operating income
   b. Average total assets
   c. Average shareholders' equity
2. Which return is more important to shareholders, return on sales or return on shareholders' equity? Why?

17-B5 Financial Ratios

Gap, Inc. is a leading global specialty apparel company with 3,263 Company-operated and franchise store locations in 2012. The company was established in 1969 and has several well-known brand names such as Gap, Banana Republic, and Old Navy. Excerpts from the company's annual report for the fiscal year ended January 28, 2012, are in Exhibit 17-9. Gap paid cash dividends of $ .45 per common share in fiscal 2012, and an average of 529 million shares were outstanding during the year.

Assume that Gap has no stock options or convertible securities. The company's market price on January 28, 2012, was $18.93 per share. Compute the following financial ratios for fiscal 2012:

1. Current ratio
2. Total debt to equity
3. Gross profit rate
4. Return on sales
5. Return on stockholders' equity
6. Earnings per share
7. Price earnings
8. Dividend yield
9. Dividend payout

Income statement for the year ended January 28, 2012

Net sales	$14,549
Cost of sales	9,275
Gross profit	$ 5,274
Operating expenses	3,836
Operating income	1,438
Interest expenses, net	69
Income before income taxes	$ 1,369
Income taxes	536
Net income	$ 833

Balance sheet	**January 28, 2012**	**January 29, 2011**
Assets		
Cash and cash equivalents	$ 1,885	$1,561
Inventories	1,615	1,620
Other current assets (summarized)	809	745
Total current assets	$ 4,309	$3,926
Property and equipment (net)	2,523	2,563
Other assets	590	576
Total assets	$ 7,422	$7,065
Liabilities and stockholders' equity		
Current liabilities (summarized)	$ 2,128	$2,095
Long-term liabilities (summarized)	2,539	890
Total liabilities	$ 4,667	$2,985
Stockholders' equity (summarized)	2,755	4,080
Total liabilities and stockholders' equity	$ 7,422	$7,065

Exhibit 17-9

Gap, Inc.

Income Statement and Balance Sheet (in millions)

Additional Assignment Material

QUESTIONS

17-1 Distinguish between trading securities and available-for-sale securities.

17-2 "An increase in the market value of available-for-sale securities is added to other comprehensive income, which in turn is added to income after taxes to get net income." Do you agree? Explain.

17-3 What is the equity method?

17-4 Contrast the market-value method and the equity method.

17-5 "The equity method is usually used for long-term investments." Do you think this is appropriate? Explain.

17-6 What criterion is used to determine whether a parent–subsidiary relationship exists?

17-7 Why have subsidiaries? Why not have the corporation take the form of a single legal entity?

17-8 "A consolidated financial statement simply adds together the separate accounts of a parent company and its subsidiaries." Do you agree? Explain.

17-9 "Consolidated income statements show more income than parent-company-only statements if the subsidiary has a positive net income." Do you agree? Explain.

17-10 What is a noncontrolling interest?

17-11 "Goodwill is the excess of purchase price over the book values of the individual assets acquired." Do you agree? Explain.

17-12 "It is better to recognize goodwill than to write up assets to their fair-market values." Do you agree? Why?

17-13 When will goodwill on a balance sheet be reduced?

17-14 "Pro forma statements are the formal financial statements that companies file with the Securities and Exchange Commission in the United States." Do you agree? Explain.

17-15 Why is it useful to analyze income statements and balance sheets by component percentages?

17-16 What does MD&A mean? Why might an investor want to read the MD&A section of an annual report or 10-K?

17-17 Name the three types of comparisons made with ratios.

17-18 Name two short-term ratios and five profitability ratios.

17-19 What two ratios are multiplied together to give the pretax operating rate of return on average total assets?

17-20 "Ratios are mechanical and incomplete." Explain.

17-21 "An efficient capital market is one where securities are traded through stockbrokers." Do you agree? Explain.

17-22 Give three sources of information for investors besides accounting information.

17-23 Evaluate the following quotation from *Forbes*: "If IBM had been forced to expense [the software development cost of] $785 million, its earnings would have been cut by 72 cents a share. With IBM selling at 14 times earnings, expensing the costs might have knocked over $10 off IBM's share price."

17-24 Suppose the president of your company wanted to switch depreciation methods to increase reported net income: "Our stock price is 10% below what I think it should be; changing depreciation method will increase income by 10%, thus getting our share price up to its proper level." How would you respond?

CRITICAL THINKING EXERCISES

17-25 Market-Value Method, Equity Method, and Total Assets

Suppose Pixar plans to buy about 20% of the common shares of a small animation company that recently went public. The management of Pixar believes that patents developed by the software company will make the company very valuable in a year or two. Near-term profits may not be high, but large increases in the share price are likely. No dividends are expected. How would the choice of accounting method, the market-value method or the equity method, affect Pixar's total assets reported on its balance sheet in the next couple years if its expectations about the software firm come true? How would Pixar achieve its preferred accounting method? Explain.

17-26 Depreciation in Consolidated Financial Statements

Suppose Company P buys 100% of the common stock of Company S for more than the book value of S. After 1 year, the consolidated entity prepares financial statements. Two expense items appear on the consolidated income statement that are not on the individual statements of P and S:

1. Depreciation on equipment in excess of that in the individual statements
2. Write-off of goodwill

Explain why these two accounts exist. That is, what was there about the acquisition that generated the need for these two accounts?

17-27 Just-in-Time (JIT) Inventory and Current Ratio
Many companies have adopted JIT inventory methods to reduce the size of their inventories. What would you expect to happen to the current ratios of such companies? Would you interpret the current ratio differently for JIT companies compared to other companies? Explain.

17-28 Market Efficiency
Suppose you are treasurer for your church or other nonprofit organization. You are responsible for investing the organization's small endowment. If you believe that capital markets are efficient, what does that imply about how you will invest the endowment funds?

GENERAL EXERCISES AND PROBLEMS

17-29 Equity Method
Kappa Company acquired 20% of the voting stock of Omega Company for $40 million cash. In year 1, Omega had a net income of $20 million and paid cash dividends of $10 million. At the end of the year, the total market value of Omega Company was $240 million. Prepare a tabulation that compares the equity method and the market-value method of accounting for Kappa's investment in Omega. Show the effects on the balance sheet equation under each method. What is the year-end balance in the Investment in Omega account under the equity method? Under the market-value method? What difference in accounting would there be if the investment were a trading security instead of an available-for-sale security?

17-30 Consolidated Financial Statements
Ace Mining Company (the parent) acquired 100% of the common stock of Alberta Development (the subsidiary) for $300,000 on January 2, 20X1. Their financial statements follow:

	Ace Mining (Parent)	Alberta Development (Subsidiary)
Balance sheets, December 31, 20X0		
Assets	$1,000,000	$ 550,000
Liabilities to creditors	$ 400,000	$ 250,000
Stockholders' equity	600,000	300,000
Total liabilities and stockholders' equity	$1,000,000	$ 550,000
Income statement for 20X1		
Revenue and "other income"	$5,500,000	$1,100,000
Expenses	5,050,000	900,000
Net income	$ 450,000	$ 200,000

1. What would be Ace Mining's net income for 20X1 if it had not purchased the Alberta Development stock?
2. After acquiring the Alberta Development stock, Ace Mining prepared its income statement by showing its claim to Alberta's income as part of "other income." Prepare a consolidated income statement for 20X1 and a consolidated balance sheet as of December 31, 20X1. Use the balance-sheet-equation format for the latter.
3. Suppose Ace Mining Company bought only 60% of Alberta Development Company for $180,000. Therefore, Ace Mining's revenue and other income for 20X1 is $5,420,000, not $5,500,000. Prepare a consolidated income statement and a consolidated balance sheet. Use the balance-sheet-equation format for the latter.

17-31 Determination of Goodwill
Refer to the preceding problem, number 2. Suppose the investment in Alberta Development was $350,000 instead of the $300,000 as stated. The fair-market values of Alberta' assets and liabilities were equal to their book values. Would the consolidated income differ? How? Be as specific as possible. Would the consolidated balance sheet differ? How? Be as specific as possible.

17-32 Purchased Goodwill

Consider the following balance sheets (in millions):

	Cloud Software Company	Tron Gaming
Cash	$ 850	$ 80
Inventories	350	70
Plant assets, net	390	60
Total assets	$1,590	$210
Common stock and paid-in capital	$ 620	$120
Retained income	970	90
Total liabilities and stockholders' equity	$1,590	$210

Cloud Software paid $300 million to Tron stockholders for all their stock. The fair value of the plant assets of Tron is $150 million. The fair value of cash and inventories is equal to their carrying amounts. Cloud and Tron still keep separate books.

1. Prepare a tabulation showing the balance sheets of Cloud, of Tron, Intercompany Eliminations, and Consolidated Balances immediately after the acquisition.
2. Suppose only $100 million rather than $150 million of the total purchase price of $300 million could be logically assigned to the plant assets. How would the consolidated accounts be affected?
3. Refer to the facts in number 1. Suppose Cloud had paid $340 million rather than $300 million. State how your tabulation in number 1 would change.

17-33 Amortization and Depreciation

Refer to the preceding problem, number 3. Suppose a year passes, and Cloud and Tron generate individual net incomes of $105 million and $35 million, respectively. The latter is after a deduction by Tron of $12 million of straight-line depreciation. Compute the consolidated net income if (1) goodwill is not impaired and (2) half of the goodwill is written off at the end of the year. Ignore income taxes.

17-34 Allocating Total Purchase Price to Assets

Two Hollywood companies had the following balance sheet accounts as of December 31, 20X0, and net income for 20X0 (in millions):

	LA Media	Beverly Communications
Cash and receivables	$ 30	$ 22
Inventories	120	3
Plant assets, net	150	95
Total assets	$300	$120
Net income for 20X0	$ 19	$ 4
Current liabilities	$ 50	$ 20
Common stock	100	10
Retained income	150	90
Total liab. and stk. eq.	$300	$120

On January 4, 20X1, these firms merged. LA issued $180 million of its shares (at market value) in exchange for all the shares of Beverly, a motion picture division of a large company. The inventory of films acquired through the combination had been fully amortized on Beverly's books. During 20X1, Beverly received revenue of $16 million from the rental of films from its inventory. LA earned $20 million on its other operations (i.e., excluding Beverly) during 20X1. Beverly broke even on its other operations (i.e., excluding the film rental contracts) during 20X1.

1. Prepare a consolidated balance sheet for the combined company immediately after the combination. Assume that $80 million of the purchase price was assigned to the inventory of films.
2. Prepare a comparison of LA's net income between 20X0 and 20X1 where the cost of the film inventories would be amortized on a straight-line basis over 4 years. What would be the net income for 20X1 if the $80 million were assigned to goodwill rather than to the inventory of films and the value of goodwill was maintained?

17-35 Preparation of Consolidated Financial Statements

The Cypress Tool & Die Company's fiscal year ends on December 31. The company had the following items on its 20X1 income statement and balance sheet (in millions):

Net sales and other operating revenue	$900
Investments in affiliated companies	100
Common stock, 11,000,000, $1 par	11
Depreciation and amortization	20
Accounts payable	210
Cash	20
Paid-in capital in excess of par	101
Interest expense	25
Retained earnings	188
Accrued income taxes payable	20
Cost of goods sold and operating expenses, exclusive of depreciation and amortization	660
Subordinated debentures, 11% interest, due December 31, 20X8	100
Noncontrolling interest in consolidated subsidiaries' net income	20
Goodwill	95
First-mortgage bonds, 10% interest, due December 31, 20X9	80
Property, plant, and equipment, net	125
Preferred stock, 2,000,000 shares, $50 par, dividend rate is $3.5 per share	100
Short-term investments at market value	45
Income tax expense	90
Accounts receivable, net	175
Noncontrolling interest in subsidiaries	90
Inventories at average cost	340
Dividends declared and paid on preferred stock	7
Equity in earnings of affiliated companies	20

Prepare Cypress's consolidated 20X1 income statement and its consolidated balance sheet for December 31, 20X1.

17-36 Intercorporate Investments and Ethics

Bud Conn and Salvador Cruz were best friends at a small college, and they fought side-by-side in Iraq. After their military service, they went their separate ways to pursue MBA degrees, Bud to a prestigious East Coast business school and Salvador to an equally prestigious West Coast school. Nearly 20 years later, their paths crossed again.

By 2006, Salvador had become president and CEO of Quantum Electronics after 13 years with the firm. Bud had started out working for Delta Airlines, but left after 7 years to start his own firm, Conn Transport. In April 2009, Conn Transport was near bankruptcy when Bud approached his old friend for help. Salvador answered his friend's call, and Quantum Electronics bought 19% of Conn Transport. In 2012, Conn was financially stable, and Quantum was struggling. Salvador Cruz thought his job as CEO might be in jeopardy if Quantum did not report income up to expectations. Late in 2012, Salvador approached Bud with a request—quadruple Conn's dividends so that Quantum could recognize $760,000 of investment income. Quantum had listed its investment in Conn as an available-for-sale security, so changes in the market value of Conn were recorded directly in stockholders' equity. However, dividends received were recognized in Quantum's income statement. Although Conn had never paid dividends of more than 25% of net income, and it had plenty of uses for excess cash, Bud felt a deep obligation to Salvador. Thus, he agreed to a $4 million dividend on net income of $4.17 million.

1. Why does the dividend policy of Conn Transport affect the income of Quantum Electronics? Is this consistent with the intent of the accounting principles relating to the market value and equity methods for intercorporate investments? Explain.
2. Comment on the ethical issues in the arrangements between Bud Conn and Salvador Cruz.

17-37 Profitability Ratios

Valencia Company had the following income statements for 20X1 and 20X2:

	20X2	20X1
Sales	$1,600	$1,500
Cost of goods sold	950	920
Gross margin	650	580
Operating expenses	224	210
Operating income	426	370
Income taxes	166	148
Net income	$ 260	$ 222

Valencia Company generally paid dividends approximately equal to its net income. This resulted in the company's stockholders' equity totaling $1,480 at the end of both 20X0 and 20X1. However, at the end of 20X2 the company's total stockholders' equity was $2,080 primarily because of a large issuance of common stock in mid-20X2.

1. Compute Valencia Company's gross margin percentage, the return on sales, and the return on stockholders' equity for 20X1 and 20X2.
2. As a stockholder, would you have been pleased about the change in performance between 20X1 and 20X2? Explain why or why not.

17-38 Financial Ratios

The annual reports of Milano SpA, an Italian clothing chain, included the following selected data (in millions):

	20X2	20X1	20X0
Annual amounts:			
Net income	€ 90*	€ 60	€ 25
Gross margin on sales	520	380	200
Cost of goods sold	980	620	300
Operating expenses	380	295	165
Income tax expense	50	25	10
Dividends declared and paid	35	15	5
End-of-year amounts:			
Long-term assets	€240	€220	€180
Long-term debt	85	65	40
Current liabilities	65	55	35
Cash	20	5	10
Accounts receivable	85	70	40
Merchandise inventory	120	85	60
Paid-in capital	205	205	205
Retained income	110	55	10

*€ is the European euro.

During each of the three years, 10 million shares of common stock were outstanding.

Assume that all sales were on account and that the applicable market prices per share of stock were € 90 for 20X1 and € 117 for 20X2.

1. Compute each of the following for each of the last two years, 20X1 and 20X2:
   a. Rate of return on sales
   b. Rate of return on stockholders' equity
   c. Current ratio
   d. Ratio of total debt to stockholders' equity
   e. Ratio of current debt to stockholders' equity
   f. Gross profit rate

   g. Average collection period for accounts receivable
   h. P/E ratio
   i. Dividend-payout percentage
   j. Dividend yield
2. Answer yes or no to each of these questions and indicate which of the computations in number 1 support your answer:
   a. Have business operations improved?
   b. Has gross profit rate improved?
   c. Has the rate of return on sales deteriorated?
   d. Has the rate of return on owners' investment increased?
   e. Is there a decrease in the effectiveness of collection efforts?
   f. Are dividends relatively more generous?
   g. Have the risks of insolvency changed significantly?
   h. Has the market price of the stock become cheaper relative to earnings?
   i. Has there been a worsening of the company's ability to pay current debts on time?
   j. Has there been a decline in the cash return on the market value of the capital stock?
   k. Did the collectibility of the receivables improve?
3. Basing your observations on only the available data and the ratios you computed, prepare some brief comments on the company's operations and financial changes during the three years.

UNDERSTANDING PUBLISHED FINANCIAL REPORTS

17-39 Meaning of Account Descriptions

The following account descriptions were found in the 2011 annual report of E. I. du Pont de Nemours & Company (in millions):

● Net income attributable to noncontrolling interests	$ 36
● Noncontrolling interests	469
● Investments in affiliates	1,117
● Equity in earnings of affiliates	191

In your own words, explain what each type of account represents. Indicate whether the item appears on the balance sheet or the income statement.

17-40 Classification on Balance Sheet

The following accounts appeared in the 2011 financial statements of the Royal Dutch Shell plc, the global energy company headquartered in The Hague, The Netherlands. Shell reports using IFRS.

1. Noncontrolling interests
2. Share of profit of equity-accounted investments
3. Prepaid pension costs
4. Taxes payable
5. Income attributable to noncontrolling interests
6. Equity-accounted investments

   Four of these items are on the balance sheet. Indicate in detail in which section of the balance sheet each account should appear. Two items are on the income statement. Indicate in detail in which section of the income statement each account should appear.

17-41 Effect of Transactions Under the Equity Method

Chevron Corporation engages in fully integrated petroleum operations, chemicals operations, mining operations, power generation, and energy services. It accounts for its investments in affiliated companies by the equity method. The following balances were reported (in millions):

	December 31	
	2011	**2010**
Investments in equity affiliates	$22,150	$20,816

   Chevron's equity in the earnings of affiliated companies in 2011 was $7,363 million. Assume that there was no additional investment in affiliates during 2011. Chevron had pretax income in 2011 of $47,634 million.

1. How much did Chevron receive in dividends from its equity affiliates in 2011?
2. What pretax income would Chevron have reported if it did not have an interest in the affiliated companies? What proportion of Chevron's pretax income came from the affiliated companies?
3. Suppose that, instead of the number you calculated in number 1, Chevron received $3,000 million in dividends from its affiliated companies in 2011. What income would Chevron recognize from its affiliated companies in 2011?

17-42 Noncontrolling Interests

Toyota Motor Company has 507 consolidated subsidiaries both inside and outside of Japan. It owns 100% of many of these companies and percentages ranging from 50% to 99% in the others. Toyota's 2011 income statement showed the following (in billions of yen):

Income (loss) before income taxes and equity in earnings of affiliated companies	¥563
Provision for income taxes	(313)
Equity in earnings of affiliated companies	215
Net income	465
Less: Net income attributable to the noncontrolling interests	(57)
Net income attributable to Toyota Motor Corporation	¥408

Toyota's 2011 balance sheet included an amount of ¥588 billion for "Noncontrolling Interest" and ¥1,827 billion in "Affiliated Companies."

1. What net income would be attributable to stockholders in Toyota have been if Toyota had owned 100% of all its subsidiaries?
2. Suppose Toyota's average ownership percentage of these consolidated subsidiaries is 90%. What was the total 2011 net income of the subsidiaries?
3. Toyota has 56 affiliated companies with a total net income of ¥642 billion. What was Toyota's average percentage ownership of these affiliated companies? What is Toyota's maximum percentage ownership of these companies?

17-43 General Electric and GECS

The consolidated financial statements of General Electric (GE) include the results of General Electric Capital Services (GECS), its 100%-owned financial services subsidiary.

Some investors think the business of a financial services subsidiary is so different from that of its parent that the two should not be consolidated. In 2011, GE reported consolidated net income of $14,443 million, and GECS reported net income of $6,637 million.

1. What would be the 2011 net income of GE if it did not consolidate GECS but accounted for it on an equity basis?
2. What would GE's 2011 net income be if it did not own GECS but all other results were as reported? What percentage of GE's net income comes from GECS?
3. What advantages does the consolidated statement have? What advantages does the unconsolidated statement that accounts for GECS on an equity basis have?

17-44 Goodwill

In 2005 Procter & Gamble (P&G) bought the Gillette Company for $53.4 billion. The purchase added $10.0 billion of tangible assets and $21.2 billion of liabilities to P&G's balance sheet. In addition, P&G identified $29.7 billion of specific intangible assets acquired. These intangible assets had lives ranging from 5 years to more than 40 years. However, assume that all had useful lives of 10 years.

1. How much goodwill did P&G record as a result of the acquisition of Gillette? How much of this goodwill was still on P&G's balance sheet in 2011, assuming P&G did not identify any impairment of the goodwill?
2. Suppose P&G had not identified the $29.7 billion of specific intangible assets but instead had recorded an extra $29.7 billion worth of goodwill. How would this affect P&G's income in 2006?
3. Why might a manager want this $29.7 billion to be recorded as goodwill rather than as part of the value of identifiable intangible assets?

17-45 Accounting for Goodwill

On February 25, 2011, Medtronic, the Minneapolis-based medical technology company, bought 100% of Jolife AB, a company that develops, manufactures, and markets the LUCAS Chest Compression System together with complementary technologies. The purchase price was $53 million.

Medtronic acquired no tangible assets, technology-based intangible assets with a useful life of 10 years that were valued at $46 million, and $11 million of tangible liabilities.

1. Compute the amount of goodwill recognized at the time of purchase.
2. Medtronic had pretax earnings of $3,723 million in fiscal 2011. Assume that these exclude earnings or losses from Jolife. Suppose that Medtronic's on-going operations (that is, excluding the results of Jolife) had the same results for fiscal 2012 as for fiscal 2011 and that Jolife had a pretax loss for fiscal 2012 of $5 million. What consolidated net income would Medtronic report for fiscal 2012? Assume that neither Medtronic nor Jolife had sales to the other.
3. How would the consolidated net income computed in number 2 change if the entire excess of the purchase price over the value of tangible assets less liabilities had been assigned to goodwill?

17-46 Income Ratios and Asset Turnover

Briggs & Stratton is the world's largest producer of air-cooled gasoline engines for outdoor power equipment. Its 2011 annual report to stockholders included the following data (in millions):

Net income	$ 24,355
Total assets	
Beginning of year	1,690,057
End of year	1,666,218
Net income as a percent of total revenue	1.15427%
Average stockholders' equity	3.50805%

Using only the data given, compute the (1) net income percent of average assets, (2) total revenues, (3) average stockholders' equity, and (4) asset turnover (using two different approaches).

17-47 Financial Ratios

Honda Motor Company is a Japanese company with sales equivalent to more than $100 billion. The company's income statement and balance sheet for the year ended March 31, 2011, are shown in Exhibit 17-10 and 17-11. Monetary amounts are in Japanese yen (¥).

Net sales	¥8,937
Cost of sales	6,497
Gross profit	¥2,440
Selling and administrative	1,383
Research and development	487
Operating income	¥ 570
Other income (expense):	
Interest income	23
Interest expense	(9)
Equity in income of affiliates	140
Other, net	46
Income before income taxes	¥ 770
Income tax expense	207
Net income	¥ 563
Amounts per share	
Net income (EPS)	¥ 296
Cash dividends	¥ 54

Exhibit 17-10

Honda Motor Company, Ltd.

Income Statement for the Year Ended March 31, 2011 (in billions, except per-share amounts)

Assets	
Current Assets	
Cash and cash equivalents	¥ 1,279
Receivables	1,919
Inventories	900
Other	592
Total current assets	¥ 4,690
Property, plant, and equipment, net	3,297
Investments	640
Other assets	2,944
Total assets	¥11,571
Liabilities and Stockholders' Equity	
Current liabilities	
Short-term debt	¥ 1,095
Payables	717
Accrued expenses	525
Current portion of long-term debt	962
Other	269
Total current liabilities	¥ 3,568
Long-term liabilities	
Long-term debt	¥ 2,043
Other	1,377
Total long-term liabilities	¥ 3,420
Stockholders' equity	
Common Stock	¥ 86
Additional paid-in capital	173
Retained earnings	5,667
Other	(1,476)
Total honda motor company shareholders' equity	4,450
Noncontrolling interests	133
Total stockholders' equity	¥ 4,583
Total liabilities and stockholders' equity	¥11,571

Exhibit 17-11
Honda Motor Company, Ltd.
Balance Sheet March 31, 2011 (in billions)

1. Prepare a common-size income statement, that is, one showing component percentages.
2. Compute the following ratios:
   a. Current ratio
   b. Total debt to equity
   c. Gross profit rate
   d. Return on stockholders' equity (March 31, 2010 stockholders' equity was ¥4,456 billion)
   e. P/E ratio (the market price on March 31, 2011, was approximately ¥2,207 per share)
   f. Dividend-payout ratio
3. What additional information would help you interpret the percentages and ratios you calculated?

NIKE 10-K PROBLEM

17-48 Using Consolidated Financial Statements

Examine Nike's Form 10-K report in Appendix C, focusing on the income statement and balance sheet. Answer the following questions:

1. Nike used the term *consolidated* to describe its financial statements. What does this mean? Does Nike have any consolidated subsidiaries in which it has less than 100% ownership? How do you know?
2. Suppose Nike's retail stores buy shoes from Converse, a wholly owned subsidiary of Nike, to resell in its stores. Suppose that at the end of fiscal 2012, Converse had recorded $10 million of such sales and all the shoes were still in Nike stores' inventories. Converse's inventory value for the shoes was $6 million. How do such sales of Converse affect the consolidated income statement and balance sheet of Nike? Ignore tax effects.
3. In Exhibit 17-8 on p. 732 you will find 10 ratios for Nike for fiscal 2010 and 2011. For each ratio, explain whether the 2011 ratio is an improvement over the 2010 value.

EXCEL APPLICATION EXERCISE

17-49 Calculating Financial Ratios

Goal: Create an Excel spreadsheet to calculate financial ratios. Use the results to answer questions about your findings.

Scenario: Gap, Inc. has asked you to calculate financial ratios for the company based on income statement and balance sheet data presented in Exhibit 17-9 on page 742.

Additional background information for your calculations appears in problem 17-B5. The formulas for the financial ratios can be found in Exhibit 17-8.

When you have completed your spreadsheet, answer the following questions:

1. Discuss Gap's current ratio calculations and their meaning. Compare the results to the rule of thumb presented in the chapter on p. 733 for this calculation.
2. Discuss Gap's total debt-to-equity calculations and their meaning. Compare the results to the rule of thumb presented in the chapter on p. 733 for this calculation.
3. Discuss the results of the dividend payout calculation and your opinion regarding its percentage.

Step-by-Step:

1. Open a new Excel spreadsheet.
2. In column A, create a bold-faced heading that contains the following:
   Row 1: Chapter 17 Decision Guideline
   Row 2: Gap, Inc.
   Row 3: Financial Ratio Analysis
   Row 4: Today's Date
3. Merge and center the four heading rows across columns A–C.
4. In row 7, create the following bold-faced column headings:
   Column A: Financial Data (in millions):
   Column B: January 28, 2012
   Column C: February 3, 2011

   Note: Adjust column widths as necessary.

5. Modify the format of the date headings in columns B and C as follows:

Number tab:	Category:	Date
Type:		March 14, 2012

6. In column A, create the following row headings:
   Row 8: Current Assets
   Row 9: Current Liabilities
   Row 10: Total Liabilities
   Row 11: Stockholders' Equity
   Row 12: Net Sales
   Row 13: Gross Profit

Row 14: Net Earnings
Row 15: Market Price of Stock
Row 16: Dividends Paid
Row 17: Avg. Common Shares Outstanding

Note: Adjust the column width as necessary.

7. Use data from Exhibit 17-9 and Problem 17-B5 to enter the amounts for rows 8–17 in columns B and C.
8. Skip a row.
9. In row 19, create the following bold-faced column heading:

Column A: Financial Ratios:

10. In column A, create the following row headings:
Row 20: Current ratio
Row 21: Total debt to equity
Row 22: Gross profit percentage
Row 23: Return on sales
Row 24: Return on stockholders' equity
Row 25: Earnings per share
Row 26: Price earnings
Row 27: Dividend yield
Row 28: Dividend payout

11. Use cell-referenced formulas to calculate the amounts in columns B and C for rows 20–28.

Hint: By using cell-referenced formulas, the data in rows 8–17 can be changed without invalidating the Excel formulas coded in rows 20–28.

Example: The Excel formula for the current ratio in cell B20 would be =B8/B9.

Note: The ratio formulas can be found in Exhibit 17-8.

12. Format amounts in column B, rows 8–15 and column C, rows 8–11 as Number tab: Category: Accounting

Decimal: 0
Symbol: $

13. Format the amount in column B, row 16 as Number tab: Category: Accounting

Decimal: 2
Symbol: $

14. Format the amount in column B, row 25 as Number tab: Category: Currency

Decimal: 2
Symbol: $
Negative numbers: Black with parentheses

15. Format amounts in columns B and C, row 20 and column B, row 26 as

Number tab: Category: Number
Decimal: 2
Negative numbers: Black with parentheses

16. Format amounts in column B, rows 21–24 and 27–28, and column C, row 21 as follows:

Number tab: Category: Percentage
Decimal: 2

17. Save your work and print a copy for your files

COLLABORATIVE LEARNING EXERCISE

17-50 Financial Ratios

Form groups of four to six persons each. Each member of the group should pick a different company and find the most recent annual report for that company. (If you do not have printed annual reports, try searching the Internet for one.)

1. Each member should compute the following ratios for his or her company:
   a. EPS
   b. P/E ratio
   c. Dividend-yield ratio
   d. Dividend-payout ratio
2. As a group, list two possible reasons that each ratio differs across the selected companies. Focus on comparing the companies with the highest and lowest values for each ratio, and explain how the nature of the company might be the reason for the differences in ratios.

INTERNET EXERCISE

17-51 General Electric's Annual Report

Go to www.ge.com and follow the link to Investor Relations, and then to Financial Reporting to see General Electric's (GE) most recent annual report.
Answer the following questions about GE:

1. Look at GE's income statement, which it calls a statement of earnings. Does GE consolidate parent and subsidiary accounts in the statement? Does GE hold less than 100% interest in any of its subsidiaries? How do you know?
2. Turn to GE's balance sheet. What does GE call this statement? GE omits some subtotals that most companies include on their balance sheets. What are these subtotals? How much "Noncontrolling interest [in equity of consolidated affiliates]" does GE show? What does this mean?
3. Does GE pay cash dividends? If so, what was the payout ratio in the most recent year?
4. Compute GE's return on shareholders' equity for the GE shareholders for the last two years. Is the change in a positive or negative direction?

Appendix A Recommended Readings

The following readings will aid readers who want to pursue some topics in more depth than is possible in this book. There is a hazard in compiling a group of recommended readings. Inevitably, we will omit some worthwhile books or periodicals. Moreover, such a list cannot include books published subsequently to the compilation date. Although this list is not comprehensive, it includes many excellent readings.

Periodicals

Professional Journals

The following professional journals are typically available in university libraries and include articles on the application of management accounting:

- *Accounting Horizons.* Published by the American Accounting Association; stresses current practice-oriented articles in all areas of accounting
- *CMA Magazine.* Published by CMA Canada; includes much practice-oriented research in management accounting
- *Cost Management.* Published by Thompson Reuters; stresses cost management tools
- *Financial Executive.* Published by Financial Executives International; emphasizes general policy issues for accounting and finance executives
- *The Journal of Corporate Accounting & Finance.* Published by Wiley; directed to corporate accounting and finance executives and outside auditors and accountants working for the corporation
- *Harvard Business Review.* Published by Harvard Business School; directed to general managers but contains excellent articles on applications of management accounting
- *Journal of Accountancy.* Published by the American Institute of CPAs; emphasizes financial accounting and is directed at the practicing CPA
- *Management Accounting Quarterly.* An online journal published by the Institute of Management Accountants; practical articles with an academic focus
- *Strategic Finance.* Published by the Institute of Management Accountants; many articles on actual applications by individual organizations
- *BusinessWeek, Forbes, Fortune, the Economist, and the Wall Street Journal.* Popular publications that cover a variety of business and economics topics; often their articles relate to management accounting

Academic Journals

The academic journal that focuses most directly on current management and cost accounting research is the *Journal of Management Accounting Research*, published by the Management Accounting section of the American Accounting Association. *The Accounting Review*, the general research publication of the American Accounting Association; *Journal of Accounting Research*, published at the University of Chicago; and *Contemporary Accounting Research*, published by the Canadian Academic Association, cover all accounting topics at a more theoretical level. *Accounting, Organizations and Society*, a British journal, publishes research on behavioral aspects of management accounting. The *Journal of Accounting and Economics* covers economics-based accounting research. *Journal of Accounting, Ethics and Public Policy* and *Research on Professional Responsibility and Ethics in Accounting* are journals devoted to ethical issues.

Books in Management Accounting

Most of the topics in this text are covered in more detail in the many books on cost accounting, including *Cost Accounting: A Managerial Emphasis*, 14th edition, by C. T. Horngren, S. Datar, and M. Rajan (Prentice Hall, 2012). You can find more advanced coverage in *Advanced Management Accounting*, 3rd edition, by R. S. Kaplan and A. A. Atkinson (Prentice Hall, 1998). Current management accounting issues are discussed in *Issues in Management Accounting* by Trevor Hopper, Robert W. Scapens, and Deryl Northcott (Prentice Hall, 2007).

Financial Executives International, 1250 Headquarters Plaza, West Tower, 7th Floor, Morristown, NJ, 07960, and the IMA, 10 Paragon Drive, Suite 1, Montvale, NJ 07645-1760, have long lists of accounting research publications.

Handbooks, General Texts, and Case Books
The books in this list have wide application to management accounting issues. The handbooks are basic references. The textbooks are designed for classroom use but may be useful for self-study. The case books present applications from real companies.

- Adkins, T. C., *Case Studies in Performance Management: A Guide from the Experts*, Hoboken, NJ: John Wiley & Sons, 2006.
- Allen, B. R., E. R. Brownlee, M. E. Haskins, L. J. Lynch, and J. W. Rotch, *Cases in Management Accounting and Control Systems*, 4th ed. Upper Saddle River, NJ: Prentice Hall, 2004.
- Bahnub, B., *Activity-Based Management for Financial Institutions: Driving Bottom-Line Results*, New York: Wiley, 2010.
- Bierman, H., Jr., and S. Smidt, *The Capital Budgeting Decision: Economic Analysis of Investment Projects*, 9th ed. Routledge, 2006. This text expands the capital budgeting discussion from Chapter 11.
- Bierman, H., Jr., and S. Smidt, *Advanced Capital Budgeting: Refinements in the Economic Analysis of Investment Projects*, Routledge, 2007.
- Groot, T., and K. Lukka (eds.), *Cases in Management Accounting: Current Practices in European Companies*, Harlow: Prentice Hall/Pearson, 2000.
- Kaplan, R., and S. Anderson, *Time-Driven Activity-Based Costing: A Simpler and More Powerful Path to Higher Profits*, Boston: Harvard Business Review Press, 2007.
- Manning, G. A., *Financial Investigation and Forensic Accounting*, 3rd ed. Boca Raton, FL: CRC Press, 2010.
- Pryor, T., et al., *Activity Dictionary: A Comprehensive Reference Tool for ABM and ABC: 2000 Edition*, Arlington, TX: ICMS, Inc., 2000.
- Render, B., R. Stair, and M. Hanna, *Quantitative Analysis for Management*, 11th ed. Prentice Hall, 2011.
- Rogers, J., *Strategy, Value, and Risk: The Real Options Approach*, 2nd Ed., Basingstoke, UK: Palgrave Macmillan, 2009.
- Seitz, N., and M. Ellison, *Capital Budgeting and Long-Term Financing Decisions*, Cincinnati, OH: South-Western, 2004.
- Shank, J., and V. Govindarajan, *Strategic Cost Management: The New Tool for Competitive Advantage*, New York: Free Press, 2008.
- Smith, J., *Handbook of Management Accounting*, 4th ed. London: CIMA, 2007.
- Weil, R., and M. Maher, *Handbook of Cost Management*, New York: Wiley, 2005.
- Young, S. M., *Readings in Management Accounting*, 6th ed. Upper Saddle River, NJ: Prentice Hall, 2012.

Accounting Ethics
Integrity is essential for accountants. An increasing emphasis on ethics has led to a number of books devoted to the subject.

- Brooks, L. J., and P. Dunn, *Business and Professional Ethics for Directors, Executives, & Accountants*, 5th ed., Mason, OH: South-Western, 2009.
- Duska, R. F., and B. S. Duska, *Accounting Ethics*, 2nd ed., Malden, MA: Wiley-Blackwell, 2011.
- Mintz, S. M., and R. E. Morris, *Ethical Obligations and Decision Making in Accounting: Text and Cases*, 2nd ed., New York: McGraw-Hill/Irwin, 2010.
- Pakaluk, M, and M. L. Cheffers, *Accounting Ethics*, Manchaug, MA: Allen David Press, 2011.

The Strategic Nature of Management Accounting
Management accountants realize that cost and performance information is most useful to organizations when it helps define strategic alternatives and helps in the management of resources

to achieve strategic objectives. The books in this list, though not necessarily accounting books, provide a valuable foundation to the interaction of strategy and accounting information.

- Ansari, S., and J. Bell, *Target Costing: The Next Frontier in Strategic Cost Management*, Mountain Valley Publishing, 2009.
- Carr, L., and A. Nanni Jr., *Delivering Results: Managing What Matters*, Springer, 2009.
- Cokins, G., *Performance Management: Integrating Strategy Execution, Methodologies, Risk, and Analytics*, New York: Wiley, 2009.
- Grant, J. L., *Foundations of Economic Value Added*, 2nd ed. New York: Wiley, 2002.
- Kaplan, R., and D. Norton, *The Execution Premium: Linking Strategy to Operations for Competitive Advantage*, Boston: Harvard Business School Press, 2008.
- Magretta, J., *Understanding Michael Porter: The Essential Guide to Competition and Strategy*, Boston: Harvard Business Review Press, 2011.
- Stern, J., J. Shiely, and I. Ross, *The EVA Challenge: Implementing Value-Added Change in an Organization*, New York: Wiley, 2003.

Modern Manufacturing

The following books provide background on the role of accounting in modern manufacturing environments.

- Atkinson, A. A., R. S. Kaplan, E. M. Matsumura, and S. M. Young, *Management Accounting*, 6th ed. Upper Saddle River, NJ: Prentice Hall, 2012.
- Byrne, A., *The Lean Turnaround: How Business Leaders Use Lean Principles to Create Value and Transform Their Company*, New York: McGraw-Hill, 2013.
- Carreira, B, and B. Trudell, *Lean Six Sigma That Works: A Powerful Action Plan for Dramatically Improving Quality, Increasing Speed, and Reducing Waste*, New York: AMACOM, 2006.
- Cooper, R., and R. Kaplan, *Design of Cost Management Systems*, 2nd ed. Upper Saddle River, NJ: Prentice Hall, 1999.
- Cox III, J., and J. Schleier, *Theory of Constraints Handbook*, New York: McGraw-Hill, 2010.
- Goldratt, E. M., *Theory of Constraints*, Croton-on-Hudson, NY: North River Press, Inc., 2000.
- Goldratt, E. M., and J. Cox, *The Goal*, 3rd ed. Croton-on-Hudson, NY: North River Press, 2004. This is a novel illustrating the new manufacturing environment.
- Jacobs, F. R., R. Chase, and N. Aquilano, *Operations and Supply Management*, 12th ed., Homewood, IL: McGraw-Hill/Irwin, 2008.
- Mann, D., *Creating a Lean Culture: Tools to Sustain Lean Conversions*, 2nd ed., London: Productivity Press, 2010.
- Morgan, J., and M. Brenig-Jones, *Lean Six Sigma for Dummies*, 2nd ed., New York: Wiley, 2012.
- Pyzdek, T., and P. Keller, *The Six Sigma Handbook*, 3rd ed. New York: McGraw-Hill, 2009.
- Rubrich, L., and M. Watson, *Implementing World Class Manufacturing*, 2nd ed., Fort Wayne, IN: WCM Associates, 2004.
- Wilson, L., *How to Implement Lean Manufacturing*, New York: McGraw-Hill, 2009.

Management Control Systems

The topics of Chapters 7–10 can be explored further in several books, including the following:

- Anthony, R. N., and V. Govindarajan, *Management Control Systems*, 12th ed. McGraw-Hill/Irwin, 2006.
- Arrow, K. J., *The Limits of Organization*, New York: Norton, 1974. [This is a readable classic by a Nobel laureate.]
- Blocher, E., D. Stout, and G. Cokins, *Cost Management: A Strategic Emphasis*, 5th ed., McGraw-Hill/Irwin, 2009.
- Eckerson, W., *Performance Dashboards: Measuring, Monitoring, and Managing Your Business*, New York: Wiley, 2010.
- Gupta, P., and A. W. Wiggenhorn, *Six Sigma Business Scorecard: Creating a Comprehensive Corporate Performance Measurement System*, 2nd ed. New York: McGraw-Hill, 2006.

- Kaplan, R. S., and D. P. Norton, *The Balanced Scorecard: Measures That Drive Performance*, Boston: Harvard Business School Press, 1996.
- Kaplan, R. S., and D. P. Norton, *Alignment: Using the Balanced Scorecard to Create Corporate Synergies*, Boston: Harvard Business School Press, 2006.
- Merchant K., and W. Van der Stede, *Management Control Systems: Performance Measurement, Evaluation and Incentives*, 3rd ed. Upper Saddle River, NJ: Prentice Hall, 2012.
- Niven, P. R., *Balanced Scorecard Step-by-Step: Maximizing Performance and Maintaining Results*, 2nd ed., Hoboken, NJ: John Wiley & Sons, 2006.
- Parmenter, D., *Key Performance Indicators (KPI): Developing, Implementing, and Using Winning KPIs*, New York: Wiley, 2010.
- Simons, R., *Performance Measurement and Control Systems for Implementing Strategy*, Upper Saddle River, NJ: Prentice Hall, 2000.
- Solomons, D., *Divisional Performance: Measurement and Control*, New York: Markus Wiener, 1983. [This is a reprint of a 1965 classic that is still relevant.]

Management Accounting in Nonprofit Organizations

Many books discuss management accounting in nonprofit organizations, especially in health care. Examples are as follows:

- Anthony, R. N., and D. W. Young, *Management Control in Nonprofit Organizations*, 7th ed. Homewood, IL: Irwin, 2003.
- Baker, J. J., and R. W. Baker, *Health Care Finance: Basic Tools for Nonfinancial Managers*, 3rd ed. Sudbury, MA: Jones and Bartlett, 2009.
- Brimson, J., and J. Antos, *Activity Based Management for Service Industries, Government Entities, and Non-Profit Organizations*, New York: John Wiley & Sons, 1998.
- Finkler, S. A., D. M. Ward, and J. J. Baker, *Essentials of Cost Accounting for Health Care Organizations*, 3rd ed. Sudbury, MA: Jones and Bartlett, 2007.
- Gapenski, L. C., *Healthcare Finance: An Introduction to Accounting and Financial Management*, 4th ed. Washington DC: Health Administration Press, 2008.
- Marr, B., *Managing and Delivering Performance: How Government, Public Sector and Not-for-Profit Organisations Can Measure and Manage What Really Matters*, Abingdon, UK: Taylor & Francis, 2009.
- Niven, P., *Balanced Scorecard: Step-by-Step for Government and Nonprofit Agencies*, 2nd ed., New York: John Wiley & Sons, 2008.
- Young, D., *Management Accounting in Health Care Organizations*, 2nd ed., Jossey-Bass, 2009.

Online Resources

The online resources related to management accounting are too extensive to create a comprehensive list. The best way to access them may be to use a good search engine. However, we list a few URLs that can help you get started.

- AICPA's Financial Management Center: Information for CPAs in business and industry, at http://fmcenter.aicpa.org/
- Balanced Scorecard Institute: Includes a variety of resources related to the balanced scorecard, at http://www.balancedscorecard.org
- CMA Canada: Many services, including strategic management accounting practices and management accounting standards, at http://www.cma-canada.org
- Consortium for Advanced Manufacturing International (CAM-I): Online library, at http://www.cam-i.org
- Financial Executives International: Information for corporate financial officers, at http://www.fei.org
- IMA: A variety of services, including an index of research publications, at http://www.imanet.org/
- Metrus Group: A variation of the balance scorecard, at http://www.metrus.com/products/balanced-scorecards.html
- Stern Stewart & Co.: Information about economic value added by the firm that developed the technique, at http://www.sternstewart.com/

Appendix B Fundamentals of Compound Interest and the Use of Present-Value Tables

The Nature of Interest

Interest is the cost of using money. A lender who loans an initial amount to a borrower now and receives repayment from the borrower later expects to receive more than the amount loaned. The difference between the initial amount loaned and the amount repaid later is interest. Interest is the rental fee for money, similar to the rental fees charged for the use of equipment or land.

Suppose you invest $10,000 in a savings account in a financial institution. In this transaction, you are lending your money to the financial institution. Your initial $10,000 investment (or loan to the financial institution) is the *principal*. Interest is the amount you earn on the investment each period. In this appendix, we focus on compound interest, where we add each period's interest to the beginning-of-the-period principal to come up with the principal for the start of the next period. For example, suppose the financial institution promised to pay 10% interest per year on your $10,000 investment. The $10\% \times \$10,000 = \$1,000$ interest the first year would create a principal of $\$10,000 + \$1,000 = \$11,000$ at the start of the second year. If you let the amount accumulate for 3 years before withdrawing the full balance of the deposit, the deposit would accumulate to $13,310:

	Principal	Compound Interest	Balance, End of Year
Year 1	$10,000	$10,000 × 0.10 = $1,000	$11,000
Year 2	11,000	11,000 × 0.10 = 1,100	12,100
Year 3	12,100	12,100 × 0.10 = 1,210	13,310

Because compound interest accumulates on both the original principal and the previously accumulated interest that has been added to principal each period, the "force" of compound interest can be staggering. For example, the $10,000 deposit would accumulate at 10% interest compounded annually as follows:

	At End of		
3 Years	10 Years	20 Years	40 Years
$13,310	$25,937	$67,275	$452,593

Step-by-step calculations of compound interest quickly become burdensome. However, the calculations can be described compactly in the formulas outlined next. These formulas are built into many handheld calculators and computer software programs. Compound interest tables show the results for various combinations of parameters.

This appendix explains how to use the two compound interest tables most commonly used in capital budgeting. Both tables allow us to calculate *present value*, the value today of a future amount. In the previous example, the $10,000 amount is a present value. The calculations showed what the future value of this amount would be after 3 years, 10 years, and so on. Another way to interpret these same calculations is that $10,000 is the present value of $13,310 to be repaid 3 years in the future, or the present value of $25,937 to be repaid 10 years in the future, or the present value of $452,593 to be repaid 40 years in the future. The remainder of this chapter explains how to use the tables to find the present value of any set of future payments.

Table B-1: Present Value of $1

How do you express a future cash inflow or outflow in terms of its equivalent today? Table B-1 provides factors that give the present value at time 0 of a single, lump-sum cash flow that you will receive or pay at the end of n periods.

Suppose you invest $1.00 today at 6% interest. It will grow to $1.06 in 1 year; that is, $\$1 \times 1.06 = \$1.06$. At the end of the second year, its value is $(\$1 \times 1.06) \times 1.06 = \$1 \times (1.06)^2 = \$1.124$; and at the end of the third year it is $\$1 \times (1.06)^3 = 1.191$. In n years at i percent interest, $1.00 grows to $\$1 \times (1 + i)^n$.

To determine the present value, you invert this accumulation process. If you will receive $1.00 in 1 year, it is worth $\$1 \div 1.06 = \$0.9434$ today at an interest rate of 6%. Stated differently, if you invest $0.9434 today, in 1 year you will have $\$0.9434 \times 1.06 = \$1.00$. Thus, $0.9434 is the present value of $1.00 a year hence at 6%.

Suppose you will receive the $1 in 2 years instead of in 1 year. Its present value is then $\$1.00 \div (1.06)^2 = \$0.8900$. The general formula for the present value (PV) of $1 is the inverse of the previous formula for the future value of $1, i.e., $\$1 \div (1 + i)^n$. If you will receive or pay an amount S in n periods at an interest rate of $i\%$ per period, the formula for present value is:

$$PV = S\frac{1}{(1 + i)^n}$$

TABLE B-1 Present Value of $1

Period	3%	4%	5%	6%	7%	8%	10%	12%	14%	16%	18%	20%	22%	24%	25%	26%	28%	30%	40%
1	.9709	.9615	.9524	.9434	.9346	.9259	.9091	.8929	.8772	.8621	.8475	.8333	.8197	.8065	.8000	.7937	.7813	.7692	.7143
2	.9426	.9246	.9070	.8900	.8734	.8573	.8264	.7972	.7695	.7432	.7182	.6944	.6719	.6504	.6400	.6299	.6104	.5917	.5102
3	.9151	.8890	.8638	.8396	.8163	.7938	.7513	.7118	.6750	.6407	.6086	.5787	.5507	.5245	.5120	.4999	.4768	.4552	.3644
4	.8885	.8548	.8227	.7921	.7629	.7350	.6830	.6355	.5921	.5523	.5158	.4823	.4514	.4230	.4096	.3968	.3725	.3501	.2603
5	.8626	.8219	.7835	.7473	.7130	.6806	.6209	.5674	.5194	.4761	.4371	.4019	.3700	.3411	.3277	.3149	.2910	.2693	.1859
6	.8375	.7903	.7462	.7050	.6663	.6302	.5645	.5066	.4556	.4104	.3704	.3349	.3033	.2751	.2621	.2499	.2274	.2072	.1328
7	.8131	.7599	.7107	.6651	.6227	.5835	.5132	.4523	.3996	.3538	.3139	.2791	.2486	.2218	.2097	.1983	.1776	.1594	.0949
8	.7894	.7307	.6768	.6274	.5820	.5403	.4665	.4039	.3506	.3050	.2660	.2326	.2038	.1789	.1678	.1574	.1388	.1226	.0678
9	.7664	.7026	.6446	.5919	.5439	.5002	.4241	.3606	.3075	.2630	.2255	.1938	.1670	.1443	.1342	.1249	.1084	.0943	.0484
10	.7441	.6756	.6139	.5584	.5083	.4632	.3855	.3220	.2697	.2267	.1911	.1615	.1369	.1164	.1074	.0992	.0847	.0725	.0346
11	.7224	.6496	.5847	.5268	.4751	.4289	.3505	.2875	.2366	.1954	.1619	.1346	.1122	.0938	.0859	.0787	.0662	.0558	.0247
12	.7014	.6246	.5568	.4970	.4440	.3971	.3186	.2567	.2076	.1685	.1372	.1122	.0920	.0757	.0687	.0625	.0517	.0429	.0176
13	.6810	.6006	.5303	.4688	.4150	.3677	.2897	.2292	.1821	.1452	.1163	.0935	.0754	.0610	.0550	.0496	.0404	.0330	.0126
14	.6611	.5775	.5051	.4423	.3878	.3405	.2633	.2046	.1597	.1252	.0985	.0779	.0618	.0492	.0440	.0393	.0316	.0254	.0090
15	.6419	.5553	.4810	.4173	.3624	.3152	.2394	.1827	.1401	.1079	.0835	.0649	.0507	.0397	.0352	.0312	.0247	.0195	.0064
16	.6232	.5339	.4581	.3936	.3387	.2919	.2176	.1631	.1229	.0930	.0708	.0541	.0415	.0320	.0281	.0248	.0193	.0150	.0046
17	.6050	.5134	.4363	.3714	.3166	.2703	.1978	.1456	.1078	.0802	.0600	.0451	.0340	.0258	.0225	.0197	.0150	.0116	.0033
18	.5874	.4936	.4155	.3503	.2959	.2502	.1799	.1300	.0946	.0691	.0508	.0376	.0279	.0208	.0180	.0156	.0118	.0089	.0023
19	.5703	.4746	.3957	.3305	.2765	.2317	.1635	.1161	.0829	.0596	.0431	.0313	.0229	.0168	.0144	.0124	.0092	.0068	.0017
20	.5537	.4564	.3769	.3118	.2584	.2145	.1486	.1037	.0728	.0514	.0365	.0261	.0187	.0135	.0115	.0098	.0072	.0053	.0012
21	.5375	.4388	.3589	.2942	.2415	.1987	.1351	.0926	.0638	.0443	.0309	.0217	.0154	.0109	.0092	.0078	.0056	.0040	.0009
22	.5219	.4220	.3418	.2775	.2257	.1839	.1228	.0826	.0560	.0382	.0262	.0181	.0126	.0088	.0074	.0062	.0044	.0031	.0006
23	.5067	.4057	.3256	.2618	.2109	.1703	.1117	.0738	.0491	.0329	.0222	.0151	.0103	.0071	.0059	.0049	.0034	.0024	.0004
24	.4919	.3901	.3101	.2470	.1971	.1577	.1015	.0659	.0431	.0284	.0188	.0126	.0085	.0057	.0047	.0039	.0027	.0018	.0003
25	.4776	.3751	.2953	.2330	.1842	.1460	.0923	.0588	.0378	.0245	.0160	.0105	.0069	.0046	.0038	.0031	.0021	.0014	.0002
26	.4637	.3607	.2812	.2198	.1722	.1352	.0839	.0525	.0331	.0211	.0135	.0087	.0057	.0037	.0030	.0025	.0016	.0011	.0002
27	.4502	.3468	.2678	.2074	.1609	.1252	.0763	.0469	.0291	.0182	.0115	.0073	.0047	.0030	.0024	.0019	.0013	.0008	.0001
28	.4371	.3335	.2551	.1956	.1504	.1159	.0693	.0419	.0255	.0157	.0097	.0061	.0038	.0024	.0019	.0015	.0010	.0006	.0001
29	.4243	.3207	.2429	.1846	.1406	.1073	.0630	.0374	.0224	.0135	.0082	.0051	.0031	.0020	.0015	.0012	.0008	.0005	.0001
30	.4120	.3083	.2314	.1741	.1314	.0994	.0573	.0334	.0196	.0116	.0070	.0042	.0026	.0016	.0012	.0010	.0006	.0004	.0000
40	.3066	.2083	.1420	.0972	.0668	.0460	.0221	.0107	.0053	.0026	.0013	.0007	.0004	.0002	.0001	.0001	.0001	.0000	.0000

Table B-1 on page A6 provides factors computed using this formula for various combinations of n and i. Each factor shows the present value of a single, lump-sum cash flow of $1 at the end of n future periods at interest rate i.

Present values are also called *discounted values*, and the process of finding the present value is called *discounting*. You can think of this as discounting (decreasing) the value of a future cash inflow or outflow. Why is the value discounted? Because you will receive or pay the cash in the future, its value today is reduced or discounted from the future amount to be received.

Assume that a municipality issues a 3-year non-interest-bearing note payable that promises to pay you a lump sum of $1,000 exactly 3 years from the issue date. You desire a rate of return of 6%, compounded annually. How much would you be willing to pay now for the 3-year note? The situation is sketched as follows:

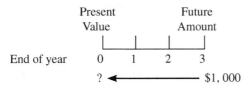

The factor in the period 3 row and 6% column of Table B-1 is 0.8396. The present value of the $1,000 payment is $1,000 × 0.8396 = $839.60. You would therefore be willing to pay $839.60 today for the $1,000 that you will receive in 3 years; $839.60 is the discounted value of the $1,000 future amount.

Compounding can occur more frequently than once per year. Suppose interest is compounded semiannually rather than annually. In our previous example, the 3 years become six semi-annual interest compounding periods. How much would you be willing to pay, assuming the rate of return you demand per semiannual period is half the annual rate, or 6% ÷ 2 = 3%? The factor in the period 6 row and 3% column of Table B-1 is 0.8375. You would be willing to pay $1,000 × 0.8375, or only $837.50.

Why is the present value lower when compounding occurs more frequently? Because money grows more quickly with more frequent compounding. Consider $1,000 invested at 6% interest compounded annually versus semi-annually:

	Annual Compounding	Semi-Annual Compounding
Year 0	$1,000.00	$1,000.00
½ year		$1,000.00 × 1.03 = $1,030.00
1 year	$1,000.00 × 1.06 = $1,060.00	$1,030.00 × 1.03 = $1,060.90
1 ½ years		$1,060.90 × 1.03 = $1,092.73
2 years	$1,060.00 × 1.06 = $1,123.60	$1,092.73 × 1.03 = $1,125.51
2 ½ years		$1,125.51 × 1.03 = $1,159.27
3 years	$1,123.60 × 1.06 = 1,190.16	$1,159.27 × 1.03 = $1,194.05

Notice that during the second half of year one, interest is paid on $1,000 with annual compounding, but interest is paid on $1,030 with semi-annual compounding. Compounding implies that interest is paid on interest, and with more frequent compounding, interest paid on interest starts sooner. Because money grows faster with semi-annual compounding, it doesn't require as many current dollars (present value) to grow to a given final value. This explains why a present value of $837.50 grows to $1,000 in 3 years at 6% compounded semi-annually, but if compounding occurs only annually, it requires a present value of $839.60 to grow to $1,000 in 3 years.

As a further check on your understanding, review the earlier example of your $10,000 investment. Suppose the financial institution promised to pay $13,310 at the end of 3 years. How much would you be willing to deposit at time zero if you required a 10% rate of return compounded annually? The period 3 row and 10% column factor is 0.7513 so the present value is this factor multiplied by the future amount of $13,310:

$$PV = 0.7513 \times \$13,310 = \$10,000$$

A diagram of this computation follows:

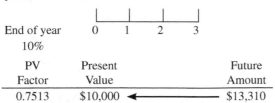

Pause for a moment. Use Table B-1 to obtain the present values of

1. $1,700 at 20% at the end of 20 years.
2. $8,300 at 10% at the end of 12 years.
3. $8,000 at 4% at the end of 4 years.

Answers:

1. $1,700 × 0.0261 = $44.37
2. $8,300 × 0.3186 = $2,644.38
3. $8,000 × 0.8548 = $6,838.40

Table B-2: Present Value of an Ordinary Annuity of $1

An annuity is a series of equal-sized cash flows spaced equally in time. An ordinary annuity has the equally spaced payments occurring at the end of each period. (We will not discuss the other type of annuity, an annuity due, which has payments at the beginning of each year.) Assume that you buy a note from a municipality that promises to pay $1,000 at the end of each of the next 3 years. How much should you be willing to pay if you desire a rate of return of 6%, compounded annually? This series of payments is a 3-year ordinary annuity. You denote the present value of an ordinary annuity as PV_A.

Before we introduce a computational method to deal with an annuity, note that you can always find the present value of the series of annuity payments by adding together the present values of the individual payments. That is, you can simply treat the annuity as a series of individual amounts, find the present values of each of the individual amounts using Table B-1, and then add the present values to find the present value of the entire series. For our example, you would be willing to pay $943.40 for the first payment, $890.00 for the second, and $839.60 for the third, so for the series of three payments, you are willing to pay a total of $2,673.00:

Payment	End of Year Table 1 Factor	0 Present Value	1	2	3
1	$\dfrac{1}{1.06} = .9434$	$ 943.40	$1,000		
2	$\dfrac{1}{(1.06)^2} = .8900$	890.00		1,000	
3	$\dfrac{1}{(1.06)^3} = .8396$	839.60			$1,000
Total		$2,673.00			

Although you can always treat an annuity as a series of individual amounts, this approach is computationally inconvenient for a long annuity. Instead, the factors in Table B-2 on page A9 provide a computational shortcut. Let's examine the conceptual basis for Table B-2 using our 3-year annuity. The three present value factors corresponding to the three annuity payments are the first three numbers from the 6% column of Table B-1. Because you multiply each of these factors by the $1,000 annuity payment, you can sum the factors and then multiply by $1,000 instead of multiplying each factor by $1,000 and then summing. For this example, the sum of the factors is .9434 + .8900 + .8396 = 2.6730, and this is the value that you find in Table B-2 for a three-period annuity with an interest rate of 6%. The present value of the annuity is simply the value from Table B-2, 2.6730, multiplied by $1,000: 2.6730 × $1,000 = $2,673.00. This shortcut is especially valuable if the cash payments or receipts extend over many periods. Consider an annual cash payment of $1,000 for 20 years at 6%. The present value, calculated from Table B-2, is $1,000 × 11.4699 = $11,469.90. To use Table B-1 for this calculation, you would have to perform 20 multiplications and then add the 20 products.

The factors in Table B-2 could be calculated by summing the factors in Table B-1, but they can instead be calculated using the following general formula:

$$PV_A = \frac{1}{i}\left[1 - \frac{1}{(1+i)^n}\right]$$

Applied to our illustration,

$$PV_A = \frac{1}{.06}\left[1 - \frac{1}{(1.06)^3}\right] = \frac{1}{.06}(1 - .8396) = \frac{.1604}{.06} = 2.6730$$

There is also a potential accuracy advantage to using annuity Table B-2 rather than summing the factors from Table B-1 for individual amounts. If you round the individual numbers before summing them, you

TABLE B-2 Present Value of Ordinary Annuity of $1

Period	3%	4%	5%	6%	7%	8%	10%	12%	14%	16%	18%	20%	22%	24%	25%	26%	28%	30%	40%
1	.9709	.9615	.9524	.9434	.9346	.9259	.9091	.8929	.8772	.8621	.8475	.8333	.8197	.8065	.8000	.7937	.7813	.7692	.7143
2	1.9135	1.8861	1.8594	1.8334	1.8080	1.7833	1.7355	1.6901	1.6467	1.6052	1.5656	1.5278	1.4915	1.4568	1.4400	1.4235	1.3916	1.3609	1.2245
3	2.8286	2.7751	2.7232	2.6730	2.6243	2.5771	2.4869	2.4018	2.3216	2.2459	2.1743	2.1065	2.0422	1.9813	1.9520	1.9234	1.8684	1.8161	1.5889
4	3.7171	3.6299	3.5460	3.4651	3.3872	3.3121	3.1699	3.0373	2.9137	2.7982	2.6901	2.5887	2.4936	2.4043	2.3616	2.3202	2.2410	2.1662	1.8492
5	4.5797	4.4518	4.3295	4.2124	4.1002	3.9927	3.7908	3.6048	3.4331	3.2743	3.1272	2.9906	2.8636	2.7454	2.6893	2.6351	2.5320	2.4356	2.0352
6	5.4172	5.2421	5.0757	4.9173	4.7665	4.6229	4.3553	4.1114	3.8887	3.6847	3.4976	3.3255	3.1669	3.0205	2.9514	2.8850	2.7594	2.6427	2.1680
7	6.2303	6.0021	5.7864	5.5824	5.3893	5.2064	4.8684	4.5638	4.2883	4.0386	3.8115	3.6046	3.4155	3.2423	3.1611	3.0833	2.9370	2.8021	2.2628
8	7.0197	6.7327	6.4632	6.2098	5.9713	5.7466	5.3349	4.9676	4.6389	4.3436	4.0776	3.8372	3.6193	3.4212	3.3289	3.2407	3.0758	2.9247	2.3306
9	7.7861	7.4353	7.1078	6.8017	6.5152	6.2469	5.7590	5.3282	4.9464	4.6065	4.3030	4.0310	3.7863	3.5655	3.4631	3.3657	3.1842	3.0190	2.3790
10	8.5302	8.1109	7.7217	7.3601	7.0236	6.7101	6.1446	5.6502	5.2161	4.8332	4.4941	4.1925	3.9232	3.6819	3.5705	3.4648	3.2689	3.0915	2.4136
11	9.2526	8.7605	8.3064	7.8869	7.4987	7.1390	6.4951	5.9377	5.4527	5.0286	4.6560	4.3271	4.0354	3.7757	3.6564	3.5435	3.3351	3.1473	2.4383
12	9.9540	9.3851	8.8633	8.3838	7.9427	7.5361	6.8137	6.1944	5.6603	5.1971	4.7932	4.4392	4.1274	3.8514	3.7251	3.6059	3.3868	3.1903	2.4559
13	10.6350	9.9856	9.3936	8.8527	8.3577	7.9038	7.1034	6.4235	5.8424	5.3423	4.9095	4.5327	4.2028	3.9124	3.7801	3.6555	3.4272	3.2233	2.4685
14	11.2961	10.5631	9.8986	9.2950	8.7455	8.2442	7.3667	6.6282	6.0021	5.4675	5.0081	4.6106	4.2646	3.9616	3.8241	3.6949	3.4587	3.2487	2.4775
15	11.9379	11.1184	10.3797	9.7122	9.1079	8.5595	7.6061	6.8109	6.1422	5.5755	5.0916	4.6755	4.3152	4.0013	3.8593	3.7261	3.4834	3.2682	2.4839
16	12.5611	11.6523	10.8378	10.1059	9.4466	8.8514	7.8237	6.9740	6.2651	5.6685	5.1624	4.7296	4.3567	4.0333	3.8874	3.7509	3.5026	3.2832	2.4885
17	13.1661	12.1657	11.2741	10.4773	9.7632	9.1216	8.0216	7.1196	6.3729	5.7487	5.2223	4.7746	4.3908	4.0591	3.9099	3.7705	3.5177	3.2948	2.4918
18	13.7535	12.6593	11.6896	10.8276	10.0591	9.3719	8.2014	7.2497	6.4674	5.8178	5.2732	4.8122	4.4187	4.0799	3.9279	3.7861	3.5294	3.3037	2.4941
19	14.3238	13.1339	12.0853	11.1581	10.3356	9.6036	8.3649	7.3658	6.5504	5.8775	5.3162	4.8435	4.4415	4.0967	3.9424	3.7985	3.5386	3.3105	2.4958
20	14.8775	13.5903	12.4622	11.4699	10.5940	9.8181	8.5136	7.4694	6.6231	5.9288	5.3527	4.8696	4.4603	4.1103	3.9539	3.8083	3.5458	3.3158	2.4970
21	15.4150	14.0292	12.8212	11.7641	10.8355	10.0168	8.6487	7.5620	6.6870	5.9731	5.3837	4.8913	4.4756	4.1212	3.9631	3.8161	3.5514	3.3198	2.4979
22	15.9369	14.4511	13.1630	12.0416	11.0612	10.2007	8.7715	7.6446	6.7429	6.0113	5.4099	4.9094	4.4882	4.1300	3.9705	3.8223	3.5558	3.3230	2.4985
23	16.4436	14.8568	13.4886	12.3034	11.2722	10.3711	8.8832	7.7184	6.7921	6.0442	5.4321	4.9245	4.4985	4.1371	3.9764	3.8273	3.5592	3.3254	2.4989
24	16.9355	15.2470	13.7986	12.5504	11.4693	10.5288	8.9847	7.7843	6.8351	6.0726	5.4509	4.9371	4.5070	4.1428	3.9811	3.8312	3.5619	3.3272	2.4992
25	17.4131	15.6221	14.0939	12.7834	11.6536	10.6748	9.0770	7.8431	6.8729	6.0971	5.4669	4.9476	4.5139	4.1474	3.9849	3.8342	3.5640	3.3286	2.4994
26	17.8768	15.9828	14.3752	13.0032	11.8258	10.8100	9.1609	7.8957	6.9061	6.1182	5.4804	4.9563	4.5196	4.1511	3.9879	3.8367	3.5656	3.3297	2.4996
27	18.3270	16.3296	14.6430	13.2105	11.9867	10.9352	9.2372	7.9426	6.9352	6.1364	5.4919	4.9636	4.5243	4.1542	3.9903	3.8387	3.5669	3.3305	2.4997
28	18.7641	16.6631	14.8981	13.4062	12.1371	11.0511	9.3066	7.9844	6.9607	6.1520	5.5016	4.9697	4.5281	4.1566	3.9923	3.8402	3.5679	3.3312	2.4998
29	19.1885	16.9837	15.1411	13.5907	12.2777	11.1584	9.3696	8.0218	6.9830	6.1656	5.5098	4.9747	4.5312	4.1585	3.9938	3.8414	3.5687	3.3317	2.4999
30	19.6004	17.2920	15.3725	13.7648	12.4090	11.2578	9.4269	8.0552	7.0027	6.1772	5.5168	4.9789	4.5338	4.1601	3.9950	3.8424	3.5693	3.3321	2.4999
40	23.1148	19.7928	17.1591	15.0463	13.3317	11.9246	9.7791	8.2438	7.1050	6.2335	5.5482	4.9966	4.5439	4.1659	3.9995	3.8458	3.5712	3.3332	2.5000

run the risk of introducing more rounding error than you would by using Table B-2, where rounding occurs only after the numbers are summed. Therefore, computations are more accurate using the annuity factors in Table B-2.

Now, use Table B-2 to obtain the present values of the following ordinary annuities:

1. $1,600 at 20% for 20 years
2. $8,300 at 10% for 12 years
3. $8,000 at 4% for 4 years

Answers:

1. $1,600 × 4.8696 = $7,791.36
2. $8,300 × 6.8137 = $56,553.71
3. $8,000 × 3.6299 = $29,039.20

Note that the higher the interest rate, the lower the present value.

Appendix C Excerpts from Form 10-K of NIKE, Inc.

UNITED STATES SECURITIES AND EXCHANGE COMMISSION
Washington, D.C. 20549

Form 10-K

(Mark One)

☑ **ANNUAL REPORT PURSUANT TO SECTION 13 OR 15(d) OF THE SECURITIES EXCHANGE ACT OF 1934**

For the fiscal year ended May 31, 2011

or

☐ **TRANSITION REPORT PURSUANT TO SECTION 13 OR 15(d) OF THE SECURITIES EXCHANGE ACT OF 1934**

For the transition period from   to   .

Commission File No. 1-10635

NIKE, Inc.

(Exact name of Registrant as specified in its charter)

Oregon	**93-0584541**
(State or other jurisdiction of incorporation)	*(IRS Employer Identification No.)*
One Bowerman Drive	**(503) 671-6453**
Beaverton, Oregon 97005-6453	*(Registrant's Telephone Number, Including Area Code)*
(Address of principal executive offices) (Zip Code)	

Securities registered pursuant to Section 12(b) of the Act:

Class B Common Stock	New York Stock Exchange
(Title of Each Class)	*(Name of Each Exchange on Which Registered)*

Securities registered pursuant to Section 12(g) of the Act:

None

DOCUMENTS INCORPORATED BY REFERENCE:

Parts of Registrant's Proxy Statement for the Annual Meeting of Shareholders to be held on September 19, 2011 are incorporated by reference into Part III of this Report.

Part I

Item 1. *Business*

GENERAL NIKE, Inc. was incorporated in 1968 under the laws of the state of Oregon. As used in this report, the terms "we", "us", "NIKE" and the "Company" refer to NIKE, Inc. and its predecessors, subsidiaries and affiliates, unless the context indicates otherwise. Our Internet address is *www.nike.com*. On our NIKE Corporate web site, located at *www.nikebiz.com*, we post the following filings as soon as reasonably practicable after they are electronically filed with or furnished to the Securities and Exchange Commission: our annual report on Form 10-K, our quarterly reports on Form 10-Q, our current reports on Form 8-K and any amendments to those reports filed or furnished pursuant to Section 13(a) or 15(d) of the Securities and Exchange Act of 1934, as amended. All such filings on our NIKE Corporate web site are available free of charge. Also available on the NIKE Corporate web site are the charters of the committees of our board of directors, as well as our corporate governance guidelines and code of ethics; copies of any of these documents will be provided in print to any shareholder who submits a request in writing to NIKE Investor Relations, One Bowerman Drive, Beaverton, Oregon 97005-6453.

Our principal business activity is the design, development and worldwide marketing and selling of high quality footwear, apparel, equipment, and accessory products. NIKE is the largest seller of athletic footwear and athletic apparel in the world. We sell our products to retail accounts, through NIKE-owned retail stores and internet sales, which we refer to as our "Direct to Consumer" operations, and through a mix of independent distributors and licensees, in over 170 countries around the world. Virtually all of our products are manufactured by independent contractors. Virtually all footwear and apparel products are produced outside the United States, while equipment products are produced both in the United States and abroad.

PRODUCTS   NIKE's athletic footwear products are designed primarily for specific athletic use, although a large percentage of the products are worn for casual or leisure purposes. We place considerable emphasis on high quality construction and innovation in products designed for men, women and children. Running, training, basketball, soccer, sport-inspired casual shoes, and kids' shoes are currently our top-selling footwear categories and we expect them to continue to lead in product sales in the near future. We also market footwear designed for baseball, cheerleading, football, golf, lacrosse, outdoor activities, skateboarding, tennis, volleyball, walking, wrestling, and other athletic and recreational uses.

We sell sports apparel and accessories covering most of the above categories, sports-inspired lifestyle apparel, as well as athletic bags and accessory items. NIKE apparel and accessories feature the same trademarks and are sold through the same marketing and distribution channels. We often market footwear, apparel and accessories in "collections" of similar design or for specific purposes. We also market apparel with licensed college and professional team and league logos.

We sell a line of performance equipment under the NIKE Brand name, including bags, socks, sport balls, eyewear, timepieces, electronic devices, bats, gloves, protective equipment, golf clubs, and other equipment designed for sports activities. We also sell small amounts of various plastic products to other manufacturers through our wholly-owned subsidiary, NIKE IHM, Inc.

In addition to the products we sell directly to customers through our Direct to Consumer operations, we have entered into license agreements that permit unaffiliated parties to manufacture and sell certain apparel, electronic devices and other equipment designed for sports activities.

Our wholly-owned subsidiary, Cole Haan ("Cole Haan"), headquartered in New York, New York, designs and distributes dress and casual footwear, apparel and accessories for men and women under the Cole Haan® trademark.

Our wholly-owned subsidiary, Converse Inc. ("Converse"), headquartered in North Andover, Massachusetts, designs, distributes and licenses athletic and casual footwear, apparel and accessories under the Converse®, Chuck Taylor®, All Star®, One Star®, Star Chevron and Jack Purcell® trademarks.

Our wholly-owned subsidiary, Hurley International LLC ("Hurley"), headquartered in Costa Mesa, California, designs and distributes a line of action sports and youth lifestyle apparel and accessories under the Hurley® trademark.

Our wholly-owned subsidiary, Umbro International Limited ("Umbro"), headquartered in Cheadle, United Kingdom, designs, distributes and licenses athletic and casual footwear, apparel and equipment, primarily for the sport of football (soccer), under the Umbro® trademark.

SALES AND MARKETING   Financial information about geographic and segment operations appears in Note 18 of the accompanying Notes to the Consolidated Financial Statements.

We experience moderate fluctuations in aggregate sales volume during the year. Historically, revenues in the first and fourth fiscal quarters have slightly exceeded those in the second and third quarters. However, the mix of product sales may vary considerably as a result of changes in seasonal and geographic demand for particular types of footwear, apparel and equipment.

Because NIKE is a consumer products company, the relative popularity of various sports and fitness activities and changing design trends affect the demand for our products. We must therefore respond to trends and shifts in consumer preferences by adjusting the mix of existing product offerings, developing new products, styles and categories, and influencing sports and fitness preferences through aggressive marketing. Failure to respond in a timely and adequate manner could have a material adverse effect on our sales and profitability. This is a continuing risk.

We report our NIKE Brand operations based on our internal geographic organization. Each NIKE Brand geography operates predominantly in one industry: the design, development, marketing and selling of athletic footwear, apparel, and equipment. Effective June 1, 2009, we began operating under our new organizational structure for the NIKE Brand, which consists of the following six geographies: North America, Western Europe, Central & Eastern Europe, Greater China, Japan, and Emerging Markets. Previously, NIKE Brand operations were organized into the following four geographic regions: U.S., Europe, Middle East and Africa (collectively, "EMEA"), Asia Pacific, and Americas. Our NIKE Brand Direct to Consumer operations are managed within each geographic segment.

UNITED STATES MARKET   In fiscal 2011, sales in the United States including U.S. sales of our Other Businesses accounted for approximately 43% of total revenues, compared to 42% in fiscal 2010 and 2009. Our Other Businesses were primarily comprised of our affiliate brands; Cole Haan, Converse, Hurley and Umbro (which was acquired on March 3, 2008); and NIKE Golf. We estimate that we sell to more than 20,000 retail accounts in the United States. The NIKE Brand domestic retail account base includes a mix of footwear stores, sporting goods stores, athletic specialty stores, department stores, skate, tennis and golf shops, and other retail accounts. During fiscal 2011, our three largest customers accounted for approximately 23% of sales in the United States.

We make substantial use of our "futures" ordering program, which allows retailers to order five to six months in advance of delivery with the commitment that their orders will be delivered within a set time period at a fixed price. In fiscal 2011, 87% of our U.S. wholesale footwear shipments (excluding our Other Businesses) were made under the futures program, compared to 89% in fiscal 2010 and 2009. In fiscal 2011, 60% of our U.S. wholesale apparel shipments (excluding our Other Businesses) were made under the futures program, compared to 62% in fiscal 2010 and 60% in fiscal 2009.

We utilize 18 NIKE sales offices to solicit sales in the United States. We also utilize 4 independent sales representatives to sell specialty products for golf and 5 for skateboarding and snowboarding products. In addition, our Direct to Consumer operations sell NIKE Brand products through our internet website, *www.nikestore.com*, and the following retail outlets in the United States:

U.S. Retail Stores	Number
NIKE factory stores	150
NIKE stores	16
NIKETOWNs	9
NIKE employee-only stores	3
Cole Haan stores (including factory stores)	107
Converse stores (including factory stores)	58
Hurley stores (including factory and employee stores)	20
Total	363

NIKE's three significant distribution centers in the United States for NIKE Brand products, including NIKE Golf, are located in Memphis, Tennessee. NIKE also operates and leases one facility in Memphis, Tennessee for NIKE Brand product returns. NIKE Brand apparel and equipment products are also shipped from our Foothill Ranch, California distribution center. Cole Haan products are distributed primarily from Greenland, New Hampshire, and Converse and Hurley products are shipped primarily from Ontario, California.

INTERNATIONAL MARKETS In fiscal 2011, non-U.S. sales (including non-U.S. sales of our Other Businesses) accounted for 57% of total revenues, compared to 58% in fiscal 2010 and 2009. We sell our products to retail accounts, through our own Direct to Consumer operations, and through a mix of independent distributors and licensees around the world. We estimate that we sell to more than 20,000 retail accounts outside the United States, excluding sales by independent distributors and licensees. We operate 16 distribution centers outside of the United States. In many countries and regions, including Canada, Asia, some Latin American countries, and Europe, we have a futures ordering program for retailers similar to the United States futures program described above. During fiscal 2011, NIKE's three largest customers outside of the U.S. accounted for approximately 9% of total non-U.S. sales.

Our Direct to Consumer business operates the following retail outlets outside the United States:

Non-U.S. Retail Stores	Number
NIKE factory stores	243
NIKE stores	50
NIKETOWNs	3
NIKE employee-only stores	13
Cole Haan stores	83
Hurley stores	1
Total	393

International branch offices and subsidiaries of NIKE are located in Argentina, Australia, Austria, Belgium, Bermuda, Brazil, Canada, Chile, China, Croatia, Cyprus, the Czech Republic, Denmark, Finland, France, Germany, Greece, Hong Kong, Hungary, Indonesia, India, Ireland, Israel, Italy, Japan, Korea, Lebanon, Macau, Malaysia, Mexico, New Zealand, the Netherlands, Norway, the Philippines, Poland, Portugal, Russia, Singapore, Slovakia, Slovenia, South Africa, Spain, Sri Lanka, Sweden, Switzerland, Taiwan, Thailand, Turkey, the United Arab Emirates, the United Kingdom, Uruguay and Vietnam.

SIGNIFICANT CUSTOMER No customer accounted for 10% or more of our net sales during fiscal 2011.

ORDERS Worldwide futures and advance orders for NIKE Brand athletic footwear and apparel, scheduled for delivery from June through November 2011, were $10.3 billion compared to $8.8 billion for the same period last year. This futures and advance order amount is calculated based upon our forecast of the actual exchange rates under which our revenues will be translated during this period, which approximate current spot rates. Reported futures and advance orders are not necessarily indicative of our expectation of revenues for this period. This is because the mix of orders can shift between futures/advance and at-once orders and the fulfillment of certain of these futures/advance orders may fall outside of the scheduled time period noted above. In addition, foreign currency exchange rate fluctuations as well as differing levels of order cancellations and discounts can cause differences in the comparisons between futures and advance orders and actual revenues. Moreover, a significant portion of our revenue is not derived from futures and advance orders, including at-once and close-out sales of NIKE Brand footwear and apparel, sales of NIKE Brand equipment, sales from our Direct to Consumer operations, and sales from our Other Businesses.

PRODUCT RESEARCH AND DEVELOPMENT We believe our research and development efforts are a key factor in our past and future success. Technical innovation in the design of footwear, apparel, and athletic equipment receive continued emphasis as NIKE strives to produce products that help to reduce injury, enhance athletic performance and maximize comfort.

In addition to NIKE's own staff of specialists in the areas of biomechanics, chemistry, exercise physiology, engineering, industrial design, and related fields, we also utilize research committees and advisory boards made up of athletes, coaches, trainers, equipment managers, orthopedists, podiatrists, and other experts who consult with us and review designs, materials, concepts for product improvements and compliance with product safety regulations around the world. Employee athletes, athletes engaged under sports marketing contracts and other athletes wear-test and evaluate products during the design and development process.

MANUFACTURING   Virtually all of our footwear is produced by factories we contract with outside of the United States. In fiscal 2011, contract factories in Vietnam, China, Indonesia, and India manufactured approximately 39%, 33%, 24% and 2% of total NIKE Brand footwear, respectively. We also have manufacturing agreements with independent factories in Argentina, Brazil, India, and Mexico to manufacture footwear for sale primarily within those countries. The largest single footwear factory that we have contracted with accounted for approximately 6% of total fiscal 2011 NIKE Brand footwear production. Almost all of NIKE Brand apparel is manufactured outside of the United States by independent contract manufacturers located in 33 countries. Most of this apparel production occurred in China, Thailand, Vietnam, Malaysia, Sri Lanka, Indonesia, Turkey, Cambodia, El Salvador, and Mexico. The largest single apparel factory that we have contracted with accounted for approximately 7% of total fiscal 2011 apparel production.

The principal materials used in our footwear products are natural and synthetic rubber, plastic compounds, foam cushioning materials, nylon, leather, canvas, and polyurethane films used to make Air-Sole cushioning components. During fiscal 2011, NIKE IHM, Inc., a wholly-owned subsidiary of NIKE, as well as independent contractors in China and Taiwan, were our largest suppliers of the Air-Sole cushioning components used in footwear. The principal materials used in our apparel products are natural and synthetic fabrics and threads, plastic and metal hardware, and specialized performance fabrics designed to repel rain, retain heat, or efficiently transport body moisture. NIKE's independent contractors and suppliers buy raw materials in bulk for the manufacturing of our footwear, apparel and equipment products. Most raw materials are available and purchased by those independent contractors and suppliers in the countries where manufacturing takes place. We have thus far experienced little difficulty in satisfying our raw material requirements.

Since 1972, Sojitz Corporation of America ("Sojitz America"), a large Japanese trading company and the sole owner of our redeemable preferred stock, has performed significant import-export financing services for us. During fiscal 2011, Sojitz America provided financing and purchasing services for NIKE Brand products sold in Argentina, Uruguay, Canada, Brazil, India, Indonesia, the Philippines, Malaysia, South Africa, China, Korea, and Thailand, excluding products produced and sold in the same country. Approximately 19% of NIKE Brand sales occurred in those countries. Any failure of Sojitz America to provide these services or any failure of Sojitz America's banks could disrupt our ability to acquire products from our suppliers and to deliver products to our customers in those jurisdictions. Such a disruption could result in cancelled orders that would adversely affect sales and profitability. However, we believe that any such disruption would be short-term in duration due to the ready availability of alternative sources of financing at competitive rates. Our current agreements with Sojitz America expire on May 31, 2014.

INTERNATIONAL OPERATIONS AND TRADE   Our international operations and sources of supply are subject to the usual risks of doing business abroad, such as possible revaluation of currencies, export and import duties, anti-dumping measures, quotas, safeguard measures, trade restrictions, restrictions on the transfer of funds and, in certain parts of the world, political instability and terrorism. We have not, to date, been materially affected by any such risk, but cannot predict the likelihood of such developments occurring.

The global economic recession resulted in a significant slow-down in international trade and a sharp rise in protectionist actions around the world. These trends are affecting many global manufacturing and service sectors, and the footwear and apparel industries, as a whole, are not immune. Companies in our industry are facing trade protectionist challenges in many different regions, and in nearly all cases we are working together to address trade issues to reduce the impact to the industry, while observing applicable competition laws. Notwithstanding our efforts, such actions, if implemented, could result in increases in the cost of our products, which could adversely affect our sales or profitability and the imported footwear and apparel industry as a whole. Accordingly, we are actively monitoring the developments described below.

FOOTWEAR IMPORTS INTO THE EUROPEAN UNION   In 2005, at the request of the European domestic footwear industry, the European Commission ("EC") initiated investigations into leather footwear imported from China and Vietnam. Together with other companies in our industry, we took the position that Special Technology Athletic Footwear (STAF) (i) should not be within the scope of the investigation, and (ii) does not meet the legal requirements of injury and price in an anti-dumping investigation. Our arguments were successful and the EU agreed in October 2006 on definitive duties of 16.5% for China and 10% for Vietnam for non-STAF leather footwear, but excluded STAF from the final measures. Prior to the scheduled expiration in October 2008 of the measures imposed on the non-STAF footwear, the domestic industry requested and the EC agreed to review a petition to extend these restrictions on non-STAF leather footwear. In December 2009, following a review of the ongoing restrictions, EU member states voted to extend the measures for an additional 15 months, until March 31, 2011. In early 2011, the EC declined to further extend the measures and since April 1, 2011 these restrictions have been terminated. The EC noted that it will be monitoring leather footwear imports from Vietnam and China over the next 12 months and it is hoped that any increases will not result in renewed trade defense actions by the EC.

On February 3, 2010, the Chinese government announced it would seek to refer the EU decision (both on the original measures and subsequent review decision) to the World Trade Organization ("WTO") for its further review and decision. On May 18, 2010, the Dispute Settlement Body of the WTO agreed to establish a panel to rule on China's claims against the EU with respect to the above anti-dumping measures. The ruling from the WTO panel is expected in late July or August 2011, after which either party may accept or appeal the findings.

FOOTWEAR, APPAREL AND EQUIPMENT IMPORTS INTO BRAZIL AND ARGENTINA At the request of certain domestic footwear industry participants, both Brazil and Argentina have initiated independent anti-dumping investigations against footwear made in China. Over the last two years, we have been working with a broad coalition of other companies in our industry to challenge these cases on the basis that the athletic footwear being imported from China (i) should not be within the scope of the investigation, and (ii) does not meet the legal requirements of injury and price in an anti-dumping investigation. In the case of Argentina, in 2010, the final determination made by the administering authorities was favorable to us. In the case of Brazil, the administering authorities agreed to impose an anti-dumping duty against nearly all footwear from China, which we believe will impact all brands in the footwear industry. Although we do not currently expect that this decision will materially affect us, we are working with the same broad coalition of footwear companies to challenge this decision in domestic Brazilian courts as well as international forums such as the WTO.

Many products, including footwear, apparel and equipment products, that we and others in our industry import into Argentina and Brazil are subject to the WTO non-automatic licensing requirements, which means that it may take up to 60 days for those products to clear customs and enter into those jurisdictions. From time to time, in addition to these WTO licensing requirements, these jurisdictions impose further importation restrictions or limitations. As a result, we have experienced delays in our ability to import our products or it has taken longer than the time allowed under the WTO for us to import our products. To date, our business has not been materially affected by these restrictions or delays. In the future, however, if we are unable to import our products into these jurisdictions due to these or other restrictions or if we experience increasing or more frequent delays beyond the WTO-permitted 60 days to import our products, our business could be materially affected.

FOOTWEAR, APPAREL AND EQUIPMENT IMPORTS INTO TURKEY In 2006, Turkey introduced safeguard measures in the form of additional duties on all imported footwear into Turkey with the goal of protecting its local shoe manufacturing industry until August 2009. In June 2009, Turkish shoe-manufacturers submitted, and the Turkish Government agreed to review, a request for extension of the safeguard measures claiming that the rehabilitation process of the local Turkish industry was interrupted due to the continuing increase of footwear imports. Despite the importers opposition to the continuation of the safeguard measures, the Turkish authorities extended these safeguard measures until August 2012, but reduced the duty from $3 per pair of footwear to $1.60 per pair of footwear.

In 2011, two new safeguard measures and reviews were initiated by the Turkish Undersecretariat of Foreign Trade ("UFT") on apparel and equipment imports. In January 2011, the UFT began an investigation on apparel imports that could result in a 20-30% increase in import duties applied to imported apparel products, regardless of country of origin and with only a few exceptions for countries that currently have a Free Trade Agreement with Turkey. A decision is expected in late July 2011 and if approved, these higher import duties will be in place through July 2014. Together with other companies in our industry, we are advocating for exclusion of certain apparel products used for sporting activities that cannot be manufactured in Turkey and therefore should not be subject to a higher import duty. In February 2011, the UFT began a review of existing safeguard measure on travel goods, handbags and similar accessories and containers listed under applicable regulations. One Turkish bag manufacturers association has requested the continuation of the safeguard measures through April 2014, with the application of an additional import duty of 2.70 USD/kg (max. 4.25 USD/unit), regardless of country of origin. Together with other companies in our industry, we are advocating for the exclusion of non-leather bags from the scope of the continued safeguards.

TRADE RELATIONS WITH CHINA China represents an important sourcing country and consumer marketing country for us. Many governments around the world are concerned about China's growing and fast-paced economy, compliance with WTO rules, currency valuation, and high trade surpluses. As a result, a wide range of legislative proposals have been introduced to address these concerns. While some of these concerns may be justified, we are working with broad coalitions of global businesses and trade associations representing a wide variety of sectors (e.g., services, manufacturing, and agriculture) to help ensure any legislation enacted and implemented (i) addresses legitimate and core concerns, (ii) is consistent with international trade rules, and (iii) reflects and considers China's domestic economy and the important role it has in the global economic community. We believe other companies in our industry as well as most other multinational companies are in a similar position regarding these trade measures.

In the event any of these trade protection measures are implemented, we believe that we have the ability to develop, over a period of time, adequate alternative sources of supply for the products obtained from our present suppliers. If events prevented us from acquiring products from our suppliers in a particular country, our operations could be temporarily disrupted and we could experience an adverse financial impact. However, we believe we could abate any such disruption, and that much of the adverse impact on supply would, therefore, be of a short-term nature. We believe our principal competitors are subject to similar risks.

COMPETITION The athletic footwear, apparel, and equipment industry is keenly competitive in the United States and on a worldwide basis. We compete internationally with a significant number of athletic and leisure shoe companies, athletic and leisure apparel companies, sports equipment companies, and large companies having diversified lines of athletic and leisure shoes, apparel, and equipment, including Adidas, Puma, and others. The intense competition and the rapid changes in technology and consumer preferences in the markets for athletic and leisure footwear and apparel, and athletic equipment, constitute significant risk factors in our operations.

NIKE is the largest seller of athletic footwear and athletic apparel in the world. Performance and reliability of shoes, apparel, and equipment, new product development, price, product identity through marketing and promotion, and customer support and service are important aspects of competition in the athletic footwear, apparel, and equipment industry. To help market our products, we contract with prominent and influential athletes, coaches, teams, colleges and sports leagues to endorse our brands and use our products, and we actively sponsor sporting events and clinics. We believe that we are competitive in all of these areas.

TRADEMARKS AND PATENTS We utilize trademarks on nearly all of our products and believe having distinctive marks that are readily identifiable is an important factor in creating a market for our goods, in identifying our brands and the Company, and in distinguishing our goods from the goods of others. We consider our NIKE® and Swoosh Design® trademarks to be among our most valuable assets and we have registered these trademarks in over 150 countries. In addition, we own many other trademarks that we utilize in marketing our products. We continue to vigorously protect our trademarks against infringement.

NIKE has an exclusive, worldwide license to make and sell footwear using patented "Air" technology. The process utilizes pressurized gas encapsulated in polyurethane. Some of the early NIKE AIR® patents have expired, which may enable competitors to use certain types of similar technology. Subsequent NIKE AIR® patents will not expire for several years. We also have hundreds of U.S. and foreign utility patents, and thousands of U.S. and foreign design patents covering components and features used in various athletic and leisure shoes, apparel, and equipment. These patents expire at various times, and patents issued for applications filed this year will last from now to 2025 for design patents, and from now to 2031 for utility patents. We believe our success depends primarily upon skills in design, research and development, production, and marketing rather than upon our patent position. However, we have followed a policy of filing applications for United States and foreign patents on inventions, designs, and improvements that we deem valuable.

EMPLOYEES As of May 31, 2011, we had approximately 38,000 employees worldwide, which includes retail and part-time employees. Management considers its relationship with employees to be excellent. None of our employees is represented by a union, except for certain employees in the Emerging Markets geography, where local law requires those employees to be represented by a trade union, and in the United States, where certain employees of Cole Haan are represented by a union. Also, in some countries outside of the United States, local laws require representation for employees by works councils (such as in certain countries in the European Union, in which they are entitled to information and consultation on certain Company decisions) or other employee representation by an organization similar to a union, and in certain European countries, we are required by local law to enter into and/or comply with (industry wide or national) collective bargaining agreements. There has never been a material interruption of operations due to labor disagreements.

EXECUTIVE OFFICERS OF THE REGISTRANT The executive officers of NIKE as of July 14, 2011 are as follows:

Philip H. Knight, Chairman of the Board—Mr. Knight, 73, a director since 1968, is a co-founder of NIKE and, except for the period from June 1983 through September 1984, served as its President from 1968 to 1990 and from June 2000 to December 2004. Prior to 1968, Mr. Knight was a certified public accountant with Price Waterhouse and Coopers & Lybrand and was an Assistant Professor of Business Administration at Portland State University.

Mark G. Parker, Chief Executive Officer and President—Mr. Parker, 55, was appointed CEO and President in January 2006. He has been employed by NIKE since 1979 with primary responsibilities in product research, design and development, marketing, and brand management. Mr. Parker was appointed divisional Vice President in charge of development in 1987, corporate Vice President in 1989, General Manager in 1993, Vice President of Global Footwear in 1998, and President of the NIKE Brand in 2001.

David J. Ayre, Vice President, Global Human Resources—Mr. Ayre, 51, joined NIKE as Vice President, Global Human Resources in 2007. Prior to joining NIKE, he held a number of senior human resource positions with PepsiCo, Inc. since 1990, most recently as head of Talent and Performance Rewards.

Donald W. Blair, Vice President and Chief Financial Officer—Mr. Blair, 53, joined NIKE in November 1999. Prior to joining NIKE, he held a number of financial management positions with PepsiCo, Inc., including Vice President, Finance of Pepsi-Cola Asia, Vice President, Planning of PepsiCo's Pizza Hut Division, and Senior Vice President, Finance of The Pepsi Bottling Group, Inc. Prior to joining PepsiCo, Mr. Blair was a certified public accountant with Deloitte, Haskins, and Sells.

Charles D. Denson, President of the NIKE Brand—Mr. Denson, 55, has been employed by NIKE since 1979. Mr. Denson held several management positions within the Company, including his appointments as Director of USA Apparel Sales in 1994, divisional Vice President, U.S. Sales in 1994, divisional Vice President European Sales in 1997, divisional Vice President and General Manager, NIKE Europe in 1998, Vice President and General Manager of NIKE USA in 2000, and President of the NIKE Brand in 2001.

Gary M. DeStefano, President, Global Operations—Mr. DeStefano, 54, has been employed by NIKE since 1982, with primary responsibilities in sales and regional administration. Mr. DeStefano was appointed Director of Domestic Sales in 1990, divisional Vice President in charge of domestic sales in 1992, Vice President of Global Sales in 1996, Vice President and General Manager of Asia Pacific in 1997, President of USA Operations in 2001, and President of Global Operations in 2006.

Trevor Edwards, Vice President, Global Brand and Category Management—Mr. Edwards, 48, joined NIKE in 1992. He was appointed Marketing Manager, Strategic Accounts, Foot Locker in 1993, Director of Marketing, the Americas in 1995, Director of Marketing, Europe in 1997,

Vice President, Marketing for Europe, Middle East and Africa in 1999, and Vice President, U.S. Brand Marketing in 2000. Mr. Edwards was appointed corporate Vice President, Global Brand Management in 2002 and Vice President, Global Brand and Category Management in 2006. Prior to NIKE, Mr. Edwards was with the Colgate-Palmolive Company.

Jeanne P. Jackson, President, Direct to Consumer—Ms. Jackson, 59, served as a member of the NIKE, Inc. Board of Directors from 2001 through 2009, when she resigned from our Board and was appointed President, Direct to Consumer. She is founder and CEO of MSP Capital, a private investment company. Ms. Jackson was CEO of Walmart.com from March 2000 to January 2002. She was with Gap, Inc., as President and CEO of Banana Republic from 1995 to 2000, also serving as CEO of Gap, Inc. Direct from 1998 to 2000. Since 1978, she has held various retail management positions with Victoria's Secret, The Walt Disney Company, Saks Fifth Avenue, and Federated Department Stores. Ms. Jackson is the past President of the United States Ski and Snowboard Foundation Board of Trustees, and is a director of McDonald's Corporation. She is a former director of Nordstrom, Inc., and Harrah's Entertainment, Inc.

Hilary K. Krane, Vice President and General Counsel—Ms. Krane, 47, joined NIKE as Vice President and General Counsel in April 2010. Prior to joining NIKE, Ms. Krane was General Counsel and Senior Vice President for Corporate Affairs at Levi Strauss & Co. where she was responsible for legal affairs and overseeing the global brand protection department from 2006 to 2010. From 1996 to 2006, she was a partner and assistant general counsel at PricewaterhouseCoopers LLP.

Bernard F. Pliska, Vice President, Corporate Controller—Mr. Pliska, 49, joined NIKE as Corporate Controller in 1995. He was appointed Vice President, Corporate Controller in 2003. Prior to NIKE, Mr. Pliska was with Price Waterhouse from 1984 to 1995. Mr. Pliska is a certified public accountant.

John F. Slusher, Vice President, Global Sports Marketing—Mr. Slusher, 42, has been employed by NIKE since 1998 with primary responsibilities in global sports marketing. Mr. Slusher was appointed Director of Sports Marketing for the Asia Pacific and Americas Regions in 2006, divisional Vice President, Asia Pacific & Americas Sports Marketing in September 2007 and Vice President, Global Sports Marketing in November 2007. Prior to joining NIKE, Mr. Slusher was an attorney at the law firm of O'Melveny & Myers from 1995 to 1998.

Eric D. Sprunk, Vice President, Merchandising and Product—Mr. Sprunk, 47, joined NIKE in 1993. He was appointed Finance Director and General Manager of the Americas in 1994, Finance Director, NIKE Europe in 1995, Regional General Manager, NIKE Europe Footwear in 1998, and Vice President & General Manager of the Americas in 2000. Mr. Sprunk was appointed corporate Vice President, Global Footwear in 2001 and Vice President, Merchandising and Product in 2009. Prior to joining NIKE, Mr. Sprunk was a certified public accountant with Price Waterhouse from 1987 to 1993.

Hans van Alebeek, Vice President, Global Operations and Technology—Mr. van Alebeek, 45, joined NIKE as Director of Operations of Europe in 1999, and was appointed Vice President, Operations & Administration in EMEA in 2001, Vice President, Global Operations in 2003, Vice President, Global Operations & Technology in 2004, and Corporate Vice President in November 2005. Prior to joining NIKE, Mr. van Alebeek worked for McKinsey & Company as a management consultant and at N.V. Indivers in business development.

Roger S. Wyett, President, Affiliates—Mr. Wyett, 54, joined NIKE in April 2005 as President and Chief Operating Officer of the Company's Hurley brand and was appointed Vice President, Global Apparel in 2006. In October 2007, Mr. Wyett returned to the Company's Hurley brand as President and Chief Executive Officer, and then in February 2011 was appointed President of Affiliates. Mr. Wyett first joined NIKE in 1994, holding a number of management positions in soccer and NIKE Team Sports. From 2000 to 2005, Mr. Wyett was employed by The Walt Disney Company where he was Senior Vice President for Global Apparel, Accessories and Footwear, and later promoted to Executive Vice President for Global Sales and Marketing for Consumer Products.

Item 2. *Properties*

The following is a summary of principal properties owned or leased by NIKE.

The NIKE World Campus, owned by NIKE and located in Beaverton, Oregon, USA, is a 176 acre facility of 18 buildings which functions as our world headquarters and is occupied by approximately 6,000 employees engaged in management, research, design, development, marketing, finance, and other administrative functions from nearly all of our divisions. We also lease various office facilities in the surrounding metropolitan area. We lease a similar, but smaller, administrative facility in Hilversum, the Netherlands, which serves as the headquarters for the Western Europe and Central & Eastern Europe geographies. There are three significant distribution and customer service facilities for NIKE Brand products, including NIKE Golf, in the United States. All three of them are located in Memphis, Tennessee, two of which are owned and one of which is leased. NIKE also operates and leases one facility in Memphis, Tennessee for NIKE Brand product returns. NIKE Brand apparel and equipment are also shipped from our Foothill Ranch, California distribution center, which we lease. Cole Haan also operates a distribution facility in Greenland, New Hampshire, which we lease. Smaller leased distribution facilities for other brands and non-NIKE Brand businesses are located in various parts of the United States. We also own or lease distribution and customer service facilities in many parts of the world, the most significant of which are the distribution facilities located in Tomisatomachi, Japan, Laakdal, Belgium, and Taicang, China, all of which we own.

We manufacture Air-Sole cushioning materials and components at NIKE IHM, Inc. manufacturing facilities located in Beaverton, Oregon and St. Charles, Missouri, which we own. We also manufacture and sell small amounts of various plastic products to other manufacturers through NIKE IHM, Inc.

Aside from the principal properties described above, we lease three production offices outside the United States, over 100 sales offices and showrooms worldwide, and approximately 65 administrative offices worldwide. We lease more than 700 retail stores worldwide, which consist primarily of factory outlet stores. See "United States Market" and "International Markets" starting on pages 2 and 3 of this Report, respectively. Our leases expire at various dates through the year 2035.

Item 7. *Management's Discussion and Analysis of Financial Condition and Results of Operations*

NIKE designs, develops, markets and sells high quality footwear, apparel, equipment and accessory products worldwide. We are the largest seller of athletic footwear and apparel in the world. We sell our products to retail accounts, through NIKE-owned retail stores and internet sales, which we refer to as our "Direct to Consumer" operations, and through a mix of independent distributors and licensees, worldwide. Our goal is to deliver value to our shareholders by building a profitable global portfolio of branded footwear, apparel, equipment and accessories businesses. Our strategy is to achieve long-term revenue growth by creating innovative, "must have" products, building deep personal consumer connections with our brands, and delivering compelling retail presentation and experiences.

In addition to achieving long-term revenue growth, we continue to strive to deliver shareholder value by driving operational excellence in several key areas:

- Making our supply chain a competitive advantage through operational discipline,
- Reducing product costs through a continued focus on lean manufacturing and product design that strives to eliminate waste,
- Improving selling and administrative expense productivity by focusing on investments that drive economic returns in the form of incremental revenue and gross margin, and leveraging existing infrastructure across our portfolio of brands to eliminate duplicative costs,
- Improving working capital efficiency, and
- Deploying capital effectively to create value for our shareholders.

Through execution of this strategy, our long-term financial goals continue to be:

- High single-digit revenue growth,
- Mid-teens earnings per share growth,
- Increased return on invested capital and accelerated cash flows, and
- Consistent results through effective management of our diversified portfolio of businesses.

Over the past ten years, we have achieved or exceeded all of these financial goals. During this time, NIKE, Inc's revenues and earnings per share have grown 8% and 15%, respectively, on an annual compounded basis. Our return on invested capital has increased from 14% to 22% and we expanded gross margins by more than 5 percentage points.

Our fiscal 2011 results demonstrated our continued focus toward meeting our financial goals, while positioning ourselves for sustainable, profitable long-term growth. Despite the uncertain macroeconomic environment in fiscal 2011, we delivered record high revenues and diluted earnings per share. Our revenues grew 10% to $20.9 billion, net income increased 12% to $2.1 billion, and we delivered diluted earnings per share of $4.39, a 14% increase from fiscal 2010.

Income before income taxes increased 13% for fiscal 2011 primarily as a result of the increase in revenues and leverage on selling and administrative expense, which more than offset a decrease in gross margin percentage. The increase in revenues is reflective of increased demand for NIKE Brand footwear and apparel products across most businesses, particularly in the North America, Emerging Markets and Greater China geographies. Demand for our NIKE Brand footwear and apparel was fueled by our innovative products as well as strong category focused retail presentations. The decrease in gross margin percentage was primarily driven by higher product input costs, increased transportation expenses and a lower mix of licensee revenue as certain markets within our Other Businesses transitioned to NIKE, Inc. owned markets. These factors more than offset the positive impact from the growth and expanding profitability of our NIKE Brand Direct to Consumer business and our ongoing product cost reduction initiatives.

Net income for fiscal 2011 was negatively impacted by a year-over-year increase of 80 basis points in our effective tax rate, driven primarily by an increase in the percentage of total pre-tax income earned from operations in the United States. The United States statutory tax rate is generally higher than the tax rate on operations outside the United States.

For the year, diluted earnings per share grew at a higher rate than net income due to a 2% decrease in the weighted average number of diluted common shares outstanding driven by our share repurchases during fiscal 2011. While we increased the use of working capital in fiscal 2011 to support the growth of our businesses, we returned larger amounts of cash to our shareholders through higher dividends and increased share repurchases compared to fiscal 2010.

While we continue to believe that the Company is well positioned from a business and financial perspective, our future performance is subject to the inherent uncertainty presented by volatile macroeconomic conditions that may have an impact on our operations around the world. Our future performance is subject to our continued ability to take appropriate actions to respond to these conditions.

RESULTS OF OPERATIONS

	Fiscal 2011	Fiscal 2010	FY11 vs. FY10 % Change	Fiscal 2009	FY10 vs. FY09 % Change
	(In millions, except per share data)				
Revenues	$20,862	$19,014	10%	$19,176	−1%
Cost of sales	11,354	10,214	11%	10,572	−3%
Gross margin	9,508	8,800	8%	8,604	2%
Gross margin %	45.6%	46.3%		44.9%	
Demand creation expense	2,448	2,356	4%	2,352	0%
Operating overhead expense	4,245	3,970	7%	3,798	5%
Total selling and administrative expense	6,693	6,326	6%	6,150	3%
% of Revenues	32.1%	33.3%		32.1%	
Restructuring charges	—	—	—	195	—
Goodwill impairment	—	—	—	199	—
Intangible and other asset impairment	—	—	—	202	—
Income before income taxes	2,844	2,517	13%	1,957	29%
Net income	2,133	1,907	12%	1,487	28%
Diluted earnings per share	4.39	3.86	14%	3.03	27%

CONSOLIDATED OPERATING RESULTS

Revenues

	Fiscal 2011	Fiscal 2010	FY11 vs. FY10 % Change	FY11 vs. FY10 % Change Excluding Currency Changes[1]	Fiscal 2009	FY10 vs. FY09 % Change	FY10 vs. FY09 % Change Excluding Currency Changes[1]
				(In millions)			
Revenues	$20,862	$19,014	10%	10%	$19,176	−1%	−2%

[1] Results have been restated using constant exchange rates for the comparative period to enhance the visibility of the underlying business trends excluding the impact of foreign currency exchange rate fluctuations.

Fiscal 2011 Compared to Fiscal 2010 On both a reported and currency neutral basis, revenues for NIKE, Inc. grew 10% for fiscal 2011, driven by increases in revenues for both the NIKE Brand and our Other Businesses. On a currency neutral basis, revenues for the NIKE Brand increased 10% for fiscal 2011, while revenues for our Other Businesses increased 8%. Excluding the effects of changes in currency exchange rates, every NIKE Brand geography except Japan delivered higher revenues for fiscal 2011, led by North America, which contributed approximately 5 percentage points to the NIKE Brand revenue increase. The Emerging Markets and Greater China contributed approximately 3 and 2 percentage points to the NIKE Brand revenue growth, respectively.

By product group, NIKE Brand footwear and apparel revenue increased 11% and 9%, respectively, while NIKE Brand equipment revenues declined 2% during fiscal 2011. Fueling the growth of our NIKE Brand footwear business was the increased demand in our performance products, including the NIKE Lunar and Free technologies which are used across multiple categories. The increase in NIKE Brand footwear revenue for fiscal 2011 was attributable to a high single-digit percentage increase in unit sales along with a low single-digit percentage increase in the average selling price per pair. The increase in unit sales was primarily driven by double-digit percentage growth in Running, Men's Training, Action Sports and Women's Training products, while the increase in average selling price per pair was primarily driven by price increases on selected products and fewer close-outs as a percentage of total sales. For NIKE Brand apparel, the increase in revenue for fiscal 2011 was primarily driven by a low double-digit percentage increase in unit sales attributable to strong category presentations and improved product lines, while the average selling price per unit was relatively flat. The increase in unit sales was driven by increased demand in all key categories.

While wholesale revenues remain the largest component of overall NIKE Brand revenues, we continue to see growth in revenue through our Direct to Consumer channels. Our NIKE Brand Direct to Consumer operations include NIKE owned in-line and factory stores, as well as online sales through NIKE owned websites. For fiscal 2011, Direct to Consumer channels represented approximately 16% of our total NIKE Brand revenues compared to 15% in fiscal 2010. On a currency neutral basis, Direct to Consumer revenues grew 16% for fiscal 2011 as we continue to expand our store network, increase comparable store sales and build our e-commerce business. Comparable store sales grew 11% for fiscal 2011. Comparable store sales include revenues from NIKE owned in-line and factory stores for which all three of the following requirements have been met: the store has been open at least one year, square footage has not changed by more than 15% within the past year, and the store has not been permanently repositioned within the past year.

Revenues for our Other Businesses consist of results from our affiliate brands; Cole Haan, Converse, Hurley and Umbro; and NIKE Golf. Excluding the impact of currency changes, revenues for these businesses increased by 8% in fiscal 2011, reflecting double-digit percentage revenue growth at Converse, Cole Haan and Hurley, and a low single-digit growth at Umbro, which more than offset a mid single-digit revenue decline at NIKE Golf.

Fiscal 2010 Compared to Fiscal 2009 Excluding the effects of changes in currency exchange rates, revenues for NIKE, Inc. declined 2%, driven primarily by a 2% decline in revenues for the NIKE Brand. All of our geographies delivered lower revenues with the exception of Emerging Markets, reflecting a challenging economic environment across most markets, most notably in our Western Europe and Central & Eastern Europe geographies. By product group, revenues for our worldwide NIKE Brand footwear business were down 1% compared to the prior year.

Worldwide NIKE Brand apparel and equipment revenues declined 5% and 7%, respectively. Our Direct to Consumer operations represented approximately 15% of our total NIKE Brand revenues in fiscal 2010 as compared to 13% in fiscal 2009.

Excluding the impact of currency changes, revenues for our Other Businesses increased by 4% for fiscal 2010, driven by increased revenues at Converse, Umbro and Hurley, which more than offset revenue declines at NIKE Golf and Cole Haan.

Futures Orders Futures and advance orders for NIKE Brand footwear and apparel scheduled for delivery from June through November 2011 were 15% higher than the orders reported for the comparable prior year period. This futures and advance order amount is calculated based upon our forecast of the actual exchange rates under which our revenues will be translated during this period, which approximate current spot rates. Excluding the impact of currency changes, futures orders increased 12%, primarily driven by a high single-digit percentage increase in unit sales volume and a low single-digit percentage increase in average price per unit for both footwear and apparel products.

By geography, futures orders growth was as follows:

	Reported Futures Orders Growth	Futures Orders Excluding Currency Changes[1]
North America	+14%	+14%
Western Europe	+11%	+1%
Central & Eastern Europe	+13%	+10%
Greater China	+24%	+17%
Japan	−13%	−6%
Emerging Markets	+25%	+23%
Total NIKE Brand Futures Orders	+15%	+12%

[1] Growth rates have been restated using constant exchange rates for the comparative period to enhance the visibility of the underlying business trends excluding the impact of foreign currency exchange rate fluctuations.

The reported futures and advance orders growth is not necessarily indicative of our expectation of revenue growth during this period. This is due to year-over-year changes in shipment timing and because the mix of orders can shift between advance/futures and at-once orders and the fulfillment of certain orders may fall outside of the schedule noted above. In addition, exchange rate fluctuations as well as differing levels of order cancellations and discounts can cause differences in the comparisons between advance/futures orders and actual revenues. Moreover, a significant portion of our revenue is not derived from futures and advance orders, including at-once and close-out sales of NIKE Brand footwear and apparel, sales of NIKE Brand equipment, sales from our Direct to Consumer operations, and sales from our Other Businesses.

Gross Margin

	Fiscal 2011	Fiscal 2010	FY11 vs. FY10 % Change	Fiscal 2009	FY10 vs. FY09 % Change
			(In millions)		
Gross Margin	$9,508	$8,800	8%	$8,604	2%
Gross Margin %	45.6%	46.3%	(70) bps	44.9%	140 bps

Fiscal 2011 Compared to Fiscal 2010 For fiscal 2011, our consolidated gross margin percentage was 70 basis points lower than the prior year. The primary factors contributing to this decrease were as follows:

- Higher input costs across most businesses,
- Increased transportation costs, including additional air freight incurred to meet strong demand for NIKE Brand products across most businesses, most notably in North America, Western Europe, and Central & Eastern Europe geographies, and
- A lower mix of licensee revenue as distribution for certain markets within our Other Businesses transitioned from licensees to operating units of NIKE, Inc.

Together, these factors decreased consolidated gross margins by approximately 130 basis points for fiscal 2011, with the most significant erosion in the second half of the fiscal year. These decreases were partially offset by the positive impact from the growth and expanding profitability of our NIKE Brand Direct to Consumer business, a higher mix of full-price sales and favorable impacts from our ongoing product cost efficiency initiatives.

As we head into fiscal 2012, we anticipate that our gross margins will continue to face pressure from macroeconomic factors, most notably rising product input costs as well as higher transportation costs, which may more than offset the favorable impact from our planned price increases and ongoing production cost efficiency initiatives.

Fiscal 2010 Compared to Fiscal 2009 For fiscal 2010, our consolidated gross margin percentage was 140 basis points higher than the prior year. The primary factors contributing to this improvement were as follows:

- Improved in-line product margins across most geographies, driven by reduced raw material and freight costs as well as favorable changes in product mix,
- Improved inventory positions, most notably in North America and Western Europe, which drove a shift in mix from discounted close-out to higher margin in-line sales, and
- Growth of NIKE-owned retail as a percentage of total revenue, across most NIKE Brand geographies, driven by an increase in both new store openings and comparable store sales.

Together, these factors increased consolidated gross margins by approximately 160 basis points for fiscal 2010. These increases were partially offset by the impact of unfavorable currency exchange rates, primarily affecting our Emerging Markets and Central & Eastern Europe geographies.

Selling and Administrative Expense

	Fiscal 2011	Fiscal 2010	FY11 vs. FY10 % Change	Fiscal 2009	FY10 vs. FY09 % Change
			(In millions)		
Demand creation expense[1]	$2,448	$2,356	4%	$2,352	0%
Operating overhead expense	4,245	3,970	7%	3,798	5%
Selling and administrative expense	$6,693	$6,326	6%	$6,150	3%
% of Revenues	32.1%	33.3%	(120) bps	32.1%	120 bps

[1] Demand creation consists of advertising and promotion expenses, including costs of endorsement contracts.

Fiscal 2011 Compared to Fiscal 2010 In fiscal 2011, the effect of changes in foreign currency exchange rates did not have a significant impact on selling and administrative expense.

Demand creation expense increased 4% compared to the prior year, primarily driven by a higher level of brand event spending around the World Cup and World Basketball Festival in the first half of fiscal 2011, as well as increased spending around key product initiatives and investments in retail product presentation with wholesale customers.

Operating overhead expense increased 7% compared to the prior year. This increase was primarily attributable to increased investments in our Direct to Consumer operations as well as growth in our wholesale operations, where we incurred higher personnel costs and travel expenses as compared to the prior year.

Fiscal 2010 Compared to Fiscal 2009 In fiscal 2010, changes in currency exchange rates had a minimal impact on demand creation expense. Demand creation expense remained flat compared to the prior year, as increases in sports marketing and digital marketing expenses were offset by reductions in advertising.

Excluding changes in exchange rates, operating overhead expense increased 4% compared to the prior year due primarily to increases in performance-based compensation and investments in our Direct to Consumer operations. These increases were partially offset by reductions in compensation spending in fiscal 2010 as a result of restructuring activities that took place in the fourth quarter of fiscal 2009.

Restructuring Charges

During fiscal 2009, we restructured the organization to streamline our management structure, enhance consumer focus, drive innovation more quickly to market and establish a more scalable cost structure. As a result of these actions, we reduced our global workforce by approximately 5% and incurred pre-tax restructuring charges of $195 million in fiscal 2009, primarily consisting of cash severance costs. These charges are included in "Corporate" for segment reporting purposes.

Goodwill, Intangibles and Other Assets Impairment

In fiscal 2009, we recognized non-cash impairment charges of $199 million and $202 million relating to Umbro's goodwill, intangibles and other assets, respectively. Although Umbro's financial performance for fiscal 2009 was slightly better than we had originally expected, projected future cash flows had fallen below the levels we expected at the time of acquisition. This erosion was a result of both the unprecedented decline in global consumer markets, particularly in the United Kingdom, and our decision to adjust the level of investment in the business.

For additional information about our impairment charges, see Note 4–Acquisition, Identifiable Intangible Assets, Goodwill and Umbro Impairment in the accompanying Notes to the Consolidated Financial Statements.

Other (Income), net

	Fiscal 2011	Fiscal 2010	FY11 vs. FY10 % Change	Fiscal 2009	FY10 vs. FY09 % Change
			(In millions)		
Other (income), net	$(33)	$(49)	−33%	$(89)	−45%

Fiscal 2011 Compared to Fiscal 2010 Other (income), net is comprised of foreign currency conversion gains and losses from the re-measurement of monetary assets and liabilities in non-functional currencies and the impact of certain foreign currency derivative instruments, as well as unusual or non-recurring transactions that are outside the normal course of business. For fiscal 2011, other (income), net was primarily comprised of net foreign currency gains.

For fiscal 2011, we estimate that the combination of translation of foreign currency-denominated profits from our international businesses and the year-over-year change in foreign currency related net gains included in other (income), net had an unfavorable impact of approximately $33 million on our income before income taxes.

Fiscal 2010 Compared to Fiscal 2009 For fiscal 2010 and 2009, other (income), net was primarily comprised of net foreign currency gains and the recognition of previously deferred licensing income related to our fiscal 2008 sale of NIKE Bauer Hockey.

For fiscal 2010, we estimate that the combination of translation of foreign currency-denominated profits from our international businesses and the year-over-year change in foreign currency related net gains included in other (income), net increased our income before income taxes by approximately $34 million.

Income Taxes

	Fiscal 2011	Fiscal 2010	FY11 vs. FY10 % Change	Fiscal 2009	FY10 vs. FY09 % Change
Effective tax rate	25.0%	24.2%	80 bps	24.0%	20 bps

Fiscal 2011 Compared to Fiscal 2010 Our effective tax rate for fiscal 2011 was 80 basis points higher than the effective rate for fiscal 2010 due primarily to the change in geographic mix of earnings. A larger percentage of our earnings in fiscal 2011 were attributable to operations in the U.S., where the statutory tax rate is generally higher than the tax rate on operations outside of the U.S. This impact was partially offset by changes to uncertain tax positions.

Fiscal 2010 Compared to Fiscal 2009 Our effective tax rate for fiscal 2010 was 20 basis points higher than the effective rate for fiscal 2009. Our effective tax rate for fiscal 2009 includes a tax benefit related to charges recorded for the impairment of Umbro's goodwill, intangible and other assets. Excluding this tax benefit, our effective rate for fiscal 2009 would have been 26.5%, 230 basis points higher than our effective tax rate for fiscal 2010. The decrease in our effective tax rate for fiscal 2010 was primarily attributable to our international operations, as tax rates for these operations are generally lower than the U.S. statutory rate.

OPERATING SEGMENTS The Company's reportable operating segments are based on our internal geographic organization. Each NIKE Brand geography operates predominantly in one industry: the design, development, marketing and selling of athletic footwear, apparel, and equipment. Our reportable operating segments for the NIKE Brand are: North America, Western Europe, Central & Eastern Europe, Greater China, Japan, and Emerging Markets. Our NIKE Brand Direct to Consumer operations are managed within each geographic segment.

As part of our centrally managed foreign exchange risk management program, standard foreign currency rates are assigned to each NIKE Brand entity in our geographic operating segments and are used to record any non-functional currency revenues or product purchases into the entity's functional currency. Geographic operating segment revenues and cost of sales reflect use of these standard rates. For all NIKE Brand operating segments, differences between assigned standard foreign currency rates and actual market rates are included in Corporate together with foreign currency hedge gains and losses generated from our centrally managed foreign exchange risk management program. Prior to fiscal 2010, all foreign currency results, including hedge results and other conversion gains and losses generated by the Western Europe and Central & Eastern Europe geographies were recorded in their respective geographic results.

Certain prior year amounts have been reclassified to conform to fiscal 2011 presentation, as South Africa became part of the Emerging Markets operating segment beginning June 1, 2010. Previously, South Africa was part of the Central & Eastern Europe operating segment.

The breakdown of revenues follows:

	Fiscal 2011	Fiscal 2010[1]	FY11 vs. FY10 % Change	FY11 vs. FY10 % Change Excluding Currency Changes[2]	Fiscal 2009[1]	FY10 vs. FY09 % Change	FY10 vs. FY09 % Change Excluding Currency Changes[2]
	(In millions)						
North America	$ 7,578	$ 6,696	13%	13%	$ 6,778	−1%	−1%
Western Europe	3,810	3,892	−2%	4%	4,139	−6%	−6%
Central & Eastern Europe	1,031	993	4%	7%	1,247	−20%	−19%
Greater China	2,060	1,742	18%	16%	1,743	0%	0%
Japan	766	882	−13%	−21%	926	−5%	−12%
Emerging Markets	2,736	2,199	24%	19%	1,828	20%	17%
Global Brand Divisions	123	105	17%	21%	96	9%	12%
Total NIKE Brand Revenues	18,104	16,509	10%	10%	16,757	−1%	−2%
Other Businesses	2,747	2,530	9%	8%	2,419	5%	4%
Corporate[3]	11	(25)	—	—	—	—	—
Total NIKE, Inc. Revenues	$20,862	$19,014	10%	10%	$19,176	−1%	−2%

[1] Certain prior year amounts have been reclassified to conform to fiscal year 2011 presentation. These changes had no impact on previously reported results of operations or shareholders' equity.

[2] Results have been restated using constant exchange rates for the comparative period to enhance the visibility of the underlying business trends excluding the impact of foreign currency exchange rate fluctuations.

[3] Corporate revenues primarily consist of foreign currency hedge gains and losses generated by entities within the NIKE Brand geographic operating segments but managed through our central foreign exchange risk management program, and foreign currency gains and losses resulting from the difference between actual foreign currency rates and standard rates assigned to these entities, which are used to record any non-functional currency revenues into the entity's functional currency.

The primary financial measure used by the Company to evaluate performance of individual operating segments is earnings before interest and taxes (commonly referred to as "EBIT") which represents net income before interest expense (income), net and income taxes in the consolidated statements of income. As discussed in Note 18—Operating Segments and Related Information in the accompanying Notes to the Consolidated Financial Statements, certain corporate costs are not included in EBIT of our operating segments.

The breakdown of earnings before interest and taxes is as follows:

	Fiscal 2011	Fiscal 2010[1]	FY11 vs. FY10 % Change	Fiscal 2009[1]	FY10 vs. FY09 % Change
			(In millions)		
North America	$1,750	$1,538	14%	$1,429	8%
Western Europe	721	856	−16%	939	−9%
Central & Eastern Europe	233	253	−8%	394	−36%
Greater China	777	637	22%	575	11%
Japan	114	180	−37%	205	−12%
Emerging Markets	688	521	32%	364	43%
Global Brand Divisions	(998)	(867)	−15%	(811)	−7%
Total NIKE Brand	3,285	3,118	5%	3,095	1%
Other Businesses	334	299	12%	(193)	—
Corporate	(771)	(894)	14%	(955)	6%
Total Consolidated Earnings Before Interest and Taxes	$2,848	$2,523	13%	$1,947	30%
Interest expense (income), net	4	6	−33%	(10)	—
Total Consolidated Income Before Income Taxes	$2,844	$2,517	13%	$1,957	29%

[1] Certain prior year amounts have been reclassified to conform to fiscal year 2011 presentation. These changes had no impact on previously reported results of operations or shareholders' equity.

North America

	Fiscal 2011	Fiscal 2010	FY11 vs. FY10 % Change	FY11 vs. FY10 % Change Excluding Currency Changes	Fiscal 2009	FY10 vs. FY09 % Change	FY10 vs. FY09 % Change Excluding Currency Changes
				(In millions)			
Revenues							
Footwear	$5,109	$4,610	11%	11%	$4,694	−2%	−2%
Apparel	2,105	1,740	21%	21%	1,740	0%	0%
Equipment	364	346	5%	5%	344	1%	0%
Total Revenues	$7,578	$6,696	13%	13%	$6,778	−1%	−1%
Earnings Before Interest and Taxes	$1,750	$1,538	14%		$1,429	8%	

Fiscal 2011 Compared to Fiscal 2010 Revenues for North America increased 13%, driven by double-digit percentage growth in both wholesale and Direct to Consumer revenues. Contributing to the wholesale revenue growth was strong product category presentations at our wholesale customers, improved product lines and earlier shipments of summer season products. North America's Direct to Consumer revenues grew 19%, which contributed approximately 4 percentage points to North America's revenue increase. The growth in the Direct to Consumer business was fueled by 14% growth in comparable store sales.

For fiscal 2011, the increase in North America footwear revenue was primarily driven by double-digit percentage growth in Running, Men's and Women's Training and Football (Soccer) categories and a single-digit percentage growth in Basketball, partially offset by a low single-digit percentage decline in sales of our NIKE Brand Sportswear products.

The year-over-year increase in North America apparel revenues was primarily driven by double-digit percentage growth in most key categories, most notably Men's Training, Running, Basketball and Women's Training.

For fiscal 2011, the increase in North America's EBIT was primarily the result of revenue growth and leverage on selling and administrative expense, which more than offset a lower gross margin percentage. The decline in gross margin percentage was due primarily to increased air freight and product input costs, which more than offset the favorable impact from the growth of our Direct to Consumer business and fewer close-out sales.

Fiscal 2010 Compared to Fiscal 2009 Excluding the changes in currency exchange rates, revenues for North America declined 1%, driven primarily by a decrease in revenue from our wholesale business. This decrease was partially offset by an increase in our NIKE-owned retail business, driven primarily by an increase in comparable store sales.

During fiscal 2010, the decrease in North America footwear revenue was primarily attributable to a low single-digit percentage decrease in unit sales, while average selling price per pair remained flat. The decline in unit sales was primarily driven by lower sales for our Kids' and Running categories in the first half of fiscal 2010.

North America apparel revenue during fiscal 2010 was flat when compared to fiscal 2009, which was reflective of a high single-digit percentage increase in average selling price per unit, offset by a low double-digit percentage decrease in unit sales. Both the increase in average selling price per unit and the decrease in unit sales were primarily a result of fewer close-out sales compared to the prior year.

For fiscal 2010, the increase in North America's EBIT was primarily the result of improved gross margins combined with a slight decrease in selling and administrative expense, driven by a reduction in demand creation expense compared to prior year. The improvement in gross margin was mainly attributable to a shift in mix from close-out to in-line sales, growth of our Direct to Consumer business as a percentage of total sales, improved in-line product margins and lower warehousing costs.

Western Europe

	Fiscal 2011	Fiscal 2010	FY11 vs. FY10 % Change	FY11 vs. FY10 % Change Excluding Currency Changes	Fiscal 2009	FY10 vs. FY09 % Change	FY10 vs. FY09 % Change Excluding Currency Changes
				(In millions)			
Revenues							
Footwear	$2,327	$2,320	0%	7%	$2,385	−3%	−3%
Apparel	1,266	1,325	−4%	2%	1,463	−9%	−9%
Equipment	217	247	−12%	−6%	291	−15%	−15%
Total Revenues	$3,810	$3,892	−2%	4%	$4,139	−6%	−6%
Earnings Before Interest and Taxes	$ 721	$ 856	−16%		$ 939	−9%	

Fiscal 2011 Compared to Fiscal 2010 On a currency neutral basis, revenues for Western Europe increased 4% for fiscal 2011, attributable to growth in most territories. Revenues for the U.K. & Ireland, the largest market in Western Europe, grew 5% for fiscal 2011. Western Europe's Direct to Consumer revenues grew 10%, which contributed approximately 1 percentage point to Western Europe's revenue increase. The growth in the Direct to Consumer business was fueled by 6% growth in comparable store sales.

Excluding changes in currency exchange rates, footwear revenue in Western Europe increased 7%, driven by double-digit percentage growth in our Running, Football (Soccer) and Action Sports categories, which more than offset a slight revenue decline in our NIKE Brand Sportswear category.

On a currency neutral basis, apparel revenue in Western Europe increased 2%, primarily driven by double-digit percentage growth in our Football (Soccer) and Running categories, which more than offset a mid single-digit revenue decline in our NIKE Brand Sportswear category.

For fiscal 2011, the decrease in Western Europe's EBIT was driven by unfavorable foreign currency translation and a lower gross margin percentage, all of which more than offset the increase in revenues and improved leverage on selling and administrative expense. The decline in the gross margin percentage was significantly impacted by the unfavorable year-over-year standard currency rates. Also contributing to the decrease in the gross margin percentage was higher product input and air freight costs, higher royalty expenses related to sales of endorsed team products and higher full price discounts. These factors more than offset the favorable impact of fewer close-out sales.

Fiscal 2010 Compared to Fiscal 2009 On a currency neutral basis, most markets in Western Europe experienced lower revenues during fiscal 2010, reflecting a difficult retail environment throughout the geography. Our largest market, the U.K. & Ireland, declined 4%.

Excluding changes in currency exchange rates, the decrease in footwear revenue during fiscal 2010 was primarily the result of low single-digit decreases in both average selling price and unit sales. The decrease in average selling price was attributable to higher customer discounts provided to manage inventory levels, while the reduction in unit sales was due to lower sales for most NIKE Brand product categories.

The year-over-year decrease in apparel revenue was primarily driven by a high single-digit decline in unit sales combined with a mid single-digit decrease in average selling price. The decrease in unit sales was due to lower sales for most NIKE Brand product categories, while the decrease in average selling price was a result of higher discounts provided to retailers to manage their inventory levels.

For fiscal 2010, EBIT for Western Europe declined at a faster rate than revenues, as the increase in selling and administrative expense as a percentage of revenues more than offset the improvements in gross margin percentage. The increase in selling administrative expense was primarily driven by a higher level of both demand creation spending around the 2010 World Cup and operating overhead expense as a result of investments in our Direct to Consumer operations and higher performance-based compensation. The gross margin improvement in fiscal 2010 was primarily attributable to higher in-line product margins, a smaller proportion of close-out sales and reduced inventory obsolescence expense as a result of our leaner inventory positions.

Central & Eastern Europe

	Fiscal 2011	Fiscal 2010	FY11 vs. FY10 % Change	FY11 vs. FY10 % Change Excluding Currency Changes	Fiscal 2009	FY10 vs. FY09 % Change	FY10 vs. FY09 % Change Excluding Currency Changes
				(In millions)			
Revenues							
Footwear	$ 600	$558	8%	11%	$ 673	−17%	−16%
Apparel	356	354	1%	4%	468	−24%	−24%
Equipment	75	81	−7%	−5%	106	−24%	−21%
Total Revenues	$1,031	$993	4%	7%	$1,247	−20%	−19%
Earnings Before Interest and Taxes	$ 233	$253	−8%		$ 394	−36%	

Fiscal 2011 Compared to Fiscal 2010 Led by Russia and Turkey, most territories within Central & Eastern Europe reported revenue growth during fiscal 2011 as economic conditions in the geography continued to show signs of recovery.

The growth in Central & Eastern Europe's footwear revenues was mainly driven by double-digit percentage growth in our Football (Soccer), Running and Action Sports categories, while the growth in apparel revenues was primarily driven by double-digit percentage growth in our Running category.

For fiscal 2011, the decrease in Central & Eastern Europe's EBIT was primarily driven by unfavorable foreign currency translation and a lower gross margin percentage, which more than offset the increase in revenues and improved leverage on selling and administrative expense. The decline in the gross margin percentage was primarily due to unfavorable year-over-year standard currency rates, higher air freight costs and an increase in product input costs.

Fiscal 2010 Compared to Fiscal 2009 Economic conditions in Central & Eastern Europe remained difficult as most markets within the geography experienced lower revenues in fiscal 2010 as compared to fiscal 2009.

The decrease in footwear revenue was due to a decline in average selling price, while unit sales remained flat compared to fiscal 2009. The decline in average selling price was primarily the result of higher discounts provided to retailers to manage their inventory levels.

The year-over-year decrease in apparel revenue was primarily driven by a double-digit decrease in average selling price and a mid single-digit decline in unit sales. The decline in average selling price was primarily the result of higher discounts provided to retailers to manage their inventory levels, while the decline in unit sales was due to lower sales in most key product categories.

The year-over-year decrease in Central & Eastern Europe's EBIT during fiscal 2010 was the result of lower revenues, a decline in gross margin percentage and higher selling and administrative expense. The decline in gross margin percentage was primarily attributable to less favorable year-over-year standard currency rates, as well as higher discounts provided to customers. The increase in selling and administrative expense was primarily due to an increase in the reserve for bad debts along with increased investments in our Direct to Consumer operations.

Greater China

	Fiscal 2011	Fiscal 2010	FY11 vs. FY10 % Change	FY11 vs. FY10 % Change Excluding Currency Changes	Fiscal 2009	FY10 vs. FY09 % Change	FY10 vs. FY09 % Change Excluding Currency Changes
				(In millions)			
Revenues							
Footwear	$1,164	$ 953	22%	19%	$ 940	1%	1%
Apparel	789	684	15%	13%	700	−2%	−3%
Equipment	107	105	2%	0%	103	2%	0%
Total Revenues	$2,060	$1,742	18%	16%	$1,743	0%	0%
Earnings Before Interest and Taxes	$ 777	$ 637	22%		$ 575	11%	

Fiscal 2011 Compared to Fiscal 2010 Excluding changes in currency exchange rates, Greater China revenues increased 16% for fiscal 2011, driven by expansion in the number of partner-owned stores selling NIKE products, as well as improvement in comparable store sales for partner-owned stores.

For fiscal 2011, the increase in Greater China's footwear revenue was primarily driven by double-digit percentage growth in our Running and NIKE Brand Sportswear categories, while the growth in apparel revenue was mainly driven by double-digit percentage increases in our NIKE Brand Sportswear, Basketball and Men's Training categories.

For fiscal 2011, EBIT for Greater China grew at a faster rate than revenue as a result of a higher gross margin percentage, improved leverage on selling and administrative expense and favorable foreign currency translation. The improvement in the gross margin percentage was primarily attributable to higher product prices, favorable product mix and lower inventory obsolescence expense, which more than offset higher product input costs and warehousing costs from our new China distribution center.

Fiscal 2010 Compared to Fiscal 2009 For fiscal 2010, revenues for Greater China were flat, primarily attributable to comparisons against strong revenue growth in the first half of fiscal 2009 driven by the Beijing Olympics. Greater China began to gain momentum in the second half of fiscal 2010, as revenues increased 11% as compared to the second half of fiscal 2009.

The increase in footwear revenue was primarily driven by a mid single-digit increase in average selling price, partially offset by a mid single-digit decrease in unit sales. The increase in average selling price was primarily due to strategic price increases, while the decrease in unit sales was primarily driven by lower discounts on in-line products compared to the prior year.

The decrease in apparel revenue for fiscal 2010 was primarily due to a mid single-digit decrease in unit sales across most major categories, which more than offset a low single-digit increase in average selling price primarily driven by strategic price increases.

EBIT for Greater China increased at a faster rate than revenue as a result of higher gross margins and reductions in demand creation spending attributable to comparisons against higher prior year spending around the Beijing Olympics.

Japan

	Fiscal 2011	Fiscal 2010	FY11 vs. FY10 % Change	FY11 vs. FY10 % Change Excluding Currency Changes	Fiscal 2009	FY10 vs. FY09 % Change	FY10 vs. FY09 % Change Excluding Currency Changes
				(In millions)			
Revenues							
Footwear	$396	$433	−9%	−16%	$430	1%	−7%
Apparel	302	357	−15%	−23%	397	−10%	−17%
Equipment	68	92	−26%	−32%	99	−7%	−13%
Total Revenues	$766	$882	−13%	−21%	$926	−5%	−12%
Earnings Before Interest and Taxes	$114	$180	−37%		$205	−12%	

Fiscal 2011 Compared to Fiscal 2010 Macroeconomic conditions in Japan remain difficult. On March 11, 2011, Japan experienced a major earthquake and resulting tsunami. While the Company's organization and assets in Japan were not materially damaged, business results for the month of March 2011 were significantly eroded by the natural disaster. As we enter fiscal 2012, we anticipate macroeconomic conditions in Japan to remain difficult as consumer confidence continues to recover.

Excluding changes in currency exchange rates, both footwear and apparel revenues in Japan declined, driven by decreases across most key categories. Partially offsetting the decreases was a double-digit percentage growth in revenues from Running apparel.

The decrease in Japan's EBIT for fiscal 2011 was primarily due to lower revenues and higher selling and administrative expense as a percentage of revenue, partially offset by an improvement in the gross margin percentage. The improvement in the gross margin percentage was primarily driven by favorable year-over-year standard currency rates and positive impacts from fewer discounts on close-out sales, which more than offset higher product input costs and inventory obsolescence expense.

Fiscal 2010 Compared to Fiscal 2009 Excluding changes in currency exchange rates, both footwear and apparel revenues in Japan declined during fiscal 2010 due to decreases in unit sales across most major categories. The decline in revenues was reflective of a difficult and highly promotional marketplace in Japan.

For fiscal 2010, the decrease in Japan's EBIT was primarily due to lower revenues and higher selling and administrative expense, driven by increased investments in our Direct to Consumer operations, which more than offset improved gross margins.

Emerging Markets

	Fiscal 2011	Fiscal 2010	FY11 vs. FY10 % Change	FY11 vs. FY10 % Change Excluding Currency Changes	Fiscal 2009	FY10 vs. FY09 % Change	FY10 vs. FY09 % Change Excluding Currency Changes
				(In millions)			
Revenues							
Footwear	$1,897	$1,458	30%	24%	$1,185	23%	20%
Apparel	657	577	14%	9%	477	21%	17%
Equipment	182	164	11%	6%	166	−1%	−3%
Total Revenues	$2,736	$2,199	24%	19%	$1,828	20%	17%
Earnings Before Interest and Taxes	$ 688	$ 521	32%		$ 364	43%	

Fiscal 2011 Compared to Fiscal 2010 Excluding the changes in currency exchange rates, revenues for Emerging Markets increased 19% for fiscal 2011. Most territories in the geography reported double-digit revenue growth for the fiscal year, led by Brazil, Argentina, Mexico, and Korea.

For fiscal 2011, both footwear and apparel revenue growth in the Emerging Markets was primarily driven by strong demand in nearly all key categories, most notably NIKE Brand Sportswear and Running.

For fiscal 2011, EBIT for Emerging Markets grew at a faster rate than revenue as a result of higher gross margin percentage, improved leverage on selling and administrative expense and favorable foreign currency translation. The increase in the gross margin percentage was primarily due to a higher mix of in-line product sales, lower warehousing costs and favorable year-over-year standard currency rates, which more than offset the increase in product input costs and higher full-price discounts.

Fiscal 2010 Compared to Fiscal 2009 Excluding changes in currency exchange rates, fiscal 2010 revenue growth for the Emerging Markets geography was driven by growth in all product categories and all territories, most notably Brazil, Mexico and Korea.

Footwear revenue growth was primarily driven by a double-digit growth in unit sales and a mid single-digit increase in average selling price per pair during fiscal 2010, reflective of strong demand for most NIKE Brand product categories in all markets within the geography.

For fiscal 2010, the increase in Emerging Markets' EBIT was primarily the result of revenue growth combined with lower selling and administrative expense, which more than offset a decrease in gross margin percentage. The decrease in selling and administrative expense was primarily due to lower operating overhead expense resulting from fiscal 2009 restructuring activities. The decline in gross margin was primarily due to less favorable year-over-year standard currency rates compared to the prior year, which more than offset improved in-line product margins.

Global Brand Divisions

	Fiscal 2011	Fiscal 2010	FY11 vs. FY10 % Change	FY11 vs. FY10 % Change Excluding Currency Changes	Fiscal 2009	FY10 vs. FY09 % Change	FY10 vs. FY09 % Change Excluding Currency Changes
				(In millions)			
Revenues	$123	$105	17%	21%	$ 96	9%	12%
(Loss) Before Interest and Taxes	(998)	(867)	−15%		(811)	−7%	

Global Brand Divisions primarily represent demand creation and operating overhead expenses that are centrally managed for the NIKE Brand. Revenues for the Global Brand Divisions are attributable to NIKE Brand licensing businesses that are not part of a geographic operating segment.

Fiscal 2011 Compared to Fiscal 2010 For fiscal 2011, the increase in Global Brand Division expense was primarily due to an increase in both operating overhead and centrally managed demand creation expense. The increase in operating overhead expense was mainly driven by increased investments in our Direct to Consumer infrastructure along with higher wages and travel expense. The increase in demand creation expense was primarily driven by a higher level of brand event spending around the World Cup and World Basketball Festival in the first half of fiscal 2011, as well as increased investments in sports marketing.

Fiscal 2010 Compared to Fiscal 2009 For fiscal 2010, the increase in Global Brand Division expense was largely due to increases in centrally managed demand creation expense and performance-based compensation, which more than offset an increase in licensing revenues. The increase in demand creation expense was primarily driven by the centralization of certain marketing production costs.

Other Businesses

	Fiscal 2011	Fiscal 2010	FY11 vs. FY10 % Change	FY11 vs. FY10 % Change Excluding Currency Changes	Fiscal 2009	FY10 vs. FY09 % Change	FY10 vs. FY09 % Change Excluding Currency Changes
				(In millions)			
Revenues							
Converse	$1,130	$ 983	15%	15%	$ 915	7%	7%
NIKE Golf	623	638	−2%	−4%	648	−2%	−4%
Cole Haan	518	463	12%	12%	472	−2%	−2%
Hurley	252	221	14%	14%	203	9%	9%
Umbro	224	225	0%	2%	174	29%	30%
Other	—	—	—	—	7	—	—
Total Revenues	$2,747	$2,530	9%	8%	$2,419	5%	4%
Earnings Before Interest and Taxes	$ 334	$ 299	12%		$(193)	—	

Fiscal 2011 Compared to Fiscal 2010 Our Other Businesses are comprised of our affiliate brands; Cole Haan, Converse, Hurley and Umbro; and NIKE Golf. The revenue growth at Converse was primarily driven by increased licensing revenue in China, as well as increased sales in the U.K. as we transitioned that market to a Converse owned distribution model. Revenues for Cole Haan increased 12%, driven by double-digit percentage growth in our wholesale operations as well as high single-digit percentage growth in our Direct to Consumer operations. Revenues declined at NIKE Golf, where we experienced significant erosion in our Japan business following the earthquake and tsunami in March 2011.

For fiscal 2011, EBIT for our Other Businesses grew at a faster rate than revenues, primarily as a result of more favorable foreign currency exchange impacts. The gross margin percentage remained relatively flat for fiscal 2011, as the favorable impact from improved product mix was offset by a lower mix of licensee revenues. Selling and administrative expense as a percentage of revenues remained relatively flat for fiscal 2011.

Fiscal 2010 Compared to Fiscal 2009 For fiscal 2010, the increase in Other Businesses' revenue was primarily driven by revenue growth at Converse, Umbro and Hurley, which more than offset the declines at NIKE Golf and Cole Haan due to reductions in consumer discretionary spending in their respective markets.

In fiscal 2009, EBIT for our Other Businesses included a $401 million pre-tax non-cash charge relating to the impairment of goodwill, intangible and other assets of Umbro. Excluding this impairment charge, EBIT for our Other Businesses would have increased 43%, as a result of higher revenues, improved gross margins across most businesses, and lower demand creation spending.

For additional information about our impairment charges, see Note 4—Identifiable Intangible Assets, Goodwill and Umbro Impairment in the Notes to the Consolidated Financial Statements.

Corporate

	Fiscal 2011	Fiscal 2010	FY11 vs. FY10 % Change	Fiscal 2009	FY10 vs. FY09 % Change
		(In millions)			
Revenues	$ 11	$(25)	—	$ —	—
(Loss) Before Interest and Taxes	(771)	(894)	14%	(955)	6%

Corporate consists largely of unallocated general and administrative expenses, which includes expenses associated with centrally managed departments, depreciation and amortization related to our corporate headquarters, unallocated insurance, benefit and compensation programs, including stock-based compensation, certain foreign currency gains and losses, including certain hedge gains and losses, corporate eliminations and other items.

Corporate revenues primarily consist of (1) foreign currency hedge gains and losses related to revenues generated by entities within the NIKE Brand geographic operating segments but managed through our central foreign exchange risk management program and (2) foreign currency gains and losses resulting from the difference between actual foreign currency rates and standard rates assigned to these entities, which are used to record any non-functional currency revenues into the entity's functional currency.

In addition to the foreign currency gains and losses recognized in Corporate revenues, foreign currency results include all other foreign currency hedge results generated through our centrally managed foreign exchange risk management program, other conversion gains and losses arising from re-measurement of monetary assets and liabilities in non-functional currencies, and gains and losses resulting from the difference between actual foreign currency rates and standard rates assigned to each entity in NIKE Brand geographic operating segments, which are used to record any non-functional currency product purchases into the entity's functional currency. Prior to fiscal 2010, all foreign currency results, including hedge results and other conversion gains and losses, generated by the Western Europe and Central & Eastern Europe geographies were recorded in their respective geographic results.

Fiscal 2011 Compared to Fiscal 2010 For fiscal 2011, the decrease in Corporate expense was primarily driven by year-over-year net foreign currency gains generated by our centrally managed foreign exchange risk management program. Also contributing to the decrease in Corporate expense for fiscal 2011 was a $54 million year-over-year reduction in stock options expense primarily due to a change in accelerated vesting provisions that took effect in the first quarter of fiscal 2011 and a lower estimated fair value for stock options granted in the current year. These benefits more than offset an increase in corporate operating overhead expenses, primarily driven by higher wage-related expense.

Fiscal 2010 Compared to Fiscal 2009 In fiscal 2009, results for Corporate included a pre-tax restructuring charge of $195 million. Excluding this restructuring charge, loss before interest and taxes for Corporate would have increased by 18% for fiscal 2010, primarily driven by an increase in performance-based compensation.

LIQUIDITY AND CAPITAL RESOURCES

Cash Flow Activity Cash provided by operations was $1.8 billion for fiscal 2011 compared to $3.2 billion for fiscal 2010. Our primary source of operating cash flow for fiscal 2011 was net income of $2.1 billion. Our working capital was a net cash outflow of $708 million for fiscal 2011 as compared to a positive net cash inflow of $694 million for fiscal 2010. Our investments in working capital increased primarily due to an increase in inventory and higher accounts receivable. Inventory at the end of fiscal 2011 increased 33% compared to fiscal 2010, primarily driven by a 15% increase in futures orders, growth in replenishment programs for high-turnover styles, early purchases of key seasonal items with longer production lead times as well as the growth of Direct to Consumer operations. Changes in currency exchange rates and higher product costs also contributed to the increase in dollar inventory. The increase in accounts receivable was mainly attributable to the increase in revenues during fiscal 2011.

Cash used by investing activities was $1.0 billion during fiscal 2011, compared to $1.3 billion for fiscal 2010. The year-over-year decrease was primarily due to lower net purchases of short-term investments. Net purchases of short-term investments were $537 million (net of sales and maturities) in fiscal 2011 compared to $937 million during fiscal 2010.

Cash used by financing activities was $2.0 billion for fiscal 2011 compared to $1.1 billion used in fiscal 2010. The increase in cash used by financing activities was primarily due to an increase in share repurchases and dividends paid, partially offset by an increase in notes payable.

In fiscal 2011, we purchased 23.8 million shares of NIKE's class B common stock for $1.9 billion. These repurchases were made under the four-year, $5 billion program approved by our Board of Directors which commenced in December 2009 and as of the end of fiscal 2011, we have repurchased 30.4 million shares for $2.3 billion under this program. We continue to expect funding of share repurchases will come from operating cash flow, excess cash, and/or debt. The timing and the amount of shares purchased will be dictated by our capital needs and stock market conditions.

Off-Balance Sheet Arrangements

In connection with various contracts and agreements, we provide routine indemnifications relating to the enforceability of intellectual property rights, coverage for legal issues that arise and other items where we are acting as the guarantor. Currently, we have several such agreements in place. However, based on our historical experience and the estimated probability of future loss, we have determined that the fair value of such indemnifications is not material to our financial position or results of operations.

Contractual Obligations

Our significant long-term contractual obligations as of May 31, 2011, and significant endorsement contracts entered into through the date of this report are as follows:

Description of Commitment	Cash Payments Due During the Year Ending May 31,						
	2012	2013	2014	2015	2016	Thereafter	Total
	(In millions)						
Operating Leases	$ 374	$ 310	$ 253	$198	$174	$ 535	$ 1,844
Long-term Debt	200	48	58	8	109	37	460
Endorsement Contracts[1]	800	806	742	615	463	1,018	4,444
Product Purchase Obligations[2]	3,175	—	—	—	—	—	3,175
Other[3]	277	137	22	4	1	—	441
Total	$4,826	$1,301	$1,075	$825	$747	$1,590	$10,364

[1] The amounts listed for endorsement contracts represent approximate amounts of base compensation and minimum guaranteed royalty fees we are obligated to pay athlete and sport team endorsers of our products. Actual payments under some contracts may be higher than the amounts listed as these contracts provide for bonuses to be paid to the endorsers based upon athletic achievements and/or royalties on product sales in future periods. Actual payments under some contracts may also be lower as these contracts include provisions for reduced payments if athletic performance declines in future periods.

In addition to the cash payments, we are obligated to furnish our endorsers with NIKE product for their use. It is not possible to determine how much we will spend on this product on an annual basis as the contracts generally do not stipulate a specific amount of cash to be spent on the product. The amount of product provided to the endorsers will depend on many factors including general playing conditions, the number of sporting events in which they participate, and our own decisions regarding product and marketing initiatives. In addition, the costs to design, develop, source, and purchase the products furnished to the endorsers are incurred over a period of time and are not necessarily tracked separately from similar costs incurred for products sold to customers.

[2] We generally order product at least 4 to 5 months in advance of sale based primarily on advanced futures orders received from customers. The amounts listed for product purchase obligations represent agreements (including open purchase orders) to purchase products in the ordinary course of business, that are enforceable and legally binding and that specify all significant terms. In some cases, prices are subject to change throughout the production process. The reported amounts exclude product purchase liabilities included in accounts payable on the consolidated balance sheet as of May 31, 2011.

[3] Other amounts primarily include service and marketing commitments made in the ordinary course of business. The amounts represent the minimum payments required by legally binding contracts and agreements that specify all significant terms, including open purchase orders for non-product purchases. The reported amounts exclude those liabilities included in accounts payable or accrued liabilities on the consolidated balance sheet as of May 31, 2011.

The total liability for uncertain tax positions was $212 million, excluding related interest and penalties, at May 31, 2011. We are not able to reasonably estimate when or if cash payments of the long-term liability for uncertain tax positions will occur.

We also have the following outstanding short-term debt obligations as of May 31, 2011. Please refer to the accompanying Notes to the Consolidated Financial Statements (Note 7—Short-Term Borrowings and Credit Lines) for further description and interest rates related to the short-term debt obligations listed below.

	Outstanding as of May 31, 2011
	(In millions)
Notes payable, due at mutually agreed-upon dates within one year of issuance or on demand	$187
Payable to Sojitz America for the purchase of inventories, generally due 60 days after shipment of goods from a foreign port	$111

As of May 31, 2011, letters of credit of $99 million were outstanding, generally for the purchase of inventory.

Capital Resources

In December 2008, we filed a shelf registration statement with the Securities and Exchange Commission under which $760 million in debt securities may be issued. As of May 31, 2011, no debt securities had been issued under this shelf registration.

As of and for the year ended May 31, 2011, we had no amounts outstanding under our multi-year, $1 billion revolving credit facility in place with a group of banks. The facility matures in December 2012. Based on our current long-term senior unsecured debt ratings of A+ and A1 from Standard and Poor's Corporation and Moody's Investor Services, respectively, the interest rate charged on any outstanding borrowings would be the prevailing London Interbank Offer Rate ("LIBOR") plus 0.15%. The facility fee is 0.05% of the total commitment.

If our long-term debt rating were to decline, the facility fee and interest rate under our committed credit facility would increase. Conversely, if our long-term debt rating were to improve, the facility fee and interest rate would decrease. Changes in our long-term debt rating would not trigger acceleration of maturity of any then outstanding borrowings or any future borrowings under the committed credit facility. Under this committed credit facility, we have agreed to various covenants. These covenants include limits on our disposal of fixed assets and the amount of debt secured by liens we may incur as well as a minimum capitalization ratio. In the event we were to have any borrowings outstanding under this facility, failed to meet any covenant, and were unable to obtain a waiver from a majority of the banks, any borrowings would become immediately due and payable. As of May 31, 2011, we were in full compliance with each of these covenants and believe it is unlikely we will fail to meet any of these covenants in the foreseeable future.

Liquidity is also provided by our $1 billion commercial paper program. As of and for the year ended May 31, 2011, no amounts were outstanding under this program. We currently have short-term debt ratings of A1 and P1 from Standard and Poor's Corporation and Moody's Investor Services, respectively.

As of May 31, 2011, we had cash, cash equivalents and short term investments totaling $4.5 billion, including amounts held in the U.S. and foreign jurisdictions. Cash equivalents and short term investments consist primarily of deposits held at major banks, money market funds, Tier-1 commercial paper, corporate notes, U.S. Treasury obligations, U.S. government agency obligations and government sponsored enterprise obligations, and other investment grade fixed income securities. Our fixed income investments are exposed to both credit and interest rate risk. All of our investments are investment grade to minimize our credit risk. While individual securities have varying durations, the average duration of our entire cash equivalents and short term investment portfolio is less than 120 days as of May 31, 2011.

Despite recent uncertainties in the financial markets, to date we have not experienced difficulty accessing the credit markets or incurred higher interest costs. Future volatility in the capital markets, however, may increase costs associated with issuing commercial paper or other debt instruments or affect our ability to access those markets. We utilize a variety of tax planning and financing strategies in an effort to manage our worldwide cash and deploy funds to locations where it is needed. We believe that existing cash, cash equivalents, short-term investments and cash generated by operations, together with access to external sources of funds as described above, will be sufficient to meet our domestic and foreign capital needs in the foreseeable future.

Item 8. *Financial Statements and Supplemental Data*

Management of NIKE, Inc. is responsible for the information and representations contained in this report. The financial statements have been prepared in conformity with the generally accepted accounting principles we considered appropriate in the circumstances and include some amounts based on our best estimates and judgments. Other financial information in this report is consistent with these financial statements.

Our accounting systems include controls designed to reasonably assure assets are safeguarded from unauthorized use or disposition and provide for the preparation of financial statements in conformity with generally accepted accounting principles. These systems are supplemented by the selection and training of qualified financial personnel and an organizational structure providing for appropriate segregation of duties.

An Internal Audit department reviews the results of its work with the Audit Committee of the Board of Directors, presently consisting of three outside directors. The Audit Committee is responsible for the appointment of the independent registered public accounting firm and reviews with the independent registered public accounting firm, management and the internal audit staff, the scope and the results of the annual examination, the effectiveness of the accounting control system and other matters relating to the financial affairs of NIKE as they deem appropriate. The independent registered public accounting firm and the internal auditors have full access to the Committee, with and without the presence of management, to discuss any appropriate matters.

Management's Annual Report on Internal Control Over Financial Reporting

Management is responsible for establishing and maintaining adequate internal control over financial reporting, as such term is defined in Rule 13a-15(f) and Rule 15d-15(f) of the Securities Exchange Act of 1934, as amended. Internal control over financial reporting is a process designed to provide reasonable assurance regarding the reliability of financial reporting and the preparation of the financial statements for external purposes in accordance with generally accepted accounting principles in the United States of America. Internal control over financial reporting includes those policies and procedures that: (i) pertain to the maintenance of records that, in reasonable detail, accurately and fairly reflect the transactions and dispositions of assets of the company; (ii) provide reasonable assurance that transactions are recorded as necessary to permit preparation of financial statements in accordance with generally accepted accounting principles, and that receipts and expenditures of the company are being made only in accordance with authorizations of our management and directors; and (iii) provide reasonable assurance regarding prevention or timely detection of unauthorized acquisition, use or disposition of assets of the company that could have a material effect on the financial statements.

While "reasonable assurance" is a high level of assurance, it does not mean absolute assurance. Because of its inherent limitations, internal control over financial reporting may not prevent or detect every misstatement and instance of fraud. Controls are susceptible to manipulation, especially in instances of fraud caused by the collusion of two or more people, including our senior management. Also, projections of any evaluation of effectiveness to future periods are subject to the risk that controls may become inadequate because of changes in conditions, or that the degree of compliance with the policies or procedures may deteriorate.

Under the supervision and with the participation of our Chief Executive Officer and Chief Financial Officer, our management conducted an evaluation of the effectiveness of our internal control over financial reporting based upon the framework in *Internal Control—Integrated Framework* issued by the Committee of Sponsoring Organizations of the Treadway Commission (COSO). Based on the results of our evaluation, our management concluded that our internal control over financial reporting was effective as of May 31, 2011.

PricewaterhouseCoopers LLP, an independent registered public accounting firm, has audited (1) the consolidated financial statements and (2) the effectiveness of our internal control over financial reporting as of May 31, 2011, as stated in their report herein.

Mark G. Parker	Donald W. Blair
Chief Executive Officer and President	Chief Financial Officer

Report of Independent Registered Public Accounting Firm

To the Board of Directors and Shareholders of NIKE, Inc.:

In our opinion, the consolidated financial statements listed in the index appearing under Item 15(a)(1) present fairly, in all material respects, the financial position of NIKE, Inc. and its subsidiaries at May 31, 2011 and 2010, and the results of their operations and their cash flows for each of the three years in the period ended May 31, 2011 in conformity with accounting principles generally accepted in the United States of America. In addition, in our opinion, the financial statement schedule listed in the appendix appearing under Item 15(a)(2) presents fairly, in all material respects, the information set forth therein when read in conjunction with the related consolidated financial statements. Also in our opinion, the Company maintained, in all material respects, effective internal control over financial reporting as of May 31, 2011, based on criteria established in *Internal Control—Integrated Framework* issued by the Committee of Sponsoring Organizations of the Treadway Commission (COSO). The Company's management is responsible for these financial statements and financial statement schedule, for maintaining effective internal control over financial reporting and for its assessment of the effectiveness of internal control over financial reporting, included in Management's Annual Report on Internal Control Over Financial Reporting appearing under Item 8. Our responsibility is to express opinions on these financial statements, on the financial statement schedule, and on the Company's internal control over financial reporting based on our integrated audits. We conducted our audits in accordance with the standards of the Public Company Accounting Oversight Board (United States). Those standards require that we plan and perform the audits to obtain reasonable assurance about whether the financial statements are free of material misstatement and whether effective internal control over financial reporting was maintained in all material respects. Our audits of the financial statements included examining, on a test basis, evidence supporting the amounts and disclosures in the financial statements, assessing the accounting principles used and significant estimates made by management, and evaluating the overall financial statement presentation. Our audit of internal control over financial reporting included obtaining an understanding of internal control over financial reporting, assessing the risk that a material weakness exists, and testing and evaluating the design and operating effectiveness of internal control based on the assessed risk. Our audits also included performing such other procedures as we considered necessary in the circumstances. We believe that our audits provide a reasonable basis for our opinions.

A company's internal control over financial reporting is a process designed to provide reasonable assurance regarding the reliability of financial reporting and the preparation of financial statements for external purposes in accordance with generally accepted accounting principles. A company's internal control over financial reporting includes those policies and procedures that (i) pertain to the maintenance of records that, in reasonable detail, accurately and fairly reflect the transactions and dispositions of the assets of the company; (ii) provide reasonable assurance that transactions are recorded as necessary to permit preparation of financial statements in accordance with generally accepted accounting principles, and that receipts and expenditures of the company are being made only in accordance with authorizations of management and directors of the company; and (iii) provide reasonable assurance regarding prevention or timely detection of unauthorized acquisition, use, or disposition of the company's assets that could have a material effect on the financial statements.

Because of its inherent limitations, internal control over financial reporting may not prevent or detect misstatements. Also, projections of any evaluation of effectiveness to future periods are subject to the risk that controls may become inadequate because of changes in conditions, or that the degree of compliance with the policies or procedures may deteriorate.

/s/ PRICEWATERHOUSECOOPERS LLP

Portland, Oregon
July 22, 2011

NIKE, INC.
CONSOLIDATED STATEMENTS OF INCOME

	Year Ended May 31,		
	2011	2010	2009
	(In millions, except per share data)		
Revenues	$20,862	$19,014	$19,176
Cost of sales	11,354	10,214	10,572
Gross margin	9,508	8,800	8,604
Demand creation expense	2,448	2,356	2,352

	Year Ended May 31,		
	2011	2010	2009
	(In millions, except per share data)		
Operating overhead expense	4,245	3,970	3,798
Total selling and administrative expense	6,693	6,326	6,150
Restructuring charges (Note 16)	—	—	195
Goodwill impairment (Note 4)	—	—	199
Intangible and other asset impairment (Note 4)	—	—	202
Interest expense (income), net (Notes 6, 7 and 8)	4	6	(10)
Other (income), net (Note 17)	(33)	(49)	(89)
Income before income taxes	2,844	2,517	1,957
Income taxes (Note 9)	711	610	470
Net income	$ 2,133	$ 1,907	$ 1,487
Basic earnings per common share (Notes 1 and 12)	$ 4.48	$ 3.93	$ 3.07
Diluted earnings per common share (Notes 1 and 12)	$ 4.39	$ 3.86	$ 3.03
Dividends declared per common share	$ 1.20	$ 1.06	$ 0.98

The accompanying notes to consolidated financial statements are an integral part of this statement.

NIKE, INC.
CONSOLIDATED BALANCE SHEETS

	May 31,	
	2011	2010
	(In millions)	
ASSETS		
Current assets:		
Cash and equivalents	$ 1,955	$ 3,079
Short-term investments (Note 6)	2,583	2,067
Accounts receivable, net (Note 1)	3,138	2,650
Inventories (Notes 1 and 2)	2,715	2,041
Deferred income taxes (Note 9)	312	249
Prepaid expenses and other current assets	594	873
Total current assets	11,297	10,959
Property, plant and equipment, net (Note 3)	2,115	1,932
Identifiable intangible assets, net (Note 4)	487	467
Goodwill (Note 4)	205	188
Deferred income taxes and other assets (Notes 9 and 17)	894	873
Total assets	$14,998	$14,419
LIABILITIES AND SHAREHOLDERS' EQUITY		
Current liabilities:		
Current portion of long-term debt (Note 8)	$ 200	$ 7
Notes payable (Note 7)	187	139
Accounts payable (Note 7)	1,469	1,255
Accrued liabilities (Notes 5 and 17)	1,985	1,904
Income taxes payable (Note 9)	117	59
Total current liabilities	3,958	3,364
Long-term debt (Note 8)	276	446
Deferred income taxes and other liabilities (Notes 9 and 17)	921	855
Commitments and contingencies (Note 15)	—	—
Redeemable Preferred Stock (Note 10)	—	—

	May 31,	
	2011	**2010**
	(In millions)	
Shareholders' equity:		
Common stock at stated value (Note 11):		
Class A convertible—90 and 90 shares outstanding	—	—
Class B—378 and 394 shares outstanding	3	3
Capital in excess of stated value	3,944	3,441
Accumulated other comprehensive income (Note 14)	95	215
Retained earnings	5,801	6,095
Total shareholders' equity	9,843	9,754
Total liabilities and shareholders' equity	$14,998	$14,419

The accompanying notes to consolidated financial statements are an integral part of this statement.

NIKE, INC.
CONSOLIDATED STATEMENTS OF CASH FLOWS

	Year Ended May 31,		
	2011	**2010**	**2009**
	(In millions)		
Cash provided by operations:			
Net income	$2,133	$1,907	$1,487
Income charges (credits) not affecting cash:			
Depreciation	335	324	335
Deferred income taxes	(76)	8	(294)
Stock-based compensation (Note 11)	105	159	171
Impairment of goodwill, intangibles and other assets (Note 4)	—	—	401
Amortization and other	23	72	48
Changes in certain working capital components and other assets and liabilities excluding the impact of acquisition and divestitures:			
(Increase) decrease in accounts receivable	(273)	182	(238)
(Increase) decrease in inventories	(551)	285	32
(Increase) decrease in prepaid expenses and other current assets	(35)	(70)	14
Increase (decrease) in accounts payable, accrued liabilities and income taxes payable	151	297	(220)
Cash provided by operations	1,812	3,164	1,736
Cash used by investing activities:			
Purchases of short-term investments	(7,616)	(3,724)	(2,909)
Maturities of short-term investments	4,313	2,334	1,280
Sales of short-term investments	2,766	453	1,110
Additions to property, plant and equipment	(432)	(335)	(456)
Disposals of property, plant and equipment	1	10	33
Increase in other assets, net of other liabilities	(30)	(11)	(47)
Settlement of net investment hedges	(23)	5	191
Cash used by investing activities	(1,021)	(1,268)	(798)
Cash used by financing activities:			
Reductions in long-term debt, including current portion	(8)	(32)	(7)
Increase (decrease) in notes payable	41	(205)	177
Proceeds from exercise of stock options and other stock issuances	345	364	187

	Year Ended May 31,		
	2011	2010	2009
	(In millions)		
Excess tax benefits from share-based payment arrangements	64	58	25
Repurchase of common stock	(1,859)	(741)	(649)
Dividends—common and preferred	(555)	(505)	(467)
Cash used by financing activities	(1,972)	(1,061)	(734)
Effect of exchange rate changes	57	(47)	(47)
Net (decrease) increase in cash and equivalents	(1,124)	788	157
Cash and equivalents, beginning of year	3,079	2,291	2,134
Cash and equivalents, end of year	$1,955	$3,079	$2,291
Supplemental disclosure of cash flow information:			
Cash paid during the year for:			
Interest, net of capitalized interest	$ 32	$ 48	$ 47
Income taxes	736	537	765
Dividends declared and not paid	145	131	121

The accompanying notes to consolidated financial statements are an integral part of this statement.

NIKE, INC.
CONSOLIDATED STATEMENTS OF SHAREHOLDERS' EQUITY

	Common Stock				Capital in Excess of Stated Value	Accumulated Other Comprehensive Income	Retained Earnings	Total
	Class A		Class B					
	Shares	Amount	Shares	Amount				
	(In millions, except per share data)							
Balance at May 31, 2008	97	$ —	394	$ 3	$ 2,498	$ 251	$ 5,073	$ 7,825
Stock options exercised			4		167			167
Conversion to Class B Common Stock	(2)		2					—
Repurchase of Class B Common Stock			(11)		(6)		(633)	(639)
Dividends on Common stock ($0.98 per share)							(475)	(475)
Issuance of shares to employees			1		45			45
Stock-based compensation (Note 11):					171			171
Forfeiture of shares from employees			—		(4)		(1)	(5)
Comprehensive income:								
Net income							1,487	1,487

NIKE, INC.
CONSOLIDATED STATEMENTS OF SHAREHOLDERS' EQUITY

	Common Stock				Capital in Excess of Stated Value	Accumulated Other Comprehensive Income	Retained Earnings	Total
	Class A		Class B					
	Shares	Amount	Shares	Amount				
					(In millions, except per share data)			
Other comprehensive income:								
Foreign currency translation and other (net of tax benefit of $178)						(335)		(335)
Net gain on cash flow hedges (net of tax expense of $168)							454	454
Net gain on net investment hedges (net of tax expense of $55)						106		106
Reclassification to net income of previously deferred net gains related to hedge derivatives (net of tax expense of $40)						(108)		(108)
Total comprehensive income						117	1,487	1,604
Balance at May 31, 2009	**95**	**$ —**	**390**	**$ 3**	**$ 2,871**	**$ 368**	**$ 5,451**	**$ 8,693**
Stock options exercised			9		380			380
Conversion to Class B Common Stock	(5)		5					—
Repurchase of Class B Common Stock			(11)		(7)		(747)	(754)
Dividends on Common stock ($1.06 per share)							(515)	(515)
Issuance of shares to employees			1		40			40
Stock-based compensation (Note 11):					159			159
Forfeiture of shares from employees			—		(2)		(1)	(3)
Comprehensive income:								
Net income							1,907	1,907
Other comprehensive income (Notes 14 and 17):								
Foreign currency translation and other (net of tax benefit of $72)						(159)		(159)
Net gain on cash flow hedges (net of tax expense of $28)						87		87

NIKE, INC.
CONSOLIDATED STATEMENTS OF SHAREHOLDERS' EQUITY

| | Common Stock | | | | Capital in Excess of Stated Value | Accumulated Other Comprehensive Income | Retained Earnings | Total |
| | Class A | | Class B | | | | | |
	Shares	Amount	Shares	Amount				
					(In millions, except per share data)			
Net gain on net investment hedges (net of tax expense of $21)						45		45
Reclassification to net income of previously deferred net gains related to hedge derivatives (net of tax expense of $42)						(122)		(122)
Reclassification of ineffective hedge gains to net income (net of tax expense of $1)						(4)		(4)
Total comprehensive income						(153)	1,907	1,754
Balance at May 31, 2010	**90**	**$ —**	**394**	**$ 3**	**$ 3,441**	**$ 215**	**$ 6,095**	**$ 9,754**
Stock options exercised			7		368			368
Repurchase of Class B Common Stock			(24)		(14)		(1,857)	(1,871)
Dividends on Common stock ($1.20 per share)							(569)	(569)
Issuance of shares to employees			1		49			49
Stock-based compensation (Note 11):					105			105
Forfeiture of shares from employees			—		(5)		(1)	(6)
Comprehensive income:								
Net income							2,133	2,133
Other comprehensive income (Notes 14 and 17):								
Foreign currency translation and other (net of tax expense of $121)						263		263
Net loss on cash flow hedges (net of tax benefit of $66)						(242)		(242)
Net loss on net investment hedges (net of tax benefit of $28)						(57)		(57)

NIKE, INC.
CONSOLIDATED STATEMENTS OF SHAREHOLDERS' EQUITY

	Common Stock				Capital in Excess of Stated Value	Accumulated Other Comprehensive Income	Retained Earnings	Total
	Class A		Class B					
	Shares	Amount	Shares	Amount				
	(In millions, except per share data)							
Reclassification to net income of previously deferred net gains related to hedge derivatives (net of tax expense of $24)						(84)		(84)
Total comprehensive income						(120)	2,133	2,013
Balance at May 31, 2011	90	$ —	378	$ 3	$ 3,944	$ 95	$ 5,801	$ 9,843

The accompanying notes to consolidated financial statements are an integral part of this statement.

NIKE, INC.
NOTES TO CONSOLIDATED FINANCIAL STATEMENTS

Note 1—Summary of Significant Accounting Policies

Description of Business

NIKE, Inc. is a worldwide leader in the design, marketing and distribution of athletic and sports-inspired footwear, apparel, equipment and accessories. Wholly-owned NIKE subsidiaries include Cole Haan, which designs, markets and distributes dress and casual shoes, handbags, accessories and coats; Converse Inc., which designs, markets and distributes athletic and casual footwear, apparel and accessories; Hurley International LLC, which designs, markets and distributes action sports and youth lifestyle footwear, apparel and accessories; and Umbro International Limited, which designs, distributes and licenses athletic and casual footwear, apparel and equipment, primarily for the sport of soccer.

Basis of Consolidation

The consolidated financial statements include the accounts of NIKE, Inc. and its subsidiaries (the "Company"). All significant intercompany transactions and balances have been eliminated.

Recognition of Revenues

Wholesale revenues are recognized when title passes and the risks and rewards of ownership have passed to the customer, based on the terms of sale. This occurs upon shipment or upon receipt by the customer depending on the country of the sale and the agreement with the customer. Retail store revenues are recorded at the time of sale. Provisions for sales discounts, returns and miscellaneous claims from customers are made at the time of sale. As of May 31, 2011 and 2010, the Company's reserve balances for sales discounts, returns and miscellaneous claims were $423 million and $371 million, respectively.

Shipping and Handling Costs

Shipping and handling costs are expensed as incurred and included in cost of sales.

Demand Creation Expense

Demand creation expense consists of advertising and promotion costs, including costs of endorsement contracts, television, digital and print advertising, brand events, and retail brand presentation. Advertising production costs are expensed the first time an advertisement is run.

Advertising placement costs are expensed in the month the advertising appears, while costs related to brand events are expensed when the event occurs. Costs related to retail brand presentation are expensed when the presentation is completed and delivered. A significant amount of the Company's promotional expenses result from payments under endorsement contracts. Accounting for endorsement payments is based upon specific contract provisions. Generally, endorsement payments are expensed on a straight-line basis over the term of the contract after giving recognition to periodic performance compliance provisions of the contracts. Prepayments made under contracts are included in prepaid expenses or other assets depending on the period to which the prepayment applies.

Through cooperative advertising programs, the Company reimburses retail customers for certain costs of advertising the Company's products. The Company records these costs in selling and administrative expense at the point in time when it is obligated to its customers for the costs, which is when the related revenues are recognized. This obligation may arise prior to the related advertisement being run.

Total advertising and promotion expenses were $2,448 million, $2,356 million, and $2,352 million for the years ended May 31, 2011, 2010 and 2009, respectively. Prepaid advertising and promotion expenses recorded in prepaid expenses and other assets totaled $291 million and $261 million at May 31, 2011 and 2010, respectively.

Cash and Equivalents

Cash and equivalents represent cash and short-term, highly liquid investments with maturities of three months or less at date of purchase. The carrying amounts reflected in the consolidated balance sheet for cash and equivalents approximate fair value.

Short-Term Investments

Short-term investments consist of highly liquid investments, including commercial paper, U.S. treasury, U.S. agency, and corporate debt securities, with maturities over three months from the date of purchase. Debt securities that the Company has the ability and positive intent to hold to maturity are carried at amortized cost. At May 31, 2011 and 2010, the Company did not hold any short-term investments that were classified as trading or held-to-maturity.

At May 31, 2011 and 2010, short-term investments consisted of available-for-sale securities. Available-for-sale securities are recorded at fair value with unrealized gains and losses reported, net of tax, in other comprehensive income, unless unrealized losses are determined to be other than temporary. The Company considers all available-for-sale securities, including those with maturity dates beyond 12 months, as available to support current operational liquidity needs and therefore classifies all securities with maturity dates beyond three months at the date of purchase as current assets within short-term investments on the consolidated balance sheet.

See Note 6—Fair Value Measurements for more information on the Company's short term investments.

Allowance for Uncollectible Accounts Receivable

Accounts receivable consists primarily of amounts receivable from customers. We make ongoing estimates relating to the collectability of our accounts receivable and maintain an allowance for estimated losses resulting from the inability of our customers to make required payments. In determining the amount of the allowance, we consider our historical level of credit losses and make judgments about the creditworthiness of significant customers based on ongoing credit evaluations. Accounts receivable with anticipated collection dates greater than 12 months from the balance sheet date and related allowances are considered non-current and recorded in other assets. The allowance for uncollectible accounts receivable was $124 million and $117 million at May 31, 2011 and 2010, respectively, of which $50 million and $43 million was classified as long-term and recorded in other assets.

Inventory Valuation

Inventories are stated at lower of cost or market and valued on a first-in, first-out ("FIFO") or moving average cost basis.

Property, Plant and Equipment and Depreciation

Property, plant and equipment are recorded at cost. Depreciation for financial reporting purposes is determined on a straight-line basis for buildings and leasehold improvements over 2 to 40 years and for machinery and equipment over 2 to 15 years. Computer software (including, in some cases, the cost of internal labor) is depreciated on a straight-line basis over 3 to 10 years.

Impairment of Long-Lived Assets

The Company reviews the carrying value of long-lived assets or asset groups to be used in operations whenever events or changes in circumstances indicate that the carrying amount of the assets might not be recoverable. Factors that would necessitate an impairment assessment include a significant adverse change in the extent or manner in which an asset is used, a significant adverse change in legal factors or the business climate that could affect the value of the asset, or a significant decline in the observable market value of an asset, among others. If such facts indicate a potential impairment, the Company would assess the recoverability of an asset group by determining if the carrying value of the asset group exceeds the sum of the projected undiscounted cash flows expected to result from the use and eventual disposition of the assets over the remaining economic life of the primary asset in the asset group. If the recoverability test indicates that the carrying value of the asset group is not recoverable, the Company will estimate the fair value of the asset group using appropriate valuation methodologies which would typically include an estimate of discounted cash flows. Any impairment would be measured as the difference between the asset groups carrying amount and its estimated fair value.

Identifiable Intangible Assets and Goodwill

The Company performs annual impairment tests on goodwill and intangible assets with indefinite lives in the fourth quarter of each fiscal year, or when events occur or circumstances change that would, more likely than not, reduce the fair value of a reporting unit or an intangible asset with an indefinite life below its carrying value. Events or changes in circumstances that may trigger interim impairment reviews include significant changes in business climate, operating results, planned investments in the reporting unit, or an expectation that the carrying amount may not be recoverable, among other factors. The impairment test requires the Company to estimate the fair value of its reporting units. If the carrying value of a reporting unit exceeds its fair value, the goodwill of that reporting unit is potentially impaired and the Company proceeds to step two of the impairment analysis. In step two of the analysis, the Company measures and records an impairment loss equal to the excess of the carrying value of the reporting unit's goodwill over its implied fair value should such a circumstance arise.

The Company generally bases its measurement of fair value of a reporting unit on a blended analysis of the present value of future discounted cash flows and the market valuation approach. The discounted cash flows model indicates the fair value of the reporting unit based on the present value of the cash flows that the Company expects the reporting unit to generate in the future. The Company's significant estimates in the discounted cash flows model include: its weighted average cost of capital; long-term rate of growth and profitability of the reporting unit's business; and working capital effects. The market valuation approach indicates the fair value of the business based on a comparison of the reporting unit to comparable publicly traded companies in similar lines of business. Significant estimates in the market valuation approach model include identifying similar companies with comparable business factors such as size, growth, profitability, risk and return on investment, and assessing comparable revenue and operating income multiples in estimating the fair value of the reporting unit.

The Company believes the weighted use of discounted cash flows and the market valuation approach is the best method for determining the fair value of its reporting units because these are the most common valuation methodologies used within its industry; and the blended use of both models compensates for the inherent risks associated with either model if used on a stand-alone basis.

Indefinite-lived intangible assets primarily consist of acquired trade names and trademarks. In measuring the fair value for these intangible assets, the Company utilizes the relief-from-royalty method. This method assumes that trade names and trademarks have value to the extent that their owner is relieved of the obligation to pay royalties for the benefits received from them. This method requires the Company to estimate the future revenue for the related brands, the appropriate royalty rate and the weighted average cost of capital.

Foreign Currency Translation and Foreign Currency Transactions

Adjustments resulting from translating foreign functional currency financial statements into U.S. dollars are included in the foreign currency translation adjustment, a component of accumulated other comprehensive income in shareholders' equity.

The Company's global subsidiaries have various assets and liabilities, primarily receivables and payables, that are denominated in currencies other than their functional currency. These balance sheet items are subject to remeasurement, the impact of which is recorded in other (income), net, within our consolidated statement of income.

Accounting for Derivatives and Hedging Activities

The Company uses derivative financial instruments to limit exposure to changes in foreign currency exchange rates and interest rates. All derivatives are recorded at fair value on the balance sheet and changes in the fair value of derivative financial instruments are either recognized in other comprehensive income (a component of shareholders' equity), debt or net income depending on the nature of the underlying exposure, whether the derivative is formally designated as a hedge, and, if designated, the extent to which the hedge is effective. The Company classifies the cash flows at settlement from derivatives in the same category as the cash flows from the related hedged items. For undesignated hedges and designated cash flow hedges, this is within the cash provided by operations component of the consolidated statements of cash flows. For designated net investment hedges, this is generally within the cash used by investing activities component of the cash flow statement. As our fair value hedges are receive-fixed, pay-variable interest rate swaps, the cash flows associated with these derivative instruments are periodic interest payments while the swaps are outstanding, which are reflected in net income within the cash provided by operations component of the cash flow statement.

See Note 17—Risk Management and Derivatives for more information on the Company's risk management program and derivatives.

Stock-Based Compensation

The Company estimates the fair value of options and stock appreciation rights granted under the NIKE, Inc. 1990 Stock Incentive Plan (the "1990 Plan") and employees' purchase rights under the Employee Stock Purchase Plans ("ESPPs") using the Black-Scholes option pricing model. The Company recognizes this fair value, net of estimated forfeitures, as selling and administrative expense in the consolidated statements of income over the vesting period using the straight-line method.

See Note 11—Common Stock and Stock-Based Compensation for more information on the Company's stock programs.

Income Taxes

The Company accounts for income taxes using the asset and liability method. This approach requires the recognition of deferred tax assets and liabilities for the expected future tax consequences of temporary differences between the carrying amounts and the tax basis of assets and liabilities. United States income taxes are provided cur.rently on financial statement earnings of non-U.S. subsidiaries that are expected to be repatriated. The Company determines annually the amount of undistributed non-U.S. earnings to invest indefinitely in its non-U.S. operations. The Company recognizes interest and penalties related to income tax matters in income tax expense.

See Note 9—Income Taxes for further discussion.

Earnings Per Share

Basic earnings per common share is calculated by dividing net income by the weighted average number of common shares outstanding during the year. Diluted earnings per common share is calculated by adjusting weighted average outstanding shares, assuming conversion of all potentially dilutive stock options and awards.

See Note 12—Earnings Per Share for further discussion.

Management Estimates

The preparation of financial statements in conformity with generally accepted accounting principles requires management to make estimates, including estimates relating to assumptions that affect the reported amounts of assets and liabilities and disclosure of contingent assets and liabilities at the date of financial statements and the reported amounts of revenues and expenses during the reporting period. Actual results could differ from these estimates.

Note 2—Inventories

Inventory balances of $2,715 million and $2,041 million at May 31, 2011 and 2010, respectively, were substantially all finished goods.

Note 3—Property, Plant and Equipment

Property, plant and equipment included the following:

	As of May 31,	
	2011	**2010**
	(In millions)	
Land	$ 237	$ 223
Buildings	1,124	952
Machinery and equipment	2,487	2,217
Leasehold improvements	931	821
Construction in process	127	177
	4,906	4,390
Less accumulated depreciation	2,791	2,458
	$2,115	$1,932

Capitalized interest was not material for the years ended May 31, 2011, 2010, and 2009.

Note 4—Identifiable Intangible Assets, Goodwill and Umbro Impairment

Identified Intangible Assets and Goodwill

The following table summarizes the Company's identifiable intangible asset balances as of May 31, 2011 and 2010:

	May 31, 2011			May 31, 2010		
	Gross Carrying Amount	Accumulated Amortization	Net Carrying Amount	Gross Carrying Amount	Accumulated Amortization	Net Carrying Amount
	(In millions)					
Amortized intangible assets:						
Patents	$ 80	$(24)	$ 56	$ 69	$(21)	$ 48
Trademarks	44	(25)	19	40	(18)	22
Other	47	(22)	25	32	(18)	14
Total	$171	$(71)	$100	$141	$(57)	$ 84
Unamortized intangible assets—Trademarks			387			383
Identifiable intangible assets, net			$487			$467

The effect of foreign exchange fluctuations for the year ended May 31, 2011 increased unamortized intangible assets by approximately $4 million.

Amortization expense, which is included in selling and administrative expense, was $16 million, $14 million, and $12 million for the years ended May 31, 2011, 2010, and 2009, respectively. The estimated amortization expense for intangible assets subject to amortization for each of the years ending May 31, 2012 through May 31, 2016 are as follows: 2012: $16 million; 2013: $14 million; 2014: $12 million; 2015: $8 million; 2016: $7 million.

All goodwill balances are included in the Company's "Other" category for segment reporting purposes. The following table summarizes the Company's goodwill balance as of May 31, 2011 and 2010:

	Goodwill	Accumulated Impairment	Goodwill, net
	(In millions)		
May 31, 2009	$393	$(199)	$194
Other[1]	(6)	—	(6)
May 31, 2010	387	(199)	188
Umbro France[2]	10	—	10
Other[1]	7	—	7
May 31, 2011	$404	$(199)	$205

[1] Other consists of foreign currency translation adjustments on Umbro goodwill.

[2] In March 2011, Umbro acquired the remaining 51% of the exclusive licensee and distributor of the Umbro brand in France for approximately $15 million.

Umbro Impairment in Fiscal 2009

The Company performs annual impairment tests on goodwill and intangible assets with indefinite lives in the fourth quarter of each fiscal year, or when events occur or circumstances change that would, more likely than not, reduce the fair value of a reporting unit or intangible assets with an indefinite life below its carrying value. As a result of a significant decline in global consumer demand and continued weakness in the macroeconomic environment, as well as decisions by Company management to adjust planned investment in the Umbro brand, the Company concluded sufficient indicators of impairment existed to require the performance of an interim assessment of Umbro's goodwill and indefinite lived intangible assets as of February 1, 2009. Accordingly, the Company performed the first step of the goodwill impairment assessment for Umbro by comparing the estimated fair value of Umbro to its carrying amount, and determined there was a potential impairment of goodwill as the carrying amount exceeded the estimated fair value. Therefore, the Company performed the second step of the assessment which compared the implied fair value of Umbro's goodwill to the book value of goodwill. The implied fair value of goodwill is determined by allocating the estimated fair value of Umbro to all of its assets and liabilities, including both recognized and unrecognized intangibles, in the same manner as goodwill was determined in the original business combination.

The Company measured the fair value of Umbro by using an equal weighting of the fair value implied by a discounted cash flow analysis and by comparisons with the market values of similar publicly traded companies. The Company believes the blended use of both models compensates for the inherent risk associated with either model if used on a stand-alone basis, and this combination is indicative of the factors a market participant would consider when performing a similar valuation. The fair value of Umbro's indefinite-lived trademark was estimated using the relief from royalty method, which assumes that the trademark has value to the extent that Umbro is relieved of the obligation to pay royalties for the benefits received from the trademark. The assessments of the Company resulted in the recognition of impairment charges of $199 million and $181 million related to Umbro's goodwill and trademark, respectively, for the year ended May 31, 2009. A tax benefit of $55 million was recognized as a result of the trademark impairment charge. In addition to the above impairment analysis, the Company determined an equity investment held by Umbro was impaired, and recognized a charge of $21 million related to the impairment of this investment. These charges are included in the Company's "Other" category for segment reporting purposes.

The discounted cash flow analysis calculated the fair value of Umbro using management's business plans and projections as the basis for expected cash flows for the next 12 years and a 3% residual growth rate thereafter. The Company used a weighted average discount rate of 14% in its analysis, which was derived primarily from published sources as well as our adjustment for increased market risk given current market conditions. Other significant estimates used in the discounted cash flow analysis include the rates of projected growth and profitability of Umbro's business and working capital effects. The market valuation approach indicates the fair value of Umbro based on a comparison of Umbro to publicly traded companies in similar lines of business. Significant estimates in the market valuation approach include identifying similar companies with comparable business factors such as size, growth, profitability, mix of revenue generated from licensed and direct distribution, and risk of return on investment.

Holding all other assumptions constant at the test date, a 100 basis point increase in the discount rate would reduce the adjusted carrying value of Umbro's net assets by an additional 12%.

Note 5—Accrued Liabilities

Accrued liabilities included the following:

	May 31,	
	2011	2010
	(In millions)	
Compensation and benefits, excluding taxes	$ 628	$ 599
Endorser compensation	284	267
Taxes other than income taxes	214	158
Fair value of derivatives	186	164
Dividends payable	145	131
Advertising and marketing	139	125
Import and logistics costs	98	80
Other[1]	291	380
	$1,985	$1,904

[1] Other consists of various accrued expenses and no individual item accounted for more than 5% of the balance at May 31, 2011 and 2010.

Note 7—Short-Term Borrowings and Credit Lines

Notes payable to banks and interest-bearing accounts payable to Sojitz Corporation of America ("Sojitz America") as of May 31, 2011 and 2010, are summarized below:

	May 31,			
	2011		2010	
	Borrowings	Interest Rate	Borrowings	Interest Rate
	(In millions)			
Notes payable:				
U.S. operations	35	—[1]	18	—[1]
Non-U.S. operations	152	7.05%[1]	121	6.35%[1]
	$187		$139	
Sojitz America	$111	0.99%	$ 88	1.07%

[1] Weighted average interest rate includes non-interest bearing overdrafts.

The carrying amounts reflected in the consolidated balance sheet for notes payable approximate fair value.

The Company purchases through Sojitz America certain athletic footwear, apparel and equipment it acquires from non-U.S. suppliers. These purchases are for the Company's operations outside of the United States, Europe and Japan. Accounts payable to Sojitz America are generally due up to 60 days after shipment of goods from the foreign port. The interest rate on such accounts payable is the 60-day London Interbank Offered Rate ("LIBOR") as of the beginning of the month of the invoice date, plus 0.75%.

As of May 31, 2011 and 2010, the Company had no amounts outstanding under its commercial paper program.

In December 2006, the Company entered into a $1 billion revolving credit facility with a group of banks. The facility matures in December 2012. Based on the Company's current long-term senior unsecured debt ratings of A+ and A1 from Standard and Poor's Corporation and Moody's Investor Services, respectively, the interest rate charged on any outstanding borrowings would be the prevailing LIBOR plus 0.15%. The facility fee is 0.05% of the total commitment. Under this agreement, the Company must maintain, among other things, certain minimum specified financial ratios with which the Company was in compliance at May 31, 2011. No amounts were outstanding under this facility as of May 31, 2011 and 2010.

Note 8—Long-Term Debt

Long-term debt, net of unamortized premiums and discounts and swap fair value adjustments, is comprised of the following:

	May 31,	
	2011	**2010**
	(In millions)	
5.66% Corporate bond, payable July 23, 2012	$ 26	$ 27
5.40% Corporate bond, payable August 7, 2012	16	16
4.70% Corporate bond, payable October 1, 2013	50	50
5.15% Corporate bond, payable October 15, 2015	114	112
4.30% Japanese Yen note, payable June 26, 2011	130	116
1.52% Japanese Yen note, payable February 14, 2012	62	55
2.60% Japanese Yen note, maturing August 20, 2001 through November 20, 2020	54	53
2.00% Japanese Yen note, maturing August 20, 2001 through November 20, 2020	24	24
Total	476	453
Less current maturities	200	7
	$276	$446

The scheduled maturity of long-term debt in each of the years ending May 31, 2012 through 2016 are $200 million, $48 million, $58 million, $8 million and $109 million, at face value, respectively.

The Company's long-term debt is recorded at adjusted cost, net of amortized premiums and discounts and interest rate swap fair value adjustments. The fair value of long-term debt is estimated based upon quoted prices for similar instruments. The fair value of the Company's long-term debt, including the current portion, was approximately $482 million at May 31, 2011 and $453 million at May 31, 2010.

In fiscal years 2003 and 2004, the Company issued a total of $240 million in medium-term notes of which $190 million, at face value, were outstanding at May 31, 2011. The outstanding notes have coupon rates that range from 4.70% to 5.66% and maturity dates ranging from July 2012 to October 2015. For each of these notes, except the $50 million note maturing in October 2013, the Company has entered into interest rate swap agreements whereby the Company receives fixed interest payments at the same rate as the notes and pays variable interest payments based on the six-month LIBOR plus a spread. Each swap has the same notional amount and maturity date as the corresponding note. At May 31, 2011, the interest rates payable on these swap agreements ranged from approximately 0.3% to 1.0%.

In June 1996, one of the Company's wholly owned Japanese subsidiaries, NIKE Logistics YK, borrowed ¥10.5 billion (approximately $130 million as of May 31, 2011) in a private placement with a maturity of June 26, 2011. Interest is paid semi-annually. The agreement provides for early retirement of the borrowing.

In July 1999, NIKE Logistics YK assumed a total of ¥13.0 billion in loans as part of its agreement to purchase a distribution center in Japan, which serves as collateral for the loans. These loans mature in equal quarterly installments during the period August 20, 2001 through November 20, 2020. Interest is also paid quarterly. As of May 31, 2011, ¥6.3 billion (approximately

$78 million) in loans remain outstanding. In February 2007, NIKE Logistics YK entered into a ¥5.0 billion (approximately $62 million as of May 31, 2011) term loan that replaced certain intercompany borrowings and matures on February 14, 2012. The interest rate on the loan is approximately 1.5% and interest is paid semi-annually.

Note 9—Income Taxes

Income before income taxes is as follows:

	Year Ended May 31,		
	2011	**2010**	**2009**
	(In millions)		
Income before income taxes:			
United States	$1,084	$ 699	$ 846
Foreign	1,760	1,818	1,111
	$2,844	$2,517	$1,957

The provision for income taxes is as follows:

	Year Ended May 31,		
	2011	**2010**	**2009**
	(In millions)		
Current:			
United States			
Federal	$289	$200	$410
State	57	50	46
Foreign	441	349	308
	787	599	764
Deferred:			
United States			
Federal	(61)	18	(251)
State	—	(1)	(8)
Foreign	(15)	(6)	(35)
	(76)	11	(294)
	$711	$610	$470

A reconciliation from the U.S. statutory federal income tax rate to the effective income tax rate follows:

	Year Ended May 31,		
	2011	**2010**	**2009**
Federal income tax rate	35.0%	35.0%	35.0%
State taxes, net of federal benefit	1.3%	1.3%	1.2%
Foreign earnings	−10.2%	−13.6%	−14.9%
Other, net	−1.1%	1.5%	2.7%
Effective income tax rate	25.0%	24.2%	24.0%

The effective tax rate for the year ended May 31, 2011 of 25.0% increased from the fiscal 2010 effective tax rate of 24.2% due primarily to the change in geographic mix of earnings. A larger percentage of our earnings before income taxes in the current year are attributable to operations in the United States where the statutory tax rate is generally higher than the tax rate on operations outside of the U.S. This impact was partially offset by changes to uncertain tax positions. Our effective tax rate for the year ended May 31, 2010 of 24.2% increased from the fiscal 2009 effective rate of 24.0%. The effective tax rate for fiscal 2009 includes a tax benefit related to charges recorded for the impairment of Umbro's goodwill, intangible and other assets.

Deferred tax assets and (liabilities) are comprised of the following:

	May 31,	
	2011	2010
	(In millions)	
Deferred tax assets:		
Allowance for doubtful accounts	$ 19	$ 17
Inventories	63	47
Sales return reserves	72	52
Deferred compensation	152	144
Stock-based compensation	148	145
Reserves and accrued liabilities	66	86
Foreign loss carry-forwards	60	26
Foreign tax credit carry-forwards	236	148
Hedges	21	1
Undistributed earnings of foreign subsidiaries	—	128
Other	86	37
Total deferred tax assets	923	831
Valuation allowance	(51)	(36)
Total deferred tax assets after valuation allowance	872	795
Deferred tax liabilities:		
Undistributed earnings of foreign subsidiaries	(40)	—
Property, plant and equipment	(151)	(99)
Intangibles	(97)	(99)
Hedges	(1)	(72)
Other	(20)	(8)
Total deferred tax liability	(309)	(278)
Net deferred tax asset	$ 563	$ 517

The following is a reconciliation of the changes in the gross balance of unrecognized tax benefits:

	May 31,		
	2011	2010	2009
	(In millions)		
Unrecognized tax benefits, as of the beginning of the period	$282	$274	$251
Gross increases related to prior period tax positions	13	87	53
Gross decreases related to prior period tax positions	(98)	(122)	(62)
Gross increases related to current period tax positions	59	52	72
Gross decreases related to current period tax positions	(6)	—	—
Settlements	(43)	(3)	(29)
Lapse of statute of limitations	(8)	(9)	(4)
Changes due to currency translation	13	3	(7)
Unrecognized tax benefits, as of the end of the period	$212	$282	$274

As of May 31, 2011, the total gross unrecognized tax benefits, excluding related interest and penalties, were $212 million, $93 million of which would affect the Company's effective tax rate if recognized in future periods. Total gross unrecognized tax benefits, excluding interest and penalties, as of May 31, 2010 and 2009 was $282 million and $274 million, respectively.

The Company recognizes interest and penalties related to income tax matters in income tax expense. The liability for payment of interest and penalties increased $10 million, $6 million, and $2 million during the years ended May 31, 2011, 2010, and 2009, respectively. As of May 31, 2011 and 2010, accrued interest and penalties related to uncertain tax positions was $91 million and $81 million, respectively (excluding federal benefit).

The Company is subject to taxation primarily in the U.S., China and the Netherlands as well as various state and other foreign jurisdictions. The Company has concluded substantially all U.S. federal income tax matters through fiscal year 2009. The Company is currently under audit by the Internal Revenue Service for the 2010 tax year. The Company's major foreign jurisdictions, China and the Netherlands, have concluded substantially all income tax matters through calendar 2000 and fiscal 2005, respectively. The Company estimates that it is reasonably possible that the total gross unrecognized tax benefits could decrease by up to $69 million within the next 12 months as a result of resolutions of global tax examinations and the expiration of applicable statutes of limitations.

The Company has indefinitely reinvested approximately $4.4 billion of the cumulative undistributed earnings of certain foreign subsidiaries. Such earnings would be subject to U.S. taxation if repatriated to the U.S. Determination of the amount of unrecognized deferred tax liability associated with the indefinitely reinvested cumulative undistributed earnings is not practicable.

A portion of the Company's foreign operations are benefitting from a tax holiday that will phase out in 2019. The decrease in income tax expense for the year ended May 31, 2011 as a result of this arrangement was approximately $36 million ($0.07 per diluted share) and $30 million ($0.06 per diluted share) for the year ended May 31, 2010.

Deferred tax assets at May 31, 2011 and 2010 were reduced by a valuation allowance relating to tax benefits of certain subsidiaries with operating losses where it is more likely than not that the deferred tax assets will not be realized. The net change in the valuation allowance was an increase of $15 million and $10 million for the years ended May 31, 2011 and 2010, respectively and a decrease of $15 million for the year ended May 31, 2009.

The Company does not anticipate that any foreign tax credit carry-forwards will expire. The Company has available domestic and foreign loss carry-forwards of $183 million at May 31, 2011. Such losses will expire as follows:

	Year Ending May 31,						
	2013	2014	2015	2016	2017-2028	Indefinite	Total
	(In millions)						
Net Operating Losses	$7	$10	$4	$10	$91	$61	$183

During the years ended May 31, 2011, 2010, and 2009, income tax benefits attributable to employee stock-based compensation transactions of $68 million, $57 million, and $25 million, respectively, were allocated to shareholders' equity.

Note 10—Redeemable Preferred Stock

Sojitz America is the sole owner of the Company's authorized Redeemable Preferred Stock, $1 par value, which is redeemable at the option of Sojitz America or the Company at par value aggregating $0.3 million. A cumulative dividend of $0.10 per share is payable annually on May 31 and no dividends may be declared or paid on the common stock of the Company unless dividends on the Redeemable Preferred Stock have been declared and paid in full. There have been no changes in the Redeemable Preferred Stock in the three years ended May 31, 2011, 2010, and 2009. As the holder of the Redeemable Preferred Stock, Sojitz America does not have general voting rights but does have the right to vote as a separate class on the sale of all or substantially all of the assets of the Company and its subsidiaries, on merger, consolidation, liquidation or dissolution of the Company or on the sale or assignment of the NIKE trademark for athletic footwear sold in the United States.

Note 11—Common Stock and Stock-Based Compensation

The authorized number of shares of Class A Common Stock, no par value, and Class B Common Stock, no par value, are 175 million and 750 million, respectively. Each share of Class A Common Stock is convertible into one share of Class B Common Stock. Voting rights of Class B Common Stock are limited in certain circumstances with respect to the election of directors.

In 1990, the Board of Directors adopted, and the shareholders approved, the NIKE, Inc. 1990 Stock Incentive Plan (the "1990 Plan"). The 1990 Plan provides for the issuance of up to 163 million previously unissued shares of Class B Common Stock in connection with stock options and other awards granted under the plan. The 1990 Plan authorizes the grant of non-statutory stock options, incentive stock options, stock appreciation rights, restricted stock, restricted stock units, and performance-based awards. The exercise price for stock options and stock appreciation rights may not be less than the fair market value of the underlying shares on the date of grant. A committee of the Board of Directors administers the 1990 Plan. The committee has the authority to determine the employees to whom awards will be made, the amount of the awards, and the other terms and conditions of the awards. Substantially all stock option grants outstanding under the 1990 Plan were granted in the first quarter of each fiscal year, vest ratably over four years, and expire 10 years from the date of grant.

The following table summarizes the Company's total stock-based compensation expense recognized in selling and administrative expense:

	Year Ended May 31,		
	2011	2010	2009
	(in millions)		
Stock options[1]	$ 77	$135	$129
ESPPs	14	14	14
Restricted stock	14	10	8
Subtotal	105	159	151
Stock options and restricted stock expense—restructuring [2]	—	—	20
Total stock-based compensation expense	$105	$159	$171

[1] Expense for stock options includes the expense associated with stock appreciation rights. Accelerated stock option expense is recorded for employees eligible for accelerated stock option vesting upon retirement. In the first quarter of fiscal 2011, the Company changed the accelerated vesting provisions of its stock option plan. Under the new provisions, accelerated stock option expense for year ended May 31, 2011 was $12 million. The accelerated stock option expense for the years ended May 31, 2010 and 2009 was $74 million and $59 million, respectively.

[2] In connection with the restructuring activities that took place during fiscal 2009, the Company recognized stock-based compensation expense relating to the modification of stock option agreements, allowing for an extended post-termination exercise period, and accelerated vesting of restricted stock as part of severance packages. See Note 16—Restructuring Charges for further details.

As of May 31, 2011, the Company had $111 million of unrecognized compensation costs from stock options, net of estimated forfeitures, to be recognized as selling and administrative expense over a weighted average period of 2.2 years.

The weighted average fair value per share of the options granted during the years ended May 31, 2011, 2010, and 2009, as computed using the Black-Scholes pricing model, was $17.68, $23.43, and $17.13, respectively. The weighted average assumptions used to estimate these fair values are as follows:

	Year Ended May 31,		
	2011	2010	2009
Dividend yield	1.6%	1.9%	1.5%
Expected volatility	31.5%	57.6%	32.5%
Weighted average expected life (in years)	5.0	5.0	5.0
Risk-free interest rate	1.7%	2.5%	3.4%

The Company estimates the expected volatility based on the implied volatility in market traded options on the Company's common stock with a term greater than one year, along with other factors. The weighted average expected life of options is based on an analysis of historical and expected future exercise patterns. The interest rate is based on the U.S. Treasury (constant maturity) risk-free rate in effect at the date of grant for periods corresponding with the expected term of the options.

The following summarizes the stock option transactions under the plan discussed above:

	Shares[1]	Weighted Average Option Price
	(In millions)	
Options outstanding May 31, 2008	36.6	$40.14
Exercised	(4.0)	35.70
Forfeited	(1.3)	51.19
Granted	7.5	58.17
Options outstanding May 31, 2009	38.8	$43.69
Exercised	(8.6)	37.64
Forfeited	(0.6)	51.92
Granted	6.4	52.79
Options outstanding May 31, 2010	36.0	$46.60
Exercised	(7.0)	42.70
Forfeited	(0.5)	58.08
Granted	6.3	69.20
Options outstanding May 31, 2011	34.8	$51.29
Options exercisable at May 31,		
2009	21.4	$36.91
2010	20.4	41.16
2011	20.1	$44.05

[1] Includes stock appreciation rights transactions.

The weighted average contractual life remaining for options outstanding and options exercisable at May 31, 2011 was 6.0 years and 4.5 years, respectively. The aggregate intrinsic value for options outstanding and exercisable at May 31, 2011 was $1,154 million and $811 million, respectively. The aggregate intrinsic value was the amount by which the market value of the underlying stock exceeded the exercise price of the options. The total intrinsic value of the options exercised during the years ended May 31, 2011, 2010, and 2009 was $267 million, $239 million, and $108 million, respectively.

In addition to the 1990 Plan, the Company gives employees the right to purchase shares at a discount to the market price under employee stock purchase plans ("ESPPs"). Employees are eligible to participate through payroll deductions up to 10% of their compensation. At the end of each six-month offering period, shares are purchased by the participants at 85% of the lower of the fair market value at the beginning or the end of the offering period. Employees purchased 0.8 million shares during the years ended May 31, 2011 and 2010, and 1.0 million shares during the year ended May 31, 2009.

From time to time, the Company grants restricted stock and unrestricted stock to key employees under the 1990 Plan. The number of shares granted to employees during the years ended May 31, 2011, 2010, and 2009 were 0.2 million, 0.5 million, and 0.1 million with weighted average values per share of $70.23, $53.16, and $56.97, respectively. Recipients of restricted shares are entitled to cash dividends and to vote their respective shares throughout the period of restriction. The value of all of the granted shares was established by the market price on the date of grant. During the years ended May 31, 2011, 2010, and 2009, the fair value of restricted shares vested was $15 million, $8 million, and $10 million, respectively, determined as of the date of vesting.

Note 12—Earnings Per Share

The following is a reconciliation from basic earnings per share to diluted earnings per share. Options to purchase an additional 0.2 million, 0.2 million, and 13.2 million shares of common stock were outstanding at May 31, 2011, 2010, and 2009, respectively, but were not included in the computation of diluted earnings per share because the options were anti-dilutive.

| | Year Ended May 31, | | |
	2011	2010	2009
	(In millions, except per share data)		
Determination of shares:			
Weighted average common shares outstanding	475.5	485.5	484.9
Assumed conversion of dilutive stock options and awards	10.2	8.4	5.8
Diluted weighted average common shares outstanding	485.7	493.9	490.7
Basic earnings per common share	$ 4.48	$ 3.93	$ 3.07
Diluted earnings per common share	$ 4.39	$ 3.86	$ 3.03

Note 13—Benefit Plans

The Company has a profit sharing plan available to most U.S.-based employees. The terms of the plan call for annual contributions by the Company as determined by the Board of Directors. A subsidiary of the Company also has a profit sharing plan available to its U.S.-based employees. The terms of the plan call for annual contributions as determined by the subsidiary's executive management. Contributions of $39 million, $35 million, and $28 million were made to the plans and are included in selling and administrative expense for the years ended May 31, 2011, 2010, and 2009, respectively. The Company has various 401(k) employee savings plans available to U.S.-based employees. The Company matches a portion of employee contributions. Company contributions to the savings plans were $39 million, $34 million, and $38 million for the years ended May 31, 2011, 2010, and 2009, respectively, and are included in selling and administrative expense.

The Company also has a Long-Term Incentive Plan ("LTIP") that was adopted by the Board of Directors and approved by shareholders in September 1997 and later amended in fiscal 2007. The Company recognized $31 million, $24 million, and $18 million of selling and administrative expense related to cash awards under the LTIP during the years ended May 31, 2011, 2010, and 2009, respectively.

The Company has pension plans in various countries worldwide. The pension plans are only available to local employees and are generally government mandated. The liability related to the unfunded pension liabilities of the plans was $93 million and $113 million at May 31, 2011 and 2010, respectively, which was primarily classified as long-term in other liabilities.

Note 14—Accumulated Other Comprehensive Income

The components of accumulated other comprehensive income, net of tax, are as follows:

| | May 31, | |
	2011	2010
	(In millions)	
Cumulative translation adjustment and other	$168	$(95)
Net deferred gain on net investment hedge derivatives	50	107
Net deferred (loss) gain on cash flow hedge derivatives	(123)	203
	$ 95	$215

Note 15—Commitments and Contingencies

The Company leases space for certain of its offices, warehouses and retail stores under leases expiring from 1 to 24 years after May 31, 2011. Rent expense was $446 million, $416 million, and $397 million for the years ended May 31, 2011, 2010 and 2009, respectively. Amounts of minimum future annual rental commitments under non-cancelable operating leases in each of the five years ending May 31, 2012 through 2016 are $374 million, $310 million, $253 million, $198 million, $174 million, respectively, and $535 million in later years.

As of May 31, 2011 and 2010, the Company had letters of credit outstanding totaling $99 million and $101 million, respectively. These letters of credit were generally issued for the purchase of inventory.

In connection with various contracts and agreements, the Company provides routine indemnifications relating to the enforceability of intellectual property rights, coverage for legal issues that arise and other items where the Company is acting as the guarantor. Currently, the Company has several such agreements in place. However, based on the Company's historical experience and the estimated probability of future loss, the Company has determined that the fair value of such indemnifications is not material to the Company's financial position or results of operations.

In the ordinary course of its business, the Company is involved in various legal proceedings involving contractual and employment relationships, product liability claims, trademark rights, and a variety of other matters. The Company does not believe there are any pending legal proceedings that will have a material impact on the Company's financial position or results of operations.

Note 16—Restructuring Charges

During fiscal 2009, the Company took necessary steps to streamline its management structure, enhance consumer focus, drive innovation more quickly to market and establish a more scalable, long-term cost structure. As a result, the Company reduced its global workforce by approximately 5% and incurred pre-tax restructuring charges of $195 million, primarily consisting of severance costs related to the workforce reduction. As nearly all of the restructuring activities were completed in fiscal 2009, the Company did not recognize additional costs relating to these actions. The restructuring charge is reflected in the corporate expense line in the segment presentation of earnings before interest and taxes in Note 18—Operating Segments and Related Information. The restructuring accrual included in accrued liabilities in the consolidated balance sheet was $3 million and $8 million as of May 31, 2011 and 2010, respectively.

Note 18—Operating Segments and Related Information

Operating Segments. The Company's operating segments are evidence of the structure of the Company's internal organization. The major segments are defined by geographic regions for operations participating in NIKE Brand sales activity excluding NIKE Golf. Each NIKE Brand geographic segment operates predominantly in one industry: the design, development, marketing and selling of athletic footwear, apparel, and equipment. In fiscal 2009, the Company initiated a reorganization of the NIKE Brand into a new model consisting of six geographies. Effective June 1, 2009, the Company's new reportable operating segments for the NIKE Brand are: North America, Western Europe, Central and Eastern Europe, Greater China, Japan, and Emerging Markets. Previously, NIKE Brand operations were organized into the following four geographic regions: U.S., Europe, Middle East and Africa (collectively, "EMEA"), Asia Pacific, and Americas. The Company's NIKE Brand Direct to Consumer operations are managed within each geographic segment.

The Company's "Other" category is broken into two components for presentation purposes to align with the way management views the Company. The "Global Brand Divisions" category primarily represents NIKE Brand licensing businesses that are not part of a geographic operating segment, selling, general and administrative expenses that are centrally managed for the NIKE Brand and costs associated with product development and supply chain operations. The "Other Businesses" category primarily consists of the activities of our affiliate brands; Cole Haan, Converse Inc., Hurley International LLC and Umbro International Limited; and NIKE Golf. Activities represented in the "Other" category are immaterial for individual disclosure.

Revenues as shown below represent sales to external customers for each segment. Intercompany revenues have been eliminated and are immaterial for separate disclosure.

Corporate consists of unallocated general and administrative expenses, which includes expenses associated with centrally managed departments, depreciation and amortization related to the Company's headquarters, unallocated insurance and benefit programs, including stock-based compensation, certain foreign currency gains and losses, including hedge gains and losses, certain corporate eliminations and other items.

Effective June 1, 2009, the primary financial measure used by the Company to evaluate performance of individual operating segments is Earnings Before Interest and Taxes (commonly referred to as "EBIT") which represents net income before interest expense (income), net and income taxes in the consolidated statements of income. Reconciling items for EBIT represent corporate expense items that are not allocated to the operating segments for management reporting. Previously, the Company evaluated performance of individual operating segments based on pre-tax income or income before income taxes.

As part of the Company's centrally managed foreign exchange risk management program, standard foreign currency rates are assigned to each NIKE Brand entity in our geographic operating segments and are used to record any non-functional currency revenues or product purchases into the entity's functional currency. Geographic operating segment revenues and cost of sales reflect use of these standard rates. For all NIKE Brand operating segments, differences between assigned standard foreign currency rates and actual market rates are included in Corporate together with foreign currency hedge gains and losses generated from the centrally managed foreign exchange risk management program and other conversion gains and losses. Prior to June 1, 2010, foreign currency results, including hedge results and other conversion gains and losses generated by the Western Europe and Central & Eastern Europe geographies were recorded in their respective geographic results.

Additions to long-lived assets as presented in the following table represent capital expenditures.

Accounts receivable, inventories and property, plant and equipment for operating segments are regularly reviewed by management and are therefore provided below.

Certain prior year amounts have been reclassified to conform to fiscal 2011 presentation, as South Africa became part of the Emerging Markets operating segment beginning June 1, 2010. Previously, South Africa was part of the Central & Eastern Europe operating segment.

	Year Ended May 31,		
	2011	2010	2009
	(In millions)		
Revenue			
North America	$ 7,578	$ 6,696	$ 6,778
Western Europe	3,810	3,892	4,139
Central & Eastern Europe	1,031	993	1,247
Greater China	2,060	1,742	1,743
Japan	766	882	926
Emerging Markets	2,736	2,199	1,828
Global Brand Divisions	123	105	96
Total NIKE Brand	18,104	16,509	16,757
Other Businesses	2,747	2,530	2,419
Corporate	11	(25)	—
Total NIKE Consolidated Revenues	$20,862	$19,014	$19,176
Earnings Before Interest and Taxes			
North America	$ 1,750	$ 1,538	$ 1,429
Western Europe	721	856	939
Central & Eastern Europe	233	253	394
Greater China	777	637	575
Japan	114	180	205
Emerging Markets	688	521	364
Global Brand Divisions	(998)	(867)	(811)
Total NIKE Brand	3,285	3,118	3,095
Other Businesses[1]	334	299	(193)
Corporate[2]	(771)	(894)	(955)

	Year Ended May 31,		
	2011	**2010**	**2009**
	(In millions)		
Total NIKE Consolidated Earnings Before Interest and Taxes	2,848	2,523	1,947
Interest expense (income), net	4	6	(10)
Total NIKE Consolidated Earnings Before Taxes	$ 2,844	$ 2,517	$ 1,957
Additions to Long-lived Assets			
North America	$ 79	$ 45	$ 99
Western Europe	75	59	70
Central & Eastern Europe	5	4	7
Greater China	43	80	59
Japan	9	12	10
Emerging Markets	21	11	12
Global Brand Divisions	44	30	37
Total NIKE Brand	276	241	294
Other Businesses	38	52	90
Corporate	118	42	72
Total Additions to Long-lived Assets	$ 432	$ 335	$ 456
Depreciation			
North America	$ 70	$ 65	$ 64
Western Europe	52	57	51
Central & Eastern Europe	4	4	4
Greater China	19	11	7
Japan	22	26	30
Emerging Markets	14	12	10
Global Brand Divisions	39	33	43
Total NIKE Brand	220	208	209
Other Businesses	44	46	38
Corporate	71	70	88
Total Depreciation	$ 335	$ 324	$ 335

[1] During the year ended May 31, 2009, the Other category included a pre-tax charge of $401 million for the impairment of goodwill, intangible and other assets of Umbro, which was recorded in the third quarter of fiscal 2009. See Note 4—Identifiable Intangible Assets, Goodwill and Umbro Impairment for more information.

[2] During the year ended May 31, 2009, Corporate expense included pre-tax charges of $195 million for the Company's restructuring activities, which were completed in the fourth quarter of fiscal 2009. See Note 16—Restructuring Charges for more information.

	Year Ended May 31,	
	2011	**2010**
	(In millions)	
Accounts Receivable, net		
North America	$1,069	$ 848
Western Europe	500	402
Central & Eastern Europe	290	271
Greater China	140	129
Japan	153	167
Emerging Markets	466	350
Global Brand Divisions	23	22
Total NIKE Brand	2,641	2,189
Other Businesses	471	442
Corporate	26	19
Total Accounts Receivable, net	$3,138	$2,650
Inventories		
North America	$1,034	$ 768
Western Europe	434	347
Central & Eastern Europe	145	102
Greater China	152	104
Japan	82	68
Emerging Markets	429	285
Global Brand Divisions	25	20
Total NIKE Brand	2,301	1,694
Other Businesses	414	347
Corporate	—	—
Total Inventories	$2,715	$2,041
Property, Plant and Equipment, net		
North America	$ 330	$325
Western Europe	338	282
Central & Eastern Europe	13	11
Greater China	179	146
Japan	360	333
Emerging Markets	58	48
Global Brand Divisions	116	99
Total NIKE Brand	1,394	1,244
Other Businesses	164	167
Corporate	557	521
Total Property, Plant and Equipment, net	$2,115	$1,932

Revenues by Major Product Lines.

Revenues to external customers for NIKE Brand products are attributable to sales of footwear, apparel and equipment. Other revenues to external customers primarily include external sales by Cole Haan, Converse, Hurley, NIKE Golf, and Umbro.

	Year Ended May 31,		
	2011	**2010**	**2009**
	(In millions)		
Footwear	$11,493	$10,332	$10,307
Apparel	5,475	5,037	5,245
Equipment	1,013	1,035	1,110
Other	2,881	2,610	2,514
	$20,862	$19,014	$19,176

Revenues and Long-Lived Assets by Geographic Area.

Geographical area information is similar to what was shown previously under operating segments with the exception of the Other activity, which has been allocated to the geographical areas based on the location where the sales originated. Revenues derived in the United States were $8,956 million, $7,914 million, and $8,020 million for the years ended May 31, 2011, 2010, and 2009, respectively. The Company's largest concentrations of long-lived assets primarily consist of the Company's world headquarters and distribution facilities in the United States and distribution facilities in Japan, Belgium and China. Long-lived assets attributable to operations in the United States, which are comprised of net property, plant & equipment, were $1,115 million, $1,070 million, and $1,143 million at May 31, 2011, 2010, and 2009, respectively. Long-lived assets attributable to operations in Japan were $363 million, $336 million, and $322 million at May 31, 2011, 2010 and 2009, respectively. Long-lived assets attributable to operations in Belgium were $182 million, $164 million, and $191 million at May 31, 2011, 2010, and 2009, respectively. Long-lived assets attributable to operations in China were $175 million, $144 million, and $76 million at May 31, 2011, 2010, and 2009, respectively.

Major Customers.

No customer accounted for 10% or more of the Company's net sales during the years ended May 31, 2011, 2010, and 2009.

Glossary

absorption approach (absorption costing) A costing approach that considers all indirect manufacturing costs (both variable and fixed) to be product (inventoriable) costs that become an expense in the form of manufacturing cost of goods sold only as sales occur (p. 184).

accelerated depreciation A pattern of depreciation that charges a larger proportion of an asset's cost to the earlier years and less to later years (p. 445).

account analysis Classifying each account as a variable cost or as a fixed cost with respect to a selected cost driver (p. 95).

account Each item in a financial statement (p. 620).

accounting rate-of-return (ARR) model A non-DCF capital-budgeting model expressed as the increase in expected average annual operating income divided by the initial required investment (p. 453).

accounting system A formal mechanism for gathering, organizing, and communicating information about an organization's activities (p. 5).

accounts payable Amounts owed to vendors for purchases on open accounts (p. 619).

accounts receivable Amounts due from customers for sales charged to an account instead of being paid for in cash (p. 619).

accrual basis A process of accounting that recognizes the impact of transactions on the financial statements in the time periods when revenues and expenses occur instead of when the company pays or receives cash (p. 624).

accrue To accumulate a receivable or payable during a given period, even though no explicit transaction occurs (p. 629).

accrued expenses Expenses reported on the income statement before a company pays for them with cash (p. 629).

accrued revenues Revenues that a company has earned but has not yet received in cash (p. 631).

accumulated depreciation The sum of all depreciation charged to past periods (p. 240).

activity analysis The process of identifying appropriate cost drivers and their effects on the costs of making a product or providing a service (p. 92).

activity-based budget (ABB) A budget that focuses on the budgeted cost of activities required to produce and sell products and services (p. 289).

activity-based costing (ABC) system A system that first accumulates indirect resource costs for each of the activities of the area being costed and then assigns the costs of each activity to the products, services, or other cost objects that require that activity (p. 135).

activity-based flexible budget A budget based on budgeted costs for each activity using the related cost driver (p. 313).

activity-based management (ABM) Using the output of an activity-based cost accounting system to aid strategic decision making and to improve operational control of an organization (p. 142).

activity-level variances The differences between the static budget amounts and the amounts in the flexible budget (p. 315).

adjustments (adjusting entries) Entries that record implicit transactions such as unpaid wages, prepaid rent, interest owed, and the like (p. 625).

after-tax cash flow The cash flow after the effect of income taxes, generally the pretax cash flow multiplied by $(1 - \text{marginal tax rate})$ (p. 445).

agency theory A theory that deals with relationships where one party (the principal) delegates decision-making authority to another party (the agent) (p. 394).

annual report A report prepared by management for the company's shareholders (p. 687).

assets Economic resources that a company owns and expects to provide future benefits (p. 620).

attention directing Reporting and interpreting information that helps managers to focus on operating problems, imperfections, inefficiencies, and opportunities (p. 5).

audit An "examination" or in-depth inspection of financial statements and companies' records made in accordance with auditing standards (p. 635).

available-for-sale securities Investments that the investor company does not intend to sell in the near future (p. 717).

avoidable costs Costs that will not continue if an ongoing operation is changed or deleted (p. 235).

backflush costing An accounting system that applies costs to products only when the production is complete (p. 598).

balanced scorecard (BSC) A performance measurement and reporting system that strikes a balance between financial and nonfinancial measures, links performance to rewards, and gives explicit recognition to the link between performance measurement and organizational goals and objectives (p. 370).

balance sheet (statement of financial position) A snapshot of the financial status of an organization at a point in time (p. 620).

behavioral implications The accounting system's effect on the behavior, specifically the decisions, of managers (p. 9).

benchmark comparisons Comparison of a company's financial ratios with general rules of thumb (p. 731).

benchmarking The continuous process of comparing products, services, and activities against the best industry standards (p. 142).

book value (net book value) The original cost of equipment less accumulated depreciation (p. 240).

break-even point The level of sales at which revenue equals total cost and net income is zero (p. 46).

budget A quantitative expression of a plan of action and an aid to coordinating and implementing the plan (p. 7).

budgetary slack (budget padding) Overstatement of budgeted cost or understatement of budgeted revenue to create a budget goal that is easier to achieve (p. 274).

budgeted factory-overhead rate The budgeted total overhead for each cost pool divided by the budgeted cost-allocation base level (p. 534).

business-to-business (B2B) Electronic commerce from one business to another business (p. 16).

business-to-consumer (B2C) Electronic commerce from business to consumer (p. 16).

business process reengineering The fundamental rethinking and radical redesign of business processes to improve performance in areas such as cost, quality, service, and speed (p. 16).

by-product A product that, like a joint product, is not individually identifiable until manufacturing reaches a split-off point, but has relatively insignificant total sales value (p. 509).

capacity costs The fixed costs of being able to achieve a desired level of production or to provide a desired level of service while maintaining product or service attributes, such as quality (p. 88).

capital budget A budget that details the planned expenditures for facilities, equipment, new products, and other long-term investments (p. 277).

capital budgeting The long-term planning for investment commitments with returns spread over time, typically over multiple years (p. 435).

capital charge Company's cost of capital × average invested capital (p. 400).

capital turnover Revenue divided by invested capital (p. 397).

capitalize To record an amount as an asset rather than as an expense (p. 665).

cash basis A process of accounting where revenue and expense recognition occur when the company receives and pays out cash (p. 624).

cash budget A statement of planned cash receipts and disbursements (p. 283).

cash dividends (dividends) Distributions of cash to stockholders that reduce retained earnings (p. 632).

cash equivalents Short-term investments that a company can easily convert into cash with little delay (p. 663).

cash flows from financing activities The section in the statement of cash flows that lists the cash-flow effects of obtaining cash from creditors and owners, repaying creditors or buying back stock from owners, and paying cash dividends (p. 675).

cash flows from investing activities The section in the statement of cash flows that lists the cash-flow effects of (1) lending and collecting on loans and (2) acquiring and selling long-term assets (p. 675).

cash flows from operating activities The section in the statement of cash flows that lists the cash-flow effects of transactions that affect the income statement (p. 675).

centralization Concentration of decision-making authority only at the highest levels of an organization (p. 391).

certified management accountant (CMA) The management accountant's counterpart to the CPA (p. 4).

certified public accountant (CPA) In the United States, independent accountants who assure the reliability of companies' published financial statements (p. 4).

chartered accountant (CA) In many countries, the equivalent to the CPA in the United States—independent accountants who assure the reliability of companies' financial statements (p. 4).

chief financial officer (CFO) The top executive who deals with all finance and accounting issues in an organization. The CFO generally oversees the accounting function (p. 14).

code of conduct A document specifying the ethical standards of an organization (p. 8).

coefficient of determination (R^2) A measurement of how much of the fluctuation of a cost is explained by changes in the cost driver (p. 101).

committed fixed costs Costs arising from the possession of facilities, equipment, and a basic organization (p. 89).

common costs Those costs of facilities and services that are shared by users (p. 235).

common stock Stock that has no predetermined rate of dividends and is the last to obtain a share in the assets when the corporation liquidates. It usually confers voting power to elect the board of directors of the corporation (p. 668).

common-size statements Financial statements expressed in component percentages (p. 730).

comparability A characteristic of information produced when all companies use similar concepts and measurements and use them consistently (p. 642).

component percentages Analysis and presentation of financial statements in percentage form to aid comparability, frequently used when companies differ in size (p. 730).

compound entry A transaction that affects more than two accounts (p. 622).

computer-aided design (CAD) The use of computer technology for the design of real or virtual objects (p. 16).

computer-aided manufacturing (CAM) The use of computer-based software tools in manufacturing or prototyping (p. 16).

computer-integrated manufacturing (CIM) systems Systems that use computer-aided design, computer-aided manufacturing, robots, and computer-controlled machines (p. 16).

confirmatory value A quality of information that allows it to confirm or change existing expectations (p. 642).

conservatism convention Selecting the method of measurement that yields the gloomiest immediate results (p. 642).

consistency Using the same accounting policies and procedures from period to period (p. 642).

consolidated financial statements Financial statements that combine the books of two or more separate legal entities into one set of financial statements (p. 716).

continuity convention (going concern convention) The assumption that an organization will continue to exist and operate (p. 641).

continuous budget (rolling budget) A common form of master budget that adds a month in the future as the month just ended is dropped (p. 277).

contribution approach A method of internal (management accounting) reporting that emphasizes the distinction between variable and fixed costs for the purpose of better decision making (p. 185).

contribution margin A term used for either total contribution margin, unit contribution margin, or contribution margin percentage (p. 49).

contribution-margin percentage Total contribution margin divided by sales or 100% minus the variable cost percentage (p. 48).

contribution-margin ratio Contribution margin percentage expressed as a ratio (p. 48).

control Implementing plans and using feedback to evaluate the attainment of objectives (p. 6).

controllable cost Any cost that a manager's decisions and actions can influence (p. 360).

controller (comptroller) The accounting officer of an organization who deals mainly with operating matters, such as aiding management decision making (p. 14).

corporation A business organized as a separate legal entity and owned by its stockholders (p. 619).

cost A sacrifice or giving up of resources for a particular purpose (p. 124).

cost accounting That part of the cost management system that measures costs for the purposes of management decision making and financial reporting (p. 124).

cost accounting systems The techniques used to determine the cost of a product, service, customer, or other cost object (p. 124).

cost accumulation Collecting costs by some natural classification, such as activities performed, labor, or materials (p. 125).

cost allocation Assigning indirect costs to cost objects in proportion to the cost object's use of a particular cost-allocation base (p. 126).

cost-allocation base A measure of input or output that determines the amount of cost to be allocated to a particular cost object. An ideal cost-allocation base measures how much of the particular cost is caused by the cost object (p. 126).

cost application The allocation of total departmental costs to the revenue-producing products or services (p. 490).

cost assignment Attaching costs to one or more cost objects, such as activities, departments, customers, or products (p. 125).

cost behavior How the activities of an organization affect its costs (p. 37).

cost-benefit balance Weighing estimated costs against probable benefits, the primary consideration in choosing among accounting systems and methods (p. 9).

cost-benefit criterion An approach that implicitly underlies the decisions about the design of accounting systems. As companies change their accounting systems, the potential benefits should exceed the costs of gathering and interpreting the information (p. 643).

cost of capital The cost of long-term liabilities and stockholders' equity weighted by their relative size (p. 400).

cost center A responsibility center in which managers are responsible for costs only (p. 360).

cost driver A measure of activities that requires the use of resources and thereby cause costs (p. 37).

cost function An algebraic equation used by managers to describe the relationship between a cost and its cost driver(s) (p. 91).

cost of goods sold The cost of the merchandise that a company acquires or produces and sells (p. 58).

cost management system (CMS) A collection of tools and techniques that identify how management's decisions affect costs (p. 123).

cost measurement Estimating or predicting costs as a function of appropriate cost drivers (p. 91).

cost object (cost objective) Anything for which decision makers desire a separate measurement of costs. Examples include departments, products, activities, and territories (p. 124).

cost pool A group of individual costs that a company allocates to cost objects using a singlecost-allocation base (p. 128).

cost of quality report A report that displays the financial impact of quality (p. 366).

cost recovery A concept in which companies carry forward as assets such items as inventories, prepayments, and equipment because they expect to recover the costs of these assets in the form of cash inflows (or reduced cash outflows) in future periods (p. 638).

cost structure The combination of variable- and fixed-cost resources used to carry out the organization's activities (p. 55).

cost-volume-profit (CVP) analysis The study of the effects of output volume on revenue (sales), expenses (costs), and net income (net profit) (p. 45).

credit An entry on the right side of an account (p. 644).

cross-sectional comparisons Comparisons of a company's financial ratios with ratios of similar companies, with industry averages, or "best-practices" ratios for the same period (p. 731).

current assets Cash and all other assets that a company reasonably expects to convert to cash or sell or consume within one year or during the normal operating cycle, if longer than a year (p. 661).

current liabilities An organization's debts that fall due within the coming year or within the normal operating cycle if longer than a year (p. 666).

currently attainable standards Levels of performance that managers can achieve by realistic levels of effort (p. 318).

cycle time (throughput time) The time taken to complete a product or service (p. 367).

debentures Formal certificates of indebtedness that are accompanied by a promise to pay interest at a specified annual rate (p. 666).

debit An entry on the left side of an account (p. 644).

decentralization The delegation of decision-making authority to lower levels of the organization. The lower in the organization that authority is delegated, the greater the decentralization (p. 391).

decision context The circumstances surrounding the decision for which the cost will be used (p. 42).

decision making Choosing among alternative courses of action designed to achieve some objective (p. 5).

decision model Any method for making a choice, sometimes requiring elaborate quantitative procedures (p. 182).

degree of operating leverage The ratio of contribution margin to profit, defined at a specific volume of sales (p. 56).

denominator level The expected cost-allocation base activity selected to determine the fixed-overhead rate (p. 543).

depreciation The periodic cost of equipment that a company spreads over the future periods in which the company will use the equipment (p. 240).

depreciation tax shield The tax savings due to depreciation deductions, generally the present value of the product of the tax rate and the depreciation deduction (p. 449).

differential analysis A decision process that compares the differential revenues and costs of alternatives (p. 227).

differential approach A method for comparing alternatives that computes the differences in cash flows between alternatives and then converts these differences in cash flows to their present values (p. 440).

differential cost The difference in total cost between two alternatives (p. 227).

differential revenue The difference in total revenue between two alternatives (p. 227).

direct costs Costs that accountants can identify specifically and exclusively with a given cost object in an economically feasible way (p. 126).

direct-labor costs The wages of all labor that a company can trace specifically and exclusively to the manufactured goods (p. 131).

direct-material costs The acquisition costs of raw materials that a company traces to the manufactured goods (p. 131).

direct method A method for allocating service department costs that ignores other service departments when allocating any given service department's costs to the operating departments (p. 487).

direct method for operating cash flows A method for computing cash flows from operating activities that subtracts operating cash disbursements from cash collections to arrive at cash flows from operations (p. 680).

discounted-cash-flow (DCF) models Capital-budgeting models that focus on cash inflows and outflows while taking into account the time value of money (p. 435).

discretionary fixed costs Costs determined by management as part of the periodic planning process in order to meet the organization's goals. They have no obvious relationship with levels of capacity or output activity (p. 89).

discriminatory pricing Charging different prices to different customers for the same product or service (p. 194).

double-entry system A method of record keeping in which each transaction affects at least two accounts (p. 644).

dysfunctional decision Any decision that is in conflict with organizational goals (p. 408).

earnings per share (EPS) Net income divided by the average number of common shares outstanding during the year (p. 671).

economic profit (residual income) After-tax operating income less a capital charge (p. 400).

economic value added (EVA) Adjusted after-tax operating income minus the weighted-average cost of capital multiplied by the adjusted average invested capital (p. 400).

effectiveness The degree to which an organization meets an objective (p. 99).

efficiency The degree to which an organization minimizes the resources used to achieve an objective (p. 319).

efficient capital market A market in which market prices fully reflect all information available to the public (p. 735).

electronic commerce (e-commerce) Conducting business online (p. 16).

engineering analysis The systematic review of materials, supplies, labor, support services, and facilities needed for products and services; measuring cost behavior according to what costs should be, not by what costs have been (p. 93).

enterprise resource planning (ERP) systems Integrated information systems that support all functional areas of a company (p. 16).

equity method A method of accounting for an investment by adjusting the acquisition cost of the investment for the investor's share of earnings or losses of the investee after the date of investment and for dividends received (p. 718).

equivalent units The number of completed (whole) units that could have been produced from the resources required for the partially completed units (p. 591).

ethics The field that deals with human conduct in relation to what is morally good and bad, right and wrong. It is the application of values to decision making. These values include honesty, fairness, responsibility, respect, and compassion (p. 18).

expected cost The cost most likely to be attained (p. 318).

expenses Decreases in ownership claims arising from delivering goods or services or using up assets (p. 622).

explicit transactions Transactions that record day-to-day routine events—such as credit sales, credit purchases, cash received on account, and cash disbursed on account—that are supported by source documents (p. 625).

eXtensible Business Reporting Language (XBRL) An XML-based accounting language that helps communicate financial information electronically (p. 16).

faithful representation A quality of information that ensures that it captures the economic substance of the transactions, events, or circumstances it describes. It requires information to be complete, neutral, and free from material errors (p. 642).

favorable cost variance A variance that occurs when actual costs are less than budgeted costs (p. 312).

favorable profit variance A variance that occurs when actual profit exceeds budgeted profit (p. 311).

favorable revenue variance A variance that occurs when actual revenue exceeds budgeted revenue (p. 312).

financial accounting The branch of accounting that develops information for external decision makers, such as stockholders, suppliers, banks, and government regulatory agencies (p. 3).

Financial Accounting Standards Board (FASB) The body that sets GAAP in the United States (p. 636).

financial budget The part of a master budget that focuses on the effects that the operating budget and other plans (such as capital budgets and repayments of debt) have on cash balances (p. 277).

financial planning model A mathematical model of the master budget that can incorporate any set of assumptions about sales, costs, or product mix (p. 290).

financial statements Summarized reports of accounting transactions (p. 619).

finished-goods inventory Goods fully completed but not yet sold (p. 132).

first-in, first-out (FIFO) An inventory method that assumes that a company sells or uses up first the stock acquired earliest (p. 693).

fiscal year The year established for accounting purposes for the preparation of annual reports (p. 663).

fixed assets (tangible assets) Physical items that a person can see and touch, such as property, plant, and equipment (p. 663).

fixed cost A cost that is not affected by changes in the cost-driver level (p. 39).

fixed-overhead rate The amount of fixed manufacturing overhead applied to each unit of production. It is determined by dividing the budgeted fixed overhead by the expected cost-allocation base activity for the budget period (p. 543).

fixed-overhead spending variance The difference between actual fixed overhead and budgeted fixed overhead (p. 329).

flexible budget (variable budget) A budget that adjusts to different levels of activity (p. 312).

flexible-budget variance The difference between actual results and the flexible budget for the actual level of output achieved (p. 315).

Foreign Corrupt Practices Act A U.S. law forbidding bribery and other corrupt practices. The law also requires all publicly held companies to maintain their accounting records in reasonable detail and accuracy and have an appropriate system of internal controls (p. 8).

free cash flow Cash flows from operations less capital expenditures (p. 685).

full cost The total of all manufacturing costs plus the total of all selling and administrative costs (p. 195).

functional budgeting Budgeting process that focuses on preparing budgets for various functions, such as production, selling, and administrative support (p. 289).

general ledger A collection of the group of accounts that supports the items shown in the major financial statements (p. 644).

generally accepted accounting principles (GAAP) A set of standards to which public companies' published financial statements must adhere (p. 8).

goal congruence A condition where employees, responding to the incentives created by the control system, make decisions that help meet the overall goals of the organization (p. 355).

goodwill The excess of the cost of an acquired company over the sum of the fair market values of its identifiable individual assets less its liabilities (p. 665).

Grenzplankostenrechnung (GPK) A German cost accounting system that goes a step further than ABC systems (p. 143).

gross book value The original cost of an asset before deducting accumulated depreciation (p. 398).

gross margin (gross profit) The excess of sales over the total cost of goods sold (p. 58).

high-low method A simple method for measuring a linear-cost function from past cost data, focusing on the highest-activity and lowest-activity points and fitting a line through these two points (p. 98).

hybrid costing systems An accounting system that is a blend of ideas from both job costing and process costing (p. 577).

IMA Statement of Ethical Professional Practice A code of conduct developed by the Institute of Management Accountants; this code includes competence, confidentiality, integrity, and credibility (p. 18).

imperfect competition A market in which the price a firm charges for a unit influences the quantity of units it sells (p. 192).

implicit transactions Transactions that record events that day-to-day recording procedures temporarily ignore, such as expiration of prepaid rent or accrual of interest due to the passage of time (p. 625).

incentives Rewards, both implicit and explicit, for managerial effort and actions (p. 393).

income (net income, profits, earnings) The excess of revenues over expenses (p. 622).

income statement A statement that summarizes a company's revenues and expenses. It measures the performance of an organization by matching its accomplishments (revenue from customers) and its efforts (cost of goods sold and other expenses) (p. 622).

incremental analysis An analysis of the incremental (additional) costs and benefits of a proposed alternative compared with the current situation (p. 227).

incremental benefits The additional revenues or reduced costs generated by the proposed alternative in comparison with the current situation (p. 227).

incremental costs The additional costs or reduced benefits generated by the proposed alternative in comparison with the current situation (p. 227).

incremental effect The change in total results (such as revenue, expenses, or income) under a new condition in comparison with some given or known condition (p. 51).

independent opinion The accountant's assurance that management's financial statements are in conformity with GAAP (p. 635).

indirect costs Costs that accountants cannot identify specifically and exclusively with a given cost object in an economically feasible way (p. 126).

indirect method for operating cash flows A method for computing cash flows from operating activities that adjusts the previously calculated accrual net income from the income statement to reflect only cash receipts and cash disbursements (p. 680).

indirect production costs (indirect manufacturing costs, factory burden, factory overhead, manufacturing overhead) All costs associated with the production process that a company cannot trace to the goods or services produced in an economically feasible way; usually all production costs except direct materials and direct labor (p. 131).

inflation The decline in the general purchasing power of the monetary unit (p. 457).

Institute of Management Accountants (IMA) The largest U.S. professional organization of accountants focused on internal accounting (p. 3).

intangible assets Long-lived assets that are not physical in nature. Examples are goodwill, franchises, patents, trademarks, and copyrights (p. 665).

internal auditors Accountants who review and evaluate accounting systems, including their internal controls (p. 8).

internal controls Policies to protect and make the most efficient use of an organization's assets (p. 8).

internal rate of return (IRR) model A capital-budgeting model that determines the interest rate, the IRR, at which the NPV equals zero (p. 438).

International Accounting Standards Board (IASB) The group that establishes international GAAP (p. 636).

inventory turnover The number of times the average inventory is sold per year (p. 237).

investment center A responsibility center where managers are responsible for investment as well as profits (p. 361).

job-cost record (job-cost sheet, job order) A document that shows all costs for a particular product, service, or batch of products (p. 577).

job-order costing (job costing) The method of allocating costs to heterogeneous products that are readily identified by individual units or batches, each of which requires differential (sometimes custom) amounts of materials, labor, and overhead (p. 577).

joint costs The costs of manufacturing joint products prior to the split-off point (p. 238).

joint products Two or more manufactured products that (1) have relatively significant sales values and (2) are not separately identifiable as individual products until their split-off point (p. 238).

just-in-time (JIT) philosophy A philosophy to eliminate waste by reducing the time products spend in the production process and eliminating the time products spend on activities that do not add value (p. 16).

kaizen costing The Japanese term for continuous improvement during manufacturing (p. 202).

key performance indicators Measures that drive the organization to achieve its goals (p. 371).

key success factors Characteristics or attributes that managers must achieve in order to drive the organization toward its goals (p. 354).

labor time tickets (time cards) The record of the time a particular direct laborer spends on each job (p. 577).

last-in, first-out (LIFO) An inventory method that assumes that a company sells or uses up the stock acquired most recently first (p. 693).

lean manufacturing Applying continuous process improvements to eliminate waste from the entire enterprise (p. 17).

least-squares regression (regression analysis) Measuring a cost function objectively by using statistics to fit a cost function to all the data (p. 100).

ledger accounts A method of keeping track of how transactions affect each particular asset, liability, revenue, and expense (p. 643).

liabilities The entity's economic obligations to nonowners (p. 620).

LIFO layers (LIFO increments) Separately identifiable additions to a LIFO inventory (p. 694).

limited liability A provision that a company's creditors cannot seek payment from stockholders as individuals if the corporation itself cannot pay its debts (p. 668).

limiting factor (scarce resource) The item that restricts or constrains the production or sale of a product or service (p. 236).

linear-cost behavior Activity that can be graphed with a straight line because costs are assumed to be either fixed or variable (p. 87).

line managers Managers who are directly involved with making and selling the organization's products or services (p. 13).

liquidation Converting assets to cash and using the cash to pay off outside claims (p. 667).

long-lived assets Assets that will provide services for more than a year (p. 626).

long-range plan Forecasted financial statements for 5- to 10-year periods (p. 277).

lower-of-cost-or-market (LCM) An inventory method in which accountants compare the current market price of inventory with its cost (derived by specific identification, FIFO, LIFO, or weighted average) and select the lower of the two as the inventory value (p. 695).

management accounting The branch of accounting that produces information for managers within an organization. It is the process of identifying, measuring, accumulating, analyzing, preparing, interpreting, and communicating information that helps managers fulfill organizational objectives (p. 3).

management audit A review to determine whether managers are implementing the policies and procedures specified by top management (p. 8).

management by exception Concentrating more on areas that deviate from the plan and less on areas that conform with plans and are presumed to be running smoothly (p. 7).

management by objectives (MBO) The joint formulation by managers and their superiors of a set of goals and plans for achieving the goals for a forthcoming period (p. 413).

management control system An integrated set of techniques for gathering and using information to make planning and control decisions, for motivating employee behavior, and for evaluating performance (p. 353).

management's discussion and analysis (MD&A) A section of annual reports and 10-K filings that concentrates on explaining the major changes in the income statement, changes in liquidity and capital resources, and the impact of inflation from one year to the next (p. 730).

managerial effort Exertion toward a goal or objective, including all conscious actions (such as supervising, planning, and thinking) that result in more efficiency and effectiveness (p. 355).

marginal cost The additional cost resulting from producing and selling one additional unit (p. 192).

marginal income tax rate The tax rate paid on incremental taxable income (p. 445).

marginal revenue The additional revenue resulting from the sale of an additional unit (p. 192).

margin of safety Planned unit sales less the break-even unit sales; a measure of how far sales can fall below the planned level before losses occur (p. 55).

market-value method The method of accounting for investments in equity securities that shows the investment on the balance sheet at market value (p. 717).

markup The amount by which price exceeds cost (p. 195).

master budget An extensive analysis of the first year of the long-range plan. It summarizes the planned activities of all subunits of an organization (p. 277).

matching The linking of revenues (as measured by the selling prices of goods and services delivered) with the expenses incurred to generate them (as measured by the cost of goods and services used) (p. 638).

materiality The accounting convention that justifies the omission of insignificant information when its omission or misstatement would not mislead a user of the financial statements (p. 642).

materials requisitions Records of materials used in particular jobs (p. 577).

measurement of cost behavior Understanding and quantifying how activities of an organization affect its levels of costs (p. 86).

mixed cost A cost that contains elements of both fixed- and variable-cost behavior (p. 44).

modified accelerated cost recovery system (MACRS) The method companies use to depreciate most assets under U.S. income tax laws (p. 448).

motivation The drive that creates effort and action toward a goal (p. 356).

net book value The original cost of an asset less any accumulated depreciation (p. 398).

net operating profit after-tax (NOPAT) Income before interest expense but after tax (p. 400).

net present value The sum of the present values of all expected cash flows (p. 436).

net-present-value (NPV) method A discounted-cash-flow approach to capital budgeting that computes the present value of all expected future cash flows using the required rate of return (p. 436).

net worth A synonym for owners' equity (p. 634).

nominal rate Interest rate that includes an inflation element (p. 457).

noncontrolling interests An account that summarizes the outside stockholders' interest, as opposed to the parent's interest, in a subsidiary corporation (p. 721).

noncurrent liabilities (long-term liabilities) An organization's debts that fall due beyond one year (p. 666).

non-value-added costs Costs that a company can eliminate without affecting a product's value to the customer (p. 142).

normal costing system The cost system in which the cost of the manufactured product is composed of actual direct material, actual direct labor, and normal applied overhead (p. 536).

operating budget (profit plan) A major part of a master budget that focuses on the income statement and its supporting schedules (p. 277).

operating cycle The time span during which a company spends cash to acquire goods and services that it uses to produce the organization's output, which it in turn sells to customers, who in turn pay for their purchases with cash (p. 661).

operating leverage The sensitivity of a firm's profit to changes in volume of sales (p. 55).

opportunity cost For a resource that a company already owns or that it has already committed to purchase, the maximum available benefit forgone (or passed up) by using such a resource for a particular purpose (p. 228).

other comprehensive income A few special types of gains and losses that do not appear on the income statement and thus do not become part of retained earnings (p. 668).

outlay cost A cost that requires a future cash disbursement (p. 227).

outsourcing Purchasing products or services from an outside supplier (p. 229).

overapplied overhead The difference between actual and applied overhead when the amount applied exceeds the amount incurred (p. 537).

owners' equity The excess of the assets over the liabilities (p. 620).

paid-in capital The ownership claim arising from funds paid in by the owners (p. 620).

parent company A company that has effective control over another company. Usually this means owning more than 50% of the company's stock (p. 719).

participative budgeting Budgets formulated with the active participation of all affected employees (p. 274).

partnership An organization that joins two or more individuals together as co-owners (p. 634).

par value (stated value) The value often printed on the face of stock certificates (p. 668).

payback period (payback time) The time it will take to recoup, in the form of cash inflows from operations, the initial dollars invested in a project (p. 452).

perfect competition A market in which a firm can sell as much of a product as it can produce, all at a single market price (p. 191).

perfection standards (ideal standards) Expressions of the most efficient performance possible under the best conceivable conditions, using existing specifications and equipment (p. 318).

performance metric A specific measure of management accomplishment (p. 393).

performance reports Feedback provided by comparing results with plans and by highlighting variances (p. 7).

period costs Costs that become expenses during the current period without becoming part of inventory (p. 131).

planning Setting objectives for an organization and determining how to attain them (p. 6).

post-audit A follow-up evaluation of capital-budgeting decisions (p. 455).

predatory pricing Establishing prices so low that they drive competitors out of the market. The predatory pricer then has no significant competition and can raise prices dramatically (p. 194).

predictive value A quality of information that allows it to help users form their expectations about the future (p. 642).

preferred stock Stock that typically has some priority over other shares in the payment of dividends or the distribution of assets upon liquidation (p. 668).

present value (PV) The value today of a future cash flow (p. 435).

price elasticity The effect of price changes on sales volume (p. 193).

price variance The difference between actual input prices and standard input prices multiplied by the actual quantity of inputs used (p. 323).

problem solving Analysis of possible courses of action and identification of the best course to follow (p. 5).

process costing The method of allocating costs to homogeneous products by averaging costs over large numbers of nearly identical products (p. 577).

process map A schematic diagram capturing interrelationships between cost objects, activities, and resources (p. 135).

producing departments Departments where employees work on the organization's products or services (p. 481).

product costs (inventoriable costs) Costs identified with goods produced or purchased for resale (p. 131).

product life cycle The various stages through which a product passes, from conception and development to introduction into the market to maturation and, finally, withdrawal from the market (p. 9).

production-volume variance A variance that appears whenever actual production deviates from the expected volume of production used in computing the fixed overhead rate. It is calculated as (actual volume – expected volume) × fixed-overhead rate (p. 543).

productivity A measure of outputs divided by inputs (p. 368).

profit center A responsibility center in which managers are responsible for revenues as well as costs—that is, profitability (p. 360).

proration To assign underapplied overhead or overapplied overhead to cost of goods sold, work-in-process inventory, and finished-goods inventory in proportion to the ending balances of each account (p. 537).

quality control The effort to ensure that products and services perform to customer requirements (p. 365).

quality-control chart The statistical plot of measures of various product quality dimensions or attributes (p. 366).

quantity variance The difference between the actual quantity of inputs used and the standard quantity allowed for the good output achieved multiplied by the standard price of the input (p. 323).

rate variance An alternative name for the price variance applied to labor (p. 326).

raw material The basic material from which a product is made (p. 131).

raw-material inventory Raw material on hand and awaiting use in the production process (p. 132).

real options model A capital-budgeting model that recognizes the value of contingent investments—that is, investments that a company can adjust as it learns more about its potential for success (p. 439).

recognition The principle that specifies when a company should record revenue in the accounting records (p. 638).

recognize To formally record in the accounting records during the current period (p. 622).

recovery period The number of years over which a company can depreciate an asset for tax purposes (p. 445).

relevance The capability of information to make a difference to the decision maker (p. 642).

relevant information The predicted future costs and revenues that will differ among alternative courses of action (p. 181).

relevant range The limits of the cost-driver level within which a specific relationship between costs and the cost driver is valid (p. 42).

required rate of return (hurdle rate, discount rate) The minimum acceptable rate of return, based on the firm's cost of capital (p. 436).

residual value The predicted sales value of a long-lived asset at the end of its useful life (p. 626).

responsibility accounting Identifying what parts of the organization have primary responsibility for each action, developing performance measures and targets, and designing reports of these measures by responsibility center (p. 360).

responsibility center A set of activities and resources assigned to a manager, a group of managers, or other employees (p. 360).

retained earnings (retained income) The ownership claim arising from the reinvestment of previous profits (p. 620).

return on investment (ROI) A measure of income divided by the investment required to obtain that income (p. 396).

return on sales Income divided by revenue (p. 397).

revenue Increases in ownership claims arising from the delivery of goods or services (p. 622).

sales-activity variances The activity-level variances when sales is used as the cost driver (p. 315).

sales budget The sales forecast that is the result of decisions to create conditions that will generate a desired level of sales (p. 276).

sales forecast A prediction of sales under a given set of conditions (p. 276).

sales mix The relative proportions or combinations of quantities of products that constitute total sales (p. 47).

sales revenue (sales) Revenue from customers (p. 622).

Sarbanes-Oxley Act A 2002 law that requires top-management oversight of a company's accounting policies and procedures (p. 8).

scorekeeping The accumulation, classification, and reporting of data that help users understand and evaluate performance (p. 5).

Securities and Exchange Commission (SEC) A government agency that regulates the financial markets in the United States, including financial reporting (p. 635).

segment autonomy The delegation of decision-making power to managers of segments in an organization (p. 392).

segments Responsibility centers for which a company develops separate measures of revenues and costs (p. 361).

sensitivity analysis The systematic varying of decision input assumptions to examine the effect on a decision (p. 293).

separable costs Any cost beyond the split-off point (p. 238).

service departments Units that exist only to support other departments or customers (p. 481).

service organizations Organizations that do not make or sell tangible goods but instead provide other forms of value (p. 15).

short-term investments Temporary investments in marketable securities (p. 663).

Six Sigma A data-driven continuous process improvement effort designed to eliminate defects and improve quality (p. 17).

sole proprietorship A business entity with a single owner (p. 634).

source documents Clear evidence of transactions, such as sales slips and purchase invoices (p. 625).

specific identification An inventory method that recognizes the actual cost paid for the specific physical item sold (p. 692).

split-off point The juncture of manufacturing where the joint products become individually identifiable (p. 238).

staff managers Managers who are advisory to the line managers. They have no authority over line managers, but they support the line managers by providing information and advice (p. 13).

standard cost A cost that should be achieved (p. 318).

statement of cash flows A statement that reports the cash receipts and cash payments of an organization during a particular period (p. 674).

statement of stockholders' equity A statement that shows the changes in each stockholders' equity account during the period (p. 634).

static budget A budget that is prepared for only one expected level of activity (p. 312).

static-budget variance The difference between actual results and the static budget for the original planned level of output (p. 314).

step cost A cost that changes abruptly at different intervals of activity because the resources and their costs come in indivisible chunks (p. 43).

step-down method A method for allocating service department costs that recognizes that some service departments support the activities in other service departments as well as those in operating departments (p. 488).

stockholders' equity The owners' equity of a corporation (p. 620).

straight-line method A method that depreciates an asset by the same amount each year (p. 627).

strategic plan A plan that sets the overall goals and objectives of the organization (p. 277).

subordinated A creditor claim that is junior to the other creditors in exercising claims against assets (p. 667).

subsidiary A company controlled by a parent company that generally owns more than 50% of its stock (p. 719).

sunk cost A historical or past cost, that is, a cost that the company has already incurred and, therefore, is irrelevant to the decision-making process (p. 240).

T-accounts Simplified versions of ledger accounts that take the form of the capital letter T (p. 643).

target costing Taking a product's market price as given and determining the maximum cost the company can spend to make the product and still achieve the desired profitability (p. 201).

timeliness The quality that information must reach decision makers while it can still influence their decisions (p. 642).

time-series comparisons Comparison of a company's financial ratios with its own historical ratios (p. 731).

total quality management (TQM) An approach to quality that focuses on prevention of defects and on customer satisfaction (p. 366).

total contribution margin Total number of units sold times the unit contribution margin (p. 48).

total project approach A method for comparing alternatives that computes the total impact on cash flows for each alternative and then converts these total cash flows to their present values (p. 440).

tracing Physically identifying the amount of a direct cost that relates exclusively to a particular cost object (p. 126).

trading securities Investments "held for current resale," that is, investments that the investor company intends to sell in the near future (p. 717).

traditional costing systems Accounting systems that do not accumulate or report costs of individual activities or processes. They often use a single cost pool for all indirect production costs with a labor-based cost-allocation base (p. 135).

transaction Any event that affects the financial position of an organization and requires recording (p. 619).

transfer price The price at which one segment of an organization sells products or services to another segment of the same organization (p. 404).

transferred-in costs In process costing, costs incurred in a previous department for items that have been received by a subsequent department (p. 596).

treasurer The executive who is concerned mainly with the company's financial matters, such as raising and managing cash (p. 14).

treasury stock A corporation's own stock that it has issued and subsequently repurchased but has not permanently retired (p. 668).

two-stage ABC system A costing system with two stages of allocation to get from the original indirect resource cost to the final product or service cost. The first stage allocates indirect resource costs to activity-cost pools. The second stage allocates activity costs to products or services (p. 138).

unallocated costs Costs that an accounting system records but does not allocate to any cost object (p. 129).

unavoidable costs Costs that will continue even if a company discontinues an operation (p. 235).

uncontrollable cost Any cost that the management of a responsibility center cannot affect within a given time span (p. 360).

underapplied overhead The difference between actual and applied overhead when the amount applied is less than the amount incurred (p. 537).

understandable A criterion that requires accountants to present information clearly and concisely (p. 642).

unearned revenue (deferred revenue) Collections from customers that companies receive and record before they earn the revenue (p. 629).

unexpired cost Any asset that managers expect to become an expense in future periods, for example, inventory and prepaid rent (p. 626).

unfavorable cost variance A variance that occurs when actual costs exceed budgeted costs (p. 312).

unfavorable profit variance A variance that occurs when actual profit falls below budgeted profit (p. 312).

unfavorable revenue variance A variance that occurs when actual revenue falls below budgeted revenue (p. 312).

unit contribution margin (marginal income per unit) The sales price per unit minus the variable cost per unit (p. 48).

usage variance (efficiency variance) Alternative names for the quantity variance (p. 326).

useful life The number of years the company expects to use an asset (p. 626).

value-added cost The necessary cost of an activity that cannot be eliminated without affecting a product's value to the customer (p. 142).

value chain The set of business functions or activities that add value to the products or services of an organization (p. 10).

value engineering A cost-reduction technique, used primarily during design, that uses information about all value-chain functions to satisfy customer needs while reducing costs (p. 202).

variable cost A cost that changes in direct proportion to changes in the cost-driver level (p. 39).

variable-cost percentage Total variable costs divided by total sales (p. 48).

variable-cost ratio Variable cost percentage expressed as a ratio (p. 48).

variable-overhead efficiency variance The difference between actual cost-driver activity and the standard amount allowed for the actual output achieved multiplied by the standard variable-overhead rate per cost-driver unit (p. 328).

variable-overhead spending variance The difference between the actual variable overhead cost and the amount predicted for the actual level of cost-driver activity (p. 328).

variances Deviations from plans (p. 7).

verifiability A characteristic of information that can be checked to ensure it is correct (p. 642).

visual-fit method A method in which the cost analyst visually fits a straight line through a plot of all the available data (p. 100).

volume variance A common name for the production-volume variance (p. 546).

weighted-average cost An inventory method that assigns the same unit cost to each unit available for sale (p. 694).

weighted-average (WA) process-costing method A process-costing method that determines total cost by adding together the cost of (1) all work done in the current period and (2) the work done in the preceding period on the current period's beginning inventory of work in process, and divides the total by the equivalent units of work done to date (p. 595).

working capital Current assets less current liabilities (p. 666).

work-in-process inventory Goods undergoing the production process but not yet fully completed (p. 132).

zero-base budget A budget that requires justification of expenditures for every activity, including continuing activities (p. 272).

Subject Index

A

absorption approach, 184, 186, 197
absorption costing. *See* absorption approach
accelerated depreciation, 445–446
account, defined, 620
account analysis, 95–96
accountants, role of, 10–12, 14
accounting
  cost, 124. *See also* cost accounting systems
  ethics in. *See* ethics
  financial, 3–4
  management, 2–3, 14
  need for, 619
  place in organizational structure, 12
  and pricing, 193–194
  purpose of, 4
accounting concepts, 641–643
  accrual basis vs. cash basis, 624–625
  conservatism convention, 642–643
  continuity or going concern, 641
  cost-benefit, 643
  materiality, 642
  relevance and faithful
    representation, 642
accounting information, 4–6
accounting rate-of-return (ARR) model, 453–454
accounting systems, 5, 8–9
accounts, 643–644
  adjustments to. *See* adjustments
  debits and credits to, 644–645
  doubtful, 663
  ledger, 643–646
accounts payable, 619, 666
accounts receivable, 619, 663
accrual basis, 624
accrue, defined, 629
accrued expenses, 629
accrued expenses payable, 666
accrued liabilities, 666
accrued revenues, 631
accumulated depreciation, 240
accumulated other comprehensive income, 668
activity analysis, 92, 94
activity-based budget (ABB), 289–290
activity-based cost accounting system,
  design of, 147–151
activity-based cost allocation (ABC), 290
  in a job-costing environment, 582–583

activity-based costing (ABC) system
  135–140, 144–146, 190
  benefits of, 142–143
  use for cost allocation, 495–498
activity-based flexible budgets, 313–314
activity-based management
  (ABM), 142, 150
  benefits of, 142–143
activity-level variances, 315–316
adjustments (adjusting entries), 625
  accrual of unrecorded expenses, 629–631
  accrual of unrecorded revenues, 631
  expiration of unexpired costs, 625–627
  recognition (earning) of unearned revenues, 629
after-tax cash flow, 445
agency theory, 394–396
Akers, John, 366
American Institute of CPAs (AICPA), 637, 733
annual reports, 687–688
Aspin, Les, 241
Assets, 620
  current, 661, 663
  expiration of, 626
  fixed, 663
  intangible, 665
  long-lived, 626
  tangible, 663
  valuation of, 398–399
attention directing, 5
audit, 635–636
  internal, 8
  management, 8
  post-audit, 455–456
authority, line and staff, 13–14
available-for-sale securities, 717
average revenue curve, 192
avoidable costs, 234–236

B

backflush costing, 598–599
bad debts, 663
balance sheets, 127, 132–133, 620–624
  budgeted, 284–285
  classified, 661–669
balanced scorecard (BSC), 370–371
Balanced Scorecard Hall of Fame (BSHF), 370
behavioral implications, 9
Beijing Olympic Games, 390

benchmarking, 142
  benchmark comparisons, 731, 733
book value, 240
break-even point, 46–47, 62
Bryant, Kobe, 390, 460
budget padding, 274
budgetary slack, 274
budgeted factory-overhead rate, 534
budgeting, 272. *See also* budgets
  advantages of, 271–273
  capital, 435, 455, 457–459
  functional, 289
  participative, 274
budgets, 6–8, 271, 413–414. *See also* budgeting
  activity-based (ABB), 289–290
  and business plans, 285
  capital, 277–278, 283
  cash, 238, 283–284
  continuous, 277
  financial, 277–278, 280, 283, 286
  as financial planning models, 290–291
  flexible, 313
  master, 277–285
  misuse of, 274–276
  operating, 277–278, 280–282, 286
  purchases, 281
  rolling, 277
  sales, 276–278, 281
  static vs. flexible, 312–315
  types of, 277–278
  variable, 313
  zero-base, 272
Buffett, Warren, 18, 688, 716, 741
business plans, 265, 285
business process reengineering, 16
Business Week, 506
business-to-business (B2B), 16
business-to-consumer (B2C), 16
by-product, 509

C

Call, Kevin, 180
capacity costs, 88
capital budget, 277–278, 283
capital budgeting, 435, 455
  and inflation, 457–459
capital charge, 400
capital in excess of stated (par) value, 668
capital market, efficient, 735
capital turnover, 397
capitalize, 665
Casey, Paul, 390
cash basis, 624
cash budget, 238, 283–284
cash dividends, 632–633

cash equivalents, 663
cash flow statement, interpreting, 685
cash flows
  after-tax, 445
  from financing activities, 675–676
  free, 685
  from investing activities, 675, 679–680
  from operating activities, 675, 680
  relevant, 443–444
centralization, 391
certified management accountants (CMAs), 4
certified public accountants (CPAs), 3–4
change, adapting to, 15–18
chartered accountants (CAs), 3–4
cheating, incentives for, 274–276. *See also* ethics
chief financial officer (CFO), 14
Clark, Richard, 637
classified balance sheet, 661–669
code of conduct, 18, 21, 26
coefficient of determination (R^2), 101
committed fixed costs, 89
common costs, 235
common stock, 668
common-size statements, 730
comparability, 642
competition
  global, 15–16
  imperfect, 192
  perfect, 191–192
competitors, actions of, 194
component percentages, 730
compound entry, 622
computer-aided design (CAD), 16
computer-aided manufacturing (CAM), 16
computer-integrated manufacturing (CIM) systems, 16
confirmatory value, 642
conservatism convention, 642–643
consistency, 642
consolidations, 717–721
Consortium for Advanced Marketing, 203
continuity convention, 641–642
continuous budget, 277
contribution approach, 185–187, 362
  to pricing, 196–198
contribution margin, 49–51, 58, 361
  contribution-margin percentage, 48
  contribution-margin ratio, 48
control, defined, 6
controllability, 360, 413
controllable cost, 360, 363
controller (comptroller), 14
cooking the books, 275
Cooper, Cynthia, 20, 22
Cornelius, James M., 402
Corporate Responsibility (CR) Magazine, 31, 637

corporation, 619
cost. *See* costs
cost accounting, 124
cost accounting systems, 124–126, 134–140
  activity-based, 135–136
  traditional, 134–135
cost accumulation, 125
cost allocation, 126–127. *See also* cost behavior; costs
  ABC costing system, 495–498
  by-product costs, 507, 509
  central corporate support costs, 506–507
  to customer cost objects, 498–503
  framework for, 481–483
  joint costs, 507–509
  methods of, 128–129
  to product or service cost objects, 490–492
  purposes of, 127–128
  refined system, 501–503
  service department costs, 483–489
cost application, 490
cost assignment, 125
cost behavior, 37, 86–88. *See also*
    cost allocation; costs
  effect of magnitude on, 44
  influence of management on, 88
  mixed cost, 44
  step cost, 43–44
  effect of time horizon on, 44
  variable vs. fixed, 39, 42
cost center, 360
cost drivers, 37–38, 87, 126
  choice of, 92–93
cost functions, 90–92
  measuring, 93–101
cost management systems (CMS), 123
cost measurement, 91
cost object (cost objective), 124
cost of capital, 400
cost of goods sold, 58, 134, 581
cost of quality report, 366
cost pool, 128
cost recovery, 638
cost structure, 55
cost-allocation base, 126
cost-benefit balance, 9
cost-benefit criterion, 643
cost-control incentives, 90
costing
  absorption, 538–544
  activity-based, 495–498
  backflush, 598–599
  kaizen, 202
  process, 577, 586–591, 595–596
  target, 201–204
  variable, 538–544

costing systems
  activity-based, 135–151, 145–146, 190
  Grenzplankostenrechnung (GPK), 143–144
  hybrid, 577
  traditional, 134–137, 145–146
cost-plus pricing, 195–197, 203–204
costs. *See also* cost allocation;
    cost behavior
  absorption, 544–548
  avoidable, 234–236
  capacity, 88
  committed fixed, 89
  common, 235
  controllable, 360, 363
  controlling, 40
  current, 398
  defined, 124
  differential, 227
  direct, 126, 128, 130
  direct-labor, 131
  direct-material, 131, 580
  discretionary fixed, 89–90
  expected, 318
  factory overhead, 580
  fixed, 39, 42–43, 188
  full cost, 195, 198
  historical, 398
  incremental, 227
  indirect, 126, 128, 130–131
  inventoriable, 131
  irrelevant, 242–244
  joint, 238–239, 507–508
  labor, 580
  of management control systems, 359
  manufacturing, 131–134
  marginal, 192
  misspecified, 242–244
  mixed, 44
  non-value-added, 142
  opportunity, 228
  outlay, 227
  overhead, 533–537
  period, 131, 133
  product, 131, 133
  production, 592–593
  resource, 40
  separable, 238
  step, 43–44
  sunk, 240–241
  transferred-in, 596–597
  types of, 88–90
  unallocated, 129–131, 363
  unavoidable, 234–236
  uncontrollable, 360, 363
  unexpired, 626

value-added, 142
variable, 39, 42–43, 188, 198, 547–548
cost-volume-profit (CVP) analysis, 45
Cox, Christopher, 733
Cracking the Value Code, 353
credit, 644, 646
cross-sectional comparisons, 731, 733
current assets, 661, 663
current liabilities, 666–667
current portion of long-term debt, 666
currently attainable standards, 318
customers
customer service, 10
demands of, 194–195
focus on, 11
profitability of, 498–503
cycle time (throughput time), 367–368

D

Danaher, John, 352
debentures, 666
debit, 644, 646
debt
bad debt, 663
long-term, 666
decentralization, 391, 404, 414
cost benefits of, 392–393
decision making, 5–6
decision context, 42
decision model, 182
dysfunctional decisions, 408
make-or-buy, 229–232
vs. performance evaluation, 244–245
about pricing, 186–187
deferred income, 663
deferred revenue, 629
deferred taxes, 696–697
degree of operating leverage, 55
Dell, Michael, 122–123
Deming, W. Edwards, 366
denominator level, 543
depreciation, 240, 626–627, 664, 686, 697. *See also* equipment
accelerated, 445–446. *See also* modified accelerated
cost recovery system (MACRS)
accumulated, 240
deductions for, 445–446
timing of, 447–448
design, 10
differential analysis, 227
differential approach, 440
differential cost, 227
differential revenue, 227
direct costs, 126, 128, 130
direct method, cost allocation, 487, 489, 680–681
direct method, cash flow statement, 680–681

direct-labor costs, 131
direct-material costs, 131, 580
discount rate, 436
discounted-cash-flow (DCF) models, 435–440, 455. *See also*
internal rate of return (IRR) model; net-present-value
(NPV) method
and technology investments, 444
discretionary fixed costs, 89–90
discriminatory pricing, 194
dividends, 632–633
double-entry system, 644
doubtful accounts, 663
downsizing, 89
Durant, Kevin, 390
dysfunctional decision, 408

E

earnings. *See also* income
before interest and taxes (EBIT), 396
before interest, taxes, depreciation and amortization
(EBITDA), 396
retained, 632–633
per share (EPS), 671
easily attainable standards, 318–319
economic profit, 400–403, 424
economic value added (EVA), 400–403, 424
effectiveness, defined, 319
efficiency, defined, 319
efficiency variance, 325
efficient capital market, 735
electronic commerce (e-commerce), 16
engineering analysis, 93–95
enterprise learning culture, 358–359
enterprise resource planning (ERP)
systems, 16, 144, 643
equipment, 662–365. *See also* depreciation
disposal of, 450–451
keeping or replacing, 240–241
equity method, 718–719
equivalent units, 591–592
Escobar, Angel R., 370
ethics, 18, 20, 59, 413–414, 637
ethical dilemmas, 20–23
expected cost, 318
expenses, 134, 622
accrued, 629
fixed, 50
prepaid, 663
explicit transactions, 625
eXtensible Business Reporting Language (XBRL), 16, 733

F

facilities
idle, 230–231
use of, 231–232

factory burden, 131
factory overhead costs, 131, 533–535, 580–581
fair value, 717
faithful representation, 642
Fastow, Andrew, 18
favorable cost variances, 312
favorable profit variance, 311–312
favorable revenue variances, 312
Federer, Roger, 390
Financial Accounting Standards Board (FASB), 8, 636–637
financial accounting
  defined, 3
  vs. management accounting, 4
financial budget, 277–278, 280, 283, 286.
  See also budgets
Financial Executive, 21
financial Executives Institute (FEI), 21, 26
financial management, 670
financial planning model, 290–291
financial reporting, 127
financial statements, 619
  analysis of, 726
  consolidated, 719–725
  preparing, 633–634
finished goods, 581
  finished-goods inventory, 132
First, Tom, 226
first-in, first-out (FIFO), 693
fiscal year, 663
fixed assets, 663
fixed cost, 39, 42–43, 188
fixed expenses, 50
fixed-overhead rate, 543
fixed-overhead spending variance, 329
flexible budgets, 313
  flexible-budget formulas, 312–313
  flexible-budget variance, 315, 322–329, 549–550
Foreign Corrupt Practices Act, 8
Fortune magazine, 358
free cash flow, 685
full cost, 195, 198
functional budgeting, 289

G

Gallaway, Ron, 203
Gamster, Scott, 444
general ledger, 644
generally accepted accounting principles (GAAP),
  8, 127–128, 635, 637–638
Gladden, Brian, 123
global competition, 15–16
goals
  goal congruence, 355
  organizational, 353–355
going concern convention, 641–642

Goodmanson, Richard, 86
goodwill, 665–666, 725–726
government contracts, 8, 241
Grenzplankostenrechnung (GPK), 143–144
gross book value, 398
gross margin (gross profit), 58, 184, 670

H

Hallin, Keith, 209
Hamilton, Frank, Jr., 587
Hasan, Malik, 352
health-care organizations, 94
Henkle, Dan, 637
high-low method, 97–100
Howard, Michael, 370
hurdle rate, 436
hybrid costing systems, 577

I

ideal standards, 318
IMA. *See* Institute of Management Accountants
Immelman, Trevor, 390
imperfect competition, 192
implicit transactions, 625
incentives, 356, 393–395, 402–403
  cost-control, 90
  from economic profit, 402–403
  income measures as, 396, 402–403
  from ROI, 399–400, 402–403
income, 402–403, 622
  deferred, 663
  measuring, 396
  from operations, 670
  other comprehensive, 668
  residual, 400
income statements, 127, 132–134, 622, 669–670
  model, 362
income taxes
  effects of, 445–450
  impact of, 62–63
  marginal rate, 445
  payable, 666
  reporting, 696–697
incremental analysis, 227
incremental costs, 227
incremental effect, 51
independent opinion, 635
indirect costs, 126, 128, 130
  manufacturing, 131
  production, 131
indirect method for operating cash flows, 680–684
Industry Norms and Key Business Ratios, 733
inflation, 457
Institute of Management Accountants (IMA), 3–4, 29, 35
  Statement of Ethical Professional Practice, 18–19

intangible assets, 665
internal auditors, 8
internal controls, 8, 636
internal rate of return (IRR) model, 438–439
International Accounting Standards Board (IASB),
    8, 636–637
Inventoriable costs, 131
inventories, 663. *See also* inventory methods
  accounting for, 691–695
  beginning, 594–597
  finished-goods, 132
  proration among, 538
  raw-material, 132
  work-in-process, 132
inventory methods. *See also* inventories
  first-in, first-out (FIFO), 693
  last-in, first-out (LIFO), 693
  LIFO increments (LIFO layers), 694
  lower-of-cost-or-market, 695
  and physical flow of inventories, 694–695
  specific identification, 692
  weighted-average cost, 694
inventory turnover, 237–238
investment center, 361
investments
  intercorporate, 717
  long-term, 665
  measuring, 397–398
  return on, 396–399
  short-term, 663
  technology, 444

J

James, LeBron, 190, 390, 460
Jensen, Michael, 274
job-cost record (job-cost sheet, job order), 577
job-order costing (job costing), 577–579
  in nonprofit organizations, 585–586
  compared to process costing, 586–591
  in service organizations, 585–586
joint costs, 238–239, 507–508
joint products, 238
just-in-time (JIT) philosophy, 16, 397
just-in-time production system (JIT), 537, 598

K

kaizen costing, 202
Kaplan, Robert, 370–371
Kapoor, Sunir, 733
Kaufman, Stephen, 356
Kertley, Todd, 230
key performance indicators, 371
key success factors, 354
Kim, Anthony, 390
Knight, Philip, 391

L

labor time tickets, 577
last-in, first-out (LIFO), 693
Lay, Kenneth, 18
League of American Communications Professionals, 688
lean manufacturing, 16–17
leasehold improvements, 664
least-squares regression method (regression analysis),
    97, 100–104
ledger accounts, 643–646
Leung, Sandra, 637
liabilities, 620, 666–668
  accrued, 666
  current, 666–667
LIFO increments (LIFO layers), 694
limited liability, 668
limiting factor, 236
line managers, 13
linear cost function, 91
linear-cost behavior, 87–88
liquidation, 667
long-lived assets, 626
long-range plan, 277
long-term liabilities, 666
lower-of-cost-or-market, 695
lying, incentives for, 274–276

M

management
  by exception, 6–8
  financial, 670
  influence on cost behavior, 88
management accounting, 14
  case study, 2–3
  defined, 3
  vs. financial accounting, 4
management audit, 8
management by objectives (MBO), 413
management control systems
  defined, 353
  designing, 355–359, 394
  future of, 373
  in government organizations, 372
  in nonprofit organizations, 372
  and operational goals, 353–354
  in service organizations, 372
  successful, 413–414
management's discussion and analysis (MD&A), 730
managerial effort, 355
managers
  and budgets, 274
  as decision makers, 363, 392–395
  line, 13
  staff, 13
manufacturing costs (overhead), 131–134

margin of safety, 55
marginal cost, 192
marginal income tax rate, 445
marginal revenue, 192
market value, 717
marketing, 10
market-value method, 717
markup, 195
master budget, 277–285
matching, 638
materiality, 642
materials requisitions, 577
measurement
   of cost behavior, 86
   of performance, 394–400
measurement principles, 638–639
misspecified costs, 242–244
mixed costs, 44
mixed-cost behavior, 88
mixed-cost function, 91
modified accelerated cost recovery system (MACRS),
   448–450
monetary unit, stable, 638–639
motivation, 356
Mulally, Alan, 37

N

Nadal, Rafael, 390
Nardelli, Bob, 359
net book value, 240, 398
net income. *See* income
net operating profit after-tax (NOPAT), 400
net worth, 634
net-present-value (NPV) method, 436–440
   use for comparison, 440–442
nominal rate, 457
noncontrolling interests, 721–725
noncurrent liabilities, 666
nonprofit organizations, 15, 53, 625
non-value-added costs, 142
normal costing system, 536
Norton, David, 370–371
notes payable, 666

O

operating budget, 277–278, 280–282, 286
operating cycle, 661
operating expense budget, 281–282
operating income, 670
operating leverage, 55
operating performance, 669–670
operating profit, 670
opportunity cost, 228
organization chart, 13
other comprehensive income, 668

Otis, Clarence, 21
outlay cost, 227
outsourcing, 230
   outsourcing decisions, 268
overhead
   fixed, 543–547
   fixed-manufacturing, 539–540
   overapplied, 537
   underapplied, 537
owners' equity, 620

P

paid-in capital, 620
par value (stated value), 668
parent company, 719
participative budgeting, 274
partnership, 634
payback period (payback time), 452–453
perfect competition, 191–192
perfection standards, 318
performance, nonfinancial, 365–370
performance evaluation, 127, 454–456
   vs. decision making, 244–245
   and budgets, 274
   performance measures, 356–3357
   performance metrics, 393–395
   performance reports, 7–8
   performance targets, 413–414
period costs, 131, 133
planning, 6–8. *See also* budgeting
   for product life cycles, 9–10
   for the value chain, 10–12
plant, 663–365
post-audit, 455–456
Powell, Ken, 618
predatory pricing, 194
predictive value, 642
preferred stock, 668
prepaid expenses, 663
present value (PV), 435
price. *See also* pricing
   price elasticity, 193
   transfer. *See* transfer price
pricing. *See also* price
   absorption-cost approach, 197
   and accounting, 193–194
   contribution approach, 196–198
   cost-plus, 194, 203–204
   discriminatory, 194
   formats for, 198–199
   influences on, 194–195
   of Microsoft Xbox 360, 199
   predatory, 194
   pricing decisions, 191–194
   of special orders, 186

prior period's results, 320–321
problem solving, 5
process costing, 577, 586–591, 596
  weighted-average method, 595
process map, 135, 137–138
producing departments, 481
products
  cost of, 131, 133
  decisions concerning, 88
  development of, 201–202
  life cycle of, 9–10
production, 10
production costs, 592–593
production-volume variance
  (volume variance), 543–544, 552–554
productivity, 368–370
profit, economic, 400–403
  profit center, 360
profit plan, 277
profitability, customer, 498–503
profits. *See* income
property, 663–365
proration, 537–538
Public Company Accounting Oversight
  Board (PCAOB), 635
purchases budget, 281

Q

quality control, 365–366
quality-control chart, 366

R

radiofrequency identification (RFID), 368
rate variance, 326
ratios, 731, 734–735
raw material, 131–132. *See also* inventory
Reagan, Ronald, 576
real options model, 439
receiving activity, 40
recognition, 638
recognize, defined, 622
reconciliation statement, 685
recovery period, 445
regression analysis, 97, 100–104
regulation, defined, 8
relevance, defined, 642
relevant cash flows, 443–444
relevant information, 181–183
relevant range, 42–43
required rate of return, 436, 348
research and development (R&D), 10, 401, 626
residual income, 400
residual value, 626
resources
  cost of, 40

linked to cost, 37–38
  scarce, 236
responsibility accounting, 360
responsibility centers, 360–361, 392–393–393
retained earnings (retained income), 620, 668
return on investment (ROI), 396–399
return on sales, 397
revenue, 622. *See also* sales
  accrued, 631
  and cost variances, 316
  deferred, 629
  differential, 227
  sales, 622
risk assessment, 439–440
rolling budget, 277
Rowan, Jim, 285

S

sales, 581. *See also* revenue
  return on, 397
  sales budget, 276–278, 281
  sales forecast, 276
  sales mix, 47
  sales revenue (sales), 622
sales-activity variances, 315–316
sales-mix analysis, 61–62
Sarbanes-Oxley Act, 8, 21
scarce resource, 236
Schuessler, Jack, 370
Schultz, Howard, 2
Schumacher, Michael, 391, 394
scorekeeping, 5
Scott, Tom, 226
Securities and Exchange Commission (SEC), 635–637, 733
segment autonomy, 392
segments, 361, 363, 404
sensitivity analysis, 292–293, 439–440
separable costs, 238
service decisions, 88
service departments, 481
service organizations, 15
Sharapova, Maria, 390
shareholder reporting, 696–697
short-term investments, 663
Simon, Neil, 262–263
Six Sigma, 17, 366–367, 383–385
Small Business Administration (SBA), 290
Smith, Jim, 14
sole proprietorship, 634
source documents, 625
specific identification, 692
split-off point, 238
spreadsheets, 53–55, 292
  spreadsheet software, 292–294
staff managers, 13

standard cost, 318
standards
  in accounting, 636–637
  easily attainable, 318–319
  of ethical conduct, 18–20
  role of, 318–319
statements. *See also* financial statements
  of cash flows, 674–684
  of financial position. *See* balance sheet
  of stockholders' equity, 634, 671
static budget, 312
static-budget variance, 314
step cost, 43–44
step-down method, 488–489
stock, 668
stockholders' equity, 620, 667–669, 671–672
straight-line method, 627
strategic plan, 277
subordinated, 667
subsidiary, 719
sunk cost, 240–241

T

T-accounts, 643–644
tangible assets, 663
target costing, 201–204
taxes, deferred, 696–697. *See also* income taxes
technology
  advances in, 16
  changes in, 733
  investments in, 444
  technology decisions, 90
throughput time, 367–368
time cards, 577
time horizon, 44
timeliness, defined, 642
time-series comparisons, 731, 733
total contribution margin, 48
total project approach, 440
total quality management (TQM), 17, 366
Toyoda, Kiichiro, 434
tracing, defined, 126
trading securities, 717
traditional costing systems, 134–137, 145–146
transaction, 619, 625
  implicit, 625
transfer price, 404–405
  and activity-based costing, 411
  market-based, 407–408
  multinational, 410–412
  negotiated, 409–410
  purposes of, 406
  rule for, 406–408
  transfers at cost, 408–409
transferred-in costs, 596–597

treasurer, 14
two-stage ABC system, 138

U

U.S. Small Business Administration (SBA), 290
unallocated costs, 129–131
unavoidable costs, 234–236
uncontrollable cost, 360, 363
underapplied overhead, 537
understandable, defined, 642
unearned revenue, 629
unexpired cost, 626
unfavorable cost variances, 312
unfavorable profit variances, 312
unfavorable revenue variances, 312
unit contribution margin (marginal income per unit), 48
usage variance, 326
useful life, 626

V

value chain, 10–12, 37–38, 88, 583
value engineering, 202
value-added cost, 142
variable budgets, 313
variable cost, 39, 42–43, 188, 198, 547–548
variable-cost percentage, 48
variable-cost ratio, 48
variable-overhead efficiency variance, 328–329
variable-overhead spending variance, 328–329
variances, 7, 311–312
  activity-level, 315
  effects of, 547–550
  efficiency, 326
  explaining, 319–320
  favorable, 311–12
  flexible-budget, 314–315, 322–329, 549–550
  investigating, 320
  production-volume, 543–544, 552–554
  rate of 326
  sales-activity, 315
  and the role of standards, 318–319
  static-budget, 314
  trade-offs among, 320
  unfavorable, 312
  variable-overhead efficiency, 328–329
  variable-overhead spending, 328–329
verifiability, defined, 642
Vick, Ralph, 270
visual-fit method, 97, 100
volume variance (production-volume variance), 546

W

wages
  accrual of, 630–631
  payment of, 630

Wall Street Journal, 366
Walton, Sam, 11
Washington Post, The, 81
Watkins, Sherron, 18, 20
Watson, Ray, 480
weighted-average (WA) cost, 694
weighted-average (WA) process-costing
    method, 595, 694
Welch, John, 358–359
Welch, Larry O., 241
Weldon, Bill, 393
whistle-blowing, 20

White, Larry, 3
Williams, Serena, 390
working capital, 666
work-in-process inventory, 132

X
XBRL (eXtensible Business Reporting Language), 16, 733
XBRL International, 733

Z
Zampino, Peter, 203
zero-base budget, 272

Company Index

A

A & P, 124
ABC, Inc., 65
Accenture, 31, 637
Ace Hardware Corporation, 229, 652
Acer, 111
Adelphia, 18
Aetna, 391
AIG, 21, 637, 661
Air France, 227, 391
Airbus, 25, 27, 36
Albertsons, 661
Allen-Bradley, 356
Allstate, 272, 371
Amazon.com, 3, 15, 28, 44, 444, 476
America West, 86
American Express Company, 371, 716, 719, 741
American Gypsum Company, 598
American Medical Systems of Ohio, 9
AmeriCorps, 372
Amgen, 632
AOL Time Warner, 444
Apple Computer, 371
Army and Air Force Exchange Service (AAFES), 370
Arrow Electronics, 356
Arthur Anderson, 22
ArvinMeritor, 30
Aswega AS, 473
AT&T, 145, 146–152, 161
AT&T Universal Card Services, 356
AXA Equitable, 391

B

Balanced Scorecard Hall of Fame, 370
Bank of America, 3, 463
Barnes & Noble, 444
Battelle, 272
Bayliner, 740–741
Ben & Jerry's, 20
Berkshire Hathaway, 14, 30, 480, 688, 716–719, 741
Best Buy, 480
Beta Alpha Psi, 33
Blockbuster Video, 59, 75
BlueCross, 306
BlueCross BlueShield of Florida (BCBSF), 136
BMW, 248
BMW Financial Services, 370

Boeing Company
  and customer input, 202
  exercises involving, 28, 30, 74
  management decisions of, 3
  market life of product, 10
  MMA Program in Integrated Defense Systems, 209
  pricing, 180
  profitability of, 36–37, 41, 52
  target costing by, 204
BorgWarner's Automotive, 135, 540
Bose, 252
Branson Gray Line Tours, 186
Briggs & Stratton, 750
Bristol-Meyers Squibb Co., 31, 637
Brunswick Corporation, 740–741
Burberry plc, 741
Burlington Northern Santa Fe Railroad, 468, 716

C

Cadbury-Schweppes, 226
Campbell Soup Co., 31, 637
Carnival Corporation, 309, 478
Caterpillar, 204, 208
Chevron Corporation, 616, 710–711, 748–749
Chrysler, 47, 143–144, 169–170
Cisco Systems, 132, 637
Citicorp, 359
City of Corpus Christi, 370
CNN, 339
Coca-Cola, 607, 716
Cole Haan, 221–222
Colgate-Palmolive Company, 224–225
Columbia Sportswear, 730
Colville Timber Resource Company, 24
ComROAD AG, 661
Comtell, 105
ConAgra, 238, 249
Continental Airlines, 217
Converse, 752
Corning, 356, 402
Costco Wholesale, 132, 208, 253, 634, 655, 711, 736
CSX Corporation, 21
Culp, 203

D

DaimlerChrysler, 47, 143–144
Dairy Queen, 716
Dana Corporation, 256–257

Darden Restaurants, 21
Dell Computers, Inc.
  use of ABC by, 582–583
  cost management systems, 122–123, 126, 128–129, 142, 176
  cost of overhead, 532–533, 536, 541
  decisions by managers, 532–533
  and design function, 10
  exercise involving, 28
  financial statements of, 575, 656
  income statement of, 546
  and IT investment, 444
  job costing at, 608–609
Delta Airlines, 37, 652, 709–710
Disney, 59
Dollar General, 480
Dow Chemical Company
  use of ABC system by, 497–498
  budget system of, 290
  controllable vs. uncontrollable costs, 360
  exercise involving, 707–708
  and joint product costs, 238–239, 507–508
  use of Six Sigma by, 367, 385
Dr. Pepper Snapple Group, 226
drkoop.com, 444
Dun & Bradstreet, 733
DuPont, 17, 748

E

E. I. du Pont de Nemours & Company, 17, 748
Eastman Kodak Company, 77, 203–204
eBay, 76, 444
Eddie Bauer, 333
Eli Lilly, 230
EncrypTix, 285
Enron, 18, 20–22, 275, 356, 414, 420, 661
Ethan Allen, 616
Expedia, 444
ExxonMobil, 254, 371

F

Fannie Mae, 21, 272
FedEx Office, 616
Financial Executives Institute (FEI), 21, 26
Ford Motor Company, 24, 28, 47, 203, 272
Freddie Mac, 21, 637, 661

Frito-Lay, 610–611
Froedtert Memorial Lutheran
    Hospital, 136
Frontier Airlines, 258
Fruit of the Loom, 716

G

Gap, Inc., 637, 741–742, 752
GEICO Insurance, 716
General Dynamics, 243
General Electric (GE)
    annual report, 754
    disposal of assets, 451
    enterprise learning culture, 358–359
    exercise involving, 24, 381
    fixed and variable costs, 42–43
    management control system, 357
    freedom of managers, 392
    pricing and accounting, 193
    use of Six Sigma by, 17, 367, 385
    subsidiary of, 749
General Electric Capital Services
    (GECS), 749
General Mills
    audit opinion, 635–636
    balance sheet, 640
    exercises involving, 25, 30, 72, 616, 713
    financial statements of, 618–619, 632,
        635–636
    management decisions, 3, 227
General Motors, 16, 47, 72, 717
Georgia State University, 605
Georgia-Pacific, 661
Gillette Company, 749
Global Crossing, 18, 22, 420
GM. *See* General Motors
GM Daewoo, 717
Goodyear, 16
Google, Inc., 404, 656, 740
Grand Canyon Railway, 180–181, 195,
    217–218
Grant Thornton, 444
Green Mountain Coffee Company, 269
Gruen Telekom, 143–144
Guidant Corporation, 402

H

Hamleys Toy Store, 248–249
Harley-Davidson, 357, 537
Harvard University, 414
Health Net, 352–353, 379
HealthSouth, 661
Hershey Foods Company, 351, 643
Hewlett-Packard Company
    and accountants, 125
    corporate citizen award, 31, 637
    exercises involving, 80, 111–112,
        570, 708

    and IT investment, 444
    and the JIT philosophy, 16
    management decisions, 123
Holiday Inn, 258
Home Depot, 359, 713
Honda Motor Company, Ltd., 688,
    750–751
Honda of America, 204
Hosparus, 94
Hospital for Sick Children, 144

I

Iberia Airlines, 391
IBM. *See* International Business
    Machines
Intel, 637, 699
Intercontinental, 300–301
Internal Revenue Service, 112
International Business Machines (IBM),
    31, 230, 366, 402, 637, 640
ITT Automotive, 202–204

J

J. Sainsbury plc, 709–710
J.C. Penney Company, 506
J.M. Smucker Company, 711
Jelly Belly Candy, 576–577
Johnson & Johnson, 393
Johnson Controls Inc., 31, 637
Jolife AB, 749–750
JP Morgan Chase & Co., 655

K

Kawasaki, 16
Kellogg's, 78
Kemps LLC, 498
KFC, 338
Kiewit Construction Co., 616
Kimberly-Clark Corp., 31, 637
Kmart, 28, 237, 480, 516
Kraft Foods, 596, 708, 726
Kroger, 361, 661

L

L.A. Darling
    use of ABC by, 495–496
    and budgeting, 507
    cost allocation, 480–481, 486, 491
    exercises involving, 504, 516–517, 567
La Brasserie, 80
Lands' End, 65, 208, 617
La-Z-Boy, 617
Lowe's Companies, 715

M

Macy's, 222, 643, 652
Marks & Spencer, 29
Marmon Group, 14, 30, 480
Marriott Corporation, 256

Marriott International, 432–433
Mars, 52
Matrix USA, 402
Matsushita Electric, 17
Mattel, Inc., 31, 229, 637
Mayo Clinic, 44
MBNA America, 372
McDonald's, 89, 310–311, 320
    balance sheet, 659, 669
Medtronic, 52, 749–750
Mercedes-Benz, 202, 204
Merck, 637
Metropolitan Transit Authority
    (MTA), 469
Michelin Group, 428
Microsoft Corporation
    annual report, 688, 733
    balanced scorecard, 371
    exercises involving, 29, 65, 73–74,
        708–709
    IT investments by, 444
    Xbox 360, 198–199
Microsoft Dynamics, 16
Micrus Semiconductors, 203
MidAmerica Energy, 716
Middleton Foods, 597
Minnesota State University, 306
Mission Foods, 27–28
Mitsubishi Chemical Corporation, 471
Mittal Steel, 24
Motorola, 17, 241, 367, 385

N

Nally & Gibson Georgetown, 586–587,
    589, 594, 607, 610
Nantucket Nectars, 226–228, 230–232,
    243, 252–253
NBA, 464
Neenah Paper Inc., 62
Nestlé Purina, 37
Netflix, 15
New York City, 378
Nike Inc.
    annual report, 660–669, 671–672
    balance sheet, 640
    budgeting assumptions at, 307–308
    corporate citizenship award, 31, 637
    cost accounting system, 176
    and decentralization, 390–392,
        394–395
    depreciation method, 476
    dysfunctional decisions, 409
    financial statement of, 717,
        728–731, 734
    form 10K, 33, 82, 613–614, 714
    form 10K, exercise involving, 752
    income statement, 656–657
    make or buy, 266, 268

and management control systems, 413
performance standards, 349
product-mix decisions, 236–237
profitability ratios, 731
R&D, 401
and segment performance, 430
and special orders, 190
statement of cash flows, 686–687
step and mixed costs and cost
  drivers, 119
subsidiary of, 573
and transfer price, 405–407, 410–412
value-chain functions, 30
Nintendo, 47
Nordstrom, 222, 648, 712, 736
Nortel Networks, 541
Northern Telecom, 541
NXP Semiconductors, 203
NYCE Payments Network, 444

O

Oracle, 16, 226, 638
Owens Corning, 272

P

Parker Hannifin Corporation, 319
Parmalat, 661
Payless Shoe Source, 480
Peace Corps, 372
PepsiCo, 393, 708
PETCO, 124
Pfizer, 10, 463
Philip Morris, 708, 726
Philips Electronics, 371
Pixar, 743
Pizza Hut, 205
Planters Specialty Products
  Company, 596
Porsche Motor Company, 27, 144
Post, 78
Process Machinery, Inc., 587
Procter & Gamble (P&G), 73–76,
  203–204, 393, 716, 749
Providence Hospital, 25
Prudential, 616

R

Radio Shack, 210
RIM, 652
Ritz-Carlton, 270–271, 274, 276
Royal Ahold, 661
Royal Dutch Shell plc, 748

S

SAAB Automobile AB, 28
Sabena, 391
Safeway, 180, 253, 361
Sage Group, 16
Saint Jude Hospital, 252

Sam's Club, 253
Samsung, 17
SAP, 16
Scottsdale Luxury Suites, 354
Sears, 28
Sears Holding Corporation, 530
7-Up Bottling, 65
Shanghai President Coffee Co., 725
Siecor, 402
Siemens Corporation, 402
Six Sigma, 17, 366–367, 383–385
Sony, 24, 39, 47
South Central Bell, 124
South China Airlines, 391
Southwest Airlines (SWA), 65, 84–85,
  121, 357
Sports Authority, 190
Sprint, 272
St. Luke's Hospital, 27
St. Mary's Hospital, 28
Stamps.com, 285
Starbucks Coffee Japan, Ltd., 725
Starbucks Coffee Korea Co., 725
Starbucks Company
  balance sheet, 723–725
  corporate citizenship award, 637
  and customer satisfaction, 11
  ethical principles of, 20
  expansion of, 2, 89
  income statement, 723–725
  irrelevance of past costs, 264
  planning and control, 6–7, 28
  and the value chain, 12
State Farm, 607
Stern Stewart, 400–402
STIHL, 144
Stomil Olsztyn, 428
SunAmerica, 285
Sunbeam, 22
Super 8, 71
Super Valu, 73, 361
SuperSol, 167–167

T

Target Corporation
  use of ABC by, 498
  cost allocation, 486, 498
  exercises involving, 27–28, 504, 700
  use of ledger accounts by, 643
  increasing turnover at, 237
Tasty Baking Company, 617
TCBY, 255
Tenneco, 68
Teva Pharmaceutical Industries Ltd., 411
Texaco, 272
3M Co., 31, 367, 385, 637
Thrift Drug Co., 506
Time Warner, Inc., 666, 669

Toyota Motor Company
  cost behavior of, 37
  lowering break-even point, 47
  depreciation of assets, 446–447, 450, 452
  exercises involving, 24, 749
  investment decisions by, 434–436,
    439–440
  use of JIT philosophy, 16
  management decisions, 227
Tyco, 17, 18, 420, 661

U

U.S. Department of Transportation, 371
U.S. Post Office, 607
UBmatrix, 733
Umbro, 573, 665
Unisys Corporation, 712–713
United Airlines, 44
United Way of America, 371
University of Michigan, 25
US Airways, 86, 91, 113

V

Verizon, 708
Vermont Teddy Bear Factory, 179
Vigor Industrial, 616
Volvo Group, 649

W

W. L. Gore & Associates, 13
Walgreen Co., 480, 486, 516, 700
Wal-Mart
  cost allocation, 480, 486
  cost behavior of, 37
  cost management systems, 124
  and customer satisfaction, 11
  exercises involving, 28, 364, 516
  lower contribution margins, 237
  and pricing, 180, 194
Walt Disney Company, 59
Washington Mutual, 637
Watkins Products, 39
WCCO, 65
Wells Fargo, 708
Wendy's International, 370
Western Area Power Authority
  (WAPA), 360
Weyerhaeuser Company, 94, 246,
  650, 661
Whirlpool Corporation, 371, 708
Wiremold, 21
WorldCom, 18, 20, 22, 275, 414, 420, 661

X

Xerox, 16, 18, 468

Y

Yahoo!, 444
Yankee 24, 444